2007 Standard Catalog of WORLD COINS 2001-DATE

Colin R. Bruce II
Senior Editor

Thomas Michael
Market Analyst

George Cuhaj
Editor

Merna Dudley
Coordinating Editor

Deborah McCue
Database Specialist

Fred J. Borgmann
New Issues Editor

Randy Thern
Numismatic Cataloging Supervisor

Special Contributors
Frank Putrow
Dr. Wolfgang Schuster

Bullion Value (BV) Market Valuations

Valuations for all platinum, gold, palladium and silver coins of the more common, basically bullion types, or those possessing only modest numismatic premiums are presented in this edition based on the market levels of:

$1,100 per ounce for **platinu**

$650 per ounce for **gold**

$300 per ounce for **palladiu**

$11.50 per ounce for **silver**

Published by

700 East State Street • Iola, WI 54990-0001
715-445-2214 • 888-457-2873

Our toll-free number to place an order or obtain
a free catalog is (800) 258-0929.

Library of Congress Catalog Number: 2006931743

ISBN 13-digit: 978-0-89689-429-7

ISBN 10-digit: 0-89689-429-0

Edited by: George Cuhaj/Thomas Michael

Designed by: Stacy Bloch

Printed in the United States of America

TABLE OF CONTENTS

Title Page I
Copyright Page II
Introduction III
Standard International Numeral Systems IV
Country Index VI
Acknowledgments X
How To Use XII
Foreign Exchange XVIII
A Guide To International Numerics 313
Numismatic Societies 314

ADVERTISER INDEX

Ponterio and Associates, Inc.. V
Pobjoy Mint VIII
Stack's IX
Universal Mint XI
I.A.P.N. XIII
Numis-Phil (s) Pte. Ltd. XVII
Mietens & Partner GmbH XIX
C.I.C.F XX

INTRODUCTION

Welcome to our all-new 21st Century edition of the Standard Catalog of World Coins. This most recent version, of our ever changing and evolving series of comprehensive reference catalogs, is designed to meet the needs of those whose interest in coins exceeds the casual jingle in your pants pocket. Perhaps you've traveled overseas and still have some coins that came home with you, maybe you read in the news about the newest Euro coins, or it could be that you are a long term collector who wants to wade out into the most current of numismatic trends. In all cases, this book is for you.

Arranged in a basic alphabetic fashion by country and with groupings for political structure, coinage type and denomination to help better organize the data, this volume is as easy to use as the phone book. You will find photographs of many 21st Century coins, plenty of information on metal content, descriptions of types and varieties, date listings and of course values presented in multiple grades of preservation. In short, just about all the information you could want on the most modern coins of our world.

Marvel at the ingenuity of today's most inventive world mints, which are striking coins in a variety of shapes and sizes, colors and textures. Enjoy the practicality of coins designed for serious circulation in durable metals. Celebrate the advent of coins made of acrylic materials and those, which house precious stones or display gold overlays. All are here in our 21st Century edition.

The accuracy of the data offered in this volume is assured through the assistance of over fifty contributing coin dealers, collectors and researchers who have lent their knowledge to the compiling of this new reference, providing our staff with information on new coinage types, new dates and accurate mintage figures. To them we offer a heartfelt "Thank you!" for their generosity and dedication to the advancement of our shared field of coin collecting.

Finally to you, the reader, we extend our wishes that you may enjoy using this catalog as much as we enjoyed it's production. Look it over, put it to good use and please let us know if you have any comments or questions.

Best Wishes,

The Editorial Staff of the Standard Catalog of World Coins

STANDARD INTERNATIONAL NUMERAL SYSTEMS

PREPARED ESPECIALLY FOR THE **STANDARD CATALOG OF WORLD COINS**

WESTERN	0	½	1	2	3	4	5	6	7	8	9	10	50	100	500	1000
ROMAN			I	II	III	IV	V	VI	VII	VIII	IX	X	L	C	D	M
ARABIC-TURKISH	٠	١/٢	١	٢	٣	٤	٥	٦	٧	٨	٩	١٠	٥٠	١٠٠	٥٠٠	١٠٠٠
MALAY-PERSIAN	٠	١/٢	١	٢	٣	۴	۵	٦ or ۶	٧	٨	٩	١٠	۵٠	١٠٠	۵٠٠	١٠٠٠
EASTERN ARABIC	۰	۱/۲	۱	۲	۳	۴	۵	۶	۷	۸	۹	۱۰	۵۰	۱۰۰	۵۰۰	۱۰۰۰
HYDERABAD ARABIC	٠	١/٢	١	٢	٣	۴	۵	٦	٧	٨	٩	١٠	۵٠	١٠٠	۵٠٠	١٠٠٠
INDIAN (Sanskrit)	०	१/२	१	२	३	४	५	६	७	८	९	१०	५०	१००	५००	१०००
ASSAMESE	০	১/২	১	২	৩	৪	৫	৬	৭	৮	৯	১০	৫০	১০০	৫০০	১০০০
BENGALI	০	১/২	১	২	৩	৪	৫	৬	৭	৮	৯	১০	৫০	১০০	৫০০	১০০০
GUJARATI	૦	૧/૨	૧	૨	૩	૪	૫	૬	૭	૮	૯	૧૦	૫૦	૧૦૦	૫૦૦	૧૦૦૦
KUTCH	०	१/२	१	२	३	४	५	६	७	८	९	१०	५०	१००	५००	१०००
DEVAVNAGRI	०	१/२	१	२	३	४	५	६ or ६	७	८	९ or ९	१०	५०	१००	५००	१०००
NEPALESE	०	१/२	१ or १	२	३	४	५ or ५	६	७	८ or ८	९ or ९ or ९	१०	५०	१००	५००	१०००
TIBETAN	༠	༡/༢	༡	༢	༣	༤	༥	༦	༧	༨	༩	༡༠	༥༠	༡༠༠	༥༠༠	༡༠༠༠
MONGOLIAN	᠐	᠑/᠒	᠑	᠒	᠓	᠔	᠕	᠖	᠗	᠘	᠙	᠑᠐	᠕᠐	᠑᠐᠐	᠕᠐᠐	᠑᠐᠐᠐
BURMESE	၀	၁/၂	၁	၂	၃	၄	၅	၆	၇	၈	၉	၁၀	၅၀	၁၀၀	၅၀၀	၁၀၀၀
THAI-LAO	๐	๑/๒	๑	๒	๓	๔	๕	๖	๗	๘	๙	๑๐	๕๐	๑๐๐	๕๐๐	๑๐๐๐
JAVANESE	꧐		꧑	꧒	꧓	꧔	꧕	꧖	꧗	꧘	꧙	꧑꧐	꧕꧐	꧑꧐꧐	꧕꧐꧐	꧑꧐꧐꧐
ORDINARY CHINESE JAPANESE-KOREAN	零	半	一	二	三	四	五	六	七	八	九	十	十五	百	百五	千
OFFICIAL CHINESE			壹	貳	叁	肆	伍	陸	柒	捌	玖	拾	拾伍	佰	佰伍	仟
COMMERCIAL CHINESE			〡	〢	〣	〤	〥	〦	〧	〨	〩	十	〥十	〡百	〥百	〡千
KOREAN		반	일	이	삼	사	오	육	칠	팔	구	십	오십	백	오백	천
GEORGIAN			ა	ბ	გ	დ	ე	ვ	ზ	ჱ	თ	ი	ნ	რ	ფ	ჩ
			11 ია	20 კ	30 ლ	40 მ	50 ნ	60 ჲ	70 ო	80 პ	90 ჟ	100 რ	200 ს 300 ტ	400 უ	600 ქ	700 ღ 800 ყ
ETHIOPIAN	◆		፩	፪	፫	፬	፭	፮	፯	፰	፱	፲	፶	፻	፭፻	፲፻
				20 ፳	30 ፴	40 ፵		60 ፷	70 ፸	80 ፹	90 ፺					
HEBREW			א	ב	ג	ד	ה	ו	ז	ח	ט	י	נ	ק	תק	
				20 כ	30 ל	40 מ		60 ס	70 ע	80 פ	90 צ		200 ר	300 ש 400 ת	600 תר	700 תש 800 תת
GREEK			Α	Β	Γ	Δ	Ε	ΣΤ	Ζ	Η	Θ	Ι	Ν	Ρ	Φ	Α
				20 Κ	30 Λ	40 Μ	60 Ξ	70 Ο	80 Π		200 Σ	300 Τ	400 Υ	600 Χ	700 Ψ	800 Ω

COUNTRY INDEX

A

Afghanistan....1
Albania....1
Alderney....2
Algeria....4
Andorra....5
Argentina....7
Armenia....7
Aruba....8
Ascension Island....10
Australia....11
Austria....23
Azerbaijan....27

B

Bahamas....28
Bahrain....28
Bangladesh....28
Barbados....29
Belarus....29
Belgium....32
Belize....34
Benin....34
Bermuda....35
Bhutan....35
Bolivia....36
Bosnia-Herzegovina....36
Brazil....36
British Virgin Islands....38
Brunei....42
Bulgaria....42
Burkina Faso....44

C

Cambodia....44
Cameroon....45
Canada....46
Cape Verde....55
Cayman Islands....55
Central African Republic....55
Central African States....56
Chad....56
Chile....57
China, People's Republic....57
China, Republic of....61
Colombia....62
Comoros....62
Congo Republic....63
Congo, Democratic Republic....63
Cook Islands....70
Costa Rica....72
Croatia....73
Cuba....74
Cyprus....80
Czech Republic....80

D

Denmark....83
Djibouti....85
Dominican Republic....85

E

East Caribbean States....86
East Timor....87
Ecuador....87
Egypt....88
Equatorial Guinea....89
Estonia....90

F

Falkland Islands....90
Fiji....95
Finland....96
France....98
French Polynesia....103

G

Gabon....103
German-Federal Republic....104
Ghana....109
Gibraltar....109
Great Britain....117
Greece....123
Guadeloupe....125
Guatemala....125
Guernsey....125
Guinea....129
Guyana....129

H

Honduras....129
Hong Kong....129
Hungary....130

I

Iceland....133
India-Republic....134
Indonesia....135
Iran....136
Iraq....136
Ireland Republic....137
Isle Of Man....138
Israel....147
Italy....150
Ivory Coast....152

J

Jamaica....153
Japan....153
Jersey....155
Jordan....157

K

Kazakhstan....157
Kenya....160
Kiribati....160
Korea-North....160
Korea-South....174
Kuwait....175
Kyrgyzstan....175

L

Lao....175

Latvia 176
Lebanon 177
Liberia 178
Libya 181
Lithuania 181
Luxembourg 182

M

Macao 183
Macedonia 184
Madagascar 185
Malawi 185
Malaysia 186
Mali 188
Malta 188
Martinique 189
Mauritania 189
Mauritius 189
Mexico 190
Moldova 194
Monaco 195
Mongolia 196
Morocco 197
Mozambique 198

N

Nagorno-Karabakh 198
Namibia 199
Nauru 199
Nepal 200
Netherlands 202
Netherlands Antilles 205
New Caledonia 206
New Zealand 207
Nicaragua 209
Niger 210
Nigeria 210
Niue 210
Norway 212

O

Oman 213

P

Pakistan 213
Palau 213
Panama 217
Papua New Guinea 217
Paraguay 218
Peru 218
Philippines 219
Pitcairn Islands 219
Poland 219
Portugal 225

Q

Qatar 227

R

Romania 227
Russia (U.S.S.R.) 229
Rwanda 239

S

Saharawi Arab Democratic Republic 239
Saint Helena 239
Samoa 241
San Marino 242
Saudi Arabia 244
Senegal 244
Serbia 244
Seychelles 245
Sierra Leone 245
Singapore 249
Slovakia 250
Slovenia 252
Solomon Islands 254
Somalia 255
Somaliland 257
South Africa 257
South Georgia And The South Sandwich Islands 260
Spain 261
Sri Lanka 264
Sudan 264
Suriname 265
Swaziland 265
Sweden 266
Switzerland 266
Syria 269

T

Tajikistan 269
Tanzania 270
Thailand 270
Togo 272
Tokelau Islands 273
Tonga 273
Transnistria 274
Trinidad & Tobago 274
Tristan Da Cunha 275
Tunisia 275
Turkey 275
Turks & Caicos Islands 280
Tuvalu 280

U

Uganda 281
Ukraine 283
United Arab Emirates 296
United States 297
Uruguay 304
Uzbekistan 304

V

Vatican City 304
Venezuela 306
Viet Nam 307

W

West African States 308

Y

Yemen Republic 308
Yugoslavia 309

Z

Zambia 309
Zimbabwe 312

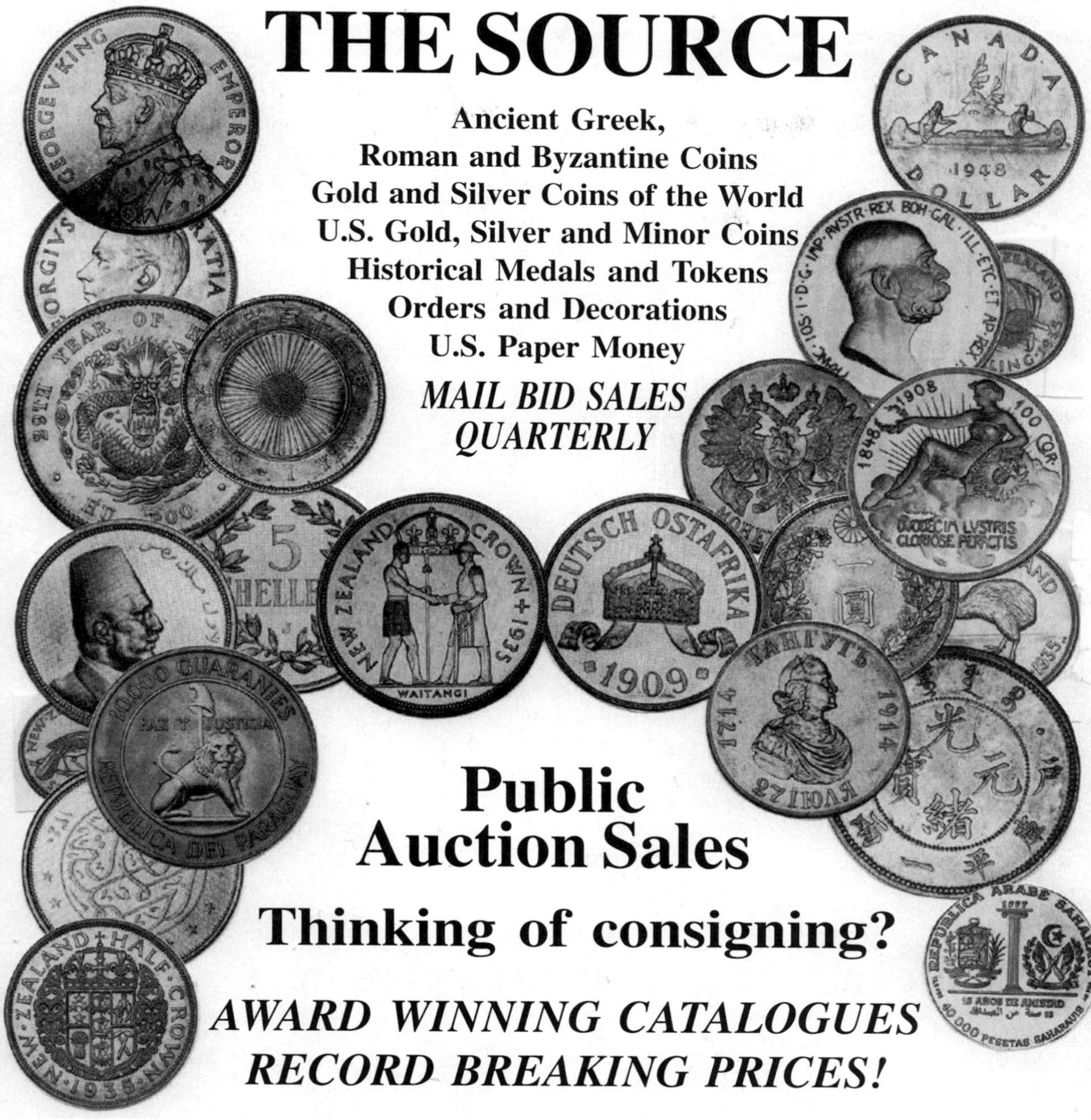

Stack's
Coin Galleries

ACKNOWLEDGMENTS

Many individuals have contributed countless changes, which have been incorporated into this first edition. While all may not be acknowledged, special appreciation is extended to the following who have exhibited a special enthusiasm for this edition.

David Addey
Esko Ahlroth
Don Bailey
Paul Baker
Yuri Barshay
Albert Beck
Richard Benson
Sharon Blocker
Joseph Boling
Al Boulanger
Mahdi Bseiso
Chris Budesa
Doru Calin
Howard A. Daniel III
Yossi Dotan
Stephen Eccles
Esko Ekman
Jack Erb
Eugene Freeman
Mark Freehill
Carman Fun Tanar
David R. Gotkin
Brian Hannon
Flemming Lyngbeck Hansen
David Harrison
Martin Rodney Hayter
Istvan Hegedus
James H. Higby
Anton Holt
Nelva G. Icaza
Dennis H. Irving
A.K. Jain
Børge R. Juul
Alex Kaglyan
Melvyn Kassenoff
Craig Keplinger
E. James Kindrake
Peter Kraneveld
Peter Krix
Matti Kuronen
Alex Lazarovici
Richard Lobel
Rudi Lotter
Enrico Manara
Ranko Mandic
Franck Medina
Juozas Minikevicius
Robert Mish
Dr. Richard Montrey
Paul Montz
Edward Moschetti
Arkady Nakhimovsky
Michael G. Nielsen
Dick Parker
Frank Passic
Kirsten F. Petersen
Jens Pilegaard
Gastone Polacco
Elena Pop
Michel Prier
Frank Putrow
Yahya Qureshi
Dr. Dennis G. Rainey
Alistair Robb
Dr. Kerry A. Rodgers
William M. Rosenblum
Egon Conti Rossini
Leon Saryan
Erwin Schaffer
Gerhard Schön
Dr. Wolfgang Schuster
Evzen Sknouril
Benjamin Swagerty
Steven Tan
Anthony Tumonis
J. J. Van Grover
Erik J. Van Loon
Carmen Viciedo
Helen Wallace
R.W. Walter
Paul Welz
Stewart Westdal
J. Brix Westergaard
J. Hugh Witherow
Joseph Zaffern

AUCTION HOUSES AND DISTRIBUTORS

Dix-Noonan-Webb
Educational Coins
Heritage World Coin Auctions
Hess-Divo Ltd.
Gerhard Hirsch
Thomas Høiland Møntauktion
Fritz Rudolf Künker
Leu Numismatik AG
Münzenhandlung Harald Möller, GmbH
Noble Numismatics, Pty. Ltd.
Omni Trading B. V.
Ponterio & Associates
Stack's
UBS, AG
World Wide Coins of California

SOCIETIES, INSTITUTIONS AND INTERNATIONAL MINTS

Africa Mint
American Numismatic Association
American Numismatic Society
Austrian Mint
British Museum
British Royal Mint
Casa de la Moneda de Cuba
Central Bank of The Russian Federation
Mint of Finland
Numismatics International
Pobjoy Mint
Royal Dutch Mint
Singapore Mint
Smithsonian Institution

PUBLICATIONS

The Statesman's Yearbook, 2004.
The Politics, Cultures and Economies of the World 140th Edition
edited by Barry Turner, Palgrave Macmillan Ltd
Houndmills, Basingstoke,
Hampshire, RG21 6XS, England
The World Factbook 2003.
By Central Intelligence Agency

A special thanks to these members of the Krause Publications production team:

Stacy Bloch Sandra Morrison

HOW TO USE THIS CATALOG

This catalog is designed to serve the needs of both the novice and advanced collectors. It is generally arranged so that persons with no more than a basic knowledge of world history and a casual acquaintance with coin collecting can consult it with confidence and ease. The following explanations summarize the general practices used in preparing this catalog's listings.

ARRANGEMENT

Countries are arranged alphabetically. Political changes within a country are arranged chronologically. In countries where Rulers are the single most significant political entity, a chronological arrangement by Ruler has been employed. Distinctive sub-geographic regions are listed alphabetically following the country's main listings.

Diverse coinage types relating to fabrication methods, revaluations, denomination systems, non-circulating categories and such have been identified, separated and arranged in logical fashion. Chronological arrangement is employed for most circulating coinage. Monetary reforms will flow in order of their institution. Non-circulating types such as Essais, Piefors, Patterns, Trial Strikes, Mint and Proof sets will follow the main listings.

Within a coinage type coins will be listed by denomination, from smallest to largest. Numbered types within a denomination will be ordered by their first date of issue.

IDENTIFICATION

The most important step in the identification of a coin is the determination of the nation of origin. This is generally easily accomplished where English-speaking lands are concerned, however, use of the country index is sometimes required.

The coins of many countries beyond the English-language realm, such as those of French, Italian or Spanish heritage, are also quite easy to identify through reference to their legends, which appear in the national languages based on Western alphabets. In many instances the name is spelled exactly the same in English as in the national language, such as France; while in other cases it varies only slightly, like Italia for Italy, Belgique or Belgie for Belgium, Brasil for Brazil and Danmark for Denmark.

This is not always the case, however, as in Norge for Norway, Espana for Spain, Sverige for Sweden and Helvetia for Switzerland. Coins bearing Cyrillic lettering are attributable to Bulgaria, Russia, the Slavic states and Mongolia; the Greek script peculiar to Greece, Crete and the Ionian Islands; the Amharic characters of Ethiopia; or Hebrew in the case of Israel.

The toughra monogram, occurs on some of the coins of Afghanistan, Egypt, Sudan, Pakistan, and Turkey. A predominant design feature on the coins of Nepal is the trident; while neighboring Tibet features a lotus blossom or lion on many of their issues.

DATING

Coin dating is the final basic attribution consideration. Here, the problem can be more difficult because the reading of a coin date is subject not only to the vagaries of numeric styling, but to calendar variations caused by the observance of various religious eras or regal periods from country to country, or even within a country. Here again, with the exception of the sphere from North Africa through the Orient, it will be found that most countries rely on Western date numerals and Christian (AD) era reckoning, although in a few instances, coin dating has been tied to the year of a reign or government. The Vatican, for example dates its coinage according to the year of reign of the current pope, in addition to the Christian-era date.

Countries in the Arabic sphere generally date their coins to the Muslim era (AH).

The following table indicates the year dating for the various eras, which correspond to 2006 in Christian calendar reckoning, but it must be remembered that there are overlaps between the eras in some instances.

Christian era (AD)	-2006
Muslim era (AH)	-AH1427
Solar year (SH)	-SH1384
Monarchic Solar era (MS)	-MS2565
Vikrama Samvat (VS)	-VS2063
Saka era (SE)	-SE1928
Buddhist era (BE)	-BE2549
Bangkok era (RS)	-RS225
Chula-Sakarat era (CS)	-CS1368
Ethiopian era (EE)	-EE2000
Korean era	-4339
Javanese Aji Saka era (AS)	-AS1939
Fasli era (FE)	-FE1416
Jewish era (JE)	-JE5766

More detailed guides to less prevalent coin dating systems, which are strictly local in nature, are presented with the appropriate listings.

Some coins carry dates according to both locally observed and Christian eras. This is particularly true in the Arabic world, where the Hejira date may be indicated in Arabic numerals and the Christian date in Western numerals, or both dates in either form.

HEJIRA DATE CONVERSION CHART

JEHIRA DATE CHART

HEJIRA (Hijira, Hegira), the name of the Muslim era (A.H. = Anno Hegirae) dates back to the Christian year 622 when Mohammed "fled" from Mecca, escaping to Medina to avoid persecution from the Koreish tribemen. Based on a lunar year the Muslim year is 11 days shorter.

*=Leap Year (Christian Calendar)

AH Hejira	AD Christian Date
1420	1999, April 17
1421	2000, April 6*
1422	2001, March 26
1423	2002, March 15
1424	2003, March 5
1425	2004, February 22*
1426	2005, February 10
1427	2006, January 31
1428	2007, January 20
1429	2008, January 10*
1430	2008, December 29
1431	2009, December 18
1432	2010, December 8
1433	2011, November 27*
1434	2012, November 15
1435	2013, November 5
1436	2014, October 25
1437	2015, October 15*
1438	2016, October 3
1439	2017, September 22
1440	2018, September 12
1441	2019, September 11*
1442	2020, August 20
1443	2021, August 10
1444	2022, July 30
1445	2023, July 19*
1446	2024, July 8
1447	2025, June 27
1448	2026, June 17
1449	2027, June 6*
1450	2028, May25

The date actually carried on a given coin is generally cataloged here in the first column (Date) to the right of the catalog number. If this date is by a non-Christian dating system, such as 'AH' (Muslim), the Christian equivalent date will appear in parentheses(), for example AH1336(1917). Dates listed alone in the date column which do not actually appear on a given coin, or dates which are known, but do not appear on the coin,

"The I.A.P.N. dealer, your guide to the world of numismatics"

More than one hundred of the world's most respected coin dealers are members of the I.A.P.N. (International Association of Professional Numismatists). I.A.P.N. members offer the collector an exceptional selection of quality material, expert cataloguing, outstanding service and realistic pricing.
The I.A.P.N. also maintains the International Bureau for the Suppression of Counterfeit Coins (I.B.S.C.C.) which for a fee can provide expert opinions on the authenticity of coins submitted to it.
A booklet listing the names, addresses and specialties of all I.A.P.N. members is available without charge by writing to the I.A.P.N. General Secretary, Jean-Luc Van der Schueren, 14 rue de la Bourse, B-1000 BRUXELLES, Belgium. Tel: +32-2-513 3400; Fax: +32-2-512 2528; E-mail: iapnsecret@compuserve.com; Web site: http://www.iapn.ch.

ARGENTINA
DERMAN, Alberto José
Avenida Corrientes 368
1043 BUENOS AIRES
AUSTRALIA
NOBLE NUMISMATICS Pty Ltd
169 Macquarie Street
SYDNEY, NSW 2000
AUSTRIA
HERINEK, Gerhard
Josefstädterstrasse 27
1080 WIEN
MOZELT Numismatik
Postfach 19
1043 WIEN
BELGIUM
FRANCESCHI & FILS, B.
Rue de la Croix-de-Fer 10
1000 BRUXELLES
JEAN ELSEN & ses Fils s.a.
Avenue de Tervueren 65
1040 BRUXELLES
VAN DER SCHUEREN, Jean-Luc
Rue de la Bourse 14
1000 BRUXELLES
CANADA
WEIR NUMISMATICS Ltd
P.O. Box 64577
UNIONVILLE, ONT. L3R 0M9
EGYPT
BAJOCCHI JEWELLERS
Abdel Khalek Sarwat Street 45
CAIRO 11511
FRANCE
BOURGEY, Sabine
Rue Drouot 7
75009 PARIS
BURGAN, Claude - Maison FLORANGE
Rue du 4 Septembre 8
75002 PARIS
MAISON PLATT S.A.
B.P. 2612
75026 PARIS Cedex 01
NUMISMATIQUE & CHANGE DE PARIS
Rue de la Bourse 3
75002 PARIS
O.G.N.
Rue de Richelieu 64
75002 PARIS
POINSIGNON-NUMISMATIQUE (A.)
Rue des Francs Bourgeois 4
67000 STRASBOURG
SILBERSTEIN, Claude - COMPTOIR de NUMISMATIQUE
Rue Vivienne 39
75002 PARIS
SPES NUMISMATIQUE
Rue de Richelieu 54
75001 PARIS
VINCHON - NUMISMATIQUE
Rue de Richelieu 77
75002 PARIS
GERMANY
DILLER, Johannes
Postfach 70 04 29
81304 MÜNCHEN
GORNY & MOSCH - GIESSENER MÜNZENHANDLUNG GmbH
Maximiliansplatz 20
D - 80333 MÜNCHEN
HIRSCH NACHF., Gerhard
Promenadeplatz 10/II
80333 MÜNCHEN
JACQUIER, Paul-Francis
Honsellstrasse 8
77694 KEHL am RHEIN
KAISER MÜNZFACHGESCHÄFT
Mittelweg 54
60318 FRANKFURT
KRICHELDORF NACHF.
Günterstalstrasse16
79102 FREIBURG i. Br.
KÜNKER MÜNZENHANDLUNG
Gutenbergstrasse 23
49076 OSNABRÜCK
KURPFÄLZISCHE MÜNZHANDLUNG
Augusta-Anlage 52
68165 MANNHEIM
LEIPZIGER MÜNZHANDLUNG
Nicolaistr. 25
04109 LEIPZIG
MEISTER, Michael
Moltkestrasse 6
D-71634 LUDWIGSBURG
MÜNZEN- UND MEDAILLENHANDLUNG STUTTGART
Charlottenstrasse 4
70182 STUTTGART
NEUMANN GmbH
Wätteplatz 6
89312 GÜNZBURG
NUMISMATIK LANZ
Luitpoldblock - Maximiliansplatz 10
80333 MÜNCHEN
OLDING, Manfred
Goldbreede 14
49078 OSNABRÜCK
PEUS NACHF.
Bornwiesenweg 34
60322 FRANKFURT / M
RITTER MÜNZHANDLUNG GmbH
Postfach 24 01 26
40090 DÜSSELDORF
TIETJEN + Co
Spitalerstrasse 30
20095 HAMBURG
WESTFÄLISCHE AUKTIONSGE-SELLSCHAFT
Nordring 22
59821 ARNSBERG
HUNGARY
NUMISMATICA EREMBOLT
Vörösmarty Tér 6
1051 BUDAPEST
ISRAEL
QEDAR, Shraga
P.O. Box 520
91004 JERUSALEM 93399
ITALY
BARANOWSKY S.A.S.
Via del Corso 184
00187 ROMA
CRIPPA NUMISMATICA S.A.S.
Via Cavalieri del S. Sepolcro 10
20121 MILANO
DE FALCO, Alberto
Corso Umberto 24
80138 NAPOLI
FALLANI, Carlo-Maria
Via del Babuino 58a
00187 ROMA
GIULIO BERNARDI S.R.L.
Casella Postale 560
34121 TRIESTE
MARCHESI GINO & FIGLIO
Viale Pietramellara 35
40121 BOLOGNA
PAOLUCCI, Raffaele
Via San Francesco 154
35121 PADOVA
RINALDI, Marco
Via Cappello 23 (Casa di Giulietta)
37121 VERONA
VARESI NUMISMATICA S.A.S.
Via Robolini 1
27100 PAVIA
JAPAN
DARUMA INTERNATIONAL GALLERIES
2-16-32-701, Takanawa, Minato-ku
TOKYO 108-0074
WORLD COINS JAPAN
1-15-5, Hamamatsu-cho, Minato-ku
TOKYO 105-0013
MONACO
EDITIONS VICTOR GADOURY
57 rue Grimaldi "Le Panorama"
98000 MONACO
NETHERLANDS
MEVIUS NUMISBOOKS INTERNATIONAL BV
Oosteinde 97
7671 AT VRIEZENVEEN
SCHULMAN BV, Laurens
Brinklaan 84a
1404 GM BUSSUM
VERSCHOOR, Munthandel
Binnensingel 3
3291 TB STRIJEN
WESTERHOF, Jille Binne
Trekpad 38-40
8742 KP BURGWERD
NORWAY
OSLO MYNTHANDEL AS
Postboks 355 Sentrum
0101 OSLO
PORTUGAL
NUMISPORTO LDA
Av. Combatentes Grande Guerra 610 Lj6
4200-186 PORTO
SINGAPORE
TAISEI STAMPS & COINS
116 Middle Road #09-02
IBC Enterpr. house
188972 SINGAPORE
SPAIN
CALICO, X. & F.
Plaza del Angel 2
08002 BARCELONA
CAYON - JANO S.L.
Alcala 35
28014 MADRID
SEGARRA, Fernando P.
Plaza Mayor 26
28012 MADRID
VICO S.A., Jesús
Jorge Juan n 83 Duplicado
28009 MADRID
SWEDEN
NORDLINDS MYNTHANDEL AB
P.O. Box 5132
102 43 STOCKHOLM
SWITZERLAND
HESS AG, Adolph
Postfach 7070
8023 ZÜRICH
HESS-DIVO AG
Postfach 7070
8023 ZÜRICH
NUMISMATICA GENEVENSIS S.A.
1 Rond-Point de Plainpalais
1205 GENEVE
LHS NUMISMATICS LTD.
P.O. Box 2553 8022 ZÜRICH
STERNBERG AG, Frank
Schanzengasse 10
8001 ZÜRICH

UNITED KINGDOM
BALDWIN & SONS Ltd
Adelphi Terrace 11
LONDON, WC2N 6BJ
DAVIES, Paul, Ltd.
P.O. Box 17
ILKLEY, W.Yorkshire LS29 8TZ
DIX NOONAN WEBB
16 Bolton Street, Piccadilly
LONDON W1J 8BQ
EIMER, Christopher
P.O. Box 352
LONDON NW11 7RF
FORMAT OF BIRMINGHAM Ltd
Burlington Court 18 Lower Temple Street
BIRMINGHAM B2 4JD
KNIGHTSBRIDGE COINS
Duke Street 43 St. James's
LONDON SW1Y 6DD
LUBBOCK & SON Ltd
P.O. Box 35732
LONDON E14 7WB
NUMISMATICA ARS CLASSICA AG
3rd Floor Genavco House
17 Waterloo Place
LONDON SW1 4AR
RASMUSSEN, MARK
P.O. Box 42
BETCHWORTH RH3 7YR
RUDD, Chris
P. O. Box 222
AYLSHAM, Norfolk NR11 6TY
SPINK & SON, Ltd
69 Southampton Row Bloomsbury
LONDON WC1B 4ET
USA
BASOK, Alexander
1954 First Street #186
HIGHLAND PARK, IL 60035
BERK, Ltd., Harlan J.
North Clark Street, 31
CHICAGO, IL 60602
BULLOWA, C.E. - COINHUNTER
1616 Walnut Street, Suite 2112
PHILADELPHIA, PA 19103
CLASSICAL NUMISMATIC GROUP
P.O. Box 479
LANCASTER, PA 17608-0479
COIN AND CURRENCY INSTITUTE, Inc.
P.O. Box 1057
CLIFTON, NJ 07014
COIN GALLERIES
123 West 57th Street
NEW YORK, NY 10019
CRAIG, Freeman
P.O. Box 4176
SAN RAFAEL, CA 94913
DAVISSON'S, LTD.
COLD SPRING, MN 56320-1050
DUNIGAN, Mike
5332 Birchman
FORT WORTH, TX 76107
FREEMAN & SEAR
P.O. Box 641352
LOS ANGELES, CA 90064-6352
FROSETH, INC.
P.O. Box 23116
MINNEAPOLIS, MN 55423
GEORGE FREDERICK KOLBE - FINE NUMISMATIC BOOKS
P.O. Drawer 3100
CRESTLINE, CA 92325-3100
GILLIO, INC.
8 West Figueroa Street
SANTA BARBARA, CA 93101
HARVEY, Stephen
P.O. Box 3778
BEVERLY HILLS, CA 90212
KERN, Jonathan K.
441 South Ashland Avenue
LEXINGTON, KY 40502-2114
KOVACS, Frank L.
P.O. Box 151790
SAN RAFAEL, CA 94915-1790
KREINDLER, B. & H.
236 Altessa Blvd.
MELVILLE, NY 11747
MALTER GALLERIES, Inc.
17003 Ventura Boulevard, Suite 205
ENCINO, CA 91316
MARGOLIS, Richard
P.O. Box 2054
TEANECK, NJ 07666
MARKOV, Dmitry
P.O. Box 950
NEW YORK, NY 10272
MILCAREK, Dr. Ron
P.O. Box 1028
GREENFIELD, MA 01302
PEGASI NUMISMATICS
P.O. Box 131040
ANN ARBOR, MI 48113
PONTERIO & ASSOCIATES, INC.
1818 Robinson Avenue
SAN DIEGO, CA 92103
RARCOA, INC.
6262 South Route 83, Suite 200
WILLOWBROOK, IL 60527-2998
RARE COIN GALLERIES
P.O. Box 569
GLENDALE, CA 91209
ROSENBLUM, William M.
P.O. Box 355
EVERGREEN, CO 80437-0355
RYNEARSON, Dr. Paul
P.O. Box 4009
MALIBU, CA 90264
STACK'S
123 West 57th Street
NEW YORK, NY 10019
STEPHENS, INC., Karl
P.O. Box 3038
FALLBROOK, CA 92088
SUBAK, INC.
22 West Monroe Street, Room 1506
CHICAGO, IL 60603
TELLER NUMISMATIC ENTERPRISES
16055 Ventura Boulevard, Suite 635
ENCINO, CA 91436
WADDELL, Edward J., Ltd.
P.O. Box 3759
FREDERICK, MD 21705-3759
WORLD-WIDE COINS OF CALIFORNIA
P.O. Box 3684
SANTA ROSA, CA 95402
VENEZUELA
NUMISMATICA GLOBUS
Apartado de Correos 50418
CARACAS 1050

are generally enclosed by parentheses with 'ND' at the left, for example ND(2001).

Timing differentials between some era of reckoning, particularly the 354-day Mohammedan and 365-day Christian years, cause situations whereby coins which carry dates for both eras exist bearing two year dates from one calendar combined with a single date from another.

Countermarked Coinage is presented with both 'Countermark Date' and 'Host Coin' date for each type. Actual date representation follows the rules outlined above.

DENOMINATIONS

The second basic consideration to be met in the attribution of a coin is the determination of denomination. Since denominations are usually expressed in numeric rather than word form on a coin, this is usually quite easily accomplished on coins from nations which use Western numerals, except in those instances where issues are devoid of any mention of face value, and denomination must be attributed by size, metallic composition or weight. Coins listed in this volume are generally illustrated in actual size.

The sphere of countries stretching from North Africa through the Orient, on which numeric symbols generally unfamiliar to Westerners are employed, often provide the collector with a much greater challenge. This is particularly true on nearly all pre-20th Century issues. On some of the more modern issues and increasingly so as the years progress, Western-style numerals usually presented in combination with the local numeric system are becoming more commonplace on these coins.

The included table of Standard International Numeral Systems presents charts of the basic numeric designations found on coins of non-Western origin. Although denomination numerals are generally prominently displayed on coins, it must be remembered that these are general representations of characters, which individual coin engravers may have rendered in widely varying styles. Where numeric or script denominations designation forms peculiar to a given coin or country apply, such as the script used on some Persian (Iranian) issues. They are so indicated or illustrated in conjunction with the appropriate listings.

MINTAGES

Quantities minted of each date are indicated where that information is available, generally stated in millions or rounded off to the nearest 10,000 pieces when more exact figures are not available. On quantities of a few thousand or less, actual mintages are generally indicated. For combined mintage figures the abbreviation "Inc. Above" means Included Above, while "Inc. Below" means Included Below. "Est." beside a mintage figure indicates the number given is an estimate or mintage limit.

METALS

Each numbered type listing will contain a description of the coins metallic content. The traditional coinage metals and their symbolic chemical abbreviations sometimes used in this catalog are:

Platinum - (PT)	Copper - (Cu)
Gold - (Au)	Brass -
Silver - (Ag)	Copper-nickel- (CN)
Billion -	Lead - (Pb)
Nickel - (Ni)	Steel -
Zinc - (Zn)	Tin - (Sn)
Bronze - (Ae)	Aluminum - (Al)

Modern commemorative coins have employed still more unusual methods such as bimetallic coins, color applications and precious metal or gem inlays.

PRECIOUS METAL WEIGHTS

Listings of weight, fineness and actual silver (ASW), gold (AGW), platinum or palladium (APW) content of most machine-struck silver, gold, platinum and palladium coins are provided in this edition. This information will be found incorporated in each separate type listing, along with other data related to the coin.

The ASW, AGW or APW figure can be multiplied by the spot price of each precious metal to determine the current intrinsic value of any coin accompanied by these designations.

As the silver and gold bullion markets have advanced and declined sharply over the years, the fineness and total precious metal content of coins has become especially significant where bullion coins - issues which trade on the basis of their intrinsic metallic content rather than numismatic value - are concerned. In many instances, such issues have become worth more in bullion form than their nominal collector values or denominations indicate.

BULLION VALUE

The simplest method for determining the bullion value of a precious metal coin is to multiply the actual precious metal weight by the current spot price for that metal. A silver coin with a .6822 actual silver weight (ASW) would have an intrinsic value of $6.65 when the spot price of silver is $9.75. If the spot price of silver rose to $11.00 that same coins intrinsic value would rise to $7.50.

Valuations for most of the silver, gold, platinum and palladium coins listed in this edition are based on assumed market values of **$9.75** per troy ounce for silver, **$550** for gold, **$1000** for platinum, and **$285** for palladium. To arrive at accurate current market indications for these issues, increase or decrease the valuations appropriately based on any variations in these indicated levels.

PHOTOGRAPHS

To assist the reader in coin identification, every effort has been made to present actual size photographs of every coinage type listed. Obverse and reverse are illustrated, except when a change in design is restricted to one side, and the coin has a diameter of 39mm or larger, in which case only the side required for identification of the type is generally illustrated. All coins up to 60mm are illustrated actual size, to the nearest 1/2mm up to 25mm, and to the nearest 1mm thereafter. Coins larger than 60mm diameter are illustrated in reduced size, with the actual size noted in the descriptive text block. Where slight change in size is important to coin type identification, actual millimeter measurements are stated.

VALUATIONS

Values quoted in this catalog represent the current market and are compiled from recommendations provided and verified through various source documents and specialized consultants. It should be stressed, however, that this book is intended to serve only as an aid for evaluating coins, actual market conditions are constantly changing and additional influences, such as particularly strong local demand for certain coin series, fluctuation of international exchange rates, changes in spot price of precious metals and worldwide collection patterns must also be considered. Publication of this catalog is not intended as a solicitation by the publisher, editors or contributors to buy or sell the coins listed at the prices indicated.

All valuations are stated in U.S. dollars, based on careful assessment of the varied international collector market. Valuations for coins priced below $100.00 are generally stated in full amounts - i.e. 37.50 or 95.00 - while valuations at or above that figure are rounded off in even dollars - i.e. $125.00 is expressed 125. A comma is added to indicate thousands of dollars in value.

For the convenience of overseas collectors and for U.S. collectors doing business with overseas dealers, the base exchange rate for the national currencies of approximately 180 countries are presented in the Foreign Exchange Table.

It should be noted that when particularly select uncirculated or proof-like examples of uncirculated coins become available they can be expected to command proportionately high premiums. Such examples in reference to choice Germanic Thalers are referred to as "erst schlage" or first strikes.

NEW ISSUES

All newly released coins dated up to the year 2006 that have been physically observed by our staff or identified by reliable sources and have been confirmed by press time have been incorporated in this edition. Exceptions exist in some countries where current date coin production lags far behind or information on current issues is less accessible.

SETS

Listings in this catalog for specimen, proof and mint sets are for official, government-produced sets. In many instances privately packaged sets also exist.

Mint Sets/Fleur de Coin Sets: Specially prepared by worldwide mints to provide banks, collectors and government dignitaries with examples of current coinage. Usually subjected to rigorous inspection to insure that top quality specimens of selected business strikes are provided.

Specimen Sets: Forerunners of today's proof sets. In most cases the coins were specially struck, perhaps even double struck, to produce a very soft or matte finish on the effigies and fields, along with high, sharp, "wire" rims. The finish is rather dull to the naked eye.

The original purpose of these sets was to provide VIPs, monarchs and mintmasters around the world with samples of the highest quality workmanship of a particular mint. These were usually housed in elaborate velvet-lined leather and metal cases.

Proof-like Sets are relatively new to the field of numismatics. During the mid 1950s the Royal Canadian Mint furnished the hobby with specially selected early business strike coins that exhibited some qualities similar to proof coinage. However, the "proof-like" fields are generally flawed and the edges are rounded. These pieces are not double struck. These are commonly encountered in cardboard holders, later in soft plastic or pliofilm packaging. Of late, the Royal Canadian Mint packages such sets in rigid plastic cases.

Many worldwide officially issued proof sets would in reality fall into this category upon careful examination of the quality of the coin's finish.

Another term encountered in this category is "Special Select," used to describe the crowns of the Union of South Africa and 100-schilling coins produced for collectors in the late 1970s by the Austrian Mint.

Proof Sets: This is undoubtedly among the most misused terms in the hobby, not only by collectors and dealers, but also by many of the world mints.

A true proof set must be at least double-struck on specially prepared polished planchets and struck using dies (often themselves polished) of the highest quality.

Modern-day proof quality consists of frosted effigies surrounded by absolute mirror-like fields.

Listings for proof sets in this catalog are for officially issued proof sets so designated by the issuing authority, and may or may not possess what are considered modern proof quality standards.

It is necessary for collectors to acquire the knowledge to allow them to differentiate true proof sets from would-be proof sets and proof-like sets which may be encountered.

CONDITIONS/GRADING

Wherever possible, coin valuations are given in four or five grades of preservation. For modern commemoratives, which do not circulate, only uncirculated values are usually sufficient. Proof issues are indicated by the word "Proof" next to the date, with valuation proceeded by the word "value" following the mintage. For very recent circulating coins and coins of limited value, one, two or three grade values are presented.

There are almost no grading guides for world coins. What follows is an attempt to help bridge that gap until a detailed, illustrated guide becomes available.

Coin Alignment

Medal Alignment

COIN vs MEDAL ALIGNMENT

Some coins are struck with obverse and reverse aligned at a rotation of 180 degrees from each other. When a coin is held for vertical viewing with the obverse design aligned upright and the index finger and thumb at the top and bottom, upon rotation from left to right for viewing the reverse, the latter will be upside down. Such alignment is called "coin rotation." Other coins are struck with the obverse and reverse designs mated on an alignment of zero or 360 degrees. If such an example is held and rotated as described, the reverse will appear upright. This is the alignment, which is generally observed in the striking of medals, and for that reason coins produced in this manner are considered struck in "medal rotation". In some instances, often through error, certain coin issues have been struck to both alignment standards, creating interesting collectible varieties, which will be found noted in some listings. In addition, some countries are now producing coins with other designated obverse to reverse alignments which are considered standard for this type.

In grading world coins, there are two elements to look for: 1) Overall wear, and 2) loss of design details, such as strands of hair, feathers on eagles, designs on coats of arms, etc.

The age, rarity or type of a coin should not be a consideration in grading.

Grade each coin by the weaker of the two sides. This method appears to give results most nearly consistent with conservative American Numismatic Association standards for U.S. coins. Split grades, i.e., F/VF for obverse and reverse, respectively, are normally no more than one grade apart. If the two sides are more than one grade apart, the series of coins probably wears differently on each side and should then be graded by the weaker side alone.

Grade by the amount of overall wear and loss of design detail evident on each side of the coin. On coins with a moderately small design element, which is prone to early wear, grade by that design alone. For example, the 5-ore (KM#554) of Sweden has a crown above the monogram on which the beads on the arches show wear most clearly. So, grade by the crown alone.

For **Brilliant Uncirculated** (BU) grades there will be no visible signs of wear or handling, even under a 30-power microscope. Full mint luster will be present. Ideally no bags marks will be evident.

For **Uncirculated** (Unc.) grades there will be no visible signs of wear or handling, even under a 30-power microscope. Bag marks may be present.

For **Almost Uncirculated** (AU), all detail will be visible. There will be wear only on the highest point of the coin. There will often be half or more of the original mint luster present.

On the **Extremely Fine** (XF or EF) coin, there will be about 95% of the original detail visible. Or, on a coin with a design with no inner detail to wear down, there will be a light wear over nearly all the coin. If a small design is used as the grading area, about 90% of the original detail will be visible. This latter rule stems from the logic that a smaller amount of detail needs to be present because a small area is being used to grade the whole coin.

The **Very Fine** (VF) coin will have about 75% of the original detail visible. Or, on a coin with no inner detail, there will be moderate wear over the entire coin. Corners of letters and numbers may be weak. A small grading area will have about 66% of the original detail.

For **Fine** (F), there will be about 50% of the original detail visible. Or, on a coin with no inner detail, there will be fairly heavy wear over all of the coin. Sides of letters will be weak. A typically uncleaned coin will often appear as dirty or dull. A small grading area will have just under 50% of the original detail.

On the **Very Good** (VG) coin, there will be about 25% of the original detail visible. There will be heavy wear on all of the coin.

The **Good** (G) coin's design will be clearly outlined but with substantial wear. Some of the larger detail may be visible. The rim may have a few weak spots of wear.

On the **About Good** (AG) coin, there will typically be only a silhouette of a large design. The rim will be worn down into the letters if any.

Strong or weak strikes, partially weak strikes, damage, corrosion, attractive or unattractive toning, dipping or cleaning should be described along with the above grades. These factors affect the quality of the coin just as do wear and loss of detail, but are easier to describe.

STANDARD INTERNATIONAL GRADING TERMINOLOGY AND ABBREVIATIONS

	PROOF	UNCIRCULATED	EXTREMELY FINE	VERY FINE
U.S. and ENGLISH SPEAKING LANDS	PRF	UNC	EF or XF	VF
BRAZIL	—	(1)FDC or FC	(3) S	(5) MBC
DENMARK	M	0	01	1+
FINLAND	00	0	01	1+
FRANCE	FB Flan Bruni	FDC Fleur de Coin	SUP Superbe	TTB Très très beau
GERMANY	PP Polierte Platte	STG Stempelglanz	VZ Vorzüglich	SS Sehr schön
ITALY	FS Fondo Specchio	FDC Fior di Conio	SPL Splendido	BB Bellissimo
JAPAN	—	未使用	極美品	美品
NETHERLANDS	— Proef	FDC Fleur de Coin	Pr. Prachtig	Z.f. Zeer fraai
NORWAY	M	0	01	1+
PORTUGAL	—	Soberba	Bela	MBC
SPAIN	Prueba	SC	EBC	MBC
SWEDEN	Polerad	0	01	1+

Sending Scanned Images by Email

Over the past 2 years or so, we have been receiving an ever-increasing flow of scanned images from sources worldwide. Unfortunately, many of these scans could not be used due to the type of scan, or simple incompatability with our systems. We appreciate the effort it takes to produce these images and accuracy they add to the catalog listings.

Here are a few simple instructions to follow when producing these scans. We encourage you to continue sending new images or upgrades to those currently illustrated and please do not hesitate to ask questions about this process.

— Scan all images within a resolution range of 200 dpi to 300 dpi
— Size setting should be at 100%
— Scan in true 4-color
— Save images as 'jpeg' or 'tiff' and name in such a way, which clearly identifies the country of origin
— Please email with a request to confirm receipt of the attachment
— Please send images to Randy.Thern@fwpubs.com

FOREIGN EXCHANGE TABLE

The latest foreign exchange fixed rates below apply to trade with banks in the country of origin. The left column shows the number of units per U.S. dollar at the official rate. The right column shows the number of units per dollar at the free market rate.

Country	Official #/$	Market #/$
Afghanistan (New Afghani)	49.6	–
Albania (Lek)	102	–
Algeria (Dinar)	70.8	–
Andorra uses Euro	.83	–
Angola (Readjust Kwanza)	80	–
Anguilla uses E.C.Dollar	2.70	–
Antigua uses E.C.Dollar	2.70	–
Argentina (Peso)	3.08	–
Armenia (Dram)	450	–
Aruba (Florin)	1.79	–
Australia (Dollar)	1.35	–
Austria (Euro)	.83	–
Azerbaijan (Manat)	4,600	–
Bahamas (Dollar)	1.00	–
Bahrain Is.(Dinar)	.377	–
Bangladesh (Taka)	68	–
Barbados (Dollar)	2.00	–
Belarus (Ruble)	2,150	–
Belgium (Euro)	.83	–
Belize (Dollar)	1.98	–
Benin uses CFA Franc West	545	–
Bermuda (Dollar)	1.00	–
Bhutan (Ngultrum)	44.3	–
Bolivia (Boliviano)	8.00	–
Bosnia-Herzegovina (Deutschmark)	1.63	–
Botswana (Pula)	5.50	–
British Virgin Islands uses U.S.Dollar	1.00	–
Brazil (Real)	2.15	–
Brunei (Dollar)	1.63	–
Bulgaria (Lev)	1.63	–
Burkina Faso uses CFA Fr.West	545	–
Burma (Kyat)	6.42	1,250
Burundi (Franc)	975	–
Cambodia (Riel)	4,100	–
Cameroon uses CFA Franc Central	545	–
Canada (Dollar)	1.14	–
Cape Verde (Escudo)	91.8	–
Cayman Is.(Dollar)	0.82	–
Central African Rep.	545	–
CFA Franc Central	545	–
CFA Franc West	545	–
CFP Franc	99.3	–
Chad uses CFA Franc Central	545	–
Chile (Peso)	525	–
China, P.R. (Renminbi Yuan)	8.037	–
Colombia (Peso)	2,255	–
Comoros (Franc)	410	–
Congo uses CFA Franc Central	545	–
Congo-Dem.Rep. (Congolese Franc)	430	–
Cook Islands (Dollar)	1.73	–
Costa Rica (Colon)	503	–
Croatia (Kuna)	6.09	–
Cuba (Peso)	1.00	27
Cyprus (Pound)	.48	–
Czech Republic (Koruna)	23.8	–
Denmark (Danish Krone)	6.21	–
Djibouti (Franc)	175	–
Dominica uses E.C.Dollar	2.70	–
Dominican Republic (Peso)	32.5	–
East Caribbean (Dollar)	2.70	–
Ecuador uses U.S. Dollar	1.00	–
Egypt (Pound)	5.74	–
El Salvador uses U.S. Dollar	1.00	–
England	.57	–
Equatorial Guinea uses CFA Franc Central	545	–
Eritrea (Nafka)	15	–
Estonia (Kroon)	13.02	–
Ethiopia (Birr)	8.73	–
Euro	.83	–
Falkland Is. (Pound)	.57	–
Faroe Islands (Krona)	6.21	–
Fiji Islands (Dollar)	1.75	–
Finland (Euro)	.83	–
France (Euro)	.83	–
French Polynesia uses CFP Franc	99.3	–
Gabon (CFA Franc)	545	–
Gambia (Dalasi)	28.3	–
Georgia (Lari)	1.83	–
Germany (Euro)	.83	–
Ghana (Cedi)	9,160	–
Gibraltar (Pound)	.57	–
Great Britain	.57	–
Greece (Euro)	.83	–
Greenland uses Danish Krone	6.21	–
Grenada uses E.C.Dollar	2.70	–
Guatemala (Quetzal)	7.63	–
Guernsey (Pound Sterling)	.57	–
Guinea Bissau (CFA Franc)	545	–
Guinea Conakry (Franc)	4475	–
Guyana (Dollar)	200	–
Haiti (Gourde)	41.9	–
Honduras (Lempira)	18.9	–
Hong Kong (Dollar)	7.76	–
Hungary (Forint)	210	–
Iceland (Krona)	66.2	–
India (Rupee)	44.3	–
Indonesia (Rupiah)	9,200	–
Iran (Rial)	9.130	–
Iraq (Dinar)	1,523	1,930
Ireland (Euro)	.83	–
Isle of Man (Pound Sterling)	.57	–
Israel (New Sheqalim)	4.71	–
Italy (Euro)	.83	–
Ivory Coast uses CFA Franc West	545	–
Jamaica (Dollar)	63	–
Japan (Yen)	117.6	–
Jersey (Pound Sterling)	.57	–
Jordan (Dinar)	.71	–
Kazakhstan (Tenge)	130	–
Kenya (Shilling)	72	–
Kiribati uses Australian Dollar	1.35	–
Korea-PDR (Won)	2.2	500
Korea-Rep. (Won)	975	–
Kuwait (Dinar)	.292	–
Kyrgyzstan (Som)	417	–
Laos (Kip)	10,400	–
Latvia (Lat)	.58	–
Lebanon (Pound)	1,500	–
Lesotho (Maloti)	6.24	–
Liberia (Dollar) "JJ"	57	-
Libya (Dinar)	1.34	–
Liechtenstein uses Swiss Franc	1.297	–
Lithuania (Litas)	2.88	–
Luxembourg (Euro)	.83	–
Macao (Pataca)	7.99	–
Macedonia (New Denar)	51	–
Madagascar (Franc)	2,220	–
Malawi (Kwacha)	135	–
Malaysia (Ringgit)	3.71	–
Maldives (Rufiya)	12.8	–
Mali uses CFA Franc West	545	–
Malta (Lira)	.36	–
Marshall Islands uses U.S.Dollar	1.00	–
Mauritania (Ouguiya)	270	–
Mauritius (Rupee)	30.7	–
Mexico (Peso)	10.69	–
Moldova (Leu)	13	–
Monaco uses Euro	.83	–
Mongolia (Tugrik)	1,200	–
Montenegro uses Euro	.83	–
Montserrat uses E.C.Dollar	2.70	–
Morocco (Dirham)	9.73	–
Mozambique (Metical)	26,850	–
Myanmar (Burma) (Kyat)	6.42	1,250
Namibia (Rand)	6.24	–
Nauru uses Australian Dollar	1.35	–
Nepal (Rupee)	70.9	–
Netherlands (Euro)	.83	–
Netherlands Antilles (Gulden)	1.79	–
New Caledonia uses CFP Franc	99.3	–
New Zealand (Dollar)	1.52	–
Nicaragua (Cordoba Oro)	17.15	–
Niger uses CFA Franc West	545	–
Nigeria (Naira)	130	–
Northern Ireland (Pound Sterling)	.57	–
Norway (Krone)	6.64	–
Oman (Rial)	.385	–
Pakistan (Rupee)	59.9	–
Palau uses U.S.Dollar	1.00	–
Panama (Balboa) uses U.S.Dollar	1.00	–
Papua New Guinea (Kina)	3.10	–
Paraguay (Guarani)	5,970	–
Peru (Nuevo Sol)	3.33	–
Philippines (Peso)	51	–
Poland (Zloty)	3.19	–
Portugal (Euro)	.83	–
Qatar (Riyal)	3.64	–
Romania (New Leu)	2.89	–
Russia (New Ruble)	27.93	–
Rwanda (Franc)	545	–
St.Helena (Pound)	.57	–
St.Kitts uses E.C.Dollar	2.70	–
St.Lucia uses E.C.Dollar	2.70	–
St.Vincent uses E.C.Dollar	2.70	–
San Marino uses Euro	.83	–
Sao Tome e Principe (Dobra)	7100	–
Saudi Arabia (Riyal)	3.751	–
Scotland (Pound Sterling)	.57	–
Senegal uses CFA Franc West	545	–
Serbia (Dinar)	72.8	–
Seychelles (Rupee)	5.52	6.40
Sierra Leone (Leone)	2,950	–
Singapore (Dollar)	1.63	–
Slovakia (Sk. Koruna)	31	–
Slovenia (Tolar)	200	–
Solomon Is.(Dollar)	7.59	–
Somalia (Shilling)	1600	–
Somaliland (Somali Shilling)	1,800	4,000
South Africa (Rand)	6.24	–
Spain (Euro)	.83	–
Sri Lanka (Rupee)	102	–
Sudan (Dinar)	230	300
Surinam (Dollar)	2.74	–
Swaziland (Lilangeni)	6.24	–
Sweden (Krona)	7.86	–
Switzerland (Franc)	1.29	–
Syria (Pound)	52.2	–
Taiwan (NT Dollar)	32.5	–
Tajikistan (Somoni)	3.21	–
Tanzania (Shilling)	1,200	–
Thailand (Baht)	38.8	–
Togo uses CFAFranc West	545	–
Tonga (Paíanga)	2.05	–
Transdniestra (Ruble)	6.51	–
Trinidad & Tobago (Dollar)	6.29	–
Tunisia (Dinar)	1.35	–
Turkey (New Lira)	1.31	–
Turkmenistan (Manat)	5,200	–
Turks & Caicos uses U.S.Dollar	1.00	–
Tuvalu uses Australian Dollar	1.35	–
Uganda (Shilling)	1,825	–
Ukraine (Hryvnia)	5.06	–
United Arab Emirates (Dirham)	3.67	–
United Kingdom (Pound Sterling)	.57	–
Uruguay (Peso Uruguayo)	24.3	–
Uzbekistan (Som)	1,200	–
Vanuatu (Vatu)	113	–
Vatican City uses Euro	.83	–
Venezuela (Bolivar)	2,150	2,000
Vietnam (Dong)	15,915	–
Western Samoa (Tala)	2.74	–
Yemen (Rial)	195	–
Zambia (Kwacha)	3,300	–
Zimbabwe (Dollar)	100,000	–

If you collect world COINS

World Coin News
FROM THE PUBLISHERS OF THE STANDARD CATALOG OF WORLD COINS
January 2005
Strong 2005 NYINC show expected

World Coin News
FROM THE PUBLISHERS OF THE STANDARD CATALOG OF WORLD COINS
February 2005
Eliasberg collection yields discovery
New book examines escudos
Antiquities Act signed by Bush
Inside:
Party like its 1984
Victorian ties remain
Russia's Paul I

Check out *World Coin News*!

World Coin News is your one-stop monthly information source for world coin information. Get new issues, mintage totals, market reports, informative articles on coins from around the globe, and a large qualified marketplace letting you buy and sell with confidence.

Credit card customers dial toll-free **800-258-0929** Offer ABBLJ6

Mon.-Fri.
7 am – 8 pm
Sat.
8 am – 2 pm, CST

❑ ***Yes!*** Send me 4 issues of ***World Coin News***

4 issues U.S. only. . . $9.95
Save $5.85 off the newsstand cost!

Name____________________
Address____________________
City____________________
State____________________
Zip____________________

❑ Check or money order
(to ***World Coin News***, payable in U.S. funds)
❑ MasterCard ❑ Visa
❑ Discover/Novus ❑ American Express

Card #____________________
Expires: Mo.__________Yr.______
Signature____________________
Phone No.____________________
E-mail address____________________

It is ok to send me offers and information via e-mail. ❑ Yes ❑ No

World Coin News
Circulation Dept. ABBLJ6, 700 E. State St., Iola, WI 54990-0001 • www.worldcoinnews.net

AFGHANISTAN

The Islamic State of Afghanistan, which occupies a mountainous region of Southwest Asia, has an area of 251,825 sq. mi. (652,090 sq. km.) and a population of 25.59 million. Presently, about a fifth of the total population lives in exile as refugees, (mostly in Pakistan). Capital: Kabul. It is bordered by Iran, Pakistan, Turkmenistan, Uzbekistan, Tajikistan, and China's Sinkiang Province. Agriculture and herding are the principal industries; textile mills and cement factories add to the industrial sector. Cotton, wool, fruits, nuts, oil, sheepskin coats and hand-woven carpets are normally exported but foreign trade has been interrupted since 1979.

Because of its strategic position astride the ancient land route to India, Afghanistan (formerly known as Aryana and Khorasan) was invaded by Darius I, Alexander the Great, various Scythian tribes, the White Huns, the Arabs, the Turks, Genghis Khan, Tamerlane, the Mughals, the Persians, and in more recent times by Great Britain and Russia.

ISLAMIC STATE

SH1373-1381 / 1994-2002AD

STANDARD COINAGE

KM# 1043 500 AFGHANIS
19.8700 g., 0.9990 Silver 0.6382 oz. ASW, 37.9 mm. **Obv:** National arms **Rev:** Soccer ball on German map **Edge:** Reeded

Date	Mintage	F	VF	XF	Unc
2001 Proof	—	Value: 40.00			

ALBANIA

The Republic of Albania, a Balkan republic bounded by Macedonia, Greece, Montenegro, and the Adriatic Sea, has an area of 11,100 sq. mi. (28,748 sq. km.) and a population of 3.49 million. Capital: Tirane. The country is predominantly agricultural, although recent progress has been made in the manufacturing and mining sectors. Petroleum, chrome, iron, copper, cotton textiles, tobacco and wood products are exported.

MINT MARKS
L – London
R - Rome
V – Vienna

MONETARY SYSTEM
100 Qindar Leku = 1 Lek
100 Qindar Ari = 1 Frang Ar = 5 Lek

REPUBLIC

STANDARD COINAGE

KM# 87 20 LEKE
8.5400 g., Brass, 26.1 mm. **Subject:** Prehistoric art **Obv:** Horseman **Rev:** Ancient coin design with Apollo portrait **Edge:** Reeded

Date	Mintage	F	VF	XF	Unc	BU
2002	—	—	—	—	3.00	4.00

KM# 81 50 LEKE
7.5000 g., Copper-Nickel, 28 mm. **Subject:** Michaelangelo's "David" **Obv:** Towered building **Rev:** Statue's head and denomination **Edge:** Reeded

Date	Mintage	F	VF	XF	Unc	BU
2001	1,000	—	—	—	6.00	7.50

KM# 88 50 LEKE
11.9200 g., Brass, 28.1 mm. **Obv:** Value **Rev:** Sami Frasheri (1860-1904) **Edge:** Reeded

Date	Mintage	F	VF	XF	Unc	BU
2002	—	—	—	—	3.00	4.00

KM# 89 50 LEKE
11.8400 g., Brass, 28 mm. **Obv:** Jeronim De Rada **Rev:** Value **Edge:** Plain

Date	Mintage	F	VF	XF	Unc	BU
2003	—	—	—	—	3.00	4.00

KM# 86 50 LEKE
5.4600 g., Copper-Nickel, 24.2 mm. **Obv:** Value and legend **Rev:** Ancient Illyrian helmet **Edge:** Reeded

Date	Mintage	F	VF	XF	Unc	BU
2003 (2004)	200,000	—	—	—	6.00	7.50

KM# 90 50 LEKE
5.5000 g., Copper-Nickel, 24.2 mm. **Obv:** Wheel design **Rev:** Ancient bust above value **Edge:** Reeded

Date	Mintage	F	VF	XF	Unc	BU
2004	—	—	—	—	3.00	4.00

KM# 91 50 LEKE
5.5000 g., Copper-Nickel, 24.2 mm. **Obv:** Soldier **Rev:** Value **Edge:** Reeded

Date	Mintage	F	VF	XF	Unc	BU
2004	—	—	—	—	3.00	4.00

KM# 82 100 LEKE
15.7000 g., 0.9250 Silver 0.4669 oz. ASW, 32.65 mm. **Subject:** Michaelangelo's "David" **Obv:** Arch of Triumph **Rev:** Statue's upper half and denomination **Edge:** Plain

Date	Mintage	F	VF	XF	Unc	BU
2001	1,000	—	—	—	30.00	32.50

KM# 84 100 LEKE
15.0000 g., 0.9250 Silver 0.4461 oz. ASW, 32 mm. **Subject:** Albanian-European Integration **Obv:** Dove in flight **Rev:** European and Albanian maps **Edge:** Reeded

Date	Mintage	F	VF	XF	Unc	BU
2001	1,000	—	—	—	25.00	27.50

KM# 83 200 LEKE
7.6500 g., 0.9000 Gold 0.2214 oz. AGW, 25.45 mm. **Subject:** Michaelangelo's "David" **Obv:** City plaza **Rev:** Statue of "David" and denomination **Edge:** Reeded

Date	Mintage	F	VF	XF	Unc	BU
2001	500	—	—	—	185	220

KM# 85 200 LEKE
15.0000 g., 0.9250 Silver 0.4461 oz. ASW, 32 mm.
Subject: Albanian-European Integration **Obv:** Dove in flight **Rev:** Adult and infant hand **Edge:** Reeded

Date	Mintage	F	VF	XF	Unc	BU
2001	1,000	—	—	—	35.00	37.50

ALDERNEY

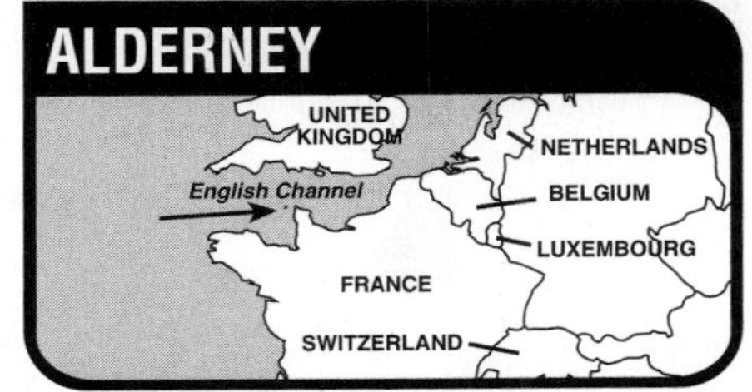

Alderney, the northernmost and third largest of the Channel Islands, separated from the coast of France by the dangerous 8-mile-wide tidal channel, has an area of 3 sq. mi. (8 km.) and a population of 1,686. It is a dependency of the British island of Guernsey, to the southwest. Capital: St. Anne. Principal industries are agriculture and raising cattle.

The Channel Islands have never been subject to the British Parliament and are self-governing units under the direct rule of the Crown acting through the Privy Council. Alderney is within the Bailiwick of Guernsey (q.v.). It is one of the nine Channel Islands, the only part of the Duchy of Normandy still belonging to the British Crown, and has been a British possession since the Norman Conquest of 1066. Legislation was only recently introduced for the issue of its own coinage, a right it now shares with Jersey and Guernsey. Alderney is a dependency of the British island of Guernsey, to the southwest.

RULERS
British

MONETARY SYSTEM
100 Pence = 1 Pound Sterling

DEPENDENCY

STANDARD COINAGE

KM# 24 5 POUNDS
28.2800 g., 0.9250 Silver 0.841 oz. ASW, 38.6 mm. **Ruler:** Elizabeth II **Subject:** Queen Elizabeth II - 50 Years of Reign **Obv:** Queen's head right **Rev:** Sword hilt and denomination with royal arms background **Rev. Designer:** Marcel Canioni **Edge:** Reeded

Date	Mintage	F	VF	XF	Unc	BU
2002 Proof	15,000	Value: 50.00				

KM# 25 5 POUNDS
28.2800 g., 0.9250 Silver 0.841 oz. ASW, 38.6 mm. **Ruler:** Elizabeth II **Subject:** Queen's Golden Jubilee **Obv:** Queen's portrait **Rev:** Honor guard and trumpets **Edge:** Reeded

Date	Mintage	F	VF	XF	Unc	BU
2002 Proof	15,000	Value: 50.00				

KM# 27 5 POUNDS
28.2800 g., Copper-Nickel, 38.6 mm. **Ruler:** Elizabeth II **Obv:** Queen's portrait **Rev:** Diana accepting flowers from girl **Edge:** Reeded

Date	Mintage	F	VF	XF	Unc	BU
2002	—	—	—	—	13.50	15.00

KM# 27a 5 POUNDS
28.2800 g., 0.9250 Silver 0.841 oz. ASW, 38.6 mm. **Ruler:** Elizabeth II **Subject:** Princess Diana **Obv:** Queen's portrait **Rev:** Diana accepting flowers from girl **Edge:** Reeded

Date	Mintage	F	VF	XF	Unc	BU
2002 Proof	20,000	Value: 45.00				

KM# 27b 5 POUNDS
39.9400 g., 0.9167 Gold 1.1771 oz. AGW, 38.6 mm. **Ruler:** Elizabeth II **Subject:** Princess Diana **Obv:** Queen's portrait **Rev:** Diana accepting flowers from girl **Edge:** Reeded

Date	Mintage	F	VF	XF	Unc	BU
2002 Proof	100	Value: 925				

KM# 29 5 POUNDS
28.2800 g., Copper-Nickel, 38.6 mm. **Ruler:** Elizabeth II **Subject:** The Duke of Wellington **Obv:** Queen's portrait **Rev:** Coat of arms, castle and portrait **Edge:** Reeded

Date	Mintage	F	VF	XF	Unc	BU
2002	—	—	—	—	12.50	14.00

KM# 29a 5 POUNDS
28.2800 g., 0.9250 Silver 0.841 oz. ASW, 38.6 mm. **Ruler:** Elizabeth II **Subject:** The Duke of Wellington **Obv:** Queen's portrait **Rev:** Multicolor coat of arms, portrait and castle **Edge:** Reeded

Date	Mintage	VG	F	VF	XF	Unc
2002 Proof	15,000	Value: 55.00				

KM# 29b 5 POUNDS
39.9400 g., 0.9167 Gold 1.1771 oz. AGW, 38.6 mm. **R uler:** Elizabeth II **Subject:** The Duke of Wellington **Obv:** Queen's portrait **Rev:** Coat of arms, castle and portrait **Edge:** Reeded

Date	Mintage	VG	F	VF	XF	Unc
2002 Proof	200	Value: 900				

KM# 44 5 POUNDS
28.2800 g., Copper-Nickel, 38.6 mm. **Ruler:** Elizabeth II **Obv:** Queen Elizabeth II **Rev:** HMS Mary Rose **Edge:** Reeded

Date	Mintage	F	VF	XF	Unc	BU
2003	—	—	—	—	12.00	13.50

KM# 44a 5 POUNDS
28.2800 g., 0.9250 Silver 0.841 oz. ASW, 38.6 mm. **Ruler:** Elizabeth II **Obv:** Queen Elizabeth II **Rev:** HMS Mary Rose below multicolor flag **Edge:** Reeded

Date	Mintage	F	VF	XF	Unc	BU
2003 Proof	15,000	Value: 60.00				

KM# 45 5 POUNDS
28.2800 g., Copper-Nickel, 38.6 mm. **Ruler:** Elizabeth II **Obv:** Queen Elizabeth II **Rev:** Alfred the Great on ship **Edge:** Reeded

Date	Mintage	F	VF	XF	Unc	BU
2003	—	—	—	—	12.00	13.50

KM# 45a 5 POUNDS
28.2800 g., 0.9250 Silver 0.841 oz. ASW, 38.6 mm. **Ruler:** Elizabeth II **Obv:** Queen Elizabeth II **Rev:** Alfred the Great on ship below multicolor flag **Edge:** Reeded

Date	Mintage	F	VF	XF	Unc	BU
2003 Proof	15,000	Value: 60.00				

KM# 45b 5 POUNDS
39.9400 g., 0.9167 Gold 1.1771 oz. AGW, 38.6 mm. **Ruler:** Elizabeth II **Obv:** Queen Elizabeth II **Rev:** Alfred the Great on ship **Edge:** Reeded

Date	Mintage	F	VF	XF	Unc	BU
2003 Proof	500	Value: 975				

KM# 31 5 POUNDS
28.2800 g., Copper-Nickel, 38.6 mm. **Ruler:** Elizabeth II **Subject:** Prince William **Obv:** Queen's portrait **Rev:** Portrait with open shirt collar **Edge:** Reeded

Date	Mintage	F	VF	XF	Unc	BU
2003	—	—	—	—	16.50	18.00

KM# 31a 5 POUNDS
28.2800 g., 0.9250 Silver 0.841 oz. ASW, 38.6 mm. **Ruler:** Elizabeth II **Subject:** Prince William **Obv:** Queen's portrait **Rev:** Portrait with open shirt collar **Edge:** Reeded

Date	Mintage	F	VF	XF	Unc	BU
2003 Proof	—	Value: 47.50				

KM# 31b 5 POUNDS
39.9400 g., 0.9166 Gold 1.177 oz. AGW, 38.6 mm. **Ruler:** Elizabeth II **Subject:** Prince Willliam **Obv:** Queen's portrait **Rev:** Portrait with open shirt collar **Edge:** Reeded

Date	Mintage	F	VF	XF	Unc	BU
2003 Proof	200	Value: 950				

KM# 35 5 POUNDS
28.2800 g., 0.9250 Silver 0.841 oz. ASW, 38.6 mm. **Ruler:** Elizabeth II **Subject:** Last Flight of the Concorde **Obv:** Elizabeth II **Rev:** Concorde in flight **Edge:** Reeded

Date	Mintage	F	VF	XF	Unc	BU
2003 Proof	5,000	Value: 70.00				

KM# 35a 5 POUNDS
39.9400 g., 0.9166 Gold 1.177 oz. AGW, 38.6 mm. **Ruler:** Elizabeth II **Obv:** Elizabeth II **Rev:** Concorde in flight **Edge:** Reeded

Date	Mintage	F	VF	XF	Unc	BU
2003 Proof	500	Value: 925				

KM# 38 5 POUNDS
28.2800 g., Copper-Nickel, 38.6 mm. **Ruler:** Elizabeth II **Obv:** Queen Elizabeth II **Rev:** Battleship and transports **Edge:** Reeded **Note:** D-Day

Date	Mintage	F	VF	XF	Unc	BU
2004	—	—	—	—	15.00	17.50

KM# 38a 5 POUNDS
28.2800 g., 0.9250 Silver 0.841 oz. ASW, 38.6 mm. **Ruler:** Elizabeth II

Date	Mintage	F	VF	XF	Unc	BU
2004 Proof	10,000	Value: 85.00				

KM# 38b 5 POUNDS
39.9400 g., 0.9167 Gold 1.1771 oz. AGW, 38.6 mm. **Ruler:** Elizabeth II

Date	Mintage	F	VF	XF	Unc	BU
2004 Proof	500	Value: 975				

KM# 42 5 POUNDS
28.2800 g., Copper-Nickel, 38.6 mm. **Ruler:** Elizabeth II **Obv:** Queen Elizabeth II **Rev:** Florence Nightingale **Edge:** Reeded

Date	Mintage	F	VF	XF	Unc	BU
2004	—	—	—	—	18.00	20.00

KM# 42a 5 POUNDS
28.2800 g., 0.9250 Silver 0.841 oz. ASW, 38.6 mm. **Ruler:** Elizabeth II **Obv:** Queen Elizabeth II **Rev:** Florence Nightingale **Edge:** Reeded

Date	Mintage	F	VF	XF	Unc	BU
2004 Proof	25,000	Value: 70.00				

KM# 43 5 POUNDS
28.2800 g., Copper-Nickel, 38.6 mm. **Ruler:** Elizabeth II **Obv:** Queen Elizabeth II **Rev:** Florence Nightingale above the Battle of Inkerman scene with one multicolor soldier **Edge:** Reeded

Date	Mintage	F	VF	XF	Unc	BU
2004	—	—	—	—	22.50	25.00

KM# 43a 5 POUNDS
28.2800 g., 0.9250 Silver 0.841 oz. ASW, 38.6 mm. **Ruler:** Elizabeth II **Obv:** Queen Elizabeth II **Rev:** Florence Nightingale above Battle of Inkerman scene with one multicolor soldier **Edge:** Reeded

Date	Mintage	F	VF	XF	Unc	BU
2004 Proof	10,000	Value: 85.00				

KM# 43b 5 POUNDS
39.9400 g., 0.9166 Gold 1.177 oz. AGW, 38.6 mm. **Ruler:** Elizabeth II **Obv:** Queen Elizabeth II **Rev:** Florence Nightingale above Battle of Inkerman scene with one multicolor soldier **Edge:** Reeded

Date	Mintage	F	VF	XF	Unc	BU
2004 Proof	500	Value: 975				

KM# 47 5 POUNDS
28.2800 g., Copper-Nickel, 38.6 mm. **Ruler:** Elizabeth II **Obv:** Queen Elizabeth II **Rev:** Locomotive, The Rocket **Edge:** Reeded

Date	Mintage	F	VF	XF	Unc	BU
2004	—	—	—	—	12.00	14.00

KM# 47a 5 POUNDS
28.2800 g., 0.9250 Silver 0.841 oz. ASW, 38.6 mm. **Ruler:** Elizabeth II **Obv:** Queen Elizabeth II **Rev:** Locomotive, The Rocket **Edge:** Reeded

Date	Mintage	F	VF	XF	Unc	BU
2004 Proof	20,000	Value: 60.00				

KM# 47b 5 POUNDS
39.9400 g., 0.9167 Gold 1.1771 oz. AGW, 38.6 mm. **Ruler:** Elizabeth II **Obv:** Queen Elizabeth II **Rev:** Locomotive, The Rocket **Edge:** Reeded

Date	Mintage	F	VF	XF	Unc	BU
2004 Proof	500	Value: 975				

KM# 48 5 POUNDS
28.2800 g., Copper-Nickel, 38.6 mm. **Ruler:** Elizabeth II **Obv:** Queen Elizabeth II **Rev:** Locomotive, The Royal Scot **Edge:** Reeded

Date	Mintage	F	VF	XF	Unc	BU
2004	—	—	—	—	12.00	14.00

KM# 48a 5 POUNDS
28.2800 g., 0.9250 Silver 0.841 oz. ASW, 38.6 mm. **Ruler:** Elizabeth II **Obv:** Queen Elizabeth II **Rev:** Locomotive, The Royal Scot **Edge:** Reeded

Date	Mintage	F	VF	XF	Unc	BU
2004 Proof	10,000	Value: 60.00				

KM# 49 5 POUNDS
28.2800 g., Copper-Nickel, 38.6 mm. **Ruler:** Elizabeth II **Obv:** Queen Elizabeth II **Rev:** Locomotive, The Merchant Navy 21C1 **Edge:** Reeded

Date	Mintage	F	VF	XF	Unc	BU
2004	—	—	—	—	12.00	14.00

KM# 49a 5 POUNDS
28.2800 g., 0.9250 Silver 0.841 oz. ASW, 38.6 mm. **Ruler:** Elizabeth II **Obv:** Queen Elizabeth II **Rev:** Locomotive, The Merchant Navy 21C1 **Edge:** Reeded

Date	Mintage	F	VF	XF	Unc	BU
2004 Proof	10,000	Value: 60.00				

KM# 53a 5 POUNDS
28.2800 g., 0.9250 Silver 0.841 oz. ASW, 38.6 mm. **Ruler:** Elizabeth II **Subject:** End of WWII **Obv:** Elizabeth II by Maklouf **Rev:** Flag waving crowd **Edge:** Reeded

Date	Mintage	F	VF	XF	Unc	BU
2005 Proof	5,000	Value: 85.00				

KM# 53b 5 POUNDS
39.9400 g., 0.9167 Gold 1.1771 oz. AGW, 38.6 mm. **Ruler:** Elizabeth II **Subject:** End of WWII **Obv:** Elizabeth II by Maklouf **Rev:** Flag waving crowd **Edge:** Reeded

Date	Mintage	F	VF	XF	Unc	BU
2005 Proof	150	Value: 1,000				

KM# 54a 5 POUNDS
39.9400 g., 0.9167 Gold 1.1771 oz. AGW, 38.6 mm. **Ruler:** Elizabeth II **Subject:** WWII Liberation **Obv:** Elizabeth II by Maklouf **Rev:** Churchill flashing the "V" sign **Edge:** Reeded

Date	Mintage	F	VF	XF	Unc	BU
2005 Proof	150	Value: 1,000				

KM# 36 10 POUNDS
155.5170 g., 0.9250 Silver 4.625 oz. ASW, 65 mm. **Ruler:** Elizabeth II **Subject:** Last Flight of the Concorde **Obv:** Elizabeth II **Rev:** Gold-plated Concorde in flight **Edge:** Reeded

Date	Mintage	F	VF	XF	Unc	BU
2003 Proof	1,969	Value: 320				

KM# 55 10 POUNDS
155.5100 g., 0.9250 Silver 4.6248 oz. ASW, 65 mm. **Ruler:** Elizabeth II **Subject:** WWII Liberation **Obv:** Elizabeth II by Maklouf sign **Rev:** Churchill flashing the "V" **Edge:** Reeded

Date	Mintage	F	VF	XF	Unc	BU
2005 Proof	1,945	Value: 350				

KM# 28 25 POUNDS
7.9800 g., 0.9167 Gold 0.2352 oz. AGW, 22.05 mm. **Ruler:** Elizabeth II **Subject:** Princess Diana **Obv:** Queen's portrait **Rev:** Diana's cameo portrait above denomination **Edge:** Reeded

Date	Mintage	VG	F	VF	XF	Unc
2002 Proof	2,500	Value: 275				

KM# 30 25 POUNDS
7.9800 g., 0.9166 Gold 0.2352 oz. AGW, 22 mm. **Ruler:** Elizabeth II **Subject:** The Duke of Wellington **Obv:** Queen's portrait **Rev:** Coat of arms, castle and portrait **Edge:** Reeded

Date	Mintage	VG	F	VF	XF	Unc
2002 Proof	2,500	Value: 300				

KM# 32 25 POUNDS
7.9800 g., 0.9166 Gold 0.2352 oz. AGW, 22 mm. **Ruler:** Elizabeth II **Subject:** Prince William **Obv:** Queen's portrait **Rev:** Portrait with open shirt collar **Edge:** Reeded

Date	Mintage	F	VF	XF	Unc	BU
2003 Proof	1,500	Value: 325				

KM# 46 25 POUNDS
7.9800 g., 0.9167 Gold 0.2352 oz. AGW, 22 mm. **Ruler:** Elizabeth II **Obv:** Queen Elizabeth II **Rev:** HMS Mary Rose **Edge:** Reeded

Date	Mintage	F	VF	XF	Unc	BU
2003 Proof	2,500	Value: 365				

KM# 39 25 POUNDS
7.9800 g., 0.9167 Gold 0.2352 oz. AGW, 22 mm. **Ruler:** Elizabeth II **Subject:** D-Day **Obv:** Queen Elizabeth II **Rev:** Battleship and transports **Edge:** Reeded

Date	Mintage	F	VF	XF	Unc	BU
2004 Proof	500	Value: 325				

KM# 50 25 POUNDS
7.9800 g., 0.9167 Gold 0.2352 oz. AGW, 22 mm. **Ruler:** Elizabeth II **Obv:** Queen Elizabeth II **Rev:** Locomotive, The Rocket **Edge:** Reeded

Date	Mintage	F	VF	XF	Unc	BU
2004 Proof	2,500	Value: 365				

KM# 51 25 POUNDS
7.9800 g., 0.9167 Gold 0.2352 oz. AGW, 22 mm. **Ruler:** Elizabeth II **Obv:** Queen Elizabeth II **Rev:** Locomotive, The Merchant Navy 21C1 **Edge:** Reeded

Date	Mintage	F	VF	XF	Unc	BU
2004 Proof	1,500	Value: 365				

KM# 33 50 POUNDS
1000.0000 g., 0.9250 Silver 29.7394 oz. ASW, 100 mm. **Ruler:** Elizabeth II **Subject:** Prince William **Obv:** Queen's portrait **Rev:** Portrait with open shirt collar **Edge:** Reeded

Date	Mintage	F	VF	XF	Unc	BU
2003 Proof	500	Value: 995				

KM# 40 50 POUNDS
1000.0000 g., 0.9250 Silver 29.7394 oz. ASW, 100 mm. **Ruler:** Elizabeth II **Subject:** D-Day **Obv:** Queen Elizabeth II **Rev:** US and British troops wading ashore **Edge:** Reeded

Date	Mintage	F	VF	XF	Unc	BU
2004 Proof	600	Value: 1,200				

KM# 34 100 POUNDS
1000.0000 g., 0.9166 Gold 29.4694 oz. AGW, 100 mm. **Ruler:** Elizabeth II **Subject:** Prince William **Obv:** Queen's portrait **Rev:** Portrait with open shirt collar **Edge:** Reeded

Date	Mintage	F	VF	XF	Unc	BU
2003 Proof	—	Value: 24,500				

KM# 37 1000 POUNDS
1090.8600 g., 0.9166 Gold 32.1469 oz. AGW, 100 mm. **Ruler:** Elizabeth II **Subject:** Last Flight of the Concorde **Obv:** Elizabeth II **Rev:** Concorde in flight **Edge:** Reeded

Date	Mintage	F	VF	XF	Unc	BU
2003 Proof	34	Value: 25,000				

KM# 41 1000 POUNDS
1000.0000 g., 0.9167 Gold 29.4726 oz. AGW, 100 mm. **Ruler:** Elizabeth II **Subject:** D-Day **Obv:** Queen Elizabeth II **Rev:** US and British troops wading ashore **Edge:** Reeded

Date	Mintage	F	VF	XF	Unc	BU
2004 Proof	60	Value: 24,000				

ALGERIA

The Democratic and Popular Republic of Algeria, a North African country fronting on the Mediterranean Sea between Tunisia and Morocco, has an area of 919,595 sq. mi. (2,381,740 sq. km.) and a population of 31.6 million. Capital: Algiers (Alger). Most of the country's working population is engaged in agriculture although a recent industrial diversification, financed by oil revenues, is making steady progress. Wines, fruits, iron and zinc ores, phosphates, tobacco products, liquified natural gas, and petroleum are exported.

MINT MARKS
Paris – Privy marks only

MONETARY SYSTEMS
100 Centimes = 1 Franc

REPUBLIC

MONETARY SYSTEM
100 Centimes = 1 Dinar

STANDARD COINAGE

KM# 127 1/4 DINAR
1.1500 g., Aluminum **Subject:** Fennec Fox

Date	Mintage	F	VF	XF	Unc	BU
2003-AH1423	—	—	0.65	1.25	2.50	—

KM# 129 DINAR
Steel **Subject:** Buffalo

Date	Mintage	F	VF	XF	Unc	BU
AH1422-2002	—	—	1.00	2.00	5.00	—
AH1423-2003	—	—	1.00	2.00	5.00	—
AH1424-2004	—	—	1.00	2.00	5.00	—

KM# 130 2 DINARS
Steel **Subject:** Camel's Head

Date	Mintage	F	VF	XF	Unc	BU
AH1422-2002	—	—	1.00	2.50	6.00	—
AH1423-2002	—	—	1.00	2.50	6.00	—
AH1424-2003	—	—	1.00	2.50	6.00	—

KM# 123 5 DINARS
Steel **Obv:** Denomination **Rev:** Elephant

Date	Mintage	F	VF	XF	Unc	BU
AH1422-2003	—	—	1.50	3.50	7.50	—
AH1423-2003	—	—	1.50	3.50	7.50	—
AH1424-2004	—	—	1.50	3.50	7.50	—

KM# 124 10 DINARS
Bi-Metallic Aluminum center in Steel ring **Obv:** Denomination **Rev:** Falcon

Date	Mintage	F	VF	XF	Unc	BU
AH1423-2002	—	—	2.00	6.00	12.00	—
AH1425-2004	—	—	2.00	6.00	12.00	—

KM# 125 20 DINARS
Bi-Metallic Brass center in Steel ring **Obv:** Denomination **Rev:** Lion

Date	Mintage	F	VF	XF	Unc	BU
AH1424-2004	—	—	3.00	7.00	15.00	—

KM# 126 50 DINARS
Bi-Metallic Steel center in Brass ring **Obv:** Denomination **Rev:** Gazelle

Date	Mintage	F	VF	XF	Unc	BU
AH1425-2004(a)	—	—	4.00	8.00	16.50	—

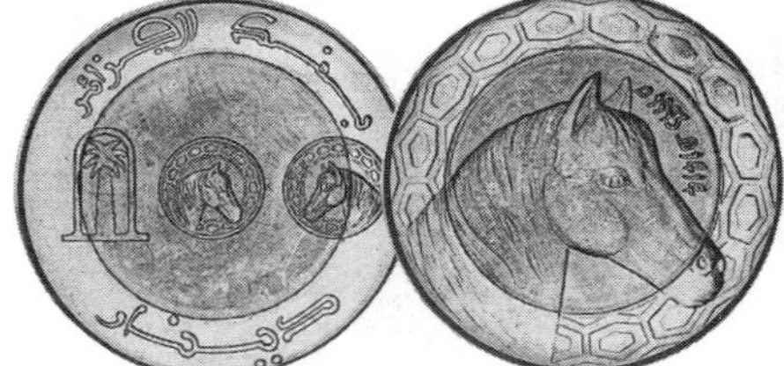

KM# 132 100 DINARS
Bi-Metallic Aluminum-Bronze center in Stainless Steel ring **Obv:** Denomination stylized with reverse design **Rev:** Horse head

Date	Mintage	F	VF	XF	Unc	BU
AH1422-2002	—	—	6.50	12.50	22.50	—
AH1423-2002(a)	—	—	6.50	12.50	22.50	—
AH1425-2004(a)	—	—	6.50	12.50	22.50	—

KM# 137 100 DINARS
11.0000 g., Bi-Metallic Brass center in Stainless Steel ring, 29.5 mm. **Subject:** 40th Anniversary of Independence **Obv:** Stylized value **Rev:** Number 40 and stylized face **Edge:** Reeded

Date	Mintage	F	VF	XF	Unc	BU
2002	—	—	—	—	27.50	—

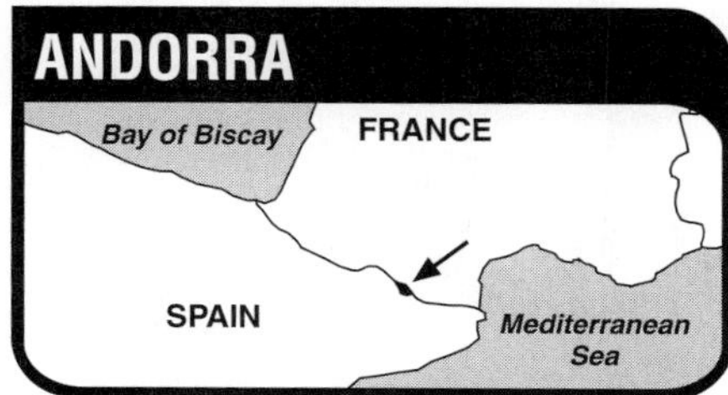

Principality of Andorra (Principat d'Andorra), situated on the southern slopes of the Pyrenees Mountains between France and Spain, has an area of 181 sq. mi. (453 sq. km.) and a population of 80,000. Capital: Andorra la Vella. Tourism is the chief source of income. Timber, cattle and derivatives, and furniture are exported.

RULER

Joan D.M. Bisbe D'Urgell I

MONETARY SYSTEM

125 Pesetas = 1 Diner, 1986-

NOTE: The Diners have been struck for collectors while the Euro is used in everyday commerce.

MINT MARK

Crowned M = Madrid

PRINCIPALITY

DECIMAL COINAGE

KM# 176 CENTIM

1.2500 g., Aluminum, 21.9 mm. **Subject:** Charlemagne **Obv:** National arms **Rev:** Crowned portrait **Edge:** Plain

Date	Mintage	F	VF	XF	Unc	BU
2002	—	—	—	—	1.00	1.50

KM# 177 CENTIM

1.2500 g., Aluminum, 21.9 mm. **Subject:** Isard **Obv:** National arms **Rev:** Mountain goat **Edge:** Plain

Date	Mintage	F	VF	XF	Unc	BU
2002	—	—	—	—	1.50	2.00

KM# 178 CENTIM

1.2500 g., Aluminum, 21.9 mm. **Subject:** Agnus Dei **Obv:** National arms **Rev:** Lamb of God **Edge:** Plain

Date	Mintage	F	VF	XF	Unc	BU
2002	—	—	—	—	1.00	1.50

KM# 198 CENTIM

Aluminum-Magnesium, 27 mm. **Obv:** Coat of arms **Rev:** A piece of the wall paintings belonging to the 12th century Romanesque church of St. Marti de la Cortinado

Date	Mintage	F	VF	XF	Unc	BU
2003	—	—	—	—	1.25	1.75

KM# 200 CENTIM

Aluminum-Magnesium, 27 mm. **Obv:** Arms **Rev:** Image of the 12th century Romanesque church of St. Miquel d'Engolasters with its bell tower, the Romanesque apse, the small portico and the large Lombard windows

Date	Mintage	F	VF	XF	Unc	BU
2003	—	—	1.25	—	—	1.75

KM# 199 CENTIM

Aluminum-Magnesium, 27 mm. **Obv:** Arms **Rev:** Pont de la Margineda, reproduction of the bridge

Date	Mintage	F	VF	XF	Unc	BU
2003	—	—	—	—	1.25	1.75

KM# 179 2 CENTIMS

Brass **Subject:** Grandalla **Obv:** National arms **Rev:** Edelweiss flower **Edge:** Plain

Date	Mintage	F	VF	XF	Unc	BU
2002	—	—	—	—	1.50	2.00

KM# 201 2 CENTIMS

Copper-Zinc-Nickel, 18.15 mm. **Obv:** Arms **Rev:** Clavell Deltoide, a flower found in Andorra

Date	Mintage	F	VF	XF	Unc	BU
2003	—	—	—	—	1.75	2.50

KM# 180 5 CENTIMS

Brass **Subject:** Esquirel **Obv:** National arms **Rev:** Squirrel on tree stump **Edge:** Plain

Date	Mintage	F	VF	XF	Unc	BU
2002	—	—	—	—	2.00	2.50

KM# 181 5 CENTIMS

Brass **Subject:** Gall Fer **Obv:** National arms **Rev:** Male capercaillie (grouse) displaying plumage **Edge:** Plain

Date	Mintage	F	VF	XF	Unc	BU
2002	—	—	—	—	2.00	2.50

KM# 203 5 CENTIMS

Copper-Zinc, 21.8 mm. **Obv:** Arms **Rev:** Wall painting from the 11th century church of Sant Serni de Nagol showing an eagle

Date	Mintage	F	VF	XF	Unc	BU
2003	—	—	—	—	2.25	2.75

KM# 202 5 CENTIMS

Copper-Zinc, 21.8 mm. **Obv:** Arms **Rev:** The cross of Seven Arms, traditional Gothic cross

Date	Mintage	F	VF	XF	Unc	BU
2003	—	—	—	—	2.25	2.75

KM# 182 10 CENTIMS

Brass **Subject:** St. Joan de Caselles **Obv:** National arms **Rev:** Tower and building **Edge:** Plain

Date	Mintage	F	VF	XF	Unc	BU
2002	—	—	—	—	3.00	4.00

KM# 204 10 CENTIMS

Copper-Nickel, 27.8 mm. **Obv:** Arms **Rev:** 12th century wood carving image from Our Lady of Meritxell

Date	Mintage	F	VF	XF	Unc	BU
2003	—	—	—	—	3.50	4.50

KM# 193 5 DINERS

1.2400 g., 0.9990 Gold 0.0398 oz. AGW, 13.92 mm. **Obv:** National arms **Rev:** The Escorial Palace in Madrid **Edge:** Reeded

Date	Mintage	F	VF	XF	Unc	BU
2004 Proof	3,000	Value: 45.00				

KM# 194 5 DINERS

1.2400 g., 0.9990 Gold 0.0398 oz. AGW, 13.92 mm. **Obv:** National arms **Rev:** Eiffel Tower, Paris **Edge:** Reeded

Date	Mintage	F	VF	XF	Unc	BU
2004 Proof	3,000	Value: 45.00				

KM# 195 5 DINERS

1.2400 g., 0.9990 Gold 0.0398 oz. AGW, 13.92 mm. **Obv:** National arms **Rev:** Atomic model monument, Brussels **Edge:** Reeded

Date	Mintage	F	VF	XF	Unc	BU
2004 Proof	3,000	Value: 45.00				

KM# 196 5 DINERS

1.2400 g., 0.9990 Gold 0.0398 oz. AGW, 13.92 mm. **Subject:** Andorran membership in the United Nations **Obv:** National arms **Rev:** Seated woman, world globe and UN logo **Edge:** Reeded

Date	Mintage	F	VF	XF	Unc	BU
2004 Proof	3,000	Value: 45.00				

KM# 172 10 DINERS

31.4700 g., 0.9250 Silver 0.9359 oz. ASW, 38.6 mm. **Subject:** Europa **Obv:** National arms **Rev:** Europa in chariot **Edge:** Reeded

Date	Mintage	F	VF	XF	Unc	BU
2001 Proof	15,000	Value: 40.00				

KM# 173 10 DINERS

31.4700 g., 0.9250 Silver 0.9359 oz. ASW, 38.6 mm. **Subject:** Concordia Europea **Obv:** National arms **Rev:** Two crowned women holding hands **Edge:** Reeded

Date	Mintage	F	VF	XF	Unc	BU
2001 Proof	15,000	Value: 40.00				

KM# 175 10 DINERS
31.4700 g., 0.9250 Silver 0.9359 oz. ASW, 38.6 mm. **Subject:** Olympics **Obv:** National arms **Rev:** Snowboarder **Edge:** Reeded

Date	Mintage	F	VF	XF	Unc	BU
2002 Proof	15,000	Value: 40.00				

KM# 183 10 DINERS
31.4700 g., 0.9250 Silver 0.9359 oz. ASW, 38.6 mm. **Subject:** Mouflon **Obv:** National arms **Rev:** Big Horn sheep **Edge:** Reeded

Date	Mintage	F	VF	XF	Unc	BU
2002 Proof	15,000	Value: 50.00				

KM# 188 10 DINERS
31.1035 g., 0.9250 Silver 0.925 oz. ASW, 38.6 mm. **Obv:** National arms **Rev:** John Paul II with doves **Edge:** Reeded

Date	Mintage	F	VF	XF	Unc	BU
2004 Proof	9,999	Value: 40.00				

KM# 189 10 DINERS
31.1035 g., 0.9250 Silver 0.925 oz. ASW, 38.6 mm. **Obv:** National arms **Rev:** John Paul II holding staff with 2 hands **Edge:** Reeded

Date	Mintage	F	VF	XF	Unc	BU
2004 Proof	9,999	Value: 40.00				

KM# 190 10 DINERS
31.1035 g., 0.9250 Silver 0.925 oz. ASW, 38.6 mm. **Obv:** National arms **Rev:** John Paul II raising a chalice **Edge:** Reeded

Date	Mintage	F	VF	XF	Unc	BU
2004 Proof	9,999	Value: 40.00				

KM# 191 10 DINERS
31.1035 g., 0.9250 Silver 0.925 oz. ASW, 38.6 mm. **Obv:** National arms **Rev:** John Paul II with hammer **Edge:** Reeded

Date	Mintage	F	VF	XF	Unc	BU
2004 Proof	9,999	Value: 40.00				

KM# 192 10 DINERS
31.1035 g., 0.9250 Silver 0.925 oz. ASW, 38.6 mm. **Obv:** National arms **Rev:** Gold-plated John Paul II writing **Edge:** Reeded

Date	Mintage	F	VF	XF	Unc	BU
2004 Proof	9,999	Value: 40.00				

KM# 174 25 DINERS
12.4414 g., 0.9990 Gold 0.3996 oz. AGW, 26 mm. **Subject:** Christmas **Obv:** National arms **Rev:** Nativity scene **Edge:** Reeded

Date	Mintage	F	VF	XF	Unc	BU
2001 Proof	3,000	Value: 300				

KM# 184 25 DINERS
10.0000 g., 0.9999 Gold 0.3215 oz. AGW, 26 mm. **Subject:** Christmas **Obv:** National arms **Rev:** Standing Christ child **Edge:** Reeded

Date	Mintage	F	VF	XF	Unc	BU
2002 Proof	2,000	Value: 275				

KM# 185 25 DINERS
7.7759 g., 0.9990 Gold 0.2498 oz. AGW, 26 mm. **Subject:** Christmas **Obv:** National arms **Rev:** Madonna-like mother and child **Edge:** Reeded

Date	Mintage	F	VF	XF	Unc	BU
2003 Proof	3,000	Value: 250				

KM# 197 25 DINERS
8.0000 g., 0.9990 Gold 0.2569 oz. AGW, 26 mm. **Obv:** National arms **Rev:** Nativity scene **Edge:** Reeded

Date	Mintage	F	VF	XF	Unc	BU
2004 Proof	5,000	Value: 225				

KM# 186 50 DINERS
159.5000 g., 0.9990 Bi-Metallic Gold And Silver .999 Silver 155.5g coin with .999 Gold 4g, 20x50mm insert 5.1229 oz., 65 mm. **Subject:** 10th Anniversary of Constitution **Obv:** National arms **Rev:** Seated allegorical woman holding scrolled constitution **Edge:** Reeded

Date	Mintage	F	VF	XF	Unc	BU
2003	3,000	—	—	—	275	300

ARGENTINA

The Argentine Republic, located in southern South America, has an area of 1,073,518 sq. mi. (3,761,274 sq. km.) and an estimated population of 37.03 million. Capital: Buenos Aires. The rolling, fertile pampas of central Argentina are ideal for agriculture and grazing, and support most of the republic's population. Meatpacking, flour milling, textiles, sugar refining and dairy products are the principal industries. Oil is found in Patagonia, but most mineral requirements must be imported.

Internal conflict through the first half century of Argentine independence resulted in a provisional national coinage, chiefly of crown-sized silver. Provincial issues mainly of minor denominations supplemented this.

REPUBLIC

REFORM COINAGE

1992; 10,000 Australes = 1 Peso

KM# 107 10 CENTAVOS
Aluminum-Bronze **Edge:** Reeded **Note:** Prev. KM#82.

Date	Mintage	F	VF	XF	Unc	BU
2004	190,000,000	—	—	—	0.65	0.85

KM# 132.1 PESO
6.3500 g., Bi-Metallic Brass center in Copper-Nickel ring, 23 mm. **Subject:** General Urquiza **Obv:** Stylized portrait **Rev:** Church tower and denomination **Edge:** Reeded

Date	Mintage	F	VF	XF	Unc	BU
2001	995,000	—	—	—	3.75	4.50

KM# 132.2 PESO
6.3500 g., Bi-Metallic Copper-Aluminum-Nickel center in Copper-Nickel ring, 23 mm. **Obv:** Gral. Justo Jose de Urquiza's portrait **Rev:** Church tower and denomination **Edge:** Plain

Date	Mintage	F	VF	XF	Unc	BU
2001	5,000	—	—	—	7.50	8.00

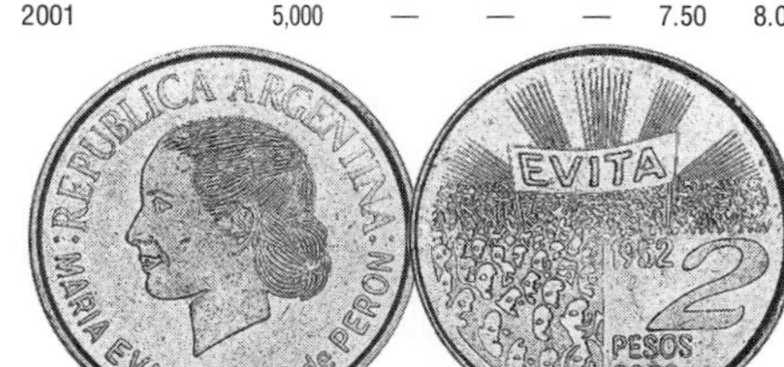

KM# 135 2 PESOS
10.4400 g., Copper-Nickel, 30.2 mm. **Obv:** Head of Eva Peron left **Rev:** Stylized crowd scene and value **Edge:** Reeded

Date	Mintage	F	VF	XF	Unc	BU
2002	—	—	—	—	7.50	9.00

KM# 133 5 PESOS
8.0640 g., 0.9000 Gold 0.2333 oz. AGW, 22 mm. **Subject:** Gral. Justo Jose de Urquiza **Obv:** Portrait **Rev:** Church tower and denomination **Edge:** Reeded

Date	Mintage	F	VF	XF	Unc	BU
2001	1,000	—	—	—	185	200

ARMENIA

The Republic of Armenia, formerly Armenian S.S.R., is bordered to the north by Georgia, the east by Azerbaijan and the south and west by Turkey and Iran. It has an area of 11,506 sq. mi. (29,800 sq. km) and an estimated population of 3.66 million. Capital: Yerevan. Agriculture including cotton, vineyards and orchards, hydroelectricity, chemicals - primarily synthetic rubber and fertilizers, vast mineral deposits of copper, zinc and aluminum, and production of steel and paper are major industries.

Fighting between Christians in Armenia and Muslim forces of Azerbaijan escalated in 1992 and continued through early 1994. Each country claimed the Nagorno-Karabakh, an Armenian ethnic enclave, in Azerbaijan. A temporary cease-fire was announced in May 1994.

MONETARY SYSTEM
100 Luma = 1 Dram

MINT NAME
Revan, (Erevan, now Yerevan)

REPUBLIC

STANDARD COINAGE

KM# 112 10 DRAM
1.3000 g., Aluminum, 20 mm. **Obv:** National arms **Rev:** Value **Edge:** Reeded

Date	Mintage	F	VF	XF	Unc	BU
2004	—	—	—	—	0.50	0.75

KM# 93 20 DRAM
2.8000 g., Copper Plated Steel, 20.5 mm. **Obv:** National arms **Rev:** Denomination **Edge:** Plain

Date	Mintage	F	VF	XF	Unc	BU
2003	—	—	—	—	1.00	1.25

KM# 94 50 DRAM
3.4500 g., Brass Plated Steel, 21.4 mm. **Obv:** National arms **Rev:** Value **Edge:** Reeded

Date	Mintage	F	VF	XF	Unc	BU
2003	—	—	—	—	1.25	1.50

KM# 86 100 DRAM
31.0400 g., 0.9990 Silver 0.997 oz. ASW, 38 mm. **Obv:** National arms **Rev:** Bust of General Garegen Nzhdeh facing at right **Edge:** Plain **Edge Lettering:** Serial number

Date	Mintage	F	VF	XF	Unc	BU
2001 Proof	170	Value: 250				

KM# 86a 100 DRAM
31.0400 g., 0.9990 Gold Plated Silver 0.997 oz. ASW AGW, 38 mm. **Obv:** National arms **Obv. Inscription:** Bust of General Garegen Nzhdeh facing at right **Edge:** Plain **Edge Lettering:** Serial number

Date	Mintage	F	VF	XF	Unc	BU
2001 Proof	30	Value: 500				

KM# 87 100 DRAM
31.0400 g., 0.9990 Silver 0.997 oz. ASW, 38 mm. **Subject:** Armenian Membership in the Council of Europe **Obv:** National arms **Rev:** Spiral design with star circle **Edge:** Plain **Edge Lettering:** Serial number

Date	Mintage	F	VF	XF	Unc	BU
2001 Proof	170	Value: 100				

KM# 98 100 DRAM
31.1000 g., 0.9250 Silver 0.9249 oz. ASW, 40 mm. **Obv:** National arms **Rev:** Aram Khachatryan **Edge:** Reeded

Date	Mintage	F	VF	XF	Unc	BU
2002	300	—	—	—	65.00	75.00

KM# 99 100 DRAM
31.1000 g., 0.9250 Silver 0.9249 oz. ASW, 40 mm. **Obv:** The Book of Sadness **Rev:** Saint Grigor Narekatsi with book and quill **Edge:** Reeded

Date	Mintage	F	VF	XF	Unc	BU
2002 Proof	500	Value: 65.00				

KM# 110 100 DRAM
33.9200 g., 0.9250 Silver 1.0088 oz. ASW, 39 mm. **Subject:** 110th Anniversary of State Banking in Armenia **Obv:** Building above value **Rev:** State Bank emblem **Edge:** Reeded

Date	Mintage	F	VF	XF	Unc	BU
2003 Proof	300	Value: 65.00				

KM# 95 100 DRAM
3.8700 g., Nickel Plated Steel, 22.4 mm. **Obv:** National arms **Rev:** Value **Edge:** Reeded

Date	Mintage	F	VF	XF	Unc	BU
2003	—	—	—	—	1.50	1.75

KM# 111 100 DRAM
28.2800 g., 0.9250 Silver 0.841 oz. ASW, 38.6 mm. **Subject:** FIFA World Cup Soccer Games - Germany **Obv:** National arms **Rev:** Three soccer players

Date	Mintage	F	VF	XF	Unc	BU
2004 Proof	50,000	Value: 45.00				

KM# 113 100 DRAM
31.1000 g., 0.9990 Silver 0.9989 oz. ASW, 38 mm.
Subject: Gandzasar Monastery **Obv:** Monastery **Rev:** Folk art crusafix and denomination

Date	Mintage	F	VF	XF	Unc	BU
2004 Proof	500	Value: 65.00				

KM# 115 100 DRAM
31.1000 g., 0.9250 Silver 0.9249 oz. ASW, 40 mm.
Subject: Anania Shirakatsi **Obv:** Profile of Shirakatsi, deep in thought **Rev:** Planets and stars, denomination

Date	Mintage	F	VF	XF	Unc	BU
2005 Proof	500	Value: 65.00				

KM# 96 200 DRAM
4.4000 g., Brass, 23.9 mm. **Obv:** National arms **Rev:** Value **Edge:** Reeded

Date	Mintage	F	VF	XF	Unc	BU
2003	—	—	—	—	2.50	3.00

KM# 106 500 DRAM
155.5000 g., 0.9250 Silver 4.6245 oz. ASW, 63 mm. **Subject:** 10th Anniversary of Independence **Obv:** National arms **Rev:** Tower with flag, logo at right

Date	Mintage	F	VF	XF	Unc	BU
2001 Proof	200	Value: 125				

KM# 97 500 DRAM
4.9300 g., Bi-Metallic Copper-Nickel center in a Brass ring, 22 mm. **Obv:** National arms **Rev:** Value **Edge:** Segmented reeding

Date	Mintage	F	VF	XF	Unc	BU
2003	—	—	—	—	4.00	5.00

KM# 109 1000 DRAM
15.5500 g., 0.5850 Gold 0.2925 oz. AGW, 26 mm.
Obv: National arms on ancient coin design **Rev:** Tigran the Great ancient coin portrait

Date	Mintage	F	VF	XF	Unc	BU
2003	500	—	—	—	235	250

KM# 117 5000 DRAMS
31.1000 g., 0.9250 Silver 0.9249 oz. ASW, 38 mm.
Subject: Armenian Armed Forces **Obv:** Order of the Combat Cross of the Second Degree and the Emblem of the Ministry of Defense of the Republic of Armenia **Obv. Designer:** H. Samuelian **Rev:** Arms, date and denomination **Shape:** Octagonal

Date	Mintage	F	VF	XF	Unc	BU
2005 Proof	5,000	Value: 65.00				

KM# 107 10000 DRAMS
8.6000 g., 0.9990 Gold 0.2762 oz. AGW, 22 mm. **Obv:** Mesrop Mashtots, creater of the Armenian Alphabet **Rev:** Armenian Alphabet

Date	Mintage	F	VF	XF	Unc	BU
2002 Proof	1,000	Value: 235				

KM# 108 10000 DRAMS
8.6000 g., 0.9990 Gold 0.2762 oz. AGW, 22 mm. **Obv:** Building above value **Rev:** Aram Khachatryan left

Date	Mintage	F	VF	XF	Unc	BU
2002 Proof	500	Value: 250				

KM# 114 10000 DRAMS
8.6000 g., 0.9990 Gold 0.2762 oz. AGW, 22 mm. **Subject:** Arshile Gorky **Obv:** Bust of Gorky **Rev:** Denomination

Date	Mintage	F	VF	XF	Unc	BU
2004 Proof	1,000	Value: 235				

KM# 116 10000 DRAMS
8.6000 g., 0.9990 Gold 0.2762 oz. AGW, 22 mm. **Subject:** Martiros Sarian **Obv:** Bust of Sarian **Rev:** Landscape, denomination

Date	Mintage	F	VF	XF	Unc	BU
2005 Proof	1,000	Value: 235				

KM# 118 50000 DRAMS
8.6000 g., 0.9990 Gold 0.2762 oz. AGW, 22 mm. **Subject:** Armenian Armed Forces **Obv:** Order of the Combat Cross of the Second Degree and the Emblem of the Ministry of Defense of the Republic of Armenia **Obv. Designer:** H. Samuelian
Rev: Arms, date and denomination

Date	Mintage	F	VF	XF	Unc	BU
2005 Proof	1,000	Value: 235				

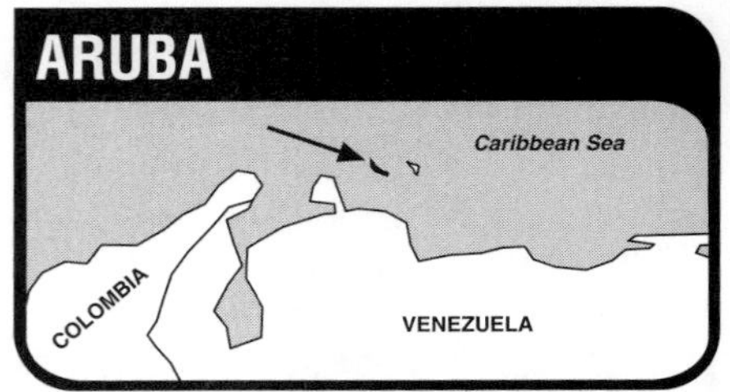

The second largest island of the Netherlands Antilles, Aruba is situated near the Venezuelan coast. The island has an area of 74-1/2 sq. mi. (193 sq. km.) and a population of 65,974. Capital: Oranjestad, named after the Dutch royal family. Aruba was important in the processing and transportation of petroleum products in the first part of the twentieth century, but today the chief industry is tourism.

For earlier issues see Curacao and the Netherlands Antilles.

RULERS
Dutch

MINT MARKS
(u) Utrecht - Privy marks only
Winetendril with grapes, 2001-
Winetendril with grapes plus star, 2002-
Sails of a clipper, 2003-

MONETARY SYSTEM
100 Cents = 1 Florin

DUTCH STATE
"Status Aparte"
REGULAR COINAGE

KM# 1 5 CENTS
2.0000 g., Nickel Bonded Steel, 16 mm. **Obv:** Arms
Rev: Geometric design **Edge:** Plain

Date	Mintage	F	VF	XF	Unc	BU
2001(u)	946,900	—	—	—	0.20	0.50
2002(u)	1,006,000	—	—	—	0.20	0.50
2003(u)	1,104,100	—	—	—	0.20	0.50
2004(u)	502,500	—	—	—	0.20	0.50
2005(u)	—	—	—	—	0.20	0.50
2006(u)	—	—	—	—	0.20	0.50

KM# 2 10 CENTS
3.0000 g., Nickel Bonded Steel, 18 mm. **Obv:** Arms
Rev: Geometric design **Edge:** Reeded

Date	Mintage	F	VF	XF	Unc	BU
2001(u)	1,006,900	—	—	—	0.30	0.50
2002(u)	1,006,000	—	—	—	0.30	0.50
2003(u)	1,004,000	—	—	—	0.30	0.50
2004(u)	402,500	—	—	—	0.30	0.50
2005(u)	—	—	—	—	0.30	0.50
2006(u)	—	—	—	—	0.30	0.50

KM# 3 25 CENTS
3.5000 g., Nickel Bonded Steel, 20 mm. **Obv:** Arms
Rev: Geometric design **Edge:** Plain

Date	Mintage	F	VF	XF	Unc	BU
2001(u)	716,900	—	—	—	0.40	0.80
2002(u)	806,000	—	—	—	0.40	0.80
2003(u)	804,000	—	—	—	0.40	0.80
2004(u)	362,500	—	—	—	0.40	0.80
2005(u)	—	—	—	—	0.40	0.80
2006(u)	—	—	—	—	0.40	0.80

KM# 4 50 CENTS
5.0000 g., Nickel Bonded Steel, 20 mm. **Obv:** Arms **Rev:** Geometric design **Edge:** Plain **Shape:** 4-sided

Date	Mintage	F	VF	XF	Unc	BU
2001(u)	506,900	—	—	0.35	0.65	0.80
2002(u)	306,000	—	—	0.35	0.65	0.80
2003(u)	279,000	—	—	—	0.65	0.80
2004(u)	402,500	—	—	—	0.65	0.80
2005(u)	—	—	—	—	0.65	0.80
2006(u)	—	—	—	—	0.65	0.80

KM# 5 FLORIN
8.5000 Nickel Bonded Steel, 26 mm. **Obv:** Head of Queen Beatrix left **Rev:** Arms **Edge:** Lettered **Edge Lettering:** GOD * ZiJ * MET * ONS

Date	Mintage	F	VF	XF	Unc	BU
2001(u)	406,900	—	—	0.65	1.25	2.25
2002(u)	206,000	—	—	0.65	1.25	2.25
2003(u)	179,000	—	—	0.70	1.35	2.35
2004(u)	410,000	—	—	0.70	1.35	2.35
2005(u)	—	—	—	0.70	1.35	2.35
2006(u)	—	—	—	0.70	1.35	2.35

KM# 6 2-1/2 FLORIN
10.3000 g., Nickel Bonded Steel, 30 mm. **Obv:** Head of Queen Beatrix left **Rev:** Arms **Edge:** Lettered **Edge Lettering:** GOD * ZiJ * MET * ONS

Date	Mintage	F	VF	XF	Unc	BU
2001(u)	6,900	—	—	—	3.50	6.00
Note: In sets only						
2002(u)	6,000	—	—	—	3.50	6.00
Note: In sets only						
2003(u)	4,000	—	—	—	3.50	6.00
Note: In sets only						
2004(u)	2,500	—	—	—	3.50	6.00
Note: In sets only						
2005(u)	—	—	—	—	3.50	6.00
Note: In sets only						
2006(u)	—	—	—	—	3.50	6.00
Note: In sets only						

KM# 12 5 FLORIN
8.6400 g., Nickel Bonded Steel, 26 mm. **Obv:** Head of Queen Beatrix left **Rev:** Arms **Edge:** Plain **Shape:** 4-sided

Date	Mintage	F	VF	XF	Unc	BU
2001(u)	6,900	—	—	—	6.00	7.50
Note: In sets only						
2002(u)	6,000	—	—	—	6.00	7.50
Note: In sets only						
2003(u)	4,000	—	—	—	5.50	7.00
Note: In sets only						
2004(u)	2,500	—	—	—	5.50	7.00
Note: In sets only						
2005(u)	2,500	—	—	—	5.50	7.00
Note: In sets only						
2006(u)	—	—	—	—	5.50	7.00
Note: In sets only						

KM# 25 5 FLORIN
11.9000 g., 0.9250 Silver 0.3539 oz. ASW, 29 mm. **Subject:** 50th Anniversary of Autonomy **Obv:** Queen left **Rev:** Royal seal

Date	Mintage	F	VF	XF	Unc	BU
2004 Proof	4,000	Value: 32.00				

KM# 34 5 FLORIN
11.9000 g., 0.9250 Silver 0.3539 oz. ASW, 29 mm. **Subject:** Queen's Silver Jubilee **Obv:** Queen left **Rev:** Flag

Date	Mintage	F	VF	XF	Unc	BU
2005(u) Proof	4,000	Value: 32.00				

KM# 20 10 FLORIN
25.0000 g., 0.9250 Silver 0.7435 oz. ASW, 38 mm. **Subject:** Green Sea Turtles **Obv:** Head of Queen Beatrix left **Rev:** Seven sea turtles **Edge:** Plain **Designer:** E. Fingal

Date	Mintage	F	VF	XF	Unc	BU
2001(u) Prooflike	2,000	—	—	—	—	40.00

KM# 24 10 FLORIN
17.8000 g., 0.9250 Silver 0.5294 oz. ASW, 33 mm. **Subject:** Crown Prince's Wedding **Obv:** Head of Queen Beatrix left **Rev:** Portraits of the prince and princess Maxima, faces right **Edge Lettering:** GOD ZIJ MET ONS **Designer:** G. Colley

Date	Mintage	F	VF	XF	Unc	BU
ND(2002)(u) Prooflike	5,000	—	—	—	—	35.00

KM# 27 10 FLORIN
25.0000 g., 0.9250 Silver 0.7435 oz. ASW **Obv:** Head of Queen Beatrix **Rev:** Sea Shells

Date	Mintage	F	VF	XF	Unc	BU
2003 Prooflike	2,000	—	—	—	—	40.00

KM# 28 10 FLORIN
25.0000 g., 0.9250 Silver 0.7435 oz. ASW **Obv:** Head of Queen Beatrix **Rev:** Snake

Date	Mintage	F	VF	XF	Unc	BU
2003 Prooflike	2,000	—	—	—	—	40.00

KM# 29 10 FLORIN
25.0000 g., 0.9250 Silver 0.7435 oz. ASW **Obv:** Head of Queen Beatrix **Rev:** Owl

Date	Mintage	F	VF	XF	Unc	BU
2003 Prooflike	1,000	—	—	—	—	45.00

KM# 30 10 FLORIN
25.0000 g., 0.9250 Silver 0.7435 oz. ASW **Obv:** Head of Queen Beatrix **Rev:** Frog

Date	Mintage	F	VF	XF	Unc	BU
2004 Prooflike	1,000	—	—	—	—	45.00

KM# 31 10 FLORIN
25.0000 g., 0.9250 Silver 0.7435 oz. ASW **Obv:** Head of Queen Beatrix **Rev:** Fish

Date	Mintage	F	VF	XF	Unc	BU
2004	1,000	—	—	—	—	45.00

KM# 33 10 FLORIN
1.2442 g., 0.9990 Gold 0.04 oz. AGW, 13.9 mm. **Subject:** Death of Juliana **Obv:** Queen left **Rev:** Juliana in center

Date	Mintage	F	VF	XF	Unc	BU
ND (2004)(u) Proof	10,000	Value: 57.00				

KM# 26 10 FLORIN
6.7200 g., 0.9000 Gold 0.1944 oz. AGW, 22.5 mm. **Subject:** 50th Anniversary of Autonomy **Obv:** Queen left **Rev:** Royal seal

Date	Mintage	F	VF	XF	Unc	BU
2004 Proof	1,000	Value: 180				

KM# 35 10 FLORIN
6.7200 g., 0.9000 Gold 0.1944 oz. AGW, 22.5 mm. **Subject:** Queen's Silver Jubilee **Obv:** Queen left **Rev:** Flag

Date	Mintage	F	VF	XF	Unc	BU
2005(u) Proof	1,500	Value: 175				

KM# 22 25 FLORIN
25.0000 g., 0.9250 Silver 0.7435 oz. ASW, 38 mm. **Subject:** 15th Anniversary of Autonomy **Obv:** Head of Queen Beatrix left **Rev:** National arms and inscription **Edge:** Plain

Date	Mintage	F	VF	XF	Unc	BU
2001(u) Proof	3,000	Value: 45.00				

KM# 32 25 FLORIN
31.1000 g., 0.9250 Silver 0.9249 oz. ASW **Obv:** Head of Queen Beatrix **Rev:** Two running athletes

Date	Mintage	F	VF	XF	Unc	BU
2004 Proof	—	Value: 40.00				

KM# 23 100 FLORIN
6.7200 g., Gold, 22.5 mm. **Subject:** Independence **Obv:** Arms, treaty name, dates **Rev:** Head of Queen Beatrix left **Edge:** Grained

Date	Mintage	F	VF	XF	Unc	BU
2001 Proof	1,000	Value: 260				

MINT SETS

KM#	Date	Mintage	Identification	Issue Price	Mkt Val
MS18	2001	—	KM#1-6, 12, with medal	15.00	14.50
MS19	2001 (7)	6,900	KM#1-6, 12	13.25	15.00
MS20	2002 (7)	6,000	KM# 1-6, 12	15.00	16.50
MS21	2003 (7)	4,000	KM# 1-6, 12	15.00	16.50
MS22	2004 (7)	2,500	KM# 1-6, 12	15.00	16.50
MS23	2005	2,500	KM# 1-6, 12	15.00	16.50
MS24	2006	—	KM# 1-6, 12	15.00	16.50

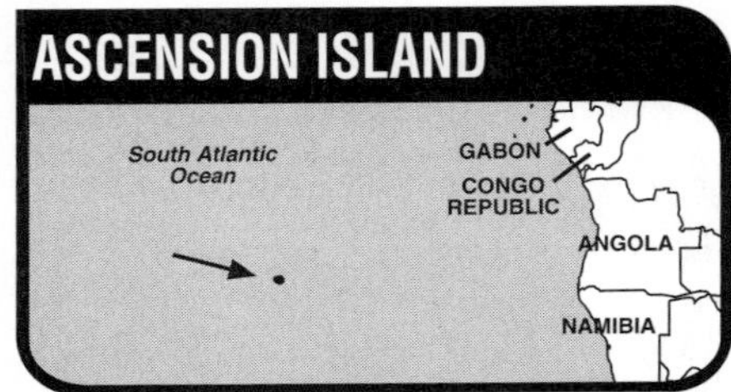

An island of volcanic origin, Ascension Island lies in the South Atlantic, 700 miles (1,100 km.) northwest of St. Helena. It has an area of 34 sq. mi. (88 sq. km.) on an island 9 miles (14 km.) long and 6 miles (10 km.) wide. Approximate population: 1,146. Although having little vegetation and scant rainfall, the island has a very healthy climate. The island is the nesting place for a large number of sea turtles and sooty terns. Phosphates and guano are the chief natural sources of income.

RULERS
British

MINT MARKS
PM - Pobjoy Mint

BRITISH ADMINISTRATION

STANDARD COINAGE

KM# 14 50 PENCE

28.6300 g., Copper-Nickel, 38.6 mm. **Subject:** Centennial - Queen Victoria's Death **Obv:** Queen's bust right **Rev:** Queen Victoria's 3/4 bust left **Edge:** Reeded

Date	Mintage	F	VF	XF	Unc	BU
2001	—	—	—	—	8.00	9.50

KM# 14a 50 PENCE

28.2800 g., 0.9250 Silver 0.841 oz. ASW, 38.6 mm. **Subject:** Centennial of Queen Victoria's Death **Obv:** Queen Elizabeth II **Rev:** Queen Victoria **Edge:** Reeded

Date	Mintage	F	VF	XF	Unc	BU
2001 Proof	10,000	Value: 50.00				

KM# 14b 50 PENCE

47.5400 g., 0.9166 Gold 1.401 oz. AGW, 38.6 mm. **Subject:** Centennial of Queen Victoria's Death **Obv:** Queen Elizabeth II **Rev:** Queen Victoria **Edge:** Reeded

Date	Mintage	F	VF	XF	Unc	BU
2001 Proof	100	Value: 1,100				

KM# 13 50 PENCE

28.6300 g., Copper-Nickel, 38.6 mm. **Subject:** 75th Birthday of Queen Elizabeth **Obv:** Queen's head right **Rev:** Crowned monogram above flowers **Edge:** Reeded

Date	Mintage	F	VF	XF	Unc	BU
2001	—	—	—	—	8.00	9.50

KM# 13a 50 PENCE

28.2800 g., 0.9250 Silver 0.841 oz. ASW, 38.6 mm. **Subject:** Queen Elizabeth II's 75th Birthday **Obv:** Queen Elizabeth II **Rev:** Crowned monogram above roses **Edge:** Reeded

Date	Mintage	F	VF	XF	Unc	BU
2001 Proof	10,000	Value: 50.00				

KM# 13b 50 PENCE

47.5400 g., 0.9166 Gold 1.401 oz. AGW, 38.6 mm. **Subject:** Queen Elizabeth II's 75th Birthday **Obv:** Queen Elizabeth II **Rev:** Crowned monogram above roses **Edge:** Reeded

Date	Mintage	F	VF	XF	Unc	BU
2001 Proof	75	Value: 1,100				

KM# 15 50 PENCE

28.3500 g., Copper-Nickel, 38.6 mm. **Subject:** Queen's Golden Jubilee **Obv:** Queen's portrait **Rev:** Westminster Abby **Edge:** Reeded

Date	Mintage	F	VF	XF	Unc	BU
ND(2002)	—	—	—	—	8.00	9.50

KM# 15a 50 PENCE

28.2800 g., 0.9250 Silver 0.841 oz. ASW, 38.6 mm. **Subject:** Queen Elizabeth II's Golden Jubilee **Obv:** Gold plated Queen Elizabeth II **Rev:** Monogram and Westminster Abbey **Edge:** Reeded

Date	Mintage	F	VF	XF	Unc	BU
ND(2002) Proof	10,000	Value: 50.00				

KM# 18 50 PENCE

28.2800 g., Copper-Nickel, 38.6 mm. **Subject:** Death of Queen Mother **Obv:** Queen Elizabeth II **Rev:** Queen Mother between her life dates **Edge:** Reeded

Date	Mintage	F	VF	XF	Unc	BU
ND(2002)	—	—	—	—	10.00	12.00

KM# 18a 50 PENCE

28.2800 g., 0.9250 Silver 0.841 oz. ASW, 38.6 mm. **Subject:** Death of Queen Mother **Obv:** Queen Elizabeth II **Rev:** Queen Mother between her life dates **Edge:** Reeded

Date	Mintage	F	VF	XF	Unc	BU
ND(2002) Proof	10,000	Value: 50.00				

KM# 16 50 PENCE

28.3600 g., Copper-Nickel, 38.6 mm. **Subject:** Coronation Jubilee **Obv:** Queen's portrait **Rev:** Coronation regalia **Edge:** Reeded

Date	Mintage	F	VF	XF	Unc	BU
ND (2003) Prooflike	—	—	—	—	10.00	12.00

KM# 16a 50 PENCE

28.2800 g., 0.9250 Silver 0.841 oz. ASW, 38.6 mm.
Subject: Queen Elizabeth II's - 50th Anniversary of Coronation **Obv:** Queen Elizabeth II **Rev:** Crown, two sceptres and the ampula **Edge:** Reeded

Date	Mintage	F	VF	XF	Unc	BU
ND(2003) Proof	5,000	Value: 50.00				

KM# 16b 50 PENCE

39.9400 g., 0.9166 Gold 1.177 oz. AGW, 38.6 mm.
Subject: Queen Elizabeth II's - 50th Anniversary of Coronation **Obv:** Queen Elizabeth II **Rev:** Crown, two sceptres and the ampula **Edge:** Reeded

Date	Mintage	F	VF	XF	Unc	BU
ND(2003) Proof	50	Value: 950				

KM# 17 50 PENCE

28.2800 g., Copper-Nickel, 38.6 mm. **Subject:** Queen Elizabeth II's- 50th Anniversary of Coronation **Obv:** Queen Elizabeth II **Rev:** Crowned monogram **Edge:** Reeded

Date	Mintage	F	VF	XF	Unc	BU
ND(2003)	—	—	—	—	10.00	12.00

KM# 17a 50 PENCE

28.2800 g., 0.9250 Silver 0.841 oz. ASW, 38.6 mm. **Subject:** Queen Elizabeth II's- 50th Anniversary of Coronation **Obv:** Queen Elizabeth II **Rev:** Crowned monogram **Edge:** Reeded

Date	Mintage	F	VF	XF	Unc	BU
ND(2003) Proof	5,000	Value: 50.00				

KM# 17b 50 PENCE

39.9400 g., 0.9166 Gold 1.177 oz. AGW, 38.6 mm. **Subject:** Queen Elizabeth II's - 50th Anniversary of Coronation **Obv:** Queen Elizabeth II **Rev:** Crowned monogram **Edge:** Reeded

Date	Mintage	F	VF	XF	Unc	BU
ND(2003) Proof	50	Value: 950				

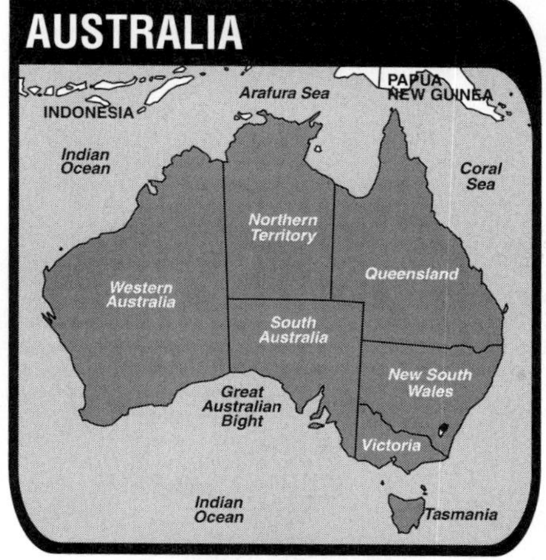

The Commonwealth of Australia, the smallest continent in the world, is located south of Indonesia between the Indian and Pacific oceans. It has an area of 2,967,893 sq. mi. (7,686,850 sq. km.) and an estimated population of 18.84 million. Capital: Canberra. Due to its early and sustained isolation, Australia is the habitat of such curious and unique fauna as the kangaroo, koala, platypus, wombat, echidna and frilled-necked lizard. The continent possesses extensive mineral deposits, the most important of which are iron ore, coal, gold, silver, nickel, uranium, lead and zinc. Raising livestock, mining and manufacturing are the principal industries. Chief exports are wool, meat, wheat, iron ore, coal and nonferrous metals.

Australia's currency system was changed from Pounds - Shillings - Pence to a decimal system of Dollars and Cents on Feb. 14, 1966.

NOTE: Home market grading of Australian coinage is generally stricter than USA practiced standards. The pricing in this catalog reflects strict home market grading standard.

RULERS

British until 1942

MONETARY SYSTEM

Decimal Coinage (Commencing 1966)

100 Cents = 1 Dollar

COMMONWEALTH OF AUSTRALIA

MINT MARKS

M – Melbourne
P – Perth
S – Sydney
(sy) - Sydney

DECIMAL COINAGE

KM# 767 CENT

2.6000 g., Bronze, 17.53 mm. **Ruler:** Elizabeth II **Obv:** Rank-Broadley head of Elizabeth II right **Rev:** Ring-tailed opossum

Date	Mintage	F	VF	XF	Unc	BU
2006	—	—	—	—	—	—

Note: In sets only

KM# 768 2 CENTS

5.2000 g., Bronze, 21.6 mm. **Ruler:** Elizabeth II **Obv:** Rank-Broadley head of Elizabeth II right **Rev:** Frilled lizard

Date	Mintage	F	VF	XF	Unc	BU
2006	—	—	—	—	—	—

Note: In sets only

KM# 401 5 CENTS

2.8300 g., Copper-Nickel, 19.4 mm. **Ruler:** Elizabeth II **Obv:** Queen's portrait by Rank-Broadley **Rev:** Short-beaked Spiny Anteater **Rev. Designer:** Stuart Devlin

Date	Mintage	F	VF	XF	Unc	BU
2001	174,579,000	—	—	—	0.20	0.50
2001 Proof	—	Value: 0.75				
2002	148,812,000	—	—	—	0.20	0.50
2002 Proof	—	Value: 0.75				
2003	115,069,000	—	—	—	0.20	0.50
2003 Proof	—	Value: 0.75				
2004	—	—	—	—	0.20	0.50
2004 Proof	—	Value: 0.75				
2005	—	—	—	—	0.20	0.50
2005 Proof	—	Value: 0.75				
2006	—	—	—	—	0.20	0.50
2006 Proof	—	Value: 0.75				

KM# 402 10 CENTS

5.6500 g., Copper-Nickel, 23.6 mm. **Ruler:** Elizabeth II **Obv:** Head of Queen Elizabeth II right by Rank-Broadley **Rev:** Superb Lyre-bird **Rev. Designer:** Stuart Devlin

Date	Mintage	F	VF	XF	Unc	BU
2001	109,357,000	—	—	—	0.50	0.80
2001 Proof	—	Value: 1.00				
2002	70,329,000	—	—	—	0.50	0.80
2002 Proof	—	Value: 1.00				
2003	53,635,000	—	—	—	0.50	0.80
2003 Proof	—	Value: 1.00				
2004	—	—	—	—	0.50	0.80
2004 Proof	—	Value: 1.00				
2005	—	—	—	—	0.50	0.80
2005 Proof	—	Value: 1.00				
2006	—	—	—	—	0.50	0.80
2006 Proof	—	Value: 1.00				

KM# 403 20 CENTS

11.3000 g., Copper-Nickel, 28.5 mm. **Ruler:** Elizabeth II **Obv:** Queen's portrait by Rank-Broadley **Rev:** Duckbill Platypus **Rev. Designer:** Stuart Devlin

Date	Mintage	F	VF	XF	Unc	BU
2001	109,467,000	—	—	—	0.60	1.00
2001 Proof	—	Value: 2.50				
2002	27,244,000	—	—	—	0.60	1.00
2002 Proof	—	Value: 2.50				
2003	7,573,000	—	—	—	0.60	1.00
2003 Proof	—	Value: 2.50				
2004	—	—	—	—	0.60	1.00
2004 Proof	—	Value: 2.50				
2005	—	—	—	—	0.60	1.00
2005 Proof	—	Value: 2.50				
2006	—	—	—	—	0.60	1.00
2006 Proof	—	Value: 2.50				

KM# 532 20 CENTS

11.3300 g., Copper-Nickel, 28.5 mm. **Subject:** Centennial of Federation - Norfolk **Obv:** Queen's head right **Rev:** Plant on island map **Rev. Designer:** Megan Cummings

Date	Mintage	F	VF	XF	Unc	BU
2001	2,200,000	—	—	—	2.25	2.50
2001 Proof	—	Value: 2.75				

KM# 550 20 CENTS

11.3000 g., Copper-Nickel, 28.5 mm. **Series:** Centenary of Federation - New South Wales **Obv:** Queen's head right **Rev:** Flower on state map **Rev. Designer:** Joseph Neve **Edge:** Reeded

Date	Mintage	F	VF	XF	Unc	BU
2001	3,200,000	—	—	—	2.25	2.50
2001 Proof	—	Value: 2.75				

KM# 554 20 CENTS

11.3000 g., Copper-Nickel, 28.5 mm. **Series:** Centenary of Federation - Queensland **Obv:** Queen's head right **Rev:** Radiant design **Edge:** Reeded

Date	Mintage	F	VF	XF	Unc	BU
2001	2,300,000	—	—	—	2.25	2.50
2001 Proof	—	Value: 2.75				

KM# 556 20 CENTS

11.3000 g., Copper-Nickel, 28.5 mm. **Series:** Centenary of Federation - Victoria **Obv:** Queen's head right **Rev:** Capital building **Rev. Designer:** Ryan Ladd & Mark Kennedy **Edge:** Reeded

Date	Mintage	F	VF	XF	Unc	BU
2001	2,900,000	—	—	—	1.75	2.00
2001 Proof	—	Value: 2.50				

KM# 558 20 CENTS

11.3000 g., Copper-Nickel, 28.5 mm. **Series:** Centenary of Federation - Northern Territory **Obv:** Queen's head right **Rev:** Two brolga cranes in ritual dance **Rev. Designer:** Lisa Brett **Edge:** Reeded

Date	Mintage	F	VF	XF	Unc	BU
2001	2,100,000	—	—	—	3.00	3.25
2001 Proof	—	Value: 3.50				

KM# 560 20 CENTS

11.3000 g., Copper-Nickel, 28.5 mm. **Series:** Centenary of Federation - South Australia **Obv:** Queen's head right **Rev:** Flower, landscape and stars **Rev. Designer:** Lisa Murphy **Edge:** Reeded

Date	Mintage	F	VF	XF	Unc	BU
2001	2,400,000	—	—	—	2.25	2.50
2001 Proof	—	Value: 2.75				

KM# 562 20 CENTS

11.3000 g., Copper-Nickel, 28.5 mm. **Series:** Centenary of Federation - Western Australia **Obv:** Queen's head right **Rev:** Rabbit-eared Bandicoot (bilby), plant and map **Rev. Designer:** Janice Ng **Edge:** Reeded

Date	Mintage	F	VF	XF	Unc	BU
2001	2,400,000	—	—	—	3.00	3.25
2001 Proof	—	Value: 3.50				

KM# 564 20 CENTS

11.3000 g., Copper-Nickel, 28.5 mm. **Series:** Centenary of Federation - Tasmania **Obv:** Queen's head right **Rev:** Tasmanian Devil on map **Rev. Designer:** Abbey MacDonald **Edge:** Reeded

Date	Mintage	F	VF	XF	Unc	BU
2001	2,200,000	—	—	—	3.00	3.25
2001 Proof	—	Value: 3.50				

KM# 552 20 CENTS

11.3000 g., Copper-Nickel, 28.5 mm. **Series:** Centenary of Federation - Australian Capital Territory **Obv:** Queen's head right **Rev:** Parliament house, map, flowers **Rev. Designer:** Stacy Jo-Ann Paine **Edge:** Reeded **Note:** Prev. KM#551.

Date	Mintage	F	VF	XF	Unc	BU
2001	2,100,000	—	—	—	2.25	2.50
2001 Proof	—	Value: 2.75				

KM# 589 20 CENTS

11.3000 g., Copper Nickel, 28.5 mm. **Subject:** Sir Donald Bradman **Obv:** Bust of Queen Elizabeth II right **Rev:** Cricket player batsman **Edge:** Reeded

Date	Mintage	F	VF	XF	Unc	BU
2001	10,000,000	—	—	—	2.00	2.25

KM# 688 20 CENTS

11.3000 g., Copper-Nickel, 28.52 mm. **Obv:** Elizabeth II **Rev:** Group of Australian Volunteers **Edge:** Reeded

Date	Mintage	F	VF	XF	Unc	BU
2003	7,600,000	—	—	—	2.00	2.25

KM# 688a 20 CENTS

11.3000 g., 0.9990 Silver 0.3629 oz. ASW, 28.52 mm. **Edge:** Reeded

Date	Mintage	F	VF	XF	Unc	BU
2003 Proof	6,500	Value: 6.50				

KM# 745 20 CENTS

11.3000 g., Copper-Nickel, 28.52 mm. **Ruler:** Elizabeth II **Obv:** Elizabeth II **Rev:** Soldier with wife and child **Edge:** Reeded

Date	Mintage	F	VF	XF	Unc	BU
2005	—	—	—	—	2.00	2.50
2005 Proof	—	Value: 3.00				

KM# 745a 20 CENTS

13.3600 g., 0.9990 Silver 0.4291 oz. ASW, 28.52 mm. **Ruler:** Elizabeth II **Obv:** Elizabeth II **Rev:** Soldier with wife and child **Edge:** Reeded

Date	Mintage	F	VF	XF	Unc	BU
2005 Proof	6,500	Value: 9.50				

KM# 745b 20 CENTS

24.3600 g., 0.9999 Gold 0.7831 oz. AGW, 28.52 mm. **Ruler:** Elizabeth II **Obv:** Elizabeth II **Rev:** Soldier with wife and child **Edge:** Reeded

Date	Mintage	F	VF	XF	Unc	BU
2005 Proof	650	Value: 625				

KM# 599 25 CENTS (The Dump)

7.7750 g., 0.9990 Silver 0.2497 oz. ASW, 24.8 mm. **Obv:** Bust of Queen Elizabeth II right **Rev:** Parliament House **Edge:** Plain **Shape:** 7-pointed star **Note:** "The Dump" portion of the "Holey Dollar" KM#598.

Date	Mintage	F	VF	XF	Unc	BU
2001 Prooflike	30,000	—	—	—	15.00	17.50

KM# 404 50 CENTS

15.5500 g., Copper-Nickel, 31.5 mm. **Obv:** Head of Queen Elizabeth II right by Rank-Broadley **Rev:** National arms

Date	Mintage	F	VF	XF	Unc	BU
2001	57,312,000	—	—	0.85	2.75	3.00
2001 Proof	—	Value: 6.50				
2002	11,507,000	—	—	0.85	2.75	3.00
2002 Proof	—	Value: 6.50				
2003	13,926,000	—	—	0.85	2.75	3.00
2003 Proof	—	Value: 6.50				
2004	—	—	—	0.85	2.75	3.00
2004 Proof	—	Value: 6.50				
2006	—	—	—	—	—	—

KM# 533 50 CENTS

15.6000 g., Copper-Nickel, 31.4 mm. **Subject:** Centennial - Norfolk Island Federation **Obv:** Queen's head right **Rev:** Norfolk Island coat of arms **Edge:** Plain **Shape:** 12-sided

Date	Mintage	F	VF	XF	Unc	BU
2001	2,200,000	—	—	—	3.00	3.50
2001 Proof	—	Value: 6.50				

KM# 535 50 CENTS

16.8860 g., 0.9990 Silver .5424 oz. ASW, 32.1 mm. **Subject:** Year of the Snake **Obv:** Bust of Queen Elizabeth II right **Rev:** Snake with eggs **Edge:** Plain

Date	Mintage	F	VF	XF	Unc	BU
2001	500,000	—	—	—	15.00	16.50
2001P Proof	5,000	Value: 36.00				

KM# 551 50 CENTS

15.5500 g., Copper-Nickel, 31.5 mm. **Series:** Centenary of Federation - New South Wales **Obv:** Queen's head right **Rev:** New South Wales state arms **Edge:** Plain **Shape:** 12-sided

Date	Mintage	F	VF	XF	Unc	BU
2001	3,000,000	—	—	—	3.00	3.50
2001 Proof	—	Value: 6.50				

KM# 553 50 CENTS

15.5500 g., Copper-Nickel, 31.5 mm. **Series:** Centenary of Federation - Australian Capital Territory **Obv:** Queen's head right **Rev:** Austrian Capital Territory arms **Edge:** Plain **Shape:** 12-sided

Date	Mintage	F	VF	XF	Unc	BU
2001	2,000,000	—	—	—	3.00	3.50
2001 Proof	—	Value: 6.50				

KM# 555 50 CENTS

15.5500 g., Copper-Nickel, 31.5 mm. **Series:** Centenary of Federation - Queensland **Obv:** Queen's head right **Rev:** Queensland state arms **Edge:** Plain **Shape:** 12-sided

Date	Mintage	F	VF	XF	Unc	BU
2001	2,300,000	—	—	—	3.00	3.50
2001 Proof	—	Value: 6.50				

KM# 557 50 CENTS
15.5500 g., Copper-Nickel, 31.5 mm. **Series:** Centenary of Federation - Victoria **Obv:** Queen's head right **Rev:** Victoria state arms **Edge:** Plain **Shape:** 12-sided

Date	Mintage	F	VF	XF	Unc	BU
2001	2,800,000	—	—	—	3.00	3.50
2001 Proof	—	Value: 6.50				

KM# 559 50 CENTS
15.5500 g., Copper-Nickel, 31.5 mm. **Series:** Centenary of Federation - Northern Territory **Obv:** Queen's head right **Rev:** Northern Territory state arms **Edge:** Plain **Shape:** 12-sided

Date	Mintage	F	VF	XF	Unc	BU
2001	2,100,000	—	—	—	3.00	3.50
2001 Proof	—	Value: 6.50				

KM# 561 50 CENTS
15.5500 g., Copper-Nickel, 31.5 mm. **Series:** Centenary of Federation - South Australia **Obv:** Queen's head right **Rev:** South Australia state arms **Edge:** Plain **Shape:** 12-sided

Date	Mintage	F	VF	XF	Unc	BU
2001	2,400,000	—	—	—	3.00	3.50
2001 Proof	—	Value: 6.50				

KM# 563 50 CENTS
15.5500 g., Copper-Nickel, 31.5 mm. **Series:** Centenary of Federation - Western Australia **Obv:** Queen's head right **Rev:** Western Australia state arms **Edge:** Plain **Shape:** 12-sided

Date	Mintage	F	VF	XF	Unc	BU
2001	2,400,000	—	—	—	3.00	3.50
2001 Proof	—	Value: 6.50				

KM# 565 50 CENTS
15.5500 g., Copper-Nickel, 31.5 mm. **Series:** Centenary of Federation - Tasmania **Obv:** Queen's head right **Rev:** Tasmania state arms **Edge:** Plain **Shape:** 12-sided

Date	Mintage	F	VF	XF	Unc	BU
2001	2,200,000	—	—	—	3.00	3.50
2001 Proof	—	Value: 6.50				

KM# 491.1 50 CENTS
Copper-Nickel, 31.5 mm. **Subject:** Centenary of Federation, 1901-2001 **Obv:** Queen's head right **Rev:** Commonwealth coat of arms **Edge:** Plain **Shape:** 12-sided **Note:** Prev. KM#491.

Date	Mintage	F	VF	XF	Unc	BU
2001	43,100,000	—	—	—	2.50	2.75

KM# 491.2a 50 CENTS
18.2400 g., 0.9990 Silver .5858 oz. ASW, 31.5 mm. **Subject:** Centenary of Federation, 1901-2001 **Obv:** Queen's head right **Rev:** Multicolored Commonwealth coat of arms **Edge:** Plain **Shape:** 12-sided **Note:** Prev. KM#491a.

Date	Mintage	F	VF	XF	Unc	BU
2001 Proof	—	Value: 27.50				

KM# 602 50 CENTS
15.5500 g., Copper-Nickel, 31.5 mm. **Subject:** The Outback Region **Obv:** Bust of Queen Elizabeth II right **Rev:** Windmill **Edge:** Plain **Shape:** 12-sided

Date	Mintage	F	VF	XF	Unc	BU
2002	11,500,000	—	—	—	3.00	3.50
2002 Proof	—	Value: 6.50				

KM# 645 50 CENTS
15.5500 g., Copper-Nickel, 31.51 mm. **Subject:** Queen's 50th Anniversary of Succession **Obv:** Queen's portrait **Rev:** Crown and star **Rev. Designer:** Peter Soobik **Shape:** 12-sided

Date	Mintage	F	VF	XF	Unc	BU
2002	—	—	—	—	4.00	4.50

KM# 645a 50 CENTS
18.2400 g., 0.9990 Silver 0.5858 oz. ASW, 31.51 mm. **Subject:** Queen's 50th Anniversary of Accession **Obv:** Queen's portrait **Rev:** Crown and star **Rev. Designer:** Peter Soobik **Shape:** 12-sided

Date	Mintage	F	VF	XF	Unc	BU
2002 Proof	19,502	Value: 40.00				

KM# 689 50 CENTS
15.5500 g., Copper-Nickel, 31.5 mm. **Obv:** Elizabeth II **Rev:** Value within circle of volunteer activities **Edge:** Plain **Shape:** 12-sided

Date	Mintage	F	VF	XF	Unc	BU
2003	13,900,000	—	—	—	3.00	3.50

KM# 689a 50 CENTS
15.5500 g., 0.9990 Silver 0.4994 oz. ASW, 31.5 mm.

Date	Mintage	F	VF	XF	Unc	BU
2003 Proof	6,500	Value: 8.50				

KM# 694 50 CENTS
15.5500 g., Copper-Nickel, 31.5 mm. **Ruler:** Elizabeth II **Obv:** Queen Elizabeth II **Rev:** Koala, Lorikeet (bird) and a Wombat **Edge:** Plain **Shape:** 12-sided

Date	Mintage	F	VF	XF	Unc	BU
2004	—	—	—	—	3.00	4.00

KM# 694a 50 CENTS
18.2400 g., 0.9990 Silver 0.5858 oz. ASW, 31.5 mm. **Ruler:** Elizabeth II **Obv:** Elizabeth II **Rev:** Wombat, lorikeet and koala **Edge:** Plain **Shape:** 12-sided

Date	Mintage	F	VF	XF	Unc	BU
2004 Proof	12,500	Value: 25.00				

KM# 746 50 CENTS
15.5500 g., Copper-Nickel, 31.51 mm. **Ruler:** Elizabeth II **Obv:** Elizabeth II **Rev:** Military cemetery scene **Edge:** Plain **Shape:** 12-sided

Date	Mintage	F	VF	XF	Unc	BU
2005	—	—	—	—	2.25	2.75
2005 Proof	—	Value: 8.00				

KM# 746a 50 CENTS
18.2400 g., 0.9990 Silver 0.5858 oz. ASW, 31.51 mm. **Ruler:** Elizabeth II **Obv:** Elizabeth II **Rev:** Military cemetery scene **Edge:** Plain **Shape:** 12-sided

Date	Mintage	F	VF	XF	Unc	BU
2005 Proof	6,500	Value: 22.50				

KM# 746b 50 CENTS
33.6300 g., 0.9999 Gold 1.0811 oz. AGW, 31.51 mm. **Ruler:** Elizabeth II **Obv:** Elizabeth II **Rev:** Military cemetery scene **Edge:** Plain **Shape:** 12-sided

Date	Mintage	F	VF	XF	Unc	BU
2005 Proof	650	Value: 850				

KM# 769 50 CENTS
Copper-Nickel **Ruler:** Elizabeth II **Subject:** Commonweath Games, Secondary School Design Competition

Date	Mintage	F	VF	XF	Unc	BU
2005	—	—	—	—	2.25	2.75
2005 Proof	10,000	Value: 35.00				

KM# 770 50 CENTS
Copper-Nickel **Ruler:** Elizabeth II **Subject:** Commonweath Games **Rev:** Basketball

Date	Mintage	F	VF	XF	Unc	BU
2006	—	—	—	—	2.50	3.00

KM# 771 50 CENTS
Copper-Nickel **Ruler:** Elizabeth II **Subject:** Commonweath Games **Rev:** Hockey

Date	Mintage	F	VF	XF	Unc	BU
2006	—	—	—	—	2.50	3.00

KM# 772 50 CENTS
Copper-Nickel **Ruler:** Elizabeth II **Subject:** Commonweath Games **Rev:** Shooting

Date	Mintage	F	VF	XF	Unc	BU
2006	—	—	—	—	2.50	3.00

KM# 773 50 CENTS
Copper-Nickel **Ruler:** Elizabeth II **Subject:** Commonweath Games **Rev:** Weightlifting

Date	Mintage	F	VF	XF	Unc	BU
2006	—	—	—	—	2.50	3.00

KM# 774 50 CENTS
Copper-Nickel **Ruler:** Elizabeth II **Subject:** Commonwealth Games **Rev:** Gymnastics

Date	Mintage	F	VF	XF	Unc	BU
2006	—	—	—	—	2.50	3.00

KM# 775 50 CENTS
Copper-Nickel **Ruler:** Elizabeth II **Subject:** Commonwealth Games **Rev:** Rugby

Date	Mintage	F	VF	XF	Unc	BU
2006	—	—	—	—	2.50	3.00

KM# 776 50 CENTS
Copper-Nickel **Ruler:** Elizabeth II **Subject:** Commonwealth Games **Rev:** Cycling

Date	Mintage	F	VF	XF	Unc	BU
2006	—	—	—	—	2.50	3.00

KM# 777 50 CENTS
Copper-Nickel **Ruler:** Elizabeth II **Subject:** Commonwealth Games **Rev:** Athletics

Date	Mintage	F	VF	XF	Unc	BU
2006	—	—	—	—	2.50	3.00

KM# 778 50 CENTS
Copper-Nickel **Ruler:** Elizabeth II **Subject:** Commonwealth Games **Rev:** Triathlon

Date	Mintage	F	VF	XF	Unc	BU
2006	—	—	—	—	2.50	3.00

KM# 779 50 CENTS

Copper-Nickel **Ruler:** Elizabeth II **Subject:** Commonwealth Games **Rev:** Netball

Date	Mintage	F	VF	XF	Unc	BU
2006	—	—	—	—	2.50	3.00

KM# 780 50 CENTS

Copper-Nickel **Ruler:** Elizabeth II **Subject:** Commonwealth Games **Rev:** Table tennis

Date	Mintage	F	VF	XF	Unc	BU
2006	—	—	—	—	2.50	3.00

KM# 781 50 CENTS

Copper-Nickel **Ruler:** Elizabeth II **Subject:** Commonwealth Games **Rev:** Aquatics

Date	Mintage	F	VF	XF	Unc	BU
2006	—	—	—	—	2.50	3.00

KM# 530 DOLLAR

9.0000 g., Nickel-Aluminum-Copper, 24.9 mm. **Subject:** Army Centennial **Obv:** Queen's head right **Rev:** Army crest **Edge:** Reeded and plain sections

Date	Mintage	F	VF	XF	Unc	BU
2001C	6,781,200	—	—	—	4.00	5.00

KM# 530a DOLLAR

11.6600 g., 0.9990 Silver .3745 oz. ASW, 24.9 mm. **Subject:** Army Centennial **Obv:** Queen's head right **Rev:** Army crest **Edge:** Reeded and plain sections

Date	Mintage	F	VF	XF	Unc	BU
2001 Proof	20,000	Value: 20.00				

KM# 531 DOLLAR

9.0000 g., Nickel-Aluminum-Copper, 24.9 mm. **Subject:** 50th Anniversary - Air Force **Obv:** Queen's head right **Rev:** Air Force badge **Edge:** Reeded and plain sections

Date	Mintage	F	VF	XF	Unc	BU
2001	6,781,200	—	—	—	4.00	5.00

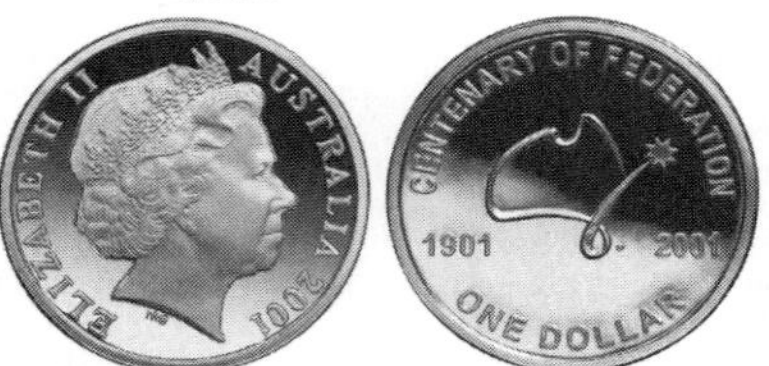

KM# 534.1 DOLLAR

9.5000 g., Nickel-Aluminum-Copper, 24.9 mm. **Subject:** Centennial - Norfolk Island Federation **Obv:** Queen's head right **Rev:** Stylized ribbon map of Australia with star **Edge:** Plain and reeded sections **Note:** Prev. KM#534.

Date	Mintage	F	VF	XF	Unc	BU
2001	6,781,200	—	—	—	4.00	5.00

KM# 534.2 DOLLAR

9.5000 g., Nickel-Aluminum-Copper, 24.9 mm. **Subject:** Centenary of Norfolk Island Federation **Obv:** Queen's head right **Rev:** Multicolor ribbon design of Australia with star **Edge:** Plain and reeded sections

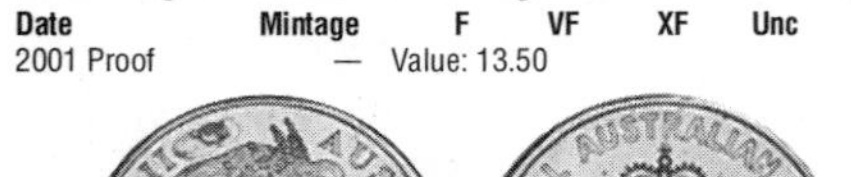

Date	Mintage	F	VF	XF	Unc	BU
2001 Proof	—	Value: 13.50				

KM# 588 DOLLAR

9.0000 g., Aluminum-Bronze, 25 mm. **Subject:** Royal Australian Navy **Obv:** Head of Queen Elizabeth II right **Rev:** Navy emblem **Edge:** Reeded and plain sections

Date	Mintage	F	VF	XF	Unc	BU
2001	6,781,200	—	—	—	4.00	5.00

KM# 594 DOLLAR

31.1035 g., 0.9990 Silver 0.999 oz. ASW, 40 mm. **Subject:** Millennium **Obv:** Bust of Queen Elizabeth II right **Rev:** Gold inset Sun on multicolor Earth above Egyptian obelisk **Edge:** Reeded

Date	Mintage	F	VF	XF	Unc	BU
2001 Prooflike	30,000	—	—	—	35.00	37.50

KM# 598 DOLLAR

31.1000 g., 0.9990 Silver 0.9989 oz. ASW, 40.4 mm. **Subject:** Centenary of Federation "Holey Dollar" **Obv:** Legend around star-shaped center hole **Rev:** Seven coats of arms around star-shaped hole **Edge:** Reeded

Date	Mintage	F	VF	XF	Unc	BU
ND(2001) Prooflike	30,000	—	—	—	40.00	42.50

KM# 682 DOLLAR

Aluminum-Bronze **Subject:** International Year of Volunteers

Date	Mintage	F	VF	XF	Unc	BU
2001	6,781,200	—	—	—	4.00	5.00

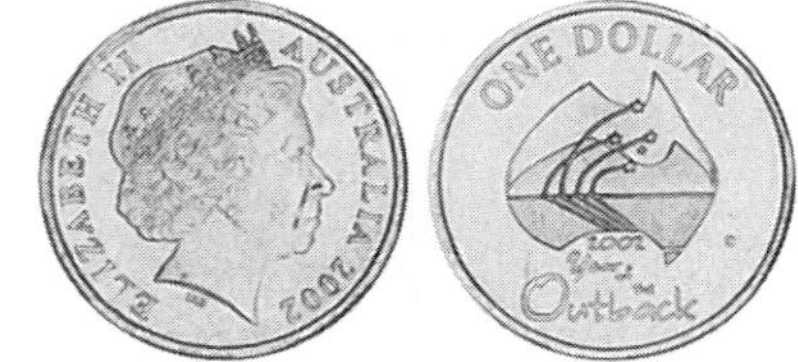

KM# 600.1 DOLLAR

9.0000 g., Aluminum-Bronze, 24.9 mm. **Subject:** Year of the Outback **Obv:** Bust of Queen Elizabeth II right **Rev:** Stylized Australian map **Edge:** Reeded and plain sections **Note:** Prev. KM#600.

Date	Mintage	F	VF	XF	Unc	BU
2002	35,373,000	—	—	—	2.50	3.00
2002 Proof	—	Value: 4.00				
2002C	—	—	—	—	2.50	3.00

KM# 600.2 DOLLAR

9.0000 g., Aluminum-Bronze, 24.9 mm. **Subject:** The Outback **Obv:** Queen's portrait **Rev:** Multicolor stylized Australian map **Edge:** Reeded and plain sections

Date	Mintage	F	VF	XF	Unc	BU
2002(c)	—	—	—	—	3.50	4.50
2002(c) Proof	—	Value: 6.00				

KM# 580a DOLLAR

31.6350 g., 0.9990 Silver, 40.6 mm. **Ruler:** Elizabeth II **Obv:** Queen Elizabeth II **Rev:** Gold-plated horse **Edge:** Reeded

Date	Mintage	F	VF	XF	Unc	BU
2002	50,000	—	—	—	45.00	47.50

KM# 632 DOLLAR

31.1035 g., 0.9990 Silver 0.999 oz. ASW, 40 mm. **Subject:** Queen's Golden Jubilee **Obv:** Queen's portrait **Rev:** Queen on horse with multicolor flag background **Edge:** Reeded

Date	Mintage	F	VF	XF	Unc	BU
2002P Proof	40,000	Value: 50.00				

KM# 660 DOLLAR

31.1035 g., 0.9990 Silver 0.999 oz. ASW, 40 mm. **Subject:** Melbourne Mint **Obv:** Queen's portrait **Rev:** Mint entrance between two gold foil inserts replicating gold sovereign reverse designs **Edge:** Reeded

Date	Mintage	F	VF	XF	Unc	BU
2002 Proof	13,328	Value: 40.00				

KM# 754 DOLLAR

9.0000 g., Aluminum-Bronze, 25 mm. **Ruler:** Elizabeth II **Subject:** Womens Suffrage **Obv:** Elizabeth II **Rev:** Suffragette talking to Britannia **Edge:** Segmented reeding

Date	Mintage	F	VF	XF	Unc	BU
2003	10,000,000	—	—	—	4.00	5.00

KM# 763 DOLLAR

13.3600 g., 0.9990 Silver 0.4291 oz. ASW, 28.5 mm. **Ruler:** Elizabeth II **Series:** Masterpieces in Silver - Port Phillip Patterns **Obv:** 1/4 Ounce design **Rev:** Kangaroo design **Edge:** Reeded

Date	Mintage	F	VF	XF	Unc	BU
2003 Proof	10,000	Value: 7.50				

KM# 663 DOLLAR

9.0000 g., Aluminum-Bronze, 25 mm. **Ruler:** Elizabeth II **Subject:** Korean War **Obv:** Queen's portrait **Rev:** Dove of Peace **Edge:** Segmented reeding

Date	Mintage	F	VF	XF	Unc	BU
2003C	14,156,000	—	—	—	4.50	5.50

KM# 663a DOLLAR

11.6600 g., 0.9990 Silver 0.3745 oz. ASW, 25 mm. **Subject:** Korean War **Obv:** Queen's portrait **Rev:** Dove of Peace **Edge:** Segmented reeding

Date	Mintage	F	VF	XF	Unc	BU
2003	15,000	Value: 30.00				

KM# 685 DOLLAR

31.1035 g., 0.9990 Silver 0.999 oz. ASW, 40.6 mm. **Subject:** 21st Birthday of William **Obv:** Queen Elizabeth II **Rev:** Multicolor Crown Prince William **Edge:** Segmented reeding

Date	Mintage	F	VF	XF	Unc	BU
ND(2003)P Proof	12,500	Value: 42.50				

KM# 690 DOLLAR
9.0000 g., Aluminum-Bronze, 25 mm. **Obv:** Elizabeth II **Rev:** Australia Volunteers logo **Edge:** Segmented reeding

Date	Mintage	F	VF	XF	Unc	BU
2003	4,100,000	—	—	—	3.50	4.50

KM# 690a DOLLAR
9.0000 g., 0.9990 Silver 0.2891 oz. ASW, 25 mm.

Date	Mintage	F	VF	XF	Unc	BU
2003 Proof	6,500	Value: 20.00				

KM# 733 DOLLAR
9.0000 g., Aluminum-Bronze, 25 mm. **Ruler:** Elizabeth II **Obv:** Elizabeth II **Rev:** Multicolor holographic five kangaroos design **Edge:** Reeded and plain sections

Date	Mintage	F	VF	XF	Unc	BU
2004 Proof	—	Value: 15.00				

KM# 725 DOLLAR
56.2300 g., 0.9990 Bi-Metallic Copper center in Silver ring 1.806 oz., 50 mm. **Ruler:** Elizabeth II **Subject:** The Last Penny **Obv:** 1964 dated penny obverse **Rev:** 1964 date penny reverse **Edge:** Reeded

Date	Mintage	F	VF	XF	Unc	BU
2004 Proof	16,437	Value: 50.00				

KM# 726 DOLLAR
9.0000 g., Aluminum-Bronze, 25 mm. **Ruler:** Elizabeth II **Subject:** Eureka Stockade **Obv:** Elizabeth II **Rev:** Stockade and stylized soldiers **Edge:** Reeded and plain sections

Date	Mintage	F	VF	XF	Unc	BU
2004 B	23,402	—	—	—	4.00	5.00
2004 C	65,088	—	—	—	4.00	5.00
2004 E	72,498	—	—	—	4.00	5.00
2004 S	33,083	—	—	—	4.00	5.00

KM# 726a DOLLAR
11.6600 g., 0.9990 Silver 0.3745 oz. ASW, 25 mm. **Ruler:** Elizabeth II **Subject:** Eureka Stockade **Obv:** Elizabeth II **Rev:** Stockade and stylized soldiers **Edge:** Reeded and Plain sections

Date	Mintage	F	VF	XF	Unc	BU
2004 Proof	16,447	Value: 20.00				

KM# 734 DOLLAR
31.1035 g., 0.9990 Silver 0.999 oz. ASW, 40 mm. **Ruler:** Elizabeth II **Subject:** First Moon Walk **Obv:** Elizabeth II **Rev:** Multicolor rocket in flight **Edge:** Reeded

Date	Mintage	F	VF	XF	Unc	BU
2004P Proof	40,000	Value: 40.00				

KM# 735 DOLLAR
31.1035 g., 0.9990 Silver 0.999 oz. ASW, 40 mm. **Ruler:** Elizabeth II **Subject:** First Moon Walk **Obv:** Elizabeth II **Rev:** Multicolor scene of astronauts planting flag on moon **Edge:** Reeded

Date	Mintage	F	VF	XF	Unc	BU
2004P Proof	40,000	Value: 40.00				

KM# 736 DOLLAR
31.1035 g., 0.9990 Silver 0.999 oz. ASW, 40 mm. **Ruler:** Elizabeth II **Subject:** First Moon Walk **Rev:** Multicolor close up of astronaut on moon **Edge:** Reeded

Date	Mintage	F	VF	XF	Unc	BU
2004P Proof	40,000	Value: 40.00				

KM# 737 DOLLAR
31.1035 g., 0.9990 Silver 0.999 oz. ASW, 40 mm. **Ruler:** Elizabeth II **Obv:** Elizabeth II **Rev:** Multicolor Antarctic view of Mawson Station and penguins **Edge:** Reeded

Date	Mintage	F	VF	XF	Unc	BU
2004P Proof	7,500	Value: 50.00				

KM# 738 DOLLAR
31.1035 g., 0.9990 Silver 0.999 oz. ASW, 40 mm. **Ruler:** Elizabeth II **Subject:** 50th Anniversary of Royal Visit **Obv:** Gold-plated bust of Elizabeth II **Rev:** Gold-plated lion and kangaroo **Edge:** Reeded

Date	Mintage	F	VF	XF	Unc	BU
ND (2004) Proof	12,500	Value: 40.00				

KM# 740 DOLLAR
24.3750 g., 0.9990 Silver Encapsulated gold nuggets center in Silver ring 0.7812 oz. ASW, 40.6 mm. **Ruler:** Elizabeth II **Obv:** Elizabeth II **Rev:** Eureka Stockade leader, miners and flag **Edge:** Reeded

Date	Mintage	F	VF	XF	Unc	BU
2004 Proof	12,500	Value: 75.00				

KM# 747 DOLLAR
9.0000 g., Aluminum-Bronze, 25 mm. **Ruler:** Elizabeth II **Obv:** Elizabeth II **Rev:** Happy man **Edge:** Segmented reeding

Date	Mintage	F	VF	XF	Unc	BU
2005	—	—	—	—	4.50	5.50
2005 Proof	—	Value: 16.00				

KM# 747a DOLLAR
11.6600 g., 0.9990 Silver 0.3745 oz. ASW, 25 mm. **Ruler:** Elizabeth II **Obv:** Elizabeth II **Rev:** Happy man **Edge:** Segmented reeding

Date	Mintage	F	VF	XF	Unc	BU
2005 Proof	6,500	Value: 42.00				

KM# 747b DOLLAR
21.5200 g., 0.9999 Gold 0.6918 oz. AGW, 25 mm. **Ruler:** Elizabeth II **Obv:** Elizabeth II **Rev:** Happy man **Edge:** Segmented reeding

Date	Mintage	F	VF	XF	Unc	BU
2005 Proof	650	Value: 550				

KM# 748 DOLLAR
9.0000 g., Aluminum-Bronze, 25 mm. **Ruler:** Elizabeth II **Subject:** Gallipoli **Obv:** Elizabeth II **Rev:** Bugler silhouette **Edge:** Segmented reeding

Date	Mintage	F	VF	XF	Unc	BU
2005B	—	—	—	—	2.00	3.00
2005C	—	—	—	—	2.00	3.00
2005G	—	—	—	—	2.00	3.00
2005M	—	—	—	—	2.00	3.00
2005S	—	—	—	—	2.00	3.00

KM# 748a DOLLAR
11.6600 g., 0.9990 Silver 0.3745 oz. ASW, 25 mm. **Ruler:** Elizabeth II **Subject:** Gallipoli **Obv:** Elizabeth II **Rev:** Bugler silhouette **Edge:** Segmented reeding

Date	Mintage	F	VF	XF	Unc	BU
2005 Proof	20,000	Value: 28.00				

KM# 749 DOLLAR
31.1035 g., 0.9990 Silver 0.999 oz. ASW, 40 mm. **Ruler:** Elizabeth II **Obv:** Elizabeth II **Rev:** Kangaroo and stars **Edge:** Reeded

Date	Mintage	F	VF	XF	Unc	BU
2005	—	—	—	—	18.00	20.00
2005 Proof	12,500	Value: 40.00				

KM# 749a DOLLAR
31.1035 g., 0.9990 Silver Partially Gold Plated 0.999 oz. ASW, 40 mm. **Ruler:** Elizabeth II **Obv:** Elizabeth II **Rev:** Kangaroo and stars **Edge:** Reeded

Date	Mintage	F	VF	XF	Unc	BU
2005 Proof	12,500	Value: 55.00				

KM# 489 DOLLAR
9.0000 g., Nickel-Aluminum-Copper, 25 mm. **Subject:** Kangaroos **Obv:** Queen's head by Rank-Broadley right **Rev:** Circle of 5 kangaroos **Edge:** Reeded and plain sections

Date	Mintage	F	VF	XF	Unc	BU
2006	—	—	—	—	—	5.00

KM# 406 2 DOLLARS
6.6000 g., Aluminum-Bronze, 20.5 mm. **Obv:** Head of Queen Elizabeth II right by Rank-Broadley **Rev:** Aboriginal man at left, stars above at right

Date	Mintage	F	VF	XF	Unc	BU
2001	3,565,000	—	—	—	4.50	5.50
2001 Proof	—	Value: 11.50				
2002	29,689,000	—	—	—	4.50	5.50
2002 Proof	—	Value: 11.50				
2003	13,656,000	—	—	—	4.50	5.50
2003 Proof	—	Value: 11.50				
2004	—	—	—	—	4.50	5.50
2004 Proof	—	Value: 11.50				
2005	—	—	—	—	4.50	5.50
2005 Proof	—	Value: 11.50				
2006	—	—	—	—	4.50	5.50
2006 Proof	—	Value: 11.50				

KM# 764 2 DOLLARS
18.2200 g., 0.9990 Silver 0.5852 oz. ASW, 32.5 mm. **Ruler:** Elizabeth II **Series:** Masterpieces in Silver - Port Phillip Patterns **Obv:** 1/2 Ounce design **Rev:** Kangaroo design **Edge:** Reeded

Date	Mintage	F	VF	XF	Unc	BU
2003 Proof	10,000	Value: 15.00				

KM# 755 2 DOLLARS
62.2700 g., 0.9990 Silver 2 oz. ASW, 50.3 mm. **Ruler:** Elizabeth II **Series:** Australian Peacekeepers **Obv:** Elizabeth II **Rev:** Australian army and color insignia **Edge:** Reeded

Date	Mintage	F	VF	XF	Unc	BU
2005P Proof	2,500	Value: 80.00				

KM# 756 2 DOLLARS
62.2700 g., 0.9990 Silver 2 oz. ASW, 50.3 mm. **Ruler:** Elizabeth II **Series:** Australian Peacekeepers **Obv:** Elizabeth II **Rev:** Australian Navy and color insignia **Edge:** Reeded

Date	Mintage	F	VF	XF	Unc	BU
2005P Proof	2,500	Value: 80.00				

KM# 757 2 DOLLARS
62.2700 g., 0.9990 Silver 2 oz. ASW, 50.3 mm. **Ruler:** Elizabeth II **Subject:** Australian Peacekeepers Set **Obv:** Elizabeth II **Rev:** Australian Airforce and color insignia **Edge:** Reeded

Date	Mintage	F	VF	XF	Unc	BU
2005P Proof	2,500	Value: 80.00				

KM# 758 2 DOLLARS
62.2700 g., 0.9990 Silver 2 oz. ASW, 50.3 mm. **Ruler:** Elizabeth II **Series:** Australian Peacekeepers **Obv:** Elizabeth II **Rev:** Australian Federal Police and color insignia **Edge:** Reeded

Date	Mintage	F	VF	XF	Unc	BU
2005P Proof	2,500	Value: 80.00				

KM# 759 2 DOLLARS
62.2700 g., 0.9990 Silver 2 oz. ASW, 50.3 mm. **Ruler:** Elizabeth II **Series:** Australian Peacekeepers **Obv:** Elizabeth II **Rev:** Australian Agency for International Development and color insignia **Edge:** Reeded

Date	Mintage	F	VF	XF	Unc	BU
2005P Proof	2,500	Value: 80.00				

KM# 591 5 DOLLARS
36.3100 g., 0.9990 Silver 1.1662 oz. ASW, 38.74 mm. **Subject:** Centennial of Federation Series Finale **Obv:** Bust of Queen Elizabeth II right **Rev:** Multicolor dual hologram: map and rotunda **Edge:** Reeded

Date	Mintage	F	VF	XF	Unc	BU
2001 Proof	—	Value: 30.00				

KM# 592 5 DOLLARS
36.3100 g., 0.9990 Silver 1.1662 oz. ASW, 38.74 mm. **Subject:** Barton and Reid **Obv:** Bust of Queen Elizabeth II right **Rev:** Portraits of Dame Flora Reid and Lady Jean Barton **Edge:** Reeded

Date	Mintage	F	VF	XF	Unc	BU
2001 Proof	—	Value: 28.00				

KM# 637 5 DOLLARS
36.3100 g., 0.9990 Silver 1.1662 oz. ASW, 38.74 mm. **Subject:** Kingston, Barton and Deakin **Obv:** Queen's portrait **Rev:** Three rectangular portraits and value **Edge:** Reeded

Date	Mintage	F	VF	XF	Unc	BU
2001 Proof	—	Value: 30.00				

KM# 638 5 DOLLARS
36.3100 g., 0.9990 Silver 1.1662 oz. ASW, 38.74 mm. **Subject:** Clark, Parkes and Griffith **Obv:** Queen's portrait **Rev:** Three rectangular portraits and value **Edge:** Reeded

Date	Mintage	F	VF	XF	Unc	BU
2001 Proof	—	Value: 30.00				

KM# 639 5 DOLLARS
36.3100 g., 0.9990 Silver 1.1662 oz. ASW, 38.74 mm. **Subject:** Spence, Nicholls and Anderson **Obv:** Queen's portrait **Rev:** Three circular portraits and value **Edge:** Reeded

Date	Mintage	F	VF	XF	Unc	BU
2001	—	Value: 30.00				

KM# 640 5 DOLLARS
36.3100 g., 0.9990 Silver 1.1662 oz. ASW, 38.74 mm. **Subject:** Reid, Forrest and Quick **Obv:** Queen's portrait **Rev:** Three rectangular portraits and value **Edge:** Reeded

Date	Mintage	F	VF	XF	Unc	BU
2001 Proof	—	Value: 30.00				

KM# 641 5 DOLLARS
36.3100 g., 0.9990 Silver 1.1662 oz. ASW, 38.74 mm. **Subject:** Bathurst Ladies Organizing Committee **Obv:** Queen's portrait **Rev:** Circular design with names above value **Edge:** Reeded

Date	Mintage	F	VF	XF	Unc	BU
2001 Proof	—	Value: 30.00				

KM# 662 5 DOLLARS
36.3100 g., 0.9990 Silver 1.1662 oz. ASW, 38.74 mm. **Subject:** Year of the Outback **Obv:** Queen's portrait **Rev:** Multicolor holographic landscape **Edge:** Reeded

Date	Mintage	F	VF	XF	Unc	BU
2001 Proof	15,000	Value: 55.00				

KM# 761 5 DOLLARS
36.3100 g., 0.9990 Silver 1.1662 oz. ASW **Ruler:** Elizabeth II **Rev:** Sir Donald Bradman

Date	Mintage	F	VF	XF	Unc	BU
2001 Proof	—	Value: 40.00				

KM# 762 5 DOLLARS
20.0000 g., Aluminum-Bronze, 38.74 mm. **Ruler:** Elizabeth II **Rev:** Sir Donald Bradman

Date	Mintage	F	VF	XF	Unc	BU
2001	—	—	—	—	8.50	9.50

KM# 601 5 DOLLARS
10.5200 g., Bi-Metallic Aluminumn-Bronze center in Stainless Steel ring, 27.8 mm. **Subject:** Battle of Sunda Strait **Obv:** Bust of Queen Elizabeth II right **Rev:** Ships bell from the "USS Houston" **Rev. Designer:** Vladimir Gottwald **Edge:** Plain **Shape:** 24-sided **Note:** Demagnetized.

Date	Mintage	F	VF	XF	Unc	BU
2002	—	—	—	—	7.50	9.50

KM# 647 5 DOLLARS
28.0000 g., Aluminum-Bronze, 38.74 mm. **Subject:** Battle of Sunda Strait **Obv:** Queen's portrait **Rev:** Two ships; USS Houston and HMS Perth **Edge:** Reeded

Date	Mintage	F	VF	XF	Unc	BU
2002 Proof	15,000	Value: 25.00				

KM# 649 5 DOLLARS
20.0000 g., Aluminum-Bronze, 38.74 mm. **Subject:** Commonwealth Games **Obv:** Queen's portrait **Rev:** Eight arms, one of which holds a tennis racket **Edge:** Reeded

Date	Mintage	F	VF	XF	Unc	BU
2002	20,000	—	—	—	8.50	9.50

KM# 650 5 DOLLARS
20.0000 g., Aluminum-Bronze, 38.74 mm. **Subject:** Commonwealth Games **Obv:** Queen's portrait **Rev:** Eight arms, one of which holds a hook **Edge:** Reeded

Date	Mintage	F	VF	XF	Unc	BU
2002	20,000	—	—	—	8.50	9.50

KM# 651 5 DOLLARS
20.0000 g., Aluminum-Bronze, 38.74 mm. **Subject:** Commonwealth Games **Obv:** Queen's portrait **Rev:** Blue games logo **Edge:** Reeded

Date	Mintage	F	VF	XF	Unc	BU
2002	20,000	—	—	—	8.50	9.50

KM# 652 5 DOLLARS
36.3100 g., 0.9990 Silver 1.1662 oz. ASW, 38.74 mm. **Subject:** Commonwealth Games **Obv:** Queen's portrait **Rev:** Victorious athletes **Edge:** Reeded

Date	Mintage	F	VF	XF	Unc	BU
2002 Proof	15,000	Value: 40.00				

KM# 653 5 DOLLARS
36.3100 g., 0.9990 Silver 1.1662 oz. ASW, 38.74 mm. **Obv:** Queen's portrait **Rev:** Dutch sailing ship, The Duyfken **Edge:** Reeded

Date	Mintage	F	VF	XF	Unc	BU
2002 Proof	10,000	Value: 28.00				

KM# 654 5 DOLLARS

36.3100 g., 0.9990 Silver 1.1662 oz. ASW, 38.74 mm. **Obv:** Queen's portrait **Rev:** HMS Endeavour sailing ship **Edge:** Reeded

Date	Mintage	F	VF	XF	Unc	BU
2002 Proof	10,000	Value: 28.00				

KM# 655 5 DOLLARS

36.3100 g., 0.9990 Silver 1.1662 oz. ASW, 38.74 mm. **Obv:** Queen's portrait **Rev:** HMS Sirius sailing ship **Edge:** Reeded

Date	Mintage	F	VF	XF	Unc	BU
2002 Proof	10,000	Value: 28.00				

KM# 656 5 DOLLARS

36.3100 g., 0.9990 Silver 1.1662 oz. ASW, 38.74 mm. **Obv:** Queen's portrait **Rev:** HMS Investigator sailing ship **Edge:** Reeded

Date	Mintage	F	VF	XF	Unc	BU
2002 Proof	10,000	Value: 28.00				

KM# 659 5 DOLLARS

31.1035 g., 0.9990 Silver 0.999 oz. ASW, 40 mm. **Subject:** Queen Mother **Obv:** Queen's portrait **Rev:** Queen Mother circa 1927 **Rev. Designer:** Stuart Devlin **Edge:** Reeded

Date	Mintage	F	VF	XF	Unc	BU
2002 Proof	30,000	Value: 30.00				

KM# 765 5 DOLLARS

36.3100 g., 0.9990 Silver 1.1662 oz. ASW, 38.7 mm. **Ruler:** Elizabeth II **Series:** Masterpieces in Silver - Port Phillip Patterns **Obv:** 1 Ounce design **Rev:** Kangaroo design **Edge:** Reeded

Date	Mintage	F	VF	XF	Unc	BU
2003 Proof	10,000	Value: 35.00				

KM# 727 5 DOLLARS

36.3100 g., 0.9990 Silver 1.1662 oz. ASW, 38.74 mm. **Ruler:** Elizabeth II **Subject:** Olympics **Obv:** Elizabeth II **Rev:** Parthenon, Sydney Opera House and shield with multicolor flag and rings **Edge:** Reeded

Date	Mintage	F	VF	XF	Unc	BU
2004 Proof	17,500	Value: 40.00				

KM# 728 5 DOLLARS

36.3100 g., 0.9990 Silver 1.1662 oz. ASW, 38.74 mm. **Ruler:** Elizabeth II **Subject:** Tasmania **Obv:** Elizabeth II **Rev:** Ship on island map **Edge:** Reeded

Date	Mintage	F	VF	XF	Unc	BU
2004 Proof	7,500	Value: 40.00				

KM# 729 5 DOLLARS

31.1035 g., 0.9990 Silver 0.999 oz. ASW, 40 mm. **Ruler:** Elizabeth II **Subject:** Adelaide to Darwin Railroad **Obv:** Elizabeth II **Rev:** Train, tracks and outline map **Edge:** Reeded

Date	Mintage	F	VF	XF	Unc	BU
2004 Proof	12,500	Value: 40.00				

KM# 730 5 DOLLARS

31.1035 g., 0.9990 Silver 0.999 oz. ASW, 40 mm. **Ruler:** Elizabeth II **Subject:** 150 Years of Australian Steam Railways **Obv:** Elizabeth II **Rev:** Old steam train **Edge:** Reeded

Date	Mintage	F	VF	XF	Unc	BU
2004 Proof	15,000	Value: 40.00				

KM# 750 5 DOLLARS

20.0000 g., Aluminum-Brass, 38.74 mm. **Ruler:** Elizabeth II **Obv:** Elizabeth II **Rev:** Tennis player **Edge:** Reeded

Date	Mintage	F	VF	XF	Unc	BU
2005	—	—	—	—	11.00	12.50

KM# 782 5 DOLLARS

36.3100 g., 0.9250 Silver 1.0798 oz. ASW, 38.74 mm. **Ruler:** Elizabeth II **Subject:** Commonwealth Games **Rev:** Melbourne - City of Sport

Date	Mintage	F	VF	XF	Unc	BU
2006 Proof	10,000	Value: 35.00				

KM# 790 5 DOLLARS

Silver **Ruler:** Elizabeth II **Subject:** Masters in Art - Drysdale

Date	Mintage	F	VF	XF	Unc	BU
2006 Proof	10,000	Value: 35.00				

KM# 786 5 DOLLARS

Aluminum-Bronze **Ruler:** Elizabeth II **Subject:** Queens Baton Relay

Date	Mintage	F	VF	XF	Unc	BU
2006	—	—	—	—	6.00	8.00

KM# 787 5 DOLLARS

Silver **Ruler:** Elizabeth II **Subject:** Masters in Art - Nolan

Date	Mintage	F	VF	XF	Unc	BU
2006 Proof	10,000	Value: 35.00				

KM# 788 5 DOLLARS

Silver **Ruler:** Elizabeth II **Subject:** Masters in Art - Siding

Date	Mintage	F	VF	XF	Unc	BU
2006 Proof	10,000	Value: 35.00				

KM# 789 5 DOLLARS

Silver **Ruler:** Elizabeth II **Subject:** Masters in Art - Whiteley

Date	Mintage	F	VF	XF	Unc	BU
2006 Proof	10,000	Value: 35.00				

KM# 786a 5 DOLLARS

Silver **Ruler:** Elizabeth II **Subject:** Queens Baton Relay

Date	Mintage	F	VF	XF	Unc	BU
2006 Proof	10,000	Value: 35.00				

KM# 783 5 DOLLARS

Aluminum-Bronze **Ruler:** Elizabeth II **Subject:** Commonwealth Games **Rev:** Games Logo

Date	Mintage	F	VF	XF	Unc	BU
2006	—	—	—	—	6.00	7.50

KM# 593 10 DOLLARS

33.1500 g., Bi-Metallic Gold plated .999 Silver center in Copper ring, 38.74 mm. **Subject:** "The Future" **Obv:** Bust of Queen Elizabeth II right **Rev:** Tree, map and denomination **Edge:** Reeded

Date	Mintage	F	VF	XF	Unc	BU
2001 Proof	20,000	Value: 40.00				

KM# 596 10 DOLLARS

311.0350 g., 0.9990 Silver 9.99 oz. ASW, 75.5 mm. **Subject:** Calendar Evolution **Obv:** Bust of Queen Elizabeth II right **Rev:** Multicolor solar system in center **Edge:** Segmented reeding **Note:** Illustration reduced.

Date	Mintage	F	VF	XF	Unc	BU
ND(2001) Proof	15,000	Value: 300				

KM# 633 10 DOLLARS

311.0350 g., 0.9990 Silver 9.99 oz. ASW, 75.5 mm. **Subject:** Evolution of Time **Obv:** Queen's portrait **Rev:** Various time keeping devices **Edge:** Segmented reeding

Date	Mintage	F	VF	XF	Unc	BU
2002P Proof	1,500	Value: 300				

KM# 661 10 DOLLARS

60.5000 g., 0.9990 Silver 1.9432 oz. ASW, 50 mm. **Subject:** The Adelaide Pound **Obv:** Queen's portrait above gold plated coin design **Rev:** Legend around gold plated coin design **Edge:** Reeded

Date	Mintage	F	VF	XF	Unc	BU
2002 Proof	10,000	Value: 65.00				

KM# 686 10 DOLLARS
311.0000 g., 0.9990 Silver 9.9889 oz. ASW, 75.5 mm. **Obv:** Queen Elizabeth II **Rev:** Alphabet Evolution design **Edge:** Reeded

Date	Mintage	F	VF	XF	Unc	BU
2003P Proof	1,500	Value: 275				

KM# 766 10 DOLLARS
36.3100 g., 0.9990 Silver 1.1662 oz. ASW, 38.7 mm. **Ruler:** Elizabeth II **Series:** Masterpieces in Silver - Port Phillip Patterns **Obv:** Elizabeth II **Rev:** Kangaroo design **Edge:** Reeded

Date	Mintage	F	VF	XF	Unc	BU
2003 Proof	10,000	Value: 70.00				

KM# 739 10 DOLLARS
311.0350 g., 0.9990 Silver 9.99 oz. ASW, 75.5 mm. **Ruler:** Elizabeth II **Subject:** Evolution of Numbers **Obv:** Elizabeth II **Rev:** Numbers, symbols, abacus and calculator **Edge:** Reeded

Date	Mintage	F	VF	XF	Unc	BU
2004 Proof	1,500	Value: 275				

KM# 744 10 DOLLARS
311.3460 g., 0.9990 Silver 10 oz. ASW, 75.5 mm. **Ruler:** Elizabeth II **Obv:** Elizabeth II **Rev:** Multicolor symbolic design **Edge:** Reeded

Date	Mintage	F	VF	XF	Unc	BU
2005 Proof	1,500	Value: 300				

KM# 751 10 DOLLARS
60.5000 g., 0.9990 Silver Partially Gold Plated 1.9432 oz. ASW, 50 mm. **Ruler:** Elizabeth II **Subject:** 150th Anniversary - Sydney Mint **Obv:** 7-line center inscription between two coin designs **Rev:** Mint building **Edge:** Reeded

Date	Mintage	F	VF	XF	Unc	BU
ND(2005) Proof	10,000	Value: 70.00				

KM# 760 20 DOLLARS
Bi-Metallic Gold center in Silver ring **Ruler:** Elizabeth II **Rev:** Sir Donald Bradman portrait

Date	Mintage	F	VF	XF	Unc	BU
2001 Proof	—	Value: 200				

KM# 595 20 DOLLARS
Bi-Metallic .999 4.5287 Silver center in .9999 9.499 Gold ring, 32.1 mm. **Subject:** Gregorian Millennium **Obv:** Bust of Queen Elizabeth II right **Rev:** Chronograph watch face with observatory in center and three depictions of the Earth's rotation **Edge:** Reeded **Note:** 14.03 grams total weight.

Date	Mintage	F	VF	XF	Unc	BU
2001 Prooflike	7,500	—	—	—	—	275

KM# 597 20 DOLLARS
Bi-Metallic .9999 8.8645 Gold center in .9999 10.7618 Silver ring, 32.1 mm. **Subject:** Centenary of Federation **Obv:** Bust of Queen Elizabeth II right **Rev:** National arms on a flowery background **Edge:** Reeded **Note:** 19.63 grams total weight.

Date	Mintage	F	VF	XF	Unc	BU
ND(2001) Prooflike	7,500	—	—	—	—	250

KM# 634 20 DOLLARS
18.3510 g., Bi-Metallic .999 Silver, 4.6655g, breast star shaped center in a .9999 Gold ,13.6855g outer ring, 32.1 mm. **Subject:** Queen's Golden Jubilee **Obv:** Queen's portrait **Rev:** Queen before Buckingham Palace **Edge:** Reeded

Date	Mintage	F	VF	XF	Unc	BU
2002P Proof	7,500	Value: 225				

KM# 687 20 DOLLARS
13.4056 g., 0.9990 Bi-Metallic .999 Gold 8.3979g Center in a .999 Silver 5.0077g Ring 0.4306 oz., 32 mm. **Subject:** Golden Jubilee of Coronation **Obv:** Queen Elizabeth II **Rev:** Four different coinage portraits of Queen Elizabeth II **Edge:** Reeded

Date	Mintage	F	VF	XF	Unc	BU
2003P Proof	7,500	Value: 450				

KM# 784 30 DOLLARS
1000.0000 g., 0.9990 Silver 32.1186 oz. ASW **Ruler:** Elizabeth II **Subject:** Commonwealth Games **Rev:** Two figures within circle of all the sports

Date	Mintage	F	VF	XF	Unc	BU
2006 Proof	500	Value: 550				

KM# 648 50 DOLLARS
36.5100 g., Tri-Metallic .9999 Gold 7.8g, 13.1 mm center in .999 Silver 13.39g, 26.85mm inner ring within a copper 15.32g, 3, 38.74 mm. **Subject:** Commonwealth Games **Obv:** Queen's portrait **Rev:** Victorious athletes within inscriptions and runners **Edge:** Reeded

Date	Mintage	F	VF	XF	Unc	BU
2002 Proof	5,000	Value: 300				

KM# 724 50 DOLLARS
36.5100 g., 0.9990 Tri-Metallic .999 Gold 7.8g center in .999 Silver 13.39g ring within .999 Copper 15.32g outer ring 1.1726 oz., 38.74 mm. **Subject:** Olympics **Obv:** Elizabeth II **Rev:** Multicolor flag above Olympic rings on shield within wreath **Edge:** Reeded

Date	Mintage	F	VF	XF	Unc	BU
2004 Proof	2,500	Value: 375				

KM# 785 50 DOLLARS
Tri-Metallic Gold center within Silver ring within Copper outer ring **Ruler:** Elizabeth II **Subject:** Commonwealth Games **Rev:** Victory wreath at center of legend

Date	Mintage	F	VF	XF	Unc	BU
2006 Proof	5,000	Value: 300				

KM# 643 100 DOLLARS
10.3678 g., 0.9999 Gold 0.3333 oz. AGW, 25 mm. **Subject:** Golden Wattle Flower **Obv:** Queen's portrait **Rev:** Flower and denomination **Edge:** Reeded

Date	Mintage	F	VF	XF	Unc	BU
2001	3,000	—	—	—	275	285
2001 Proof	2,500	Value: 300				

KM# 646 100 DOLLARS
31.4000 g., 0.9999 Gold 1.0094 oz. AGW, 34.1 mm. **Subject:** Queen's 50th Anniversary of Accession **Obv:** Queen's portrait **Rev:** Silhouette of George VI, Queen's portrait and denomination **Rev. Designer:** Peter Soobik **Edge:** Reeded

Date	Mintage	F	VF	XF	Unc	BU
2002 Proof	2,002	Value: 800				

Note: In sets only

KM# 657 100 DOLLARS
10.3678 g., 0.9999 Gold 0.3333 oz. AGW, 25 mm. **Obv:** Queen's portrait **Rev:** Sturt's Desert Rose **Edge:** Reeded

Date	Mintage	F	VF	XF	Unc	BU
2002	3,000	—	—	—	275	285
2002 Proof	2,500	Value: 300				

KM# 635 100 DOLLARS
31.1035 g., 0.9999 Gold 0.9999 oz. AGW, 32.1 mm. **Subject:** Gold Panning **Obv:** Queen's potrait **Rev:** Two prospectors dry panning for gold with color highlighted pans and dust **Edge:** Reeded

Date	Mintage	F	VF	XF	Unc	BU
2002P Proof	1,500	Value: 775				

KM# 636 100 DOLLARS
31.1035 g., 0.9995 Platinum 0.9995 oz. APW, 32.1 mm. **Subject:** Multiculturalism **Obv:** Queen's portrait **Rev:** Six racially diverse portraits against a blue background **Edge:** Reeded

Date	Mintage	F	VF	XF	Unc	BU
2002P Proof	1,000	Value: 1,450				

KM# 741 100 DOLLARS
31.1035 g., 0.9999 Gold 0.9999 oz. AGW, 32 mm. **Ruler:** Elizabeth II **Obv:** Elizabeth II **Rev:** Eureka Stockade leader Peter Lalor and blue flag **Edge:** Reeded

Date	Mintage	F	VF	XF	Unc	BU
2004P Proof	1,500	Value: 1,000				

KM# 742 100 DOLLARS
31.1035 g., 0.9995 Platinum 0.9995 oz. APW, 32.1 mm. **Ruler:** Elizabeth II **Obv:** Elizabeth II **Rev:** Four different sport athletes and multicolor background **Edge:** Reeded

Date	Mintage	F	VF	XF	Unc	BU
2004P Proof	1,000	Value: 1,900				

KM# 644 150 DOLLARS
15.5517 g., 0.9999 Gold 0.4999 oz. AGW, 30 mm. **Obv:** Queen's portrait **Rev:** Golden Wattle Flower, value **Edge:** Reeded

Date	Mintage	F	VF	XF	Unc	BU
2001 Proof	1,500	Value: 400				

KM# 658 150 DOLLARS
15.5517 g., 0.9999 Gold 0.4999 oz. AGW, 30 mm. **Subject:** Sturt's Desert Rose Flower **Obv:** Queen's portrait **Rev:** Flowers **Edge:** Reeded

Date	Mintage	F	VF	XF	Unc	BU
2002 Proof	1,500	Value: 400				

KM# 731 150 DOLLARS
10.3678 g., 0.9990 Gold 0.333 oz. AGW, 25 mm. **Ruler:** Elizabeth II **Obv:** Elizabeth II **Rev:** Cassowary bird **Edge:** Reeded

Date	Mintage	F	VF	XF	Unc	BU
2004 Proof	2,500	Value: 275				

KM# 752 150 DOLLARS
10.3678 g., 0.9999 Gold 0.3333 oz. AGW, 25 mm. **Ruler:** Elizabeth II **Obv:** Elizabeth II **Rev:** Malleefowl bird **Edge:** Reeded

Date	Mintage	F	VF	XF	Unc	BU
2005 Proof	2,500	Value: 335				

KM# 732 200 DOLLARS
15.5518 g., 0.9990 Gold 0.4995 oz. AGW, 30 mm. **Ruler:** Elizabeth II **Obv:** Elizabeth II **Rev:** Cassowary bird **Edge:** Reeded

Date	Mintage	F	VF	XF	Unc	BU
2004 Proof	2,500	Value: 385				

KM# 753 200 DOLLARS
15.5518 g., 0.9999 Gold 0.5 oz. AGW, 30 mm. **Ruler:** Elizabeth II **Obv:** Elizabeth II **Rev:** Malleefowl bird **Edge:** Reeded

Date	Mintage	F	VF	XF	Unc	BU
2005 Proof	2,500	Value: 480				

SILVER BULLION - KANGAROO

KM# 590 DOLLAR
31.1035 g., 0.9990 Silver 0.999 oz. ASW, 40 mm. **Obv:** Bust of Queen Elizabeth II right **Rev:** Aboriginal kangaroo design with dots **Rev. Designer:** Jeanette Timbery **Edge:** Reeded

Date	Mintage	F	VF	XF	Unc	BU
2001 Frosted Unc	—				15.00	
2001 Proof	—	Value: 25.00				

KM# 642 DOLLAR
31.1035 g., 0.9990 Silver 0.999 oz. ASW, 40 mm. **Obv:** Queen's portrait **Rev:** Aboriginal style kangaroo with wavy line background **Edge:** Reeded

Date	Mintage	F	VF	XF	Unc	BU
2002	—	—	—	—	24.00	26.00
2002 Proof	—	Value: 35.00				

KM# 723 DOLLAR
31.1035 g., 0.9990 Silver 0.999 oz. ASW, 40 mm. **Obv:** Elizabeth II **Rev:** Kangaroo with semi-circle background **Edge:** Reeded

Date	Mintage	F	VF	XF	Unc	BU
2004 Frosted Finish	—	—	—	—	18.00	20.00
2004 Proof	12,500	Value: 40.00				

KM# 723a DOLLAR
31.1035 g., 0.9990 Silver 0.999 oz. ASW, 40 mm. **Edge:** Reeded **Note:** Partially gold plated.

Date	Mintage	F	VF	XF	Unc	BU
2004 Frosted finish	—	—	—	—	55.00	60.00

SILVER BULLION - KOOKABURRA

KM# 684 50 CENTS
15.5500 g., 0.9990 Silver 0.4994 oz. ASW, 32.1 mm. **Obv:** Queen Elizabeth II **Rev:** Two Kookaburras **Edge:** Reeded **Shape:** Square with rounded corners

Date	Mintage	F	VF	XF	Unc	BU
2003P Proof	30,000	Value: 32.50				

KM# 479 DOLLAR
31.9700 g., 0.9990 Silver 1.0268 oz. ASW **Obv:** Queen's head right **Rev:** Two Kookaburras back to back on branch

Date	Mintage	F	VF	XF	Unc	BU
2001	—	—	—	—	22.50	25.00

KM# 618 DOLLAR
31.1035 g., 0.9990 Silver 0.999 oz. ASW, 40.4 mm. **Subject:** U.S. State Quarter - New York

Date	Mintage	F	VF	XF	Unc	BU
2001	75,000	—	—	—	24.50	27.50

KM# 619 DOLLAR
31.1035 g., 0.9990 Silver 0.999 oz. ASW, 40.4 mm. **Subject:** U.S. State Quarter - North Carolina

Date	Mintage	F	VF	XF	Unc	BU
2001	75,000	—	—	—	24.50	27.50

KM# 620 DOLLAR
31.1035 g., 0.9990 Silver 0.999 oz. ASW, 40.4 mm. **Subject:** U.S. State Quarter - Rhode Island

Date	Mintage	F	VF	XF	Unc	BU
2001	75,000	—	—	—	24.50	27.50

KM# 621 DOLLAR
31.1035 g., 0.9990 Silver 0.999 oz. ASW, 40.4 mm. **Subject:** U.S. State Quarter - Vermont

Date	Mintage	F	VF	XF	Unc	BU
2001	75,000	—	—	—	24.50	27.50

KM# 622 DOLLAR
31.1035 g., 0.9990 Silver 0.999 oz. ASW, 40.4 mm. **Subject:** U.S. State Quarter - Kentucky

Date	Mintage	F	VF	XF	Unc	BU
2001	75,000	—	—	—	24.50	27.50

KM# 691.1 DOLLAR
31.6200 g., 0.9990 Silver 1.0156 oz. ASW, 40.5 mm. **Ruler:** Elizabeth II **Obv:** Elizabeth II right **Rev:** Kookaburra flying over Australia **Edge:** Reeded

Date	Mintage	F	VF	XF	Unc	BU
2002	—	—	—	—	20.00	22.50

KM# 691.2 DOLLAR
31.6200 g., 0.9990 Silver 1.0156 oz. ASW, 40.5 mm. **Ruler:** Elizabeth II **Obv:** Queen Elizabeth II **Rev:** Multicolor US flag above a kookaburra flying over Australia **Edge:** Reeded

Date	Mintage	F	VF	XF	Unc	BU
2002	—	—	—	—	25.00	28.00

KM# 625 DOLLAR
31.1035 g., 0.9990 Silver 0.999 oz. ASW, 40.4 mm. **Subject:** U.S. State Quarter - Tennessee

Date	Mintage	F	VF	XF	Unc	BU
2002	75,000	—	—	—	24.50	27.50

KM# 626 DOLLAR
31.1035 g., 0.9990 Silver 0.999 oz. ASW, 40.4 mm. **Subject:** U.S. State Quarter - Ohio

Date	Mintage	F	VF	XF	Unc	BU
2002	75,000	—	—	—	24.50	27.50

KM# 627 DOLLAR
31.1035 g., 0.9990 Silver 0.999 oz. ASW, 40.4 mm. **Subject:** U.S. State Quarter - Louisiana

Date	Mintage	F	VF	XF	Unc	BU
2002	75,000	—	—	—	24.50	27.50

KM# 628 DOLLAR
31.1035 g., 0.9990 Silver 0.999 oz. ASW, 40.4 mm. **Subject:** U.S. State Quarter - Indiana

Date	Mintage	F	VF	XF	Unc	BU
2002	75,000	—	—	—	24.50	27.50

KM# 629 DOLLAR
31.1035 g., 0.9990 Silver 0.999 oz. ASW, 40.4 mm. **Subject:** U.S. State Quarter - Mississippi

Date	Mintage	F	VF	XF	Unc	BU
2002	75,000	—	—	—	24.50	27.50

KM# 666 DOLLAR
31.6200 g., 0.9990 Silver 1.0156 oz. ASW, 40.3 mm. **Obv:** Queen's portrait **Rev:** Kookaburra perched on branch **Edge:** Reeded

Date	Mintage	F	VF	XF	Unc	BU
2003	—	—	—	—	22.50	25.00

KM# 683 DOLLAR
31.5600 g., 0.9990 Silver 1.0137 oz. ASW, 40.5 mm. **Obv:** Queen Elizabeth II **Rev:** Two gold-plated kookaburra birds **Edge:** Reeded

Date	Mintage	F	VF	XF	Unc	BU
2004 Proof	15,000	Value: 35.00				

KM# 720 DOLLAR
1.0350 g., 0.9990 Silver 0.0332 oz. ASW **Ruler:** Elizabeth II **Rev:** Kookabarra

Date	Mintage	F	VF	XF	Unc	BU
2005	—	—	—	—	20.00	22.50

KM# 623.1 2 DOLLARS
62.8500 g., 0.9990 Silver 2.0187 oz. ASW, 50 mm. **Obv:** Queen's portrait **Rev:** Two Kookaburras back to back **Edge:** Reeded

Date	Mintage	F	VF	XF	Unc	BU
2001	—	—	—	—	40.00	45.00

KM# 623.2 2 DOLLARS
62.2070 g., 0.9990 Silver 1.998 oz. ASW **Subject:** USA State Quarters - 2001 **Obv:** Queen's head right **Rev:** Two kookaburras on branch with five state quarter designs added **Edge:** Reeded and plain sections **Note:** Prev. KM#623

Date	Mintage	F	VF	XF	Unc	BU
2001	10,000	—	—	—	150	165

KM# 678 2 DOLLARS
62.8500 g., 0.9990 Silver 2.0187 oz. ASW, 50 mm. **Obv:** Queen's portrait **Rev:** Kookaburra flying over Australian map **Edge:** Reeded

Date	Mintage	F	VF	XF	Unc	BU
2002	—	—	—	—	40.00	45.00

KM# 603 10 DOLLARS
311.0350 g., 0.9990 Silver 9.99 oz. ASW, 74.9 mm. **Subject:** Kookaburra **Obv:** Queen's portrait **Rev:** Flying bird over map **Edge:** Reeded

Date	Mintage	F	VF	XF	Unc	BU
2002 Proof	—	Value: 150				

KM# 630 20 DOLLARS
62.2070 g., 0.9990 Silver 1.998 oz. ASW **Subject:** USA State Quarters - 2002 **Obv:** Queen's head right **Rev:** Kookaburra on branch with five state quarter designs added below **Edge:** Reeded and plain sections

Date	Mintage	F	VF	XF	Unc	BU
2002	10,000	—	—	—	42.00	45.00

KM# 624 30 DOLLARS
1002.5020 g., 0.9990 Silver 32.1989 oz. ASW **Subject:** USA State Quarters - 2001 **Obv:** Queen's head right **Rev:** Two kookaburras on branch with five state quarter designs added below **Edge:** Reeded and plain sections

Date	Mintage	F	VF	XF	Unc	BU
2001	1,000	—	—	—	—	500

KM# 631 30 DOLLARS
1002.5020 g., 0.9990 Silver 32.1989 oz. ASW **Subject:** USA State Quarters - 2002 **Obv:** Queen's head right **Rev:** Kookaburra on branch with five state quarter designs added below **Edge:** Reeded and plain sections

Date	Mintage	F	VF	XF	Unc	BU
2002	1,000	—	—	—	—	500

KM# 680 30 DOLLARS
1000.0000 g., 0.9990 Silver 32.1186 oz. ASW, 101 mm. **Obv:** Queen's portrait **Rev:** Kookaburra in flight above Australian map **Edge:** Segmented reeding

Date	Mintage	F	VF	XF	Unc	BU
2002	—	—	—	—	—	550

BULLION - LUNAR YEAR

KM# 579 50 CENTS
15.5518 g., 0.9990 Silver 0.4995 oz. ASW, 32.1 mm. **Subject:** Year of the Horse **Obv:** Bust of Queen Elizabeth II right **Rev:** Horse running left **Edge:** Reeded

Date	Mintage	F	VF	XF	Unc	BU
2002P Proof	5,000	Value: 28.00				

KM# 664 50 CENTS
16.4000 g., 0.9990 Silver 0.5267 oz. ASW, 31.9 mm. **Subject:** Year of the Goat **Obv:** Queen's portrait **Rev:** Two goats **Edge:** Reeded

Date	Mintage	F	VF	XF	Unc	BU
2003	—	—	—	—	12.00	14.00

KM# 673 50 CENTS
15.5518 g., 0.9990 Silver 0.4995 oz. ASW, 32.1 mm. **Subject:** Year of the Monkey **Obv:** Queen's portrait **Rev:** Monkey sitting on branch **Edge:** Reeded

Date	Mintage	F	VF	XF	Unc	BU
2004(2003) Proof	11,000	Value: 25.00				

KM# 536 DOLLAR
31.1035 g., 0.9990 Silver 1. oz. ASW, 40.6 mm. **Subject:** Year of the Snake **Obv:** Bust of Queen Elizabeth II right **Rev:** Snake with eggs **Edge:** Reeded

Date	Mintage	F	VF	XF	Unc	BU
2001	300,000	—	—	—	25.00	28.00
2001P Proof	2,500	Value: 42.00				

KM# 536a DOLLAR
31.6350 g., 0.9990 Silver, 40.6 mm. **Ruler:** Elizabeth II **Obv:** Queen Elizabeth II **Rev:** Gold-plated snake **Edge:** Reeded

Date	Mintage	F	VF	XF	Unc	BU
2001	50,000	—	—	—	45.00	50.00

KM# 580 DOLLAR
31.1035 g., 0.9990 Silver 0.999 oz. ASW, 40.6 mm. **Subject:** Year of the Horse **Obv:** Bust of Queen Elizabeth II right **Rev:** Horse running left **Edge:** Reeded

Date	Mintage	F	VF	XF	Unc	BU
2002P	—	—	—	—	25.00	28.00
2002P Proof	2,500	Value: 42.00				

KM# 665 DOLLAR
31.6200 g., 0.9990 Silver 1.0156 oz. ASW, 40.3 mm. **Subject:** Year of the Goat **Obv:** Queen's portrait **Rev:** Two goats **Edge:** Reeded

Date	Mintage	F	VF	XF	Unc	BU
2003	—	—	—	—	22.50	25.00

KM# 674 DOLLAR
31.1035 g., 0.9990 Silver 0.999 oz. ASW, 40.6 mm. **Ruler:** Elizabeth II **Subject:** Year of the Monkey **Obv:** Queen's portrait **Rev:** Monkey sitting on branch **Edge:** Reeded

Date	Mintage	F	VF	XF	Unc	BU
2004(2003)	—	—	—	—	22.50	25.00
2004(2003) Proof	8,500	Value: 35.00				

KM# 665a DOLLAR
31.6350 g., 0.9990 Silver, 40.6 mm. **Ruler:** Elizabeth II **Obv:** Queen Elizabeth II **Rev:** Gold-plated goat **Edge:** Reeded

Date	Mintage	F	VF	XF	Unc	BU
2003	50,000	—	—	—	50.00	55.00

KM# 674a DOLLAR
31.6350 g., 0.9990 Silver, 40.6 mm. **Ruler:** Elizabeth II **Obv:** Queen Elizabeth II **Rev:** Gold-plated Monkey **Edge:** Reeded

Date	Mintage	F	VF	XF	Unc	BU
2004	50,000	—	—	—	50.00	55.00

KM# 695 DOLLAR
31.6350 g., 0.9990 Silver 1.0161 oz. ASW, 40.5 mm. **Ruler:** Elizabeth II **Obv:** Queen Elizabeth II **Rev:** Rooster **Edge:** Reeded

Date	Mintage	F	VF	XF	Unc	BU
2005	—	—	—	—	22.50	25.00

KM# 695a.1 DOLLAR
31.6350 g., 0.9990 Silver 1.0161 oz. ASW, 40.5 mm. **Ruler:** Elizabeth II **Obv:** Queen Elizabeth II **Rev:** Gold-plated Rooster on polished surface **Edge:** Reeded

Date	Mintage	F	VF	XF	Unc	BU
2005	47,200	—	—	—	45.00	50.00

KM# 695a.2 DOLLAR
31.6350 g., 0.9990 Silver 1.0161 oz. ASW, 40.5 mm. **Ruler:** Elizabeth II **Obv:** Queen Elizabeth II **Rev:** Gold-plated Rooster on matte surface **Edge:** Reeded

Date	Mintage	F	VF	XF	Unc	BU
2005	2,800	—	—	—	175	185

KM# 537 2 DOLLARS
62.2070 g., 0.9990 Silver 2. oz. ASW, 50.3 mm. **Subject:** Year of the Snake **Obv:** Queen's head right **Rev:** Snake with eggs **Edge:** Segmented reeding

Date	Mintage	F	VF	XF	Unc	BU
2001	—	—	—	—	40.00	45.00
2001P Proof	1,000	Value: 100				

KM# 581 2 DOLLARS
62.2070 g., 0.9990 Silver 1.998 oz. ASW, 50 mm. **Subject:** Year of the Horse **Obv:** Bust of Queen Elizabeth II right **Rev:** Horse running left **Edge:** Reeded

Date	Mintage	F	VF	XF	Unc	BU
2002	—	—	—	—	40.00	45.00
2002P Proof	1,000	Value: 100				

KM# 679 2 DOLLARS
62.8500 g., 0.9990 Silver 2.0187 oz. ASW, 50 mm. **Subject:** Year of the Goat **Obv:** Queen's portrait **Rev:** Two goats **Edge:** Reeded

Date	Mintage	F	VF	XF	Unc	BU
2003	—	—	—	—	40.00	45.00

KM# 675 2 DOLLARS
62.2070 g., 0.9990 Silver 1.998 oz. ASW, 50 mm. **Subject:** Year of the Monkey **Obv:** Queen's portrait **Rev:** Monkey sitting on branch **Edge:** Reeded

Date	Mintage	F	VF	XF	Unc	BU
2004(2003)	—	—	—	—	37.50	40.00
2004(2003) Proof	7,000	Value: 90.00				

KM# 538 5 DOLLARS
1.5710 g., 0.9990 Gold .0500 oz. AGW, 14.1 mm. **Subject:** Year of the Snake **Obv:** Queen's head right **Rev:** Snake in tree **Edge:** Reeded

Date	Mintage	F	VF	XF	Unc	BU
2001	100,000	—	—	—	—	40.00
2001P Proof	100,000	Value: 50.00				

KM# 582 5 DOLLARS
1.5552 g., 0.9990 Gold 0.05 oz. AGW, 14.1 mm. **Subject:** Year of the Horse **Obv:** Bust of Queen Elizabeth II right **Rev:** Horse galloping towards us **Edge:** Reeded

Date	Mintage	F	VF	XF	Unc	BU
2002P	100,000	—	—	—	—	50.00

KM# 668 5 DOLLARS
1.5710 g., 0.9999 Gold 0.0505 oz. AGW, 14.1 mm. **Subject:** Year of the Monkey **Obv:** Queen's portrait **Rev:** Monkey **Edge:** Reeded

Date	Mintage	F	VF	XF	Unc	BU
2004(2003)P Proof	100,000	Value: 50.00				

KM# 743 8 DOLLARS
155.5175 g., 0.9990 Silver 4.995 oz. ASW, 65 mm. **Ruler:** Elizabeth II **Obv:** Elizabeth II **Rev:** Gold-plated seated monkey and multicolored ornamentation **Edge:** Reeded

Date	Mintage	F	VF	XF	Unc	BU
2004	6,000	—	—	—	—	200

KM# 539 10 DOLLARS
311.0350 g., 0.9990 Silver 10.0000 oz. ASW, 75.5 mm. **Subject:** Year of the Snake **Obv:** Queen's head right **Rev:** Snake with eggs **Edge:** Segmented reeding

Date	Mintage	F	VF	XF	Unc	BU
2001	—	—	—	—	160	175
2001P Proof	250	Value: 300				

KM# 583 10 DOLLARS
311.0350 g., 0.9990 Silver 9.99 oz. ASW, 75.5 mm. **Subject:** Year of the Horse **Obv:** Bust of Queen Elizabeth II right **Rev:** Horse running left **Edge:** Segmented reeding

Date	Mintage	F	VF	XF	Unc	BU
2002	—	—	—	—	165	185
2002P Proof	500	Value: 285				

KM# 676 10 DOLLARS
311.0350 g., 0.9990 Silver 9.99 oz. ASW, 75.5 mm. **Subject:** Year of the Monkey **Obv:** Queen's portrait **Rev:** Monkey sitting on branch **Edge:** Segmented reeding

Date	Mintage	F	VF	XF	Unc	BU
2004(2003)	—	—	—	—	160	175
2004(2003) Proof	5,000	Value: 275				

KM# 710 10 DOLLARS
311.0350 g., 0.9990 Silver 9.99 oz. ASW **Ruler:** Elizabeth II **Rev:** Goat

Date	Mintage	F	VF	XF	Unc	BU
2003	—	—	—	—	160	175
2003 Proof	—	Value: 285				

KM# 696 10 DOLLARS
311.0350 g., 0.9990 Silver 9.99 oz. ASW **Ruler:** Elizabeth II **Rev:** Rooster

Date	Mintage	F	VF	XF	Unc	BU
2005	—	—	—	—	160	175
2005 Proof	—	Value: 285				

KM# 540 15 DOLLARS
3.1103 g., 0.9990 Gold .1000 oz. AGW, 16.1 mm. **Subject:** Year of the Snake **Obv:** Queen's head right **Rev:** Snake in tree **Edge:** Reeded

Date	Mintage	F	VF	XF	Unc	BU
2001	80,000	—	—	—	—	85.00
2001P Proof	7,000	Value: 100				

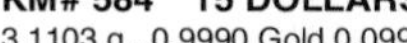

KM# 584 15 DOLLARS
3.1103 g., 0.9990 Gold 0.0999 oz. AGW, 16.1 mm. **Subject:** Year of the Horse **Obv:** Bust of Queen Elizabeth II right **Rev:** Horse galloping left **Edge:** Reeded

Date	Mintage	F	VF	XF	Unc	BU
2002P	—	—	—	—	—	85.00
2002P Proof	7,000	Value: 100				

KM# 669 15 DOLLARS
3.1103 g., 0.9999 Gold 0.1 oz. AGW, 16.1 mm. **Subject:** Year of the Monkey **Obv:** Queen's portrait **Rev:** Monkey **Edge:** Reeded

Date	Mintage	F	VF	XF	Unc	BU
2004P	—	—	—	—	—	85.00
2004(2003)P Proof	80,000	Value: 115				

KM# 711 15 DOLLARS
3.1100 g., 0.9999 Gold 0.1 oz. AGW **Ruler:** Elizabeth II **Rev:** Goat

Date	Mintage	F	VF	XF	Unc	BU
2003	—	—	—	—	—	85.00
2003 Proof	—	Value: 100				

KM# 541 25 DOLLARS
7.7508 g., 0.9990 Gold .2500 oz. AGW, 20.1 mm. **Subject:** Year of the Snake **Obv:** Queen's head right **Rev:** Snake in tree **Edge:** Reeded

Date	Mintage	F	VF	XF	Unc	BU
2001	60,000	—	—	—	—	185
2001P Proof	7,000	Value: 225				

KM# 585 25 DOLLARS
7.7759 g., 0.9990 Gold 0.2498 oz. AGW, 20.1 mm. **Subject:** Year of the Horse **Obv:** Bust of Queen Elizabeth II right **Rev:** Horse galloping half left **Edge:** Reeded

Date	Mintage	F	VF	XF	Unc	BU
2002P	—	—	—	—	—	185
2002P Proof	7,000	Value: 225				

KM# 670 25 DOLLARS
7.7508 g., 0.9999 Gold 0.2492 oz. AGW, 20.1 mm. **Subject:** Year of the Monkey **Obv:** Queen's portrait **Rev:** Monkey **Edge:** Reeded

Date	Mintage	F	VF	XF	Unc	BU
2004P	—	—	—	—	—	190
2004(2003)P Proof	60,000	Value: 300				

KM# 712 25 DOLLARS
7.7500 g., 0.9999 Gold 0.2491 oz. AGW **Ruler:** Elizabeth II **Rev:** Goat

Date	Mintage	F	VF	XF	Unc	BU
2003	—	—	—	—	—	185
2003 Proof	—	Value: 225				

KM# 542 30 DOLLARS
1002.5020 g., 0.9990 Silver 32.2312 oz. ASW, 101 mm. **Subject:** Year of the Snake **Obv:** Queen's head right **Rev:** Snake with eggs **Edge:** Segmented reeding

Date	Mintage	F	VF	XF	Unc	BU
2001	—	—	—	—	—	500
2001P Proof	250	Value: 550				

KM# 586 30 DOLLARS
1002.5020 g., 0.9990 Silver 32.1989 oz. ASW, 101 mm. **Subject:** Year of the Horse **Obv:** Bust of Queen Elizabeth II right **Rev:** Horse running left **Edge:** Segmented reeding **Note:** Illustration reduced.

Date	Mintage	F	VF	XF	Unc	BU
2002	—	—	—	—	—	500
2002P Proof	250	Value: 550				

KM# 677.1 30 DOLLARS
1000.0000 g., 0.9990 Silver 32.1186 oz. ASW, 101 mm. **Subject:** Year of the Monkey **Obv:** Queen's portrait **Rev:** Monkey sitting on branch **Edge:** Segmented reeding

Date	Mintage	F	VF	XF	Unc	BU
2004(2003)	—	—	—	—	—	500
2004(2003) Proof	5,250	Value: 585				

KM# 677.2 30 DOLLARS
1000.0000 g., 0.9990 Silver 32.1186 oz. ASW, 101 mm. **Subject:** Year of the Monkey **Obv:** Queen's portrait **Rev:** Multicolor ornamentation and Monkey with diamond chip eyes sitting on branch **Edge:** Segmented reeding **Note:** Illustration reduced.

Date	Mintage	F	VF	XF	Unc	BU
2004(2003) Proof	5,000	Value: 600				

KM# 681 30 DOLLARS
1000.0000 g., 0.9990 Silver 32.1186 oz. ASW, 101 mm. **Subject:** Year of the Goat **Obv:** Queen's portrait **Rev:** Nanny goat and kid **Edge:** Segmented reeding

Date	Mintage	F	VF	XF	Unc	BU
2003	—	—	—	—	—	500
2003P Proof	—	Value: 550				

KM# 697 30 DOLLARS
1000.0000 g., 0.9990 Silver 32.1186 oz. ASW **Ruler:** Elizabeth II **Rev:** Rooster

Date	Mintage	F	VF	XF	Unc	BU
2005	—	—	—	—	—	500
2005 Proof	—	Value: 600				

KM# 671 50 DOLLARS
15.5940 g., 0.9999 Gold 0.5013 oz. AGW, 25.1 mm. **Subject:** Year of the Monkey **Obv:** Queen's portrait **Rev:** Monkey **Edge:** Reeded

Date	Mintage	F	VF	XF	Unc	BU
2004(2003)P Proof	40,000	Value: 385				

KM# 543 100 DOLLARS
31.1035 g., 0.9990 Gold 1. oz. AGW, 32.1 mm. **Subject:** Year of the Snake **Obv:** Queen's head right **Rev:** Snake in tree **Edge:** Reeded

Date	Mintage	F	VF	XF	Unc	BU
2001	30,000	—	—	—	—	725
2001P Proof	—	Value: 825				

KM# 587 100 DOLLARS
31.1035 g., 0.9990 Gold 0.999 oz. AGW, 32.1 mm. **Subject:** Year of the Horse **Obv:** Bust of Queen Elizabeth II right **Rev:** Horse running left **Edge:** Reeded

Date	Mintage	F	VF	XF	Unc	BU
2002	—	—	—	—	—	725
2002P Proof	—	Value: 800				

KM# 672 100 DOLLARS
31.1035 g., 0.9999 Gold 0.9999 oz. AGW, 32.1 mm. **Subject:** Year of the Monkey **Obv:** Queen's portrait **Rev:** Monkey **Edge:** Reeded

Date	Mintage	F	VF	XF	Unc	BU
2004	—	—	—	—	—	725
2004(2003)P Proof	30,000	Value: 800				

KM# 713 100 DOLLARS
31.1035 g., 0.9999 Gold 0.9999 oz. AGW **Ruler:** Elizabeth II **Rev:** Goat

Date	Mintage	F	VF	XF	Unc	BU
2003	—	—	—	—	—	725
2003 Proof	—	Value: 800				

KM# 704 200 DOLLARS
62.2140 g., 0.9999 Gold 2 oz. AGW **Ruler:** Elizabeth II **Rev:** Snake

Date	Mintage	F	VF	XF	Unc	BU
2001 Proof	—	Value: 1,500				

KM# 707 200 DOLLARS
62.2140 g., 0.9999 Gold 2 oz. AGW **Ruler:** Elizabeth II **Rev:** Horse

Date	Mintage	F	VF	XF	Unc	BU
2002 Proof	—	Value: 1,500				

KM# 714 200 DOLLARS
62.2140 g., 0.9999 Gold 2 oz. AGW **Ruler:** Elizabeth II **Rev:** Goat

Date	Mintage	F	VF	XF	Unc	BU
2003 Proof	—	Value: 1,500				

KM# 717 200 DOLLARS
62.2100 g., 0.9999 Gold 1.9999 oz. AGW **Ruler:** Elizabeth II **Rev:** Monkey

Date	Mintage	F	VF	XF	Unc	BU
2004 Proof	—	Value: 1,500				

KM# 698 200 DOLLARS
62.2100 g., 0.9999 Gold 1.9999 oz. AGW **Ruler:** Elizabeth II **Rev:** Rooster

Date	Mintage	F	VF	XF	Unc	BU
2005 Proof	—	Value: 1,500				

KM# 705 1000 DOLLARS
311.0480 g., 0.9999 Gold 9.9994 oz. AGW **Ruler:** Elizabeth II **Rev:** Snake

Date	Mintage	F	VF	XF	Unc	BU
2001	—	—	—	—	—	7,500

KM# 708 1000 DOLLARS
311.0480 g., 0.9999 Gold 9.9994 oz. AGW **Ruler:** Elizabeth II **Rev:** Horse

Date	Mintage	F	VF	XF	Unc	BU
2002	—	—	—	—	—	7,500

KM# 715 1000 DOLLARS
311.0480 g., 0.9999 Gold 9.9994 oz. AGW **Ruler:** Elizabeth II **Rev:** Goat

Date	Mintage	F	VF	XF	Unc	BU
2003	—	—	—	—	—	7,500

KM# 718 1000 DOLLARS
311.0480 g., 0.9999 Gold 9.9994 oz. AGW **Ruler:** Elizabeth II **Rev:** Monkey

Date	Mintage	F	VF	XF	Unc	BU
2004	—	—	—	—	—	7,500

KM# 699 1000 DOLLARS
311.0480 g., 0.9999 Gold 9.9994 oz. AGW **Ruler:** Elizabeth II **Rev:** Rooster

Date	Mintage	F	VF	XF	Unc	BU
2005	—	—	—	—	—	7,500

KM# 706 3000 DOLLARS
1000.0000 g., 0.9999 Gold 32.1475 oz. AGW **Ruler:** Elizabeth II **Rev:** Snake

Date	Mintage	F	VF	XF	Unc	BU
2001	—	—	—	—BV+10%		—

KM# 709 3000 DOLLARS
1000.0000 g., 0.9999 Gold 32.1475 oz. AGW **Ruler:** Elizabeth II **Rev:** Horse

Date	Mintage	F	VF	XF	Unc	BU
2002	—	—	—	—BV+10%		—

KM# 716 3000 DOLLARS
1000.0000 g., 0.9999 Gold 32.1475 oz. AGW **Ruler:** Elizabeth II **Rev:** Goat

Date	Mintage	F	VF	XF	Unc	BU
2003	—	—	—	—BV+10%		—

KM# 719 3000 DOLLARS
1000.0000 g., 0.9999 Gold 32.1475 oz. AGW **Ruler:** Elizabeth II **Rev:** Monkey

Date	Mintage	F	VF	XF	Unc	BU
2004	—	—	—	—BV+10%		—

KM# 700 3000 DOLLARS
1000.0000 g., 0.9999 Gold 32.1475 oz. AGW **Ruler:** Elizabeth II **Rev:** Rooster

Date	Mintage	F	VF	XF	Unc	BU
2005	—	—	—	—BV+10%		—

GOLD BULLION - KANGAROO

KM# 692 50 DOLLARS
15.5540 g., 0.9999 Gold 0.5 oz. AGW, 25.1 mm. **Ruler:** Elizabeth II **Obv:** Queen Elizabeth II **Rev:** Two kangaroos on map above silver Liberty Bell insert **Edge:** Reeded

Date	Mintage	F	VF	XF	Unc	BU
2002	—	—	—	—	—	400

KM# 693 100 DOLLARS
31.1070 g., 0.9999 Gold 1 oz. AGW, 32.1 mm. **Ruler:** Elizabeth II **Obv:** Queen Elizabeth II **Rev:** Two kangaroos on map above silver Liberty Bell insert **Edge:** Reeded

Date	Mintage	F	VF	XF	Unc	BU
2002	—	—	—	—	—	750

MINT SETS

KM#	Date	Mintage	Identification	Issue Price	Mkt Val
MS39	2001 (3)	—	KM532-533, 534.1	7.80	7.50
MS40	2001 (3)	—	KM534.1, 550-551	7.80	7.50
MS41	2001 (3)	—	KM534.1, 552-553	7.80	7.50
MS42	2001 (3)	—	KM534.1, 554-555	7.80	7.50
MS43	2001 (3)	—	KM534.1, 556-557	7.80	7.50
MS44	2001 (3)	—	KM534.1, 558-559	7.80	7.50
MS45	2001 (3)	—	KM534.1, 560-561	7.80	7.50
MS46	2001 (3)	—	KM534.1, 562-563	7.80	7.50
MS47	2001 (3)	—	KM534.1, 564-565	7.80	7.50
MS48	2001 (20)	—	KM532-533, 534.1, 491.1, 550-565	43.68	70.00
MS49	2001 (6)	—	KM#401-403,406,491.1,492	—	—
MS50	2002 (6)	—	KM#401-403, 406, 600.1, 602	—	15.00
MS51	2002 (3)	—	KM#691, 692, 693	—	1,000
MS52	2003 (6)	—		—	15.00
MS53	2004 (6)	—		—	15.00
MS55	2006	—	KM#767, 768, 401-404, 489, 406 40 Years of Decimal Currency	—	—

PROOF SETS

KM#	Date	Mintage	Identification	Issue Price	Mkt Val
PS107	2001 (3)	—	KM532-533, 534.2	21.00	22.50
PS108	2001 (3)	—	KM534.2, 550-551	21.00	22.50
PS109	2001 (3)	—	KM534.2, 552-553	21.00	22.50
PS110	2001 (3)	—	KM534.2, 554-555	21.00	22.50
PS111	2001 (3)	—	KM534.2, 556-557	21.00	22.50
PS112	2001 (3)	—	KM534.2, 558-559	21.00	22.50
PS113	2001 (3)	—	KM534.2, 560-561	21.00	22.50
PS114	2001 (3)	—	KM534.2, 562-563	21.00	22.50
PS115	2001 (3)	—	KM534.2, 564-565	21.00	22.50
PS116	2001 (20)	—	KM532-533, 534.2, 549.2, 550-565	120	200
PS117	2003 (4)	10,000	KM763-766	118	128

The Republic of Austria, a parliamentary democracy located in mountainous central Europe, has an area of 32,374 sq. mi. (83,850 sq. km.) and a population of 8.08 million. Capital: Wien (Vienna). Austria is primarily an industrial country. Machinery, iron, steel, textiles, yarns and timber are exported.

REPUBLIC

POST WWII DECIMAL COINAGE

100 Groschen - 1 Schilling

KM# 2878 10 GROSCHEN

Aluminum **Edge:** Plain **Designer:** Hans Köttenstorfer

Date	Mintage	F	VF	XF	Unc	BU
2001	—	—	—	—	0.45	—
2001 Proof	75,000	Value: 1.50				

KM# 2885 50 GROSCHEN

Aluminum-Bronze **Obv. Designer:** Hans Köttenstorfer **Rev. Designer:** Ferdinand Welz

Date	Mintage	F	VF	XF	Unc	BU
2001	—	—	—	—	0.45	—
2001 Proof	75,000	Value: 2.00				

Note: In sets only

KM# 2886 SCHILLING

Aluminum-Bronze **Obv. Designer:** Edwin Grienauer **Rev:** Edelweiss flower **Rev. Designer:** Ferdinand Welz **Edge:** Plain

Date	Mintage	F	VF	XF	Unc	BU
2001	—	—	—	—	1.25	—
2001 Proof	75,000	Value: 2.00				

Note: In sets only

KM# 2889a 5 SCHILLING

Copper-Nickel **Obv. Designer:** Hans Köttenstorfer **Rev. Designer:** Josef Köblinger **Edge:** Plain

Date	Mintage	F	VF	XF	Unc	BU
2001	—	—	—	—	2.00	—
2001 Proof	75,000	Value: 2.50				

Note: In sets only

KM# 2918 10 SCHILLING

Copper-Nickel Plated Nickel **Obv. Designer:** Kurt Bodlak **Rev:** Woman of Wachau **Rev. Designer:** Ferdinand Welz

Date	Mintage	F	VF	XF	Unc	BU
2001	—	—	—	—	2.00	—
2001 Proof; in sets only	75,000	Value: 2.50				

KM# 3075 20 SCHILLING

8.1300 g., Brass, 27.8 mm. **Subject:** Johann Nepomuk Nestroy **Obv:** Denomination **Rev:** Bust of Nestroy half facing left **Edge:** Plain **Designer:** Herbert Wähner

Date	Mintage	F	VF	XF	Unc	BU
2001	300,000	—	—	—	4.50	—
2001 Proof	75,000	Value: 10.00				

KM# 3076 50 SCHILLING

8.1100 g., Bi-Metallic Copper-Nickel clad Nickel center in Aluminumn-Bronze ring, 26.5 mm. **Subject:** The Schilling Era **Obv:** Denomination and shields **Rev:** Four old coin designs **Edge:** Plain

Date	Mintage	F	VF	XF	Unc	BU
2001	600,000	—	—	—	7.50	—
2001 Special Unc.	100,000	—	—	—	9.50	—

KM# 3073 100 SCHILLING

Ring Weight: 7.0000 g. **Ring Composition:** 0.9000 Silver .2604 oz. ASW **Center Weight:** 3.7500 g. **Center Composition:** Titanium, 34 mm. **Subject:** Transportation **Obv:** Automobile engine **Obv. Designer:** Thomas Pesendorfer **Rev:** Car, train, truck, and plane **Rev. Designer:** Andreas Zanaschka **Edge:** Plain

Date	Mintage	F	VF	XF	Unc	BU
2001 Proof	50,000	Value: 40.00				

KM# 3077 100 SCHILLING

20.0000 g., 0.9000 Silver .5209 oz. ASW, 34 mm. **Subject:** Charlemagne **Obv:** Holy Roman Emperor's crown above denomination **Obv. Designer:** Thomas Pesendorfer **Rev:** Bust of Charlemagne facing half right holding scepter **Rev. Designer:** Herbert Wähner **Edge:** Reeded

Date	Mintage	F	VF	XF	Unc	BU
2001 Proof	30,000	Value: 40.00				

KM# 3079 100 SCHILLING

20.0000 g., 0.9000 Silver .5209 oz. ASW, 34 mm. **Subject:** Duke Rudolf IV **Obv:** University teaching scene **Obv. Designer:** Thomas Pesendorfer **Rev:** Bust of Duke Rudolf IV at right facing half left, St. Stephen's Cathedral at left **Rev. Designer:** Herbert Wähner **Edge:** Reeded

Date	Mintage	F	VF	XF	Unc	BU
2001 Proof	30,000	Value: 40.00				

KM# 3074 500 SCHILLING

10.1400 g., 0.9860 Gold .3170 oz. AGW, 22 mm. **Subject:** 2000 Years of Christianity - Bible **Obv:** Bible and symbols of the saints: Matthew, Luke, Mark, and John **Rev:** St. Paul reading from a scroll to two listeners **Edge:** Reeded **Designer:** Thomas Pesendorfer

Date	Mintage	F	VF	XF	Unc	BU
2001	50,000	—	—	—	—	235

KM# 3078 500 SCHILLING

24.0000 g., 0.9250 Silver .7137 oz. ASW, 37 mm. **Subject:** Kufstein Castle **Obv:** Castle view above denomination **Rev:** Emperor Maximilian being shown one of his new cannons **Edge:** Lettered **Designer:** Thomas Pesendorfer

Date	Mintage	F	VF	XF	Unc	BU
2001	95,000	—	—	—	45.00	—
2001 Special Unc.	25,000	—	—	—	50.00	—
2001 Proof	50,000	Value: 60.00				

KM# 3080 500 SCHILLING

24.0000 g., 0.9250 Silver .7137 oz. ASW, 37 mm. **Subject:** Schattenburg Castle **Obv:** Castle view **Obv. Designer:** Thomas Pesendorfer **Rev:** Two medieval armourers at work **Rev. Designer:** Helmut Andexlinger **Edge:** Lettered

Date	Mintage	F	VF	XF	Unc	BU
2001	95,000	—	—	—	42.00	—
2001 Special Unc	15,000	—	—	—	50.00	—
2001 Proof	43,000	Value: 60.00				

KM# 3081 1000 SCHILLING

16.2200 g., 0.9860 Gold .5072 oz. AGW, 30 mm. **Subject:** Austrian National Library **Obv:** Archduke Maximilian as a student **Obv. Designer:** Thomas Pesendorfer **Rev:** Library interior view **Rev. Designer:** Herbert Wähner **Edge:** Reeded

Date	Mintage	F	VF	XF	Unc	BU
2001	30,000	—	—	—	—	375

BULLION COINAGE

Philharmonic Issues

KM# 3004 200 SCHILLING

3.1100 g., 0.9999 Gold .1000 oz. AGW **Series:** Vienna Philharmonic Orchestra **Obv:** Building **Rev:** Instruments **Designer:** Thomas Pesendorfer

Date	Mintage	F	VF	XF	Unc	BU
2001	26,400	—	—	—	BV+13%	—

KM# 2989 500 SCHILLING

7.7760 g., 0.9999 Gold .2505 oz. AGW **Series:** Vienna Philharmonic Orchestra **Obv:** Similar to 2000 Schilling, KM#2990 **Designer:** Thomas Pesendorfer

Date	Mintage	F	VF	XF	Unc	BU
2001	25,800	—	—	—	BV+10%	—

KM# 3031 1000 SCHILLING

15.5500 g., 0.9999 Gold .5000 oz. AGW **Series:** Vienna Philharmonic Orchestra **Designer:** Thomas Pesendorfer

Date	Mintage	F	VF	XF	Unc	BU
2001	26,800	—	—	—	BV+8%	—

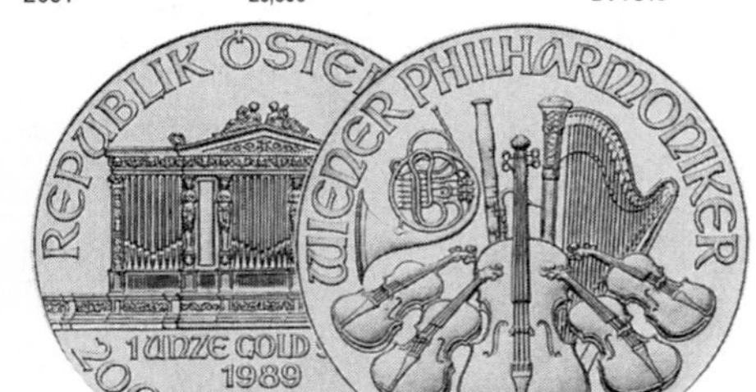

KM# 2990 2000 SCHILLING

31.1035 g., 0.9999 Gold 1.0002 oz. AGW **Series:** Vienna Philharmonic Orchestra **Designer:** Thomas Pesendorfer

Date	Mintage	F	VF	XF	Unc	BU
2001	51,700	—	—	—	BV+4%	—

EURO COINAGE

European Economic Community Issues

KM# 3082 EURO CENT

2.2700 g., Copper Plated Steel, 16.2 mm. **Obv:** Gentian flower **Obv. Designer:** Josef Kaiser **Rev:** Denomination and globe **Rev. Designer:** Luc Luyex **Edge:** Plain

Date	Mintage	F	VF	XF	Unc	BU
2002	378,500,000	—	—	—	0.35	0.50
2002 Proof	10,000	Value: 15.00				
2003	10,925,000	—	—	—	0.35	0.50
2003 Proof	25,000	Value: 3.00				
2004	115,100,000	—	—	—	—	0.35
2004 Proof	20,000	Value: 3.00				
2005	122,900,000	—	—	—	—	0.35
2005 Proof	20,000	Value: 4.00				
2006	—	—	—	—	—	0.35

KM# 3083 2 EURO CENTS

3.0300 g., Copper Plated Steel, 18.7 mm. **Obv:** Edelweiss flower in inner circle, stars in outer circle **Obv. Designer:** Josef Kaiser **Rev:** Denomination and globe **Rev. Designer:** Luc Luyex **Edge:** Grooved

Date	Mintage	F	VF	XF	Unc	BU
2002	326,500,000	—	—	—	0.50	0.65
2002 Proof	10,000	Value: 20.00				
2003	118,625,000	—	—	—	0.50	0.65
2003 Proof	25,000	Value: 5.00				
2004	156,500,000	—	—	—	—	0.50
2004 Proof	20,000	Value: 5.00				
2005	112,900,000	—	—	—	—	0.50
2005 Proof	20,000	Value: 6.00				
2006	—	—	—	—	—	0.50

KM# 3084 5 EURO CENTS

3.8600 g., Copper Plated Steel, 21.2 mm. **Obv:** Alpine prim rose flower in inner ring, stars in outer ring **Obv. Designer:** Josef Kaiser **Rev:** Denomination and globe **Rev. Designer:** Luc Luycx **Edge:** Plain

Date	Mintage	F	VF	XF	Unc	BU
2002	217,100,000	—	—	—	0.75	1.00
2002 Proof	10,000	Value: 30.00				
2003	108,625,000	—	—	—	0.75	1.00
2003 Proof	25,000	Value: 8.50				
2004	89,400,000	—	—	—	—	0.75
2004 Proof	20,000	Value: 9.00				
2005	66,200,000	—	—	—	—	0.75
2005 Proof	20,000	Value: 10.00				
2006	—	—	—	—	—	0.75

KM# 3085 10 EURO CENTS

4.0700 g., Brass, 19.7 mm. **Obv:** St. Stephen's Cathedral spires **Obv. Designer:** Josef Kaiser **Rev:** Denomination and map **Rev. Designer:** Luc Luycx **Edge:** Reeded

Date	Mintage	F	VF	XF	Unc	BU
2002	441,700,000	—	—	—	0.75	1.00
2002 Proof	10,000	Value: 45.00				
2003	125,000	—	—	—	0.75	1.00
2003 Proof	25,000	Value: 8.50				
2004	5,300,000	—	—	—	—	0.75
2004 Proof	20,000	Value: 9.00				
2005	5,200,000	—	—	—	—	0.75
2005 Proof	20,000	Value: 10.00				
2006	—	—	—	—	—	0.75

KM# 3086 20 EURO CENTS

5.7300 g., Brass, 22.1 mm. **Obv:** Belvedere Palace gate **Obv. Designer:** Josef Kaiser **Rev:** Denomination and map **Rev. Designer:** Luc Luycx **Edge:** Notched

Date	Mintage	F	VF	XF	Unc	BU
2002	203,500,000	—	—	—	1.00	1.25
2002 Proof	10,000	Value: 60.00				
2003	51,038,200	—	—	—	1.00	1.25
2003 Proof	25,000	Value: 10.00				
2004	54,900,000	—	—	—	—	1.00
2004 Proof	20,000	Value: 11.50				
2005	4,100,000	—	—	—	—	1.00
2005 Proof	20,000	Value: 12.50				
2006	—	—	—	—	—	1.00

KM# 3087 50 EURO CENTS

7.8100 g., Brass, 24.2 mm. **Obv:** Secession building in Vienna **Obv. Designer:** Josef Kaiser **Rev:** Denomination and map **Rev. Designer:** Luc Luycx **Edge:** Reeded

Date	Mintage	F	VF	XF	Unc	BU
2002	169,200,000	—	—	—	1.25	1.50
2002 Proof	10,000	Value: 75.00				
2003	9,199,000	—	—	—	1.25	1.50
2003 Proof	25,000	Value: 12.50				
2004	3,200,000	—	—	—	—	1.25
2004 Proof	20,000	Value: 13.50				
2005	3,100,000	—	—	—	—	1.25
2005 Proof	20,000	Value: 15.00				
2006	—	—	—	—	—	1.25

KM# 3088 EURO

7.5000 g., Bi-Metallic Copper-Nickel center in Brass ring, 23.2 mm. **Obv:** Bust of Mozart right within inner circle, stars in outer circle **Obv. Designer:** Josef Kaiser **Rev:** Denomination and map **Rev. Designer:** Luc Luycx **Edge:** Reeded and plain sections

Date	Mintage	F	VF	XF	Unc	BU
2002	223,600,000	—	—	—	2.50	2.75
2002 Proof	10,000	Value: 100				
2003	125,000	—	—	—	2.50	2.75
2003 Proof	25,000	Value: 16.50				
2004	2,700,000	—	—	—	—	2.50
2004 Proof	20,000	Value: 17.50				
2005	2,600,000	—	—	—	—	2.50
2005 Proof	20,000	Value: 18.50				
2006	—	—	—	—	—	2.50

KM# 3089 2 EUROS

8.5200 g., Bi-Metallic Brass center in Copper-Nickel ring, 25.7 mm. **Obv:** Bust of Bertha von Suttner, Novelist and winner of 1905 Peace Prize, at right facing left in inner circle, stars in outer circle **Obv. Designer:** Joaef Kaiser **Rev:** Denomination and map **Rev. Designer:** Luc Luycx **Edge:** Reeded and lettered: 2 EURO (star) (star) (star) (star)

Date	Mintage	F	VF	XF	Unc	BU
2002	196,500,000	—	—	—	3.75	4.00
2002 Proof	10,000	Value: 125				
2003	4,804,500	—	—	—	3.75	4.00
2003 Proof	25,000	Value: 25.00				
2004	2,600,000	—	—	—	—	3.75
2004 Proof	20,000	Value: 27.50				
2005	6,900,000	—	—	—	—	3.75
2005 Proof	20,000	Value: 30.00				
2006	—	—	—	—	—	3.75

KM# 3124 2 EUROS

8.5200 g., Bi-Metallic Brass center in Copper-Nickel ring, 25.7 mm. **Subject:** 50th Anniversary of the State Treaty **Obv:** Treaty seals and signatures **Rev:** Value and map **Edge:** Reeding over lettering **Edge Lettering:** "2 EURO" and 3 stars repeated four times **Note:** No country name on this coin!

Date	Mintage	F	VF	XF	Unc	BU
2005	—	—	—	—	5.00	6.00

KM# 3091 5 EURO

8.0000 g., 0.8000 Silver 0.2058 oz. ASW, 29 mm. **Subject:** Schoenbrunn Zoo **Obv:** Circle of provincial arms around denomination **Rev:** Building and animals **Edge:** Plain **Shape:** 9-sided

Date	Mintage	F	VF	XF	Unc	BU
ND(2002)	500,000	—	—	—	12.50	—
ND(2002) Special Unc	100,000	—	—	—	22.50	—

KM# 3105 5 EURO
10.0500 g., 0.8000 Silver 0.2585 oz. ASW, 28.1 mm. **Subject:** Water Power **Obv:** Denomination **Rev:** Dam with turbine, electric power plant and fish **Edge:** Plain **Shape:** 9-sided

Date	Mintage	F	VF	XF	Unc	BU
2003	500,000	—	—	—	10.00	—
2003 Special Unc	100,000	—	—	—	15.00	—

KM# 3122 5 EURO
10.0000 g., 0.8000 Silver 0.2572 oz. ASW, 28.5 mm. **Subject:** Enlargement of the European Union **Obv:** Value in circle of provincial arms **Rev:** Map of Europe above country names **Edge:** Plain **Shape:** 9-sided

Date	Mintage	F	VF	XF	Unc	BU
2004 Special select	125,000	—	—	—	12.50	—
2004	275,000	—	—	—	9.00	—

KM# 3113 5 EURO
8.0000 g., 0.8000 Silver 0.2058 oz. ASW, 28.5 mm. **Obv:** Provincial arms around value **Rev:** Soccer player scoring a goal **Edge:** Plain **Shape:** 9-sided **Note:** Centennial of Austrian Soccer

Date	Mintage	F	VF	XF	Unc	BU
2004	500,000	—	—	—	9.00	—
2004 Special select	100,000	—	—	—	12.00	—

KM# 3117 5 EURO
10.0000 g., 0.8000 Silver 0.2572 oz. ASW, 28.5 mm. **Subject:** Centennial of sport Skiing **Obv:** Value encircled in provincial arms **Rev:** Skier **Edge:** Plain **Shape:** 9-sided

Date	Mintage	F	VF	XF	Unc	BU
2005	100,000	—	—	—	12.50	14.50

KM# 3120 5 EURO
10.0000 g., 0.8000 Silver 0.2572 oz. ASW, 28.5 mm. **Subject:** 10th Anniversary of Austrian E U Membership **Obv:** Value in circle of arms **Rev:** Carinthian Gate Theater and Beethoven cameo portrait **Edge:** Plain **Shape:** 9-sided

Date	Mintage	F	VF	XF	Unc	BU
2005	100,000	—	—	—	12.50	14.50

KM# 3131 5 EURO
10.0800 g., 0.8000 Silver 0.2593 oz. ASW, 28.5 mm. **Subject:** Mozart **Obv:** Value in circle of provincial arms **Rev:** Mozart and the Salzburg Cathedral **Edge:** Plain **Shape:** Nine sided

Date	Mintage	F	VF	XF	Unc	BU
2006	125,000	—	—	—	15.00	17.50

KM# 3096 10 EURO
16.0000 g., 0.9250 Silver 0.4758 oz. ASW, 32 mm. **Subject:** Ambras Palace **Obv:** Palace **Rev:** Three strolling musicians **Edge:** Reeded

Date	Mintage	F	VF	XF	Unc	BU
2002	130,000	—	—	—	15.00	—
2002 Special Unc	20,000	—	—	—	30.00	—
2002 Proof	50,000	Value: 40.00				

KM# 3099 10 EURO
16.0000 g., 0.9250 Silver 0.4758 oz. ASW, 32 mm. **Subject:** Eggenberg Palace and Johannes Kepler **Obv:** Palace **Rev:** Portrait **Edge:** Reeded

Date	Mintage	F	VF	XF	Unc	BU
2002	130,000	—	—	—	17.50	—
2002 Proof	50,000	Value: 32.50				
2002 Special Select	20,000	—	—	—	30.00	—

KM# 3103 10 EURO
16.0000 g., 0.9250 Silver 0.4758 oz. ASW, 32 mm. **Subject:** Schloss Hof **Obv:** Baroque fountain and palace **Rev:** Two gardeners at work **Edge:** Reeded

Date	Mintage	F	VF	XF	Unc	BU
2003	130,000	—	—	—	17.50	—
2003 Special Select	20,000	—	—	—	30.00	—
2003 Proof	50,000	Value: 32.50				

KM# 3106 10 EURO
16.0000 g., 0.9250 Silver 0.4758 oz. ASW, 32 mm. **Subject:** Schoenbrunn Palace **Obv:** Fountain with palace background **Rev:** Palmenhaus greenhouse **Edge:** Reeded

Date	Mintage	F	VF	XF	Unc	BU
2003	100,000	—	—	—	17.50	—
2003 Special Select	40,000	—	—	—	27.50	—
2003 Proof	60,000	Value: 30.00				

KM# 3111 10 EURO
17.2973 g., 0.9250 Silver 0.5144 oz. ASW, 32 mm.
Obv: Hellbrunn Palace **Rev:** Archbishop Marcus Sitticus and Hellbrunn's "Roman Theatre" **Edge:** Reeded

Date	Mintage	F	VF	XF	Unc	BU
2004 Special Select	40,000	—	—	—	25.00	—
2004 Proof	60,000	Value: 30.00				
2004	130,000	—	—	—	15.00	—

KM# 3115 10 EURO
17.2973 g., 0.9250 Silver 0.5144 oz. ASW, 32 mm. **Obv:** Artstetten Palace **Rev:** Crypt entrance behind portraits of Franz Ferdinand and Sophie **Edge:** Reeded

Date	Mintage	F	VF	XF	Unc	BU
2004 Special Select	40,000	—	—	—	25.00	—
2004 Proof	60,000	Value: 30.00				
2004	130,000	—	—	—	15.00	—

KM# 3121 10 EURO
17.3000 g., 0.9250 Silver 0.5145 oz. ASW, 32 mm. **Subject:** 60th Anniversary of the Republic **Obv:** Statue of Athena and nine provincial shields **Rev:** Parliament building, broken chain and a crowd of people **Edge:** Reeded

Date	Mintage	F	VF	XF	Unc	BU
2005	40,000	—	—	—	25.00	—
2005 Proof	60,000	Value: 35.00				

KM# 3125 10 EURO
17.3000 g., 0.9250 Silver 0.5145 oz. ASW, 32 mm. **Subject:** Reopening of the Burg Theater and Opera **Obv:** Two large buildings **Rev:** Comedy and Tragedy Masks **Edge:** Reeded

Date	Mintage	F	VF	XF	Unc	BU
2005	40,000	—	—	—	25.00	—
2005 Proof	60,000	Value: 35.00				

KM# 3129 10 EURO
17.2973 g., 0.9250 Silver 0.5144 oz. ASW, 32 mm.
Subject: Nonnenberg Abbey **Obv:** Abbey view **Rev:** Statue of St. Erentrudis **Edge:** Reeded

Date	Mintage	F	VF	XF	Unc	BU
2006	40,000	—	—	—	—	25.00
2006 Proof	60,000	Value: 35.00				

KM# 3097 20 EURO
18.0000 g., 0.9000 Silver 0.5208 oz. ASW, 34 mm. **Subject:** Ferdinand I - Renaissance **Obv:** Hofburg Palace "Swiss Gate" with two guards **Rev:** Ferdinand I and coat of arms **Edge:** Reeded

Date	Mintage	F	VF	XF	Unc	BU
2002 Proof	50,000	Value: 37.50				

KM# 3098 20 EURO
18.0000 g., 0.9000 Silver 0.5208 oz. ASW, 34 mm. **Subject:** Prince Eugen - Baroque Period **Obv:** Baroque staircase with statues **Rev:** Portrait **Edge:** Reeded

Date	Mintage	F	VF	XF	Unc	BU
2002 Proof	50,000	Value: 42.00				

KM# 3104 20 EURO
18.0000 g., 0.9000 Silver 0.5208 oz. ASW, 34 mm.
Subject: Prince Metternich **Obv:** Early steam locomotive **Rev:** Portrait with map background **Edge:** Reeded

Date	Mintage	F	VF	XF	Unc	BU
2003 Proof	50,000	Value: 45.00				

KM# 3107 20 EURO
18.0000 g., 0.9000 Silver 0.5208 oz. ASW, 34 mm.
Obv: Republic of Austria arms **Rev:** Four men in a jeep **Edge:** Reeded **Note:** Post War Austrian Reconstruction

Date	Mintage	F	VF	XF	Unc	BU
2003 Proof	50,000	Value: 50.00				

KM# 3112 20 EURO
20.0000 g., 0.9000 Silver 0.5787 oz. ASW, 34 mm. **Obv:** S.M.S Novara under sail in Chinese waters **Rev:** Standing figures of Duke Ferdinand Maximilian and Commodore von Wullerstorf-Urbair behind table with globe and microscope **Edge:** Reeded **Note:** First Global Circumnavigation by an Austrian ship.

Date	Mintage	F	VF	XF	Unc	BU
2004 Proof	50,000	Value: 50.00				

KM# 3114 20 EURO
20.0000 g., 0.9000 Silver 0.5787 oz. ASW, 34 mm. **Obv:** SMS Erzherzog Ferdinand Max sailing to the Battle of Lissa **Rev:** Sailors at the wheel with Admiral Tegetthof in background **Edge:** Reeded

Date	Mintage	F	VF	XF	Unc	BU
2004 Proof	50,000	Value: 52.50				

KM# 3126 20 EURO
20.0000 g., 0.9000 Silver 0.5787 oz. ASW, 34 mm. **Obv:** Ship, "Admiral Tegetthoff" in arctic waters **Rev:** Expedition leaders, von Payer and Weyprecht with their icebound ship behind them **Edge:** Reeded

Date	Mintage	F	VF	XF	Unc	BU
2005 Proof	50,000	Value: 50.00				

KM# 3127 20 EURO
20.0000 g., 0.9000 Silver 0.5787 oz. ASW, 34 mm. **Obv:** SMS St. George sailing past the Statue of Liberty **Rev:** Shipyard at Pola **Edge:** Reeded

Date	Mintage	F	VF	XF	Unc	BU
2005 Proof	50,000	Value: 50.00				

KM# 3101 25 EURO
16.1500 g., Bi-Metallic 7.15g pure Niobium (Columbium) blue color center in a 9 g., .900 Silver ring, 34 mm. **Subject:** City of Hall in Tyrol **Obv:** Satellite mapping the city from outer space **Rev:** Depiction of the die face used to strike the 1486 guldiner coin **Edge:** Plain

Date	Mintage	F	VF	XF	Unc	BU
2003 Proof	50,000	Value: 125				

KM# 3109 25 EURO
16.1500 g., Bi-Metallic Niobium center (7.15) in .900 SILVER 9g, ring, 34 mm. **Subject:** Semmering Alpine Railway **Obv:** Modern and antique locomotives **Rev:** Steam train **Edge:** Plain

Date	Mintage	F	VF	XF	Unc	BU
2004 Proof	50,000	Value: 100				

KM# 3119 25 EURO
16.1500 g., Bi-Metallic Purple color pure Niobium 7.15g center in .900 Silver 9g, ring, 34 mm. **Subject:** 50 Years Austrian Television **Obv:** The original test pattern of the 1950's **Rev:** World globe behind "rabbit ear" antenna. Television developmental milestones from 7-1 oclock **Edge:** Plain

Date	Mintage	F	VF	XF	Unc	BU
2005 Proof	65,000	Value: 60.00				

KM# 3090 50 EURO
10.0000 g., 0.9860 Gold 0.317 oz. AGW, 22 mm. **Subject:** Saints Benedict and Scholastica **Obv:** St. Benedict and his sister St. Scholastica **Rev:** Monk copying a manuscript **Edge:** Reeded

Date	Mintage	F	VF	XF	Unc	BU
2002	50,000	—	—	—	—	235

KM# 3102 50 EURO
10.1420 g., 0.9860 Gold 0.3215 oz. AGW, 22 mm. **Subject:** Christian Charity **Obv:** Nursing Sister with hospital patient **Rev:** The Good Samaritan **Edge:** Reeded

Date	Mintage	F	VF	XF	Unc	BU
2003	50,000	—	—	—	—	245

KM# 3110 50 EURO
10.1420 g., 0.9860 Gold 0.3215 oz. AGW, 22 mm. **Obv:** Esterhazy Palace **Rev:** Joseph Hayden (1732-1809) **Edge:** Reeded

Date	Mintage	F	VF	XF	Unc	BU
2004 Proof	50,000	Value: 245				

KM# 3118 50 EURO
10.1420 g., 0.9860 Gold 0.3215 oz. AGW, 22 mm.
Obv: Lobkowitz Palace above value and document **Rev:** Ludwig Van Beethoven (1770-1827) **Edge:** Reeded

Date	Mintage	F	VF	XF	Unc	BU
2005 Proof	50,000	Value: 245				

KM# 3130 50 EURO
10.1420 g., 0.9860 Gold 0.3215 oz. AGW, 22 mm.
Subject: Mozart **Obv:** Mozart's birthplace **Rev:** Leopold and Wolfgang Mozart **Edge:** Reeded

Date	Mintage	F	VF	XF	Unc	BU
2006 Proof	50,000	Value: 300				

KM# 3100 100 EURO
16.2272 g., 0.9860 Gold 0.5072 oz. AGW, 30 mm. **Subject:** Raphael Donner **Obv:** Portrait in front of building **Rev:** Providentia Fountain **Edge:** Reeded

Date	Mintage	F	VF	XF	Unc	BU
2002	30,000	—	—	—	—	375

KM# 3108 100 EURO
16.2272 g., 0.9860 Gold 0.5072 oz. AGW, 30 mm. **Obv:** Gustav Klimt standing **Rev:** Klimt's painting "The Kiss" **Edge:** Reeded

Date	Mintage	F	VF	XF	Unc	BU
2003	30,000	—	—	—	—	400

KM# 3116 100 EURO
16.2272 g., 0.9860 Gold 0.5144 oz. AGW, 30 mm. **Obv:** Secession Exhibit Hall in Vienna **Rev:** Knight in armor, "strength" with two women, "ambition and sympathy" **Edge:** Reeded

Date	Mintage	F	VF	XF	Unc	BU
2004 Proof	30,000	Value: 400				

KM# 3128 100 EURO
16.2272 g., 0.9860 Gold 0.5144 oz. AGW, 30 mm. **Subject:** St. Leopold's Church at Steinhof **Obv:** Domed church building **Rev:** Two angels and stained glass portrait **Edge:** Reeded

Date	Mintage	F	VF	XF	Unc	BU
2005 Proof	30,000	Value: 450				

EURO BULLION COINAGE

Philharmonic Orchestra

KM# 3092 10 EURO
3.1210 g., 0.9999 Gold 0.1003 oz. AGW, 16 mm. **Subject:** Vienna Philharmonic **Obv:** The Golden Hall organ **Rev:** Musical instruments **Edge:** Segmented reeding

Date	Mintage	F	VF	XF	Unc	BU
2002	75,800	—	—	—	—	BV+13%
2003	59,700	—	—	—	—	BV+13%
2004	68,100	—	—	—	—	BV+13%
2005	—	—	—	—	—	BV+13%
2006	—	—	—	—	—	BV+13%

KM# 3093 25 EURO
7.7760 g., 0.9999 Gold 0.25 oz. AGW, 22 mm. **Subject:** Vienna Philharmonic **Obv:** The Golden Hall organ **Rev:** Musical instruments **Edge:** Segmented reeding

Date	Mintage	F	VF	XF	Unc	BU
2002	40,800	—	—	—	—	BV+10%
2003	34,000	—	—	—	—	BV+10%
2004	26,600	—	—	—	—	BV+10%
2005	—	—	—	—	—	BV+10%
2006	—	—	—	—	—	BV+10%

KM# 3094 50 EURO
15.5520 g., 0.9999 Gold 0.5 oz. AGW, 28 mm. **Subject:** Vienna Philharmonic **Obv:** The Golden Hall organ **Rev:** Musical instruments **Edge:** Segmented reeding

Date	Mintage	F	VF	XF	Unc	BU
2002	40,900	—	—	—	—	BV+8%
2003	26,800	—	—	—	—	BV+8%
2004	21,800	—	—	—	—	BV+8%
2005	—	—	—	—	—	BV+8%
2006	—	—	—	—	—	BV+8%

KM# 3095 100 EURO
31.1035 g., 0.9999 Gold 0.9999 oz. AGW, 37 mm.
Subject: Vienna Philharmonic **Obv:** The Golden Hall organ **Rev:** Musical instruments **Edge:** Segmented reeding

Date	Mintage	F	VF	XF	Unc	BU
2002	164,100	—	—	—	—	BV+4%
2003	179,900	—	—	—	—	BV+4%
2004	169,800	—	—	—	—	BV+4%
2005	—	—	—	—	—	BV+4%
2006	—	—	—	—	—	BV+4%

KM# 3123 100000 EURO
31103.5000 g., 0.9999 Gold 999.9 oz. AGW **Subject:** World's Largest Gold Bullion Coin **Obv:** Pipe organ **Rev:** Musical instruments **Edge:** Reeded

Date	Mintage	F	VF	XF	Unc	BU
2004 Proof	—	—	—	—	—	BV+3%

MINT SETS

KM#	Date	Mintage	Identification	Issue Price	Mkt Val
MS10	2001 (6)	75,000	KM#2878, 2885, 2886, 2889a, 2918, 3075	25.00	25.00
MS11	2002 (8)	100,000	KM#3082-3089	22.50	45.00
MS12	2003 (8)	125,000	KM#3082-3089	22.50	35.00
MS13	2004 (8)	—	KM#3082-3089	—	35.00
MS14	2005 (8)	—	KM#3082-3089	—	35.00
MS15	2006 (8)	—	KM#3082-3089	—	35.00

PROOF SETS

KM#	Date	Mintage	Identification	Issue Price	Mkt Val
PS63	2002 (8)	10,000	KM#3082-3089	85.00	470
PS64	2003 (8)	25,000	KM#3082-3089	85.00	90.00
PS65	2004 (8)	20,000	KM#3082-3089	—	95.00
PS66	2005 (8)	20,000	KM#3082-3089	—	100

AZERBAIJAN

The Republic of Azerbaijan (formerly Azerbaijan S.S.R.) includes the Nakhichevan Autonomous Republic. Situated in the eastern area of Transcaucasia, it is bordered in the west by Armenia, in the north by Georgia and Dagestan, to the east by the Caspian Sea and to the south by Iran. It has an area of 33,430 sq. mi. (86,600 sq. km.) and a population of 7.8 million. Capital: Baku. The area is rich in mineral deposits of aluminum, copper, iron, lead, salt and zinc, with oil as its leading industry. Agriculture and livestock follow in importance.

MONETARY SYSTEM
100 Qapik = 1 Manat

REPUBLIC

DECIMAL COINAGE

KM# 39 QAPIK
2.7300 g., Copper Plated Steel, 16.2 mm. **Obv:** Map above value **Rev:** Value and musical instruments **Edge:** Plain

Date	Mintage	F	VF	XF	Unc	BU
ND (2006)	—	—	—	—	—	0.75

KM# 40 3 QAPIK
3.3600 g., Copper-Plated-Steel, 17.9 mm. **Obv:** Map above value **Rev:** Value above books **Edge:** Grooved

Date	Mintage	F	VF	XF	Unc	BU
ND (2006)	—	—	—	—	—	1.00

KM# 41 5 QAPIK
4.7200 g., Copper-Plated-Steel, 29.75 mm. **Obv:** Map above value **Rev:** Building above value **Edge:** Reeded

Date	Mintage	F	VF	XF	Unc	BU
ND (2006)	—	—	—	—	—	1.25

KM# 42 10 QAPIK
5.1000 g., Brass-Plated Steel, 22.2 mm. **Obv:** Map above value **Rev:** Dome shaped object to right of value **Edge:** Notched

Date	Mintage	F	VF	XF	Unc	BU
ND (2006)	—	—	—	—	—	1.50

KM# 43 20 QAPIK
6.3500 g., Brass Plated Steel, 24.2 mm. **Obv:** Map above value **Rev:** Value and spiral staircase **Edge:** Segmented reeding

Date	Mintage	F	VF	XF	Unc	BU
ND (2006)	—	—	—	—	—	1.75

KM# 44 50 QAPIK
7.4200 g., Bi-Metallic Brass plated Steel center in Stainless Steel ring, 25.4 mm. **Obv:** Map above value **Rev:** Two oil wells **Edge:** Reeding over lettering

Date	Mintage	F	VF	XF	Unc	BU
ND (2006)	—	—	—	—	—	2.50

KM# 37 50 MANAT
28.3400 g., 0.9250 Silver 0.8428 oz. ASW, 38.6 mm.
Obv: National map **Rev:** Heydar Aliyev **Edge:** Reeded

Date	Mintage	F	VF	XF	Unc	BU
2004 Proof	2,000	Value: 65.00				

BAHAMAS

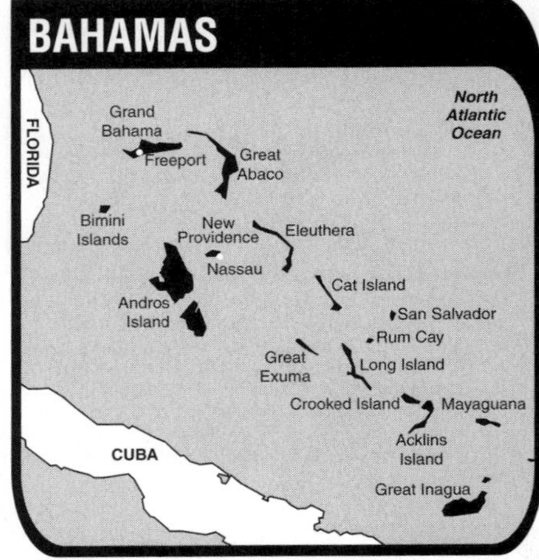

The Commonwealth of the Bahamas is an archipelago of about 3,000 islands, cays and rocks located in the Atlantic Ocean east of Florida and north of Cuba. The total land area of the 800 mile (1,287 km.) long chain of islands is 5,382 sq. mi. (13,935 sq. km.). They have a population of 302,000. Capital: Nassau. The Bahamas import most of their food and manufactured products and export cement, refined oil, pulpwood and lobsters. Tourism is the principal industry.

The coinage of Great Britain was legal tender in the Bahamas from 1825 to the issuing of a definitive coinage in 1966.

RULERS

British

MONETARY SYSTEM

12 Pence = 1 Shilling

COMMONWEALTH

DECIMAL COINAGE

100 Cents = 1 Dollar

KM# 59a CENT

Copper Plated Zinc

Date	Mintage	F	VF	XF	Unc	BU
2000	—	—	—	0.10	0.25	0.75
2001	—	—	—	0.10	0.25	0.75

BAHRAIN

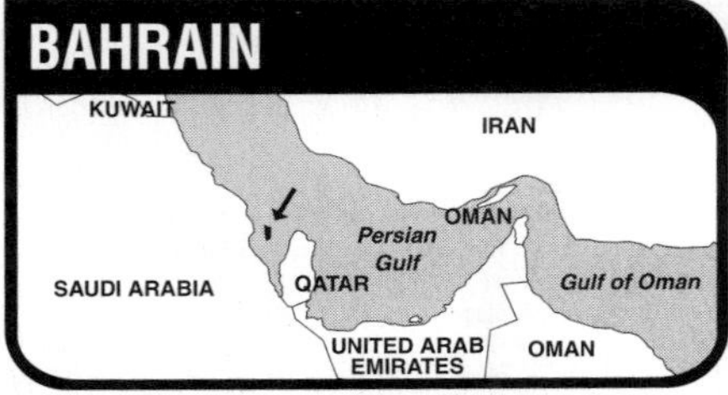

The Kingdom of Bahrain, a group of islands in the Persian Gulf off Saudi Arabia, has an area of 268 sq. mi. (622 sq. km.) and a population of 618,000. Capital: Manama. Prior to the depression of the 1930's, the economy was based on pearl fishing. Petroleum and aluminum industries and transit trade are the vital factors in the economy today.

The coinage of the Kingdom of Bahrain was struck at the Royal Mint, London, England.

RULERS

Al Khalifa Dynasty

Hamed Bin Isa, 1999-

MONETARY SYSTEM

1000 Fils = 1 Dinar

KINGDOM OF BAHRAIN

STANDARD COINAGE

KM# 28 10 FILS

3.3500 g., Brass, 21 mm. **Ruler:** Hamed Bin Isa **Obv:** Palm Tree, "Kingdom Of Bahrain" **Rev:** Value **Edge:** Plain

Date	Mintage	F	VF	XF	Unc	BU
AH 1423-2002	—	—	—	—	0.75	1.00

KM# 24 25 FILS

3.5300 g., Copper-Nickel, 19.8 mm. **Obv:** Similar to KM-18 except for legend **Obv. Legend:** KINGDOM OF BAHRAIN **Rev:** Same as KM#18 **Edge:** Reeded

Date	Mintage	F	VF	XF	Unc	BU
AH1423-2002	—	—	—	—	1.25	1.50

KM# 25 50 FILS

4.4700 g., Copper-Nickel, 21.8 mm. **Subject:** Kingdom **Obv:** Similar to KM-19 except for legend **Obv. Legend:** KINGDOM OF BAHRAIN **Rev:** Same as KM-19 **Edge:** Reeded

Date	Mintage	F	VF	XF	Unc	BU
AH1423-2002	—	—	—	—	1.50	1.75

KM# 26 100 FILS

5.9500 g., Bi-Metallic Copper-Nickel center in Brass ring, 23.9 mm. **Subject:** Kingdom **Obv:** Similar to KM-20 except for legend **Obv. Legend:** KINGDOM OF BAHRAIN **Rev:** Same as KM-20 **Edge:** Reeded

Date	Mintage	F	VF	XF	Unc	BU
AH1423-2002	—	—	—	—	3.50	4.00

KM# 29 100 FILS

5.9500 g., Bi-Metallic Copper-Nickel center in Brass ring, 23.9 mm. **Subject:** 1st Bahrain Grand Prix **Obv:** Ornamental design **Rev:** Value **Edge:** Reeded

Date	Mintage	F	VF	XF	Unc	BU
AH1425-2004	3,000	—	—	—	65.00	75.00

KM# 22 500 FILS

Bi-Metallic Brass center in Copper-Nickel ring, 27 mm. **Obv:** Monument and inscription **Obv. Inscription:** STATE OF BAHRAIN **Rev:** Denomination **Edge:** Reeded **Note:** Total weight: 9.05 grams.

Date	Mintage	F	VF	XF	Unc	BU
2001	—	—	—	—	6.00	7.50

KM# 27 500 FILS

9.0500 g., Bi-Metallic Brass center Copper-Nickel ring, 27 mm. **Subject:** Kingdom **Obv:** Similar to KM-22 except for legend **Obv. Legend:** KINGDOM OF BAHRAIN **Rev:** Same as KM#22 **Edge:** Reeded

Date	Mintage	F	VF	XF	Unc	BU
AH1423-2002	—	—	—	—	6.50	8.00

BANGLADESH

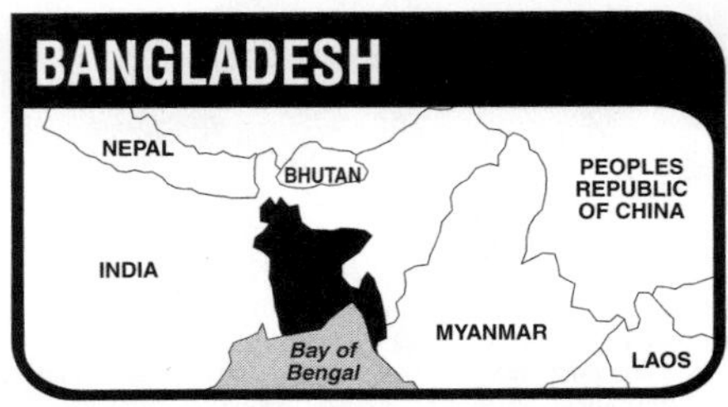

The Peoples Republic of Bangladesh (formerly East Pakistan), a parliamentary democracy located on the Bay of Bengal bordered by India and Burma, has an area of 55,598 sq. mi. (143,998 sq. km.) and a population of 128.1 million. Capital: Dhaka. The economy is predominantly agricultural. Jute products, jute and tea are exported.

Bangladesh is a member of the Commonwealth of Nations. The president is the Head of State and the Government.

MONETARY SYSTEM

100 Poisha = 1 Taka

DATING

Christian era using Bengali numerals.

PEOPLES REPUBLIC

STANDARD COINAGE

KM# 24 50 POISHA

2.6000 g., Stainless Steel, 19.3 mm. **Obv:** Fish, chicken and produce **Rev:** Water lily **Edge:** Plain **Shape:** Octagonal

Date	Mintage	F	VF	XF	Unc	BU
2001	—	—	—	—	1.50	—

KM# 9.5 TAKA

Stainless Steel

Date	Mintage	F	VF	XF	Unc	BU
2002	—	—	0.20	0.65	1.75	—

BARBADOS

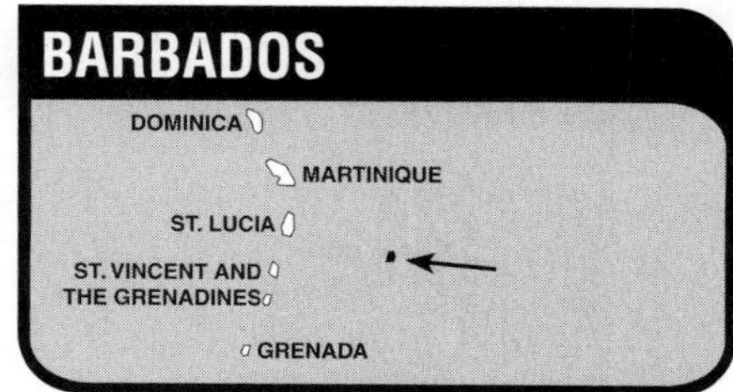

Barbados, an independent state within the British Commonwealth, is located in the Windward Islands of the West Indies east of St. Vincent. The coral island has an area of 166 sq. mi. (430 sq. km.) and a population of 269,000. Capital: Bridgetown. The economy is based on sugar and tourism. Sugar, petroleum products, molasses, and rum are exported.

MONETARY SYSTEM
100 Cents = 1 Dollar

INDEPENDENT SOVEREIGN STATE
within the British Commonwealth

DECIMAL COINAGE

KM# 10a CENT
Copper Plated Zinc **Edge:** Plain

Date	Mintage	F	VF	XF	Unc	BU
2001	—	—	—	0.10	0.25	0.75

KM# 11 5 CENTS
Brass **Rev:** South Point Lighthouse **Edge:** Plain

Date	Mintage	F	VF	XF	Unc	BU
2001	—	—	—	—	0.25	0.75

KM# 12 10 CENTS
Copper-Nickel **Rev:** Laughing Gull **Edge:** Reeded

Date	Mintage	F	VF	XF	Unc	BU
2001	—	—	0.10	0.15	0.50	1.50

KM# 69 5 DOLLARS
28.2700 g., 0.9250 Silver 0.8407 oz. ASW, 38.6 mm.
Subject: UNICEF **Obv:** National arms **Rev:** Three boys playing cricket **Edge:** Reeded

Date	Mintage	F	VF	XF	Unc	BU
2001 Proof	—	Value: 40.00				

BELARUS

Belarus (Byelorussia, Belorussia, or White Russia- formerly the Belorussian S.S.R.) is situated along the western Dvina and Dnieper Rivers, bounded in the west by Poland, to the north by Latvia and Lithuania, to the east by Russia and the south by the Ukraine. It has an area of 80,154 sq. mi. (207,600 sq. km.) and a population of 4.8 million. Capital: Minsk. Chief products: peat, salt, and agricultural products including flax, fodder and grasses for cattle breeding and dairy products.

MONETARY SYSTEM
100 Kapeek = 1 Rouble

REPUBLIC

STANDARD COINAGE

KM# 47 ROUBLE
13.1400 g., Copper-Nickel, 31.9 mm. **Obv:** National arms **Rev:** Bison **Edge:** Reeded

Date	Mintage	F	VF	XF	Unc	BU
2001 Proof	—	Value: 15.00				

KM# 50 ROUBLE
12.8000 g., Copper-Nickel, 28.6 mm. **Subject:** 2002 Winter Olympics **Obv:** National arms **Rev:** Two freestyle skiers **Edge:** Reeded

Date	Mintage	F	VF	XF	Unc	BU
2001 Proof	—	Value: 10.00				

KM# 44 ROUBLE
13.1400 g., Copper-Nickel, 31.9 mm. **Obv:** National arms **Rev:** Beaver and young **Edge:** Reeded

Date	Mintage	F	VF	XF	Unc	BU
2002 Proof	—	Value: 15.00				

KM# 61 ROUBLE
12.5000 g., Copper-Nickel, 32 mm. **Obv:** National arms **Rev:** Wrestlers **Edge:** Reeded

Date	Mintage	F	VF	XF	Unc	BU
2003 Proof	—	Value: 10.00				

KM# 54 ROUBLE
13.1200 g., Copper-Nickel, 31.9 mm. **Obv:** National arms **Rev:** Mute swans **Edge:** Reeded

Date	Mintage	F	VF	XF	Unc	BU
2003 Proof	—	Value: 15.00				

KM# 55 ROUBLE
13.1000 g., Copper-Nickel, 31.9 mm. **Obv:** State arms **Rev:** Herring Gull in flight **Edge:** Reeded

Date	Mintage	F	VF	XF	Unc	BU
2003 Proof	—	Value: 15.00				

KM# 56 ROUBLE
13.1000 g., Copper-Nickel, 32 mm. **Obv:** National arms **Rev:** Church of the Savior and Transfiguration **Edge:** Reeded

Date	Mintage	F	VF	XF	Unc	BU
2003	2,000	—	—	—	12.00	—

KM# 60 ROUBLE
13.1000 g., Copper-Nickel, 31.9 mm. **Obv:** National arms **Rev:** Two Common Cranes **Edge:** Reeded

Date	Mintage	F	VF	XF	Unc	BU
2004 Proof	—	Value: 15.00				

KM# 75 ROUBLE
15.9200 g., Copper-Nickel Antiqued Finish, 33 mm.
Subject: "Kupalle" **Obv:** Folk art cross design **Rev:** Flower above ferns **Edge:** Reeded

Date	Mintage	F	VF	XF	Unc	BU
2004	5,000	—	—	—	10.00	—

KM# 76 ROUBLE
15.9200 g., Copper-Nickel, 33 mm. **Subject:** "Kalyady"
Obv: Folk art cross design **Rev:** Stylized sun flower **Edge:** Reeded

Date	Mintage	F	VF	XF	Unc	BU
2004	5,000	—	—	—	10.00	—

KM# 78 ROUBLE
15.9000 g., Copper-Nickel, 33 mm. **Obv:** National arms
Rev: Radziwill's Castle in Neswizh **Edge:** Reeded

Date	Mintage	F	VF	XF	Unc	BU
2004 Proof-like	2,000	—	—	—	—	12.50

KM# 80 ROUBLE

15.9000 g., Copper-Nickel, 33 mm. **Subject:** Defenders of Brest **Obv:** Soviet Patriotic War Order **Rev:** "Courage" monument **Edge:** Reeded

Date	Mintage	F	VF	XF	Unc	BU
2004	5,000	—	—	—	12.50	—

KM# 64 10 ROUBLES

16.8200 g., 0.9250 Silver 0.5002 oz. ASW, 32.9 mm. **Obv:** National arms **Rev:** Jakub Kolas (1882-1956) **Edge:** Reeded

Date	Mintage	F	VF	XF	Unc	BU
2002 Proof	—	Value: 27.50				

KM# 46 20 ROUBLES

33.7300 g., 0.9250 Silver 1.0031 oz. ASW, 38.6 mm. **Subject:** Wildlife **Obv:** National arms **Rev:** Bison **Edge:** Reeded

Date	Mintage	F	VF	XF	Unc	BU
2001 Proof	—	Value: 45.00				

KM# 49 20 ROUBLES

28.3200 g., 0.9250 Silver 0.8422 oz. ASW, 38.6 mm. **Subject:** 2002 Winter Olympics **Obv:** National arms **Rev:** Marksman **Edge:** Reeded

Date	Mintage	F	VF	XF	Unc	BU
2001 Proof	—	Value: 42.50				

KM# 51 20 ROUBLES

33.6500 g., 0.9250 Silver 1.0007 oz. ASW, 38.6 mm. **Subject:** 2002 Winter Olympics **Obv:** National arms **Rev:** Two freestyle skiers **Edge:** Reeded

Date	Mintage	F	VF	XF	Unc	BU
2001 Proof	—	Value: 47.50				

KM# 45 20 ROUBLES

33.7300 g., 0.9250 Silver 1.0031 oz. ASW, 38.8 mm. **Obv:** National arms **Rev:** Beaver and young **Edge:** Reeded

Date	Mintage	F	VF	XF	Unc	BU
2002 Proof	—	Value: 45.00				

KM# 59 20 ROUBLES

28.6300 g., 0.9250 Silver 0.8514 oz. ASW, 38.6 mm. **Obv:** National arms **Rev:** Arctic bear with two cubs **Edge:** Reeded

Date	Mintage	F	VF	XF	Unc	BU
2002 Proof	—	Value: 45.00				

KM# 70 20 ROUBLES

33.8500 g., 0.9250 Silver 1.0067 oz. ASW, 33.43 mm. **Obv:** National arms **Rev:** 80th Anniversary - National Savings Bank **Edge:** Reeded

Date	Mintage	F	VF	XF	Unc	BU
2002 Proof	1,000	Value: 40.00				

KM# 53 20 ROUBLES

33.8400 g., 0.9250 Silver 1.0064 oz. ASW, 38.5 mm. **Obv:** State arms **Rev:** Two Mute swans in pond **Edge:** Reeded

Date	Mintage	F	VF	XF	Unc	BU
2003 Proof	2,000	Value: 45.00				

KM# 57 20 ROUBLES

31.1000 g., 0.9250 Silver 0.9249 oz. ASW, 38.6 mm. **Obv:** National arms **Rev:** Church of the Savior and Transfiguration **Edge:** Reeded

Date	Mintage	F	VF	XF	Unc	BU
2003 Proof	2,000	Value: 50.00				

KM# 71 20 ROUBLES

31.1000 g., 0.9250 Silver 0.9249 oz. ASW, 38.6 mm. **Subject:** "Kupalle" **Obv:** Folk art design **Rev:** Fern flower with inset red synthetic crystal **Edge:** Reeded

Date	Mintage	F	VF	XF	Unc	BU
2004 Antique finish	3,000	—	—	—	45.00	—

KM# 72 20 ROUBLES

31.1000 g., 0.9250 Silver 0.9249 oz. ASW, 38.6 mm. **Subject:** Defense of Brest **Obv:** Multicolor Soviet Order of the Patriotic War **Rev:** "Courage" monument **Edge:** Reeded

Date	Mintage	F	VF	XF	Unc	BU
2004 Proof	3,000	Value: 50.00				

KM# 73 20 ROUBLES

31.1000 g., 0.9250 Silver 0.9249 oz. ASW, 38.6 mm. **Obv:** National arms **Rev:** 2 common cranes **Edge:** Reeded

Date	Mintage	F	VF	XF	Unc	BU
2004 Proof	2,000	Value: 40.00				

KM# 77 20 ROUBLES
31.1000 g., 0.9250 Silver 0.9249 oz. ASW, 38.6 mm. **Subject:** "Kalyady" **Obv:** Folk art cross design **Rev:** Stylized sunflower with inset blue synthetic crystal **Edge:** Reeded

Date	Mintage	F	VF	XF	Unc	BU
2004 Antique finish	5,000	—	—	—	45.00	—

KM# 79 20 ROUBLES
31.1000 g., 0.9250 Silver 0.9249 oz. ASW, 38.6 mm. **Obv:** National arms **Rev:** Radziwill's Castle in Neswizh **Edge:** Reeded

Date	Mintage	F	VF	XF	Unc	BU
2004 Proof	2,000	Value: 50.00				

KM# 82 20 ROUBLES
28.7200 g., 0.9250 Silver 0.8541 oz. ASW, 38.6 mm. **Subject:** WW II Victory **Obv:** Multicolor Soviet Order of Victory **Rev:** Soviet soldiers raising their flag in the Reichstag in Berlin **Edge:** Reeded

Date	Mintage	F	VF	XF	Unc	BU
2005 Proof	12,000	Value: 50.00				

KM# 92 20 ROUBLES
28.6300 g., 0.9250 Silver 0.8514 oz. ASW, 38.6 mm. **Obv:** Two children sitting on crescent moon **Rev:** Violinist and inset orange color glass crystal **Edge:** Plain

Date	Mintage	F	VF	XF	Unc	BU
2005 Antique finish	20,000	—	—	—	50.00	—

KM# 93 20 ROUBLES
28.6300 g., 0.9250 Silver 0.8514 oz. ASW, 38.6 mm. **Subject:** Kalyady's star **Obv:** Two children sitting on a crescent moon **Rev:** Blue glass crystal inset on forehead, flower **Edge:** Plain

Date	Mintage	F	VF	XF	Unc	BU
2005 Antique finish	20,000	—	—	—	50.00	—

KM# 94 20 ROUBLES
28.6300 g., 0.9250 Silver 0.8514 oz. ASW, 38.6 mm. **Obv:** Two children sitting on a crescent moon **Rev:** White glass crystal inset above landscape with fox **Edge:** Plain

Date	Mintage	F	VF	XF	Unc	BU
2005 Antique finish	20,000	—	—	—	50.00	—

KM# 95 20 ROUBLES
28.6300 g., 0.9250 Silver 0.8514 oz. ASW **Obv:** Two children sitting on a crescent moon **Rev:** Yellow glass crystal inset in flower design **Edge:** Plain

Date	Mintage	F	VF	XF	Unc	BU
2005 Antique finish	20,000	—	—	—	50.00	—

KM# 96 20 ROUBLES
33.6600 g., 0.9250 Silver 1.001 oz. ASW, 38.6 mm. **Obv:** Quilted star design **Rev:** Yellow glass crystal inset in candle flame above basket **Edge:** Reeded

Date	Mintage	F	VF	XF	Unc	BU
2005 Antique finish	5,000	—	—	—	50.00	—

KM# 58 100 ROUBLES
155.5000 g., 0.9250 Silver 4.6245 oz. ASW, 64 mm. **Obv:** Theater building **Rev:** Two ballet dancers **Edge:** Reeded **Note:** Illustration reduced.

Date	Mintage	F	VF	XF	Unc	BU
2003 Proof	1,000	Value: 150				

KM# 74 1000 ROUBLES
1000.0000 g., 0.9990 Silver 32.1186 oz. ASW, 100 mm. **Subject:** 2004 Olympics **Obv:** National arms **Rev:** Ancient charioteer **Note:** Illustration reduced.

Date	Mintage	F	VF	XF	Unc	BU
2004 Proof	650	Value: 500				

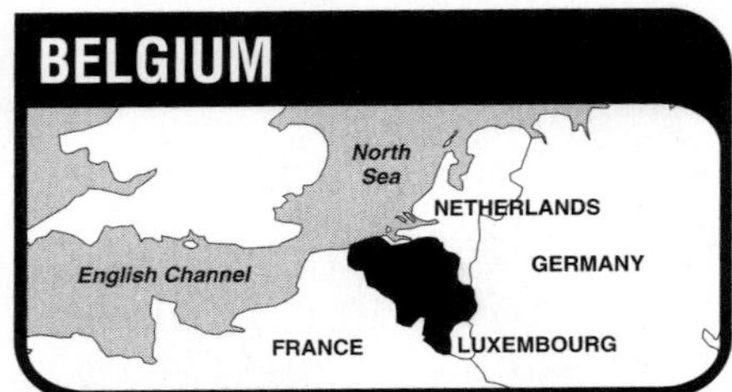

The Kingdom of Belgium, a constitutional monarchy in northwest Europe, has an area of 11,780 sq. mi. (30,519 sq. km.) and a population of 10.1 million, chiefly Dutch-speaking Flemish and French-speaking Walloons. Capital: Brussels. Agriculture, dairy farming, and the processing of raw materials for re-export are the principal industries. Beurs voor Diamant in Antwerp is the world's largest diamond trading center. Iron and steel, machinery motor vehicles, chemicals, textile yarns and fabrics comprise the principal exports.

RULERS
Albert II, 1993-

MINT MARKS
Angel head - Brussels

MINTMASTERS' INITIALS & PRIVY MARKS
(b) - bird - Vogelier
Lamb head – Lambret

NOTE: Beginning in 1987, the letters "qp" appear on the coins - (quality proof)

MONETARY SYSTEM
100 Centimes = 1 Franc
1 Euro = 100 Cents

LEGENDS
Belgian coins are usually inscribed either in Dutch, French or both. However some modern coins are being inscribed in Latin or German. The language used is best told by noting the spelling of the name of the country.
(Fr) French: BELGIQUE or BELGES
(Du) Dutch: BELGIE or BELGEN
(La) Latin: BELGICA
(Ge) German: BELGIEN

KINGDOM

DECIMAL COINAGE

KM# 148.1 50 CENTIMES

Bronze **Obv:** Legend in French **Obv. Legend:** BELGIQUE **Rev:** Helmeted mine worker, miner's lamp at right, smaller head, tip of neck 1mm from rim **Edge:** Plain

Date	Mintage	F	VF	XF	Unc	BU
2001	60,000	—	—	—	2.00	—

Note: In sets only

Date	Mintage	F	VF	XF	Unc	BU
2001	Inc. above	—	—	—	25.00	—

Note: Medal alignment

KM# 149.1 50 CENTIMES

Bronze **Rev:** Helmeted mint worker, miner's lamp at r. Smaller head, legend in Dutch **Rev. Legend:** BELGIE **Edge:** Plain

Date	Mintage	F	VF	XF	Unc	BU
2001	60,000	—	—	—	2.00	—

Note: In sets only

Date	Mintage	F	VF	XF	Unc	BU
2001	Inc. above	—	—	—	25.00	—

Note: Medal alignment

KM# 188 FRANC

Nickel Plated Iron **Rev:** Legend in Dutch **Rev. Legend:** BELGIE

Date	Mintage	F	VF	XF	Unc	BU
2001	60,000	—	—	—	3.00	—

Note: In sets only

Date	Mintage	F	VF	XF	Unc	BU
2001	Inc. above	—	—	—	25.00	—

Note: Medal alignment

KM# 187 FRANC

Nickel Plated Iron **Obv:** Albert II **Rev:** Legend in French **Rev. Legend:** BELGIQUE **Note:** Struck at Brussels Mint. Mint mark - Angel Head. Unknown mintmaster's privy mark - scales.

Date	Mintage	F	VF	XF	Unc	BU
2001	60,000	—	—	—	2.00	—

Note: In sets only

Date	Mintage	F	VF	XF	Unc	BU
2001	Inc. above	—	—	—	25.00	—

Note: Medal alignment

KM# 189 5 FRANCS - 5 FRANK (Un / Een Belga)

Aluminum-Bronze **Obv:** Albert II **Rev:** Legend in French **Rev. Legend:** BELGIQUE **Note:** Struck at Brussels Mint. Mint mark - Angel head. Mintmaster R. Coenen's privy mark - Scale.

Date	Mintage	F	VF	XF	Unc	BU
2001	60,000	—	—	—	4.00	—

Note: In sets only

KM# 190 5 FRANCS - 5 FRANK (Un / Een Belga)

Aluminum-Bronze **Rev:** Legend in Dutch **Rev. Legend:** BELGIE **Note:** Struck at Brussels Mint. Mint mark - Angel head. Mintmaster R. Coenen's privy mark - Scale.

Date	Mintage	F	VF	XF	Unc	BU
2001	60,000	—	—	—	2.00	—

Note: In sets only

KM# 191 20 FRANCS - 20 FRANK (Vier / Quatre Belgas)

Nickel-Bronze **Obv:** Albert II **Rev:** Legend in French **Rev. Legend:** BELGIQUE **Note:** Struck at Brussels Mint. Mint mark - Angel head. Mintmaster R. Coenen's privy mark - Scale.

Date	Mintage	F	VF	XF	Unc	BU
2001	60,000	—	—	—	5.00	—

Note: In sets only

KM# 192 20 FRANCS - 20 FRANK (Vier / Quatre Belgas)

Nickel-Bronze **Rev:** Legend in Dutch **Rev. Legend:** BELGIE **Note:** Struck at Brussels Mint. Mint mark - Angel head. Mintmaster R. Coenen's privy mark - Scale.

Date	Mintage	F	VF	XF	Unc	BU
2001	60,000	—	—	—	5.00	—

Note: In sets only

KM# 193 50 FRANCS (50 Frank)

Nickel **Obv:** Albert II **Rev:** Legend in French **Rev. Legend:** BELGIQUE **Note:** Struck at Brussels Mint. Mint mark - Angel head. Mintmaster R. Coenen's privy mark - Scale.

Date	Mintage	F	VF	XF	Unc	BU
2001	60,000	—	—	—	8.00	—

Note: In sets only

KM# 194 50 FRANCS (50 Frank)

Nickel **Obv:** Albert II **Rev:** Legend in Dutch **Rev. Legend:** BELGIE **Note:** Struck at Brussels Mint. Mint mark - Angel head. Mintmaster R. Coenen's privy mark - Scale.

Date	Mintage	F	VF	XF	Unc	BU
2001	60,000	—	—	—	8.00	—

Note: In sets only

KM# 222 500 FRANCS (500 Frank)

22.8500 g., 0.9250 Silver .6795 oz. ASW, 37 mm. **Subject:** Europe: Europa and the Bull **Obv:** Map and denomination **Rev:** Europa sitting on a bull **Edge:** Plain

Date	Mintage	F	VF	XF	Unc	BU
2001 (qp) Proof	40,000	Value: 50.00				

KM# 223 5000 FRANCS

15.5500 g., 0.9990 Gold .4994 oz. AGW, 29 mm. **Subject:** Europe: Europa and the Bull **Obv:** Map and denomination **Rev:** Europa sitting on a bull **Edge:** Plain

Date	Mintage	F	VF	XF	Unc	BU
2001 (qp) Proof	2,000	Value: 500				

EURO COINAGE

European Economic Community Issues

KM# 224 EURO CENT

2.2700 g., Copper Plated Steel, 16.2 mm. **Ruler:** Albert II **Obv:** King's portrait **Obv. Designer:** Jan Alfons Keustermans **Rev:** Denomination and globe **Rev. Designer:** Luc Luycx **Edge:** Plain

Date	Mintage	F	VF	XF	Unc	BU
2001	99,840,000	—	—	—	0.60	1.00
2001 Proof	15,000	Value: 15.00				
2002	140,000	—	—	—	18.50	22.50
2002 Proof	15,000	Value: 20.00				
2003	10,135,000	—	—	—	0.35	0.75
2003 Proof	15,000	Value: 15.00				
2004	180,000,000	—	—	—	0.35	0.75
2004 Proof	—	Value: 15.00				
2005	—	—	—	—	0.35	0.75
2005 Proof	3,000	Value: 15.00				

KM# 225 2 EURO CENTS

3.0300 g., Copper Plated Steel, 18.7 mm. **Ruler:** Albert II **Obv:** King's portrait **Obv. Designer:** Jan Alfons Keustermans **Rev:** Denomination and globe **Rev. Designer:** Luc Luycx **Edge:** Grooved

Date	Mintage	F	VF	XF	Unc	BU
2001	40,000	—	—	—	7.00	9.00

Note: Only available in sets at present, circulation strikes not yet released

Date	Mintage	F	VF	XF	Unc	BU
2001 Proof	15,000	Value: 20.00				
2002	140,000	—	—	—	3.50	6.50

Date	Mintage	F	VF	XF	Unc	BU
2002 Proof	15,000	Value: 15.00				
2003	40,135,000	—	—	—	0.50	1.00
2003 Proof	15,000	Value: 15.00				
2004	140,000,000	—	—	—	0.50	1.00

KM# 226 5 EURO CENTS

3.8600 g., Copper Plated Steel, 21.2 mm. **Ruler:** Albert II **Obv:** King's portrait **Obv. Designer:** Jan Alfons Keustermans **Rev:** Denomination and globe **Rev. Designer:** Luc Luycx **Edge:** Plain

Date	Mintage	F	VF	XF	Unc	BU
2001	40,000	—	—	—	10.00	12.50
2001 Proof	15,000	Value: 18.00				
2002	140,000	—	—	—	6.00	8.00
2002 Proof	15,000	Value: 18.00				
2003	30,135,000	—	—	—	1.00	1.50
2003 Proof	15,000	Value: 16.00				
2004	97,000,000	—	—	—	1.00	1.50
2004 Proof	—	Value: 16.00				
2005	—	—	—	—	1.00	1.50
2005 Proof	3,000	Value: 16.00				

KM# 227 10 EURO CENTS

4.0700 g., Brass, 19.7 mm. **Ruler:** Albert II **Obv:** King's portrait **Obv. Designer:** Jan Alfons Keustermans **Rev:** Denomination and map **Rev. Designer:** Luc Luycx **Edge:** Reeded

Date	Mintage	F	VF	XF	Unc	BU
2001	145,790,000	—	—	—	0.75	1.25
2001 Proof	15,000	Value: 16.00				
2002	140,000	—	—	—	6.00	8.00
2002 Proof	15,000	Value: 18.00				
2003	135,000	—	—	—	6.00	8.00
2003 Proof	15,000	Value: 18.00				
2004	20,000,000	—	—	—	1.00	1.50
2004 Proof	—	Value: 18.00				
2005	—	—	—	—	1.00	1.50
2005 Proof	3,000	Value: 18.00				

KM# 228 20 EURO CENTS

5.7300 g., Brass, 22.1 mm. **Ruler:** Albert II **Obv:** King's portrait **Obv. Designer:** Jan Alfons Keustermans **Rev:** Denomination and map **Rev. Designer:** Luc Luycx **Edge:** Notched

Date	Mintage	F	VF	XF	Unc	BU
2001	40,000	—	—	—	10.00	12.50

Note: Only available in sets at present, circulation strikes not yet released

Date	Mintage	F	VF	XF	Unc	BU
2001 Proof	15,000	Value: 20.00				
2002	104,140,000	—	—	—	1.00	1.50
2002 Proof	15,000	Value: 16.00				
2003	30,135,000	—	—	—	1.25	1.75
2003 Proof	15,000	Value: 16.00				
2004	109,550,000	—	—	—	1.25	1.75
2004 Proof	—	Value: 16.00				
2005	—	—	—	—	1.25	1.75
2005 Proof	3,000	Value: 16.00				

KM# 229 50 EURO CENTS

7.8100 g., Brass, 24.2 mm. **Ruler:** Albert II **Obv:** King's portrait **Obv. Designer:** Jan Alfons Keustermans **Rev:** Denomination and map **Rev. Designer:** Luc Luycx **Edge:** Reeded

Date	Mintage	F	VF	XF	Unc	BU
2001	40,000	—	—	—	10.00	12.50
2001 Proof	15,000	Value: 18.00				
2002	50,040,000	—	—	—	1.00	1.50
2002 Proof	15,000	Value: 16.00				
2003	135,000	—	—	—	1.25	1.75
2003 Proof	15,000	Value: 16.00				
2004	15,000,000	—	—	—	1.25	1.75
2004 Proof	—	Value: 16.00				
2005	—	—	—	—	1.25	1.75
2005 Proof	3,000	Value: 16.00				

KM# 230 EURO

7.5000 g., Bi-Metallic Copper-Nickel center in Brass ring, 23.2 mm. **Ruler:** Albert II **Obv:** King's portrait **Obv. Designer:** Jan Alfons Keustermans **Rev:** Denominaton and map **Rev. Designer:** Luc Luycx **Edge:** Reeded and plain sections

Date	Mintage	F	VF	XF	Unc	BU
2001	40,000	—	—	—	12.50	15.00

Note: Only available in sets at present, circulation strikes not yet released

Date	Mintage	F	VF	XF	Unc	BU
2001 Proof	15,000	Value: 20.00				
2002	90,640,000	—	—	—	3.00	5.00

Note: Only a fraction of the mintage released at present

Date	Mintage	F	VF	XF	Unc	BU
2002 Proof	15,000	Value: 18.00				
2003	135,000	—	—	—	3.00	5.00
2003 Proof	15,000	Value: 18.00				
2004	15,000,000	—	—	—	3.00	5.00
2004 Proof	—	Value: 18.00				
2005	—	—	—	—	3.00	5.00
2005 Proof	3,000	Value: 18.00				

KM# 231 2 EURO

8.5200 g., Bi-Metallic Brass center in Copper-Nickel ring, 25.7 mm. **Obv:** King's portrait **Obv. Designer:** Jan Alfons Keustermans **Rev:** Denomination and map **Rev. Designer:** Luc Luycx **Edge:** Reeded with 2's and stars

Date	Mintage	F	VF	XF	Unc	BU
2001	40,000	—	—	—	12.50	15.00

Note: Only available in sets at present, circulation strikes not yet released

Date	Mintage	F	VF	XF	Unc	BU
2001 Proof	15,000	Value: 25.00				
2002	50,140,000	—	—	—	3.75	6.00
2002 Proof	15,000	Value: 22.50				
2003	30,135,000	—	—	—	3.75	6.00
2003 Proof	15,000	Value: 22.50				
2004	65,500,000	—	—	—	3.75	6.00
2004 Proof	—	Value: 22.50				
2005	—	—	—	—	3.75	6.00
2005 Proof	3,000	Value: 22.50				

KM# 240 2 EURO

8.5200 g., Bi-Metallic Brass center in Copper-Nickel ring, 25.7 mm. **Ruler:** Albert II **Subject:** Schengen Agreement **Obv:** Albert II of Belgium and Henri of Luxembourg **Rev:** Value and map **Edge:** Reeding over stars

Date	Mintage	F	VF	XF	Unc	BU
2005	6,020,000	—	—	—	5.00	7.50
2005 Proof	3,000	Value: 25.00				

KM# 241 2 EURO

8.5200 g., Bi-Metallic Brass center in Copper-Nickel ring, 25.7 mm. **Ruler:** Albert II **Obv:** Atomic model **Rev:** Value and map **Edge:** Reeding over stars and 2's

Date	Mintage	F	VF	XF	Unc	BU
2006	—	—	—	—	—	3.50

KM# 233 10 EURO

18.9300 g., 0.9250 Silver 0.563 oz. ASW, 32.9 mm. **Subject:** Belgian Railway System **Obv:** Value, head at right transposed on map **Rev:** Train exiting tunnel **Edge:** Reeded

Date	Mintage	F	VF	XF	Unc	BU
ND (2002) Proof	50,000	Value: 40.00				

KM# 235 10 EURO

18.9300 g., 0.9250 Silver 0.563 oz. ASW, 32.9 mm. **Subject:** "Simenon" **Edge:** Reeded

Date	Mintage	F	VF	XF	Unc	BU
2003 Proof	50,000	Value: 40.00				

KM# 236 10 EURO

18.9300 g., 0.9250 Silver 0.563 oz. ASW, 32.9 mm. **Ruler:** Albert II **Subject:** "Tintin" **Edge:** Reeded

Date	Mintage	F	VF	XF	Unc	BU
2004 Proof	50,000	Value: 75.00				

KM# 234 10 EURO

18.7500 g., 0.9250 Silver 0.5576 oz. ASW, 33 mm. **Ruler:** Albert II **Obv:** Value **Rev:** Western Europe map and Goddess Europa riding a bull **Edge:** Reeded

Date	Mintage	F	VF	XF	Unc	BU
2004 Proof	50,000	Value: 40.00				

KM# 237 100 EURO

15.5500 g., 0.9990 Gold 0.4994 oz. AGW, 29 mm. **Subject:** Founding Fathers

Date	Mintage	F	VF	XF	Unc	BU
2002 Proof	5,000	Value: 550				

KM# 238 100 EURO

15.5500 g., 0.9990 Gold 0.4994 oz. AGW, 29 mm. **Subject:** 10th Anniversary of Reign

Date	Mintage	F	VF	XF	Unc	BU
2003 Proof	5,000	Value: 475				

KM# 239 100 EURO

15.5500 g., 0.9990 Gold 0.4994 oz. AGW, 29 mm. **Subject:** Franc Germinal

Date	Mintage	F	VF	XF	Unc	BU
2004 Proof	5,000	Value: 475				

PROOF SETS

KM#	Date	Mintage	Identification	Issue Price	Mkt Val
PS10	2001 (8)	—	KM#224-231	80.00	150
PS11	2002 (8)	—	KM#224-231	80.00	145
PS12	2003 (8)	—	KM#224-231	80.00	135

BELIZE

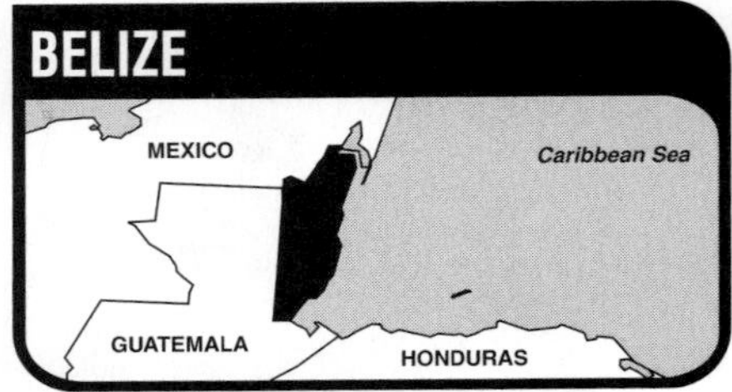

Belize, formerly British Honduras, but now an independent member of the British Commonwealth, is situated in Central America south of Mexico and east and north of Guatemala, with an area of 8,867 sq. mi. (22,960 sq. km.) and a population of *242,000. Capital: Belmopan. Tourism now augments Belize's economy, in addition to sugar, citrus fruits, chicle and hardwoods which are exported.

MONETARY SYSTEM

Commencing 1864
100 Cents = 1 Dollar

BRITISH COLONIAL & CONSTITUTIONAL

DECIMAL COINAGE

KM# 114 CENT
Aluminum **Obv:** New portrait of Queen Elizabeth II

Date	Mintage	F	VF	XF	Unc	BU
2002	—	—	—	0.10	0.15	0.45

KM# 115 5 CENTS
Aluminum

Date	Mintage	F	VF	XF	Unc	BU
2002	—	—	—	0.10	0.20	0.40

KM# 134 DOLLAR
30.9400 g., 0.9990 Silver 0.9937 oz. ASW, 39.9 mm. **Subject:** Mayan King **Obv:** National arms **Rev:** Mayan portrait in ornate headdress **Edge:** Reeded

Date	Mintage	F	VF	XF	Unc	BU
2002	—	—	—	—	35.00	37.50

BENIN

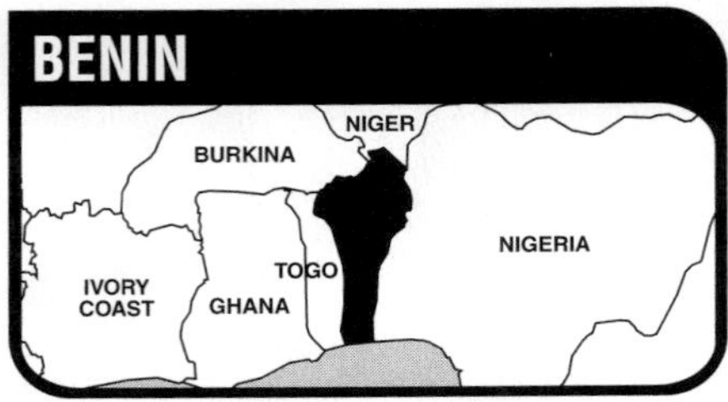

The Republic of Benin (formerly the Republic of Dahomey), located on the south side of the African bulge between Togo and Nigeria, has an area of 43,500 sq. mi. (112,620 sq. km.) and a population of 5.5 million. Capital: Porto-Novo. The principal industry of Benin, one of the poorest countries of West Africa, is the processing of palm oil products. Palm kernel oil, peanuts, cotton, and coffee are exported.

PEOPLES REPUBLIC

STANDARD COINAGE

KM# 38 1000 FRANCS
20.0000 g., 0.9990 Silver 0.6424 oz. ASW, 37.9 mm. **Subject:** Endangered Species **Obv:** National arms **Rev:** Two zebras grazing **Edge:** Reeded

Date	Mintage	F	VF	XF	Unc	BU
2001 Proof	—	Value: 40.00				

KM# 37 1000 FRANCS
14.9500 g., 0.9990 Silver .4802 oz. ASW, 35 mm. **Subject:** Leif Ericksson **Obv:** National arms **Rev:** Head of Eriksson at left, Viking ship at right **Edge:** Plain

Date	Mintage	F	VF	XF	Unc	BU
2001 Proof	—	Value: 30.00				

KM# 49 1000 FRANCS
20.1100 g., 0.9990 Silver 0.6459 oz. ASW, 40 mm. **Obv:** National arms **Rev:** Soccer player and wall of flags **Edge:** Reeded

Date	Mintage	F	VF	XF	Unc	BU
2002 Proof	—	Value: 40.00				

KM# 40 1500 CFA FRANCS - 1 AFRICA
7.3000 g., Nickel Plated Steel, 25.9 mm. **Obv:** Buffalo and two birds **Rev:** Elephant head on map **Edge:** Plain

Date	Mintage	F	VF	XF	Unc	BU
2003	1,200	—	—	—	20.00	—

KM# 40a 1500 CFA FRANCS - 1 AFRICA
0.9250 Silver, 25.9 mm. **Edge:** Plain

Date	Mintage	F	VF	XF	Unc	BU
2003	5	—	—	—	250	—

KM# 44 1500 CFA FRANCS - 1 AFRICA
7.3000 g., Nickel Plated Steel, 26 mm. **Obv:** European Union map **Rev:** Elephant head on map **Edge:** Plain

Date	Mintage	F	VF	XF	Unc	BU
2005	2,005	—	—	—	9.00	—

KM# 44a 1500 CFA FRANCS - 1 AFRICA
9.5000 g., 0.9990 Silver 0.3051 oz. ASW, 26 mm. **Obv:** European Union map **Rev:** Elephant head on map **Edge:** Plain

Date	Mintage	F	VF	XF	Unc	BU
2005	10	—	—	—	400	—

KM# 41 6000 CFA FRANCS - 4 AFRICA
10.1000 g., Bi-Metallic Copper-Nickel center in Brass ring, 28.3 mm. **Obv:** Map left of President **Rev:** Elephant head on map **Edge:** Plain

Date	Mintage	F	VF	XF	Unc	BU
2003	500	—	—	—	40.00	—

KM# 45 6000 CFA FRANCS - 4 AFRICA
10.1000 g., Bi-Metallic Copper-Nickel center in Brass ring, 28.3 mm. **Obv:** Olympic athletic figures **Rev:** Elephant head on map **Edge:** Plain

Date	Mintage	F	VF	XF	Unc	BU
2005	1,200	—	—	—	40.00	—

KM# 45a 6000 CFA FRANCS - 4 AFRICA
11.0000 g., 0.9990 Bi-Metallic .999 Silver center in .999 Gold ring 0.3533 oz., 28.3 mm. **Obv:** Olympic athletic figures **Rev:** Elephant head on map **Edge:** Plain

Date	Mintage	F	VF	XF	Unc	BU
2005	10	—	—	—	400	—

KM# 45b 6000 CFA FRANCS - 4 AFRICA
13.2000 g., 0.9990 Silver 0.424 oz. ASW, 28.3 mm. **Obv:** Olympic athletic figures **Rev:** Elephant head on map **Edge:** Plain

Date	Mintage	F	VF	XF	Unc	BU
2005	10	—	—	—	400	—

KM# 46 6000 CFA FRANCS - 4 AFRICA
10.1000 g., Bi-Metallic Copper-Nickel center in Brass ring, 28.3 mm. **Obv:** Papal Visit scene **Rev:** Elephant head on map **Edge:** Plain

Date	Mintage	F	VF	XF	Unc	BU
2005	1,200	—	—	—	40.00	—

KM# 46a 6000 CFA FRANCS - 4 AFRICA
11.0000 g., 0.9990 Bi-Metallic .999 Silver center in .999 Gold ring 0.3533 oz., 28.3 mm. **Obv:** Papal Visit scene **Rev:** Elephant head on map **Edge:** Plain

Date	Mintage	F	VF	XF	Unc	BU
2005	10	—	—	—	400	—

KM# 46b 6000 CFA FRANCS - 4 AFRICA
13.2000 g., 0.9990 Silver 0.424 oz. ASW, 28.3 mm. **Obv:** Papal Visit scene **Rev:** Elephant head on map **Edge:** Plain

Date	Mintage	F	VF	XF	Unc	BU
2005	10	—	—	—	400	—

KM# 42 150000 CFA FRANCS - 100 AFRICA
13.2000 g., 0.9990 Silver **Obv:** Map left of President **Rev:** Elephant head on map

Date	Mintage	F	VF	XF	Unc	BU
2003	25	—	—	—	250	—

KM# 42a 150000 CFA FRANCS - 100 AFRICA
0.9990 Gold Plated Silver

Date	Mintage	F	VF	XF	Unc	BU
2003	25	—	—	—	275	—

BERMUDA

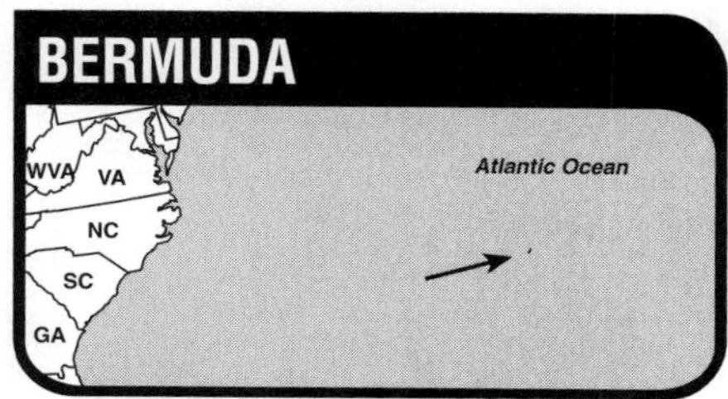

The Parliamentary British Colony of Bermuda, situated in the western Atlantic Ocean 660 miles (1,062 km.) east of North Carolina, has an area of 20.6 sq. mi. (53 sq. km.) and a population of 61,600. Capital: Hamilton. Concentrated essences, beauty preparations, and cut flowers are exported. Most Bermudians derive their livelihood from tourism. The British monarch is the head of state and is represented by a governor.

RULERS
British

BRITISH ADMINISTRATION

DECIMAL COINAGE

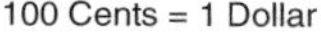

100 Cents = 1 Dollar

KM# 107 CENT
Copper Plated Zinc **Obv:** Queen's portrait **Obv. Designer:** Rank-Broadley **Rev:** Wild boar

Date	Mintage	F	VF	XF	Unc	BU
2001	1,600,000	—	—	—	0.50	0.75
2002	1,120,000	—	—	—	0.50	0.75
2003	800,000	—	—	—	0.50	0.75
2004	1,600,000	—	—	—	0.50	0.75
2005	3,200,000	—	—	—	0.50	0.75

KM# 108 5 CENTS
Copper-Nickel **Obv:** Queen's portrait **Obv. Designer:** Rank-Broadley **Rev:** Queen angel fish

Date	Mintage	F	VF	XF	Unc	BU
2001	1,000,000	—	—	—	0.75	1.00
2002	700,000	—	—	—	0.75	1.00
2003	700,000	—	—	—	0.75	1.00
2004	700,000	—	—	—	0.75	1.00
2005	600,000	—	—	—	0.75	1.00

KM# 109 10 CENTS
Copper-Nickel **Obv:** Queen's portrait **Obv. Designer:** Rank-Broadley **Rev:** Bermuda lily

Date	Mintage	F	VF	XF	Unc	BU
2001	1,400,000	—	—	—	0.85	1.00
2002	800,000	—	—	—	0.85	1.00
2003	600,000	—	—	—	0.85	1.00
2004	800,000	—	—	—	0.85	1.00
2005	800,000	—	—	—	0.85	1.00

KM# 110 25 CENTS
Copper-Nickel **Obv:** Queen's portrait **Obv. Designer:** Rank-Broadley **Rev:** Yellow-billed tropical bird

Date	Mintage	F	VF	XF	Unc	BU
2001	800,000	—	—	—	1.50	2.00
2002	800,000	—	—	—	1.50	2.00
2003	800,000	—	—	—	1.50	2.00
2004	800,000	—	—	—	1.50	2.00
2005	1,440,000	—	—	—	1.50	2.00

KM# 139 DOLLAR
28.2800 g., Copper-Nickel, 38.6 mm. **Obv:** Elizabeth II **Rev:** 4 Gombey dancers **Edge:** Reeded

Date	Mintage	F	VF	XF	Unc	BU
2001	—	—	—	—	10.00	12.00

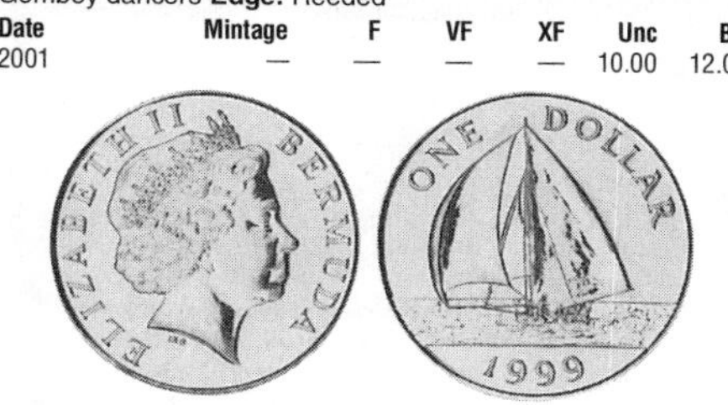

KM# 111 DOLLAR
Nickel-Brass **Obv:** Queen's portrait **Obv. Designer:** Rank-Broadley **Rev:** Sailboat **Rev. Designer:** Eldron Trimingham III

Date	Mintage	F	VF	XF	Unc	BU
2001	—	—	—	—	3.00	3.50
2002	12,000	—	—	—	3.00	3.50
2003	12,000	—	—	—	3.00	3.50
2004	12,000	—	—	—	3.00	3.50
2005	240,000	—	—	—	3.00	3.50

KM# 124 DOLLAR
28.4100 g., Copper-Nickel, 38.5 mm. **Subject:** Queen's Jubilee **Obv:** Queen's portrait **Rev:** Stylized trumpeters **Edge:** Reeded

Date	Mintage	F	VF	XF	Unc	BU
2002	—	—	—	—	10.00	12.00

KM# 120 5 DOLLARS
28.2800 g., 0.9250 Silver .8410 oz. ASW, 38.6 mm. **Subject:** Gombey Dancers **Obv:** Queen's head right **Rev:** Multicolor costumed dancers **Edge:** Reeded

Date	Mintage	F	VF	XF	Unc	BU
2001 Proof	3,500	Value: 50.00				

KM# 129 5 DOLLARS
28.2800 g., 0.9250 Silver 0.841 oz. ASW, 38.6 mm.
Subject: Queen's Jubilee **Obv:** Gold-plated bust of Elizabeth II **Rev:** Trumpeters **Edge:** Reeded

Date	Mintage	F	VF	XF	Unc	BU
2002 Proof	20,000	Value: 40.00				

KM# 130 5 DOLLARS
28.2800 g., 0.9250 Silver 0.841 oz. ASW, 38.6 mm.
Subject: Queen's Jubilee **Obv:** Gold-plated bust of Elizabeth II **Rev:** Royal visit scene **Edge:** Reeded

Date	Mintage	F	VF	XF	Unc	BU
2003 Proof	20,000	Value: 40.00				

KM# 128 5 DOLLARS
28.2800 g., 0.9250 Silver 0.841 oz. ASW, 38.6 mm.
Obv: Elizabeth II **Rev:** 2 fitted racing dinghys with multicolor sails **Edge:** Reeded

Date	Mintage	F	VF	XF	Unc	BU
ND (2003) Proof	3,500	Value: 60.00				

KM# 131 5 DOLLARS
28.2800 g., 0.9250 Silver 0.841 oz. ASW, 38.6 mm. **Obv:** Queen Elizabeth II **Rev:** Bermudan stone quarrying scene **Edge:** Reeded

Date	Mintage	F	VF	XF	Unc	BU
2004 Proof	3,500	Value: 60.00				

BHUTAN

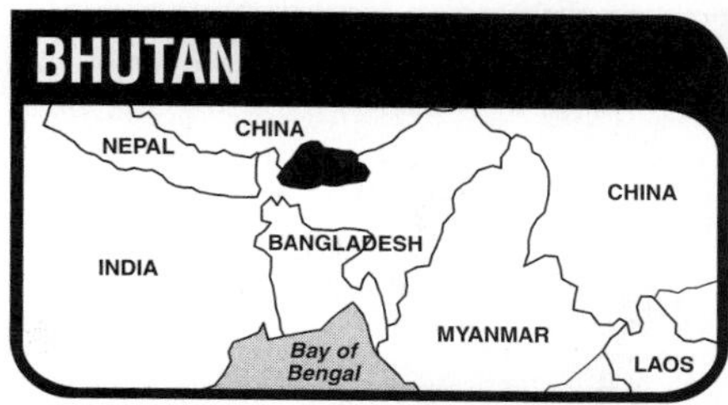

The Kingdom of Bhutan, a landlocked Himalayan country bordered by Tibet and India, has an area of 18,150 sq. mi. (47,000 sq. km.) and a population of *2.03 million. Capital: Thimphu. Virtually the entire population is engaged in agricultural and pastoral activities. Rice, wheat, barley, and yak butter are produced in sufficient quantity to make the country self-sufficient in food. The economy of Bhutan is primitive and many transactions are conducted on a barter basis.

RULERS
Jigme Singye Wangchuck, 1972-

KINGDOM

REFORM COINAGE

Commencing 1974; 100 Chetrums (Paisa) = 1 Ngultrum (Rupee); 100 Ngultrums = 1 Sertum

KM# 105 5 CHHERTUM
3.8600 g., Brass, 21.9 mm. **Obv:** Monkey **Rev:** Inscription above value **Edge:** Plain

Date	Mintage	F	VF	XF	Unc	BU
2003	—	—	—	—	0.25	0.40

BOLIVIA

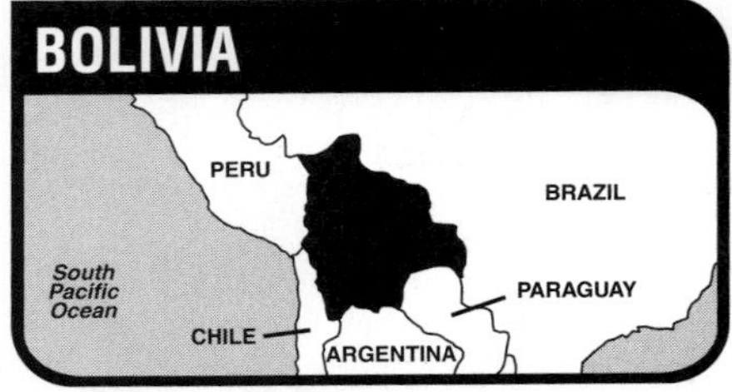

The Republic of Bolivia, a landlocked country in west central South America, has an area of 424,165 sq. mi. (1,098,580 sq. km.) and a population of *8.33 million. Its capitals are: La Paz (administrative) and Sucre (constitutional). Principal exports are tin, zinc, antimony, tungsten, petroleum, natural gas, cotton and coffee.

Much of present day Bolivia was first dominated by the Tiahuanaco Culture ca.400 BC. It had in turn been incorporated into the Inca Empire by 1440AD prior to the arrival of the Spanish, in 1535, who reduced the Indian population to virtual slavery. When Joseph Napoleon was placed upon the throne of occupied Spain in 1809, a fervor of revolutionary activity quickened throughout Alto Peru - culminating in the 1809 Proclamation of Liberty. Sixteen bloody years of struggle ensued before the republic, named for the famed liberator Simon Bolivar, was established on August 6, 1825. Since then Bolivia has survived more than 16 constitutions, 78 Presidents, 3 military juntas and over 160 revolutions.

REPUBLIC

REFORM COINAGE

1987-; 1,000,000 Peso Bolivianos = 1 Boliviano; 100 Centavos = 1 Boliviano

KM# 204 50 CENTAVOS
Stainless Steel **Edge:** Plain

Date	Mintage	F	VF	XF	Unc	BU
2001	—	—	—	—	0.75	1.00

KM# 212 5 BOLIVIANOS
Center Weight: 5.0000 g. **Center Composition:** Brass Clad Steel, 23 mm. **Obv:** National arms **Rev:** Denomination within inner ring **Edge:** Reeded

Date	Mintage	F	VF	XF	Unc	BU
2001	—	—	—	—	3.50	5.00

BOSNIA AND HERZEGOVINA

The Republic of Bosnia and Herzegovina borders Croatia to the north and west, Serbia to the east and Montenegro in the southeast with only 12.4 mi. of coastline. The total land area is 19,735 sq. mi. (51,129 sq. km.). They have a population of *4.34 million. Capital: Sarajevo. Electricity, mining and agriculture are leading industries.

MONETARY SYSTEM
1 Convertible Marka = 100 Convertible Feniga = 1 Deutschemark 1998-
NOTE: German Euros circulate freely.

REPUBLIC

STANDARD COINAGE

KM# 115 10 FENINGA
Copper-Plated-Steel **Obv:** Denomination on map **Rev:** Triangle and stars

Date	Mintage	F	VF	XF	Unc	BU
2004	—	—	—	—	0.50	0.75

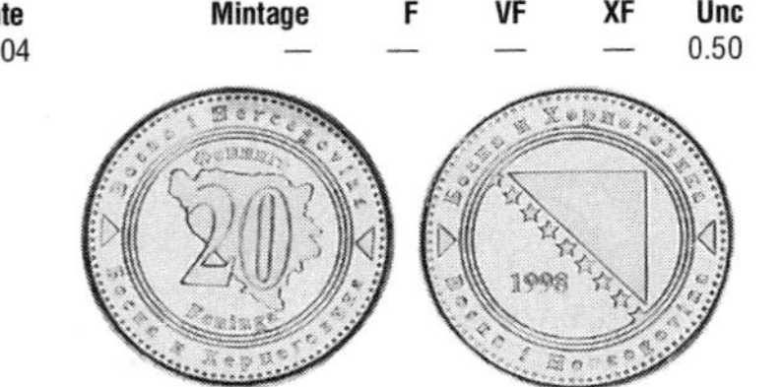

KM# 116 20 FENINGA
Copper-Plated-Steel **Obv:** Denomination on map **Rev:** Triangle and stars

Date	Mintage	F	VF	XF	Unc	BU
2004	—	—	—	—	1.00	1.25

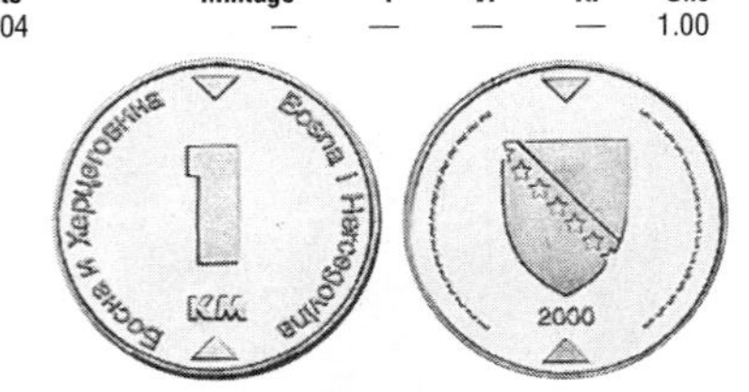

KM# 118 KONVERTIBLE MARKA
4.9000 g., Nickel Plated Steel, 23.23 mm. **Obv:** Denomination **Rev:** Coat of arms above date **Edge:** Reeded and plain sections

Date	Mintage	F	VF	XF	Unc	BU
2003	—	—	—	—	5.50	6.00

KM# 119 2 KONVERTIBLE MARKA
6.9000 g., Bi-Metallic Copper-Nickel center in Nickel-Brass ring, 25.75 mm. **Obv:** Denomination **Rev:** Dove of peace **Edge:** Reeded and plain sections

Date	Mintage	F	VF	XF	Unc	BU
2003	—	—	—	—	12.50	13.50

BRAZIL

The Federative Republic of Brazil, which comprises half the continent of South America and is the only Latin American country deriving its culture and language from Portugal, has an area of 3,286,488 sq. mi. (8,511,965 sq. km.) and a population of *169.2 million. Capital: Brasilia. The economy of Brazil is as varied and complex as any in the developing world. Agriculture is a mainstay of the economy, while only 4 percent of the area is under cultivation. Known mineral resources are almost unlimited in variety and size of reserves. A large, relatively sophisticated industry ranges from basic steel and chemical production to finished consumer goods. Coffee, cotton, iron ore and cocoa are the chief exports.

MINT MARKS
(a) - Paris, privy marks only
B - Bahia

FEDERAL REPUBLIC

REFORM COINAGE

1994-present

2750 Cruzeiros Reais = 1 Real; 100 Centavos = 1 Real

KM# 668 REAL
6.9100 g., Bi-Metallic Stainless Steel center in Brass plated Stainless Steel ring, 27.1 mm. **Subject:** 40th Anniversary of Central Bank **Obv:** Monument **Rev:** Value on flag **Edge:** Segmented reeding

Date	Mintage	F	VF	XF	Unc	BU
2005	—	—	—	—	5.00	6.50

REPUBLIC

REFORM COINAGE

1994-present

2750 Cruzeiros Reais = 1 Real; 100 Centavos = 1 Real

KM# 647 CENTAVO
Copper Plated Steel **Obv:** Cabral bust at right **Rev:** Denomination **Edge:** Plain

Date	Mintage	F	VF	XF	Unc	BU
2001	—	—	—	—	0.10	0.20
2002	—	—	—	—	0.10	0.20
2003	—	—	—	—	0.10	0.20
2004	—	—	—	—	0.10	0.20

KM# 648 5 CENTAVOS
Copper Plated Steel **Obv:** Tiradente bust at right **Rev:** Denomination **Edge:** Plain

Date	Mintage	F	VF	XF	Unc	BU
2001	—	—	—	—	0.45	0.65
2002	—	—	—	—	0.45	0.65

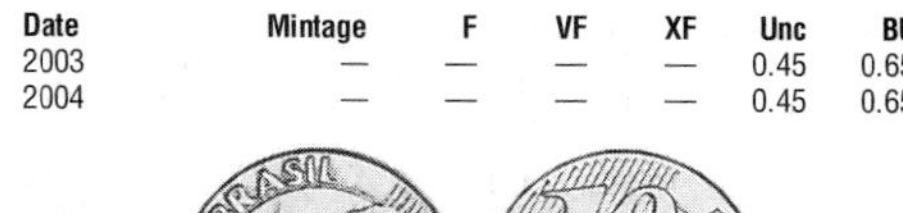

Date	Mintage	F	VF	XF	Unc	BU
2003	—	—	—	—	0.45	0.65
2004	—	—	—	—	0.45	0.65

KM# 649.2 10 CENTAVOS

Brass Plated Steel **Obv:** Bust of Pedro, horseman with sword in right hand **Edge:** Plain

Date	Mintage	F	VF	XF	Unc	BU
2001	—	—	—	—	0.60	0.80
2002	—	—	—	—	0.60	0.80
2003	—	—	—	—	0.60	0.80
2004	—	—	—	—	0.60	0.80

KM# 650 25 CENTAVOS

Brass Plated Steel **Obv:** Deodoro bust at right, national emblem **Rev:** Denomination **Edge:** Plain

Date	Mintage	F	VF	XF	Unc	BU
2001	—	—	—	—	0.75	1.00
2002	—	—	—	—	0.75	1.00
2003	—	—	—	—	0.75	1.00
2004	—	—	—	—	0.75	1.00

KM# 651 50 CENTAVOS

Copper-Nickel **Obv:** Rio Branco bust at right **Rev:** Denomination **Edge Lettering:** BRASIL ORDEM E PROGRESSO

Date	Mintage	F	VF	XF	Unc	BU
2001	—	—	—	—	1.25	1.50
2002	—	—	—	—	1.25	1.50
2003	—	—	—	—	1.25	1.50

KM# 651a 50 CENTAVOS

Stainless Steel

Date	Mintage	F	VF	XF	Unc	BU
2002	—	—	—	—	1.25	1.50

KM# 652 REAL

Bi-Metallic Copper-Nickel center in Brass ring **Obv:** Allegorical portrait **Rev:** Denomination **Edge:** Alternating reeded and plain **Note:** Total coin weight 7.8 grams.

Date	Mintage	F	VF	XF	Unc	BU
2002	—	—	—	—	3.00	4.50

KM# 652a REAL

Bi-Metallic Stainless Steel center in Brass Plated Steel ring, 26.9 mm. **Obv:** Allegorical portrait **Rev:** Denomination **Edge:** Reeded and plain sections **Note:** Total coin weight 7.0 grams.

Date	Mintage	F	VF	XF	Unc	BU
2002	—	—	—	—	3.00	4.00

KM# 656 REAL

7.0000 g., Bi-Metallic Stainless Steel center in Brass Plated Steel ring, 26.9 mm. **Subject:** Centennial of Juscelino Kubitschek, president **Obv:** Portrait **Obv. Designer:** Alzira Duim **Rev:** Denomination **Edge:** Reeded and plain sections

Date	Mintage	F	VF	XF	Unc	BU
2002	50,000,000	—	—	—	3.00	4.00

KM# 657 2 REAIS

28.0000 g., 0.9990 Silver 0.8993 oz. ASW, 40 mm. **Subject:** Centennial - Carlos Drummond de Andrade **Obv:** Denomination and writer **Rev:** Stylized portrait **Edge:** Reeded

Date	Mintage	F	VF	XF	Unc	BU
ND(2002) Proof	7,000	Value: 60.00				

KM# 658 2 REAIS

28.0000 g., 0.9990 Silver 0.8993 oz. ASW, 40 mm. **Subject:** Centennial - Juscelino Kubitschek **Obv:** Portrait **Rev:** Denomination **Edge:** Reeded

Date	Mintage	F	VF	XF	Unc	BU
2002 Proof	20,000	Value: 55.00				

KM# 663 2 REAIS

27.0000 g., 0.9250 Silver 0.803 oz. ASW, 40 mm. **Obv:** Value and piano player **Rev:** Ary Barroso singing **Edge:** Reeded

Date	Mintage	F	VF	XF	Unc	BU
ND(2003) Proof	7,000	Value: 45.00				

KM# 665 2 REAIS

27.0000 g., 0.9250 Silver 0.803 oz. ASW, 40 mm. **Subject:** Centennial - Portinari **Obv:** Starving family scene, value and country name **Rev:** Portinari's portrait, stars in squares design **Edge:** Reeded

Date	Mintage	F	VF	XF	Unc	BU
ND(2003) Proof	2,000	Value: 50.00				

KM# 666 2 REAIS

27.0000 g., 0.9250 Silver 0.803 oz. ASW, 40 mm. **Obv:** Soccer ball and value **Rev:** Center part of a Brazilian flag and stars **Edge:** Reeded

Date	Mintage	F	VF	XF	Unc	BU
2004 Proof	—	Value: 55.00				

KM# 661 5 REAIS

28.0000 g., 0.9990 Silver 0.8993 oz. ASW, 40 mm. **Obv:** Soccer player and Brazilian flag **Rev:** Soccer ball and value **Edge:** Reeded

Date	Mintage	F	VF	XF	Unc	BU
2002 Proof	10,000	Value: 45.00				

KM# 659 20 REAIS

8.0000 g., 0.9000 Gold 0.2315 oz. AGW, 22 mm. **Obv:** Juscelino Kubitschek de Oliveira's portrait **Rev:** Value **Edge:** Reeded

Date	Mintage	F	VF	XF	Unc	BU
2002 Proof	2,500	Value: 235				

KM# 660 20 REAIS

8.0000 g., 0.9000 Gold 0.2315 oz. AGW, 22 mm. **Obv:** Carlos Drummond de Andrade portrait and value **Rev:** Andrade caricature, name and dates **Edge:** Reeded

Date	Mintage	F	VF	XF	Unc	BU
ND(2002) Proof	2,500	Value: 235				

KM# 662 20 REAIS

8.0000 g., 0.9000 Gold 0.2315 oz. AGW, 22 mm. **Obv:** Soccer player **Rev:** Value, inscription and shooting stars **Edge:** Reeded

Date	Mintage	F	VF	XF	Unc	BU
2002	2,500	Value: 235				

KM# 664 20 REAIS

8.0000 g., 0.9000 Gold 0.2315 oz. AGW, 22 mm. **Subject:** Centennial - Ary Barroso **Obv:** Piano keyboard and music above value **Rev:** Caricature of Ary Barroso **Edge:** Reeded

Date	Mintage	F	VF	XF	Unc	BU
ND(2003) Proof	2,500	Value: 235				

BRITISH VIRGIN ISLANDS

The Colony of the Virgin Islands, a British colony situated in the Caribbean Sea northeast of Puerto Rico and west of the Leeward Islands, has an area of 59 sq. mi. (155 sq. km.) and a population of 13,000. Capital: Road Town. The principal islands of the 36-island group are Tortola, Virgin Gorda, Anegada, and Jost Van Dyke. The chief industries are fishing and stock raising. Fish, livestock and bananas are exported.

BRITISH COLONY

STANDARD COINAGE

KM# 196 DOLLAR

28.2800 g., Copper-Nickel, 38.6 mm. **Subject:** Queen's Golden Jubilee **Obv:** Bust of Queen Elizabeth II right **Rev:** Carnival dancers **Edge:** Reeded

Date	Mintage	F	VF	XF	Unc	BU
2002	—	—	—	—	7.50	9.50

KM# 180 DOLLAR

28.2800 g., Copper-Nickel, 25.7 mm. **Subject:** Sir Francis Drake **Obv:** Bust of Queen Elizabeth II right **Rev:** Ship, portrait and map **Edge:** Reeded

Date	Mintage	F	VF	XF	Unc	BU
2002	—	—	—	—	7.50	9.50

KM# 183 DOLLAR

28.2800 g., Copper-Nickel, 38.6 mm. **Subject:** Sir Walter Raleigh **Obv:** Bust of Queen Elizabeth II right **Rev:** Ship, portrait and map **Edge:** Reeded

Date	Mintage	F	VF	XF	Unc	BU
2002	—	—	—	—	7.50	9.50

KM# 187 DOLLAR

28.2800 g., Copper-Nickel, 38.6 mm. **Subject:** Queen's Golden Jubilee **Obv:** Bust of Queen Elizabeth II right **Rev:** Queen on horse **Edge:** Reeded

Date	Mintage	F	VF	XF	Unc	BU
2002	—	—	—	—	7.50	9.50

KM# 190 DOLLAR

28.2800 g., Copper-Nickel, 38.6 mm. **Subject:** Queen's Golden Jubilee **Obv:** Bust of Queen Elizabeth II right **Rev:** Queen on throne **Edge:** Reeded

Date	Mintage	F	VF	XF	Unc	BU
2002	—	—	—	—	7.50	9.50

KM# 193 DOLLAR

28.2800 g., Copper-Nickel, 38.6 mm. **Subject:** Queen's Golden Jubilee **Obv:** Bust of Queen Elizabeth II right **Rev:** Queen with President Ronald Reagan and First Lady Nancy Reagan **Edge:** Reeded

Date	Mintage	F	VF	XF	Unc	BU
2002	—	—	—	—	7.50	9.50

KM# 199 DOLLAR

28.2800 g., Copper-Nickel, 38.6 mm. **Subject:** Teddy Bear Centennial **Obv:** Bust of Queen Elizabeth II right **Rev:** Teddy bear **Edge:** Reeded

Date	Mintage	F	VF	XF	Unc	BU
2002	—	—	—	—	8.50	10.00

KM# 204 DOLLAR

28.2800 g., Copper-Nickel, 38.6 mm. **Subject:** Princess Diana **Obv:** Bust of Queen Elizabeth II right **Rev:** Diana's portrait **Edge:** Reeded

Date	Mintage	F	VF	XF	Unc	BU
2002	—	—	—	—	7.50	9.50

KM# 207 DOLLAR

28.2800 g., Copper-Nickel, 38.6 mm. **Subject:** September 11, 2001 **Obv:** Bust of Queen Elizabeth II right **Rev:** World Trade Center twin towers **Edge:** Reeded

Date	Mintage	F	VF	XF	Unc	BU
2002	—	—	—	—	12.00	13.50

KM# 210 DOLLAR

28.2800 g., Copper-Nickel, 38.6 mm. **Subject:** September 11, 2001 **Obv:** Bust of Queen Elizabeth II right **Rev:** Statue of Liberty **Edge:** Reeded

Date	Mintage	F	VF	XF	Unc	BU
2002	—	—	—	—	12.00	13.50

KM# 213 DOLLAR

28.2800 g., Copper-Nickel, 38.6 mm. **Subject:** Queen Mother **Obv:** Queen's portrait **Rev:** Queen Mother and a young Prince Charles **Edge:** Reeded

Date	Mintage	F	VF	XF	Unc	BU
2002	—	—	—	—	10.00	12.00

KM# 216 DOLLAR

28.2800 g., Copper-Nickel, 38.6 mm. **Subject:** Queen Mother **Obv:** Queen's portrait **Rev:** Queen Mother with four grandchildren **Edge:** Reeded

Date	Mintage	F	VF	XF	Unc	BU
2002	—	—	—	—	10.00	12.00

KM# 219 DOLLAR

28.2800 g., Copper-Nickel, 38.6 mm. **Subject:** Queen Mother Series **Obv:** Queen's portrait **Rev:** Queen Mother with uniformed Prince Charles **Edge:** Reeded

Date	Mintage	F	VF	XF	Unc	BU
2002	—	—	—	—	10.00	12.00

KM# 222 DOLLAR

28.2800 g., Copper-Nickel, 38.6 mm. **Subject:** Queen Mother Series **Obv:** Queen's portrait **Rev:** Queen Mother's coffin **Edge:** Reeded

Date	Mintage	F	VF	XF	Unc	BU
2002	—	—	—	—	10.00	12.00

KM# 303 DOLLAR

28.2800 g., Copper-Nickel, 38.6 mm. **Subject:** 2004 Athens Olympics **Obv:** Elizabeth II **Rev:** Ancient athlete's bust right, runners at lower right, ancient coin with owl at upper right coin **Edge:** Reeded

Date	Mintage	F	VF	XF	Unc	BU
2003	—	—	—	—	10.00	12.00

KM# 306 DOLLAR

28.2800 g., Copper-Nickel, 38.6 mm. **Subject:** 2004 Athens Olympics **Obv:** Elizabeth II **Rev:** Ancient athlete bust left, chariot race at lower left, ancient coin at upper left **Edge:** Reeded

Date	Mintage	F	VF	XF	Unc	BU
2003	—	—	—	—	10.00	12.00

KM# 225 DOLLAR

28.4400 g., Copper Nickel, 38.6 mm. **Subject:** Kennedy Assassination **Obv:** Queen's portrait **Rev:** President Kennedy's portrait **Edge:** Reeded

Date	Mintage	F	VF	XF	Unc	BU
2003	—	—	—	—	10.00	12.00

KM# 229 DOLLAR

28.2800 g., Copper-Nickel, 38.6 mm. **Subject:** Powered Flight Centennial **Obv:** Queen's portrait **Rev:** Three historic airplanes and rocket **Edge:** Reeded

Date	Mintage	F	VF	XF	Unc	BU
2003	—	—	—	—	10.00	12.00

KM# 232 DOLLAR

28.2800 g., Copper-Nickel, 38.6 mm. **Obv:** Queen's portrait **Rev:** Henry VIII and Elizabeth I **Edge:** Reeded

Date	Mintage	F	VF	XF	Unc	BU
2003	—	—	—	—	10.00	12.00

KM# 235 DOLLAR

28.2800 g., Copper-Nickel, 38.6 mm. **Obv:** Queen's portrait **Rev:** Matthew Parker, Archbishop of Canterbury **Edge:** Reeded

Date	Mintage	F	VF	XF	Unc	BU
2003	—	—	—	—	10.00	12.00

KM# 238 DOLLAR

28.2800 g., Copper-Nickel, 38.6 mm. **Obv:** Queen's portrait **Rev:** Sir Francis Drake and ships **Edge:** Reeded

Date	Mintage	F	VF	XF	Unc	BU
2003	—	—	—	—	10.00	12.00

KM# 241 DOLLAR

28.2800 g., Copper-Nickel, 38.6 mm. **Obv:** Queen's portrait **Rev:** Sir Walter Raleigh **Edge:** Reeded

Date	Mintage	F	VF	XF	Unc	BU
2003	—	—	—	—	10.00	12.00

KM# 244 DOLLAR

28.2800 g., Copper-Nickel, 38.6 mm. **Obv:** Queen's portrait **Rev:** Sir William Shakespeare **Edge:** Reeded

Date	Mintage	F	VF	XF	Unc	BU
2003	—	—	—	—	10.00	12.00

KM# 247 DOLLAR

28.2800 g., Copper-Nickel, 38.6 mm. **Obv:** Queen's portrait **Rev:** Elizabeth I above her funeral procession **Edge:** Reeded

Date	Mintage	F	VF	XF	Unc	BU
2003	—	—	—	—	10.00	12.00

KM# 250 DOLLAR

28.2800 g., Copper-Nickel, 38.6 mm. **Subject:** Olympics **Obv:** Queen's portrait **Rev:** Ancient bust, runners and coin **Edge:** Reeded

Date	Mintage	F	VF	XF	Unc	BU
2003	—	—	—	—	10.00	12.00

KM# 253 DOLLAR

28.2800 g., Copper-Nickel, 38.6 mm. **Subject:** Olympics **Obv:** Queen's portrait **Rev:** Ancient bust, charioteer and coin **Edge:** Reeded

Date	Mintage	F	VF	XF	Unc	BU
2003	—	—	—	—	10.00	12.00

KM# 265 DOLLAR

28.2800 g., Copper-Nickel, 38.6 mm. **Obv:** Queen Elizabeth II **Rev:** Sir Francis Drake, ship and map **Edge:** Reeded

Date	Mintage	F	VF	XF	Unc	BU
2004	—	—	—	—	10.00	12.00

KM# 267.1 DOLLAR

28.2800 g., Copper-Nickel, 38.6 mm. **Obv:** Queen Elizabeth II **Rev:** Peter Rabbit **Edge:** Reeded

Date	Mintage	F	VF	XF	Unc	BU
2004	—	—	—	—	15.00	17.00

KM# 267.2 DOLLAR

28.2800 g., Copper-Nickel, 38.6 mm. **Obv:** Queen Elizabeth II **Rev:** Multicolor Peter Rabbit **Edge:** Reeded

Date	Mintage	F	VF	XF	Unc	BU
2004	—	—	—	—	20.00	22.00

KM# 268 DOLLAR

3.1100 g., 0.9990 Silver 0.0999 oz. ASW, 18 mm. **Obv:** Queen Elizabeth II **Rev:** Peter Rabbit **Edge:** Reeded

Date	Mintage	F	VF	XF	Unc	BU
2004 Proof	10,000	Value: 25.00				

KM# 281 DOLLAR

28.2800 g., Copper-Nickel, 38.6 mm. **Obv:** Elizabeth II **Rev:** Sailor above two D-Day landing craft **Edge:** Reeded

Date	Mintage	F	VF	XF	Unc	BU
2004	—	—	—	—	10.00	12.00

KM# 297 DOLLAR

28.2800 g., Copper-Nickel, 38.6 mm. **Obv:** Elizabeth II **Rev:** Soldier above tank and jeeps **Edge:** Reeded

Date	Mintage	F	VF	XF	Unc	BU
2004	—	—	—	—	10.00	12.00

KM# 300 DOLLAR

28.2800 g., Copper-Nickel, 38.6 mm. **Obv:** Elizabeth II **Rev:** Pilot and planes above D-Day landing **Edge:** Reeded

Date	Mintage	F	VF	XF	Unc	BU
2004	—	—	—	—	10.00	12.00

KM# 286 DOLLAR

28.2800 g., Copper-Nickel, 38.6 mm. **Obv:** Elizabeth II **Rev:** Dolphin **Edge:** Reeded

Date	Mintage	F	VF	XF	Unc	BU
2004	—	—	—	—	10.00	12.00

KM# 278 2 DOLLARS

58.0000 g., Bronze, 50 mm. **Obv:** Elizabeth II **Rev:** 1896 Olympic medal design **Edge:** Reeded

Date	Mintage	F	VF	XF	Unc	BU
2004 Proof	3,500	Value: 20.00				

KM# 269.1 2.50 DOLLARS

7.7758 g., 0.9990 Silver 0.2497 oz. ASW, 26 mm. **Obv:** Queen Elizabeth II **Rev:** Peter Rabbit **Edge:** Reeded

Date	Mintage	F	VF	XF	Unc	BU
2004 Proof	—	Value: 15.00				

KM# 269.2 2.50 DOLLARS

7.7758 g., 0.9990 Silver 0.2497 oz. ASW, 26 mm. **Obv:** Queen Elizabeth II **Rev:** Multicolor Peter Rabbit **Edge:** Reeded

Date	Mintage	F	VF	XF	Unc	BU
2004 Proof	7,500	Value: 25.00				

KM# 284 5 DOLLARS

10.0000 g., 0.9900 Titanium 0.3183 oz., 36.1 mm. **Obv:** Elizabeth II **Rev:** British Guiana stamp design **Edge:** Reeded

Date	Mintage	F	VF	XF	Unc	BU
2004 Proof	7,500	Value: 65.00				

KM# 181 10 DOLLARS

28.2800 g., 0.9250 Silver 0.841 oz. ASW, 38.6 mm. **Subject:** Sir Francis Drake **Obv:** Bust of Queen Elizabeth II right **Rev:** Ship, portrait and map **Edge:** Reeded

Date	Mintage	F	VF	XF	Unc	BU
2002 Proof	—	Value: 40.00				

KM# 184 10 DOLLARS

28.2800 g., 0.9250 Silver 0.841 oz. ASW, 38.6 mm.
Subject: Sir Walter Raleigh **Obv:** Bust of Queen Elizabeth II right **Rev:** Ship, portrait and map **Edge:** Reeded

Date	Mintage	F	VF	XF	Unc	BU
2002 Proof	—	Value: 40.00				

KM# 214 10 DOLLARS

28.2800 g., 0.9250 Silver 0.841 oz. ASW, 38.6 mm.
Subject: Queen Mother **Obv:** Queen's portrait **Rev:** Queen Mother with young Prince Charles **Edge:** Reeded

Date	Mintage	F	VF	XF	Unc	BU
2002 Proof	10,000	Value: 40.00				

KM# 217 10 DOLLARS

28.2800 g., 0.9250 Silver 0.841 oz. ASW, 38.6 mm.
Subject: Queen Mother Series **Obv:** Queen's portrait
Rev: Queen Mother with four grandchildren **Edge:** Reeded

Date	Mintage	F	VF	XF	Unc	BU
2002 Proof	10,000	Value: 40.00				

KM# 220 10 DOLLARS

28.2800 g., 0.9250 Silver 0.841 oz. ASW, 38.6 mm.
Subject: Queen Mother Series **Obv:** Queen's portrait
Rev: Queen Mother with uniformed Prince Charles **Edge:** Reeded

Date	Mintage	F	VF	XF	Unc	BU
2002 Proof	10,000	Value: 40.00				

KM# 223 10 DOLLARS

28.2800 g., 0.9250 Silver 0.841 oz. ASW, 38.6 mm.
Subject: Queen Mother Series **Obv:** Queen's portrait
Rev: Queen Mother's coffin **Edge:** Reeded

Date	Mintage	F	VF	XF	Unc	BU
2002 Proof	10,000	Value: 40.00				

KM# 188 10 DOLLARS

28.2800 g., 0.9250 Gold Clad Silver 0.841 oz., 38.6 mm.
Subject: Queen's Golden Jubilee **Obv:** Bust of Queen Elizabeth II right **Rev:** Queen on horse trotting left **Edge:** Reeded

Date	Mintage	F	VF	XF	Unc	BU
2002 Proof	10,000	Value: 40.00				

KM# 191 10 DOLLARS

28.2800 g., 0.9250 Gold Clad Silver 0.841 oz., 38.6 mm.
Subject: Queen's Golden Jubilee **Obv:** Bust of Queen Elizabeth II right **Rev:** 3/4-length Queen seated on throne **Edge:** Reeded

Date	Mintage	F	VF	XF	Unc	BU
2002 Proof	10,000	Value: 45.00				

KM# 194 10 DOLLARS

28.2800 g., 0.9250 Gold Clad Silver 0.841 oz., 38.6 mm.
Subject: Queen's Golden Jubilee **Obv:** Bust of Queen Elizabeth II right **Rev:** Queen with President Ronald Reagan and First Lady Nancy Reagan **Edge:** Reeded

Date	Mintage	F	VF	XF	Unc	BU
2002 Proof	10,000	Value: 45.00				

KM# 197 10 DOLLARS

28.2800 g., 0.9250 Gold Clad Silver 0.841 oz., 38.6 mm.
Subject: Queen's Golden Jubilee **Obv:** Bust of Queen Elizabeth II right **Rev:** Carnival dancers **Edge:** Reeded

Date	Mintage	F	VF	XF	Unc	BU
2002 Proof	10,000	Value: 45.00				

KM# 200 10 DOLLARS

28.2800 g., 0.9250 Silver 0.841 oz. ASW, 38.6 mm.
Subject: Teddy Bear Centennial **Obv:** Bust of Queen Elizabeth II right **Rev:** Teddy bear **Edge:** Reeded

Date	Mintage	F	VF	XF	Unc	BU
2002 Proof	10,000	Value: 40.00				

KM# 205 10 DOLLARS

28.2800 g., 0.9250 Silver 0.841 oz. ASW, 38.6 mm.
Subject: Princess Diana **Obv:** Bust of Queen Elizabeth II right
Rev: Diana's portrait **Edge:** Reeded

Date	Mintage	F	VF	XF	Unc	BU
2002 Proof	10,000	Value: 40.00				

KM# 208.1 10 DOLLARS

28.2800 g., 0.9250 Silver 0.841 oz. ASW, 38.6 mm.
Subject: September 11, 2001 **Obv:** Bust of Queen Elizabeth II right **Rev:** World Trade Center twin towers **Edge:** Reeded

Date	Mintage	F	VF	XF	Unc	BU
2002 Proof	10,000	Value: 40.00				

KM# 208.2 10 DOLLARS

28.2800 g., 0.9250 Silver 0.841 oz. ASW, 38.6 mm.
Subject: September 11, 2001 **Obv:** Bust of Queen Elizabeth II right **Rev:** Holographic multicolor World Trade Center twin towers **Edge:** Reeded

Date	Mintage	F	VF	XF	Unc	BU
2002 Proof	10,000	Value: 45.00				

KM# 211 10 DOLLARS

28.2800 g., 0.9250 Silver 0.841 oz. ASW, 38.6 mm.
Subject: September 11, 2001 **Obv:** Bust of Queen Elizabeth II right **Rev:** Statue of Liberty **Edge:** Reeded

Date	Mintage	F	VF	XF	Unc	BU
2002 Proof	10,000	Value: 40.00				

KM# 226 10 DOLLARS
28.2800 g., 0.9250 Silver 0.841 oz. ASW, 38.6 mm.
Subject: Kennedy Assassination **Obv:** Queen's portrait **Rev:** President Kennedy's head left **Edge:** Reeded

Date	Mintage	F	VF	XF	Unc	BU
2003 Proof	10,000	Value: 40.00				

KM# 230 10 DOLLARS
28.2800 g., 0.9250 Silver 0.841 oz. ASW, 38.6 mm.
Subject: Powered Flight Centennial **Obv:** Queen's portrait **Rev:** Three historic airplanes and rocket **Edge:** Reeded

Date	Mintage	F	VF	XF	Unc	BU
2003 Proof	10,000	Value: 45.00				

KM# 233 10 DOLLARS
28.2800 g., 0.9250 Silver 0.841 oz. ASW, 38.6 mm. **Obv:** Queen's portrait **Rev:** Henry VIII and Elizabeth I **Edge:** Reeded

Date	Mintage	F	VF	XF	Unc	BU
2003 Proof	10,000	Value: 40.00				

KM# 236 10 DOLLARS
28.2800 g., 0.9250 Silver 0.841 oz. ASW, 38.6 mm.
Obv: Queen's portrait **Rev:** Matthew Parker, Archbishop of Canterbury **Edge:** Reeded

Date	Mintage	F	VF	XF	Unc	BU
2003 Proof	10,000	Value: 40.00				

KM# 239 10 DOLLARS
28.2800 g., 0.9250 Silver 0.841 oz. ASW, 38.6 mm. **Obv:** Queen's portrait **Rev:** Sir Francis Drake and ships **Edge:** Reeded

Date	Mintage	F	VF	XF	Unc	BU
2003 Proof	10,000	Value: 40.00				

KM# 242 10 DOLLARS
28.2800 g., 0.9250 Silver 0.841 oz. ASW, 38.6 mm.
Obv: Queen's portrait **Rev:** Sir Walter Raleigh **Edge:** Reeded

Date	Mintage	F	VF	XF	Unc	BU
2003 Proof	10,000	Value: 40.00				

KM# 245 10 DOLLARS
28.2800 g., 0.9250 Silver 0.841 oz. ASW, 38.6 mm. **Obv:** Queen's portrait **Rev:** Sir William Shakespeare **Edge:** Reeded

Date	Mintage	F	VF	XF	Unc	BU
2003 Proof	10,000	Value: 40.00				

KM# 248 10 DOLLARS
28.2800 g., 0.9250 Silver 0.841 oz. ASW, 38.6 mm.
Obv: Queen's portrait **Rev:** Elizabeth I above her funeral procession **Edge:** Reeded

Date	Mintage	F	VF	XF	Unc	BU
2003 Proof	10,000	Value: 40.00				

KM# 251 10 DOLLARS
28.2800 g., 0.9250 Silver 0.841 oz. ASW, 38.6 mm. **Subject:** Olympics **Obv:** Queen's portrait **Rev:** Ancient bust, runners and coin **Edge:** Reeded

Date	Mintage	F	VF	XF	Unc	BU
2003 Proof	10,000	Value: 40.00				

KM# 254 10 DOLLARS
28.2800 g., 0.9250 Silver 0.841 oz. ASW, 38.6 mm.
Subject: Olympics **Obv:** Queen's portrait **Rev:** Ancient bust, charioteer and coin **Edge:** Reeded

Date	Mintage	F	VF	XF	Unc	BU
2003 Proof	10,000	Value: 40.00				

KM# 266 10 DOLLARS
28.2800 g., 0.9250 Silver 0.841 oz. ASW, 38.6 mm. **Obv:** Queen Elizabeth II **Rev:** Sir Francis Drake, ship and map **Edge:** Reeded

Date	Mintage	F	VF	XF	Unc	BU
2004 Proof	10,000	Value: 45.00				

KM# 270.1 10 DOLLARS
28.2800 g., 0.9250 Silver 0.841 oz. ASW, 38.6 mm. **Obv:** Queen Elizabeth II **Rev:** Peter Rabbit **Edge:** Reeded

Date	Mintage	F	VF	XF	Unc	BU
2004 Proof	5,000	Value: 47.50				

KM# 270.2 10 DOLLARS
28.2800 g., 0.9250 Silver 0.841 oz. ASW, 38.6 mm. **Obv:** Queen Elizabeth II **Rev:** Multicolor Peter Rabbit **Edge:** Reeded

Date	Mintage	F	VF	XF	Unc	BU
2004 Proof	—	Value: 65.00				

KM# 274 10 DOLLARS
1.2440 g., 0.9999 Gold 0.04 oz. AGW, 14 mm. **Obv:** Elizabeth II **Rev:** Hernando Pizarro **Edge:** Reeded

Date	Mintage	F	VF	XF	Unc	BU
2004 Proof	350	Value: 75.00				

KM# 282 10 DOLLARS
28.2800 g., 0.9250 Silver 0.841 oz. ASW, 38.6 mm.
Obv: Elizabeth II **Rev:** Sailor above two D-Day landing craft **Edge:** Reeded

Date	Mintage	F	VF	XF	Unc	BU
2004 Proof	10,000	Value: 50.00				

KM# 298 10 DOLLARS
28.2800 g., 0.9250 Silver 0.841 oz. ASW, 38.6 mm. **Obv:** Elizabeth II **Rev:** Soldier above tank and jeeps **Edge:** Reeded

Date	Mintage	F	VF	XF	Unc	BU
2004 Proof	10,000	Value: 50.00				

KM# 301 10 DOLLARS
28.2800 g., 0.9250 Silver 0.841 oz. ASW, 38.6 mm.
Obv: Elizabeth II **Rev:** Pilot and planes above D-Day landing **Edge:** Reeded

Date	Mintage	F	VF	XF	Unc	BU
2004 Proof	10,000	Value: 50.00				

KM# 304 10 DOLLARS
28.2800 g., 0.9250 Silver 0.841 oz. ASW, 38.6 mm.
Obv: Elizabeth II **Rev:** Ancient Olympic bust, runners and owl coin **Edge:** Reeded

Date	Mintage	F	VF	XF	Unc	BU
2004 Proof	10,000	Value: 50.00				

KM# 307 10 DOLLARS
28.2800 g., 0.9250 Silver 0.841 oz. ASW, 38.6 mm.
Obv: Elizabeth II **Rev:** Ancient Olympic bust, charioteer and Zeus coin **Edge:** Reeded

Date	Mintage	F	VF	XF	Unc	BU
2004 Proof	10,000	Value: 50.00				

KM# 287 10 DOLLARS
31.1035 g., 0.9990 Silver 0.999 oz. ASW, 38.6 mm.
Obv: Elizabeth II **Rev:** Dolphin **Edge:** Reeded

Date	Mintage	F	VF	XF	Unc	BU
2004 Proof	10,000	Value: 50.00				

KM# 288 10 DOLLARS
1.2440 g., 0.9999 Gold 0.04 oz. AGW, 14 mm. **Obv:** Elizabeth II **Rev:** Dolphin **Edge:** Reeded

Date	Mintage	F	VF	XF	Unc	BU
2004 Proof	10,000	Value: 55.00				

KM# 201 20 DOLLARS
1.2441 g., 0.9999 Gold 0.04 oz. AGW, 13.92 mm.
Subject: Teddy Bear Centennial **Obv:** Bust of Queen Elizabeth II right **Rev:** Teddy bear **Edge:** Reeded

Date	Mintage	F	VF	XF	Unc	BU
2002 Proof	10,000	Value: 45.00				

KM# 227 20 DOLLARS
1.2400 g., 0.9999 Gold 0.0399 oz. AGW, 13.92 mm.
Subject: Kennedy Assasination **Obv:** Queen's portrait **Rev:** President Kennedy's portrait **Edge:** Reeded

Date	Mintage	F	VF	XF	Unc	BU
2003 Proof	10,000	Value: 45.00				

KM# 271 20 DOLLARS
1.2440 g., 0.9999 Gold 0.04 oz. AGW, 14 mm. **Obv:** Elizabeth II **Rev:** Peter Rabbit **Edge:** Reeded

Date	Mintage	F	VF	XF	Unc	BU
2004 Proof	5,000	Value: 50.00				

KM# 279 20 DOLLARS
58.0000 g., 0.9990 Silver 1.8629 oz. ASW, 50 mm. **Obv:** Elizabeth II **Rev:** 1896 Olympic medal design **Edge:** Reeded

Date	Mintage	F	VF	XF	Unc	BU
2004 Proof	2,004	Value: 75.00				

KM# 275 25 DOLLARS
3.1100 g., 0.9999 Gold 0.1 oz. AGW, 18 mm. **Obv:** Elizabeth II **Rev:** Hernando Pizarro portrait and life events pictorial **Edge:** Reeded

Date	Mintage	F	VF	XF	Unc	BU
2004 Proof	350	Value: 125				

KM# 289 25 DOLLARS
3.1100 g., 0.9999 Gold 0.1 oz. AGW, 18 mm. **Obv:** Elizabeth II **Rev:** Dolphin **Edge:** Reeded

Date	Mintage	F	VF	XF	Unc	BU
2004 Proof	6,000	Value: 115				

KM# 202 50 DOLLARS
3.1104 g., 0.9999 Gold 0.1 oz. AGW, 17.95 mm. **Subject:** Teddy Bear Centennial **Obv:** Bust of Queen Elizabeth II right **Rev:** Teddy bear **Edge:** Reeded

Date	Mintage	F	VF	XF	Unc	BU
2002 Proof	7,000	Value: 85.00				

KM# 272 50 DOLLARS
3.1100 g., 0.9999 Gold 0.1 oz. AGW, 18 mm. **Obv:** Elizabeth II **Rev:** Peter Rabbit **Edge:** Reeded

Date	Mintage	F	VF	XF	Unc	BU
2004 Proof	3,000	Value: 100				

KM# 276 50 DOLLARS
6.2200 g., 0.9999 Gold 0.2 oz. AGW, 22 mm. **Obv:** Elizabeth II **Rev:** Treasure ship with blue color sail **Edge:** Reeded

Date	Mintage	F	VF	XF	Unc	BU
2004 Proof	350	Value: 225				

KM# 290 50 DOLLARS
6.2200 g., 0.9999 Gold 0.2 oz. AGW, 22 mm. **Obv:** Elizabeth II **Rev:** Dolphin **Edge:** Reeded

Date	Mintage	F	VF	XF	Unc	BU
2004 Proof	3,500	Value: 215				

KM# 285 75 DOLLARS
11.0000 g., Bi-Metallic .990 Titanium 2g center in .9999 Gold 9g ring, 36.5 mm. **Obv:** Elizabeth II **Rev:** British Guiana stamp design **Edge:** Reeded

Date	Mintage	F	VF	XF	Unc	BU
2004 Proof	2,500	Value: 300				

KM# 182 100 DOLLARS
6.2200 g., 0.9990 Gold 0.1998 oz. AGW, 22 mm. **Subject:** Sir Francis Drake **Obv:** Bust of Queen Elizabeth II right **Rev:** Ship, portrait and map **Edge:** Reeded

Date	Mintage	F	VF	XF	Unc	BU
2002 Proof	5,000	Value: 185				

KM# 185 100 DOLLARS
6.2200 g., 0.9990 Gold 0.1998 oz. AGW, 22 mm. **Subject:** Sir Walter Raleigh **Obv:** Bust of Queen Elizabeth II right **Rev:** Ship, portrait and map **Edge:** Reeded

Date	Mintage	F	VF	XF	Unc	BU
2002 Proof	5,000	Value: 185				

KM# 189 100 DOLLARS
6.2208 g., 0.9999 Gold 0.2 oz. AGW, 22 mm. **Subject:** Queen's Golden Jubilee **Obv:** Bust of Queen Elizabeth II right **Rev:** Queen on horse **Edge:** Reeded

Date	Mintage	F	VF	XF	Unc	BU
2002 Proof	2,002	Value: 185				

KM# 192 100 DOLLARS
6.2208 g., 0.9999 Gold 0.2 oz. AGW, 22 mm. **Subject:** Queen's Golden Jubilee **Obv:** Bust of Queen Elizabeth II right **Rev:** Queen on throne **Edge:** Reeded

Date	Mintage	F	VF	XF	Unc	BU
2002 Proof	2,002	Value: 185				

KM# 195 100 DOLLARS
6.2208 g., 0.9999 Gold 0.2 oz. AGW, 22 mm. **Subject:** Queen's Golden Jubilee **Obv:** Bust of Queen Elizabeth II right **Rev:** Queen with President Ronald Reagan and Mrs. Nancy Reagan **Edge:** Reeded

Date	Mintage	F	VF	XF	Unc	BU
2002 Proof	2,002	Value: 185				

KM# 198 100 DOLLARS
6.2208 g., 0.9999 Gold 0.2 oz. AGW, 22 mm. **Subject:** Queen's Golden Jubilee **Obv:** Bust of Queen Elizabeth II right **Rev:** Carnival dancers **Edge:** Reeded

Date	Mintage	F	VF	XF	Unc	BU
2002 Proof	2,002	Value: 185				

KM# 203 100 DOLLARS
6.2200 g., 0.9999 Gold 0.2 oz. AGW, 22 mm. **Subject:** Teddy Bear Centennial **Obv:** Bust of Queen Elizabeth II right **Rev:** Teddy bear **Edge:** Reeded

Date	Mintage	F	VF	XF	Unc	BU
2002 Proof	5,000	Value: 185				

KM# 206 100 DOLLARS
6.2200 g., 0.9999 Gold 0.2 oz. AGW, 22 mm. **Subject:** Princess Diana **Obv:** Bust of Queen Elizabeth II right **Rev:** Diana's portrait **Edge:** Reeded

Date	Mintage	F	VF	XF	Unc	BU
2002 Proof	5,000	Value: 185				

KM# 209.1 100 DOLLARS
6.2200 g., 0.9999 Gold 0.2 oz. AGW, 22 mm. **Subject:** September 11, 2001 **Obv:** Bust of Queen Elizabeth II right **Rev:** World Trade Center twin towers **Edge:** Reeded

Date	Mintage	F	VF	XF	Unc	BU
2002 Proof	5,000	Value: 185				

KM# 209.2 100 DOLLARS
6.2200 g., 0.9999 Gold 0.2 oz. AGW, 22 mm. **Subject:** September 11, 2001 **Obv:** Bust of Queen Elizabeth II right **Rev:** Holographic multicolor World Trade Center twin towers **Edge:** Reeded

Date	Mintage	F	VF	XF	Unc	BU
2002 Proof	5,000	Value: 185				

KM# 212 100 DOLLARS
6.2200 g., 0.9999 Gold 0.2 oz. AGW, 22 mm. **Subject:** September 11, 2001 **Obv:** Bust of Queen Elizabeth II right **Rev:** Statue of Liberty **Edge:** Reeded

Date	Mintage	F	VF	XF	Unc	BU
2002 Proof	5,000	Value: 185				

KM# 215 100 DOLLARS
6.2200 g., 0.9999 Gold 0.2 oz. AGW, 22 mm. **Subject:** Queen Mother Series **Obv:** Queen's portrait **Rev:** Queen Mother with young Prince Charles **Edge:** Reeded

Date	Mintage	F	VF	XF	Unc	BU
2002 Proof	5,000	Value: 185				

KM# 218 100 DOLLARS
6.2200 g., 0.9999 Gold 0.2 oz. AGW, 22 mm. **Subject:** Queen Mother Series **Obv:** Queen's portrait **Rev:** Queen Mother with four grandchildren **Edge:** Reeded

Date	Mintage	F	VF	XF	Unc	BU
2002 Proof	5,000	Value: 185				

KM# 221 100 DOLLARS
6.2200 g., 0.9999 Gold 0.2 oz. AGW, 22 mm. **Subject:** Queen Mother Series **Obv:** Queen's portrait **Rev:** Queen Mother with uniformed Prince Charles **Edge:** Reeded

Date	Mintage	F	VF	XF	Unc	BU
2002 Proof	5,000	Value: 185				

KM# 224 100 DOLLARS
6.2200 g., 0.9999 Gold 0.2 oz. AGW, 22 mm. **Subject:** Queen Mother Series **Obv:** Queen's portrait **Rev:** Queen Mother's coffin **Edge:** Reeded

Date	Mintage	F	VF	XF	Unc	BU
2002 Proof	5,000	Value: 185				

KM# 228 100 DOLLARS
6.2200 g., 0.9999 Gold 0.2 oz. AGW, 22 mm. **Subject:** Kennedy Assasination **Obv:** Queen's portrait **Rev:** President Kennedy's portrait **Edge:** Reeded

Date	Mintage	F	VF	XF	Unc	BU
2003 Proof	5,000	Value: 185				

KM# 231 100 DOLLARS
15.5500 g., 0.9999 Gold 0.4999 oz. AGW, 30 mm. **Subject:** Powered Flight Centennial **Obv:** Queen's portrait **Rev:** Three historic airplanes and rocket **Edge:** Reeded

Date	Mintage	F	VF	XF	Unc	BU
2003 Proof	—	Value: 375				

KM# 234 100 DOLLARS
6.2200 g., 0.9999 Gold 0.2 oz. AGW, 22 mm. **Obv:** Queen's portrait **Rev:** Henry VIII and Elizabeth I **Edge:** Reeded

Date	Mintage	F	VF	XF	Unc	BU
2003 Proof	5,000	Value: 185				

KM# 237 100 DOLLARS
6.2200 g., 0.9999 Gold 0.2 oz. AGW, 22 mm. **Obv:** Queen's portrait **Rev:** Matthew Parker, Archbishop of Canterbury **Edge:** Reeded

Date	Mintage	F	VF	XF	Unc	BU
2003 Proof	5,000	Value: 185				

KM# 240 100 DOLLARS
6.2200 g., 0.9999 Gold 0.2 oz. AGW, 22 mm. **Obv:** Queen's portrait **Rev:** Sir Francis Drake and ships **Edge:** Reeded

Date	Mintage	F	VF	XF	Unc	BU
2003 Proof	5,000	Value: 185				

KM# 243 100 DOLLARS
6.2200 g., 0.9999 Gold 0.2 oz. AGW, 22 mm. **Obv:** Queen's portrait **Rev:** Sir Walter Raleigh **Edge:** Reeded

Date	Mintage	F	VF	XF	Unc	BU
2003 Proof	5,000	Value: 185				

KM# 246 100 DOLLARS
6.2200 g., 0.9999 Gold 0.2 oz. AGW, 22 mm. **Obv:** Queen's portrait **Rev:** Sir William Shakespeare **Edge:** Reeded

Date	Mintage	F	VF	XF	Unc	BU
2003 Proof	5,000	Value: 185				

KM# 249 100 DOLLARS
6.2200 g., 0.9999 Gold 0.2 oz. AGW, 22 mm. **Obv:** Queen's portrait **Rev:** Elizabeth I above her funeral procession **Edge:** Reeded

Date	Mintage	F	VF	XF	Unc	BU
2003 Proof	5,000	Value: 185				

KM# 252 100 DOLLARS
6.2200 g., 0.9999 Gold 0.2 oz. AGW, 22 mm. **Subject:** Olympics **Obv:** Queen's portrait **Rev:** Ancient bust, runners and coin **Edge:** Reeded

Date	Mintage	F	VF	XF	Unc	BU
2003 Proof	5,000	Value: 185				

KM# 255 100 DOLLARS
6.2200 g., 0.9999 Gold 0.2 oz. AGW, 22 mm. **Subject:** Olympics **Obv:** Queen's portrait **Rev:** Ancient bust, charioteer and coin **Edge:** Reeded

Date	Mintage	F	VF	XF	Unc	BU
2003 Proof	5,000	Value: 185				

KM# 273.1 100 DOLLARS
6.2200 g., 0.9999 Gold 0.2 oz. AGW, 22 mm. **Obv:** Elizabeth II **Rev:** Peter Rabbit **Edge:** Reeded

Date	Mintage	F	VF	XF	Unc	BU
2004 Proof	2,000	Value: 185				

KM# 273.2 100 DOLLARS
6.2200 g., 0.9999 Gold 0.2 oz. AGW, 22 mm. **Obv:** Elizabeth II **Rev:** Multicolor Peter Rabbit **Edge:** Reeded

Date	Mintage	F	VF	XF	Unc	BU
2004 Proof	—	Value: 240				

KM# 283 100 DOLLARS
6.2200 g., 0.9999 Gold 0.2 oz. AGW, 22 mm. **Obv:** Elizabeth II **Rev:** Sailor above two D-Day landing craft **Edge:** Reeded

Date	Mintage	F	VF	XF	Unc	BU
2004 Proof	5,000	Value: 185				

KM# 299 100 DOLLARS
6.2200 g., 0.9999 Gold 0.2 oz. AGW, 22 mm. **Obv:** Elizabeth II **Rev:** Soldier above tank and jeeps **Edge:** Reeded

Date	Mintage	F	VF	XF	Unc	BU
2004 Proof	5,000	Value: 185				

KM# 302 100 DOLLARS
6.2200 g., 0.9999 Gold 0.2 oz. AGW, 22 mm. **Obv:** Elizabeth II **Rev:** Pilot and planes above D-Day landing **Edge:** Reeded

Date	Mintage	F	VF	XF	Unc	BU
2004 Proof	5,000	Value: 185				

KM# 305 100 DOLLARS
6.2200 g., 0.9999 Gold 0.2 oz. AGW, 22 mm. **Obv:** Elizabeth II **Rev:** Ancient Olympic bust, runners and owl coin **Edge:** Reeded

Date	Mintage	F	VF	XF	Unc	BU
2004 Proof	5,000	Value: 185				

KM# 308 100 DOLLARS
6.2200 g., 0.9999 Gold 0.2 oz. AGW, 22 mm. **Obv:** Elizabeth II **Rev:** Ancient Olympic bust, charioteer and Zeus coin **Edge:** Reeded

Date	Mintage	F	VF	XF	Unc	BU
2004 Proof	5,000	Value: 185				

KM# 309 250 DOLLARS
15.5517 g., 0.9990 Gold 0.4995 oz. AGW, 30 mm. **Obv:** Elizabeth II **Rev:** Statue of Liberty and the date "11 Sept. 2001" **Edge:** Reeded

Date	Mintage	F	VF	XF	Unc	BU
2002	250	Value: 375				

KM# 280 250 DOLLARS
58.0000 g., 0.5000 Gold 0.9324 oz. AGW, 50 mm. **Obv:** Elizabeth II **Rev:** 1896 Olympic medal design **Edge:** Reeded

Date	Mintage	F	VF	XF	Unc	BU
2004 Proof	1,000	Value: 700				

KM# 277 500 DOLLARS
5000.0000 g., 0.9999 Silver 160.738 oz. ASW, 150 mm. **Obv:** Elizabeth II **Rev:** Gold-plated portrait of Hernando Pizarro, small inset emerald above Pizarro's life events pictoral **Edge:** Reeded

Date	Mintage	F	VF	XF	Unc	BU
2004 Proof	500	Value: 2,250				

BRUNEI

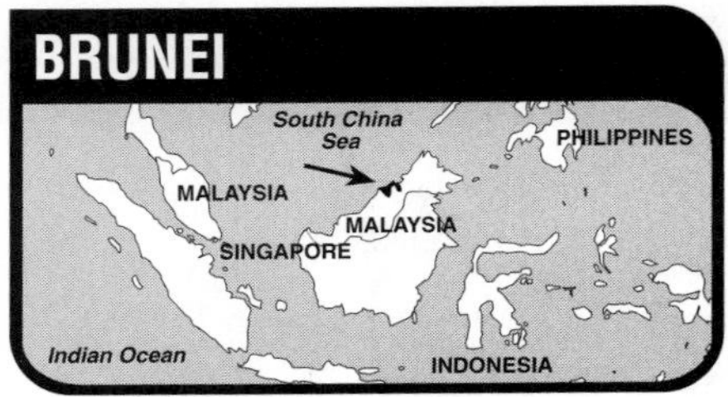

Negara Brunei Darussalam (State of Brunei), an independent sultanate on the northwest coast of the island of Borneo, has an area of 2,226 sq. mi. (5,765 sq. km.) and a population of *326,000. Capital: Bandar Seri Begawan. Crude oil and rubber are exported.

RULERS
Sultan Hassanal Bolkiah I, 1967-

SULTANATE

DECIMAL COINAGE

100 Sen = 1 Dollar (Ringgit)

KM# 34 SEN
Copper Clad Steel

Date	Mintage	F	VF	XF	Unc	BU
2001	576,000	—	—	—	0.35	0.50
2002	804,900	—	—	—	0.35	0.50

KM# 35 5 SEN
Copper-Nickel

Date	Mintage	F	VF	XF	Unc	BU
2001	808,000	—	—	—	0.50	0.75
2002	1,418,178	—	—	—	0.50	0.75

KM# 36 10 SEN
Copper-Nickel

Date	Mintage	F	VF	XF	Unc	BU
2001	164,000	—	—	—	0.65	1.00
2002	476,452	—	—	—	0.65	1.00

KM# 37 20 SEN
Copper-Nickel

Date	Mintage	F	VF	XF	Unc	BU
2001	270,647	—	—	—	1.00	1.50
2002	597,272	—	—	—	1.00	1.50

KM# 38 50 SEN
Copper-Nickel **Edge:** Reeded and security edge

Date	Mintage	F	VF	XF	Unc	BU
2001	50,000	—	—	—	2.50	3.00
2002	1,325	—	—	—	3.50	5.00

KM# 77 3 DOLLARS
24.0000 g., Copper-Nickel, 40 mm. **Ruler:** Sultan Hassanal Bolkiah **Obv:** Sultan in uniform **Rev:** Radiant globe **Edge:** Reeded
Note: Commonwealth Finance Ministers Meeting

Date	Mintage	F	VF	XF	Unc	BU
ND(2003) Proof	4,000	Value: 25.00				

BULGARIA

The Republic of Bulgaria, formerly the Peoples Republic of Bulgaria, a Balkan country on the Black Sea in southeastern Europe, has an area of 42,855 sq. mi. (110,910 sq. km.) and a population of *8.31 million. Capital: Sofia. Agriculture remains a key component of the economy but industrialization, particularly heavy industry, has been emphasized since the late 1940s. Machinery, tobacco and cigarettes, wines and spirits, clothing and metals are the chief exports.

MONETARY SYSTEM
100 Stotinki = 1 Lev

REPUBLIC

REFORM COINAGE

KM# 237 STOTINKA
Brass **Obv:** Madara horseman **Rev:** Denomination **Edge:** Plain

Date	Mintage	F	VF	XF	Unc	BU
2002 Proof	10,000	Value: 1.00				

KM# 238 2 STOTINKI
Brass **Obv:** Madara horseman **Rev:** Denomination **Edge:** Plain

Date	Mintage	F	VF	XF	Unc	BU
2002 Proof	10,000	Value: 1.50				

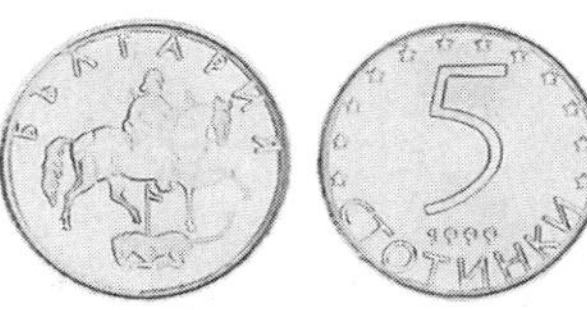

KM# 239 5 STOTINKI
Brass **Obv:** Madara horseman **Rev:** Denomination **Edge:** Plain
Note: Prev. KM#A239.

Date	Mintage	F	VF	XF	Unc	BU
2002 Proof	10,000	Value: 2.00				

KM# 240 10 STOTINKI
Copper-Nickel **Obv:** Madara horseman **Rev:** Denomination
Edge: Reeded

Date	Mintage	F	VF	XF	Unc	BU
2002 Proof	10,000	Value: 2.50				

KM# 241 20 STOTINKI
Copper-Nickel **Obv:** Madara horseman **Rev:** Denomination
Edge: Reeded

Date	Mintage	F	VF	XF	Unc	BU
2002 Proof	10,000	Value: 3.00				

KM# 242 50 STOTINKI
Copper-Nickel **Obv:** Madara horseman **Rev:** Denomination **Edge:** Reeded

Date	Mintage	F	VF	XF	Unc	BU
2002 Proof	10,000	Value: 5.00				

KM# 272 50 STOTINKI
Copper-Nickel **Obv:** Stylized Bulgarian arms, lion left, NATO - 2004 under lion **Rev:** Value **Edge:** Reeded

Date	Mintage	F	VF	XF	Unc	BU
2004	—	—	—	—	2.00	3.00

KM# 274 50 STOTINKI
5.0300 g., Copper-Nickel, 22.6 mm. **Obv:** European Union seated woman allegory **Rev:** Value **Edge:** Reeded

Date	Mintage	F	VF	XF	Unc	BU
2005	—	—	—	—	1.25	1.75

KM# 254 LEV
7.0300 g., Bi-Metallic Copper-Nickel center in Brass ring, 24.3 mm. **Obv:** St. Ivan of Rila **Rev:** Denomination **Edge:** Reeded and plain sections

Date	Mintage	F	VF	XF	Unc	BU
2002	24,842,000	—	—	—	3.00	3.50
2002 Proof	10,000	Value: 10.00				

KM# 257 LEV
15.5500 g., 0.9990 Gold 0.4994 oz. AGW **Obv:** St. Ivan of Rila **Rev:** Large number one **Edge:** Plain

Date	Mintage	F	VF	XF	Unc	BU
2002 Proof	2,000	Value: 450				

KM# 258 5 LEVA
1.2400 g., 0.9990 Gold 0.0398 oz. AGW **Obv:** Value **Rev:** Olympic archer **Edge:** Plain

Date	Mintage	F	VF	XF	Unc	BU
2002 Proof	12,000	Value: 47.50				

KM# 259 5 LEVA
1.2400 g., 0.9990 Gold 0.0398 oz. AGW **Obv:** Value **Rev:** Olympic cyclist **Edge:** Plain

Date	Mintage	F	VF	XF	Unc	BU
2002 Proof	12,000	Value: 47.50				

KM# 260 5 LEVA
1.2400 g., 0.9990 Gold 0.0398 oz. AGW **Obv:** Value **Rev:** Olympic fencing **Edge:** Plain

Date	Mintage	F	VF	XF	Unc	BU
2002 Proof	12,000	Value: 47.50				

KM# 261 5 LEVA
1.2400 g., 0.9990 Gold 0.0398 oz. AGW **Obv:** Value **Rev:** Olympic wrestling **Edge:** Plain

Date	Mintage	F	VF	XF	Unc	BU
2002 Proof	12,000	Value: 47.50				

KM# 262 5 LEVA
1.2400 g., 0.9990 Gold 0.0398 oz. AGW, 14 mm. **Obv:** Value **Rev:** Olympic gymnastics **Edge:** Plain

Date	Mintage	F	VF	XF	Unc	BU
2002 Proof	12,000	Value: 47.50				

KM# 263 5 LEVA
1.2400 g., 0.9990 Gold 0.0398 oz. AGW, 14 mm. **Obv:** Value **Rev:** Olympics founder Pierre du Coubertin **Edge:** Plain

Date	Mintage	F	VF	XF	Unc	BU
2002 Proof	17,000	Value: 47.50				

KM# 264 5 LEVA
1.2400 g., 0.9990 Gold 0.0398 oz. AGW, 14 mm. **Obv:** Value **Rev:** Olympic running **Edge:** Plain

Date	Mintage	F	VF	XF	Unc	BU
2002 Proof	12,000	Value: 47.50				

KM# 265 5 LEVA
1.2400 g., 0.9990 Gold 0.0398 oz. AGW, 14 mm. **Obv:** Value **Rev:** Olympic swimming **Edge:** Plain

Date	Mintage	F	VF	XF	Unc	BU
2002 Proof	12,000	Value: 47.50				

KM# 266 5 LEVA
1.2400 g., 0.9990 Gold 0.0398 oz. AGW, 14 mm. **Obv:** Value **Rev:** Olympic tennis **Edge:** Plain

Date	Mintage	F	VF	XF	Unc	BU
2002 Proof	12,000	Value: 47.50				

KM# 267 5 LEVA
1.2400 g., 0.9990 Gold 0.0398 oz. AGW, 14 mm. **Obv:** Value **Rev:** Olympic weight lifting **Edge:** Plain

Date	Mintage	F	VF	XF	Unc	BU
2002 Proof	12,000	Value: 47.50				

KM# 268 5 LEVA
28.2800 g., 0.9250 Silver 0.841 oz. ASW, 38.5 mm. **Obv:** Value **Rev:** FIFA Soccer trophy cup **Edge:** Plain

Date	Mintage	F	VF	XF	Unc	BU
2003 Proof	50,000	Value: 37.50				

KM# 275 5 LEVA
15.0000 g., Copper-Nickel, 34.2 mm. **Obv:** National arms **Rev:** Multicolor child on rocking horse **Edge:** Plain

Date	Mintage	F	VF	XF	Unc	BU
2003 Proof	—	Value: 15.00				

KM# 247 10 LEVA
23.3300 g., 0.9250 Silver 0.6938 oz. ASW, 38.5 mm. **Subject:** Olympics **Obv:** National arms **Rev:** Ski jumper **Edge:** Plain with serial number

Date	Mintage	F	VF	XF	Unc	BU
2001 Proof	25,000	Value: 50.00				

KM# 246 10 LEVA
23.6000 g., 0.9250 Silver 0.7019 oz. ASW, 38.5 mm. **Subject:** Higher Education **Obv:** National arms **Rev:** Graduate before building **Edge:** Plain

Date	Mintage	F	VF	XF	Unc	BU
2001 Proof	10,000	Value: 40.00				

KM# 270 10 LEVA
23.3300 g., 0.9990 Silver 0.7493 oz. ASW, 38.6 mm. **Subject:** National Theater Centennial **Edge:** Plain

Date	Mintage	F	VF	XF	Unc	BU
2004 Proof	5,000	Value: 40.00				

KM# 273 10 LEVA
23.2000 g., 0.9250 Silver 0.69 oz. ASW, 38.5 mm. **Obv:** National arms **Rev:** St. Nikolay Mirlikiisky Chudofvorez with gold plated crosses and halo **Edge:** Plain

Date	Mintage	F	VF	XF	Unc	BU
2004 Proof	10,000	Value: 40.00				

KM# 269 20 LEVA
1.5500 g., 0.9990 Gold 0.0498 oz. AGW, 16 mm. **Obv:** Value **Rev:** Mother of God **Edge:** Plain

Date	Mintage	F	VF	XF	Unc	BU
2003 Proof	20,000	Value: 55.00				

KM# 271 125 LEVA
7.7800 g., 0.9990 Gold 0.2499 oz. AGW, 21 mm. **Subject:** Bulgarian National Bank 125th Anniversary

Date	Mintage	F	VF	XF	Unc	BU
2004 Proof	3,000	Value: 250				

PIEFORTS

KM#	Date	Mintage	Identification	Mkt Val
P4	2004	5,000	10 Leva. 0.9990 Silver. 46.6600 g. 100 Years - National Theatre, 38.61mm.	75.00

PROOF SETS

KM#	Date	Mintage	Identification	Issue Price	Mkt Val
PS8	2002 (7)	10,000	KM#237-242, 254	—	25.00

DEMOCRATIC REPUBLIC

INSTITUT MONETAIRE

KM# 1 6000 CFA FRANCS - 4 AFRICA
10.1000 g., Bi-Metallic Copper-Nickel center in Brass ring, 28.3 mm. **Obv:** Bird and rhinoceros **Rev:** Elephant head on map **Edge:** Plain

Date	Mintage	F	VF	XF	Unc	BU
2003	1,200	—	—	—	40.00	—

KM# 1a 6000 CFA FRANCS - 4 AFRICA
13.2000 g., 0.9990 Silver, 28.3 mm. **Edge:** Plain

Date	Mintage	F	VF	XF	Unc	BU
2003	5	—	—	—	135	—

KM# 1b 6000 CFA FRANCS - 4 AFRICA
11.0000 g., 0.9990 Bi-Metallic .999 Silver center in Gold ring 0.3533 oz., 28.3 mm. **Obv:** Bird and Rhinoceros **Rev:** Elephant head on map **Edge:** Plain

Date	Mintage	F	VF	XF	Unc	BU
2003	5	—	—	—	450	—

REPUBLIC

INSTITUT MONETAIRE

KM# 2 6000 CFA FRANCS - 4 AFRICA
11.0000 g., 0.9990 Silver 0.3533 oz. ASW, 28.4 mm. **Obv:** Rhinoceros and bird **Rev:** Elephant head on full African map within Presidential legend **Edge:** Plain

Date	Mintage	F	VF	XF	Unc	BU
2003	5	—	—	—	480	—

KM# 2a 6000 CFA FRANCS - 4 AFRICA
11.0000 g., 0.9990 Bi-Metallic .999 Silver center in .999 Gold plated .999 Silver ring 0.3533 oz., 28.4 mm. **Obv:** Rhinocerous and bird **Rev:** Elephant head on full African map within Presidential legend **Edge:** Plain

Date	Mintage	F	VF	XF	Unc	BU
2003	5	—	—	—	480	—

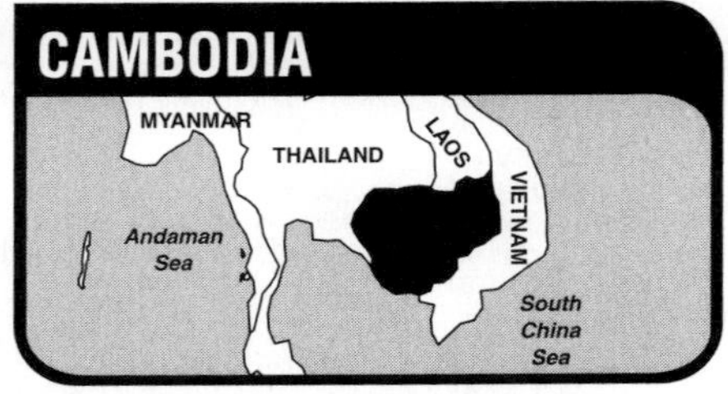

The State of Cambodia, formerly Democratic Kampuchea and the Khmer Republic, a land of paddy fields and forest-clad hills located on the Indo-Chinese peninsula, fronting on the Gulf of Thailand, has an area of 70,238 sq. mi. (181,040 sq. km.) and a population of *11.21 million. Capital: Phnom Penh. Agriculture is the basis of the economy, with rice the chief crop. Native industries include cattle breeding, weaving and rice milling. Rubber, cattle, corn, and timber are exported.

RULERS
Kings of Cambodia
Norodom Sihanouk, 1991-1993
Chairman, Supreme National Council
King, 1993-

KINGDOM OF CAMBODIA

1993 -

DECIMAL COINAGE

KM# 98 500 RIELS
19.9200 g., Brass, 38.7 mm. **Subject:** Angkor Wat **Obv:** Armless statue of Jayavarman VII **Rev:** View of Angkor Wat in center **Edge:** Reeded

Date	Mintage	F	VF	XF	Unc	BU
2001	28,000	—	—	—	7.50	10.00

KM# 99 3000 RIELS
1.2441 g., 0.9999 Gold 0.04 oz. AGW, 13.92 mm. **Subject:** Angkor Wat **Obv:** Armless statue of Jayavarman VII **Rev:** View of Angkor Wat in center **Edge:** Reeded

Date	Mintage	F	VF	XF	Unc	BU
2001	28,000	—	—	—	45.00	55.00

KM# 100 3000 RIELS
20.0000 g., 0.9250 Silver 0.5948 oz. ASW, 38.7 mm. **Subject:** Buddha **Obv:** Armless statue of Jayavarman VII **Rev:** Radiant Buddha next to a carved Buddha face **Edge:** Reeded

Date	Mintage	F	VF	XF	Unc	BU
2001 Proof	10,000	Value: 45.00				

KM# 101 3000 RIELS
20.0000 g., 0.9250 Silver 0.5948 oz. ASW, 38.7 mm. **Subject:** Apsara Dance **Obv:** Armless statue of Jayavarman VII **Rev:** Dancer next to multicolor wall **Edge:** Reeded

Date	Mintage	F	VF	XF	Unc	BU
2001 Proof	10,000	Value: 50.00				

KM# 103 3000 RIELS
20.0000 g., 0.9990 Silver 0.6424 oz. ASW, 38.7 mm. **Obv:** King Jayavarman VII (1162-1201) **Rev:** Multicolor Tutankhamen's mask **Edge:** Reeded

Date	Mintage	F	VF	XF	Unc	BU
2004 Proof	9,100	Value: 50.00				

KM# 104 3000 RIELS
1.2440 g., 0.9990 Gold 0.04 oz. AGW, 13.92 mm. **Obv:** King Jayavarman VII (1162-1201) **Rev:** Sphinx and pyramid **Edge:** Reeded

Date	Mintage	F	VF	XF	Unc	BU
2004 Proof	27,900	Value: 45.00				

KM# 102 10000 RIELS
31.1035 g., 0.9990 Silver .9990 oz. ASW **Center Weight:** 3.5000 g. **Center Composition:** 0.9999 Gold 0.1125 oz. AGW, 40.7 mm. **Subject:** Angkor Wat **Obv:** Armless statue of Jayavarman **Rev:** Multicolor holographic view of Angkor Wat in center **Edge:** Reeded

Date	Mintage	F	VF	XF	Unc	BU
2001 Proof	3,000	Value: 90.00				

KM# 105 10000 RIELS
31.1035 g., 0.9990 Silver 0.999 oz. ASW, 40.7 mm. **Obv:** King Jayavarman VII (1162-1201) **Rev:** Sphinx and pyramid on holographic gold insert **Edge:** Reeded

Date	Mintage	F	VF	XF	Unc	BU
2004 Proof	2,100	Value: 80.00				

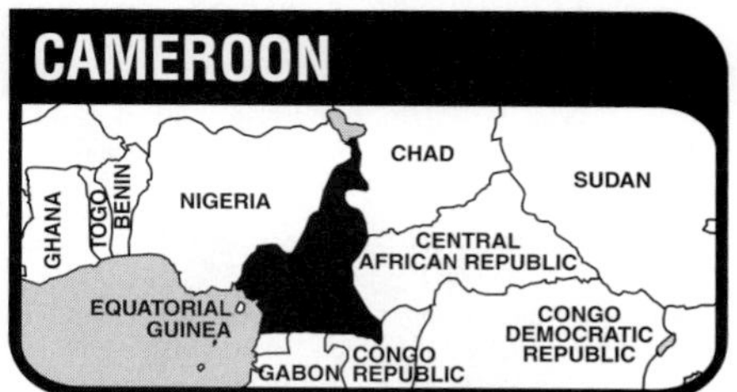

The Republic of Cameroon, located in west-central Africa on the Gulf of Guinea, has an area of 183,569 sq. mi. (475,445 sq. km.) and a population of *15.13 million. Capital: Yaounde. About 90 percent of the labor force is employed on the land; cash crops account for 80 percent of the country's export revenue. Cocoa, coffee, aluminum, cotton, rubber, and timber are exported.

MINT MARKS

(a) - Paris, privy marks only
SA - Pretoria, 1943

MONETARY SYSTEM

100 Centimes = 1 Franc

REPUBLIC

INSTITUT MONETAIRE

KM# 25 750 CFA FRANCS - 1/2 AFRICA

5.1700 g., Iron - Blued Cobalt plated Iron, 20 mm. **Obv:** Standing Pygmy **Rev:** Elephant head on full Africa map **Edge:** Plain

Date	Mintage	F	VF	XF	Unc	BU
2005	2,500	—	—	—	20.00	—

KM# 25a 750 CFA FRANCS - 1/2 AFRICA

5.2400 g., Bi-Metallic Copper-Nickel center in Brass ring, 20 mm. **Obv:** Standing Pygmy **Rev:** Elephant head on full Africa map **Edge:** Plain

Date	Mintage	F	VF	XF	Unc	BU
2005	2,005	—	—	—	55.00	—

KM# 25b 750 CFA FRANCS - 1/2 AFRICA

0.9990 Silver, 20 mm. **Obv:** Standing Pygmy **Rev:** Elephant head on full Africa map

Date	Mintage	F	VF	XF	Unc	BU
2005	25	—	—	—	475	—

KM# 26 1500 CFA FRANCS - 1 AFRICA

7.4000 g., Nickel Plated Iron, 26 mm. **Obv:** "Mambila" (Iron double hoe money) **Rev:** Elephant head on full Africa map **Edge:** Plain

Date	Mintage	F	VF	XF	Unc	BU
2005	2,005	—	—	—	20.00	—

KM# 26a 1500 CFA FRANCS - 1 AFRICA

0.9990 Silver, 26 mm. **Obv:** "Mambila" (Iron double hoe money) **Rev:** Elephant head on full Africa map

Date	Mintage	F	VF	XF	Unc	BU
2005	25	—	—	—	365	—

KM# 29 1500 CFA FRANCS - 1 AFRICA

7.3000 g., Nickel Plated Iron, 26 mm. **Obv:** Soccer player at left, Brandenburg Gate at back, African map at right **Rev:** Elephant head on full African map **Edge:** Plain

Date	Mintage	F	VF	XF	Unc	BU
2006	5,000	—	—	—	20.00	—

KM# 29a 1500 CFA FRANCS - 1 AFRICA

12.0000 g., 0.9990 Silver 0.3854 oz. ASW, 26 mm. **Obv:** Soccer player at left, Brandenburg Gate at back, African map at right **Rev:** Elephant head on full African map **Edge:** Plain

Date	Mintage	F	VF	XF	Unc	BU
2006	25	—	—	—	425	—

KM# 30 1500 CFA FRANCS - 1 AFRICA

7.3000 g., Nickel Plated Iron, 26 mm. **Obv:** Soccer player at left, Brandenburg Gate at back, African map at right **Rev:** Elephant head on full African map **Edge:** Plain

Date	Mintage	F	VF	XF	Unc	BU
2006	5,000	—	—	—	20.00	—

KM# 30a 1500 CFA FRANCS - 1 AFRICA

9.0000 g., Bi-Metallic Gold Plated Copper center in Brass ring, 26 mm. **Obv:** Soccer player at left, Brandenburg Gate at back, African map at right **Rev:** Elephant head on full African map **Edge:** Plain

Date	Mintage	F	VF	XF	Unc	BU
2006	10	—	—	—	765	—

KM# 30b 1500 CFA FRANCS - 1 AFRICA

12.0000 g., Silver, 26 mm. **Obv:** Soccer player at left, Brandenburg Gate at back, African map at right **Rev:** Elephant head on full African map **Edge:** Plain

Date	Mintage	F	VF	XF	Unc	BU
2006	25	—	—	—	425	—

KM# 24 4500 CFA FRANCS - 3 AFRICA

7.5000 g., Bi-Metallic Copper-Nickel center in Brass ring, 26 mm. **Obv:** Pope Benedict XVI **Rev:** Elephant head on Central Africa map **Edge:** Segmented reeding

Date	Mintage	F	VF	XF	Unc	BU
2005	2,005	—	—	—	55.00	—

KM# 24a 4500 CFA FRANCS - 3 AFRICA

Bi-Metallic .999 Silver center in .999 Gold plated .999 Silver ring, 26 mm. **Obv:** Pope Benedict XVI **Rev:** Elephant head on Central Africa map

Date	Mintage	F	VF	XF	Unc	BU
2005	25	—	—	—	550	—

KM# 24b 4500 CFA FRANCS - 3 AFRICA

0.9990 Silver, 26 mm. **Obv:** Pope Benedict XVI **Rev:** Elephant head on Central Africa map

Date	Mintage	F	VF	XF	Unc	BU
2005	25	—	—	—	550	—

KM# 27 6000 CFA FRANCS - 4 AFRICA

10.1300 g., Bi-Metallic Copper-Nickel center in Brass ring, 28.4 mm. **Obv:** President and map **Rev:** Elephant head on Central Africa map **Edge:** Plain

Date	Mintage	F	VF	XF	Unc	BU
ND (2003)	500	—	—	—	80.00	—

KM# 27a 6000 CFA FRANCS - 4 AFRICA

0.9990 Silver **Obv:** President and map **Rev:** Elephant head on Central Africa map

Date	Mintage	F	VF	XF	Unc	BU
2003	25	—	—	—	320	—

KM# 31 7500 CFA - 5 AFRICA

12.5000 g., Silver Plated Brass, 30.5 mm. **Obv:** Two wedding rings **Rev:** Elephant head on full African map **Edge:** Segmented reeding

Date	Mintage	F	VF	XF	Unc	BU
2006	1,500	—	—	—	45.00	—

KM# 31a 7500 CFA - 5 AFRICA

12.5000 g., Gold Plated Brass, 30.5 mm. **Obv:** Two wedding rings **Rev:** Elephant head on full African map **Edge:** Segmented reeding

Date	Mintage	F	VF	XF	Unc	BU
2006	1,500	—	—	—	45.00	—

KM# 31b 7500 CFA - 5 AFRICA

15.6000 g., 0.9990 Silver 0.501 oz. ASW, 30.5 mm. **Obv:** Two wedding rings **Rev:** Elephant head on full African map **Edge:** Segmented reeding

Date	Mintage	F	VF	XF	Unc	BU
2006	25	—	—	—	485	—

KM# 28 150000 CFA FRANCS - 100 AFRICA

0.9990 Silver **Obv:** President and map **Rev:** Elephant head on Central Africa map

Date	Mintage	F	VF	XF	Unc	BU
2003	25	—	—	—	320	—

KM# 28a 150000 CFA FRANCS - 100 AFRICA

Bi-Metallic .999 Silver center in .999 Gold plated .999 Silver ring **Obv:** President and map **Rev:** Elephant head on Central Africa map

Date	Mintage	F	VF	XF	Unc	BU
2003	25	—	—	—	320	—

Canada is located to the north of the United States, and spans the full breadth of the northern portion of North America from Atlantic to Pacific oceans, except for the State of Alaska. It has a total area of 3,850,000 sq. mi. (9,971,550 sq. km.) and a population of 30.29 million. Capital: Ottawa.

Jacques Cartier, a French explorer, took possession of Canada for France in 1534, and for more than a century the history of Canada was that of a French colony. Samuel de Champlain helped to establish the first permanent colony in North America, in 1604 at Port Royal, Acadia – now Annapolis Royal, Nova Scotia. Four years later he founded the settlement in Quebec.

The British settled along the coast to the south while the French, motivated by a grand design, pushed into the interior. France's plan for a great American empire was to occupy the Mississippi heartland of the country, and from there to press in upon the narrow strip of English coastal settlements from the west. Inevitably, armed conflict erupted between the French and the British; consequently, Britain acquired Hudson Bay, Newfoundland and Nova Scotia from the French in 1713. British control of the rest of New France was secured in 1763, largely because of James Wolfe's great victory over Montcalm near Quebec in 1759.

During the American Revolution, Canada became a refuge for great numbers of American Royalists, most of whom settled in Ontario, thereby creating an English majority west of the Ottawa River. The ethnic imbalance contravened the effectiveness of the prevailing French type of government, and in 1791 the Constitutional act was passed by the British parliament, dividing Canada at the Ottawa River into two parts, each with its own government: Upper Canada, chiefly English and consisting of the southern section of what is now Ontario; and Lower Canada, chiefly French and consisting principally of the southern section of Quebec. Subsequent revolt by dissidents in both sections caused the British government to pass the Union Act, July 23, 1840, which united Lower and Upper Canada (as Canada East and Canada West) to form the Province of Canada, with one council and one assembly in which the two sections had equal numbers.

The union of the two provinces did not encourage political stability; the equal strength of the French and British made the task of government all but impossible. A further change was made with the passage of the British North American Act, which took effect on July 1, 1867, and established Canada as the first federal union in the British Empire. Four provinces entered the union at first: Upper Canada as Ontario, Lower Canada as Quebec, Nova Scotia and New Brunswick. The Hudson Bay Company's territories were acquired in 1869 out of which were formed the provinces of Manitoba, Saskatchewan and Alberta. British Columbia joined in 1871 and Prince Edward Island in 1873. Canada took over the Arctic Archipelago in 1895. In 1949 Newfoundland came into the confederation.

In the early years, Canada's coins were struck in England at the Royal Mint in London or at the Heaton Mint in Birmingham. Issues struck at the Royal Mint do not bear a mint mark, but those produced by Heaton carry an "H". All Canadian coins have been struck since January 2, 1908, at the Royal Canadian Mints at Ottawa and recently at Winnipeg except for some 1968 pure nickel dimes struck at the U.S. Mint in Philadelphia, and do not bear mint marks. Ottawa's mint mark (C) does not appear on some 20th Century Newfoundland issues, however, as it does on English type sovereigns struck there from 1908 through 1918.

Canada is a member of the Commonwealth of Nations. Elizabeth II is Head of State as Queen of Canada.

RULERS:
British 1763-

MONETARY SYSTEM
1 Dollar = 100 Cents

CONFEDERATION

CIRCULATION COINAGE

KM# 289 CENT **Composition:** Copper Plated Zinc **Edge:** Round and plain

Date	Mintage	VG-8	F-12	VF-20	XF-40	MS-60	MS-63	Proof
2001	919,358,000	—	—	—	—	—	0.10	—
2001 Proof	—	—	—	—	—	—	—	4.00
2003	92,219,775	—	—	—	—	—	0.10	—
2003 Proof	—	—	—	—	—	—	—	4.00
2003P	235,936,799	—	—	—	—	—	1.75	—

KM# 445 CENT **Composition:** Bronze-Plated Zinc **Subject:** Elizabeth II Golden Jubilee **Obverse:** Queen, Jubilee commemorative dates 1952-2002 **Edge:** Plain

Date	Mintage	VG-8	F-12	VF-20	XF-40	MS-60	MS-63	Proof
ND(2002)	716,366,000	—	—	—	—	—	0.75	—
ND(2002)P	114,212,000	—	—	—	—	—	1.00	—
ND(2002) In proof sets only	32,642	—	—	—	—	—	—	2.50

KM# 445a CENT **Composition:** 0.9250 Silver **Subject:** Elizabeth II Golden Jubilee **Obverse:** Queen, Jubilee commemorative dates 1952-2002 **Obv. Designer:** Dora dePedery-Hunt **Rev. Designer:** George E. Kruger-Gray

Date	Mintage	MS-63	Proof
ND(2002) In sets only	100,000	—	3.00

KM# 468 CENT **Composition:** Copper **Subject:** 50th Anniversary of the Coronation of Elizabeth II **Obverse:** 1953 effigy of the Queen, Jubilee commemorative dates 1952-2002

Date	Mintage	MS-63	Proof
ND(2003) In Coronation Proof sets only	—	2.50	—

KM# 490 CENT **Composition:** Bronze-Plated Zinc **Obverse:** New effigy of Queen Elizabeth II **Obv. Designer:** Susanna Blunt **Edge:** Plain

Date	Mintage	VG-8	F-12	VF-20	XF-40	MS-60	MS-63	Proof
2003	56,877,144	—	—	—	—	—	0.25	—
2004	645,220,000	—	—	—	—	—	0.25	—
2004 Proof	—	—	—	—	—	—	—	2.50
2005	—	—	—	—	—	—	0.25	—
2006	—	—	—	—	—	—	0.25	—

KM# 410 3 CENTS **Weight:** 3.1100 g. **Composition:** 0.9250 Gold Plated Silver .1600 oz. ASW AGW **Subject:** 1st Canadian Postage Stamp **Obverse:** Queen's head right **Obv. Designer:** Dora dePedery-Hunt **Reverse:** Partial stamp design **Rev. Designer:** Sandford Fleming **Edge:** Plain **Size:** 21.1 mm.

Date	Mintage	MS-63	Proof
2001 Proof	90,000	—	20.00

KM# 182 5 CENTS **Composition:** Copper-Nickel **Obverse:** Elizabeth II effigy **Obv. Designer:** Dora dePedery-Hunt **Rev. Designer:** George E. Kruger-Gray

Date	Mintage	VG-8	F-12	VF-20	XF-40	MS-60	MS-63	Proof
2001	166,672,000	—	—	—	—	0.15	0.30	—
2001 Proof	—	—	—	—	—	—	—	5.00
2003	—	—	—	—	—	0.15	0.30	—

KM# 182a 5 CENTS **Weight:** 5.3500 g. **Composition:** 0.9250 Silver 0.1591 oz. ASW **Obv. Designer:** Dora dePedery-Hunt **Rev. Designer:** George E. Kruger-Gray

Date	Mintage	MS-63	Proof
2001 Proof	—	—	5.00
2003 Proof	—	—	5.00

KM# 182b 5 CENTS **Weight:** 3.9000 g. **Composition:** Nickel Plated Steel **Obverse:** Queen's head right **Obv. Designer:** Dora dePedery-Hunt **Reverse:** Beaver **Rev. Designer:** George E. Kruger-Gray **Edge:** Plain **Size:** 21.2 mm.

Date	Mintage	VG-8	F-12	VF-20	XF-40	MS-60	MS-63	Proof
2001 P	136,650	—	—	—	—	0.20	0.35	—
2003 P	31,388,921	—	—	—	—	—	0.35	—

KM# 413 5 CENTS **Weight:** 5.3500 g. **Composition:** 0.9250 Silver .1591 oz. ASW **Subject:** Royal Military College **Obverse:** Queen's head right **Reverse:** Marching cadets and arch **Rev. Designer:** Gerald T. Locklin **Edge:** Plain **Size:** 21.2 mm.

Date	Mintage	MS-63	Proof
2001 Proof	25,834	—	8.50

KM# 453 5 CENTS **Composition:** 0.9250 Silver **Subject:** Vimy Ridge - WWI **Obverse:** Queen's head right **Reverse:** Vimy Ridge Memorial, allegorical figure and dates 1917-2003 **Rev. Designer:** S. A. Allward

Date	Mintage	MS-63	Proof
ND(2003) Proof	22,646	—	12.50

KM# 446 5 CENTS **Composition:** Copper-Nickel **Subject:** Elizabeth II Golden Jubilee **Obverse:** Queen, Jubilee commemorative dates 1952-2002 **Obv. Designer:** Dora dePedery-Hunt **Rev. Designer:** George E. Kruger-Gray **Note:** Magnetic.

Date	Mintage	MS-63	Proof
ND(2002)P	134,362,000	0.75	—
ND(2002)P Proof	32,642	—	5.00

KM# 446a 5 CENTS **Composition:** 0.9250 Silver **Subject:** Elizabeth II Golden Jubilee **Obverse:** Queen, Jubilee commemorative dates 1952-2002

Date	Mintage	MS-63	Proof
ND(2002) In proof sets only	100,000	—	11.50

KM# 469 5 CENTS **Composition:** 0.9250 Silver **Subject:** 50th Anniversary of the Coronation of Elizabeth II **Obverse:** 1953 effigy of the Queen, Jubilee commemorative dates 1952-2002

Date	Mintage	MS-63	Proof
ND(2003) In Coronation Proof sets only	30,000	11.50	—

KM# 491 5 CENTS **Composition:** Nickel Plated Steel **Obverse:** New effigy of Queen Elizabeth II **Obv. Designer:** Susanna Blunt **Rev. Designer:** George E. Kruger-Gray **Note:** Magnetic.

Date	Mintage	MS-63	Proof
2003	61,392,180	1.50	—
2004	123,085,000	0.50	—
2005	—	0.50	—
2006	—	0.50	—

KM# 491a 5 CENTS **Weight:** 5.3500 g. **Composition:** 0.9250 Silver 0.1591 oz. ASW **Ruler:** Elizabeth II **Obverse:** Elizabeth II by Suanne Blunt **Reverse:** Beaver **Edge:** Plain **Size:** 21.1 mm.

Date	Mintage	MS-63	Proof
2004 Proof	—	—	3.00

KM# 506 5 CENTS **Weight:** 5.3500 g. **Composition:** 0.9250 Silver 0.1591 oz. ASW **Obverse:** Queen Elizabeth II **Reverse:** "Victory " design of the KM-40 reverse **Edge:** 12-sided plain **Size:** 21.3 mm.

Date	Mintage	MS-63	Proof
ND(2004) Proof	20,000	—	11.50

KM# 183a 10 CENTS **Weight:** 2.4000 g. **Composition:** 0.9250 Silver 0.0713 oz. ASW

Date	Mintage	MS-63	Proof
2001 Proof	—	—	5.00
2002 Proof	—	—	5.00
2003 Proof	—	—	5.00

KM# 183b 10 CENTS **Composition:** Nickel Plated Steel **Obverse:** Queen's head right **Obv. Designer:** Dora dePedery-Hunt **Reverse:** Sailboat **Rev. Designer:** Emanuel Hahn **Edge:** Reeded **Size:** 18 mm.

Date	Mintage	MS-63	Proof
2001 P	266,000,000	0.45	—
2003 P	162,398,000	0.20	—

KM# 412 10 CENTS **Weight:** 1.7700 g. **Composition:** Nickel Plated Steel **Subject:** Year of the Volunteer **Obverse:** Queen's head right **Reverse:** Three portraits and radiant sun **Rev. Designer:** R. C. M. Staff **Edge:** Reeded **Size:** 18 mm.

Date	Mintage	MS-63	Proof
2001P Proof	—	—	8.50

KM# 412a 10 CENTS **Weight:** 2.4000 g. **Composition:** 0.9250 Silver .0714 oz. ASW **Subject:** Year of the Volunteer **Obverse:** Queen's head right **Reverse:** 3 conjoined busts above banner, radiant sun below **Edge:** Reeded **Size:** 18 mm.

Date	Mintage	MS-63	Proof
2001P Proof	50,000	—	12.50

KM# 447 10 CENTS **Composition:** Nickel Plated Steel **Subject:** Elizabeth II Golden Jubilee **Obverse:** Queen, Jubilee commemorative dates 1952-2002

Date	Mintage	MS-63	Proof
ND(2002)P	251,278,000	1.00	—
ND(2002) Proof	32,642	—	2.50

KM# 447a 10 CENTS **Composition:** 0.9250 Silver **Subject:** Elizabeth II Golden Jubilee **Obverse:** Queen, Jubilee commemorative dates 1952-2002

Date	Mintage	MS-63	Proof
ND(2002) In proof sets only	100,000	—	12.50

KM# 470 10 CENTS **Composition:** 0.9250 Silver **Subject:** 50th Anniversary of the Coronation of Elizabeth II

Date	Mintage	MS-63	Proof
ND(2003) In Coronation Proof sets only	30,000	12.00	—

KM# 492 10 CENTS **Composition:** Nickel Plated Steel **Obverse:** New effigy of Queen Elizabeth II **Obv. Designer:** Susanna Blunt

Date	Mintage	MS-63	Proof
2003P	—	1.50	—
2004P	211,924,000	0.60	—
2005P	—	0.60	—
2006P	—	0.60	—

KM# 524 10 CENTS **Weight:** 2.4000 g. **Composition:** 0.9250 Silver 0.0714 oz. ASW **Ruler:** Elizabeth II **Subject:** Golf, Championship of Canada, Centennial.

Date	Mintage	MS-63	Proof
2004	—	12.50	—

KM# 492a 10 CENTS **Weight:** 2.4000 g. **Composition:** 0.9250 Silver 0.0714 oz. ASW **Ruler:** Elizabeth II **Obverse:** Elizabeth II by Suanne Blunt **Reverse:** Sailboat **Edge:** Reeded **Size:** 18 mm.

Date	Mintage	MS-63	Proof
2004 Proof	—	—	5.00

KM# 184 25 CENTS **Composition:** Nickel **Obverse:** Elizabeth II effigy **Obv. Designer:** Dora dePedery-Hunt **Rev. Designer:** Emanuel Hahn

Date	Mintage	VG-8	F-12	VF-20	XF-40	MS-60	MS-63	Proof
2001	64,182,000	—	—	—	—	—	4.00	—
2001 Proof	—	—	—	—	—	—	—	6.00

KM# 184a 25 CENTS **Weight:** 5.9000 g. **Composition:** 0.9250 Silver 0.1754 oz. ASW

Date	Mintage	VG-8	F-12	VF-20	XF-40	MS-60	MS-63	Proof
2001 Proof	—	—	—	—	—	—	—	6.50
2003 Proof	—	—	—	—	—	—	—	6.50

KM# 184b 25 CENTS **Composition:** Nickel Plated Steel

Date	Mintage	VG-8	F-12	VF-20	XF-40	MS-60	MS-63	Proof
2001 P	52,153,000	—	—	—	—	0.35	0.70	—
2002 P	—	—	—	—	—	—	0.50	—
2003 P	15,905,090	—	—	—	—	—	0.50	—

KM# 419 25 CENTS **Weight:** 5.0600 g. **Composition:** Nickel Plated Steel **Subject:** Spirit of Canada **Obverse:** Queen's head right **Reverse:** Maple leaf at center, children holding hands below **Rev. Designer:** Silke Ware **Edge:** Reeded **Size:** 23.9 mm.

Date	Mintage	MS-63	Proof
2001	96,352	7.00	—

KM# 451 25 CENTS **Weight:** 4.4000 g. **Composition:** Nickel Plated Steel **Subject:** Canada Day **Obverse:** Queen's portrait **Reverse:** Human figures with large red maple leaf **Edge:** Reeded **Size:** 23.88 mm.

Date	Mintage	MS-63	Proof
2002	49,903	6.75	—

KM# 448 25 CENTS **Composition:** Nickel Plated Steel **Subject:** Elizabeth II Golden Jubilee **Note:** Double-dated 1952-2002.

Date	Mintage	MS-63	Proof
ND(2002)P	152,485,000	2.00	—
ND(2002) Proof	32,642	—	6.00

KM# 448a 25 CENTS **Composition:** 0.9250 Silver **Subject:** Elizabeth II Golden Jubilee **Obverse:** Queen, Jubilee commemorative dates 1952-2002

Date	Mintage	MS-63	Proof
ND(2002) Proof	100,000	—	12.50

KM# 493 25 CENTS **Composition:** Nickel Plated Steel **Obverse:** New effigy of Queen Elizabeth II **Obv. Designer:** Susanna Blunt

Date	Mintage	VG-8	F-12	VF-20	XF-40	MS-60	MS-63	Proof
2003P	66,861,633	—	—	—	—	—	3.00	—
2004P	159,465,000	—	—	—	—	—	1.00	—
2005P	—	—	—	—	—	—	1.00	—
2006P	—	—	—	—	—	—	1.00	—

KM# 471 25 CENTS **Composition:** 0.9250 Silver **Subject:** 50th Anniversary of the Coronation of Elizabeth II **Obverse:** 1953 effigy of the Queen, Jubilee commemorative dates 1952-2002

Date	Mintage	MS-63	Proof
ND(2003) In coronation proof sets only	30,000	12.50	—

KM# 474 25 CENTS **Composition:** 0.9250 Silver **Obverse:** Queen's head right **Reverse:** Polar bear and red colored maple leaves

Date	Mintage	MS-63	Proof
2003 Proof	—	—	7.50

KM# 510 25 CENTS **Weight:** 4.4000 g. **Composition:** Nickel Plated Steel **Ruler:** Elizabeth II **Obverse:** Elizabeth II **Reverse:** Red Poppy in center of maple leaf **Edge:** Reeded **Size:** 23.9 mm.

Date	Mintage	MS-63	Proof
2004	—	8.00	—

KM# 510a 25 CENTS **Composition:** 0.9250 Silver **Ruler:** Elizabeth II **Obverse:** Elizabeth II **Reverse:** Gold-plated poppy in maple leaf **Edge:** Reeded **Size:** 23.9 mm.

Date	Mintage	MS-63	Proof
2004 Proof	15,000	—	20.00

KM# 525 25 CENTS **Composition:** Nickel Plated Steel **Ruler:** Elizabeth II **Subject:** Celebration! Maple leaf, colorized

Date	Mintage	MS-63	Proof
2004	—	8.00	—

KM# 493a 25 CENTS **Weight:** 5.9000 g. **Composition:** 0.9250 Silver 0.1755 oz. ASW **Ruler:** Elizabeth II **Obverse:** Elizabeth II by Suanne Blunt **Reverse:** Caribou **Edge:** Reeded **Size:** 23.6 mm.

Date	Mintage	MS-63	Proof
2004 Proof	—	—	6.50

KM# 529 25 CENTS **Composition:** Nickel Plated Steel **Ruler:** Elizabeth II **Subject:** WWII **Reverse:** Three soldiers and flag

Date	Mintage	MS-63	Proof
2005	—	20.00	—

KM# 530 25 CENTS **Composition:** Nickel Plated Steel **Ruler:** Elizabeth II **Subject:** Alberta

Date	Mintage	MS-63	Proof
2005	—	8.50	—

KM# 531 25 CENTS **Composition:** Nickel Plated Steel **Ruler:** Elizabeth II **Subject:** Canada Day **Reverse:** Beaver, colorized

Date	Mintage	MS-63	Proof
2005	—	8.50	—

KM# 532 25 CENTS **Composition:** Nickel Plated Steel **Ruler:** Elizabeth II **Subject:** Saskatchewan

Date	Mintage	MS-63	Proof
2005	—	8.50	—

KM# 533 25 CENTS **Composition:** Nickel Plated Steel **Ruler:** Elizabeth II **Reverse:** Stuffed bear in Christmas stocking, colorized

Date	Mintage	MS-63	Proof
2005	—	8.50	—

KM# 535 25 CENTS **Composition:** Nickel Plated Steel **Ruler:** Elizabeth II **Subject:** Year of the Veteran **Reverse:** Profile of young and old soldier

Date	Mintage	MS-63	Proof
2005	—	8.50	—

KM# 575 25 CENTS **Composition:** Nickel Plated Steel **Ruler:** Elizabeth II **Subject:** Montreal Canadiens **Reverse:** Colorized logo

Date	Mintage	MS-63	Proof
2006P	—	8.50	—

KM# 576 25 CENTS **Composition:** Nickel Plated Steel **Ruler:** Elizabeth II **Subject:** Quebec Winter Carnival **Reverse:** Snowman, colorized

Date	Mintage	MS-63	Proof
2006	—	8.50	—

KM# 534 25 CENTS **Composition:** Nickel Plated Steel **Ruler:** Elizabeth II **Subject:** Toronto Maple Leafs **Reverse:** Colorized team logo

Date	Mintage	MS-63	Proof
2006P	—	8.50	—

KM# 290b 50 CENTS **Composition:** Nickel Plated Steel **Reverse:** Redesigned arms

Date	Mintage	MS-63	Proof
2001 P	389,000	1.25	—
2003 P	—	1.00	—

KM# 290a 50 CENTS **Weight:** 11.6380 g. **Composition:** 0.9250 Silver .3461 oz. ASW

Date	Mintage	MS-63	Proof
2001 Proof	—	—	10.00
2003 Proof	—	—	10.00

KM# 420 50 CENTS **Weight:** 9.3000 g. **Composition:** 0.9250 Silver .2766 oz. ASW **Series:** Festivals - Quebec **Obverse:** Queen's head right **Reverse:** Snowman and Chateau Frontenac **Rev. Designer:** Sylvie Daigneault **Edge:** Reeded **Size:** 27.13 mm.

Date	Mintage	MS-63	Proof
2001 Proof	58,123	—	11.50

KM# 421 50 CENTS **Weight:** 9.3000 g. **Composition:** 0.9250 Silver .2766 oz. ASW **Series:** Festivals - Nunavut **Obverse:** Queen's head right **Reverse:** Dancer, dog sled and snowmobiles **Rev. Designer:** John Mardon **Edge:** Reeded **Size:** 27.13 mm.

Date	Mintage	MS-63	Proof
2001 Proof	58,123	—	11.50

KM# 422 50 CENTS **Weight:** 9.3000 g. **Composition:** 0.9250 Silver .2766 oz. ASW **Series:** Festivals - Newfoundland **Obverse:** Queen's head right **Reverse:** Sailor and musical people **Rev. Designer:** David Craig **Edge:** Reeded **Size:** 27.13 mm.

Date	Mintage	MS-63	Proof
2001 Proof	58,123	—	11.50

KM# 423 50 CENTS **Weight:** 9.3000 g. **Composition:** 0.9250 Silver .2766 oz. ASW **Series:** Festivals - Prince Edward Island **Obverse:** Queen's head right **Reverse:** Family, juggler and building **Rev. Designer:** Brenda Whiteway **Edge:** Reeded **Size:** 27.13 mm.

Date	Mintage	MS-63	Proof
2001 Proof	58,123	—	11.50

KM# 424 50 CENTS **Weight:** 9.3000 g. **Composition:** 0.9250 Silver .2766 oz. ASW **Series:** Folklore - The Sled **Obverse:** Queen's head right **Reverse:** Family scene **Rev. Designer:** Valentina Hotz-Entin **Edge:** Reeded **Size:** 27.13 mm.

Date	Mintage	MS-63	Proof
2001 Proof	28,979	—	12.50

KM# 425 50 CENTS **Weight:** 9.3000 g. **Composition:** 0.9250 Silver .2766 oz. ASW **Series:** Folklore - The Maiden's Cave **Obverse:** Queen's head right **Reverse:** Woman shouting **Rev. Designer:** Peter Kiss **Edge:** Reeded **Size:** 27.13 mm.

Date	Mintage	MS-63	Proof
2001 Proof	28,979	—	12.50

KM# 426 50 CENTS **Weight:** 9.3000 g. **Composition:** 0.9250 Silver .2766 oz. ASW **Series:** Folklore - The Small Jumpers **Obverse:** Queen's head right **Reverse:** Jumping children on seashore **Rev. Designer:** Miynki Tanobe **Edge:** Reeded **Size:** 27.13 mm.

Date	Mintage	MS-63	Proof
2001 Proof	28,979	—	12.50

KM# 509 50 CENTS **Weight:** 6.9000 g. **Composition:** Nickel Plated Steel **Ruler:** Elizabeth II **Obverse:** Queen Elizabeth II **Reverse:** National arms **Edge:** Reeded **Size:** 27.13 mm.

Date	Mintage	MS-63	Proof
ND(2001) P	—	1.50	—

KM# 444 50 CENTS **Weight:** 6.8300 g. **Composition:** Nickel Plated Steel **Subject:** Queen's Golden Jubilee **Obverse:** Bust of Queen Elizabeth II right and monogram **Reverse:** Canadian arms **Rev. Designer:** Bursey Sabourin **Edge:** Reeded **Size:** 27 mm.

Date	Mintage	MS-63	Proof
ND(2002)P	1,440,000	2.00	—

KM# 461 50 CENTS **Composition:** 0.9250 Silver **Series:** Canadian Folklore and Legends **Subject:** The Pig That Wouldn't Get Over the Stile **Rev. Designer:** Laura Jolicoeur

Date	Mintage	MS-63	Proof
2002 Proof	19,267	—	13.50

KM# 458 50 CENTS **Composition:** 0.9250 Silver **Subject:** Squamish Days Logger Sports **Rev. Designer:** Jose Osio

Date	Mintage	MS-63	Proof
2002 Proof	59,998	—	12.00

KM# 456 50 CENTS **Composition:** 0.9250 Silver **Subject:** Folklorama **Rev. Designer:** William Woodruff

Date	Mintage	MS-63	Proof
2002 Proof	59,998	—	12.00

KM# 460 50 CENTS **Composition:** 0.9250 Silver **Series:** Canadian Folklore and Legends **Subject:** The Ghost Ship **Rev. Designer:** Colette Boivin

Date	Mintage	MS-63	Proof
2002 Proof	19,267	—	13.50

KM# 457 50 CENTS **Composition:** 0.9250 Silver **Subject:** Calgary Stampede **Rev. Designer:** Stan Witten

Date	Mintage	MS-63	Proof
2002 Proof	59,998	—	12.00

KM# 454 50 CENTS **Composition:** 0.9250 Silver **Subject:** Annapolis Valley Apple Blossom Festival **Rev. Designer:** Bonnie Ross

Date	Mintage	MS-63	Proof
2002 Proof	59,998	—	12.00

KM# 459 50 CENTS **Composition:** 0.9250 Silver **Series:** Canadian Folklore and Legends **Obverse:** Queen's head right **Reverse:** The Shoemaker in Heaven **Rev. Designer:** Francine Gravel

Date	Mintage	MS-63	Proof
2002 Proof	19,267	—	13.50

KM# 455 50 CENTS **Composition:** 0.9250 Silver **Subject:** Stratford Festival **Obverse:** Queen's head right **Reverse:** Couple with building in background **Rev. Designer:** Laurie McGaw

Date	Mintage	MS-63	Proof
2002 Proof	59,998	—	12.00

KM# 444a 50 CENTS **Composition:** 0.9250 Silver **Subject:** Elizabeth II Golden Jubilee **Obverse:** Queen, Jubilee commemorative dates 1952-2002

Date	Mintage	MS-63	Proof
ND(2002) In proof sets only	100,000	—	17.50

KM# 444b 50 CENTS **Composition:** Gold Plated Silver **Subject:** Queen's Golden Jubilee **Obverse:** Bust of Queen Elizabeth II right and monogram **Reverse:** Canadian arms **Edge:** Reeded **Size:** 27 mm. **Note:** Special 24 karat gold plated issue of KM#444.

Date	Mintage	MS-63	Proof
ND(2002) Proof	32,642	—	35.00

KM# 290 50 CENTS **Composition:** Nickel **Obv. Designer:** Dora dePedery-Hunt **Reverse:** Redesigned arms **Rev. Designer:** Cathy Bursey-Sabourin

Date	Mintage	VG-8	F-12	VF-20	XF-40	MS-60	MS-63	Proof
2003	—	—	—	—	—	—	1.00	—

KM# 494 50 CENTS **Composition:** Nickel Plated Steel **Obverse:** New effigy of Queen Elizabeth II **Obv. Designer:** Susanna Blunt **Rev. Designer:** Cathy Bursey-Sabourin

Date	Mintage	VG-8	F-12	VF-20	XF-40	MS-60	MS-63	Proof
2003W	—	—	—	—	—	—	1.50	—
2004	—	—	—	—	—	—	1.50	—

Date	Mintage	VG-8	F-12	VF-20	XF-40	MS-60	MS-63	Proof
2005	—	—	—	—	—	—	1.50	—
2006	—	—	—	—	—	—	1.50	—

KM# 494a 50 CENTS **Weight:** 11.6380 g. **Composition:** 0.9250 Silver 0.3461 oz. ASW **Ruler:** Elizabeth II **Obverse:** Elizabeth II by Suanne Blunt **Reverse:** Canadian coat of arms **Edge:** Reeded **Size:** 27 mm.

Date	Mintage	MS-63	Proof
2004 Proof	—	—	10.00

KM# 472 50 CENTS **Composition:** 0.9250 Silver **Subject:** 50th Anniversary of the Coronation of Elizabeth II **Obverse:** 1953 effigy of the Queen, Jubilee commemorative dates 1952-2002

Date	Mintage	MS-63	Proof
ND(2003) In coronation proof sets only	30,000	15.00	—

KM# 478 50 CENTS **Composition:** 0.9250 Silver **Subject:** Back to batoche

Date	Mintage	MS-63	Proof
2003 Proof	—	—	16.50

KM# 475 50 CENTS **Composition:** 0.9250 Silver **Reverse:** Golden daffodil

Date	Mintage	MS-63	Proof
2003 Proof	55,000	—	25.00

KM# 479 50 CENTS **Composition:** 0.9250 Silver **Subject:** Great Northern Arts Festival

Date	Mintage	MS-63	Proof
2003 Proof	—	—	16.50

KM# 476 50 CENTS **Composition:** 0.9250 Silver **Subject:** Yukon International Storytelling Festival

Date	Mintage	MS-63	Proof
2003 Proof	—	—	16.50

KM# 477 50 CENTS **Composition:** 0.9250 Silver **Subject:** Festival Acadien de Caraquet **Obverse:** Queen's head right **Reverse:** Sailboat and couple

Date	Mintage	MS-63	Proof
2003 Proof	—	—	16.50

KM# 606 50 CENTS **Composition:** Silver **Ruler:** Elizabeth II **Reverse:** Sulphur Butterfly, hologram

Date	Mintage	MS-63	Proof
2004 Proof	—	—	35.00

KM# 536 50 CENTS **Composition:** Silver With Partial Gold Plating **Ruler:** Elizabeth II **Subject:** Golden rose

Date	Mintage	MS-63	Proof
2005 Proof	—	—	32.50

KM# 537 50 CENTS **Composition:** Silver **Ruler:** Elizabeth II **Subject:** Great Spangled Fritillary butterfly, hologram

Date	Mintage	MS-63	Proof
2005 Proof	—	—	35.00

KM# 538 50 CENTS **Composition:** Silver **Ruler:** Elizabeth II **Subject:** Toronto Maple Leafs **Reverse:** Darryl Sittler

Date	Mintage	MS-63	Proof
2005	—	25.00	—

KM# 539 50 CENTS **Composition:** Silver **Ruler:** Elizabeth II **Subject:** Toronto Maple Leafs **Reverse:** Dave Keon

Date	Mintage	MS-63	Proof
2005	—	25.00	—

KM# 540 50 CENTS **Composition:** Silver **Ruler:** Elizabeth II **Subject:** Toronto Maple Leafs **Reverse:** Jonny Bover

Date	Mintage	MS-63	Proof
2005	—	25.00	—

KM# 541 50 CENTS **Composition:** Silver **Ruler:** Elizabeth II **Subject:** Toronto Maple Leafs **Reverse:** Tim Horton

Date	Mintage	MS-63	Proof
2005	—	25.00	—

KM# 544 50 CENTS **Composition:** Silver **Ruler:** Elizabeth II **Subject:** WWII - Battle of Scheldt **Reverse:** Four soldiers walking down road

Date	Mintage	MS-63	Proof
2005	—	22.50	—

KM# 545 50 CENTS **Composition:** Silver **Ruler:** Elizabeth II **Subject:** WWII - Battle of the Atlantic **Reverse:** Merchant ship sinking

Date	Mintage	MS-63	Proof
2005	—	22.50	—

KM# 546 50 CENTS **Composition:** Silver **Ruler:** Elizabeth II **Subject:** WWII - Conquest of Sicily **Reverse:** Tank among town ruins

Date	Mintage	MS-63	Proof
2005	—	22.50	—

KM# 547 50 CENTS **Composition:** Silver **Ruler:** Elizabeth II **Subject:** WWII - Liberation of the Netherlands **Reverse:** Soldiers in parade, one holding flag

Date	Mintage	MS-63	Proof
2005	—	22.50	—

KM# 548 50 CENTS **Composition:** Silver **Ruler:** Elizabeth II **Subject:** WWII - Raid of Dieppe **Reverse:** Three soldiers comming off landing craft

Date	Mintage	MS-63	Proof
2005	—	22.50	—

KM# 577 50 CENTS **Composition:** Silver **Ruler:** Elizabeth II **Subject:** Montreal Canadiens **Reverse:** Guy LaFleur

Date	Mintage	MS-63	Proof
2005	—	25.00	—

KM# 578 50 CENTS **Composition:** Silver **Ruler:** Elizabeth II **Subject:** Montreal Canadiens **Reverse:** Jaque Plante

Date	Mintage	MS-63	Proof
2005	—	25.00	—

KM# 579 50 CENTS **Composition:** Silver **Ruler:** Elizabeth II **Subject:** Montreal Canadiens **Reverse:** Jean Beliveau

Date	Mintage	MS-63	Proof
2005	—	25.00	—

KM# 580 50 CENTS **Composition:** Silver **Ruler:** Elizabeth II **Subject:** Montreal Canadiens **Reverse:** Maurice Richard

Date	Mintage	MS-63	Proof
2005	—	25.00	—

KM# 599 50 CENTS **Composition:** Silver **Ruler:** Elizabeth II **Subject:** Monarch Butterfly, hologram

Date	Mintage	MS-63	Proof
2005 Proof	—	—	35.00

KM# 186 DOLLAR **Composition:** Aureate-Bronze Plated Nickel **Obverse:** Elizabeth II effigy **Obv. Designer:** Dora dePedery-Hunt **Reverse:** Loon **Rev. Designer:** Robert R. Carmichael **Shape:** 11-sided

Date	Mintage	MS-63	Proof
2001	—	2.00	—
2001 Proof	—	—	8.00
2002	—	6.00	—
2002 Proof	—	—	—
2003	—	6.00	—
2003 Proof	100,000	—	12.00

KM# 414 DOLLAR **Weight:** 25.1750 g. **Composition:** 0.9250 Silver 0.7487 oz. ASW **Subject:** National Ballet **Obverse:** Queen's head right **Reverse:** Ballet dancers **Rev. Designer:** Scott McKowen **Edge:** Reeded **Size:** 36 mm.

Date	Mintage	MS-63	P/L	Proof
2001	65,000	9.00	12.00	—
2001 Proof	225,000	—	—	21.50

KM# 434 DOLLAR **Weight:** 25.1750 g. **Composition:** 0.9250 Silver 0.7487 oz. ASW **Obverse:** Bust of Queen Elizabeth II right. **Reverse:** Recycled 1911 pattern dollar design: denomination, country name and dates in crowned wreath. **Edge:** Reeded. **Size:** 36 mm.

Date	Mintage	MS-63	P/L	Proof
ND(2001) Proof	25,000	—	—	55.00

KM# 443 DOLLAR **Weight:** 25.1750 g. **Composition:** 0.9250 Silver 0.7487 oz. ASW **Subject:** Queen's Golden Jubilee **Obverse:** Queen's portrait with anniversary date **Reverse:** Queen in her coach and a view of the coach **Edge:** Reeded **Size:** 36 mm.

Date	Mintage	MS-63	P/L	Proof
ND(2002)	—	—	12.00	—
ND(2002) Proof	—	—	—	21.50

KM# 443a DOLLAR **Composition:** Gold Plated Silver **Subject:** Queen's Golden Jubilee **Obverse:** Queen's portrait with anniversary date **Reverse:** Queen in her coach and a view of the coach **Edge:** Reeded **Size:** 36 mm. **Note:** Special 24 karat gold plated issue of KM#443.

Date	Mintage	MS-63	Proof
ND(2002) Proof	32,642	—	40.00

KM# 186a DOLLAR **Composition:** Gold Plated **Subject:** Olympic Win

Date	Mintage	MS-63	Proof
2002 Proof	—	—	40.00

KM# 467 DOLLAR **Composition:** Nickel **Subject:** Elizabeth II Golden Jubilee **Obverse:** Queen, Jubilee commemorative dates 1952-2002

Date	Mintage	MS-63	Proof
ND(2002)	—	2.50	—
ND(2002) Proof	—	—	8.00

KM# 462 DOLLAR **Composition:** Aureate-Bronze Plated Nickel **Obverse:** Commemorative dates 1952-2002 **Reverse:** Family of Loons

Date	Mintage	MS-63	Proof
ND(2002) In Specimen Sets only	75,000	10.00	—

KM# 503 DOLLAR **Weight:** 25.1750 g. **Composition:** 0.9250 Silver 0.7487 oz. ASW **Subject:** Queen Mother **Obverse:** Queen's head right **Obv. Designer:** Dora de Pedery-Hunt **Reverse:** Queen Mother facing **Size:** 36 mm.

Date	Mintage	MS-63	Proof
2002 Proof	9,984	—	200

KM# 473 DOLLAR **Composition:** 0.9999 Silver **Subject:** 50th Anniversary of the Coronation of Elizabeth II **Obverse:** 1953 effigy of the Queen, Jubilee commemorative dates 1952-2002 **Reverse:** Voyageur design similar to KM#54

Date	Mintage	MS-63	Proof
ND(2003) In coronation proof sets only	30,000	35.00	—

KM# 495 DOLLAR **Composition:** Aureate-Bronze Plated Nickel **Obverse:** New effigy of Queen Elizabeth II **Obv. Designer:** Susanna Blunt **Rev. Designer:** Robert R. Carmichael

Date	Mintage	MS-63	Proof
2003	5,102,000	6.00	—
2004	3,409,000	3.00	—
2004 Proof	—	—	12.00
2005	—	3.00	—
2006	—	3.00	—

KM# 450 DOLLAR **Weight:** 25.1750 g. **Composition:** 0.9999 Silver 0.8093 oz. ASW **Subject:** Cobalt Mining Centennial **Obverse:** Queen's portrait **Reverse:** Mine tower and fox **Edge:** Reeded **Size:** 36 mm.

Date	Mintage	MS-63	Proof
ND(2003)	75,000	20.00	—
ND(2003) Proof	125,000	—	28.00

KM# 480 DOLLAR **Composition:** 0.9999 Silver **Subject:** Coronation of Queen Elizabeth II

Date	Mintage	MS-63	Proof
2003 Proof	30,000	—	38.00

KM# 507 DOLLAR **Weight:** 6.9500 g. **Composition:** Aureate-Bronze Plated Nickel **Obverse:** Queen Elizabeth II **Reverse:** Loon **Edge:** Plain **Shape:** 11-sided **Size:** 26.5 mm.

Date	Mintage	MS-63	Proof
2004 Proof	—	—	12.50

KM# 512 DOLLAR **Weight:** 25.1750 g. **Composition:** 0.9999 Silver 0.8093 oz. ASW **Ruler:** Elizabeth II **Subject:** First French Settlement in America **Obverse:** Elizabeth II **Reverse:** Sailing ship **Edge:** Reeded **Size:** 36 mm.

Date	Mintage	MS-63	Proof
2004 Proof	10,400	—	42.50

KM# 513 DOLLAR **Weight:** 6.9500 g. **Composition:** Aureate-Bronze Plated Nickel **Ruler:** Elizabeth II **Subject:** Olympics **Obverse:** Elizabeth II **Reverse:** Maple leaf, Olympic flame and rings above loon **Edge:** Plain **Shape:** 11-sided **Size:** 26.5 mm.

Date	Mintage	MS-63	Proof
2004	—	12.50	—

KM# 513a DOLLAR **Weight:** 9.3100 g. **Composition:** 0.9250 Silver 0.2769 oz. ASW **Ruler:** Elizabeth II **Subject:** Olympics **Obverse:** Elizabeth II **Reverse:** Multicolor maple leaf, Olympic flame and rings above loon **Edge:** Plain **Shape:** 11-sided **Size:** 26.5 mm.

Date	Mintage	MS-63	Proof
2004 Proof	20,000	—	50.00

KM# 549 DOLLAR **Composition:** Silver **Ruler:** Elizabeth II **Subject:** 40th Anniversary of National Flag

Date	Mintage	MS-63	Proof
2005	—	22.50	—
2005 Proof	—	—	32.50

KM# 552 DOLLAR **Composition:** Aureate-Bronze Plated Nickel **Ruler:** Elizabeth II **Subject:** Terry Fox

Date	Mintage	MS-63	Proof
2005	—	3.50	—

KM# 553 DOLLAR **Composition:** Aureate-Bronze Plated Nickel **Ruler:** Elizabeth II **Subject:** Tuffed Puffin

Date	Mintage	MS-63	Proof
2005 In specimen sets only	—	30.00	—

KM# 549a DOLLAR **Composition:** Silver With Partial Gold Plating **Ruler:** Elizabeth II **Subject:** 40th Anniversary of National Flag

Date	Mintage	MS-63	Proof
2005	—	65.00	—

KM# 581 DOLLAR **Composition:** Aureate-Bronze Plated Nickel **Ruler:** Elizabeth II **Reverse:** Loon and moon, teddy bear in stars

Date	Mintage	MS-63	Proof
2006	—	3.50	—

KM# 582 DOLLAR **Composition:** Aureate-Bronze Plated Nickel **Ruler:** Elizabeth II **Subject:** Snowy owl

Date	Mintage	MS-63	Proof
2006 In specimen sets only	40,000	30.00	—

KM# 583 DOLLAR **Composition:** Silver **Ruler:** Elizabeth II **Subject:** Victoria Cross

Date	Mintage	MS-63	Proof
2006	—	27.50	—
2006 Proof	—	—	35.00

KM# 583a DOLLAR **Composition:** Silver With Partial Gold Plating **Ruler:** Elizabeth II **Subject:** Victoria Cross

Date	Mintage	MS-63	Proof
2006 Proof	—	—	60.00

KM# 270 2 DOLLARS **Composition:** Bi-Metallic **Obv. Designer:** Dora dePedery-Hunt **Reverse:** Polar bear **Rev. Designer:** Brent Townsend **Size:** 28 mm.

Date	Mintage	MS-63	Proof
2001	27,008,000	3.25	—
2002	11,910,000	3.25	—
2003	—	3.25	—

KM# 270c 2 DOLLARS **Composition:** Bi-Metallic Gold And Silver **Reverse:** Polar bear **Note:** Silver ring; Gold plated silver center. 8.83g., .925 silver, .2626 ASW.

Date	Mintage	MS-63	Proof
2001 Proof	—	—	12.00

KM# 449 2 DOLLARS **Weight:** 7.3000 g. **Composition:** Bi-Metallic **Subject:** Elizabeth II Golden Jubilee **Obverse:** Queen, Jubilee commemorative dates 1952-2002

Date	Mintage	MS-63	Proof
ND(2002)	27,008,000	4.00	—

KM# 449a 2 DOLLARS **Composition:** Bi-Metallic **Subject:** Elizabeth II Golden Jubilee **Obverse:** Queen, Jubilee commemorative dates 1952-2002

Date	Mintage	MS-63	Proof
ND(2002) In proof sets only	100,000	—	14.00

KM# 496 2 DOLLARS **Composition:** Bi-Metallic **Obverse:** New effigy of Queen Elizabeth II **Obv. Designer:** Susanna Blunt **Rev. Designer:** Brent Townsend

Date	Mintage	MS-63	Proof
2003	—	3.50	—
2004	—	3.50	—
2005	—	3.50	—
2006	—	3.50	—

KM# 270d 2 DOLLARS **Composition:** Bi-Metallic **Subject:** 100th Anniversary of the Cobalt Silver Strike

Date	Mintage	MS-63	Proof
2003 In proof sets only	100,000	—	25.00

KM# 496a 2 DOLLARS **Weight:** 10.8414 g. **Composition:** 0.9250 Bi-Metallic Gold And Silver 0.3224 oz. **Ruler:** Elizabeth II **Obverse:** Elizabeth II by Suanne Blunt **Reverse:** Polar Bear **Edge:** Segmented reeding **Size:** 28 mm.

Date	Mintage	MS-63	Proof
2004 Proof	—	—	25.00

KM# 584 2 DOLLARS **Composition:** Bi-Metallic **Ruler:** Elizabeth II **Subject:** 10th Anniversary of Polar Bear $2.00

Date	Mintage	MS-63	Proof
2006 Proof	3,000	—	385

KM# 435 5 DOLLARS **Weight:** 16.8600 g. **Composition:** 0.9250 Silver 0.5014 oz. ASW **Subject:** Guglielmo Marconi **Obverse:** Bust of Queen Elizabeth II right **Reverse:** Gold-plated cameo portrait of Marconi **Rev. Designer:** Cosme Saffioti **Edge:** Reeded **Size:** 28.4 mm. **Note:** Only issued in two coin set with British 2 pounds KM#1014a.

Date	Mintage	MS-63	Proof
ND(2001) Proof	30,000	—	33.50

KM# 519 5 DOLLARS **Weight:** 8.3600 g. **Composition:** 0.9000 Gold 0.2419 oz. AGW **Ruler:** Elizabeth II **Obverse:** Elizabeth II **Reverse:** National arms **Edge:** Reeded **Size:** 21.6 mm.

Date	Mintage	MS-63	Proof
ND (2002) Proof	2,002	—	230

KM# 518 5 DOLLARS **Weight:** 31.3900 g. **Composition:** 0.9999 Silver 1.0091 oz. ASW **Ruler:** Elizabeth II **Subject:** World Cup Soccer , Germany 2006 **Obverse:** Elizabeth II and value **Reverse:** Goalie on knees **Edge:** Reeded **Size:** 38 mm.

Date	Mintage	MS-63	Proof
2003 Proof	50,000	—	32.50

KM# 514 5 DOLLARS **Weight:** 31.1200 g. **Composition:** 0.9999 Silver 1.0287 oz. ASW **Ruler:** Elizabeth II **Obverse:** Elizabeth II **Reverse:** Moose **Edge:** Reeded **Size:** 38 mm.

Date	Mintage	MS-63	Proof
2004 Proof	25,555	—	120

KM# 607 5 DOLLARS **Composition:** Silver **Ruler:** Elizabeth II **Reverse:** Maple leaf, winter colors

Date	Mintage	MS-63	Proof
2004	—	35.00	—

KM# 527 5 DOLLARS **Composition:** Silver **Ruler:** Elizabeth II **Subject:** Golf, Championship of Canada, Centennial

Date	Mintage	MS-63	Proof
2004 Proof	—	—	20.00

KM# 554 5 DOLLARS **Composition:** 0.9999 Silver **Ruler:** Elizabeth II **Subject:** Alberta

Date	Mintage	MS-63	Proof
2005 Proof	—	—	42.50

KM# 555 5 DOLLARS **Composition:** 0.9999 Silver **Ruler:** Elizabeth II **Subject:** Saskatchewan

Date	Mintage	MS-63	Proof
2005 Proof	—	—	42.50

KM# 556 5 DOLLARS **Composition:** Silver **Ruler:** Elizabeth II **Subject:** WWII Veterans **Reverse:** Large V and three portraits

Date	Mintage	MS-63	Proof
2005	—	35.00	—

KM# 557 5 DOLLARS **Composition:** Silver **Ruler:** Elizabeth II **Subject:** Walrus and calf

Date	Mintage	MS-63	Proof
2005 Proof	—	—	45.00

KM# 558 5 DOLLARS **Composition:** Silver **Ruler:** Elizabeth II **Subject:** White tailed deer

Date	Mintage	MS-63	Proof
2005 Proof	—	—	45.00

KM# 585 5 DOLLARS **Composition:** 0.9999 Silver **Ruler:** Elizabeth II **Subject:** Peregrine Falcon

Date	Mintage	MS-63	Proof
2006 Proof	—	—	50.00

KM# 586 5 DOLLARS **Composition:** 0.9999 Silver **Ruler:** Elizabeth II **Subject:** Sable Island horse and foal

Date	Mintage	MS-63	Proof
2006 Proof	—	—	50.00

KM# 515 8 DOLLARS **Weight:** 32.0000 g. **Composition:** 0.9999 Silver 1.0287 oz. ASW **Ruler:** Elizabeth II **Obverse:** Elizabeth II **Reverse:** Grizzly bear walking left **Edge:** Reeded **Size:** 40 mm.

Date	Mintage	MS-63	Proof
2004 Proof	25,888	—	50.00

KM# 597 8 DOLLARS **Composition:** Silver **Ruler:** Elizabeth II **Subject:** Canadian Pacific Railway, 120th Anniversary **Reverse:** Railway bridge

Date	Mintage	MS-63	Proof
2005 Proof	—	—	55.00

KM# 598 8 DOLLARS **Composition:** Silver **Ruler:** Elizabeth II **Subject:** Canadian Pacific Railway, 120th Anniversary **Reverse:** Chinese worker

Date	Mintage	MS-63	Proof
2005 Proof	—	—	55.00

KM# 520 10 DOLLARS **Weight:** 16.7200 g. **Composition:** 0.9000 Gold 0.4838 oz. AGW **Ruler:** Elizabeth II **Obverse:** Elizabeth II **Reverse:** National arms **Edge:** Reeded **Size:** 26.92 mm.

Date	Mintage	MS-63	Proof
ND (2002) Proof	2,002	—	465

KM# 559 10 DOLLARS **Composition:** 0.9999 Silver **Ruler:** Elizabeth II **Subject:** Pope John Paul II

Date	Mintage	MS-63	Proof
2005 Proof	—	—	45.00

KM# 415 15 DOLLARS **Weight:** 33.6300 g. **Composition:** 0.9250 Silver 1 oz. ASW **Subject:** Year of the Snake **Obverse:** Queen's head right **Reverse:** Snake within circle of lunar calendar signs **Rev. Designer:** Harvey Chain **Edge:** Reeded **Size:** 40 mm.

Date	Mintage	MS-63	Proof
2001 Proof	60,754	—	37.50

KM# 463 15 DOLLARS **Composition:** 0.9250 Silver **Subject:** Year of the Horse **Rev. Designer:** Harvey Chain

Date	Mintage	MS-63	Proof
2002 Proof	59,395	—	60.00

KM# 481 15 DOLLARS **Composition:** 0.9250 Silver **Subject:** Year of the Sheep **Rev. Designer:** Harvey Chain **Size:** 40 mm.

Date	Mintage	MS-63	Proof
2003 Proof	68,888	—	60.00

KM# 610 15 DOLLARS **Composition:** Silver **Ruler:** Elizabeth II **Subject:** Year of the Monkey

Date	Mintage	MS-63	Proof
2004 Proof	—	—	85.00

KM# 560 15 DOLLARS **Composition:** Silver With Partial Gold Plating **Ruler:** Elizabeth II **Subject:** Year of the Rooster

Date	Mintage	MS-63	Proof
2005 Proof	—	—	75.00

KM# 587 15 DOLLARS **Composition:** Silver With Partial Gold Plating **Ruler:** Elizabeth II **Subject:** Year of the Dog

Date	Mintage	MS-63	Proof
2006 Proof	48,888	—	80.00

KM# 411 20 DOLLARS **Weight:** 31.1035 g. **Composition:** 0.9250 Silver .9250 oz. ASW **Subject:** First Canadian Steel Boiler Steam Locomotive **Obverse:** Queen's head right **Reverse:** Locomotive and cameo hologram **Rev. Designer:** Don Curely **Edge:** Reeded and plain sections **Size:** 38 mm.

Date	Mintage	MS-63	Proof
2001 Proof	15,000	—	40.00

KM# 427 20 DOLLARS **Weight:** 31.1030 g. **Composition:** 0.9250 Silver .9250 oz. ASW **Series:** Transportation - The Marco Polo **Obverse:** Queen's head right **Reverse:** Sailship with hologram cameo **Rev. Designer:** J. Franklin Wright **Edge:** Reeded and plain sections **Size:** 38 mm.

Date	Mintage	MS-63	Proof
2001 Proof	15,000	—	40.00

KM# 428 20 DOLLARS **Weight:** 31.1030 g. **Composition:** 0.9250 Silver .9250 oz. ASW **Series:** Transportation - Russell Touring Car **Obverse:** Queen's head right **Reverse:** Russell touring car with hologram cameo **Rev. Designer:** John Mardon **Edge:** Reeded and plain sections **Size:** 38 mm.

Date	Mintage	MS-63	Proof
2001 Proof	15,000	—	40.00

KM# 464 20 DOLLARS **Composition:** 0.9250 Silver **Obverse:** Queen's head right **Reverse:** Gray-Dort Model 25-SM with cameo hologram **Rev. Designer:** John Mardon

Date	Mintage	MS-63	Proof
2002 Proof	Est. 15,000	—	45.00

KM# 465 20 DOLLARS **Composition:** 0.9250 Silver **Reverse:** Sailing ship William D. Lawrence **Rev. Designer:** Bonnie Ross

Date	Mintage	MS-63	Proof
2002 Proof	15,000	—	45.00

KM# 523 20 DOLLARS **Composition:** 0.9250 Silver **Ruler:** Elizabeth II **Subject:** Canadian Rockies, colorized

Date	Mintage	MS-63	Proof
2003 Proof	—	—	55.00

KM# 483 20 DOLLARS **Composition:** 0.9250 Silver **Subject:** The HMCS Bras d'or (FHE-400)

Date	Mintage	MS-63	Proof
2003 Proof	15,000	—	45.00

KM# 484 20 DOLLARS **Composition:** 0.9250 Silver **Subject:** Canadian National FA-1 diesel-electric locomotive

Date	Mintage	MS-63	Proof
2003 Proof	15,000	—	45.00

KM# 485 20 DOLLARS **Composition:** Silver With Partial Gold Plating **Obverse:** Queens head right **Reverse:** The Bricklin SV-1

Date	Mintage	MS-63	Proof
2003 Proof	Est. 15,000	—	50.00

KM# 482 20 DOLLARS **Composition:** 0.9999 Silver **Obverse:** Queens head right **Reverse:** Niagara Falls hologram

Date	Mintage	MS-63	Proof
2003 Proof	Est. 30,000	—	70.00

KM# 611 20 DOLLARS **Composition:** Silver **Ruler:** Elizabeth II **Reverse:** Iceburg, hologram

Date	Mintage	MS-63	Proof
2004 Proof	—	—	60.00

KM# 561 20 DOLLARS **Weight:** 31.1050 g. **Composition:** 0.9999 Silver 1. oz. ASW **Ruler:** Elizabeth II **Subject:** Three-masted sailing ship, hologram

Date	Mintage	MS-63	Proof
2005 Proof	—	—	60.00

KM# 562 20 DOLLARS **Weight:** 31.3900 g. **Composition:** 0.9990 Silver **Ruler:** Elizabeth II **Subject:** Northwest Territories Diamonds **Obverse:** Elizabeth II **Reverse:** Multicolor diamond hologram on landscape **Edge:** Reeded **Size:** 38 mm.

Date	Mintage	MS-63	Proof
2005	25,000	—	45.00

KM# 563 20 DOLLARS **Weight:** 31.1050 g. **Composition:** 0.9999 Silver 1. oz. ASW **Ruler:** Elizabeth II **Subject:** Mingan Archepelago

Date	Mintage	MS-63	Proof
2005 Proof	—	—	62.50

KM# 564 20 DOLLARS **Weight:** 31.1050 g. **Composition:** 0.9999 Silver 1. oz. ASW **Ruler:** Elizabeth II **Subject:** Rainforests of the Pacific Northwest

Date	Mintage	MS-63	Proof
2005 Proof	—	—	60.00

KM# 565 20 DOLLARS **Composition:** Silver **Ruler:** Elizabeth II **Subject:** Toronto Island National Park **Reverse:** Toronto Island Lighthouse

Date	Mintage	MS-63	Proof
2005 Proof	—	—	62.50

KM# 588 20 DOLLARS **Weight:** 31.1050 g. **Composition:** 0.9999 Silver 1. oz. ASW **Ruler:** Elizabeth II **Subject:** Georgian Bay National Park

Date	Mintage	MS-63	Proof
2006 Proof	—	—	65.00

KM# 589 20 DOLLARS **Composition:** 0.9999 Silver **Ruler:** Elizabeth II **Subject:** Notre Dame Basilica, hologram

Date	Mintage	MS-63	Proof
2006 Proof	15,000	—	65.00

KM# 590 30 DOLLARS **Composition:** Silver **Ruler:** Elizabeth II **Subject:** Pacific Northwest Wood Carvings **Reverse:** Welcome figure totem pole

Date	Mintage	MS-63	Proof
2006 Proof	—	—	67.50

KM# 543 50 DOLLARS **Composition:** Silver **Ruler:** Elizabeth II **Subject:** WWII - Battle of Britain **Reverse:** Fighter plane in sky

Date	Mintage	MS-63	Proof
2005	—	22.50	—

KM# 566 50 DOLLARS **Composition:** Gold **Ruler:** Elizabeth II **Subject:** WWII **Reverse:** Large V and three portraits

Date	Mintage	MS-63	Proof
2005 Proof	—	—	275

KM# 567 75 DOLLARS **Composition:** 0.9999 Gold **Ruler:** Elizabeth II **Subject:** Pope John Paul II

Date	Mintage	MS-63	Proof
2005 Proof	—	—	425

KM# 416 100 DOLLARS **Weight:** 13.3375 g. **Composition:** 0.5830 Gold 0.2500 oz. AGW **Subject:** Library of Parliament **Obverse:** Queen's portrait **Reverse:** Statue in domed building **Rev. Designer:** Robert R. Carmichael **Edge:** Reeded **Size:** 27 mm.

Date	Mintage	MS-63	Proof
2001 Proof	8,080	—	185

KM# 452 100 DOLLARS **Weight:** 13.3380 g. **Composition:** 0.5833 Gold 0.2501 oz. AGW **Subject:** Discovery of Oil in Alberta **Obverse:** Queen's portrait **Reverse:** Oil well with black oil spill on ground **Rev. Designer:** John Marden **Edge:** Reeded **Size:** 27 mm.

Date	Mintage	MS-63	Proof
2002 Proof	9,992	—	275

KM# 486 100 DOLLARS **Composition:** Gold **Subject:** 100th Anniversary of the Discovery of Marquis Wheat

Date	Mintage	MS-63	Proof
2003 Proof	10,000	—	225

KM# 528 100 DOLLARS **Weight:** 13.3375 g. **Composition:** 0.5830 Gold 0.25 oz. AGW **Ruler:** Elizabeth II **Subject:** St. Lawrence Seaway, 50th Anniversary

Date	Mintage	MS-63	Proof
2004 Proof	—	—	235

KM# 616 100 DOLLARS **Composition:** Gold **Ruler:** Elizabeth II **Subject:** Supreme Court **Reverse:** Draped figure with sword

Date	Mintage	MS-63	Proof
2005 Proof	—	—	275

KM# 591 100 DOLLARS **Composition:** Gold **Ruler:** Elizabeth II **Subject:** 75th Anniversary, Hockey Classic between Royal Military College and U.S. Military Academy

Date	Mintage	MS-63	Proof
2006 Proof	—	—	285

KM# 417 150 DOLLARS **Weight:** 13.6100 g. **Composition:** 0.7500 Gold .3282 oz. AGW **Subject:** Year of the Snake **Obverse:** Queen's head right **Reverse:** Multicolor snake hologram **Edge:** Reeded **Size:** 28 mm.

Date	Mintage	MS-63	Proof
2001 Proof	6,571	—	285

KM# 604 150 DOLLARS **Composition:** Gold **Ruler:** Elizabeth II **Reverse:** Year of the Horse, hologram

Date	Mintage	MS-63	Proof
2002 Proof	6,843	—	320

KM# 487 150 DOLLARS **Composition:** Gold **Subject:** Year of the Sheep **Rev. Designer:** Harvey Chan

Date	Mintage	MS-63	Proof
2003 Proof	6,888	—	325

KM# 614 150 DOLLARS **Composition:** Gold **Ruler:** Elizabeth II **Reverse:** Year of the Monkey, hologram

Date	Mintage	MS-63	Proof
2004 Proof	—	—	345

KM# 568 150 DOLLARS **Composition:** Gold **Ruler:** Elizabeth II **Subject:** Year of the Rooster

Date	Mintage	MS-63	Proof
2005 Proof	—	—	380

KM# 592 150 DOLLARS **Composition:** Gold **Ruler:** Elizabeth II **Subject:** Year of the Dog, hologram

Date	Mintage	MS-63	Proof
2006 Proof	4,888	—	385

KM# 418 200 DOLLARS **Weight:** 17.1350 g. **Composition:** 0.9170 Gold 0.5115 oz. AGW **Subject:** Cornelius D. Krieghoff's "The Habitant farm" **Obverse:** Queen's head right **Edge:** Reeded **Size:** 29 mm.

Date	Mintage	MS-63	Proof
2001 Proof	5,406	—	345

KM# 466 200 DOLLARS **Weight:** 17.1350 g. **Composition:** 0.9170 Gold .5115 oz. AGW **Subject:** Thomas Thompson "The Jack Pine" (1916-17)

Date	Mintage	MS-63	Proof
2002 Proof	5,264	—	350

KM# 488 200 DOLLARS **Weight:** 17.1350 g. **Composition:** 0.9170 Gold .5115 oz. AGW **Ruler:** Elizabeth II **Subject:** Fitzgerald's "Houses" (1929)

Date	Mintage	MS-63	Proof
2003 Proof	10,000	—	360

KM# 516 200 DOLLARS **Weight:** 16.0000 g. **Composition:** 0.9167 Gold 0.4716 oz. AGW **Ruler:** Elizabeth II **Subject:** "Fragments" **Obverse:** Elizabeth II **Edge:** Reeded **Size:** 29 mm.

Date	Mintage	MS-63	Proof
2004 Proof	—	—	360

KM# 569 200 DOLLARS **Composition:** Gold **Ruler:** Elizabeth II **Subject:** Fur traders

Date	Mintage	MS-63	Proof
2005 Proof	—	—	420

KM# 593 200 DOLLARS **Composition:** Gold **Ruler:** Elizabeth II **Subject:** 130th Anniversary, Supreme Court

Date	Mintage	MS-63	Proof
2006 Proof	—	—	420

KM# 594 200 DOLLARS **Composition:** Gold **Ruler:** Elizabeth II **Subject:** Timber trade **Reverse:** Lumberjacks felling tree

Date	Mintage	MS-63	Proof
2006 Proof	—	—	420

KM# 501 300 DOLLARS **Weight:** 60.0000 g. **Composition:** Bi-Metallic Gold And Silver **Obverse:** Triple cameo portraits of Queen Elizabeth II by Gillick, Machin and de Pedery-Hunt, each in 14K gold, rose in center **Reverse:** Dates "1952-2002" and denomination in legend, rose in center **Size:** 50 mm. **Note:** Housed in anodized gold-colored aluminum box with cherrywood stained siding

Date	Mintage	MS-63	Proof
ND(2002) Proof	993	—	1,150

KM# 517 300 DOLLARS **Weight:** 60.0000 g. **Composition:** 0.5833 Gold 1.1252 oz. AGW **Ruler:** Elizabeth II **Obverse:** Four coinage portraits of Elizabeth II **Reverse:** Canadian arms above value **Edge:** Plain **Size:** 50 mm.

Date	Mintage	MS-63	Proof
2004 Proof	1,000	—	1,200

KM# 570 300 DOLLARS **Composition:** Gold **Ruler:** Elizabeth II **Subject:** Standard Time

Date	Mintage	MS-63	Proof
2005 Proof	—	—	1,200

KM# 596 300 DOLLARS **Composition:** Gold **Ruler:** Elizabeth II **Subject:** Shinplaster **Reverse:** Britannia bust, spear over shoulder

Date	Mintage	MS-63	Proof
2005 Proof	—	—	1,100

KM# 600 300 DOLLARS **Composition:** Gold **Ruler:** Elizabeth II **Subject:** Welcome figure totem pole

Date	Mintage	MS-63	Proof
2005 Proof	—	—	1,150

KM# 595 300 DOLLARS **Composition:** Gold **Ruler:** Elizabeth II **Subject:** The Shinplaster **Reverse:** Seated Britannia with shield

Date	Mintage	MS-63	Proof
2006 Proof	—	—	1,250

KM# 433 350 DOLLARS **Weight:** 38.0500 g. **Composition:** 0.9999 Gold 1.2233 oz. AGW **Subject:** The Mayflower Flower **Obverse:** Queen's portrait **Reverse:** Two flowers **Rev. Designer:** Bonnie Ross **Edge:** Reeded **Size:** 34 mm.

Date	Mintage	MS-63	Proof
2001 Proof	—	—	900

KM# 502 350 DOLLARS **Weight:** 38.0500 g. **Composition:** 0.9999 Gold 1.2232 oz. AGW **Subject:** The Wild Rose **Obverse:** Queen's portrait **Obv. Designer:** Dora de Pedery-Hunt **Reverse:** Wild rose plant **Rev. Designer:** Dr. Andreas Kare Hellum **Size:** 34 mm.

Date	Mintage	MS-63	Proof
2002 Proof	1,803	—	925

KM# 504 350 DOLLARS **Weight:** 38.0500 g. **Composition:** 9999.0000 Gold 12232.1 oz. AGW **Subject:** The White Trillium **Obverse:** Queen's portrait **Obv. Designer:** Dora de Pedery-Hunt **Reverse:** White Trillium **Size:** 34 mm.

Date	Mintage	MS-63	Proof
2003 Proof	3,003	—	925

KM# 601 350 DOLLARS **Composition:** Gold **Ruler:** Elizabeth II **Subject:** Western Red Lilly

Date	Mintage	MS-63	Proof
2005 Proof	—	—	975

KM# 626 350 DOLLARS **Weight:** 38.0500 g. **Composition:** 0.9999 Gold 1.2232 oz. AGW **Ruler:** Elizabeth II **Subject:** Iris Vericolor **Obverse:** Queen's portrait **Reverse:** Iris **Size:** 34 mm.

Date	Mintage	MS-63	Proof
2006 Proof	—	—	1,100

SILVER BULLION COINAGE

KM# 617 DOLLAR **Weight:** 1.5550 g. **Composition:** 0.9999 Silver 0.05 oz. ASW **Ruler:** Elizabeth II **Obverse:** Elizabeth II **Reverse:** Maple leaf **Edge:** Reeded **Size:** 17 mm.

Date	Mintage	MS-63	Proof
2003	—	—	—

KM# 621 DOLLAR **Weight:** 1.5550 g. **Composition:** 0.9999 Silver 0.05 oz. ASW **Ruler:** Elizabeth II **Obverse:** Elizabeth II **Reverse:** Maple leaf and mint logo privy mark **Edge:** Reeded **Size:** 17 mm.

Date	Mintage	MS-63	Proof
2004 Proof	25,000	—	4.50

KM# 618 2 DOLLARS **Weight:** 3.1100 g. **Composition:** 0.9999 Silver 0.1 oz. ASW **Ruler:** Elizabeth II **Obverse:** Elizabeth II **Reverse:** Maple leaf **Edge:** Reeded **Size:** 21 mm.

Date	Mintage	MS-63	Proof
2003	—	—	—

KM# 622 2 DOLLARS **Weight:** 3.1100 g. **Composition:** 0.9999 Silver 0.1 oz. ASW **Ruler:** Elizabeth II **Obverse:** Elizabeth II **Reverse:** Maple leaf and mint logo privy mark **Edge:** Reeded **Size:** 21 mm.

Date	Mintage	MS-63	Proof
2004 Proof	25,000	—	7.50

KM# 571 2 DOLLARS **Weight:** 3.1050 g. **Composition:** 0.9999 Silver .1000 oz. ASW **Ruler:** Elizabeth II **Reverse:** Lynx

Date	Mintage	MS-63	Proof
2005 Proof	—	—	7.50

KM# 619 3 DOLLARS **Weight:** 7.7760 g. **Composition:** 0.9999 Silver 0.25 oz. ASW **Ruler:** Elizabeth II **Obverse:** Elizabeth II **Reverse:** Maple leaf **Edge:** Reeded **Size:** 27 mm.

Date	Mintage	MS-63	Proof
2003	—	—	—

KM# 623 3 DOLLARS **Weight:** 7.7760 g. **Composition:** 0.9999 Silver 0.25 oz. ASW **Ruler:** Elizabeth II **Obverse:** Elizabeth II **Reverse:** Maple leaf and mint logo privy mark **Edge:** Reeded **Size:** 27 mm.

Date	Mintage	MS-63	Proof
2004 Proof	25,000	—	12.50

KM# 572 3 DOLLARS **Composition:** 0.9999 Silver .2500 oz. ASW **Ruler:** Elizabeth II **Reverse:** Lynx

Date	Mintage	MS-63	Proof
2005 Proof	—	—	12.50

KM# 620 4 DOLLARS **Composition:** 0.9999 Silver 1.0000 oz. ASW **Ruler:** Elizabeth II **Obverse:** Elizabeth II **Reverse:** Maple leaf **Edge:** Reeded **Size:** 34 mm.

Date	Mintage	MS-63	Proof
2003	—	30.00	—

KM# 624 4 DOLLARS **Weight:** 15.5500 g. **Composition:** 0.9999 Silver 0.4999 oz. ASW **Ruler:** Elizabeth II **Obverse:** Elizabeth II **Reverse:** Maple leaf and mint logo privy mark **Edge:** Reeded **Size:** 34 mm.

Date	Mintage	MS-63	Proof
2004 Proof	25,000	—	25.00

KM# 573 4 DOLLARS **Composition:** 0.9999 Silver .5000 oz. ASW **Ruler:** Elizabeth II **Reverse:** Lynx

Date	Mintage	MS-63	Proof
2005 Proof	—	—	22.50

KM# 187 5 DOLLARS **Weight:** 31.1000 g. **Composition:** 0.9999 Silver 1.0000 oz. ASW **Obverse:** Elizabeth II effigy **Obv. Designer:** Dora de Pedery-Hunt **Reverse:** Maple leaf

Date	Mintage	MS-63	Proof
2001 Snake privy mark	25,000	22.00	—
2001	398,563	15.00	—
2002	576,196	15.00	—
2002 Horse privy mark	25,000	22.00	—
2003	—	15.00	—
2003 Sheep privy mark	25,000	18.00	—

KM# 436 5 DOLLARS **Weight:** 31.1035 g. **Composition:** 0.9999 Silver 0.9999 oz. ASW **Obverse:** Queen's portrait **Reverse:** Three maple leaves in autumn colors **Rev. Designer:** Debbie Adams **Edge:** Reeded **Size:** 38 mm.

Date	Mintage	MS-63	Proof
2001	49,900	32.50	—

KM# 437 5 DOLLARS **Weight:** 31.1035 g. **Composition:** 0.9999 Silver 0.9999 oz. ASW **Subject:** Multicolor Holographic Maple Leaf **Obverse:** Queen's portrait **Reverse:** Radiant maple leaf hologram with date privy mark **Edge:** Reeded **Size:** 38 mm.

Date	Mintage	MS-63	Proof
2001	29,906	75.00	—

KM# 505 5 DOLLARS **Weight:** 31.2800 g. **Composition:** 0.9999 Silver 1.0056 oz. ASW **Obverse:** Queen Elizabeth II **Reverse:** Two maple leaves in spring color (green) **Edge:** Reeded **Size:** 38 mm.

Date	Mintage	MS-63	Proof
2002 Proof	—	—	35.00

KM# 603 5 DOLLARS **Composition:** 0.9999 Silver **Ruler:** Elizabeth II **Subject:** Loon, hologram

Date	Mintage	MS-63	Proof
2002 Satin Proof	30,000	—	45.00

KM# 521 5 DOLLARS **Composition:** 0.9999 Silver **Ruler:** Elizabeth II **Reverse:** Maple leaf, summer colors

Date	Mintage	MS-63	Proof
2003	—	35.00	—

KM# 522 5 DOLLARS **Weight:** 31.1050 g. **Composition:** 0.9999 Silver 0.9999 oz. ASW **Ruler:** Elizabeth II **Subject:** Colorized maple leaf

Date	Mintage	MS-63	Proof
2003	—	32.50	—

KM# 625 5 DOLLARS **Weight:** 31.1035 g. **Composition:** 0.9999 Silver 0.9999 oz. ASW **Ruler:** Elizabeth II **Obverse:** Elizabeth II **Reverse:** Maple leaf and mint logo privy mark **Edge:** Reeded **Size:** 38 mm.

Date	Mintage	MS-63	Proof
2004 Proof	25,000	—	35.00

KM# 508 5 DOLLARS **Weight:** 31.1200 g. **Composition:** 0.9999 Silver 1.0004 oz. ASW **Obverse:** Queen Elizabeth II **Reverse:** Maple leaf **Edge:** Reeded **Size:** 38 mm.

Date	Mintage	MS-63	Proof
2004	—	35.00	—

KM# 550 5 DOLLARS **Weight:** 31.1050 g. **Composition:** 0.9999 Silver 1. oz. ASW **Ruler:** Elizabeth II **Subject:** Big Leaf Maple, colorized

Date	Mintage	MS-63	Proof
2005	25,000	35.00	—

KM# 574 5 DOLLARS **Composition:** 0.9999 Silver 1.0000 oz. ASW **Ruler:** Elizabeth II **Reverse:** Lynx

Date	Mintage	MS-63	Proof
2005 Proof	—	—	35.00

GOLD BULLION COINAGE

KM# 526 50 CENTS **Weight:** 1.2700 g. **Composition:** 0.9999 Gold .0425 oz. AGW **Ruler:** Elizabeth II **Subject:** Moose **Reverse:** Moose head facing right **Size:** 14 mm.

Date	Mintage	MS-63	Proof
2004 Proof	—	—	85.00

KM# 542 50 CENTS **Composition:** 0.9999 Gold .0425 oz. AGW **Ruler:** Elizabeth II **Subject:** Voyageurs

Date	Mintage	MS-63	Proof
2005 Proof	—	—	65.00

KM# 438 DOLLAR **Weight:** 1.5810 g. **Composition:** 0.9990 Gold 0.0508 oz. AGW **Subject:** Holographic Maple Leaves **Obverse:** Queen's portrait **Reverse:** Three maple leaves multicolor hologram **Edge:** Reeded. **Size:** 14.1 mm.

Date	Mintage	MS-63	Proof
2001 in sets only	600	75.00	—

KM# 439 5 DOLLARS **Weight:** 3.1310 g. **Composition:** 0.9999 Gold 0.1007 oz. AGW **Subject:** Holographic Maple Leaves **Obverse:** Queen's portrait **Reverse:** Three maple leaves multicolor hologram **Edge:** Reeded **Size:** 16 mm.

Date	Mintage	MS-63	Proof
2001 in sets only	600	150	—

KM# 440 10 DOLLARS **Weight:** 7.7970 g. **Composition:** 0.9999 Gold 0.2507 oz. AGW **Subject:** Holographic Maples Leaves **Obverse:** Queen's portrait **Reverse:** Three maple leaves multicolor hologram **Edge:** Reeded **Size:** 20 mm.

Date	Mintage	MS-63	Proof
2001	15,000	180	—

KM# 441 20 DOLLARS **Weight:** 15.5840 g. **Composition:** 0.9999 Gold 0.501 oz. AGW **Subject:** Holographic Maples Leaves **Obverse:** Queen's portrait **Reverse:** Three maple leaves multicolor hologram **Edge:** Reeded **Size:** 25 mm.

Date	Mintage	MS-63	Proof
2001 in sets only	600	675	—

KM# 442 50 DOLLARS **Weight:** 31.1500 g. **Composition:** 0.9999 Gold 1.0014 oz. AGW **Subject:** Holographic Maples Leaves **Obverse:** Queen's portrait **Reverse:** Three maple leaves multicolor hologram **Edge:** Reeded **Size:** 30 mm.

Date	Mintage	MS-63	Proof
2001 in sets only	600	1,350	—

PLATINUM BULLION COINAGE

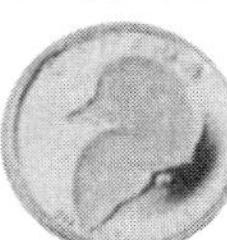

KM# 429 30 DOLLARS **Weight:** 3.1100 g. **Composition:** 0.9995 Platinum .1000 oz. APW **Reverse:** Harlequin duck's head **Rev. Designer:** Cosme Saffioti and Susan Taylor **Edge:** Reeded **Size:** 16 mm.

Date	Mintage	MS-63	Proof
2001 Proof	448	—	150

KM# 430 75 DOLLARS **Weight:** 7.7760 g. **Composition:** 0.9995 Platinum .2500 oz. APW **Reverse:** Harlequin duck in flight **Rev. Designer:** Cosme Saffioti and Susan Taylor **Edge:** Reeded **Size:** 20 mm.

Date	Mintage	MS-63	Proof
2001 Proof	448	—	375

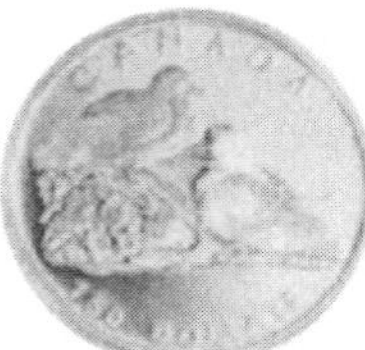

KM# 431 150 DOLLARS **Weight:** 15.5500 g. **Composition:** 0.9995 Platinum .5000 oz. APW **Reverse:** Two harlequin ducks **Rev. Designer:** Cosme Saffioti and Susan Taylor **Edge:** Reeded **Size:** 25 mm.

Date	Mintage	MS-63	Proof
2001 Proof	448	—	700

KM# 432 300 DOLLARS **Weight:** 31.1035 g. **Composition:** 0.9995 Platinum 1.0000 oz. APW **Obverse:** Queen's head right **Reverse:** Two standing harlequin ducks **Rev. Designer:** Cosme Saffioti and Susan Taylor **Edge:** Reeded **Size:** 30 mm.

Date	Mintage	MS-63	Proof
2001 Proof	448	—	1,300

MINT SETS

KM	Date	Mintage	Identification	Issue Price	Mkt Val
MS8	2001	600	KM438-442	1,996	2,450
MS9	2002	135,000	Double-dated 1952-2002, KM#444-449, 467	11.75	11.00
MS10	2002	—	KM#444-449, 467	17.00	16.00
MS11	2002	—	KM#444-449, 467	17.00	16.00
MS12	2003	135,000	KM#289, 182b, 183b, 184b, 290, 186, 270	12.00	12.00
MS13	2003	75,000	KM#490-496	13.25	14.00
MS14	2003	—	KM#289, 182-184, 290, 186, 270	17.75	16.00
MS15	2003	—	KM#289, 182-184, 290, 186, 270	17.75	16.00

PROOF SETS

KM	Date	Mintage	Identification	Issue Price	Mkt Val
PS51	2001	—	KM429, 430, 431, 432	—	2,300
PS52	2002	100,000	KM#443, 444a,445,446a-449a, 467	60.00	70.00
PS53	2002	—	KM#459-461	57.50	55.00
PS54	2002	—	KM#519, 520	750	725
PS55	2003	100,000	KM#182a,183a,184a, 186, 270d, 289, 290a, 450	62.50	80.00
PS56	2003	30,000	KM#468-473	75.00	80.00
PS57	2004	—	KM#490, 491a-494a, 495, 496a, 512	—	90.00
PS58	2004	25,000	KM#621-625	—	145

SPECIMEN SETS (SS)

KM	Date	Mintage	Identification	Issue Price	Mkt Val
SS90	2002	75,000	KM#444-449,462	30.00	22.50
SS91	2003	75,000	KM#182-184, 186, 270, 289, 290	30.00	27.50

CAPE VERDE

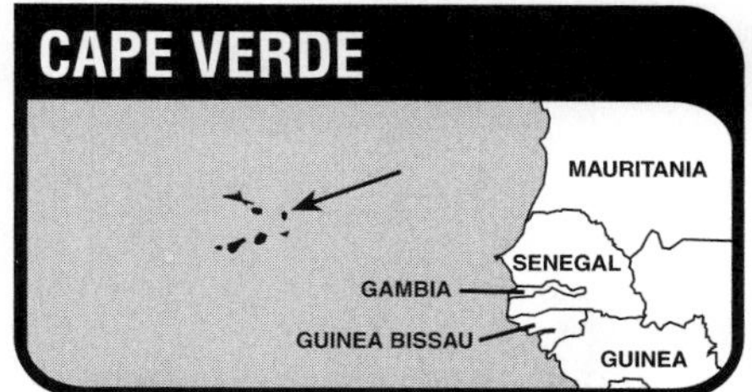

The Republic of Cape Verde, Africa's smallest republic, is located in the Atlantic Ocean, about 370 miles (595 km.) west of Dakar, Senegal, off the coast of Africa. The 14-island republic has an area of 1,557 sq. mi. (4,033 sq. km.) and a population of 435,983. Capital: Praia. The refueling of ships and aircraft is the chief economic function of the country. Fishing is important and agriculture is widely practiced, but the Cape Verdes are not self-sufficient in food. Fish products, salt, bananas, and shellfish are exported.

The date of discovery of the islands is uncertain. Possibly they were visited by Venetian captain Alvise Cadamosto in 1456. Portuguese navigator Diogo Gomes claimed them for Portugal in May of 1460. Settlement began two years later. The early importance and wealth of the islands, which caused them to be attacked by Sir Francis Drake and the Dutch, resulted from the monopoly of the Guinea slave trade granted the inhabitants in 1466. Poverty and famine occasioned by frequent periods of severe drought have marked the history of the country since abolition of the slave trade in 1876.

After 500 years of Portuguese rule, the Cape Verdes became independent on July 5, 1975. At the first general election, all seats of the new national assembly were won by the Party for the Independence of Guinea-Bissau and Cape Verde (PAIGC). The PAIGC linked the two former colonies into one state. Antonio Mascarenhas Monteiro won the first free presidential election in 1991.

RULERS
Portuguese, until 1975

MONETARY SYSTEM
100 Centavos = 1 Escudo

REPUBLIC

DECIMAL COINAGE

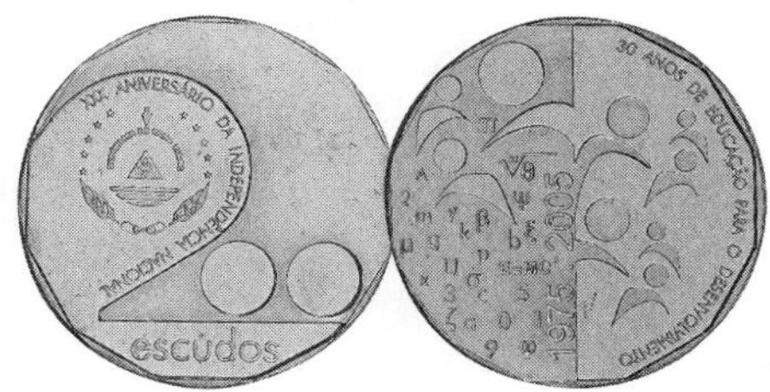

KM# 45 200 ESCUDOS
7.8000 g., Copper-Nickel, 29.5 mm. **Subject:** 30th Anniversary of Independence **Obv:** National arms in number 2 of 200 **Rev:** Symbolic education design **Edge:** Reeded **Shape:** Round

Date	Mintage	F	VF	XF	Unc	BU
2005	—	—	—	—	8.50	10.00

CAYMAN ISLANDS

MEXICO BAHAMAS CUBA HAITI DOM. REP. JAMAICA

The Cayman Islands is a dependent territory of the United Kingdom with the British monarch as head of state. It is situated about 180 miles (290 km.) northwest of Jamaica, consists of three islands: Grand Cayman, Little Cayman, and Cayman Brac. The islands have an area of 102 sq. mi. (259 sq. km.) and a population of 33,200. Capital: George Town. Seafaring, commerce, banking, and tourism are the principal industries. Rope, turtle shells, and sharkskins are exported.

RULERS
British

MONETARY SYSTEM
100 Cents = 1 Dollar

BRITISH COLONY

DECIMAL COINAGE

KM# 131 CENT
2.5300 g., Bronze Plated Steel, 17 mm. **Obv:** Queen's head right **Rev:** Great Caiman thrush **Rev. Designer:** Stuart Devlin

Date	Mintage	F	VF	XF	Unc	BU
2002	—	—	—	—	0.50	1.00

KM# 135 2 DOLLARS
28.2800 g., 0.9250 Sterling Silver 0.841 oz. ASW, 38.6 mm. **Subject:** 500th Anniversary - Christopher Columbus First Recorded Sighting of the Cayman Islands **Obv:** Head of Queen Elizabeth II right **Rev:** Quincentennial Celebrations Logo in color

Date	Mintage	F	VF	XF	Unc	BU
2003 Proof	1,500	Value: 75.00				

CENTRAL AFRICAN REPUBLIC

CHAD SUDAN NIGERIA CAMEROON CONGO DEMOCRATIC REPUBLIC GABON

The Central African Republic, a landlocked country in Central Africa, bounded by Chad on the north, Cameroon on the west, Congo (Brazzaville) and Congo Democratic Republic, (formerly Zaire) on the south and the Sudan on the east, has an area of 240,324 sq. mi. (622,984 sq. km.) and a population of 3.2 million. Capital: Bangui. Deposits of uranium, iron ore, manganese and copper remain to be developed. Diamonds, cotton, timber and coffee are exported.

NOTE: For earlier coinage see French Equatorial Africa and Equatorial African States including later coinage as listed in Central African States.

MINT MARKS
(a) - Paris, privy marks only

MONETARY SYSTEM
100 Centimes = 1 Franc

SECOND REPUBLIC

INSTITUT MONETAIRE

KM# 12 1500 CFA FRANCS - 1 AFRICA
7.3200 g., Nickel Plated Iron, 25.9 mm. **Obv:** Crossed lances **Rev:** Elephant head on full Africa map **Edge:** Plain

Date	Mintage	F	VF	XF	Unc	BU
2005	2,005	—	—	—	20.00	—

KM# 12a 1500 CFA FRANCS - 1 AFRICA
0.9990 Silver, 26 mm. **Obv:** Crossed lances **Rev:** Elephant head on full Africa map

Date	Mintage	F	VF	XF	Unc	BU
2005	25	—	—	—	360	—

CENTRAL AFRICAN STATES

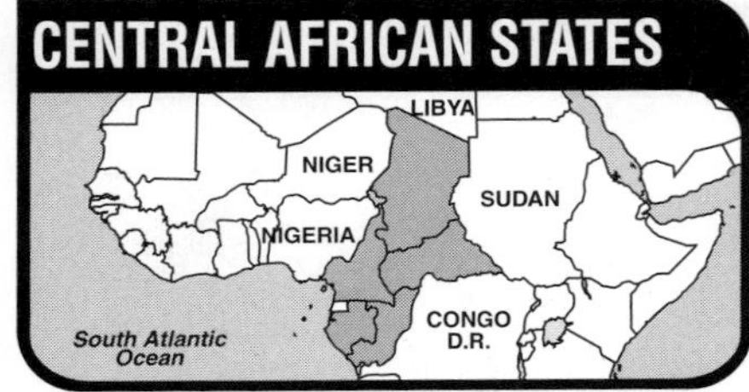

The Central African States, a monetary union comprised of Equatorial Guinea (a former Spanish possession), the former French possessions and now independent states of the Republic of Congo (Brazzaville), Gabon, Central African Republic, Chad and Cameroon, issues a common currency for the member states from a common central bank. The monetary unit, the African Financial Community franc, is tied to and supported by the French franc.

In 1960, an attempt was made to form a union of the newly independent republics of Chad, Congo, Central Africa and Gabon. The proposal was discarded when Chad refused to become a constituent member. The four countries then linked into an Equatorial Customs Unit, to which Cameroon became an associate member in 1961. A more extensive cooperation of the five republics, identified as the Central African Customs and Economic Union, was entered into force at the beginning of 1966.

In 1974 the Central Bank of the Equatorial African States, which had issued coins and paper currency in its own name and with the names of the constituent member nations, changed its name to the Bank of the Central African States. Equatorial Guinea converted to the CFA currency system issuing its first 100 Franc in 1985.

For earlier coinage see French Equatorial Africa.

MONETARY UNION

STANDARD COINAGE

KM# 9 10 FRANCS

Aluminum-Bronze **Obv:** Three giant eland **Obv. Designer:** G. B. L. Bazor **Rev:** Denomination

Date	Mintage	F	VF	XF	Unc	BU
2003 (a)	—	0.20	0.35	0.75	1.50	—

KM# 11 50 FRANCS

Nickel **Obv:** Three giant eland **Rev:** Denomination **Obv. Designer:** G.B.L. Bazor **Note:** Starting in 1996 an extra flora item was added where the mint mark was formerly located

Date	Mintage	F	VF	XF	Unc	BU
2003 (a)	—	0.75	1.50	3.50	6.00	—

KM# 15 100 FRANCS

6.0000 g., Bi-Metallic Stainless Steel center in Brass ring, 23.9 mm. **Obv:** Bank name **Rev:** Value above produce **Edge:** Reeded

Date	Mintage	F	VF	XF	Unc	BU
2006 (a)	—	—	—	—	5.00	6.50

CHAD

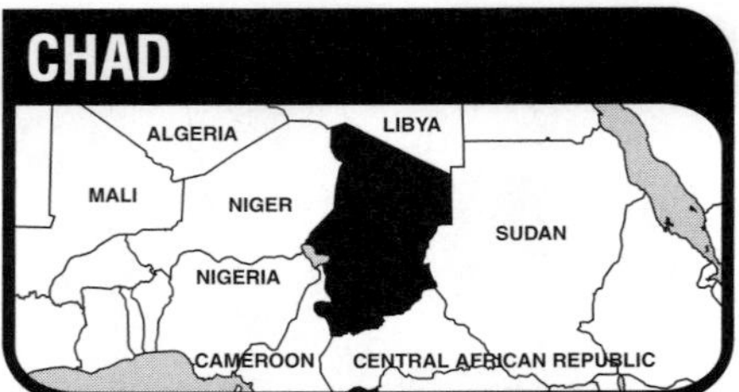

The Republic of Chad, a landlocked country of central Africa, is the largest country of former French Equatorial Africa. It has an area of 495,755 sq. mi. (1,284,000 sq. km.) and a population of *7.27 million. Capital: N'Djamena. An expanding livestock industry produces camels, cattle and sheep. Cotton (the chief product), ivory and palm oil are important exports.

NOTE: For earlier and related coinage see French Equatorial Africa and the Equatorial African States. For later coinage see Central African States.

MINT MARKS

(a) - Paris, privy marks only

(b) = Brussels

NI - Numismatic Italiana, Arezzo, Italy

REPUBLIC

DECIMAL COINAGE

KM# 20 1000 FRANCS

15.0000 g., 0.9990 Silver 0.4818 oz. ASW, 35 mm. **Obv:** Native portrait **Rev:** Ancient Arabic war ship **Edge:** Plain

Date	Mintage	F	VF	XF	Unc	BU
2001 Proof	—	Value: 35.00				

KM# 21 1000 FRANCS

25.1000 g., 0.9990 Silver 0.8062 oz. ASW, 40 mm. **Obv:** Native portrait **Rev:** Soccer player and stadium **Edge:** Reeded

Date	Mintage	F	VF	XF	Unc	BU
2001 Proof	—	Value: 40.00				

KM# 22 1000 FRANCS

20.0000 g., 0.9990 Silver 0.6424 oz. ASW, 40 mm. **Obv:** Native portrait **Rev:** Horizontal soccer player above stadium **Edge:** Reeded

Date	Mintage	F	VF	XF	Unc	BU
2002 Proof	—	Value: 40.00				

KM# 23 1000 FRANCS

20.1500 g., 0.9990 Silver 0.6472 oz. ASW, 40 mm. **Obv:** Native portrait **Rev:** Soccer player and Arch of Triumph **Edge:** Reeded

Date	Mintage	F	VF	XF	Unc	BU
2002 Proof	—	Value: 40.00				

INSTITUT MONETAIRE

KM# 19 1500 CFA FRANCS - 1 AFRICA

7.2200 g., Nickel Plated Iron, 26 mm. **Obv:** "Manilla" bracelet **Rev:** Elephant head on full Africa map **Edge:** Plain

Date	Mintage	F	VF	XF	Unc	BU
2005	2,005	—	—	—	20.00	—

KM# 19a 1500 CFA FRANCS - 1 AFRICA

0.9990 Silver, 22 mm. **Obv:** "Manilla" bracelet **Rev:** Elephant head on full Africa map

Date	Mintage	F	VF	XF	Unc	BU
2005	25	—	—	—	365	—

KM# 18 4500 CFA FRANCS - 3 AFRICA

7.5100 g., Bi-Metallic Copper-Nickel center in Brass ring, 26.1 mm. **Obv:** Lamb above oil can **Rev:** Elephant head on full African map **Edge:** Segmented reeding

Date	Mintage	F	VF	XF	Unc	BU
2005	2,005	—	—	—	55.00	—

KM# 18a 4500 CFA FRANCS - 3 AFRICA

0.9990 Bi-Metallic .999 Silver center in .999 Gold plated .999 Silver ring, 26 mm. **Obv:** Lamb above oil can **Rev:** Elephant head on full African map

Date	Mintage	F	VF	XF	Unc	BU
2005	25	—	—	—	550	—

KM# 18b 4500 CFA FRANCS - 3 AFRICA

0.9990 Silver, 26 mm. **Obv:** Lamb above oil can **Rev:** Elephant head on full African map

Date	Mintage	F	VF	XF	Unc	BU
2005	25	—	—	—	550	—

The Republic of Chile, a ribbon-like country on the Pacific coast of southern South America, has an area of 292,135 sq. mi. (756,950 sq. km.) and a population of *15.21 million. Capital: Santiago. Historically, the economic base of Chile has been the rich mineral deposits of its northern provinces. Copper has accounted for more than 75 percent of Chile's export earnings in recent years. Other important mineral exports are iron ore, iodine and nitrate of soda. Fresh fruits and vegetables, as well as wine are increasingly significant in inter-hemispheric trade.

MINT MARKS

So - Santiago

REPUBLIC

REFORM COINAGE

100 Centavos = 1 Peso; 1000 Old Escudos = 1 Peso

KM# 231 PESO

Aluminum **Shape:** 8-sided **Note:** Varieties exist.

Date	Mintage	F	VF	XF	Unc	BU
2001	—	—	—	—	0.10	0.20
2002	—	—	—	—	0.10	0.20
2003	—	—	—	—	0.10	0.20
2004	—	—	—	—	0.10	0.20
2005	—	—	—	—	0.10	0.20

KM# 232 5 PESOS

Aluminum-Bronze **Shape:** 8-sided **Note:** Varieties exist.

Date	Mintage	F	VF	XF	Unc	BU
2001 Narrow date	—	—	—	0.10	0.35	0.60
2001 (sa) Wide date	—	—	—	0.15	0.50	0.75
Note: Without name of sculptor						
2002 Narrow date	—	—	—	0.10	0.35	0.60
2002A Narrow date	—	—	—	0.15	0.50	0.75
2003	—	—	—	0.10	0.35	0.60
2004	—	—	—	0.10	0.35	0.60
2005	—	—	—	0.10	0.35	0.60

KM# 228.2 10 PESOS

Nickel-Brass **Obv:** Large bust of Bernardo O'Higgins right, normal rim **Note:** All 9's are curl tail 9's except for the 1999 date, these are straight tail 9's.

Date	Mintage	F	VF	XF	Unc	BU
2002	—	—	0.10	0.20	0.50	0.65
2003	—	—	0.10	0.20	0.50	0.65
2004	—	—	0.10	0.20	0.50	0.65
2005	—	—	0.10	0.20	0.50	0.65

KM# 219.2 50 PESOS

Aluminum-Bronze **Shape:** 10-sided **Note:** Narrow date.

Date	Mintage	F	VF	XF	Unc	BU
2001	—	—	0.25	0.50	1.25	1.50
2002	—	—	0.25	0.50	1.25	1.50
2005	—	—	0.25	0.50	1.00	1.25

KM# 236 100 PESOS

Bi-Metallic Copper-nickel center in Brass ring, 23.5 mm. **Subject:** Native people **Obv:** Bust of native Mapuche girl facing **Rev:** National arms above denomination **Edge:** Reeded and striated sections

Date	Mintage	F	VF	XF	Unc	BU
2001	—	—	—	—	2.50	3.00
2003	—	—	—	—	2.50	3.00
2004	—	—	—	—	2.50	3.00
2005	—	—	—	—	2.50	3.00

KM# 235 500 PESOS

6.5000 g., Bi-Metallic Aluminum-bronze center in Copper-nickel ring, 25.9 mm. **Subject:** Cardinal Raul Silva Henriquez **Obv:** Bust of Henriquez in inner ring facing left **Rev:** Denomination with date below **Edge:** Reeded

Date	Mintage	F	VF	XF	Unc	BU
2001	—	—	—	—	6.00	6.50
2002 4.1mm date	—	—	—	—	6.00	6.50
2002 5.2mm date	—	—	—	—	6.00	6.50
2003	—	—	—	—	6.00	6.50

The Peoples Republic of China, located in eastern Asia, has an area of 3,696,100 sq. mi. (9,596,960 sq. km.) (including Manchuria and Tibet) and a population of *1.20 billion. Capital: Peking (Beijing). The economy is based on agriculture, mining, and manufacturing. Textiles, clothing, metal ores, tea and rice are exported.

MONETARY SYSTEM

After 1949

10 Fen (Cents) = 1 Jiao

10 Jiao = 1 Renminbi Yuan

MINT MARKS

(b) - Beijing (Peking)

(s) - Shanghai

(y) - Shenyang (Mukden)

PEOPLES REPUBLIC

STANDARD COINAGE

Y# 1068 JIAO

Aluminum, 18.9 mm. **Obv:** Denomination **Rev:** Orchid **Edge:** Plain

Date	Mintage	F	VF	XF	Unc	BU
2001	—	—	—	—	0.50	—
2002	—	—	—	—	0.50	—
2003	—	—	—	—	0.50	—

Y# 329 5 JIAO

3.8300 g., Brass, 20.5 mm. **Edge:** Segmented reeding

Date	Mintage	F	VF	XF	Unc	BU
2001	—	—	—	—	1.00	—

Y# 1106 5 JIAO

3.8000 g., Brass, 20.5 mm. **Obv:** Denomination **Rev:** Flower **Edge:** Reeded and plain sections

Date	Mintage	F	VF	XF	Unc	BU
2002	—	—	—	—	1.50	—
2003	—	—	—	—	1.50	—

Y# 1069 YUAN

Nickel Plated Steel, 24.9 mm. **Obv:** Denomination **Rev:** Chrysanthemum **Edge:** "RMB" three times

Date	Mintage	F	VF	XF	Unc	BU
2001	—	—	—	—	2.00	—
2002	—	—	—	—	2.00	—
2003	—	—	—	—	2.00	—
2004	—	—	—	—	2.00	—

Y# 1125 YUAN

6.8500 g., Brass, 25 mm. **Obv:** Value **Rev:** Celebrating child and ram **Edge:** Lettered **Edge Lettering:** "R M B" three times

Date	Mintage	F	VF	XF	Unc	BU
2003	—	—	—	—	5.00	—

Y# 1208 YUAN

5.9600 g., Nickel Clad Steel, 25 mm. **Obv:** Building **Rev:** Bust of Chenyun **Edge:** Lettered

Date	Mintage	F	VF	XF	Unc	BU
2005	—	—	—	—	3.50	—

Y# 1109 5 YUAN

12.3000 g., Brass, 30 mm. **Subject:** Revolution: 90th Anniversary **Obv:** State emblem **Rev:** Battle scene **Edge:** Reeded

Date	Mintage	F	VF	XF	Unc	BU
2001	—	—	—	—	7.50	—

Y# 1126 5 YUAN

12.8000 g., Brass, 30 mm. **Subject:** 50th Anniversary - Chinese Occupation of Tibet **Obv:** National emblem **Rev:** Potala Palace, value and two dancers **Edge:** Reeded

Date	Mintage	F	VF	XF	Unc	BU
2001(y)	10,000,000	—	—	—	7.00	—

Y# 1107 5 YUAN

12.9000 g., Brass, 29.9 mm. **Subject:** The Great Wall **Obv:** State arms. Microscopic inscription repeated four times on the inner raised rim **Obv. Inscription:** SHI JIE WEN HUA YI CHAN **Rev:** Two views of the Great Wall **Edge:** Reeded

Date	Mintage	F	VF	XF	Unc	BU
2002	—	—	—	—	7.00	—

Y# 1108 5 YUAN

12.8200 g., Brass, 29.9 mm. **Subject:** Terra Cotta Army **Obv:** State arms and the microscopic inscription repeated four times on the raised inner rim. **Obv. Inscription:** SHI JIE WEN HUA YI CHAN **Rev:** Terra Cotta Soldier close-up with many more in background **Edge:** Reeded

Date	Mintage	F	VF	XF	Unc	BU
2002	—	—	—	—	7.00	—

Y# 1230 5 YUAN

12.8000 g., Brass, 30 mm. **Subject:** Chaotian Temple in Beijing **Obv:** State emblem **Rev:** Buildings **Edge:** Reeded

Date	Mintage	F	VF	XF	Unc	BU
2003	10,000,000	—	—	—	7.00	—

Y# 1127 5 YUAN

12.8000 g., Brass, 30 mm. **Obv:** National emblem **Rev:** Chaotian Temple in Beigang Taiwan **Edge:** Reeded

Date	Mintage	F	VF	XF	Unc	BU
2003	10,000,000	—	—	—	7.00	—

Y# 1128 5 YUAN

12.8000 g., Brass, 30 mm. **Obv:** National emblem **Rev:** Chikan Tower on Treasure Island Taiwan **Edge:** Reeded

Date	Mintage	F	VF	XF	Unc	BU
2003(y)	10,000,000	—	—	—	7.00	—

Y# 1201 5 YUAN

12.7000 g., Brass, 30 mm. **Obv:** State arms **Rev:** Peking Man bust and discovery site view **Edge:** Reeded

Date	Mintage	F	VF	XF	Unc	BU
2004	6,000,000	—	—	—	6.00	—

Y# 1202 5 YUAN

12.7000 g., Brass, 30 mm. **Obv:** State arms **Rev:** Pavilion and bridge **Edge:** Reeded

Date	Mintage	F	VF	XF	Unc	BU
2004	6,000,000	—	—	—	6.00	—

Y# 1209 5 YUAN

12.9200 g., Brass, 30 mm. **Obv:** National arms **Rev:** Lijiang building **Edge:** Reeded

Date	Mintage	F	VF	XF	Unc	BU
2005	—	—	—	—	6.00	—

Y# 1210 5 YUAN

12.9200 g., Brass, 30 mm. **Obv:** National arms **Rev:** Green City Hall **Edge:** Reeded

Date	Mintage	F	VF	XF	Unc	BU
2005	—	—	—	—	6.00	—

Y# 1231 5 YUAN

12.8000 g., Brass, 30 mm. **Subject:** "Taiwan" **Obv:** State emblem **Rev:** Tower and terrace **Edge:** Reeded

Date	Mintage	F	VF	XF	Unc	BU
2005	—	—	—	—	6.00	—

Y# 1103 10 YUAN

31.1035 g., 0.9990 Silver 0.999 oz. ASW, 40 mm. **Subject:** 2008 Olympics to be in Beijing **Obv:** Gold-plated "v" design **Rev:** Radiant Temple of Heaven **Edge:** Reeded

Date	Mintage	F	VF	XF	Unc	BU
2001 Proof	60,000	Value: 50.00				

Y# 1233 10 YUAN

31.1035 g., 0.9990 Silver, 40 mm. **Subject:** Shanghai World Expo of 2010 **Obv:** Flower design with inset pearl **Rev:** 2010 Logo incorporating a tower **Edge:** Reeded

Date	Mintage	F	VF	XF	Unc	BU
2002 Proof	50,000	Value: 50.00				

Y# 1132 10 YUAN

31.1035 g., 0.9990 Silver 0.999 oz. ASW, 40 mm. **Obv:** Stylized forest **Rev:** Cyclists in forest **Edge:** Reeded

Date	Mintage	F	VF	XF	Unc	BU
2003 Proof	30,000	Value: 50.00				

Y# 1133 10 YUAN

31.1035 g., 0.9990 Silver 0.999 oz. ASW, 40 mm. **Obv:** Stylized forest **Rev:** Birds flying over forest **Edge:** Reeded

Date	Mintage	F	VF	XF	Unc	BU
2003(y) Proof	30,000	Value: 50.00				

Y# 1134 10 YUAN

31.1035 g., 0.9990 Silver 0.999 oz. ASW, 40 mm. **Obv:** Solar system design **Rev:** Multicolor Chinese Astronaut **Edge:** Reeded

Date	Mintage	F	VF	XF	Unc	BU
2003(y) Proof	60,000	Value: 60.00				

Y# 1214 10 YUAN

31.1035 g., 0.9990 Silver, 40 mm. **Obv:** Monkey King leading the Master over bridge **Rev:** Multicolor Monkey King fighting the "Ox Fiend" **Edge:** Reeded

Date	Mintage	F	VF	XF	Unc	BU
2004 Proof	38,000	Value: 55.00				

Y# 1215 10 YUAN

31.1035 g., 0.9990 Silver 0.999 oz. ASW, 40 mm. **Obv:** Monkey King leading the Master over bridge **Rev:** Multicolor Pig carrying Monkey King piggy-back style **Edge:** Reeded

Date	Mintage	F	VF	XF	Unc	BU
2004 Proof	38,000	Value: 55.00				

Y# 1219 10 YUAN

31.1035 g., Silver **Obv:** Qing Yuan Gate of the China Great Wall **Rev:** 2 dogs at play **Shape:** 30° Fan

Date	Mintage	F	VF	XF	Unc	BU
2006 Proof	66,000	Value: 65.00				

Y# 1221 10 YUAN

31.1035 g., Silver, 40 mm. **Obv:** Belt-hook in dog shape from Chinese ancient bronze ware and a decorative design of dog tail-shaped plant leaves **Rev:** 2 dogs at play

Date	Mintage	F	VF	XF	Unc	BU
2006 Proof	100,000	Value: 50.00				

Y# 1223 10 YUAN

31.1035 g., Silver, 40 mm. **Obv:** Dog-shaped belt-hook depicted from ancient Chinese bronze ware and a decorative design of dog tail-shaped plant leaves **Rev:** 2 smart dogs **Shape:** Scalloped

Date	Mintage	F	VF	XF	Unc	BU
2006 Proof	60,000	Value: 55.00				

Y# 1082 20 YUAN

62.2070 g., 0.9990 Silver 1.998 oz. ASW, 40 mm. **Subject:** Mogao Grottos **Obv:** 8-story building **Rev:** Buddha-like statue **Edge:** Reeded

Date	Mintage	F	VF	XF	Unc	BU
2001 Proof	30,000	Value: 100				

Y# 1083 50 YUAN

155.5175 g., 0.9990 Silver 4.995 oz. ASW, 70 mm. **Subject:** Mogao Grottoes **Obv:** Eight story building. **Rev:** Four musicians. **Edge:** Reeded.

Date	Mintage	F	VF	XF	Unc	BU
2001 Proof	8,000	Value: 200				

Y# 1084 50 YUAN

3.1104 g., 0.9990 Gold 0.0999 oz. AGW **Subject:** Mogao Grottoes **Obv:** Eight story building. **Rev:** Buddha-like statue. **Edge:** Reeded.

Date	Mintage	F	VF	XF	Unc	BU
2001 Proof	50,000	Value: 85.00				

Y# 1104 50 YUAN

155.5175 g., 0.9990 Silver 4.995 oz. ASW **Subject:** Han Xizai's Dinner Party **Obv:** Tang dynasty buildings **Rev:** Multicolor "Five Dynasties" painting **Edge:** Plain **Shape:** Rectangular **Note:** Illustration reduced. Actual size: 90x40mm.

Date	Mintage	F	VF	XF	Unc	BU
2001 Proof	18,800	Value: 175				

Y# 1139 50 YUAN

15.5500 g., 0.9990 Gold 0.4994 oz. AGW **Subject:** Bird **Note:** Multicolored

Date	Mintage	F	VF	XF	Unc	BU
2001	8,800	—	—	—	—	875

Y# 1140 50 YUAN

15.5500 g., 0.9990 Gold 0.4994 oz. AGW **Subject:** Caveman art **Note:** Multicolored

Date	Mintage	F	VF	XF	Unc	BU
2001	8,800	—	—	—	—	660

Y# 1234 50 YUAN

3.1104 g., 0.9990 Gold 0.0999 oz. AGW, 18 mm. **Obv:** Putuo Mountain Pilgrimage Gate **Rev:** Seated Kuanyin with holographic background **Edge:** Reeded

Date	Mintage	F	VF	XF	Unc	BU
2003 Proof	33,000	Value: 85.00				

Y# 1237 50 YUAN

3.1100 g., 0.9990 Gold .0999 oz. AGW, 18 mm. **Obv:** Putuo Mountain Pilgrimage Gate **Rev:** Kuanyin and value **Edge:** Reeded

Date	Mintage	F	VF	XF	Unc	BU
2004 Proof	33,000	Value: 85.00				

Y# 1216 50 YUAN

155.5175 g., 0.9990 Silver 4.995 oz. ASW, 80x50 mm. **Obv:** Monkey King leading the Master over bridge **Rev:** Multicolor Monkey King fighting the Pig Demon of Bones **Edge:** Plain **Shape:** ingot

Date	Mintage	F	VF	XF	Unc	BU
2004 Proof	10,000	Value: 300				

Y# 1222 50 YUAN

3.1103 g., 0.9990 Gold 0.0999 oz. AGW, 18 mm. **Obv:** Dog-shaped belt-hook , an ancient Chinese bronze ware, decorative disign of dog tail-shaped plant leaves **Rev:** 2 dogs at play

Date	Mintage	F	VF	XF	Unc	BU
2006 Proof	30,000	Value: 85.00				

Y# 1238 100 YUAN

3.1100 g., 0.9995 Platinum APW, 18 mm. **Obv:** Putuo Mountain Pilgrimage Gate **Rev:** Kuanyin and value **Edge:** Reeded

Date	Mintage	F	VF	XF	Unc	BU
2004 Proof	33,000	Value: 150				

Y# 1211 100 YUAN

15.5500 g., 0.9990 Palladium 0.4994 oz., 27 mm. **Obv:** Temple of Heaven **Rev:** Panda mother and cub, "kissing pandas" **Edge:** Reeded

Date	Mintage	F	VF	XF	Unc	BU
2004 Proof	8,000	Value: 375				

Y# 1085 200 YUAN

15.5518 g., 0.9990 Gold 0.4995 oz. AGW, 27 mm. **Subject:** Mogao Grottoes **Obv:** Eight story building. **Rev:** Dancing drummer. **Edge:** Reeded.

Date	Mintage	F	VF	XF	Unc	BU
2001 Proof	8,800	Value: 375				

Y# 1087 200 YUAN

15.5518 g., 0.9990 Gold 0.4995 oz. AGW, 27 mm. **Subject:** 50th Anniversary Chinese Occupation of Tibet **Obv:** Five stars. **Rev:** Denomination in flower. **Edge:** Reeded.

Date	Mintage	F	VF	XF	Unc	BU
2001 Proof	15,000	Value: 360				

Y# 1142 200 YUAN

15.5517 g., 0.9999 Gold 0.4999 oz. AGW, 27 mm. **Subject:** Awarding of 2008 Olympics to Bjing

Date	Mintage	F	VF	XF	Unc	BU
2001	15,000	—	—	—	—	350

Y# 1145 200 YUAN

15.5500 g., 0.9990 Gold 0.4994 oz. AGW, 27 mm. **Subject:** Budda

Date	Mintage	F	VF	XF	Unc	BU
2002	8,800	—	—	—	—	375

Y# 1146 200 YUAN

15.5000 g., 0.9990 Gold 0.4978 oz. AGW **Subject:** Peking Opera

Date	Mintage	F	VF	XF	Unc	BU
2002	8,000	—	—	—	—	825

Y# 1147 200 YUAN

15.5000 g., 0.9990 Gold 0.4978 oz. AGW **Subject:** Dream of the Red Mansion **Shape:** Octagon

Date	Mintage	F	VF	XF	Unc	BU
2002 Proof	8,000	Value: 550				

Y# 1149 200 YUAN

15.5000 g., 0.9990 Gold 0.4978 oz. AGW **Subject:** Ceremonial Mask

Date	Mintage	F	VF	XF	Unc	BU
2002	5,000	—	—	—	—	385

Y# 1148 200 YUAN

15.5000 g., 0.9990 Gold 0.4978 oz. AGW **Subject:** Cave man art **Note:** Multicolor

Date	Mintage	F	VF	XF	Unc	BU
2002 Proof	8,800	Value: 525				

Y# 1159 200 YUAN

15.5519 g., 0.9999 Gold 0.5 oz. AGW **Subject:** Pilgrimage to the West

Date	Mintage	F	VF	XF	Unc	BU
2003	—	—	—	—	—	375

Y# 1160 200 YUAN

15.5519 g., 0.9999 Gold 0.5 oz. AGW **Subject:** Chinese Mythical Folk Tales

Date	Mintage	F	VF	XF	Unc	BU
2003	—	—	—	—	—	375

Y# 1217 200 YUAN

15.5500 g., 0.9990 Gold 0.4994 oz. AGW, 27 mm. **Obv:** Monkey King leading the Master over bridge **Rev:** Multicolor Monkey King on one knee meeting the Master **Edge:** Reeded

Date	Mintage	F	VF	XF	Unc	BU
2004 Proof	11,800	Value: 470				

Y# 1213 200 YUAN

15.5500 g., 0.9990 Gold 0.4994 oz. AGW, 27 mm. **Obv:** National arms above People's Congress Hall and ornamental column **Rev:** Multicolor hologram depicting the hall's overhead lighting **Edge:** Reeded

Date	Mintage	F	VF	XF	Unc	BU
2004 Proof	5,000	Value: 550				

Y# 1220 200 YUAN

15.6300 g., Gold **Obv:** Qing Yuan Gate of the China Great Wall **Rev:** 2 dogs at play **Shape:** 30° Fan

Date	Mintage	F	VF	XF	Unc	BU
2006 Proof	6,600	Value: 485				

Y# 1224 200 YUAN

15.6300 g., Gold, 27 mm. **Obv:** Dog-shaped belt-hook from ancient Chinese bronze ware, decorative design of dog tail-shaped plant leaves **Rev:** 2 smart dogs **Shape:** Scalloped

Date	Mintage	F	VF	XF	Unc	BU
2006 Proof	8,000	Value: 485				

Y# 1227 300 YUAN

32.1500 g., Silver, 100 mm. **Obv:** Dog-shaped belt-hook from ancient Chinese bronze ware, decorative design of dog tail-shaped plant leaves **Rev:** 2 dogs

Date	Mintage	F	VF	XF	Unc	BU
2006 Proof	3,800	Value: 65.00				

Y# 1086 2000 YUAN

155.5175 g., 0.9990 Gold 4.995 oz. AGW, 60 mm. **Subject:** Mogao Grottoes **Obv:** Eight story building. **Rev:** Two dancers. **Edge:** Reeded.

Date	Mintage	F	VF	XF	Unc	BU
2001 Proof	288	Value: 3,500				

Y# 1151 2000 YUAN

155.5175 g., 0.9990 Gold 4.995 oz. AGW, 60 mm. **Subject:** Buddest Ceremony

Date	Mintage	F	VF	XF	Unc	BU
2002	288	—	—	—	—	4,250

Y# 1206 2000 YUAN
155.5175 g., 0.9990 Gold 4.995 oz. AGW, 60 mm. **Subject:** Maijishan Grottos **Obv:** Grotto view **Rev:** Buddha portrait within halo of flying devatas **Edge:** Reeded

Date	Mintage	F	VF	XF	Unc	BU
2004(y) Proof	288	Value: 3,500				

Y# 1218 2000 YUAN
155.5175 g., 0.9990 Gold 4.995 oz. AGW, 64x40 mm. **Obv:** Monkey King leading Master over bridge **Rev:** Multicolor Monkey King fighting the Pig "Demon of Bones" **Edge:** Plain **Shape:** Ingot

Date	Mintage	F	VF	XF	Unc	BU
2004 Proof	500	Value: 5,300				

SILVER BULLION COINAGE

Lunar Series

Y# 1042 10 YUAN
31.1035 g., 0.9990 Silver 1.0000 oz. ASW **Subject:** Year of the Snake **Shape:** Fan-like

Date	Mintage	F	VF	XF	Unc	BU
2001	66,000	—	—	—	35.00	—

Y# 1041 10 YUAN
30.8400 g., 0.9990 Silver .9905 oz. ASW, 39.9 mm. **Subject:** Year of the Snake **Obv:** Traditional style building **Rev:** Snake **Edge:** Scalloped

Date	Mintage	F	VF	XF	Unc	BU
2001 Proof	6,800	Value: 65.00				

Y# 1232 10 YUAN
31.1035 g., 0.9990 Silver, 40 mm. **Subject:** Year of the Horse **Obv:** Da Zheng Hall **Rev:** Stylized horse head **Edge:** Reeded

Date	Mintage	F	VF	XF	Unc	BU
2002	50,000	—	—	—	—	50.00

Y# 1225 10 YUAN
31.1035 g., Silver, 40 mm. **Obv:** Dog-shaped belt-hook from ancient Chinese bronze ware, decorative design of dog tail-shaped plant leaves **Rev:** 2 smart dogs

Date	Mintage	F	VF	XF	Unc	BU
2006	80,000	—	—	—	—	45.00

Y# 1040 50 YUAN
155.4400 g., 0.9990 Silver 4.9925 oz. ASW, 80.6 x 50.5 mm. **Subject:** Year of the Snake **Obv:** Traditional style building **Rev:** Snake **Edge:** Plain **Note:** Illustration reduced.

Date	Mintage	F	VF	XF	Unc	BU
2001 Proof	1,888,000	Value: 245				

SILVER BULLION COINAGE

Panda Series

Y# 1111 10 YUAN
31.1035 g., 0.9990 Silver 0.999 oz. ASW, 40 mm. **Obv:** Temple of Heaven with incuse legend **Rev:** Panda walking left through bamboo **Edge:** Reeded **Note:** Large and Small date varieties exist.

Date	Mintage	F	VF	XF	Unc	BU
2001	250,000	—	—	—	25.00	—
2001 D	—	—	—	—	25.00	—

Note: Domestic issue

Y# 1097a 10 YUAN
31.3200 g., 0.9990 Silver 1.006 oz. ASW, 40 mm. **Obv:** Temple of Heaven **Rev:** Two tone gold-plated Panda walking left in bamboo forest **Edge:** Slant reeding **Note:** Large and Small date varieties exist.

Date	Mintage	F	VF	XF	Unc	BU
2002 Proof	—	Value: 55.00				

Note: Privately gold plated

Y# 1097 10 YUAN
31.3200 g., 0.9990 Silver 1.006 oz. ASW, 40 mm. **Obv:** Temple of Heaven and incuse legend **Rev:** Panda walking left in bamboo forest **Edge:** Slanted reeding **Note:** Large and Small date varieties exist.

Date	Mintage	F	VF	XF	Unc	BU
2002	—	—	—	—	22.00	—

Y# 1098 10 YUAN
31.2300 g., 0.9990 Silver 1.0031 oz. ASW, 40 mm. **Obv:** Temple of Heaven, incuse legend **Rev:** Multicolor panda walking in bamboo **Edge:** Slanted reeding **Note:** Large and Small date varieties exist.

Date	Mintage	F	VF	XF	Unc	BU
2002 Proof	—	Value: 55.00				

Note: Privately colored

Y# 1116 300 YUAN
1007.7534 g., 0.9990 Silver 32.3676 oz. ASW, 100 mm. **Subject:** Panda Coinage 20th Anniversary **Obv:** Temple of Heaven **Rev:** Two gold inserts with the 1982 and 2002 panda designs on bamboo leaves **Edge:** Plain **Note:** Large and Small date varieties exist.

Date	Mintage	F	VF	XF	Unc	BU
2002 Proof	6,000	Value: 675				

GOLD BULLION COINAGE

Panda Series

Y# 1112 20 YUAN
1.5600 g., 0.9990 Gold 0.0501 oz. AGW, 14 mm. **Obv:** Temple of Heaven **Rev:** Panda walking left through bamboo **Edge:** Reeded **Note:** Large and Small date varieties exist.

Date	Mintage	F	VF	XF	Unc	BU
2001	100,000	—	—	—	—	37.50
2001 D	200,000	—	—	—	—	37.50

Y# 1154 20 YUAN
3.1103 g., 0.9999 Gold 0.1 oz. AGW **Subject:** Panda **Note:** Large and Small date varieties exist.

Date	Mintage	F	VF	XF	Unc	BU
2003	—	—	—	—	—	70.00

Y# 1172 20 YUAN
1.5552 g., 0.9999 Gold 0.05 oz. AGW **Subject:** Panda **Note:** Large and Small date varieties exist.

Date	Mintage	F	VF	XF	Unc	BU
2004	—	—	—	—	—	37.50

Y# 1113 50 YUAN
3.1103 g., 0.9990 Gold 0.0999 oz. AGW, 18 mm. **Obv:** Temple of Heaven **Rev:** Panda walking left through bamboo **Edge:** Reeded **Note:** Large and Small date varieties exist.

Date	Mintage	F	VF	XF	Unc	BU
2001	50,000	—	—	—	—	70.00
2001 D	150,000	—	—	—	—	70.00

Y# 1157 50 YUAN
3.1103 g., 0.9999 Gold 0.1 oz. AGW **Subject:** Panda **Note:** Large and Small date varieties exist.

Date	Mintage	F	VF	XF	Unc	BU
2003	—	—	—	—	—	70.00

Y# 1173 50 YUAN
3.1103 g., 0.9999 Gold 0.1 oz. AGW **Subject:** Panda **Note:** Large and Small date varieties exist.

Date	Mintage	F	VF	XF	Unc	BU
2004	—	—	—	—	—	70.00

Y# 1114 100 YUAN
7.7759 g., 0.9990 Gold 0.2498 oz. AGW, 22 mm. **Obv:** Temple of Heaven **Rev:** Panda walking left through bamboo **Edge:** Reeded **Note:** Large and Small date varieties exist.

Date	Mintage	F	VF	XF	Unc	BU
2001	30,000	—	—	—	—	175
2001 D	100,000	—	—	—	—	175

Y# 1158 100 YUAN
7.7759 g., 0.9999 Gold 0.25 oz. AGW **Subject:** Panda **Note:** Large and Small date varieties exist.

Date	Mintage	F	VF	XF	Unc	BU
2003	—	—	—	—	—	175

Y# 1174 100 YUAN
7.7759 g., 0.9999 Gold 0.25 oz. AGW **Subject:** Panda **Note:** Large and Small date varieties exist.

Date	Mintage	F	VF	XF	Unc	BU
2004	—	—	—	—	—	175

Y# 1105 200 YUAN
15.5518 g., 0.9990 Gold 0.4995 oz. AGW, 27 mm. **Obv:** Temple of Heaven **Rev:** Panda in bamboo forest **Edge:** Slanted reeding **Note:** Illustration reduced. Large and Small date varieties exist.

Date	Mintage	F	VF	XF	Unc	BU
2001	—	—	—	—	—	335
2001 D	100,000	—	—	—	—	335

Y# 1162 200 YUAN
15.5519 g., 0.9999 Gold 0.5 oz. AGW **Subject:** Panda **Note:** Large and Small date varieties exist.

Date	Mintage	F	VF	XF	Unc	BU
2003	—	—	—	—	—	335

Y# 1175 200 YUAN
15.5519 g., 0.9990 Gold 0.4995 oz. AGW **Subject:** Panda **Note:** Large and Small date varieties exist.

Date	Mintage	F	VF	XF	Unc	BU
2004	—	—	—	—	—	335

Y# 1164 500 YUAN
31.1320 g., 0.9999 Gold 1.0008 oz. AGW **Subject:** Panda **Note:** Large and Small date varieties exist.

Date	Mintage	F	VF	XF	Unc	BU
2003	—	—	—	—	—	650

Y# 1176 500 YUAN
31.1035 g., 0.9999 Gold 0.9999 oz. AGW **Subject:** Panda **Note:** Large and Small date varieties exist.

Date	Mintage	F	VF	XF	Unc	BU
2004	—	—	—	—	—	650

Y# 1138 10000 YUAN
321.5000 g., 0.9999 Gold 10.3354 oz. AGW **Subject:** Panda **Note:** Large and Small date varieties exist.

Date	Mintage	F	VF	XF	Unc	BU
2001	68	—	—	—	—	17,000

Y# 1165 10000 YUAN
1000.0000 g., 0.9999 Gold 32.1475 oz. AGW **Subject:** Panda **Note:** Large and Small date varieties exist.

Date	Mintage	F	VF	XF	Unc	BU
2003	—	—	—	—	—	BV+25%

Y# 1177 10000 YUAN
1000.0000 g., 0.9999 Gold 32.1475 oz. AGW **Subject:** Panda **Note:** Large and Small date varieties exist.

Date	Mintage	F	VF	XF	Unc	BU
2004	68	—	—	—	—	BV+25%

GOLD BULLION COINAGE

Lunar Series

Y# 1141.1 50 YUAN
3.1103 g., 0.9990 Gold 0.0999 oz. AGW **Subject:** Year of the Snake

Date	Mintage	F	VF	XF	Unc	BU
2001	48,000	—	—	—	—	110

Y# 1141.2 50 YUAN
3.1105 g., 0.9999 Gold 0.1 oz. AGW **Subject:** Year of the Snake **Note:** Multicolor

Date	Mintage	F	VF	XF	Unc	BU
2001	30,000	—	—	—	—	140

Y# 1043 50 YUAN
3.1104 g., 0.9990 Gold .1000 oz. AGW **Subject:** Year of the Snake

Date	Mintage	F	VF	XF	Unc	BU
2001	48,000	—	—	—	—	95.00

Y# 1143.2 50 YUAN
3.1050 g., 0.9999 Gold 0.0998 oz. AGW **Subject:** Year of the Horse **Note:** Multicolor

Date	Mintage	F	VF	XF	Unc	BU
2002	30,000	—	—	—	—	275

Y# 1143.1 50 YUAN
3.1050 g., 0.9999 Gold 0.0998 oz. AGW **Subject:** Year of the Horse

Date	Mintage	F	VF	XF	Unc	BU
2002	48,000	—	—	—	—	140

Y# 1144 50 YUAN
15.5500 g., 0.9990 Gold 0.4994 oz. AGW **Subject:** Year of the Horse **Shape:** Fan

Date	Mintage	F	VF	XF	Unc	BU
2002	6,600	—	—	—	—	650

Y# 1155.1 50 YUAN
3.1103 g., 0.9999 Gold 0.1 oz. AGW **Subject:** Year of the Goat

Date	Mintage	F	VF	XF	Unc	BU
2003	48,000	—	—	—	—	110

Y# 1156 50 YUAN
15.5517 g., 0.9999 Gold 0.4999 oz. AGW **Subject:** Year of the Goat

Date	Mintage	F	VF	XF	Unc	BU
2003	6,600	—	—	—	—	475

Y# 1155.2 50 YUAN
3.1105 g., 0.9999 Gold 0.1 oz. AGW **Subject:** Year of the Goat **Note:** Multicolor

Date	Mintage	F	VF	XF	Unc	BU
2003	30,000	—	—	—	—	195

Y# 1167.2 50 YUAN
3.1103 g., 0.9999 Gold 0.1 oz. AGW **Subject:** Year of the Monkey **Note:** Multicolor.

Date	Mintage	F	VF	XF	Unc	BU
2004	30,000	—	—	—	—	275

Y# 1167.1 50 YUAN
3.1103 g., 0.9999 Gold 0.1 oz. AGW **Subject:** Year of the Monkey

Date	Mintage	F	VF	XF	Unc	BU
2004	48,000	—	—	—	—	140

Y# 1226 50 YUAN
3.1103 g., 0.9990 Gold 0.0999 oz. AGW, 18 mm. **Obv:** Dog-shaped belt-hook from ancient Chinese bronze ware, decorative design of dog tail-shaped plant leaves **Rev:** 2 smart dogs

Date	Mintage	F	VF	XF	Unc	BU
2006	60,000	—	—	—	—	110

Y# 1044 200 YUAN
15.5518 g., 0.9990 Gold .5000 oz. AGW **Subject:** Year of the Snake

Date	Mintage	F	VF	XF	Unc	BU
2001	6,600	—	—	—	—	400

Y# 1045 200 YUAN
15.5518 g., 0.9990 Gold .5000 oz. AGW **Subject:** Year of the Snake **Shape:** Scalloped

Date	Mintage	F	VF	XF	Unc	BU
2001 Proof	2,300	Value: 385				

Y# 1150 200 YUAN
15.5000 g., 0.9990 Gold 0.4978 oz. AGW **Subject:** Year of the Horse

Date	Mintage	F	VF	XF	Unc	BU
2002	2,300	—	—	—	—	650

Y# 1161 200 YUAN
15.5519 g., 0.9999 Gold 0.5 oz. AGW **Subject:** Year of the Goat

Date	Mintage	F	VF	XF	Unc	BU
2003	2,300	—	—	—	—	475

Y# 1169 200 YUAN
15.5519 g., 0.9999 Gold 0.5 oz. AGW **Subject:** Year of the Monkey

Date	Mintage	F	VF	XF	Unc	BU
2004	2,300	—	—	—	—	750

Y# 1088 500 YUAN
31.1035 g., 0.9990 Gold 0.999 oz. AGW, 32 mm. **Obv:** Temple of Heaven **Rev:** Panda walking through bamboo **Edge:** Reeded

Date	Mintage	F	VF	XF	Unc	BU
2001	—	—	—	—	—	BV+15%
2001 D	150,000	—	—	—	—	BV+15%

Y# 1168 500 YUAN
15.5519 g., 0.9999 Gold 0.5 oz. AGW **Subject:** Year of the Monkey **Shape:** Fan

Date	Mintage	F	VF	XF	Unc	BU
2004	6,600	—	—	—	—	535

Y# 1046 2000 YUAN
155.5175 g., 0.9990 Gold 5.0000 oz. AGW **Subject:** Year of the Snake **Shape:** Rectangle

Date	Mintage	F	VF	XF	Unc	BU
2001 Proof	118	Value: 3,450				

Y# 1152 2000 YUAN
155.5175 g., 0.9999 Gold 4.9995 oz. AGW **Subject:** Year of the Horse

Date	Mintage	F	VF	XF	Unc	BU
2002	—	—	—	—	—	4,750

Y# 1163 2000 YUAN
155.5190 g., 0.9999 Gold 4.9995 oz. AGW **Subject:** Year of the Goat

Date	Mintage	F	VF	XF	Unc	BU
2003	—	—	—	—	—	4,250

Y# 1170 2000 YUAN
155.1750 g., 0.9999 Gold 4.9885 oz. AGW **Subject:** Year of the Monkey

Date	Mintage	F	VF	XF	Unc	BU
2004	—	—	—	—	—	4,750

Y# 1047 10000 YUAN
1000.2108 g., 0.9990 Gold 32.1575 oz. AGW **Subject:** Year of the Snake **Shape:** Scalloped

Date	Mintage	F	VF	XF	Unc	BU
2001 Proof	15	Value: 28,000				

Y# 1153 10000 YUAN
1000.0000 g., 0.9999 Gold 32.1475 oz. AGW **Subject:** Year of the Horse **Shape:** Scalloped

Date	Mintage	F	VF	XF	Unc	BU
2002	15	—	—	—	—	35,000

Y# 1166 10000 YUAN
1000.0000 g., 0.9999 Gold 32.1475 oz. AGW **Subject:** Year of the Goat

Date	Mintage	F	VF	XF	Unc	BU
2003	15	—	—	—	—	35,000

Y# 1171 10000 YUAN
1000.0000 g., 0.9999 Gold 32.1475 oz. AGW **Subject:** Year of the Monkey

Date	Mintage	F	VF	XF	Unc	BU
2004	15	—	—	—	—	35,000

PLATINUM BULLION COINAGE

Panda Series

Y# 1115 100 YUAN
3.1103 g., 0.9995 Platinum 0.0999 oz. APW, 18 mm. **Subject:** Panda Coinage 20th Anniversary **Obv:** Seated panda design of 1982 **Rev:** Walking panda design of 2002 **Edge:** Reeded

Date	Mintage	F	VF	XF	Unc	BU
2002 Proof	20,000	Value: 200				

REPUBLIC OF CHINA

East China Sea
JAPAN
CHINA
Philippine Sea

The Republic of China, comprising Taiwan (an island located 90 miles (145 km.) off the southeastern coast of mainland China), the offshore islands of Quemoy and Matsu and nearby islets of the Pescadores chain, has an area of 14,000 sq. mi. (35,980 sq. km.) and a population of 20.2 million. Capital: Taipei. During the past decade, manufacturing has replaced agriculture in importance. Fruits, vegetables, plywood, textile yarns and fabrics and clothing are exported.

The coins of Nationalist China do not carry A.D. dating, but are dated according to the year of the republic, which was established in 1911. However, republican years are added to 1911 to find the western year. Thus republican year 90 plus 1911 equals Gregorian calendar year 2001AD.

TAIWAN

REPUBLIC

STANDARD COINAGE

Y# 550 5 CHIAO
Bronze

Date	Mintage	F	VF	XF	Unc	BU
92(2003)	—	—	0.15	0.30	1.00	1.25
92(2003) Proof	—	Value: 10.00				

Y# 551 YUAN
Bronze **Obv:** Bust of Chiang Kai-shek left

Date	Mintage	F	VF	XF	Unc	BU
92(2003)	—	—	—	0.15	0.30	0.45
92(2003) Proof	—	Value: 12.50				

Y# 552 5 YUAN
Copper-Nickel

Date	Mintage	F	VF	XF	Unc	BU
92(2003)	—	—	0.15	0.25	0.50	0.75
92(2003) Proof	—	Value: 12.50				

Y# 567 10 YUAN
7.4300 g., Copper-Nickel, 26 mm. **Subject:** 90th Anniversary of the Republic **Obv:** Bust of Sun Yat-sen facing **Rev:** Holographic design and denomination **Edge:** Reeded

Date	Mintage	F	VF	XF	Unc	BU
90 (2001)	30,000,000	—	—	—	2.50	3.00

Y# 553 10 YUAN
Copper-Nickel **Obv:** Bust of Chiang Kai-shek left

Date	Mintage	F	VF	XF	Unc	BU
92(2003)	—	—	0.25	0.45	0.75	1.00
92(2003) Proof	—	Value: 15.00				

Y# 565 20 YUAN
Ring Composition: Brass **Center Weight:** 8.4000 g. **Center Composition:** Copper-Nickel, 26.8 mm. **Obv:** Male portrait. **Rev:** Three boats. **Edge:** Reeded.

Date	Mintage	F	VF	XF	Unc	BU
90 (2001)	—	—	—	—	3.50	4.50
92(2003)	—	—	—	—	3.50	4.50
92(2003) Proof	—	Value: 18.00				

Y# 570 50 YUAN
15.5680 g., 0.9990 Silver 0.5 oz. ASW, 33 mm. **Subject:** World Cup Baseball **Obv:** Player at bat with ball background **Rev:** Mount Jade above denomination **Edge:** Reeded

Date	Mintage	F	VF	XF	Unc	BU
90 (2001)	130,000	—	—	—	25.00	27.50

Y# 568 50 YUAN
10.0000 g., Brass, 28 mm. **Obv:** Bust **Rev:** Denomination above latent image denomination **Edge:** Reeding and denomination

Date	Mintage	F	VF	XF	Unc	BU
91-2002	—	—	—	—	7.50	10.00
92-2003	—	—	—	—	7.50	10.00
92-2003 Proof	—	Value: 20.00				

Y# 569 50 YUAN
15.5680 g., 0.9990 Silver 0.5 oz. ASW, 33 mm. **Subject:** 90th Anniversary of the Republic **Obv:** Portrait of Sun Yat-sen **Rev:** Latent image above denomination **Edge:** Reeded

Date	Mintage	F	VF	XF	Unc	BU
90(2001)	230,000	—	—	—	25.00	27.50

Y# 571 50 YUAN
31.1035 g., 0.9990 Silver 0.999 oz. ASW, 38 mm. **Subject:** Third National Expressway **Obv:** Multicolor island map **Rev:** Kao Ping Hsi bridge **Edge:** Reeded

Date	Mintage	F	VF	XF	Unc	BU
Yr 93- 2004	20,000	—	—	—	40.00	—

MINT SETS

KM#	Date	Mintage	Identification	Issue Price	Mkt Val
MS4	92(2003) (6)	—	Y550, 551, 552, 553, 565, 568 plus C-N Year of the Goat medal	—	—

PROOF SETS

KM#	Date	Mintage	Identification	Issue Price	Mkt Val
PS10	90(2001) (5)	150,000	Y#550-554	29.40	35.00
PS12	92(2003) (6)	—	Y550, 551, 552, 553, 565, 568 plus silver Year of the Goat Medal	—	—

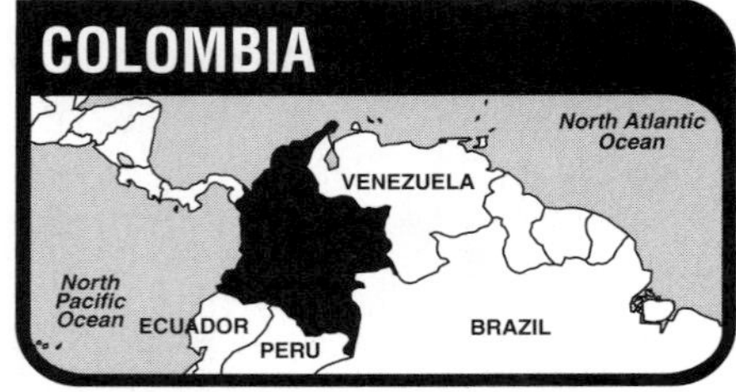

The Republic of Colombia, in the northwestern corner of South America, has an area of 440,831 sq. mi. (1,138,910 sq. km.) and a population of*42.3 million. Capital: Bogota. The economy is primarily agricultural with a mild, rich coffee being the chief crop. Colombia has the world's largest platinum deposits and important reserves of coal, iron ore, petroleum and limestone; other precious metals and emeralds are also mined. Coffee, crude oil, bananas, sugar and emeralds are exported.

REPUBLIC

DECIMAL COINAGE

100 Centavos = 1 Peso

KM# 282.2 20 PESOS
Copper-Aluminum-Nickel **Obv:** 68 beads circle around the rim

Date	Mintage	F	VF	XF	Unc	BU
2003	—	—	—	—	0.50	0.75

KM# 294 20 PESOS
2.0000 g., Brass, 17.2 mm. **Obv:** Simon Bolivar left **Rev:** Value **Edge:** Reeded

Date	Mintage	F	VF	XF	Unc	BU
2004	—	—	—	—	0.15	0.25

KM# 283.2 50 PESOS
Copper-Nickel-Zinc **Rev:** 72 beads circle around rim

Date	Mintage	F	VF	XF	Unc	BU
2003	—	—	—	—	1.00	1.25

KM# 286 500 PESOS
Aluminum-Bronze center in Copper-Nickel ring **Rev:** Guacari tree

Date	Mintage	F	VF	XF	Unc	BU
2004	—	—	—	—	4.00	4.50

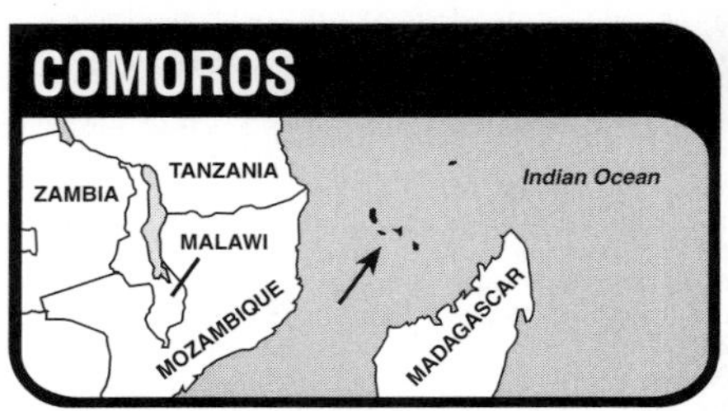

The Federal Islamic Republic of the Comoros, a volcanic archipelago located in the Mozambique Channel of the Indian Ocean 300 miles (483 km.) northwest of Madagascar, has an area of 719 sq. mi. (2,171 sq. km.) and a population of *714,000. Capital: Moroni. The economy of the islands is based on agriculture. There are practically no mineral resources. Vanilla, essence for perfumes, copra, and sisal are exported.

Ancient Phoenician traders were probably the first visitors to the Comoro Islands, but the first detailed knowledge of the area was gathered by Arab sailors. Arab dominion and culture were firmly established when the Portuguese, Dutch, and French arrived in the 16th century. In 1843 a Malagasy ruler ceded the island of Mayotte to France; the other three principal islands of the archipelago-Anjouan, Moheli, and Grand Comore came under French protection in 1886. The islands were joined administratively with Madagascar in 1912. The Comoros became partially autonomous, with the status of a French overseas territory, in 1946, and achieved complete internal autonomy in 1961. On Dec. 31, 1975, after 133 years of French association, the Comoro Islands became the independent Republic of the Comoros.

Mayotte retained the option of determining its future ties and in 1976 voted to remain French. Its present status is that of a French Territorial Collectivity. French currency now circulates there.

MINT MARKS

- Paris, privy marks only
- Paris, horseshoe privy mark (2001)
A - Paris

MONETARY SYSTEM

100 Centimes = 1 Franc

FEDERAL ISLAMIC REPUBLIC

BANQUE CENTRAL COINAGE

KM# 14 25 FRANCS
Nickel **Series:** F.A.O. **Obv:** Chickens

Date	Mintage	F	VF	XF	Unc	BU
2001(a) Horseshoe	—	0.20	0.40	0.80	2.00	—

KM# 16 50 FRANCS
Nickel

Date	Mintage	F	VF	XF	Unc	BU
2001(a)	—	0.50	0.80	1.50	2.50	3.50

The Republic of the Congo (formerly the Peoples Republic of the Congo), located on the equator in west-central Africa, has an area of 132,047 sq. mi. (342,000 sq. km.) and a population of *2.98 million. Capital: Brazzaville. Agriculture forestry, mining, and food processing are the principal industries. Timber, industrial diamonds, potash, peanuts, and cocoa beans are exported.

NOTE: For earlier and related coinage see French Equatorial Africa and the Equatorial African States. For later coinage see Central African States.

RULERS
French until 1960

MINT MARKS
(a) - Paris, privy marks only

MONETARY SYSTEM
100 Centimes = 1 Franc

REPUBLIC
Republique du Congo
DECIMAL COINAGE

KM# 47 1000 FRANCS
15.0000 g., 0.9990 Silver 0.4818 oz. ASW, 35 mm. **Obv:** Seated woman with tablet **Rev:** Two soccer players and colosseum **Edge:** Plain

Date	Mintage	F	VF	XF	Unc	BU
2001 Proof	—	Value: 40.00				

KM# 48 1000 FRANCS
20.0000 g., 0.9990 Silver 0.6424 oz. ASW, 38 mm. **Obv:** Seated woman with tablet **Rev:** Two soccer players and Mexican pyramid **Edge:** Reeded

Date	Mintage	F	VF	XF	Unc	BU
2001 Proof	—	Value: 40.00				

INSTITUT MONETAIRE

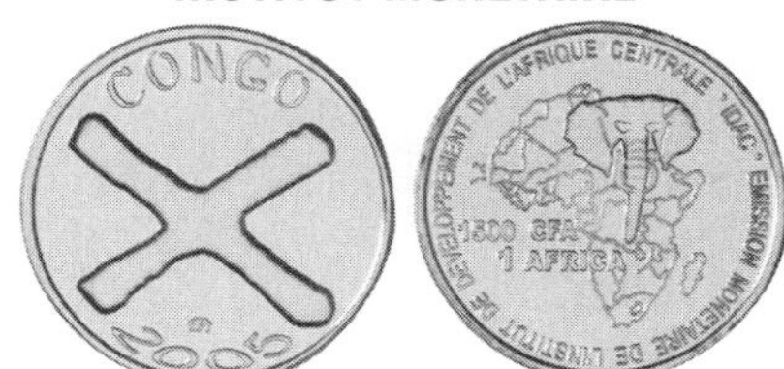

KM# 46 1500 CFA FRANCS - 1 AFRICA
7.3400 g., Nickel Plated Iron, 25.9 mm. **Obv:** Katanga Cross **Rev:** Elephant head on full Africa map **Edge:** Plain

Date	Mintage	F	VF	XF	Unc	BU
2005	2,005	—	—	—	20.00	—

KM# 46a 1500 CFA FRANCS - 1 AFRICA
0.9990 Silver, 26 mm. **Obv:** Katanga Cross **Rev:** Elephant head on full Africa map

Date	Mintage	F	VF	XF	Unc	BU
2005	25	—	—	—	360	—

The Democratic Republic of the Congo (formerly the Republic of Zaire, and earlier the Belgian Congo), located in the south-central part of Africa, has an area of 905,568 sq. mi. (2,345,410 sq. km.) and a population of *47.4 million. Capital: Kinshasa. The mineral-rich country produces copper, tin, diamonds, gold, zinc, cobalt and uranium.

DEMOCRATIC REPUBLIC
1998 -
REFORM COINAGE

KM# 76 25 CENTIMES
0.8500 g., Aluminum, 20 mm. **Obv:** Lion **Rev:** Weasel **Edge:** Plain

Date	Mintage	F	VF	XF	Unc	BU
2002	—	—	—	—	0.75	1.00

KM# 77 25 CENTIMES
0.8500 g., Aluminum, 20 mm. **Obv:** Lion **Rev:** Ram **Edge:** Plain

Date	Mintage	F	VF	XF	Unc	BU
2002	—	—	—	—	0.75	1.00

KM# 83 25 CENTIMES
1.3000 g., Aluminum, 20 mm. **Obv:** Lion **Rev:** Wild dog **Edge:** Plain

Date	Mintage	F	VF	XF	Unc	BU
2002	—	—	—	—	0.75	1.00

KM# 75 50 CENTIMES
2.1600 g., Aluminum, 27 mm. **Obv:** Lion **Rev:** Soccer player **Edge:** Plain

Date	Mintage	F	VF	XF	Unc	BU
2002	—	—	—	—	1.25	1.50

KM# 78 50 CENTIMES
2.1600 g., Aluminum, 27 mm. **Obv:** Lion **Rev:** Giraffe **Edge:** Plain

Date	Mintage	F	VF	XF	Unc	BU
2002	—	—	—	—	1.25	1.50

KM# 79 50 CENTIMES
2.1600 g., Aluminum, 27 mm. **Obv:** Lion **Rev:** Gorilla **Edge:** Plain

Date	Mintage	F	VF	XF	Unc	BU
2002	—	—	—	—	1.00	1.25

KM# 80 50 CENTIMES
2.1600 g., Aluminum, 27 mm. **Obv:** Lion **Rev:** Butterfly **Edge:** Plain

Date	Mintage	F	VF	XF	Unc	BU
2002	—	—	—	—	1.50	1.75

KM# 123 50 CENTIMES
3.9200 g., Stainless Steel, 21.9 mm. **Obv:** Lion above denomination **Rev:** Verney L. Cameron **Edge:** Plain

Date	Mintage	F	VF	XF	Unc	BU
2002	—	—	—	—	1.00	1.25

KM# 81 FRANC
4.5700 g., Brass, 22 mm. **Obv:** Lion **Rev:** Turtle **Edge:** Plain

Date	Mintage	F	VF	XF	Unc	BU
2002	—	—	—	—	1.25	1.50

KM# 82 FRANC
4.5700 g., Brass, 22 mm. **Obv:** Lion **Rev:** Chicken **Edge:** Plain

Date	Mintage	F	VF	XF	Unc	BU
2002	—	—	—	—	1.50	1.75

KM# 156 FRANC
5.0000 g., Nickel Clad Steel, 24.7 mm. **Obv:** Lion **Rev:** Pope John Paul II as a priest in 1946 **Edge:** Plain

Date	Mintage	F	VF	XF	Unc	BU
2004	—	—	—	—	2.00	2.50

KM# 157 FRANC
5.0000 g., Nickel Clad Steel, 24.7 mm. **Obv:** Lion **Rev:** Pope John Paul II as a Cardinal in 1967 **Edge:** Plain

Date	Mintage	F	VF	XF	Unc	BU
2004	—	—	—	—	2.00	2.50

KM# 158 FRANC
5.0000 g., Nickel Clad Steel, 24.7 mm. **Obv:** Lion **Rev:** Pope John Paul II as newly elected pope in 1978 **Edge:** Plain

Date	Mintage	F	VF	XF	Unc	BU
2004	—	—	—	—	2.00	2.50

KM# 159 FRANC
5.0000 g., Nickel Clad Steel, 24.7 mm. **Obv:** Lion **Rev:** Pope John Paul II wearing a mitre **Edge:** Plain

Date	Mintage	F	VF	XF	Unc	BU
2004	—	—	—	—	2.00	2.50

KM# 174 FRANC
6.0000 g., Copper-Nickel, 21 mm. **Obv:** Lion **Rev:** African Golden Cat **Edge:** Plain

Date	Mintage	F	VF	XF	Unc	BU
2004	5,000	—	—	—	7.25	9.00

KM# 174a FRANC
8.0000 g., 0.9990 Silver 0.2569 oz. ASW, 21 mm. **Obv:** Lion **Rev:** African Golden Cat **Edge:** Plain

Date	Mintage	F	VF	XF	Unc	BU
2004	25	—	—	—	270	—

KM# 56 5 FRANCS
22.4000 g., Copper-Nickel, 39.8 mm. **Series:** Wild Life Protection **Obv:** Lion **Rev:** Multicolor swallowtail butterfly hologram **Edge:** Reeded **Note:** Prev. KM#79.

Date	Mintage	F	VF	XF	Unc	BU
2002(2001)	20,000	—	—	—	30.00	—

KM# 57 5 FRANCS
22.4000 g., Copper Nickel, 39.8 mm. **Series:** Wild Life Protection **Obv:** Lion **Rev:** Multicolor dark greenish butterfly hologram **Edge:** Reeded **Note:** Prev. KM#80.

Date	Mintage	F	VF	XF	Unc	BU
2002(2001)	20,000	—	—	—	30.00	—

KM# 58 5 FRANCS
22.4000 g., Copper Nickel, 39.8 mm. **Series:** Wild Life Protection **Obv:** Lion **Rev:** Multicolor red and black butterfly hologram **Edge:** Reeded **Note:** Prev. KM#81.

Date	Mintage	F	VF	XF	Unc	BU
2002(2001)	20,000	—	—	—	30.00	—

KM# 170 5 FRANCS
24.3000 g., Copper-Nickel, 38.5 mm. **Obv:** Lion **Rev:** Multicolor German 1 mark coin dated 2001 **Edge:** Reeded

Date	Mintage	F	VF	XF	Unc	BU
2002	—	—	—	—	15.00	—

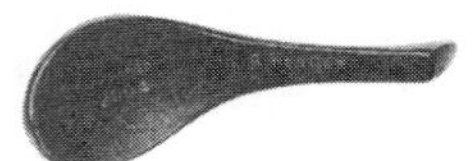

KM# 128 5 FRANCS
8.0000 g., Iron, 27.26x14.13 mm. **Obv:** Country name, lion and date in the bowl part of the spoon; value on the handle part **Edge:** Reeded **Note:** This is the Spoon part of the Compass and Spoon set. (The spoon is the compass needle.)

Date	Mintage	F	VF	XF	Unc	BU
2004	5,000	—	—	—	15.00	—

KM# 146 5 FRANCS
27.0000 g., Copper-Nickel, 38.6 mm. **Obv:** Lion **Rev:** Multicolor Quetzal bird **Edge:** Reeded

Date	Mintage	F	VF	XF	Unc	BU
2004 Proof	5,000	Value: 25.00				

KM# 147 5 FRANCS
27.0000 g., Copper-Nickel, 38.6 mm. **Obv:** Lion **Rev:** Multicolor Bird of Paradise **Edge:** Reeded

Date	Mintage	F	VF	XF	Unc	BU
2004 Proof	5,000	Value: 25.00				

KM# 148 5 FRANCS
27.0000 g., Copper-Nickel, 38.6 mm. **Obv:** Lion **Rev:** Multicolor Kingfisher bird **Edge:** Reeded

Date	Mintage	F	VF	XF	Unc	BU
2004 Proof	5,000	Value: 25.00				

KM# 164 5 FRANCS
25.4000 g., Copper-Nickel, 38.8 mm. **Subject:** Papal Visit **Obv:** Lion **Rev:** Pope John Paul II **Edge:** Reeded

Date	Mintage	F	VF	XF	Unc	BU
ND (2004) Proof	—	Value: 15.00				

KM# 165 5 FRANCS
49.5000 g., Copper-Nickel, 45.1 mm. **Obv:** Lion **Rev:** Rotating 50 year calender **Edge:** Reeded

Date	Mintage	F	VF	XF	Unc	BU
ND Matte	—	—	—	—	75.00	—

KM# 166 5 FRANCS
2.1600 g., Wood Maple wood, 39.4 mm. **Obv:** Lion, brown ink **Rev:** Gorilla, brown ink **Edge:** Plain

Date	Mintage	F	VF	XF	Unc	BU
2005	2,000	—	—	—	22.50	—

KM# 72 10 FRANCS
20.0000 g., 0.9250 Silver 0.5948 oz. ASW, 40.1 mm. **Series:** Airplanes **Obv:** Lion **Rev:** Mikoyan-Gurevich Mig 21 fighter **Edge:** Reeded

Date	Mintage	F	VF	XF	Unc	BU
2001 Proof	—	Value: 40.00				

KM# 74 10 FRANCS
31.1035 g., 0.9990 Silver 0.999 oz. ASW, 40 mm. **Subject:** 2004 Olympics **Obv:** Lion **Rev:** Convex chariot **Edge:** Reeded

Date	Mintage	F	VF	XF	Unc	BU
2001 Antique Finish	15,000	—	—	—	37.50	—

KM# 167 10 FRANCS
20.0000 g., 0.9250 Silver 0.5948 oz. ASW, 40.1 mm. **Obv:** Lion **Rev:** SS Bremen ship **Edge:** Reeded

Date	Mintage	F	VF	XF	Unc	BU
2001 Proof	—	Value: 30.00				

KM# 168 10 FRANCS
20.0000 g., 0.9250 Silver 0.5948 oz. ASW, 40.1 mm. **Obv:** Lion **Rev:** RMS Queen Elizabeth 2 **Edge:** Reeded

Date	Mintage	F	VF	XF	Unc	BU
2001 Proof	—	Value: 30.00				

KM# 169 10 FRANCS
20.0000 g., 0.9250 Silver 0.5948 oz. ASW, 30 mm. **Obv:** Lion **Rev:** Sail Ship America **Edge:** Reeded

Date	Mintage	F	VF	XF	Unc	BU
2001 Proof	—	Value: 30.00				

KM# 61 10 FRANCS
25.9500 g., 0.9250 Silver .7717 oz. ASW, 39.9 mm. **Series:** Wild Life Protection **Obv:** Lion **Rev:** Multicolor red and black butterfly hologram **Edge:** Reeded **Note:** Prev. KM#84.

Date	Mintage	F	VF	XF	Unc	BU
2002 (2001) Proof	15,000	Value: 65.00				

KM# 65 10 FRANCS
20.0000 g., 0.9250 Silver 0.5948 oz. ASW, 40.1 mm. **Series:** Airplanes **Obv:** Lion **Rev:** Vickers Vimy twin engine biplane **Edge:** Reeded **Note:** Prev. KM#88.

Date	Mintage	F	VF	XF	Unc	BU
2001 Proof	—	Value: 40.00				

KM# 66 10 FRANCS
20.0000 g., 0.9250 Silver 0.5948 oz. ASW, 40.1 mm. **Series:** Airplanes **Obv:** Lion **Rev:** Fokker DR1 triplane **Edge:** Reeded **Note:** Prev. KM#89.

Date	Mintage	F	VF	XF	Unc	BU
2001 Proof	—	Value: 40.00				

KM# 67 10 FRANCS
20.0000 g., 0.9250 Silver 0.5948 oz. ASW, 40.1 mm. **Series:** Airplanes **Obv:** Lion **Rev:** Lockheed Vega **Edge:** Reeded **Note:** Prev. KM#90.

Date	Mintage	F	VF	XF	Unc	BU
2001 Proof	—	Value: 40.00				

KM# 68 10 FRANCS
20.0000 g., 0.9250 Silver 0.5948 oz. ASW, 40.1 mm. **Series:** Airplanes **Obv:** Lion **Rev:** Boeing 314 Clipper **Edge:** Reeded **Note:** Prev. KM#91.

Date	Mintage	F	VF	XF	Unc	BU
2001 Proof	—	Value: 40.00				

KM# 69 10 FRANCS
20.0000 g., 0.9250 Silver 0.5948 oz. ASW, 40.1 mm. **Series:** Airplanes **Obv:** Lion **Rev:** Junkers JU-87 Stuka in a dive **Edge:** Reeded **Note:** Prev. KM#92.

Date	Mintage	F	VF	XF	Unc	BU
2001 Proof	—	Value: 40.00				

KM# 70 10 FRANCS
20.0000 g., 0.9250 Silver 0.5948 oz. ASW, 40.1 mm. **Series:** Airplanes **Obv:** Lion **Rev:** B-29 Enola Gay **Edge:** Reeded **Note:** Prev. KM#93.

Date	Mintage	F	VF	XF	Unc	BU
2001 Proof	—	Value: 40.00				

KM# 71 10 FRANCS
20.0000 g., 0.9250 Silver 0.5948 oz. ASW, 40.1 mm. **Series:** Airplanes **Obv:** Lion **Rev:** Bell X-1 rocket plane **Edge:** Reeded **Note:** Prev. KM#94.

Date	Mintage	F	VF	XF	Unc	BU
2001 Proof	—	Value: 40.00				

KM# 38 10 FRANCS
31.3000 g., 0.9250 Silver .9308 oz. ASW, 27 x 47.1 mm. **Subject:** Illusion **Obv:** Lion **Rev:** Multicolor couple in flower picture **Edge:** Plain **Shape:** Rectangular **Note:** Prev. KM#61.

Date	Mintage	F	VF	XF	Unc	BU
2001 Proof	—	Value: 50.00				

KM# 59 10 FRANCS
25.9500 g., 0.9250 Silver .7717 oz. ASW, 39.9 mm. **Series:** Wild Life Protection **Obv:** Lion **Rev:** Multicolor swallowtail butterfly hologram **Edge:** Reeded **Note:** Prev. KM#82.

Date	Mintage	F	VF	XF	Unc	BU
2002 (2001) Proof	15,000	Value: 65.00				

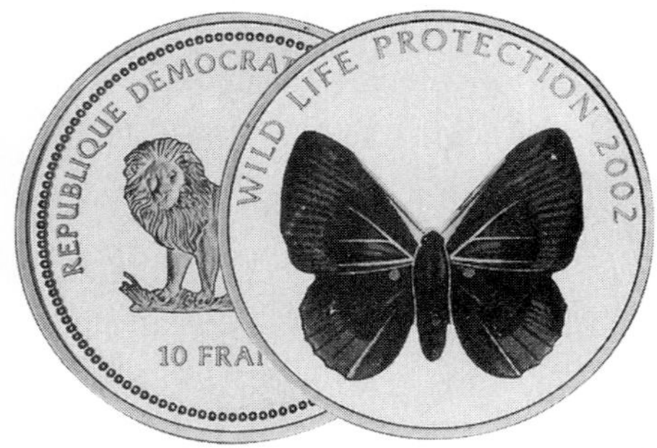

KM# 60 10 FRANCS
25.9500 g., 0.9250 Silver .7717 oz. ASW, 39.9 mm.
Series: Wild Life Protection **Obv:** Lion **Rev:** Multicolor dark greenish butterfly hologram **Edge:** Reeded **Note:** Prev. KM#83.

Date	Mintage	F	VF	XF	Unc	BU
2002 (2001) Proof	15,000	Value: 65.00				

KM# 175 10 FRANCS
25.8300 g., Silver, 40 mm. **Obv:** Lion **Rev:** 3 players **Edge:** Reeded

Date	Mintage	F	VF	XF	Unc	BU
2001	—	—	—	—	—	50.00

KM# 91 10 FRANCS
31.1000 g., 0.9990 Silver 0.9989 oz. ASW, 40 mm.
Subject: Olympics **Obv:** Lion **Rev:** Ancient athlete incuse design **Edge:** Plain **Note:** Design hubs with the design of the 500 sika coin KM-42 of Ghana

Date	Mintage	F	VF	XF	Unc	BU
2002 Antiqued finish	—	—	—	—	37.50	—

KM# 124 10 FRANCS
26.0000 g., 0.9250 Silver 0.7732 oz. ASW, 40 mm.
Subject: Field Marshal Erwin Rommel **Obv:** Lion above value **Rev:** Rommel, tank and map **Edge:** Reeded

Date	Mintage	F	VF	XF	Unc	BU
2002 Proof	15,000	Value: 40.00				

KM# 125 10 FRANCS
26.0000 g., 0.9250 Silver 0.7732 oz. ASW, 40 mm.
Subject: Field Marshal Erwin Rommel **Obv:** Lion above value **Rev:** Patton, tank and map **Edge:** Reeded

Date	Mintage	F	VF	XF	Unc	BU
2002 Proof	15,000	Value: 40.00				

KM# 162 10 FRANCS
20.2000 g., 0.9990 Silver 0.6488 oz. ASW, 40 mm. **Obv:** Lion **Rev:** Space shuttle and five astronauts **Edge:** Reeded

Date	Mintage	F	VF	XF	Unc	BU
2002 Proof	—	Value: 40.00				

KM# 93 10 FRANCS
31.2300 g., 0.9990 Silver 1.0031 oz. ASW, 38.7 mm. **Obv:** Lion **Rev:** Bearded portrait of Verney L. Camereon **Edge:** Reeded

Date	Mintage	F	VF	XF	Unc	BU
2002	—	—	—	—	35.00	40.00

KM# 94 10 FRANCS
26.1500 g., Copper Nickel, 40.3 mm. **Subject:** Historic Automobiles **Obv:** Lion **Rev:** 1908 Berliet car **Edge:** Reeded

Date	Mintage	F	VF	XF	Unc	BU
2002 Proof	—	Value: 18.00				

KM# 95 10 FRANCS
26.1500 g., Copper Nickel, 40.3 mm. **Subject:** Historic Automobiles **Obv:** Lion **Rev:** 1919 Hispano Suiza H6 car **Edge:** Reeded

Date	Mintage	F	VF	XF	Unc	BU
2002 Proof	—	Value: 18.00				

KM# 96 10 FRANCS
32.0000 g., Silver Plated Copper, 40 mm. **Subject:** World Cup Soccer **Obv:** Lion **Rev:** Soccer player and multicolor American flag **Edge:** Reeded

Date	Mintage	F	VF	XF	Unc	BU
2002 Proof	20,000	Value: 50.00				

KM# 97 10 FRANCS
32.0000 g., Silver Plated Copper, 40 mm. **Subject:** World Cup Soccer **Obv:** Lion **Rev:** Two soccer players and multicolor flag of Ecuador **Edge:** Reeded

Date	Mintage	F	VF	XF	Unc	BU
2002 Proof	20,000	Value: 50.00				

KM# 103 10 FRANCS
19.0000 g., 0.9990 Silver 0.6103 oz. ASW, 40 mm. **Subject:** Gotha Ursinus G **Obv:** Lion **Rev:** WWI German bomber **Edge:** Reeded

Date	Mintage	F	VF	XF	Unc	BU
2002 Proof	—	Value: 40.00				

KM# 104 10 FRANCS
19.0000 g., 0.9990 Silver 0.6103 oz. ASW, 40 mm. **Obv:** Lion **Rev:** WWII ME 109 German fighter plane **Edge:** Reeded

Date	Mintage	F	VF	XF	Unc	BU
2002 Proof	—	Value: 40.00				

KM# 105 10 FRANCS
19.0000 g., 0.9990 Silver 0.6103 oz. ASW, 40 mm. **Obv:** Lion **Rev:** Savoia-Marchetti S 55 flying seaplane **Edge:** Reeded

Date	Mintage	F	VF	XF	Unc	BU
2002 Proof	—	Value: 40.00				

KM# 106 10 FRANCS
19.0000 g., 0.9990 Silver 0.6103 oz. ASW, 40 mm. **Obv:** Lion **Rev:** B-58 Hustler Delta wing bomber in flight **Edge:** Reeded

Date	Mintage	F	VF	XF	Unc	BU
2002 Proof	—	Value: 40.00				

KM# 107 10 FRANCS
19.0000 g., 0.9990 Silver 0.6103 oz. ASW, 40 mm. **Obv:** Lion **Rev:** CF-105 Arrow jet fighter plane in flight **Edge:** Reeded

Date	Mintage	F	VF	XF	Unc	BU
2002 Proof	—	Value: 40.00				

KM# 108 10 FRANCS
19.0000 g., 0.9990 Silver 0.6103 oz. ASW, 40 mm. **Obv:** Lion **Rev:** XB-70 Valkyrie experimental jet bomber in flight **Edge:** Reeded

Date	Mintage	F	VF	XF	Unc	BU
2002 Proof	—	Value: 40.00				

KM# 109 10 FRANCS
19.0000 g., 0.9990 Silver 0.6103 oz. ASW, 40 mm. **Obv:** Lion **Rev:** 14 BIS early aircraft in flight **Edge:** Reeded

Date	Mintage	F	VF	XF	Unc	BU
2003 Proof	—	Value: 40.00				

KM# 110 10 FRANCS
19.0000 g., 0.9990 Silver 0.6103 oz. ASW, 40 mm. **Obv:** Lion **Rev:** WWI Sopwith Camel fighter plane **Edge:** Reeded

Date	Mintage	F	VF	XF	Unc	BU
2003 Proof	—	Value: 40.00				

KM# 111 10 FRANCS
19.0000 g., 0.9990 Silver 0.6103 oz. ASW, 40 mm. **Obv:** Lion **Rev:** Curtiss NC-4 early seaplane **Edge:** Reeded

Date	Mintage	F	VF	XF	Unc	BU
2003 Proof	—	Value: 40.00				

KM# 112 10 FRANCS
19.0000 g., 0.9990 Silver 0.6103 oz. ASW, 40 mm. **Obv:** Lion **Rev:** Macchi-Castoldi MC-72 seaplane **Edge:** Reeded

Date	Mintage	F	VF	XF	Unc	BU
2003 Proof	—	Value: 40.00				

KM# 113 10 FRANCS
19.0000 g., 0.9990 Silver 0.6103 oz. ASW, 40 mm. **Obv:** Lion **Rev:** WWII CA-12 Boomerang fighter plane **Edge:** Reeded

Date	Mintage	F	VF	XF	Unc	BU
2003 Proof	—	Value: 40.00				

KM# 114 10 FRANCS
19.0000 g., 0.9990 Silver 0.6103 oz. ASW, 40 mm. **Obv:** Lion **Rev:** B-50A Superfortress bomber in flight **Edge:** Reeded

Date	Mintage	F	VF	XF	Unc	BU
2003 Proof	—	Value: 40.00				

KM# 115 10 FRANCS
19.0000 g., 0.9990 Silver 0.6103 oz. ASW, 40 mm. **Obv:** Lion **Rev:** WWII Heinkel-178 German jet plane **Edge:** Reeded

Date	Mintage	F	VF	XF	Unc	BU
2003 Proof	—	Value: 40.00				

KM# 116 10 FRANCS
19.0000 g., 0.9990 Silver 0.6103 oz. ASW, 40 mm. **Obv:** Lion **Rev:** Early De Havilland Comet jet liner **Edge:** Reeded

Date	Mintage	F	VF	XF	Unc	BU
2003 Proof	—	Value: 40.00				

KM# 117 10 FRANCS
19.0000 g., 0.9990 Silver 0.6103 oz. ASW, 40 mm. **Obv:** Lion **Rev:** Panavia Tornado jet fighter-bomber **Edge:** Reeded

Date	Mintage	F	VF	XF	Unc	BU
2003 Proof	—	Value: 40.00				

KM# 118 10 FRANCS
19.0000 g., 0.9990 Silver 0.6103 oz. ASW, 40 mm. **Obv:** Lion **Rev:** Hindustan HF24 jet fighter **Edge:** Reeded

Date	Mintage	F	VF	XF	Unc	BU
2003 Proof	—	Value: 40.00				

KM# 119 10 FRANCS
19.0000 g., 0.9990 Silver 0.6103 oz. ASW, 40 mm. **Obv:** Lion **Rev:** Lockheed F-117 Stealth fighter **Edge:** Reeded

Date	Mintage	F	VF	XF	Unc	BU
2003 Proof	—	Value: 40.00				

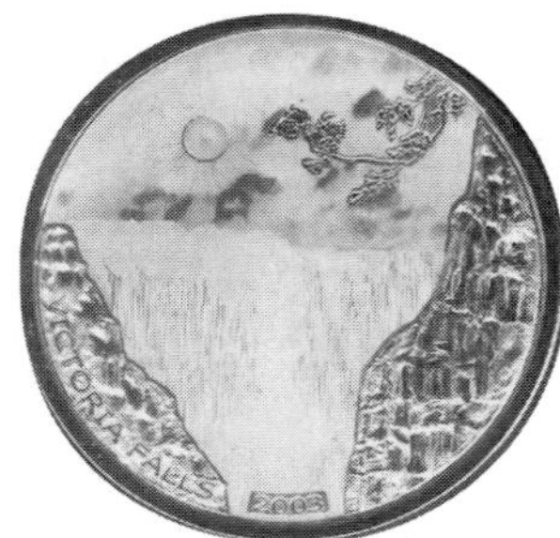

KM# 120 10 FRANCS
19.0000 g., 0.9990 Silver 0.6103 oz. ASW, 40 mm. **Obv:** Lion **Rev:** North American X-15 experimental rocket plane **Edge:** Reeded

Date	Mintage	F	VF	XF	Unc	BU
2003 Proof	—	Value: 40.00				

KM# 122 10 FRANCS
25.0000 g., 0.9250 Silver 0.7435 oz. ASW, 38.6 mm. **Obv:** Lion **Rev:** Multicolor 3D hologram view of Victoria Falls **Edge:** Reeded

Date	Mintage	F	VF	XF	Unc	BU
2003 Proof	5,000	Value: 40.00				

KM# 99.1 10 FRANCS
24.9100 g., 0.9250 Silver 0.7408 oz. ASW, 38.6 mm. **Obv:** Lion **Rev:** Chameleon **Edge:** Reeded

Date	Mintage	F	VF	XF	Unc	BU
2003 Proof	—	Value: 40.00				

KM# 99.2 10 FRANCS
24.9100 g., 0.9250 Silver 0.7408 oz. ASW, 38.6 mm. **Obv:** Lion **Rev:** Multicolor chameleon **Edge:** Reeded

Date	Mintage	F	VF	XF	Unc	BU
2003 Proof	—	Value: 50.00				

KM# 100 10 FRANCS
24.9100 g., 0.9250 Silver 0.7408 oz. ASW, 38.6 mm. **Obv:** Lion **Rev:** Skunk **Edge:** Reeded

Date	Mintage	F	VF	XF	Unc	BU
2003 Proof	—	Value: 40.00				

KM# 101 10 FRANCS
24.9100 g., 0.9250 Silver 0.7408 oz. ASW, 38.6 mm. **Obv:** Lion **Rev:** Porcupine **Edge:** Reeded

Date	Mintage	F	VF	XF	Unc	BU
2003 Proof	—	Value: 37.50				

KM# 102 10 FRANCS
24.9100 g., 0.9250 Silver 0.7408 oz. ASW, 38.6 mm. **Obv:** Lion **Rev:** Giant anteater **Edge:** Reeded

Date	Mintage	F	VF	XF	Unc	BU
2003 Proof	—	Value: 40.00				

KM# 132 10 FRANCS
25.0000 g., 0.9000 Silver 0.7234 oz. ASW, 40 mm. **Obv:** Lion **Rev:** Multicolor dolphin **Edge:** Reeded

Date	Mintage	F	VF	XF	Unc	BU
2003 Proof	5,000	Value: 50.00				

KM# 133 10 FRANCS
25.0000 g., 0.9000 Silver 0.7234 oz. ASW, 40 mm. **Obv:** Lion **Rev:** Multicolor sea turtle **Edge:** Reeded

Date	Mintage	F	VF	XF	Unc	BU
2003 Proof	5,000	Value: 50.00				

KM# 134 10 FRANCS
25.0000 g., 0.9000 Silver 0.7234 oz. ASW, 40 mm. **Obv:** Lion **Rev:** Multicolor killer whale **Edge:** Reeded

Date	Mintage	F	VF	XF	Unc	BU
2003 Proof	5,000	Value: 50.00				

KM# 135 10 FRANCS
26.0000 g., 0.9990 Silver 0.8351 oz. ASW, 40 mm. **Obv:** Lion **Rev:** Pope John Paul II **Edge:** Reeded

Date	Mintage	F	VF	XF	Unc	BU
2003 Proof	—	Value: 50.00				

KM# 163 10 FRANCS
39.1000 g., Acrylic, 49.9 mm. **Obv:** Butterfly above lion and value **Rev:** Rear view of the obverse **Edge:** Plain

Date	Mintage	F	VF	XF	Unc	BU
2003	—	—	—	—	75.00	—

KM# 171 10 FRANCS
39.1000 g., Acrylic, 49.9 mm. **Obv:** Gorch Fock sail ship above lion and value **Rev:** Rear view of the obverse design **Edge:** Plain

Date	Mintage	F	VF	XF	Unc	BU
2003	1,000	—	—	—	75.00	—

KM# 126 10 FRANCS

25.0000 g., 0.9250 Silver 0.7435 oz. ASW, 38.6 mm. **Obv:** Lion above value **Rev:** Sundial face with collapsible gnomon **Edge:** Reeded

Date	Mintage	F	VF	XF	Unc	BU
2004 Proof	5,000	Value: 50.00				

KM# 127 10 FRANCS

25.0000 g., 0.9250 Silver 0.7435 oz. ASW, 38.6 mm. **Obv:** Lion above value **Rev:** Compass face **Edge:** Reeded **Note:** Compass part of the Compass and Spoon set

Date	Mintage	F	VF	XF	Unc	BU
2004 Proof	5,000	Value: 50.00				

KM# 141 10 FRANCS

25.0000 g., 0.9250 Silver 0.7435 oz. ASW, 38.6 mm. **Obv:** Lion **Rev:** Multicolor Emperor fish **Edge:** Reeded

Date	Mintage	F	VF	XF	Unc	BU
2004 Proof	5,000	Value: 45.00				

KM# 142 10 FRANCS

25.0000 g., 0.9250 Silver 0.7435 oz. ASW, 38.6 mm. **Obv:** Lion **Rev:** Multicolor octopus **Edge:** Reeded

Date	Mintage	F	VF	XF	Unc	BU
2004 Proof	5,000	Value: 50.00				

KM# 143 10 FRANCS

25.0000 g., 0.9250 Silver 0.7435 oz. ASW, 38.6 mm. **Obv:** Lion **Rev:** Formula 1 and GT race cars **Edge:** Reeded

Date	Mintage	F	VF	XF	Unc	BU
2004 Proof	5,000	Value: 45.00				

KM# 145 10 FRANCS

25.0000 g., 0.9250 Silver 0.7435 oz. ASW, 27x47 mm. **Obv:** Lion **Rev:** Pope with crucifix **Edge:** Plain

Date	Mintage	F	VF	XF	Unc	BU
2004 Proof	5,000	Value: 45.00				

KM# 149 10 FRANCS

25.0000 g., 0.9250 Silver 0.7435 oz. ASW, 38.6 mm. **Obv:** Lion **Rev:** Multicolor Quetzal bird **Edge:** Reeded

Date	Mintage	F	VF	XF	Unc	BU
2004 Proof	5,000	Value: 45.00				

KM# 150 10 FRANCS

25.0000 g., 0.9250 Silver 0.7435 oz. ASW, 38.6 mm. **Obv:** Lion **Rev:** Multicolor Bird of Paradise **Edge:** Reeded

Date	Mintage	F	VF	XF	Unc	BU
2004 Proof	5,000	Value: 45.00				

KM# 151 10 FRANCS

25.0000 g., 0.9250 Silver 0.7435 oz. ASW, 38.6 mm. **Obv:** Lion **Rev:** Multicolor Kingfisher bird **Edge:** Reeded

Date	Mintage	F	VF	XF	Unc	BU
2004 Proof	5,000	Value: 45.00				

KM# 155 10 FRANCS

Acrylic Clear, 50 mm. **Obv:** Etched nine-masted sailing junk above lion, value and country name **Edge:** Plain

Date	Mintage	F	VF	XF	Unc	BU
2004	2,000	—	—	—	25.00	—

KM# 172 10 FRANCS

25.0000 g., Silver, 38.6 mm. **Obv:** Lion **Rev:** Pope waving half facing at left, cross at upper right, Vatican at lower right

Date	Mintage	F	VF	XF	Unc	BU
2005 Proof	3,000	Value: 50.00				

KM# 136 20 FRANCS

1.2440 g., 0.9999 Gold 0.04 oz. AGW, 13.92 mm. **Obv:** Lion **Rev:** Pope John Paul II **Edge:** Plain

Date	Mintage	F	VF	XF	Unc	BU
2003 Proof	—	Value: 55.00				

KM# 137 20 FRANCS

1.2440 g., 0.9999 Gold 0.04 oz. AGW, 13.92 mm. **Obv:** Lion **Rev:** Skunk **Edge:** Plain

Date	Mintage	F	VF	XF	Unc	BU
2003 Proof	25,000	Value: 55.00				

KM# 138 20 FRANCS

1.2440 g., 0.9999 Gold 0.04 oz. AGW, 13.92 mm. **Obv:** Lion **Rev:** Giant anteater **Edge:** Plain

Date	Mintage	F	VF	XF	Unc	BU
2003 Proof	25,000	Value: 55.00				

KM# 139 20 FRANCS

1.2440 g., 0.9999 Gold 0.04 oz. AGW, 13.92 mm. **Obv:** Lion **Rev:** Porcupine **Edge:** Plain

Date	Mintage	F	VF	XF	Unc	BU
2003 Proof	25,000	Value: 55.00				

KM# 140 20 FRANCS

1.2440 g., 0.9999 Gold 0.04 oz. AGW, 13.92 mm. **Obv:** Lion **Rev:** Chameleon **Edge:** Plain

Date	Mintage	F	VF	XF	Unc	BU
2003 Proof	25,000	Value: 55.00				

KM# 144 20 FRANCS
1.2440 g., 0.9999 Gold 0.04 oz. AGW, 13.92 mm. **Obv:** Lion **Rev:** Ferrari coat of arms **Edge:** Plain

Date	Mintage	F	VF	XF	Unc	BU
2004 Proof	5,000	Value: 55.00				

KM# 173 20 FRANCS
1.5300 g., 0.9990 Gold 0.0491 oz. AGW, 13.9 mm. **Obv:** Lion **Rev:** Pope waving at left, cross at upper right, Vatican at lower right

Date	Mintage	F	VF	XF	Unc	BU
2005 Proof	25,000	Value: 60.00				

KM# 129 100 FRANCS
31.1000 g., 0.9999 Gold 0.9998 oz. AGW, 40 mm. **Obv:** Lion **Rev:** Reflective multicolor swallowtail butterfly **Edge:** Reeded

Date	Mintage	F	VF	XF	Unc	BU
2002 Proof	50	Value: 1,000				

KM# 130 100 FRANCS
31.1000 g., 0.9999 Gold 0.9998 oz. AGW, 40 mm. **Obv:** Lion **Rev:** Reflective multicolor dark greenish butterfly **Edge:** Reeded

Date	Mintage	F	VF	XF	Unc	BU
2002 Proof	50	Value: 1,000				

KM# 131 100 FRANCS
31.1000 g., 0.9999 Gold 0.9998 oz. AGW, 40 mm. **Obv:** Lion **Rev:** Reflective multicolor red and black butterfly **Edge:** Reeded

Date	Mintage	F	VF	XF	Unc	BU
2002 Proof	50	Value: 1,000				

KM# 152 100 FRANCS
31.1035 g., 0.9999 Gold 0.9999 oz. AGW, 38.6 mm. **Obv:** Lion **Rev:** Multicolor Quetzal bird **Edge:** Reeded

Date	Mintage	F	VF	XF	Unc	BU
2004 Proof	25	Value: 1,200				

KM# 153 100 FRANCS
31.1035 g., 0.9999 Gold 0.9999 oz. AGW, 38.6 mm. **Obv:** Lion **Rev:** Multicolor Bird of Paradise **Edge:** Reeded

Date	Mintage	F	VF	XF	Unc	BU
2004 Proof	25	Value: 1,200				

KM# 154 100 FRANCS
31.1035 g., 0.9999 Gold 0.9999 oz. AGW, 38.6 mm. **Obv:** Lion **Rev:** Multicolor Kingfisher bird **Edge:** Reeded

Date	Mintage	F	VF	XF	Unc	BU
2004 Proof	25	Value: 1,200				

COOK ISLANDS

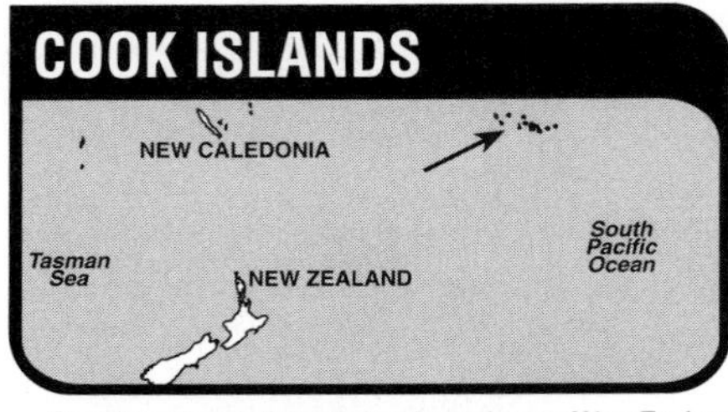

Cook Islands, a self-governing dependency of New Zealand consisting of 15 islands, is located in the South Pacific Ocean about 2,000 miles (3,218 km.) northeast of New Zealand. It has an area of 93 sq. mi. (234 sq. km.) and a population of 17,185. Capital: Avarua. The United States claims the islands of Danger, Manahiki, Penrhyn, and Rakahanga atolls. Citrus and canned fruits and juices, copra, clothing, jewelry, and mother-of-pearl shell are exported.

RULERS
British

MINT MARKS
PM - Pobjoy Mint

MONETARY SYSTEM
100 Cents = 1 Dollar

DEPENDENCY OF NEW ZEALAND

DECIMAL COINAGE

KM# 419 CENT
1.4400 g., Aluminum, 21.9 mm. **Obv:** Queen Elizabeth II **Rev:** Capt. James Cook **Edge:** Plain

Date	Mintage	F	VF	XF	Unc	BU
2003	—	—	—	—	1.50	1.75

KM# 420 CENT
1.4400 g., Aluminum, 21.9 mm. **Obv:** Queen Elizabeth II **Rev:** Collie dog **Edge:** Plain

Date	Mintage	F	VF	XF	Unc	BU
2003	—	—	—	—	1.00	1.25

KM# 421 CENT
1.4400 g., Aluminum, 21.9 mm. **Obv:** Queen Elizabeth II **Rev:** Pointer dog **Edge:** Plain

Date	Mintage	F	VF	XF	Unc	BU
2003	—	—	—	—	1.00	1.25

KM# 422 CENT
1.4400 g., Aluminum, 21.9 mm. **Obv:** Queen Elizabeth II **Rev:** Rooster **Edge:** Plain

Date	Mintage	F	VF	XF	Unc	BU
2003	—	—	—	—	1.00	1.25

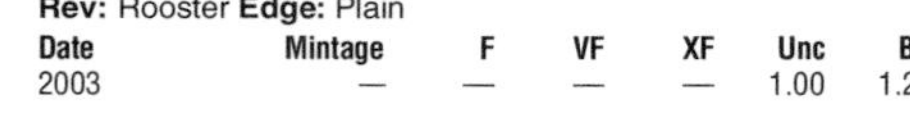

KM# 423 CENT
1.4400 g., Aluminum, 22 mm. **Obv:** Queen Elizabeth II **Rev:** Monkey on branch **Edge:** Plain

Date	Mintage	F	VF	XF	Unc	BU
2003	—	—	—	—	1.00	1.25

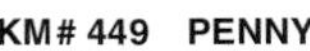

KM# 449 PENNY
0.4800 g., 0.9990 Silver 0.0154 oz. ASW, 11.1 mm. **Subject:** Maundy **Obv:** Elizabeth II **Rev:** Crowned value **Edge:** Plain

Date	Mintage	F	VF	XF	Unc	BU
2002 Proof	—	Value: 15.00				

KM# 450 2 PENCE
0.9400 g., 0.9990 Silver 0.0302 oz. ASW, 13.4 mm. **Subject:** Maundy **Obv:** Elizabeth II **Rev:** Crowned value **Edge:** Plain

Date	Mintage	F	VF	XF	Unc	BU
2002 Proof	—	Value: 20.00				

KM# 451 3 PENCE
1.4400 g., 0.9990 Silver 0.0463 oz. ASW, 16.1 mm. **Subject:** Maundy **Obv:** Elizabeth II **Rev:** Crowned value **Edge:** Plain

Date	Mintage	F	VF	XF	Unc	BU
2002 Proof	—	Value: 25.00				

KM# 452 4 PENCE
1.9300 g., 0.9990 Silver 0.062 oz. ASW, 17.5 mm. **Subject:** Maundy **Obv:** Elizabeth II **Rev:** Crowned value **Edge:** Plain

Date	Mintage	F	VF	XF	Unc	BU
2002 Proof	—	Value: 30.00				

KM# 396 DOLLAR
24.8828 g., 0.9990 Silver with Acrylic capsule center containing tiny rubies, sapphires and cubic zirconias 0.7992 oz. ASW, 40.6 mm. **Subject:** Crown Jewels **Obv:** Queen's portrait and legend **Rev:** Crowns and royal regalia **Edge:** Reeded

Date	Mintage	F	VF	XF	Unc	BU
2002 Proof	50,000	Value: 12.50				

KM# 416 DOLLAR
10.7500 g., Copper-Nickel, 28.5 mm. **Obv:** Queen's new portrait **Rev:** Tangaroa statue and value **Edge:** Scalloped

Date	Mintage	F	VF	XF	Unc	BU
2003	—	—	—	—	3.00	3.50

KM# 424 DOLLAR
8.5000 g., 0.9990 Silver 0.273 oz. ASW, 25.1 mm. **Subject:** Zodiac Gemstones - Cancer **Obv:** Queen Elizabeth II above ornamental center **Rev:** Encapsulated emeralds above Crab (Cancer) **Edge:** Reeded

Date	Mintage	F	VF	XF	Unc	BU
ND(2003) Proof	10,000	Value: 25.00				

KM# 424a DOLLAR
8.5000 g., 0.9990 Gold Plated Silver 0.273 oz. ASW, 25.1 mm.

Date	Mintage	F	VF	XF	Unc	BU
ND(2003) Proof	10,000	Value: 30.00				

KM# 425 DOLLAR
8.5000 g., 0.9990 Silver 0.273 oz. ASW, 25.1 mm. **Subject:** Zodiac Gemstones - Aquarius **Obv:** Queen Elizabeth II above ornamental center **Rev:** Encapsulated garnets with Aquarious in background **Edge:** Reeded

Date	Mintage	F	VF	XF	Unc	BU
ND(2004) Proof	10,000	Value: 25.00				

KM# 425a DOLLAR
8.5000 g., 0.9990 Gold Plated Silver 0.273 oz. ASW, 25.1 mm.

Date	Mintage	F	VF	XF	Unc	BU
ND(2003) Proof	10,000	Value: 30.00				

KM# 426 DOLLAR
8.5000 g., 0.9990 Silver 0.273 oz. ASW, 25.1 mm. **Subject:** Zodiac Gemstones - Aries **Obv:** Queen Elizabeth II above ornamental center **Rev:** Encapsulated Bloodstones in center with ram at left **Edge:** Reeded

Date	Mintage	F	VF	XF	Unc	BU
ND(2003) Proof	10,000	Value: 25.00				

KM# 426a DOLLAR
8.5000 g., 0.9990 Gold Plated Silver 0.273 oz. ASW, 25.1 mm.

Date	Mintage	F	VF	XF	Unc	BU
ND(2003) Proof	10,000	Value: 30.00				

KM# 427 DOLLAR
8.5000 g., 0.9990 Silver 0.273 oz. ASW, 25.1 mm. **Subject:** Zodiac Gemstones - Taurus **Obv:** Queen Elizabeth II above ornamental center **Rev:** Encapsulated Sapphires with bull in background **Edge:** Reeded

Date	Mintage	F	VF	XF	Unc	BU
ND(2003) Proof	10,000	Value: 25.00				

KM# 427a DOLLAR
8.5000 g., 0.9990 Gold Plated Silver 0.273 oz. ASW, 25.1 mm. **Subject:** Zodiac Gemstones - Taurus **Obv:** Queen Elizabeth II above ornamental center **Rev:** Encapsulated Sapphires with bull in background **Edge:** Reeded

Date	Mintage	F	VF	XF	Unc	BU
ND(2003) Proof	10,000	Value: 30.00				

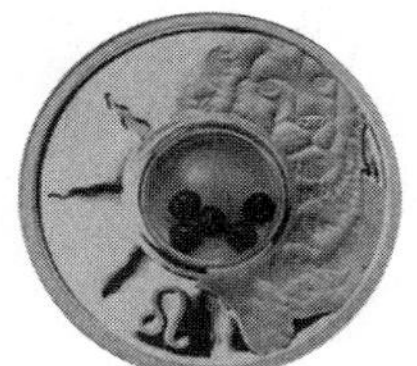

KM# 428 DOLLAR
8.5000 g., 0.9990 Silver 0.273 oz. ASW, 25.1 mm. **Obv:** Queen Elizabeth II above ornamental center **Rev:** Encapsulated Agates between twins **Edge:** Reeded

Date	Mintage	F	VF	XF	Unc	BU
ND(2003) Proof	10,000	Value: 25.00				

KM# 428a DOLLAR
8.5000 g., 0.9990 Gold Plated Silver 0.273 oz. ASW, 25.1 mm. **Obv:** Queen Elizabeth II above ornamental center **Rev:** Encapsulated Agates between twins **Edge:** Reeded

Date	Mintage	F	VF	XF	Unc	BU
ND(2003) Proof	10,000	Value: 30.00				

KM# 429 DOLLAR
8.5000 g., 0.9990 Silver 0.273 oz. ASW, 25.1 mm. **Obv:** Queen Elizabeth II above ornamental center **Rev:** Encapsulated Onyx stones with lion at right **Edge:** Reeded

Date	Mintage	F	VF	XF	Unc	BU
ND(2003) Proof	10,000	Value: 25.00				

KM# 429a DOLLAR
8.5000 g., 0.9990 Gold Plated Silver 0.273 oz. ASW, 25.1 mm. **Obv:** Queen Elizabeth II above ornamental center **Rev:** Encapsulated Onyx stones with lion at right **Edge:** Reeded

Date	Mintage	F	VF	XF	Unc	BU
ND(2003) Proof	10,000	Value: 30.00				

KM# 430 DOLLAR
8.5000 g., 0.9990 Silver 0.273 oz. ASW, 25.1 mm. **Subject:** Zodiac Gemstones - Virgo **Obv:** Queen Elizabeth II above ornamented center **Rev:** Encapsulated Carnelian stones with woman at right **Edge:** Reeded

Date	Mintage	F	VF	XF	Unc	BU
ND(2003) Proof	10,000	Value: 25.00				

KM# 430a DOLLAR
8.5000 g., 0.9990 Gold Plated Silver 0.273 oz. ASW, 25.1 mm. **Subject:** Zodiac Gemstones - Virgo **Obv:** Queen Elizabeth II above ornamented center **Rev:** Encapsulated Carnelian stones with Virgo at right **Edge:** Reeded

Date	Mintage	F	VF	XF	Unc	BU
ND(2003) Proof	10,000	Value: 30.00				

KM# 431 DOLLAR
8.5000 g., 0.9990 Silver 0.273 oz. ASW, 25.1 mm. **Subject:** Zodiac Gemstones - Libra **Obv:** Queen Elizabeth II above ornamented center **Rev:** Encapsulated Peridot stones with balance scale **Edge:** Reeded

Date	Mintage	F	VF	XF	Unc	BU
ND(2003) Proof	10,000	Value: 25.00				

KM# 431a DOLLAR
8.5000 g., 0.9990 Gold Plated Silver 0.273 oz. ASW, 25.1 mm. **Subject:** Zodiac Gemstones - Libra **Obv:** Queen Elizabeth II above ornamented center **Rev:** Encapsulated Peridot stones with balance scale **Edge:** Reeded

Date	Mintage	F	VF	XF	Unc	BU
ND(2003) Proof	10,000	Value: 30.00				

KM# 432 DOLLAR
8.5000 g., 0.9990 Silver 0.273 oz. ASW, 25.1 mm. **Subject:** Zodiac Gemstones - Scorpio **Obv:** Queen Elizabeth II above ornamented center **Rev:** Encapsulated Aquamarine stones with scorpion at lower right **Edge:** Reeded

Date	Mintage	F	VF	XF	Unc	BU
ND(2003) Proof	10,000	Value: 25.00				

KM# 432a DOLLAR
8.5000 g., 0.9990 Gold Plated Silver 0.273 oz. ASW, 25.1 mm. **Subject:** Zodiac Gemstones - Scorpio **Obv:** Queen Elizabeth II above ornamented center **Rev:** Encapsulated Aquamarine stones with scorpion at lower right **Edge:** Reeded

Date	Mintage	F	VF	XF	Unc	BU
ND(2003) Proof	10,000	Value: 30.00				

KM# 433 DOLLAR
8.5000 g., 0.9990 Silver 0.273 oz. ASW, 25.1 mm. **Subject:** Zodiac Gemstones - Sagittarius **Obv:** Queen Elizabeth II above ornamented center **Rev:** Encapsulated Topaz stones with centaur at right **Edge:** Reeded

Date	Mintage	F	VF	XF	Unc	BU
ND(2003) Proof	10,000	Value: 25.00				

KM# 433a DOLLAR
8.5000 g., 0.9990 Gold Plated Silver 0.273 oz. ASW, 25.1 mm. **Subject:** Zodiac Gemstones - Sagittarius **Obv:** Queen Elizabeth II above ornamented center **Rev:** Encapsulated Topaz stones with centaur at right **Edge:** Reeded

Date	Mintage	F	VF	XF	Unc	BU
ND(2003) Proof	10,000	Value: 30.00				

KM# 434 DOLLAR
8.5000 g., 0.9990 Silver 0.273 oz. ASW, 25.1 mm. **Subject:** Zodiac Gemstones - Capricorn **Obv:** Queen Elizabeth II above ornamental center **Rev:** Encapsulated rubies with goat at right **Edge:** Reeded

Date	Mintage	F	VF	XF	Unc	BU
ND(2003) Proof	10,000	Value: 25.00				

KM# 434a DOLLAR
8.5000 g., 0.9990 Gold Plated Silver 0.273 oz. ASW, 25.1 mm. **Subject:** Zodiac Gemstones - Capricorn **Obv:** Queen Elizabeth II above ornamented center **Rev:** Encapsulated Rubies with goat at right **Edge:** Reeded

Date	Mintage	F	VF	XF	Unc	BU
ND(2003) Proof	10,000	Value: 30.00				

KM# 435 DOLLAR
8.5000 g., 0.9990 Silver 0.273 oz. ASW, 25.1 mm. **Subject:** Zodiac Gemstones - Pices **Obv:** Queen Elizabeth II above ornamented center **Rev:** Encapsulated Amethyst stones and two fish **Edge:** Reeded

Date	Mintage	F	VF	XF	Unc	BU
ND(2003) Proof	10,000	Value: 25.00				

KM# 435a DOLLAR
8.5000 g., 0.9990 Gold Plated Silver 0.273 oz. ASW, 25.1 mm. **Subject:** Zodiac Gemstones - Pices **Obv:** Queen Elizabeth II above ornamented center **Rev:** Encapsulated Amethyst stones and 2 fish **Edge:** Reeded

Date	Mintage	F	VF	XF	Unc	BU
ND(2003) Proof	10,000	Value: 30.00				

KM# 438 DOLLAR
31.1035 g., 0.9990 Silver 0.999 oz. ASW, 40.5 mm.
Obv: Elizabeth II **Rev:** Multicolor Deng Xiaoping on Chinese map **Edge:** Plain **Shape:** As a map

Date	Mintage	F	VF	XF	Unc	BU
2004	20,000	—	—	—	30.00	—

KM# 454 DOLLAR
27.5300 g., 0.9990 Silver Clad Copper-Nickel, 38.6 mm.
Subject: 60th Anniversary - D-Day Invasion **Obv:** Bust of Queen Elizabeth II right **Rev:** Invasion scene of soldiers storming the beaches (Sword, Gold, Juno, Omaha, and Utah) of Normandy

Date	Mintage	F	VF	XF	Unc	BU
2004	—	—	—	—	12.00	14.00

KM# 443 DOLLAR
23.9000 g., Copper-Nickel, 38.5 mm. **Subject:** Battle of Trafalgar **Obv:** Elizabeth II **Rev:** HMS Victory and color portrait of Nelson **Edge:** Reeded

Date	Mintage	F	VF	XF	Unc	BU
2005	—	—	—	—	10.00	11.50

KM# 417 2 DOLLARS
7.5500 g., Copper-Nickel, 26 mm. **Obv:** Queen's new portrait **Rev:** Bottle on table, value above **Edge:** Triangular

Date	Mintage	F	VF	XF	Unc	BU
2003	—	—	—	—	3.00	3.50

KM# 418 5 DOLLARS
14.0000 g., Aluminum-Bronze, 31.5 mm. **Obv:** Queen's new portrait **Rev:** Conch shell and value **Shape:** 12-sided

Date	Mintage	F	VF	XF	Unc	BU
2003	—	—	—	—	7.00	9.00

KM# 453 10 DOLLARS
186.8300 g., 0.9990 Gold Plated Silver 6.0007 oz. ASW AGW, 89 mm. **Obv:** Elizabeth II above value **Rev:** Queen Victoria standing with lion **Edge:** Reeded **Note:** Illustration reduced.

Date	Mintage	F	VF	XF	Unc	BU
2003 Proof	198	Value: 315				

KM# 439 30 DOLLARS
10.0000 g., 0.9999 Gold 0.3215 oz. AGW, 16.1 mm.
Obv: Elizabeth II **Rev:** Multicolor Peony flower **Edge:** Reeded

Date	Mintage	F	VF	XF	Unc	BU
2004	10,000	—	—	—	—	225

KM# 440 35 DOLLARS
10.0000 g., 0.9999 Gold 0.3215 oz. AGW, 16.1 mm. **Obv:** Elizabeth II **Rev:** Multicolor Chinese man beating a tiger **Edge:** Reeded

Date	Mintage	F	VF	XF	Unc	BU
2004	6,000	—	—	—	—	225

KM# 441 35 DOLLARS
10.0000 g., 0.9999 Gold 0.3215 oz. AGW, 16.1 mm. **Obv:** Elizabeth II **Rev:** Multicolor Chinese man riding a horse **Edge:** Reeded

Date	Mintage	F	VF	XF	Unc	BU
2004	10,000	—	—	—	—	225

KM# 442 35 DOLLARS
10.0000 g., 0.9999 Gold 0.3215 oz. AGW, 25 x 15 mm.
Obv: Elizabeth II **Rev:** Multicolor "Eight immortals crossing the sea" **Edge:** Plain **Shape:** Ingot

Date	Mintage	F	VF	XF	Unc	BU
2004	3,000	—	—	—	—	225

KM# 397 100 DOLLARS
23.3276 g., 0.9999 Gold Acrylic capsule center containing tiny diamonds, rubies and sapphires 0.7499 oz. AGW, 32.1 mm.
Subject: Crown Jewels **Obv:** Queen's portrait and legend **Rev:** Crowns and royal regalia **Edge:** Reeded

Date	Mintage	F	VF	XF	Unc	BU
2002 Proof	5,000	Value: 500				

KM# 389 500 DOLLARS
1723.1259 g., 0.9990 Silver 55.3443 oz. ASW, 115.2 mm.
Subject: Moby Dick **Obv:** Queen's portrait **Rev:** Whale jumping over a six-man rowboat **Edge:** Plain **Note:** Illustration reduced.

Date	Mintage	F	VF	XF	Unc	BU
2001 Proof	—	Value: 850				

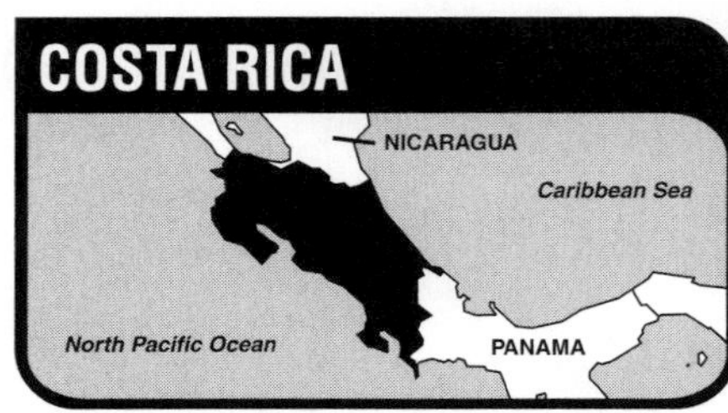

The Republic of Costa Rica, located in southern Central America between Nicaragua and Panama, has an area of 19,730 sq. mi. (51,100 sq. km.) and a population of 3.4 million. Capital: San Jose. Agriculture predominates; tourism and coffee, bananas, beef and sugar contribute heavily to the country's export earnings.

REPUBLIC

REFORM COINAGE

100 Centimos = 1 Colon

KM# 227 5 COLONES
Brass Plated Steel **Obv:** National arms **Rev:** Denomination

Date	Mintage	F	VF	XF	Unc	BU
2001	—	—	—	0.25	0.75	—

KM# 227a.1 5 COLONES
4.0000 g., Brass, 21.6 mm. **Obv:** Smaller letters in legend **Rev:** Smaller letters in legend **Edge:** Segmented reeding

Date	Mintage	F	VF	XF	Unc	BU
2001	—	—	—	—	0.65	—

KM# 229a 25 COLONES
7.0000 g., Brass, 25.4 mm. **Obv:** National arms **Rev:** Value **Edge:** Segmented reeding

Date	Mintage	F	VF	XF	Unc	BU
2001	—	—	—	—	2.50	—

KM# 239.1 500 COLONES
11.0000 g., Copper-Aluminum-Nickel, 32.9 mm. **Obv:** National arms **Rev:** Value in thick numerals **Edge:** Segmented reeding

Date	Mintage	F	VF	XF	Unc	BU
2003	—	—	—	—	3.00	—

KM# 239.2 500 COLONES
11.0000 g., Copper-Aluminum-Nickel, 32.9 mm. **Obv:** National arms **Rev:** Value in thin numerals **Edge:** Segmented reeding

Date	Mintage	F	VF	XF	Unc	BU
2003	100	—	—	120	200	—

The Republic of Croatia, (Hrvatska) bordered on the west by the Adriatic Sea and the northeast by Hungary, has an area of 21,829 sq. mi. (56,538 sq. km.) and a population of 4.7 million. Capital: Zagreb.

NOTE: Coin dates starting with 1994 are followed with a period. Example: 1994.

REPUBLIC

REFORM COINAGE

May 30, 1994 - 1000 Dinara = 1 Kuna; 100 Lipa = 1 Kuna

For the circulating minor coins, the reverse legend (name of item) is in Croatian for odd dated years and Latin for even dated years.

KM# 3 LIPA

0.7000 g., Aluminum, 17 mm. **Rev:** Ears of corn
Designer: Kuzma Kovacic

Date	Mintage	F	VF	XF	Unc	BU
2001.	2,000,000	—	—	0.20	0.50	—
2001. Proof	1,000	Value: 2.50				
2003.	1,500,000	—	—	0.20	0.50	—
2003. Proof	1,000	Value: 2.50				
2005.	—	—	—	0.20	0.50	—
2005. Proof	—	Value: 2.00				

KM# 12 LIPA

0.7000 g., Aluminum, 17 mm. **Rev:** Ears of corn
Rev. Legend: ZEA MAYS

Date	Mintage	F	VF	XF	Unc	BU
2002.	3,000,000	—	—	0.40	1.00	—
2002. Proof	1,000	Value: 2.50				
2004.	2,000,000	—	—	0.40	1.00	—
2004. Proof	2,000	Value: 1.50				

KM# 4 2 LIPE

0.9200 g., Aluminum, 19 mm. **Rev:** Grapevine

Date	Mintage	F	VF	XF	Unc	BU
2001.	2,986,000	—	—	0.40	1.00	—
2001. Proof	1,000	Value: 3.00				
2003.	2,000,000	—	—	0.40	1.00	—
2003. Proof	1,000	Value: 3.00				
2005.	—	—	—	0.40	1.00	—
2005. Proof	—	Value: 3.00				

KM# 14 2 LIPE

0.9200 g., Aluminum, 19 mm. **Rev:** Grapevine
Rev. Legend: VITIS VINIFERA **Designer:** Kuzma Kovacic

Date	Mintage	F	VF	XF	Unc	BU
2002.	2,000,000	—	—	0.80	2.00	—
2002. Proof	1,000	Value: 3.00				
2004.	2,000,000	—	—	0.80	2.00	—
2004. Proof	2,000	Value: 2.50				

KM# 5 5 LIPA

2.5000 g., Brass Plated Steel, 18 mm. **Rev:** Oak leaves
Designer: Kuzma Kovacic

Date	Mintage	F	VF	XF	Unc	BU
2001.	6,598,000	—	—	0.40	1.00	—
2001. Proof	1,000	Value: 4.00				
2003.	13,000,000	—	—	0.40	1.00	—
2003. Proof	2,000	Value: 3.50				
2005.	—	—	—	0.40	1.00	—
2005. Proof	—	Value: 3.50				

KM# 15 5 LIPA

Brass Plated Steel, 18 mm. **Rev:** Oak leaves **Rev. Legend:** QUERCUS ROBUR **Designer:** Kuzma Kovacic

Date	Mintage	F	VF	XF	Unc	BU
2002.	3,500,000	—	—	0.80	2.00	—
2002. Proof	1,000	Value: 4.00				
2004.	2,000,000	—	—	0.80	2.00	—
2004. Proof	2,000	Value: 3.00				

KM# 6 10 LIPA

Brass Plated Steel, 20 mm. **Rev:** Tobacco plant
Designer: Kuzma Kovacic

Date	Mintage	F	VF	XF	Unc	BU
2001.	31,500,000	—	—	0.40	1.50	—
2001. Proof	1,000	Value: 5.00				
2003.	12,000,000	—	—	0.40	1.50	—
2003. Proof	1,000	Value: 5.00				
2005.	—	—	—	0.40	1.50	—
2005. Proof	—	Value: 5.00				

KM# 16 10 LIPA

Brass Plated Steel, 20 mm. **Rev:** Tobacco plant **Rev. Legend:** NICOTIANA TABACUM **Designer:** Kuzma Kovacic

Date	Mintage	F	VF	XF	Unc	BU
2002.	2,000,000	—	—	0.80	2.50	—
2002. Proof	1,000	Value: 5.00				
2004.	2,000,000	—	—	0.80	2.50	—
2004. Proof	2,000	Value: 4.50				

KM# 7 20 LIPA

2.9000 g., Nickel Plated Steel, 18.5 mm. **Rev:** Olive branch
Designer: Kuzma Kovacic

Date	Mintage	F	VF	XF	Unc	BU
2001.	23,000,000	—	—	0.45	1.50	—
2001. Proof	1,000	Value: 5.00				
2003.	12,500,000	—	—	0.45	1.50	—
2003. Proof	1,000	Value: 5.00				
2005.	—	—	—	0.45	1.50	—
2005. Proof	—	Value: 5.00				

KM# 17 20 LIPA

Nickel Plated Steel **Rev:** Olive branch **Rev. Legend:** OLEA EUROPAEA

Date	Mintage	F	VF	XF	Unc	BU
2002.	2,000,000	—	—	0.80	2.50	—
2002. Proof	1,000	Value: 5.00				
2004.	2,000,000	—	—	0.80	2.50	—
2004. Proof	2,000	Value: 4.50				

KM# 8 50 LIPA

3.6500 g., Nickel Plated Steel, 20.5 mm. **Rev:** Flowers
Designer: Kuzma Kovacic

Date	Mintage	F	VF	XF	Unc	BU
2001.	5,500,000	—	—	0.60	1.50	—
2001. Proof	1,000	Value: 5.50				
2003.	8,000,000	—	—	0.60	1.50	—
2003. Proof	1,000	Value: 5.50				
2005.	—	—	—	0.60	1.50	—
2005. Proof	—	Value: 5.00				

KM# 19 50 LIPA

3.6500 g., Nickel Plated Steel, 20.5 mm. **Rev:** Flowers **Rev. Legend:** DEGENIA VELEBITICA **Designer:** Kuzma Kovacic

Date	Mintage	F	VF	XF	Unc	BU
2002.	2,000,000	—	—	0.80	2.50	—
2002. Proof	1,000	Value: 5.00				
2004.	2,000,000	—	—	0.80	2.50	—
2004. Proof	2,000	Value: 4.50				

KM# 9.1 KUNA

5.0000 g., Copper-Nickel, 22.5 mm. **Rev:** Nightingale
Designer: Kusma Kovacic

Date	Mintage	F	VF	XF	Unc	BU
2001.	1,000,000	—	—	0.75	1.50	—
2001. Proof	1,000	Value: 4.50				
2003.	2,000,000	—	—	0.75	1.50	—
2003. Proof	1,000	Value: 4.50				
2005.	—	—	—	0.75	1.50	—
2005. Proof	—	Value: 4.50				

KM# 20.1 KUNA

5.0000 g., Copper-Nickel, 22.5 mm. **Obv:** Value and marten **Rev:** Nightingale **Rev. Legend:** Error spelling "LUSCINNIA" MEGARHYNCHOS **Designer:** Kuzma Kovacic **Note:** Formerly KM-20

Date	Mintage	F	VF	XF	Unc	BU
2002.	—	—	—	—	—	—

KM# 20.2 KUNA

5.0000 g., Copper-Nickel, 22.5 mm. **Obv:** Value and marten **Rev:** Nightingale **Rev. Legend:** Correct spelling "LUSCINIA" MEGARHYNCHOS **Edge:** Reeded **Designer:** Kuzma Kovacic

Date	Mintage	F	VF	XF	Unc	BU
2002.	1,000,000	—	—	1.00	3.00	—
2002. Proof	1,000	Value: 5.00				

KM# 79 KUNA

5.0000 g., Copper Nickel **Subject:** 10th Anniversary of National Currency **Rev:** Nightingale

Date	Mintage	F	VF	XF	Unc	BU
ND(2004)	30,000	—	—	1.00	3.00	—
ND(2004) Proof	2,000	Value: 5.00				

KM# 10 2 KUNE

6.2000 g., Copper-Nickel, 24.5 mm. **Rev:** Bluefin tuna
Designer: Kuzma Kovacic

Date	Mintage	F	VF	XF	Unc	BU
2001.	1,250,000	—	—	1.00	2.00	—
2001. Proof	1,000	Value: 6.50				

Date	Mintage	F	VF	XF	Unc	BU
2003.	7,250,000	—	—	1.00	2.00	—
2003. Proof	1,000	Value: 6.50				
2005.	—	—	—	1.00	2.00	—
2005. Proof	—	Value: 6.50				

KM# 21 2 KUNE
6.2000 g., Copper-Nickel, 24.5 mm. **Rev:** Bluefin tuna **Rev. Legend:** THUNNUS - THYNNUS **Designer:** Kuzma Kovacic

Date	Mintage	F	VF	XF	Unc	BU
2002.	1,000,000	—	—	1.50	3.00	—
2002. Proof	1,000	Value: 6.00				
2004.	2,000,000	—	—	1.50	3.00	—
2004. Proof	2,000	Value: 5.50				

KM# 11 5 KUNA
Copper-Nickel **Rev:** Brown bear

Date	Mintage	F	VF	XF	Unc	BU
2001.	17,300,000	—	—	1.50	3.00	5.00
2001. Proof	1,000	Value: 8.00				
2003.	1,000,000	—	—	1.50	3.00	5.00
2003. Proof	1,000	Value: 8.00				
2005.	—	—	—	1.50	3.00	5.00
2005. Proof	—	Value: 8.00				

KM# 23 5 KUNA
Copper-Nickel **Rev:** Brown bear **Rev. Legend:** URSUS ARCTOS

Date	Mintage	F	VF	XF	Unc	BU
2002.	2,000,000	—	—	2.00	4.00	6.00
2002. Proof	1,000	Value: 9.00				
2004.	2,000,000	—	—	2.00	4.00	6.00
2004. Proof	2,000	Value: 8.00				

KM# 66 25 KUNA
Bi-Metallic Brass center in Copper-Nickel ring, 31 mm. **Subject:** 10th Anniversary of International Recognition **Obv:** Denomination **Rev:** National map **Edge:** Plain **Shape:** 12-sided

Date	Mintage	F	VF	XF	Unc	BU
ND(2002)	200,000	—	—	—	8.50	—

KM# 78 25 KUNA
12.6500 g., Bi-Metallic, 31 mm. **Subject:** Croatian European Union Candidacy **Obv:** Value **Rev:** Joined squares in star circle **Edge:** Plain **Shape:** 12-sided

Date	Mintage	F	VF	XF	Unc	BU
ND (2004)	30,000	—	—	—	10.00	—
ND (2004) Proof	—	Value: 25.00				

MINT SETS

KM#	Date	Mintage	Identification	Issue Price	Mkt Val
MS2	2002 (9)	—	KM#12, 14-17, 19-21, 23	—	15.00

CUBA

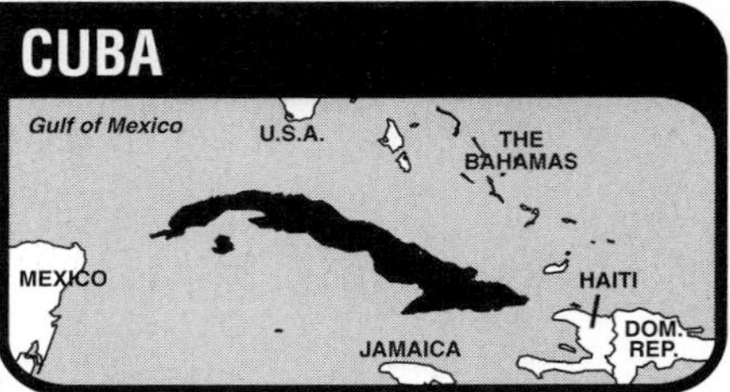

The Republic of Cuba, situated at the northern edge of the Caribbean Sea about 90 miles (145 km.) south of Florida, has an area of 42,804 sq. mi. (110,860 sq. km.) and a population of *11.2 million. Capital: Havana. The Cuban economy is based on the cultivation and refining of sugar, which provides 80 percent of export earnings.

MINT MARKS
Key - Havana, 1977-

MONETARY SYSTEM
100 Centavos = 1 Peso

SECOND REPUBLIC
1962 - Present

DECIMAL COINAGE

KM# 33.3 CENTAVO
0.7500 g., Aluminum, 16.76 mm. **Obv:** Cuban arms **Rev:** Wide "1" in star

Date	Mintage	F	VF	XF	Unc	BU
2001	—	—	0.10	0.40	0.80	1.75
2002	—	—	0.10	0.40	0.80	1.75
2003	—	—	0.10	0.40	0.80	1.75
2003	—	—	0.10	0.40	0.80	1.75
2004	—	—	0.10	0.40	0.80	1.75
2005	—	—	0.10	0.40	0.80	1.75

KM# 34 5 CENTAVOS
Aluminum

Date	Mintage	F	VF	XF	Unc	BU
2001	—	—	0.10	0.25	0.75	1.50
2002	—	—	0.10	0.25	0.75	1.50
2003	—	—	0.10	0.25	0.75	1.50
2004	—	—	0.10	0.25	0.75	1.50

KM# 35.1 20 CENTAVOS
2.0000 g., Aluminum, 24 mm.

Date	Mintage	F	VF	XF	Unc	BU
2002	—	—	0.50	1.00	2.00	4.00
2003	—	—	0.50	1.00	2.00	4.00
2005	—	—	0.50	1.00	2.00	4.00
2006	—	—	0.50	1.00	2.00	4.00

KM# 347 PESO
Brass Plated Steel **Subject:** Jose Marti **Rev. Legend:** PATRIA O MUERTE

Date	Mintage	F	VF	XF	Unc	BU
2001	—	—	—	1.00	2.00	—
2002	—	—	—	1.00	2.00	—

KM# 346a 3 PESOS
8.2000 g., Nickel Clad Steel, 26.5 mm. **Obv:** Cuban arms **Rev:** Che

Date	Mintage	F	VF	XF	Unc	BU
2002	—	—	—	2.50	5.00	—

KM# 739 5 PESOS
1.2400 g., Gold, 14 mm. **Obv:** Cuban arms **Rev:** Ancient lighthouse of Alexandria

Date	Mintage	F	VF	XF	Unc	BU
2005 Proof	5,000	Value: 40.00				

KM# 740 5 PESOS
1.2400 g., Gold, 14 mm. **Obv:** Cuban arms **Rev:** Colossus of Rhodes

Date	Mintage	F	VF	XF	Unc	BU
2005 Proof	5,000	Value: 40.00				

KM# 741 5 PESOS
1.2400 g., Gold, 14 mm. **Obv:** Cuban arms **Rev:** Hanging Gardens of Babylon

Date	Mintage	F	VF	XF	Unc	BU
2005 Proof	5,000	Value: 40.00				

KM# 742 5 PESOS
1.2400 g., Gold, 14 mm. **Obv:** Cuban arms **Rev:** Egyptian Pyramids

Date	Mintage	F	VF	XF	Unc	BU
2005	5,000	Value: 40.00				

KM# 743 5 PESOS
1.2400 g., Gold, 14 mm. **Obv:** Cuban arms **Rev:** Temple of Artemis

Date	Mintage	F	VF	XF	Unc	BU
2005 Proof	5,000	Value: 40.00				

KM# 744 5 PESOS
1.2400 g., Gold, 14 mm. **Obv:** Cuban arms **Rev:** Statue of Jupiter

Date	Mintage	F	VF	XF	Unc	BU
2005	5,000	Value: 40.00				

KM# 745 5 PESOS
1.2400 g., Gold, 14 mm. **Obv:** Cuban arms **Rev:** Mausoleum of Halicarnas

Date	Mintage	F	VF	XF	Unc	BU
2005 Proof	5,000	Value: 40.00				

KM# 746 5 PESOS
1.2400 g., Gold, 14 mm. **Obv:** Cuban arms **Rev:** Cortes, Montezuma and Aztec Pyramid

Date	Mintage	F	VF	XF	Unc	BU
2005 Proof	15,000	Value: 40.00				

KM# 763 10 PESOS
20.0000 g., 0.9990 Silver 0.6424 oz. ASW, 38 mm. **Subject:** Third Globalization Conference **Obv:** Cuban arms **Rev:** World map

Date	Mintage	F	VF	XF	Unc	BU
2001 Proof	100	Value: 45.00				

KM# 764 10 PESOS
20.0000 g., 0.9990 Silver 0.6424 oz. ASW, 38 mm. **Subject:** 40th Anniversary - Battle of Giron **Obv:** Cuban arms **Rev:** Soldiers on tank

Date	Mintage	F	VF	XF	Unc	BU
2001 Proof	3,000	Value: 45.00				

KM# 765 10 PESOS
31.1035 g., 0.9990 Silver, 38 mm. **Subject:** 106th Anniversary - Jose Marti's **Obv:** Cuban arms **Rev:** Monument

Date	Mintage	F	VF	XF	Unc	BU
2001 Proof	2,000	Value: 50.00				

KM# 762 10 PESOS
31.1035 g., 0.9990 Silver 0.999 oz. ASW, 38 mm. **Obv:** Cuban arms **Rev:** Two hummingbirds

Date	Mintage	F	VF	XF	Unc	BU
2001 Proof	20,000	Value: 40.00				

KM# 766 10 PESOS
15.0000 g., 0.9990 Silver 0.4818 oz. ASW, 35 mm. **Obv:** Cuban arms **Rev:** Multicolor Avellanedas butterfly

Date	Mintage	F	VF	XF	Unc	BU
2001 Proof	5,000	Value: 35.00				

KM# 767 10 PESOS
15.0000 g., 0.9990 Silver 0.4818 oz. ASW, 35 mm. **Obv:** Cuban arms **Rev:** Multicolor Cotorra parrot

Date	Mintage	F	VF	XF	Unc	BU
2001 Proof	5,000	Value: 35.00				

KM# 768 10 PESOS
15.0000 g., 0.9990 Silver 0.4818 oz. ASW, 35 mm. **Obv:** Cuban arms **Rev:** Multicolor woodpecker

Date	Mintage	F	VF	XF	Unc	BU
2001 Proof	5,000	Value: 35.00				

KM# 769 10 PESOS
15.0000 g., 0.9990 Silver 0.4818 oz. ASW, 35 mm. **Obv:** Cuban arms **Rev:** Multicolor white orchid

Date	Mintage	F	VF	XF	Unc	BU
2001 Proof	5,000	Value: 35.00				

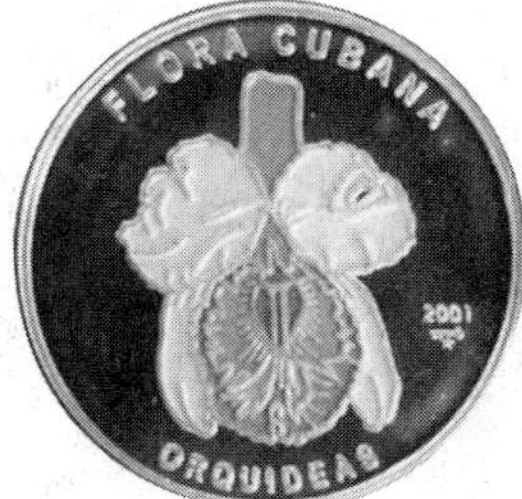

KM# 770 10 PESOS
15.0000 g., 0.9990 Silver 0.4818 oz. ASW, 35 mm. **Obv:** Cuban arms **Rev:** Multicolor yellow orchid

Date	Mintage	F	VF	XF	Unc	BU
2001 Proof	5,000	Value: 35.00				

KM# 771 10 PESOS
15.0000 g., 0.9990 Silver 0.4818 oz. ASW, 35 mm. **Obv:** Cuban arms **Rev:** Multicolor pink orchid

Date	Mintage	F	VF	XF	Unc	BU
2001 Proof	5,000	Value: 35.00				

KM# 772 10 PESOS
31.1035 g., 0.9990 Silver 0.999 oz. ASW, 38 mm. **Obv:** Cuban arms **Rev:** Multicolor Santa Maria

Date	Mintage	F	VF	XF	Unc	BU
2001 Proof	4,000	Value: 50.00				

KM# 773 10 PESOS
15.0000 g., 0.9990 Silver 0.4818 oz. ASW, 35 mm. **Subject:** Soccer - Uruguay 1930 **Obv:** Cuban arms **Rev:** Soccer player and stadium

Date	Mintage	F	VF	XF	Unc	BU
2001 Proof	7,500	Value: 35.00				

KM# 774 10 PESOS
20.0000 g., 0.9990 Silver 0.6424 oz. ASW, 38 mm. **Obv:** Cuban arms **Rev:** Trinidad street view

Date	Mintage	F	VF	XF	Unc	BU
2001 Proof	5,000	Value: 45.00				

KM# 775 10 PESOS
20.0000 g., 0.9990 Silver 0.6424 oz. ASW, 38 mm. **Obv:** Cuban arms **Rev:** Havana Cathedral

Date	Mintage	F	VF	XF	Unc	BU
2001 Proof	5,000	Value: 45.00				

KM# 776 10 PESOS
20.0000 g., 0.9990 Silver 0.6424 oz. ASW, 38 mm. **Obv:** Cuban arms **Rev:** Templete building

Date	Mintage	F	VF	XF	Unc	BU
2001 Proof	5,000	Value: 45.00				

KM# 777 10 PESOS
31.1035 g., 0.9990 Silver 0.999 oz. ASW, 38 mm. **Obv:** Cuban arms **Rev:** Bolivar standing at his birth place

Date	Mintage	F	VF	XF	Unc	BU
2001 Proof	5,000	Value: 50.00				

KM# 783 10 PESOS
20.0000 g., 0.9990 Silver 0.6424 oz. ASW, 38 mm. **Obv:** Cuban arms **Rev:** Americo Vespucio and ship

Date	Mintage	F	VF	XF	Unc	BU
2001 Proof	5,000	Value: 45.00				

KM# 778 10 PESOS
31.1035 g., 0.9990 Silver 0.999 oz. ASW, 38 mm. **Obv:** Cuban arms **Rev:** Bolivar and map of South America

Date	Mintage	F	VF	XF	Unc	BU
2001 Proof	5,000	Value: 50.00				

KM# 779 10 PESOS
31.1035 g., 0.9990 Silver 0.999 oz. ASW, 38 mm. **Obv:** Cuban arms **Rev:** Bolivar leading troops

Date	Mintage	F	VF	XF	Unc	BU
2001 Proof	5,000	Value: 50.00				

KM# 734 10 PESOS
20.0000 g., 0.9990 Silver 0.6424 oz. ASW, 37.9 mm. **Subject:** Olympics **Obv:** National arms **Rev:** Runner and ancient ruins **Edge:** Reeded

Date	Mintage	F	VF	XF	Unc	BU
2002 Proof	—	Value: 45.00				

KM# 782 10 PESOS
20.0000 g., 0.9990 Silver 0.6424 oz. ASW, 38 mm. **Obv:** Cuban arms **Rev:** Vasco De Gama and ship

Date	Mintage	F	VF	XF	Unc	BU
2002 Proof	5,000	Value: 45.00				

KM# 784 10 PESOS
31.1035 g., 0.9990 Silver 0.999 oz. ASW, 38 mm. **Obv:** Cuban arms **Rev:** Mao Tse Tung

Date	Mintage	F	VF	XF	Unc	BU
2002 Proof	2,000	Value: 50.00				

KM# 785 10 PESOS
31.1035 g., 0.9990 Silver 0.999 oz. ASW, 38 mm. **Obv:** Cuban arms **Rev:** Carl Marx

Date	Mintage	F	VF	XF	Unc	BU
2002 Proof	2,000	Value: 50.00				

KM# 786 10 PESOS
31.1035 g., 0.9990 Silver 0.999 oz. ASW, 38 mm. **Obv:** Cuban arms **Rev:** V.I. Lenin

Date	Mintage	F	VF	XF	Unc	BU
2002 Proof	2,000	Value: 50.00				

KM# 787 10 PESOS
31.1035 g., 0.9990 Silver 0.999 oz. ASW, 38 mm. **Obv:** Cuban arms **Rev:** Friedrich Engels

Date	Mintage	F	VF	XF	Unc	BU
2002 Proof	2,000	Value: 50.00				

KM# 788 10 PESOS
27.0000 g., 0.9990 Silver 0.8672 oz. ASW, 40 mm. **Obv:** Circle of arms around Cuban arms **Rev:** Santisima Trinidad ship

Date	Mintage	F	VF	XF	Unc	BU
2002 Proof	14,000	Value: 75.00				

KM# 780 10 PESOS
20.0000 g., 0.9990 Silver 0.6424 oz. ASW, 38 mm. **Obv:** Cuban arms **Rev:** Soccer player and map above "CHILE 1962"

Date	Mintage	F	VF	XF	Unc	BU
2002 Proof	7,500	Value: 45.00				

KM# 781 10 PESOS

20.0000 g., 0.9990 Silver 0.6424 oz. ASW, 38 mm. **Obv:** Cuban arms **Rev:** Soccer player and "CUAUHTEMOC" below "MEXICO 1970"

Date	Mintage	F	VF	XF	Unc	BU
2002 Proof	7,500	Value: 45.00				

KM# 794 10 PESOS

20.0000 g., 0.9990 Silver 0.6424 oz. ASW, 38 mm. **Obv:** Cuban arms **Rev:** Crocodile

Date	Mintage	F	VF	XF	Unc	BU
2003 Proof	5,000	Value: 45.00				

KM# 795 10 PESOS

20.0000 g., 0.9990 Silver 0.6424 oz. ASW, 38 mm. **Obv:** Cuban arms **Rev:** Ocelot

Date	Mintage	F	VF	XF	Unc	BU
2003 Proof	5,000	Value: 45.00				

KM# 792 10 PESOS

20.0000 g., 0.9990 Silver 0.6424 oz. ASW, 38 mm. **Obv:** Cuban arms **Rev:** Che Guevara

Date	Mintage	F	VF	XF	Unc	BU
2003 Proof	5,000	Value: 45.00				

KM# 791 10 PESOS

20.0000 g., 0.9990 Silver 0.6424 oz. ASW, 38 mm. **Obv:** Cuban arms **Rev:** Sailing ship, Sovereign of the Seas

Date	Mintage	F	VF	XF	Unc	BU
2003 Proof	5,000	Value: 45.00				

KM# 790 10 PESOS

20.0000 g., 0.9990 Silver 0.6424 oz. ASW, 38 mm. **Obv:** Cuban arms **Rev:** Ferdinand Magellan, ship, and astrolab

Date	Mintage	F	VF	XF	Unc	BU
2003 Proof	5,000	Value: 45.00				

KM# 789 10 PESOS

31.1035 g., 0.9990 Silver 0.999 oz. ASW, 38 mm. **Subject:** Jose Marti's 150th Birthday **Obv:** Cuban arms **Rev:** Numbered infield behind Marti's

Date	Mintage	F	VF	XF	Unc	BU
2003 Proof	150	Value: 50.00				

KM# 793 10 PESOS

31.1000 g., 0.9990 Silver 0.9989 oz. ASW, 38 mm. **Subject:** World Cup Soccer - Germany 2006 **Obv:** Cuban arms **Rev:** 5 soccer players

Date	Mintage	F	VF	XF	Unc	BU
2003 Proof	50,000	Value: 50.00				

KM# 796 10 PESOS

20.0000 g., 0.9990 Silver 0.6424 oz. ASW, 38 mm. **Obv:** Cuban arms **Rev:** John Cabot's portrait above ship

Date	Mintage	F	VF	XF	Unc	BU
2004 Proof	5,000	Value: 45.00				

KM# 797 10 PESOS

15.0000 g., 0.9990 Silver 0.4818 oz. ASW, 35 mm. **Subject:** Hippocampus Kuda **Obv:** Cuban arms **Rev:** Multicolor seahorse

Date	Mintage	F	VF	XF	Unc	BU
2004 Proof	5,000	Value: 35.00				

KM# 798 10 PESOS

20.0000 g., 0.9990 Silver 0.6424 oz. ASW, 38 mm. **Obv:** Cuban arms **Rev:** Murphy's Petrel bird on rock

Date	Mintage	F	VF	XF	Unc	BU
2004 Proof	5,000	Value: 45.00				

KM# 799 10 PESOS

20.0000 g., 0.9990 Silver 0.6424 oz. ASW, 38 mm. **Obv:** Cuban arms **Rev:** Iguana on branch

Date	Mintage	F	VF	XF	Unc	BU
2004 Proof	5,000	Value: 45.00				

KM# 800 10 PESOS

31.1000 g., 0.9990 Silver 0.9989 oz. ASW, 38 mm. **Obv:** Cuban arms **Rev:** Imperial eagle perched on branch

Date	Mintage	F	VF	XF	Unc	BU
2004 Proof	1,000	Value: 50.00				

KM# 801 10 PESOS
31.1000 g., 0.9990 Silver .9989 oz. ASW, 38 mm. **Obv:** Cuban arms **Rev:** Osprey in flight

Date	Mintage	F	VF	XF	Unc	BU
2004 Proof	1,000	Value: 50.00				

KM# 802 10 PESOS
31.1000 g., 0.9990 Silver 0.9989 oz. ASW, 38 mm. **Obv:** Cuban arms **Rev:** Iberian Lynx

Date	Mintage	F	VF	XF	Unc	BU
2004 Proof	1,000	Value: 50.00				

KM# 803 10 PESOS
31.1000 g., 0.9990 Silver 0.9989 oz. ASW, 38 mm. **Obv:** Cuban arms **Rev:** 2 grey wolves

Date	Mintage	F	VF	XF	Unc	BU
2004 Proof	1,000	Value: 50.00				

KM# 804 10 PESOS
31.1000 g., 0.9990 Silver 0.9989 oz. ASW, 38 mm. **Obv:** Cuban arms **Rev:** Brown bear

Date	Mintage	F	VF	XF	Unc	BU
2004 Proof	1,000	Value: 50.00				

KM# 805 10 PESOS
31.1000 g., 0.9990 Silver 0.9989 oz. ASW, 38 mm. **Obv:** Cuban arms **Rev:** Pilgrim hawk perches on branch

Date	Mintage	F	VF	XF	Unc	BU
2004 Proof	1,000	Value: 50.00				

KM# 806 10 PESOS
20.0000 g., 0.9990 Silver 0.6424 oz. ASW, 38 mm. **Obv:** Cuban arms **Rev:** University of Havana building

Date	Mintage	F	VF	XF	Unc	BU
2004 Proof	1,500	Value: 45.00				

KM# 807 10 PESOS
20.0000 g., 0.9990 Silver 0.6424 oz. ASW, 38 mm. **Obv:** Cuban arms **Rev:** Fountain of India

Date	Mintage	F	VF	XF	Unc	BU
2004 Proof	1,500	Value: 45.00				

KM# 808 10 PESOS
20.0000 g., 0.9990 Silver 0.6424 oz. ASW, 38 mm.

Date	Mintage	F	VF	XF	Unc	BU
2004 Proof	1,500	Value: 45.00				

KM# 809 10 PESOS
27.0000 g., 0.9250 Silver 0.803 oz. ASW, 40 mm. **Obv:** Cuban arms within circle of arms **Rev:** Portions of the old Havana Wall

Date	Mintage	F	VF	XF	Unc	BU
2005 Proof	12,000	Value: 75.00				

KM# 810 10 PESOS
20.0000 g., 0.9990 Silver 0.6424 oz. ASW, 38 mm. **Subject:** Tobacco **Obv:** Cuban arms **Rev:** Indian showing tobacco to Columbus, ship in background

Date	Mintage	F	VF	XF	Unc	BU
2005 Proof	50	Value: 45.00				

KM# 811 10 PESOS
20.0000 g., 0.9990 Silver 0.6424 oz. ASW, 38 mm. **Obv:** Cuban arms **Rev:** The Santa Maria under sail

Date	Mintage	F	VF	XF	Unc	BU
2005 Proof	50	Value: 45.00				

KM# 812 10 PESOS
20.0000 g., 0.9990 Silver 0.6424 oz. ASW, 38 mm. **Obv:** Cuban arms **Rev:** The Nina under sail

Date	Mintage	F	VF	XF	Unc	BU
2005 Proof	50	Value: 45.00				

KM# 813 10 PESOS
20.0000 g., 0.9990 Silver 0.6424 oz. ASW, 38 mm. **Obv:** Cuban arms **Rev:** The Pinta under sail

Date	Mintage	F	VF	XF	Unc	BU
2005 Proof	50	Value: 45.00				

KM# 814 10 PESOS
20.0000 g., 0.9990 Silver 0.6424 oz. ASW, 38 mm. **Obv:** Cuban arms **Rev:** Cuban Solenodon on branch

Date	Mintage	F	VF	XF	Unc	BU
2005 Proof	150	Value: 45.00				

KM# 815 10 PESOS
15.0000 g., 0.9990 Silver 0.4818 oz. ASW, 35 mm. **Obv:** Cuban arms **Rev:** Multicolor Solenodon on branch

Date	Mintage	F	VF	XF	Unc	BU
2005 Proof	2,000	Value: 35.00				

KM# 816 10 PESOS
15.0000 g., 0.9990 Silver 0.4818 oz. ASW, 35 mm. **Obv:** Cuban arms **Rev:** Multicolor Reef Triggerfish

Date	Mintage	F	VF	XF	Unc	BU
2005 Proof	150	Value: 35.00				

KM# 817 10 PESOS
15.0000 g., 0.9990 Silver 0.4818 oz. ASW, 35 mm. **Obv:** Cuban arms **Rev:** Black and blue striped Moorish Idol fish

Date	Mintage	F	VF	XF	Unc	BU
2005 Proof	100	Value: 35.00				

KM# 818 10 PESOS
15.0000 g., 0.9990 Silver 0.4818 oz. ASW, 35 mm. **Subject:** Pyglopites Diacanthus **Obv:** Cuban arms **Rev:** Multicolor angel fish

Date	Mintage	F	VF	XF	Unc	BU
2005 Proof	25	Value: 35.00				

KM# 819 10 PESOS
31.1000 g., 0.9990 Silver 0.9989 oz. ASW, 38 mm. **Obv:** Cuban arms **Rev:** Don Quijote and Sancho looking at two wind mills

Date	Mintage	F	VF	XF	Unc	BU
2005 Proof	4,000	Value: 50.00				

KM# 820 10 PESOS
31.1000 g., 0.9990 Silver 0.9989 oz. ASW, 38 mm. **Subject:** Maximo Gomez Centennial of Death **Obv:** Cuban arms **Rev:** Gomez, numbered behind neck

Date	Mintage	F	VF	XF	Unc	BU
2005 Proof	3,000	Value: 50.00				

KM# 821 10 PESOS
20.0000 g., 0.9990 Silver 0.6424 oz. ASW, 38 mm. **Subject:** XXIX Olympics **Obv:** Cuban arms **Rev:** Baseball player with bat, baseball background

Date	Mintage	F	VF	XF	Unc	BU
2006 Proof	2,000	Value: 45.00				

KM# 822 100 PESOS
31.1000 g., 0.9990 Gold 0.9989 oz. AGW, 38 mm. **Subject:** 100th Anniversary - Death of Marti **Obv:** Cuban arms **Rev:** Monument

Date	Mintage	F	VF	XF	Unc	BU
2001 Proof	100	Value: 750				

PESO CONVERTIBLE SERIES

KM# 733 CENTAVO
0.7500 g., Aluminum, 16.75 mm. **Obv:** National arms **Rev:** Tower and denomination **Edge:** Plain

Date	Mintage	F	VF	XF	Unc	BU
2001	—	—	—	—	2.00	—
2002	—	—	—	—	2.00	—
2003	—	—	—	—	2.00	—
2005	—	—	—	—	2.00	—

KM# 733a CENTAVO
1.7000 g., Copper Plated Steel, 14.8 mm. **Obv:** National arms **Rev:** Tower **Edge:** Reeded

Date	Mintage	F	VF	XF	Unc	BU
2002	—	—	—	—	2.50	—

KM# 729 CENTAVO
1.7000 g., Copper Plated Steel, 15 mm. **Obv:** National arms **Rev:** Tower and denomination **Edge:** Reeded

Date	Mintage	F	VF	XF	Unc	BU
2002	—	—	—	—	3.00	—

KM# 575.2 5 CENTAVOS
2.6500 g., Nickel-Plated Steel, 18 mm. **Obv:** National arms **Rev:** Casa Colonial **Note:** Coin alignment, recut designs.

Date	Mintage	F	VF	XF	Unc	BU
2002	—	—	—	—	1.00	—
2006	—	—	—	—	1.00	—

KM# 576.2 10 CENTAVOS
Nickel Plated Steel **Obv:** National arms **Rev:** Castillo de la Fuerza **Note:** Coin alignment, recut designs.

Date	Mintage	F	VF	XF	Unc	BU
2002	—	—	—	—	2.00	—

KM# 577.2 25 CENTAVOS
5.6500 g., Nickel Plated Steel, 23 mm. **Obv:** National arms **Rev:** Trinidad **Note:** Coin alignment.

Date	Mintage	F	VF	XF	Unc	BU
2001	—	—	—	—	3.00	—
2002	—	—	—	—	3.00	—
2003	—	—	—	—	3.00	—
2006	—	—	—	—	3.00	—

KM# 578a 50 CENTAVOS
7.5000 g., Nickel Plated Steel, 25 mm. **Obv:** Cuban arms **Rev:** Havana Cathedral

Date	Mintage	F	VF	XF	Unc	BU
2002	—	—	—	—	5.00	—

KM# 579.2 PESO
8.5000 g., Nickel Plated Steel, 27 mm. **Obv:** National arms **Rev:** Guama **Note:** Coin alignment.

Date	Mintage	F	VF	XF	Unc	BU
2001	—	—	—	—	5.00	—

CYPRUS

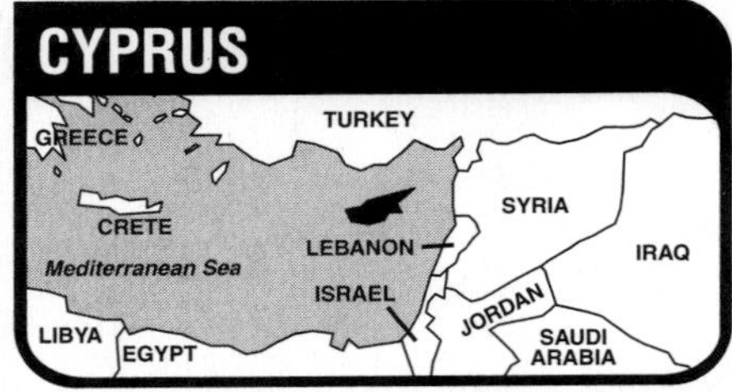

The island of Cyprus lies in the eastern Mediterranean Sea 44 miles (71 km.) south of Turkey and 60 miles (97 km.) off the Syrian coast. It is the third largest island in the Mediterranean Sea, having an area of 3,572 sq. mi. (9,251 sq. km.) and a population of 736,636. Capital: Nicosia. Agriculture, light manufacturing and tourism are the chief industries. Citrus fruit, potatoes, footwear and clothing are exported

Cyprus is a member of the Commonwealth of Nations. The president is Chief of State and Head of Government.

REPUBLIC

REFORM COINAGE

100 Cents = 1 Pound

KM# 53.3 CENT

Nickel-Brass **Rev:** Stylized bird on a branch; altered wreath around arms

Date	Mintage	F	VF	XF	Unc	BU
2003	5,000,000	—	—	0.10	0.20	0.30
2004	—	—	—	0.10	0.20	0.30

KM# 54.3 2 CENTS

Nickel-Brass **Obv:** Stylized goats, altered wreath around arms

Date	Mintage	F	VF	XF	Unc	BU
2003	5,000,000	—	—	0.15	0.25	0.35
2004	—	—	—	0.15	0.25	0.35

KM# 55.3 5 CENTS

Nickel-Brass **Obv:** Altered wreath around arms

Date	Mintage	F	VF	XF	Unc	BU
2001	15,000,000	—	—	0.20	0.50	0.75
2004	—	—	—	0.20	0.50	0.75

KM# 56.3 10 CENTS

Nickel-Brass **Obv:** Altered wreath around arms

Date	Mintage	F	VF	XF	Unc	BU
2002	10,000,000	—	—	0.35	0.75	1.00
2004	—	—	—	0.35	0.75	1.00

KM# 62.2 20 CENTS

Nickel-Brass **Obv:** Zenon Kitieus head left, altered wreath around arms

Date	Mintage	F	VF	XF	Unc	BU
2001	15,000,000	—	—	—	1.00	1.50
2004	—	—	—	—	1.00	1.50

KM# 66 50 CENTS

Copper-Nickel **Subject:** Abduction of Europa **Shape:** 7-sided

Date	Mintage	F	VF	XF	Unc	BU
2002	7,000,000	—	—	—	2.50	3.25
2004	—	—	—	—	2.50	3.25

KM# 75 POUND

28.2800 g., Copper-Nickel, 38.6 mm. **Subject:** Cyprus Joins the European Union **Obv:** National arms **Rev:** Map in center with Triton trumpeting through a seashell **Edge:** Plain

Date	Mintage	F	VF	XF	Unc	BU
2004	6,000	—	—	—	15.00	18.00

KM# 75a POUND

28.2800 g., 0.9250 Silver 0.841 oz. ASW, 38.6 mm. **Subject:** Cyprus Joins the European Union **Obv:** National arms **Rev:** Map and Triton trumpeting through a sea shell **Edge:** Plain

Date	Mintage	F	VF	XF	Unc	BU
2004 Proof	3,000	Value: 45.00				

KM# 76 POUND

28.2700 g., Copper-Nickel, 38.5 mm. **Obv:** National arms **Rev:** Mediterranean Monk Seal **Edge:** Plain

Date	Mintage	F	VF	XF	Unc	BU
2005 Proof	—	Value: 20.00				

CZECH REPUBLIC

The Czech Republic was formerly united with Slovakia as Czechoslovakia. It is bordered in the west by Germany, to the north by Poland, to the east by Slovakia and to the south by Austria. It consists of 3 major regions: Bohemia, Moravia and Silesia and has an area of 30,450 sq. mi. (78,864 sq. km.) and a population of 10.4 million. Capital: Prague (Praha). Agriculture and livestock are chief occupations while coal deposits are the main mineral resources.

MONETARY SYSTEM

1 Czechoslovak Koruna (Kcs) = 1 Czech Koruna (Kc)

1 Koruna = 100 Haleru

REPUBLIC

STANDARD COINAGE

KM# 6 10 HALERU

0.9900 Aluminum 0.6 oz., 15.5 mm. **Obv:** Crowned Czech lion **Rev:** Value and stylized river **Edge:** Plain **Designer:** Jiri Pradler **Note:** Two varieties of mint marks exist for 1994.

Date	Mintage	F	VF	XF	Unc	BU
2001(m)	41,525,000	—	—	—	0.20	—
2001(m) Proof	2,500	Value: 2.00				
2002(m)	81,496,000	—	—	—	0.20	—
2002(m) Proof	3,490	Value: 2.00				
2003(m)	3,022,350	—	—	—	0.20	—
2003(l) Proof	3,000	Value: 2.00				
2004(m)	—	—	—	—	0.20	—
2004(m) Proof	3,000	Value: 2.00				

KM# 2.3 20 HALERU

Aluminum **Rev:** Open 2 in denomination, "h" above angle line **Note:** Medallic coin alignment.

Date	Mintage	F	VF	XF	Unc	BU
2001(m)	44,425,000	—	—	—	0.30	—
2001(m) Proof	2,500	Value: 3.00				
2002(m)	20,000	—	—	—	0.30	—
2002(m) Proof	3,490	Value: 3.00				
2003(m)	22,200	—	—	—	0.30	—
2003(m) Proof	3,000	Value: 3.00				
2004(m)	—	—	—	—	0.30	—
2004(m) Proof	3,000	Value: 3.00				

KM# 3.1 50 HALERU

Aluminum 0.9 oz., 19 mm. **Obv:** Crowned Czech lion **Rev:** Large value **Edge:** Part plain, part milled repeated **Designer:** Vladimir Oppl **Note:** Two styles of "9" exist for 1994; prev. KM#3.

Date	Mintage	F	VF	XF	Unc	BU
2001(m)	20,000,000	—	—	—	0.50	—
2001(m) Proof	3,000	Value: 3.00				

KM# 3.2 50 HALERU

0.9000 g., Aluminum, 19 mm. **Subject:** Outlined lettering and larger mint mark

Date	Mintage	F	VF	XF	Unc	BU
2001(m)	21,425,000	—	—	—	0.50	—
2001(m) Proof	2,500	Value: 3.00				

Date	Mintage	F	VF	XF	Unc	BU
2002(m)	26,246,298	—	—	—	0.50	—
2002(m) Proof	2,500	Value: 3.00				
2003(m)	41,548,000	—	—	—	0.50	—
2003(m) Proof	3,490	Value: 3.00				
2004(m)	931,145	—	—	—	0.50	—
2004(m) Proof	3,000	Value: 3.00				
2005(m)	—	—	—	—	0.50	—
2005(m) Proof	—	Value: 3.00				

KM# 7 KORUNA

Nickel Clad Steel, 20 mm. **Obv:** Crowned Czech lion **Rev:** Value above crown **Edge:** Milled **Designer:** Jarmila Truhlikova-Spevakova **Note:** Two varieties of mint marks exist for 1996. 2000-03 have two varieties in the artisit monogram.

Date	Mintage	F	VF	XF	Unc	BU
2001(m)	15,938,353	—	—	—	0.60	—
2001(m) Proof	2,500	Value: 4.00				
2002(m)	26,244,666	—	—	—	0.60	—
2002(m) Proof	3,490	Value: 4.00				
2003(m)	36,877,440	—	—	—	0.60	—
2003(m) Proof	3,000	Value: 4.00				
2004(m)	30,500	—	—	—	0.60	—
2004(m) Proof	4,000	Value: 4.00				
2005(m)	—	—	—	—	0.60	—
2005(m) Proof	—	Value: 6.00				

KM# 9 2 KORUN

3.7000 g., Nickel Clad Steel, 21.5 mm. **Obv:** Crowned Czech lion **Edge:** Plain **Shape:** 11-sided **Designer:** Jarmila Truhlikova-Spevakova **Note:** Two varieties of designer monograms exist for 2001-04.

Date	Mintage	F	VF	XF	Unc	BU
2001(m)	26,117,000	—	—	—	0.65	—
2001(m) Proof	2,500	Value: 5.00				
2002(m)	20,941,084	—	—	—	0.65	—
2002(m) Proof	3,490	Value: 5.00				
2003(m)	20,955,000	—	—	—	0.65	—
2003(m) Proof	3,000	Value: 5.00				
2004(m)	15,658,556	—	—	—	0.65	—
2004(m) Proof	4,000	Value: 5.00				
2005(m)	—	—	—	—	0.65	—
2005(m) Proof	—	Value: 5.00				

KM# 8 5 KORUN

4.8000 g., Nickel Plated Steel, 23 mm. **Obv:** Crowned Czech lion **Rev:** Large value, Charles bridge and linden leaf **Edge:** Plain **Designer:** Jiri Harcuba

Date	Mintage	F	VF	XF	Unc	BU
2001(m)	25,000	—	—	—	1.00	—
2001(m) Proof	2,500	Value: 6.00				
2002(m)	21,344,995	—	—	—	1.00	—
2002(m) Proof	3,490	Value: 6.00				
2003(m)	22,000	—	—	—	1.00	—
2003(m) Proof	3,000	Value: 6.00				
2004(m)	34,940	—	—	—	1.00	—
2004(m) Proof	4,000	Value: 6.00				
2005(m)	—	—	—	—	1.00	—
2005(m) Proof	—	Value: 6.00				

KM# 4 10 KORUN

7.6200 g., Copper Plated Steel, 24.5 mm. **Obv:** Crowned Czech lion **Rev:** Brno Cathedral **Edge:** Milled **Designer:** Ladislav Kozak **Note:** Position of designer's initials on reverse change during the 1995 strike.

Date	Mintage	F	VF	XF	Unc	BU
2001(m)	25,000	—	—	—	1.50	—
2001(m) Proof	2,500	Value: 7.00				

Date	Mintage	F	VF	XF	Unc	BU
2002(m)	20,156	—	—	—	1.50	—
2002(m) Proof	3,490	Value: 7.00				
2003(m)	18,747,000	—	—	—	1.50	—
2003(m) Proof	3,000	Value: 7.00				
2004(m)	2,255,740	—	—	—	1.50	—
2004(m) Proof	4,000	Value: 7.00				
2005(m)	—	—	—	—	1.50	—
2005(m) Proof	—	Value: 7.00				

KM# 5 20 KORUN

8.4300 g., Brass Plated Steel, 26 mm. **Obv:** Crowned Czech lion **Rev:** St. Wenceslas (Duke Vaclav) on horse **Edge:** Plain **Shape:** 13-sided **Designer:** Vladimir Oppl **Note:** Two varieties of mint marks and style of 9's exist for 1997.

Date	Mintage	F	VF	XF	Unc	BU
2001(m)	25,000	—	—	—	2.50	—
2001(m) Proof	2,500	Value: 10.00				
2002(m)	20,996,500	—	—	—	2.50	—
2002(m) Proof	3,490	Value: 10.00				
2003(m)	22,000	—	—	—	2.50	—
2003(m) Proof	3,000	Value: 10.00				
2004(m)	8,249,507	—	—	—	2.50	—
2004(m) Proof	4,000	Value: 10.00				

KM# 1 50 KORUN

9.7000 g., Bi-Metallic Brass plated Steel center in Copper plated Steel ring, 27.5 mm. **Obv:** Crowned Czech lion **Rev:** Prague city view **Edge:** Plain **Designer:** Ladislav Kozak

Date	Mintage	F	VF	XF	Unc	BU
2001(m)	16,000	—	—	—	9.00	—
2001(m) Proof	2,500	Value: 20.00				
2002(m)	16,771	—	—	—	9.00	—
2002(m) Proof	3,490	Value: 20.00				
2003(m)	22,000	—	—	—	9.00	—
2003(m) Proof	3,000	Value: 20.00				
2004(m)	34,555	—	—	—	9.00	—
2004(m) Proof	4,000	Value: 20.00				
2005(m)	—	—	—	—	9.00	—
2005(m) Proof	—	Value: 20.00				

KM# 58 200 KORUN

13.0000 g., 0.9000 Silver 0.3762 oz. ASW, 31 mm. **Subject:** Frantisek Skroup **Obv:** National arms **Rev:** Portrait and name **Designer:** Jiri Harcuba

Date	Mintage	F	VF	XF	Unc	BU
ND(2001)	12,909	—	—	—	15.00	17.00
Note: Reeded edge						
ND(2001) Proof	3,200	Value: 30.00				
Note: CESKA NARODNI BANKA * 0.900 *						

KM# 51 200 KORUN

13.0000 g., 0.9000 Silver 0.3762 oz. ASW, 31 mm. **Subject:** Jaroslav Seifert **Obv:** National arms **Rev:** Head of Jaroslav Seifert right **Designer:** Ladislav Kozak

Date	Mintage	F	VF	XF	Unc	BU
ND(2001)	12,870	—	—	—	15.00	17.00
Note: Reeded edge						
ND(2001) Proof	3,199	Value: 30.00				
Note: CESKA NARODNI BANKA * 0.900 *						

KM# 52 200 KORUN

13.0000 g., 0.9000 Silver 0.3762 oz. ASW, 31 mm. **Subject:** Soccer **Obv:** National arms **Rev:** Rampant lion on soccer ball **Designer:** Milena Blaskova

Date	Mintage	F	VF	XF	Unc	BU
ND(2001)	13,324	—	—	—	15.00	17.00
Note: Reeded edge						
ND(2001) Proof	3,900	Value: 28.00				
Note: CESKA NARODNI BANKA * 0.900 *						

KM# 53 200 KORUN

13.0000 g., 0.9000 Silver 0.3762 oz. ASW, 31 mm. **Subject:** 250th Anniversary - Death of Kilian Ignac Dientzenhofer **Obv:** National arms, denomination **Rev:** Doorway and caliper **Designer:** Petr Pyciak

Date	Mintage	F	VF	XF	Unc	BU
ND(2001)	12,744	—	—	—	15.00	17.00
Note: Reeded edge						
ND(2001) Proof	3,373	Value: 30.00				
Note: CESKA NARODNI BANKA * 0.900 *						

KM# 54 200 KORUN

13.0000 g., 0.9000 Silver 0.3762 oz. ASW, 31 mm. **Subject:** Euro Currency System **Obv:** National arms **Rev:** Prague gros coin design **Designer:** Josef Safarik

Date	Mintage	F	VF	XF	Unc	BU
ND(2001)	13,867	—	—	—	15.00	17.00
Note: Reeded edge						
ND(2001) Proof	4,000	Value: 28.00				
Note: CESKA NARODNI BANKA * 0.900 *						

KM# 55 200 KORUN

13.0000 g., 0.9000 Silver 0.3762 oz. ASW, 31 mm. **Subject:** St. Zdislava **Obv:** National arms **Rev:** Saint feeding sick person **Designer:** Michal Vitanovsky

Date	Mintage	F	VF	XF	Unc	BU
ND(2002)	12,706	—	—	—	15.00	17.00
Note: Reeded edge						
ND(2002) Proof	3,600	Value: 28.00				
Note: CESKA NARODNI BANKA * 0.900 *						

KM# 56 200 KORUN
13.0000 g., 0.9000 Silver 0.3762 oz. ASW, 30.9 mm. **Subject:** Emil Holub **Obv:** National arms **Rev:** Traveller and African dancers **Designer:** Ladislav Kozak

Date	Mintage	F	VF	XF	Unc	BU
ND(2002)	12,635	—	—	—	15.00	17.00
Note: Reeded edge						
ND(2002) Proof	3,600	Value: 28.00				
Note: CESKA NARODNI BANKA * 0.900 *						

KM# 57 200 KORUN
13.0000 g., 0.9000 Silver 0.3762 oz. ASW, 30.9 mm. **Subject:** Jiri of Podebrady **Obv:** Overlapped arms **Rev:** Head of Podebrady

Date	Mintage	F	VF	XF	Unc	BU
ND(2002)	12,750	—	—	—	15.00	17.00
Note: Reeded edge						
ND(2002) Proof	3,600	Value: 28.00				
Note: CESKA NARDONI BANKA * 0.900 *						

KM# 59 200 KORUN
13.0000 g., 0.9000 Silver 0.3762 oz. ASW, 31 mm. **Subject:** Mikolas Ales **Obv:** Four coats of arms above denomination **Rev:** Horse and rider **Edge:** Reeded

Date	Mintage	F	VF	XF	Unc	BU
ND(2002)	12,473	—	—	—	15.00	17.00
ND(2002)(m) Proof	4,400	Value: 28.00				

KM# 60 200 KORUN
13.1400 g., 0.9000 Silver 0.3802 oz. ASW, 31 mm. **Subject:** Jaroslav Vrchlicky **Obv:** Denomination and quill **Rev:** Portrait with hat

Date	Mintage	F	VF	XF	Unc	BU
ND(2003)	11,975	—	—	—	15.00	17.00
Note: Reeded						
ND(2003) Proof	3,700	Value: 28.00				
Note: Plain with CESKA NARODNI BANKA *Ag 0.900* 13g*						

KM# 62 200 KORUN
13.0000 g., 0.9000 Silver 0.3762 oz. ASW, 30.9 mm. **Subject:** Josef Thomayer **Obv:** National arms **Rev:** Portrait **Edge:** Reeded

Date	Mintage	F	VF	XF	Unc	BU
ND(2003)	11,975	—	—	—	15.00	17.00
ND(2003) Proof	4,000	Value: 28.00				

KM# 63 200 KORUN
13.0000 g., 0.9000 Silver 0.3762 oz. ASW, 31 mm. **Subject:** Tabor-Bechyne Electric Railway **Obv:** Portrait **Rev:** Railroad station scene

Date	Mintage	F	VF	XF	Unc	BU
ND(2003)	11,975	—	—	—	16.00	18.00
Note: Reeded edge						
ND(2003) Proof	4,100	Value: 28.00				
Note: Plain edge with CESKA NARODNI BANKA * Ag 0.900, * 13g						

KM# 64 200 KORUN
13.0000 g., 0.9000 Silver 0.3762 oz. ASW, 31 mm. **Subject:** Bohemian Skiers' Union **Obv:** Portrait **Rev:** Skier **Edge:** Reeded

Date	Mintage	F	VF	XF	Unc	BU
ND(2003) Reeded edge	11,975	—	—	—	16.00	18.00
ND(2003) Proof	4,300	Value: 28.00				
Note: Plain edge with CESKA NARODNI BANKA * Ag 0.900, * 13g						

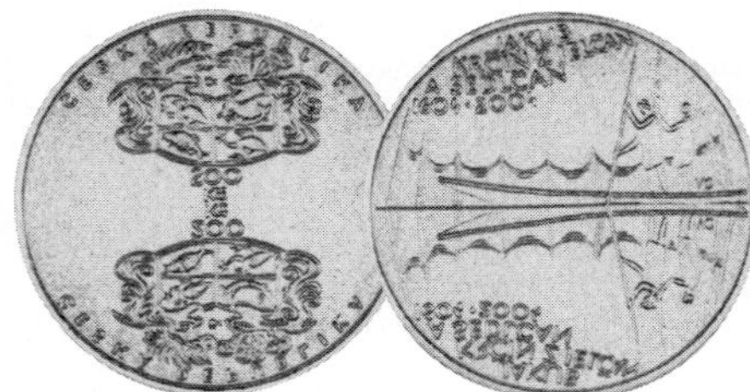

KM# 70 200 KORUN
13.1000 g., 0.9000 Silver 0.3791 oz. ASW, 30.8 mm. **Subject:** 300th Anniversary - Death of Pond builder Jakub Krcin **Obv:** Coat of arms above value with reflected design below **Rev:** Two fishermen in boat with reflection on water below

Date	Mintage	F	VF	XF	Unc	BU
ND(2004)(m)	11,975	—	—	—	16.00	18.00
Note: Reeded						
ND(2004) Proof	4,000	Value: 28.00				
Note: Plain with CESKA NARODNI BANKA *Ag 0.900* 13g*						

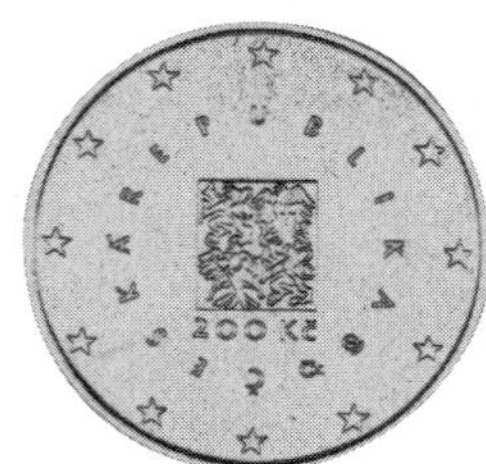

KM# 71 200 KORUN
13.1000 g., 0.9000 Silver 0.3791 oz. ASW **Subject:** Entry into the European Union

Date	Mintage	F	VF	XF	Unc	BU
2004	10,000	—	—	—	16.00	18.00
Note: Reeded						
2004 Proof	8,800	Value: 28.00				

KM# 72 200 KORUN
13.1000 g., 0.9000 Silver 0.3791 oz. ASW **Subject:** Prokop Divis

Date	Mintage	F	VF	XF	Unc	BU
2004	10,975	—	—	—	16.00	18.00
Note: Reeded						
2004 Proof	3,900	Value: 28.00				

KM# 73 200 KORUN
13.1000 g., 0.9000 Silver 0.3791 oz. ASW **Subject:** Leos Janacek

Date	Mintage	F	VF	XF	Unc	BU
2004	10,975	—	—	—	16.00	18.00
Note: Reeded						
2004 Proof	4,100	Value: 28.00				

KM# 74 200 KORUN
13.1000 g., 0.9000 Silver 0.3791 oz. ASW **Subject:** Kralice Bible

Date	Mintage	F	VF	XF	Unc	BU
2004	10,975	—	—	—	16.00	18.00
Note: Reeded						
2004 Proof	5,000	Value: 28.00				

KM# 75.1 2000 KORUN
6.2200 g., 0.9999 Gold 0.2 oz. AGW, 20 mm. **Obv:** Ornamental porch below three heraldic animals **Rev:** Hluboka Castle with coat of arms in foreground **Edge:** Reeded

Date	Mintage	F	VF	XF	Unc	BU
2004	2,500	—	—	—	—	145

KM# 75.2 2000 KORUN
6.2200 g., 0.9999 Gold 0.2 oz. AGW, 20 mm. **Edge:** Plain

Date	Mintage	F	VF	XF	Unc	BU
2004 Proof	3,500	Value: 165				

KM# 76 2500 KORUN
31.1040 g., 0.9990 Bi-Metallic Gold And Silver .9999 Gold 7.776g center in .999 Silver 23.328g ring 0.999 oz., 40 mm. **Subject:** Czech entry into the European Union **Obv:** Value within circle of shields **Rev:** "1.5.2004" within circle of dates and text **Edge:** Lettered **Edge Lettering:** " CNB * Ag 0.999 * 23,328 g * Au 999.9 * 7,776g * "

Date	Mintage	F	VF	XF	Unc	BU
ND (2004) Proof	10,000	Value: 265				

GOLD BULLION COINAGE

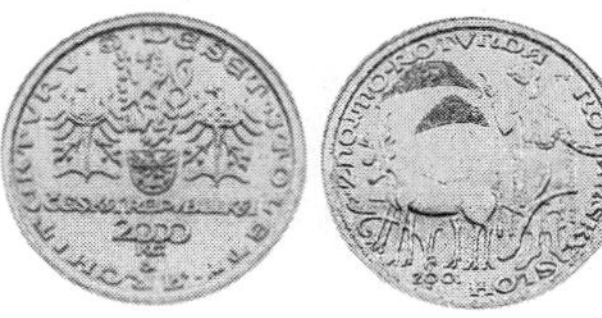

KM# 65 2000 KORUN
6.2200 g., 0.9999 Gold 0.2 oz. AGW, 20 mm. **Subject:** Znojmo Rotunda **Obv:** Three heraldic animals **Rev:** Farmer and round building

Date	Mintage	F	VF	XF	Unc	BU
ND(2001)	2,197	—	—	—	—	145
Note: Reeded edge						
ND(2001) Proof	2,997	Value: 165				
Note: Plain edge						

KM# 66 2000 KORUN
6.2200 g., 0.9999 Gold 0.2 oz. AGW, 20 mm. **Subject:** Vyssi Brod Monastery **Obv:** Three heraldic animals above Gothic design **Rev:** Man holding church building model

Date	Mintage	F	VF	XF	Unc	BU
2001	2,197	—	—	—	—	145
Note: Reeded edge						
2001 Proof	2,997	Value: 165				
Note: Plain edge						

KM# 67 2000 KORUN
6.2200 g., 0.9999 Gold 0.2 oz. AGW, 20 mm. **Subject:** Kutna Hora Fountain **Obv:** Three heraldic animals **Rev:** Fountain enclosure

Date	Mintage	F	VF	XF	Unc	BU
2002	2,197	—	—	—	—	145
Note: Reeded edge						

Date	Mintage	F	VF	XF	Unc	BU
2002	2,997	Value: 165				

Note: Plain edge

KM# 61 2000 KORUN

6.2200 g., 0.9999 Gold 0.2 oz. AGW, 20 mm. **Subject:** Litomysl Castle **Obv:** Three heraldic animals above mermaid **Rev:** Aerial castle view and mythical creature

Date	Mintage	F	VF	XF	Unc	BU
2002	2,097	—	—	—	—	150
Note: Reeded edge						
2002 Proof	3,097	Value: 175				
Note: Plain edge						

KM# 68 2000 KORUN

6.2200 g., 0.9999 Gold 0.2 oz. AGW, 20 mm. **Subject:** Slavonice House Gables **Obv:** Three heraldic animals above city view **Rev:** City arms

Date	Mintage	F	VF	XF	Unc	BU
2003	1,997	—	—	—	—	145
Note: Reeded edge						
2003 Proof	2,997	Value: 165				
Note: Plain edge						

KM# 69 2000 KORUN

6.2200 g., 0.9999 Gold 0.2 oz. AGW, 20 mm. **Subject:** Buchlovice Palace **Obv:** Three heraldic animals above palace **Rev:** Palace view

Date	Mintage	F	VF	XF	Unc	BU
2003	1,997	—	—	—	—	145
Note: Reeded						
2003 Proof	3,197	Value: 165				
Note: Plain edge						

DENMARK

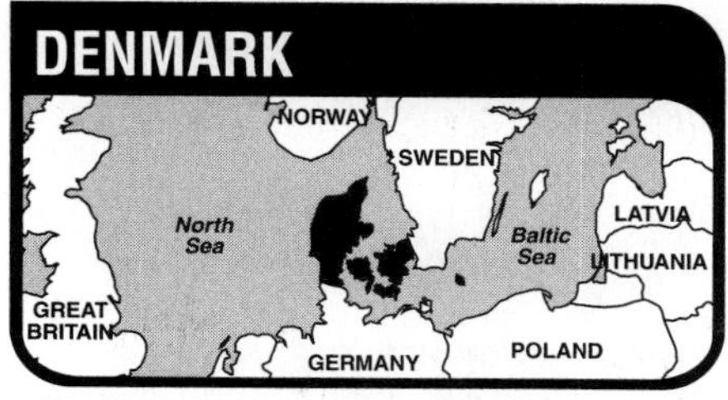

The Kingdom of Denmark (Danmark), a constitutional monarchy located at the mouth of the Baltic Sea, has an area of 16,639 sq. mi. (43,070 sq. km.) and a population of 5.2 million. Capital: Copenhagen. Most of the country is arable. Agriculture is conducted by large farms served by cooperatives. The largest industries are food processing, iron and metal, and shipping. Machinery, meats (chiefly bacon), dairy products and chemicals are exported.

As a result of a referendum held September 28, 2000, the currency of the European Monetary Union, the Euro, will not be introduced in Denmark in the foreseeable future.

RULERS

Margrethe II, 1972—

MINT MARKS

(h) - Copenhagen, heart

MINT OFFICIALS' INITIALS

Copenhagen

Letter	Date	Name
LG	1989-2001	Laust Grove

MONEYERS' INITIALS

Copenhagen

Letter	Date	Name
A	1986-	Johan Alkjaer (designer)
HV	1986-	Hanne Varming (sculptor)
JP	1989-	Jan Petersen

MONETARY SYSTEM

100 Øre = 1 Krone

KINGDOM

DECIMAL COINAGE

100 Øre = 1 Krone; 1874-present

KM# 868.1 25 ORE

2.8000 g., Bronze **Ruler:** Margrethe II **Obv:** Date above large crown, country name below, initial A to right **Rev:** Large heart above value, mint mark and initials LG-JP below **Note:** Beginning in 1996 and ending with 1998, the words "DANMARK" and "ØRE" have raised edges. Heart mint mark under "ØRE"; Prev. KM#868.

Date	Mintage	F	VF	XF	Unc	BU
2001 LG; JP; A	10,530,000	—	—	—	0.15	—

KM# 868.2 25 ORE

2.8000 g., Bronze, 17.5 mm. **Ruler:** Margrethe II **Obv:** Crown **Rev:** Value **Edge:** Plain **Note:** Without initials

Date	Mintage	F	VF	XF	Unc	BU
2002	12,000,000	—	—	—	0.15	—
2003	17,590,000	—	—	—	0.15	—
2004	7,040,304	—	—	—	0.15	—
2004 Proof	3,000	Value: 12.00				
2005	—	—	—	—	0.15	—
2005 Proof	—	Value: 12.00				
2006	—	—	—	—	0.15	—
2006 Proof	—	Value: 12.00				

KM# 866.2 50 ORE

4.3000 g., Bronze **Ruler:** Margrethe II **Obv:** Date above large crown, country name below, initial A to right **Rev:** Large heart above value, mint mark and initials LG-JP below **Note:** Beginning in 1996 and ending with 1998, the words "DANMARK" and "ØRE" have raised edges. Heart mint mark under the word "ØRE".

Date	Mintage	F	VF	XF	Unc	BU
2001 LG; JP; A	12,270,000	—	—	—	0.20	—

KM# 866.3 50 ORE

4.3000 g., Bronze **Ruler:** Margrethe II **Note:** No initials

Date	Mintage	F	VF	XF	Unc	BU
2002	3,900,000	—	—	—	0.20	—
2003	8,817,000	—	—	—	0.20	—
2004	10,040,706	—	—	—	0.20	—
2004 Proof	3,000	Value: 15.00				
2005	—	—	—	—	0.20	—
2005 Proof	—	Value: 15.00				
2006	—	—	—	—	0.20	—
2006 Proof	—	Value: 15.00				

KM# 873.1 KRONE

3.6000 g., Copper-Nickel **Ruler:** Margrethe II **Obv:** 3 crowned MII monograms, date, mint mark and initials LG-JP-A below **Rev:** Value, country name, ornaments around center hole **Note:** Prev. KM#873.

Date	Mintage	F	VF	XF	Unc	BU
2001 LG; JP; A	14,640,000	—	—	—	0.30	—

KM# 873.2 KRONE

3.6000 g., Copper-Nickel, 20.2 mm. **Ruler:** Margrethe II **Obv:** 3 crowns and MII monograms, date and mint mark **Rev:** Value and country name **Edge:** Reeded **Note:** Without initials

Date	Mintage	F	VF	XF	Unc	BU
2002	9,000,000	—	—	—	0.30	—
2003	5,231,000	—	—	—	0.30	—
2004	16,139,596	—	—	—	0.30	—
2004 Proof	3,000	Value: 18.00				
2005	—	—	—	—	0.30	—
2005 Proof	—	Value: 18.00				
2006	—	—	—	—	0.30	—
2006 Proof	—	Value: 18.00				

KM# 874.1 2 KRONER

Copper-Nickel **Ruler:** Margrethe II **Obv:** Value, country name, ornaments around center hole **Rev:** 3 crowned MII monograms around center hole, date and initials LG-JP-A below **Note:** Prev. KM#874.

Date	Mintage	F	VF	XF	Unc	BU
2001 LG; JP; A	11,180,000	—	—	—	0.50	—

KM# 874.2 2 KRONER

5.9400 g., Copper-Nickel, 24.5 mm. **Ruler:** Margrethe II **Obv:** 3 crowned MII monograms around center hole, date below **Rev:** Value, country name, ornaments around center hole **Edge:** Reeded and plain sections **Note:** Without initials

Date	Mintage	F	VF	XF	Unc	BU
2002	60,159,000	—	—	—	0.50	—
2004	7,381,531	—	—	—	0.50	—
2004 Proof	3,000	Value: 22.00				
2005	—	—	—	—	0.50	—
2005 Proof	—	Value: 22.00				
2006	—	—	—	—	0.50	—
2006 Proof	—	Value: 22.00				

KM# 869.1 5 KRONER

9.2000 g., Copper-Nickel **Ruler:** Margrethe II **Obv:** 3 crowned MII monograms around center hole, dates and initials LG-JP-A below **Rev:** Value, country name, ornaments around center hole **Note:** Large and small date varieties exist.

Date	Mintage	F	VF	XF	Unc	BU
2001 LG; JP; A	5,700,000	—	—	—	1.40	—

KM# 869.2 5 KRONER

9.2000 g., Copper Nickel, 28.5 mm. **Ruler:** Margrethe II **Obv:** 3 crowned MII monograms around center hole, dates below **Rev:** Value, country name, ornaments around center hole **Edge:** Reeded **Note:** Without initials

Date	Mintage	F	VF	XF	Unc	BU
2002	5,980,000	—	—	—	1.40	—
2004	1,415,925	—	—	—	1.40	—
2004 Proof	3,000	Value: 25.00				
2005	—	—	—	—	1.40	—
2005 Proof	—	Value: 25.00				
2006	—	—	—	—	1.40	—
2006 Proof	—	Value: 25.00				

KM# 887.1 10 KRONER

7.0000 g., Aluminum-Bronze, 23.4 mm. **Ruler:** Margrethe II **Obv:** Crowned head of Queen Margrethe II right within inner circle, date, initials LG-JP-A below, mint mark after II in title **Rev:** Crowned arms above denomination **Edge:** Plain **Designer:** Mogens Moeller

Date	Mintage	F	VF	XF	Unc	BU
2001 LG; JP; A	4,800,000	—	—	—	2.75	—

KM# 887.2 10 KRONER

7.0000 g., Aluminum-Bronze, 23.4 mm. **Ruler:** Margrethe II **Obv:** Crowned head of Queen Margrethe II right, mint mark after II in title **Rev:** Crowned arms and value **Edge:** Plain **Designer:** Mogens Moeller **Note:** Without initials

Date	Mintage	F	VF	XF	Unc	BU
2002	7,299,900	—	—	—	2.75	—

KM# 896 10 KRONER

Aluminum-Bronze **Ruler:** Margrethe II **Obv:** Queen's portrait **Rev:** Similar to KM#891.

Date	Mintage	F	VF	XF	Unc	BU
2004	5,835,426	—	—	—	2.50	—
2004 Proof	—	Value: 30.00				
2005	—	—	—	—	2.50	—
2005 Proof	—	Value: 30.00				
2006	—	—	—	—	2.50	—
2006 Proof	—	Value: 30.00				

KM# 898 10 KRONER

7.0000 g., Copper-Aluminum-Nickel, 23.4 mm. **Ruler:** Margrethe II **Subject:** Hans Christian Andersen, Ugly duckling story **Obv:** Margrethe II **Rev:** Swan on water **Edge:** Plain

Date	Mintage	F	VF	XF	Unc	BU
2005	1,200,000	—	—	—	4.50	—

KM# 898a 10 KRONER

31.1000 g., 0.9990 Silver 0.9989 oz. ASW **Ruler:** Margrethe II **Subject:** Hans Christian Andersen, Ugly Duckling **Rev:** Swan

Date	Mintage	F	VF	XF	Unc	BU
2005	75,000	—	—	—	—	30.00

KM# 898b 10 KRONER

8.6500 g., 0.9000 Gold 0.2503 oz. AGW **Ruler:** Margrethe II **Subject:** Hans Christian Andersen, Ugly Duckling

Date	Mintage	F	VF	XF	Unc	BU
2005	7,000	—	—	—	—	300

KM# 900 10 KRONER

7.0000 g., Aluminum-Bronze, 23.4 mm. **Ruler:** Margrethe II **Subject:** Hans Christian Andersen **Rev:** Little Mermaid

Date	Mintage	F	VF	XF	Unc	BU
2005	1,200,000	—	—	—	—	4.25

KM# 900a 10 KRONER

31.1000 g., 0.9990 Silver 0.9989 oz. ASW **Ruler:** Margrethe II **Subject:** Hans Christian Andersen **Rev:** Little Mermaid

Date	Mintage	F	VF	XF	Unc	BU
2005	60,000	—	—	—	—	30.00

KM# 900b 10 KRONER

7.6500 g., 0.9000 Gold 0.2214 oz. AGW **Ruler:** Margrethe II **Subject:** Hans Christian Andersen **Rev:** Little Mermaid

Date	Mintage	F	VF	XF	Unc	BU
2005	6,000	—	—	—	—	300

KM# 903a 10 KRONER

Silver **Ruler:** Margrethe II **Subject:** H.C. Andersen **Rev:** Skyggen

Date	Mintage	F	VF	XF	Unc	BU
2006	—	—	—	—	—	—

KM# 903b 10 KRONER

Gold **Ruler:** Margrethe II **Subject:** H.C. Andersen **Rev:** Skyggen

Date	Mintage	F	VF	XF	Unc	BU
2006	—	—	—	—	—	—

KM# 903 10 KRONER

Aluminum-Bronze **Ruler:** Margrethe II **Subject:** H.C. Andersen story "Skyggen" **Rev:** Skyggen **Note:** 3rd H.C. Andersen coin

Date	Mintage	F	VF	XF	Unc	BU
2006	—	—	—	—	4.50	—

KM# 888.1 20 KRONER

9.3000 g., Aluminum-Bronze **Ruler:** Margrethe II **Obv:** Crowned head of Queen Margrethe II right within inner circle, date and initials LG-JP-A below, mint mark after II in legend **Rev:** Crowned arms within ornaments and value **Edge:** Alternate reeded and plain sections **Designer:** Mogens Moeller

Date	Mintage	F	VF	XF	Unc	BU
2001(h) LG; JP; A	2,900,000	—	—	—	4.50	—

KM# 888.2 20 KRONER

9.3000 g., Aluminum-Bronze, 26.9 mm. **Ruler:** Margrethe II **Obv:** Crowned head of Queen Margrethe II right within inner circle, mint mark after II in legend **Rev:** Crowned arms within ornaments and value **Edge:** Alternate reeded and plain sections **Note:** Without initials.

Date	Mintage	F	VF	XF	Unc	BU
2002	5,500,000	—	—	—	4.50	—

KM# 889 20 KRONER

9.3000 g., Aluminum-Bronze **Ruler:** Margrethe II **Subject:** Arhus City Hall **Obv:** Queen's portrait, mint mark after II in legend **Rev:** Tower, without initials **Edge:** Reeded and plain sections

Date	Mintage	F	VF	XF	Unc	BU
2002	1,000,000	—	—	—	4.50	—
2003	—	—	—	—	4.50	—

KM# 890 20 KRONER

9.3000 g., Aluminum-Bronze, 26.8 mm. **Ruler:** Margrethe II **Subject:** Danish towers **Obv:** Queen's portrait, mint mark and date **Rev:** Copenhagen Old Stock Exchange spire with four intertwined dragon tails **Edge:** Alternate reeded and plain sections

Date	Mintage	F	VF	XF	Unc	BU
2003	1,000,000	—	—	—	4.50	—

KM# 891 20 KRONER

9.3000 g., Aluminum-Bronze, 26.8 mm. **Ruler:** Margrethe II **Obv:** Queen's portrait, mint mark and date **Rev:** Crowned arms above denomination **Edge:** Alternate reeded and plain sections

Date	Mintage	F	VF	XF	Unc	BU
2003	5,720,000	—	—	—	4.50	—
2004	6,922,182	—	—	—	4.50	—
2004 Proof	3,000	Value: 40.00				
2005	—	—	—	—	4.50	—
2005	—	Value: 45.00				
2006	—	—	—	—	4.50	—
2006 Proof	—	Value: 45.00				

KM# 892 20 KRONER

9.3100 g., Aluminum-Bronze, 26.8 mm. **Ruler:** Margrethe II **Subject:** Danish towers **Obv:** Queen Margrethe II, mint mark and date **Rev:** Christiansborg Castle (parliment) tower and Danish flag **Edge:** Alternate reeded and plain sections

Date	Mintage	F	VF	XF	Unc	BU
2003	1,000,000	—	—	—	4.50	—

KM# 893 20 KRONER

9.3100 g., Aluminum-Bronze, 26.8 mm. **Ruler:** Margrethe II **Subject:** Danish towers **Obv:** Queen Margrethe II **Rev:** Gåsetårnet tower **Edge:** Alternate reeded and plain sections

Date	Mintage	F	VF	XF	Unc	BU
2004	1,200,000	—	—	—	4.50	—

KM# 894 20 KRONER

9.3100 g., Aluminum-Bronze, 26.8 mm. **Ruler:** Margrethe II **Subject:** Crown Prince's Wedding **Obv:** Queen Margrethe II **Rev:** Crown Prince Frederik and Crown Princess Mary **Edge:** Alternate reeded and plain sections

Date	Mintage	F	VF	XF	Unc	BU
2004	1,200,000	—	—	—	4.50	—

KM# 897 20 KRONER

Aluminum-Bronze, 26.8 mm. **Ruler:** Margrethe II **Subject:** Danish towers **Obv:** Queen Margrethe II **Rev:** Svaneke water tower, Bornholm **Edge:** Alternate reeded and plain sections

Date	Mintage	F	VF	XF	Unc	BU
2004	1,200,000	—	—	—	4.50	—

KM# 904 20 KRONER

9.7300 g., Nickel-Brass, 27.4 mm. **Ruler:** Margrethe II **Subject:** 150 Years of Railway

Date	Mintage	F	VF	XF	Unc	BU
2004	—	—	—	—	10.00	—

KM# 899 20 KRONER

9.3000 g., Copper-Aluminum-Nickel, 26.8 mm. **Ruler:** Margrethe II **Obv:** Margrethe II **Rev:** Landet Kirke, with elements from the story of Elvira Madigan and Sixten Sparre, including a revolver among leaves of chestnut-trees **Edge:** Segmented reeding

Date	Mintage	F	VF	XF	Unc	BU
2005	1,200,000	—	—	—	8.00	—

KM# 901 20 KRONER
9.3000 g., Aluminum-Bronze, 26.8 mm. **Ruler:** Margrethe II **Rev:** Lighthouse of Nolsoy (Faeroe Islands)

Date	Mintage	F	VF	XF	Unc	BU
2005	1,200,000	—	—	—	8.00	—

KM# 902 20 KRONER
9.3300 g., Brass, 26.9 mm. **Ruler:** Margrethe II **Obv:** Queen **Rev:** Grasten Slut Bell Tower **Edge:** Segmented reeding

Date	Mintage	F	VF	XF	Unc	BU
2006(h)	—	—	—	—	—	7.50

KM# 905 20 KRONER
9.7300 g., Nickel-Brass, 27.4 mm. **Ruler:** Margrethe II **Subject:** Henrik Ibsen

Date	Mintage	F	VF	XF	Unc	BU
2006	—	—	—	—	10.00	—

KM# 895 200 KRONER
31.1000 g., 0.9990 Silver 0.9989 oz. ASW, 38.3 mm. **Ruler:** Margrethe II **Subject:** Wedding of Crown Prince **Obv:** Queen Margrethe II **Rev:** Crown Prince Frederik and Crown Princess Mary **Edge:** Plain **Note:** No initials.

Date	Mintage	F	VF	XF	Unc	BU
2004	125,000	—	—	—	50.00	—

MINT SETS

KM#	Date	Mintage	Identification	Issue Price	Mkt Val
MS46	2001 (7)	28,000	KM866.2, 868, 869, 873, 874, 887, 888	15.00	25.00
MS47	2002 (7)	28,000	KM866.3, 868.2, 869.2, 873.2, 874.2, 887.2, 888.2	17.50	20.00
MS48	2003 (6)	35,000	KM866.3, 868.2, 873.2, 889, 890, 891	17.50	20.00
MS49	2004 (8)	35,000	KM#866.3, 868.2, 869.2, 873.2, 874.2, 891, 895, 896, plus medal in Nordic gold	34.50	35.00
MS50	2005 (8)	31,000	KM#866.3, 868.2, 869.2, 873.2, 874.2, 869.2, 896, 891, 898.	34.50	35.00
MS51	2006 (8)	—	KM#868.2, 866.3, 873.2, 874.2, 869.2, 896, 902, plus silver medal	40.00	—

PROOF SETS

KM#	Date	Mintage	Identification	Issue Price	Mkt Val
PS1	2004 (8)	3,000	KM#866.3, 868.2, 869.2, 873.2, 874.2, 896, 891, plus Wedding medal in .925 Silver	150	190
PS2	2005 (9)	3,500	KM866.2, 868.2, 873.2, 874.2, 869.2, 896, 891, 898, and 1801 Battle of Copenhagen medal.	150	165

DJIBOUTI

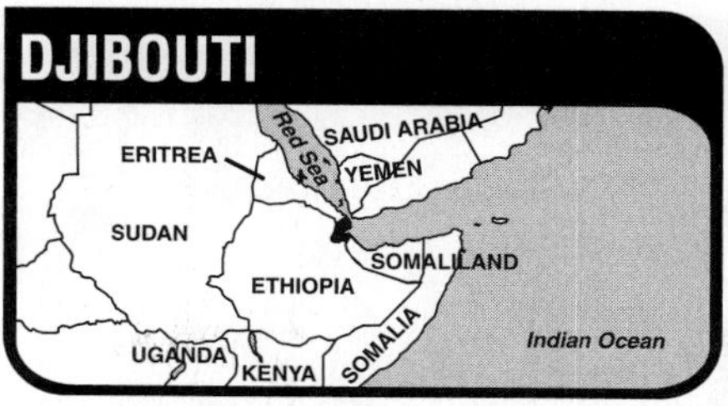

The Republic of Djibouti (formerly French Somaliland and the French Overseas Territory of Afars and Issas), located in northeast Africa at the Bab el Mandeb Strait connecting the Suez Canal and the Red Sea with the Gulf of Aden and the Indian Ocean, has an area of 8,950 sq. mi. (22,000 sq. km.) and a population of 421,320. Capital: Djibouti. The tiny nation has less than one sq. mi. of arable land, and no natural resources except salt, sand, and camels. The commercial activities of the transshipment port of Djibouti and the Addis Abada-Djibouti railroad are the basis of the economy. Salt, fish and hides are exported.

REPUBLIC

STANDARD COINAGE

KM# 34 10 FRANCS
3.4000 g., Copper-Nickel, 20.9 mm. **Obv:** National arms **Rev:** Chimpanzee **Edge:** Plain

Date	Mintage	F	VF	XF	Unc	BU
2003	—	—	—	—	1.00	2.00

DOMINICAN REPUBLIC

The Dominican Republic, which occupies the eastern two-thirds of the island of Hispaniola, has an area of 18,704 sq. mi. (48,734 sq. km.) and a population of 7.9 million. Capital: Santo Domingo. The largely agricultural economy produces sugar, coffee, tobacco and cocoa. Tourism and casino gaming are also a rising source of revenue.

REPUBLIC

REFORM COINAGE

1937

100 Centavos = 1 Peso Oro

KM# 80.1 PESO
Copper-Zinc **Subject:** Juan Pablo Duarte **Countermark:** 11-sided **Obv:** Denomination, national arms **Rev:** DUARTE on bust **Note:** Coin die alignment.

Date	Mintage	F	VF	XF	Unc	BU
2002	—	—	—	—	2.00	2.50

KM# 80.2 PESO
Copper-Zinc **Subject:** Juan Pablo Duarte **Obv:** Denomination, national arms **Rev:** DUARTE below bust

Date	Mintage	F	VF	XF	Unc	BU
2002	—	—	—	—	2.00	2.50

KM# 90 PESO
12.5000 g., Copper-Nickel, 30.6 mm. **Obv:** Pan American Games logo **Rev:** Value and national arms **Edge:** Reeded

Date	Mintage	F	VF	XF	Unc	BU
2003 Proof	—	Value: 15.00				

KM# 89 5 PESOS
5.9500 g., Bi-Metallic Stainless Steel center in Brass ring, 23 mm. **Subject:** Sanchez **Obv:** National arms and denomination **Rev:** Portrait **Edge:** Segmented reeding

Date	Mintage	F	VF	XF	Unc	BU
2002	—	—	—	—	2.50	3.00

KM# 91 10 PESOS
2.4500 g., 0.9990 Silver 0.0787 oz. ASW, 18 mm. **Obv:** National arms **Rev:** St. Andrews Chapel

Date	Mintage	F	VF	XF	Unc	BU
2002 Proof	—	Value: 15.00				

KM# 92 10 PESOS
2.4500 g., 0.9990 Silver 0.0787 oz. ASW, 18 mm. **Obv:** National arms **Rev:** Our Lady of Carmen Church

Date	Mintage	F	VF	XF	Unc	BU
2002 Proof	—	Value: 15.00				

KM# 93 10 PESOS
2.4500 g., 0.9990 Silver 0.0787 oz. ASW, 18 mm. **Obv:** National arms **Rev:** Regina Angelorum Church

Date	Mintage	F	VF	XF	Unc	BU
2002 Proof	—	Value: 15.00				

KM# 94 10 PESOS
2.4500 g., 0.9990 Silver 0.0787 oz. ASW, 18 mm. **Obv:** National arms **Rev:** Chapel of the Remedies

Date	Mintage	F	VF	XF	Unc	BU
2002 Proof	—	Value: 15.00				

KM# 95 10 PESOS
2.4500 g., 0.9990 Silver 0.0787 oz. ASW, 18 mm. **Obv:** National arms **Rev:** St. Lazarus Church

Date	Mintage	F	VF	XF	Unc	BU
2002 Proof	—	Value: 15.00				

KM# 96 10 PESOS
2.4500 g., 0.9990 Silver 0.0787 oz. ASW, 18 mm. **Obv:** National arms **Rev:** St. Michael's Church

Date	Mintage	F	VF	XF	Unc	BU
2002 Proof	—	Value: 15.00				

KM# 97 10 PESOS
2.4500 g., 0.9990 Silver 0.0787 oz. ASW, 18 mm. **Obv:** National arms **Rev:** Church of Santa Barbara

Date	Mintage	F	VF	XF	Unc	BU
2002 Proof	—	Value: 15.00				

KM# 98 10 PESOS
2.4500 g., 0.9990 Silver 0.0787 oz. ASW, 18 mm. **Obv:** National arms **Rev:** Our Lady of the Rosary Church

Date	Mintage	F	VF	XF	Unc	BU
2002 Proof	—	Value: 15.00				

KM# 99 10 PESOS
2.4500 g., 0.9990 Silver 0.0787 oz. ASW, 18 mm. **Obv:** National arms **Rev:** Church of Banica

Date	Mintage	F	VF	XF	Unc	BU
2002 Proof	—	Value: 15.00				

KM# 100 10 PESOS
2.4500 g., 0.9990 Silver 0.0787 oz. ASW, 18 mm. **Obv:** National arms **Rev:** Church of Boya

Date	Mintage	F	VF	XF	Unc	BU
2002 Proof	—	Value: 15.00				

KM# 101 10 PESOS
2.4500 g., 0.9990 Silver 0.0787 oz. ASW, 18 mm. **Obv:** National arms **Rev:** Santo Domingo Cathedral

Date	Mintage	F	VF	XF	Unc	BU
2002 Proof	—	Value: 15.00				

KM# 102 10 PESOS
2.4500 g., 0.9990 Silver 0.0787 oz. ASW, 18 mm. **Obv:** National arms **Rev:** Holy Cross Cathedral of El Seibo

Date	Mintage	F	VF	XF	Unc	BU
2002 Proof	—	Value: 15.00				

KM# 103 10 PESOS
2.4500 g., 0.9990 Silver 0.0787 oz. ASW, 18 mm. **Obv:** National arms **Rev:** Higney Sanctuary

Date	Mintage	F	VF	XF	Unc	BU
2002 Proof	—	Value: 15.00				

PROOF SETS

KM#	Date	Mintage	Identification	Issue Price	Mkt Val
PS32	2002 (13)	—	KM#91-103	—	195

The East Caribbean States, formerly the British Caribbean Territories (Eastern group), formed a currency board in 1950 to provide the constituent territories of Trinidad & Tobago, Barbados, British Guiana (now Guyana), British Virgin Islands, Anguilla, St. Kitts, Nevis, Antigua, Dominica, St. Lucia, St. Vincent and Grenada with a common currency, thereby permitting withdrawal of the regular British Pound currency. This was dissolved in 1965 and after the breakup, the East Caribbean Territories, a grouping including Barbados, the Leeward and Windward Islands, came into being. Coinage of the dissolved 'Eastern Group' continues to circulate. Paper currency of the East Caribbean Authority was first issued in 1965 and although Barbados withdrew from the group they continued using them prior to 1973 when Barbados issued a decimal coinage.

A series of 4-dollar coins tied to the FAO coinage program were released in 1970 under the name of the Caribbean Development Bank by eight loosely federated island groupings in the eastern Caribbean. These issues are listed individually in this volume under Antigua, Barbados, Dominica, Grenada, Montserrat, St. Kitts, St. Lucia and St. Vincent.

RULERS
British

EAST CARIBBEAN STATES

British Administration

STANDARD COINAGE

100 Cents = 1 Dollar

KM# 34 CENT
1.0300 g., Aluminum, 18.42 mm. **Obv:** Queen's new portrait **Rev:** Denomination **Edge:** Plain

Date	Mintage	F	VF	XF	Unc	BU
2002	—	—	—	—	0.20	0.30

KM# 35 2 CENTS
1.4200 g., Aluminum, 21.46 mm. **Obv:** Queen's new portrait **Rev:** Denomination **Edge:** Plain

Date	Mintage	F	VF	XF	Unc	BU
2002	—	—	—	—	0.25	0.35

KM# 36 5 CENTS
1.7400 g., Aluminum, 23.11 mm. **Obv:** Queen's new portrait **Rev:** Denomination **Edge:** Plain

Date	Mintage	F	VF	XF	Unc	BU
2002	—	—	—	—	0.30	0.45

KM# 37 10 CENTS
Copper-Nickel, 18.06 mm. **Obv:** Queen's new portrait **Rev:** Sir Francis Drake's Golden Hind and denomination **Edge:** Reeded

Date	Mintage	F	VF	XF	Unc	BU
2002	—	—	—	—	0.40	0.60

KM# 38 25 CENTS
6.4800 g., Copper-Nickel, 23.98 mm. **Obv:** Queen's new portrait **Rev:** Sir Francis Drake's Golden Hind **Edge:** Reeded

Date	Mintage	F	VF	XF	Unc	BU
2002	—	—	—	—	0.50	0.75

KM# 39 DOLLAR
7.9800 g., Copper-Nickel, 26.5 mm. **Obv:** Queen's new portrait **Rev:** Sir Francis Drake's Golden Hind and denomination **Edge:** Alternating plain and reeded

Date	Mintage	F	VF	XF	Unc	BU
2002	—	—	—	—	2.00	3.00

KM# 40 DOLLAR
28.2800 g., Gold Plated Copper-Nickel, 38.6 mm. **Subject:** Golden Jubilee Monarchs **Obv:** Queen's portrait **Rev:** Henry III (1216-1277) **Edge:** Reeded

Date	Mintage	F	VF	XF	Unc	BU
2002	5,000	—	—	—	22.50	25.00

KM# 42 DOLLAR
28.2800 g., Gold Plated Copper-Nickel, 38.6 mm. **Subject:** Golden Jubilee Monarchs **Obv:** Queen's portrait **Rev:** Edward III (1327-1377) **Edge:** Reeded

Date	Mintage	F	VF	XF	Unc	BU
2002	5,000	—	—	—	22.50	25.00

KM# 44 DOLLAR
28.2800 g., Gold Plated Copper-Nickel, 38.6 mm. **Subject:** Golden Jubilee Monarchs **Obv:** Queen's portrait **Rev:** George III (1760-1820) **Edge:** Reeded

Date	Mintage	F	VF	XF	Unc	BU
2002	5,000	—	—	—	22.50	25.00

KM# 46 DOLLAR
28.2800 g., Gold Plated Copper-Nickel, 38.6 mm. **Subject:** Golden Jubilee Monarchs **Obv:** Queen's portrait **Rev:** Queen Victoria (1837-1901) **Edge:** Reeded

Date	Mintage	F	VF	XF	Unc	BU
2002	5,000	—	—	—	22.50	25.00

KM# 48 DOLLAR
28.2800 g., Gold Plated Copper-Nickel, 38.6 mm. **Subject:** Golden Jubilee Monarchs **Obv:** Queen's portrait **Rev:** Queen Elizabeth II (1952-) **Edge:** Reeded

Date	Mintage	F	VF	XF	Unc	BU
2002	5,000	—	—	—	22.50	25.00

KM# 86 DOLLAR
27.7300 g., Copper-Nickel, 38.5 mm. **Subject:** Coronation Jubilee **Obv:** Queen's portrait **Rev:** Fireworks display above building **Edge:** Reeded

Date	Mintage	F	VF	XF	Unc	BU
2002	—	—	—	—	10.00	12.00

KM# 51 2 DOLLARS
56.5600 g., Gold Plated Copper-Nickel, 38.6 mm. **Subject:** British Military Leaders **Obv:** Queen's portrait **Rev:** Wellington's portrait and battle scene **Edge:** Reeded

Date	Mintage	F	VF	XF	Unc	BU
2002 Proof	10,000	Value: 45.00				

KM# 54 2 DOLLARS
56.5600 g., Gold Plated Copper-Nickel, 38.6 mm. **Subject:** British Military Leaders **Obv:** Queen's portrait **Rev:** Admiral Nelson's portrait and naval battle scene **Edge:** Reeded

Date	Mintage	F	VF	XF	Unc	BU
2003 Proof	10,000	Value: 45.00				

KM# 57 2 DOLLARS
56.5600 g., Gold Plated Copper-Nickel, 38.6 mm. **Subject:** British Military Leaders **Obv:** Queen's portrait **Rev:** Churchill's portrait and air battle scene **Edge:** Reeded

Date	Mintage	F	VF	XF	Unc	BU
2003 Proof	10,000	Value: 45.00				

KM# 41 10 DOLLARS
28.2800 g., 0.9250 Silver with gold cameo 0.841 oz. ASW, 38.6 mm. **Subject:** Golden Jubilee Monarchs **Obv:** Queen's portrait **Rev:** Henry III (1216-1272) **Edge:** Reeded

Date	Mintage	F	VF	XF	Unc	BU
2002 Proof	10,000	Value: 65.00				

KM# 41a 10 DOLLARS
39.9400 g., 0.9166 Gold 1.177 oz. AGW, 38.6 mm. **Subject:** Golden Jubilee Monarchs **Obv:** Queen's portrait **Rev:** Henry III (1216-1272) **Edge:** Reeded

Date	Mintage	F	VF	XF	Unc	BU
2002 Proof	100	Value: 1,100				

KM# 43 10 DOLLARS
28.2800 g., 0.9250 Silver 0.841 oz. ASW, 38.6 mm. **Subject:** Golden Jubile Monarchs **Obv:** Queen's portrait **Rev:** Edward III (1327-1377) **Edge:** Reeded

Date	Mintage	F	VF	XF	Unc	BU
2002 Proof	10,000	Value: 65.00				

KM# 43a 10 DOLLARS
39.9400 g., 0.9166 Gold 1.177 oz. AGW, 38.6 mm. **Subject:** Golden Jubilee Monarchs **Obv:** Queen's portrait **Rev:** Edward III (1327-1377) **Edge:** Reeded

Date	Mintage	F	VF	XF	Unc	BU
2002 Proof	100	Value: 1,100				

KM# 45 10 DOLLARS
28.2800 g., 0.9250 Silver with gold cameo 0.841 oz. ASW, 38.6 mm. **Subject:** Golden Jubilee Monarchs **Obv:** Queen's portrait **Rev:** George III (1760-1820) **Edge:** Reeded

Date	Mintage	F	VF	XF	Unc	BU
2002 Proof	10,000	Value: 65.00				

KM# 45a 10 DOLLARS
39.9400 g., 0.9166 Gold 1.177 oz. AGW, 38.6 mm. **Subject:** Golden Jubilee Monarchs **Obv:** Queen's portrait **Rev:** George III (1760-1820) **Edge:** Reeded

Date	Mintage	F	VF	XF	Unc	BU
2002 Proof	100	Value: 1,100				

KM# 47 10 DOLLARS
28.2800 g., 0.9250 Silver With Partial Gold Plating 0.841 oz., 38.6 mm. **Subject:** Golden Jubilee Monarchs **Obv:** Queen's portrait **Rev:** Queen Victoria (1837-1901) **Edge:** Reeded

Date	Mintage	F	VF	XF	Unc	BU
2002 Proof	10,000	Value: 65.00				

KM# 47a 10 DOLLARS
39.9400 g., 0.9166 Gold 1.177 oz. AGW, 38.6 mm. **Subject:** Golden Jubilee Monarchs **Obv:** Queen's portrait **Rev:** Queen Victoria (1837-1901) **Edge:** Reeded

Date	Mintage	F	VF	XF	Unc	BU
2002 Proof	100	Value: 1,100				

KM# 49 10 DOLLARS
28.2800 g., 0.9250 Silver with gold cameo 0.841 oz. ASW, 38.6 mm. **Subject:** Golden Jubilee Monarchs **Obv:** Queen's portrait **Rev:** Queen Elizabeth II (1952-) **Edge:** Reeded

Date	Mintage	F	VF	XF	Unc	BU
2002 Proof	10,000	Value: 65.00				

KM# 49a 10 DOLLARS
39.9400 g., 0.9166 Gold 1.177 oz. AGW, 38.6 mm. **Subject:** Golden Jubilee Monarchs **Obv:** Queen's portrait **Rev:** Queen Elizabeth II (1952-) **Edge:** Reeded

Date	Mintage	F	VF	XF	Unc	BU
2002 Proof	100	Value: 1,100				

EAST TIMOR

ATAURO ISLAND
Diui
OCUSSI (Okusi)
EAST TIMOR
WESTERN TIMOR (Indonesian)
Timor Sea

East Timor, population: 522,433, area: 7332 sq. miles, capital: Dili, is primarily located on the eastern half of the island of Timor, just northwest of Australia at the eastern end of the Indonesian archipelago. Formerly a Portuguese colony, Timor declared its independence from Portugal on November 28, 1975. After nine short days of fledgling autonomy, a guerilla faction sympathetic to the Indonesian territorial claim to East Timor seized the government. On July 17, 1976 the Provisional government enacted a law, which dissolved the free republic and made East Timor the 24th province of Indonesia. Violent rule and civil unrest plagued the province, with great loss of life and extreme damage to property and natural resources until independence was again achieved with United Nations assistance during a period from 1999 to 2002. Emerging as the Democratic Republic of Timor-Leste and commonly known as East Timor the country has worked, with international assistance to rebuild its decimated infrastructure. Natural resources waiting to be tapped include rich oil reserves, though current exports are most dependent on coffee, sandalwood and marble. The first coins of the new republic were issued in 2003.

DEMOCRATIC REPUBLIC OF TIMOR-LESTE

DECIMAL COINAGE

KM# 1 CENTAVO
3.1000 g., Nickel Clad Steel, 17 mm. **Obv:** Nautilus **Rev:** Value **Edge:** Plain

Date	Mintage	F	VF	XF	Unc	BU
2003	1,500,000	—	—	—	1.50	2.50
2003 Proof	12,500	Value: 7.00				
2004	1,500,000	—	—	—	1.50	2.50

KM# 2 5 CENTAVOS
4.0500 g., Nickel Clad Steel, 18.8 mm. **Obv:** Rice plant **Rev:** Value **Edge:** Plain

Date	Mintage	F	VF	XF	Unc	BU
2003	1,500,000	—	—	—	2.00	3.00
2003 Proof	12,500	Value: 9.00				
2004	1,500,000	—	—	—	2.00	3.00

KM# 3 10 CENTAVOS
5.1100 g., Nickel Clad Steel, 20.8 mm. **Obv:** Rooster **Rev:** Value **Edge:** Plain

Date	Mintage	F	VF	XF	Unc	BU
2003	2,500,000	—	—	—	2.50	4.00
2003 Proof	12,500	Value: 12.00				
2004	2,500,000	—	—	—	2.50	4.00

KM# 4 25 CENTAVOS
5.8700 g., Copper-Zinc-Nickel, 21.3 mm. **Obv:** Sail boat **Rev:** Value **Edge:** Reeded

Date	Mintage	F	VF	XF	Unc	BU
2003	1,500,000	—	—	—	3.50	5.00
2003 Proof	12,500	Value: 15.00				
2004	1,500,000	—	—	—	3.50	5.00

KM# 5 50 CENTAVOS
6.5000 g., Copper-Zinc-Nickel, 25 mm. **Obv:** Coffee plant with beans **Rev:** Value **Edge:** Reeded

Date	Mintage	F	VF	XF	Unc	BU
2003	1,000,000	—	—	—	5.00	7.00
2003 Proof	12,500	Value: 20.00				
2004	1,000,000	—	—	—	5.00	7.00

MINT SETS

KM#	Date	Mintage	Identification	Issue Price	Mkt Val
MS1	2003 (5)	25,000	KM#1 - KM#5	27.84	35.00

PROOF SETS

KM#	Date	Mintage	Identification	Issue Price	Mkt Val
PS1	2003 (5)	12,500	KM#1 - KM#5	57.25	65.00

ECUADOR

North Pacific Ocean
COLOMBIA
BRAZIL
PERU

The Republic of Ecuador, located astride the equator on the Pacific Coast of South America, has an area of 105,037 sq. mi. (283,560 sq. km.) and a population of 10.9 million. Capital: Quito. Agriculture is the mainstay of the economy but there are appreciable deposits of minerals and petroleum. It is one of the world's largest exporters of bananas and balsa wood. Coffee, cacao, sugar and petroleum are also valuable exports.

REPUBLIC

DECIMAL COINAGE

10 Centavos = 1 Decimo; 10 Decimos = 1 Sucre;
25 Sucres = 1 Condor

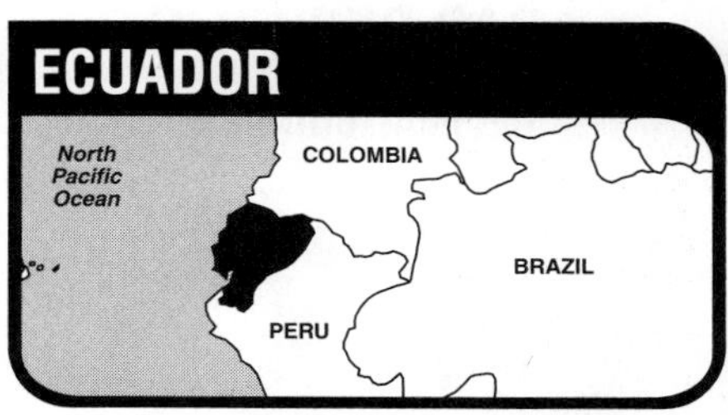

KM# 104 CENTAVO (Un)
2.5200 g., Brass, 19 mm. **Obv:** Map of the Americas **Rev:** Denomination **Edge:** Plain

Date	Mintage	F	VF	XF	Unc	BU
2003	—	—	—	—	0.20	0.40
2004	—	—	—	—	0.20	0.40

KM# 104a CENTAVO (Un)
2.4200 g., Copper Plated Steel, 19 mm. **Obv:** Map **Rev:** Value **Edge:** Plain

Date	Mintage	F	VF	XF	Unc	BU
2003	—	—	—	—	0.30	0.50

The Arab Republic of Egypt, located on the northeastern corner of Africa, has an area of 385,229 sq. mi. (1,1001,450 sq. km.) and a population of 62.4 million. Capital: Cairo. Although Egypt is an almost rainless expanse of desert, its economy is predominantly agricultural. Cotton, rice and petroleum are exported. Other main sources of income are revenues from the Suez Canal, remittances of Egyptian workers abroad and tourism.

ARAB REPUBLIC

AH1391- / 1971- AD

DECIMAL COINAGE

KM# 922 10 PIASTRES
4.5200 g., Copper-Nickel, 24.8 mm. **Subject:** National Women's Council **Obv:** Value **Rev:** Woman standing next to Sphinx **Edge:** Reeded

Date	Mintage	F	VF	XF	Unc
AH1425-2004	—	—	—	—	1.50

KM# 923 20 PIASTRES
6.0000 g., Copper-Nickel, 26.8 mm. **Subject:** National Women's Council **Obv:** Value **Rev:** Woman standing next to Sphinx **Edge:** Reeded

Date	Mintage	F	VF	XF	Unc
AH1425-2004	—	—	—	—	2.50

KM# 903 1/2 POUND
4.0000 g., 0.8750 Gold 0.1125 oz. AGW, 18 mm. **Subject:** Egyptian Museum Centennial **Obv:** Value **Rev:** Building **Edge:** Reeded

Date	Mintage	F	VF	XF	Unc
AH1423-2002	—	—	—	—	250

KM# 930 POUND
15.0000 g., 0.7200 Silver 0.3472 oz. ASW, 35 mm. **Subject:** National Women's Council **Obv:** Value **Rev:** Woman standing next to Sphinx **Edge:** Reeded

Date	Mintage	F	VF	XF	Unc
AH1421-2001	600	—	—	—	45.00

KM# 904 POUND
15.0000 g., 0.7200 Silver 0.3472 oz. ASW, 35 mm. **Subject:** Egyptian Museum Centennial **Obv:** Value **Rev:** Building **Edge:** Reeded

Date	Mintage	F	VF	XF	Unc
AH1423-2002	1,500	—	—	—	35.00

KM# 905 POUND
8.0000 g., 0.8750 Gold 0.2251 oz. AGW, 24 mm. **Subject:** Egyptian Museum Centennial **Obv:** Value **Rev:** Building **Edge:** Reeded

Date	Mintage	F	VF	XF	Unc
AH1423-2002	—	—	—	—	400

KM# 909 POUND
15.0000 g., 0.7200 Silver 0.3472 oz. ASW, 35 mm. **Subject:** International Ear, Nose and Throat Conference **Obv:** King Tut's Gold Mask **Rev:** "IFOS" on world map **Edge:** Reeded

Date	Mintage	F	VF	XF	Unc
AH1423-2002	2,500	—	—	—	30.00

KM# 910 POUND
14.9400 g., 0.7200 Silver 0.3458 oz. ASW, 34.9 mm. **Subject:** 50th Anniversary of Egyptian Revolution **Obv:** Value **Rev:** Soldier with flag **Edge:** Reeded

Date	Mintage	F	VF	XF	Unc
AH1423-2002	1,500	—	—	—	35.00

KM# 912 POUND
15.0000 g., 0.7200 Silver 0.3472 oz. ASW, 35 mm. **Obv:** Legend and inscription **Rev:** Inscribed arches above Alexandria library roof **Edge:** Reeded

Date	Mintage	F	VF	XF	Unc
AH1423-2002	—	—	—	—	30.00

KM# 913 POUND
15.0000 g., 0.7200 Silver 0.3472 oz. ASW, 35 mm. **Subject:** Body Building Championships **Obv:** Arabic and English legends **Rev:** Mr. Universe cartoon **Edge:** Reeded

Date	Mintage	F	VF	XF	Unc
AH1423-2002	800	—	—	—	30.00

KM# 915 POUND
15.0000 g., 0.7200 Silver 0.3472 oz. ASW, 35 mm. **Subject:** 30th Anniversary of the October War **Obv:** Value, dates and legend **Rev:** Soldier with flag above pyramids **Edge:** Reeded

Date	Mintage	F	VF	XF	Unc
AH1424-2003	—	—	—	—	30.00

KM# 917 POUND
15.0000 g., 0.7200 Silver 0.3472 oz. ASW, 35 mm. **Subject:** 25th Anniversary of the Commerce Society **Obv:** Value, dates and legend **Rev:** Radiant sun above lattice work **Edge:** Reeded

Date	Mintage	F	VF	XF	Unc
AH1424-2003	—	—	—	—	30.00

KM# 924 POUND
15.0000 g., 0.7200 Silver 0.3472 oz. ASW, 35 mm. **Obv:** Value **Rev:** Navy pilot's wings **Edge:** Reeded

Date	Mintage	F	VF	XF	Unc
AH1425-2004	—	—	—	—	30.00

KM# 934 POUND
Silver, 35 mm. **Subject:** Golden Jubilee - Military Production Day

Date	Mintage	F	VF	XF	Unc
AH1425-2004	—	—	—	—	30.00

KM# 931 5 POUNDS
17.5000 g., 0.7200 Silver 0.4051 oz. ASW, 37 mm. **Subject:** National Women's Council **Obv:** Value **Rev:** Woman standing next to Sphinx **Edge:** Reeded

Date	Mintage	F	VF	XF	Unc
AH1421-2001	600	—	—	—	55.00

KM# 932 5 POUNDS
17.5000 g., 0.7200 Silver 0.4051 oz. ASW, 37 mm. **Subject:** 50th Anniversary of the National Police **Obv:** Value and police logo **Rev:** Ceremonial design **Edge:** Reeded

Date	Mintage	F	VF	XF	Unc
AH1422-2002	—	—	—	—	45.00

KM# 906 5 POUNDS
17.5000 g., 0.7200 Silver 0.4051 oz. ASW, 37 mm. **Subject:** Egyptian Museum Centennial **Obv:** Value **Rev:** Building **Edge:** Reeded

Date	Mintage	F	VF	XF	Unc
AH1423-2002	1,500	—	—	—	40.00

KM# 907 5 POUNDS
26.0000 g., 0.8750 Gold 0.7314 oz. AGW, 33 mm. **Subject:** Egyptian Museum Centennial **Obv:** Value **Rev:** Building **Edge:** Reeded

Date	Mintage	F	VF	XF	Unc
AH1423-2002	—	—	—	—	520

KM# 911 5 POUNDS
17.5500 g., 0.9250 Silver 0.5219 oz. ASW, 37 mm.
Subject: 50th Anniversary of the Egyptian Revolution **Obv:** Value **Rev:** Soldier with flag **Edge:** Reeded

Date	Mintage	F	VF	XF	Unc
AH1423-2002	1,500	—	—	—	40.00

KM# 914 5 POUNDS
17.5000 g., 0.7200 Silver 0.4051 oz. ASW, 37 mm.
Subject: Body Building Championships **Obv:** Arabic and English legends **Rev:** Mr. Universe cartoon **Edge:** Reeded

Date	Mintage	F	VF	XF	Unc
AH1423-2002	800	—	—	—	35.00

KM# 916 5 POUNDS
17.5000 g., 0.7200 Silver 0.4051 oz. ASW, 37 mm. **Subject:** 30th Anniversary of the October War **Obv:** Value and legend **Rev:** Soldier with flag above pyramids **Edge:** Reeded

Date	Mintage	F	VF	XF	Unc
AH1424-2003	—	—	—	—	35.00

KM# 918 5 POUNDS
17.5000 g., 0.7200 Silver 0.4051 oz. ASW, 37 mm. **Obv:** Value and legend **Rev:** Geo-Physical Institute **Edge:** Reeded

Date	Mintage	F	VF	XF	Unc
AH1424-2003	—	—	—	—	35.00

KM# 919 5 POUNDS
17.5000 g., 0.7200 Silver 0.4051 oz. ASW, 37 mm.
Subject: 50th Anniversary of the Republic **Obv:** Value and legend **Rev:** Portrait and building **Edge:** Reeded

Date	Mintage	F	VF	XF	Unc
AH1424-2003	—	—	—	—	35.00

KM# 920 5 POUNDS
17.5000 g., 0.7200 Silver 0.4051 oz. ASW, 37 mm.
Subject: 25th Anniversary of the Delta Bank **Obv:** Value and legend **Rev:** Delta on world globe **Edge:** Reeded

Date	Mintage	F	VF	XF	Unc
AH1424-2004	—	—	—	—	35.00

KM# 925 5 POUNDS
17.5000 g., 0.7200 Silver 0.4051 oz. ASW, 37 mm. **Obv:** Value **Rev:** Balance scale **Edge:** Reeded

Date	Mintage	F	VF	XF	Unc
AH1425-2004	—	—	—	—	35.00

KM# 933 5 POUNDS
Silver, 37 mm. **Subject:** 90th Anniversary - Egyptian Scouts Organization - 1914-2004

Date	Mintage	F	VF	XF	Unc
AH1425-2004	—	—	—	—	35.00

KM# 935 5 POUNDS
Silver, 37 mm. **Subject:** Golden Jubilee - Military Production Day

Date	Mintage	F	VF	XF	Unc
AH1425-2004	—	—	—	—	35.00

KM# 908 10 POUNDS
40.0000 g., 0.8750 Gold 1.1253 oz. AGW, 37 mm.
Subject: Egyptian Museum Centennial **Obv:** Denomination **Rev:** Building **Edge:** Reeded

Date	Mintage	F	VF	XF	Unc
AH1423-2002	—	—	—	—	750

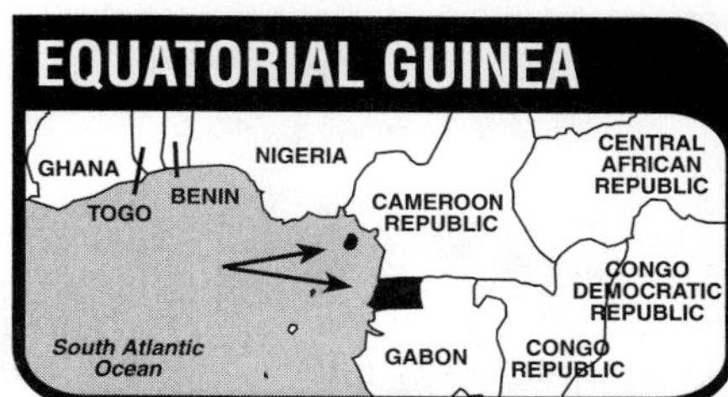

The Republic of Equatorial Guinea (formerly Spanish Guinea) consists of Rio Muni, located on the coast of West-Central Africa between Cameroon and Gabon, and the off-shore islands of Fernando Po, Annobon, Corisco, Elobey Grande and Elobey Chico. The equatorial country has an area of 10,831 sq. mi. (28,050 sq. km.) and a population of 420,293. Capital: Malabo. The economy is based on agriculture and forestry. Cacao, wood and coffee are exported.

MINT MARKS
(a) - Paris, privy marks only

REPUBLIC

INSTITUT MONETAIRE

KM# 124 1500 CFA FRANCS - 1 AFRICA
Nickel Plated Iron, 26 mm. **Obv:** Cowry shells **Rev:** Elephant head on full Africa map **Edge:** Plain

Date	Mintage	F	VF	XF	Unc	BU
2005	2,005	—	—	—	20.00	—

KM# 124a 1500 CFA FRANCS - 1 AFRICA
0.9990 Silver, 26 mm. **Obv:** Cowry shells **Rev:** Elephant head on full Africa map

Date	Mintage	F	VF	XF	Unc	BU
2005	25	—	—	—	360	—

ESTONIA

The Republic of Estonia (formerly the Estonian Soviet Socialist Republic of the U.S.S.R.) is the northernmost of the three Baltic States in Eastern Europe. It has an area of 17,462 sq. mi. (45,100 sq. km.) and a population of 1.6 million. Capital: Tallinn. Agriculture and dairy farming are the principal industries. Butter, eggs, bacon, timber and petroleum are exported.

MODERN REPUBLIC
1991 - present

STANDARD COINAGE

KM# 22 10 SENTI
Copper-Aluminum-Nickel, 17.2 mm. **Edge:** Plain

Date	Mintage	F	VF	XF	Unc	BU
2002	—	—	—	—	0.34	—

KM# 23a 20 SENTI
2.0000 g., Nickel Plated Steel, 18.9 mm. **Edge:** Plain

Date	Mintage	F	VF	XF	Unc	BU
2003	—	—	—	—	0.65	—
2004	—	—	—	—	0.65	—

KM# 24 50 SENTI
3.0000 g., Brass, 19.5 mm. **Edge:** Plain

Date	Mintage	F	VF	XF	Unc	BU
2004	—	—	—	—	1.00	—

KM# 35 KROON
5.0000 g., Brass, 23.25 mm. **Edge:** Three reeded and plain sections

Date	Mintage	F	VF	XF	Unc	BU
2001	—	—	—	—	1.25	—
2003	—	—	—	—	1.25	—

FALKLAND ISLANDS

The Colony of the Falkland Islands and Dependencies, a British colony located in the South Atlantic about 500 miles northeast of Cape Horn, has an area of 4,700 sq. mi. (12,170 sq. km.) and a population of 2,121. East Falkland, West Falkland, South Georgia, and South Sandwich are the largest of the 200 islands. Capital: Stanley. Sheep grazing is the main industry. Wool, whale oil, and seal oil are exported.

RULERS
British

MONETARY SYSTEM
100 Pence = 1 Pound

BRITISH COLONY
DECIMAL COINAGE

KM# 70 50 PENCE
29.1000 g., Copper-Nickel, 38.6 mm. **Subject:** Centennial of Queen Victoria's Death **Obv:** Queen Elizabeth's portrait **Rev:** Queen Victoria's portrait **Edge:** Reeded

Date	Mintage	F	VF	XF	Unc	BU
2001	—	—	—	—	6.00	—

KM# 70a 50 PENCE
28.2800 g., 0.9250 Silver 0.841 oz. ASW, 38.6 mm. **Edge:** Reeded

Date	Mintage	F	VF	XF	Unc	BU
2001 Proof	10,000	Value: 50.00				

KM# 70b 50 PENCE
47.5400 g., 0.9166 Gold 1.401 oz. AGW, 38.6 mm. **Subject:** Centennial of Queen Victoria's Death **Obv:** Queen Elizabeth II **Rev:** Queen Victoria **Edge:** Reeded

Date	Mintage	F	VF	XF	Unc	BU
2001 Proof	100	Value: 950				

KM# 86 50 PENCE
28.2800 g., Copper-Nickel, 38.6 mm. **Obv:** Queen Elizabeth II **Rev:** Edward IV (1461-83) with Rose Ryal gold coin design **Edge:** Reeded

Date	Mintage	F	VF	XF	Unc	BU
2001	—	—	—	—	9.00	—

KM# 86a 50 PENCE
28.2800 g., 0.9250 Silver 0.841 oz. ASW, 38.6 mm. **Obv:** Queen Elizabeth II **Rev:** Edward IV (1461-83) with gold-plated Rose Ryal gold coin design **Edge:** Reeded

Date	Mintage	F	VF	XF	Unc	BU
2001 Proof	5,000	Value: 50.00				

KM# 87 50 PENCE
28.2800 g., Copper-Nickel, 38.6 mm. **Obv:** Queen Elizabeth II **Rev:** Henry VII (1485-1509) with 1489 Gold Sovereign coin design **Edge:** Reeded

Date	Mintage	F	VF	XF	Unc	BU
2001	—	—	—	—	9.00	—

KM# 87a 50 PENCE
28.2800 g., 0.9250 Silver 0.841 oz. ASW, 38.6 mm. **Obv:** Queen Elizabeth II **Rev:** Henry VII (1485-1509) with gold-plated 1489 gold Sovereign coin design **Edge:** Reeded

Date	Mintage	F	VF	XF	Unc	BU
2001 Proof	5,000	Value: 50.00				

KM# 88 50 PENCE
28.2800 g., Copper-Nickel, 38.6 mm. **Obv:** Queen Elizabeth II **Rev:** Charles II (1660-85) with 1663 gold Guinea coin design **Edge:** Reeded

Date	Mintage	F	VF	XF	Unc	BU
2001	—	—	—	—	9.00	—

KM# 88a 50 PENCE
28.2800 g., 0.9250 Silver 0.841 oz. ASW, 38.6 mm. **Obv:** Queen Elizabeth II **Rev:** Charles II (1660-85) with gold-plated Gold Guinea coin design **Edge:** Reeded

Date	Mintage	F	VF	XF	Unc	BU
2001 Proof	5,000	Value: 50.00				

KM# 89 50 PENCE
28.2800 g., Copper-Nickel, 38.6 mm. **Obv:** Queen Elizabeth II **Rev:** Queen Victoria with Gold Sovereign coin design **Edge:** Reeded

Date	Mintage	F	VF	XF	Unc	BU
2001	—	—	—	—	9.00	—

KM# 89a 50 PENCE
28.2800 g., 0.9250 Silver 0.841 oz. ASW, 38.6 mm. **Obv:** Queen Elizabeth II **Rev:** Queen Victoria with gold-plated Gold Sovereign coin design **Edge:** Reeded

Date	Mintage	F	VF	XF	Unc	BU
2001 Proof	5,000	Value: 50.00				

KM# 71 50 PENCE

29.1000 g., Copper-Nickel, 38.6 mm. **Subject:** Queen Elizabeth's 75th Birthday **Obv:** Queen's crowned portrait **Rev:** Uncrowned portrait **Edge:** Reeded

Date	Mintage	F	VF	XF	Unc	BU
2001	—	—	—	—	6.00	—

KM# 71b 50 PENCE

47.5400 g., 0.9160 Gold 1.4001 oz. AGW **Subject:** Queen Elizabeth's 75th Birthday **Obv:** Queen's crowned portrait **Rev:** Uncrowned portrait

Date	Mintage	F	VF	XF	Unc	BU
2001 Proof	Est. 100	Value: 975				

KM# 73.1 50 PENCE

28.1300 g., Copper-Nickel, 38.6 mm. **Subject:** Queen's Golden Jubilee **Obv:** Bust of Queen Elizabeth II right **Rev:** Queen Elizabeth II on throne in inner circle below multicolor bunting **Edge:** Reeded

Date	Mintage	F	VF	XF	Unc	BU
2002(2001) Proof	—	Value: 6.00				

KM# 73.2 50 PENCE

Copper-Nickel **Rev:** With plain bunting

Date	Mintage	F	VF	XF	Unc	BU
2002	—	—	—	—	6.00	—

KM# 73a.1 50 PENCE

28.2800 g., 0.9250 Silver 0.841 oz. ASW, 38.6 mm. **Subject:** Queen's Golden Jubilee **Rev:** Queen on throne below multicolor bunting **Edge:** Reeded

Date	Mintage	F	VF	XF	Unc	BU
2002 Proof	25,000	Value: 45.00				

KM# 73a.2 50 PENCE

Silver **Rev:** With plain bunting

Date	Mintage	F	VF	XF	Unc	BU
2002 Proof	—	Value: 45.00				

KM# 73b.1 50 PENCE

39.9400 g., 0.9166 Gold 1.177 oz. AGW, 38.6 mm. **Obv:** Queen Elizabeth II **Rev:** Crowned queen with scepter and orb below multicolor bunting **Edge:** Reeded

Date	Mintage	F	VF	XF	Unc	BU
2002 Proof	150	Value: 925				

KM# 74.1 50 PENCE

28.1300 g., Copper-Nickel, 38.6 mm. **Subject:** Queen's Golden Jubilee **Obv:** Bust of Queen Elizabeth II right **Rev:** Queen on horse half left in inner circle below multicolor bunting **Edge:** Reeded

Date	Mintage	F	VF	XF	Unc	BU
2002(2001) Proof	—	Value: 6.00				

KM# 74.2 50 PENCE

Copper-Nickel **Rev:** With plain bunting

Date	Mintage	F	VF	XF	Unc	BU
2002	—	—	—	—	6.00	—

KM# 74a.1 50 PENCE

28.2800 g., 0.9250 Silver 0.841 oz. ASW, 38.6 mm. **Subject:** Queen's Golden Jubilee **Rev. Designer:** Queen on horse below multicolor bunting **Edge:** Reeded

Date	Mintage	F	VF	XF	Unc	BU
2002 Proof	25,000	Value: 45.00				

KM# 74a.2 50 PENCE

0.9250 Silver **Rev:** With plain bunting

Date	Mintage	F	VF	XF	Unc	BU
2002 Proof	—	Value: 45.00				

KM# 74b.1 50 PENCE

39.9400 g., 0.9166 Gold 1.177 oz. AGW, 38.6 mm. **Subject:** Queen's Golden Jubilee **Obv:** Queen Elizabeth II **Rev:** Queen on horseback below multicolored bunting **Edge:** Reeded

Date	Mintage	F	VF	XF	Unc	BU
2002 Proof	150	Value: 925				

KM# 74b.2 50 PENCE

Gold **Rev:** With plain bunting

Date	Mintage	F	VF	XF	Unc	BU
2002 Proof	—	Value: 925				

KM# 75.1 50 PENCE

28.1300 g., Copper-Nickel, 38.6 mm. **Subject:** Queen's Golden Jubilee **Obv:** Bust of Queen Elizabeth II right **Rev:** Queen Elizabeth II talking into microphone below multicolor bunting **Edge:** Reeded

Date	Mintage	F	VF	XF	Unc	BU
2002(2001) Proof	—	Value: 6.00				

KM# 75.2 50 PENCE

Copper-Nickel **Rev:** With plain bunting

Date	Mintage	F	VF	XF	Unc	BU
2002	—	—	—	—	6.00	—

KM# 75a.1 50 PENCE

28.2800 g., 0.9250 Silver 0.841 oz. ASW, 38.6 mm. **Subject:** Queen's Golden Jubilee **Rev:** Queen speaking into a radio microphone below multicolored bunting **Edge:** Reeded

Date	Mintage	F	VF	XF	Unc	BU
2002 Proof	25,000	Value: 45.00				

KM# 75a.2 50 PENCE

Silver **Rev:** With plain bunting

Date	Mintage	F	VF	XF	Unc	BU
2002 Proof	—	Value: 45.00				

KM# 75b.1 50 PENCE

39.9400 g., 0.9166 Gold 1.177 oz. AGW, 38.6 mm. **Subject:** Queen's Golden Jubilee **Obv:** Queen Elizabeth II **Rev:** Elizabeth speaking into a radio microphone below multicolored bunting **Edge:** Reeded

Date	Mintage	F	VF	XF	Unc	BU
2002 Proof	50	Value: 925				

KM# 75b.2 50 PENCE

Gold **Rev:** With plain bunting

Date	Mintage	F	VF	XF	Unc	BU
2002 Proof	—	Value: 925				

KM# 76.1 50 PENCE

28.1300 g., Copper-Nickel, 38.6 mm. **Subject:** Queen's Golden Jubilee **Obv:** Bust of Queen Elizabeth II right **Rev:** Queen walking to left in front of a crowd below multicolored bunting **Edge:** Reeded

Date	Mintage	F	VF	XF	Unc	BU
2002(2001) Proof	—	Value: 6.00				

KM# 76.2 50 PENCE

Copper-Nickel **Rev:** With plain bunting

Date	Mintage	F	VF	XF	Unc	BU
2002	—	—	—	—	6.00	—

KM# 76a.1 50 PENCE

28.2800 g., 0.9250 Silver 0.841 oz. ASW, 38.6 mm. **Subject:** Queen's Golden Jubilee **Rev:** Queen standing before crowd below multicolored bunting **Edge:** Reeded

Date	Mintage	F	VF	XF	Unc	BU
2002 Proof	15,000	Value: 45.00				

KM# 76a.2 50 PENCE

Silver **Rev:** With plain bunting

Date	Mintage	F	VF	XF	Unc	BU
2002 Proof	—	Value: 45.00				

KM# 76b.1 50 PENCE

39.9400 g., 0.9166 Gold 1.177 oz. AGW, 38.6 mm. **Subject:** Queen's Golden Jubilee **Obv:** Queen Elizabeth II **Rev:** Queen standing before a crowd below multicolored bunting **Edge:** Reeded

Date	Mintage	F	VF	XF	Unc	BU
2002 Proof	50	Value: 925				

KM# 76b.2 50 PENCE

Gold **Rev:** With plain bunting

Date	Mintage	F	VF	XF	Unc	BU
2002 Plain	—	Value: 925				

KM# 77.1 50 PENCE

28.1300 g., Copper-Nickel, 38.6 mm. **Subject:** Queen's Golden Jubilee **Obv:** Bust of Queen Elizabeth II right **Rev:** Conjoined busts of Queen Elizabeth, Prince Charles, Prince William facing left in inner circle below multicolor bunting **Edge:** Reeded

Date	Mintage	F	VF	XF	Unc	BU
2002(2001) Proof	—	Value: 6.00				

KM# 77.2 50 PENCE

Copper-Nickel **Rev:** With plain bunting

Date	Mintage	F	VF	XF	Unc	BU
2002	—	—	—	—	6.00	—

KM# 77a.1 50 PENCE

28.2800 g., 0.9250 Silver 0.841 oz. ASW, 38.6 mm. **Subject:** Queen's Golden Jubilee **Rev:** Queen, Crown Prince and Prince William below multicolor bunting **Edge:** Reeded

Date	Mintage	F	VF	XF	Unc	BU
2002 Proof	15,000	Value: 45.00				

KM# 77a.2 50 PENCE

Silver **Rev:** With plain bunting

Date	Mintage	F	VF	XF	Unc	BU
2002 Proof	—	Value: 45.00				

KM# 77b.1 50 PENCE

39.9400 g., 0.9166 Gold 1.177 oz. AGW, 38.6 mm. **Subject:** Queen's Golden Jubilee **Obv:** Queen Elizabeth II **Rev:** Elizabeth II, Prince Charles and his son William below multicolored bunting **Edge:** Reeded

Date	Mintage	F	VF	XF	Unc	BU
2002 Proof	50	Value: 925				

KM# 77b.2 50 PENCE

Gold **Rev:** With plain bunting

Date	Mintage	F	VF	XF	Unc	BU
2002 Proof	—	Value: 925				

KM# 78.1 50 PENCE

28.1300 g., Copper-Nickel, 38.6 mm. **Subject:** Queen's Golden Jubilee **Obv:** Bust of Queen Elizabeth right **Rev:** Royal coach below multicolor bunting **Edge:** Reeded

Date	Mintage	F	VF	XF	Unc	BU
2002 Proof	—	Value: 6.00				

KM# 78.2 50 PENCE

Copper-Nickel **Rev:** With plain bunting

Date	Mintage	F	VF	XF	Unc	BU
2002	—	—	—	—	6.00	—

KM# 78a.1 50 PENCE

28.2800 g., 0.9250 Silver 0.841 oz. ASW, 38.6 mm. **Subject:** Queen's Golden Jubilee **Rev:** Coronation coach below multicolor bunting **Edge:** Reeded

Date	Mintage	F	VF	XF	Unc	BU
2002 Proof	15,000	Value: 45.00				

KM# 78a.2 50 PENCE

Gold **Rev:** With plain bunting

Date	Mintage	F	VF	XF	Unc	BU
2002 Proof	—	Value: 925				

KM# 78b.1 50 PENCE
39.9400 g., 0.9166 Gold 1.177 oz. AGW, 38.6 mm.
Subject: Queen's Golden Jubilee **Obv:** Queen Elizabeth II **Rev:** Coronation coach below multicolor bunting **Edge:** Reeded

Date	Mintage	F	VF	XF	Unc	BU
2002 Proof	150	Value: 925				

KM# 78b.2 50 PENCE
Gold **Rev:** With plain bunting

Date	Mintage	F	VF	XF	Unc	BU
2002 Proof	—	Value: 925				

KM# 79.1 50 PENCE
28.1300 g., Copper-Nickel, 38.6 mm. **Subject:** Queen's Golden Jubilee **Obv:** Bust of Queen Elizabeth right **Rev:** Scepter and orb below multicolor bunting **Edge:** Reeded

Date	Mintage	F	VF	XF	Unc	BU
2002 Proof	—	Value: 6.00				

KM# 79.2 50 PENCE
Copper-Nickel **Rev:** With plain bunting

Date	Mintage	F	VF	XF	Unc	BU
2002	—	—	—	—	6.00	—

KM# 79a.1 50 PENCE
28.2800 g., 0.9250 Silver 0.841 oz. ASW, 38.6 mm.
Subject: Queen's Golden Jubilee **Rev:** Orb and scepter below multicolor bunting **Edge:** Reeded

Date	Mintage	F	VF	XF	Unc	BU
2002 Proof	15,000	Value: 45.00				

KM# 79a.2 50 PENCE
Silver **Rev:** With plain bunting

Date	Mintage	F	VF	XF	Unc	BU
2002 Proof	—	Value: 45.00				

KM# 79b.1 50 PENCE
39.9400 g., 0.9166 Gold 1.177 oz. AGW, 38.6 mm.
Subject: Queen's Golden Jubilee **Obv:** Queen Elizabeth II **Rev:** Orb and scepter below multicolor bunting **Edge:** Reeded

Date	Mintage	F	VF	XF	Unc	BU
2002 Proof	150	Value: 925				

KM# 79b.2 50 PENCE
Gold **Rev:** With plain bunting

Date	Mintage	F	VF	XF	Unc	BU
2002 Proof	—	Value: 925				

KM# 80.1 50 PENCE
28.1300 g., Copper-Nickel, 38.6 mm. **Subject:** Queen's Golden Jubilee **Obv:** Bust of Queen Elizabeth right **Rev:** Crown below multicolor bunting **Edge:** Reeded

Date	Mintage	F	VF	XF	Unc	BU
2002 Proof	—	Value: 6.00				

KM# 80.2 50 PENCE
Copper-Nickel **Rev:** With plain bunting

Date	Mintage	F	VF	XF	Unc	BU
2002	—	—	—	—	6.00	—

KM# 80a.1 50 PENCE
28.2800 g., 0.9250 Silver 0.841 oz. ASW, 38.6 mm.
Subject: Queen's Golden Jubilee **Rev:** Crown below multicolor bunting **Edge:** Reeded

Date	Mintage	F	VF	XF	Unc	BU
2002 Proof	15,000	Value: 45.00				

KM# 80a.2 50 PENCE
Silver **Rev:** With plain bunting

Date	Mintage	F	VF	XF	Unc	BU
2002 Proof	—	Value: 45.00				

KM# 80b.1 50 PENCE
39.9400 g., 0.9166 Gold 1.177 oz. AGW, 38.6 mm.
Subject: Queen's Golden Jubilee **Obv:** Queen Elizabeth II **Rev:** Crown below multicolor bunting **Edge:** Reeded

Date	Mintage	F	VF	XF	Unc	BU
2002 Proof	150	Value: 925				

KM# 80b.2 50 PENCE
Gold **Rev:** With plain bunting

Date	Mintage	F	VF	XF	Unc	BU
2002 Proof	—	Value: 925				

KM# 81.1 50 PENCE
28.1300 g., Copper-Nickel, 38.6 mm. **Subject:** Queen's Golden Jubilee **Obv:** Bust of Queen Elizabeth right **Rev:** Throne below multicolor bunting **Edge:** Reeded

Date	Mintage	F	VF	XF	Unc	BU
2002 Proof	—	Value: 6.00				

KM# 81.2 50 PENCE
Copper-Nickel **Rev:** With plain bunting

Date	Mintage	F	VF	XF	Unc	BU
2002	—	—	—	—	6.00	—

KM# 81a.1 50 PENCE
28.2800 g., 0.9250 Silver 0.841 oz. ASW, 38.6 mm.
Subject: Queen's Golden Jubilee **Rev:** Coronation throne below multicolor bunting **Edge:** Reeded

Date	Mintage	F	VF	XF	Unc	BU
2002 Proof	15,000	Value: 45.00				

KM# 81a.2 50 PENCE
Silver **Rev:** With plain bunting

Date	Mintage	F	VF	XF	Unc	BU
2002 Proof	—	Value: 45.00				

KM# 81b.1 50 PENCE
39.9400 g., 0.9166 Gold 1.177 oz. AGW, 38.6 mm. **Subject:** Queen's Golden Jubilee **Obv:** Queen Elizabeth II **Rev:** Coronation Throne below multicolored bunting **Edge:** Reeded

Date	Mintage	F	VF	XF	Unc	BU
2002 Proof	150	Value: 925				

KM# 81b.2 50 PENCE
Gold **Rev:** With plain bunting

Date	Mintage	F	VF	XF	Unc	BU
2002 Proof	—	Value: 925				

KM# 82.1 50 PENCE
28.1300 g., Copper-Nickel, 38.6 mm. **Subject:** Queen's Golden Jubilee **Obv:** Bust of Queen Elizabeth right **Rev:** Queen on throne below multicolor bunting **Edge:** Reeded

Date	Mintage	F	VF	XF	Unc	BU
2002 Proof	—	—	—	—	6.00	—

KM# 82.2 50 PENCE
Copper-Nickel **Rev:** With plain bunting

Date	Mintage	F	VF	XF	Unc	BU
2002	—	—	—	—	6.00	—

KM# 82a.1 50 PENCE
28.2800 g., 0.9250 Silver 0.841 oz. ASW, 38.6 mm. **Subject:** Queen's Golden Jubilee **Rev:** Queen on throne below multicolor bunting **Edge:** Reeded

Date	Mintage	F	VF	XF	Unc	BU
2002 Proof	15,000	Value: 45.00				

KM# 82a.2 50 PENCE
Silver **Rev:** With plain bunting

Date	Mintage	F	VF	XF	Unc	BU
2002 Proof	—	Value: 45.00				

KM# 82b.1 50 PENCE
39.9400 g., 0.9166 Gold 1.177 oz. AGW, 38.6 mm. **Subject:** Queen's Golden Jubilee **Obv:** Queen Elizabeth II **Rev:** Queen seated on throne below multicolor bunting **Edge:** Reeded

Date	Mintage	F	VF	XF	Unc	BU
2002 Proof	50	Value: 925				

KM# 82b.2 50 PENCE
Gold **Rev:** With plain bunting

Date	Mintage	F	VF	XF	Unc	BU
2002 Proof	—	Value: 925				

KM# 83.1 50 PENCE
28.1300 g., Copper-Nickel, 38.6 mm. **Subject:** Queen's Golden Jubilee **Obv:** Bust of Queen Elizabeth right **Rev:** Queen and young family below multicolor bunting **Edge:** Reeded

Date	Mintage	F	VF	XF	Unc	BU
2002 Proof	—	—	—	—	6.00	—

KM# 83.2 50 PENCE
Gold **Rev:** With plain bunting

Date	Mintage	F	VF	XF	Unc	BU
2002 Proof	—	Value: 925				

KM# 83a.1 50 PENCE
28.2800 g., 0.9250 Silver 0.841 oz. ASW, 38.6 mm.
Subject: Queen's Golden Jubilee **Rev:** Royal family below multicolor bunting **Edge:** Reeded

Date	Mintage	F	VF	XF	Unc	BU
2002 Proof	15,000	Value: 45.00				

KM# 83a.2 50 PENCE
Silver **Rev:** With plain bunting

Date	Mintage	F	VF	XF	Unc	BU
2002 Proof	—	Value: 45.00				

KM# 83b.1 50 PENCE
39.9400 g., 0.9166 Gold 1.177 oz. AGW, 38.6 mm.
Subject: Queen's Golden Jubilee **Obv:** Queen Elizabeth II **Rev:** Royal Family below multicolor bunting **Edge:** Reeded

Date	Mintage	F	VF	XF	Unc	BU
2002 Proof	50	Value: 925				

KM# 83b.2 50 PENCE
Gold **Rev:** With plain bunting

Date	Mintage	F	VF	XF	Unc	BU
2002 Proof	—	Value: 925				

KM# 84.1 50 PENCE
28.1300 g., Copper-Nickel, 38.6 mm. **Subject:** Queen's Golden Jubilee **Obv:** Bust of Queen Elizabeth right **Rev:** Queen and tree house below multicolor bunting **Edge:** Reeded

Date	Mintage	F	VF	XF	Unc	BU
2002 Proof	—	Value: 6.00				

KM# 84.2 50 PENCE
Copper-Nickel **Rev:** With plain bunting

Date	Mintage	F	VF	XF	Unc	BU
2002	—	—	—	—	6.00	—

KM# 84a.1 50 PENCE
28.2800 g., 0.9250 Silver 0.841 oz. ASW, 38.6 mm.
Subject: Queen's Golden Jubilee **Rev:** Queen and tree house below multicolor bunting **Edge:** Reeded

Date	Mintage	F	VF	XF	Unc	BU
2002 Proof	25,000	Value: 45.00				

KM# 84a.2 50 PENCE
Silver **Rev:** With plain bunting

Date	Mintage	F	VF	XF	Unc	BU
2002 Proof	—	Value: 45.00				

KM# 84b.1 50 PENCE
39.9400 g., 0.9166 Gold 1.177 oz. AGW, 38.6 mm. **Subject:** Queen's Golden Jubilee **Obv:** Queen Elizabeth II **Rev:** Queen and tree house below multicolor bunting **Edge:** Reeded

Date	Mintage	F	VF	XF	Unc	BU
2002 Proof	50	Value: 925				

KM# 84b.2 50 PENCE
Gold **Rev:** With plain bunting

Date	Mintage	F	VF	XF	Unc	BU
2002 Proof	—	Value: 925				

KM# 90 50 PENCE

28.2800 g., Copper-Nickel, 38.6 mm. **Obv:** Queen Elizabeth II **Rev:** Elizabeth and Philip below multicolor bunting **Edge:** Reeded

Date	Mintage	F	VF	XF	Unc	BU
2002	—	—	—	—	6.00	—

KM# 90a.1 50 PENCE

28.2800 g., 0.9250 Silver 0.841 oz. ASW, 38.6 mm. **Obv:** Queen Elizabeth II **Rev:** Elizabeth and Philip below multicolor bunting **Edge:** Reeded

Date	Mintage	F	VF	XF	Unc	BU
2002 Proof	15,000	Value: 45.00				

KM# 90a.2 50 PENCE

28.2800 g., 0.9250 Silver 0.841 oz. ASW, 38.6 mm. **Rev:** With plain bunting

Date	Mintage	F	VF	XF	Unc	BU
2002 Proof	—	Value: 45.00				

KM# 90b.1 50 PENCE

39.9400 g., 0.9160 Gold 1.1762 oz. AGW, 38.6 mm. **Obv:** Queen Elizabeth II **Rev:** Elizabeth and Philip below multicolor bunting **Edge:** Reeded

Date	Mintage	F	VF	XF	Unc	BU
2002 Proof	50	Value: 925				

KM# 90b.2 50 PENCE

39.9400 g., 0.9160 Gold 1.1762 oz. AGW, 38.6 mm. **Rev:** With plain bunting **Edge:** Reeded

Date	Mintage	F	VF	XF	Unc	BU
2002 Proof	—	Value: 925				

KM# 91 50 PENCE

28.2800 g., Copper-Nickel, 38.6 mm. **Obv:** Queen Elizabeth II **Rev:** Queen and Aborigine dancers below multicolor bunting **Edge:** Reeded

Date	Mintage	F	VF	XF	Unc	BU
2002	—	—	—	—	6.00	—

KM# 91a.1 50 PENCE

28.2800 g., 0.9250 Silver 0.841 oz. ASW, 38.6 mm. **Obv:** Queen Elizabeth II **Rev:** Queen and Aborigine dancers below multicolor bunting **Edge:** Reeded

Date	Mintage	F	VF	XF	Unc	BU
2002 Proof	15,000	Value: 45.00				

KM# 91a.2 50 PENCE

28.2800 g., 0.9250 Silver 0.841 oz. ASW, 38.6 mm. **Rev:** With plain bunting **Edge:** Reeded

Date	Mintage	F	VF	XF	Unc	BU
2002 Proof	—	Value: 45.00				

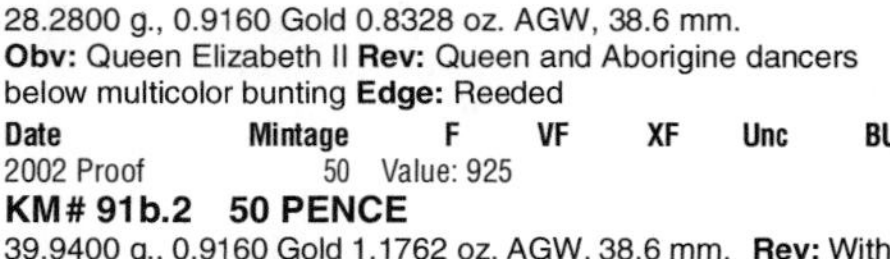

KM# 91b.1 50 PENCE

28.2800 g., 0.9160 Gold 0.8328 oz. AGW, 38.6 mm. **Obv:** Queen Elizabeth II **Rev:** Queen and Aborigine dancers below multicolor bunting **Edge:** Reeded

Date	Mintage	F	VF	XF	Unc	BU
2002 Proof	50	Value: 925				

KM# 91b.2 50 PENCE

39.9400 g., 0.9160 Gold 1.1762 oz. AGW, 38.6 mm. **Rev:** With plain bunting **Edge:** Reeded

Date	Mintage	F	VF	XF	Unc	BU
2002 Proof	—	Value: 925				

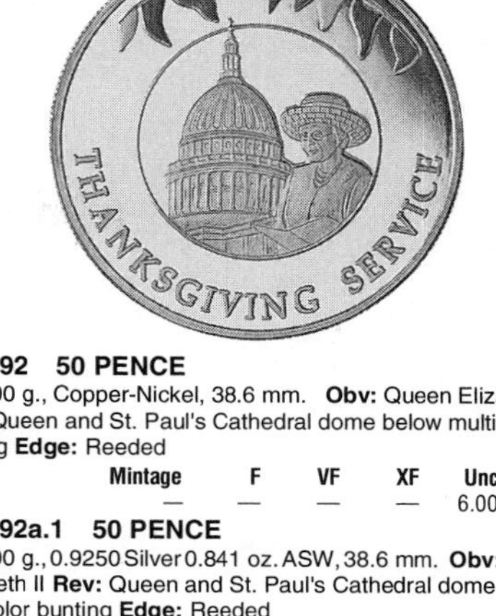

KM# 92 50 PENCE

28.2800 g., Copper-Nickel, 38.6 mm. **Obv:** Queen Elizabeth II **Rev:** Queen and St. Paul's Cathedral dome below multicolor bunting **Edge:** Reeded

Date	Mintage	F	VF	XF	Unc	BU
2002	—	—	—	—	6.00	—

KM# 92a.1 50 PENCE

28.2800 g., 0.9250 Silver 0.841 oz. ASW, 38.6 mm. **Obv:** Queen Elizabeth II **Rev:** Queen and St. Paul's Cathedral dome below multicolor bunting **Edge:** Reeded

Date	Mintage	F	VF	XF	Unc	BU
2002 Proof	15,000	Value: 45.00				

KM# 92a.2 50 PENCE

28.2800 g., 0.9250 Silver 0.841 oz. ASW, 38.6 mm. **Rev:** With plain bunting **Edge:** Reeded

Date	Mintage	F	VF	XF	Unc	BU
2002 Proof	—	Value: 45.00				

KM# 92b.1 50 PENCE

39.9400 g., 0.9160 Gold 1.1762 oz. AGW, 38.6 mm. **Obv:** Queen Elizabeth II **Rev:** Queen and St. Paul's Cathedral dome below multicolor bunting **Edge:** Reeded

Date	Mintage	F	VF	XF	Unc	BU
2002 Proof	50	Value: 925				

KM# 92b.2 50 PENCE

39.9400 g., 0.9160 Gold 1.1762 oz. AGW, 38.6 mm. **Rev:** With plain bunting **Edge:** Reeded

Date	Mintage	F	VF	XF	Unc	BU
2002 Proof	—	Value: 925				

KM# 93 50 PENCE

28.2800 g., Copper-Nickel, 38.6 mm. **Obv:** Queen Elizabeth II **Rev:** Elizabeth and Philip in coronation coach below multicolor bunting **Edge:** Reeded

Date	Mintage	F	VF	XF	Unc	BU
2002	—	—	—	—	6.00	—

KM# 93a.1 50 PENCE

28.2800 g., 0.9250 Silver 0.841 oz. ASW, 38.6 mm. **Obv:** Queen Elizabeth II **Rev:** Elizabeth and Philip in coronation coach below multicolor bunting **Edge:** Reeded

Date	Mintage	F	VF	XF	Unc	BU
2002 Proof	15,000	Value: 45.00				

KM# 93a.2 50 PENCE

28.2800 g., 0.9250 Silver 0.841 oz. ASW, 38.6 mm. **Rev:** With plain bunting **Edge:** Reeded

Date	Mintage	F	VF	XF	Unc	BU
2002 Proof	—	Value: 45.00				

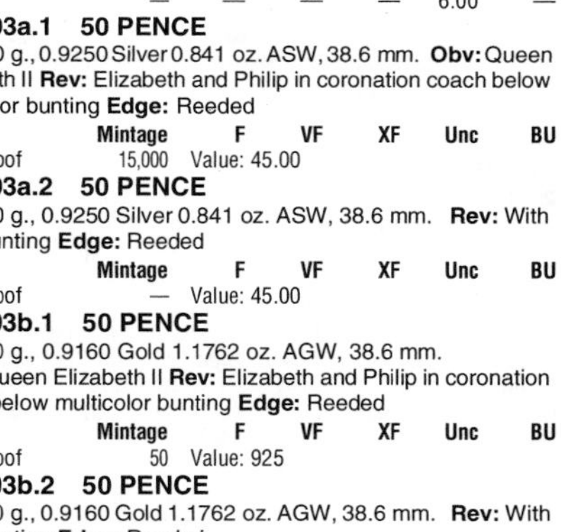

KM# 93b.1 50 PENCE

39.9400 g., 0.9160 Gold 1.1762 oz. AGW, 38.6 mm. **Obv:** Queen Elizabeth II **Rev:** Elizabeth and Philip in coronation coach below multicolor bunting **Edge:** Reeded

Date	Mintage	F	VF	XF	Unc	BU
2002 Proof	50	Value: 925				

KM# 93b.2 50 PENCE

39.9400 g., 0.9160 Gold 1.1762 oz. AGW, 38.6 mm. **Rev:** With plain bunting **Edge:** Reeded

Date	Mintage	F	VF	XF	Unc	BU
2002 Proof	—	Value: 925				

KM# 94 50 PENCE

28.2800 g., Copper-Nickel, 38.6 mm. **Obv:** Queen Elizabeth II **Rev:** Elizabeth and Prince Charles at flower show below multicolor bunting **Edge:** Reeded

Date	Mintage	F	VF	XF	Unc	BU
2002	—	—	—	—	6.00	—

KM# 94a.1 50 PENCE

28.2800 g., 0.9250 Silver 0.841 oz. ASW, 38.6 mm. **Obv:** Queen Elizabeth II **Rev:** Queen and Prince Charles at flower show below multicolor bunting **Edge:** Reeded

Date	Mintage	F	VF	XF	Unc	BU
2002 Proof	15,000	Value: 45.00				

KM# 94a.2 50 PENCE

28.2800 g., 0.9250 Silver 0.841 oz. ASW, 38.6 mm. **Rev:** With plain bunting **Edge:** Reeded

Date	Mintage	F	VF	XF	Unc	BU
2002 Proof	—	Value: 45.00				

KM# 94b.1 50 PENCE

39.9400 g., 0.9160 Gold 1.1762 oz. AGW, 38.6 mm. **Obv:** Queen Elizabeth II **Rev:** Queen and Prince Charles at flower show below multicolor bunting **Edge:** Reeded

Date	Mintage	F	VF	XF	Unc	BU
2002 Proof	50	Value: 925				

KM# 94b.2 50 PENCE

39.9400 g., 0.9160 Gold 1.1762 oz. AGW, 38.6 mm. **Rev:** With plain bunting **Edge:** Reeded

Date	Mintage	F	VF	XF	Unc	BU
2002 Proof	—	Value: 925				

KM# 95 50 PENCE

28.2800 g., Copper-Nickel, 38.6 mm. **Obv:** Queen Elizabeth II **Rev:** Elizabeth and Philip on balcony below multicolor bunting **Edge:** Reeded

Date	Mintage	F	VF	XF	Unc	BU
2002	—	—	—	—	6.00	—

KM# 95a.1 50 PENCE

28.2800 g., 0.9250 Silver 0.841 oz. ASW, 38.6 mm. **Obv:** Queen Elizabeth II **Rev:** Elizabeth and Philip on balcony **Edge:** Reeded

Date	Mintage	F	VF	XF	Unc	BU
2002 Proof	15,000	Value: 45.00				

KM# 95a.2 50 PENCE

28.2800 g., 0.9250 Silver 0.841 oz. ASW, 38.6 mm. **Rev:** With plain bunting **Edge:** Reeded

Date	Mintage	F	VF	XF	Unc	BU
2002 Proof	—	Value: 45.00				

KM# 95b.1 50 PENCE

39.9400 g., 0.9160 Gold 1.1762 oz. AGW, 38.6 mm. **Obv:** Queen Elizabeth II **Rev:** Elizabeth and Philip on balcony below multicolor bunting **Edge:** Reeded

Date	Mintage	F	VF	XF	Unc	BU
2002 Proof	50	Value: 925				

KM# 95b.2 50 PENCE

39.9400 g., 0.9160 Gold 1.1762 oz. AGW, 38.6 mm. **Rev:** With plain bunting **Edge:** Reeded

Date	Mintage	F	VF	XF	Unc	BU
2002 Proof	—	Value: 925				

KM# 96 50 PENCE

28.2800 g., Copper-Nickel, 38.6 mm. **Obv:** Queen Elizabeth II **Rev:** Multicolor jets below multicolor bunting **Edge:** Reeded

Date	Mintage	F	VF	XF	Unc	BU
2002	—	—	—	—	6.00	—

KM# 96a.1 50 PENCE

28.2800 g., 0.9250 Silver 0.841 oz. ASW, 38.6 mm. **Obv:** Queen Elizabeth II **Rev:** Multicolor jets below multicolor bunting **Edge:** Reeded

Date	Mintage	F	VF	XF	Unc	BU
2002 Proof	15,000	Value: 45.00				

KM# 96a.2 50 PENCE

28.2800 g., 0.9250 Silver 0.841 oz. ASW, 38.6 mm. **Rev:** With plain bunting **Edge:** Reeded

Date	Mintage	F	VF	XF	Unc	BU
2002 Proof	—	Value: 45.00				

KM# 96b.1 50 PENCE

39.9400 g., 0.9160 Gold 1.1762 oz. AGW, 38.6 mm. **Obv:** Queen Elizabeth II **Rev:** Multicolor jets below multicolor bunting **Edge:** Reeded

Date	Mintage	F	VF	XF	Unc	BU
2002 Proof	50	Value: 925				

KM# 96b.2 50 PENCE

39.9400 g., 0.9160 Gold 1.1762 oz. AGW, 38.6 mm. **Rev:** With plain bunting **Edge:** Reeded

Date	Mintage	F	VF	XF	Unc	BU
2002 Proof	—	Value: 925				

KM# 98 50 PENCE

28.2800 g., Copper-Nickel, 38.6 mm. **Obv:** Queen Elizabeth II **Rev:** UK map and flags below multicolor bunting **Edge:** Reeded

Date	Mintage	F	VF	XF	Unc	BU
2002	—	—	—	—	6.00	—

KM# 98a.1 50 PENCE

28.2800 g., 0.9250 Silver 0.841 oz. ASW, 38.6 mm. **Obv:** Queen Elizabeth II **Rev:** UK and four flags below multicolor bunting **Edge:** Reeded

Date	Mintage	F	VF	XF	Unc	BU
2002 Proof	15,000	Value: 45.00				

KM# 98a.2 50 PENCE

28.2800 g., 0.9250 Silver 0.841 oz. ASW, 38.6 mm. **Rev:** With plain bunting **Edge:** Reeded

Date	Mintage	F	VF	XF	Unc	BU
2002 Proof	—	Value: 45.00				

KM# 98b.1 50 PENCE

39.9400 g., 0.9160 Gold 1.1762 oz. AGW, 38.6 mm. **Obv:** Queen Elizabeth II **Rev:** UK map and four flags below multicolor bunting **Edge:** Reeded

Date	Mintage	F	VF	XF	Unc	BU
2002 Proof	50	Value: 925				

KM# 98b.2 50 PENCE

39.9400 g., 0.9160 Gold 1.1762 oz. AGW, 38.6 mm. **Rev:** With plain bunting **Edge:** Reeded

Date	Mintage	F	VF	XF	Unc	BU
2002 Proof	—	Value: 925				

KM# 100 50 PENCE

28.2800 g., Copper-Nickel, 38.6 mm. **Obv:** Queen Elizabeth II **Rev:** Royal Ascot Carriage scene below multicolor bunting **Edge:** Reeded

Date	Mintage	F	VF	XF	Unc	BU
2002	—	—	—	—	6.00	—

KM# 100a.1 50 PENCE

28.2800 g., 0.9250 Silver 0.841 oz. ASW, 38.6 mm. **Obv:** Queen Elizabeth II **Rev:** Royal Ascot Carriage scene below multicolor bunting **Edge:** Reeded

Date	Mintage	F	VF	XF	Unc	BU
2002 Proof	15,000	Value: 45.00				

KM# 100a.2 50 PENCE

28.2800 g., 0.9250 Silver 0.841 oz. ASW, 38.6 mm. **Rev:** With plain bunting **Edge:** Reeded

Date	Mintage	F	VF	XF	Unc	BU
2002 Proof	—	Value: 45.00				

KM# 100b.1 50 PENCE

39.9400 g., 0.9160 Gold 1.1762 oz. AGW, 38.6 mm. **Obv:** Queen Elizabeth II **Rev:** Royal Ascot Carriage scene below multicolor bunting **Edge:** Reeded

Date	Mintage	F	VF	XF	Unc	BU
2002 Proof	50	Value: 925				

KM# 100b.2 50 PENCE

39.9400 g., 0.9160 Gold 1.1762 oz. AGW, 38.6 mm. **Rev:** With plain bunting **Edge:** Reeded

Date	Mintage	F	VF	XF	Unc	BU
2002 Proof	—	Value: 925				

KM# 97 50 PENCE

28.2800 g., Copper-Nickel, 38.6 mm. **Obv:** Queen Elizabeth II **Rev:** Queen and fireworks below multicolor bunting **Edge:** Reeded

Date	Mintage	F	VF	XF	Unc	BU
2002	—	—	—	—	6.00	—

KM# 97a.1 50 PENCE

28.2800 g., 0.9250 Copper-Nickel 0.841 oz., 38.6 mm. **Obv:** Queen Elizabeth II **Rev:** Queen and fireworks below multicolor bunting **Edge:** Reeded

Date	Mintage	F	VF	XF	Unc	BU
2002 Proof	15,000	Value: 45.00				

KM# 97a.2 50 PENCE

28.2800 g., 0.9250 Silver 0.841 oz. ASW, 38.6 mm. **Rev:** With plain bunting **Edge:** Reeded

Date	Mintage	F	VF	XF	Unc	BU
2002 Proof	—	Value: 45.00				

KM# 97b.1 50 PENCE

39.9400 g., 0.9160 Gold 1.1762 oz. AGW, 38.6 mm. **Obv:** Queen Elizabeth II **Rev:** Queen and fireworks below multicolor bunting **Edge:** Reeded

Date	Mintage	F	VF	XF	Unc	BU
2002 Proof	50	Value: 925				

KM# 97b.2 50 PENCE

39.9400 g., 0.9160 Gold 1.1762 oz. AGW, 38.6 mm. **Rev:** With plain bunting **Edge:** Reeded

Date	Mintage	F	VF	XF	Unc	BU
2002 Proof	—	Value: 925				

KM# 99 50 PENCE

28.2800 g., Copper-Nickel, 38.6 mm. **Obv:** Queen Elizabeth II **Rev:** Queen and two Commonwealth Games athletes below multicolor bunting **Edge:** Reeded

Date	Mintage	F	VF	XF	Unc	BU
2002	—	—	—	—	6.00	—

KM# 99a.1 50 PENCE

28.2800 g., 0.9250 Silver 0.841 oz. ASW, 38.6 mm. **Obv:** Queen Elizabeth II **Rev:** Queen and two Commonwealth Games athletes below multicolor bunting **Edge:** Reeded

Date	Mintage	F	VF	XF	Unc	BU
2002 Proof	15,000	Value: 45.00				

KM# 99a.2 50 PENCE

28.2800 g., 0.9250 Silver 0.841 oz. ASW, 38.6 mm. **Rev:** With plain bunting **Edge:** Reeded

Date	Mintage	F	VF	XF	Unc	BU
2002 Proof	—	Value: 45.00				

KM# 99b.1 50 PENCE

39.9400 g., 0.9160 Gold 1.1762 oz. AGW, 38.6 mm. **Obv:** Queen Elizabeth II **Rev:** Queen and two Commonwealth Games athletes below multicolor bunting **Edge:** Reeded

Date	Mintage	F	VF	XF	Unc	BU
2002 Proof	50	Value: 925				

KM# 99b.2 50 PENCE

39.9400 g., 0.9160 Gold 1.1762 oz. AGW, 38.6 mm. **Rev:** With plain bunting **Edge:** Reeded

Date	Mintage	F	VF	XF	Unc	BU
2002 Proof	—	Value: 925				

KM# 101 50 PENCE

28.2800 g., Copper-Nickel, 38.6 mm. **Obv:** Queen Elizabeth II **Rev:** Queen and two hockey players below multicolor bunting **Edge:** Reeded

Date	Mintage	F	VF	XF	Unc	BU
2002	—	—	—	—	6.00	—

KM# 101a.1 50 PENCE

28.2800 g., 0.9250 Silver 0.841 oz. ASW, 38.6 mm. **Obv:** Queen Elizabeth II **Rev:** Queen and two hockey players below multicolor bunting **Edge:** Reeded

Date	Mintage	F	VF	XF	Unc	BU
2002 Proof	15,000	Value: 45.00				

KM# 101a.2 50 PENCE

28.2800 g., 0.9250 Silver 0.841 oz. ASW, 38.6 mm. **Rev:** With plain bunting **Edge:** Reeded

Date	Mintage	F	VF	XF	Unc	BU
2002 Proof	—	Value: 45.00				

KM# 101b.1 50 PENCE

39.9400 g., 0.9160 Gold 1.1762 oz. AGW, 38.6 mm. **Obv:** Queen Elizabeth II **Rev:** Queen and two hockey players below multicolor bunting **Edge:** Reeded

Date	Mintage	F	VF	XF	Unc	BU
2002 Proof	50	Value: 925				

KM# 101b.2 50 PENCE

39.9400 g., 0.9160 Gold 1.1762 oz. AGW, 38.6 mm. **Rev:** With plain bunting **Edge:** Reeded

Date	Mintage	F	VF	XF	Unc	BU
2002 Proof	—	Value: 925				

KM# 102 50 PENCE
28.2800 g., Copper-Nickel, 38.6 mm. **Obv:** Queen Elizabeth II **Rev:** Queen Mother as a young lady and as an elderly lady **Edge:** Reeded

Date	Mintage	F	VF	XF	Unc	BU
ND(2002)	—	—	—	—	9.00	—

KM# 102a 50 PENCE
28.2800 g., 0.9250 Silver 0.841 oz. ASW, 38.6 mm. **Obv:** Queen Elizabeth II **Rev:** Queen Mother as a young lady and as an elderly lady **Edge:** Reeded

Date	Mintage	F	VF	XF	Unc	BU
ND(2002) Proof	10,000	Value: 50.00				

KM# 103 25 POUNDS
7.8100 g., 0.9999 Gold 0.2511 oz. AGW, 22 mm. **Obv:** Queen Elizabeth II **Rev:** Queen Mother as a young lady and as an elderly lady **Edge:** Reeded

Date	Mintage	F	VF	XF	Unc	BU
ND(2002) Proof	1,000	Value: 185				

PIEFORTS

KM#	Date	Mintage	Identification	Mkt Val
P4	2001	500	50 Pence. 0.9250 Silver. 56.5600 g. 38.6 mm. Reeded edge.	100
P5	2001	500	50 Pence. 0.9250 Silver. 56.5600 g. 38.6 mm. Reeded edge. Proof KM#70a.	100
P6	2002	500	50 Pence. 0.9250 Silver. 56.5600 g. 38.6 mm. Reeded edge. Proof KM#73a.	90.00
P7	2002	500	50 Pence. 0.9250 Silver. 56.5600 g. 38.6 mm. Reeded edge. Proof KM#74a.	90.00
P8	2002	500	50 Pence. 0.9250 Silver. 56.5600 g. 38.6 mm. Reeded edge. Proof KM#75a.	90.00
P9	2002	500	50 Pence. 0.9250 Silver. 56.5600 g. 38.6 mm. Reeded edge. Proof KM#76a.	90.00
P10	2002	500	50 Pence. 0.9250 Silver. 56.5600 g. 38.6 mm. Reeded edge. Proof KM#77a.	90.00
P11	2002	500	50 Pence. 0.9250 Silver. 56.5600 g. 38.6 mm. Reeded edge. Proof KM#78a.	90.00
P12	2002	500	50 Pence. 0.9250 Silver. 56.5600 g. 38.6 mm. Reeded edge. Proof KM#79a.	90.00
P13	2002	500	50 Pence. 0.9250 Silver. 56.5600 g. 38.6 mm. Reeded edge. Proof KM#80a.	90.00
P14	2002	500	50 Pence. 0.9250 Silver. 56.5600 g. 38.6 mm. Reeded edge. Proof KM#81a.	90.00
P15	2002	500	50 Pence. 0.9250 Silver. 56.5600 g. 38.6 mm. Reeded edge. Proof KM#82a.	90.00
P16	2002	500	50 Pence. 0.9250 Silver. 56.5600 g. 38.6 mm. Reeded edge. Proof KM#83a.	90.00
P17	2002	500	50 Pence. 0.9250 Silver. 56.5600 g. 38.6 mm. Reeded edge. Proof KM#84a.	90.00
P18	2001	500	50 Pence. 0.9250 Silver. 56.5600 g. 38.6 mm. Reeded edge. Proof KM#86a.	90.00
P19	2001	500	50 Pence. 0.9250 Silver. 56.5600 g. 38.6 mm. Reeded edge.	90.00
P20	2001	500	50 Pence. 0.9250 Silver. 56.5600 g. 38.6 mm. Reeded edge.	90.00
P21	2001	500	50 Pence. 0.9250 Silver. 56.5600 g. 38.6 mm. Reeded edge.	90.00
P22	ND(2002)	500	50 Pence. 0.9250 Silver. 56.5600 g. 38.6 mm. Reeded edge. Proof KM#102a.	90.00

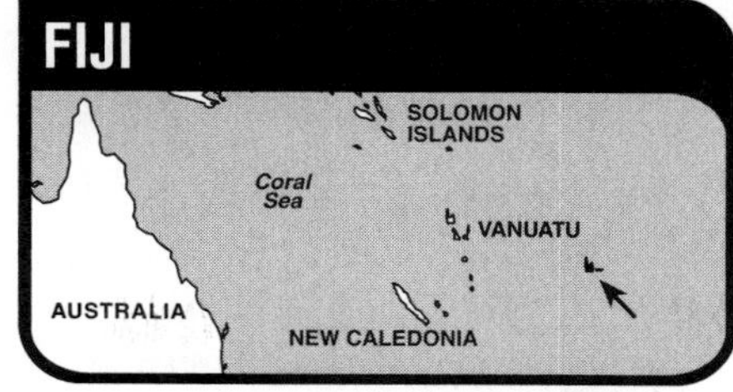

The Republic of Fiji, consists of about 320 islands located in the southwestern Pacific 1,100 miles (1,770 km.) north of New Zealand. The islands have a combined area of 7,056 sq. mi. (18,274 sq. km.) and a population of 772,891. Capital: Suva. Fiji's economy is based on agriculture and mining. Sugar, coconut products, manganese, and gold are exported.

MINT MARKS

(o) - Royal Canadian Mint, Ottawa

REPUBLIC

DECIMAL COINAGE

100 Cents = 1 Dollar

KM# 49a CENT
Copper Plated Zinc

Date	Mintage	F	VF	XF	Unc	BU
2001	—	—	—	—	0.25	0.75
2002(o)	5,880,000	—	—	—	0.25	0.75
2003(o)	8,030,000	—	—	—	0.25	0.75
2005(o)	9,720,000	—	—	—	0.25	0.75

KM# 50a 2 CENTS
Copper Plated Zinc

Date	Mintage	F	VF	XF	Unc	BU
2001(o)	2,830,000	—	—	—	0.35	1.00
2002(o)	5,000,000	—	—	—	0.35	1.00
2003(o)	6,410,000	—	—	—	0.35	1.00
2004(o)	7,050,000	—	—	—	0.35	1.00
2005(o)	7,760,000	—	—	—	0.35	1.00

KM# 95 20 CENTS
11.2400 g., Copper-Nickel, 28.4 mm. **Obv:** Queen Elizabeth II **Rev:** South Pacific Games flame logo **Edge:** Reeded

Date	Mintage	F	VF	XF	Unc	BU
2003	1,540,000	—	—	—	2.50	3.00

KM# 93 5 DOLLARS
1.5550 g., 0.9999 Gold 0.05 oz. AGW **Obv:** Queen's portrait right **Rev:** Arms

Date	Mintage	F	VF	XF	Unc	BU
2002	3,000	Value: 35.00				

KM# 82 10 DOLLARS
31.6200 g., 0.9250 Silver .9404 oz. ASW, 38.6 mm. **Obv:** Queen's portrait **Rev:** Sail-powered war ship - HMS Providence **Edge:** Reeded

Date	Mintage	F	VF	XF	Unc	BU
2001 Proof	—	Value: 15.00				

KM# 83 10 DOLLARS
28.2800 g., 0.9250 Silver 0.841 oz. ASW, 38.6 mm. **Subject:** Queen Elizabeth II - 50 Years of Reign **Obv:** Queen's head right, gilded **Rev:** Cloth draped sword hilt, legend and denomination **Rev. Legend:** Defender of the Faith... **Rev. Designer:** Robert Low **Edge:** Reeded

Date	Mintage	F	VF	XF	Unc	BU
2002 Proof	15,000	Value: 15.00				

KM# 84 10 DOLLARS
28.2800 g., 0.9250 Silver 0.841 oz. ASW, 38.6 mm. **Subject:** Queen Elizabeth II - 50th Year of Reign **Obv:** Queen's head right, gilded **Rev:** Four man chorus, legend, and denomination
Rev. Legend: Westminster Abbey June 1953.
Rev. Designer: Robert Low **Edge:** Reeded

Date	Mintage	F	VF	XF	Unc	BU
2002 Proof	15,000	Value: 15.00				

KM# 94 10 DOLLARS
3.1100 g., 0.9999 Gold 0.1 oz. AGW **Obv:** Queen's portrait right **Rev:** Arms **Edge:** Reeded

Date	Mintage	F	VF	XF	Unc	BU
2002 Proof	2,000	Value: 75.00				

KM# 101 10 DOLLARS
31.1000 g., 0.9990 Silver 0.9989 oz. ASW, 40 mm. **Obv:** Elizabeth II **Rev:** Sperm Whale on Mother of Pearl insert **Edge:** Plain

Date	Mintage	F	VF	XF	Unc	BU
2002 Proof	2,000	Value: 60.00				

KM# 99 100 DOLLARS
7.7800 g., 0.5850 Gold 0.1463 oz. AGW **Subject:** 2006 FIFA World Cup - Germany **Obv:** Queen's portrait **Rev:** World Cup **Edge:** Reeded

Date	Mintage	F	VF	XF	Unc	BU
2003 Proof	25,000	Value: 125				

FINLAND

The Republic of Finland, the third most northerly state of the European continent, has an area of 130,559 sq. mi. (338,127 sq. km.) and a population of 5.1 million. Capital: Helsinki. Lumbering, shipbuilding, metal and woodworking are the leading industries. Paper, timber, woodpulp, plywood and metal products are exported.

MONETARY SYSTEM
100 Pennia = 1 Markka

MINT MARKS
No mm – Helsinki

MINT OFFICIALS' INITIALS

Letter	Date	Name
K-M	2004	Heli Kauhaneu & Raimo Makkonen
M-M	2004	Perth Mäkinen & Raimo Makkonen
P-M	2003	Matti Peltokangas & Raimo Makkonen
S-M	2003	Anneli Sijriläinen & Raimo Makkonen
W-M	2002	Erkki Vainio & Hannu Veijalainen & Raimo Makkonen

REPUBLIC

REFORM COINAGE

100 Old Markka = 1 New Markka 1963

KM# 65 10 PENNIA
1.8000 g., Copper-Nickel, 16.3 mm. **Obv:** Flower pods and stems **Designer:** Antti Neuvonen

Date	Mintage	F	VF	XF	Unc	BU
2001 M	25,000,000	—	—	—	1.00	—
2001 M Proof	—	Value: 7.00				

KM# 66 50 PENNIA
3.3000 g., Copper-Nickel, 19.7 mm. **Obv:** Polar bear **Designer:** Antti Neuvonen

Date	Mintage	F	VF	XF	Unc	BU
2001 M	200,000	—	—	0.20	0.75	—

KM# 76 MARKKA
4.9000 g., Aluminum-Bronze, 22 mm.

Date	Mintage	F	VF	XF	Unc	BU
2001 M	200,000	—	—	0.35	0.75	—
2001 M Proof	—	Value: 10.00				

KM# 106 MARKKA
6.1000 g., Copper-Nickel, 24 mm. **Subject:** Remembrance Markka **Obv:** National arms **Rev:** Denomination and pine tree **Edge:** Plain **Designer:** Anth' Neuvoneu. **Note:** This coin is encased in acrylic resin and sealed in a display card.

Date	Mintage	F	VF	XF	Unc	BU
2001 N-M	500,000	—	—	—	5.00	6.50

KM# 95 MARKKA
8.6400 g., 0.7500 Gold .2083 oz. AGW, 22 mm. **Subject:** Last Markka Coin **Obv:** National arms **Rev:** Stylized tree with roots **Edge:** Reeded

Date	Mintage	F	VF	XF	Unc	BU
2001 P-M Proof	55,000	Value: 250				

KM# 73 5 MARKKAA
5.5000 g., Copper-Aluminum-Nickel, 24.5 mm. **Obv:** Lake Saimaa ringed seal

Date	Mintage	F	VF	XF	Unc	BU
2001 M	200,000	—	—	—	2.50	4.50
2001 M Proof	—	Value: 12.00				

KM# 77 10 MARKKAA
8.8000 g., Bi-Metallic Brass center in Copper-Nickel ring, 27.25 mm. **Obv:** Capercaillie bird

Date	Mintage	F	VF	XF	Unc	BU
2001 M	200,000	—	—	3.00	6.50	7.00
2001 M Proof	—	Value: 18.00				

KM# 96 25 MARKKAA
20.2000 g., Bi-Metallic Brass center in Copper-Nickel ring, 35 mm. **Subject:** First Nordic Ski Championship, "Lahti 2001" **Obv:** Stylized woman's face **Rev:** Female torso, landscape **Edge:** Plain **Designer:** Jarkko Roth

Date	Mintage	F	VF	XF	Unc	BU
2001 Prooflike	100,000	—	—	—	—	25.00

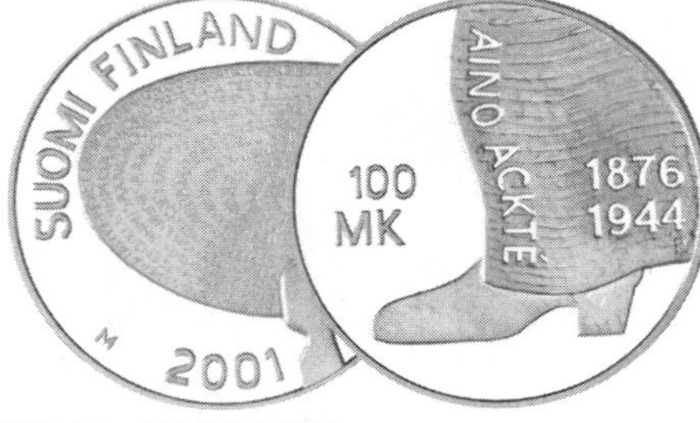

KM# 97 100 MARKKAA
31.0000 g., 0.9250 Silver 0.9219 oz. ASW, 35 mm. **Subject:** Aino Ackte **Obv:** Partial portrait **Rev:** High heel shoe and trouser bottom **Edge:** Plain **Designer:** Timo Rythönen.

Date	Mintage	F	VF	XF	Unc	BU
2001	33,000	—	—	—	35.00	40.00
2001 Proof	12,000	Value: 50.00				

KM# 93 100 MARKKAA
22.0000 g., 0.9250 Silver .6543 oz. ASW **Subject:** 450th Anniversary - Helsinki Cultural Capital **Obv:** Symbolic column design **Rev:** Carved city view **Edge:** Plain **Designer:** Teijo Paavilainen

Date	Mintage	F	VF	XF	Unc	BU
2000 P-M Proof	8,000	Value: 80.00				

EURO COINAGE

European Economic Community Issues

KM# 98 EURO CENT
2.2700 g., Copper Plated Steel, 16.3 mm. **Obv:** Rampant lion surrounded by stars **Obv. Designer:** Heikki Haivaoja **Rev:** Value and globe **Rev. Designer:** Luc Luycx **Edge:** Plain

Date	Mintage	F	VF	XF	Unc	BU
2001	570,000	—	—	—	10.00	—
2001 Proof	—	—	—	—	—	—
2002	734,000	—	—	—	5.00	—
2002 Proof	16,000	Value: 15.00				
2003	6,790,000	—	—	—	5.00	—
2003 Proof	—	Value: 15.00				
2004	9,690,000	—	—	—	5.00	—
2004 Proof	—	Value: 15.00				
2005	—	—	—	—	5.00	—

KM# 99 2 EURO CENTS
3.0000 g., Copper Plated Steel, 18.7 mm. **Obv:** Rampant lion surrounded by stars **Obv. Designer:** Heikki Haivaoja **Rev:** Value and globe **Rev. Designer:** Luc Luycx **Edge:** Grooved

Date	Mintage	F	VF	XF	Unc	BU
2001	570,000	—	—	—	10.00	—
2001 Proof	—	—	—	—	—	—
2002	734,000	—	—	—	5.00	—
2002 Proof	16,000	Value: 15.00				
2003	6,790,000	—	—	—	5.00	—
2003 Proof	—	Value: 15.00				
2004	8,024,000	—	—	—	5.00	—
2004 Proof	—	Value: 15.00				
2005	—	—	—	—	5.00	—

KM# 100 5 EURO CENTS
3.8600 g., Copper Plated Steel, 21.2 mm. **Obv:** Rampant lion surrounded by stars **Obv. Designer:** Heikki Haivaoja **Rev:** Value and globe **Rev. Designer:** Luc Luycx **Edge:** Plain

Date	Mintage	F	VF	XF	Unc	BU
2001	213,826,000	—	—	—	0.50	—
2001 Proof	—	—	—	—	—	—
2002	101,899,000	—	—	—	0.50	—
2002 Proof	16,000	Value: 15.00				
2003	790,000	—	—	—	1.00	—
2003 Proof	—	Value: 15.00				
2004	629,000	—	—	—	1.00	—
2004 Proof	—	Value: 15.00				
2005	—	—	—	—	1.00	—

KM# 101 10 EURO CENTS

4.0000 g., Brass, 19.7 mm. **Obv:** Rampant lion surrounded by stars **Obv. Designer:** Heikki Haivaoja **Rev:** Value and map **Rev. Designer:** Luc Luycx **Edge:** Reeded

Date	Mintage	F	VF	XF	Unc	BU
2001	14,800,000	—	—	—	10.00	—
2001 Proof	—	—	—	—	—	—
2002	1,574,000	—	—	—	2.50	—
2002 Proof	16,000	Value: 18.00				
2003	790,000	—	—	—	2.50	—
2003 Proof	—	Value: 18.00				
2004	629,000	—	—	—	2.50	—
2004 Proof	—	Value: 18.00				
2005	—	—	—	—	2.50	—

KM# 102 20 EURO CENTS

5.7300 g., Brass, 22.2 mm. **Obv:** Rampant lion surrounded by stars **Obv. Designer:** Heikki Haivaoja **Rev:** Value and map **Rev. Designer:** Luc Luycx **Edge:** Notched

Date	Mintage	F	VF	XF	Unc	BU
2001	121,833,000	—	—	—	1.75	—
2001 Proof	—	—	—	—	—	—
2002	100,834,000	—	—	—	1.75	—
2002 Proof	16,000	Value: 20.00				
2003	790,000	—	—	—	1.75	—
2003 Proof	—	Value: 20.00				
2004	629,000	—	—	—	1.75	—
2004 Proof	—	Value: 20.00				
2005	—	—	—	—	1.75	—

KM# 103 50 EURO CENTS

7.8100 g., Brass, 24.2 mm. **Obv:** Rampant lion surrounded by stars **Obv. Designer:** Heikki Haivaoja **Rev:** Value and map **Rev. Designer:** Luc Luycx **Edge:** Reeded

Date	Mintage	F	VF	XF	Unc	BU
2001	4,502,000	—	—	—	7.50	—
2001 Proof	—	—	—	—	—	—
2002	1,222,000	—	—	—	5.00	—
2002 Proof	16,000	Value: 22.00				
2003	790,000	—	—	—	5.00	—
2003 Proof	—	Value: 22.00				
2004	629,000	—	—	—	5.00	—
2004 Proof	—	Value: 22.00				
2005	—	—	—	—	5.00	—

KM# 104 EURO

7.5000 g., Bi-Metallic Copper-nickel center in Brass ring, 23.2 mm. **Obv:** 2 flying swans surrounded by stars on outer ring **Obv. Designer:** Pertti Maekinen **Rev:** Value and map **Rev. Designer:** Luc Luycx **Edge:** Reeded and plain sections

Date	Mintage	F	VF	XF	Unc	BU
2001	13,932,000	—	—	—	3.00	—
2001 Proof	—	—	—	—	—	—
2002	14,189,000	—	—	—	6.50	—
2002 Proof	16,000	Value: 25.00				
2003	790,000	—	—	—	6.50	—
2003 Proof	—	Value: 25.00				
2004	5,529,000	—	—	—	6.50	—
2004 Proof	—	Value: 25.00				
2005	—	—	—	—	6.50	—

KM# 105 2 EURO

8.5200 g., Bi-Metallic Brass center in Copper-nickel ring, 25.6 mm. **Obv:** 2 cloudberry flowers surrounded by stars on outer ring **Obv. Designer:** Raimo Heino **Rev:** Value and map **Rev. Designer:** Luc Luycx **Edge:** Reeded and lettered **Edge Lettering:** SUOMI FINLAND

Date	Mintage	F	VF	XF	Unc	BU
2001	29,202,000	—	—	—	4.00	—
2001 Proof	—	—	—	—	—	—
2002	1,461,000	—	—	—	7.50	—
2002 Proof	16,000	Value: 30.00				
2003	9,080,000	—	—	—	5.00	—
2003 Proof	—	Value: 30.00				
2004	10,029,000	—	—	—	5.00	—
2004 Proof	—	Value: 30.00				
2005	—	—	—	—	5.00	—

KM# 114 2 EURO

8.5200 g., Bi-Metallic, 25.6 mm. **Obv:** Stylized flower **Rev:** Value and map **Edge:** Reeded and lettered

Date	Mintage	F	VF	XF	Unc	BU
2004	1,100,000	—	—	—	10.00	11.50

KM# 119 2 EURO

8.5200 g., Bi-Metallic Brass center in Copper-Nickel ring, 25.6 mm. **Subject:** 60th Anniversary - Finland - UN **Obv:** Dove on a puzzle **Rev:** Value over map **Edge:** Reeded and lettered **Edge Lettering:** "YK 1945-2005 FN"

Date	Mintage	F	VF	XF	Unc	BU
2005	2,000,000	—	—	—	6.00	7.50

KM# 111 5 EURO

20.1000 g., Bi-Metallic Copper-Nickel center in Brass ring, 34.9 mm. **Subject:** Ice Hockey World Championships **Obv:** Summer landscape **Rev:** Three hockey sticks and a puck **Edge:** Plain **Designer:** Pertti Makinen

Date	Mintage	F	VF	XF	Unc	BU
2003 M-M	150,000	—	—	—	15.00	20.00

KM# 118 5 EURO

19.8000 g., Bi-Metallic Brass center in Copper-Nickel ring, 35 mm. **Obv:** Female javelin thrower **Rev:** Running feet **Edge:** Plain

Date	Mintage	F	VF	XF	Unc	BU
2005	170,000	—	—	—	15.00	20.00
2005 Proof	5,000	Value: 25.00				

KM# 107 10 EURO

27.4000 g., 0.9250 Silver 0.8149 oz. ASW, 38.6 mm. **Subject:** 50th Anniversary - Helsinki Olympics **Obv:** Flames and denomination above globe with map of Finland **Obv. Designer:** Erkki Vainio **Rev:** Tower and partial coin design **Rev. Designer:** Hannu Veijalainen **Edge:** Plain

Date	Mintage	F	VF	XF	Unc	BU
2002 W-M	10,000	—	—	—	32.00	35.00
2002 W-M Proof	34,800	Value: 40.00				

KM# 108 10 EURO

27.4000 g., 0.9250 Silver 0.803 oz. ASW, 38.6 mm. **Subject:** Elias Lönnrot **Obv:** Ribbon with stars **Rev:** Quill and signature **Edge:** Plain **Designer:** Perth Mäkinen.

Date	Mintage	F	VF	XF	Unc	BU
2002 M-M	40,000	—	—	—	32.00	35.00
2002 M-M Proof	40,000	Value: 40.00				

KM# 110 10 EURO

27.4000 g., 0.9250 Silver 0.8327 oz. ASW, 38.6 mm. **Subject:** Anders Chydenius **Obv:** Stylized design **Rev:** Name and book **Edge:** Plain

Date	Mintage	F	VF	XF	Unc	BU
2003 L-M	30,000	—	—	—	32.00	35.00
2003 Proof	30,000	Value: 40.00				

KM# 112 10 EURO

27.4000 g., 0.9250 Silver 0.8149 oz. ASW, 38.6 mm. **Subject:** Mannerheim and St. Petersburg **Obv:** Fortress **Rev:** Carl Gustaf Emil Mannerheim **Designer:** Anueli Sijrilainen

Date	Mintage	F	VF	XF	Unc	BU
2003 S-M Proof	27,900	Value: 55.00				
2003 S-M	7,100	—	—	—	35.00	37.50

KM# 115 10 EURO

27.4000 g., 0.9250 Silver 0.8149 oz. ASW, 38.6 mm. **Subject:** 200th Birthday of Johan Ludwig Runeberg **Obv:** Head of Runeberg **Rev:** Text of 1831 Helsingfors Tidningar newspaper

Date	Mintage	F	VF	XF	Unc	BU
2004 K-M	30,000	—	—	—	35.00	37.50
2004 Proof	25,000	Value: 45.00				

KM# 116 10 EURO
27.4000 g., 0.9250 Silver 0.8149 oz. ASW, 38.6 mm.
Subject: Tove Jansson **Obv:** Three "muumi" figures **Rev:** Head of Tove Jansson

Date	Mintage	F	VF	XF	Unc	BU
2004 M-M	50,000	—	—	—	35.00	37.50
2004 M-M Proof	20,000	Value: 45.00				

KM# 120 10 EURO
25.5000 g., 0.9250 Silver 0.7584 oz. ASW **Subject:** 60 years of Peace **Obv:** Dove of peace **Rev:** Flowering plant

Date	Mintage	F	VF	XF	Unc	BU
2005 M-M	55,000	—	—	—	35.00	37.50
2005 Proof	5,000	Value: 45.00				

KM# 121 20 EURO
1.7300 g., 0.9000 Gold 0.0501 oz. AGW **Subject:** 10th Anniversary - IAAF World Championships in Athletics
Obv: Helsinki Stadium **Rev:** Two faces

Date	Mintage	F	VF	XF	Unc	BU
2005 M-M Proof	30,000	Value: 125				

KM# 113 50 EURO
13.2000 g., Bi-Metallic Gold And Silver **Ring Composition:** 0.9250 Silver **Center Composition:** 0.7500 Gold, 27/8.25 mm.
Subject: Finnish art and design **Designer:** Matti Peltokangas

Date	Mintage	F	VF	XF	Unc	BU
2003 P-M Proof	20,000	Value: 300				

KM# 109 100 EURO
8.6400 g., 0.9000 Gold 0.25 oz. AGW, 22 mm. **Subject:** Lapland **Obv:** Small tree and mountain stream **Rev:** Lake landscape beneath the midnight sun **Edge:** Plain with serial number **Designer:** Toivo Jaatinen

Date	Mintage	F	VF	XF	Unc	BU
2002 J-M Proof	25,000	Value: 270				

KM# 117 100 EURO
8.6400 g., 0.9000 Gold 0.25 oz. AGW, 22 mm. **Subject:** 150th Birthday of Albert Edelfelt **Obv:** Flower **Rev:** Head of Edelfelt

Date	Mintage	F	VF	XF	Unc	BU
2004 M-M Proof	8,500	Value: 280				

MINT SETS

KM#	Date	Mintage	Identification	Issue Price	Mkt Val
MS58	2001 (5)	20,000	KM#65, 66, 73, 76, 77 plus 1865 coin design medal	18.00	20.00
MS59	2001 (5)	—	KM#65, 66, 73, 76, 77, medal (Johan Vilhelm Snellman)	—	22.50
MS60	2002 (8)	—	KM#98-105, medal (Church)	—	35.00

PROOF SETS

KM#	Date	Mintage	Identification	Issue Price	Mkt Val
PS9	2001 (5)	—	KM#65-66, 73, 76-77, medal (Suomen Markka 1864-2001)	—	60.00
PS10	2002 (8)	8,000	KM#98-105, gold medal (National Theater)	—	525
PS11	2002 (8)	—	KM#98-105, Silver medal	—	160

The French Republic, largest of the West European nations, has an area of 210,026 sq. mi. (547,030 sq. km.) and a population of 58.1 million. Capital: Paris. Agriculture, manufacturing, tourist industry and financial services are the most important elements of France's diversified economy. Textiles and clothing, steel products, machinery and transportation equipment, chemicals, pharmaceuticals, nuclear electricity, agricultural products and wine are exported.

RULERS
Fifth Republic, 1959—

21st Century Engraver General's Privy Marks

Desc.	Date	Name
Horseshoe	2000-2002	Gérard Buquoy
SL Heart-shaped monogram	2002-2003	Serge Levet
French horn w/starfish in water	2003	Hubert Lariviére

MINT DIRECTOR'S PRIVY MARKS
Some modern coins struck from dies produced at the Paris Mint have the 'A' mint mark. In the absence of a mint mark, the cornucopia privy mark serves to attribute a coin to Paris design.

A – Paris, Central Mint

MONETARY SYSTEM
(Commencing 2002)
100 Euro Cents = 1 Euro

MODERN REPUBLICS
1870-
REFORM COINAGE
(Commencing 1960)

1 Old Franc = 1 New Centime; 100 New Centimes = 1 New Franc

KM# 928 CENTIME
Chrome-Steel **Note:** 1991-1993 dated coins, non-Proof, exist in both coin and medal alignment. Values given here are for medal alignment examples. Pieces struck in coin alignment have been traded for as much as $50.00.

Date	Mintage	F	VF	XF	Unc	BU
2001	—	—	—	—	1.00	—
Note: In sets only						
2001 Proof	—	Value: 2.00				

KM# 928a CENTIME
2.5000 g., 0.7500 Gold .0603 oz. AGW **Obv:** Medallic alignment **Rev:** Medallic alignment **Edge:** Plain **Note:** Last Centime.

Date	Mintage	F	VF	XF	Unc	BU
2001	Est. 7,492	—	—	—	—	75.00

KM# 933 5 CENTIMES
Aluminum-Bronze **Obv. Designer:** Henri Lagriffoul
Rev. Designer: Adrien Dieudonne **Note:** 1991-1993 dated coins, non-Proof exist in both coin and medal alignment.

Date	Mintage	F	VF	XF	Unc	BU
2001	—	—	—	—	1.50	—
Note: In sets only						
2001 Proof	—	Value: 1.00				

KM# 929 10 CENTIMES
Aluminum-Bronze **Obv. Designer:** Henri Lagriffoul
Rev. Designer: Adrien Dieudonne **Note:** Without mint mark. 1991-1993 dated coins, non-Proof, exist in both coin and medal alignment.

Date	Mintage	F	VF	XF	Unc	BU
2001	—	—	—	—	2.00	—
Note: In sets only						
2001 Proof	—	Value: 1.00				

KM# 930 20 CENTIMES
Aluminum-Bronze **Obv. Designer:** Henri Lagriffoul
Rev. Designer: Adrien Dieudonne **Note:** Without mint mark. 1991-1993 dated coins, non-Proof, exist in both coin and medal alignment.

Date	Mintage	F	VF	XF	Unc	BU
2001	—	—	—	—	2.00	—
Note: In sets only						
2001 Proof	—	Value: 1.00				

KM# 931.2 1/2 FRANC
Nickel **Obv:** Modified sower, engraver's signature: "O. ROTY" preceded by "D'AP" **Edge:** Plain

Date	Mintage	F	VF	XF	Unc	BU
2001	—	—	—	—	0.40	—
2001 Proof	—	Value: 1.50				

KM# 931.1 1/2 FRANC
Nickel **Obv:** Sower **Edge:** Reeded **Designer:** Louis Oscar Roty **Note:** Without mint mark.

Date	Mintage	F	VF	XF	Unc	BU
2001	—	—	—	—	2.00	—
Note: In sets only						

KM# 925.1 FRANC
Nickel, 24 mm. **Obv:** Sower **Obv. Designer:** Louis Oscar Roty **Edge:** Reeded **Note:** Without mint mark.

Date	Mintage	F	VF	XF	Unc	BU
2001	20,000,000	—	—	—	0.40	—

KM# 925.1a FRANC
8.0000 g., 0.7500 Gold .1929 oz. AGW **Obv:** Sower **Edge:** Reeded **Designer:** Louis Oscar Roty **Note:** Medallic alignment. Struck at Paris Mint.

Date	Mintage	F	VF	XF	Unc	BU
2001	Est. 9,941	—	—	—	145	165

KM# 925.2 FRANC
Nickel **Obv:** Modified sower, engraver's signature: O. ROTY, preceded by D'AP **Edge:** Plain

Date	Mintage	F	VF	XF	Unc	BU
2001	—	—	—	—	0.40	—
2001 Proof	—	Value: 2.50				

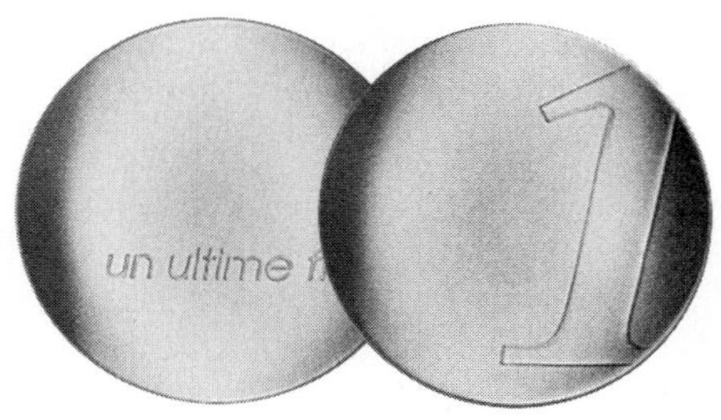

KM# 1290 FRANC

17.7700 g., 0.9800 Silver .5599 oz. ASW **Subject:** The Last Franc **Obv. Legend:** UN ULTIME FRANC **Rev:** Number "1" **Edge Lettering:** REPUBLIQUE FRANCAISE STARCK LIBERTE EGALITE FRATERNITE (2001). **Note:** The coin is intentionally warped and the edge inscription is very faint. Struck at Paris Mint.

Date	Mintage	F	VF	XF	Unc	BU
2001 Matte	49,838	Value: 65.00				

KM# 1290a FRANC

26.1000 g., 0.7500 Gold .6294 oz. AGW **Subject:** The Last Franc **Obv. Legend:** UN ULTIME FRANC **Rev:** Number 1 **Edge Lettering:** REPUBLIQUE FRANCAISE. STARCK. LIBERTE. EGALITE. FRATERNITE (cornucopia) 2001 **Note:** This coin has an intentionally warped surface and the edge inscription is very weak.

Date	Mintage	F	VF	XF	Unc	BU
2001 Matte	4,963	—	—	—	450	475

KM# 942.1 2 FRANCS

Nickel **Obv:** Sower **Edge:** Reeded **Designer:** Louis Oscar Roty

Date	Mintage	F	VF	XF	Unc	BU
2001 Bee	—	—	—	—	0.75	—

KM# 942.2 2 FRANCS

Nickel **Edge:** Plain

Date	Mintage	F	VF	XF	Unc	BU
2001	—	—	—	—	0.75	—
2001 Proof	—	Value: 3.50				

KM# 1309 5 FRANCS

12.0000 g., 0.9000 Silver 0.3472 oz. ASW, 29 mm. **Subject:** Last Year of the Franc **Obv:** The seed sower **Rev:** Value **Edge:** Lettered **Edge Lettering:** " * LIBERTY * EGALITE * FRATERNITE * "

Date	Mintage	F	VF	XF	Unc	BU
2001	25,000	—	—	—	25.00	—

KM# 926a.1 5 FRANCS

Nickel Clad Copper-Nickel **Obv:** Sower **Edge:** Reeded **Designer:** Louis Oscar Roty

Date	Mintage	F	VF	XF	Unc	BU
2001	—	—	—	—	5.00	—

Note: In sets only

KM# 926a.2 5 FRANCS

Nickel Clad Copper-Nickel **Obv:** Modified sower, engraver's signature: "O. ROTY" preceded by "D'AP" **Edge:** Plain

Date	Mintage	F	VF	XF	Unc	BU
2001	—	—	—	—	1.65	—
2001 Proof	—	Value: 6.50				

KM# 1265.1 6.55957 FRANCS

13.0000 g., 0.9000 Silver .3762 oz. ASW **Subject:** Last Year of the French Franc **Obv:** French and other European euro currency equivalents **Rev:** Similar to KM#1258 but with addition of "last year of the franc" logo after the date **Edge:** Reeded

Date	Mintage	F	VF	XF	Unc	BU
2001	Est. 20,000	—	—	—	18.00	20.00

KM# 1265.2 6.55957 FRANCS

22.2000 g., 0.9000 Silver .6424 oz. ASW **Edge:** Plain

Date	Mintage	F	VF	XF	Unc	BU
2001 Proof	Est. 10,000	Value: 35.00				

KM# 1276 6.55957 FRANCS

22.2000 g., 0.9000 Silver .6424 oz. ASW **Subject:** Mottos **Obv:** Denomination **Rev:** FRATERNITE in red letters **Edge:** Reeded

Date	Mintage	F	VF	XF	Unc	BU
2001 Proof	2,171	Value: 40.00				

KM# 1277 6.55957 FRANCS

22.2000 g., 0.9000 Silver .6424 oz. ASW **Subject:** Mottos **Rev:** EGALITE in white letters

Date	Mintage	F	VF	XF	Unc	BU
2001 Proof	2,190	Value: 40.00				

KM# 1278 6.55957 FRANCS

22.2000 g., 0.9000 Silver .6424 oz. ASW **Subject:** Mottos **Rev:** LIBERTE in white letters

Date	Mintage	F	VF	XF	Unc	BU
2001 Proof	2,259	Value: 40.00				

KM# 964.2 10 FRANCS

Aluminum-Bronze **Edge:** Plain

Date	Mintage	F	VF	XF	Unc	BU
2001	—	—	—	—	6.00	7.00
2001 Proof	—	Value: 15.00				

KM# 1268 10 FRANCS

22.2000 g., 0.9000 Silver .6424 oz. ASW **Subject:** Monuments of France - Palace of Versailles **Obv:** Stylized French map **Rev:** 1/2 bust of Louis XIV at right, internal and external palace views at left **Edge:** Plain

Date	Mintage	F	VF	XF	Unc	BU
2001 Proof	Est. 2,561	Value: 35.00				

KM# 1270 10 FRANCS

22.2000 g., 0.9000 Silver .6424 oz. ASW **Subject:** Monuments of France - Arch of Triumph **Obv:** Stylized French map **Rev:** Arch of Triumph on the Champs Elysees partial close up and aerial views

Date	Mintage	F	VF	XF	Unc	BU
2001 Proof	Est. 2,882	Value: 35.00				

KM# 1272 10 FRANCS

22.2000 g., 0.9000 Silver .6424 oz. ASW **Subject:** Monuments of France - Notre Dame Cathedral **Obv:** Stylized French map **Rev:** Gargoyle at left, cathedral views at right

Date	Mintage	F	VF	XF	Unc	BU
2001 Proof	Est. 2,877	Value: 35.00				

KM# 1274 10 FRANCS

22.2000 g., 0.9000 Silver .6424 oz. ASW **Subject:** Monuments of France - Eiffel Tower **Obv:** Stylized French map **Rev:** Two tower views

Date	Mintage	F	VF	XF	Unc	BU
2001 Proof	Est. 3,888	Value: 35.00				

KM# 1008.2 20 FRANCS

Tri-Metallic Copper-Aluminum-Nickel center plug, Nickel inner ring, Copper-Aluminum-Nickel outer ring **Edge:** 5 milled bands

Date	Mintage	F	VF	XF	Unc	BU
2001	—	—	—	—	8.00	9.00
2001 Proof	—	Value: 25.00				

KM# 1266 65.5997 FRANCS

8.4500 g., 0.9200 Gold .2499 oz. AGW **Subject:** Last Year of the French Franc **Obv:** French and other European euro currency equivalents **Rev:** Similar to KM#1258 but with addition of "last year of the franc" logo after the date **Edge:** Reeded

Date	Mintage	F	VF	XF	Unc	BU
2001 Proof	3,000	Value: 200				

KM# 1269 100 FRANCS

17.0000 g., 0.9200 Gold .5028 oz. AGW **Subject:** Palace of Versailles **Obv:** Stylized French map **Rev:** Louis XIV with internal and external palace views **Edge:** Plain

Date	Mintage	F	VF	XF	Unc	BU
2001 Proof	105	Value: 350				

KM# 1271 100 FRANCS

17.0000 g., 0.9200 Gold .5028 oz. AGW **Obv:** Champs-Elysees **Rev:** Arch of Triumph partial close up and aerial views

Date	Mintage	F	VF	XF	Unc	BU
2001 Proof	115	Value: 365				

KM# 1273 100 FRANCS

17.0000 g., 0.9200 Gold .5028 oz. AGW **Obv:** Notre-Dame Cathedral **Rev:** Gargoyle and cathedral views

Date	Mintage	F	VF	XF	Unc	BU
2001 Proof	116	Value: 375				

KM# 1275 100 FRANCS

17.0000 g., 0.9200 Gold .5028 oz. AGW **Obv:** Eiffel Tower **Rev:** Two tower views

Date	Mintage	F	VF	XF	Unc	BU
2001 Proof	170	Value: 375				

KM# 1267 655.957 FRANCS
31.1035 g., 0.9990 Gold 1.0000 oz. AGW **Subject:** Last Year of the French Franc **Obv:** French and other European euro currency equivalents **Rev:** Similar to KM#1258 but with addition of "last year of the franc" logo after the date **Edge:** Plain

Date	Mintage	F	VF	XF	Unc	BU
2001 Proof	2,000	Value: 675				

KM# 1267.1 655.957 FRANCS
155.5175 g., 0.9990 Gold 5.0000 oz. AGW **Edge:** Plain

Date	Mintage	F	VF	XF	Unc	BU
2001 Proof	99	Value: 4,000				

KM# 1279 655.957 FRANCS
17.0000 g., 0.9200 Gold .5028 oz. AGW **Subject:** Motto Series **Obv:** Denomination **Rev:** FRATERNITE **Edge:** Reeded

Date	Mintage	F	VF	XF	Unc	BU
2001 Proof	62	Value: 375				

KM# 1280 655.957 FRANCS
17.0000 g., 0.9200 Gold .5028 oz. AGW **Subject:** Motto Series **Obv:** Denomination **Rev:** EGALITE

Date	Mintage	F	VF	XF	Unc	BU
2001 Proof	64	Value: 375				

KM# 1281 655.957 FRANCS
17.0000 g., 0.9200 Gold .5028 oz. AGW **Subject:** Motto Series **Obv:** Denomination **Rev:** LIBERTE

Date	Mintage	F	VF	XF	Unc	BU
2001 Proof	63	Value: 375				

EURO COINAGE

European Economic Community Issues

KM# 1282 EURO CENT
2.2700 g., Copper Plated Steel, 16.3 mm. **Obv:** Human face **Obv. Designer:** Fabienne Courtiade **Rev:** Denomination and globe **Rev. Designer:** Luc Luycx **Edge:** Plain

Date	Mintage	F	VF	XF	Unc	BU
2001	300,681,580	—	—	—	0.35	0.50
2001 Proof	Est. 15,000	Value: 10.00				
2002	200,000	—	—	—	7.50	10.00
2002 Proof	Est. 40,000	Value: 8.00				
2003	160,175,000	—	—	—	1.00	1.50
2003 Proof	20,000	Value: 10.00				
2004	—	—	—	—	—	1.00
2005	—	—	—	—	—	1.00
2006	—	—	—	—	—	1.00

KM# 1283 2 EURO CENTS
3.0300 g., Copper-Plated-Steel, 18.7 mm. **Obv:** Human face **Obv. Designer:** Fabienne Courtiade **Rev:** Denomination and globe **Rev. Designer:** Luc Luycx **Edge:** Grooved

Date	Mintage	F	VF	XF	Unc	BU
2001	249,101,580	—	—	—	0.50	0.75
2001 Proof	Est. 15,000	Value: 10.00				
2002	100,000	—	—	—	10.00	12.50
Note: In sets only						
2002 Proof	Est. 40,000	Value: 8.00				
2003	160,175,000	—	—	—	1.25	2.00
2003 Proof	20,000	Value: 10.00				
2004	—	—	—	—	—	1.00
2005	—	—	—	—	—	1.00
2006	—	—	—	—	—	1.00

KM# 1284 5 EURO CENTS
3.8600 g., Copper-Plated-Steel, 21.2 mm. **Obv:** Human face **Obv. Designer:** Fabienne Courtiade **Rev. Designer:** Luc Luycx

Date	Mintage	F	VF	XF	Unc	BU
2001	217,324,477	—	—	—	0.75	1.25
2001 Proof	Est. 15,000	Value: 12.00				
2002	186,400,000	—	—	—	0.75	1.25
2002 Proof	Est. 40,000	Value: 10.00				
2003	101,175,000	—	—	—	1.00	1.50
2003 Proof	20,000	Value: 12.00				
2004	—	—	—	—	—	1.25
2005	—	—	—	—	—	1.25
2006	—	—	—	—	—	1.25

KM# 1285 10 EURO CENTS
4.0700 g., Brass, 19.7 mm. **Obv:** Sower **Obv. Designer:** Laurent Jorb **Rev:** Denomination and map **Rev. Designer:** Luc Luycx **Edge:** Reeded

Date	Mintage	F	VF	XF	Unc	BU
2001	144,513,261	—	—	—	1.25	2.00
2001 Proof	Est. 15,000	Value: 12.00				
2002	206,700,000	—	—	—	0.75	1.25
2002 Proof	Est. 40,000	Value: 10.00				
2003	180,875,000	—	—	—	1.25	2.00
2003 Proof	20,000	Value: 12.00				
2004	—	—	—	—	—	1.50
2005	—	—	—	—	—	1.50
2006	—	—	—	—	—	1.50

KM# 1286 20 EURO CENTS
5.7300 g., Brass, 22.2 mm. **Obv:** Sower **Obv. Designer:** Laurent Jorb **Rev. Designer:** Luc Luycx **Edge:** Notched

Date	Mintage	F	VF	XF	Unc	BU
2001	256,342,108	—	—	—	1.00	1.50
2001 Proof	Est. 15,000	Value: 14.00				
2002	192,100,000	—	—	—	1.00	1.50
2002 Proof	Est. 40,000	Value: 12.00				
2003	100,000	—	—	—	6.50	9.50
2003 Proof	20,000	Value: 14.00				
2004	—	—	—	—	—	1.50
2005	—	—	—	—	—	1.50
2006	—	—	—	—	—	1.50

KM# 1293 1/4 EURO
12.5000 g., Copper, 30 mm. **Subject:** Childrens Design **Obv:** Euro globe with children **Rev:** Denomination and stars **Edge:** Plain

Date	Mintage	F	VF	XF	Unc	BU
2002	1,000,000	—	—	—	6.50	8.50

KM# 1300 1/4 EURO
13.0000 g., 0.9000 Silver 0.3762 oz. ASW, 30 mm. **Subject:** Europa **Obv:** Eight French euro coin designs **Rev:** Portrait and flags design of 6.55957 francs coin KM-1265 **Edge:** Reeded

Date	Mintage	F	VF	XF	Unc	BU
2002	20,000	—	—	—	18.00	22.00

KM# 1293a 1/4 EURO
13.0000 g., 0.9000 Silver 0.3762 oz. ASW, 30 mm. **Subject:** Childrens Design **Obv:** Euro globe with children **Rev:** Value **Edge:** Plain

Date	Mintage	F	VF	XF	Unc	BU
2002 Proof	10,000	Value: 45.00				

KM# 1331 1/4 EURO
3.1100 g., 0.9990 Gold 0.0999 oz. AGW, 15 mm. **Subject:** Children's Design **Obv:** Euro globe with children **Rev:** Value **Edge:** Plain

Date	Mintage	F	VF	XF	Unc	BU
2002 Proof	5,000	Value: 135				

KM# 1350 1/4 EURO
3.1100 g., 0.9999 Gold 0.1 oz. AGW, 15 mm. **Obv:** Obverse design of first one franc coin **Rev:** Reverse design of first one franc coin **Edge:** Plain

Date	Mintage	F	VF	XF	Unc	BU
2003 Proof	5,000	Value: 125				

KM# 1372 1/4 EURO
22.2000 g., 0.9000 Silver 0.6424 oz. ASW, 37 mm. **Obv:** Sammuel de Champlain **Rev:** Sail ship **Edge:** Plain

Date	Mintage	F	VF	XF	Unc	BU
2004	20,000	—	—	—	27.50	32.50

KM# 1390 1/4 EURO
13.0000 g., 0.9000 Silver 0.3762 oz. ASW, 30 mm. **Subject:** European Union Expansion **Obv:** Partial face and flags **Rev:** Puzzel map **Edge:** Plain

Date	Mintage	F	VF	XF	Unc	BU
2004	20,000	—	—	—	20.00	25.00

KM# 1287 50 EURO CENTS
7.8100 g., Brass, 24.2 mm. **Obv:** Sower **Obv. Designer:** Laurent Jorb **Rev. Designer:** Luc Luycx **Edge:** Reeded

Date	Mintage	F	VF	XF	Unc	BU
2001	276,287,274	—	—	—	1.25	2.00
2001 Proof	Est. 15,000	Value: 15.00				
2002	226,500,000	—	—	—	1.25	2.00
2002 Proof	Est. 40,000	Value: 14.00				
2003	100,000	—	—	—	7.50	11.50
2003 Proof	20,000	Value: 15.00				
2004	—	—	—	—	—	2.00
2005	—	—	—	—	—	2.00
2006	—	—	—	—	—	2.00

KM# 1288 EURO
7.5000 g., Bi-Metallic Copper-Nickel center in Brass ring, 23.3 mm. **Obv:** Stylized tree **Obv. Designer:** Joaquin Jimenez **Rev:** Denomination and map **Rev. Designer:** Luc Luycx **Edge:** Reeded and plain sections

Date	Mintage	F	VF	XF	Unc	BU
2001	150,251,624	—	—	—	2.75	4.00
2001 Proof	Est. 15,000	Value: 18.00				
2002	129,400,000	—	—	—	2.50	3.75
2002 Proof	Est. 40,000	Value: 16.00				
2003	100,000	—	—	—	8.00	12.50
2003 Proof	20,000	Value: 18.00				
2004	—	—	—	—	—	2.50
2005	—	—	—	—	—	2.50
2006	—	—	—	—	—	2.50

KM# 1332 1-1/2 EURO
22.2000 g., 0.9000 Silver 0.6424 oz. ASW, 37 mm. **Obv:** Victor Hugo, value and map **Rev:** Multicolor "Gavroche" **Edge:** Plain

Date	Mintage	F	VF	XF	Unc	BU
2002 Proof	10,000	Value: 52.50				

KM# 1301 1-1/2 EURO
22.2000 g., 0.9000 Silver 0.6424 oz. ASW, 37 mm. **Subject:** Europa **Obv:** Eight French euro coins design **Rev:** Portrait and flags design of 6.55957 francs KM-1265 **Edge:** Plain

Date	Mintage	F	VF	XF	Unc	BU
2002 Proof	50,000	Value: 40.00				

KM# 1305 1-1/2 EURO
22.2000 g., 0.9000 Silver 0.6424 oz. ASW, 37 mm. **Subject:** French Landmarks **Obv:** French map **Rev:** Le Mont St. Michel **Edge:** Plain

Date	Mintage	F	VF	XF	Unc	BU
2002 Proof	10,000	Value: 42.50				

KM# 1307 1-1/2 EURO
22.2000 g., 0.9000 Silver 0.6424 oz. ASW, 37 mm. **Subject:** French Landmarks **Obv:** French map **Rev:** La Butte Montmartre **Edge:** Plain

Date	Mintage	F	VF	XF	Unc	BU
2002 Proof	10,000	Value: 42.50				

KM# 1310 1-1/2 EURO
22.2000 g., 0.9000 Silver 0.6424 oz. ASW, 37 mm. **Subject:** First West to East Transatlantic Flight **Obv:** Value, map and Lindbergh portrait **Rev:** Spirit of St. Louis (airplane) and map **Edge:** Plain

Date	Mintage	F	VF	XF	Unc	BU
2002 Proof	10,000	Value: 45.00				

KM# 1321 1-1/2 EURO
22.2000 g., 0.9000 Silver 0.6424 oz. ASW, 37 mm. **Obv:** Tour de France logo **Rev:** Cyclist going left **Edge:** Plain

Date	Mintage	F	VF	XF	Unc	BU
2003 Proof	150,000	Value: 50.00				

KM# 1322 1-1/2 EURO
22.2000 g., 0.9000 Silver 0.6424 oz. ASW, 37 mm. **Obv:** Tour de France logo **Rev:** Group of cyclists and Arch de Triumph **Edge:** Plain

Date	Mintage	F	VF	XF	Unc	BU
2003A Proof	150,000	Value: 50.00				

KM# 1323 1-1/2 EURO
22.2000 g., 0.9000 Silver 0.6424 oz. ASW, 37 mm. **Obv:** Tour de France logo **Rev:** Two cyclists and spectators **Edge:** Plain

Date	Mintage	F	VF	XF	Unc	BU
2003A Proof	150,000	Value: 50.00				

KM# 1324 1-1/2 EURO
22.2000 g., 0.9000 Silver 0.6424 oz. ASW, 37 mm. **Obv:** Tour de France logo **Rev:** Two groups of cyclists **Edge:** Plain

Date	Mintage	F	VF	XF	Unc	BU
2003A Proof	150,000	Value: 50.00				

KM# 1325 1-1/2 EURO
22.2000 g., 0.9000 Silver 0.6424 oz. ASW, 37 mm. **Obv:** Tour de France logo **Rev:** Cyclists, stopwatch and gears **Edge:** Plain

Date	Mintage	F	VF	XF	Unc	BU
2003A Proof	150,000	Value: 50.00				

KM# 1336 1-1/2 EURO
22.2000 g., 0.9000 Silver 0.6424 oz. ASW, 37 mm. **Obv:** Jefferson and Napoleon with Louisiana Purchase map **Rev:** Jazz musician, mansion and river boat **Edge:** Plain

Date	Mintage	F	VF	XF	Unc	BU
2003 Proof	10,000	Value: 47.50				

KM# 1338 1-1/2 EURO
22.2000 g., 0.9000 Silver 0.6424 oz. ASW, 37 mm. **Obv:** Curved cross design with multiple values **Rev:** Goddess Europa and flags **Edge:** Plain

Date	Mintage	F	VF	XF	Unc	BU
2003 Proof	40,000	Value: 47.50				

KM# 1341 1-1/2 EURO
22.2000 g., 0.9000 Silver 0.6424 oz. ASW, 37 mm. **Obv:** Value and compass face **Rev:** SS Normandie and New York City **Edge:** Plain

Date	Mintage	F	VF	XF	Unc	BU
2003 Proof	15,000	Value: 50.00				

KM# 1343 1-1/2 EURO
22.2000 g., 0.9000 Silver 0.6424 oz. ASW, 37 mm. **Obv:** Value and compass face **Rev:** Airplane and Tokyo Geisha **Edge:** Plain

Date	Mintage	F	VF	XF	Unc	BU
2003 Proof	15,000	Value: 50.00				

KM# 1345 1-1/2 EURO
22.2000 g., 0.9000 Silver 0.6424 oz. ASW, 37 mm. **Obv:** Paul Gauguin **Rev:** Native woman **Edge:** Plain

Date	Mintage	F	VF	XF	Unc	BU
2003 Proof	15,000	Value: 50.00				

KM# 1351 1-1/2 EURO
22.2000 g., 0.9000 Silver 0.6424 oz. ASW, 37 mm. **Obv:** Obverse design of first one franc coin **Rev:** Reverse design of first one franc coin **Edge:** Plain

Date	Mintage	F	VF	XF	Unc	BU
2003 Proof	15,000	Value: 47.50				

KM# 1353 1-1/2 EURO
22.2000 g., 0.9000 Silver 0.6424 oz. ASW, 37 mm. **Obv:** Mona Lisa **Rev:** Leonardo da Vinci **Edge:** Plain

Date	Mintage	F	VF	XF	Unc	BU
2003 Proof	10,000	Value: 50.00				

KM# 1355 1-1/2 EURO
22.2000 g., 0.9000 Silver 0.6424 oz. ASW, 37 mm. **Obv:** Map and value **Rev:** Chateau Chambord **Edge:** Plain

Date	Mintage	F	VF	XF	Unc	BU
2003 Proof	10,000	Value: 47.50				

KM# 1357 1-1/2 EURO
22.2000 g., 0.9000 Silver 0.6424 oz. ASW, 37 mm. **Obv:** Value in swirling design **Rev:** Multicolor Hansel and Gretel, witch and house **Edge:** Plain

Date	Mintage	F	VF	XF	Unc	BU
2003 Proof	10,000	Value: 50.00				

KM# 1359 1-1/2 EURO
22.2000 g., 0.9000 Silver 0.6424 oz. ASW, 37 mm. **Obv:** Value in swirling design **Rev:** Multicolor Alice in Wonderland **Edge:** Plain

Date	Mintage	F	VF	XF	Unc	BU
2003 Proof	10,000	Value: 50.00				

KM# 1361 1-1/2 EURO
22.2000 g., 0.9000 Silver 0.6424 oz. ASW, 37 mm. **Obv:** Pierre de Coubertin **Rev:** Olympic runners **Edge:** Plain

Date	Mintage	F	VF	XF	Unc	BU
2003 Proof	50,000	Value: 47.50				

KM# 1364 1-1/2 EURO
22.2000 g., 0.9000 Silver 0.6424 oz. ASW, 37 mm. **Obv:** Map with value **Rev:** Avignon Popes Palace **Edge:** Plain

Date	Mintage	F	VF	XF	Unc	BU
2004 Proof	10,000	Value: 47.50				

KM# 1373 1-1/2 EURO
22.2000 g., 0.9000 Silver 0.6424 oz. ASW, 37 mm. **Obv:** Emile Loubet and King Edward VII **Rev:** Marianne and Britannia **Edge:** Plain

Date	Mintage	F	VF	XF	Unc	BU
2004 Proof	10,000	Value: 45.00				

KM# 1374 1-1/2 EURO
22.2000 g., 0.9000 Silver 0.6424 oz. ASW, 37 mm. **Obv:** Soccer ball and value **Rev:** Rooster and quill **Edge:** Plain

Date	Mintage	F	VF	XF	Unc	BU
2004 Proof	25,000	Value: 50.00				

KM# 1378 1-1/2 EURO
22.2000 g., 0.9000 Silver 0.6424 oz. ASW, 37 mm. **Obv:** Compass rose **Rev:** Ocean liner **Edge:** Plain

Date	Mintage	F	VF	XF	Unc	BU
2004 Proof	10,000	Value: 45.00				

KM# 1380 1-1/2 EURO
22.2000 g., 0.9000 Silver 0.6424 oz. ASW, 37 mm. **Obv:** Compass rose **Rev:** Trans-Siberian Railroad **Edge:** Plain

Date	Mintage	F	VF	XF	Unc	BU
2004 Proof	10,000	Value: 45.00				

KM# 1382 1-1/2 EURO
22.2000 g., 0.9000 Silver 0.6424 oz. ASW, 37 mm. **Obv:** Compass rose **Rev:** Half-track vehicle **Edge:** Plain

Date	Mintage	F	VF	XF	Unc	BU
2004 Proof	10,000	Value: 45.00				

KM# 1384 1-1/2 EURO
22.2000 g., 0.9000 Silver 0.6424 oz. ASW, 37 mm. **Obv:** Compass rose **Rev:** Biplane airliner **Edge:** Plain

Date	Mintage	F	VF	XF	Unc	BU
2004 Proof	10,000	Value: 45.00				

KM# 1379 1-1/2 EURO
17.0000 g., 0.9200 Gold 0.5028 oz. AGW, 31 mm. **Obv:** Compass rose **Rev:** Ocean liner **Edge:** Plain

Date	Mintage	F	VF	XF	Unc	BU
2004 Proof	1,000	Value: 550				

KM# 1386 1-1/2 EURO
22.2000 g., 0.9000 Silver 0.6424 oz. ASW, 37 mm. **Obv:** Statue of Liberty **Rev:** F.A. Bartholdi **Edge:** Plain

Date	Mintage	F	VF	XF	Unc	BU
2004 Proof	15,000	Value: 45.00				

KM# 1391 1-1/2 EURO
22.2000 g., 0.9000 Silver 0.6424 oz. ASW, 37 mm. **Subject:** European Union Expansion **Obv:** Partial face and flags **Rev:** Puzzle map **Edge:** Plain

Date	Mintage	F	VF	XF	Unc	BU
2004 Proof	40,000	Value: 40.00				

KM# 1366 1-1/2 EURO
22.2000 g., 0.9000 Silver 0.6424 oz. ASW, 37 mm. **Obv:** Book, eagle and value **Rev:** Napoleon and coronation scene in background **Edge:** Plain

Date	Mintage	F	VF	XF	Unc	BU
2004 Proof	20,000	Value: 45.00				

KM# 1369 1-1/2 EURO
22.2000 g., 0.9000 Silver 0.6424 oz. ASW, 37 mm. **Obv:** Soldiers and Normandy invasion scene **Rev:** "D-DAY" above value **Edge:** Plain

Date	Mintage	F	VF	XF	Unc	BU
2004 Proof	20,000	Value: 45.00				

KM# 1289 2 EUROS
8.5200 g., Bi-Metallic Brass center in Copper-Nickel ring, 25.6 mm. **Obv:** Stylized tree **Obv. Designer:** Joaquin Jimenez **Rev. Designer:** Luc Luycx **Edge:** Reeding with 2's and stars

Date	Mintage	F	VF	XF	Unc	BU
2001	237,950,793	—	—	—	3.75	6.00
2001 Proof	Est. 15,000	Value: 20.00				
2002	153,700,000	—	—	—	3.75	6.00
2002 Proof	Est. 40,000	Value: 18.00				
2003	100,000	—	—	—	8.50	13.50
2003 Proof	20,000	Value: 20.00				
2004	—	—	—	—	—	5.00
2005	—	—	—	—	—	5.00
2006	—	—	—	—	—	5.00

KM# 1347 5 EURO
24.9000 g., 0.9000 Bi-Metallic Gold And Silver .900 Silver 22.2g planchet with .750 Gold 2.7 insert 0.7205 oz., 37 mm. **Obv:** Sower on gold insert **Rev:** Value and map **Edge:** Plain

Date	Mintage	F	VF	XF	Unc	BU
2003 Proof	10,000	Value: 475				

KM# 1371 5 EURO
24.9000 g., Bi-Metallic Gold And Silver .750 Gold 2.7 g insert on .900 Silver 22.2g planchet, 37 mm. **Obv:** Sower on gold insert **Rev:** French face map and value **Edge:** Plain

Date	Mintage	F	VF	XF	Unc	BU
2004 Proof	3,000	Value: 475				

KM# 1302 10 EURO
8.4500 g., 0.9990 Gold 0.2714 oz. AGW, 22 mm. **Subject:** Europa **Obv:** Eight French euro coin designs **Rev:** Portrait and flags design of 6.55957 francs KM-1265 **Edge:** Reeded

Date	Mintage	F	VF	XF	Unc	BU
2002 Proof	3,000	Value: 285				

KM# 1326 10 EURO
8.4500 g., 0.9200 Gold 0.2499 oz. AGW, 22 mm. **Obv:** Tour de France logo **Rev:** Cyclist going left **Edge:** Reeded

Date	Mintage	F	VF	XF	Unc	BU
2003A Proof	5,000	Value: 200				

KM# 1327 10 EURO
8.4500 g., 0.9200 Gold 0.2499 oz. AGW, 22 mm. **Obv:** Tour de France logo **Rev:** Group of cyclists and Arch de Triumph **Edge:** Reeded

Date	Mintage	F	VF	XF	Unc	BU
2003A Proof	5,000	Value: 200				

KM# 1328 10 EURO
8.4500 g., 0.9200 Gold 0.2499 oz. AGW, 22 mm. **Obv:** Tour de France logo **Rev:** Two cyclists and spectators **Edge:** Reeded

Date	Mintage	F	VF	XF	Unc	BU
2003A Proof	5,000	Value: 200				

KM# 1329 10 EURO
8.4500 g., 0.9200 Gold 0.2499 oz. AGW, 22 mm. **Obv:** Tour de France logo **Rev:** Two groups of cyclists **Edge:** Reeded

Date	Mintage	F	VF	XF	Unc	BU
2003A Proof	5,000	Value: 200				

KM# 1330 10 EURO
8.4500 g., 0.9200 Gold 0.2499 oz. AGW, 22 mm. **Obv:** Tour de France logo **Rev:** Cyclist, stop watch and gears **Edge:** Reeded

Date	Mintage	F	VF	XF	Unc	BU
2003A Proof	5,000	Value: 200				

KM# 1348 10 EURO
8.4500 g., 0.9200 Gold 0.2499 oz. AGW, 22 mm. **Obv:** Sower **Rev:** Value and map **Edge:** Plain

Date	Mintage	F	VF	XF	Unc	BU
2003 Proof	15,000	Value: 265				

KM# 1352 10 EURO
8.4500 g., 0.9200 Gold 0.2499 oz. AGW, 22 mm. **Obv:** Obverse design of first one franc coin **Rev:** Reverse design of first one franc coin **Edge:** Plain

Date	Mintage	F	VF	XF	Unc	BU
2003 Proof	10,000	Value: 265				

KM# 1362 10 EURO
8.4500 g., 0.9200 Gold 0.2499 oz. AGW, 22 mm. **Obv:** Pierre de Coubertin **Rev:** Olympic runners **Edge:** Plain

Date	Mintage	F	VF	XF	Unc	BU
2003 Proof	15,000	Value: 285				

KM# 1367 10 EURO
6.4100 g., 0.9000 Gold 0.1855 oz. AGW, 22 mm. **Obv:** Book, value and eagle **Rev:** Napoleon and coronation scene **Edge:** Plain

Date	Mintage	F	VF	XF	Unc	BU
2004 Proof	5,000	Value: 300				

KM# 1375 10 EURO
8.4500 g., 0.9200 Gold 0.2499 oz. AGW, 22 mm. **Obv:** Half soccer ball and value **Rev:** Eiffel tower and soccer balls **Edge:** Plain

Date	Mintage	F	VF	XF	Unc	BU
2004 Proof	10,000	Value: 300				

KM# 1392 10 EURO
8.4500 g., 0.9200 Gold 0.2499 oz. AGW, 22 mm. **Subject:** European Union Expansion **Obv:** Partial face and flags **Rev:** Puzzle map **Edge:** Reeded

Date	Mintage	F	VF	XF	Unc	BU
2004 Proof	5,000	Value: 245				

KM# 1306 20 EURO
17.0000 g., 0.9200 Gold 0.5028 oz. AGW, 31 mm. **Subject:** French Landmarks **Obv:** French map **Rev:** Le Mont St. Michel **Edge:** Plain

Date	Mintage	F	VF	XF	Unc	BU
2002 Proof	1,000	Value: 550				

KM# 1308 20 EURO
17.0000 g., 0.9200 Gold 0.5028 oz. AGW, 31 mm. **Subject:** French Landmarks **Obv:** French map **Rev:** La Butte Montmartre **Edge:** Plain

Date	Mintage	F	VF	XF	Unc	BU
2002 Proof	1,000	Value: 550				

KM# 1333 20 EURO
17.0000 g., 0.9200 Gold 0.5028 oz. AGW, 31 mm. **Obv:** Victor Hugo, value and map **Rev:** "Gavroche" **Edge:** Plain

Date	Mintage	F	VF	XF	Unc	BU
2002 Proof	2,000	Value: 475				

KM# 1334 20 EURO
17.0000 g., 0.9200 Gold 0.5028 oz. AGW, 31 mm. **Obv:** Tour de France logo **Rev:** Cyclist going left **Edge:** Plain

Date	Mintage	F	VF	XF	Unc	BU
2003 Proof	5,000	Value: 475				

KM# 1337 20 EURO
17.0000 g., 0.9200 Gold 0.5028 oz. AGW, 31 mm. **Obv:** Jefferson and Napoleon with Louisiana Purchase map **Rev:** Jazz musician, mansion and river boat **Edge:** Plain

Date	Mintage	F	VF	XF	Unc	BU
2003 Proof	1,000	Value: 525				

KM# 1339 20 EURO
17.0000 g., 0.9200 Gold 0.5028 oz. AGW, 31 mm. **Obv:** Curved cross design with multiple values **Rev:** Goddess Europa and flags **Edge:** Plain

Date	Mintage	F	VF	XF	Unc	BU
2003 Proof	3,000	Value: 525				

KM# 1342 20 EURO
17.0000 g., 0.9200 Gold 0.5028 oz. AGW, 31 mm. **Obv:** Value and compass face **Rev:** SS Normandie and New York City skyline **Edge:** Plain

Date	Mintage	F	VF	XF	Unc	BU
2003 Proof	1,000	Value: 525				

KM# 1344 20 EURO
17.0000 g., 0.9200 Gold 0.5028 oz. AGW, 31 mm. **Obv:** Value and compass face **Rev:** Airplane and Tokyo Geisha **Edge:** Plain

Date	Mintage	F	VF	XF	Unc	BU
2003 Proof	1,000	Value: 525				

KM# 1346 20 EURO
17.0000 g., 0.9200 Gold 0.5028 oz. AGW, 31 mm. **Obv:** Paul Gauguin **Rev:** Native woman **Edge:** Plain

Date	Mintage	F	VF	XF	Unc	BU
2003 Proof	2,000	Value: 545				

KM# 1349 20 EURO
17.0000 g., 0.9200 Gold 0.5028 oz. AGW, 31 mm. **Obv:** Sower **Rev:** Value and map **Edge:** Plain

Date	Mintage	F	VF	XF	Unc	BU
2003 Proof	5,000	Value: 575				

KM# 1354 20 EURO
17.0000 g., 0.9200 Gold 0.5028 oz. AGW, 31 mm. **Obv:** Mona Lisa **Rev:** Leonardo da Vinci and value **Edge:** Plain

Date	Mintage	F	VF	XF	Unc	BU
2003 Proof	1,000	Value: 545				

KM# 1356 20 EURO
17.0000 g., 0.9200 Gold 0.5028 oz. AGW, 31 mm. **Obv:** Map and value **Rev:** Chateau Chambord **Edge:** Plain

Date	Mintage	F	VF	XF	Unc	BU
2003 Proof	1,000	Value: 525				

KM# 1358 20 EURO
17.0000 g., 0.9200 Gold 0.5028 oz. AGW, 31 mm. **Obv:** Value in swirling design **Rev:** Hansel and Gretel, witch and house **Edge:** Plain

Date	Mintage	F	VF	XF	Unc	BU
2003 Proof	1,000	Value: 545				

KM# 1360 20 EURO
17.0000 g., 0.9200 Gold 0.5028 oz. AGW, 31 mm. **Obv:** Value in swirling design **Rev:** Alice in Wonderland **Edge:** Plain

Date	Mintage	F	VF	XF	Unc	BU
2003 Proof	1,000	Value: 545				

KM# 1363 20 EURO
17.0000 g., 0.9200 Gold 0.5028 oz. AGW, 31 mm. **Obv:** Pierre de Coubertin **Rev:** Olympic runners **Edge:** Plain

Date	Mintage	F	VF	XF	Unc	BU
2003 Proof	3,000	Value: 525				

KM# 1365 20 EURO
17.0000 g., 0.9200 Gold 0.5028 oz. AGW, 31 mm. **Obv:** Map with value **Rev:** Avignon Popes Palace **Edge:** Plain

Date	Mintage	F	VF	XF	Unc	BU
2004 Proof	1,000	Value: 600				

KM# 1370 20 EURO
17.0000 g., 0.9200 Gold 0.5028 oz. AGW, 31 mm. **Obv:** Soldiers and Normandy invasion scene **Rev:** "D-DAY" above value **Edge:** Plain

Date	Mintage	F	VF	XF	Unc	BU
2004 Proof	2,000	Value: 600				

KM# 1376 20 EURO
17.0000 g., 0.9200 Gold 0.5028 oz. AGW, 31 mm. **Obv:** Sower **Rev:** Value and French map face design **Edge:** Plain

Date	Mintage	F	VF	XF	Unc	BU
2004 Proof	3,000	Value: 575				

KM# 1381 20 EURO
17.0000 g., 0.9200 Gold 0.5028 oz. AGW, 31 mm. **Obv:** Compass rose **Rev:** Trans-Siberian Railroad **Edge:** Plain

Date	Mintage	F	VF	XF	Unc	BU
2004 Proof	1,000	Value: 535				

KM# 1383 20 EURO
17.0000 g., 0.9200 Gold 0.5028 oz. AGW, 31 mm. **Obv:** Compass rose **Rev:** Half-track vehicle **Edge:** Plain

Date	Mintage	F	VF	XF	Unc	BU
2004 Proof	1,000	Value: 535				

KM# 1385 20 EURO
17.0000 g., 0.9200 Gold 0.5028 oz. AGW, 31 mm. **Obv:** Compass rose **Rev:** Biplane airliner **Edge:** Plain

Date	Mintage	F	VF	XF	Unc	BU
2004 Proof	1,000	Value: 535				

KM# 1387 20 EURO
155.5000 g., 0.9500 Silver 4.7495 oz. ASW, 50 mm. **Obv:** Statue of Liberty **Rev:** F. A. Bartholdi **Edge:** Plain

Date	Mintage	F	VF	XF	Unc	BU
2004 Proof	999	Value: 175				

KM# 1388 20 EURO
17.0000 g., 0.9200 Gold 0.5028 oz. AGW, 31 mm. **Obv:** Statue of Liberty **Rev:** F. A. Bartholdi **Edge:** Plain

Date	Mintage	F	VF	XF	Unc	BU
2004 Proof	2,000	Value: 550				

KM# 1393 20 EURO
17.0000 g., 0.9200 Gold 0.5028 oz. AGW, 31 mm. **Subject:** European Union Expansion **Obv:** Partial face and flags **Rev:** Puzzle map **Edge:** Plain

Date	Mintage	F	VF	XF	Unc	BU
2004 Proof	3,000	Value: 550				

KM# 1303 50 EURO
31.0000 g., 0.9990 Gold 0.9957 oz. AGW, 37 mm. **Subject:** Europa **Obv:** Eight French euro coin designs **Rev:** Portrait and flags design of 6.55957 francs KM-1265 **Edge:** Plain

Date	Mintage	F	VF	XF	Unc	BU
2002 Proof	2,000	Value: 925				

KM# 1335 50 EURO
31.1000 g., 0.9990 Gold 0.9989 oz. AGW, 37 mm. **Obv:** Tour de France logo **Rev:** Cyclist going left **Edge:** Plain

Date	Mintage	F	VF	XF	Unc	BU
2003 Proof	5,000	Value: 875				

KM# 1340 50 EURO
1000.0000 g., 0.9500 Silver 30.5432 oz. ASW, 100 mm. **Obv:** Curved cross design with multiple values **Rev:** Goddess Europa and flags **Edge:** Plain with three line inscription at six o'clock

Date	Mintage	F	VF	XF	Unc	BU
2003 Proof	2,000	Value: 650				

KM# 1368 50 EURO
31.1000 g., 0.9990 Gold 0.9989 oz. AGW, 37 mm. **Obv:** Book, value and eagle **Rev:** Napoleon and coronation scene **Edge:** Plain

Date	Mintage	F	VF	XF	Unc	BU
2004 Proof	2,000	Value: 990				

KM# 1394 50 EURO
31.1040 g., 0.9990 Gold 0.999 oz. AGW, 37 mm. **Subject:** European Union Expansion **Obv:** Partial face and flags **Rev:** Puzzle map **Edge:** Plain

Date	Mintage	F	VF	XF	Unc	BU
2004 Proof	2,000	Value: 950				

KM# 1304 100 EURO
155.5175 g., 0.9990 Gold 4.995 oz. AGW, 50 mm. **Subject:** Europa **Obv:** Eight French euro coin designs **Rev:** Portrait and flags design of 6.55957 francs KM-1265 **Edge:** Plain

Date	Mintage	F	VF	XF	Unc	BU
2002 Proof	99	Value: 5,750				

KM# 1377 100 EURO
155.5175 g., 0.9990 Gold 4.995 oz. AGW, 50 mm. **Subject:** D-Day 60th Anniversary **Obv:** Soldiers and Normandy invasion scene **Rev:** "D-Day" inscription above value **Edge:** Plain

Date	Mintage	F	VF	XF	Unc	BU
2004 Proof	299	Value: 4,000				

KM# 1389 100 EURO
155.5000 g., 0.9990 Gold 4.9944 oz. AGW, 50 mm. **Obv:** Statue of Liberty **Rev:** F. A. Bartholdi **Edge:** Plain

Date	Mintage	F	VF	XF	Unc	BU
2004 Proof	99	Value: 4,000				

KM# 1395 100 EURO
155.5500 g., 0.9990 Gold 4.996 oz. AGW, 50 mm. **Subject:** European Union Expansion **Obv:** Partial face and flags **Rev:** Puzzle map **Edge:** Plain

Date	Mintage	F	VF	XF	Unc	BU
2004 Proof	99	Value: 4,000				

KM# 1396 500 EURO
1000.0000 g., 0.9990 Gold 32.1186 oz. AGW, 85 mm. **Subject:** European Union Expansion **Obv:** Partial face and flags **Rev:** Puzzle map **Edge:** Plain

Date	Mintage	F	VF	XF	Unc	BU
2004 Proof, Rare	20	—	—	—	—	—

MINT SETS

KM#	Date	Mintage	Identification	Issue Price	Mkt Val
MS20	2001 (2)	10,000	KM#925.1a, 928a	—	190
MS21	2001 (8)	35,000	KM#1282-1289	20.25	50.00
MS22	2002 (8)	35,000	KM#1282-1289	20.25	40.00
MS23	2004 (8)	—	KM#1282-1289	—	—
MS24	2005 (8)	—	KM#1282-1289	—	—
MS25	2006 (8)	—	KM#1282-1289	—	—

PROOF SETS

KM#	Date	Mintage	Identification	Issue Price	Mkt Val
PS21	2001 (8)	15,000	KM#1282-1289	59.00	110
PS22	2002 (8)	40,000	KM#1282-1289	59.00	95.00
PS23	2003 (5)	150,000	KM#1321, 1322, 1323, 1324, 1325	—	250
PS24	2003 (5)	5,000	KM#1326, 1327, 1328, 1329, 1330	—	875

FRENCH POLYNESIA

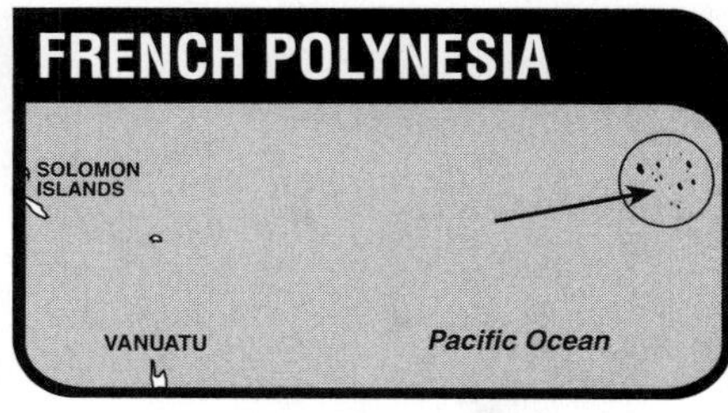

The Territory of French Polynesia (formerly French Oceania) has an area of 1,544 sq. mi. (3,941 sq. km.) and a population of 220,000. It is comprised of the same five archipelagoes that were grouped administratively to form French Oceania.

The colony of French Oceania became the Territory of French Polynesia by act of the French National Assembly in March, 1957. In Sept. of 1958 it voted in favor of the new constitution of the Fifth Republic, thereby electing to remain within the new French Community.

Picturesque, mountainous Tahiti, the setting of many tales of adventure and romance, is one of the most inspiringly beautiful islands in the world. Robert Louis Stevenson called it 'God's sweetest works'. It was there that Paul Gaugin, one of the pioneers of the Impressionist movement, painted the brilliant, exotic pictures that later made him famous. The arid coral atolls of Tuamotu comprise the most economically valuable area of French Polynesia. Pearl oysters thrive in the warm, limpid lagoons, and extensive portions of the atolls are valuable phosphate rock.

MINT MARKS

(a) - Paris, privy marks only

MONETARY SYSTEM

100 Centimes = 1 Franc

FRENCH OVERSEAS TERRITORY

DECIMAL COINAGE

KM# 11 FRANC

Aluminum **Obv:** Legend added flanking figure's feet **Obv. Legend:** I. E. O. M. **Designer:** G. B. L. Bazor

Date	Mintage	F	VF	XF	Unc	BU
2001(a)	2,900,000	—	—	—	0.20	0.50
2002(a)	1,600,000	—	—	—	0.20	0.50
2003(a)	4,200,000	—	—	—	0.20	0.50

KM# 10 2 FRANCS

Aluminum **Obv:** Legend added flanking figure's feet **Obv. Legend:** I. E. O. M. **Designer:** G. B. L. Bazor

Date	Mintage	F	VF	XF	Unc	BU
2001(a)	2,400,000	—	—	—	0.35	0.75
2002(a)	2,500,000	—	—	—	0.35	0.75
2003(a)	3,200,000	—	—	—	0.35	0.75

KM# 12 5 FRANCS

Aluminum **Obv:** Legend added flanking figure's feet **Obv. Legend:** I. E. O. M. **Designer:** G. B. L. Bazor

Date	Mintage	F	VF	XF	Unc	BU
2001(a)	1,600,000	—	—	—	0.50	1.00
2002(a)	400,000	—	—	—	0.50	1.00
2003(a)	1,000,000	—	—	—	0.50	1.00

KM# 8 10 FRANCS

Nickel **Obv:** Legend below head **Obv. Legend:** I. E. O. M. **Obv. Designer:** R. Joly **Rev. Designer:** A. Guzman

Date	Mintage	F	VF	XF	Unc	BU
2001(a)	500,000	—	—	—	0.75	1.50
2002(a)	600,000	—	—	—	0.75	1.50
2003(a)	1,000,000	—	—	—	0.70	1.25

KM# 9 20 FRANCS

Nickel **Obv:** Legend below head **Obv. Legend:** I. E. O. M. **Obv. Designer:** R. Joly **Rev. Designer:** A. Guzman

Date	Mintage	F	VF	XF	Unc	BU
2001(a)	500,000	—	—	—	1.25	1.75
2002(a)	—	—	—	—	1.25	1.75
2003(a)	700,000	—	—	—	1.00	1.50

KM# 13 50 FRANCS

Nickel **Obv:** Legend below head **Obv. Legend:** I. E. O. M. **Obv. Designer:** R. Joly **Rev. Designer:** A. Guzman

Date	Mintage	F	VF	XF	Unc	BU
2001(a)	300,000	—	—	—	1.50	2.00
2002(a)	—	—	—	—	1.50	2.00
2003(a)	240,000	—	—	—	1.25	1.75

KM# 14 100 FRANCS

Nickel-Bronze **Obv. Designer:** R. Joly **Rev. Designer:** A. Guzman

Date	Mintage	F	VF	XF	Unc	BU
2001(a)	200,000	—	—	—	2.00	3.50
2002(a)	—	—	—	—	2.00	3.50
2003(a)	600,000	—	—	—	1.75	2.50

MINT SETS

KM#	Date	Mintage	Identification	Issue Price	Mkt Val
MS1	2001 (7)	3,000	KM#8-14	—	28.00
MS2	2002 (7)	5,000	KM#8-14	—	28.00
MS3	2003 (7)	3,000	KM#8-14	—	25.00

GABON

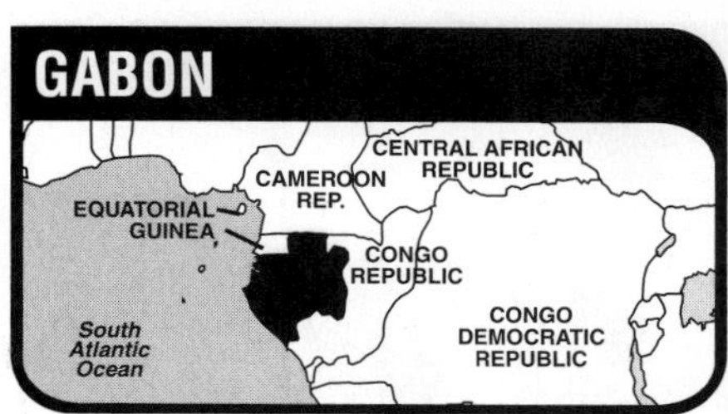

The Gabonese Republic, a member of the French Community, straddles the equator on the west coast of Africa. The hot and humid rain forest country has an area of 103,347 sq. mi. (267,670 sq. km.) and a population of 1.2 million, almost all of Bantu origin. Capital: Libreville. Extravagantly rich in resources, Gabon exports crude oil, manganese ore, gold and timbers.

For earlier coinage see French Equatorial Africa, Central African States and the Equatorial African States.

MINT MARKS

(a) - Paris, privy marks only

(t) - Poissy, privy marks only, thunderbolt

REPUBLIC

INSTITUT MONETAIRE

KM# 16 1500 CFA FRANCS - 1 AFRICA

7.3200 g., Nickel Plated Iron, 26 mm. **Obv:** Throwing knife **Rev:** Elephant head on full Africa map **Edge:** Plain

Date	Mintage	F	VF	XF	Unc	BU
2005	2,005	—	—	—	18.00	—

KM# 16a 1500 CFA FRANCS - 1 AFRICA

0.9990 Silver, 22 mm. **Obv:** Throwing knife **Rev:** Elephant head on a full Africa map

Date	Mintage	F	VF	XF	Unc	BU
2005	25	—	—	—	360	—

KM# 15 4500 CFA FRANCS - 3 AFRICA

7.5400 g., Bi-Metallic Copper-Nickel center in Brass ring, 26 mm. **Obv:** Oil drop on map **Rev:** Elephant head on full African map **Edge:** Segmented reeding

Date	Mintage	F	VF	XF	Unc	BU
2005	2,005	—	—	—	55.00	—

KM# 15a 4500 CFA FRANCS - 3 AFRICA

Bi-Metallic .999 Silver center in .999Gold plated .999 Silver ring, 26 mm. **Obv:** Oil drop on map **Rev:** Elephant head on full African map

Date	Mintage	F	VF	XF	Unc	BU
2005	25	—	—	—	540	—

KM# 15b 4500 CFA FRANCS - 3 AFRICA

0.9990 Silver, 26 mm. **Obv:** Oil drop on map **Rev:** Elephant head on full African map

Date	Mintage	F	VF	XF	Unc	BU
2005	25	—	—	—	540	—

GERMANY-FEDERAL REP.

The Federal Republic of Germany, located in north-central Europe, has an area of 137,744 sq. mi. (356,910sq. km.) and a population of 81.1 million. Capital: Berlin. The economy centers about one of the world's foremost industrial establishments. Machinery, motor vehicles, iron, steel, yarns and fabrics are exported.

MINT MARKS

A - Berlin
D - Munich
F - Stuttgart
G - Karlsruhe
J - Hamburg

MONETARY SYSTEM

100 Pfennig = 1 Deutsche Mark (DM)

FEDERAL REPUBLIC

STANDARD COINAGE

KM# 105 PFENNIG

Copper Plated Steel **Obv. Legend:** BUNDES REPUBLIK DEUTSCHLAND **Note:** Federal Republic.

Date	Mintage	F	VF	XF	Unc	BU
2001A	130,000	—	—	—	5.00	—
Note: In sets only						
2001A Proof	78,000	Value: 5.00				
2001D	130,000	—	—	—	5.00	—
Note: In sets only						
2001D Proof	78,000	Value: 5.00				
2001F	130,000	—	—	—	5.00	—
Note: In sets only						
2001F Proof	78,000	Value: 5.00				
2001G	130,000	—	—	—	5.00	—
Note: In sets only						
2001G Proof	78,000	Value: 5.00				
2001J	130,000	—	—	—	5.00	—
Note: In sets only						
2001J Proof	78,000	Value: 5.00				

KM# 106a 2 PFENNIG

Bronze Clad Steel

Date	Mintage	F	VF	XF	Unc	BU
2001A	130,000	—	—	—	5.00	—
Note: In sets only						
2001A Proof	78,000	Value: 5.00				
2001D	130,000	—	—	—	5.00	—
Note: In sets only						
2001D Proof	78,000	Value: 5.00				
2001F	130,000	—	—	—	5.00	—
Note: In sets only						
2001F Proof	78,000	Value: 5.00				
2001G	130,000	—	—	—	5.00	—
Note: In sets only						
2001G Proof	78,000	Value: 5.00				
2001J	130,000	—	—	—	5.00	—
Note: In sets only						
2001J Proof	78,000	Value: 5.00				

KM# 107 5 PFENNIG

Brass Plated Steel **Obv. Legend:** BUNDES REPUBLIK DEUTSCHLAND

Date	Mintage	F	VF	XF	Unc	BU
2001A	130,000	—	—	—	5.00	—
Note: In sets only						
2001A Proof	78,000	Value: 5.00				
2001D	130,000	—	—	—	5.00	—
Note: In sets only						
2001D Proof	78,000	Value: 5.00				
2001F	130,000	—	—	—	5.00	—
Note: In sets only						
2001F Proof	78,000	Value: 5.00				
2001G	130,000	—	—	—	5.00	—
Note: In sets only						
2001G Proof	78,000	Value: 5.00				
2001J	130,000	—	—	—	5.00	—
Note: In sets only						
2001J Proof	78,000	Value: 5.00				

KM# 108 10 PFENNIG

Brass Plated Steel **Obv. Legend:** BUNDES REPUBLIK DEUTSCHLAND **Edge:** Plain

Date	Mintage	F	VF	XF	Unc	BU
2001A	130,000	—	—	—	5.00	—
Note: In sets only						
2001A Proof	78,000	Value: 5.00				
2001D	130,000	—	—	—	5.00	—
Note: In sets only						
2001D Proof	78,000	Value: 5.00				
2001F	130,000	—	—	—	5.00	—
Note: In sets only						
2001F Proof	78,000	Value: 5.00				
2001G	130,000	—	—	—	5.00	—
Note: In sets only						
2001G Proof	78,000	Value: 5.00				
2001J	130,000	—	—	—	5.00	—
Note: In sets only						
2001J Proof	78,000	Value: 5.00				

KM# 109.2 50 PFENNIG

Copper-Nickel **Edge:** Plain **Note:** Counterfeits of 1972 dated coins with reeded edges exist.

Date	Mintage	F	VF	XF	Unc	BU
2001A	130,000	—	—	—	10.00	—
Note: In sets only						
2001A Proof	78,000	Value: 10.00				
2001D	130,000	—	—	—	10.00	—
Note: In sets only						
2001D Proof	78,000	Value: 10.00				
2001F	130,000	—	—	—	10.00	—
Note: In sets only						
2001F Proof	78,000	Value: 10.00				
2001G	130,000	—	—	—	10.00	—
Note: In sets only						
2001G Proof	78,000	Value: 10.00				
2001J	130,000	—	—	—	10.00	—
Note: In sets only						
2001J Proof	78,000	Value: 10.00				

KM# 203 MARK

11.8500 g., 0.9990 Gold .3806 oz. AGW, 23.5 mm. **Subject:** Retirement of the Mark Currency **Obv:** Eagle **Rev:** Denomination **Edge:** Lettered

Date	Mintage	F	VF	XF	Unc	BU
2001A Proof	200,000	Value: 335				
2001D Proof	200,000	Value: 335				
2001G Proof	200,000	Value: 335				
2001J Proof	200,000	Value: 335				
2001F Proof	200,000	Value: 335				

KM# 110 MARK

Copper-Nickel **Note:** Federal Republic.

Date	Mintage	F	VF	XF	Unc	BU
2001A	130,000	—	—	—	15.00	—
Note: In sets only						
2001A Proof	78,000	Value: 15.00				
2001D	130,000	—	—	—	15.00	—
Note: In sets only						
2001D Proof	78,000	Value: 15.00				
2001F	130,000	—	—	—	15.00	—
Note: In sets only						
2001F Proof	78,000	Value: 15.00				
2001G	130,000	—	—	—	15.00	—
Note: In sets only						
2001G Proof	78,000	Value: 15.00				
2001J	130,000	—	—	—	15.00	—
Note: In sets only						
2001J Proof	78,000	Value: 15.00				

KM# 170 2 MARK

Copper-Nickel Clad Nickel **Rev:** Head of Ludwig Erhard facing forward

Date	Mintage	F	VF	XF	Unc	BU
2001A	130,000	—	—	—	10.00	—
Note: In sets only						
2001A Proof	78,000	Value: 10.00				
2001D	130,000	—	—	—	10.00	—
Note: In sets only						
2001D Proof	78,000	Value: 10.00				
2001F	130,000	—	—	—	10.00	—
Note: In sets only						
2001F Proof	78,000	Value: 10.00				
2001G	130,000	—	—	—	10.00	—
Note: In sets only						
2001G Proof	78,000	Value: 10.00				
2001J	130,000	—	—	—	10.00	—
Note: In sets only						
2001J Proof	78,000	Value: 10.00				

KM# 175 2 MARK

Copper-Nickel Clad Nickel **Rev:** Head of Franz Joseph Strauss facing left

Date	Mintage	F	VF	XF	Unc	BU
2001A	130,000	—	—	—	10.00	—
Note: In sets only						
2001A Proof	78,000	Value: 10.00				
2001D	130,000	—	—	—	10.00	—
Note: In sets only						
2001D Proof	78,000	Value: 10.00				
2001F	130,000	—	—	—	10.00	—
Note: In sets only						
2001F Proof	78,000	Value: 10.00				
2001G	130,000	—	—	—	10.00	—
Note: In sets only						
2001G Proof	78,000	Value: 10.00				
2001J	130,000	—	—	—	10.00	—
Note: In sets only						
2001J Proof	78,000	Value: 10.00				

KM# 183 2 MARK
Copper-Nickel Clad Nickel **Rev:** Head of Willy Brandt facing forward

Date	Mintage	F	VF	XF	Unc	BU
2001A	130,000	—	—	—	10.00	—
Note: In sets only						
2001A Proof	78,000	Value: 10.00				
2001D	130,000	—	—	—	10.00	—
Note: In sets only						
2001D Proof	78,000	Value: 10.00				
2001F	130,000	—	—	—	10.00	—
Note: In sets only						
2001F Proof	78,000	Value: 10.00				
2001G	130,000	—	—	—	10.00	—
Note: In sets only						
2001G Proof	78,000	Value: 10.00				
2001J	130,000	—	—	—	10.00	—
Note: In sets only						
2001J Proof	78,000	Value: 10.00				

KM# 140.1 5 MARK
10.0000 g., Copper-Nickel Clad Nickel

Date	Mintage	F	VF	XF	Unc	BU
2001A	130,000	—	—	—	30.00	—
Note: In sets only						
2001A Proof	78,000	Value: 30.00				
2001D	130,000	—	—	—	30.00	—
Note: In sets only						
2001D Proof	78,000	Value: 30.00				
2001F	130,000	—	—	—	30.00	—
Note: In sets only						
2001F Proof	78,000	Value: 30.00				
2001G	130,000	—	—	—	30.00	—
Note: In sets only						
2001G Proof	78,000	Value: 30.00				
2001J	130,000	—	—	—	30.00	—
Note: In sets only						
2001J Proof	78,000	Value: 30.00				

COMMEMORATIVE COINAGE

KM# 204 10 MARK
15.5000 g., 0.9250 Silver .4610 oz. ASW, 32.5 mm.
Rev: Naval Museum, Stralsund **Edge Lettering:** "OHNE WASSER KEIN LEBEN"

Date	Mintage	F	VF	XF	Unc	BU
2001A	2,500,000	—	—	—	9.00	—
2001A Proof	160,000	Value: 22.50				
2001D Proof	160,000	Value: 22.50				
2001F Proof	160,000	Value: 22.50				
2001G Proof	160,000	Value: 22.50				
2001J Proof	160,000	Value: 22.50				

KM# 205 10 MARK
15.5000 g., 0.9250 Silver .4610 oz. ASW, 32.5 mm. **Subject:** 200th Anniversary - Birth of Albert Gustav Lortzing **Obv:** Stylized eagle **Rev:** Portrait and music **Edge Lettering:** "WILDSCHUET * UNDINE" ZAR UND ZIMMERMANN"

Date	Mintage	F	VF	XF	Unc	BU
2001A Proof	160,000	Value: 22.50				
2001D Proof	160,000	Value: 22.50				
2001F Proof	160,000	Value: 22.50				
2001G Proof	160,000	Value: 22.50				
2001J	2,500,000	—	—	—	9.00	—
2001J Proof	160,000	Value: 22.50				

KM# 206 10 MARK
15.5000 g., 0.9250 Silver .4610 oz. ASW, 32.5 mm. **Subject:** Federal Court of Constitution: 50th Anniversary **Obv:** Stylized eagle **Rev:** Justice holding books and scale **Edge:** Lettered

Date	Mintage	F	VF	XF	Unc	BU
2001A Proof	160,000	Value: 22.50				
2001D Proof	160,000	Value: 22.50				
2001F Proof	160,000	Value: 22.50				
2001G	2,500,000	—	—	—	9.00	—
2001G Proof	160,000	Value: 22.50				
2001J Proof	160,000	Value: 22.50				

EURO COINAGE

European Economic Community Issues

KM# 207 EURO CENT
2.2700 g., Copper Plated Steel, 16.3 mm. **Obv:** Oak leaves **Obv. Designer:** Rolf Lederbogen **Rev:** Denomination and globe **Rev. Designer:** Luc Luycx **Edge:** Plain

Date	Mintage	F	VF	XF	Unc	BU
2002A	770,000,000	—	—	—	0.35	—
2002A Proof	130,000	Value: 1.00				
2002D	805,350,000	—	—	—	0.35	—
2002D Proof	130,000	Value: 1.00				
2002F	902,660,000	—	—	—	0.35	—
2002F Proof	130,000	Value: 1.00				
2002G	537,100,000	—	—	—	0.35	—
2002G Proof	130,000	Value: 1.00				
2002J	833,100,000	—	—	—	0.35	—
2002J Proof	130,000	Value: 1.00				
2003A	180,000	—	—	—	4.50	—
2003A Proof	150,000	Value: 1.00				
2003D	180,000	—	—	—	4.50	—
2003D Proof	150,000	Value: 1.00				
2003F	180,000	—	—	—	4.50	—
2003F Proof	150,000	Value: 1.00				
2003G	180,000	—	—	—	4.50	—
2003G Proof	150,000	Value: 1.00				
2003J	180,000	—	—	—	4.50	—
2003J Proof	150,000	Value: 1.00				
2004A	—	—	—	—	2.50	—
2004A Proof	—	Value: 1.00				
2004D	—	—	—	—	2.50	—
2004D Proof	—	Value: 1.00				
2004F	—	—	—	—	2.50	—
2004F Proof	—	Value: 1.00				
2004G	—	—	—	—	2.50	—
2004G Proof	—	Value: 1.00				
2004J	—	—	—	—	2.50	—
2004J Proof	—	Value: 1.00				
2005A	—	—	—	—	0.35	—
2005A Proof	—	Value: 1.00				
2005D	—	—	—	—	0.35	—
2005D Proof	—	Value: 1.00				
2005F	—	—	—	—	0.35	—
2005F Proof	—	Value: 1.00				
2005G	—	—	—	—	0.35	—
2005G Proof	—	Value: 1.00				
2005J	—	—	—	—	0.35	—
2005J Proof	—	Value: 1.00				

KM# 208 2 EURO CENTS
3.0000 g., Copper Plated Steel, 18.7 mm. **Obv:** Oak leaves **Obv. Designer:** Rolf Lederbogen **Rev:** Denomination and globe **Rev. Designer:** Luc Luycx **Edge:** Grooved

Date	Mintage	F	VF	XF	Unc	BU
2002A	460,000,000	—	—	—	0.50	—
2002A Proof	130,000	Value: 1.50				
2002D	436,100,000	—	—	—	0.50	—
2002D Proof	130,000	Value: 1.50				
2002F	495,960,000	—	—	—	0.50	—
2002F Proof	130,000	Value: 1.50				
2002G	311,900,000	—	—	—	0.50	—
2002G Proof	130,000	Value: 1.50				
2002J	419,274,000	—	—	—	0.50	—
2002J Proof	130,000	Value: 1.50				
2003A	100,000,000	—	—	—	0.50	—
2003A Proof	150,000	Value: 1.50				
2003D	151,855,000	—	—	—	0.50	—
2003D Proof	150,000	Value: 1.50				
2003F	175,400,000	—	—	—	0.50	—
2003F Proof	150,000	Value: 1.50				
2003G	80,200,000	—	—	—	0.50	—
2003G Proof	150,000	Value: 1.50				
2003J	168,681,000	—	—	—	0.50	—
2003J Proof	150,000	Value: 1.50				
2004A	—	—	—	—	0.50	—
2004A Proof	—	Value: 1.50				
2004D	—	—	—	—	0.50	—
2004D Proof	—	Value: 1.50				
2004F	—	—	—	—	0.50	—
2004F Proof	—	Value: 1.50				
2004G	—	—	—	—	0.50	—
2004G Proof	—	Value: 1.50				
2004J	—	—	—	—	0.50	—
2004J Proof	—	Value: 1.50				
2005A	—	—	—	—	0.50	—
2005A Proof	—	Value: 1.50				
2005D	—	—	—	—	0.50	—
2005D Proof	—	Value: 1.50				
2005F	—	—	—	—	0.50	—
2005F Proof	—	Value: 1.50				
2005G	—	—	—	—	0.50	—
2005G Proof	—	Value: 1.50				
2005J	—	—	—	—	0.50	—
2005J Proof	—	Value: 1.50				

KM# 209 5 EURO CENTS
3.8600 g., Copper Plated Steel, 21.2 mm. **Obv:** Oak leaves **Obv. Designer:** Rolf Lederbogen **Rev:** Denomination and globe **Rev. Designer:** Luc Luycx **Edge:** Plain

Date	Mintage	F	VF	XF	Unc	BU
2002A	475,000,000	—	—	—	0.75	—
2002A Proof	130,000	Value: 2.00				
2002D	495,700,000	—	—	—	0.75	—
2002D Proof	130,000	Value: 2.00				
2002F	563,710,000	—	—	—	0.75	—
2002F Proof	130,000	Value: 2.00				
2002G	328,400,000	—	—	—	0.75	—
2002G Proof	130,000	Value: 2.00				
2002J	501,850,000	—	—	—	0.75	—
2002J Proof	130,000	Value: 2.00				
2003A	180,000	—	—	—	4.50	—
2003A Proof	150,000	Value: 2.00				
2003D	180,000	—	—	—	4.50	—
2003D Proof	150,000	Value: 2.00				
2003F	180,000	—	—	—	4.50	—
2003F Proof	150,000	Value: 2.00				
2003G	180,000	—	—	—	4.50	—
2003G Proof	150,000	Value: 2.00				
2003J	180,000	—	—	—	4.50	—
2003J Proof	150,000	Value: 2.00				
2004A	—	—	—	—	2.50	—
2004A Proof	—	Value: 2.00				
2004D	—	—	—	—	2.50	—
2004D Proof	—	Value: 2.00				
2004F	—	—	—	—	2.50	—
2004F Proof	—	Value: 2.00				
2004G	—	—	—	—	2.50	—
2004G Proof	—	Value: 2.00				
2004J	—	—	—	—	2.50	—
2004J Proof	—	Value: 2.00				
2005A	—	—	—	—	0.75	—
2005A Proof	—	Value: 2.00				
2005D	—	—	—	—	0.75	—
2005D Proof	—	Value: 2.00				
2005F	—	—	—	—	0.75	—
2005F Proof	—	Value: 2.00				
2005G	—	—	—	—	0.75	—
2005G Proof	—	Value: 2.00				
2005J	—	—	—	—	0.75	—
2005J Proof	—	Value: 2.00				

KM# 210 10 EURO CENTS
4.0000 g., Brass, 19.7 mm. **Obv:** Brandenburg Gate **Obv. Designer:** Reinhard Heinsdorff **Rev:** Denomination and map **Rev. Designer:** Luc Luycx **Edge:** Reeded

Date	Mintage	F	VF	XF	Unc	BU
2002A	696,000,000	—	—	—	0.75	—
2002A Proof	130,000	Value: 2.00				
2002D	722,050,000	—	—	—	0.75	—
2002D Proof	130,000	Value: 2.00				
2002F	788,860,000	—	—	—	0.75	—
2002F Proof	130,000	Value: 2.00				
2002G	545,500,000	—	—	—	0.75	—
2002G Proof	130,000	Value: 2.00				
2002J	694,150,000	—	—	—	0.75	—
2002J Proof	130,000	Value: 2.00				
2003A	15,000,000	—	—	—	1.25	—
2003A Proof	150,000	Value: 2.00				
2003D	9,000,000	—	—	—	1.25	—
2003D Proof	150,000	Value: 2.00				
2003F	1,500,000	—	—	—	1.50	—
2003F Proof	150,000	Value: 2.00				
2003G	9,450,000	—	—	—	1.25	—
2003G Proof	150,000	Value: 2.00				
2003J	89,405,000	—	—	—	1.25	—
2003J Proof	150,000	Value: 2.00				
2004A	—	—	—	—	1.25	—
2004A Proof	—	Value: 2.00				
2004D	—	—	—	—	1.25	—
2004D Proof	—	Value: 2.00				
2004F	—	—	—	—	1.25	—
2004F Proof	—	Value: 2.00				
2004G	—	—	—	—	1.25	—
2004G Proof	—	Value: 2.00				
2004J	—	—	—	—	1.25	—
2004J Proof	—	Value: 2.00				
2005A	—	—	—	—	1.25	—
2005A Proof	—	Value: 2.00				
2005D	—	—	—	—	1.25	—
2005D Proof	—	Value: 2.00				
2005F	—	—	—	—	1.25	—
2005F Proof	—	Value: 2.00				
2005G	—	—	—	—	1.25	—
2005G Proof	—	Value: 2.00				
2005J	—	—	—	—	1.25	—
2005J Proof	—	—	—	—	—	—

KM# 211 20 EURO CENTS

5.7300 g., Brass, 22.2 mm. **Obv:** Brandenburg Gate **Obv. Designer:** Reinhard Heinsdorff **Rev:** Denomination and map **Rev. Designer:** Luc Luycx **Edge:** Notched

Date	Mintage	F	VF	XF	Unc	BU
2002A	378,000,000	—	—	—	1.00	—
2002A Proof	130,000	Value: 3.00				
2002D	367,100,000	—	—	—	1.00	—
2002D Proof	130,000	Value: 3.00				
2002F	423,760,000	—	—	—	1.00	—
2002F Proof	130,000	Value: 3.00				
2002G	252,100,000	—	—	—	1.00	—
2002G Proof	130,000	Value: 3.00				
2002J	441,000,000	—	—	—	1.00	—
2002J Proof	130,000	Value: 3.00				
2003A	42,000,000	—	—	—	1.00	—
2003A Proof	150,000	Value: 3.00				
2003D	24,100,000	—	—	—	1.00	—
2003D Proof	150,000	Value: 3.00				
2003F	82,000,000	—	—	—	1.00	—
2003F Proof	150,000	Value: 3.00				
2003G	24,829,000	—	—	—	1.00	—
2003G Proof	150,000	Value: 3.00				
2003J	180,000	—	—	—	4.50	—
2003J Proof	150,000	Value: 3.00				
2004A	—	—	—	—	2.50	—
2004A Proof	—	Value: 3.00				
2004D	—	—	—	—	2.50	—
2004D Proof	—	Value: 3.00				
2004F	—	—	—	—	2.50	—
2004F Proof	—	Value: 3.00				
2004G	—	—	—	—	2.50	—
2004G Proof	—	Value: 3.00				
2004J	—	—	—	—	2.50	—
2004J Proof	—	Value: 3.00				
2005A	—	—	—	—	1.00	—
2005A Proof	—	Value: 3.00				
2005D	—	—	—	—	1.00	—
2005D Proof	—	Value: 3.00				
2005F	—	—	—	—	1.00	—
2005F Proof	—	Value: 3.00				
2005G	—	—	—	—	1.00	—
2005G Proof	—	Value: 3.00				
2005J	—	—	—	—	1.00	—
2005J Proof	—	Value: 3.00				

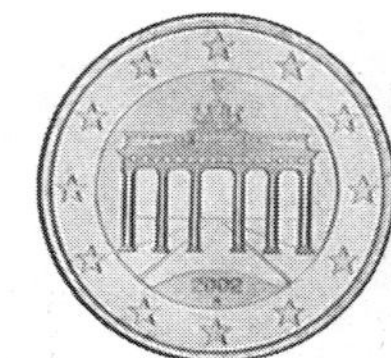

KM# 212 50 EURO CENTS

7.8100 g., Brass, 24.2 mm. **Obv:** Brandenburg Gate **Obv. Designer:** Reinhard Heinsdorff **Rev:** Denomination and map **Rev. Designer:** Luc Luycx **Edge:** Reeded

Date	Mintage	F	VF	XF	Unc	BU
2002A	337,600,000	—	—	—	1.75	—
2002A Proof	130,000	Value: 4.00				
2002D	370,340,000	—	—	—	1.75	—
2002D Proof	130,000	Value: 4.00				
2002F	432,000,000	—	—	—	1.75	—
2002F Proof	130,000	Value: 4.00				
2002G	257,860,000	—	—	—	1.75	—
2002G Proof	130,000	Value: 4.00				
2002J	375,467,000	—	—	—	1.75	—
2002J Proof	130,000	Value: 4.00				
2003A	180,000	—	—	—	4.50	—
2003A Proof	150,000	Value: 4.00				
2003D	180,000	—	—	—	4.50	—
2003D Proof	150,000	Value: 4.00				
2003F	180,000	—	—	—	4.50	—
2003F Proof	150,000	Value: 4.00				
2003G	180,000	—	—	—	4.50	—
2003G Proof	150,000	Value: 4.00				
2003J	54,400,000	—	—	—	1.75	—
2003J Proof	150,000	Value: 4.00				
2004A	—	—	—	—	1.75	—
2004A Proof	—	Value: 4.00				
2004D	—	—	—	—	1.75	—
2004D Proof	—	Value: 4.00				
2004F	—	—	—	—	1.75	—
2004F Proof	—	Value: 4.00				
2004G	—	—	—	—	1.75	—
2004G Proof	—	Value: 4.00				
2004J	—	—	—	—	1.75	—
2004J Proof	—	Value: 4.00				
2005A	—	—	—	—	1.00	—
2005A Proof	—	Value: 3.00				
2005D	—	—	—	—	1.00	—
2005D Proof	—	Value: 3.00				
2005F	—	—	—	—	1.00	—
2005F Proof	—	Value: 3.00				
2005G	—	—	—	—	1.00	—
2005G Proof	—	Value: 3.00				
2005J	—	—	—	—	1.00	—
2005J Proof	—	Value: 3.00				

KM# 213 EURO

7.5000 g., Bi-Metallic Copper-Nickel center in Brass ring, 23.3 mm. **Obv:** Stylized eagle **Obv. Designer:** Heinz Sneschana Russewa-Hover **Rev:** Denomination over map **Rev. Designer:** Luc Luycx **Edge:** Three normally reeded and three very finely reeded sections

Date	Mintage	F	VF	XF	Unc	BU
2002A	367,750,000	—	—	—	2.50	—
2002A Proof	130,000	Value: 6.50				
2002D	372,700,000	—	—	—	2.50	—
2002D Proof	130,000	Value: 6.50				
2002F	440,910,000	—	—	—	2.50	—
2002F Proof	130,000	Value: 6.50				
2002G	266,975,000	—	—	—	2.50	—
2002G Proof	130,000	Value: 6.50				
2002J	433,000,000	—	—	—	2.50	—
2002J Proof	130,000	Value: 6.50				
2003A	36,750,000	—	—	—	2.50	—
2003A Proof	150,000	Value: 6.50				
2003D	180,000	—	—	—	5.50	—
2003D Proof	150,000	Value: 6.50				
2003F	375,000	—	—	—	5.50	—
2003F Proof	150,000	Value: 6.50				
2003G	180,000	—	—	—	5.50	—
2003G Proof	150,000	Value: 6.50				
2003J	975,000	—	—	—	2.50	—
2003J Proof	150,000	Value: 6.50				
2004A	—	—	—	—	2.50	—
2004A Proof	—	Value: 6.50				
2004D	—	—	—	—	2.50	—
2004D Proof	—	Value: 6.50				
2004F	—	—	—	—	2.50	—
2004F Proof	—	Value: 6.50				
2004G	—	—	—	—	2.50	—
2004G Proof	—	Value: 6.50				
2004J	—	—	—	—	2.50	—
2004J Proof	—	Value: 6.50				
2005A	—	—	—	—	2.50	—
2005A Proof	—	Value: 5.00				
2005D	—	—	—	—	2.50	—
2005D Proof	—	Value: 5.00				
2005F	—	—	—	—	2.50	—
2005F Proof	—	Value: 5.00				
2005G	—	—	—	—	2.50	—
2005G Proof	—	Value: 5.00				
2005J	—	—	—	—	2.50	—
2005J Proof	—	Value: 5.00				

KM# 214 2 EUROS

8.5200 g., Bi-Metallic Brass center in Copper-Nickel ring, 25.6 mm. **Obv:** Stylized eagle **Obv. Designer:** Heinz Sneschana Russewa-Hover **Rev:** Denomination and map **Rev. Designer:** Luc Luycx **Edge:** Reeded and "EINIGKEIT UND RECHT UND FREIHEIT"

Date	Mintage	F	VF	XF	Unc	BU
2002A	238,775,000	—	—	—	4.50	—
2002A Proof	130,000	Value: 12.50				
2002D	231,400,000	—	—	—	4.50	—
2002D Proof	130,000	Value: 12.50				
2002F	264,610,000	—	—	—	4.50	—
2002F Proof	130,000	Value: 12.50				
2002G	181,050,000	—	—	—	4.50	—
2002G Proof	130,000	Value: 12.50				
2002J	257,718,000	—	—	—	4.50	—
2002J Proof	130,000	Value: 12.50				
2003A	20,475,000	—	—	—	4.50	—
2003A Proof	150,000	Value: 12.50				
2003D	30,300,000	—	—	—	4.50	—
2003D Proof	150,000	Value: 12.50				
2003F	74,000,000	—	—	—	4.50	—
2003F Proof	150,000	Value: 12.50				
2003G	13,950,000	—	—	—	4.50	—
2003G Proof	150,000	Value: 12.50				
2003J	6,450,000	—	—	—	4.50	—
2003J Proof	150,000	Value: 12.50				
2004A	—	—	—	—	4.50	—
2004A Proof	—	Value: 12.50				
2004D	—	—	—	—	4.50	—
2004D Proof	—	Value: 12.50				
2004F	—	—	—	—	4.50	—
2004F Proof	—	Value: 12.50				
2004G	—	—	—	—	4.50	—
2004G Proof	—	Value: 12.50				
2004J	—	—	—	—	4.50	—
2004J Proof	—	Value: 12.50				
2005A	—	—	—	—	4.50	—
2005A Proof	—	Value: 10.00				
2005D	—	—	—	—	4.50	—
2005D Proof	—	Value: 10.00				
2005F	—	—	—	—	4.50	—
2005F Proof	—	Value: 10.00				
2005G	—	—	—	—	4.50	—
2005G Proof	—	Value: 10.00				
2005J	—	—	—	—	4.50	—
2005J Proof	—	Value: 10.00				

KM# 215 10 EURO

18.0000 g., 0.9250 Silver 0.5353 oz. ASW, 32.5 mm. **Subject:** Introduction of the Euro Currency **Obv:** Stylized round eagle **Rev:** Euro symbol and map **Edge Lettering:** IM ZEICHEN DER EINIGUNG EUROPAS

Date	Mintage	F	VF	XF	Unc	BU
2002F	2,000,000	—	—	—	20.00	—
2002F Proof	400,000	Value: 25.00				

KM# 216 10 EURO
18.0000 g., 0.9250 Silver 0.5353 oz. ASW, 32.5 mm.
Subject: Berlin Subway Centennial **Obv:** Stylized squarish eagle **Rev:** Elevated and subterranean train views
Edge Lettering: HISTORISCH UND

Date	Mintage	F	VF	XF	Unc	BU
2002D	2,000,000	—	—	—	20.00	—
2002D Proof	400,000	Value: 25.00				

KM# 217 10 EURO
18.0000 g., 0.9250 Silver 0.5353 oz. ASW, 32.5 mm.
Subject: "Documenta Kassel" Art Exposition **Obv:** Stylized eagle above inscription **Rev:** Exposition logo **Edge Lettering:** ART (in nine languages)

Date	Mintage	F	VF	XF	Unc	BU
2002J	2,000,000	—	—	—	20.00	—
2002J Proof	400,000	Value: 25.00				

KM# 218 10 EURO
18.0000 g., 0.9250 Silver 0.5353 oz. ASW, 32.5 mm. **Subject:** Museum Island, Berlin **Obv:** Stylized eagle **Rev:** Aerial view of museum complex **Edge:** Lettered

Date	Mintage	F	VF	XF	Unc	BU
2002A	2,000,000	—	—	—	20.00	—
2002A Proof	280,000	Value: 30.00				

KM# 219 10 EURO
18.0000 g., 0.9250 Silver 0.5353 oz. ASW, 32.5 mm. **Subject:** 50 Years - German Television **Obv:** Stylized eagle silhouette **Rev:** Television screen silhouette **Edge Lettering:** BILDUNG UNTERHALTUNG INFORMATION

Date	Mintage	F	VF	XF	Unc	BU
2002G	2,000,000	—	—	—	20.00	—
2002G Proof	290,000	Value: 30.00				

KM# 222 10 EURO
18.0000 g., 0.9250 Silver 0.5353 oz. ASW, 32.5 mm. **Subject:** Justus von Liebig **Obv:** Eagle above denomination **Rev:** Liebig's portrait **Edge Lettering:** FORSCHEN . LEHREN . ANWENDEN ..

Date	Mintage	F	VF	XF	Unc	BU
2003J	2,050,000	—	—	—	20.00	—
2003J Proof	350,000	Value: 30.00				

KM# 227 10 EURO
18.0000 g., 0.9250 Silver 0.5353 oz. ASW, 32.5 mm.
Obv: Stylized eagle **Rev:** Gottfried Semper and floor plan
Edge: Lettered **Edge Lettering:** "ARCHITEKT. FORSCHER. KOSMOPOLIT. DEMOKRAT."

Date	Mintage	F	VF	XF	Unc	BU
2003G	2,050,000	—	—	—	18.50	—
2003G Proof	350,000	Value: 22.50				

KM# 223 10 EURO
18.0000 g., 0.9250 Silver 0.5353 oz. ASW, 32.5 mm. **Subject:** World Cup Soccer **Obv:** Stylized round eagle **Rev:** German map on soccer ball **Edge:** Lettered **Edge Lettering:** "DIE WELT ZU GAST BEI FREUNDEN A. D. F. G.J ." **Note:** Mint is determined by which letter "E" in the edge inscription has a short center bar. If the first letter "E" has the short center bar the coin is from the Berlin mint. Second "E"= Munich, third "E"=Stuttgart, fourth "E"=Karlsruhe, fifth "E"=Hamburg

Date	Mintage	F	VF	XF	Unc	BU
2003A	710,000	—	—	—	20.00	—
2003A Proof	80,000	Value: 30.00				
2003D	710,000	—	—	—	20.00	—
2003D Proof	80,000	Value: 30.00				
2003F	710,000	—	—	—	20.00	—
2003F Proof	80,000	Value: 30.00				
2003G	710,000	—	—	—	20.00	—
2003G Proof	80,000	Value: 30.00				
2003J	710,000	—	—	—	20.00	—
2003J Proof	80,000	Value: 30.00				

KM# 224 10 EURO
18.0000 g., 0.9250 Silver 0.5353 oz. ASW, 32.5 mm. **Subject:** Ruhr Industrial District **Obv:** Stylized eagle **Rev:** Various city views **Edge:** Lettered **Edge Lettering:** "RUHRPOTT KULTURLANDSCHAFT"

Date	Mintage	F	VF	XF	Unc	BU
2003F	2,050,000	—	—	—	20.00	—
2003F Proof	350,000	Value: 30.00				

KM# 225 10 EURO
18.0000 g., 0.9250 Silver 0.5353 oz. ASW, 32.5 mm.
Subject: German Museum Centennial **Obv:** Stylized eagle
Rev: Abstract design **Edge:** Lettered **Edge Lettering:** "SAMMELN. AUSSTELLEN. FORSCHEN. BILDEN."

Date	Mintage	F	VF	XF	Unc	BU
2003D Proof	350,000	Value: 30.00				
2003D	2,050,000	—	—	—	20.00	—

KM# 226 10 EURO
18.0000 g., 0.9250 Silver 0.5353 oz. ASW, 32.5 mm.
Subject: 50th Anniversary of the Ill-fated East German Revolution **Obv:** Stylized eagle **Rev:** Tank tracks over slogans
Edge: Lettered **Edge Lettering:** "ERINNERUNG AN DEN VOLKSAUFSTAND IN DER DDR"

Date	Mintage	F	VF	XF	Unc	BU
2003A	2,050,000	—	—	—	20.00	—
2003A Proof	350,000	Value: 30.00				

KM# 229 10 EURO
18.0000 g., 0.9250 Silver 0.5353 oz. ASW, 32.5 mm. **Obv:** Stylized eagle **Rev:** Soccer ball orbiting the earth **Edge:** Lettered **Edge Lettering:** "DIE WELT ZU GAST BEI FREUNDEN A D F G J" **Note:** Soccer Series:Mint determination same as KM-223

Date	Mintage	F	VF	XF	Unc	BU
2004A	800,000	—	—	—	15.00	—
2004A Proof	80,000	Value: 20.00				
2004D	800,000	—	—	—	15.00	—
2004D Proof	80,000	Value: 20.00				
2004F	800,000	—	—	—	15.00	—
2004F Proof	80,000	Value: 20.00				
2004G	800,000	—	—	—	15.00	—
2004G Proof	80,000	Value: 20.00				
2004J	800,000	—	—	—	15.00	—
2004J Proof	80,000	Value: 20.00				

KM# 230 10 EURO
18.0000 g., 0.9250 Silver 0.5353 oz. ASW, 32.5 mm.
Obv: Stylized eagle, stars and value **Rev:** Bauhaus Dessau geometric shapes design **Edge:** Lettered **Edge Lettering:** "KUNST TECHNIK LEHRE"

Date	Mintage	F	VF	XF	Unc	BU
2004A	1,800,000	—	—	—	15.00	—
2004A Proof	300,000	Value: 20.00				

KM# 231 10 EURO
18.0000 g., 0.9250 Silver 0.5353 oz. ASW, 32.5 mm.
Obv: Stylized eagle above value **Rev:** European Union country names and dates **Edge:** Lettered **Edge Lettering:** "FREUDE SCHONER GOTTERFUNKEN"

Date	Mintage	F	VF	XF	Unc	BU
2004F	—	—	—	—	15.00	—
2004F Proof	—	Value: 20.00				
2004G	—	—	—	—	15.00	—
2004G Proof	—	Value: 20.00				

KM# 232 10 EURO
18.0000 g., 0.9250 Silver 0.5353 oz. ASW, 32.5 mm.
Obv: Stylized eagle and value **Rev:** Geese flying over Wattenmeer National Park **Edge:** Lettered **Edge Lettering:** "MEERESGRUND TRIFFT HORIZONT"

Date	Mintage	F	VF	XF	Unc	BU
2004J	—	—	—	—	15.00	—
2004J Proof	—	Value: 20.00				

KM# 233 10 EURO
18.0000 g., 0.9250 Silver 0.5353 oz. ASW, 32.5 mm.
Obv: Stylized eagle **Rev:** Eduard Moerike **Edge:** Lettered **Edge Lettering:** "OHNE DAS SCHONE WAS SOLL DER GEWINN"

Date	Mintage	F	VF	XF	Unc	BU
2004F	—	—	—	—	15.00	—
2004F Proof	—	Value: 20.00				

KM# 234 10 EURO
18.0000 g., 0.9250 Silver 0.5353 oz. ASW, 32.5 mm. **Obv:** Stylized eagle **Rev:** Space station above the earth **Edge:** Lettered **Edge Lettering:** "RAUMFAHRT VERBINDET DIE WELT"

Date	Mintage	F	VF	XF	Unc	BU
2004D	1,800,000	—	—	—	15.00	—
2004D Proof	300,000	Value: 20.00				

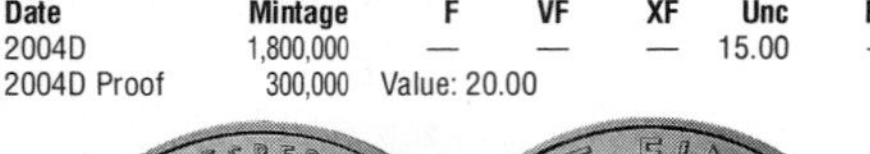

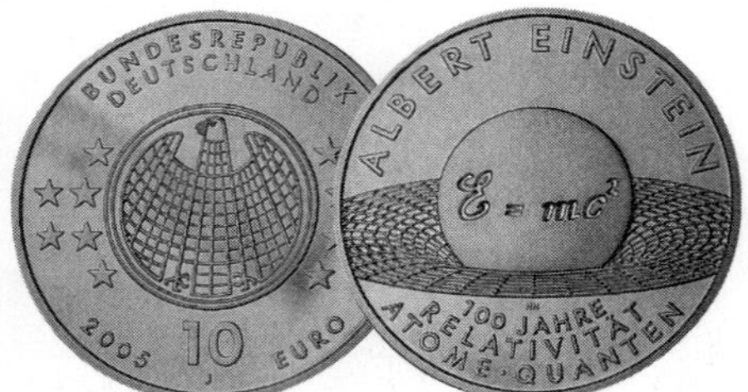

KM# 238 10 EURO
18.0000 g., 0.9250 Silver 0.5353 oz. ASW, 32.5 mm. **Subject:** Albert Einstein **Obv:** Stylized eagle **Rev:** E=mc2 on a sphere resting on a net **Edge Lettering:** "NICHT AUFHOREN ZU FRAGEN"

Date	Mintage	F	VF	XF	Unc	BU
2005J	1,800,000	—	—	—	15.00	—
2005J Proof	300,000	Value: 20.00				

KM# 239 10 EURO
18.0000 g., 0.9250 Silver 0.5353 oz. ASW, 32.5 mm. **Subject:** Friedrich von Schiller **Obv:** Stylized eagle **Rev:** Schiller portrait **Edge Lettering:** "ERNST IST DAS LEBEN. HEITER IST DIE KUNST"

Date	Mintage	F	VF	XF	Unc	BU
2005G	1,800,000	—	—	—	15.00	—
2005G Proof	300,000	Value: 20.00				

KM# 240 10 EURO
18.0000 g., 0.9250 Silver 0.5353 oz. ASW, 32.5 mm.
Subject: Magdeburg **Obv:** Stylized eagle **Rev:** Church flanked by landmarks and objects **Edge Lettering:** MAGADOBURG 805..MAGDEBURG 2005..

Date	Mintage	F	VF	XF	Unc	BU
2005A	1,800,000	—	—	—	15.00	—
2005A Proof	300,000	Value: 20.00				

KM# 241 10 EURO
18.0000 g., 0.9250 Silver 0.5353 oz. ASW, 32.5 mm.
Subject: Bavarian Forest National Park **Obv:** Stylized eagle **Rev:** Various park scenes **Edge:** Lettered

Date	Mintage	F	VF	XF	Unc	BU
2005D	1,800,000	—	—	—	15.00	—
2005D Proof	300,000	Value: 20.00				

KM# 242 10 EURO
18.0000 g., 0.9250 Silver 0.5353 oz. ASW, 32.5 mm.
Subject: Bertha von Suttner **Obv:** Stylized eagle above stars **Rev:** Suttner's portrait **Edge:** Lettered

Date	Mintage	F	VF	XF	Unc	BU
2005F	1,800,000	—	—	—	15.00	—
2005F Proof	300,000	Value: 20.00				

KM# 243 10 EURO
18.0000 g., 0.9250 Silver 0.5353 oz. ASW, 32.5 mm. **Subject:** World Cup Soccer **Obv:** Round Stylized eagle **Rev:** Ball and legs seen through a net **Edge Lettering:** DIE WELT ZU GAST BEI FREUNDEN

Date	Mintage	F	VF	XF	Unc	BU
2005A	800,000	—	—	—	15.00	—
2005A Proof	80,000	Value: 20.00				
2005D	800,000	—	—	—	15.00	—
2005D Proof	80,000	Value: 20.00				
2005F	800,000	—	—	—	15.00	—
2005F Proof	80,000	Value: 20.00				
2005G	800,000	—	—	—	15.00	—
2005G Proof	80,000	Value: 20.00				
2005J	800,000	—	—	—	15.00	—
2005J Proof	80,000	Value: 20.00				

KM# 245 10 EURO
18.0000 g., 0.9250 Silver 0.5353 oz. ASW, 32.5 mm. **Subject:** Karl Friedrich Schinkel **Obv:** Stylized eagle **Rev:** Kneeling brick layer **Edge Lettering:** DER MENSCH BILDE SICH IN ALLEM SCHON

Date	Mintage	F	VF	XF	Unc	BU
2006F	1,600,000	—	—	—	20.00	—
2006F Proof	300,000	Value: 25.00				

KM# 246 10 EURO
18.0000 g., 0.9250 Silver 0.5353 oz. ASW, 32.5 mm. **Subject:** Dresden **Obv:** Stylized eagle **Rev:** City view and reflection **Edge Lettering:** 1206 1485 1547 1697 1832 1945 1989 2006

Date	Mintage	F	VF	XF	Unc	BU
2006A	—	—	—	—	15.00	—
2006A Proof	—	Value: 20.00				

KM# 247 10 EURO
18.0000 g., 0.9250 Silver 0.5353 oz. ASW, 32.5 mm. **Subject:** Hanseatic League **Obv:** Stylized eagle **Rev:** Old sail boat **Edge Lettering:** Wandel durch Handel - von der Hanse nach Europa

Date	Mintage	F	VF	XF	Unc	BU
2006J	—	—	—	—	15.00	—
2006J Proof	—	Value: 20.00				

KM# 248 10 EURO
18.0000 g., 0.9250 Silver 0.5353 oz. ASW, 32.5 mm.
Subject: Mozart **Obv:** Stylized eagle and music **Rev:** Mozart **Edge Lettering:** -- MOZART -- DIE WELT HAT EINEN SINN

Date	Mintage	F	VF	XF	Unc	BU
2006D	—	—	—	—	15.00	—
2006D Proof	—	Value: 20.00				

KM# 249 10 EURO
18.0000 g., 0.9250 Silver 0.5353 oz. ASW, 32.5 mm.
Subject: World Cup Soccer **Obv:** Stylized eagle
Rev: Brandenburg Gate on ball on globe

Date	Mintage	F	VF	XF	Unc	BU
2006A	800,000	—	—	—	15.00	—
2006A Proof	80,000	Value: 20.00				
2006D	800,000	—	—	—	15.00	—
2006D Proof	80,000	Value: 20.00				
2006F	800,000	—	—	—	15.00	—
2006F Proof	80,000	Value: 20.00				
2006G	800,000	—	—	—	15.00	—
2006G Proof	80,000	Value: 20.00				
2006J	800,000	—	—	—	15.00	—
2006J Proof	80,000	Value: 20.00				

KM# 220 100 EURO
15.5500 g., 0.9990 Gold 0.4994 oz. AGW, 28 mm.
Subject: Introduction of the Euro Currency **Obv:** Stylized round eagle **Rev:** Euro symbol and arches **Edge:** Reeded

Date	Mintage	F	VF	XF	Unc	BU
2002A Proof	100,000	Value: 375				
2002D Proof	100,000	Value: 375				
2002F Proof	100,000	Value: 375				
2002G Proof	100,000	Value: 375				
2002J Proof	100,000	Value: 375				

KM# 228 100 EURO
15.5000 g., 0.9999 Gold 0.4983 oz. AGW, 28 mm. **Obv:** Stylized eagle **Rev:** Quedlinburg Abbey in monogram **Edge:** Reeded

Date	Mintage	F	VF	XF	Unc	BU
2003A Proof	100,000	Value: 365				
2003D Proof	100,000	Value: 365				
2003F Proof	100,000	Value: 365				
2003G Proof	100,000	Value: 365				
2003J Proof	100,000	Value: 365				

KM# 235 100 EURO
15.5500 g., 0.9999 Gold 0.4999 oz. AGW, 28 mm. **Obv:** Stylized eagle **Rev:** Bamberg city view **Edge:** Reeded

Date	Mintage	F	VF	XF	Unc	BU
2004A Proof	80,000	Value: 350				
2004D Proof	80,000	Value: 350				
2004F Proof	80,000	Value: 350				
2004G Proof	80,000	Value: 350				
2004J Proof	80,000	Value: 350				

KM# 236 100 EURO
15.5500 g., 0.9990 Gold 0.4994 oz. AGW **Subject:** UNESCO - Weimar **Obv:** Stylized eagle **Rev:** Historical City of Weimar buildings

Date	Mintage	F	VF	XF	Unc	BU
2005A	80,000	—	—	—	—	350
2005D	80,000	—	—	—	—	350
2005F	80,000	—	—	—	—	350
2005G	80,000	—	—	—	—	350
2005J	80,000	—	—	—	—	350

KM# 237 100 EURO
15.5500 g., 0.9990 Gold 0.4994 oz. AGW **Subject:** Soccer - Germany 2006 **Obv:** Round stylized eagle **Rev:** Aerial view of stadium

Date	Mintage	F	VF	XF	Unc	BU
2005A	70,000	—	—	—	—	360
2005D	70,000	—	—	—	—	360
2005F	70,000	—	—	—	—	360
2005G	70,000	—	—	—	—	360
2005J	70,000	—	—	—	—	360

KM# 221 200 EURO
31.1000 g., 0.9990 Gold 0.9989 oz. AGW, 32.5 mm.
Subject: Introduction of the Euro Currency **Obv:** Stylized round eagle **Rev:** Euro symbol and arches **Edge Lettering:** IM...ZEICHEN...DER...EINIGUNG...EUROPAS

Date	Mintage	F	VF	XF	Unc	BU
2002A Proof	20,000	Value: 1,250				
2002D Proof	20,000	Value: 1,250				
2002F Proof	20,000	Value: 1,250				
2002G Proof	20,000	Value: 1,250				
2002J Proof	20,000	Value: 1,250				

KM# 250 200 EURO

31.1000 g., 0.9990 Gold 0.9989 oz. AGW **Subject:** Quedlinburg Abbey

Date	Mintage	F	VF	XF	Unc	BU
2003A Proof	—	Value: 950				
2003D Proof	—	Value: 950				
2003F Proof	—	Value: 950				
2003G Proof	—	Value: 950				
2003J Proof	—	Value: 950				

KM# 251 200 EURO

31.1000 g., 0.9990 Gold 0.9989 oz. AGW **Subject:** City of Bamberg

Date	Mintage	F	VF	XF	Unc	BU
2004A Proof	—	Value: 850				
2004D Proof	—	Value: 850				
2004F Proof	—	Value: 850				
2004G Proof	—	Value: 850				
2004J Proof	—	Value: 850				

KM# 252 200 EURO

31.1000 g., 0.9990 Gold 0.9989 oz. AGW **Subject:** 2006 World Cup - Soccer

Date	Mintage	F	VF	XF	Unc	BU
2005A Proof	—	Value: 900				
2005D Proof	—	Value: 900				
2005F Proof	—	Value: 900				
2005G Proof	—	Value: 900				
2005J Proof	—	Value: 900				

MINT SETS

KM#	Date	Mintage	Identification	Issue Price	Mkt Val
MS119	2001A (10)	130,000	KM105,106a,107-108,109.2,110,140.1,170,175,183	—	40.00
MS120	2001D (10)	130,000	KM105,106a,107-108,109.2,110,140.1,170,175,183	—	40.00
MS121	2001F (10)	130,000	KM105,106a,107-108,109.2,110,140.1,170,175,183	—	40.00
MS122	2001G (10)	130,000	KM105,106a,107-108,109.2,110,140.1,170,175,183	—	40.00
MS123	2001J (10)	130,000	KM105,106a,107-108,109.2,110,140.1,170,175,183	—	40.00
MS124	2002A (8)	145,000	KM#207-214	—	27.50
MS125	2002D (8)	145,000	KM#207-214	—	27.50
MS126	2002F (8)	145,000	KM#207-214	—	27.50
MS127	2002G (8)	145,000	KM#207-214	—	27.50
MS128	2002J (8)	145,000	KM#207-214	—	27.50
MS129	2003A (8)	180,000	KM#207-214	—	27.50
MS130	2003D (8)	180,000	KM#207-214	—	27.50
MS131	2003F (8)	180,000	KM#207-214	—	27.50
MS132	2003G (8)	180,000	KM#207-214	—	27.50
MS133	2003J (8)	180,000	KM#207-214	—	27.50
MS134	2004A (8)	—	KM#207-214	—	27.50
MS135	2004D (8)	—	KM#207-214	—	27.50
MS136	2004F (8)	—	KM#207-214	—	27.50
MS137	2004G (8)	—	KM#207-214	—	27.50
MS138	2004J (8)	—	KM#207-214	—	27.50
MS139	2005A (8)	—	KM#207-214	—	25.00
MS140	2005D (8)	—	KM#207-214	—	25.00
MS141	2005F (8)	—	KM#207-214	—	25.00
MS142	2005G (8)	—	KM#207-214	—	25.00
MS143	2005J (8)	—	KM#207-214	—	25.00

PROOF SETS

KM#	Date	Mintage	Identification	Issue Price	Mkt Val
PS150	2001A (10)	78,000	KM105,106a,107-108,109.2,110,140.1,170,175,183	—	70.00
PS151	2001D (10)	78,000	KM105,106a,107-108,109.2,110,140.1,170,175,183	—	70.00
PS152	2001F (10)	78,000	KM105,106a,107-108,110,140.1,170,175,183	—	70.00
PS153	2001G (10)	78,000	KM105,106a,107-108,109.2,110,140.1,170,175,183	—	70.00
PS154	2001J (10)	78,000	KM105,106a,107-108,109.2,110,140.1,170,175,183	—	70.00
PS155	2002A (8)	130,000	KM#207-214	—	35.00
PS156	2002D (8)	130,000	KM#207-214	—	35.00
PS157	2002F (8)	130,000	KM#207-214	—	35.00
PS158	2002G (8)	130,000	KM#207-214	—	35.00
PS159	2002J (8)	130,000	KM#207-214	—	35.00
PS160	2003A (8)	150,000	KM#207-214	—	35.00
PS161	2003D (8)	150,000	KM#207-214	—	35.00
PS162	2003F (8)	150,000	KM#207-214	—	35.00
PS163	2003G (8)	150,000	KM#207-214	—	35.00
PS164	2003J (8)	150,000	KM#207-214	—	35.00
PS165	2004A (8)	—	KM#207-214	—	35.00
PS166	2004D (8)	—	KM#207-214	—	35.00
PS167	2004F (8)	—	KM#207-214	—	35.00
PS168	2004G (8)	—	KM#207-214	—	35.00
PS169	2004J (8)	—	KM#207-214	—	35.00
PS170	2005A (8)	—	KM#207-214	—	35.00
PS171	2005D (8)	—	KM#207-214	—	35.00
PS173	2005F (8)	—	KM#207-214	—	35.00
PS174	2005G (8)	—	KM#207-214	—	35.00
PS175	2005J (8)	—	KM#207-214	—	35.00

GHANA

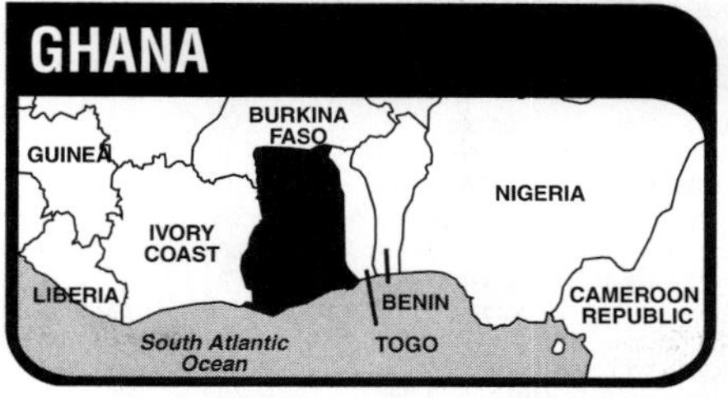

The Republic of Ghana, a member of the Commonwealth of Nations situated on the West Coast of Africa between Ivory Coast and Togo, has an area of 92,100 sq. mi. (238,540 sq. km.) and a population of 14 million, almost entirely African. Capital: Accra. Cocoa (the major crop), coconuts, palm kernels and coffee are exported. Mining, second in importance to agriculture, is concentrated on gold, manganese and industrial diamonds.

MONETARY SYSTEM

1 Cedi = 100 Pesewas, 1965-

REPUBLIC

DECIMAL COINAGE

KM# 36 10 CEDIS

4.4100 g., Copper-Nickel, 22.9 mm. **Obv:** National arms **Rev:** Gorilla family **Edge:** Reeded

Date	Mintage	F	VF	XF	Unc	BU
2003	—	—	—	—	0.75	1.00

GIBRALTAR

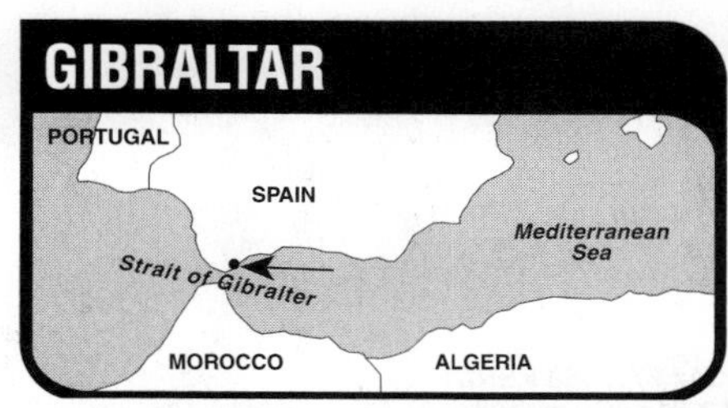

The British Colony of Gibraltar, located at the southernmost point of the Iberian Peninsula, has an area of 2.25sq. mi. (6.5 sq. km.) and a population of 29,651. Capital (and only town): Gibraltar. Aside from its strategic importance as guardian of the western entrance to the Mediterranean Sea, Gibraltar is also a free port and a British naval base.

RULERS

British

MINT MARKS

PM - Pobjoy Mint

MINT PRIVY MARKS

U - Unc finish

MONETARY SYSTEM

100 Pence = 1 Crown

BRITISH COLONY

DECIMAL COINAGE

KM# 773 PENNY

Bronze Plated Steel **Obv:** Portrait of Queen Elizabeth II **Obv. Designer:** Rank-Broadley **Rev:** Barbary partridge

Date	Mintage	F	VF	XF	Unc	BU
2001PMM AA	—	—	—	—	0.35	0.50
2002PMM AA	—	—	—	—	0.35	0.50

KM# 774 2 PENCE

Bronze Plated Steel **Obv:** Portrait of Queen Elizabeth II **Obv. Designer:** Rank-Broadley

Date	Mintage	F	VF	XF	Unc	BU
2001 AA	—	—	—	—	0.50	0.75
2001PM AB	—	—	—	—	0.50	0.75

KM# 1044 2 PENCE

7.0400 g., Copper-Plated-Steel, 25.4 mm. **Subject:** 200th Anniversary **Obv:** Elizabeth II **Rev:** Four old keys **Edge:** Plain

Date	Mintage	F	VF	XF	Unc	BU
2004	—	—	—	—	0.50	0.65

KM# 775 5 PENCE

Copper-Nickel **Obv:** Portrait of Queen Elizabeth II **Obv. Designer:** Rank-Broadley

Date	Mintage	F	VF	XF	Unc	BU
2001	—	—	—	—	0.60	0.75

KM# 776 10 PENCE

Copper-Nickel **Obv:** Portrait of Queen Elizabeth II **Obv. Designer:** Rank-Broadley

Date	Mintage	F	VF	XF	Unc	BU
2001	—	—	—	—	1.00	1.25

KM# 777 20 PENCE

Copper-Nickel **Obv:** Portrait of Queen Elizabeth II **Obv. Designer:** Rank-Broadley **Rev:** Our Lady of Europa **Rev. Designer:** Alfred Ryman

Date	Mintage	F	VF	XF	Unc	BU
2001	—	—	—	—	1.50	2.00

KM# 778 50 PENCE

8.0000 g., Copper-Nickel, 27.3 mm. **Obv:** Portrait of Queen Elizabeth II **Obv. Designer:** Rank-Broadley **Rev:** Dolphins **Edge:** Plain **Shape:** 7-sided

Date	Mintage	F	VF	XF	Unc	BU
2001 AA	—	—	—	—	4.50	5.00
2001 AB	—	—	—	—	4.50	5.00

KM# 971 50 PENCE
8.0000 g., Copper-Nickel, 27.3 mm. **Subject:** Christmas **Obv:** Queen's portrait **Rev:** Three wise men **Edge:** Plain **Shape:** 7-sided

Date	Mintage	F	VF	XF	Unc	BU
2001 BB	30,000	—	—	—	10.00	12.00

KM# 971a 50 PENCE
8.0000 g., 0.9250 Silver .2379 oz. ASW, 27.3 mm. **Edge:** Plain **Shape:** 7-sided

Date	Mintage	F	VF	XF	Unc	BU
2001 Proof	5,000	Value: 35.00				

KM# 971b 50 PENCE
8.0000 g., 0.9167 Gold .2358 oz. AGW, 27.3 mm. **Edge:** Plain **Shape:** 7-sided

Date	Mintage	F	VF	XF	Unc	BU
2001 Proof	250	Value: 645				

KM# 1026 50 PENCE
8.0000 g., Copper-Nickel, 27.3 mm. **Subject:** Christmas **Obv:** Queen's portrait **Rev:** Shepherds **Edge:** Plain **Shape:** 7-sided

Date	Mintage	F	VF	XF	Unc	BU
2002PM BB	30,000	—	—	—	10.00	12.00

KM# 1026a 50 PENCE
8.0000 g., 0.9250 Silver 0.2379 oz. ASW, 27.3 mm. **Subject:** Christmas **Obv:** Queen's portrait **Rev:** Two Shepherds **Edge:** Plain **Shape:** 7-sided

Date	Mintage	F	VF	XF	Unc	BU
2002PM Proof	2,002	Value: 35.00				

KM# 988 1/25 CROWN
1.2240 g., 0.9990 Gold 0.0393 oz. AGW, 13.92 mm. **Subject:** Peter Rabbit Centennial **Obv:** Bust of Queen Elizabeth II right **Rev:** Peter Rabbit **Edge:** Reeded

Date	Mintage	F	VF	XF	Unc	BU
2002 Proof	5,000	Value: 50.00				

KM# 988a 1/25 CROWN
1.2240 g., 0.9990 Platinum 0.0393 oz. APW, 13.92 mm. **Subject:** Peter Rabbit Centennial **Obv:** Bust of Queen Elizabeth II right **Rev:** Peter Rabbit **Edge:** Reeded

Date	Mintage	F	VF	XF	Unc	BU
2002 Proof	3,000	Value: 65.00				

KM# 1016 1/25 CROWN
1.2441 g., 0.9999 Gold 0.04 oz. AGW, 13.92 mm. **Subject:** Peter Pan **Obv:** Bust of Queen Elizabeth II right. **Rev:** Peter Pan and Tinkerbell flying above city. **Edge:** Reeded.

Date	Mintage	F	VF	XF	Unc	BU
2002 Proof	10,000	Value: 50.00				

KM# 989 1/10 CROWN
3.1100 g., 0.9990 Gold 0.0990 oz. AGW, 17.95 mm. **Subject:** Peter Rabbit Centennial **Obv:** Bust of Queen Elizabeth II right **Rev:** Peter Rabbit **Edge:** Reeded

Date	Mintage	F	VF	XF	Unc	BU
2002 Proof	5,000	Value: 95.00				

KM# 989a 1/10 CROWN
3.1100 g., 0.9990 Platinum 0.0999 oz. APW, 17395 mm. **Subject:** Peter Rabbit Centennial **Obv:** Bust of Queen Elizabeth II right **Rev:** Peter Rabbit **Edge:** Reeded

Date	Mintage	F	VF	XF	Unc	BU
2002 Proof	2,000	Value: 145				

KM# 1017 1/10 CROWN
3.1104 g., 0.9999 Gold 0.1 oz. AGW, 17.95 mm. **Subject:** Peter Pan **Obv:** Bust of Queen Elizabeth II right. **Rev:** Peter Pan and Tinkerbell flying above city. **Edge:** Reeded.

Date	Mintage	F	VF	XF	Unc	BU
2002 Proof	7,500	Value: 95.00				

KM# 902 1/5 CROWN
6.2200 g., 0.9999 Gold .2000 oz. AGW, 22 mm. **Subject:** Queen Mother **Obv:** Queen's portrait **Rev:** 1953 Coronation scene **Edge:** Reeded

Date	Mintage	F	VF	XF	Unc	BU
2001 Proof	5,000	Value: 175				

KM# 903 1/5 CROWN
6.2200 g., 0.9999 Gold .2000 oz. AGW **Obv:** Queen's portrait **Rev:** Queen Mother and Prince Charles in 1954

Date	Mintage	F	VF	XF	Unc	BU
2001 Proof	5,000	Value: 175				

KM# 909 1/5 CROWN
6.2200 g., 0.9999 Gold .2000 oz. AGW, 22 mm. **Series:** Victorian Era **Subject:** Victoria's Coronation 1838 **Obv:** Queen's portrait **Rev:** 1838 Coronation scene **Edge:** Reeded

Date	Mintage	F	VF	XF	Unc	BU
2001 Proof	5,000	Value: 175				

KM# 909.1 1/5 CROWN
6.2200 g., 0.9999 Gold .2000 oz. AGW, 22 mm. **Series:** Victorian Era **Rev:** 1838 Coronation scene with a tiny emerald set in the field below the 1838 date **Edge:** Reeded

Date	Mintage	F	VF	XF	Unc	BU
2001 Proof	2,001	Value: 200				

KM# 911.1 1/5 CROWN
6.2200 g., 0.9999 Gold .2000 oz. AGW, 22 mm. **Series:** Victorian Era **Subject:** Empress of India 1876 **Obv:** Queen's portrait **Rev:** Crowned portrait of Victoria and two elephants **Edge:** Reeded

Date	Mintage	F	VF	XF	Unc	BU
2001 Proof	5,000	Value: 175				

KM# 911.2 1/5 CROWN
6.2200 g., 0.9999 Gold .2000 oz. AGW, 22 mm. **Series:** Victorian Era **Rev:** Same but with a tiny ruby set in the field behind Victoria's head **Edge:** Reeded

Date	Mintage	F	VF	XF	Unc	BU
2001 Proof	2,001	Value: 200				

KM# 913.1 1/5 CROWN
6.2200 g., 0.9999 Gold .2000 oz. AGW, 22 mm. **Series:** Victorian Era **Subject:** Diamond Jubilee 1897 **Obv:** Queen's portrait **Rev:** Victoria's cameo portrait above naval ships **Edge:** Reeded

Date	Mintage	F	VF	XF	Unc	BU
2001 Proof	5,000	Value: 175				

KM# 913.2 1/5 CROWN
6.2200 g., 0.9999 Gold .2000 oz. AGW, 22 mm. **Series:** Victorian Era **Rev:** Same but with a tiny diamond set at the top of the fourth mast **Edge:** Reeded

Date	Mintage	F	VF	XF	Unc	BU
2001 Proof	2,001	Value: 200				

KM# 915.1 1/5 CROWN
6.2200 g., 0.9999 Gold .2000 oz. AGW, 22 mm. **Series:** Victorian Era **Subject:** Victoria's Death 1901 **Obv:** Queen's portrait **Rev:** Victoria's cameo portrait and Osborne Manor **Edge:** Reeded

Date	Mintage	F	VF	XF	Unc	BU
2001 Proof	5,000	Value: 175				

KM# 915.2 1/5 CROWN
6.2200 g., 0.9999 Gold .2000 oz. AGW, 22 mm. **Series:** Victorian Era **Rev:** Same but with a tiny sapphire set in the field between the towers **Edge:** Reeded

Date	Mintage	F	VF	XF	Unc	BU
2001 Proof	2,001	Value: 200				

KM# 917 1/5 CROWN
6.2200 g., 0.9999 Gold .2000 oz. AGW, 22 mm. **Series:** Victorian Era **Subject:** Prince Albert and the Great Exhibition 1851 **Obv:** Queen's portrait **Rev:** Albert's cameo portrait and the exhibit hall **Edge:** Reeded

Date	Mintage	F	VF	XF	Unc	BU
2001 Proof	5,000	Value: 175				

KM# 919 1/5 CROWN
6.2200 g., 0.9999 Gold .2000 oz. AGW, 22 mm. **Series:** Victorian Era **Subject:** Isambard K. Brunel **Obv:** Queen's portrait **Rev:** Portrait in top hat and railroad bridge **Edge:** Reeded

Date	Mintage	F	VF	XF	Unc	BU
2001 Proof	5,000	Value: 175				

KM# 921 1/5 CROWN
6.2200 g., 0.9999 Gold .2000 oz. AGW, 22 mm. **Series:** Victorian Era **Subject:** Charles Dickens **Obv:** Queen's portrait **Rev:** Portrait and scene from "Oliver Twist" **Edge:** Reeded

Date	Mintage	F	VF	XF	Unc	BU
2001 Proof	5,000	Value: 175				

KM# 923 1/5 CROWN
6.2200 g., 0.9999 Gold .2000 oz. AGW, 22 mm. **Series:** Victorian Era **Subject:** Charles Darwin **Obv:** Queen's portrait **Rev:** Portrait, ship and a squatting aboriginal figure **Edge:** Reeded

Date	Mintage	F	VF	XF	Unc	BU
2001 Proof	5,000	Value: 175				

KM# 925 1/5 CROWN
6.2200 g., 0.9999 Gold .2000 oz. AGW, 22 mm. **Series:** Mythology of the Solar System **Obv:** Queen's portrait **Rev:** Standing goddess with snake basket **Edge:** Reeded

Date	Mintage	F	VF	XF	Unc	BU
2001 Proof	5,000	Value: 175				

KM# 926 1/5 CROWN
Bi-metallic, 0.925 Silver center in 0.999 Gold ring, 32.25 mm. **Series:** Mythology of the Solar System **Subject:** Solar System **Obv:** Queen's portrait **Rev:** Standing goddess with snake basket **Edge:** Reeded

Date	Mintage	F	VF	XF	Unc	BU
2001 In Proof sets only	999	Value: 350				

KM# 929.1 1/5 CROWN
6.2200 g., 0.9999 Gold .2000 oz. AGW, 22 mm. **Series:** Mythology of the Solar System **Subject:** Sun **Obv:** Queen's portrait **Rev:** Helios in chariot and the sun **Edge:** Reeded

Date	Mintage	F	VF	XF	Unc	BU
2001 Proof	5,000	Value: 175				

KM# 929.2 1/5 CROWN
6.2200 g., 0.9999 Gold .2000 oz. AGW, 22 mm. **Series:** Mythology of the Solar System **Rev:** Similar but with a fiery hologram in the sun **Edge:** Reeded

Date	Mintage	F	VF	XF	Unc	BU
2001 In Proof sets only	999	Value: 350				

KM# 931.1 1/5 CROWN
6.2200 g., 0.9999 Gold .2000 oz. AGW, 22 mm. **Series:** Mythology of the Solar System **Subject:** Moon **Obv:** Queen's portrait **Rev:** Goddess Diana and the moon **Edge:** Reeded

Date	Mintage	F	VF	XF	Unc	BU
2001 Proof	5,000	Value: 175				

KM# 931.2 1/5 CROWN
6.2200 g., 0.9999 Gold .2000 oz. AGW, 22 mm. **Series:** Mythology of the Solar System **Rev:** Similar but with a small pearl set in the moon **Edge:** Reeded

Date	Mintage	F	VF	XF	Unc	BU
2001 In Proof sets only	999	Value: 350				

KM# 933.1 1/5 CROWN
6.2200 g., 0.9999 Gold .2000 oz. AGW, 22 mm. **Series:** Mythology of the Solar System **Subject:** Earth **Obv:** Queen's portrait **Rev:** Atlas carrying the earth **Edge:** Reeded

Date	Mintage	F	VF	XF	Unc	BU
2001 Proof	5,000	Value: 175				

KM# 933.2 1/5 CROWN
6.2200 g., 0.9999 Gold .2000 oz. AGW, 22 mm. **Series:** Mythology of the Solar System **Rev:** Similar but with a tiny diamond set in the earth **Edge:** Reeded

Date	Mintage	F	VF	XF	Unc	BU
2001 In Proof sets only	999	Value: 350				

KM# 935 1/5 CROWN
6.2200 g., 0.9999 Gold .2000 oz. AGW, 22 mm. **Series:** Mythology of the Solar System **Subject:** Neptune **Obv:** Queen's portrait **Rev:** Seated god with trident and ringed planet **Edge:** Reeded

Date	Mintage	F	VF	XF	Unc	BU
2001 Proof	5,000	Value: 175				

KM# 937 1/5 CROWN
6.2200 g., 0.9999 Gold .2000 oz. AGW, 22 mm. **Series:** Mythology of the Solar System **Subject:** Jupiter **Obv:** Queen's portrait **Rev:** Seated god with lightening bolts and a planet **Edge:** Reeded

Date	Mintage	F	VF	XF	Unc	BU
2001 Proof	5,000	Value: 175				

KM# 939 1/5 CROWN
6.2200 g., 0.9999 Gold .2000 oz. AGW, 22 mm. **Series:** Mythology of the Solar System **Subject:** Mars **Obv:** Queen's portrait **Rev:** Standing Roman solider and a planet **Edge:** Reeded

Date	Mintage	F	VF	XF	Unc	BU
2001 Proof	5,000	Value: 175				

KM# 941 1/5 CROWN
6.2200 g., 0.9999 Gold .2000 oz. AGW, 22 mm. **Series:** Mythology of the Solar System **Subject:** Mercury **Obv:** Queen's portrait **Rev:** Seated god with caduceus and a planet **Edge:** Reeded

Date	Mintage	F	VF	XF	Unc	BU
2001 Proof	5,000	Value: 175				

KM# 943 1/5 CROWN
6.2200 g., 0.9999 Gold .2000 oz. AGW, 22 mm. **Series:** Mythology of the Solar System **Subject:** Uranus **Obv:** Queen's portrait **Rev:** Seated god with scepter **Edge:** Reeded

Date	Mintage	F	VF	XF	Unc	BU
2001 Proof	5,000	Value: 175				

KM# 945 1/5 CROWN
6.2200 g., 0.9999 Gold .2000 oz. AGW, 22 mm. **Series:** Mythology of the Solar System **Subject:** Saturn **Obv:** Queen's portrait **Rev:** Seated god with long handled sickle and a ringed planet **Edge:** Reeded

Date	Mintage	F	VF	XF	Unc	BU
2001 Proof	5,000	Value: 175				

KM# 947 1/5 CROWN
6.2200 g., 0.9999 Gold .2000 oz. AGW, 22 mm. **Series:** Mythology of the Solar System **Subject:** Pluto **Obv:** Queen's portrait **Rev:** Seated god with dogs and a planet **Edge:** Reeded

Date	Mintage	F	VF	XF	Unc	BU
2001 Proof	5,000	Value: 175				

KM# 949 1/5 CROWN
6.2200 g., 0.9999 Gold .2000 oz. AGW, 22 mm. **Series:** Mythology of the Solar System **Subject:** Venus **Obv:** Queen's portrait **Rev:** Goddess seated on a half shell **Edge:** Reeded

Date	Mintage	F	VF	XF	Unc	BU
2001 Proof	5,000	Value: 175				

KM# 951 1/5 CROWN
6.2200 g., 0.9999 Gold .2000 oz. AGW, 22 mm. **Subject:** Queen's 76th Birthday **Obv:** Queen's portrait **Rev:** Queen in Order of the Garter robes with a tiny inset diamond **Edge:** Reeded

Date	Mintage	F	VF	XF	Unc	BU
2001 Proof	2,001	Value: 200				

KM# 954 1/5 CROWN
6.2200 g., 0.9999 Gold .2000 oz. AGW, 22 mm. **Series:** Victorian Age Part II **Subject:** Victoria's Accession to the Throne **Obv:** Queen's portrait **Rev:** Victoria learning of her accession **Edge:** Reeded

Date	Mintage	F	VF	XF	Unc	BU
2001 Proof	5,000	Value: 175				

KM# 956 1/5 CROWN
6.2200 g., 0.9999 Gold .2000 oz. AGW, 22 mm. **Series:** Victorian Age Part II **Subject:** Royal Family **Rev:** Victoria and Albert seated with children **Edge:** Reeded

Date	Mintage	F	VF	XF	Unc	BU
2001 Proof	5,000	Value: 175				

KM# 958 1/5 CROWN
6.2200 g., 0.9999 Gold .2000 oz. AGW, 22 mm. **Series:** Victorian Age Part II **Subject:** Victoria in Scotland **Rev:** Victoria on horse and servant **Edge:** Reeded

Date	Mintage	F	VF	XF	Unc	BU
2001 Proof	5,000	Value: 175				

KM# 960 1/5 CROWN

6.2200 g., 0.9999 Gold .2000 oz. AGW, 22 mm.
Series: Victorian Age Part II **Rev:** Portraits of Gladstone and Disaraeli **Edge:** Reeded

Date	Mintage	F	VF	XF	Unc	BU
2001 Proof	5,000	Value: 175				

KM# 962 1/5 CROWN

6.2200 g., 0.9999 Gold .2000 oz. AGW, 22 mm.
Series: Victorian Age Part II **Rev:** Florence Nightingale holding lantern **Edge:** Reeded

Date	Mintage	F	VF	XF	Unc	BU
2001 Proof	5,000	Value: 175				

KM# 964 1/5 CROWN

6.2200 g., 0.9999 Gold .2000 oz. AGW, 22 mm.
Series: Victorian Age Part II **Rev:** Lord Tennyson with the Light Brigade in background **Edge:** Reeded

Date	Mintage	F	VF	XF	Unc	BU
2001 Proof	5,000	Value: 175				

KM# 966 1/5 CROWN

6.2200 g., 0.9999 Gold .2000 oz. AGW, 22 mm. **Series:** Victorian Age Part II **Rev:** Stanley meeting Dr. Livingstone **Edge:** Reeded

Date	Mintage	F	VF	XF	Unc	BU
2001 Proof	5,000	Value: 175				

KM# 968 1/5 CROWN

6.2200 g., 0.9999 Gold .2000 oz. AGW, 22 mm. **Series:** Victorian Age Part II **Rev:** Bronte sisters **Edge:** Reeded

Date	Mintage	F	VF	XF	Unc	BU
2001 Proof	5,000	Value: 175				

KM# 978 1/5 CROWN

6.2200 g., 0.9990 Gold 0.1998 oz. AGW, 22 mm.
Subject: Queen Mother's Life **Obv:** Bust of Queen Elizabeth II right **Rev:** Prince William's christening scene **Edge:** Reeded

Date	Mintage	F	VF	XF	Unc	BU
2002 Proof	5,000	Value: 175				

KM# 980 1/5 CROWN

6.2200 g., 0.9999 Gold 0.2 oz. AGW, 22 mm. **Subject:** World Cup Soccer **Obv:** Bust of Queen Elizabeth II right **Rev:** Two players about to collide **Edge:** Reeded

Date	Mintage	F	VF	XF	Unc	BU
2002 Proof	5,000	Value: 175				

KM# 982 1/5 CROWN

6.2200 g., 0.9999 Gold 0.2 oz. AGW, 22 mm. **Subject:** World Cup Soccer **Obv:** Bust of Queen Elizabeth II right **Rev:** Two players facing viewer **Edge:** Reeded

Date	Mintage	F	VF	XF	Unc	BU
2002 Proof	5,000	Value: 175				

KM# 984 1/5 CROWN

6.2200 g., 0.9999 Gold 0.2 oz. AGW, 22 mm. **Subject:** World Cup Soccer **Obv:** Bust of Queen Elizabeth II right **Rev:** Two horizontal players **Edge:** Reeded

Date	Mintage	F	VF	XF	Unc	BU
2002 Proof	5,000	Value: 175				

KM# 986 1/5 CROWN

6.2200 g., 0.9999 Gold 0.2 oz. AGW, 22 mm. **Subject:** World Cup Soccer **Obv:** Bust of Queen Elizabeth II right **Rev:** Two players moving to the left **Edge:** Reeded

Date	Mintage	F	VF	XF	Unc	BU
2002 Proof	5,000	Value: 175				

KM# 990 1/5 CROWN

6.2200 g., 0.9990 Gold 0.1998 oz. AGW, 22 mm. **Subject:** Peter Rabbit Centennial **Obv:** Bust of Queen Elizabeth II right **Rev:** Peter Rabbit **Edge:** Reeded

Date	Mintage	F	VF	XF	Unc	BU
2002 Proof	3,500	Value: 175				

KM# 990a 1/5 CROWN

6.2200 g., 0.9990 Platinum 0.1998 oz. APW, 22 mm.
Subject: Peter Rabbit Centennial **Obv:** Bust of Queen Elizabeth II right **Rev:** Peter Rabbit **Edge:** Reeded

Date	Mintage	F	VF	XF	Unc	BU
2002 Proof	1,500	Value: 275				

KM# 993 1/5 CROWN

6.2200 g., 0.3750 Gold 0.075 oz. AGW, 22 mm.
Subject: Queen's Golden Jubilee **Obv:** Bust of Queen Elizabeth II right **Rev:** Royal couple and tree house **Edge:** Reeded

Date	Mintage	F	VF	XF	Unc	BU
2002 Proof	5,000	Value: 75.00				

KM# 993a 1/5 CROWN

6.2200 g., 0.9999 Gold 0.2 oz. AGW, 22 mm. **Subject:** Queen's Golden Jubilee **Obv:** Bust of Queen Elizabeth II right **Rev:** Royal couple and tree house **Edge:** Reeded

Date	Mintage	F	VF	XF	Unc	BU
2002 Proof	2,002	Value: 175				

KM# 995 1/5 CROWN

6.2200 g., 0.3750 Gold 0.075 oz. AGW, 22 mm. **Subject:** Queen's Golden Jubilee **Obv:** Bust of Queen Elizabeth II right **Rev:** Royal coach **Edge:** Reeded

Date	Mintage	F	VF	XF	Unc	BU
2002 Proof	5,000	Value: 75.00				

KM# 995a 1/5 CROWN

6.2200 g., 0.9999 Gold 0.2 oz. AGW, 22 mm. **Subject:** Queen's Golden Jubilee **Obv:** Bust of Queen Elizabeth II right **Rev:** Royal coach **Edge:** Reeded

Date	Mintage	F	VF	XF	Unc	BU
2002 Proof	2,002	Value: 175				

KM# 997 1/5 CROWN

6.2200 g., 0.3750 Gold 0.075 oz. AGW, 22 mm. **Subject:** Queen's Golden Jubilee **Obv:** Bust of Queen Elizabeth II right **Rev:** Queen holding baby **Edge:** Reeded

Date	Mintage	F	VF	XF	Unc	BU
2002 Proof	5,000	Value: 75.00				

KM# 997a 1/5 CROWN

6.2200 g., 0.9999 Gold 0.2 oz. AGW, 22 mm. **Subject:** Queen's Golden Jubilee **Obv:** Bust of Queen Elizabeth II right **Rev:** Queen holding baby **Edge:** Reeded

Date	Mintage	F	VF	XF	Unc	BU
2002 Proof	2,002	Value: 175				

KM# 999 1/5 CROWN

6.2200 g., 0.3750 Gold 0.075 oz. AGW, 22 mm. **Subject:** Queen's Golden Jubilee **Obv:** Bust of Queen Elizabeth II right **Rev:** Yacht under Tower bridge **Edge:** Reeded

Date	Mintage	F	VF	XF	Unc	BU
2002 Proof	5,000	Value: 75.00				

KM# 999a 1/5 CROWN

6.2200 g., 0.9999 Gold 0.2 oz. AGW, 22 mm. **Subject:** Queen's Golden Jubilee **Obv:** Bust of Queen Elizabeth II right **Rev:** Yacht under Tower bridge **Edge:** Reeded

Date	Mintage	F	VF	XF	Unc	BU
2002 Proof	2,002	Value: 175				

KM# 1001 1/5 CROWN

6.2200 g., 0.9999 Gold 0.2 oz. AGW, 22 mm. **Subject:** Queen's Golden Jubilee **Obv:** Bust of Queen Elizabeth II right **Rev:** Crown jewels inset with a tiny diamond, ruby, sapphire and emerald **Edge:** Reeded

Date	Mintage	F	VF	XF	Unc	BU
2002 Proof	2,002	Value: 175				

KM# 1003 1/5 CROWN

3.1100 g., 0.9990 Gold-Silver 0.0999 oz., 22 mm. **Series:** Electrum **Obv:** Bust of Queen Elizabeth II right **Rev:** Athena **Edge:** Reeded

Date	Mintage	F	VF	XF	Unc	BU
2002 Proof	3,500	Value: 95.00				

KM# 1005 1/5 CROWN

3.1100 g., 0.9990 Gold-Silver 0.0999 oz., 22 mm. **Series:** Electrum **Obv:** Bust of Queen Elizabeth II right **Rev:** Hercules **Edge:** Reeded

Date	Mintage	F	VF	XF	Unc	BU
2002 Proof	3,500	Value: 95.00				

KM# 1007 1/5 CROWN

3.1100 g., 0.9990 Gold-Silver 0.0999 oz., 22 mm. **Series:** Electrum **Obv:** Bust of Queen Elizabeth II right **Rev:** Pegasus **Edge:** Reeded

Date	Mintage	F	VF	XF	Unc	BU
2002 Proof	3,500	Value: 95.00				

KM# 1009 1/5 CROWN

3.1100 g., 0.9990 Gold-Silver 0.0999 oz., 22 mm. **Series:** Electrum **Obv:** Bust of Queen Elizabeth II right **Rev:** Lion and bull **Edge:** Reeded

Date	Mintage	F	VF	XF	Unc	BU
2002 Proof	3,500	Value: 95.00				

KM# 1012 1/5 CROWN

6.2200 g., 0.9999 Gold 0.2 oz. AGW, 22 mm. **Subject:** Queen Mother **Obv:** Bust of Queen Elizabeth II right **Rev:** Queen Mother trout fishing **Edge:** Reeded

Date	Mintage	F	VF	XF	Unc	BU
2002 Proof	5,000	Value: 175				

KM# 1014 1/5 CROWN

6.2200 g., 0.9999 Gold 0.2 oz. AGW, 22 mm. **Subject:** Princess Diana **Obv:** Bust of Queen Elizabeth II right **Rev:** Diana's portrait **Edge:** Reeded

Date	Mintage	F	VF	XF	Unc	BU
2002 Proof	5,000	Value: 175				

KM# 1018 1/5 CROWN

6.2200 g., 0.9999 Gold 0.2 oz. AGW, 22 mm. **Subject:** Peter Pan **Obv:** Bust of Queen Elizabeth II right **Rev:** Peter Pan and Tinkerbell flying above city **Edge:** Reeded

Date	Mintage	F	VF	XF	Unc	BU
2002 Proof	5,000	Value: 175				

KM# 1020 1/5 CROWN

6.2200 g., 0.9999 Gold 0.2 oz. AGW, 22 mm. **Subject:** Grand Masonic Lodge **Obv:** Bust of Queen Elizabeth II right **Rev:** Masonic seal above Gibraltar **Edge:** Reeded

Date	Mintage	F	VF	XF	Unc	BU
2002 Proof	5,000	Value: 175				

KM# 991 1/2 CROWN

15.5500 g., 0.9990 Gold 0.4994 oz. AGW, 30 mm.
Subject: Peter Rabbit Centennial **Obv:** Bust of Queen Elizabeth II right **Rev:** Peter Rabbit **Edge:** Reeded

Date	Mintage	F	VF	XF	Unc	BU
2002 Proof	1,000	Value: 350				

KM# 1002 1/2 CROWN

15.5500 g., 0.9999 Gold 0.4999 oz. AGW, 30 mm.
Subject: Queen's Golden Jubilee **Obv:** Bust of Queen Elizabeth II right **Rev:** Crown jewels inset with a tiny diamond, ruby, sapphire and emerald **Edge:** Reeded

Date	Mintage	F	VF	XF	Unc	BU
2002 Proof	999	Value: 350				

KM# 1004 1/2 CROWN

7.7750 g., 0.9990 Gold-Silver 0.2497 oz., 32.2 mm.
Series: Electrum **Obv:** Bust of Queen Elizabeth II right **Rev:** Head of Athena left **Edge:** Reeded

Date	Mintage	F	VF	XF	Unc	BU
2002 Proof	2,000	Value: 220				

KM# 1006 1/2 CROWN

7.7750 g., 0.9990 Gold-Silver 0.2497 oz., 32.2 mm.
Series: Electrum **Obv:** Bust of Queen Elizabeth II right **Rev:** Head of Hercules right **Edge:** Reeded

Date	Mintage	F	VF	XF	Unc	BU
2002 Proof	2,000	Value: 220				

KM# 1008 1/2 CROWN

7.7750 g., 0.9990 Gold-Silver 0.2497 oz., 32.2 mm.
Series: Electrum **Obv:** Bust of Queen Elizabeth II right
Rev: Pegasus **Edge:** Reeded

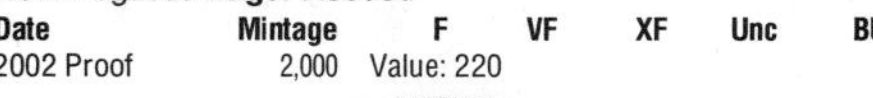

Date	Mintage	F	VF	XF	Unc	BU
2002 Proof	2,000	Value: 220				

KM# 1010 1/2 CROWN

7.7750 g., 0.9990 Gold-Silver 0.2497 oz., 32.2 mm.
Series: Electrum. **Obv:** Bust of Queen Elizabeth II right
Rev: Lion and bull **Edge:** Reeded

Date	Mintage	F	VF	XF	Unc	BU
2002 Proof	2,000	Value: 220				

KM# 904 CROWN

28.2800 g., Copper-Nickel, 38.6 mm. **Subject:** The Life of Queen Elizabeth - The Queen Mother **Obv:** Queen's portrait **Rev:** 1953 Coronation scene **Edge:** Reeded

Date	Mintage	F	VF	XF	Unc	BU
2001	—	—	—	—	10.00	12.00

KM# 904a CROWN
28.2800 g., 0.9250 Silver .8410 oz. ASW, 38.6 mm. **Subject:** The Life of Queen Elizabeth - The Queen Mother **Obv:** Queen's portrait **Rev:** 1953 Coronation scene **Edge:** Reeded

Date	Mintage	F	VF	XF	Unc	BU
2001 Proof	10,000	Value: 47.50				

KM# 905 CROWN
28.2800 g., Copper-Nickel, 38.6 mm. **Subject:** The Life of Queen Elizabeth - The Queen Mother **Obv:** Queen's portrait **Rev:** Queen Mother with Prince Charles in 1954 **Edge:** Reeded

Date	Mintage	F	VF	XF	Unc	BU
2001	—	—	—	—	10.00	12.00

KM# 905a CROWN
28.2800 g., 0.9250 Silver .8410 oz. ASW, 38.6 mm. **Subject:** The Life of Queen Elizabeth - The Queen Mother **Obv:** Queen's portrait **Rev:** Queen Mother with Prince Charles in 1954 **Edge:** Reeded

Date	Mintage	F	VF	XF	Unc	BU
2001 Proof	10,000	Value: 47.50				

KM# 906 CROWN
28.2800 g., Copper-Nickel, 38.6 mm. **Subject:** 21st Century **Obv:** Queen's portrait **Rev:** Celtic cross, Viking ship and modern technological items **Edge:** Reeded

Date	Mintage	F	VF	XF	Unc	BU
2001	—	—	—	—	10.00	12.00

KM# 906a CROWN
31.1035 g., 0.9990 Silver 1.0000 oz. ASW, 38.6 mm. **Subject:** 21st Century **Obv:** Queen's portrait **Rev:** Celtic cross, Viking ship and modern technological items **Edge:** Reeded **Note:** 31.1035 .999 Silver, 1.0000 ASW with a gold plated inner ring and a blackened outer ring.

Date	Mintage	F	VF	XF	Unc	BU
2001 Proof	2,001	Value: 47.50				

KM# 906b CROWN
31.1000 g., Tri-Metallic Center .9995 Platinum 5.2g. Inner Ring .9999 Gold 14.2g. Outer Ring .999 Silver 11.7g

Date	Mintage	F	VF	XF	Unc	BU
2001 Proof	999	Value: 600				

KM# 910 CROWN
28.2800 g., Copper-Nickel, 38.6 mm. **Series:** The Victorian Age **Obv:** Queen's portrait **Rev:** 1838 Coronation of Queen Victoria **Edge:** Reeded

Date	Mintage	F	VF	XF	Unc	BU
2001	—	—	—	—	10.00	12.00

KM# 910a CROWN
28.2800 g., 0.9250 Silver .8410 oz. ASW, 38.6 mm. **Series:** Victorian Era **Obv:** Queen's portrait **Rev:** 1838 Coronation scene **Edge:** Reeded

Date	Mintage	F	VF	XF	Unc	BU
2001 Proof	10,000	Value: 47.50				

KM# 912 CROWN
Copper-Nickel **Series:** Victorian Era **Subject:** Empress of India 1876 **Obv:** Queen's portrait **Rev:** Crowned portrait of Victoria and two elephants

Date	Mintage	F	VF	XF	Unc	BU
2001	—	—	—	—	10.00	12.00

KM# 912a CROWN
28.2800 g., 0.9250 Silver .8410 oz. ASW **Series:** The Victorian Age **Subject:** Empress of India 1876 **Obv:** Queen's portrait **Rev:** Crowned portrait of Victoria and two elephants

Date	Mintage	F	VF	XF	Unc	BU
2001 Proof	10,000	Value: 47.50				

KM# 914 CROWN
Copper-Nickel **Series:** Victorian Era **Subject:** Diamond Jubilee 1897 **Obv:** Queen's portrait **Rev:** Victoria's cameo portrait above naval ships

Date	Mintage	F	VF	XF	Unc	BU
2001	—	—	—	—	10.00	12.00

KM# 914a CROWN
28.2800 g., 0.9250 Silver .8410 oz. ASW **Series:** The Victorian Age **Subject:** Diamond Jubilee 1897 **Obv:** Queen's portrait **Rev:** Victoria's cameo above naval ships, Spithead Review

Date	Mintage	F	VF	XF	Unc	BU
2001 Proof	10,000	Value: 47.50				

KM# 916 CROWN
Copper-Nickel **Series:** The Victorian Age **Subject:** Victoria's Death 1901 **Obv:** Queen's portrait **Rev:** Victoria's cameo portrait and Osborne Manor

Date	Mintage	F	VF	XF	Unc	BU
2001	—	—	—	—	10.00	12.00

KM# 916a CROWN
28.2800 g., 0.9250 Silver .8410 oz. ASW **Series:** The Victorian Age **Subject:** Victoria's Death 1901 **Obv:** Queen's portrait **Rev:** Victoria's cameo portrait and Osborne Manor

Date	Mintage	F	VF	XF	Unc	BU
2001 Proof	10,000	Value: 47.50				

KM# 918 CROWN
Copper-Nickel **Series:** The Victorian Age **Subject:** Prince Albert and the Great Exhibition 1851 **Obv:** Queen's portrait **Rev:** Albert's cameo portrait and the exhibit hall

Date	Mintage	F	VF	XF	Unc	BU
2001 Proof	5,000	Value: 175				

KM# 918a CROWN
28.2800 g., 0.9250 Silver .8410 oz. ASW **Series:** The Victorian Age **Subject:** Prince Albert and the Great Exhibition 1851 **Obv:** Queen's portrait **Rev:** Albert's cameo portrait and the exhibit hall

Date	Mintage	F	VF	XF	Unc	BU
2001 Proof	10,000	Value: 47.50				

KM# 920 CROWN
Copper-Nickel **Series:** The Victorian Age **Obv:** Queen's portrait **Rev:** 1/2 bust of Isambard K. Brunel half left in front of railroad bridge

Date	Mintage	F	VF	XF	Unc	BU
2001	—	—	—	—	10.00	12.00

KM# 920a CROWN
28.2800 g., 0.9250 Silver .8410 oz. ASW **Series:** Victorian Era **Subject:** Isambard K. Brunel **Obv:** Queen's portrait **Rev:** Portrait in top hat and railroad bridge

Date	Mintage	F	VF	XF	Unc	BU
2001 Proof	10,000	Value: 47.50				

KM# 922 CROWN
Copper-Nickel **Series:** The Victorian Age **Obv:** Queen's portrait **Rev:** 1/2 length bust of Charles Dickens half left, scene from "Oliver Twist" in background

Date	Mintage	F	VF	XF	Unc	BU
2001	—	—	—	—	10.00	12.00

KM# 922a CROWN
28.2800 g., 0.9250 Silver .8410 oz. ASW **Series:** The Victorian Age **Obv:** Queen's portrait **Rev:** 1/2 length bust of Charles Dickens half left, scene from "Oliver Twist" in background

Date	Mintage	F	VF	XF	Unc	BU
2001 Proof	10,000	Value: 47.50				

KM# 924 CROWN
Copper-Nickel **Series:** The Victorian Age **Obv:** Queen's portrait **Rev:** 3/4-length figure of Charles Darwin right, ship and a squatting aboriginal figure

Date	Mintage	F	VF	XF	Unc	BU
2001	—	—	—	—	10.00	12.00

KM# 924a CROWN

28.2800 g., 0.9250 Silver .8410 oz. ASW **Series:** The Victorian Age **Obv:** Queen's portrait **Rev:** 3/4-length figure of Charles Darwin right, ship and a squatting aboriginal figure

Date	Mintage	F	VF	XF	Unc	BU
2001 Proof	10,000	Value: 47.50				

KM# 927 CROWN

28.2800 g., Copper-Nickel, 38.6 mm. **Series:** Mythology of the Solar System **Obv:** Queen's portrait **Rev:** Standing goddess with snake basket **Edge:** Reeded

Date	Mintage	F	VF	XF	Unc	BU
2001	—	—	—	—	10.00	12.00

KM# 927a CROWN

28.2800 g., 0.9250 Silver .8410 oz. ASW, 38.6 mm. **Series:** Mythology of the Solar System **Obv:** Queen's portrait **Rev:** Standing goddess with snake basket **Edge:** Reeded

Date	Mintage	F	VF	XF	Unc	BU
2001 Proof	10,000	Value: 47.50				

KM# 928 CROWN

Bi-metallic, Titanium center in Silver ring, 32.25 mm. **Series:** Mythology of the Solar System **Obv:** Queen's portrait **Rev:** Standing goddess with snake basket **Edge:** Reeded

Date	Mintage	F	VF	XF	Unc	BU
2001 In Proof sets only	2,001	Value: 87.50				

KM# 930 CROWN

Copper-Nickel **Series:** Mythology of the Solar System **Obv:** Queen's portrait **Rev:** Helios in chariot and the sun

Date	Mintage	F	VF	XF	Unc	BU
2001	—	—	—	—	10.00	12.00

KM# 930a CROWN

28.2800 g., 0.9250 Silver .8410 oz. ASW **Series:** Mythology of the Solar System **Obv:** Queen's portrait **Rev:** Helios in chariot and the sun

Date	Mintage	F	VF	XF	Unc	BU
2001 Proof	10,000	Value: 47.50				

KM# 930a.1 CROWN

28.2800 g., 0.9250 Silver .8410 oz. ASW **Series:** Mythology of the Solar System **Rev:** Similar but with a fiery hologram in the sun

Date	Mintage	F	VF	XF	Unc	BU
2001 In Proof sets only	2,001	Value: 87.50				

KM# 932 CROWN

Copper-Nickel **Series:** Mythology of the Solar System **Subject:** Moon **Obv:** Queen's portrait **Rev:** Goddess Diana and the moon

Date	Mintage	F	VF	XF	Unc	BU
2001	—	—	—	—	10.00	12.00

KM# 932a CROWN

28.2800 g., 0.9250 Silver .8410 oz. ASW **Series:** Mythology of the Solar System **Subject:** Moon **Obv:** Queen's portrait **Rev:** Goddess Diana and the moon

Date	Mintage	F	VF	XF	Unc	BU
2001 Proof	10,000	Value: 47.50				

KM# 932a.1 CROWN

28.2800 g., 0.9250 Silver .8410 oz. ASW **Series:** Mythology of the Solar System **Rev:** Similar but with a small pearl set in the moon

Date	Mintage	F	VF	XF	Unc	BU
2001 In Proof sets only	2,001	Value: 87.50				

KM# 934 CROWN

Copper-Nickel **Series:** Mythology of the Solar System **Obv:** Queen's portrait **Rev:** Atlas carrying the earth

Date	Mintage	F	VF	XF	Unc	BU
2001	—	—	—	—	10.00	12.00

KM# 934a CROWN

28.2800 g., 0.9250 Silver .8410 oz. ASW **Series:** Mythology of the Solar System **Obv:** Queen's portrait **Rev:** Atlas carrying the earth

Date	Mintage	F	VF	XF	Unc	BU
2001 Proof	10,000	Value: 47.50				

KM# 934a.1 CROWN

28.2800 g., 0.9250 Silver .8410 oz. ASW **Series:** Mythology of the Solar System **Rev:** Similar but with a fancy diamond set in the earth

Date	Mintage	F	VF	XF	Unc	BU
2001 In Proof sets only	2,001	Value: 87.50				

KM# 936 CROWN

Copper-Nickel **Series:** Mythology of the Solar System **Obv:** Queen's portrait **Rev:** Seated Neptune with trident and ringed planet

Date	Mintage	F	VF	XF	Unc	BU
2001	—	—	—	—	10.00	12.00

KM# 936a CROWN

28.2800 g., 0.9250 Silver .8410 oz. ASW **Series:** Mythology of the Solar System **Obv:** Queen's portrait **Rev:** Seated Neptune with trident and ringed planet

Date	Mintage	F	VF	XF	Unc	BU
2001 Proof	10,000	Value: 47.50				

KM# 938 CROWN

Copper-Nickel **Series:** Mythology of the Solar System **Obv:** Queen's portrait **Rev:** Seated Jupiter with lightening bolts and a planet

Date	Mintage	F	VF	XF	Unc	BU
2001	—	—	—	—	10.00	12.00

KM# 938a CROWN

28.2800 g., 0.9250 Silver .8410 oz. ASW **Series:** Mythology of the Solar System **Obv:** Queen's portrait **Rev:** Seated Jupiter with lightening bolts and a planet

Date	Mintage	F	VF	XF	Unc	BU
2001 Proof	10,000	Value: 47.50				

KM# 940 CROWN

Copper-Nickel **Series:** Mythology of the Solar System **Subject:** Mars **Obv:** Queen's portrait **Rev:** Standing Roman soldier and a planet

Date	Mintage	F	VF	XF	Unc	BU
2001	—	—	—	—	10.00	12.00

KM# 940a CROWN

28.2800 g., 0.9250 Silver .8410 oz. ASW **Series:** Mythology of the Solar System **Subject:** Mars **Obv:** Queen's portrait **Rev:** Standing Roman soldier and a planet

Date	Mintage	F	VF	XF	Unc	BU
2001 Proof	10,000	Value: 47.50				

KM# 942 CROWN

Copper-Nickel **Series:** Mythology of the Solar System **Obv:** Queen's portrait **Rev:** Seated Mercury with caduceus and a planet

Date	Mintage	F	VF	XF	Unc	BU
2001	—	—	—	—	10.00	12.00

KM# 942a CROWN

28.2800 g., 0.9250 Silver .8410 oz. ASW **Series:** Mythology of the Solar System **Obv:** Queen's portrait **Rev:** Seated Mercury with caduceus and a planet

Date	Mintage	F	VF	XF	Unc	BU
2001 Proof	10,000	Value: 47.50				

KM# 944 CROWN

Copper-Nickel **Series:** Mythology of the Solar System **Obv:** Queen's portrait **Rev:** Seated Uranus with scepter

Date	Mintage	F	VF	XF	Unc	BU
2001	—	—	—	—	10.00	12.00

KM# 944a CROWN

28.2800 g., 0.9250 Silver .8410 oz. ASW **Series:** Mythology of the Solar System **Obv:** Queen's portrait **Rev:** Seated Uranus with scepter

Date	Mintage	F	VF	XF	Unc	BU
2001 Proof	10,000	Value: 47.50				

KM# 946 CROWN

Copper-Nickel **Series:** Mythology of the Solar System **Obv:** Queen's portrait **Rev:** Seated Saturn with long handled sickle and a ringed planet

Date	Mintage	F	VF	XF	Unc	BU
2001	—	—	—	—	10.00	12.00

KM# 946a CROWN

28.2800 g., 0.9250 Silver .8410 oz. ASW **Series:** Mythology of the Solar System **Obv:** Queen's portrait **Rev:** Seated Saturn with long handled sickle and a ringed planet

Date	Mintage	F	VF	XF	Unc	BU
2001 Proof	10,000	Value: 47.50				

KM# 948 CROWN

Copper-Nickel **Series:** Mythology of the Solar System **Obv:** Queen's portrait **Rev:** Seated Pluto with dogs and planet

Date	Mintage	F	VF	XF	Unc	BU
2001	—	—	—	—	10.00	12.00

KM# 948a CROWN

28.2800 g., 0.9250 Silver .8410 oz. ASW **Series:** Mythology of the Solar System **Obv:** Queen's portrait **Rev:** Seated Pluto with dogs and planet

Date	Mintage	F	VF	XF	Unc	BU
2001 Proof	10,000	Value: 47.50				

KM# 950 CROWN

Copper-Nickel **Series:** Mythology of the Solar System **Obv:** Queen's portrait **Rev:** Venus seated on a half shell

Date	Mintage	F	VF	XF	Unc	BU
2001	—	—	—	—	10.00	12.00

KM# 950a CROWN

28.2800 g., 0.9250 Silver .8410 oz. ASW **Series:** Mythology of the Solar System **Obv:** Queen's portrait **Rev:** Venus seated on a half shell

Date	Mintage	F	VF	XF	Unc	BU
2001 Proof	10,000	Value: 47.50				

KM# 952 CROWN

28.2800 g., Copper-Nickel, 38.6 mm. **Subject:** Queen's 75th Birthday **Obv:** Queen's portrait **Rev:** Queen in Order of Garter robes **Edge:** Reeded

Date	Mintage	F	VF	XF	Unc	BU
2001	—	—	—	—	10.00	12.00

KM# 952a CROWN

28.2800 g., 0.9250 Silver .8410 oz. ASW, 38.6 mm. **Subject:** Queen's 75th Birthday **Obv:** Queen's portrait **Rev:** Queen in Order of Garter robes **Edge:** Reeded

Date	Mintage	F	VF	XF	Unc	BU
2001 Proof	10,000	Value: 47.50				

KM# 955 CROWN

28.2800 g., Copper-Nickel, 38.6 mm. **Series:** Victorian Age Part II **Obv:** Queen's portrait **Rev:** Victoria learning of her accession **Edge:** Reeded

Date	Mintage	F	VF	XF	Unc	BU
2001	—	—	—	—	10.00	12.00

KM# 955a CROWN

28.2800 g., 0.9250 Silver .8410 oz. ASW, 38.6 mm. **Series:** Victorian Age Part II **Obv:** Queen's portrait **Rev:** Victoria learning of her accession **Edge:** Reeded

Date	Mintage	F	VF	XF	Unc	BU
2001 Proof	10,000	Value: 47.50				

KM# 957 CROWN

Copper-Nickel, 38.6 mm. **Series:** Victorian Age Part II **Subject:** Royal Family **Rev:** Victoria and Albert seated with children **Edge:** Reeded

Date	Mintage	F	VF	XF	Unc	BU
2001	—	—	—	—	10.00	12.00

KM# 957a CROWN

28.2800 g., 0.9250 Silver .8410 oz. ASW, 38.6 mm. **Series:** Victorian Age Part II **Subject:** Royal Family **Rev:** Victoria and Albert seated with children **Edge:** Reeded

Date	Mintage	F	VF	XF	Unc	BU
2001 Proof	10,000	Value: 47.50				

KM# 959 CROWN

Copper-Nickel, 38.6 mm. **Series:** Victorian Age Part II **Subject:** Victoria in Scotland **Rev:** Victoria on horse with servant **Edge:** Reeded

Date	Mintage	F	VF	XF	Unc	BU
2001	2,001	—	—	—	10.00	12.00

KM# 959a CROWN

28.2800 g., 0.9250 Silver .8410 oz. ASW, 38.6 mm. **Series:** Victorian Age Part II **Subject:** Victoria in Scotland **Rev:** Victoria on horse with servant **Edge:** Reeded

Date	Mintage	F	VF	XF	Unc	BU
2001 Proof	10,000	Value: 47.50				

KM# 961 CROWN

Copper-Nickel, 38.6 mm. **Series:** Victorian Age Part II **Subject:** Gladstone and Disraeli **Rev:** Portraits of both politicians **Edge:** Reeded

Date	Mintage	F	VF	XF	Unc	BU
2001	—	—	—	—	10.00	12.00

KM# 961a CROWN

28.2800 g., 0.9250 Silver .8410 oz. ASW, 38.6 mm. **Series:** Victorian Age Part II **Subject:** Gladstone and Disraeli **Rev:** Portraits of both politicians **Edge:** Reeded

Date	Mintage	F	VF	XF	Unc	BU
2001 Proof	10,000	Value: 47.50				

KM# 963 CROWN

Copper-Nickel, 38.6 mm. **Series:** Victorian Age Part II **Rev:** Florence Nightingale holding lantern **Edge:** Reeded

Date	Mintage	F	VF	XF	Unc	BU
2001	—	—	—	—	10.00	12.00

KM# 963a CROWN

28.2800 g., 0.9250 Silver .8410 oz. ASW, 38.6 mm. **Series:** Victorian Age Part II **Rev:** Florence Nightingale holding lantern **Edge:** Reeded

Date	Mintage	F	VF	XF	Unc	BU
2001 Proof	10,000	Value: 47.50				

KM# 965 CROWN

Copper-Nickel, 38.6 mm. **Series:** Victorian Age Part II **Rev:** Lord Tennyson with the Light Brigade in background **Edge:** Reeded

Date	Mintage	F	VF	XF	Unc	BU
2001	—	—	—	—	10.00	12.00

KM# 965a CROWN

28.2800 g., 0.9250 Silver .8410 oz. ASW, 38.6 mm. **Series:** Victorian Age Part II **Rev:** Lord Tennyson with the Light Brigade in background **Edge:** Reeded

Date	Mintage	F	VF	XF	Unc	BU
2001 Proof	10,000	Value: 47.50				

KM# 967 CROWN

Copper-Nickel, 38.6 mm. **Series:** Victorian Age Part II **Rev:** Stanley meeting Dr. Livingstone **Edge:** Reeded

Date	Mintage	F	VF	XF	Unc	BU
2001	—	—	—	—	10.00	12.00

KM# 967a CROWN

28.2800 g., 0.9250 Silver .8410 oz. ASW, 38.6 mm. **Series:** Victorian Age Part II **Rev:** Stanley meeting Dr. Livingstone **Edge:** Reeded

Date	Mintage	F	VF	XF	Unc	BU
2001 Proof	10,000	Value: 47.50				

KM# 969 CROWN

Copper-Nickel, 38.6 mm. **Series:** Victorian Age Part II **Rev:** Bronte sisters **Edge:** Reeded

Date	Mintage	F	VF	XF	Unc	BU
2001	—	—	—	—	10.00	12.00

KM# 969a CROWN

28.2800 g., 0.9250 Silver .8410 oz. ASW, 38.6 mm. **Series:** Victorian Age Part II **Rev:** Bronte sisters **Edge:** Reeded

Date	Mintage	F	VF	XF	Unc	BU
2001 Proof	10,000	Value: 47.50				

KM# 979 CROWN

28.2800 g., Copper-Nickel, 38.6 mm. **Subject:** Queen Mother's Life **Obv:** Bust of Queen Elizabeth II right **Rev:** Christening of Prince William **Edge:** Reeded

Date	Mintage	F	VF	XF	Unc	BU
2002	—	—	—	—	10.00	12.00

KM# 979a CROWN

28.2800 g., 0.9250 Silver 0.841 oz. ASW, 38.6 mm. **Subject:** Queen Mother's Life **Obv:** Bust of Queen Elizabeth II right **Rev:** Prince William's christening scene **Edge:** Reeded

Date	Mintage	F	VF	XF	Unc	BU
2002 Proof	10,000	Value: 47.50				

KM# 981 CROWN

28.2800 g., Copper-Nickel, 38.6 mm. **Subject:** World Cup Soccer **Obv:** Bust of Queen Elizabeth II right **Rev:** Two players about to collide **Edge:** Reeded

Date	Mintage	F	VF	XF	Unc	BU
2002	—	—	—	—	10.00	11.50

KM# 981a CROWN

28.2800 g., 0.9250 Silver 0.841 oz. ASW, 38.6 mm. **Subject:** World Cup Soccer **Obv:** Bust of Queen Elizabeth II right **Rev:** Two players about to collide **Edge:** Reeded

Date	Mintage	F	VF	XF	Unc	BU
2002 Proof	10,000	Value: 47.50				

KM# 983 CROWN

28.2800 g., Copper-Nickel, 38.6 mm. **Subject:** World Cup Soccer **Obv:** Bust of Queen Elizabeth II right **Rev:** Two players facing viewer **Edge:** Reeded

Date	Mintage	F	VF	XF	Unc	BU
2002	—	—	—	—	10.00	11.50

KM# 983a CROWN

28.2800 g., 0.9250 Silver 0.841 oz. ASW, 38.6 mm. **Subject:** World Cup Soccer **Obv:** Bust of Queen Elizabeth II right **Rev:** Two players facing viewer **Edge:** Reeded

Date	Mintage	F	VF	XF	Unc	BU
2002 Proof	10,000	Value: 47.50				

KM# 985 CROWN

28.2800 g., Copper-Nickel, 38.6 mm. **Subject:** World Cup Soccer **Obv:** Bust of Queen Elizabeth II right **Rev:** Two horizontal players **Edge:** Reeded

Date	Mintage	F	VF	XF	Unc	BU
2002	—	—	—	—	10.00	11.50

KM# 985a CROWN

28.2800 g., 0.9250 Silver 0.841 oz. ASW, 38.6 mm. **Subject:** World Cup Soccer **Obv:** Bust of Queen Elizabeth II right **Rev:** Two horizontal players **Edge:** Reeded

Date	Mintage	F	VF	XF	Unc	BU
2002 Proof	10,000	Value: 47.50				

KM# 987 CROWN

28.2800 g., Copper-Nickel, 38.6 mm. **Subject:** World Cup Soccer **Obv:** Bust of Queen Elizabeth II right **Rev:** Two players moving to left **Edge:** Reeded

Date	Mintage	F	VF	XF	Unc	BU
2002	—	—	—	—	10.00	11.50

KM# 987a CROWN

28.2800 g., 0.9250 Silver 0.841 oz. ASW, 38.6 mm. **Subject:** World Cup Soccer **Obv:** Bust of Queen Elizabeth II right **Rev:** Two players moving to left **Edge:** Reeded

Date	Mintage	F	VF	XF	Unc	BU
2002 Proof	10,000	Value: 47.50				

KM# 992 CROWN

28.2800 g., Copper-Nickel, 38.6 mm. **Subject:** Peter Rabbit Centennial **Obv:** Bust of Queen Elizabeth II right. **Rev:** Peter Rabbit **Edge:** Reeded

Date	Mintage	F	VF	XF	Unc	BU
2002	—	—	—	—	10.00	12.00

KM# 992a CROWN

28.2800 g., 0.9250 Silver 0.841 oz. ASW, 38.6 mm. **Subject:** Peter Rabbit Centennial **Obv:** Bust of Queen Elizabeth II right **Rev:** Peter Rabbit **Edge:** Reeded

Date	Mintage	F	VF	XF	Unc	BU
2002 Proof	10,000	Value: 47.50				

KM# 994 CROWN

28.2800 g., Copper-Nickel, 38.6 mm. **Subject:** Queen's Golden Jubilee **Obv:** Bust of Queen Elizabeth II right **Rev:** Royal couple and tree house **Edge:** Reeded

Date	Mintage	F	VF	XF	Unc	BU
2002	—	—	—	—	10.00	12.00

KM# 994a CROWN

Yellow Brass **Subject:** Queen's Golden Jubilee **Obv:** Bust of Queen Elizabeth II right **Rev:** Royal couple and tree house **Edge:** Reeded

Date	Mintage	F	VF	XF	Unc	BU
2002 Proof	15,000	Value: 20.00				

KM# 994b CROWN

28.2800 g., 0.9250 Gold Clad Silver 0.841 oz., 38.6 mm. **Subject:** Queen's Golden Jubilee **Obv:** Bust of Queen Elizabeth II right **Rev:** Royal couple and tree house **Edge:** Reeded

Date	Mintage	F	VF	XF	Unc	BU
2002 Proof	10,000	Value: 50.00				

KM# 996 CROWN

28.2800 g., Copper-Nickel, 38.6 mm. **Subject:** Queen's Golden Jubilee **Obv:** Bust of Queen Elizabeth II right **Rev:** Royal coach **Edge:** Reeded

Date	Mintage	F	VF	XF	Unc	BU
2002	—	—	—	—	10.00	12.00

KM# 996a CROWN

Yellow Brass **Subject:** Queen's Golden Jubilee **Obv:** Bust of Queen Elizabeth II right **Rev:** Royal coach **Edge:** Reeded

Date	Mintage	F	VF	XF	Unc	BU
2002 Proof	15,000	Value: 20.00				

KM# 996b CROWN

28.2800 g., 0.9250 Gold Clad Silver 0.841 oz., 38.6 mm. **Subject:** Queen's Golden Jubilee **Obv:** Bust of Queen Elizabeth II right **Rev:** Royal coach **Edge:** Reeded

Date	Mintage	F	VF	XF	Unc	BU
2002 Proof	10,000	Value: 50.00				

KM# 998 CROWN

28.2800 g., Copper-Nickel, 38.6 mm. **Subject:** Queen's Golden Jubilee **Obv:** Bust of Queen Elizabeth II right **Rev:** Royal couple with baby **Edge:** Reeded

Date	Mintage	F	VF	XF	Unc	BU
2002	—	—	—	—	10.00	12.00

KM# 998a CROWN

Yellow Brass **Subject:** Queen's Golden Jubilee **Obv:** Bust of Queen Elizabeth II right **Rev:** Royal couple with baby **Edge:** Reeded

Date	Mintage	F	VF	XF	Unc	BU
2002 Proof	15,000	Value: 20.00				

KM# 998b CROWN

28.2800 g., 0.9250 Gold Clad Silver 0.841 oz., 38.6 mm. **Subject:** Queen's Golden Jubilee **Obv:** Bust of Queen Elizabeth II right **Rev:** Royal couple with baby **Edge:** Reeded

Date	Mintage	F	VF	XF	Unc	BU
2002 Proof	1,000	Value: 50.00				

KM# 1000 CROWN

28.2800 g., Copper-Nickel, 38.6 mm. **Subject:** Queen's Golden Jubilee **Obv:** Bust of Queen Elizabeth II right **Rev:** Royal yacht under Tower bridge **Edge:** Reeded

Date	Mintage	F	VF	XF	Unc	BU
2002	—	—	—	—	10.00	12.00

KM# 1000a CROWN

Yellow Brass **Subject:** Queen's Golden Jubilee **Obv:** Bust of Queen Elizabeth II right **Rev:** Royal yacht under Tower bridge **Edge:** Reeded

Date	Mintage	F	VF	XF	Unc	BU
2002 Proof	15,000	Value: 20.00				

KM# 1000b CROWN

28.2800 g., 0.9250 Gold Clad Silver 0.841 oz., 38.6 mm. **Subject:** Queen's Golden Jubilee **Obv:** Bust of Queen Elizabeth II right **Rev:** Royal yacht under Tower bridge **Edge:** Reeded

Date	Mintage	F	VF	XF	Unc	BU
2002 Proof	10,000	Value: 50.00				

KM# 1013 CROWN

28.2800 g., Blackened Copper-Nickel, 38.6 mm. **Subject:** Queen Mother **Obv:** Bust of Queen Elizabeth II right **Rev:** Queen Mother trout fishing **Edge:** Reeded

Date	Mintage	F	VF	XF	Unc	BU
2002	—	—	—	—	10.00	12.00

KM# 1013a CROWN

28.2800 g., 0.9250 Silver 0.841 oz. ASW, 38.6 mm. **Subject:** Queen Mother **Obv:** Bust of Queen Elizabeth II right **Rev:** Queen Mother trout fishing **Edge:** Reeded **Note:** Obv. and rev. have blackened legends.

Date	Mintage	F	VF	XF	Unc	BU
2002 Proof	5,000	Value: 175				

KM# 1015 CROWN

28.2800 g., Copper-Nickel, 38.6 mm. **Subject:** Princess Diana **Obv:** Bust of Queen Elizabeth II right **Rev:** Diana's portrait **Edge:** Reeded

Date	Mintage	F	VF	XF	Unc	BU
2002	—	—	—	—	10.00	12.00

KM# 1015a CROWN

28.2800 g., 0.9250 Silver 0.841 oz. ASW, 38.6 mm. **Subject:** Princess Diana **Obv:** Bust of Queen Elizabeth II right **Rev:** Diana's portrait **Edge:** Reeded

Date	Mintage	F	VF	XF	Unc	BU
2002 Proof	10,000	Value: 47.50				

KM# 1019 CROWN

28.2800 g., Copper-Nickel, 38.6 mm. **Subject:** Peter Pan **Obv:** Bust of Queen Elizabeth II right. **Rev:** Peter Pan and Tinkerbell flying above city **Edge:** Reeded

Date	Mintage	F	VF	XF	Unc	BU
2002	—	—	—	—	10.00	12.00

KM# 1019a CROWN

28.2800 g., 0.9250 Silver 0.841 oz. ASW, 38.6 mm. **Subject:** Peter Pan **Obv:** Bust of Queen Elizabeth II right **Rev:** Peter Pan and Tinkerbell flying above city **Edge:** Reeded

Date	Mintage	F	VF	XF	Unc	BU
2002 Proof	10,000	Value: 47.50				

KM# 1021 CROWN

28.2800 g., Copper-Nickel, 38.6 mm. **Subject:** Grand Masonic Lodge **Obv:** Bust of Queen Elizabeth II right **Rev:** Masonic seal above Gibraltar **Edge:** Reeded

Date	Mintage	F	VF	XF	Unc	BU
2002 Proof	5,000	Value: 10.00				

KM# 1021a CROWN

28.2800 g., 0.9250 Silver 0.841 oz. ASW, 38.6 mm. **Subject:** Grand Masonic Lodge **Obv:** Bust of Queen Elizabeth II right **Rev:** Masonic seal above Gibraltar **Edge:** Reeded

Date	Mintage	F	VF	XF	Unc	BU
2002 Proof	10,000	Value: 47.50				

KM# 1025 CROWN

28.2800 g., Copper Nickel, 38.6 mm. **Subject:** Calpe Conference **Obv:** Queen's portrait **Rev:** Crossed flags and arms **Edge:** Reeded

Date	Mintage	F	VF	XF	Unc	BU
2002PM	—	—	—	—	10.00	12.00

KM# 1025a CROWN

28.2800 g., 0.9250 Silver 0.841 oz. ASW, 38.6 mm. **Subject:** Calpe Conference **Obv:** Queen's portrait **Rev:** Crossed flags and arms **Edge:** Reeded

Date	Mintage	F	VF	XF	Unc	BU
2002PM Proof	10,000	Value: 47.50				

KM# 1035 CROWN

28.2800 g., Copper-Nickel, 38.6 mm. **Subject:** 1700th Anniversary - Death of St. George **Obv:** Queen's portrait **Rev:** St. George and the dragon **Edge:** Reeded

Date	Mintage	F	VF	XF	Unc	BU
2003	—	—	—	—	9.00	10.00

KM# 1035a CROWN

28.2800 g., 0.9250 Silver 0.841 oz. ASW, 38.6 mm. **Subject:** 1700th Anniversary - Death of St. George **Obv:** Queen's portrait **Rev:** St. George and the dragon **Edge:** Reeded

Date	Mintage	F	VF	XF	Unc	BU
2003 Proof	10,000	Value: 47.50				

KM# 1039 CROWN

28.3000 g., Copper-Nickel, 38.6 mm. **Subject:** Peter Rabbit **Obv:** Queen's portrait **Rev:** Peter Rabbit holding carrot **Edge:** Reeded

Date	Mintage	F	VF	XF	Unc	BU
2003PM	—	—	—	—	9.00	10.00

KM# 1040 CROWN

28.2800 g., Copper-Nickel, 38.6 mm. **Subject:** Centennial of Powered Flight **Obv:** Queen Elizabeth II **Rev:** Stealth bomber within circles of WWI and WWII planes **Edge:** Reeded

Date	Mintage	F	VF	XF	Unc	BU
2003PM	—	—	—	—	10.00	12.00

KM# 1040a CROWN

31.1000 g., Tri-Metallic .9995 Platinum 5.2g center in .9999 Gold 14.2 g ring within .999 Silver 11.7 g outer ring, 38.6 mm. **Subject:** Centennial of Powered Flight **Obv:** Queen Elizabeth II **Rev:** Stealth bomber within circles of WWI and WWII planes **Edge:** Reeded

Date	Mintage	F	VF	XF	Unc	BU
2003PM Proof	999	Value: 600				

KM# 1041 CROWN

28.2800 g., Copper-Nickel, 38.6 mm. **Subject:** 50th Anniversary of Coronation **Obv:** Queen Elizabeth II **Rev:** Buckingham Palace **Edge:** Reeded

Date	Mintage	F	VF	XF	Unc	BU
2003PM	—	—	—	—	10.00	12.00

KM# 1034 2 CROWN

41.5000 g., Bi-Metallic .999 Silver 11.5g. star shaped center in Copper outer ring, 50 mm. **Subject:** Euro's First Anniversary **Obv:** Queen's portrait **Rev:** Europa riding a bull **Edge:** Reeded

Date	Mintage	F	VF	XF	Unc	BU
2003PM Proof	3,500	Value: 100				

KM# 1034a 2 CROWN

50.0000 g., Bi-Metallic .9999 Gold 20g star shaped center in Copper outer ring, 50 mm. **Subject:** 1st Anniversary - Euro **Obv:** Queen's portrait **Rev:** Europa riding the bull **Edge:** Reeded

Date	Mintage	F	VF	XF	Unc	BU
2003PM Proof	2,003	Value: 775				

KM# 1034b 2 CROWN

56.3000 g., Bi-Metallic .9999 Gold 20.8g star shaped center in a .999 Silver 35.5g outer ring, 50 mm. **Subject:** 1st Anniversary - Euro **Obv:** Queen's portrait **Rev:** Europa riding the bull **Edge:** Reeded

Date	Mintage	F	VF	XF	Unc	BU
2003PM Proof	2,003	Value: 800				

KM# 907 5 CROWN

Tri-Metallic Center .9995 Platinum 26.9g. Inner Ring .9999 Gold 73.41g. Outer Ring .999 Silver 55.19g, 50 mm. **Subject:** 21st Century **Obv:** Like Crown KM#906 **Rev:** Like Crown KM#906 **Edge:** Reeded

Date	Mintage	F	VF	XF	Unc	BU
2001 Proof	199	Value: 2,500				

KM# 1042 5 CROWN

155.5500 g., 0.9990 Silver 4.996 oz. ASW, 65 mm. **Subject:** 50th Anniversary of Coronation **Obv:** Queen Elizabeth II **Rev:** Buckingham Palace with tiny .01ct ruby, diamond and sapphire inserts above the main entrance **Edge:** Reeded

Date	Mintage	F	VF	XF	Unc	BU
2003PM Proof	2,003	Value: 175				

KM# 1045 32 CROWNS

1000.0000 g., 0.9990 Silver 32.1186 oz. ASW **Subject:** Beatrix Potter's Peter Rabbit **Obv:** Bust of Queen Elizabeth II right **Obv. Designer:** Ian Rank-Broadley **Rev:** Multicolor Peter Rabbit holding carrot, with blue coat and red slippers

Date	Mintage	F	VF	XF	Unc	BU
2003 Proof	1,000	Value: 750				

KM# 869 POUND

Nickel-Brass **Obv:** Portrait of Queen Elizabeth II **Obv. Designer:** Rank-Broadley **Rev:** Gibraltar castle and key

Date	Mintage	F	VF	XF	Unc	BU
2001 AA	—	—	—	—	3.50	4.50
2001PM AB	—	—	—	—	3.50	4.50

KM# 1036 POUND

9.5000 g., Nickel-Brass, 22 mm. **Subject:** 1700th Anniversary - Death of St. George **Obv:** Queen's portrait **Rev:** St. George and the dragon **Edge:** Reeded

Date	Mintage	F	VF	XF	Unc	BU
2003	—	—	—	—	9.00	10.00

KM# 970 2 POUNDS

Bi-Metallic Steel Copper-Nickel center in Brass ring, 28.4 mm. **Subject:** Bicentennial of the Union Jack **Obv:** Queen's portrait **Rev:** Standing Britannia wearing flag as a cape **Edge:** Reeded

Date	Mintage	F	VF	XF	Unc	BU
2001	—	—	—	—	10.00	12.00

KM# 970a 2 POUNDS

12.0000 g., 0.9990 Bi-Metallic Silver center in Gold plated Silver ring, 28.4 mm. **Subject:** Bicentennial of the Union Jack **Obv:** Queen's portrait **Rev:** Standing Britannia wearing flag as a cape **Edge:** Reeded

Date	Mintage	F	VF	XF	Unc	BU
2001	7,500	—	—	—	30.00	35.00

KM# 1043 2 POUNDS

12.0600 g., Bi-Metallic Copper-Nickel center in Brass ring, 28.3 mm. **Obv:** Elizabeth II **Rev:** Old cannon **Edge:** Reeded

Date	Mintage	F	VF	XF	Unc	BU
2003PM	—	—	—	—	10.00	12.00

KM# 953 5 POUNDS

20.0000 g., Virenium, 36.1 mm. **Subject:** Gibraltar Chronicle 200 Years **Obv:** Queen's portrait **Rev:** Naval battle scene with newspaper in background **Edge:** Reeded

Date	Mintage	F	VF	XF	Unc	BU
2001	—	—	—	—	15.00	18.00

KM# 953a 5 POUNDS

23.5000 g., 0.9250 Silver .6989 oz. ASW, 36.1 mm. **Subject:** Gibraltar Chronicle 200 Years **Obv:** Queen's portrait **Rev:** Naval battle scene with newspaper in background **Edge:** Reeded

Date	Mintage	F	VF	XF	Unc	BU
2001 Proof	10,000	Value: 50.00				

KM# 953b 5 POUNDS

39.8300 g., 0.9167 Gold 1.1739 oz. AGW, 36.1 mm. **Edge:** Reeded

Date	Mintage	F	VF	XF	Unc	BU
2001 Proof	850	Value: 885				

KM# 1011 5 POUNDS

20.0000 g., Virenium, 36.1 mm. **Subject:** Queen's Golden Jubilee **Obv:** Bust of Queen Elizabeth II right **Rev:** Coronation scene **Edge:** Reeded

Date	Mintage	F	VF	XF	Unc	BU
2002	—	—	—	—	15.00	18.00

KM# 1011a 5 POUNDS

23.5000 g., 0.9250 Silver 0.6989 oz. ASW, 36.1 mm. **Subject:** Queen's Golden Jubilee **Obv:** Bust of Queen Elizabeth II right **Rev:** Coronation scene **Edge:** Reeded

Date	Mintage	F	VF	XF	Unc	BU
2002 Proof	10,000	Value: 50.00				

KM# 1011b 5 POUNDS

39.8300 g., 0.9166 Gold 1.1738 oz. AGW, 36.1 mm. **Subject:** Queen's Golden Jubilee **Obv:** Bust of Queen Elizabeth II right **Rev:** Coronation scene **Edge:** Reeded

Date	Mintage	F	VF	XF	Unc	BU
2002 Proof	850	Value: 885				

SOVEREIGN COINAGE

KM# 1037 1/5 SOVEREIGN

1.2200 g., 0.9999 Gold 0.0392 oz. AGW, 13.92 mm. **Subject:** Death of St. George **Obv:** Queen's portrait **Rev:** St. George and the dragon **Edge:** Reeded

Date	Mintage	F	VF	XF	Unc	BU
2003 Proof	10,000	Value: 50.00				

KM# 1038 SOVEREIGN

6.2200 g., 0.9999 Gold 0.2 oz. AGW, 22 mm. **Subject:** Death of St. George **Obv:** Queen's portrait **Rev:** St. George and the dragon **Edge:** Reeded

Date	Mintage	F	VF	XF	Unc	BU
2003 Proof	5,000	Value: 185				

ROYAL COINAGE

KM# 896 1/25 ROYAL

1.2441 g., 0.9999 Gold .0400 oz. AGW, 13.92 mm. **Subject:** Bullion **Obv:** Queen's portrait **Rev:** Two cherubs **Edge:** Reeded

Date	Mintage	F	VF	XF	Unc	BU
2001	—	—	—	—	35.00	—
2001 In Proof sets only	1,000	Value: 50.00				

KM# 972 1/25 ROYAL

1.2440 g., 0.9990 Gold 0.04 oz. AGW, 13.92 mm. **Subject:** Cherubs **Obv:** Queen Elizabeth II's bust right **Rev:** Two cherubs shooting arrrows **Edge:** Reeded

Date	Mintage	F	VF	XF	Unc	BU
2002	—	—	—	—	35.00	—
2002 Proof	1,000	Value: 50.00				

KM# 1027 1/25 ROYAL

1.2440 g., 0.9999 Gold 0.04 oz. AGW, 13.92 mm. **Obv:** Queen's portrait **Rev:** Cherub with crossed arms **Edge:** Reeded

Date	Mintage	F	VF	XF	Unc	BU
2003PM	—	—	—	—	35.00	—
2003PM Proof	—	Value: 50.00				

KM# 897 1/10 ROYAL
3.1100 g., 0.9999 Gold .1000 oz. AGW, 18 mm. **Subject:** Bullion **Obv:** Queen's portrait **Rev:** Two cherubs **Edge:** Reeded

Date	Mintage	F	VF	XF	Unc	BU
2001	—	—	—	—	75.00	—
2001 Proof	1,000	Value: 100				

KM# 973 1/10 ROYAL
3.1100 g., 0.9990 Gold 0.0999 oz. AGW, 17.95 mm. **Subject:** Cherubs **Obv:** Queen Elizabeth II's bust right **Rev:** Two cherubs shooting arrows **Edge:** Reeded

Date	Mintage	F	VF	XF	Unc	BU
2002	—	—	—	—	75.00	—
2002 Proof	1,000	Value: 100				

KM# 1028 1/10 ROYAL
3.1100 g., 0.9999 Gold 0.1 oz. AGW, 17.95 mm. **Obv:** Queen's portrait **Rev:** Cherub with crossed arms **Edge:** Reeded

Date	Mintage	F	VF	XF	Unc	BU
2003PM	—	—	—	—	75.00	—
2003PM Proof	—	Value: 100				

KM# 898 1/5 ROYAL
6.2200 g., 0.9990 Gold .2000 oz. AGW, 22 mm. **Subject:** Bullion **Obv:** Queen's portrait **Rev:** Two cherubs **Edge:** Reeded

Date	Mintage	F	VF	XF	Unc	BU
2001	—	—	—	—	145	—
2001 Proof	1,000	Value: 185				

KM# 974 1/5 ROYAL
6.2200 g., 0.9990 Gold 0.1998 oz. AGW, 22 mm. **Obv:** Queen Elizabeth II's bust right **Rev:** Two cherubs shooting arrows **Edge:** Reeded

Date	Mintage	F	VF	XF	Unc	BU
2002	—	—	—	—	145	—
2002 Proof	1,000	Value: 185				

KM# 1029 1/5 ROYAL
6.2200 g., 0.9999 Gold 0.2 oz. AGW, 22 mm. **Obv:** Queen's portrait **Rev:** Cherub with crossed arms **Edge:** Reeded

Date	Mintage	F	VF	XF	Unc	BU
2003PM	—	—	—	—	145	—
2003PM Proof	—	Value: 215				

KM# 899 1/2 ROYAL
15.5517 g., 0.9999 Gold .5000 oz. AGW, 30 mm. **Subject:** Bullion **Obv:** Queen's portrait **Rev:** Two cherubs **Edge:** Reeded

Date	Mintage	F	VF	XF	Unc	BU
2001	—	—	—	—	335	—
2001 Proof	1,000	Value: 375				

KM# 975 1/2 ROYAL
15.5510 g., 0.9990 Gold 0.4995 oz. AGW, 30 mm. **Obv:** Queen Elizabeth II's bust right **Rev:** Two cherubs shooting arrows **Edge:** Reeded

Date	Mintage	F	VF	XF	Unc	BU
2002	—	—	—	—	335	—
2002 Proof	1,000	Value: 375				

KM# 1030 1/2 ROYAL
15.5510 g., 0.9999 Gold 0.4999 oz. AGW, 30 mm. **Obv:** Queen's portrait **Rev:** Cherub with crossed arms **Edge:** Reeded

Date	Mintage	F	VF	XF	Unc	BU
2003PM	—	—	—	—	335	—
2003PM Proof	—	Value: 400				

KM# 900 ROYAL
28.2800 g., Copper-Nickel, 38.6 mm. **Obv:** Queen's portrait **Rev:** Two cherubs **Edge:** Reeded

Date	Mintage	F	VF	XF	Unc	BU
2001	—	—	—	—	10.00	12.00

KM# 900a ROYAL
31.1035 g., 0.9990 Silver 1.0000 oz. ASW

Date	Mintage	F	VF	XF	Unc	BU
2001 Proof	10,000	Value: 47.50				

KM# 901 ROYAL
31.1035 g., 0.9999 Gold 1.0000 oz. AGW, 32.7 mm. **Subject:** Bullion **Obv:** Queen's portrait **Rev:** Two cherubs **Edge:** Reeded

Date	Mintage	F	VF	XF	Unc	BU
2001	—	—	—	—	650	675
2001 In Proof sets only	1,000	Value: 725				

KM# 976 ROYAL
28.2800 g., Copper-Nickel, 38.6 mm. **Obv:** Queen Elizabeth II's bust right **Rev:** Two cherubs shooting arrows **Edge:** Reeded

Date	Mintage	F	VF	XF	Unc	BU
2002	—	—	—	—	10.00	12.00

KM# 976a ROYAL
31.1035 g., 0.9990 Silver 0.999 oz. ASW **Obv:** Bust of Queen Elizabeth II right **Rev:** Two cherubs shooting arrows **Edge:** Reeded

Date	Mintage	F	VF	XF	Unc	BU
2002 Proof	1,000	Value: 47.50				

KM# 977 ROYAL
31.1035 g., 0.9990 Gold 0.999 oz. AGW, 32.7 mm. **Obv:** Queen Elizabeth II's bust right **Rev:** Two cherubs shooting arrows **Edge:** Reeded

Date	Mintage	F	VF	XF	Unc	BU
2002	—	—	—	—	650	675
2002 Proof	1,000	Value: 725				

KM# 1031 ROYAL
28.2800 g., Copper-Nickel, 38.6 mm. **Obv:** Queen's portrait **Rev:** Cherub with crossed arms **Edge:** Reeded

Date	Mintage	F	VF	XF	Unc	BU
2003PM	—	—	—	—	10.00	12.00

KM# 1031a ROYAL
28.2800 g., 0.9990 Silver 0.9083 oz. ASW, 38.6 mm. **Subject:** Cherub **Obv:** Queen's portrait **Rev:** Cherub with crossed arms **Edge:** Reeded

Date	Mintage	F	VF	XF	Unc	BU
2003PM Proof	10,000	Value: 47.50				

KM# 1032 ROYAL
31.1035 g., 0.9999 Gold 0.9999 oz. AGW, 32.7 mm. **Subject:** Cherub **Obv:** Queen's portrait **Rev:** Cherub with crossed arms **Edge:** Reeded

Date	Mintage	F	VF	XF	Unc	BU
2003PM	—	—	—	—	650	675
2003PM Proof	—	Value: 725				

PROOF SETS

KM#	Date	Mintage	Identification	Issue Price	Mkt Val
PS27	2001 (4)	999	KM#665, 668.1, 670.1, 672.1	1,400	—
PS28	2001 (4)	2,001	KM#667, 669a.1, 671a.1, 673a.1	350	—
PS29	2001 (5)	1,000	KM#896-899, 901	—	1,350
PS30	2003 (5)	1,000	KM#1027-30, 1032	—	1,400
PS31	2003 (5)	1,000	KM#1161-1164, 1166	—	1,400

GREAT BRITAIN

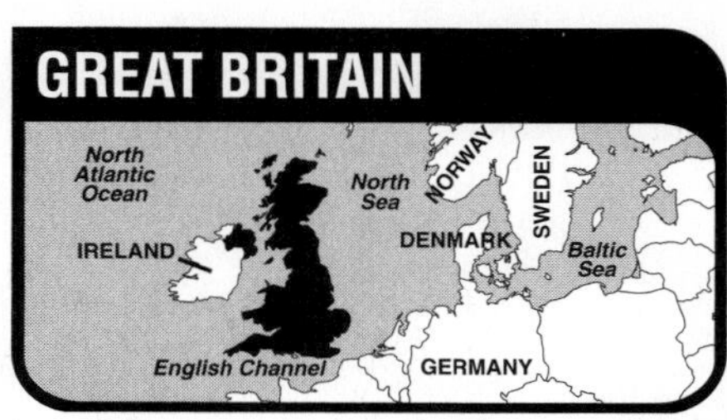

The United Kingdom of Great Britain and Northern Ireland, located off the northwest coast of the European continent, has an area of 94,227sq. mi. (244,820 sq. km.) and a population of 54 million. Capital: London. The economy is based on industrial activity and trading. Machinery, motor vehicles, chemicals, and textile yarns and fabrics are exported.

By the mid-20th century, most of the territories formerly comprising the British Empire had gained independence, and the empire had evolved into the Commonwealth of Nations, an association of equal and autonomous states, which enjoy special trade interests. The Commonwealth is presently composed of 54 member nations, including the United Kingdom. All recognize the British monarch as head of the Commonwealth. Fifteen continue to recognize the British monarch as Head of State. They are: United Kingdom, Antigua and Barbuda, Australia, Bahamas, Barbados, Belize, Canada, Grenada, Jamaica, New Zealand, Papua New Guinea, St. Christopher & Nevis, Saint Lucia, Saint Vincent and the Grenadines, Solomon Islands, and Tuvalu. Elizabeth II is personally, and separately, the Queen of the sovereign, independent countries just mentioned. There is no other British connection between the several individual, national sovereignties, except that High Commissioners represent them each instead of ambassadors in each other's countries.

RULERS
Elizabeth II, 1952--

MINT MARKS
H - Heaton
KN - King's Norton

KINGDOM

POUND COINAGE

KM# 898 PENNY
0.4713 g., 0.9250 Silver .0140 oz. ASW **Ruler:** Elizabeth II **Obv. Designer:** Mary Gillick

Date	Mintage	F	VF	XF	Unc	BU
2001 Prooflike	1,132	—	—	—	50.00	—
2002 Prooflike	1,681	—	—	—	50.00	—
2003 Prooflike	1,601	—	—	—	55.00	—
2004 Prooflike	1,611	—	—	—	55.00	—
2005 Prooflike	—	—	—	—	55.00	—
2006 Prooflike	—	—	—	—	55.00	—

KM# 899 2 PENCE
0.9426 g., 0.9250 Silver .0280 oz. ASW **Ruler:** Elizabeth II **Obv:** Legend without BRITT OMN **Obv. Designer:** Mary Gillick

Date	Mintage	F	VF	XF	Unc	BU
2001 Prooflike	1,132	—	—	—	60.00	—
2002 Prooflike	1,681	—	—	—	60.00	—
2003 Prooflike	1,601	—	—	—	65.00	—
2004 Prooflike	1,611	—	—	—	65.00	—
2005 Prooflike	—	—	—	—	65.00	—
2006 Prooflike	—	—	—	—	65.00	—

KM# 901 3 PENCE
1.4138 g., 0.9250 Silver .0420 oz. ASW **Ruler:** Elizabeth II **Obv:** Legend without BRITT OMN **Obv. Designer:** Mary Gillick

Date	Mintage	F	VF	XF	Unc	BU
2001 Prooflike	1,132	—	—	—	60.00	—
2002 Prooflike	1,681	—	—	—	60.00	—
2003 Prooflike	1,601	—	—	—	65.00	—
2004 Prooflike	1,611	—	—	—	65.00	—
2006 Prooflike	—	—	—	—	65.00	—

KM# 902 4 PENCE (Groat)

1.8851 g., 0.9250 Silver .0561 oz. ASW **Ruler:** Elizabeth II **Obv:** Legend without BRITT OMN

Date	Mintage	F	VF	XF	Unc	BU
2001 Prooflike	1,132	—	—	—	60.00	—
2002 Prooflike	1,681	—	—	—	60.00	—
2003 Prooflike	1,601	—	—	—	60.00	—
2004 Prooflike	—	—	—	—	65.00	—
2005 Prooflike	—	—	—	—	65.00	—
2006 Prooflike	—	—	—	—	65.00	—

SOVEREIGN COINAGE

KM# 1001 1/2 SOVEREIGN

3.9900 g., 0.9170 Gold .1176 oz. AGW **Ruler:** Elizabeth II **Obv:** Portrait of Queen Elizabeth II **Obv. Designer:** Ian Rank-Broadley **Rev:** St. George slaying the dragon

Date	Mintage	F	VF	XF	Unc	BU
2001	94,736	—	—	—	90.00	—
2001 Proof	10,000	Value: 145				
2002	59,568	—	—	—	90.00	—
2003	47,805	—	—	—	90.00	—
2003 Proof	14,750	Value: 145				
2004	28,821	—	—	—	90.00	—
2006	—	—	—	—	100	—
2006 Proof	8,500	Value: 170				

KM# 1025 1/2 SOVEREIGN

3.9900 g., 0.9167 Gold 0.1176 oz. AGW, 19.3 mm. **Ruler:** Elizabeth II **Subject:** Queen Elizabeth II's Golden Jubilee **Obv:** Queen's head right **Obv. Designer:** Ian Rank-Broadley **Rev:** Crowned arms **Edge:** Reeded

Date	Mintage	F	VF	XF	Unc	BU
2002 Proof	18,000	Value: 145				

KM# 1002 SOVEREIGN

7.9881 g., 0.9170 Gold .2354 oz. AGW **Ruler:** Elizabeth II **Obv:** Portrait of Queen Elizabeth II **Obv. Designer:** Ian Rank-Broadley **Rev:** St. George slaying the dragon

Date	Mintage	F	VF	XF	Unc	BU
2001	49,458	—	—	—	165	—
2001 Proof	15,000	Value: 225				
2002	71,815	—	—	—	165	—
2003	43,208	—	—	—	165	—
2003 Proof	19,750	Value: 225				
2004	28,821	—	—	—	165	—
2006	—	—	—	—	195	—
2006 Proof	16,000	Value: 315				

KM# 1026 SOVEREIGN

7.9800 g., 0.9167 Gold 0.2352 oz. AGW, 22 mm. **Ruler:** Elizabeth II **Subject:** Queen Elizabeth II's Golden Jubilee **Obv:** Queen's head right **Obv. Designer:** Ian Rank-Broadley **Rev:** Crowned arms **Edge:** Reeded

Date	Mintage	F	VF	XF	Unc	BU
2002	71,815	—	—	—	165	—
2002 Proof	20,500	Value: 225				

KM# 1027 2 POUNDS

15.9700 g., 0.9167 Gold 0.4707 oz. AGW, 28.4 mm. **Ruler:** Elizabeth II **Subject:** Queen Elizabeth II's Golden Jubilee **Obv:** Queen's head right **Obv. Designer:** Ian Rank-Broadley **Rev:** Crowned arms **Edge:** Reeded **Note:** In proof sets only.

Date	Mintage	F	VF	XF	Unc	BU
2002	8,000	Value: 435				

KM# 1003 5 POUNDS

39.9400 g., 0.9170 Gold 1.1775 oz. AGW, 36 mm. **Ruler:** Elizabeth II **Obv:** Portrait of Queen Elizabeth II **Obv. Designer:** Ian Rank-Broadley **Rev:** St. George slaying dragon **Edge:** Reeded

Date	Mintage	F	VF	XF	Unc	BU
2001 Proof	1,000	Value: 900				
2003 Proof	2,250	Value: 925				
2004	1,000	—	—	—	1,500	—
2006 Proof	1,750	Value: 1,160				
2006 Proof	1,750	Value: 1,160				

KM# 1028 5 POUNDS

39.9400 g., 0.9167 Gold 1.1771 oz. AGW, 36 mm. **Ruler:** Elizabeth II **Subject:** Queen Elizabeth II's Golden Jubilee **Obv:** Queen's head right **Obv. Designer:** Ian Rank-Broadley **Rev:** Crowned arms **Edge:** Reeded

Date	Mintage	F	VF	XF	Unc	BU
2002	3,000	Value: 875				

KM# 1003 5 POUNDS

39.9400 g., 0.9170 Gold 1.1775 oz. AGW, 36 mm. **Ruler:** Elizabeth II **Obv:** Portrait of Queen Elizabeth II **Obv. Designer:** Ian Rank-Broadley **Rev:** St. George slaying dragon **Edge:** Reeded

Date	Mintage	F	VF	XF	Unc	BU
2001 Proof	1,000	Value: 900				
2003 Proof	2,250	Value: 925				
2004	1,000	—	—	—	1,500	—
2006 Proof	1,750	Value: 1,160				
2006 Proof	1,750	Value: 1,160				

DECIMAL COINAGE

1971-1981, 100 New Pence = 1 Pound; 1982, 100 Pence = 1 Pound

KM# 986a PENNY

Bronze, 20.3 mm. **Ruler:** Elizabeth II **Obv:** Queen Elizabeth II **Rev:** Crowned portcullis **Edge:** Plain **Note:** Issued in sets only

Date	Mintage	F	VF	XF	Unc	BU
2001	—	—	—	—	0.20	—
2001 Proof	100,000	Value: 2.50				
2002 Proof	—	Value: 2.00				
2003 Proof	—	Value: 2.00				
2004 Proof	100,000	Value: 2.00				

KM# 986 PENNY

Copper Plated Steel **Ruler:** Elizabeth II **Obv:** Effigy of Queen Elizabeth II **Obv. Designer:** Ian Rank-Broadley **Rev:** Crowned portcullis **Rev. Designer:** Christopher Ironside

Date	Mintage	F	VF	XF	Unc	BU
2001	928,802,000	—	—	—	0.20	—
2002	601,446,000	—	—	—	0.20	—
2003	539,436,000	—	—	—	0.20	—
2004	530,110,000	—	—	—	0.20	—
2004 Proof	—	Value: 3.25				
2005	—	—	—	—	0.20	—
2005 Proof	—	Value: 3.25				
2006	—	—	—	—	0.20	—
2006 Proof	—	Value: 3.25				

KM# 987a 2 PENCE

Bronze **Ruler:** Elizabeth II **Obv:** Effigy of Queen Elizabeth II **Obv. Designer:** Ian Rank-Broadley **Rev:** Prince of Wales badge **Rev. Designer:** Christopher Ironside

Date	Mintage	F	VF	XF	Unc	BU
2001	—	—	—	—	0.25	—
2001 Proof	Est. 100,000	Value: 2.50				
2002 Proof	—	Value: 2.50				
2003 Proof	—	Value: 2.50				
2004 Proof	100,000	Value: 2.50				

KM# 987 2 PENCE

Copper Plated Steel **Ruler:** Elizabeth II **Obv:** Effigy of Queen Elizabeth II **Obv. Designer:** Ian Rank-Broadley **Rev:** Prince of Wales badge **Rev. Designer:** Christopher Ironside

Date	Mintage	F	VF	XF	Unc	BU
2001	551,886,000	—	—	—	0.25	—
2002	168,556,000	—	—	—	0.25	—
2003	260,225,000	—	—	—	0.25	—
2004	265,571,000	—	—	—	0.25	—
2004 Proof	—	Value: 3.25				
2005	—	—	—	—	0.25	—
2005 Proof	—	Value: 3.25				
2006	—	—	—	—	0.25	—
2006 Proof	—	Value: 3.25				

KM# 988 5 PENCE

Copper-Nickel **Ruler:** Elizabeth II **Obv:** Effigy of Queen Elizabeth II **Obv. Designer:** Ian Rank-Broadley **Rev:** Crowned Scottish thistle

Date	Mintage	F	VF	XF	Unc	BU
2001	320,330,000	—	—	—	0.30	—
2001 Proof	Est. 100,000	Value: 3.00				
2002	219,258,000	—	—	—	0.30	—
2002 Proof	—	Value: 3.00				
2003	333,230,000	—	—	—	0.30	—
2003 Proof	—	Value: 3.00				
2004	222,606,000	—	—	—	0.30	—
2004 Proof	100,000	Value: 3.00				
2005	—	—	—	—	0.30	—
2005 Proof	—	Value: 3.00				
2006	—	—	—	—	0.30	—
2006 Proof	—	Value: 3.00				

KM# 989 10 PENCE

Copper-Nickel **Ruler:** Elizabeth II **Obv:** Effigy of Queen Elizabeth II **Obv. Designer:** Ian Rank-Broadley **Rev:** Crowned lion **Rev. Designer:** Christopher Ironside

Date	Mintage	F	VF	XF	Unc	BU
2001	82,081,000	—	—	—	0.40	—
2001 Proof	Est. 100,000	Value: 3.25				
2002	80,934,000	—	—	—	0.40	—
2002 Proof	—	Value: 3.25				
2003	88,118,000	—	—	—	0.40	—
2003 Proof	—	Value: 3.25				
2004	77,601,000	—	—	—	0.40	—
2004 Proof	100,000	Value: 3.25				
2005	—	—	—	—	0.40	—
2005 Proof	—	Value: 3.25				
2006	—	—	—	—	0.40	—
2006 Proof	—	Value: 3.25				

KM# 990 20 PENCE
Copper-Nickel **Ruler:** Elizabeth II **Obv:** Effigy of Queen Elizabeth II **Obv. Designer:** Ian Rank-Broadley **Rev:** Crowned rose **Rev. Designer:** William Gardner **Shape:** 7-sided

Date	Mintage	F	VF	XF	Unc	BU
2001	148,122,500	—	—	—	0.60	—
2001 Proof	Est. 100,000	Value: 3.25				
2002	93,360,000	—	—	—	0.60	—
2002 Proof	100,000	Value: 3.25				
2003	153,383,750	—	—	—	0.60	—
2003 Proof	—	Value: 3.25				
2004	76,551,250	—	—	—	0.60	—
2004 Proof	100,000	Value: 3.25				
2005	—	—	—	—	0.60	—
2005 Proof	—	Value: 3.25				
2006	—	—	—	—	0.60	—
2006 Proof	—	Value: 3.25				

KM# 991 50 PENCE
Copper-Nickel **Ruler:** Elizabeth II **Obv:** Portrait of Queen Elizabeth II **Obv. Designer:** Ian Rank-Broadley **Rev:** Seated Brittania **Rev. Designer:** Christopher Ironside **Shape:** 7-sided

Date	Mintage	F	VF	XF	Unc	BU
2001	84,999,500	—	—	—	1.75	—
2001 Proof	Est. 100,000	Value: 2.50				
2002	23,757,500	—	—	—	1.75	—
2002 Proof	—	Value: 2.50				
2003	26,557,030	—	—	—	1.75	—
2003 Proof	—	Value: 2.50				
2004	Est. 33,478,000	—	—	—	1.75	—
2004 Proof	100,000	Value: 2.50				
2005	—	—	—	—	1.75	—
2005 Proof	—	Value: 2.50				
2006	—	—	—	—	1.75	—
2006 Proof	—	Value: 2.50				

KM# 1017 50 PENCE
8.1100 g., 0.9584 Silver .2499 oz. ASW, 22 mm. **Ruler:** Elizabeth II **Subject:** Britannia Bullion **Obv:** Queen's portrait **Rev:** Stylized "Britannia and the Lion" **Edge:** Reeded

Date	Mintage	F	VF	XF	Unc	BU
2001 Proof	5,000	Value: 25.00				

KM# 1036 50 PENCE
8.0000 g., Copper Nickel, 27.3 mm. **Ruler:** Elizabeth II **Subject:** Woman's Suffrage **Obv:** Queen's portrait **Rev:** Standing woman with banner **Edge:** Plain **Shape:** 7-sided

Date	Mintage	F	VF	XF	Unc	BU
2003	Est. 5,000,000	—	—	—	2.50	—
2003 Proof	—	Value: 9.50				

KM# 1036a 50 PENCE
8.0000 g., 0.9250 Silver 0.2379 oz. ASW, 27.3 mm. **Ruler:** Elizabeth II **Edge:** Plain **Shape:** 7-sided

Date	Mintage	F	VF	XF	Unc	BU
2003 Proof	15,000	Value: 45.00				

KM# 1036b 50 PENCE
15.5000 g., 0.9166 Gold 0.4568 oz. AGW, 27.3 mm. **Ruler:** Elizabeth II **Edge:** Plain **Shape:** 7-sided

Date	Mintage	F	VF	XF	Unc	BU
2003 Proof	1,000	Value: 475				

KM# 1047 50 PENCE
8.0000 g., Copper-Nickel, 27.3 mm. **Ruler:** Elizabeth II **Subject:** The First Four Minute Mile **Obv:** Queen Elizabeth II **Rev:** Running legs, stop watch and value **Edge:** Plain

Date	Mintage	F	VF	XF	Unc	BU
2004	Est. 5,000,000	—	—	—	5.00	6.00
2004 Proof	100,000	Value: 7.50				

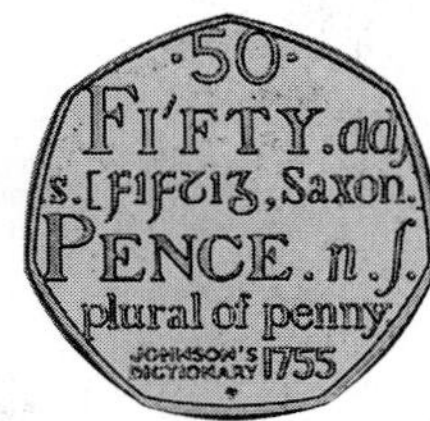

KM# 1050 50 PENCE
8.0000 g., Copper-Nickel, 27.3 mm. **Ruler:** Elizabeth II **Obv:** Queen Elizabeth II **Rev:** Text from the first English dictionary by Samuel Johnson **Edge:** Plain

Date	Mintage	F	VF	XF	Unc	BU
2005	—	—	—	—	2.50	3.50
2005 Proof	50,000	Value: 6.00				

KM# 1057 50 PENCE
8.0000 g., Copper-Nickel, 27.3 mm. **Ruler:** Elizabeth II **Obv:** Queen Elizabeth II **Rev:** Victoria Cross obverse and reverse views **Edge:** Plain **Shape:** 7-sided

Date	Mintage	F	VF	XF	Unc	BU
2006	—	—	—	—	5.00	6.00
2006 Proof	50,000	Value: 7.50				

KM# 1058 50 PENCE
8.0000 g., Copper-Nickel, 27.3 mm. **Ruler:** Elizabeth II **Obv:** Queen Elizabeth II **Rev:** Heroic Act scene with cross shape in background **Edge:** Plain **Shape:** 7-sided

Date	Mintage	F	VF	XF	Unc	BU
2006	—	—	—	—	5.00	6.00
2006 Proof	50,000	Value: 7.50				

KM# 1013a POUND
9.5000 g., 0.9250 Silver 0.2825 oz. ASW, 22.5 mm. **Ruler:** Elizabeth II **Subject:** Northern Ireland **Obv:** Queen's new portrait **Obv. Designer:** Rank-Broadley **Rev:** Celtic cross design **Edge:** Reeded **Edge Lettering:** DECUS ET TUTAMEN

Date	Mintage	F	VF	XF	Unc	BU
2001 Proof	25,000	Value: 40.00				

KM# 1013 POUND
9.5000 g., Nickel-Brass, 22.5 mm. **Ruler:** Elizabeth II **Subject:** Northern Ireland **Obv:** Queen's new portrait **Obv. Designer:** Ian Rank-Broadley **Rev:** Celtic style cross **Rev. Designer:** Norman Sillman **Edge:** Reeding **Edge Lettering:** DEBUS ET TUTAMEN

Date	Mintage	F	VF	XF	Unc	BU
2001 Proof	—	Value: 6.00				
2001	58,093,731	—	—	—	3.50	5.00

KM# 1030 POUND
9.5000 g., Nickel-Brass, 22.5 mm. **Ruler:** Elizabeth II **Obv:** Queen's new portrait **Obv. Designer:** Ian Rank-Broadley **Rev:** Three lions **Rev. Designer:** Norman Sillman **Edge:** Reeded **Edge Lettering:** DECUS ET TUTAMEN

Date	Mintage	F	VF	XF	Unc	BU
2002	77,818,000	—	—	—	3.50	5.00
2002 Proof	100,000	Value: 6.00				

KM# 1030a POUND
9.5000 g., 0.9250 Silver 0.2825 oz. ASW **Ruler:** Elizabeth II **Obv:** Queen's new portrait **Obv. Designer:** Ian Rank-Broadley **Rev:** Three lions **Edge:** Reeded **Edge Lettering:** DECUS ET TUTAMEN

Date	Mintage	F	VF	XF	Unc	BU
2002 Proof	—	Value: 40.00				

KM# 1046 POUND
16.2200 g., 0.9584 Silver 0.4998 oz. ASW, 27 mm. **Ruler:** Elizabeth II **Obv:** Queen Elizabeth II **Rev:** Britannia portrait behind wavy lines **Edge:** Reeded

Date	Mintage	F	VF	XF	Unc	BU
2003 Proof	5,000	Value: 50.00				

KM# 993 POUND
Nickel-Brass **Ruler:** Elizabeth II **Obv:** Portrait of Queen Elizabeth II **Obv. Designer:** Ian Rank-Broadley **Rev:** Shield of Great Britian within Garter, all crowned and supported **Rev. Designer:** Eric Sewell **Edge Lettering:** DECUS ET TUTAMEN

Date	Mintage	F	VF	XF	Unc	BU
2003	61,596,500	—	—	—	4.50	6.00
2003 Proof	—	Value: 7.50				

KM# 1048 POUND
9.5000 g., Nickel-Brass, 22.5 mm. **Ruler:** Elizabeth II **Obv:** Queen Elizabeth II **Rev:** "Forth Rail Bridge" in Scotland **Edge:** Reeded and lettered **Edge Lettering:** "NEMO ME IMPUNE LACESSIT"

Date	Mintage	F	VF	XF	Unc	BU
2004	37,286,000	—	—	—	6.00	7.50
2004 Proof	100,000	Value: 9.00				

KM# 1051 POUND
9.5000 g., Nickel-Brass, 22.5 mm. **Ruler:** Elizabeth II **Obv:** Queen Elizabeth II **Rev:** Menai Bridge in Wales **Edge:** Reeded and lettered **Edge Lettering:** "PLEIDOL WYF I'M GWLAD"

Date	Mintage	F	VF	XF	Unc	BU
2005	—	—	—	—	3.00	4.00
2005 Proof	50,000	Value: 5.00				

KM# 1059 POUND
9.5000 g., Nickel-Brass, 22.5 mm. **Ruler:** Elizabeth II **Obv:** Queen Elizabeth II **Rev:** Egyptian Arch Bridge at Newry, Northern Ireland **Edge:** Reeded and lettered

Date	Mintage	F	VF	XF	Unc	BU
2006	—	—	—	—	8.00	9.00
2006 Proof	50,000	Value: 10.00				

KM# 1014 2 POUNDS
11.9700 g., Bi-Metallic Copper-Nickel center in Nickel-Brass ring, 28.4 mm. **Ruler:** Elizabeth II **Subject:** First Transatlantic Radio Transmission **Obv:** Queen's portrait **Obv. Designer:** Ian Rank-Broadley **Rev:** Symbolic design **Rev. Designer:** Robert Evans **Edge:** Reeded and inscribed

Date	Mintage	F	VF	XF	Unc	BU
2001	5,000,000	—	—	—	5.00	6.50
2001 Proof	—	Value: 10.00				

KM# 1014a 2 POUNDS
24.0000 g., 0.9250 Silver Gold plated ring .7137 oz. ASW, 28.4 mm. **Ruler:** Elizabeth II **Edge:** Reeded and inscribed **Edge Lettering:** "WIRELESS BRIDGES THE ATLANTIC...MARCONI 1901..."

Date	Mintage	F	VF	XF	Unc	BU
2001 Proof	25,000	Value: 33.50				

KM# 1014b 2 POUNDS
15.9700 g., 0.9166 Gold Yellow gold plated Red Gold center in Red Gold ring .4706 oz. AGW, 28.4 mm. **Ruler:** Elizabeth II

Date	Mintage	F	VF	XF	Unc	BU
2001 Proof	1,500	Value: 445				

KM# 994 2 POUNDS
Bi-Metallic Copper-Nickel center in Nickel-Brass ring, 28.35 mm. **Ruler:** Elizabeth II **Obv:** Portrait of Queen Elizabeth II **Obv. Designer:** Ian Rank-Broadley **Rev:** Celtic design **Rev. Designer:** Bruce Rushin **Edge Lettering:** STANDING ON THE SHOULDERS OF GIANTS

Date	Mintage	F	VF	XF	Unc	BU
2001	37,843,500	—	—	—	6.00	8.50
2001 Proof	—	Value: 10.00				
2002	15,521,000	—	—	—	6.00	8.50
2002 Proof	—	Value: 10.00				
2003	21,830,250	—	—	—	6.00	8.50
2003 Proof	—	Value: 10.00				
2004	13,904,500	—	—	—	6.00	8.50
2004 Proof	100,000	Value: 10.00				
2005	—	—	—	—	6.00	8.50
2005 Proof	—	Value: 10.00				
2006	—	—	—	—	6.00	8.50
2006 Proof	—	Value: 10.00				

KM# 1019 2 POUNDS
32.4500 g., 0.9584 Silver .9999 oz. ASW, 40 mm. **Ruler:** Elizabeth II **Subject:** Britannia Bullion **Obv:** Queen's portrait **Rev:** Stylized "Britannia and the Lion" **Edge:** Reeded

Date	Mintage	F	VF	XF	Unc	BU
2001	100,000	—	—	—	25.00	30.00
2001 Proof	10,000	Value: 55.00				

KM# 1031 2 POUNDS
12.0000 g., Bi-Metallic Copper-Nickel center in Nickel-Brass ring, 28.4 mm. **Ruler:** Elizabeth II **Subject:** Commonwealth Games - England **Obv:** Head of Queen Elizabeth II right **Obv. Designer:** Ian Rank-Broadley **Rev:** Runner breaking ribbon at finish line **Rev. Designer:** Mathew Bonaccorsi **Edge:** Reeded and lettered

Date	Mintage	F	VF	XF	Unc	BU
2002	—	—	—	—	5.00	6.00
2002 Proof	—	Value: 8.75				

KM# 1031a 2 POUNDS
12.0000 g., Silver Gold plated ring, 28.4 mm. **Ruler:** Elizabeth II **Subject:** Commonwealth Games - England **Obv:** Head of Queen Elizabeth II right **Rev:** Runner breaking ribbon at finish line **Edge:** Reeded and lettered

Date	Mintage	F	VF	XF	Unc	BU
2002 Proof	10,000	—	—	—	30.00	35.00

KM# 1031b 2 POUNDS
15.9800 g., 0.9160 Gold Yellow gold center in Red Gold ring, 28.4 mm. **Ruler:** Elizabeth II **Subject:** Commonwealth Games - England **Obv:** Head of Queen Elizabeth II right **Rev:** Runner breaking ribbon at finish line **Edge:** Reeded and lettered

Date	Mintage	F	VF	XF	Unc	BU
2002 Proof	500	Value: 500				

KM# 1032 2 POUNDS
12.0000 g., Bi-Metallic Copper-Nickel center in Nickel-Brass ring, 28.4 mm. **Ruler:** Elizabeth II **Subject:** Commonwealth Games - Scotland **Obv:** Head of Queen Elizabeth II right **Obv. Designer:** Ian Rank-Broadley **Rev:** Runner breaking ribbon at finish line **Rev. Designer:** Matthew Bonaccorsi **Edge:** Reeded and lettered

Date	Mintage	F	VF	XF	Unc	BU
2002	—	—	—	—	5.00	6.00
2002 Proof	—	Value: 8.75				

KM# 1032a 2 POUNDS
Bi-metallic, Silver center with Gold plated ring, 28.4 mm. **Ruler:** Elizabeth II **Subject:** Commonwealth Games - Scotland **Obv:** Head of Queen Elizabeth II right **Rev:** Runner breaking ribbon at finish line **Edge:** Reeded and lettered

Date	Mintage	F	VF	XF	Unc	BU
2002 Proof	10,000	Value: 30.00				

KM# 1032b 2 POUNDS
15.9800 g., 0.9160 Gold Yellow gold center in Red Gold ring, 28.4 mm. **Ruler:** Elizabeth II **Subject:** Commonwealth Games - Scotland **Obv:** Head of Queen Elizabeth II right **Rev:** Runner breaking ribbon at finish line **Edge:** Reeded and lettered

Date	Mintage	F	VF	XF	Unc	BU
2002 Proof	500	Value: 500				

KM# 1033 2 POUNDS
12.0000 g., Bi-Metallic Copper-Nickel center in Nickel-Brass ring, 28.4 mm. **Ruler:** Elizabeth II **Subject:** Commonwealth Games - Wales **Obv:** Head of Queen Elizabeth II right **Rev:** Runner breaking ribbon at finish line **Rev. Designer:** Matthew Bonaccorsi **Edge:** Reeded and lettered

Date	Mintage	F	VF	XF	Unc	BU
2002	—	—	—	—	5.00	6.00
2002 Proof	—	Value: 8.75				

KM# 1033a 2 POUNDS
12.0000 g., Silver Silver center in Gold plated ring, 28.4 mm. **Ruler:** Elizabeth II **Subject:** Commonwealth Games - Wales **Obv:** Head of Queen Elizabeth II right **Rev:** Runner breaking ribbon at finish line **Edge:** Reeded and lettered

Date	Mintage	F	VF	XF	Unc	BU
2002 Proof	10,000	Value: 30.00				

KM# 1033b 2 POUNDS
15.9800 g., 0.9160 Gold Yellow Gold center in Red Gold ring, 28.4 mm. **Ruler:** Elizabeth II **Subject:** Commonwealth Games - Wales **Obv:** Head of Queen Elizabeth II right **Rev:** Runner breaking ribbon at finish line **Edge:** Reeded and lettered

Date	Mintage	F	VF	XF	Unc	BU
2002 Proof	500	Value: 500				

KM# 1034 2 POUNDS
12.0000 g., Bi-Metallic Copper-Nickel center in Nickel-Brass ring, 28.4 mm. **Ruler:** Elizabeth II **Subject:** Commonwealth Games - Northern Ireland **Obv:** Head of Queen Elizabeth II right **Rev:** Runner breaking ribbon at finish line **Rev. Designer:** Matthew Bonaccorsi **Edge:** Reeded and lettered

Date	Mintage	F	VF	XF	Unc	BU
2002	—	—	—	—	5.00	6.00
2002 Proof	—	Value: 8.75				

KM# 1034a 2 POUNDS
12.0000 g., Silver Silver center in Gold plated ring, 28.4 mm. **Ruler:** Elizabeth II **Subject:** Commonwealth Games - Northern Ireland **Obv:** Head of Queen Elizabeth II right **Rev:** Runner breaking ribbon at finish line **Edge:** Reeded and lettered

Date	Mintage	F	VF	XF	Unc	BU
2002 Proof	10,000	Value: 30.00				

KM# 1034b 2 POUNDS
15.9800 g., 0.9160 Gold Yellow Gold center in Red Gold ring, 28.4 mm. **Ruler:** Elizabeth II **Subject:** Commonwealth Games - Northern Ireland **Obv:** Head of Queen Elizabeth II right **Rev:** Runner breaking ribbon at finish line **Edge:** Reeded and lettered

Date	Mintage	F	VF	XF	Unc	BU
2002 Proof	500	Value: 500				

KM# 1037 2 POUNDS
12.0000 g., Bi-Metallic Copper-Nickel center in Nickel-Brass ring, 28.4 mm. **Ruler:** Elizabeth II **Subject:** D N A **Obv:** Queen's portrait **Rev:** DNA Double Helix **Edge:** Reeded and inscribed

Date	Mintage	F	VF	XF	Unc	BU
ND(2003)	—	—	—	—	5.00	6.50
ND(2003) Proof	—	Value: 10.00				

KM# 1037a 2 POUNDS
12.0000 g., 0.9250 Silver Silver center in Gold plated silver ring 0.3569 oz. ASW, 28.4 mm. **Ruler:** Elizabeth II **Obv:** Queen Elizabeth II **Rev:** DNA Double Helix **Edge:** Reeded and lettered

Date	Mintage	F	VF	XF	Unc	BU
ND(2003) Proof	10,000	Value: 30.00				

KM# 1037b 2 POUNDS
15.9800 g., 0.9167 Gold Yellow gold center in Red gold ring 0.471 oz. AGW, 28.4 mm. **Ruler:** Elizabeth II **Obv:** Queen Elizabeth II **Rev:** DNA Double Helix **Edge:** Reeded and lettered

Date	Mintage	F	VF	XF	Unc	BU
ND(2003) Proof	6,250	Value: 550				

KM# 1049 2 POUNDS
12.0000 g., Bi-Metallic Nickel-Brass center in Copper-Nickel ring, 28.4 mm. **Ruler:** Elizabeth II **Obv:** Queen Elizabeth II **Rev:** First steam locomotive **Edge:** Reeded and lettered

Date	Mintage	F	VF	XF	Unc	BU
2004	—	—	—	—	7.50	8.50
2004 Proof	100,000	Value: 10.00				

KM# 1049a 2 POUNDS
12.0000 g., 0.9250 Bi-Metallic .925 Silver center in Gold Plated .925 Silver ring 0.3569 oz., 28.4 mm. **Ruler:** Elizabeth II **Obv:** Queen Elizabeth II **Rev:** First steam locomotive **Edge:** Reeded and lettered

Date	Mintage	F	VF	XF	Unc	BU
2004 Proof	25,000	Value: 30.00				

KM# 1049b 2 POUNDS
15.9800 g., 0.9166 Bi-Metallic .9166 Yellow Gold center in .9166 Red Gold ring 0.4709 oz., 28.4 mm. **Ruler:** Elizabeth II **Obv:** Queen Elizabeth II **Rev:** First steam locomotive **Edge:** Reeded and lettered

Date	Mintage	F	VF	XF	Unc	BU
2004 Proof	1,500	Value: 450				

KM# 1052 2 POUNDS
12.0000 g., Bi-Metallic Nickel-Brass center in Copper-Nickel ring, 28.4 mm. **Ruler:** Elizabeth II **Subject:** 400th Anniversary - The Gunpowder Plot **Obv:** Queen Elizabeth II **Rev:** Circular design of Royal scepters, swords and crosiers **Edge:** Reeded and lettered

Date	Mintage	F	VF	XF	Unc	BU
ND(2005)	—	—	—	—	6.00	7.00
ND(2005) Proof	50,000	Value: 9.00				

KM# 1056 2 POUNDS

12.0000 g., 0.9250 Silver Gold plated outer ring 0.3569 oz. ASW, 28.4 mm. **Ruler:** Elizabeth II **Subject:** End of WW II **Obv:** Elizabeth II **Rev:** St. Paul's Cathedral amid search light beams **Edge:** Reeded and lettered **Edge Lettering:** "IN VICTORY MAGNANIMITY IN PEACE GOODWILL"

Date	Mintage	F	VF	XF	Unc	BU
ND (2005) Proof	25,000	Value: 30.00				

KM# 1061 2 POUNDS

12.0000 g., Bi-Metallic Copper-Nickel center in Nickel-Brass ring, 28.4 mm. **Ruler:** Elizabeth II **Obv:** Queen Elizabeth II **Rev:** Paddington Station structural supports **Edge:** Lettered

Date	Mintage	F	VF	XF	Unc	BU
2006	—	—	—	—	16.00	17.50
2006 Proof	50,000	Value: 20.00				

KM# 1015a 5 POUNDS

28.2800 g., 0.9250 Silver 0.841 oz. ASW, 38.6 mm. **Ruler:** Elizabeth II **Subject:** Centennial of Queen Victoria **Obv:** Queen Elizabeth's portrait **Obv. Designer:** Ian Rank-Broadley **Rev:** Queen Victoria's portrait **Rev. Designer:** Mary Milner Dickens

Date	Mintage	F	VF	XF	Unc	BU
2001 Proof	—	Value: 65.00				

KM# 1015 5 POUNDS

28.2800 g., Copper-Nickel, 38.6 mm. **Ruler:** Elizabeth II **Subject:** Centennial of Queen Victoria **Obv:** Queen Elizabeth's portrait **Obv. Designer:** Ian Rank-Broadley **Rev:** Queen Victoria's portrait **Rev. Designer:** Mary Milner Dickens **Edge:** Reeded

Date	Mintage	F	VF	XF	Unc	BU
2001	851,491	—	—	—	14.00	16.00
2001 Proof	—	Value: 20.00				

KM# 1015b 5 POUNDS

39.9400 g., 0.9167 Gold 1.1771 oz. AGW **Ruler:** Elizabeth II

Date	Mintage	F	VF	XF	Unc	BU
2001 Proof	1,000	Value: 1,000				

KM# 1024 5 POUNDS

28.2800 g., Copper-Nickel, 38.6 mm. **Ruler:** Elizabeth II **Subject:** Queen's Golden Jubilee of Reign **Obv:** Queen's portrait **Rev:** Queen on horse **Edge:** Reeded

Date	Mintage	F	VF	XF	Unc	BU
2002	3,468,210	—	—	—	12.50	14.50
2002 Proof	—	Value: 20.00				

KM# 1024a 5 POUNDS

28.2800 g., 0.9250 Silver .8410 oz. ASW, 38.6 mm. **Ruler:** Elizabeth II **Edge:** Reeded

Date	Mintage	F	VF	XF	Unc	BU
2002 Proof	—	Value: 50.00				

KM# 1024b 5 POUNDS

39.9400 g., 0.9167 Gold 1.0003 oz. AGW, 38.6 mm. **Ruler:** Elizabeth II **Edge:** Reeded

Date	Mintage	F	VF	XF	Unc	BU
2002 Proof	—	Value: 950				

KM# 1035 5 POUNDS

28.2800 g., Copper Nickel, 38.6 mm. **Ruler:** Elizabeth II **Subject:** Queen Mother **Obv:** Bust of Queen Elizabeth II right **Rev:** Queen Mother's portrait in wreath **Edge:** Reeded

Date	Mintage	F	VF	XF	Unc	BU
ND(2002) Proof	—	Value: 20.00				

KM# 1035a 5 POUNDS

28.2800 g., Silver, 38.6 mm. **Ruler:** Elizabeth II **Subject:** Queen Mother **Obv:** Bust of Queen Elizabeth II right **Rev:** Queen Mother's portrait in wreath **Edge:** Reeded

Date	Mintage	F	VF	XF	Unc	BU
ND(2002) Proof	25,000	Value: 50.00				

KM# 1035b 5 POUNDS

39.9400 g., 0.9167 Gold 1.1771 oz. AGW, 38.6 mm. **Ruler:** Elizabeth II **Subject:** Queen Mother **Obv:** Bust of Queen Elizabeth II right **Rev:** Queen Mother's portrait in wreath **Edge:** Reeded

Date	Mintage	F	VF	XF	Unc	BU
ND(2002) Proof	3,000	Value: 950				

KM# 1038 5 POUNDS

28.2800 g., Copper Nickel, 38.6 mm. **Ruler:** Elizabeth II **Subject:** Queen's Golden Jubilee **Obv:** Queen's stylized portrait **Rev:** Childlike lettering **Edge:** Reeded

Date	Mintage	F	VF	XF	Unc	BU
2003	1,307,010	—	—	—	12.50	14.50
2003 Proof	—	Value: 20.00				

KM# 1038a 5 POUNDS

28.2800 g., 0.9250 Silver 0.841 oz. ASW, 38.6 mm. **Ruler:** Elizabeth II **Edge:** Reeded

Date	Mintage	F	VF	XF	Unc	BU
2003 Proof	50,000	Value: 50.00				

KM# 1038b 5 POUNDS

39.9400 g., 0.9166 Gold 1.177 oz. AGW, 38.6 mm. **Ruler:** Elizabeth II **Edge:** Reeded

Date	Mintage	F	VF	XF	Unc	BU
2003 Proof	2,750	Value: 950				

KM# 1055 5 POUNDS

28.2800 g., Copper-Nickel, 38.6 mm. **Ruler:** Elizabeth II **Subject:** Entente Cordiale **Obv:** Elizabeth II **Rev:** Britannia and Marianne **Edge:** Reeded

Date	Mintage	F	VF	XF	Unc	BU
2004	1,205,158	—	—	—	15.00	17.50
2004 Proof	—	Value: 20.00				

KM# 1055a 5 POUNDS

28.2800 g., 0.9250 Silver 0.841 oz. ASW, 38.6 mm. **Ruler:** Elizabeth II **Subject:** Entente Cordiale **Obv:** Elizabeth II **Rev:** Britannia and Marianne **Edge:** Reeded

Date	Mintage	F	VF	XF	Unc	BU
2004 Proof	15,000	Value: 50.00				

KM# 1055b 5 POUNDS

39.9400 g., 0.9167 Gold 1.1771 oz. AGW, 38.6 mm. **Ruler:** Elizabeth II **Subject:** Entente Cordiale **Obv:** Elizabeth II **Rev:** Britannia and Marianne **Edge:** Reeded

Date	Mintage	F	VF	XF	Unc	BU
2004 Proof	1,500	Value: 1,000				

KM# 1055c 5 POUNDS

94.2000 g., 0.9995 Platinum 3.0271 oz. APW, 38.6 mm. **Ruler:** Elizabeth II **Subject:** Entente Cordiale **Obv:** Elizabeth II **Rev:** Britannia and Marianne **Edge:** Reeded

Date	Mintage	F	VF	XF	Unc	BU
2004 Proof	501	Value: 4,000				

KM# 1053 5 POUNDS

28.2800 g., Copper-Nickel, 38.6 mm. **Ruler:** Elizabeth II **Subject:** Battle of Trafalgar **Obv:** Queen Elizabeth II **Rev:** HMS Victory and HMS Temeraire at Trafalgar **Edge:** Reeded

Date	Mintage	F	VF	XF	Unc	BU
2005	—	—	—	—	15.00	16.50
2005 Proof	50,000	Value: 18.50				

KM# 1054 5 POUNDS

28.2800 g., Copper-Nickel, 38.6 mm. **Ruler:** Elizabeth II **Obv:** Queen Elizabeth II **Rev:** Admiral Horatio Nelson in uniform **Edge:** Reeded

Date	Mintage	F	VF	XF	Unc	BU
2005	—	—	—	—	15.00	16.50
2005 Proof	50,000	Value: 18.50				

KM# 1053a 5 POUNDS

28.2800 g., 0.9250 Silver 0.841 oz. ASW, 38.6 mm. **Ruler:** Elizabeth II **Subject:** Battle of Trafalgar **Obv:** Queen Elizabeth II **Rev:** Ships HMS Victory and Temeraire at Trafalgar **Edge:** Reeded

Date	Mintage	F	VF	XF	Unc	BU
2005 Proof	30,000	Value: 60.00				

KM# 1053b 5 POUNDS

39.9400 g., 0.9167 Gold 1.1771 oz. AGW, 38.6 mm. **Ruler:** Elizabeth II **Subject:** Battle of Trafalgar **Obv:** Queen Elizabeth II **Rev:** Ships HMS Victory and Temeraire at Trafalgar **Edge:** Reeded

Date	Mintage	F	VF	XF	Unc	BU
2005 Proof	1,805	Value: 1,100				

KM# 1062 5 POUNDS

28.2800 g., Copper-Nickel, 38.6 mm. **Ruler:** Elizabeth II **Obv:** Queen Elizabeth II **Rev:** Three bannered trumpets **Edge:** Reeded

Date	Mintage	F	VF	XF	Unc	BU
2006	—	—	—	—	20.00	22.00
2006 Proof	50,000	Value: 27.00				

KM# 1060 25 POUNDS (1/4 Ounce - Britannia)

12.0000 g., Bi-Metallic Copper-Nickel center in Nickel-Brass ring, 28.4 mm. **Ruler:** Elizabeth II **Obv:** Queen Elizabeth II **Rev:** Isambard Brunel **Edge:** Lettered

Date	Mintage	F	VF	XF	Unc	BU
2006	—	—	—	—	16.00	18.00
2006 Proof	50,000	Value: 35.00				

BULLION COINAGE

All proof issues have designers name as P. Nathan. The uncirculated issues use only Nathan.

KM# 1016 20 PENCE
3.2400 g., 0.9584 Silver .0998 oz. ASW, 16.5 mm.
Ruler: Elizabeth II **Subject:** Britannia Bullion **Obv:** Queen's portrait **Rev:** Stylized "Britannia and the Lion" **Edge:** Reeded

Date	Mintage	F	VF	XF	Unc	BU
2001 Proof	15,000	Value: 25.00				

KM# 1044 20 PENCE
3.2400 g., 0.9584 Silver 0.0998 oz. ASW, 16.5 mm.
Ruler: Elizabeth II **Obv:** Queen Elizabeth II **Rev:** Britannia portrait behind wavy lines **Edge:** Reeded

Date	Mintage	F	VF	XF	Unc	BU
2003 Proof	5,000	Value: 35.00				

KM# 1045 50 PENCE
8.1100 g., 0.9584 Silver 0.2499 oz. ASW, 22 mm.
Ruler: Elizabeth II **Obv:** Queen Elizabeth II **Rev:** Britannia portrait behind wavy lines **Edge:** Reeded

Date	Mintage	F	VF	XF	Unc	BU
2003 Proof	5,000	Value: 35.00				

KM# 1064 1/2 SOVEREIGN
3.9940 g., 0.9167 Gold 0.1177 oz. AGW, 19.3 mm.
Ruler: Elizabeth II **Obv:** Elizabeth II **Rev:** Knight fighting dragon with sword **Edge:** Reeded

Date	Mintage	F	VF	XF	Unc	BU
2005 Proof	12,500	Value: 175				

KM# 1065 SOVEREIGN
7.9880 g., 0.9176 Gold 0.2357 oz. AGW, 22.05 mm. **Ruler:** Elizabeth II **Obv:** Elizabeth II **Rev:** Knight fighting dragon with sword **Edge:** Reeded

Date	Mintage	F	VF	XF	Unc	BU
2005	75,000	—	—	—	—	175
2005 Proof	17,500	Value: 275				

KM# 1018 POUND
16.2200 g., 0.9584 Silver .4998 oz. ASW, 27 mm. **Ruler:** Elizabeth II **Subject:** Britannia Bullion **Obv:** Queen's portrait **Rev:** Stylized "Britannia and the Lion" **Edge:** Reeded

Date	Mintage	F	VF	XF	Unc	BU
2001 Proof	5,000	Value: 40.00				

KM# 1029 2 POUNDS
32.5400 g., 0.9580 Silver .9995 oz. ASW, 40 mm.
Ruler: Elizabeth II **Subject:** Britannia Bullion **Obv:** Queen's portrait **Obv. Designer:** Iran Rank-Braodley **Rev:** Standing Britannia **Edge:** Reeded

Date	Mintage	F	VF	XF	Unc	BU
2002	36,543	—	—	—	20.00	22.00
2004	100,000	—	—	—	20.00	22.00
2006	100,000	—	—	—	20.00	22.00

KM# 1039 2 POUNDS
32.4500 g., 0.9580 Silver 0.9995 oz. ASW, 40 mm.
Ruler: Elizabeth II **Subject:** Britannia Bullion **Obv:** Queen's portrait **Rev:** Britannia portrait behind wavy puzzle-like lines **Rev. Designer:** Philip Nathan **Edge:** Reeded

Date	Mintage	F	VF	XF	Unc	BU
2003	73,271	—	—	—	—	20.00
2003 Proof	1,833	Value: 60.00				

KM# 1063 2 POUNDS
32.4500 g., 0.9580 Silver 0.9995 oz. ASW, 40 mm. **Ruler:** Elizabeth II **Obv:** Elizabeth II **Rev:** Seated Britannia **Edge:** Reeded

Date	Mintage	F	VF	XF	Unc	BU
2005	100,000	—	—	—	—	25.00
2005 Proof	2,500	Value: 65.00				

KM# 1066 2 POUNDS
15.9760 g., 0.9167 Gold 0.4709 oz. AGW, 28.4 mm.
Ruler: Elizabeth II **Obv:** Elizabeth II **Rev:** Knight fighting dragon with sword **Edge:** Reeded

Date	Mintage	F	VF	XF	Unc	BU
2005 Proof	5,000	Value: 450				

KM# 1000a 2 POUNDS
32.4500 g., 0.9580 Silver 0.9995 oz. ASW, 40 mm. **Ruler:** Elizabeth II **Subject:** Golden Silhouette Britannias **Obv:** Queen Elizabeth II **Rev:** Gold plated Britannia in chariot **Edge:** Reeded

Date	Mintage	F	VF	XF	Unc	BU
2006 Proof	3,000	Value: 100				

KM# 1012a 2 POUNDS
32.4500 g., 0.9580 Silver 0.9995 oz. ASW, 40 mm.
Ruler: Elizabeth II **Subject:** Golden Silhouette Britannias **Obv:** Queen Elizabeth II **Rev:** Gold plated Britannia standing with shield **Edge:** Reeded

Date	Mintage	F	VF	XF	Unc	BU
2006 Proof	3,000	Value: 100				

KM# 1018a 2 POUNDS
32.4500 g., 0.9580 Silver 0.9995 oz. ASW, 40 mm. **Ruler:** Elizabeth II **Subject:** Golden Silhouette Britannias **Obv:** Queen Elizabeth II **Rev:** Gold plated Britannia and Lion **Edge:** Reeded

Date	Mintage	F	VF	XF	Unc	BU
2006 Proof	3,000	Value: 100				

KM# 1039a 2 POUNDS
32.4500 g., 0.9580 Silver 0.9995 oz. ASW, 40 mm. **Ruler:** Elizabeth II **Subject:** Golden Silhouette Britannias **Obv:** Queen Elizabeth II **Rev:** Gold plated Britannia head **Edge:** Reeded

Date	Mintage	F	VF	XF	Unc	BU
2006 Proof	3,000	Value: 100				

KM# 1063a 2 POUNDS
32.4500 g., 0.9580 Gold 0.9995 oz. AGW, 40 mm. **Ruler:** Elizabeth II **Subject:** Golden Silhouette Britannias **Obv:** Queen Elizabeth II **Rev:** Gold plated Britannia seated **Edge:** Reeded

Date	Mintage	F	VF	XF	Unc	BU
2006 Proof	3,000	Value: 100				

KM# 1072 2 POUNDS
15.9700 g., 0.9167 Gold 0.4707 oz. AGW, 28.4 mm.
Ruler: Elizabeth II **Obv:** Elizabeth II by Ian Rank-Broadley **Rev:** St. George slaying the Dragon **Edge:** Reeded

Date	Mintage	F	VF	XF	Unc	BU
2006 Proof	3,500	Value: 450				

KM# 1067 5 POUNDS
39.9400 g., 0.9167 Gold 1.1771 oz. AGW, 36 mm.
Ruler: Elizabeth II **Obv:** Elizabeth II **Rev:** Knight fighting dragon with sword **Edge:** Reeded

Date	Mintage	F	VF	XF	Unc	BU
2005 Proof	2,500	Value: 950				

KM# 1020 10 POUNDS (1/10 Ounce - Britannia)
3.4100 g., 0.9167 Gold .1005 oz. AGW, 16.5 mm. **Ruler:** Elizabeth II **Subject:** Britannia Bullion **Obv:** Queen's portrait **Rev:** Stylized "Britannia and the Lion" **Edge:** Reeded

Date	Mintage	F	VF	XF	Unc	BU
2001	1,100	—	—	—	BV+16%	—
2001 Proof	1,557	Value: 115				

KM# 1008 10 POUNDS (1/10 Ounce - Britannia)
3.4100 g., 0.9167 Gold .1005 oz. AGW **Ruler:** Elizabeth II **Rev:** Britannia standing **Edge:** Reeded

Date	Mintage	F	VF	XF	Unc	BU
2002 Proof	1,500	Value: 115				
2004	—	—	—	—	—	—
2004 Proof	—	Value: 200				

KM# 1040 10 POUNDS (1/10 Ounce - Britannia)
3.4100 g., 0.9167 Gold 0.1005 oz. AGW, 16.5 mm.
Ruler: Elizabeth II **Obv:** Queen Elizabeth II **Rev:** Britannia portrait behind wavy lines **Edge:** Reeded

Date	Mintage	F	VF	XF	Unc	BU
2003	—	—	—	—	BV+16%	—
2003 Proof	4,000	Value: 115				

KM# 1068 10 POUNDS (1/10 Ounce - Britannia)
3.4100 g., 0.9167 Gold 0.1005 oz. AGW, 16.5 mm. **Ruler:** Elizabeth II **Obv:** Elizabeth II **Rev:** Seated Britannia **Edge:** Reeded

Date	Mintage	F	VF	XF	Unc	BU
2005 Proof	3,500	Value: 150				

KM# 1021 25 POUNDS (1/4 Ounce - Britannia)
8.5100 g., 0.9167 Gold .2508 oz. AGW, 22 mm. **Ruler:** Elizabeth II **Subject:** Britannia Bullion **Obv:** Queen's portrait **Rev:** Stylized "Britannia and the Lion" **Edge:** Reeded

Date	Mintage	F	VF	XF	Unc	BU
2001	1,100	—	—	—	BV+35%	—
2001 Proof	1,500	Value: 225				

KM# 1009 25 POUNDS (1/4 Ounce - Britannia)
8.5100 g., 0.9167 Gold .2508 oz. AGW **Ruler:** Elizabeth II **Rev:** Britannia standing **Edge:** Reeded

Date	Mintage	F	VF	XF	Unc	BU
2002 Proof	750	Value: 225				
2004	—	—	—	—	—	—
2004 Proof	—	Value: 350				

KM# 1041 25 POUNDS (1/4 Ounce - Britannia)
8.5100 g., 0.9167 Gold 0.2508 oz. AGW, 22 mm. **Ruler:** Elizabeth II **Obv:** Queen Elizabeth II **Rev:** Britannia portrait behind wavy lines **Edge:** Reeded

Date	Mintage	F	VF	XF	Unc	BU
2003	604	—	—	—	BV+35%	—
2003 Proof	3,250	Value: 225				

KM# 1069 25 POUNDS (1/4 Ounce - Britannia)
8.5100 g., 0.9167 Gold 0.2508 oz. AGW, 22 mm. **Ruler:** Elizabeth II **Obv:** Elizabeth II **Rev:** Seated Britannia **Edge:** Reeded

Date	Mintage	F	VF	XF	Unc	BU
2005 Proof	2,750	Value: 300				

KM# 1022 50 POUNDS (1/2 Ounce - Britannia)
17.0200 g., 0.9167 Gold .5016 oz. AGW, 27 mm. **Ruler:** Elizabeth II **Subject:** Britannia Bullion **Obv:** Queen's portrait **Rev:** Stylized "Britannia and the Lion" **Rev. Designer:** Philip Nathan **Edge:** Reeded

Date	Mintage	F	VF	XF	Unc	BU
2001	600	—	—	—	BV+35%	—
2001 Proof	1,000	Value: 435				

KM# 1010 50 POUNDS (1/2 Ounce - Britannia)
17.0300 g., 0.9167 Gold .5019 oz. AGW **Ruler:** Elizabeth II **Rev:** Britannia standing **Edge:** Reeded

Date	Mintage	F	VF	XF	Unc	BU
2002 Proof	1,000	Value: 445				
2004	—	—	—	—	—	—
2004 Proof	—	Value: 500				

KM# 1042 50 POUNDS (1/2 Ounce - Britannia)
17.0200 g., 0.9167 Gold 0.5016 oz. AGW, 27 mm.
Ruler: Elizabeth II **Obv:** Queen Elizabeth II **Rev:** Britannia portrait behind wavy lines **Edge:** Reeded

Date	Mintage	F	VF	XF	Unc	BU
2003	—	—	—	—	BV+25%	—
2003 Proof	2,500	Value: 450				

KM# 1070 50 POUNDS (1/2 Ounce - Britannia)
17.0300 g., 0.9167 Gold 0.5019 oz. AGW, 27 mm. **Ruler:** Elizabeth II **Obv:** Elizabeth II **Rev:** Seated Britannia **Edge:** Reeded

Date	Mintage	F	VF	XF	Unc	BU
2005 Proof	2,000	Value: 450				

KM# 1023 100 POUNDS (1 Ounce - Britannia)
34.0500 g., 0.9167 Gold 1.0035 oz. AGW, 32.7 mm.
Ruler: Elizabeth II **Subject:** Britannia Bullion **Obv:** Queen's portrait **Rev:** Stylized "Britannia and the Lion" **Edge:** Reeded

Date	Mintage	F	VF	XF	Unc	BU
2001	900	—	—	—	BV+15%	—
2001 Proof	1,000	Value: 875				

KM# 1011 100 POUNDS (1 Ounce - Britannia)
34.0500 g., 0.9167 Gold 1.0035 oz. AGW **Ruler:** Elizabeth II **Rev:** Britannia standing **Edge:** Reeded

Date	Mintage	F	VF	XF	Unc	BU
2002 Proof	1,000	Value: 900				
2004	—	—	—	—	—	—
2004 Proof	—	Value: 875				

KM# 1043 100 POUNDS (1 Ounce - Britannia)
34.0500 g., 0.9167 Gold 1.0035 oz. AGW, 32.7 mm.
Ruler: Elizabeth II **Obv:** Queen Elizabeth II **Rev:** Britannia portrait behind wavy lines **Edge:** Reeded

Date	Mintage	F	VF	XF	Unc	BU
2003	—	—	—	—	BV+15%	—
2003 Proof	1,500	Value: 900				

KM# 1071 100 POUNDS (1 Ounce - Britannia)
34.0500 g., 0.9167 Gold 1.0035 oz. AGW, 32.7 mm. **Ruler:** Elizabeth II **Obv:** Elizabeth II **Rev:** Seated Britannia **Edge:** Reeded

Date	Mintage	F	VF	XF	Unc	BU
2005 Proof	1,500	Value: 875				

PIEFORTS

KM#	Date	Mintage	Identification	Mkt Val
P32	2004	10,000	2 Pounds. 0.9250 Bi-Metallic. 24.0000 g. 28.4 mm. Queen Elizabeth II. First steam locomotive. Reeded and lettered edge.	—

MAUNDY SETS

KM#	Date	Mintage	Identification	Issue Price	Mkt Val
MDS260	2001 (4)	1,132	KM#898-899, 901-902.	—	225
MDS261	2002 (4)	1,681	KM#898-899, 901-902.	—	225
MDS262	2003 (4)	1,608	KM#898-899, 901-902.	—	245
MDS263	2004 (4)	1,611	KM#898-899, 901-902.	—	245
MDS264	2005 (4)	—	KM#898-899,901-902	—	250
MDS265	2006 (4)	—	KM#898-899, 901-902	—	250

MINT SETS

KM#	Date	Mintage	Identification	Issue Price	Mkt Val
MS129	2001 (9)	57,741	KM#986-991, 994, 1013-1015 B.U. set	22.50	—
MS130	2001 (9)	—	KM#986-991, 994, 1013-1014 Wedding Collection	27.50	—
MS131	2001 (9)	—	KM#986-991, 994, 1013-1014 Baby Gift Set	27.50	—
MS132	2002 (8)	60,539	KM#986-991, 994, 1030	22.50	25.00
MS133	2002 (8)	—	KM#986-991, 994, 1030 Wedding Collection	27.50	28.00
MS134	2002 (8)	—	KM#986-991, 994, 1030 Baby Gift Set	27.50	28.00
MS135	2003 (10)	—	KM#986-991, 993, 994, 1036-1037 Brilliant Uncirclulated Set	22.50	—
MS136	2003 (10)	—	KM#986-991, 993, 994, 1036-1037 Wedding Collection	27.50	—
MS137	2003 (10)	—	KM#986-991, 993, 994, 1036-1037 Baby Gift Set	27.50	—
MS138	2005 (10)	—	KM#986-991, 994, 1050-1052	26.50	30.00
MS139	2005 (10)	—	KM#986-991, 994, 1050-1052 Baby Gift Set	36.50	37.50
MS140	2005 (3)	—	KM#1050-1052 New Coinage Set	16.25	17.50
MS141	2005 (2)	—	KM#1053-1054 Trafalgar Set	36.00	40.00
MS142	2006 (10)	—	KM#986-990, 1057-1061	30.00	30.00
MS143	2006 (10)	—	KM#986-990, 1057-1061 Baby Gift Set	38.50	38.50

PROOF SETS

KM#	Date	Mintage	Identification	Issue Price	Mkt Val
PS116	2001 (3)	1,500	KM#1001-1002, 1014a	795	—
PS117	2001 (4)	1,000	KM#1001-1003,1014a	1,645	—
PS118	2001 (4)	5,000	KM#1016-1019	—	140
PSA119	2001 (3)	1,500	KM#1001, 1002, 1014b	—	—
PSB119	2001 (4)	1,000	KM#1001, 1002, 1014b, 1015b	—	—
PS119	2001 (4)	1,000	KM#1020-1023	1,595	—
PS120	2002 (3)	5,000	KM#1025-1027	795	—
PS121	2002 (4)	3,000	KM#1025-1028	1,645	—
PS122	2002 (4)	3,358	KM#1031-1034; Standard Set	34.95	—
PS123	2002 (4)	673	KM#1031-1034; Display Set	44.95	—
PS124	2002 (4)	2,553	KM#1031a-1034a; Display Set	120	—
PS125	2002 (4)	315	KM#1031b-1034b; Display Set	1,675	—
PS126	2002 (4)	1,000	KM#1008-1011	1,600	1,625
PS127	2001 (10)	10,000	KM#986-991, 994, 1013-1015 Executive Proof Set in display case	115	—
PS128	2001 (10)	30,000	KM#986-991, 994, 1013-1015 Deluxe Proof Set in red leather case	72.50	—
PS129	2001 (10)	28,244	KM#986-991, 994, 1013-1015 Standard Proof Set in simple case	50.00	—
PS130	2001 (10)	1,351	KM#986-991, 994, 1013-1015 Gift Proof Set with a pack of occasion cards	65.00	—
PS131	2002 (9)	5,000	KM#986-991, 994, 1024, 1030 Executive Proof Set	100	100
PS132	2002 (9)	30,000	KM#986-991, 994, 1024, 1030 Deluxe Proof Set	70.00	75.00
PS133	2002 (9)	30,884	KM#986-991, 994, 1024, 1030 Standard Proof Set	48.00	50.00
PS134	2002 (9)	1,544	KM#986-991, 994, 1024, 1030 Gift Proof Set	62.40	65.00
PS135	2003 (11)	—	KM#986-991, 993, 994, 1036-1038 Executive Proof Set	100	—
PS136	2003 (11)	—	KM#986-991, 993, 994, 1036-1038 Deluxe Proof Set	72.00	—
PS137	2003 (11)	23,305	KM#986-991, 993, 994, 1036-1038 Standard Proof Set	50.00	—
PS138	2005 (12)	5,000	KM#986-991, 994, 1050-1054 Executive Set	146	150
PS139	2005 (12)	20,000	KM#986-991, 994, 1050-1054 Deluxe Proof Set	80.00	90.00
PS140	2005	25,000	KM#986-991, 994, 1050-1054	60.00	70.00
PS141	2005 (3)	2,000	KM#1068-1070	850	875
PS142	2005 (4)	1,500	KM#1068-1071	1,895	1,900
PS143	2005 (3)	2,500	KM#1064-1066	820	825
PS144	2005 (4)	2,500	KM#1064-1067	1,925	1,950
PS145	2006 (13)	5,000	KM#986-991, 994, 1057-1062 Executive Proof Set, wooden case	—	100
PS146	2006 (13)	15,000	KM#986-991, 994, 1057-1062 Deluxe Proof Set	82.50	85.00
PS147	2006 (13)	30,000	KM#986-991, 994, 1057-1062 Standard Proof Set	65.00	65.00
PS148	2006 (5)	3,000	KM#1000a, 1012a, 1018a, 1039, 1063a	475	500
PS149	2006 (3)	1,750	KM#1001, 1002, 1072	1,015	1,025
PS150	2006 (4)	1,750	KM#1001-1003, 1072	2,091	2,100

The Hellenic (Greek) Republic is situated in southeastern Europe on the southern tip of the Balkan Peninsula. The republic includes many islands, the most important of which are Crete and the Ionian Islands. Greece (including islands) has an area of 50,944 sq. mi. (131,940 sq. km.) and a population of 10.3 million. Capital: Athens. Greece is still largely agricultural. Tobacco, cotton, fruit and wool are exported.

MONETARY SYSTEM

Commencing 1831

100 Lepta = 1 Drachma

Commencing 2003

1 Euro = 100 Euro Cent

REPUBLIC

DECIMAL COINAGE

KM# 132 10 DRACHMES
Copper-Nickel **Obv:** Atom above value **Rev:** Democritus head left

Date	Mintage	F	VF	XF	Unc	BU
2002	—	—	0.25	0.50	1.25	2.50

EURO COINAGE

European Economic Community Issues

KM# 181 EURO CENT
2.2700 g., Copper Plated Steel, 16.2 mm. **Subject:** Euro Coinage **Obv:** Ancient Athenian trireme **Obv. Designer:** George Stamatopoulos **Rev:** Denomination and globe **Rev. Designer:** Luc Luycx **Edge:** Plain

Date	Mintage	F	VF	XF	Unc	BU
2002	88,000,000	—	—	—	0.35	—
2002 F in star	15,000,000	—	—	—	1.25	—
2003	7,000,000	—	—	—	0.35	—
2003 Proof	—	—	—	—	—	—
2004	45,000,000	—	—	—	0.35	—
2004 Proof	—	—	—	—	—	—
2005	—	—	—	—	0.35	—
2005 Proof	—	—	—	—	—	—

KM# 182 2 EURO CENTS
3.0300 g., Copper Plated Steel, 18.7 mm. **Subject:** Euro Coinage **Obv:** Corvette sailing ship **Obv. Designer:** George Stamatopoulos **Rev:** Denomination and globe **Rev. Designer:** Luc Luycx **Edge:** Grooved

Date	Mintage	F	VF	XF	Unc	BU
2002	172,000,000	—	—	—	0.50	—
2002 F in star	18,000,000	—	—	—	1.00	—
2003	9,000,000	—	—	—	0.50	—
2003 Proof	—	—	—	—	—	—
2004	25,000,000	—	—	—	0.50	—
2004 Proof	—	—	—	—	—	—
2005	—	—	—	—	0.50	—
2005 Proof	—	—	—	—	—	—

KM# 183 5 EURO CENTS

3.8600 g., Copper Plated Steel, 21.2 mm. **Subject:** Euro Coinage **Obv:** Freighter **Obv. Designer:** George Stamatopoulos **Rev:** Denomination and globe **Rev. Designer:** Luc Luycx **Edge:** Plain

Date	Mintage	F	VF	XF	Unc	BU
2002	288,000,000	—	—	—	1.00	—
2002 F in star	18,000,000	—	—	—	1.25	—
2003	400,000	—	—	—	1.00	—
2003 Proof	—	—	—	—	—	—
2004	250,000	—	—	—	1.00	—
2004 Proof	—	—	—	—	—	—
2005	—	—	—	—	1.00	—
2005 Proof	—	—	—	—	—	—

KM# 184 10 EURO CENTS

4.0700 g., Brass, 19.7 mm. **Subject:** Euro Coinage **Obv:** Bust of Rhgas Feriaou's half right **Obv. Designer:** George Stamatopoulos **Rev:** Denominaton and map **Rev. Designer:** Luc Luycx **Edge:** Reeded

Date	Mintage	F	VF	XF	Unc	BU
2002	257,000,000	—	—	—	1.25	—
2002 F in star	24,000,000	—	—	—	2.00	—
2003	330,000	—	—	—	1.25	—
2003 Proof	—	—	—	—	—	—
2004	—	—	—	—	1.25	—
2004 Proof	—	—	—	—	—	—
2005	—	—	—	—	1.25	—
2005 Proof	—	—	—	—	—	—

KM# 185 20 EURO CENTS

5.7300 g., Brass, 22.1 mm. **Subject:** Euro Coinage **Obv:** Bust of John Kapodistrias' half right **Obv. Designer:** George Stamatopoulos **Rev:** Denomination and map **Rev. Designer:** Luc Luycx **Edge:** Notched

Date	Mintage	F	VF	XF	Unc	BU
2002	370,000,000	—	—	—	1.25	—
2002 E in star	21,000,000	—	—	—	2.25	—
2003	330,000	—	—	—	1.25	—
2003 Proof	—	—	—	—	—	—
2004	400,000	—	—	—	1.25	—
2004 Proof	—	—	—	—	—	—
2005	—	—	—	—	1.25	—
2005 Proof	—	—	—	—	—	—

KM# 186 50 EURO CENTS

7.8100 g., Brass, 24.2 mm. **Subject:** Euro Coinage **Obv:** Bust of El. Venizelos half left **Obv. Designer:** George Stamatopoulos **Rev:** Denomination and map **Rev. Designer:** Luc Luycx **Edge:** Reeded

Date	Mintage	F	VF	XF	Unc	BU
2002	145,000,000	—	—	—	1.50	—
2002 F in star	18,000,000	—	—	—	2.50	—
2003	330,000	—	—	—	1.50	—
2003 Proof	—	—	—	—	—	—
2004	400,000	—	—	—	1.50	—
2004 Proof	—	—	—	—	—	—
2005	—	—	—	—	1.50	—
2005 Proof	—	—	—	—	—	—

KM# 187 EURO

7.5000 g., Bi-Metallic Copper-Nickel center in Brass ring, 23.2 mm. **Subject:** Euro Coinage **Obv:** Ancient Athenian coin design **Obv. Designer:** George Stamatopoulos **Rev:** Denomination and map **Rev. Designer:** Luc Luycx **Edge:** Reeded and plain sections

Date	Mintage	F	VF	XF	Unc	BU
2002	118,000,000	—	—	—	4.00	—
2002 S in star	15,000,000	—	—	—	4.50	—
2003	1,650,000	—	—	—	4.00	—
2003 Proof	—	—	—	—	—	—
2004	10,000,000	—	—	—	4.00	—
2004 Proof	—	—	—	—	—	—
2005	—	—	—	—	4.00	—
2005 Proof	—	—	—	—	—	—

KM# 188 2 EUROS

8.5200 g., Bi-Metallic Brass center in Coper-Nickel ring, 25.7 mm. **Subject:** Euro Coinage **Obv:** Europa seated on a bull **Obv. Designer:** George Stamatopoulos **Rev:** Denomination and map **Rev. Designer:** Luc Luycx **Edge:** Reeded with Greek letters and stars

Date	Mintage	F	VF	XF	Unc	BU
2002	162,000,000	—	—	—	4.00	—
2002 S in star	6,000,000	—	—	—	6.50	—
2003	540,000	—	—	—	4.00	—
2003 Proof	—	—	—	—	—	—
2004	—	—	—	—	4.00	—
2005	—	—	—	—	4.00	—
2005 Proof	—	—	—	—	—	—

KM# 209 2 EUROS

8.5200 g., Bi-Metallic Brass center in Copper-Nickel ring, 25.7 mm. **Subject:** 2004 Olympics **Obv:** Discus thrower **Rev:** Value on map **Edge:** Reeded and lettered **Edge Lettering:** Greek

Date	Mintage	F	VF	XF	Unc	BU
2004	50,000,000	—	—	—	4.00	6.00

KM# 191 10 EURO

34.0000 g., 0.9250 Silver 1.0111 oz. ASW, 40 mm. **Subject:** Olympics **Obv:** Olympic rings in wreath above value within circle of stars **Rev:** Ancient and modern discus throwers **Edge:** Plain

Date	Mintage	F	VF	XF	Unc	BU
ND(2003) Proof	68,000	Value: 60.00				

KM# 193 10 EURO

34.0000 g., 0.9250 Silver 1.0111 oz. ASW, 40 mm. **Subject:** Olympics **Obv:** Olympic rings in wreath above value within circle of stars **Rev:** Ancient and modern javelin throwers **Edge:** Plain

Date	Mintage	F	VF	XF	Unc	BU
ND(2003) Proof	68,000	Value: 60.00				

KM# 194 10 EURO

34.0000 g., 0.9250 Silver 1.0111 oz. ASW, 40 mm. **Subject:** Olympics **Obv:** Olympic rings in wreath above value within circle of stars **Rev:** Ancient and modern long jumpers **Edge:** Plain

Date	Mintage	F	VF	XF	Unc	BU
ND(2003) Proof	68,000	Value: 60.00				

KM# 196 10 EURO

34.0000 g., 0.9250 Silver 1.0111 oz. ASW, 40 mm. **Subject:** Olympics **Obv:** Olympic rings in wreath above value within circle of stars **Rev:** Ancient and modern relay runners **Edge:** Plain

Date	Mintage	F	VF	XF	Unc	BU
ND(2003) Proof	68,000	Value: 60.00				

KM# 197 10 EURO

34.0000 g., 0.9250 Silver 1.0111 oz. ASW, 40 mm. **Subject:** Olympics **Obv:** Olympic rings in wreath above value within circle of stars **Rev:** Ancient and modern horsemen **Edge:** Plain

Date	Mintage	F	VF	XF	Unc	BU
ND(2003) Proof	68,000	Value: 60.00				

KM# 199 10 EURO

34.0000 g., 0.9250 Silver 1.0111 oz. ASW, 40 mm. **Subject:** Olympics **Obv:** Olympic rings in wreath above value within circle of stars **Rev:** Modern ribbon dancer and two ancient female acrobats **Edge:** Plain

Date	Mintage	F	VF	XF	Unc	BU
ND(2003) Proof	68,000	Value: 60.00				

KM# 200 10 EURO

34.0000 g., 0.9250 Silver 1.0111 oz. ASW, 40 mm. **Subject:** Olympics **Obv:** Olympic rings in wreath above value within a circle of stars **Rev:** Ancient and modern female swimmers **Edge:** Plain

Date	Mintage	F	VF	XF	Unc	BU
ND(2003) Plain	68,000	Value: 60.00				

KM# 208 10 EURO

9.7500 g., 0.9250 Silver 0.29 oz. ASW, 28.25 mm. **Subject:** Greek Presidency of E. U. **Obv:** National arms in wreath above value **Rev:** Stylized document design **Edge:** Notched

Date	Mintage	F	VF	XF	Unc	BU
2003 Proof	50,000	Value: 50.00				

KM# 190 10 EURO

34.0000 g., 0.9250 Silver 1.0111 oz. ASW, 40 mm. **Subject:** Olympics **Obv:** Olympic rings in wreath above value within circle of stars **Rev:** Ancient and modern runners **Edge:** Plain **Note:** Olympics

Date	Mintage	F	VF	XF	Unc	BU
ND (2003) Proof	68,000	Value: 60.00				

KM# 202 10 EURO

34.0000 g., 0.9250 Silver 1.0111 oz. ASW, 40 mm. **Subject:** Olympics **Obv:** Olympic rings in wreath above value within circle of stars **Rev:** Ancient and modern weight lifters **Edge:** Plain

Date	Mintage	F	VF	XF	Unc	BU
ND(2004) Proof	68,000	Value: 60.00				

KM# 203 10 EURO

34.0000 g., 0.9250 Silver 1.0111 oz. ASW, 40 mm. **Subject:** Olympics **Obv:** Olympic rings in wreath above value within circle of stars **Rev:** Ancient and modern wrestlers **Edge:** Plain

Date	Mintage	F	VF	XF	Unc	BU
ND(2004) Proof	68,000	Value: 60.00				

KM# 205 10 EURO

34.0000 g., 0.9250 Silver 1.0111 oz. ASW, 40 mm. **Subject:** Olympics **Obv:** Olympic rings in wreath above value within circle of stars **Rev:** Ancient and modern handball players **Edge:** Plain

Date	Mintage	F	VF	XF	Unc	BU
ND(2004) Proof	68,000	Value: 60.00				

KM# 206 10 EURO

34.0000 g., 0.9250 Silver 1.0111 oz. ASW, 40 mm. **Subject:** Olympics **Obv:** Olympic rings in wreath above value within circle of stars **Rev:** Ancient and modern soccer players **Edge:** Plain

Date	Mintage	F	VF	XF	Unc	BU
ND(2004) Proof	68,000	Value: 60.00				

KM# 210 20 EURO

24.0000 g., 0.9250 Silver 0.7137 oz. ASW, 37 mm. **Subject:** Bank of Greece 75th Anniversary **Obv:** Value **Rev:** Flag

Date	Mintage	F	VF	XF	Unc	BU
2003	10,000	—	—	—	—	25.00
2003 Proof	1,000	Value: 50.00				

KM# 192 100 EURO

0.9999 Gold, 25 mm. **Subject:** Olympics **Obv:** Olympic rings in wreath above value within circle of stars **Rev:** Knossos Palace **Edge:** Plain

Date	Mintage	F	VF	XF	Unc	BU
ND(2003) Proof	28,000	Value: 565				

KM# 195 100 EURO

10.0000 g., 0.9999 Gold 0.3215 oz. AGW, 25 mm. **Subject:** Olympics **Obv:** Olympic rings in wreath above value within circle of stars **Rev:** Krypte archway **Edge:** Plain

Date	Mintage	F	VF	XF	Unc	BU
ND(2003) Proof	28,000	Value: 565				

KM# 198 100 EURO

10.0000 g., 0.9999 Gold 0.3215 oz. AGW, 25 mm. **Subject:** Olympics **Obv:** Olympic rings in wreath above value within circle of stars **Rev:** Panathenean Stadium **Edge:** Plain

Date	Mintage	F	VF	XF	Unc	BU
ND(2003) Proof	28,000	Value: 565				

KM# 201 100 EURO

10.0000 g., 0.9999 Gold 0.3215 oz. AGW, 25 mm. **Subject:** Olympics **Obv:** Olympic rings in wreath above value within circle of stars **Rev:** Zappeion Mansion **Edge:** Plain

Date	Mintage	F	VF	XF	Unc	BU
ND(2003) Proof	28,000	Value: 565				

KM# 204 100 EURO

10.0000 g., 0.9999 Gold 0.3215 oz. AGW, 25 mm. **Subject:** Olympics **Obv:** Olympic rings in wreath above value within circle of stars **Rev:** Acropolis **Edge:** Plain

Date	Mintage	F	VF	XF	Unc	BU
ND(2004) Proof	28,000	Value: 565				

KM# 207 100 EURO

10.0000 g., 0.9999 Gold 0.3215 oz. AGW, 25 mm. **Subject:** Olympics **Obv:** Olympic rings in wreath above value within circle of stars **Rev:** Academy of Athens **Edge:** Plain

Date	Mintage	F	VF	XF	Unc	BU
ND(2004) Proof	28,000	Value: 565				

MINT SETS

KM#	Date	Mintage	Identification	Issue Price	Mkt Val
MS6	2002 (8)	—	KM#181-188	—	50.00
MS7	2003 (8)	—	KM#181-188	—	45.00
MS8	2004 (8)	—	KM#181-188	—	—
MS9	2005 (8)	—	KM#181-188	—	—

GUADELOUPE

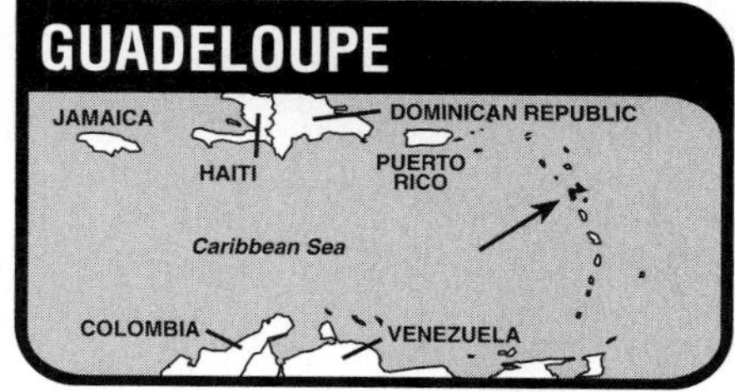

The French Overseas Department of Guadeloupe, located in the Leeward Islands of the West Indies about 300 miles (493 km.) southeast of Puerto Rico, has an area of 687 sq. mi. (1,780 sq. km.) and a population of 306,000. Actually it is two islands separated by a narrow saltwater stream: volcanic Basse-Terre to the west and the flatter limestone formation of Grande-Terre to the east. Capital: Basse-Terre, on the island of that name. The principal industries are agriculture, the distillation of liquors, and tourism. Sugar, bananas, and rum are exported.

RULERS

French 1816-

MONETARY SYSTEM

100 Centimes = 1 Franc

FRENCH OVERSEAS DEPARTMENT

ESSAIS

KM# E6 1/4 EURO

7.8000 g., 0.9990 Silver 0.2505 oz. ASW, 27.2 mm. **Obv:** Louis O. Roty **Rev:** Seated angel **Edge:** Reeded

Date	Mintage	F	VF	XF	Unc	BU
2004 Proof	2,000	Value: 20.00				

KM# E7 1-1/2 EURO

31.6000 g., 0.9990 Silver 1.0149 oz. ASW, 39.1 mm. **Obv:** Sun across sugar cane **Rev:** Sail ship Cuirasse Gloire **Edge:** Reeded and lettered **Edge Lettering:** "NWTM ONE OZ..999"

Date	Mintage	F	VF	XF	Unc	BU
2004 Proof	2,000	Value: 30.00				

KM# E8 20 EURO

7.8000 g., 0.9990 Gold 0.2505 oz. AGW, 27 mm. **Obv:** Sun across sugar cane **Rev:** Brown pelican **Edge:** Reeded

Date	Mintage	F	VF	XF	Unc	BU
2004 Proof	300	Value: 300				

GUATEMALA

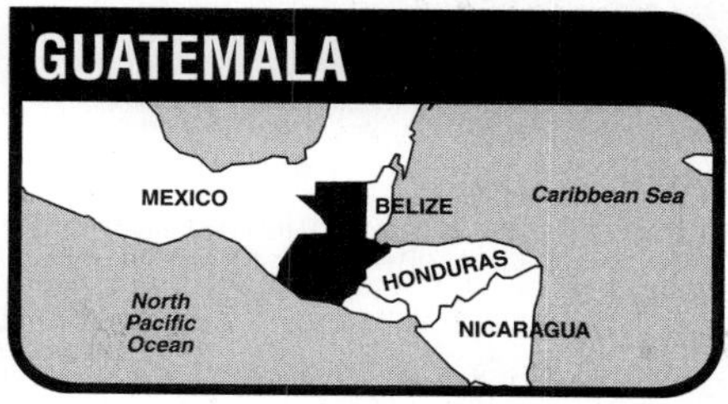

The Republic of Guatemala, the northernmost of the five Central American republics, has an area of 42,042 sq. mi. (108,890 sq. km.) and a population of 10.7 million. Capital: Guatemala City. The economy of Guatemala is heavily dependent on agriculture, however, the country is rich in nickel resources which are being developed. Coffee, cotton and bananas are exported.

Guatemala, once the site of an ancient Mayan civilization, was conquered by Pedro de Alvarado, the resourceful lieutenant of Cortes who undertook the conquest from Mexico. Cruel but strategically skillful, he progressed rapidly along the Pacific coastal lowlands to the highland plain of Quetzaltenango where the decisive battle for Guatemala was fought. After routing the Indian forces, he established the city of Guatemala in 1524. The Spanish Captaincy-General of Guatemala included all Central America but Panama. Guatemala declared its independence of Spain in 1821 and was absorbed into the Mexican empire of Augustin Iturbide (1822-23). From1823 to 1839 Guatemala was a constituent state of the Central American Republic. Upon dissolution of that confederation, Guatemala proclaimed itself an independent republic. Like El Salvador, Guatemala suffered from internal strife between right-wing, US-backed military government and leftist indigenous peoples from ca. 1954 to ca. 1997.

REPUBLIC

REFORM COINAGE

100 Centavos = 1 Quetzal

KM# 283 50 CENTAVOS

5.5400 g., Brass, 24.2 mm. **Obv:** National arms **Rev:** Whitenun orchid (lycaste skinneri var. alba) **Edge:** Reeded

Date	Mintage	F	VF	XF	Unc	BU
2001	—	—	—	0.50	1.25	1.75

KM# 284 QUETZAL

11.1000 g., Brass **Obv:** National arms **Rev:** PAX above stylized dove **Edge:** Reeded

Date	Mintage	F	VF	XF	Unc	BU
2001 Small letters	—	—	—	1.00	2.50	3.00

KM# 287 QUETZAL

31.1035 g., 0.9999 Silver 0.9999 oz. ASW, 30 mm. **Subject:** Cannonization of Brother Pedro Betancourt **Obv:** National arms **Rev:** Standing monk **Edge:** Plain

Date	Mintage	F	VF	XF	Unc	BU
ND(2002) Proof	6,000	Value: 50.00				

GUERNSEY

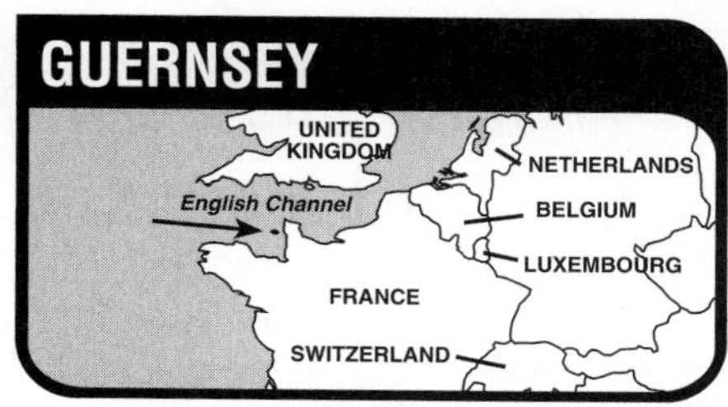

The Bailiwick of Guernsey, a British crown dependency located in the English Channel 30 miles (48 km.) west of Normandy, France, has an area of 30 sq. mi. (194 sq. km.)(including the isles of Alderney, Jethou, Herm, Brechou, and Sark), and a population of 54,000. Capital: St. Peter Port. Agriculture and cattle breeding are the main occupations.

Militant monks from the duchy of Normandy established the first permanent settlements on Guernsey prior to the Norman invasion of England, but the prevalence of prehistoric monuments suggests an earlier occupancy. The island, the only part of the duchy of Normandy belonging to the British crown, has been a possession of Britain since the Norman Conquest of 1066. During the Anglo-French wars, the harbors of Guernsey were employed in the building and out-fitting of ships for the English privateers preying on French shipping. Guernsey is administered by its own laws and customs. Unless the island is mentioned specifically, acts passed by the British Parliament are not applicable to Guernsey. During World War II, German troops occupied the island from June 30, 1940 till May 9,1945.

RULERS

British

MONETARY SYSTEM

100 Pence = 1 Pound

BRITISH DEPENDENCY

STANDARD COINAGE

KM# 169a 5 POUNDS

39.9400 g., 0.9167 Gold 1.1771 oz. AGW, 38.6 mm. **Ruler:** Elizabeth II **Subject:** WWII Liberation **Obv:** Elizabeth II by Broadley **Rev:** Soldiers and waving crowd **Edge:** Reeded

Date	Mintage	F	VF	XF	Unc	BU
2005 Proof	150	Value: 1,000				

KM# 168b 5 POUNDS

39.9400 g., 0.9167 Gold 1.1771 oz. AGW, 38.6 mm. **Ruler:** Elizabeth II **Subject:** End of WWII **Obv:** Elizabeth II by Broadley **Rev:** Churchill and George VI **Edge:** Reeded

Date	Mintage	F	VF	XF	Unc	BU
2005 Proof	150	Value: 1,000				

DECIMAL COINAGE

100 Pence = 1 Pound

KM# 89 PENNY

Copper Plated Steel **Obv:** Head of Queen Elizabeth II right **Obv. Designer:** Rank-Broadley **Rev:** Edible crab **Rev. Designer:** Robert Elderton

Date	Mintage	F	VF	XF	Unc	BU
2003	1,302,600	—	—	—	0.35	0.75

KM# 96 2 PENCE

7.2000 g., Copper Plated Steel **Obv:** Queen's new portrait **Obv. Designer:** Rank-Broadley **Rev:** Guernsey cow **Rev. Designer:** Robert Elderton **Edge:** Plain

Date	Mintage	F	VF	XF	Unc	BU
2003	662,600	—	—	—	0.50	0.75

KM# 97 5 PENCE

3.2600 g., Copper-Nickel **Obv:** Queen's new portrait **Obv. Designer:** Rank-Broadley **Rev:** Sailboat **Rev. Designer:** Robert Elderton **Edge:** Reeded

Date	Mintage	F	VF	XF	Unc	BU
2003	292,600	—	—	—	0.45	0.65

KM# 149 10 PENCE

6.5000 g., Copper-Nickel, 24.5 mm. **Obv:** Queen's new portrait **Rev:** Tomato plant **Rev. Designer:** Robert Elderton **Edge:** Reeded

Date	Mintage	F	VF	XF	Unc	BU
2003	32,600	—	—	—	0.60	0.85

KM# 90 20 PENCE

Copper-Nickel **Obv:** Bust of Queen Elizabeth II **Obv. Designer:** Rank-Broadley **Rev:** Island map within cogwheel **Rev. Designer:** Robert Elderton **Shape:** 7-sided

Date	Mintage	F	VF	XF	Unc	BU
2003	732,600	—	—	—	0.90	1.25

KM# 145 50 PENCE

7.9700 g., Copper-Nickel, 27.3 mm. **Subject:** Coronation Jubilee **Obv:** Queen's portrait **Rev:** Queen on horseback **Edge:** Plain **Shape:** 7-sided

Date	Mintage	F	VF	XF	Unc	BU
2003	—	—	—	—	1.50	2.50

KM# 45.2 50 PENCE

Copper-Nickel, 27.3 mm. **Obv:** Queen's portrait **Rev:** Freesia flowers **Rev. Designer:** Robert Elderton **Shape:** 7-sided

Date	Mintage	F	VF	XF	Unc	BU
2003	323,600	—	—	—	2.00	3.00

KM# 145a 50 PENCE

8.1000 g., 0.9250 Silver 0.2409 oz. ASW, 27.3 mm. **Subject:** Coronation Jubilee **Obv:** Queen's portrait **Rev:** Queen on horseback **Edge:** Plain **Shape:** 7-sided

Date	Mintage	F	VF	XF	Unc	BU
2003 Proof	—	Value: 25.00				

KM# 146 50 PENCE

7.9700 g., Copper-Nickel, 27.3 mm. **Subject:** Coronation Jubilee **Obv:** Queen's portrait **Rev:** Queen on throne **Edge:** Plain **Shape:** 7-sided

Date	Mintage	F	VF	XF	Unc	BU
2003	—	—	—	—	1.50	2.50

KM# 146a 50 PENCE

8.1000 g., 0.9250 Silver 0.2409 oz. ASW, 27.3 mm. **Subject:** Coronation Jubilee **Obv:** Queen's portrait **Rev:** Queen on throne **Edge:** Plain **Shape:** 7-sided

Date	Mintage	F	VF	XF	Unc	BU
2003 Proof	—	Value: 25.00				

KM# 147 50 PENCE

7.9700 g., Copper-Nickel, 27.3 mm. **Subject:** Coronation Jubilee **Obv:** Queen's portrait **Rev:** Crown **Edge:** Plain **Shape:** 7-sided

Date	Mintage	F	VF	XF	Unc	BU
2003	—	—	—	—	1.50	2.50

KM# 147a 50 PENCE

8.1000 g., 0.9250 Silver 0.2409 oz. ASW, 27.3 mm. **Subject:** Coronation Jubilee **Obv:** Queen's portrait **Rev:** Crown **Edge:** Plain **Shape:** 7-sided

Date	Mintage	F	VF	XF	Unc	BU
2003 Proof	—	Value: 25.00				

KM# 148 50 PENCE

7.9700 g., Copper-Nickel, 27.3 mm. **Subject:** Coronation Jubilee **Obv:** Queen's portrait **Rev:** Crowned ERII monogram **Edge:** Plain **Shape:** 7-sided

Date	Mintage	F	VF	XF	Unc	BU
2003	—	—	—	—	1.50	2.50

KM# 148a 50 PENCE

8.1000 g., 0.9250 Silver 0.2409 oz. ASW, 27.3 mm. **Subject:** Coronation Jubilee **Obv:** Queen's portrait **Rev:** Crowned ERII monogram **Edge:** Plain **Shape:** 7-sided

Date	Mintage	F	VF	XF	Unc	BU
2003 Proof	—	Value: 25.00				

KM# 156 50 PENCE

7.9700 g., Copper-Nickel, 27.3 mm. **Ruler:** Elizabeth II **Obv:** Queen's new portrait **Rev:** Crossed flowers **Edge:** Plain **Shape:** 7-sided

Date	Mintage	F	VF	XF	Unc	BU
2003	—	—	—	—	1.75	2.75

KM# 110 POUND

9.5000 g., Copper-Nickel-Zinc, 22.5 mm. **Subject:** Circulation Type **Obv:** Queen's new portrait **Rev:** Denomination **Edge:** Reeded

Date	Mintage	F	VF	XF	Unc	BU
2001	175,000	—	—	—	2.50	3.50
2003	46,600	—	—	—	2.50	3.50

KM# 111 POUND

9.5000 g., 0.9250 Silver .2825 oz. ASW, 22.5 mm. **Subject:** Queen's 75th Birthday **Obv:** Queen's portrait **Rev:** Queen's portrait in wreath **Edge:** Reeded

Date	Mintage	F	VF	XF	Unc	BU
2001 Proof	50,000	Value: 25.00				

KM# 142 POUND

30.9300 g., 0.9250 Silver 0.9198 oz. ASW, 38.6 mm. **Obv:** Head of Queen Elizabeth II right **Rev:** 1/2-bust of William, Duke of Normandy holding sword at left **Edge:** Reeded

Date	Mintage	F	VF	XF	Unc	BU
2002	—	—	—	—	35.00	45.00

KM# 83 2 POUNDS

Bi-Metallic Copper-Nickel center in Nickel-Brass ring **Obv:** Bust of Queen Elizabeth II right **Obv. Designer:** Rank-Broadley **Rev:** Latent image arms on cross **Edge:** Bailiwick of Guernsey

Date	Mintage	F	VF	XF	Unc	BU
2003	19,600	—	—	—	8.50	10.00

KM# 106 5 POUNDS

28.2800 g., Copper-Nickel, 38.6 mm. **Subject:** Queen Victoria Centennial **Obv:** Bust of Queen Elizabeth right **Rev:** Bust of Queen Victoria left **Edge:** Reeded

Date	Mintage	F	VF	XF	Unc	BU
2001	12,754	—	—	—	7.50	8.50
2001 Proof	30,000	Value: 20.00				

KM# 106a 5 POUNDS

28.2800 g., 0.9250 Silver .8410 oz. ASW, 38.6 mm. **Subject:** Queen Victoria 1837-1901 **Obv:** Bust of Queen Elizabeth II right **Rev:** Bust of Queen Victoria left **Edge:** Reeded

Date	Mintage	F	VF	XF	Unc	BU
2001 Proof	10,000	Value: 47.50				

KM# 108 5 POUNDS

28.0000 g., Copper-Nickel, 38.6 mm. **Subject:** Queen Elizabeth's 75th Birthday **Obv:** Queen Elizabeth's portrait **Rev:** Queen's portrait in wreath **Edge:** Reeded

Date	Mintage	F	VF	XF	Unc	BU
2001	14,000	—	—	—	6.00	7.00

KM# 108a 5 POUNDS

28.2800 g., 0.9250 Silver .8410 oz. ASW, 38.6 mm. **Subject:** Queen's 75th Birthday **Obv:** Queen's portrait **Rev:** Queen's portrait in wreath **Edge:** Reeded

Date	Mintage	F	VF	XF	Unc	BU
2001 Proof	20,000	Value: 55.00				

KM# 114 5 POUNDS

28.2800 g., Copper-Nickel, 38.6 mm. **Subject:** 19th Century Monarchy **Obv:** Queen's portrait **Rev:** Four portraits **Edge:** Reeded

Date	Mintage	F	VF	XF	Unc	BU
2001	5,700	—	—	—	11.50	12.50

KM# 114a 5 POUNDS

28.2800 g., 0.9250 Silver .8410 oz. ASW, 38.6 mm. **Edge:** Reeded

Date	Mintage	F	VF	XF	Unc	BU
2001 Proof	10,000	Value: 55.00				

KM# 115 5 POUNDS

1.1300 g., 0.9170 Gold .0333 oz. AGW, 13.9 mm. **Subject:** 19th Century Monarchy **Obv:** Bust of Queen Elizabeth II right **Rev:** Four portraits **Edge:** Reeded

Date	Mintage	F	VF	XF	Unc	BU
2001 Proof	—	Value: 65.00				

KM# 117 5 POUNDS

1.1300 g., 0.9170 Gold .0333 oz. AGW, 13.9 mm. **Subject:** Queen Victoria 1837-1901 **Obv:** Queen's portrait **Rev:** Queen Victoria's portrait **Edge:** Reeded

Date	Mintage	F	VF	XF	Unc	BU
2001 Proof	300	Value: 65.00				

KM# 118 5 POUNDS

1.1300 g., 0.9170 Gold .0333 oz. AGW, 13.9 mm. **Subject:** Queen's 75th Birthday **Obv:** Queen's portrait **Rev:** Queen's portrait in wreath **Edge:** Reeded

Date	Mintage	F	VF	XF	Unc	BU
2001 Proof	250	Value: 65.00				

KM# 114b 5 POUNDS

39.9400 g., 0.9166 Gold 1.177 oz. AGW, 38.6 mm. **Subject:** 19th Century Monarchy **Obv:** Queen's portrait **Rev:** Four royal portraits **Edge:** Reeded

Date	Mintage	F	VF	XF	Unc	BU
2001 Proof	200	Value: 900				

KM# 119 5 POUNDS

27.7100 g., Copper-Nickel 0.8018 oz., 38.6 mm. **Subject:** The Golden Jubilee **Obv:** Head of Queen Elizabeth II right **Rev:** The queen in her coach **Edge:** Reeded

Date	Mintage	F	VF	XF	Unc	BU
2002	9,250	—	—	—	16.50	18.00

KM# 119a 5 POUNDS

28.2800 g., Gold-Plated Base Metal Gold plated copper-nickel, 38.6 mm. **Subject:** Golden Jubilee **Obv:** Queen's portrait **Rev:** Queen in coach **Edge:** Reeded

Date	Mintage	F	VF	XF	Unc	BU
2002	50,000	—	—	—	15.00	16.50

KM# 119b 5 POUNDS

28.2800 g., 0.9250 Silver 0.841 oz. ASW, 38.6 mm. **Subject:** Queen's Golden Jubilee **Obv:** Bust of Queen Elizabeth II right **Rev:** Queen in her coach **Edge:** Reeded **Note:** Prev. KM#119a.

Date	Mintage	F	VF	XF	Unc	BU
2002 Proof	20,000	Value: 50.00				

KM# 119c 5 POUNDS

39.9400 g., 0.9166 Gold 1.177 oz. AGW, 38.6 mm. **Subject:** Golden Jubilee **Obv:** Queen's portrait **Rev:** Queen in coach **Edge:** Reeded

Date	Mintage	F	VF	XF	Unc	BU
2002 Proof	250	Value: 875				

KM# 121 5 POUNDS
27.7100 g., Copper Nickel, 38.6 mm. **Subject:** Queen's Golden Jubilee **Obv:** Bust of Queen Elizabeth II right **Rev:** Trooping the Colors scene **Edge:** Reeded

Date	Mintage	F	VF	XF	Unc	BU
2002	2,000	—	—	—	17.50	20.00

KM# 121a 5 POUNDS
28.2800 g., 0.9250 Silver 0.841 oz. ASW, 38.6 mm. **Subject:** Queen's Golden Jubilee **Obv:** Bust of Queen Elizabeth II right **Rev:** Trooping the Colors scene **Edge:** Reeded

Date	Mintage	F	VF	XF	Unc	BU
2002 Proof	20,000	Value: 50.00				

KM# 121b 5 POUNDS
39.9400 g., 0.9166 Gold 1.177 oz. AGW, 38.6 mm. **Subject:** Golden Jubilee **Obv:** Queen's portrait **Rev:** Trooping the Colors scene **Edge:** Reeded

Date	Mintage	F	VF	XF	Unc	BU
2002 Proof	250	Value: 875				

KM# 122 5 POUNDS
28.2800 g., Copper Nickel, 38.6 mm. **Subject:** Princess Diana **Obv:** Queen's portrait **Rev:** World and children behind cameo portrait of Diana **Edge:** Reeded

Date	Mintage	F	VF	XF	Unc	BU
2002	4,231	—	—	—	13.50	15.00

KM# 122a 5 POUNDS
28.2800 g., 0.9250 Silver .841 oz. ASW **Subject:** Princess Diana **Obv:** Queen's portrait **Rev:** World and children behind Diana's cameo portrait **Edge:** Reeded

Date	Mintage	F	VF	XF	Unc	BU
2002 Proof	20,000	Value: 45.00				

KM# 122b 5 POUNDS
39.9400 g., 0.9167 Gold 1.1771 oz. AGW, 1.1771 mm. **Subject:** Princess Diana **Obv:** Queen's portrait **Rev:** World and children behind Diana's cameo portrait **Edge:** Reeded

Date	Mintage	F	VF	XF	Unc	BU
2002 Proof	100	Value: 950				

KM# 124 5 POUNDS
28.2800 g., Copper Nickel, 38.6 mm. **Subject:** 18th Century British Monarchy **Obv:** Queen's portrait **Rev:** Five royal portraits **Edge:** Reeded

Date	Mintage	F	VF	XF	Unc	BU
2002	1,300	—	—	—	15.00	16.50

KM# 124a 5 POUNDS
28.2800 g., 0.9250 Silver 0.841 oz. ASW, 38.6 mm. **Subject:** 18th Century British Monarchy **Obv:** Queen's portrait **Rev:** Five royal portraits **Edge:** Reeded

Date	Mintage	F	VF	XF	Unc	BU
2002 Proof	10,000	Value: 50.00				

KM# 124b 5 POUNDS
39.9400 g., 0.9166 Gold 1.177 oz. AGW, 38.6 mm. **Subject:** 18th Century British Monarchy **Obv:** Queen's portrait **Rev:** Five royal portraits **Edge:** Reeded

Date	Mintage	F	VF	XF	Unc	BU
2002 Proof	200	Value: 900				

KM# 125 5 POUNDS
1.1300 g., 0.9166 Gold 0.0333 oz. AGW, 13.9 mm. **Subject:** 18th Century British Monarchy **Obv:** Queen's portrait **Rev:** Five royal portraits **Edge:** Reeded **Note:** Prev. KM#124b.

Date	Mintage	F	VF	XF	Unc	BU
2002 Proof	55	Value: 70.00				

KM# 127 5 POUNDS
28.2800 g., Copper-Nickel, 38.6 mm. **Subject:** Queen Mother **Obv:** Queen's portrait **Rev:** The late Queen Mother's portrait **Edge:** Reeded

Date	Mintage	F	VF	XF	Unc	BU
2002	1,750	—	—	—	15.00	16.50
2002 Proof	1,680	Value: 20.00				

KM# 127a 5 POUNDS
28.2800 g., 0.9250 Silver 0.841 oz. ASW, 38.6 mm. **Subject:** Queen Mother **Obv:** Queen's portrait **Rev:** The late Queen Mother's portrait **Edge:** Reeded

Date	Mintage	F	VF	XF	Unc	BU
2002 Proof	15,000	Value: 50.00				

KM# 127b 5 POUNDS
39.9400 g., 0.9166 Gold 1.177 oz. AGW, 38.6 mm. **Subject:** Queen Mother **Obv:** Queen's portrait **Rev:** Queen Mother's portrait **Edge:** Reeded

Date	Mintage	F	VF	XF	Unc	BU
2002 Proof	250	Value: 875				

KM# 128 5 POUNDS
1.1300 g., 0.9166 Gold 0.0333 oz. AGW, 13.9 mm. **Subject:** Queen Mother **Obv:** Queen's portrait **Rev:** The late Queen Mother's portrait **Edge:** Reeded

Date	Mintage	F	VF	XF	Unc	BU
2002 Proof	—	Value: 65.00				

KM# 129 5 POUNDS
28.2800 g., Copper-Nickel, 38.6 mm. **Subject:** The Duke of Wellington **Obv:** Queen's portrait **Rev:** Portrait with mounted dragoons in background **Edge:** Reeded

Date	Mintage	F	VF	XF	Unc	BU
2002	675	—	—	—	22.50	25.00

KM# 129a 5 POUNDS
28.2800 g., 0.9250 Silver 0.841 oz. ASW, 38.6 mm. **Subject:** The Duke of Wellington **Obv:** Queen's portrait **Rev:** Portrait with multicolor mounted dragoons in background **Edge:** Reeded

Date	Mintage	F	VF	XF	Unc	BU
2002 Proof	15,000	Value: 50.00				

KM# 129b 5 POUNDS
39.9400 g., 0.9166 Gold 1.177 oz. AGW, 38.6 mm. **Subject:** Duke of Wellington **Obv:** Queen's portrait **Rev:** Wellington's portrait with multicolor cavalry scene **Edge:** Reeded

Date	Mintage	F	VF	XF	Unc	BU
2002 Proof	200	Value: 900				

KM# 130 5 POUNDS
1.1300 g., 0.9166 Gold 0.0333 oz. AGW, 13.9 mm. **Subject:** The Duke of Wellington **Obv:** Queen's portrait **Rev:** Portrait with mounted dragoons in background **Edge:** Reeded

Date	Mintage	F	VF	XF	Unc	BU
2002 Proof	—	Value: 65.00				

KM# 143 5 POUNDS
28.2800 g., Copper-Nickel, 38.6 mm. **Obv:** Head of Queen Elizabeth II right **Rev:** Prince William wearing sweater **Edge:** Reeded

Date	Mintage	F	VF	XF	Unc	BU
2003	3,700	—	—	—	17.50	20.00

KM# 143a 5 POUNDS
28.2800 g., 0.9250 Silver 0.841 oz. ASW, 38.6 mm. **Obv:** Head of Queen Elizabeth II right **Rev:** Prince William wearing sweater **Edge:** Reeded

Date	Mintage	F	VF	XF	Unc	BU
2003 Proof	5,000	Value: 47.50				

KM# 143b 5 POUNDS
39.9400 g., 0.9166 Gold 1.177 oz. AGW, 38.6 mm. **Obv:** Head of Queen Elizabeth II right **Rev:** Prince William wearing sweater **Edge:** Reeded

Date	Mintage	F	VF	XF	Unc	BU
2003 Proof	200	Value: 900				

KM# 158 5 POUNDS
Copper-Nickel **Ruler:** Elizabeth II **Subject:** Golden Hind

Date	Mintage	F	VF	XF	Unc	BU
2003	300	—	—	—	—	25.00

KM# 159 5 POUNDS
Copper-Nickel **Ruler:** Elizabeth II **Subject:** 17th Century Monarchs

Date	Mintage	F	VF	XF	Unc	BU
2003	500	—	—	—	—	22.50

KM# 160 5 POUNDS
Copper-Nickel **Ruler:** Elizabeth II **Subject:** Royal Navy - H. Nelson

Date	Mintage	F	VF	XF	Unc	BU
2003	550	—	—	—	—	22.50

KM# 161 5 POUNDS
Copper-Nickel **Ruler:** Elizabeth II **Subject:** 16th Century Monarchs

Date	Mintage	F	VF	XF	Unc	BU
2004	500	—	—	—	—	22.50

KM# 162 5 POUNDS
Copper-Nickel **Ruler:** Elizabeth II **Subject:** Mallard Locomotive

Date	Mintage	F	VF	XF	Unc	BU
2004	2,193	—	—	—	—	17.50

KM# 163 5 POUNDS
Copper-Nickel **Ruler:** Elizabeth II **Subject:** City of Truro Train

Date	Mintage	F	VF	XF	Unc	BU
2004	500	—	—	—	—	22.50

KM# 164 5 POUNDS
Copper-Nickel **Ruler:** Elizabeth II **Subject:** The Boat Train

Date	Mintage	F	VF	XF	Unc	BU
2004	250	—	—	—	—	25.00

KM# 165 5 POUNDS
Copper-Nickel **Subject:** Train Spotter

Date	Mintage	F	VF	XF	Unc	BU
2004	300	—	—	—	—	25.00

KM# 166 5 POUNDS
Copper-Nickel **Ruler:** Elizabeth II **Subject:** Royal Navy - Henry VIII

Date	Mintage	F	VF	XF	Unc	BU
2004	300	—	—	—	—	25.00

KM# 167 5 POUNDS
Copper-Nickel **Ruler:** Elizabeth II **Subject:** Royal Navy - Invinvible

Date	Mintage	F	VF	XF	Unc	BU
2004	300	—	—	—	—	25.00

KM# 150 5 POUNDS
28.2800 g., Copper-Nickel, 38.6 mm. **Subject:** D-Day **Obv:** Queen Elizabeth II **Rev:** British troops storming ashore **Edge:** Reeded

Date	Mintage	F	VF	XF	Unc	BU
2004	65,611	—	—	—	15.00	16.50

KM# 154 5 POUNDS
28.2800 g., 0.9250 Silver 0.841 oz. ASW, 38.6 mm.
Subject: D-Day **Obv:** Queen Elizabeth II **Rev:** British soldier advancing to left **Edge:** Reeded

Date	Mintage	F	VF	XF	Unc	BU
2004 Proof	10,000	Value: 85.00				

KM# 154a 5 POUNDS
39.9400 g., 0.9167 Gold 1.1771 oz. AGW, 38.6 mm.
Subject: D-Day **Obv:** Queen Elizabeth II **Rev:** British soldier advancing to left **Edge:** Reeded

Date	Mintage	F	VF	XF	Unc	BU
2004 Proof	500	Value: 1,000				

KM# 155 5 POUNDS
28.2800 g., Copper-Nickel, 38.6 mm. **Ruler:** Elizabeth II
Obv: Queen Elizabeth II **Rev:** Sgt. Luke O'Connor , first army Victoria Cross winner, above Battle of Alma scene with multicolor flag **Edge:** Reeded

Date	Mintage	F	VF	XF	Unc	BU
2004	1,060	—	—	—	25.00	27.50

KM# 155a 5 POUNDS
28.2800 g., 0.9250 Silver 0.841 oz. ASW, 38.6 mm.
Ruler: Elizabeth II **Obv:** Queen Elizabeth II **Rev:** Sgt. Luke O'Conner, first army Victoria Cross winner, above Battle of Alma scene with multicolor flag **Edge:** Reeded

Date	Mintage	F	VF	XF	Unc	BU
2004 Proof	10,000	Value: 85.00				

KM# 155b 5 POUNDS
39.9400 g., 0.9166 Gold 1.177 oz. AGW, 38.6 mm.
Ruler: Elizabeth II **Obv:** Queen Elizabeth II **Rev:** Sgt. Luke O'Connor, first army Victoria Cross winner, above Battle of Alma scene with multicolor flag **Edge:** Reeded

Date	Mintage	F	VF	XF	Unc	BU
2004 Proof	500	Value: 1,000				

KM# 168a 5 POUNDS
28.2800 g., 0.9250 Silver 0.841 oz. ASW, 38.6 mm.
Subject: End of WWII **Obv:** Elizabeth II by Broadley
Rev: Churchill and George VI **Edge:** Reeded

Date	Mintage	F	VF	XF	Unc	BU
2005 Proof	5,000	Value: 85.00				

KM# 116 10 POUNDS
141.7500 g., 0.9990 Silver 4.5528 oz. ASW, 65 mm.
Subject: 19th Century Monarchy **Obv:** Queen's portrait
Rev: Four portraits **Edge:** Reeded

Date	Mintage	F	VF	XF	Unc	BU
2001 Proof	950	Value: 200				

KM# 126 10 POUNDS
155.5175 g., 0.9990 Silver 4.995 oz. ASW, 65 mm.
Subject: British Monarchy 18th Century **Obv:** Queen's portrait
Rev: Five royal portraits **Edge:** Reeded

Date	Mintage	F	VF	XF	Unc	BU
2002 Proof	950	Value: 200				

KM# 151 10 POUNDS
155.5170 g., 0.9250 Silver 4.625 oz. ASW, 65 mm. **Subject:** D-Day **Obv:** Queen Elizabeth II **Rev:** British troops storming ashore **Edge:** Reeded

Date	Mintage	F	VF	XF	Unc	BU
2004 Proof	1,944	Value: 400				

KM# 107 25 POUNDS
7.8100 g., 0.9170 Gold .2303 oz. AGW, 22 mm. **Subject:** Queen Victoria Centennial **Obv:** Queen Elizabeth's portrait **Rev:** Queen Victoria's portrait **Edge:** Reeded

Date	Mintage	F	VF	XF	Unc	BU
2001 Proof	2,500	Value: 270				

KM# 112 25 POUNDS
7.8100 g., 0.9170 Gold .2303 oz. AGW, 22 mm.
Subject: Queen's 75th Birthday **Obv:** Queen's portrait
Rev: Queen's portrait in wreath **Edge:** Reeded

Date	Mintage	F	VF	XF	Unc	BU
2001 Proof	5,000	Value: 235				

KM# 123 25 POUNDS
7.9800 g., 0.9167 Gold 0.2352 oz. AGW, 22.05 mm. **Subject:** Princess Diana **Obv:** Queen's portrait **Rev:** Diana's cameo portrait in wreath **Edge:** Reeded

Date	Mintage	F	VF	XF	Unc	BU
2002 Proof	2,500	Value: 285				

KM# 131 25 POUNDS
7.8100 g., 0.9166 Gold 0.2302 oz. AGW, 22 mm. **Subject:** The Duke of Wellington **Obv:** Queen's portrait **Rev:** Portrait with mounted dragoons in the background **Edge:** Reeded

Date	Mintage	F	VF	XF	Unc	BU
2002 Proof	2,500	Value: 235				

KM# 139 25 POUNDS
7.9800 g., 0.9166 Gold 0.2352 oz. AGW, 22 mm. **Subject:** Golden Jubilee **Obv:** Queen's portrait **Rev:** Queen in coach **Edge:** Reeded

Date	Mintage	F	VF	XF	Unc	BU
2002 Proof	5,000	Value: 300				

KM# 140 25 POUNDS
7.9800 g., 0.9166 Gold 0.2352 oz. AGW, 22 mm. **Subject:** Queen Mother **Obv:** Queen's portrait **Rev:** Queen Mother's portrait **Edge:** Reeded

Date	Mintage	F	VF	XF	Unc	BU
2002 Proof	2,500	Value: 300				

KM# 141 25 POUNDS
7.9800 g., 0.9166 Gold 0.2352 oz. AGW, 22 mm. **Subject:** Golden Jubilee **Obv:** Queen's portrait **Rev:** Trooping the Colors scene **Edge:** Reeded

Date	Mintage	F	VF	XF	Unc	BU
2003 Proof	5,000	Value: 300				

KM# 152 25 POUNDS
7.9800 g., 0.9167 Gold 0.2352 oz. AGW, 22 mm. **Subject:** D-Day **Obv:** Queen Elizabeth II **Rev:** Advancing British soldier **Edge:** Reeded

Date	Mintage	F	VF	XF	Unc	BU
2004 Proof	500	Value: 325				

KM# 144 50 POUNDS
1000.0000 g., 0.9250 Silver 29.7394 oz. ASW, 100 mm.
Obv: Queen's portrait **Rev:** Prince William wearing sweater **Edge:** Reeded

Date	Mintage	F	VF	XF	Unc	BU
2003 Proof	500	Value: 995				

KM# 153 50 POUNDS
1000.0000 g., 0.9250 Silver 29.7394 oz. ASW, 100 mm.
Subject: D-Day **Obv:** Queen Elizabeth II **Rev:** British troops storming ashore **Edge:** Reeded

Date	Mintage	F	VF	XF	Unc	BU
2004 Proof	600	Value: 1,200				

PIEFORTS

KM#	Date	Mintage	Identification	Mkt Val
P3	2002	100	5 Pounds. 0.9166 Gold. 56.5600 g. 38.6 mm. Queen's portrait. Queen in coach. Reeded edge. Not a full weight piefort.	1,400

MINT SETS

KM#	Date	Mintage	Identification	Issue Price	Mkt Val
MS10	2003 (8)	—	KM#89,96,97,149,90,148,110,83	—	20.00

The Republic of Guinea-Bissau, formerly Portuguese Guinea, an overseas province on the west coast of Africa between Senegal and Guinea, has an area of 13,948 sq. mi. (36,120sq. km.) and a population of 1.1 million. Capital: Bissau. The country has undeveloped deposits of oil and bauxite. Peanuts, oil-palm kernels and hides are exported.

REPUBLIC OF GUINEA-BISSAU

INSTITUT MONETAIRE

KM# 40 6000 CFA FRANCS - 4 AFRICA
10.2000 g., Bi-Metallic Copper-Nickel center in Brass ring, 28.4 mm. **Obv:** Gazelle **Rev:** Elephant head on Central Africa map **Edge:** Plain

Date	Mintage	F	VF	XF	Unc	BU
2004	1,200	—	—	—	55.00	—

KM# 40a 6000 CFA FRANCS - 4 AFRICA
Bi-Metallic .999Silver center in .999Gold plated .999 Silver ring, 28.4 mm. **Obv:** Gazelle **Rev:** Elephant head on Central Africa map

Date	Mintage	F	VF	XF	Unc	BU
2004	25	—	—	—	475	—

KM# 40b 6000 CFA FRANCS - 4 AFRICA
0.9990 Silver, 28.4 mm. **Obv:** Gazelle **Rev:** Elephant head on Central Africa map

Date	Mintage	F	VF	XF	Unc	BU
2004	25	—	—	—	420	—

The Cooperative Republic of Guyana, is situated on the northeast coast of South America, has an area of 83,000 sq. mi. (214,970 sq. km.) and a population of 729,000. Capital: Georgetown. The economy is basically agrarian. Sugar, rice and bauxite are exported.

The original area of Essequibo and Demerary, which included present-day Suriname, French Guiana, and parts of Brazil and Venezuela was sighted by Columbus in 1498. Guyana became a republic on Feb. 23, 1970. It is a member of the Commonwealth of Nations. The president is the Chief of State. The prime minister is the Head of Government. Guyana is a member of the Caribbean Community and Common Market (CARICOM).

REPUBLIC OF GUYANA

DECIMAL COINAGE

KM# 50 DOLLAR
Copper Plated Steel **Rev:** Hand gathering rice

Date	Mintage	F	VF	XF	Unc	BU
2001	—	—	—	—	0.50	0.65
2002	—	—	—	—	0.50	0.65

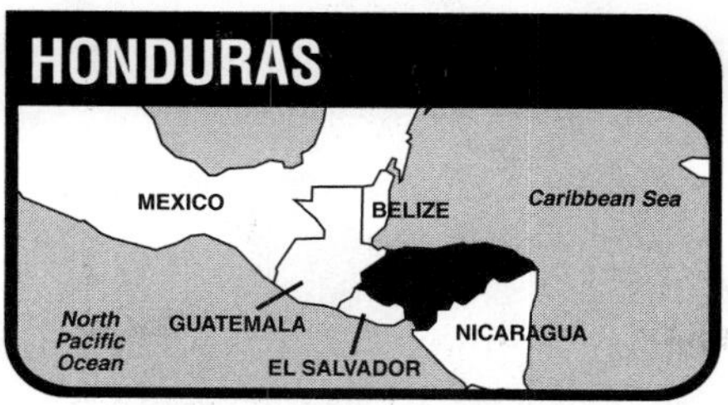

The Republic of Honduras, situated in Central America alongside El Salvador, between Nicaragua and Guatemala, has an area of 43,277sq. mi. (112,090 sq. km.) and a population of 5.6 million. Capital: Tegucigalpa. Agriculture, mining (gold and silver), and logging are the major economic activities, with increasing tourism and emerging petroleum resource discoveries. Precious metals, bananas, timber and coffee are exported.

The eastern part of Honduras was part of the ancient Mayan Empire; however, the largest Indian community in Honduras was the not too well known Lencas. Columbus claimed Honduras for Spain in 1502, during his last voyage to the Americas. Cristobal de Olid established the first settlement under orders from Hernando Cortes, then in Mexico. The area, regarded as one of the most promising sources of gold and silver in the New World, was a part of the Captaincy General of Guatemala throughout the colonial period. After declaring its independence from Spain on September 15, 1821, Honduras fell under the Mexican empire of Augustin de Iturbide, and then joined the Central American Republic (1823-39). Upon the effective dissolution of that federation (ca. 1840), Honduras reclaimed its independence as a self-standing republic. 1876 to 1933 saw a period of instability. From 1933 to 1940 General Tiburcio Carias Andino was dictator president of the Republic. Since 1990 democratic practices have become more consistent.

REPUBLIC

REFORM COINAGE

100 Centavos = 1 Lempira

KM# 72.4 5 CENTAVOS
Brass **Obv:** Without clouds behind pyramids

Date	Mintage	F	VF	XF	Unc	BU
2003	—	—	0.10	0.15	0.35	—

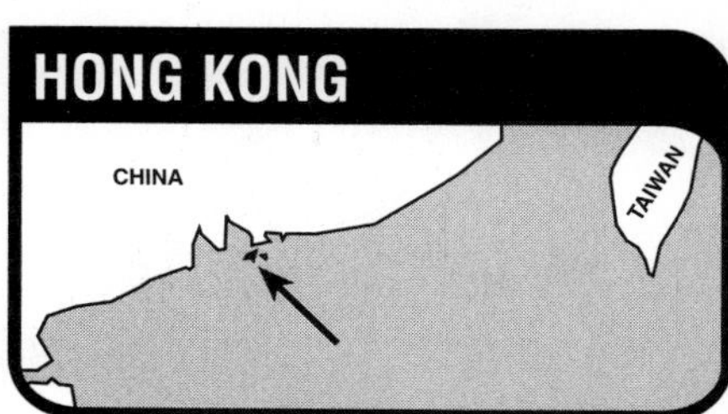

Hong Kong, a former British colony, reverted to control of the People's Republic of China on July 1, 1997 as a Special Administrative Region. It is situated at the mouth of the Canton or Pearl River 90 miles (145 km.) southeast of Canton, has an area of 403 sq. mi. (1,040 sq. km.) and an estimated population of 6.3 million. Capital: Victoria. The free port of Hong Kong, the commercial center of the Far East, is a trans-shipment point for goods destined for China and the countries of the Pacific Rim. Light manufacturing and tourism are important components of the economy.

The legends on Hong Kong coinage are bilingual: English and Chinese. The rare 1941 cent was dispatched to Hong Kong in several shipments. One fell into Japanese hands, while another was melted down by the British and a third was sunk during enemy action.

HONG KONG S.A.R.

DECIMAL COINAGE

KM# 80 50 DOLLARS
35.4300 g., 0.9250 Bi-Metallic Gold plated .925 Silver center in .925 Silver ring 1.0536 oz., 40 mm. **Subject:** "May your wishes come true" **Obv:** Bauhinia flower **Rev:** Jade Ju-I

Date	Mintage	F	VF	XF	Unc	BU
2002 Proof	60,000	Value: 60.00				

KM# 81 50 DOLLARS
35.4300 g., 0.9250 Bi-Metallic Gold plated .925 Silver center in .925 Silver ring 1.0536 oz., 40 mm. **Obv:** Bauhinia flower **Rev:** Fish

Date	Mintage	F	VF	XF	Unc	BU
2002 Proof	60,000	Value: 60.00				

KM# 82 50 DOLLARS
35.2500 g., 0.9250 Bi-Metallic Gold plated .925 Silver center in .925 Silver ring 1.0483 oz., 40 mm. **Obv:** Bauhinia flower **Rev:** Horses

Date	Mintage	F	VF	XF	Unc	BU
2002 Proof	60,000	Value: 60.00				

KM# 83 50 DOLLARS

35.3400 g., 0.9250 Bi-Metallic Gold plated .925 Silver center in .925 Silver ring 1.0510 oz., 40 mm. **Obv:** Bauhinia flower **Rev:** Peony flower

Date	Mintage	F	VF	XF	Unc	BU
2002 Proof	60,000	Value: 60.00				

KM# 84 50 DOLLARS

35.1400 g., 0.9250 Bi-Metallic Gold plated .925 Silver center in .925 Silver ring 1.0450 oz., 40 mm. **Obv:** Bauhinia flower **Rev:** Windmills

Date	Mintage	F	VF	XF	Unc	BU
2002 Proof	60,000	Value: 60.00				

PROOF SETS

KM#	Date	Mintage	Identification	Issue Price	Mkt Val
PS7	2002 (6)	60,000	KM#80-84 plus gold medal	370	300

HUNGARY

The Republic of Hungary, located in central Europe, has an area of 35,929 sq. mi. (93,030 sq. km.) and a population of 10.7 million. Capital: Budapest. The economy is based on agriculture, bauxite and a rapidly expanding industrial sector. Machinery, chemicals, iron and steel, and fruits and vegetables are exported.

MINT MARKS

B, K, KB - Kremnitz (Kormoczbanya)
BP - Budapest

MONETARY SYSTEM

Commencing 1946
100 Filler = 1 Forint

SECOND REPUBLIC
1989-present

DECIMAL COINAGE

KM# 692 FORINT

2.0500 g., Brass **Obv:** Arms of the Republic **Rev:** Value

Date	Mintage	F	VF	XF	Unc	BU
2001	—	—	—	—	0.25	—
2001 Proof	3,000	Value: 3.75				
2002	—	—	—	—	0.25	—
2002BP Proof	3,000	Value: 3.75				
2003BP	—	—	—	—	0.25	—
2003BP Proof	7,000	Value: 3.50				
2004BP	—	—	—	—	0.25	—
2004BP Proof	7,000	Value: 3.50				
2005	—	—	—	—	0.25	—
2005 Proof	—	Value: 3.50				

KM# 693 2 FORINT

3.1000 g., Copper-Nickel **Obv:** Native flower: Colchicum Hungaricum **Rev:** Value

Date	Mintage	F	VF	XF	Unc	BU
2001	—	—	—	—	0.35	—
2001 Proof	3,000	Value: 4.25				
2002BP	—	—	—	—	0.35	—
2002BP Proof	3,000	Value: 4.25				
2003BP	—	—	—	—	0.35	—
2003BP Proof	7,000	Value: 4.00				
2004BP	—	—	—	—	0.35	—
2004BP Proof	7,000	Value: 4.00				
2005	—	—	—	—	0.35	—
2005 Proof	—	Value: 4.00				

KM# 694 5 FORINT

4.2000 g., Brass **Obv:** Great White Egret

Date	Mintage	F	VF	XF	Unc	BU
2001	—	—	—	—	1.00	—
2001 Proof	3,000	Value: 5.00				
2002BP	—	—	—	—	1.00	—
2002BP Proof	3,000	Value: 5.00				
2003BP	—	—	—	—	1.00	—
2003BP Proof	7,000	Value: 4.50				
2004BP	—	—	—	—	1.00	—
2004BP Proof	7,000	Value: 4.50				
2005	—	—	—	—	1.00	—
2005 Proof	—	Value: 4.50				

KM# 695 10 FORINT

6.1000 g., Copper-Nickel Clad Brass **Obv:** Arms of the Republic **Rev:** Value

Date	Mintage	F	VF	XF	Unc	BU
2001	—	—	—	—	2.50	—
2001 Proof	3,000	Value: 5.50				
2002BP	—	—	—	—	2.50	—
2002BP Proof	3,000	Value: 5.50				
2003BP	—	—	—	—	2.50	—
2003BP Proof	7,000	Value: 5.00				
2004BP	—	—	—	—	2.50	—
2004BP Proof	7,000	Value: 5.00				
2005	—	—	—	—	2.50	—
2005 Proof	—	Value: 5.00				

KM# 779 10 FORINT

6.1000 g., Copper-Nickel, 24.8 mm. **Obv:** Jozsef Attila **Rev:** Value **Edge:** Segmented reeding

Date	Mintage	F	VF	XF	Unc	BU
2005BP	27,000	—	—	—	2.50	—
2005BP Proof	15,000	Value: 3.50				

KM# 696 20 FORINT

6.9000 g., Nickel-Brass **Obv:** Hungarian Iris **Rev:** Value

Date	Mintage	F	VF	XF	Unc	BU
2001	—	—	—	—	1.50	2.00
2001 Proof	3,000	Value: 4.50				
2002BP	—	—	—	—	1.50	2.00
2002BP Proof	3,000	Value: 4.50				
2003BP	—	—	—	—	1.50	2.00
2003BP Proof	7,000	Value: 4.00				
2004BP	—	—	—	—	1.50	2.00
2004BP Proof	7,000	Value: 4.00				
2005	—	—	—	—	1.50	2.00
2005 Proof	—	Value: 4.00				

KM# 768 20 FORINT

6.9400 g., Nickel-Brass, 26.4 mm. **Obv:** Deak Ferenc **Rev:** Value **Edge:** Reeded

Date	Mintage	F	VF	XF	Unc	BU
2003BP	1,000,000	—	—	—	1.50	2.00
2003BP Proof	7,000	Value: 4.00				

KM# 697 50 FORINT

7.7000 g., Copper-Nickel Clad Brass **Obv:** Saker falcon **Rev:** Value

Date	Mintage	F	VF	XF	Unc	BU
2001	—	—	—	—	3.00	3.50
2001 Proof	3,000	Value: 5.50				
2002BP	—	—	—	—	3.00	3.50
2002BP Proof	3,000	Value: 5.50				
2003BP	—	—	—	—	3.00	3.50
2003BP Proof	7,000	Value: 5.00				
2004BP	—	—	—	—	3.00	3.50
2004BP Proof	7,000	Value: 5.00				
2005	—	—	—	—	3.00	3.50
2005 Proof	—	Value: 5.00				

KM# 773 50 FORINT
7.7000 g., Copper-Nickel Clad Brass, 27.5 mm. **Obv:** National arms above Euro Union star circle **Rev:** Value **Edge:** Plain

Date	Mintage	F	VF	XF	Unc	BU
2004BP	1,000,000	—	—	—	3.00	3.50
2004BP Proof	7,000	Value: 6.00				

KM# 780 50 FORINT
7.7000 g., Copper-Nickel, 27.4 mm. **Subject:** International Childrens Safety Service **Obv:** Stylized crying child **Rev:** Value **Edge:** Plain

Date	Mintage	F	VF	XF	Unc	BU
2005BP	2,000,000	—	—	—	3.00	3.50
2005BP Proof	12,000	Value: 5.00				

KM# 760 100 FORINT
8.0000 g., Bi-Metallic Stainless Steel center in Brass plated Steel ring, 23.7 mm. **Obv:** Head of Kossuth right in inner circle **Rev:** Value **Edge:** Reeded

Date	Mintage	F	VF	XF	Unc	BU
2002 Proof	10,000	Value: 5.00				

KM# 721 100 FORINT (Szaz)
Bi-Metallic Brass plated Steel center in Stainless Steel ring **Obv:** Crowned arms **Rev:** Denomination in inner circle

Date	Mintage	F	VF	XF	Unc	BU
2001	—	—	—	—	5.00	—
2001 Proof	3,000	Value: 8.00				
2002	—	—	—	—	5.00	—
2002 Proof	3,000	Value: 8.00				
2003BP	—	—	—	—	5.00	—
2003BP Proof	7,000	Value: 7.50				
2004BP	—	—	—	—	5.00	—
2004BP Proof	7,000	Value: 7.50				
2005	—	—	—	—	5.00	—
2005 Proof	—	Value: 7.50				

KM# 754 200 FORINT
9.4000 g., Brass, 29.2 mm. **Subject:** Childrens Literature: Ludas Matyi **Obv:** Denomination **Rev:** Man holding a goose **Edge:** Plain

Date	Mintage	F	VF	XF	Unc	BU
2001	12,000	—	—	—	6.50	7.50
2001 Proof	5,000	Value: 12.50				

KM# 755 200 FORINT
Brass, 29.2 mm. **Subject:** Childrens Literature: Janos Vitez **Obv:** Denomination **Rev:** Soldier riding a flying bird **Edge:** Plain

Date	Mintage	F	VF	XF	Unc	BU
2001	12,000	—	—	—	6.50	7.50
2001 Proof	5,000	Value: 12.50				

KM# 756 200 FORINT
Brass, 29.2 mm. **Subject:** Childrens Literature: Toldi **Obv:** Denomination **Rev:** Knight kicking a boat off the shore **Edge:** Plain

Date	Mintage	F	VF	XF	Unc	BU
2001	12,000	—	—	—	6.50	7.50
2001 Proof	5,000	Value: 12.50				

KM# 757 200 FORINT
Brass, 29.2 mm. **Subject:** Childrens Literature: A Pal Utcai Fiuk **Obv:** Denomination **Rev:** Two men and cordwood **Edge:** Plain

Date	Mintage	F	VF	XF	Unc	BU
2001	12,000	—	—	—	6.50	7.50
2001 Proof	5,000	Value: 12.50				

KM# 764 500 FORINT
13.9000 g., Copper Nickel, 29 mm. **Subject:** Farkas Kempelen's Chess Machine **Obv:** Denomination **Rev:** Robotic human form chess playing machine built in 1769 **Edge:** Plain **Shape:** Square

Date	Mintage	F	VF	XF	Unc	BU
2002BP	5,000	—	—	—	12.50	15.00
2002BP Proof	5,000	Value: 25.00				

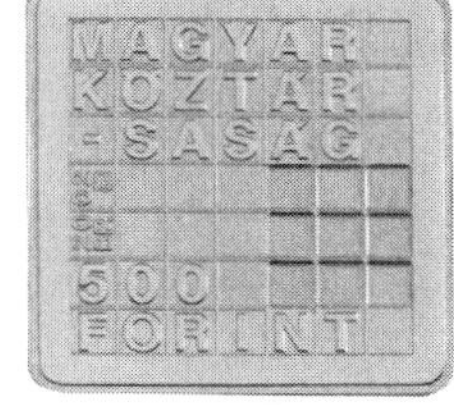

KM# 765 500 FORINT
13.8000 g., Copper Nickel, 29 mm. **Subject:** Rubik's Cube **Obv:** Inscription on Rubik's Cube design **Rev:** Rubik's Cube with inscription **Edge:** Plain **Shape:** Square

Date	Mintage	F	VF	XF	Unc	BU
2002BP	5,000	—	—	—	12.50	15.00
2002BP Proof	5,000	Value: 25.00				

KM# 781 500 FORINT
14.0000 g., Copper-Nickel **Obv:** Old wheel **Rev:** First Hungarian Post Office motor vehicle **Edge:** Plain **Shape:** Square
Note: 28.43 x 28.43mm

Date	Mintage	F	VF	XF	Unc	BU
2005BP	5,000	—	—	—	—	15.00
2005BP Proof	10,000	Value: 25.00				

KM# 766 1000 FORINT
19.5000 g., Bronze Hollow coin unscrews to open **Obv:** Denomination and satellite dish **Rev:** Mercury

Date	Mintage	F	VF	XF	Unc	BU
2002BP	15,000	—	—	—	15.00	16.50

KM# 752 3000 FORINT
31.4600 g., 0.9250 Silver .9356 oz. ASW, 28.5 mm. **Subject:** Hungarian Silver Coinage Millennium **Obv:** Denomination in ornamental frame **Rev:** Thaler design circa 1500 portraying Ladislaus I (1077-95) with the title of saint **Edge:** Reeding over "1001-2001" **Edge Lettering:** "BP.NX.KB.HX.GY.F.AF.MM.C+"

Date	Mintage	F	VF	XF	Unc	BU
2001	5,000	—	—	—	35.00	37.50
2001 Proof	5,000	Value: 40.00				

KM# 759 3000 FORINT
31.8000 g., 0.9250 Silver .9457 oz. ASW, 38.7 mm. **Subject:** Centennial of First Hungarian Film "The Dance" **Obv:** Denomination **Rev:** Two dancers on film **Edge:** Reeded

Date	Mintage	F	VF	XF	Unc	BU
2001	3,500	—	—	—	37.50	40.00
2001 Proof	3,500	Value: 45.00				

KM# 761 3000 FORINT
31.3300 g., 0.9250 Silver 0.9317 oz. ASW, 38.6 mm. **Subject:** Hortobagy National Park **Obv:** Landscape **Rev:** Hungarian Grey Longhorn bull **Edge:** Reeded

Date	Mintage	F	VF	XF	Unc	BU
2002	5,000	—	—	—	30.00	32.00
2002 Proof	5,000	Value: 35.00				

KM# 767 3000 FORINT
31.4600 g., 0.9250 Silver 0.9356 oz. ASW **Subject:** 100th Anniversary - Birth of Kovacs Margit (1902-1977) **Obv:** Denomination **Rev:** The "Trumpet of Judgement Day"

Date	Mintage	F	VF	XF	Unc	BU
2002BP	4,000	—	—	—	38.00	40.00
2002BP Proof	4,000	Value: 48.00				

KM# 762 3000 FORINT
31.4600 g., 0.9250 Silver 0.9356 oz. ASW, 38.5 mm. **Subject:** 200th Anniversary - National Library **Obv:** Small coat of arms in fancy frame **Rev:** Interior view of library **Edge:** Reeded

Date	Mintage	F	VF	XF	Unc	BU
2002BP	3,000	—	—	—	35.00	37.50
2002BP Proof	3,000	Value: 40.00				

KM# 763 3000 FORINT
31.4600 g., 0.9250 Silver 0.9356 oz. ASW, 38.5 mm.
Subject: Janos Bolyai's publication of his "Appendix"
Obv: Circular graph **Rev:** Signature above seven line inscription, name and dates **Edge:** Reeded

Date	Mintage	F	VF	XF	Unc	BU
2002BP	3,000	—	—	—	35.00	37.50
2002BP Proof	3,000	Value: 40.00				

KM# 751 4000 FORINT
31.4600 g., 0.9250 Silver .9356 oz. ASW, 26.4 x 39.6 mm. **Subject:** Godollo Artist Colony Centennial **Obv:** Denomination **Rev:** "Sisters" stained glass window design **Edge:** Plain **Shape:** 4-sided

Date	Mintage	F	VF	XF	Unc	BU
2001	4,000	—	—	—	40.00	42.50
2001 Proof	4,000	Value: 50.00				

KM# 769 5000 FORINT
31.4600 g., 0.9250 Silver 0.9356 oz. ASW, 38.6 mm. **Subject:** Budapest Philharmonic Orchestra **Obv:** Crowned arms in wreath **Rev:** Four coin-like portraits of Erkel, Dohnanyi, Bartók and Kodaly **Edge:** Reeded

Date	Mintage	F	VF	XF	Unc	BU
2003BP	4,000	—	—	—	37.50	40.00
2003BP Proof	4,000	Value: 42.50				

KM# 770 5000 FORINT
31.4600 g., 0.9250 Silver 0.9356 oz. ASW, 38.6 mm. **Subject:** 100th Anniversary - Birth of Neumann Janos **Obv:** Denomination and binary number date **Rev:** Neumann Janos **Edge:** Reeded

Date	Mintage	F	VF	XF	Unc	BU
2003BP	3,000	—	—	—	40.00	42.50
2003BP Proof	3,000	Value: 45.00				

KM# 771 5000 FORINT
31.4600 g., 0.9250 Silver 0.9356 oz. ASW, 38.6 mm. **Subject:** Rakoczi's War of Liberation **Obv:** Transylvanian ducat design above country name, value and date **Rev:** Kuruc cavalryman with sword and trumpet **Edge:** Reeded

Date	Mintage	F	VF	XF	Unc	BU
2003BP	3,000	—	—	—	45.00	47.50
2003BP Proof	3,000	Value: 50.00				

KM# 772 5000 FORINT
31.4600 g., 0.9250 Silver 0.9356 oz. ASW, 38.6 mm. **Subject:** World Heritage in Hungary - Holloko **Obv:** Holloko castle ruins above country name, value and date **Rev:** Village view behind woman in folk costume **Edge:** Reeded

Date	Mintage	F	VF	XF	Unc	BU
2003BP	5,000	—	—	—	42.50	45.00
2003BP Proof	5,000	Value: 50.00				

KM# 774 5000 FORINT
31.4600 g., 0.9250 Silver 0.9356 oz. ASW, 38.6 mm.
Obv: Value **Rev:** Two Olympic boxers **Edge:** Reeded

Date	Mintage	F	VF	XF	Unc	BU
2004BP	3,000	—	—	—	45.00	47.50
2004BP Proof	9,000	Value: 50.00				

KM# 775 5000 FORINT
31.4600 g., 0.9250 Silver 0.9356 oz. ASW, 38.6 mm.
Obv: "Solomon Tower" above value **Rev:** Visegrad Castle with the Solomon Tower **Edge:** Reeded

Date	Mintage	F	VF	XF	Unc	BU
2004BP	4,000	—	—	—	45.00	47.50
2004BP Proof	4,000	Value: 50.00				

KM# 776 5000 FORINT
31.4600 g., 0.9250 Silver 0.9356 oz. ASW, 38.6 mm. **Obv:** Value and country name above Euro Union stars **Rev:** Mythical stag seen through an ornate window **Edge:** Reeded

Date	Mintage	F	VF	XF	Unc	BU
2004BP Proof	10,000	Value: 50.00				

KM# 778 5000 FORINT
31.4600 g., 0.9250 Silver 0.9356 oz. ASW, 38.6 mm. **Subject:** Ancient Christian Necropolis at Pecs **Obv:** Value and ancient artifact **Rev:** Interior view of tomb **Edge:** Reeded

Date	Mintage	F	VF	XF	Unc	BU
2004BP	5,000	—	—	—	40.00	42.00
2004BP Proof	5,000	Value: 45.00				

KM# 782 5000 FORINT
, 38.6 mm. **Obv:** Bat flying above value **Rev:** Interior cave view **Edge:** Reeded

Date	Mintage	F	VF	XF	Unc	BU
2005BP	5,000	—	—	—	45.00	47.50
2005BP Proof	5,000	Value: 50.00				

KM# 783 5000 FORINT
31.4600 g., 0.9250 Silver 0.9356 oz. ASW, 38.6 mm. **Obv:** Hungarian National Bank building **Rev:** Ignac Alpar and life dates **Edge:** Reeded

Date	Mintage	F	VF	XF	Unc	BU
ND (2005)BP	3,000	—	—	—	45.00	47.50
ND (2005)BP Proof	3,000	Value: 50.00				

KM# 784 5000 FORINT
31.4600 g., 0.9250 Silver 0.9356 oz. ASW, 38.6 mm. **Obv:** Knight on horse with lance **Rev:** Diosgyor Castle **Edge:** Reeded

Date	Mintage	F	VF	XF	Unc	BU
2005BP	4,000	—	—	—	45.00	47.50
2005BP Proof	4,000	Value: 50.00				

KM# 785 5000 FORINT
31.4600 g., 0.9250 Silver 0.9356 oz. ASW, 38.6 mm. **Obv:** Large building above value **Rev:** Karoli Gaspar Reformed (Calvinist) University seal **Edge:** Reeded

Date	Mintage	F	VF	XF	Unc	BU
2005BP	3,000	—	—	—	45.00	47.50
2005BP Proof	3,000	Value: 50.00				

KM# 786 5000 FORINT
31.4600 g., 0.9250 Silver 0.9356 oz. ASW, 38.6 mm. **Obv:** Coin design of a Transylvanian KM-10 thaler reverse dated 1605 **Rev:** Stephan Bocskai (1557-1606) **Edge:** Reeded

Date	Mintage	F	VF	XF	Unc	BU
2005BP	3,000	—	—	—	—	45.00
2005BP Proof	3,000	Value: 50.00				

KM# 753 20000 FORINT
6.9820 g., 0.9860 Gold .2213 oz. AGW, 22 mm. **Subject:** Hungarian Coinage Millennium **Obv:** Denomination **Rev:** Hammered coinage minting scene above old coin design **Edge:** Plain

Date	Mintage	F	VF	XF	Unc	BU
2001 Proof	3,000	Value: 220				

KM# 777 50000 FORINT
13.9640 g., 0.9860 Gold 0.4427 oz. AGW, 25 mm. **Obv:** Value and country name above Euro Union stars **Rev:** Mythical stag seen through ornate window **Edge:** Reeded

Date	Mintage	F	VF	XF	Unc	BU
2004BP Proof	7,000	Value: 450				

KM# 758 100000 FORINT
31.1040 g., 0.9860 Gold .9860 oz. AGW, 37 mm. **Subject:** Saint Stephen **Obv:** Angels crowning coat of arms **Rev:** King seated on throne **Edge:** Reeded

Date	Mintage	F	VF	XF	Unc	BU
2001 Proof	3,000	Value: 675				

MINT SETS

KM#	Date	Mintage	Identification	Issue Price	Mkt Val
MS32	2001 (7)	—	KM#692-697, 721	—	16.50
MS33	2002 (8)	—	KM#692, 693, 694, 695, 696, 697, 721, 760	—	—
MS34	2003 (8)	—	KM#692, 693, 694, 695, 696, 697, 721, 768	—	—
MS35	2004 (8)	—	KM#692, 693, 694, 695, 696, 697, 721, 773	—	—

PROOF SETS

KM#	Date	Mintage	Identification	Issue Price	Mkt Val
PS26	2001 (7)	—	KM#692-697, 721	35.00	37.50
PS27	2002 (8)	—	KM#692-697, 721, 760	—	—
PS28	2003 (8)	—	KM#692-697, 721, 768	—	—
PS29	2004 (8)	—	KM#692-697, 721, 773	—	—
PS30	2005 (8)	7,000	KM#692-697, 721, 779	—	—

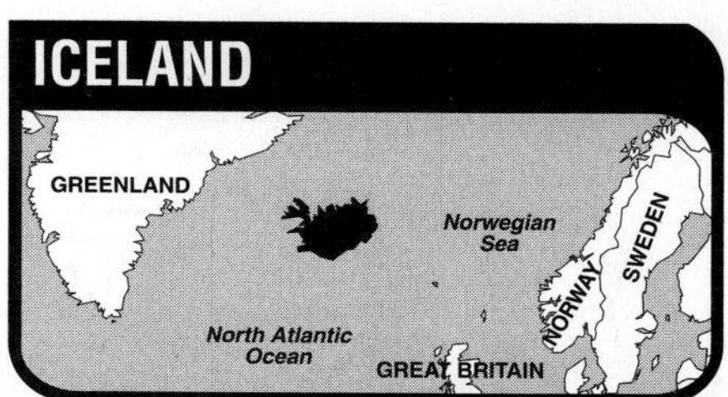

The Republic of Iceland, an island of recent volcanic origin in the North Atlantic east of Greenland and immediately south of the Arctic Circle, has an area of 39,768 sq. mi. (103,000 sq. km.) and a population of just over 300,000. Capital: Reykjavik. Fishing is the chief industry and accounts for a little less than 60 percent of the exports followed by tourism and industry.

REPUBLIC

REFORM COINAGE

100 Old Kronur = 1 New Krona

KM# 27a KRONA
4.0000 g., Nickel Coated Steel, 21.5 mm. **Rev:** Cod **Edge:** Reeded

Date	Mintage	F	VF	XF	Unc	BU
2003	5,144,000	—	—	—	0.75	1.25
2005	5,000,000	—	—	—	0.75	1.25
2006	10,000,000	—	—	—	0.75	1.25

KM# 28a 5 KRONUR
5.6000 g., Nickel Clad Steel, 24.5 mm. **Obv:** Four national icons **Rev:** Two dolphins, denomination **Edge:** Reeded

Date	Mintage	F	VF	XF	Unc	BU
2005	2,000,000	—	—	—	2.00	3.00

KM# 29.1a 10 KRONUR
8.0000 g., Nickel Clad Steel, 27.5 mm. **Obv:** Four national icons **Rev:** Four capelins, denomination **Edge:** Reeded

Date	Mintage	F	VF	XF	Unc	BU
2004	2,000,000	—	—	—	1.75	2.50
2005	4,505,000	—	—	—	1.75	2.50

KM# 31 50 KRONUR
8.2500 g., Nickel-Brass, 23 mm. **Rev:** Northern shrimp **Edge:** Reeded

Date	Mintage	F	VF	XF	Unc	BU
2001	2,000,000	—	—	—	4.00	5.00
2005	2,000,000	—	—	—	4.00	5.00

KM# 35 100 KRONUR
8.5000 g., Nickel-Brass, 25.5 mm. **Rev:** Lumpfish **Edge:** Reeded

Date	Mintage	F	VF	XF	Unc	BU
2001	2,140,000	—	—	—	6.00	7.00
2004	2,400,000	—	—	—	6.00	7.00

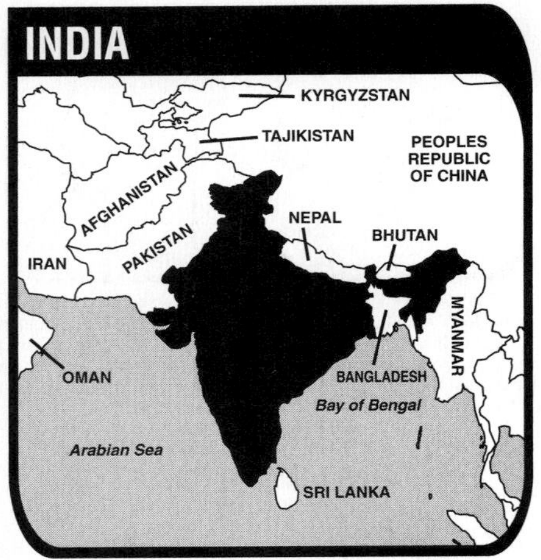

The Republic of India, a subcontinent jutting southward from the mainland of Asia, has an area of 1,269,346 sq. mi. (3,287,590 sq. km.) and a population of over 900 million, second only to that of the People's Republic of China. Capital: New Delhi. India's economy is based on agriculture and industrial activity. Engineering goods, cotton apparel and fabrics, handicrafts, tea, iron and steel are exported.

The Republic of India is a member of the Common-wealth of Nations. The president is the Chief of State. The prime minister is the Head of Government.

MINT MARKS

(Mint marks usually appear directly below the date.)

B -- Mumbai (Bombay), proof issues only
(B) - Mumbai (Bombay), diamond
C - Ottawa
(1985 25 Paise; 1988 10, 25 & 50 Paise)
(C) - Calcutta, no mint mark
(H) - Hyderabad, star (1963--)
(Hd) - Hyderabad, diamond split vertically (1953-1960)
(Hy) - Hyderabad, incuse dot in diamond (1960-1968)
(K) - Kremnica, Slovakia, MK in circle
(L) - London, diamond below first date digit
M - Mumbai (Bombay), proof only after 1996
(M) - Mexico City, M beneath O
(N) - Noida, dot
(P) - Pretoria, M in oval
(R) – Moscow, MMD in oval
(T) - Taegu (Korea), star below first date digit

REPUBLIC

DECIMAL COINAGE

100 Paise = 1 Rupee (1964-)

NOTE: The Paisa was at first called Naya Paisa (= New Paisa), so that people would distinguish from the old non-decimal Paisa (or Pice, equal to 1/64 Rupee). After 7 years, the word new was dropped, and the coin was simply called a Paisa.

KM# 54 25 PAISE

Stainless Steel **Note:** Varieties of date size exist.

Date	Mintage	F	VF	XF	Unc	BU
2001(B)	—	—	0.10	0.20	1.00	—
2001(C)	—	—	0.10	0.20	1.00	—
2001(H)	—	—	0.15	0.25	1.00	—
2002(B)	—	—	0.15	0.25	1.00	—
2002(C)	—	—	0.15	0.25	1.00	—
2002(H)	—	—	0.25	0.40	1.00	—

KM# 69 50 PAISE

3.8000 g., Stainless Steel, 22 mm. **Subject:** Parliament Building in New Delhi

Date	Mintage	F	VF	XF	Unc	BU
2001(B)	—	—	0.15	0.25	0.50	—
2001(C)	—	—	0.15	0.25	0.50	—
2001(H)	—	—	0.20	0.40	0.75	—
2001(N)	—	—	0.15	0.25	0.50	—
2002(B)	—	—	0.15	0.25	0.50	—
2002(C)	—	—	0.15	0.25	0.50	—

Date	Mintage	F	VF	XF	Unc	BU
2002(H)	—	—	0.15	0.25	0.50	—
2002(N)	—	—	0.15	0.25	0.50	—
2003(B)	—	—	0.15	0.25	0.50	—
2003(C)	—	—	0.15	0.25	0.50	—

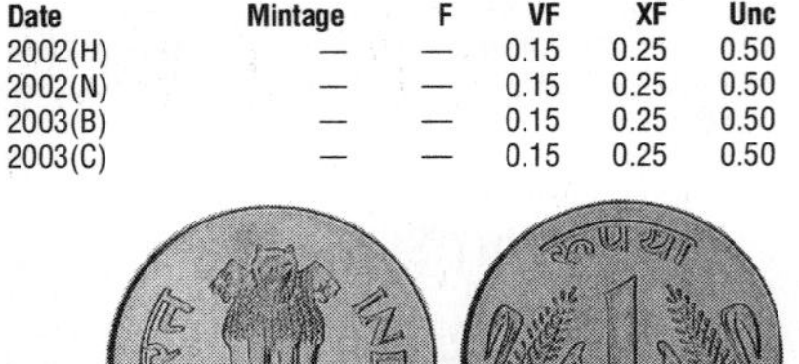

KM# 92.2 RUPEE

4.8500 g., Stainless Steel **Edge:** Plain

Date	Mintage	F	VF	XF	Unc	BU
2001(B)	—	—	0.15	0.30	0.45	—
2001(C)	—	—	0.15	0.30	0.45	—
2001(H)	—	—	0.15	0.30	0.45	—
Note: Small and large mint mark exist, doubled left or right of wheat stalks						
2001(K)	—	—	0.15	0.30	0.45	—
2001(N)	—	—	0.15	0.30	0.45	—
2002(B)	—	—	0.15	0.30	0.45	—
2002(C)	—	—	0.15	0.30	0.45	—
2002(H)	—	—	0.15	0.30	0.45	—
2002(N)	—	—	0.15	0.30	0.45	—
2003(B)	—	—	0.15	0.30	0.45	—
2003(C)	—	—	0.15	0.30	0.45	—
2003(H)	—	—	0.15	0.30	0.45	—
2003(N)	—	—	0.15	0.30	0.45	—
2004(B)	—	—	0.15	0.30	0.45	—

KM# 313 RUPEE

4.9500 g., Stainless Steel, 25 mm. **Obv:** Asoka column above date **Rev:** Jaya Prakash Narayan above date **Edge:** Plain

Date	Mintage	F	VF	XF	Unc	BU
2002(B)	—	—	0.45	0.75	1.00	—

KM# 314 RUPEE

5.0000 g., Stainless Steel, 25 mm. **Subject:** Maharana Pratap

Date	Mintage	F	VF	XF	Unc	BU
2003(B)	—	—	0.45	0.75	1.00	—

KM# 316 RUPEE

5.0000 g., Stainless Steel, 25 mm. **Obv:** Asoka lions **Rev:** Veer Durgadass with spear **Edge:** Plain

Date	Mintage	F	VF	XF	Unc	BU
2003(H)	—	—	0.50	0.80	1.25	—

KM# 303 2 RUPEES

6.2400 g., Copper-Nickel, 25.7 mm. **Subject:** Dr. Syama P. Mookerjee **Obv:** Type B **Rev:** Bust of Dr. Mookerjee half right **Edge:** Plain

Date	Mintage	F	VF	XF	Unc	BU
2001(C)	—	—	1.25	2.00	3.00	—
Note: Some specimens exhibit a die defect to the right of the face						
2001 Proof	—	Value: 7.50				

KM# 121.5 2 RUPEES

Copper-Nickel **Obv:** Type C

Date	Mintage	F	VF	XF	Unc	BU
2001(B)	—	—	0.30	0.50	1.00	—
2001(N)	—	—	0.30	0.50	1.00	—
2001(H)	—	—	0.30	0.50	1.00	—
2002(B)	—	—	0.30	0.50	1.00	—
2002(N)	—	—	0.30	0.50	1.00	—
2002(H)	—	—	0.30	0.50	1.00	—
2003(B)	—	—	0.30	0.50	1.00	—
2003(N)	—	—	0.30	0.50	1.00	—

KM# 121.3 2 RUPEES

Copper-Nickel, 26 mm. **Obv:** Type A **Note:** Reduced size.

Date	Mintage	F	VF	XF	Unc	BU
2001(B)	—	—	0.30	0.50	1.00	—
2001(C)	—	—	0.30	0.50	1.00	—
2002(C)	—	—	0.30	0.50	1.00	—
2003(C)	—	—	0.30	0.50	1.00	—

KM# A306 2 RUPEES

Copper-Nickel **Subject:** Saint Tukaram **Rev:** St. Tukaram seated facing, playing the mandolin

Date	Mintage	F	VF	XF	Unc	BU
2002	—	—	1.25	2.00	3.00	—

KM# 306 2 RUPEES

Copper Nickel **Subject:** Sant Tukaram

Date	Mintage	F	VF	XF	Unc	BU
2002(C)	—	—	1.25	2.00	3.00	—

KM# 305 2 RUPEES

6.1000 g., Copper-Nickel, 25.7 mm. **Subject:** St. Tukaram **Obv:** Asoka column above value **Rev:** Seated musician **Shape:** Eleven sided

Date	Mintage	F	VF	XF	Unc	BU
2002	—	—	0.75	1.25	2.00	—

KM# 307 2 RUPEES

6.0500 g., Copper Nickel **Subject:** 150th Anniversary - Indian Railways **Obv:** Asoka column above value **Rev:** Cartoon elephant holding railroad lantern **Edge:** Plain **Shape:** Eleven sided

Date	Mintage	F	VF	XF	Unc	BU
2003(C)	—	—	0.75	1.25	2.00	—

KM# 304 5 RUPEES

9.0700 g., Copper Nickel, 23.2 mm. **Subject:** Bhagwan Mahavir, 2600th Anniversary **Obv:** Asoka column above denomination **Rev:** Swastika above hand in irregular frame **Edge:** Security

Date	Mintage	F	VF	XF	Unc	BU
2001(B)	—	—	1.00	2.00	3.00	—
2001(B) Proof	—	Value: 6.50				

KM# 154.1 5 RUPEES

Copper-Nickel **Note:** (C) - Calcutta mint has issued 2 distinctly different security edge varieties every year 1992-2003.

Date	Mintage	F	VF	XF	Unc	BU
2001(B)	—	—	0.25	0.50	1.00	—
2001(C) Plain 1	—	—	0.25	0.50	1.00	—
2001(C) Serif 1	—	—	1.00	2.00	3.00	—
2001(H)	—	—	0.35	0.60	1.50	—
2001(N)	—	—	0.25	0.50	1.00	—
2002(C)	—	—	0.25	0.50	1.00	—
2002(N)	—	—	0.25	0.50	1.00	—
2003(N)	—	—	0.25	0.50	1.00	—

KM# 154.2 5 RUPEES

Copper-Nickel **Edge:** Milled

Date	Mintage	F	VF	XF	Unc	BU
2001(C)	—	—	8.00	10.00	15.00	—
2002(C)	—	—	8.00	10.00	15.00	—
2003(C)	—	—	8.00	10.00	15.00	—

KM# 154.4 5 RUPEES

Copper Nickel **Obv:** Similar to KM#121.5

Date	Mintage	F	VF	XF	Unc	BU
2001(B)	—	—	0.25	0.50	1.00	—

Date	Mintage	F	VF	XF	Unc	BU
2002(B)	—	—	0.25	0.50	1.00	—
2003(B)	—	—	0.25	0.50	1.00	—
2004(B)	—	—	0.25	0.50	1.00	—

KM# 308 5 RUPEES

8.9200 g., Copper Nickel, 23.1 mm. **Subject:** Dadabhai Naroji **Obv:** Asoka column above value **Rev:** Bearded portrait above dates **Edge:** Security

Date	Mintage	F	VF	XF	Unc	BU
ND(2003)(B)	—	—	1.00	1.75	3.00	—

KM# 317.1 5 RUPEES

8.8000 g., Copper-Nickel, 23.1 mm. **Obv:** Asoka lions **Rev:** K. Kamaraj above life dates **Edge:** Security

Date	Mintage	F	VF	XF	Unc	BU
ND (2003)(H)	—	—	1.25	2.00	3.50	—
ND (2003)(B)	—	—	1.00	1.75	3.00	—

KM# 317.2 5 RUPEES

8.8000 g., Copper-Nickel, 23.1 mm. **Edge:** Reeded

Date	Mintage	F	VF	XF	Unc	BU
ND (2003)(H)	—	—	5.00	7.00	11.00	—

KM# 309 10 RUPEES

12.5000 g., Copper-Nickel, 31 mm. **Obv:** Ashoka pillar **Rev:** Dr. Syama Prasad Mookerjee **Edge:** Reeded

Date	Mintage	F	VF	XF	Unc	BU
2001 Proof	—	Value: 15.00				

KM# 319 10 RUPEES

12.5000 g., Copper-Nickel, 31 mm. **Obv:** Arms **Rev:** Bust of Maharana Pratap left

Date	Mintage	F	VF	XF	Unc	BU
2003	—	—	—	—	12.00	—

KM# 310 50 RUPEES

30.0000 g., Copper-Nickel, 39 mm. **Obv:** Ashoka pillar **Rev:** Dr. Syama Prasad Mookerjee **Edge:** Reeded

Date	Mintage	F	VF	XF	Unc	BU
2001 Proof	—	Value: 30.00				

KM# 311 100 RUPEES

Silver, 44 mm. **Obv:** Ashoka pillar **Rev:** Dr. Syama Prasad Mookerjee **Edge:** Reeded

Date	Mintage	F	VF	XF	Unc	BU
2001 Proof	—	Value: 50.00				

KM# 312 100 RUPEES

35.0000 g., 0.5000 Silver 0.5626 oz. ASW, 44 mm. **Obv:** Asoka column **Rev:** Swastika above hand in irregular frame **Edge:** Reeded

Date	Mintage	F	VF	XF	Unc	BU
2001(B)	—	—	—	—	35.00	—
2001(B) Proof	—	Value: 50.00				

KM# 315 100 RUPEES

Silver **Subject:** 2600th Anniversary - Bhaglan Mahaxir

Date	Mintage	F	VF	XF	Unc	BU
2001	—	—	—	—	30.00	—

KM# 318 100 RUPEES

35.0000 g., 0.5000 Silver 0.5626 oz. ASW, 44 mm. **Obv:** Asoka lions **Rev:** K. Kamaraj above life dates **Edge:** Reeded

Date	Mintage	F	VF	XF	Unc	BU
ND (2003)(B)	—	—	—	—	35.00	—

KM# 320 100 RUPEES

35.0000 g., Silver, Copper Alloying, 44 mm. **Obv:** Arms **Rev:** Bust of Maharana Pratap left

Date	Mintage	F	VF	XF	Unc	BU
2003	—	—	—	—	30.00	—

PROOF SETS

KM#	Date	Mintage	Identification	Issue Price	Mkt Val
PS56	2001 (4)	—	KM#303, 309, 310, 311	—	100

The Republic of Indonesia, the world's largest archipelago, extends for more than 3,000 miles (4,827 km.) along the equator from the mainland of southeast Asia to Australia. The 17,508 islands comprising the archipelago have a combined area of 788,425 sq. mi. (1,919,440 sq.km.) and a population of 205 million, including East Timor. On August 30, 1999, the Timorese majority voted for independence. The Inter FET (International Forces for East Timor) is now in charge of controlling the chaotic situation. Capitol: Jakarta. Petroleum, timber, rubber, and coffee are exported.

Modern coinage issued by the Republic of Indonesia includes separate series for West Irian and for the Riau Archipelago, an area of small islands between Singapore and Sumatra.

MONETARY SYSTEM

100 Sen = 1 Rupiah

REPUBLIC

STANDARD COINAGE

100 Sen = 1 Rupiah

KM# 60 50 RUPIAH

Aluminum **Obv:** National arms **Rev:** Denomination and Black-naped Oriole

Date	Mintage	F	VF	XF	Unc	BU
2001	—	—	—	—	0.30	0.75
2002	—	—	—	—	0.30	0.75

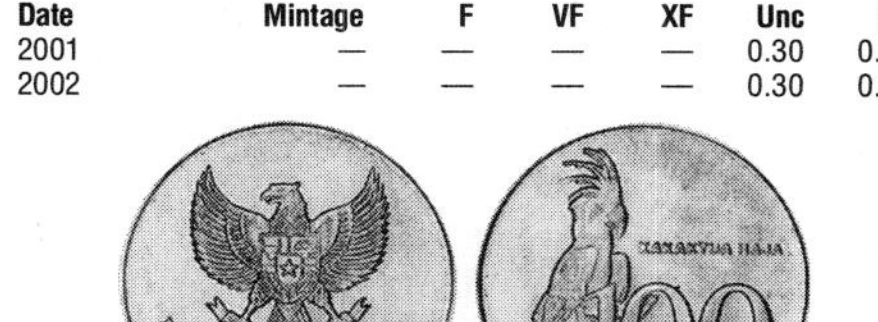

KM# 61 100 RUPIAH

Aluminum **Obv:** National arms **Rev:** Denomination and palm cockatoo

Date	Mintage	F	VF	XF	Unc	BU
2001	—	—	—	—	0.75	1.25
2002	—	—	—	—	0.75	1.25
2003	—	—	—	—	0.75	1.25
2004	—	—	—	—	0.75	1.25

KM# 66 200 RUPIAH

2.4000 g., Aluminum, 25 mm. **Obv:** National arms **Rev:** Balinese starling bird above value **Edge:** Plain

Date	Mintage	F	VF	XF	Unc	BU
2003	—	—	—	—	1.00	1.50

KM# 59 500 RUPIAH

Aluminum-Bronze **Obv:** National emblem **Rev:** Denomination

Date	Mintage	F	VF	XF	Unc	BU
2001	—	—	—	—	2.00	2.50
2002	—	—	—	—	2.00	2.50

KM# 67 500 RUPIAH

3.1100 g., Aluminum, 27.2 mm. **Obv:** National arms **Rev:** Jasmine flower above value **Edge:** Segmented reeding

Date	Mintage	F	VF	XF	Unc	BU
2003	—	—	—	—	2.00	2.50

KM# 64 25000 RUPIAH

28.2800 g., 0.9250 Silver 0.841 oz. ASW, 38.6 mm. **Subject:** Centennial of Sukarno's Birth **Obv:** National arms **Rev:** Uniformed bust of Sukarno **Edge:** Reeded

Date	Mintage	F	VF	XF	Unc	BU
2001 Proof	500	Value: 100				

KM# 65 500,000 RUPIAH

15.0000 g., 0.9990 Gold 0.4818 oz. AGW, 28.2 mm. **Subject:** Centennial of Sukarno's Birth **Obv:** National arms **Rev:** Head of Sukarno left **Edge:** Reeded

Date	Mintage	F	VF	XF	Unc	BU
2001 Proof	500	Value: 375				

IRAN

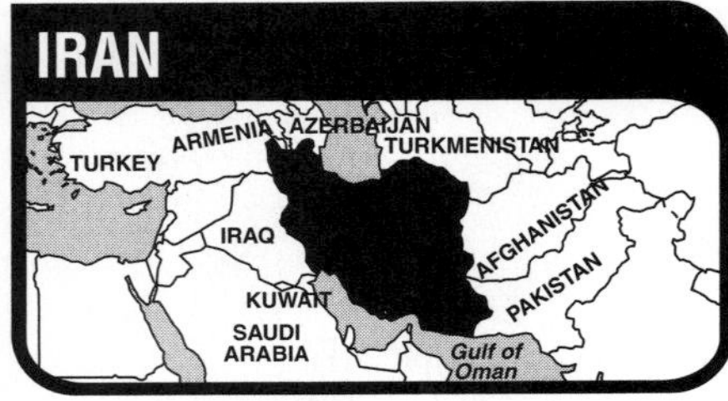

The Islamic Republic of Iran, located between the Caspian Sea and the Persian Gulf in southwestern Asia, has an area of 636,296 sq. mi. (1,648,000 sq. km.) and a population of 59.7 million. Capital: Tehran. Although predominantly an agricultural state, Iran depends heavily on oil for foreign exchange. Crude oil, carpets and agricultural products are exported.

In 1931 the Kingdom of Persia became known as the Kingdom of Iran. In 1979 the monarchy was toppled and an Islamic Republic proclaimed.

COIN DATING

Iranian coins were dated according to the Moslem lunar calendar until March 21, 1925 (AD), when dating was switched to a new calendar based on the solar year, indicated by the notation SH. The monarchial calendar system was adopted in 1976 = MS2535 and was abandoned in 1978 = MS2537. The previously used solar year calendar was restored at that time.

ISLAMIC REPUBLIC

MILLED COINAGE

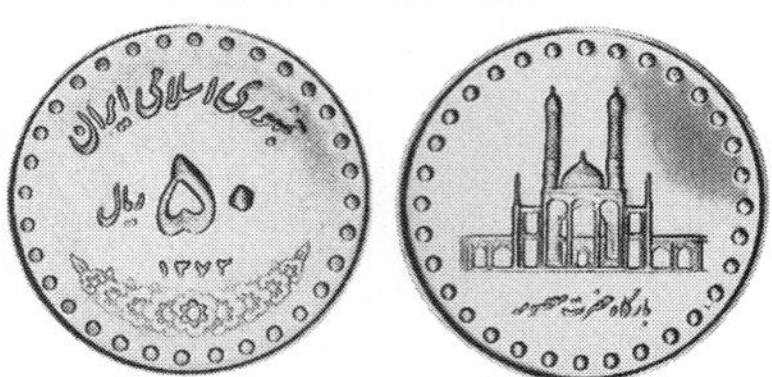

KM# 1260 50 RIALS
Copper-Nickel **Reverse:** Shrine of Hazrat Masumah **Edge:** Reeded

Date	Mintage	F	VF	XF	Unc
SH1380 (2001)	—	—	2.50	3.50	5.00

KM# 1266 50 RIALS
3.5100 g., Aluminum-Bronze, 20.1 mm. **Obverse:** Value **Reverse:** Hazrat Masumah Shrine **Edge:** Reeded **Mint:** Tehran

Date	Mintage	F	VF	XF	Unc
SH1383(2004)	—	—	—	—	5.00

KM# 1261.2 100 RIALS
Copper-Nickel **Obverse:** Thick denomination, numerals

Date	Mintage	F	VF	XF	Unc
SH1380 (2001)	—	—	—	—	6.50

KM# 1267 100 RIALS
4.6200 g., Aluminum-Bronze, 22.9 mm. **Obverse:** Value **Reverse:** Imam Reza Shrine **Edge:** Reeded **Mint:** Tehran

Date	Mintage	F	VF	XF	Unc
SH1383(2004)	—	—	—	—	6.50

KM# 1262 250 RIALS
Bi-Metallic Copper-Nickel center in Brass ring **Reverse:** Stylized flower

Date	Mintage	F	VF	XF	Unc
SH1381 (2002)	—	—	—	—	7.50
SH1382 (2003)	—	—	—	—	7.50

KM# 1268 250 RIALS
5.4200 g., Copper-Nickel, 24.2 mm. **Obverse:** Value **Reverse:** Stylized flower **Edge:** Plain **Mint:** Tehran

Date	Mintage	F	VF	XF	Unc
SH 1383(2004)	—	—	—	—	7.25

KM# 1269 500 RIALS
8.9100 g., Bi-Metallic Alumium-Bronze center in Copper-Nickel ring, 27.1 mm. **Obverse:** Value **Reverse:** Bird and flowers **Edge:** Reeded **Mint:** Tehran

Date	Mintage	F	VF	XF	Unc
SH 1383(2004)	—	—	—	—	8.50

BULLION COINAGE

Issued by the National Bank of Iran

KM# 1250.2 1/2 AZADI
4.0680 g., 0.9000 Gold .1177 oz. AGW **Obverse:** Legend larger **Obv. Legend:** "Spring of Freedom"

Date	Mintage	F	VF	XF	Unc
SH1381 (2002)	—	—	—	—	95.00

IRAQ

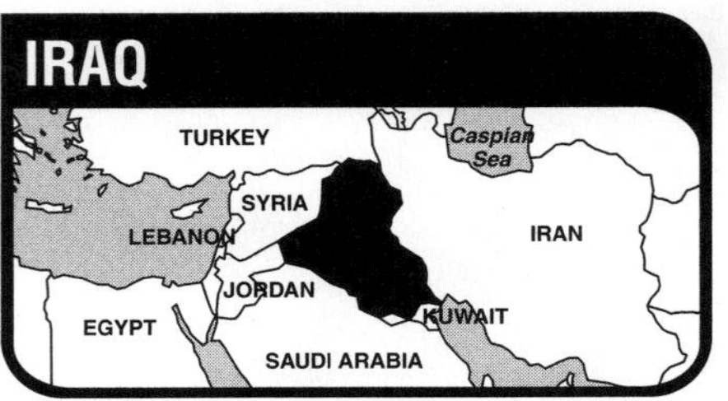

The Republic of Iraq, historically known as Mesopotamia, is located in the Near East and is bordered by Kuwait, Iran, Turkey, Syria, Jordan and Saudi Arabia. It has an area of 167,925 sq. mi. (434,920 sq. km.) and a population of 19 million. Capital: Baghdad. The economy of Iraq is based on agriculture and petroleum. Crude oil accounted for 94 percent of the exports before the war with Iran began in 1980.

Mesopotamia was the site of a number of flourishing civilizations of antiquity - Sumeria, Assyria, Babylonia, Parthia, Persia and the Biblical cities of Ur, Ninevehand and Babylon. Desired because of its favored location, which embraced the fertile alluvial plains of the Tigris and Euphrates Rivers, Mesopotamia - 'land between the rivers'- was conquered by Cyrus the Great of Persia, Alexander of Macedonia and by Arabs who made the legendary city of Baghdad the capital of the ruling caliphate. Suleiman the Magnificent conquered Mesopotamia for Turkey in1534, and it formed part of the Ottoman Empire until 1623, and from 1638 to 1917. Great Britain, given a League of Nations mandate over the territory in 1920, recognized Iraq as a kingdom in 1922. Iraq became an independent constitutional monarchy presided over by the Hashemite family, direct descendants of the prophet Mohammed, in 1932. In 1958, the army-led revolution of July 14 overthrew the monarchy and proclaimed a republic.

NOTE: The 'I' mintmark on 1938 and 1943 issues appears on the obverse near the point of the bust. Some of the issues of 1938 have a dot to denote a composition change from nickel to copper-nickel.

MONETARY SYSTEM

Falus, Fulus — Fals, Fils — Falsan

50 Fils = 1 Dirham
200 Fils = 1 Riyal
1000 Fils = 1 Dinar (Pound)

REPUBLIC

DECIMAL COINAGE

KM# 175 25 DINARS
2.5000 g., Copper-Plated-Steel, 17.4 mm. **Obv:** Value **Rev:** Map **Edge:** Plain

Date	Mintage	F	VF	XF	Unc
2004-1425	—	—	—	—	0.50

KM# 176 100 DINARS
4.3000 g., Stainless Steel, 22 mm. **Obv:** Value **Rev:** Map **Edge:** Reeded

Date	Mintage	F	VF	XF	Unc
2004-1425	—	—	—	—	1.00

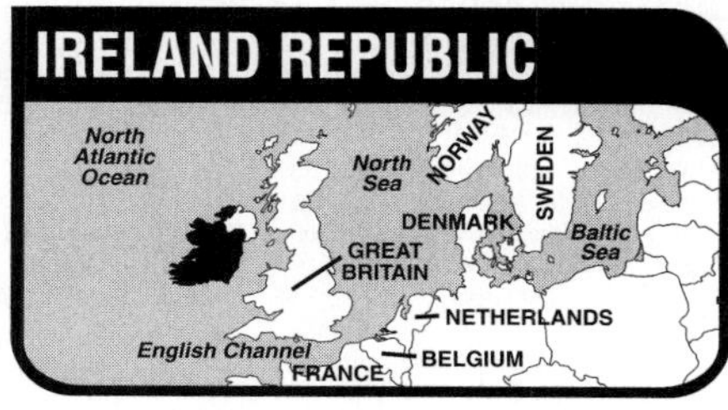

The Republic of Ireland, which occupies five-sixths of the island of Ireland located in the Atlantic Ocean west of Great Britain, has an area of 27,136 sq. mi. (70,280 sq. km.) and a population of 4.3 million. Capital: Dublin. Agriculture and dairy farming are the principal industries. Meat, livestock, dairy products and textiles are exported.

NOTE: This section has been renumbered to segregate the coinage of the Irish Free State from the earlier crown coinage of Ireland.

REPUBLIC

EURO COINAGE

European Economic Community Issues

KM# 32 EURO CENT

2.2700 g., Copper Plated Steel, 16.25 mm. **Obv:** Harp **Obv. Designer:** Jarlath Hayes **Rev:** Denomination and globe **Rev. Designer:** Luc Luycx **Edge:** Plain

Date	Mintage	VG	F	VF	XF	Unc
2002	404,000,000	—	—	—	—	0.35
2003	31,946,000	—	—	—	—	0.35
2004	180,254	—	—	—	—	0.35
2005	—	—	—	—	—	0.35
2006	—	—	—	—	—	0.35

KM# 33 2 EURO CENT

3.0000 g., Copper Plated Steel, 18.75 mm. **Obv:** Harp **Obv. Designer:** Jarlath Hayes **Rev:** Denomination and globe **Rev. Designer:** Luc Luycx **Edge:** Plain

Date	Mintage	VG	F	VF	XF	Unc
2002	355,643,000	—	—	—	—	0.50
2003	123,380,000	—	—	—	—	0.50
2004	100,300	—	—	—	—	0.50
2005	—	—	—	—	—	0.50
2006	—	—	—	—	—	0.50

KM# 34 5 EURO CENT

3.8600 g., Copper-Plated-Steel, 21.25 mm. **Obv:** Harp **Obv. Designer:** Jarlath Hayes **Rev:** Denomination and globe **Rev. Designer:** Luc Luycx **Edge:** Plain

Date	Mintage	VG	F	VF	XF	Unc
2002	443,685,000	—	—	—	—	0.75
2003	1,000,000	—	—	—	—	0.75
2004	100,200	—	—	—	—	0.75
2005	—	—	—	—	—	0.75
2006	—	—	—	—	—	0.75

KM# 35 10 EURO CENT

4.0700 g., Aluminum-Bronze, 19.75 mm. **Obv:** Harp **Obv. Designer:** Jarlath Hayes **Rev:** Denomination and map **Rev. Designer:** Luc Luycx **Edge:** Reeded

Date	Mintage	VG	F	VF	XF	Unc
2002	275,913,000	—	—	—	—	1.00
2003	48,647,000	—	—	—	—	1.00
2004	100,100	—	—	—	—	1.00
2005	—	—	—	—	—	1.00
2006	—	—	—	—	—	1.00

KM# 36 20 EURO CENT

5.7300 g., Aluminum-Bronze, 22.25 mm. **Obv:** Harp **Obv. Designer:** Jarlath Hayes **Rev:** Denomination and map **Rev. Designer:** Luc Luycx **Edge:** Notched

Date	Mintage	VG	F	VF	XF	Unc
2002	234,556,000	—	—	—	—	1.25
2003	12,541,000	—	—	—	—	1.25
2004	100,300	—	—	—	—	1.25
2005	—	—	—	—	—	1.25
2006	—	—	—	—	—	1.25

KM# 37 50 EURO CENT

7.8100 g., Aluminum-Bronze, 24.25 mm. **Obv:** Harp **Obv. Designer:** Jarlath Hayes **Rev. Designer:** Luc Luycx **Edge:** Reeded

Date	Mintage	VG	F	VF	XF	Unc
2002	139,462,000	—	—	—	—	1.50
2003	1,509,000	—	—	—	—	1.50
2004	100,200	—	—	—	—	1.50
2005	—	—	—	—	—	1.50
2006	—	—	—	—	—	1.50

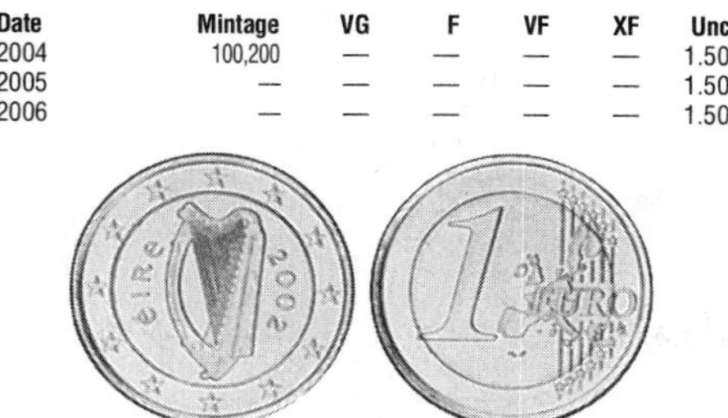

KM# 38 EURO

7.5000 g., Bi-Metallic Copper-Nickel center in Brass ring, 23.25 mm. **Obv:** Harp **Obv. Designer:** Jarlath Hayes **Rev:** Denomination and map **Rev. Designer:** Luc Luycx **Edge:** Reeded and plain sections

Date	Mintage	VG	F	VF	XF	Unc
2002	124,082,000	—	—	—	—	2.75
2003	1,520,000	—	—	—	—	2.75
2004	100,300	—	—	—	—	2.75
2005	—	—	—	—	—	2.75
2006	—	—	—	—	—	2.75

KM# 39 2 EUROS

8.5200 g., Bi-Metallic Brass center in Copper-Nickel ring, 25.7 mm. **Obv:** Harp **Obv. Designer:** Jarlath Hayes **Rev:** Denomination and map **Rev. Designer:** Luc Luycx **Edge:** Reeded with 2's and stars

Date	Mintage	VG	F	VF	XF	Unc
2002	87,449,000	—	—	—	—	4.00
2003	1,575,000	—	—	—	—	4.00
2004	53,683	—	—	—	—	4.00
2005	—	—	—	—	—	4.00
2006	—	—	—	—	—	4.00

KM# 40 5 EURO

14.1900 g., Copper-Nickel, 28.4 mm. **Subject:** Special Olympics **Obv:** Harp **Obv. Designer:** Jarlath Hayes **Rev:** Multicolor games logo **Edge:** Reeded

Date	Mintage	F	VF	XF	Unc	BU
2003	35,000	—	—	—	15.00	18.00
2003 Proof	25,000	Value: 25.00				

KM# 41 10 EURO

28.3000 g., 0.9250 Silver 0.8416 oz. ASW, 38.6 mm. **Subject:** Special Olympics **Obv:** Gold highlighted harp **Obv. Designer:** Jarlath Hayes **Rev:** Gold highlighted games logo **Edge:** Reeded

Date	Mintage	F	VF	XF	Unc	BU
2003 Proof	30,000	Value: 40.00				

KM# 42 10 EURO

28.3400 g., 0.9250 Silver 0.8428 oz. ASW, 38.6 mm. **Obv:** Harp **Rev:** Stylized Celtic swan **Edge:** Reeded

Date	Mintage	F	VF	XF	Unc	BU
2004 Proof	50,000	Value: 50.00				

KM# 44 10 EURO

28.2800 g., 0.9250 Silver 0.841 oz. ASW, 38.6 mm. **Subject:** Sir William R. Hamilton **Obv:** Harp **Rev:** Triangle in circle of Greek letters used as math symbols **Edge:** Reeded

Date	Mintage	F	VF	XF	Unc	BU
2005 Proof	30,000	Value: 50.00				

MINT SETS

KM#	Date	Mintage	Identification	Issue Price	Mkt Val
MS9	2002 (8)	20,000	KM#32,33,34,35,36,37,38,39	10.00	200
MS10	2003 (8)	30,000	KM#32-39	10.00	75.00
MS11	2003 (9)	—	KM#32-40 Special Olympics	—	90.00
MS12	2004 (8)	—	KM#32-39	—	45.00
MS13	2005 (8)	—	KM#32-39	—	45.00
MS14	2006 (8)	—	KM#32-39	—	45.00

ISLE OF MAN

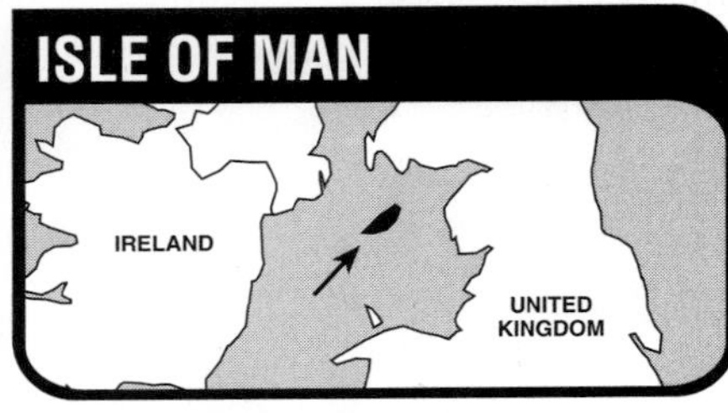

The Isle of Man, a dependency of the British Crown located in the Irish Sea equidistant from Ireland, Scotland and England, has an area of 227 sq. mi. (588 sq. km.) and a population of 68,000. Capital: Douglas. Agriculture, dairy farming, fishing and tourism are the chief industries.

MINT MARKS
PM - Pobjoy Mint

BRITISH DEPENDENCY

DECIMAL COINAGE

5 New Pence = 1 Shilling; 25 New Pence = 1 Crown; 100 New Pence = 1 Pound

KM# 1036 PENNY
3.5300 g., Bronze Plated Steel **Obv:** Queen's portrait **Rev:** Ruins **Edge:** Plain

Date	Mintage	F	VF	XF	Unc	BU
2001PM AA	—	—	—	—	0.25	0.45
2002PM AA	—	—	—	—	0.25	0.45
2003PM	—	—	—	—	0.25	0.45

KM# 1253 PENNY
3.5300 g., Copper-Plated-Steel, 20.3 mm. **Ruler:** Elizabeth II **Obv:** Elizabeth II **Rev:** Stanton War Memorial **Edge:** Reeded

Date	Mintage	F	VF	XF	Unc	BU
2004PM	—	—	—	—	0.25	0.45

KM# 1037 2 PENCE
7.1000 g., Brass Plated Steel **Obv:** Queen's portrait **Rev:** Sailboat **Edge:** Plain

Date	Mintage	F	VF	XF	Unc	BU
2001PM AA	—	—	—	—	0.40	0.60
2001PM AB	—	—	—	—	0.40	0.60
2002PM AA	—	—	—	—	0.40	0.60
2002PM AC	—	—	—	—	0.40	0.60
2003PM	—	—	—	—	0.40	0.60

KM# 1254 2 PENCE
7.1000 g., Copper-Plated-Steel, 25.9 mm. **Ruler:** Elizabeth II **Obv:** Elizabeth II **Rev:** Albert Tower **Edge:** Reeded

Date	Mintage	F	VF	XF	Unc	BU
2004	—	—	—	—	0.40	0.60

KM# 1038 5 PENCE
3.2400 g., Copper-Nickel **Obv:** Queen's portrait **Rev:** Gaut's Cross **Edge:** Reeded

Date	Mintage	F	VF	XF	Unc	BU
2001PM AA	—	—	—	—	0.75	1.00
2002PM AA	—	—	—	—	0.75	1.00
2003PM	—	—	—	—	0.75	1.00

KM# 1255 5 PENCE
3.2400 g., Copper-Nickel, 18 mm. **Ruler:** Elizabeth II **Obv:** Elizabeth II **Rev:** Tower of Refuge **Edge:** Reeded

Date	Mintage	F	VF	XF	Unc	BU
2004PM	—	—	—	—	0.75	1.00

KM# 1039 10 PENCE
3.2500 g., Copper-Nickel, 24.5 mm. **Obv:** Queen's portrait **Rev:** St. Germain's Cathedral **Edge:** Reeded

Date	Mintage	F	VF	XF	Unc	BU
2001PM AA	—	—	—	—	1.00	1.50
2002PM AA	—	—	—	—	1.00	1.50
2003PM	—	—	—	—	1.00	1.50

KM# 1256 10 PENCE
6.5500 g., Copper-Nickel, 24.5 mm. **Ruler:** Elizabeth II **Obv:** Elizabeth II **Rev:** Chicken Rock Lighthouse **Edge:** Reeded

Date	Mintage	F	VF	XF	Unc	BU
2004PM	—	—	—	—	1.00	1.50

KM# 1040 20 PENCE
5.0000 g., Copper-Nickel, 21.5 mm. **Subject:** Rushen Abbey **Obv:** Queen's portrait **Rev:** Monk writing **Edge:** Plain **Shape:** 7-sided

Date	Mintage	F	VF	XF	Unc	BU
2001PM AA	—	—	—	—	1.50	2.00
2002PM AA	—	—	—	—	1.50	2.00
2003PM	—	—	—	—	1.50	2.00

KM# 1257 20 PENCE
4.9100 g., Copper-Nickel, 21.5 mm. **Ruler:** Elizabeth II **Obv:** Elizabeth II **Rev:** Castle Rushen Clock **Edge:** Plain **Shape:** 7-sided

Date	Mintage	F	VF	XF	Unc	BU
2004PM	—	—	—	—	1.50	2.00

KM# 1041 50 PENCE
8.0000 g., Copper-Nickel **Obv:** Queen's portrait **Rev:** Stylized crucifix **Edge:** Plain **Shape:** 7-sided

Date	Mintage	F	VF	XF	Unc	BU
2001PM AA	—	—	—	—	2.25	2.75
2003PM	—	—	—	—	2.25	2.75

KM# 1105 50 PENCE
8.0000 g., Copper-Nickel, 27.3 mm. **Subject:** Christmas **Obv:** Queen's portrait **Rev:** Postman and children **Edge:** Plain **Shape:** 7-sided

Date	Mintage	F	VF	XF	Unc	BU
2001 BB	30,000	—	—	—	10.00	11.50

KM# 1105a 50 PENCE
8.0000 g., 0.9250 Silver .2379 oz. ASW, 27.3 mm. **Edge:** Plain **Shape:** 7-sided

Date	Mintage	F	VF	XF	Unc	BU
2001 Proof	5,000	Value: 35.00				

KM# 1105b 50 PENCE
8.0000 g., 0.9167 Gold .2358 oz. AGW, 27.3 mm. **Edge:** Plain **Shape:** 7-sided

Date	Mintage	F	VF	XF	Unc	BU
2001 Proof	250	Value: 550				

KM# 1160 50 PENCE
8.0000 g., Copper Nickel, 27.3 mm. **Subject:** Christmas **Obv:** Queen's portrait **Rev:** Scrooge in bed **Edge:** Plain **Shape:** 7-sided

Date	Mintage	F	VF	XF	Unc	BU
2002BB PM	30,000	—	—	—	10.00	11.50

KM# 1160a 50 PENCE
8.0000 g., 0.9250 Silver 0.2379 oz. ASW, 27.3 mm. **Subject:** Christmas **Obv:** Queen's portrait **Rev:** Scrooge in bed **Edge:** Plain **Shape:** 7-sided

Date	Mintage	F	VF	XF	Unc	BU
2002PM Proof	5,000	Value: 35.00				

KM# 1160b 50 PENCE
8.0000 g., 0.9167 Gold 0.2358 oz. AGW, 27.3 mm. **Subject:** Christmas **Obv:** Queen's portrait **Rev:** Scrooge in bed **Edge:** Plain **Shape:** 7-sided

Date	Mintage	F	VF	XF	Unc	BU
2002PM Proof	250	Value: 550				

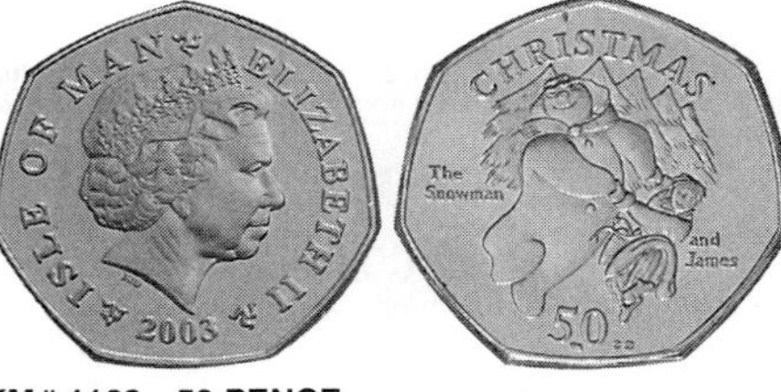

KM# 1183 50 PENCE
8.0000 g., Copper-Nickel, 27.3 mm. **Obv:** Queen Elizabeth II **Rev:** "The Snowman and James" **Edge:** Plain **Shape:** 7-sided

Date	Mintage	F	VF	XF	Unc	BU
2003PM	10,000	—	—	—	10.00	11.50

KM# 1183a 50 PENCE
8.0000 g., 0.9250 Silver 0.2379 oz. ASW, 27.3 mm. **Subject:** Christmas **Obv:** Queen Elizabeth II **Rev:** "The Snowman and James" **Edge:** Plain **Shape:** 7-sided

Date	Mintage	F	VF	XF	Unc	BU
2003PM Proof	3,000	Value: 35.00				

Note: Seven sided

KM# 1183b 50 PENCE
8.0000 g., 0.9167 Gold 0.2358 oz. AGW, 27.3 mm. **Obv:** Queen Elizabeth II **Rev:** "The Snowman and James" **Edge:** Plain **Shape:** 7-sided

Date	Mintage	F	VF	XF	Unc	BU
2003PM Proof	100	Value: 500				

KM# 1258 50 PENCE
7.9400 g., Copper-Nickel, 21.5 mm. **Ruler:** Elizabeth II **Obv:** Elizabeth II **Rev:** Milner's Tower **Edge:** Plain **Shape:** 7-sided

Date	Mintage	F	VF	XF	Unc	BU
2004PM	—	—	—	—	2.25	2.75

KM# 1262 50 PENCE
7.9400 g., Copper-Nickel, 27.3 mm. **Ruler:** Elizabeth II **Subject:** Christmas **Obv:** Elizabeth II **Rev:** Laxey Wheel **Edge:** Plain **Shape:** 7-sided

Date	Mintage	F	VF	XF	Unc	BU
2004PM	30,000	—	—	—	6.00	7.00

KM# 1262a 50 PENCE
9.1852 g., 0.9250 Silver 0.2732 oz. ASW, 27.3 mm. **Ruler:** Elizabeth II **Subject:** Christmas **Obv:** Elizabeth II **Rev:** Laxey Wheel **Edge:** Plain **Shape:** 7-sided

Date	Mintage	F	VF	XF	Unc	BU
2004PM Proof	5,000	Value: 35.00				

KM# 1262b 50 PENCE
15.4074 g., 0.9167 Gold 0.4541 oz. AGW, 27.3 mm. **Ruler:** Elizabeth II **Subject:** Christmas **Obv:** Elizabeth II **Rev:** Laxey Wheel **Edge:** Plain **Shape:** 7-sided

Date	Mintage	F	VF	XF	Unc	BU
2004PM Proof	250	Value: 645				

KM# 1128 60 PENCE
, 38.6 mm. **Subject:** Euro Currency Converter **Obv:** Bust of Queen Elizabeth II right **Rev:** Rotating map with cut out arrow revealing the Euro equivalent of the country's currency to which the arrow is pointed **Edge:** Reeded **Note:** Bronze finished base metal with a silver finished rotator on reverse.

Date	Mintage	F	VF	XF	Unc	BU
2002	15,000	—	—	—	20.00	22.50

KM# 1042 POUND
9.5000 g., Brass **Subject:** Millennium Bells **Obv:** Queen's portrait **Rev:** Triskeles and three bells **Edge:** Reeded and plain sections

Date	Mintage	F	VF	XF	Unc	BU
2001PM AA	—	—	—	—	4.00	5.00

Date	Mintage	F	VF	XF	Unc	BU
2002PM AA	—	—	—	—	4.00	5.00
2003PM	—	—	—	—	4.00	5.00

KM# 1259 POUND

9.5000 g., Nickel-Brass, 22.5 mm. **Ruler:** Elizabeth II **Obv:** Elizabeth II **Rev:** St. John's Chapel **Edge:** Reeded and Plain Sections

Date	Mintage	F	VF	XF	Unc	BU
2004PM	—	—	—	—	4.00	5.00

KM# 1043 2 POUNDS

12.0000 g., Bi-Metallic Copper-Nickel center in Brass ring **Subject:** Thorwald's Cross **Obv:** Queen's portrait **Rev:** Ancient drawing **Edge:** Reeded

Date	Mintage	F	VF	XF	Unc	BU
2001PM AA	—	—	—	—	6.50	7.50
2002PM AA	—	—	—	—	6.50	7.50
2003PM	—	—	—	—	6.50	7.50

KM# 1260 2 POUNDS

12.0000 g., Bi-Metallic Copper-Nickel center in Brass ring, 28.4 mm. **Ruler:** Elizabeth II **Obv:** Elizabeth II **Rev:** Round Tower of Peel Castle **Edge:** Reeded

Date	Mintage	F	VF	XF	Unc	BU
2004PM	—	—	—	—	6.50	7.50

KM# 1044 5 POUNDS

20.1000 g., Virenium **Subject:** St. Patrick's Hymn **Obv:** Queen's portrait **Rev:** Stylized cross design **Edge:** Reeded and plain sections

Date	Mintage	F	VF	XF	Unc	BU
2001PM AA	—	—	—	—	15.00	16.50
2002PM AA	—	—	—	—	15.00	16.50

KM# 1261 5 POUNDS

20.1000 g., Virenium, 36 mm. **Ruler:** Elizabeth II **Obv:** Elizabeth II **Rev:** Laxey Wheel **Edge:** Reeded

Date	Mintage	F	VF	XF	Unc	BU
2004PM	—	—	—	—	15.00	16.50

KM# 1129 1/32 CROWN

1.0000 g., 0.9720 Gold 0.0313 oz. AGW, 9.8 mm. **Subject:** Queen's Golden Jubilee **Obv:** Bust of Queen Elizabeth II right **Rev:** Seated crowned Queen holding sceptre at her coronation **Edge:** Plain

Date	Mintage	F	VF	XF	Unc	BU
2002 Prooflike	—	—	—	—	—	35.00

KM# 1058 1/25 CROWN

1.2440 g., 0.9999 Gold .0400 oz. AGW, 13.92 mm. **Subject:** Year of the Snake **Obv:** Queen's portrait **Rev:** Snake **Edge:** Reeded

Date	Mintage	F	VF	XF	Unc	BU
2001 Proof	20,000	Value: 45.00				

KM# 1067 1/25 CROWN

1.2440 g., 0.9999 Gold .0400 oz. AGW, 13.9 mm. **Subject:** Somali Kittens **Obv:** Queen's portrait **Rev:** Two kittens **Edge:** Reeded

Date	Mintage	F	VF	XF	Unc	BU
2001	—	—	—	—	32.00	—
2001 Proof	1,000	Value: 50.00				

KM# 1067a 1/25 CROWN

1.2441 g., 0.9995 Platinum .0400 oz. APW, 13.9 mm. **Subject:** Somali Kittens **Obv:** Queen's portrait **Rev:** Two kittens **Edge:** Reeded

Date	Mintage	F	VF	XF	Unc	BU
2001	—	—	—	—	65.00	—

KM# 1086 1/25 CROWN

1.2441 g., 0.9999 Gold .0400 oz. AGW, 13.9 mm. **Subject:** Harry Potter **Obv:** Queen's portrait **Rev:** Boy with magic wand **Edge:** Reeded

Date	Mintage	F	VF	XF	Unc	BU
2001 Proof	10,000	Value: 49.50				

KM# 1088 1/25 CROWN

1.2441 g., 0.9999 Gold .0400 oz. AGW, 13.9 mm. **Series:** Harry Potter **Subject:** Journey to Hogwarts School **Obv:** Queen's portrait **Rev:** Boat full of children going to Hogwarts School **Edge:** Reeded

Date	Mintage	F	VF	XF	Unc	BU
2001 Proof	10,000	Value: 49.50				

KM# 1090 1/25 CROWN

1.2441 g., 0.9999 Gold .0400 oz. AGW, 13.9 mm. **Series:** Harry Potter **Subject:** First Quidditch Match **Obv:** Queen's portrait **Rev:** Harry flying a broom **Edge:** Reeded

Date	Mintage	F	VF	XF	Unc	BU
2001 Proof	10,000	Value: 49.50				

KM# 1092 1/25 CROWN

1.2441 g., 0.9999 Gold .0400 oz. AGW, 13.9 mm. **Series:** Harry Potter **Subject:** Birth of Norbert **Obv:** Queen's portrait **Edge:** Reeded

Date	Mintage	F	VF	XF	Unc	BU
2001 Proof	10,000	Value: 49.50				

KM# 1094 1/25 CROWN

1.2441 g., 0.9999 Gold .0400 oz. AGW, 13.9 mm. **Series:** Harry Potter **Subject:** School **Obv:** Queen's portrait **Rev:** Harry in Potions class **Edge:** Reeded

Date	Mintage	F	VF	XF	Unc	BU
2001 Proof	10,000	Value: 49.50				

KM# 1096 1/25 CROWN

1.2441 g., 0.9999 Gold .0400 oz. AGW, 13.9 mm. **Series:** Harry Potter **Subject:** Keys **Obv:** Queen's portrait **Rev:** Harry chasing a quiditch **Edge:** Reeded

Date	Mintage	F	VF	XF	Unc	BU
2001 Proof	10,000	Value: 49.50				

KM# 1098 1/25 CROWN

1.2441 g., 0.9999 Gold .0400 oz. AGW, 13.9 mm. **Subject:** Year of the Horse **Obv:** Queen's portrait **Rev:** Two horses **Edge:** Reeded

Date	Mintage	F	VF	XF	Unc	BU
2002 Proof	20,000	Value: 49.50				

KM# 1143 1/25 CROWN

1.2440 g., 0.9999 Gold 0.04 oz. AGW, 13.92 mm. **Subject:** Harry Potter **Obv:** Queen's portrait **Rev:** Tom Riddle twirling Harry's magic wand **Edge:** Reeded

Date	Mintage	F	VF	XF	Unc	BU
2002PM Proof	10,000	Value: 55.00				

KM# 1147 1/25 CROWN

1.2440 g., 0.9999 Gold .04 oz. AGW **Subject:** Harry Potter **Obv:** Queen's portrait **Rev:** Harry arrives at the Burrow in a flying car **Edge:** Reeded

Date	Mintage	F	VF	XF	Unc	BU
2002PM Proof	10,000	Value: 55.00				

KM# 1149 1/25 CROWN

1.2440 g., 0.9999 Gold 0.04 oz. AGW, 13.92 mm. **Subject:** Harry Potter Series **Obv:** Queen's portrait **Rev:** Harry retrieves Gryffindor sword from snake **Edge:** Reeded

Date	Mintage	F	VF	XF	Unc	BU
2002PM Proof	10,000	Value: 55.00				

KM# 1151 1/25 CROWN

1.2240 g., 0.9999 Gold 0.0393 oz. AGW, 13.92 mm. **Series:** Harry Potter **Obv:** Queen's portrait **Rev:** Harry and Ron encounter the spider Aragog **Edge:** Reeded

Date	Mintage	F	VF	XF	Unc	BU
2002PM Proof	10,000	Value: 55.00				

KM# 1153 1/25 CROWN

1.2440 g., 0.9999 Gold 0.04 oz. AGW, 13.92 mm. **Series:** Harry Potter **Obv:** Queen's portrait **Rev:** Harry in hospital **Edge:** Reeded

Date	Mintage	F	VF	XF	Unc	BU
2002PM Proof	10,000	Value: 55.00				

KM# 1107 1/25 CROWN

1.2440 g., 0.9990 Gold 0.04 oz. AGW, 13.92 mm. **Subject:** Bengal Cat **Obv:** Queen Elizabeth's bust right **Rev:** Cat and kitten **Edge:** Reeded

Date	Mintage	F	VF	XF	Unc	BU
2002	—	—	—	—	32.00	—
2002 Proof	1,000	Value: 49.50				

KM# 1107a 1/25 CROWN

1.2440 g., 0.9990 Platinum 0.04 oz. APW, 13.92 mm. **Subject:** Bengal Cat **Obv:** Bust of Queen Elizabeth II right **Rev:** Cat and kitten **Edge:** Reeded

Date	Mintage	F	VF	XF	Unc	BU
2002 Proof	—	Value: 60.00				

KM# 1145 1/25 CROWN

1.2440 g., 0.9999 Gold 0.04 oz. AGW, 13.92 mm. **Subject:** Harry Potter Series **Obv:** Queen's portrait **Rev:** Harry and friends making Polyjuice potion **Edge:** Reeded

Date	Mintage	F	VF	XF	Unc	BU
2002PM Proof	10,000	Value: 55.00				

KM# 1161 1/25 CROWN

1.2440 g., 0.9999 Gold 0.04 oz. AGW, 13.92 mm. **Subject:** Cat **Obv:** Bust of Queen Elizabeth II right **Rev:** Two Balinese kittens **Edge:** Reeded

Date	Mintage	F	VF	XF	Unc	BU
2003PM	—	—	—	—	35.00	—
2003PM Proof	—	Value: 49.50				

KM# 1161a 1/25 CROWN

1.2440 g., 0.9995 Platinum 0.04 oz. APW, 13.92 mm. **Subject:** Cat **Obv:** Bust of Queen Elizabeth II right **Rev:** Two Balinese kittens **Edge:** Reeded

Date	Mintage	F	VF	XF	Unc	BU
2003PM	—	—	—	—	60.00	—

KM# 1167 1/25 CROWN

1.2441 g., 0.9999 Gold 0.04 oz. AGW, 13.9 mm. **Subject:** Year of the Goat **Obv:** Bust of Queen Elizabeth II right **Rev:** Three goats **Edge:** Reeded

Date	Mintage	F	VF	XF	Unc	BU
2003PM Proof	20,000	Value: 49.50				

KM# 1186 1/25 CROWN

1.2440 g., 0.9999 Gold 0.04 oz. AGW, 13.9 mm. **Subject:** Lord of the Rings **Obv:** Bust of Queen Elizabeth II right **Rev:** Man with short sword **Edge:** Reeded

Date	Mintage	F	VF	XF	Unc	BU
2003PM Proof	6,000	Value: 50.00				

KM# 1203 1/25 CROWN

1.2440 g., 0.9999 Gold 0.04 oz. AGW, 14 mm. **Ruler:** Elizabeth II **Obv:** Bust of Queen Elizabeth II right **Rev:** Harry Potter and patron fighting off a spectre **Edge:** Reeded

Date	Mintage	F	VF	XF	Unc	BU
2004PM Proof	2,500	Value: 50.00				

KM# 1205 1/25 CROWN

1.2440 g., 0.9999 Gold 0.04 oz. AGW, 14 mm. **Ruler:** Elizabeth II **Obv:** Bust of Queen Elizabeth II right **Rev:** Harry Potter in the shrieking shack **Edge:** Reeded

Date	Mintage	F	VF	XF	Unc	BU
2004PM Proof	2,500	Value: 50.00				

KM# 1207 1/25 CROWN

1.2440 g., 0.9999 Gold 0.04 oz. AGW, 14 mm. **Ruler:** Elizabeth II **Obv:** Bust of Queen Elizabeth II right **Rev:** Harry Potter and Professor Dumbledore **Edge:** Reeded

Date	Mintage	F	VF	XF	Unc	BU
2004PM Proof	2,500	Value: 50.00				

KM# 1209 1/25 CROWN

1.2440 g., 0.9999 Gold 0.04 oz. AGW, 14 mm. **Ruler:** Elizabeth II **Obv:** Bust of Queen Elizabeth II right **Rev:** Sirius Black on flying griffin **Edge:** Reeded

Date	Mintage	F	VF	XF	Unc	BU
2004PM Proof	2,500	Value: 50.00				

KM# 1211 1/25 CROWN

1.2440 g., 0.9999 Gold 0.04 oz. AGW, 14 mm. **Ruler:** Elizabeth II **Obv:** Bust of Queen Elizabeth II right **Rev:** Three Olympic Swimmers **Edge:** Reeded

Date	Mintage	F	VF	XF	Unc	BU
2004PM Proof	5,000	Value: 50.00				

KM# 1213 1/25 CROWN

1.2440 g., 0.9999 Gold 0.04 oz. AGW, 14 mm. **Ruler:** Elizabeth II **Obv:** Bust of Queen Elizabeth II right **Rev:** Three Olympic Cyclists **Edge:** Reeded

Date	Mintage	F	VF	XF	Unc	BU
2004PM Proof	5,000	Value: 50.00				

KM# 1215 1/25 CROWN

1.2440 g., 0.9999 Gold 0.04 oz. AGW, 14 mm. **Ruler:** Elizabeth II **Obv:** Bust of Queen Elizabeth II right **Rev:** Three Olympic Runners **Edge:** Reeded

Date	Mintage	F	VF	XF	Unc	BU
2004PM Proof	5,000	Value: 50.00				

KM# 1217 1/25 CROWN

1.2440 g., 0.9999 Gold 0.04 oz. AGW, 14 mm. **Ruler:** Elizabeth II **Obv:** Bust of Queen Elizabeth II right **Rev:** Three Olympic Sail Boarders **Edge:** Reeded

Date	Mintage	F	VF	XF	Unc	BU
2004PM Proof	5,000	Value: 50.00				

KM# 1240 1/25 CROWN

1.2440 g., 0.9999 Gold 0.04 oz. AGW, 14 mm. **Ruler:** Elizabeth II **Obv:** Bust of Queen Elizabeth II right **Rev:** Monkey **Edge:** Reeded

Date	Mintage	F	VF	XF	Unc	BU
2004PM Proof	20,000	Value: 50.00				

KM# 1247 1/25 CROWN

1.2440 g., 0.9999 Gold 0.04 oz. AGW, 14 mm. **Ruler:** Elizabeth II **Obv:** Bust of Queen Elizabeth II right **Rev:** Two Tonkinese cats **Edge:** Reeded

Date	Mintage	F	VF	XF	Unc	BU
2004PM	—	—	—	—	35.00	—
2004PM Proof	1,000	Value: 50.00				

KM# 1059 1/10 CROWN

3.1100 g., 0.9999 Gold .1000 oz. AGW, 17.95 mm. **Subject:** Year of the Snake **Obv:** Bust of Queen Elizabeth II right **Rev:** Snake **Edge:** Reeded

Date	Mintage	F	VF	XF	Unc	BU
2001 Proof	15,000	Value: 95.00				

KM# 1068 1/10 CROWN

3.1100 g., 0.9999 Gold .1000 oz. AGW, 18 mm. **Obv:** Bust of Queen Elizabeth II right **Rev:** Somali kittens **Edge:** Reeded

Date	Mintage	F	VF	XF	Unc	BU
2001	—	—	—	—	70.00	—
2001 Proof	1,000	Value: 95.00				

KM# 1068a 1/10 CROWN

3.1100 g., 0.9995 Platinum .1000 oz. APW, 18 mm. **Obv:** Bust of Queen Elizabeth II right **Rev:** Somali kittens **Edge:** Reeded

Date	Mintage	F	VF	XF	Unc	BU
2001	—	—	—	—	130	—

KM# 1099 1/10 CROWN

3.1100 g., 0.9999 Gold .1000 oz. AGW, 17.95 mm. **Subject:** Year of the Horse **Obv:** Bust of Queen Elizabeth II right **Rev:** Two horses **Edge:** Reeded

Date	Mintage	F	VF	XF	Unc	BU
2002 Proof	15,000	Value: 95.00				

KM# 1108 1/10 CROWN

3.1100 g., 0.9990 Gold 0.0999 oz. AGW, 17.95 mm. **Subject:** Bengal Cat **Obv:** Bust of Queen Elizabeth II right **Rev:** Cat and kitten **Edge:** Reeded

Date	Mintage	VG	F	VF	XF	Unc
2002	—	—	—	—	—	70.00
2002 Proof	—	Value: 95.00				

KM# 1108a 1/10 CROWN

3.1100 g., 0.9990 Platinum 0.0999 oz. APW, 17.95 mm. **Subject:** Bengal Cat **Obv:** Bust of Queen Elizabeth II right **Rev:** Cat and kitten **Edge:** Reeded

Date	Mintage	F	VF	XF	Unc	BU
2002	—	—	—	—	120	—

KM# 1162 1/10 CROWN

3.1100 g., 0.9999 Gold 0.1 oz. AGW, 17.95 mm. **Subject:** Cat **Obv:** Bust of Queen Elizabeth II right **Rev:** Two Balinese kittens **Edge:** Reeded

Date	Mintage	F	VF	XF	Unc	BU
2003PM	—	—	—	—	70.00	—
2003PM Proof	—	Value: 95.00				

KM# 1162a 1/10 CROWN

3.1100 g., 0.9995 Platinum 0.0999 oz. APW, 17.95 mm. **Subject:** Cat **Obv:** Bust of Queen Elizabeth II right **Rev:** Two Balinese kittens **Edge:** Reeded

Date	Mintage	F	VF	XF	Unc	BU
2003PM	—	—	—	—	120	—

KM# 1187 1/10 CROWN

3.1100 g., 0.9999 Gold 0.1 oz. AGW, 18 mm. **Subject:** Lord of the Rings **Obv:** Bust of Queen Elizabeth II right **Rev:** Aragorn with broad sword **Edge:** Reeded

Date	Mintage	F	VF	XF	Unc	BU
2003PM Proof	4,500	Value: 85.00				

KM# 1241 1/10 CROWN

3.1100 g., 0.9999 Gold 0.1 oz. AGW, 18 mm. **Ruler:** Elizabeth II **Obv:** Bust of Queen Elizabeth II right **Rev:** Monkey **Edge:** Reeded

Date	Mintage	F	VF	XF	Unc	BU
2004PM Proof	15,000	Value: 95.00				

KM# 1248 1/10 CROWN

3.1100 g., 0.9999 Gold 0.1 oz. AGW, 18 mm. **Ruler:** Elizabeth II **Obv:** Bust of Queen Elizabeth II right **Rev:** Two Tonkinese cats **Edge:** Reeded

Date	Mintage	F	VF	XF	Unc	BU
2004PM	—	—	—	—	75.00	—
2004PM Proof	1,000	Value: 95.00				

KM# 1168 1/10 CROWN

3.1100 g., 0.9999 Gold 0.1 oz. AGW, 17.95 mm. **Subject:** Year of the Goat **Obv:** Bust of Queen Elizabeth II right **Rev:** Three goats **Edge:** Reeded

Date	Mintage	F	VF	XF	Unc	BU
2003PM Proof	—	Value: 95.00				

KM# 1060 1/5 CROWN

6.2200 g., 0.9999 Gold .2000 oz. AGW, 22 mm. **Subject:** Year of the Snake **Obv:** Bust of Queen Elizabeth II right **Rev:** Snake **Edge:** Reeded

Date	Mintage	F	VF	XF	Unc	BU
2001 Proof	12,000	Value: 175				

KM# 1069 1/5 CROWN

6.2200 g., 0.9999 Gold .2000 oz. AGW, 22 mm. **Obv:** Bust of Queen Elizabeth II right **Rev:** Two Somali kittens **Edge:** Reeded

Date	Mintage	F	VF	XF	Unc	BU
2001	—	—	—	—	125	—
2001 Proof	1,000	Value: 175				

KM# 1069a 1/5 CROWN

6.2200 g., 0.9995 Platinum .2000 oz. APW, 22 mm. **Obv:** Bust of Queen Elizabeth II right **Rev:** Somali kittens **Edge:** Reeded

Date	Mintage	F	VF	XF	Unc	BU
2001	—	—	—	—	250	—

KM# 1074 1/5 CROWN

6.2200 g., 0.9999 Gold .2000 oz. AGW, 22 mm. **Subject:** Queen Mother **Obv:** Bust of Queen Elizabeth II right **Rev:** 1948 Silver wedding anniversary **Edge:** Reeded

Date	Mintage	F	VF	XF	Unc	BU
2001 Proof	5,000	Value: 175				

KM# 1075 1/5 CROWN

6.2200 g., 0.9999 Gold .2000 oz. AGW, 22 mm. **Subject:** Queen Mother **Obv:** Bust of Queen Elizabeth II right **Rev:** 1948 holding baby Prince Charles **Edge:** Reeded

Date	Mintage	F	VF	XF	Unc	BU
2001 Proof	5,000	Value: 175				

KM# 1078 1/5 CROWN

6.2200 g., 0.9999 Gold .2000 oz. AGW, 22 mm. **Subject:** Martin Frobisher **Obv:** Bust of Queen Elizabeth II right **Rev:** Portrait, ship and map **Edge:** Reeded

Date	Mintage	F	VF	XF	Unc	BU
2001 Proof	5,000	Value: 175				

KM# 1079 1/5 CROWN

6.2200 g., 0.9999 Gold .2000 oz. AGW, 22 mm. **Subject:** Ronald Amundsen **Obv:** Bust of Queen Elizabeth II right **Rev:** Portrait, ship and dirigible **Edge:** Reeded

Date	Mintage	F	VF	XF	Unc	BU
2001 Proof	5,000	Value: 175				

KM# 1082 1/5 CROWN

6.2200 g., 0.9999 Gold .2000 oz. AGW, 22 mm. **Subject:** Queen's 75th Birthday **Obv:** Bust of Queen Elizabeth II right **Rev:** Flower bouquet with a tiny diamond mounted on the bow of the ribbon **Edge:** Reeded

Date	Mintage	F	VF	XF	Unc	BU
2001 Proof	2,000	Value: 300				

KM# 1117 1/5 CROWN

6.2200 g., 0.9990 Gold 0.1998 oz. AGW, 22 mm. **Subject:** Queen Mother's Love of Horses **Obv:** Bust of Queen Elizabeth II right **Rev:** Queen Mother and horse **Edge:** Reeded

Date	Mintage	F	VF	XF	Unc	BU
2002 Proof	5,000	Value: 175				

KM# 1109 1/5 CROWN

6.2200 g., 0.9990 Gold 0.1998 oz. AGW, 22 mm. **Subject:** Bengal Cat **Obv:** Bust of Queen Elizabeth II right **Rev:** Cat and kitten **Edge:** Reeded

Date	Mintage	VG	F	VF	XF	Unc
2002	—	—	—	—	—	125
2002 Proof	1,000	Value: 175				

KM# 1109a 1/5 CROWN

6.2200 g., 0.9990 Platinum 0.1998 oz. APW, 22 mm. **Subject:** Bengal Cat **Obv:** Bust of Queen Elizabeth II right. **Rev:** Cat and kitten **Edge:** Reeded

Date	Mintage	F	VF	XF	Unc	BU
2002	—	—	—	—	250	—

KM# 1100 1/5 CROWN

6.2200 g., 0.9999 Gold .2000 oz. AGW, 22 mm. **Subject:** Year of the Horse **Obv:** Bust of Queen Elizabeth II right **Rev:** Two horses **Edge:** Reeded

Date	Mintage	F	VF	XF	Unc	BU
2002 Proof	12,000	Value: 175				

KM# 1113 1/5 CROWN

6.2200 g., 0.9990 Gold 0.1998 oz. AGW, 22 mm. **Subject:** Olympics - Salt Lake City **Obv:** Bust of Queen Elizabeth II right **Rev:** Skier, torch and flag **Edge:** Reeded

Date	Mintage	F	VF	XF	Unc	BU
2002 Proof	5,000	Value: 175				

KM# 1114 1/5 CROWN

6.2200 g., 0.9990 Gold 0.1998 oz. AGW **Subject:** Olympics - Salt Lake City **Obv:** Bust of Queen Elizabeth II right **Rev:** Bobsled, torch and stadium **Edge:** Reeded

Date	Mintage	F	VF	XF	Unc	BU
2002 Proof	5,000	Value: 175				

KM# 1120 1/5 CROWN

6.2200 g., 0.9990 Gold 0.1998 oz. AGW, 22 mm. **Subject:** World Cup 2002 Japan - Korea **Obv:** Bust of Queen Elizabeth II right **Rev:** Player running right **Edge:** Reeded

Date	Mintage	F	VF	XF	Unc	BU
2002 Proof	5,000	Value: 175				

KM# 1122 1/5 CROWN

6.2200 g., 0.9990 Gold 0.1998 oz. AGW, 22 mm. **Subject:** World Cup 2002 Japan - Korea **Obv:** Bust of Queen Elizabeth II right **Rev:** Player kicking to right **Edge:** Reeded

Date	Mintage	F	VF	XF	Unc	BU
2002 Proof	5,000	Value: 175				

KM# 1124 1/5 CROWN

6.2200 g., 0.9990 Gold 0.1998 oz. AGW, 22 mm. **Subject:** World Cup 2002 Japan - Korea **Obv:** Bust of Queen Elizabeth II right **Rev:** Player kicking to left **Edge:** Reeded

Date	Mintage	F	VF	XF	Unc	BU
2002 Proof	5,000	Value: 175				

KM# 1126 1/5 CROWN

6.2200 g., 0.9990 Gold 0.1998 oz. AGW, 22 mm. **Subject:** World Cup 2002 Japan - Korea **Obv:** Bust of Queen Elizabeth II right **Rev:** Player running to left **Edge:** Reeded

Date	Mintage	F	VF	XF	Unc	BU
2002 Proof	5,000	Value: 175				

KM# 1130 1/5 CROWN

6.2200 g., 0.3750 Gold 0.075 oz. AGW, 22 mm. **Subject:** Queen Elizabeth II's Golden Jubilee **Obv:** Bust of Queen Elizabeth II right **Rev:** Seated crowned Queen holding scepter at her coronation **Edge:** Reeded

Date	Mintage	F	VF	XF	Unc	BU
2002 Proof	2,002	Value: 60.00				

KM# 1132 1/5 CROWN

6.2200 g., 0.3750 Gold 0.075 oz. AGW, 22 mm. **Subject:** Queen Elizabeth II's Golden Jubilee **Obv:** Bust of Queen Elizabeth II right **Rev:** Queen on horse **Edge:** Reeded

Date	Mintage	F	VF	XF	Unc	BU
2002 Proof	2,002	Value: 60.00				

KM# 1134 1/5 CROWN

6.2200 g., 0.3750 Gold 0.075 oz. AGW, 22 mm. **Subject:** Queen Elizabeth II's Golden Jubilee **Obv:** Bust of Queen Elizabeth II right **Rev:** Queen with dog **Edge:** Reeded

Date	Mintage	F	VF	XF	Unc	BU
2002 Proof	2,002	Value: 60.00				

KM# 1136 1/5 CROWN

6.2200 g., 0.3750 Gold 0.075 oz. AGW, 22 mm. **Subject:** Queen Elizabeth II's Golden Jubilee **Obv:** Bust of Queen Elizabeth II right **Rev:** Queen at war memorial **Edge:** Reeded

Date	Mintage	F	VF	XF	Unc	BU
2002 Proof	2,002	Value: 60.00				

KM# 1138 1/5 CROWN

6.2200 g., 0.9990 Gold 0.1998 oz. AGW, 22 mm. **Subject:** Queen Mother **Obv:** Bust of Queen Elizabeth II right **Rev:** Queen Mother and Castle May **Edge:** Reeded

Date	Mintage	F	VF	XF	Unc	BU
2002 Proof	5,000	Value: 175				

KM# 1140 1/5 CROWN

6.2200 g., 0.9999 Gold 0.2 oz. AGW, 22 mm. **Subject:** Princess Diana **Obv:** Bust of Queen Elizabeth II right **Rev:** Diana's portrait **Edge:** Reeded

Date	Mintage	F	VF	XF	Unc	BU
2002 Proof	5,000	Value: 175				

KM# 1163 1/5 CROWN

6.2200 g., 0.9999 Gold 0.2 oz. AGW, 22 mm. **Subject:** Cat **Obv:** Bust of Queen Elizabeth II right **Rev:** Two Balinese kittens **Edge:** Reeded

Date	Mintage	F	VF	XF	Unc	BU
2003PM	—	—	—	—	125	—
2003PM Proof	—	Value: 175				

KM# 1163a 1/5 CROWN

6.2200 g., 0.9995 Platinum 0.1999 oz. APW, 22 mm. **Subject:** Cat **Obv:** Bust of Queen Elizabeth II right **Rev:** Two Balinese kittens **Edge:** Reeded

Date	Mintage	F	VF	XF	Unc	BU
2003PM	—	—	—	—	200	—

KM# 1169 1/5 CROWN

6.2200 g., 0.9999 Gold 0.2 oz. AGW, 22 mm. **Subject:** Year of the Goat **Obv:** Bust of Queen Elizabeth II right **Rev:** Three goats **Edge:** Reeded

Date	Mintage	F	VF	XF	Unc	BU
2003PM Proof	—	Value: 175				

KM# 1175 1/5 CROWN

6.2200 g., 0.9999 Gold 0.2 oz. AGW, 22 mm. **Subject:** Olympics **Obv:** Bust of Queen Elizabeth II right **Rev:** Swimmers **Edge:** Reeded

Date	Mintage	F	VF	XF	Unc	BU
2003PM Proof	5,000	Value: 175				

KM# 1177 1/5 CROWN

6.2200 g., 0.9999 Gold 0.2 oz. AGW, 22 mm. **Subject:** Olympics **Obv:** Bust of Queen Elizabeth II right **Rev:** Runners **Edge:** Reeded

Date	Mintage	F	VF	XF	Unc	BU
2003PM Proof	5,000	Value: 175				

KM# 1179 1/5 CROWN

6.2200 g., 0.9999 Gold 0.2 oz. AGW, 22 mm. **Subject:** Olympics **Obv:** Bust of Queen Elizabeth II right **Rev:** Bicyclists **Edge:** Reeded

Date	Mintage	F	VF	XF	Unc	BU
2003PM Proof	5,000	Value: 175				

KM# 1181 1/5 CROWN

6.2200 g., 0.9999 Gold 0.2 oz. AGW, 22 mm. **Subject:** Olympics **Obv:** Bust of Queen Elizabeth II right **Rev:** Sail Boarders **Edge:** Reeded

Date	Mintage	F	VF	XF	Unc	BU
2003PM Proof	—	Value: 175				

KM# 1188 1/5 CROWN

6.2200 g., 0.9999 Gold 0.2 oz. AGW, 22 mm. **Subject:** Lord of the Rings **Obv:** Bust of Queen Elizabeth II right **Rev:** Legolas **Edge:** Reeded

Date	Mintage	F	VF	XF	Unc	BU
2003PM Proof	3,500	Value: 175				

KM# 1223 1/5 CROWN

6.2200 g., 0.9999 Gold 0.2 oz. AGW, 22 mm. **Ruler:** Elizabeth II **Obv:** Bust of Queen Elizabeth II right **Rev:** D-Day Invasion Plan Map **Edge:** Reeded

Date	Mintage	F	VF	XF	Unc	BU
2004PM Proof	5,000	Value: 175				

KM# 1225 1/5 CROWN

6.2200 g., 0.9999 Gold 0.2 oz. AGW, 22 mm. **Ruler:** Elizabeth II **Obv:** Bust of Queen Elizabeth II right **Rev:** Victoria Cross and battle scene **Edge:** Reeded

Date	Mintage	F	VF	XF	Unc	BU
2004PM Proof	5,000	Value: 175				

KM# 1227 1/5 CROWN

6.2200 g., 0.9999 Gold 0.2 oz. AGW, 22 mm. **Ruler:** Elizabeth II **Obv:** Bust of Queen Elizabeth II right **Rev:** Silver Star and battle scene **Edge:** Reeded

Date	Mintage	F	VF	XF	Unc	BU
2004PM Proof	5,000	Value: 175				

KM# 1229 1/5 CROWN

6.2200 g., 0.9999 Gold 0.2 oz. AGW, 22 mm. **Ruler:** Elizabeth II **Obv:** Bust of Queen Elizabeth II right **Rev:** George Cross and rescue scene **Edge:** Reeded

Date	Mintage	F	VF	XF	Unc	BU
2004PM Proof	5,000	Value: 175				

KM# 1231 1/5 CROWN

6.2200 g., 0.9999 Gold 0.2 oz. AGW, 22 mm. **Ruler:** Elizabeth II **Obv:** Bust of Queen Elizabeth II right **Rev:** White Rose of Finland Medal and battle scene **Edge:** Reeded

Date	Mintage	F	VF	XF	Unc	BU
2004PM Proof	5,000	Value: 175				

KM# 1233 1/5 CROWN

6.2200 g., 0.9999 Gold 0.2 oz. AGW, 22 mm. **Ruler:** Elizabeth II **Obv:** Bust of Queen Elizabeth II right **Rev:** The Norwegian War Medal and naval battle scene **Edge:** Reeded

Date	Mintage	F	VF	XF	Unc	BU
2004PM Proof	5,000	Value: 175				

KM# 1235 1/5 CROWN

6.2200 g., 0.9999 Gold 0.2 oz. AGW, 22 mm. **Ruler:** Elizabeth II **Obv:** Bust of Queen Elizabeth II right **Rev:** French Croix de Guerre and Partisan battle scene **Edge:** Reeded

Date	Mintage	F	VF	XF	Unc	BU
2004PM Proof	5,000	Value: 175				

KM# 1249.1 1/5 CROWN

6.2200 g., 0.9999 Gold 0.2 oz. AGW, 22 mm. **Ruler:** Elizabeth II **Obv:** Bust of Queen Elizabeth II right **Rev:** Two Tonkinese cats **Edge:** Reeded

Date	Mintage	F	VF	XF	Unc	BU
2004PM	—	—	—	—	135	—
2004PM Proof	1,000	Value: 175				

KM# 1249.2 1/5 CROWN

6.2200 g., 0.9999 Gold 0.2 oz. AGW, 22 mm. **Ruler:** Elizabeth II **Obv:** Bust of Queen Elizabeth II right **Rev:** Two multicolor Tonkinese cats **Edge:** Reeded

Date	Mintage	F	VF	XF	Unc	BU
2004PM Proof	—	Value: 180				

KM# 1198 1/5 CROWN

6.2200 g., 0.9990 Palladium 0.1998 oz., 22 mm. **Ruler:** Elizabeth II **Subject:** Palladium Bicentennial **Obv:** Bust of Queen Elizabeth II right **Rev:** Athena **Edge:** Reeded

Date	Mintage	F	VF	XF	Unc	BU
2004PM Proof	999	Value: 300				

KM# 1061 1/2 CROWN

15.5517 g., 0.9999 Gold .5000 oz. AGW, 30 mm. **Subject:** Year of the Snake **Obv:** Bust of Queen Elizabeth II right **Rev:** Snake **Edge:** Reeded

Date	Mintage	F	VF	XF	Unc	BU
2001 Proof	6,000	Value: 325				

KM# 1070 1/2 CROWN

15.5517 g., 0.9999 Gold .5000 oz. AGW, 30 mm. **Obv:** Bust of Queen Elizabeth II right **Rev:** Two Somali kittens **Edge:** Reeded

Date	Mintage	F	VF	XF	Unc	BU
2001	—	—	—	—	325	—
2001 Proof	1,000	Value: 350				

KM# 1071 1/2 CROWN

15.5517 g., 0.9995 Platinum .5000 oz. APW, 27 mm. **Obv:** Bust of Queen Elizabeth II right **Rev:** Two Somali kittens **Edge:** Reeded

Date	Mintage	F	VF	XF	Unc	BU
2001	—	—	—	—	625	—

KM# 1110 1/2 CROWN

15.5510 g., 0.9990 Gold 0.4995 oz. AGW, 30 mm. **Subject:** Bengal Cat **Obv:** Queen Elizabeth's bust right **Rev:** Cat and kitten **Edge:** Reeded

Date	Mintage	VG	F	VF	XF	Unc
2002	—	—	—	—	—	325
2002 Proof	1,000	Value: 350				

KM# 1101 1/2 CROWN

15.5500 g., 0.9999 Gold .4999 oz. AGW, 30 mm. **Subject:** Year of the Horse **Obv:** Bust of Queen Elizabeth II right **Rev:** Two horses **Edge:** Reeded

Date	Mintage	F	VF	XF	Unc	BU
2002 Proof	6,000	Value: 350				

KM# 1110a 1/2 CROWN

6.2200 g., 0.9990 Platinum 0.1998 oz. APW, 30 mm. **Subject:** Bengal Cat **Obv:** Bust of Queen Elizabeth II right **Rev:** Cat and kitten **Edge:** Reeded

Date	Mintage	F	VF	XF	Unc	BU
2002	—	—	—	—	375	—

KM# 1164 1/2 CROWN

15.5510 g., 0.9999 Gold 0.4999 oz. AGW, 30 mm. **Subject:** Cat **Obv:** Bust of Queen Elizabeth II right **Rev:** Two Balinese kittens **Edge:** Reeded

Date	Mintage	F	VF	XF	Unc	BU
2003PM	—	—	—	—	325	—
2003PM Proof	—	Value: 350				

KM# 1164a 1/2 CROWN

15.5510 g., 0.9995 Platinum 0.4997 oz. APW, 30 mm. **Subject:** Cat **Obv:** Bust of Queen Elizabeth II right **Rev:** Two Balinese kittens **Edge:** Reeded

Date	Mintage	F	VF	XF	Unc	BU
2003PM	—	—	—	—	625	—

KM# 1170 1/2 CROWN

15.5500 g., 0.9999 Gold 0.4999 oz. AGW, 30 mm. **Subject:** Year of the Goat **Obv:** Bust of Queen Elizabeth II right **Rev:** Three goats **Edge:** Reeded

Date	Mintage	F	VF	XF	Unc	BU
2003PM Proof	—	Value: 350				

KM# 1189 1/2 CROWN

15.5510 g., 0.9999 Gold 0.4999 oz. AGW, 30 mm. **Subject:** Lord of the Rings **Obv:** Queen Elizabeth II **Rev:** Gimli with two battle axes **Edge:** Reeded

Date	Mintage	F	VF	XF	Unc	BU
2003PM Proof	1,000	Value: 350				

KM# 1243 1/2 CROWN

15.5520 g., 0.9999 Gold 0.5 oz. AGW, 30 mm. **Ruler:** Elizabeth II **Obv:** Bust of Queen Elizabeth II right **Rev:** Monkey **Edge:** Reeded

Date	Mintage	F	VF	XF	Unc	BU
2004PM Proof	6,000	Value: 350				

KM# 1250 1/2 CROWN

15.5520 g., 0.9999 Gold 0.5 oz. AGW, 30 mm. **Ruler:** Elizabeth II **Obv:** Bust of Queen Elizabeth II right **Rev:** Two Tonkinese cats **Edge:** Reeded

Date	Mintage	F	VF	XF	Unc	BU
2004PM	—	—	—	—	325	—
2004PM Proof	1,000	Value: 350				

KM# 1199 1/2 CROWN

15.5500 g., 0.9990 Bi-Metallic .999 Palladium 6.3g center in .9999 Gold 9.25 g ring 0.4994 oz., 30 mm. **Ruler:** Elizabeth II **Subject:** Palladium Bicentennial **Obv:** Bust of Queen Elizabeth II right **Rev:** Athena **Edge:** Reeded

Date	Mintage	F	VF	XF	Unc	BU
2004PM Proof	500	Value: 600				

KM# 1062 CROWN

28.2800 g., Copper-Nickel, 38.6 mm. **Subject:** Year of the Snake **Obv:** Bust of Queen Elizabeth II right **Rev:** Snake **Edge:** Reeded

Date	Mintage	F	VF	XF	Unc	BU
2001	—	—	—	—	10.00	12.00

KM# 1062a CROWN

28.2800 g., 0.9250 Silver .8410 oz. ASW, 38.6 mm. **Subject:** Year of the Snake **Obv:** Bust of Queen Elizabeth II right **Rev:** Snake **Edge:** Reeded

Date	Mintage	F	VF	XF	Unc	BU
2001 Proof	30,000	Value: 47.50				

KM# 1063 CROWN

31.1035 g., 0.9999 Gold 1.0000 oz. AGW, 32.7 mm. **Subject:** Year of the Snake **Obv:** Bust of Queen Elizabeth II right **Rev:** Snake **Edge:** Reeded

Date	Mintage	F	VF	XF	Unc	BU
2001 Proof	2,000	Value: 650				

KM# 1072 CROWN

28.2800 g., Copper-Nickel, 38.6 mm. **Subject:** Somali Kittens **Obv:** Bust of Queen Elizabeth II right **Rev:** Two kittens **Edge:** Reeded

Date	Mintage	F	VF	XF	Unc	BU
2001	—	—	—	—	9.00	12.00

KM# 1072a CROWN

31.1035 g., 0.9990 Silver 1.0000 oz. ASW, 38.6 mm. **Subject:** Somali Kittens **Obv:** Bust of Queen Elizabeth II right **Rev:** Two kittens **Edge:** Reeded

Date	Mintage	F	VF	XF	Unc	BU
2001 Proof	50,000	Value: 47.50				

KM# 1073 CROWN

31.1035 g., 0.9999 Gold 1.0000 oz. AGW, 32.7 mm. **Subject:** Somali Kittens **Obv:** Bust of Queen Elizabeth II right **Rev:** Two kittens **Edge:** Reeded

Date	Mintage	F	VF	XF	Unc	BU
2001	—	—	—	—	625	—
2001 Proof	1,000	Value: 650				

KM# 1076 CROWN

28.2800 g., Copper-Nickel, 38.6 mm. **Subject:** Queen Mother **Obv:** Bust of Queen Elizabeth II right **Rev:** 1948 Silver wedding anniversary **Edge:** Reeded

Date	Mintage	F	VF	XF	Unc	BU
2001	—	—	—	—	10.00	12.00

KM# 1076a CROWN

28.2800 g., 0.9250 Silver .8410 oz. ASW, 38.6 mm. **Subject:** Queen Mother **Obv:** Bust of Queen Elizabeth II right **Rev:** 1948 Silver wedding anniversary **Edge:** Reeded

Date	Mintage	F	VF	XF	Unc	BU
2001 Proof	10,000	Value: 47.50				

KM# 1077 CROWN

Copper-Nickel, 38.6 mm. **Subject:** Queen Mother **Obv:** Bust of Queen Elizabeth II right **Rev:** 1948 holding baby Prince Charles **Edge:** Reeded

Date	Mintage	F	VF	XF	Unc	BU
2001	—	—	—	—	10.00	12.00

KM# 1077a CROWN

28.2800 g., 0.9250 Silver .8410 oz. ASW, 38.6 mm. **Subject:** Queen Mother **Obv:** Bust of Queen Elizabeth II right **Rev:** 1948 holding baby Prince Charles **Edge:** Reeded

Date	Mintage	F	VF	XF	Unc	BU
2001 Proof	10,000	Value: 47.50				

KM# 1080 CROWN

Copper-Nickel, 38.6 mm. **Subject:** Martin Frobisher **Obv:** Bust of Queen Elizabeth II right **Rev:** Bust at left, ship at right and map below **Edge:** Reeded

Date	Mintage	F	VF	XF	Unc	BU
2001	—	—	—	—	10.00	12.00

KM# 1080a CROWN

28.2800 g., 0.9250 Silver .8410 oz. ASW, 38.6 mm. **Subject:** Martin Frobisher **Obv:** Bust of Queen Elizabeth II right **Rev:** Bust at left, ship at right and map below **Edge:** Reeded

Date	Mintage	F	VF	XF	Unc	BU
2001 Proof	10,000	Value: 47.50				

KM# 1081 CROWN

Copper-Nickel, 38.6 mm. **Subject:** Roald Amundsen **Obv:** Bust of Queen Elizabeth II right **Rev:** Bust at right, ship at center, dirigible above at left **Edge:** Reeded

Date	Mintage	F	VF	XF	Unc	BU
2001	—	—	—	—	10.00	12.00

KM# 1081a CROWN

28.2800 g., 0.9250 Silver .8410 oz. ASW, 38.6 mm. **Subject:** Roald Amundsen **Obv:** Bust of Queen Elizabeth II right **Rev:** Bust at right, ship at center, dirigible at upper left **Edge:** Reeded

Date	Mintage	F	VF	XF	Unc	BU
2001 Proof	10,000	Value: 47.50				

KM# 1085 CROWN

28.2800 g., Copper-Nickel, 38.6 mm. **Subject:** Joey Dunlop (1952-2000) **Obv:** Bust of Queen Elizabeth II right **Rev:** Motorcycle racer **Edge:** Reeded

Date	Mintage	F	VF	XF	Unc	BU
2001 Black finish	—	—	—	—	10.00	12.00

KM# 1085a CROWN

28.2800 g., 0.9250 Silver .8410 oz. ASW, 38.6 mm. **Subject:** Joey Dunlop (1952-2000) **Obv:** Bust of Queen Elizabeth II right **Rev:** Motorcycle racer **Edge:** Reeded

Date	Mintage	F	VF	XF	Unc	BU
2001 Proof	10,000	Value: 47.50				

KM# 1083 CROWN

28.2800 g., Copper-Nickel, 38.6 mm. **Subject:** Queen's 75th Birthday **Obv:** Bust of Queen Elizabeth II right **Rev:** Flower bouquet **Edge:** Reeded

Date	Mintage	F	VF	XF	Unc	BU
2001	—	—	—	—	14.00	16.00

KM# 1083a CROWN

28.2800 g., 0.9250 Silver .8410 oz. ASW, 38.6 mm. **Subject:** Queen's 75th Birthday **Obv:** Bust of Queen Elizabeth II right **Rev:** Flower bouquet **Edge:** Reeded

Date	Mintage	F	VF	XF	Unc	BU
2001 Proof	10,000	Value: 49.00				

KM# 1087 CROWN

28.2800 g., Copper-Nickel, 38.6 mm. **Series:** Harry Potter **Obv:** Bust of Queen Elizabeth II right **Rev:** Harry with magic wand **Edge:** Reeded

Date	Mintage	F	VF	XF	Unc	BU
2001	—	—	—	—	10.00	12.00

KM# 1087a CROWN

28.2800 g., 0.9250 Silver .8410 oz. ASW, 38.6 mm. **Series:** Harry Potter **Obv:** Bust of Queen Elizabeth II right **Rev:** Harry with magic wand **Edge:** Reeded

Date	Mintage	F	VF	XF	Unc	BU
2001 Proof	15,000	Value: 47.50				

KM# 1089 CROWN

28.2800 g., Copper-Nickel, 38.6 mm. **Series:** Harry Potter **Subject:** Journey to Hogwart's **Obv:** Bust of Queen Elizabeth II right **Rev:** Boat full of children going to Hogwart's **Edge:** Reeded

Date	Mintage	F	VF	XF	Unc	BU
2001	—	—	—	—	10.00	12.00

KM# 1089a CROWN

28.2800 g., 0.9250 Silver .8410 oz. ASW, 38.6 mm. **Series:** Harry Potter **Obv:** Bust of Queen Elizabeth II right **Rev:** Boat full of children going to Hogwart's **Edge:** Reeded

Date	Mintage	F	VF	XF	Unc	BU
2001 Proof	15,000	Value: 47.50				

KM# 1091 CROWN

Copper-Nickel **Series:** Harry Potter **Subject:** First Quidditch Match **Obv:** Bust of Queen Elizabeth II right **Rev:** Harry flying his Nimbus 2000

Date	Mintage	F	VF	XF	Unc	BU
2001	—	—	—	—	10.00	12.00

KM# 1091a CROWN

28.2800 g., 0.9250 Silver .8410 oz. ASW **Series:** Harry Potter **Subject:** First Quidditch Match **Obv:** Bust of Queen Elizabeth II right **Rev:** Harry flying his Nimbus 2000

Date	Mintage	F	VF	XF	Unc	BU
2001 Proof	15,000	Value: 47.50				

KM# 1093 CROWN

Copper-Nickel **Series:** Harry Potter **Subject:** Birth of Norbert **Obv:** Bust of Queen Elizabeth II right **Rev:** Hagrid and children watching Norbert hatch

Date	Mintage	F	VF	XF	Unc	BU
2001	—	—	—	—	10.00	12.00

KM# 1093a CROWN

28.2800 g., 0.9250 Silver .8410 oz. ASW **Series:** Harry Potter **Subject:** Birth of Norbert **Obv:** Bust of Queen Elizabeth II right **Rev:** Hagrid and children watching Norbert hatch

Date	Mintage	F	VF	XF	Unc	BU
2001 Proof	15,000	Value: 47.50				

KM# 1095 CROWN

Copper-Nickel **Series:** Harry Potter **Subject:** School **Obv:** Bust of Queen Elizabeth II right **Rev:** Harry in Potions class

Date	Mintage	F	VF	XF	Unc	BU
2001	—	—	—	—	10.00	12.00

KM# 1095a CROWN

28.2800 g., 0.9250 Silver .8410 oz. ASW **Series:** Harry Potter **Subject:** School **Obv:** Bust of Queen Elizabeth II right **Rev:** Harry in Potions class

Date	Mintage	F	VF	XF	Unc	BU
2001 Proof	15,000	Value: 47.50				

KM# 1097 CROWN

Copper-Nickel **Series:** Harry Potter **Subject:** Keys **Obv:** Bust of Queen Elizabeth II right **Rev:** Harry catching a flying key

Date	Mintage	F	VF	XF	Unc	BU
2001	—	—	—	—	10.00	12.00

KM# 1097a CROWN

28.2800 g., 0.9250 Silver .8410 oz. ASW **Series:** Harry Potter **Subject:** Keys **Obv:** Bust of Queen Elizabeth II right **Rev:** Harry catching a flying quidditch

Date	Mintage	F	VF	XF	Unc	BU
2001 Proof	15,000	Value: 47.50				

KM# 1118 CROWN

28.2800 g., Copper-Nickel, 38.6 mm. **Subject:** Queen Mother's Love of Horses **Obv:** Bust of Queen Elizabeth II right **Rev:** Queen Mother and horse **Edge:** Reeded

Date	Mintage	F	VF	XF	Unc	BU
2002	—	—	—	—	10.00	12.00

KM# 1118a CROWN

28.2800 g., Silver, 38.6 mm. **Subject:** Queen Mother's Love of Horses **Obv:** Bust of Queen Elizabeth II right **Rev:** Queen Mother and horse **Edge:** Reeded

Date	Mintage	F	VF	XF	Unc	BU
2002 Proof	10,000	Value: 47.50				

KM# 1119 CROWN

35.0000 g., 0.7500 Gold 0.844 oz. AGW, 38.6 mm. **Subject:** Golden Jubilee **Obv:** Bust of Queen Elizabeth II right **Rev:** Queen Elizabeth II's young bust right **Edge:** Reeded **Note:** Red Gold center in a White Gold inner ring within a Yellow Gold outer ring.

Date	Mintage	F	VF	XF	Unc	BU
2002 Proof	999	Value: 550				

KM# 1144 CROWN

28.2800 g., Copper Nickel, 38.6 mm. **Series:** Harry Potter **Obv:** Bust of Queen Elizabeth II right **Rev:** Tom Riddle twirling Harry's magic wand **Edge:** Reeded

Date	Mintage	F	VF	XF	Unc	BU
2002PM	—	—	—	—	10.00	12.00

KM# 1144a CROWN

28.2800 g., 0.9250 Silver 0.841 oz. ASW, 28.6 mm. **Series:** Harry Potter **Obv:** Bust of Queen Elizabeth II right **Rev:** Tom Riddle twirling Harry's magic wand **Edge:** Reeded

Date	Mintage	F	VF	XF	Unc	BU
2002PM Proof	15,000	Value: 49.00				

KM# 1146 CROWN

28.2800 g., Copper-Nickel, 38.6 mm. **Series:** Harry Potter **Obv:** Bust of Queen Elizabeth II right **Rev:** Harry and friends making Polyjuice potion **Edge:** Reeded

Date	Mintage	F	VF	XF	Unc	BU
2002PM	—	—	—	—	10.00	12.00

KM# 1146a CROWN

28.2800 g., 0.9250 Silver 0.841 oz. ASW, 38.6 mm. **Series:** Harry Potter **Obv:** Bust of Queen Elizabeth II right **Rev:** Harry Potter and friends making Polyjuice potion **Edge:** Reeded

Date	Mintage	F	VF	XF	Unc	BU
2002PM Proof	15,000	Value: 49.00				

KM# 1148 CROWN

28.2800 g., Copper Nickel, 38.6 mm. **Series:** Harry Potter **Obv:** Bust of Queen Elizabeth II right **Rev:** Harry arrives at the Burrow in a flying car **Edge:** Reeded

Date	Mintage	F	VF	XF	Unc	BU
2002PM	—	—	—	—	10.00	12.00

KM# 1148a CROWN

28.2800 g., 0.9250 Silver 0.841 oz. ASW, 38.6 mm. **Series:** Harry Potter **Obv:** Bust of Queen Elizabeth II right **Rev:** Harry arrives at the Burrow in a flying car **Edge:** Reeded

Date	Mintage	F	VF	XF	Unc	BU
2002PM Proof	15,000	Value: 49.00				

KM# 1150 CROWN

28.2800 g., Copper-Nickel, 38.6 mm. **Series:** Harry Potter **Obv:** Bust of Queen Elizabeth II right **Rev:** Harry retrieves Gryffindor sword from snake **Edge:** Reeded

Date	Mintage	F	VF	XF	Unc	BU
2002PM	—	—	—	—	10.00	12.00

KM# 1150a CROWN

28.2800 g., 0.9250 Silver 0.841 oz. ASW, 38.6 mm. **Series:** Harry Potter **Obv:** Bust of Queen Elizabeth II right **Rev:** Harry retrieves Gryffindor sword from snake **Edge:** Reeded

Date	Mintage	F	VF	XF	Unc	BU
2002PM Proof	15,000	Value: 49.00				

KM# 1152 CROWN

28.2800 g., Copper-Nickel, 38.6 mm. **Series:** Harry Potter **Obv:** Bust of Queen Elizabeth II right **Rev:** Harry and Ron encounter the spider Aragog **Edge:** Reeded

Date	Mintage	F	VF	XF	Unc	BU
2002PM	—	—	—	—	10.00	12.00

KM# 1152a CROWN

28.2800 g., 0.9250 Silver 0.841 oz. ASW, 38.6 mm. **Series:** Harry Potter **Obv:** Bust of Queen Elizabeth II right **Rev:** Harry and Ron encounter the spider Aragog **Edge:** Reeded

Date	Mintage	F	VF	XF	Unc	BU
2002PM Proof	15,000	Value: 49.00				

KM# 1154 CROWN

28.2800 g., Copper Nickel, 38.6 mm. **Series:** Harry Potter **Obv:** Bust of Queen Elizabeth II right **Rev:** Harry in hospital **Edge:** Reeded

Date	Mintage	F	VF	XF	Unc	BU
2002PM	—	—	—	—	10.00	12.00

KM# 1154a CROWN

28.2800 g., 0.9250 Silver 0.841 oz. ASW, 38.6 mm. **Series:** Harry Potter **Obv:** Bust of Queen Elizabeth II right **Rev:** Harry in hospital **Edge:** Reeded

Date	Mintage	F	VF	XF	Unc	BU
2002PM Proof	15,000	Value: 49.00				

KM# 1102 CROWN

28.2800 g., Copper-Nickel, 38.6 mm. **Subject:** Year of the Horse **Obv:** Bust of Queen Elizabeth II right **Rev:** Two horses **Edge:** Reeded

Date	Mintage	F	VF	XF	Unc	BU
2002	—	—	—	—	9.00	12.00

KM# 1102a CROWN

28.2800 g., 0.9250 Silver .8410 oz. ASW, 38.6 mm. **Subject:** Year of the Horse **Obv:** Bust of Queen Elizabeth II right **Rev:** Two horses **Edge:** Reeded

Date	Mintage	F	VF	XF	Unc	BU
2002 Proof	30,000	Value: 47.50				

KM# 1103 CROWN

31.1000 g., 0.9999 Gold .9998 oz. AGW **Subject:** Year of the Horse

Date	Mintage	F	VF	XF	Unc	BU
2002 Proof	2,000	Value: 650				

KM# 1111 CROWN

28.2800 g., Copper-Nickel, 38.6 mm. **Subject:** Bengal Cat **Obv:** Queen Elizabeth II bust right **Rev:** Cat and kitten **Edge:** Reeded

Date	Mintage	VG	F	VF	XF	Unc
2002	—	—	—	—	—	12.00

KM# 1111a CROWN

31.1035 g., 0.9990 Silver 0.999 oz. ASW, 38.6 mm. **Subject:** Bengal Cat **Obv:** Bust of Queen Elizabeth II right **Rev:** Cat and kitten **Edge:** Reeded

Date	Mintage	F	VF	XF	Unc	BU
2002 Proof	10,000	Value: 47.50				

KM# 1112 CROWN

31.1035 g., 0.9990 Gold 0.999 oz. AGW **Subject:** Bengal Cat **Obv:** Queen Elizabeth II bust right **Rev:** Cat and kitten **Edge:** Reeded

Date	Mintage	VG	F	VF	XF	Unc
2002	—	—	—	—	—	625
2002 Proof	1,000	Value: 650				

KM# 1115 CROWN

28.2800 g., Copper-Nickel, 38.6 mm. **Subject:** Olympics - Salt Lake City **Obv:** Bust of Queen Elizabeth II right **Rev:** Skier, torch and flag **Edge:** Reeded

Date	Mintage	F	VF	XF	Unc	BU
2002	—	—	—	—	10.00	12.00

KM# 1115a CROWN

28.2800 g., 0.9250 Silver 0.841 oz. ASW, 38.6 mm. **Subject:** Olympics - Salt Lake City **Obv:** Bust of Queen Elizabeth II right **Rev:** Skier, torch and flag **Edge:** Reeded

Date	Mintage	F	VF	XF	Unc	BU
2002 Proof	10,000	—	—	—	47.50	—

KM# 1116 CROWN

28.2800 g., Copper-Nickel, 38.6 mm. **Subject:** Olympics - Salt Lake City **Obv:** Bust of Queen Elizabeth II right **Rev:** Bobsled, torch and stadium **Edge:** Reeded

Date	Mintage	F	VF	XF	Unc	BU
2002	—	—	—	—	10.00	12.00

KM# 1116a CROWN

28.2800 g., 0.9250 Silver 0.841 oz. ASW, 38.6 mm. **Subject:** Olympics - Salt Lake City **Obv:** Bust of Queen Elizabeth II right **Rev:** Bobsled, torch and stadium **Edge:** Reeded

Date	Mintage	F	VF	XF	Unc	BU
2002 Proof	10,000	Value: 47.50				

KM# 1121 CROWN

28.2800 g., Copper-Nickel, 38.6 mm. **Subject:** World Cup 2002 Japan - Korea **Obv:** Bust of Queen Elizabeth II right **Rev:** Player running right **Edge:** Reeded

Date	Mintage	F	VF	XF	Unc	BU
2002	—	—	—	—	10.00	12.00

KM# 1121a CROWN

28.2800 g., 0.9250 Silver 0.841 oz. ASW, 38.6 mm. **Subject:** World Cup 2002 Japan - Korea **Obv:** Bust of Queen Elizabeth II right **Rev:** Player running right **Edge:** Reeded

Date	Mintage	F	VF	XF	Unc	BU
2002 Proof	10,000	Value: 47.50				

KM# 1123 CROWN

28.2800 g., Copper-Nickel, 38.6 mm. **Subject:** World Cup 2002 Japan - Korea **Obv:** Bust of Queen Elizabeth II right **Rev:** Player kicking to right **Edge:** Reeded

Date	Mintage	F	VF	XF	Unc	BU
2002	—	—	—	—	10.00	12.00

KM# 1123a CROWN

28.2800 g., 0.9250 Silver 0.841 oz. ASW, 38.6 mm. **Subject:** World Cup 2002 Japan - Korea **Obv:** Bust of Queen Elizabeth II right **Rev:** Player kicking to right **Edge:** Reeded

Date	Mintage	F	VF	XF	Unc	BU
2002 Proof	10,000	Value: 47.50				

KM# 1125 CROWN

28.2800 g., Copper-Nickel, 38.6 mm. **Subject:** World Cup 2002 Japan - Korea **Obv:** Bust of Queen Elizabeth II right **Rev:** Player kicking to left **Edge:** Reeded

Date	Mintage	F	VF	XF	Unc	BU
2002	—	—	—	—	10.00	12.00

KM# 1125a CROWN

28.2800 g., 0.9250 Silver 0.841 oz. ASW, 38.6 mm. **Subject:** World Cup 2002 Japan - Korea **Obv:** Bust of Queen Elizabeth II right **Rev:** Player kicking to left **Edge:** Reeded

Date	Mintage	F	VF	XF	Unc	BU
2002 Proof	10,000	Value: 47.50				

KM# 1127 CROWN

28.2800 g., Copper-Nickel, 38.6 mm. **Subject:** World Cup 2002 Japan - Korea **Obv:** Bust of Queen Elizabeth II right **Rev:** Player running to left **Edge:** Reeded

Date	Mintage	F	VF	XF	Unc	BU
2002	—	—	—	—	10.00	12.00

KM# 1127a CROWN

28.2800 g., 0.9250 Silver 0.841 oz. ASW, 38.6 mm. **Subject:** World Cup 2002 Japan - Korea **Obv:** Bust of Queen Elizabeth II right **Rev:** Player running to left **Edge:** Reeded

Date	Mintage	F	VF	XF	Unc	BU
2002 Proof	10,000	Value: 47.50				

KM# 1131 CROWN

28.2800 g., Copper-Nickel, 38.6 mm. **Subject:** Queen Elizabeth II's Golden Jubilee **Obv:** Bust of Queen Elizabeth II right **Rev:** Seated crowned Queen holding scepter at her coronation **Edge:** Reeded

Date	Mintage	F	VF	XF	Unc	BU
2002	—	—	—	—	10.00	12.00

KM# 1131a CROWN

28.2800 g., Gold Color Base Metal, 38.6 mm. **Subject:** Queen Elizabeth II's Golden Jubilee **Obv:** Bust of Queen Elizabeth II right **Rev:** Seated crowned Queen holding scepter at her coronation **Edge:** Reeded

Date	Mintage	F	VF	XF	Unc	BU
2002	15,000	—	—	—	10.00	12.00

KM# 1131b CROWN

28.2800 g., 0.9250 Gold Clad Silver 0.841 oz., 38.6 mm. **Subject:** Queen Elizabeth II's Golden Jubilee **Obv:** Bust of Queen Elizabeth II right **Rev:** Seated crowned Queen holding scepter at her coronation **Edge:** Reeded

Date	Mintage	F	VF	XF	Unc	BU
2002 Proof	10,000	Value: 47.50				

KM# 1133 CROWN

28.2800 g., Copper-Nickel, 38.6 mm. **Subject:** Queen Elizabeth II's Golden Jubilee **Obv:** Bust of Queen Elizabeth II right **Rev:** Queen on horse **Edge:** Reeded

Date	Mintage	F	VF	XF	Unc	BU
2002	—	—	—	—	10.00	12.00

KM# 1133a CROWN

28.2800 g., Gold Color Base Metal, 38.6 mm. **Subject:** Queen Elizabeth II's Golden Jubilee **Obv:** Bust of Queen Elizabeth II right **Rev:** Queen on horse **Edge:** Reeded

Date	Mintage	F	VF	XF	Unc	BU
2002	15,000	—	—	—	10.00	12.00

KM# 1133b CROWN

28.2800 g., 0.9250 Gold Clad Silver 0.841 oz., 38.6 mm. **Subject:** Queen Elizabeth II's Golden Jubilee **Obv:** Bust of Queen Elizabeth II right **Rev:** Queen on horse half left **Edge:** Reeded

Date	Mintage	F	VF	XF	Unc	BU
2002 Proof	10,000	Value: 47.50				

KM# 1135 CROWN

28.2800 g., Copper-Nickel, 38.6 mm. **Subject:** Queen Elizabeth II's Golden Jubilee **Obv:** Bust of Queen Elizabeth II right **Rev:** Queen with her pet Corgi **Edge:** Reeded

Date	Mintage	F	VF	XF	Unc	BU
2002	—	—	—	—	10.00	12.00

KM# 1135a CROWN

28.2800 g., Gold Color Base Metal, 38.6 mm. **Subject:** Queen Elizabeth II's Golden Jubilee **Obv:** Bust of Queen Elizabeth II right **Rev:** Seated Queen with her pet Corgi **Edge:** Reeded

Date	Mintage	F	VF	XF	Unc	BU
2002	15,000	—	—	—	10.00	12.00

KM# 1135b CROWN

28.2800 g., 0.9250 Gold Clad Silver 0.841 oz., 38.6 mm. **Subject:** Queen Elizabeth II's Golden Jubilee **Obv:** Bust of Queen Elizabeth II right **Rev:** Queen with her pet Corgi **Edge:** Reeded

Date	Mintage	F	VF	XF	Unc	BU
2002 Proof	10,000	Value: 47.50				

KM# 1137 CROWN

28.2800 g., Copper-Nickel, 38.6 mm. **Subject:** Queen Elizabeth II's Golden Jubilee **Obv:** Bust of Queen Elizabeth II right **Rev:** Queen at war memorial **Edge:** Reeded

Date	Mintage	F	VF	XF	Unc	BU
2002	—	—	—	—	10.00	12.00

KM# 1137a CROWN

28.2800 g., Gold Color Base Metal, 38.6 mm. **Subject:** Queen Elizabeth II's Golden Jubilee **Obv:** Bust of Queen Elizabeth II right **Rev:** Queen at war memorial **Edge:** Reeded

Date	Mintage	F	VF	XF	Unc	BU
2002	15,000	—	—	—	10.00	12.00

KM# 1137b CROWN

28.2800 g., Gold Clad Silver, 38.6 mm. **Subject:** Queen Elizabeth II's Golden Jubilee **Obv:** Bust of Queen Elizabeth II right **Rev:** Queen at war memorial **Edge:** Reeded

Date	Mintage	F	VF	XF	Unc	BU
2002 Proof	10,000	Value: 47.50				

KM# 1139 CROWN

Blackened Copper-Nickel, 38.6 mm. **Subject:** Queen Mother **Obv:** Bust of Queen Elizabeth II right **Rev:** Queen Mother and Castle May **Edge:** Reeded

Date	Mintage	F	VF	XF	Unc	BU
2002	—	—	—	—	10.00	12.00

KM# 1139a CROWN

28.2800 g., 0.9250 Silver 0.841 oz. ASW, 38.6 mm. **Obv:** Bust of Queen Elizabeth II right with blackened legends **Rev:** Queen Mother standing at left in front of Castle May with blackened legends

Date	Mintage	F	VF	XF	Unc	BU
2002 Proof	10,000	Value: 47.50				

KM# 1141 CROWN

28.2800 g., Copper Nickel, 38.6 mm. **Subject:** Princess Diana **Obv:** Bust of Queen Elizabeth II right **Rev:** Diana's bust facing **Edge:** Reeded

Date	Mintage	F	VF	XF	Unc	BU
2002	—	—	—	—	10.00	—

KM# 1141a CROWN

28.2800 g., 0.9250 Silver 0.841 oz. ASW, 38.6 mm. **Subject:** Princess Diana **Obv:** Bust of Queen Elizabeth II right **Rev:** Diana facing **Edge:** Reeded

Date	Mintage	F	VF	XF	Unc	BU
2002 Proof	10,000	Value: 47.50				

KM# 1165 CROWN

28.2800 g., Copper-Nickel, 38.6 mm. **Subject:** Cat **Obv:** Bust of Queen Elizabeth II right **Rev:** Two Balinese kittens **Edge:** Reeded

Date	Mintage	F	VF	XF	Unc	BU
2003PM	—	—	—	—	10.00	12.00

KM# 1165a CROWN

31.1035 g., 0.9990 Silver 0.999 oz. ASW, 38.6 mm. **Subject:** Cat **Obv:** Bust of Queen Elizabeth II right **Rev:** Two Balinese kittens **Edge:** Reeded

Date	Mintage	F	VF	XF	Unc	BU
2003PM Proof	50,000	Value: 47.50				

KM# 1166 CROWN

31.1035 g., 0.9999 Gold 0.9999 oz. AGW, 32.7 mm. **Subject:** Cat **Obv:** Bust of Queen Elizabeth II right **Rev:** Two Balinese kittens **Edge:** Reeded

Date	Mintage	F	VF	XF	Unc	BU
2003PM	—	—	—	—	625	—
2003PM Proof	—	Value: 650				

KM# 1171 CROWN

28.2800 g., Copper-Nickel, 38.6 mm. **Subject:** Year of the Goat **Obv:** Bust of Queen Elizabeth II right **Rev:** Three goats **Edge:** Reeded

Date	Mintage	F	VF	XF	Unc	BU
2003PM	—	—	—	—	10.00	12.00

KM# 1171a CROWN

28.2800 g., 0.9250 Silver 0.841 oz. ASW, 38.6 mm. **Subject:** Year of the Goat **Obv:** Bust of Queen Elizabeth II right **Rev:** Three goats **Edge:** Reeded

Date	Mintage	F	VF	XF	Unc	BU
2003PM Proof	30,000	Value: 47.50				

KM# 1172 CROWN

31.1035 g., 0.9999 Gold 0.9999 oz. AGW, 32.7 mm. **Subject:** Year of the Goat **Obv:** Bust of Queen Elizabeth II right **Rev:** Three goats **Edge:** Reeded

Date	Mintage	F	VF	XF	Unc	BU
2003PM Proof	2,000	Value: 625				

KM# 1174 CROWN

28.5300 g., Copper-Nickel, 38.6 mm. **Obv:** Bust of Queen Elizabeth II right **Rev:** The Star of India sailing ship **Edge:** Reeded

Date	Mintage	F	VF	XF	Unc	BU
2003PM	—	—	—	—	10.00	12.00

KM# 1176 CROWN

28.2800 g., Copper-Nickel, 38.6 mm. **Subject:** Olympics **Obv:** Bust of Queen Elizabeth II right **Rev:** Swimmers **Edge:** Reeded

Date	Mintage	F	VF	XF	Unc	BU
2003PM	—	—	—	—	10.00	12.00

KM# 1176a CROWN

28.2800 g., 0.9250 Silver 0.841 oz. ASW, 38.6 mm. **Subject:** Olympics **Obv:** Bust of Queen Elizabeth II right **Rev:** Swimmers **Edge:** Reeded

Date	Mintage	F	VF	XF	Unc	BU
2003PM Proof	10,000	Value: 47.50				

KM# 1178 CROWN

28.2800 g., Copper-Nickel, 38.6 mm. **Subject:** Olympics **Obv:** Bust of Queen Elizabeth II right **Rev:** Runners **Edge:** Reeded

Date	Mintage	F	VF	XF	Unc	BU
2003PM	—	—	—	—	10.00	12.00

KM# 1178a CROWN

28.2800 g., 0.9250 Silver 0.841 oz. ASW, 38.6 mm. **Subject:** Olympics **Obv:** Bust of Queen Elizabeth II right **Rev:** Runners **Edge:** Reeded

Date	Mintage	F	VF	XF	Unc	BU
2003PM Proof	10,000	Value: 47.50				

KM# 1180 CROWN

28.2800 g., Copper-Nickel, 38.6 mm. **Subject:** Olympics **Obv:** Bust of Queen Elizabeth II right **Rev:** Bicyclists **Edge:** Reeded

Date	Mintage	F	VF	XF	Unc	BU
2003PM	—	—	—	—	10.00	12.00

KM# 1180a CROWN

28.2800 g., 0.9250 Silver 0.841 oz. ASW, 38.6 mm. **Subject:** Olympics **Obv:** Bust of Queen Elizabeth II right **Rev:** Bicyclists **Edge:** Reeded

Date	Mintage	F	VF	XF	Unc	BU
2003PM Proof	10,000	Value: 47.50				

KM# 1182 CROWN

28.2800 g., Copper-Nickel, 38.6 mm. **Subject:** Olympics **Obv:** Bust of Queen Elizabeth II right **Rev:** Sail Boarders **Edge:** Reeded

Date	Mintage	F	VF	XF	Unc	BU
2003PM	—	—	—	—	10.00	12.00

KM# 1182a CROWN

28.2800 g., 0.9250 Silver 0.841 oz. ASW, 38.6 mm. **Subject:** Olympics **Obv:** Bust of Queen Elizabeth II right **Rev:** Sail Boarders **Edge:** Reeded

Date	Mintage	F	VF	XF	Unc	BU
2003PM Proof	10,000	Value: 47.50				

KM# 1196 CROWN

28.4400 g., Copper-Nickel, 38.6 mm. **Obv:** Bust of Queen Elizabeth II right **Rev:** Four pre-1918 airplanes **Edge:** Reeded

Date	Mintage	F	VF	XF	Unc	BU
2003PM	—	—	—	—	10.00	12.00

KM# 1197 CROWN

28.4400 g., Copper-Nickel, 38.6 mm. **Obv:** Bust of Queen Elizabeth II right **Rev:** Propeller plain, Zeppelin and two jet airliners **Edge:** Reeded

Date	Mintage	F	VF	XF	Unc	BU
2003PM	—	—	—	—	10.00	12.00

KM# 1185 CROWN

28.2800 g., Copper-Nickel, 38.6 mm. **Obv:** Bust of Queen Elizabeth II right **Rev:** Lord of the Rings characters **Edge:** Reeded

Date	Mintage	F	VF	XF	Unc	BU
2003PM	100,000	—	—	—	12.50	14.50

KM# 1185a CROWN

28.2800 g., 0.9250 Silver 0.841 oz. ASW, 38.6 mm. **Obv:** Bust of Queen Elizabeth II right **Rev:** Lord of the Rings characters **Edge:** Reeded

Date	Mintage	F	VF	XF	Unc	BU
2003PM Proof	10,000	Value: 50.00				

KM# 1190 CROWN

31.1035 g., 0.9999 Gold 0.9999 oz. AGW, 32.7 mm. **Subject:** Lord of the Rings **Obv:** Bust of Queen Elizabeth II right **Rev:** Man on horse **Edge:** Reeded

Date	Mintage	F	VF	XF	Unc	BU
2003PM Proof	1,000	Value: 650				

KM# 1191 CROWN

28.2800 g., 0.9250 Silver 0.841 oz. ASW, 38.6 mm. **Subject:** Lord of the Rings **Obv:** Bust of Queen Elizabeth II right **Rev:** Man with short sword **Edge:** Reeded

Date	Mintage	F	VF	XF	Unc	BU
2003PM Proof	5,000	Value: 47.50				

KM# 1192 CROWN

28.2800 g., 0.9250 Silver 0.841 oz. ASW, 38.6 mm. **Subject:** Lord of the Rings **Obv:** Bust of Queen Elizabeth II right **Rev:** Aragorn with broadsword **Edge:** Reeded

Date	Mintage	F	VF	XF	Unc	BU
2003PM Proof	5,000	Value: 47.50				

KM# 1193 CROWN

28.2800 g., 0.9250 Silver 0.841 oz. ASW, 38.6 mm. **Subject:** Lord of the Rings **Obv:** Bust of Queen Elizabeth II right **Rev:** Legolas **Edge:** Reeded

Date	Mintage	F	VF	XF	Unc	BU
2003PM Proof	5,000	Value: 47.50				

KM# 1194 CROWN

28.2800 g., 0.9250 Silver 0.841 oz. ASW, 38.6 mm. **Subject:** Lord of the Rings **Obv:** Bust of Queen Elizabeth II right **Rev:** Gimli with two battle axes **Edge:** Reeded

Date	Mintage	F	VF	XF	Unc	BU
2003PM Proof	5,000	Value: 47.50				

KM# 1195 CROWN

28.2800 g., 0.9250 Silver 0.841 oz. ASW, 38.6 mm. **Subject:** Lord of the Rings **Obv:** Bust of Queen Elizabeth II right **Rev:** Man on horse **Edge:** Reeded

Date	Mintage	F	VF	XF	Unc	BU
2003PM Proof	5,000	Value: 47.50				

KM# 1201 CROWN

28.2800 g., Copper-Nickel, 38.6 mm. **Ruler:** Elizabeth II **Obv:** Bust of Queen Elizabeth II right **Rev:** European Union map within hand held rope circle **Edge:** Reeded

Date	Mintage	F	VF	XF	Unc	BU
2004PM	—	—	—	—	10.00	12.00

KM# 1201a CROWN

28.2800 g., 0.9250 Silver 0.841 oz. ASW, 38.6 mm. **Ruler:** Elizabeth II **Obv:** Bust of Queen Elizabeth II right **Rev:** European Union map within a hand held rope circle **Edge:** Reeded

Date	Mintage	F	VF	XF	Unc	BU
2004PM Proof	10,000	Value: 50.00				

KM# 1202 CROWN

28.2800 g., Copper-Nickel, 38.6 mm. **Ruler:** Elizabeth II **Obv:** Bust of Queen Elizabeth II right **Rev:** Harry Potter and patron fighting off a spectre **Edge:** Reeded

Date	Mintage	F	VF	XF	Unc	BU
2004PM	—	—	—	—	15.00	17.00

KM# 1202a CROWN

28.2800 g., 0.9250 Silver 0.841 oz. ASW, 38.6 mm. **Ruler:** Elizabeth II **Obv:** Bust of Queen Elizabeth II right **Rev:** Harry Potter and patron fighting off a spectre **Edge:** Reeded

Date	Mintage	F	VF	XF	Unc	BU
2004PM Proof	10,000	Value: 50.00				

KM# 1204 CROWN

28.2800 g., Copper-Nickel, 38.6 mm. **Ruler:** Elizabeth II **Obv:** Bust of Queen Elizabeth II right **Rev:** Harry Potter in the shrieking shed **Edge:** Reeded

Date	Mintage	F	VF	XF	Unc	BU
2004PM	—	—	—	—	15.00	17.00

KM# 1204a CROWN

28.2800 g., 0.9250 Silver 0.841 oz. ASW, 38.6 mm. **Ruler:** Elizabeth II **Obv:** Bust of Queen Elizabeth II right **Rev:** Harry Potter in the shrieking shack **Edge:** Reeded

Date	Mintage	F	VF	XF	Unc	BU
2004PM Proof	10,000	Value: 50.00				

KM# 1206 CROWN

28.2800 g., Copper-Nickel, 38.6 mm. **Ruler:** Elizabeth II **Obv:** Bust of Queen Elizabeth II right **Rev:** Harry Potter and Professor Dumbledore **Edge:** Reeded

Date	Mintage	F	VF	XF	Unc	BU
2004PM	—	—	—	—	15.00	17.00

KM# 1206a CROWN

28.2800 g., 0.9250 Silver 0.841 oz. ASW, 38.6 mm. **Ruler:** Elizabeth II **Obv:** Bust of Queen Elizabeth II right **Rev:** Harry Potter and Professor Dumbledore **Edge:** Reeded

Date	Mintage	F	VF	XF	Unc	BU
2004PM Proof	10,000	Value: 50.00				

KM# 1208 CROWN

28.2800 g., Copper-Nickel, 38.6 mm. **Ruler:** Elizabeth II **Obv:** Bust of Queen Elizabeth II right **Rev:** Sirius Black on flying griffin **Edge:** Reeded

Date	Mintage	F	VF	XF	Unc	BU
2004PM	—	—	—	—	15.00	17.00

KM# 1208a CROWN

28.2800 g., 0.9250 Silver 0.841 oz. ASW, 38.6 mm. **Ruler:** Elizabeth II **Obv:** Bust of Queen Elizabeth II right **Rev:** Sirius Black on flying griffin **Edge:** Reeded

Date	Mintage	F	VF	XF	Unc	BU
2004PM Proof	10,000	Value: 50.00				

KM# 1210 CROWN

28.2800 g., Copper-Nickel, 38.6 mm. **Ruler:** Elizabeth II **Obv:** Bust of Queen Elizabeth II right **Rev:** Three Olympic Swimmers **Edge:** Reeded

Date	Mintage	F	VF	XF	Unc	BU
2004PM	—	—	—	—	10.00	12.00

KM# 1210a CROWN

28.2800 g., 0.9250 Silver 0.841 oz. ASW, 38.6 mm. **Ruler:** Elizabeth II **Obv:** Bust of Queen Elizabeth II right **Rev:** Three Olympic Swimmers **Edge:** Reeded

Date	Mintage	F	VF	XF	Unc	BU
2004PM Proof	10,000	Value: 50.00				

KM# 1212 CROWN

28.2800 g., Copper-Nickel, 38.6 mm. **Ruler:** Elizabeth II **Obv:** Bust of Queen Elizabeth II right **Rev:** Three Olympic Cyclists **Edge:** Reeded

Date	Mintage	F	VF	XF	Unc	BU
2004PM	—	—	—	—	10.00	12.00

KM# 1212a CROWN

28.2800 g., 0.9250 Silver 0.841 oz. ASW, 38.6 mm. **Ruler:** Elizabeth II **Obv:** Bust of Queen Elizabeth II right **Rev:** Three Olympic Cyclists **Edge:** Reeded

Date	Mintage	F	VF	XF	Unc	BU
2004PM Proof	10,000	Value: 50.00				

KM# 1214 CROWN

28.2800 g., Copper-Nickel, 38.6 mm. **Ruler:** Elizabeth II **Obv:** Bust of Queen Elizabeth II right **Rev:** Three Olympic Runners **Edge:** Reeded

Date	Mintage	F	VF	XF	Unc	BU
2004PM	—	—	—	—	10.00	12.00

KM# 1214a CROWN

28.2800 g., 0.9250 Silver 0.841 oz. ASW, 38.6 mm. **Ruler:** Elizabeth II **Obv:** Bust of Queen Elizabeth II right **Rev:** Three Olympic Runners **Edge:** Reeded

Date	Mintage	F	VF	XF	Unc	BU
2004PM Proof	10,000	Value: 50.00				

KM# 1216 CROWN

28.2800 g., Copper-Nickel, 38.6 mm. **Ruler:** Elizabeth II **Obv:** Bust of Queen Elizabeth II right **Rev:** Three Olympic Sail Boarders **Edge:** Reeded

Date	Mintage	F	VF	XF	Unc	BU
2004PM	—	—	—	—	10.00	12.00

KM# 1216a CROWN

28.2800 g., 0.9250 Silver 0.841 oz. ASW, 38.6 mm. **Ruler:** Elizabeth II **Obv:** Elizabeth Bust of Queen Elizabeth II right **Rev:** Three Olympic Sail Boarders **Edge:** Reeded

Date	Mintage	F	VF	XF	Unc	BU
2004PM Proof	10,000	Value: 50.00				

KM# 1218 CROWN

28.2800 g., Copper-Nickel, 38.6 mm. **Ruler:** Elizabeth II **Obv:** Bust of Queen Elizabeth II right **Rev:** Ocean Liner Queen Mary 2 **Edge:** Reeded

Date	Mintage	F	VF	XF	Unc	BU
2004PM	—	—	—	—	15.00	17.00

KM# 1220 CROWN

28.2800 g., Copper-Nickel, 38.6 mm. **Ruler:** Elizabeth II **Obv:** Bust of Queen Elizabeth II right **Rev:** Lt. Quillan portrait above Battle of Trafalgar scene **Edge:** Reeded

Date	Mintage	F	VF	XF	Unc	BU
2004PM	—	—	—	—	15.00	17.00

KM# 1220a CROWN

28.2800 g., 0.9250 Silver 0.841 oz. ASW, 38.6 mm. **Ruler:** Elizabeth II **Obv:** Bust of Queen Elizabeth II right **Rev:** Lt. Quillan portrait above Battle of Trafalgar scene **Edge:** Reeded

Date	Mintage	F	VF	XF	Unc	BU
2004PM Proof	10,000	Value: 50.00				

KM# 1221 CROWN
28.2800 g., Copper-Nickel, 38.6 mm. **Ruler:** Elizabeth II **Obv:** Bust of Queen Elizabeth II right **Rev:** Napoleon and Nelson portraits above Battle of Trafalgar scene **Edge:** Reeded

Date	Mintage	F	VF	XF	Unc	BU
2004PM	—	—	—	—	15.00	17.00

KM# 1221a CROWN
28.2800 g., 0.9990 Silver 0.9083 oz. ASW, 38.6 mm. **Ruler:** Elizabeth II **Obv:** Bust of Queen Elizabeth II right **Rev:** Napoleon and Nelson portraits above Battle of Trafalgar scene **Edge:** Reeded

Date	Mintage	F	VF	XF	Unc	BU
2004PM Proof	10,000	Value: 50.00				

KM# 1222 CROWN
28.2800 g., Copper-Nickel, 38.6 mm. **Ruler:** Elizabeth II **Obv:** Bust of Queen Elizabeth II right **Rev:** D-Day Invasion Plan Map **Edge:** Reeded

Date	Mintage	F	VF	XF	Unc	BU
2004PM	—	—	—	—	15.00	17.00

KM# 1222a CROWN
28.2800 g., 0.9250 Silver 0.841 oz. ASW, 38.6 mm. **Ruler:** Elizabeth II **Obv:** Bust of Queen Elizabeth II right **Rev:** D-Day Invasion Plan Map **Edge:** Reeded

Date	Mintage	F	VF	XF	Unc	BU
2004PM Proof	10,000	Value: 50.00				

KM# 1224 CROWN
28.2800 g., Copper-Nickel, 38.6 mm. **Ruler:** Elizabeth II **Obv:** Bust of Queen Elizabeth II right **Rev:** Victoria Cross and battle scene **Edge:** Reeded

Date	Mintage	F	VF	XF	Unc	BU
2004PM	—	—	—	—	15.00	17.00

KM# 1224a CROWN
28.2800 g., 0.9250 Silver 0.841 oz. ASW, 38.6 mm. **Ruler:** Elizabeth II **Obv:** Bust of Queen Elizabeth II right **Rev:** Victoria Cross and battle scene **Edge:** Reeded

Date	Mintage	F	VF	XF	Unc	BU
2004PM Proof	10,000	Value: 50.00				

KM# 1226 CROWN
28.2800 g., Copper-Nickel, 38.6 mm. **Ruler:** Elizabeth II **Obv:** Bust of Queen Elizabeth II right **Rev:** Silver Star and battle scene **Edge:** Reeded

Date	Mintage	F	VF	XF	Unc	BU
2004PM	—	—	—	—	15.00	17.00

KM# 1226a CROWN
28.2800 g., 0.9250 Silver 0.841 oz. ASW, 38.6 mm. **Ruler:** Elizabeth II **Obv:** Bust of Queen Elizabeth II right **Rev:** Silver Star and battle scene **Edge:** Reeded

Date	Mintage	F	VF	XF	Unc	BU
2004PM Proof	10,000	Value: 50.00				

KM# 1228 CROWN
28.2800 g., Copper-Nickel, 38.6 mm. **Ruler:** Elizabeth II **Obv:** Bust of Queen Elizabeth II right **Rev:** George Cross and rescue scene **Edge:** Reeded

Date	Mintage	F	VF	XF	Unc	BU
2004PM	—	—	—	—	15.00	17.00

KM# 1228a CROWN
28.2800 g., 0.9250 Silver 0.841 oz. ASW, 38.6 mm. **Ruler:** Elizabeth II **Obv:** Bust of Queen Elizabeth II right **Rev:** George Cross and rescue scene **Edge:** Reeded

Date	Mintage	F	VF	XF	Unc	BU
2004PM Proof	10,000	Value: 50.00				

KM# 1230 CROWN
28.2800 g., Copper-Nickel, 38.6 mm. **Ruler:** Elizabeth II **Obv:** Bust of Queen Elizabeth II right **Rev:** White Rose of Finland Medal and battle scene **Edge:** Reeded

Date	Mintage	F	VF	XF	Unc	BU
2004PM	—	—	—	—	15.00	17.00

KM# 1230a CROWN
28.2800 g., 0.9250 Silver 0.841 oz. ASW, 38.6 mm. **Ruler:** Elizabeth II **Obv:** Bust of Queen Elizabeth II right **Rev:** White Rose of Finland Medal and battle scene **Edge:** Reeded

Date	Mintage	F	VF	XF	Unc	BU
2004PM Proof	10,000	Value: 50.00				

KM# 1232 CROWN
28.2800 g., Copper-Nickel, 38.6 mm. **Ruler:** Elizabeth II **Obv:** Bust of Queen Elizabeth II right **Rev:** The Norwegian War Medal and naval battle scene **Edge:** Reeded

Date	Mintage	F	VF	XF	Unc	BU
2004PM	—	—	—	—	15.00	17.00

KM# 1232a CROWN
28.2800 g., 0.9250 Silver 0.841 oz. ASW, 38.6 mm. **Ruler:** Elizabeth II **Obv:** Bust of Queen Elizabeth II right **Rev:** The Norwegian War Medal and a naval battle scene **Edge:** Reeded

Date	Mintage	F	VF	XF	Unc	BU
2004PM Proof	10,000	Value: 50.00				

KM# 1234 CROWN
28.2800 g., Copper-Nickel, 38.6 mm. **Ruler:** Elizabeth II **Obv:** Bust of Queen Elizabeth II right **Rev:** French Croix de Guerre and Partisian battle scene **Edge:** Reeded

Date	Mintage	F	VF	XF	Unc	BU
2004PM	—	—	—	—	15.00	17.00

KM# 1234a CROWN
28.2800 g., 0.9250 Silver 0.841 oz. ASW, 38.6 mm. **Ruler:** Elizabeth II **Obv:** Bust of Queen Elizabeth II right **Rev:** French Croix de Guerre and partisan battle scene **Edge:** Reeded

Date	Mintage	F	VF	XF	Unc	BU
2004PM Proof	10,000	Value: 50.00				

KM# 1236 CROWN
28.2800 g., Copper-Nickel, 38.6 mm. **Ruler:** Elizabeth II **Obv:** Bust of Queen Elizabeth II right **Rev:** Multicolor cartoon soccer player **Edge:** Reeded

Date	Mintage	F	VF	XF	Unc	BU
2004PM	—	—	—	—	10.00	12.00

KM# 1236a CROWN
28.2800 g., 0.9250 Silver 0.841 oz. ASW, 38.6 mm. **Ruler:** Elizabeth II **Obv:** Bust of Queen Elizabeth II right **Rev:** Multicolor cartoon soccer player **Edge:** Reeded

Date	Mintage	F	VF	XF	Unc	BU
2004PM Proof	7,500	Value: 50.00				

KM# 1237 CROWN
28.2800 g., Copper-Nickel, 38.6 mm. **Ruler:** Elizabeth II **Obv:** Bust of Queen Elizabeth II right **Rev:** Soccer ball in flight **Edge:** Reeded

Date	Mintage	F	VF	XF	Unc	BU
2004PM	—	—	—	—	10.00	12.00

KM# 1237a CROWN
28.2800 g., 0.9250 Silver 0.841 oz. ASW, 38.6 mm. **Ruler:** Elizabeth II **Obv:** Bust of Queen Elizabeth II right **Rev:** Soccer ball in flight **Edge:** Reeded

Date	Mintage	F	VF	XF	Unc	BU
2004PM Proof	7,500	Value: 50.00				

KM# 1238 CROWN
28.2800 g., Copper-Nickel, 38.6 mm. **Ruler:** Elizabeth II **Obv:** Bust of Queen Elizabeth II right **Rev:** Monkey **Edge:** Reeded

Date	Mintage	F	VF	XF	Unc	BU
2004PM	—	—	—	—	10.00	12.00

KM# 1238a CROWN
28.2800 g., 0.9250 Silver 0.841 oz. ASW, 38.6 mm. **Ruler:** Elizabeth II **Obv:** Bust of Queen Elizabeth II right **Rev:** Monkey **Edge:** Reeded

Date	Mintage	F	VF	XF	Unc	BU
2004PM Proof	30,000	Value: 50.00				

KM# 1239 CROWN
31.1035 g., 0.9999 Gold 0.9999 oz. AGW, 32.7 mm. **Ruler:** Elizabeth II **Obv:** Bust of Queen Elizabeth II right **Rev:** Monkey **Edge:** Reeded

Date	Mintage	F	VF	XF	Unc	BU
2004PM Proof	2,000	Value: 675				

KM# 1242 CROWN
6.2200 g., 0.9999 Gold 0.2 oz. AGW, 22 mm. **Ruler:** Elizabeth II **Obv:** Bust of Queen Elizabeth II right **Rev:** Monkey **Edge:** Reeded

Date	Mintage	F	VF	XF	Unc	BU
2004PM Proof	12,000	Value: 175				

KM# 1245 CROWN
28.2800 g., Copper-Nickel, 38.6 mm. **Ruler:** Elizabeth II **Subject:** Lord of the Rings **Obv:** Bust of Queen Elizabeth II right **Rev:** Nine characters **Edge:** Reeded

Date	Mintage	F	VF	XF	Unc	BU
2004PM	100,000	—	—	—	15.00	17.00

KM# 1245a CROWN
28.2800 g., 0.9250 Silver 0.841 oz. ASW, 38.6 mm. **Ruler:** Elizabeth II **Subject:** Lord of the Rings **Obv:** Bust of Queen Elizabeth II right **Rev:** Nine characters **Edge:** Reeded

Date	Mintage	F	VF	XF	Unc	BU
2004PM Proof	10,000	Value: 50.00				

KM# 1246 CROWN
28.2800 g., Copper-Nickel, 38.6 mm. **Ruler:** Elizabeth II **Obv:** Bust of Queen Elizabeth II right **Rev:** Two Tonkinese cats **Edge:** Reeded

Date	Mintage	F	VF	XF	Unc	BU
2004PM	—	—	—	—	15.00	17.00

KM# 1246a CROWN
31.1035 g., 0.9990 Silver 0.999 oz. ASW, 38.6 mm. **Ruler:** Elizabeth II **Obv:** Bust of Queen Elizabeth II right **Rev:** Two Tonkinese cats **Edge:** Reeded

Date	Mintage	F	VF	XF	Unc	BU
2004PM Proof	50,000	Value: 50.00				

KM# 1246a.1 CROWN
31.1035 g., 0.9990 Silver 0.999 oz. ASW, 38.6 mm. **Ruler:** Elizabeth II **Obv:** Bust of Queen Elizabeth II right **Rev:** Two multicolor Tonkinese cats **Edge:** Reeded

Date	Mintage	F	VF	XF	Unc	BU
2004PM Proof	—	Value: 55.00				

KM# 1251 CROWN
31.1035 g., 0.9999 Gold 0.9999 oz. AGW, 32.7 mm. **Ruler:** Elizabeth II **Obv:** Bust of Queen Elizabeth II right **Rev:** Two Tonkinese cats **Edge:** Reeded

Date	Mintage	F	VF	XF	Unc	BU
2004PM	—	—	—	—	650	—
2004PM Proof	1,000	Value: 750				

KM# 1266 CROWN
28.3300 g., Copper-Nickel, 38.7 mm. **Ruler:** Elizabeth II **Obv:** Elizabeth II **Rev:** Himalayan cat with two kittens **Edge:** Reeded

Date	Mintage	F	VF	XF	Unc	BU
2005PM	—	—	—	—	10.00	12.00

KM# 1200 2 CROWNS
62.2000 g., 0.9990 Palladium 1.9978 oz., 40 mm. **Subject:** Discovery of Palladium Bicentennial **Obv:** Bust of Queen Elizabeth II right **Rev:** Pallas Athena left **Edge:** Reeded

Date	Mintage	F	VF	XF	Unc	BU
2004PM Proof	300	Value: 800				

KM# 1064 5 CROWN
155.5175 g., 0.9999 Gold 5.0000 oz. AGW, 65 mm. **Subject:** Year of the Snake **Obv:** Bust of Queen Elizabeth II right **Rev:** Snake **Edge:** Reeded

Date	Mintage	F	VF	XF	Unc	BU
2001 Proof	250	Value: 3,250				

KM# 1104 5 CROWN
155.5100 g., 0.9999 Gold 4.9993 oz. AGW, 65 mm. **Subject:** Year of the Horse **Obv:** Bust of Queen Elizabeth II right **Rev:** Two horses **Edge:** Reeded

Date	Mintage	F	VF	XF	Unc	BU
2002 Proof	250	Value: 3,250				

KM# 1173 5 CROWN
155.5100 g., 0.9999 Gold 4.9993 oz. AGW, 65 mm. **Subject:** Year of the Goat **Obv:** Bust of Queen Elizabeth II right **Rev:** Three goats **Edge:** Reeded

Date	Mintage	F	VF	XF	Unc	BU
2003PM Proof	250	Value: 3,250				

KM# 1244 5 CROWN
155.5175 g., 0.9999 Gold 4.9995 oz. AGW, 65 mm. **Ruler:** Elizabeth II **Obv:** Bust of Queen Elizabeth II right **Rev:** Monkey **Edge:** Reeded

Date	Mintage	F	VF	XF	Unc	BU
2004PM Proof	250	Value: 3,250				

KM# 1219 64 CROWNS
2000.0000 g., 0.9990 Silver 64.2371 oz. ASW, 140 mm. **Ruler:** Elizabeth II **Obv:** Bust of Queen Elizabeth II right **Rev:** Ocean Liner Queen Mary 2 **Edge:** Reeded

Date	Mintage	F	VF	XF	Unc	BU
2004PM Proof	500	Value: 750				

KM# 1142 100 CROWNS
3000.0000 g., 0.9999 Silver 96.4425 oz. ASW, 130 mm. **Subject:** Queen's Golden Jubilee **Obv:** Bust of Queen Elizabeth II right **Rev:** Queen on horse **Edge:** Reeded **Note:** Illustration reduced.

Date	Mintage	F	VF	XF	Unc	BU
2002 Proof	500	Value: 1,250				

KM# 1184 130 CROWNS
4000.0000 g., 0.9990 Silver 128.474 oz. ASW, 130 mm. **Obv:** Bust of Queen Elizabeth II right **Rev:** Gold clad cameo portrait of Elizabeth I with a .035ct ruby inset on her forehead all within a circle of portraits **Edge:** Reeded

Date	Mintage	F	VF	XF	Unc	BU
2003PM Proof	500	Value: 1,600				

GOLD BULLION COINAGE

Angel Issues

KM# 1106 1/20 ANGEL

1.5552 g., 0.9999 Gold .0500 oz. AGW, 15 mm. **Obv:** Bust of Queen Elizabeth II right **Rev:** St. Michael slaying dragon, three crown privy mark at right **Edge:** Reeded **Note:** New likeness of the Queen.

Date	Mintage	F	VF	XF	Unc	BU
2001 (3c) Proof	1,000	Value: 50.00				
2002 Proof	—	Value: 50.00				

Note: With candy cane privy mark

KM# 1252 1/20 ANGEL

1.5550 g., 0.9999 Gold 0.05 oz. AGW, 15 mm. **Ruler:** Elizabeth II **Obv:** Bust of Queen Elizabeth II right **Rev:** St. Michael and Christmas privy mark **Edge:** Reeded

Date	Mintage	F	VF	XF	Unc	BU
2004PM Proof	1,000	Value: 60.00				

MINT SETS

KM#	Date	Mintage	Identification	Issue Price	Mkt Val
MS30	2004 (8)	—	KM#1253, 1254, 1255, 1256, 1257, 1258, 1259, 1260	—	25.00
MS31	2004 (9)	—	KM#1253, 1254, 1255, 1256, 1257, 1258, 1259, 1260, 1261	—	40.00

PROOF SETS

KM#	Date	Mintage	Identification	Issue Price	Mkt Val
PS55	2001 (5)	1,000	KM#1067-1070, 1073	—	1,310
PS60	2003 (3)	—	KM#1186, 1187, 1188	—	320
PS61	2003 (5)	—	KM#1186, 1187, 1188, 1189, 1190 w/gold ring	—	1,350
PS62	2003 (5)	—	KM#1191, 1192, 1193, 1194, 1195 w/gold-plated silver ring	—	240
PS63	2004 (5)	1,000	KM#1247, 1248, 1249.1, 1250, 1251	—	1,425

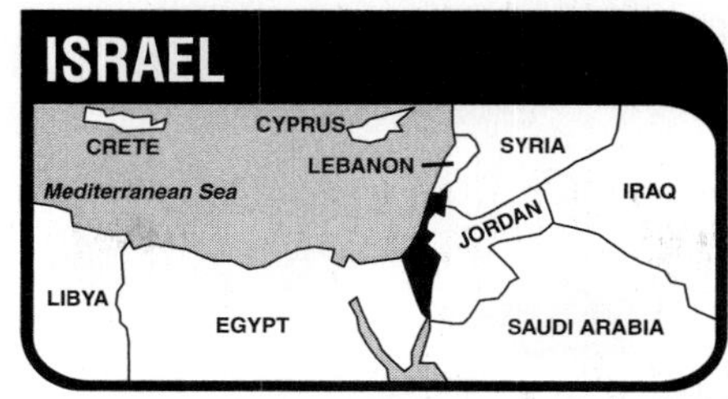

The state of Israel, a Middle Eastern republic at the eastern end of the Mediterranean Sea, bounded by Lebanon on the north, Syria on the northeast, Jordan on the east, and Egypt on the southwest, has an area of 9,000sq. mi. (20,770 sq. km.) and a population of 6 million. Capital: Jerusalem. Finished diamonds, chemicals, citrus, textiles, minerals, electronic and transportation equipment are exported.

HEBREW COIN DATING

Modern Israel's coins carry Hebrew dating formed from a combination of the 22 consonant letters of the Hebrew alphabet and read from right to left. The Jewish calendar dates back more than 5700 years; but five millenniums are assumed in the dating of coins (until 1981). Thus, the year 5735 (1975AD) appears as 735, with the first two characters from the right indicating the number of years in hundreds; tav (400), plus shin (300). The next is lamedh (30), followed by a separation mark which has the appearance of double quotation marks, then heh (5).

The Star of David is not a mintmark. It appears only on some coins sold by the Israel Government Coins and Medals Corporation Ltd., which is owned by the Israel government, and is a division of the Prime Minister's office and sole distributor to collectors. The Star of David was first used in 1971 on the science coin to signify that it was minted in Jerusalem, but was later used by different mint facilities.

AD Date		Jewish Era
2001	התשס״א	5761
2002	התשס״ב	5762
2003	התשס״ג	5763
2004	התשס״ד	5764
2005	התשס״ה	5765

MINT MARKS

(o) - Ottawa
(s) - San Francisco
None – Jerusalem

REPUBLIC

REFORM COINAGE

10 Sheqalim = 1 Agora; 1000 Sheqalim = 1 New Sheqel

September 4, 1985

KM# 157 5 AGOROT

Aluminum-Bronze

Date	Mintage	F	VF	XF	Unc	BU
JE5761 (2001)	6,144,000	—	—	0.10	0.15	—
JE5762 (2002)	6,144,000	—	—	0.10	0.15	—
JE5764 (2004)	—	—	—	0.10	0.15	—
JE5765 (2005)	—	—	—	0.10	0.15	—

KM# 172 5 AGOROT

Aluminum-Bronze **Subject:** Hanukkah **Note:** JE5754-5765 coins contain the Star of David mint mark; the JE5747-5753 coins do not.

Date	Mintage	F	VF	XF	Unc	BU
JE5761 (2001)	4,000	—	—	—	2.50	—
Note: In sets only						
JE5762 (2002)	4,000	—	—	—	2.50	—
Note: In sets only						
JE5763 (2003)	3,000	—	—	—	2.50	—
Note: In sets only						
JE5764 (2004)	3,000	—	—	—	2.50	—
Note: In sets only						

Date	Mintage	F	VF	XF	Unc	BU
JE5765 (2005)	2,500	—	—	—	2.50	—
Note: In sets only						

KM# 158 10 AGOROT

Aluminum-Bronze **Obv:** Menorah

Date	Mintage	F	VF	XF	Unc	BU
JE5761 (2001)	78,396,000	—	—	0.10	0.20	—
Note: Coins struck at Seoul and Santiago Mints						
JE5762 (2002)	4,608,000	—	—	0.10	0.20	—
JE5763 (2003)	22,980,000	—	—	0.10	0.20	—
Note: Struck at Seoul mint						
JE5764 (2004)	—	—	—	0.10	0.20	—

KM# 173 10 AGOROT

Aluminum-Bronze **Subject:** Hanukka **Obv:** Menorah **Note:** JE5754-5765 have the Star of David mint mark, JE5747-5753 coins do not.

Date	Mintage	F	VF	XF	Unc	BU
JE5761 (2001)	4,000	—	—	—	2.50	—
Note: In sets only						
JE5762 (2002)	4,000	—	—	—	2.50	—
Note: In sets only						
JE5763 (2003)	3,000	—	—	—	2.50	—
Note: In sets only						
JE5764 (2004)	3,000	—	—	—	2.50	—
Note: In sets only						
JE5765 (2005)	2,500	—	—	—	2.50	—
Note: In sets only						

KM# 354 1/2 NEW SHEQEL

6.5000 g., Copper-Aluminum-Nickel, 25.5 mm. **Subject:** Hanukka **Obv:** Denomination **Rev:** Curacao Hanukka lamp **Edge:** Plain **Shape:** 12-sided

Date	Mintage	F	VF	XF	Unc	BU
JE5761 (2001)	4,000	—	—	—	8.00	—

KM# 174 1/2 NEW SHEQEL

Aluminum-Bronze **Subject:** Hanukka **Rev:** Lyre **Note:** Coins dated JE5754-5765 have the Star of David mint mark; the coins from JE5747-5753 do not.

Date	Mintage	F	VF	XF	Unc	BU
JE5761 (2001)	4,000	—	—	—	2.50	—
Note: In sets only						
JE5762 (2002)	4,000	—	—	—	2.50	—
Note: In sets only						
JE5763 (2003)	3,000	—	—	—	2.50	—
Note: In sets only						
JE5764 (2004)	3,000	—	—	—	2.50	—
Note: In sets only						
JE5765 (2005)	2,500	—	—	—	2.50	—
Note: In sets only						

KM# 355 1/2 NEW SHEQEL

6.5000 g., Copper-Aluminum-Nickel, 25.5 mm. **Obv:** Value **Rev:** Yemenite Hanukka Lamp **Edge:** Twelve plain sections

Date	Mintage	F	VF	XF	Unc	BU
JE5762 (2002)	4,000	—	—	—	8.00	—

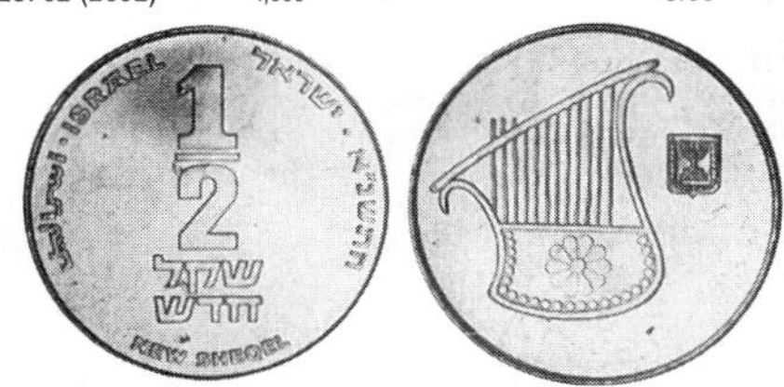

KM# 159 1/2 NEW SHEQEL

Aluminum-Bronze **Rev:** Lyre

Date	Mintage	F	VF	XF	Unc	BU
JE5762 (2002)	8,640,000	—	—	0.35	0.75	—

Date	Mintage	F	VF	XF	Unc	BU

Note: Struck at the Santiago and Vantaa Mints. Exist with 4 and 4.5mm long fraction line between 1 and 2 of value.

Date	Mintage	F	VF	XF	Unc	BU
JE5763 (2003)	—	—	—	0.35	0.75	—
JE5764 (2004)	2,640,000	—	—	0.35	0.75	—

KM# 389 1/2 NEW SHEQEL

6.5000 g., Copper-Aluminum-Nickel, 25.5 mm. **Obv:** Value **Rev:** Polish Hanukka Lamp **Edge:** Plain **Shape:** 12-sided

Date	Mintage	F	VF	XF	Unc	BU
JE5763 (2003) In sets only	3,000	—	—	—	8.00	—

KM# 390 1/2 NEW SHEQEL

6.5000 g., Copper-Aluminum-Nickel, 25.5 mm. **Obv:** Value **Rev:** Iraqi Hanukka Lamp **Edge:** Plain **Shape:** 12-sided

Date	Mintage	F	VF	XF	Unc	BU
JE5764 (2004) In sets only	3,000	—	—	—	8.00	—

KM# 391 1/2 NEW SHEQEL

6.5000 g., Copper-Aluminum-Nickel, 25.5 mm. **Obv:** Value **Rev:** Syrian Hanukka Lamp **Edge:** Plain **Shape:** 12-sided

Date	Mintage	F	VF	XF	Unc	BU
JE5765 (2005) In sets only	2,500	—	—	—	8.00	—

KM# 160a NEW SHEQEL

Nickel Clad Steel

Date	Mintage	F	VF	XF	Unc	BU
JE5761 (2001)	9,648,000	—	—	—	1.00	—
JE5762 (2002)	18,816,000	—	—	—	1.00	—
JE5763 (2003)	10,198,500	—	—	—	1.00	—
JE5765 (2005)	—	—	—	—	1.00	—

KM# 344 NEW SHEQEL

14.4000 g., 0.9250 Silver .4282 oz. ASW, 30 mm. **Subject:** Anniversary - Independence Day and Education **Obv:** Denomination **Rev:** Pomegranate full of symbols - Hebrew 'ABC-123', etc. **Rev. Designer:** Asher Kalderon **Edge:** Plain

Date	Mintage	F	VF	XF	Unc	BU
JE5761-2001 Prooflike	1,653	—	—	—	—	25.00

KM# 351 NEW SHEQEL

14.4000 g., 0.9250 Silver 0.4282 oz. ASW, 30 mm. **Subject:** Music **Obv:** National arms and denomination **Rev:** Musical instruments **Edge:** Plain

Date	Mintage	F	VF	XF	Unc	BU
JE5761-2001	1,182	—	—	—	25.00	—

KM# 163 NEW SHEQEL

Copper-Nickel **Subject:** Hanukkah **Note:** Coins dated JE5754-5765 have the Star of David mint mark; the JE5746-5753 coins do not.

Date	Mintage	F	VF	XF	Unc	BU
JE5761 (2001) Note: In sets only	4,000	—	—	—	2.50	—
JE5762 (2002) Note: In sets only	4,000	—	—	—	2.50	—
JE5763 (2003) Note: In sets only	3,000	—	—	—	2.50	—
JE5764 (2004) Note: In sets only	3,000	—	—	—	2.50	—
JE5765 (2005) Note: In sets only	2,500	—	—	—	2.50	—

KM# 356 NEW SHEQEL

14.4000 g., 0.9250 Silver 0.4282 oz. ASW, 30 mm. **Subject:** Independence - Volunteering **Obv:** Denomination **Rev:** Heart in hands **Edge:** Plain

Date	Mintage	F	VF	XF	Unc	BU
JE5762-2002 Prooflike	1,364	—	—	—	—	25.00

KM# 359 NEW SHEQEL

14.4000 g., 0.9250 Silver 0.4282 oz. ASW, 30 mm. **Subject:** Tower of Babel **Obv:** National arms in spiral inscription **Rev:** Tower of Hebrew verses **Edge:** Plain

Date	Mintage	F	VF	XF	Unc	BU
JE5762 (2002) Prooflike	1,312	—	—	—	—	25.00

KM# 371 NEW SHEQEL

14.4000 g., 0.9250 Silver 0.4282 oz. ASW, 30 mm. **Subject:** Space Exploration **Obv:** "Ofeq" satellite in orbit **Rev:** "Shavit" rocket **Edge:** Plain

Date	Mintage	F	VF	XF	Unc	BU
JE5763-2003	Est. 2,500	—	—	—	25.00	—

KM# 374 NEW SHEQEL

14.4000 g., 0.9250 Silver 0.4282 oz. ASW, 30 mm. **Obv:** Value **Rev:** Jacob and Rachel floating in air **Edge:** Plain

Date	Mintage	F	VF	XF	Unc	BU
JE5763-2003	Est. 2,000	—	—	—	25.00	—

KM# 377 NEW SHEQEL

14.4000 g., 0.9250 Silver 0.4282 oz. ASW, 30 mm. **Obv:** Value **Rev:** Architectural design **Edge:** Plain

Date	Mintage	F	VF	XF	Unc	BU
JE5764-2004	Est. 2,500	—	—	—	25.00	—

KM# 380 NEW SHEQEL

14.4000 g., 0.9250 Silver 0.4282 oz. ASW, 30 mm. **Obv:** Value **Rev:** Parent and child **Edge:** Plain

Date	Mintage	F	VF	XF	Unc	BU
JE5764-2004	Est. 2,500	—	—	—	25.00	—

KM# 383 NEW SHEQEL

14.4000 g., 0.9250 Silver 0.4282 oz. ASW, 30 mm. **Obv:** Four windsurfers, value and national arms **Rev:** Eight windsurfers **Edge:** Reeded

Date	Mintage	F	VF	XF	Unc	BU
JE5764-2004 Prooflike	Est. 2,000	—	—	—	—	25.00

KM# 386 NEW SHEQEL

14.4000 g., 0.9250 Silver 0.4282 oz. ASW, 30 mm. **Subject:** Biblical Burning Bush **Obv:** Burning twig and value **Rev:** Burning Bush **Edge:** Plain

Date	Mintage	F	VF	XF	Unc	BU
JE5764-2004	Est. 1,800	—	—	—	25.00	—

KM# 345 2 NEW SHEQALIM

28.8000 g., 0.9250 Silver .8564 oz. ASW, 38.7 mm. **Subject:** Independence Day and Education **Obv:** Denomination **Rev:** Pomegranate full of symbols **Edge:** Reeded **Designer:** Asher Kalderon

Date	Mintage	F	VF	XF	Unc	BU
JE5761-2001 Proof	1,847	Value: 45.00				

KM# 349 2 NEW SHEQALIM

28.8000 g., 0.9250 Silver .8564 oz. ASW, 38.7 mm. **Subject:** Wildlife **Obv:** Acacia tree **Rev:** Ibex **Edge:** Reeded

Date	Mintage	F	VF	XF	Unc	BU
JE5761-2001 Prooflike	2,000	—	—	—	50.00	—

KM# 352 2 NEW SHEQALIM

28.8000 g., 0.9250 Silver 0.8565 oz. ASW, 38.7 mm. **Subject:** Music **Obv:** National arms and denomination **Rev:** Musical instruments **Edge:** Reeded

Date	Mintage	F	VF	XF	Unc	BU
JE5761-2001 Proof	1,747	Value: 45.00				

KM# 357 2 NEW SHEQALIM

28.8000 g., 0.9250 Silver 0.8565 oz. ASW, 38.7 mm. **Subject:** Independence - Volunteering **Obv:** Denomination **Rev:** Heart in hands **Edge:** Reeded

Date	Mintage	F	VF	XF	Unc	BU
JE5762-2002 Proof	1,426	Value: 45.00				

KM# 360 2 NEW SHEQALIM

28.8000 g., 0.9250 Silver 0.8565 oz. ASW, 38.7 mm. **Subject:** Tower of Babel **Obv:** National arms in spiral inscription **Rev:** Tower of Hebrew verses **Edge:** Reeded

Date	Mintage	F	VF	XF	Unc	BU
JE5762-2002 Proof	1,295	Value: 50.00				

KM# 372 2 NEW SHEQALIM
28.8000 g., 0.9250 Silver 0.8565 oz. ASW, 38.7 mm. **Subject:** Space Exploration **Obv:** "Amos" satellite in orbit **Rev:** "Shavit" rocket **Edge:** Reeded

Date	Mintage	F	VF	XF	Unc	BU
JE5763-2003 Proof	Est. 2,500	Value: 45.00				

KM# 375 2 NEW SHEQALIM
28.8000 g., 0.9250 Silver 0.8565 oz. ASW, 38.7 mm. **Obv:** Value **Rev:** Jacob and Rachel floating in air **Edge:** Reeded

Date	Mintage	F	VF	XF	Unc	BU
JE5763-2003 Proof	Est. 2,000	Value: 45.00				

KM# 378 2 NEW SHEQALIM
28.8000 g., 0.9250 Silver 0.8565 oz. ASW, 38.7 mm. **Obv:** Value and colored shapes **Rev:** Architectural design **Edge:** Reeded

Date	Mintage	F	VF	XF	Unc	BU
JE5764-2004 Proof	Est. 2,500	Value: 45.00				

KM# 381 2 NEW SHEQALIM
28.8000 g., 0.9250 Silver 0.8565 oz. ASW, 38.7 mm. **Obv:** Value **Rev:** Parent and child **Edge:** Reeded

Date	Mintage	F	VF	XF	Unc	BU
JE5764-2004 Proof	Est. 2,500	Value: 45.00				

KM# 384 2 NEW SHEQALIM
28.8000 g., 0.9250 Silver 0.8565 oz. ASW, 38.7 mm. **Obv:** Four windsurfers, value and national arms **Rev:** Eight windsurfers **Edge:** Reeded

Date	Mintage	F	VF	XF	Unc	BU
JE5764-2004 Proof	Est. 2,000	Value: 45.00				

KM# 387 2 NEW SHEQALIM
28.8000 g., 0.9250 Silver 0.8565 oz. ASW, 38.7 mm. **Subject:** Biblical Burning Bush **Obv:** Burning twig and value **Rev:** Burning Bush **Edge:** Reeded

Date	Mintage	F	VF	XF	Unc	BU
JE5764-2004 Proof	Est. 1,800	Value: 45.00				

KM# 350 5 NEW SHEQALIM
8.6300 g., 0.9000 Gold .2497 oz. AGW, 22 mm. **Subject:** Wildlife **Obv:** Ocacia tree **Rev:** Ibex **Edge:** Reeded

Date	Mintage	F	VF	XF	Unc	BU
JE5761-2001 Proof	600	Value: 325				

KM# 217 5 NEW SHEQALIM
Copper-Nickel **Subject:** Hanukka **Rev:** Ancient column
Note: Coins dated JE5754-5765 have the Star of David mint mark; the JE5751-5753 coins do not.

Date	Mintage	F	VF	XF	Unc	BU
JE5762 (2002)	4,000	—	—	—	3.75	—
Note: In sets only						
JE5763 (2003)	3,000	—	—	—	3.75	—
Note: In sets only						
JE5764 (2004)	3,000	—	—	—	3.75	—
Note: In sets only						
JE5765 (2005)	2,500	—	—	—	3.75	—
Note: In sets only						

KM# 207 5 NEW SHEQALIM
Copper-Nickel **Shape:** 12-sided

Date	Mintage	F	VF	XF	Unc	BU
JE5762 (2002)	4,464,000	—	—	—	3.75	—
JE5765 (2005)	—	—	—	—	3.00	—

KM# 315 10 NEW SHEQALIM
Bi-Metallic Aureate bonded Bronze center in Nickel bonded Steel ring **Subject:** Hanukka **Obv:** Denomination **Rev:** Palm tree and baskets

Date	Mintage	F	VF	XF	Unc	BU
JE5761 (2001)	4,000	—	—	—	8.00	—
Note: In sets only						
JE5762 (2002)	4,000	—	—	—	8.00	—
Note: In sets only						
JE5763 (2003)	3,000	—	—	—	8.00	—
Note: In sets only						
JE5764 (2004)	3,000	—	—	—	8.00	—
Note: In sets only						
JE5765 (2005)	2,500	—	—	—	8.00	—
Note: In sets only						

KM# 346 10 NEW SHEQALIM
16.9600 g., 0.9170 Gold .5000 oz. AGW, 30 mm. **Subject:** Independence Day and Education **Obv:** Denomination **Rev:** Pomegranate full of symbols - Hebrew for 'ABC - 123', etc. **Edge:** Reeded **Designer:** Asher Kalderon

Date	Mintage	F	VF	XF	Unc	BU
JE5761-2001 Proof	660	Value: 650				

KM# 353 10 NEW SHEQALIM
16.9600 g., 0.9170 Gold 0.5 oz. AGW, 30 mm. **Subject:** Music **Obv:** National arms and denomination **Rev:** Musical instruments **Edge:** Reeded

Date	Mintage	F	VF	XF	Unc	BU
JE5761-2001 Proof	766	Value: 600				

KM# 358 10 NEW SHEQALIM
16.9600 g., 0.9166 Gold 0.4998 oz. AGW, 30 mm. **Subject:** Independence - Volunteering **Obv:** Denomination **Rev:** Heart in hands **Edge:** Reeded

Date	Mintage	F	VF	XF	Unc	BU
JE5762-2002 Proof	617	Value: 575				

KM# 361 10 NEW SHEQALIM
16.9600 g., 0.9170 Gold 0.5 oz. AGW, 30 mm. **Subject:** Tower of Babel **Obv:** National arms in spiral inscription **Rev:** Tower of Hebrew verses **Edge:** Reeded

Date	Mintage	F	VF	XF	Unc	BU
JE5762-2002 Proof	750	Value: 650				

KM# 270 10 NEW SHEQALIM
Bi-Metallic Aureate bonded Bronze center in Nickel bonded Steel ring

Date	Mintage	F	VF	XF	Unc	BU
JE5762 (2002)	4,749,000	—	—	—	7.50	—
JE5765 (2005)	—	—	—	—	7.00	—

KM# 373 10 NEW SHEQALIM
16.9600 g., 0.9170 Gold 0.5 oz. AGW, 30 mm. **Subject:** Space Exploration **Obv:** "Eros" satellite in orbit **Rev:** "Shavit" rocket **Edge:** Reeded

Date	Mintage	F	VF	XF	Unc	BU
JE5763-2003 Proof	575	Value: 600				

KM# 376 10 NEW SHEQALIM

16.9600 g., 0.9170 Gold 0.5 oz. AGW, 30 mm. **Obv:** Value **Rev:** Jacob and Rachel floating in air **Edge:** Reeded

Date	Mintage	F	VF	XF	Unc	BU
JE5763-2003 Proof	555	Value: 650				

KM# 379 10 NEW SHEQALIM

16.9600 g., 0.9170 Gold 0.5 oz. AGW, 30 mm. **Obv:** Value **Rev:** Architectural design **Edge:** Reeded

Date	Mintage	F	VF	XF	Unc	BU
JE5764-2004 Proof	555	Value: 650				

KM# 382 10 NEW SHEQALIM

16.9600 g., 0.9170 Gold 0.5 oz. AGW, 30 mm. **Obv:** Value **Rev:** Parent and child **Edge:** Reeded

Date	Mintage	F	VF	XF	Unc	BU
JE5764-2004 Proof	555	Value: 625				

KM# 385 10 NEW SHEQALIM

16.9600 g., 0.9170 Gold 0.5 oz. AGW, 30 mm. **Obv:** Four windsurfers, value and national arms **Rev:** Eight windsurfers **Edge:** Reeded

Date	Mintage	F	VF	XF	Unc	BU
JE5764-2004 Proof	555	Value: 650				

KM# 388 10 NEW SHEQALIM

16.9600 g., 0.9170 Gold 0.5 oz. AGW, 30 mm. **Subject:** Biblical Burning Bush **Obv:** Burning twig and value **Rev:** Burning Bush **Edge:** Reeded

Date	Mintage	F	VF	XF	Unc	BU
JE5764-2004 Proof	555	Value: 600				

MINT SETS

Non-standard Metals

KM#	Date	Mintage	Identification	Issue Price	Mkt Val
MS58	JE5761-62 (2001-02) (9)	3,000	KM#157 (2 pcs), 158 (2 pcs), 159, 160a (2 pcs), 207, 270 mixed date set	—	—
MS59	JE5761 (2001) (7)	4,000	KM#163, 172-174, 217, 315, 354	39.00	40.00
MS60	JE5761 (2002) (7)	4,000	KM#163, 172-174, 217, 315, 355	—	—
MS61	JE5763 (2003) (7)	3,000	KM#163, 172-174, 217, 315, 389	39.00	40.00
MS62	JE5764 (2004) (7)	3,000	KM#163, 172-174, 217, 315, 390	—	—
MS63	JE5765 (2005) (7)	2,500	KM#163, 172-174, 315, 391	39.00	40.00

The Italian Republic, a 700-mile-long peninsula extending into the heart of the Mediterranean Sea, has an area of 116,304 sq. mi. (301,230 sq. km.) and a population of 60 million. Capital: Rome. The economy centers around agriculture, manufacturing, forestry and fishing. Machinery, textiles, clothing and motor vehicles are exported.

REPUBLIC

DECIMAL COINAGE

KM# 219 LIRA

11.0000 g., 0.8350 Silver 0.2953 oz. ASW, 29 mm. **Subject:** History of the Lira - Lira of 1946 (KM#87) **Obv:** Allegorical portrait left **Rev:** Apple on branch **Edge:** Reeded **Note:** This is a Lira Series reproducing an old coin design in the center of each coin.

Date	Mintage	F	VF	XF	Unc	BU
2001	—	—	—	—	40.00	—
2001 Proof	—	Value: 60.00				

KM# 220 LIRA

6.0000 g., 0.8350 Silver 0.1611 oz. ASW, 24 mm. **Subject:** History of the Lira - Lira of 1951 (KM#91) **Obv:** Balance scale **Rev:** Denomination and cornucopia **Edge:** Reeded **Note:** This is a Lira Series reproducing an old coin design in the center of each coin.

Date	Mintage	F	VF	XF	Unc	BU
2001	—	—	—	—	40.00	—
2001 Proof	—	Value: 60.00				

KM# 91 LIRA

Aluminum **Obv:** Balance scales **Rev:** Cornucopia **Designer:** Giuseppe Romagnoli **Note:** The 1968-1969 and 1982-1999 dates were issued in sets only.

Date	Mintage	F	VF	XF	Unc	BU
2001R	—	—	—	—	12.00	—
2001R Proof	—	Value: 16.00				

KM# 91a LIRA

4.0000 g., 0.9000 Gold 0.1157 oz. AGW, 17.2 mm. **Obv:** Scale **Rev:** Value and cornucopia **Edge:** Plain **Note:** Official Restrike

Date	Mintage	F	VF	XF	Unc	BU
1951 (2006)R Proof	1,999	Value: 75.00				

KM# 87a LIRA

8.0000 g., 0.9000 Gold 0.2315 oz. AGW, 21.6 mm. **Obv:** Ceres **Rev:** Orange on branch **Edge:** Plain **Note:** Official Restrike

Date	Mintage	F	VF	XF	Unc	BU
1946 (2006)R Proof	1,999	Value: 150				

KM# 94 2 LIRE

Aluminum **Obv:** Honey bee (apis mellifica) **Rev:** Olive branch (olea europa) **Note:** The 1968-1969 and 1982-1999 dates were issued in sets only.

Date	Mintage	F	VF	XF	Unc	BU
2001R	—	—	—	—	4.00	—
2001R Proof	—	Value: 6.00				

KM# 94a 2 LIRE

5.0000 g., 0.9000 Gold 0.1447 oz. AGW, 18.3 mm. **Obv:** Honey bee **Rev:** Olive branch **Edge:** Reeded **Note:** Official Restrike

Date	Mintage	F	VF	XF	Unc	BU
1953 (2006)R Proof	1,999	Value: 95.00				

KM# 88a 2 LIRE

11.0000 g., 0.9000 Gold 0.3183 oz. AGW, 24.1 mm. **Obv:** Farmer plowing field **Rev:** Wheat ear **Edge:** Plain **Note:** Official Restrike

Date	Mintage	F	VF	XF	Unc	BU
1946 (2006)R Proof	1,999	Value: 210				

KM# 90a 10 LIRE

19.0000 g., 0.9000 Gold 0.5498 oz. AGW, 29 mm. **Obv:** Pegasus **Rev:** Olive branch **Edge:** Lettered **Edge Lettering:** REPVBBLICA ITALIANA **Note:** Official Restrike

Date	Mintage	F	VF	XF	Unc	BU
1946 (2006)R Proof	1,999	Value: 365				

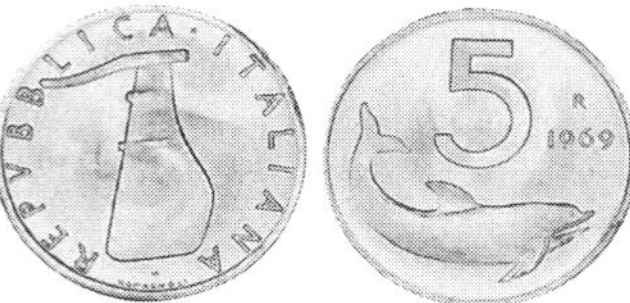

KM# 92 5 LIRE

Aluminum **Obv:** Rudder **Rev:** Dolphin (delphinus delphis) **Designer:** Giuseppe Romagnoli

Date	Mintage	F	VF	XF	Unc	BU
2001R	100,000	—	—	—	8.00	—
2001R Proof	—	Value: 15.00				

KM# 92a 5 LIRE

6.0000 g., 0.9000 Gold 0.1736 oz. AGW, 20.2 mm. **Obv:** Rudder **Rev:** Dolphin **Edge:** Plain **Note:** Official Restrike

Date	Mintage	F	VF	XF	Unc	BU
1951 (2006)R Proof	1,999	Value: 115				

KM# 89a 5 LIRE

16.0000 g., 0.9000 Gold 0.463 oz. AGW, 26.7 mm. **Obv:** Italia with torch **Rev:** Bunch of grapes **Edge:** Reeded **Note:** Official Restrike

Date	Mintage	F	VF	XF	Unc	BU
1946 (2006)R Proof	1,999	Value: 300				

KM# 93 10 LIRE

Aluminum **Obv:** Plough **Rev:** Two wheat ears **Designer:** Giuseppe Romagnoli

Date	Mintage	F	VF	XF	Unc	BU
2001R	100,000	—	—	—	12.00	—
2001R Proof	—	Value: 8.00				

KM# 93a 10 LIRE

10.0000 g., 0.9000 Gold 0.2894 oz. AGW, 23.3 mm. **Obv:** Plow **Rev:** Value and two wheat ears **Edge:** Plain **Note:** Official Restrike

Date	Mintage	F	VF	XF	Unc	BU
1951 (2006)R Proof	1,999	Value: 195				

KM# 97.2 20 LIRE

Aluminum-Bronze **Rev:** Oak leaves **Edge:** Plain **Designer:** Pietro Giampaoli

Date	Mintage	F	VF	XF	Unc	BU
2001R	100,000	—	—	—	7.50	—
2001R Proof	—	Value: 8.00				

KM# 97.1a 20 LIRE
8.0000 g., 0.9000 Gold 0.2315 oz. AGW, 21.3 mm. **Obv:** Ceres **Rev:** Oak leaves **Edge:** Reeded **Note:** Official Restrike

Date	Mintage	F	VF	XF	Unc	BU
1957 (2006)R Proof	1,999	Value: 150				

KM# 183 50 LIRE
Copper-Nickel **Designer:** L. Cretara

Date	Mintage	F	VF	XF	Unc	BU
2001R	100,000	—	—	—	12.00	—
2001R Proof	—	Value: 18.00				

KM# 95.1a 50 LIRE
8.0000 g., 0.9000 Gold 0.2315 oz. AGW, 24.8 mm. **Obv:** Italia **Rev:** Vulcan **Edge:** Reeded **Note:** Official Restrike

Date	Mintage	F	VF	XF	Unc	BU
1954 (2006)R Proof	1,999	Value: 240				

KM# 183a 50 LIRE
9.0000 g., 0.9000 Gold 0.2604 oz. AGW, 19.2 mm. **Obv:** Roma **Rev:** Value in wreath **Edge:** Plain **Note:** Official Restrike

Date	Mintage	F	VF	XF	Unc	BU
1996 (2006)R Proof	1,999	Value: 175				

KM# 159 100 LIRE
Copper-Nickel **Designer:** Laura Cretara

Date	Mintage	F	VF	XF	Unc	BU
2001R Proof	100,000	Value: 10.00				
2001R	—	0.15	0.25	0.35	0.75	—

KM# 159a 100 LIRE
9.0000 g., 0.9000 Gold 0.2604 oz. AGW, 22 mm. **Obv:** Roma **Rev:** Value **Edge:** Segmented reeding **Note:** Official Restrike

Date	Mintage	F	VF	XF	Unc	BU
1993 (2006)R Proof	1,999	Value: 175				

KM# 96.1a 100 LIRE
18.0000 g., 0.9000 Gold 0.5208 oz. AGW, 27.8 mm. **Obv:** Ancient athlete **Rev:** Minerva standing **Edge:** Reeded **Note:** Official Restrike

Date	Mintage	F	VF	XF	Unc	BU
1955 (2006)R Proof	1,999	Value: 350				

KM# 105 200 LIRE
Aluminum-Bronze **Designer:** M. Vallucci

Date	Mintage	F	VF	XF	Unc	BU
2001R	100,000	—	—	—	7.50	—
2001R Proof	—	Value: 12.50				

KM# 105a 200 LIRE
11.0000 g., 0.9000 Gold 0.3183 oz. AGW, 24 mm. **Obv:** Italia **Rev:** Value in gear wheel **Edge:** Reeded **Note:** Official Restrike

Date	Mintage	F	VF	XF	Unc	BU
1977 (2006)R Proof	1,999	Value: 210				

KM# 98 500 LIRE
11.0000 g., 0.8350 Silver .2953 oz. ASW **Obv:** Columbus' ships **Obv. Designer:** Guido Veroi **Rev. Designer:** Pietro Giampaoli **Edge:** Dates in raised lettering

Date	Mintage	F	VF	XF	Unc	BU
2001R	100,000	—	—	—	40.00	—
2001R Proof	10,000	Value: 45.00				

KM# 98a 500 LIRE
18.0000 g., 0.9000 Gold 0.5208 oz. AGW, 29 mm. **Obv:** Columbus' ships **Rev:** Lady **Edge:** Lettered **Edge Lettering:** REPVBBLICA ITALIANA *** 1958*** **Note:** Official Restrike

Date	Mintage	F	VF	XF	Unc	BU
1958 (2006)R Proof	1,999	Value: 350				

KM# 111 500 LIRE
Bi-Metallic Bronzital center in Acmonital ring **Designer:** Cretara

Date	Mintage	F	VF	XF	Unc	BU
2001R	100,000	—	—	—	15.00	—
2001R Proof	8,600	Value: 30.00				

KM# 111a 500 LIRE
14.0000 g., Bi-Metallic .750 Gold center in .900 Gold ring, 25.8 mm. **Obv:** Italia **Rev:** Quirinala Piazza **Edge:** Segmented reeding **Note:** Official Restrike

Date	Mintage	F	VF	XF	Unc	BU
1982 (2006)R Proof	1,999	Value: 245				

KM# 99a 500 LIRE
18.0000 g., 0.9000 Gold 0.5208 oz. AGW, 29 mm. **Obv:** Seated Italia **Rev:** Lady **Edge:** Lettered **Edge Lettering:** "1 CENTENARIO VNITA'D'ITALIA * 1861-1961* " **Note:** Official Restrike

Date	Mintage	F	VF	XF	Unc	BU
1961 (2006)R Proof	1,999	Value: 350				

KM# 100a 500 LIRE
18.0000 g., 0.9000 Gold 0.5208 oz. AGW, 29 mm. **Obv:** Dante **Rev:** Hell **Edge:** Lettered **Edge Lettering:** "7 CENTENARIO DELLA NASCITA DI DANTE" **Note:** Official Restrike

Date	Mintage	F	VF	XF	Unc	BU
1965 (2006)R Proof	1,999	Value: 350				

KM# 236 1000 LIRE
14.6000 g., 0.8350 Silver 0.3919 oz. ASW, 31.4 mm. **Obv:** Giuseppe Verdi **Rev:** Building

Date	Mintage	F	VF	XF	Unc	BU
2001R	—	—	—	—	80.00	—
2001R Proof	—	Value: 130				

KM# 194 1000 LIRE
Bi-Metallic Copper-Nickel center in Aluminum-Bronze ring **Subject:** European Union **Obv:** Allegorical portrait **Obv. Designer:** Laura Cretara **Rev:** Corrected map with United Germany **Rev. Designer:** Pernazza

Date	Mintage	F	VF	XF	Unc	BU
2001R	100,000	—	—	—	15.00	—
2001R Proof	10,000	Value: 25.00				

KM# 101a 1000 LIRE
24.0000 g., 0.9000 Gold 0.6945 oz. AGW, 31.4 mm. **Obv:** Concordia **Rev:** Geometric shape above value **Edge:** Lettered **Edge Lettering:** "REPVBBLICA ITALIANA"

Date	Mintage	F	VF	XF	Unc	BU
1970 (2006)R Proof	1,999	Value: 450				

KM# 190a 1000 LIRE
17.0000 g., Bi-Metallic .750 Gold center in .900 Gold ring, 27 mm. **Obv:** Roma **Rev:** European map **Edge:** Segmented reeding **Note:** Official Restrike

Date	Mintage	F	VF	XF	Unc	BU
1997 (2006)R Proof	1,999	Value: 275				

KM# 234 50000 LIRE
7.5000 g., 0.9000 Gold 0.217 oz. AGW, 20 mm. **Subject:** 250th Anniversary - Palace of Caserta **Obv:** Front view of palace **Rev:** Fountain, date and denomination

Date	Mintage	F	VF	XF	Unc	BU
2001R Proof	—	Value: 320				

KM# 233 100000 LIRE
15.0000 g., 0.9000 Gold 0.434 oz. AGW, 25 mm. **Subject:** 700th Anniversary - Pulpit at the Church of St. Andrea a Pistoia **Obv:** Full pulpit **Rev:** Enlarged detail of the pulpit

Date	Mintage	F	VF	XF	Unc	BU
2001R Proof	—	Value: 600				

EURO COINAGE

European Economic Community Issues

KM# 210 EURO CENT
2.2700 g., Copper Plated Steel, 16.2 mm. **Obv:** Castle del Monte **Obv. Designer:** Eugenio Drutti **Rev:** Denomination and globe **Rev. Designer:** Luc Luycx **Edge:** Plain

Date	Mintage	F	VF	XF	Unc	BU
2002	1,348,000,000	—	—	—	0.25	—
2003	9,479,000	—	—	—	0.35	—
2004	14,418,000	—	—	—	0.35	—
2005	—	—	—	—	0.35	—

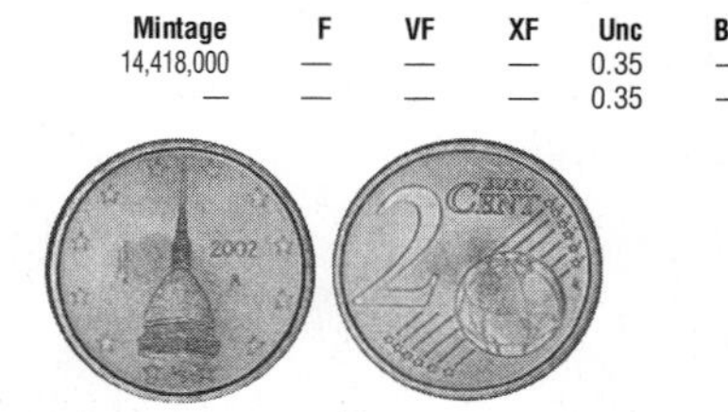

KM# 211 2 EURO CENTS
3.0300 g., Copper Plated Steel, 18.7 mm. **Obv:** Observation tower in Turin **Obv. Designer:** Luciana de Simoni **Rev:** Denomination and globe **Rev. Designer:** Luc Luycx **Edge:** Grooved

Date	Mintage	F	VF	XF	Unc	BU
2002	1,100,000,000	—	—	—	0.25	—
2003	21,667,000	—	—	—	0.50	—
2004	32,620,000	—	—	—	0.50	—

KM# 212 5 EURO CENTS
3.8600 g., Copper Plated Steel, 21.2 mm. **Obv:** Colosseum **Obv. Designer:** Lorenzo Frapiccini **Rev:** Denomination and globe **Rev. Designer:** Luc Luycx **Edge:** Plain

Date	Mintage	F	VF	XF	Unc	BU
2002	1,341,000,000	—	—	—	0.25	—
2003	1,956,000	—	—	—	0.75	—
2004	2,936,000	—	—	—	0.75	—

KM# 213 10 EURO CENTS
4.0700 g., Brass, 19.7 mm. **Obv:** Venus by Botticelli **Obv. Designer:** Claudia Momoni **Rev:** Denomination and map **Rev. Designer:** Luc Luycx **Edge:** Reeded

Date	Mintage	F	VF	XF	Unc	BU
2002	1,142,000,000	—	—	—	0.25	—
2003	29,826,000	—	—	—	0.75	—
2004	44,741,000	—	—	—	0.75	—

KM# 214 20 EURO CENTS
5.7300 g., Brass, 22.1 mm. **Obv:** Futuristic sculpture **Obv. Designer:** Maria Cassol **Rev:** Denomination and map **Rev. Designer:** Luc Luycx **Edge:** Notched

Date	Mintage	F	VF	XF	Unc	BU
2002	1,411,000,000	—	—	—	0.30	—
2003	26,005,000	—	—	—	1.00	—
2004	39,008,000	—	—	—	1.00	—

KM# 215 50 EURO CENTS
7.8100 g., Brass, 24.2 mm. **Obv:** Sculpture of Marcus Aurelius on horseback **Obv. Designer:** Roberto Mauri **Rev:** Denomination and map **Rev. Designer:** Luc Luycx **Edge:** Reeded

Date	Mintage	F	VF	XF	Unc	BU
2002	1,136,000,000	—	—	—	0.80	—
2003	44,675,000	—	—	—	1.25	—
2004	67,013,000	—	—	—	1.25	—

KM# 216 EURO

7.5000 g., Bi-Metallic Copper-Nickel center in Brass ring, 23.2 mm. **Obv:** Male figure drawing by Leonardo da Vinci **Obv. Designer:** Laura Cretara **Rev:** Denomination and map **Rev. Designer:** Luc Luycx **Edge:** Reeded and plain sections

Date	Mintage	F	VF	XF	Unc	BU
2002	965,875,000	—	—	—	1.60	—
2003	66,342,000	—	—	—	2.50	—
2004	99,516,000	—	—	—	2.50	—

KM# 217 2 EUROS

8.5200 g., Bi-Metallic Brass center in Copper-Nickel ring, 25.7 mm. **Obv:** Bust of Dante Aligheri **Obv. Designer:** Maria Colanieri **Rev:** Denomination and map **Rev. Designer:** Luc Luycx **Edge:** Reeded **Edge Lettering:** 2's and stars

Date	Mintage	F	VF	XF	Unc	BU
2002	463,552,000	—	—	—	3.50	—
2003	36,210,000	—	—	—	3.75	—
2004	54,315,000	—	—	—	3.75	—

KM# 237 2 EUROS

8.5300 g., Bi-Metallic Aluminum-Bronze center in Copper-Nickel ring, 25.7 mm. **Obv:** World Food Program globe **Rev:** Value and map **Edge:** Reeded and lettered **Edge Lettering:** 2's and stars

Date	Mintage	F	VF	XF	Unc	BU
2004R	—	—	—	—	5.75	—

KM# 245 2 EUROS

8.5200 g., Bi-Metallic Brass center in Copper-Nickel ring, 25.6 mm. **Subject:** European Constitution **Obv:** Europa holding an open book while sitting on a bull **Rev:** Value over map **Edge:** Reeding over stars and 2's

Date	Mintage	F	VF	XF	Unc	BU
2005R	—	—	—	—	6.00	—

KM# 246 2 EUROS

8.5100 g., Bi-Metallic Brass center in Copper-Nickel ring, 25.7 mm. **Subject:** Torino Winter Olympics **Obv:** Skier **Rev:** Value **Edge:** Reeded with stars and 2's

Date	Mintage	F	VF	XF	Unc	BU
2006	—	—	—	—	5.00	—

KM# 238 5 EURO

18.0000 g., 0.9250 Silver 0.5353 oz. ASW, 32 mm. **Subject:** World Cup Soccer - Germany 2006 **Obv:** St. Croce Square in Florence **Rev:** Soccer ball and world globe design

Date	Mintage	F	VF	XF	Unc	BU
2004R Proof	35,000	Value: 95.00				

KM# 239 5 EURO

18.0000 g., 0.9250 Silver 0.5353 oz. ASW, 32 mm. **Subject:** Madam Butterfly **Obv:** Large building **Rev:** Geisha

Date	Mintage	F	VF	XF	Unc	BU
2004R	30,000	—	—	—	27.50	—
2004R Proof	12,000	Value: 37.50				

KM# 240 10 EURO

22.0000 g., 0.9250 Silver 0.6543 oz. ASW, 34 mm. **Subject:** City of Genoa **Obv:** Sculpture and art works **Rev:** Tower and harbor map

Date	Mintage	F	VF	XF	Unc	BU
2004R	30,000	—	—	—	40.00	—
2004R Proof	12,000	Value: 55.00				

KM# 241 10 EURO

22.0000 g., 0.9250 Silver 0.6543 oz. ASW, 34 mm. **Subject:** Giacomo Puccini **Obv:** Pucini wearing hat **Rev:** Stage, music and quill

Date	Mintage	F	VF	XF	Unc	BU
2004R Proof	12,000	Value: 75.00				

KM# 242 20 EURO

6.4510 g., 0.9000 Gold 0.1867 oz. AGW, 21 mm. **Obv:** European ship of state **Rev:** Flying bird obscuring a man's face

Date	Mintage	F	VF	XF	Unc	BU
2004R Proof	6,000	Value: 250				

KM# 243 20 EURO

6.4510 g., 0.9000 Gold 0.1867 oz. AGW, 21 mm. **Subject:** World Cup Soccer - Germany 2006 **Obv:** Mascot **Rev:** Soccer ball and world globe

Date	Mintage	F	VF	XF	Unc	BU
2004R Proof	7,500	Value: 300				

KM# 244 50 EURO

16.1300 g., 0.9000 Gold 0.4667 oz. AGW, 28 mm. **Obv:** European ship of state **Rev:** Angel carrying away two children

Date	Mintage	F	VF	XF	Unc	BU
2004R Proof	6,000	Value: 575				

MINT SETS

KM#	Date	Mintage	Identification	Issue Price	Mkt Val
MS39	2001 (12)	—	KM#91-94, 97.2, 98, 105, 111, 159, 183, 194, 236	—	100

PROOF SETS

KM#	Date	Mintage	Identification	Issue Price	Mkt Val
PS25	2001 (12)	—	KM#91-94, 97.2, 98, 105, 111, 159, 183, 194, 236	—	180

IVORY COAST

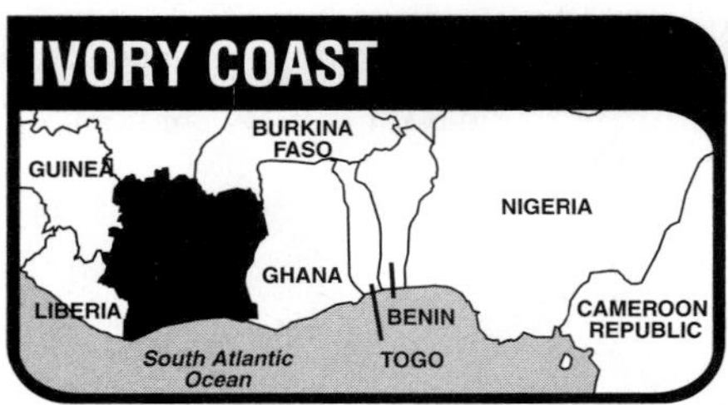

The Republic of the Ivory Coast, (Cote d'Ivoire), a former French Overseas territory located on the south side of the African bulge between Liberia and Ghana, has an area of 124,504 sq. mi. (322,463 sq. km.) and a population of 11.8 million. Capital: Yamoussoukro. The predominantly agricultural economy is one of Africa's most prosperous. Coffee, tropical woods, cocoa, and bananas are exported.

REPUBLIC

DECIMAL COINAGE

KM# 6 1500 CFA FRANCS - 1 AFRICA

7.3000 g., Nickel Plated Steel, 25.9 mm. **Obv:** Fighting elephants **Rev:** Elephant head on map **Edge:** Plain

Date	Mintage	F	VF	XF	Unc	BU
2003	1,200	—	—	—	20.00	—

KM# 6a 1500 CFA FRANCS - 1 AFRICA

0.9990 Silver, 25.9 mm. **Edge:** Plain

Date	Mintage	F	VF	XF	Unc	BU
2003	5	—	—	—	120	—

KM# 7 6000 CFA FRANCS - 4 AFRICA

10.1000 g., Bi-Metallic Copper-Nickel center in Brass ring, 28.3 mm. **Obv:** Map at left, President at right **Rev:** Elephant head on map **Edge:** Plain

Date	Mintage	F	VF	XF	Unc	BU
ND(2003)	500	—	—	—	40.00	—

KM# 8 150000 CFA FRANCS - 100 AFRICA

13.2000 g., 0.9990 Silver, 28.4 mm. **Obv:** Map left of President **Rev:** Elephant head on map

Date	Mintage	F	VF	XF	Unc	BU
ND(2003)	25	—	—	—	250	—

KM# 8a 150000 CFA FRANCS - 100 AFRICA

13.2000 g., 0.9990 Gold Plated Silver, 28.4 mm.

Date	Mintage	F	VF	XF	Unc	BU
ND(2003)	25	—	—	—	250	—

JAMAICA

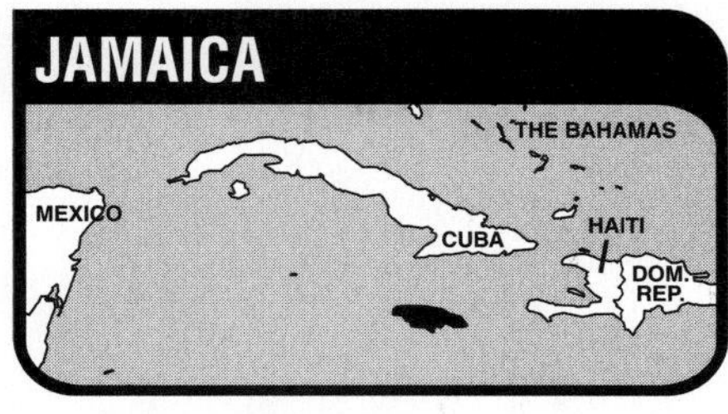

Jamaica is situated in the Caribbean Sea 90 miles south of Cuba, has an area of 4,244 sq. mi. (10,990 sq. km.) and a population of 2.1 million. Capital: Kingston. The economy is founded chiefly on mining, tourism and agriculture. Aluminum, bauxite, sugar, rum and molasses are exported.

MINT MARKS

C - Royal Canadian Mint, Ottawa

MONETARY SYSTEM

(Commencing 1969)

100 Cents = 1 Dollar

COMMONWEALTH

DECIMAL COINAGE

KM# 64 CENT

Aluminum **Series:** F.A.O. **Rev:** Ackee fruit (blighia sapida) **Shape:** 12-sided **Designer:** Christopher Ironside

Date	Mintage	F	VF	XF	Unc	BU
2002	—	—	—	—	0.50	0.75
2002 Proof	500	Value: 1.00				

KM# 146.2 10 CENTS

Copper Plated Steel **Note:** Reduced size.

Date	Mintage	F	VF	XF	Unc	BU
2002	—	—	—	—	0.25	0.50
2002 Proof	500	Value: 2.00				

KM# 167 25 CENTS

Copper Plated Steel

Date	Mintage	F	VF	XF	Unc	BU
2002	—	—	—	—	0.50	0.75
2002 Proof	500	Value: 3.00				

KM# 164 DOLLAR

Nickel Clad Steel **Shape:** 7-sided

Date	Mintage	F	VF	XF	Unc	BU
2002	—	—	—	—	1.00	1.50
2002 Proof	500	Value: 4.00				

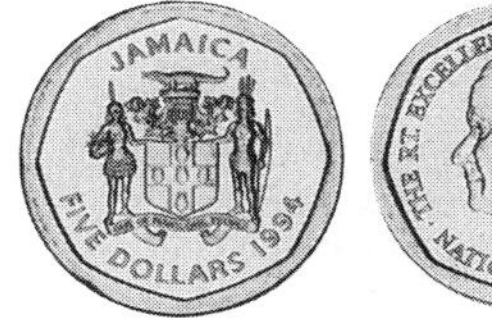

KM# 163 5 DOLLARS

Steel **Note:** National Hero - Norman Manley

Date	Mintage	F	VF	XF	Unc	BU
2002	—	—	—	—	2.50	3.50
2002 Proof	500	Value: 5.00				

KM# 181 10 DOLLARS

Stainless Steel **Obv:** National arms **Rev:** Portrait of George William Gordon **Shape:** Scalloped

Date	Mintage	F	VF	XF	Unc	BU
2002	—	—	—	—	3.00	4.00
2002 Proof	500	Value: 9.00				

KM# 182 20 DOLLARS

Ring Composition: Brass **Center Composition:** Copper-Nickel, 23 mm. **Obv:** National arms, denomination above **Rev:** Marcus Garvey **Edge:** Reeded

Date	Mintage	F	VF	XF	Unc	BU
2002	—	—	—	—	3.00	4.00
2002 Proof	500	Value: 15.00				

KM# 186 25 DOLLARS

28.2800 g., 0.9250 Silver 0.841 oz. ASW, 38.6 mm. **Subject:** UNICEF **Obv:** National arms **Rev:** Two boys above "Pals" **Edge:** Reeded

Date	Mintage	F	VF	XF	Unc	BU
2001 Proof	—	Value: 50.00				

KM# 185 25 DOLLARS

28.2800 g., 0.9250 Silver 0.841 oz. ASW, 38.6 mm. **Subject:** IAAF World Junior Championships **Obv:** National arms and denomination **Rev:** Female runner **Edge:** Reeded

Date	Mintage	F	VF	XF	Unc	BU
2002 Proof	5,500	Value: 50.00				

KM# 184 50 DOLLARS

28.4500 g., 0.9250 Silver .8461 oz. ASW, 38.6 mm. **Subject:** Millennium **Obv:** National arms **Rev:** Family and radiant sun **Edge:** Reeded

Date	Mintage	F	VF	XF	Unc	BU
ND(2002) Proof	5,000	Value: 50.00				

PROOF SETS

KM#	Date	Mintage	Identification	Issue Price	Mkt Val
PS33	2002 (8)	500	KM#64, 146.2, 163, 164, 167, 181, 182, 185	99.00	—

JAPAN

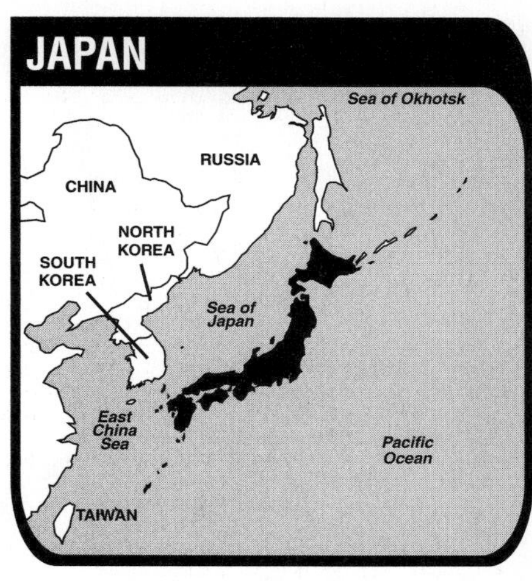

Japan, a constitutional monarchy situated off the east coast of Asia, has an area of 145,809 sq. mi. (377,835 sq. km.) and a population of 123.2 million. Capital: Tokyo. Japan, one of the major industrial nations of the world, exports machinery, motor vehicles, electronics and chemicals.

Japanese coinage of concern to this catalog includes those issued for the Ryukyu Islands (also called Liuchu), a chain of islands extending southwest from Japan toward Taiwan (Formosa), before the Japanese government converted the islands into a prefecture under the name Okinawa. Many of the provinces of Japan issued their own definitive coinage under the Shogunate.

RULERS

Emperors

Akihito (Heisei), 1989-

Years 1 – 平成

NOTE: The personal name of the emperor is followed by the name that he chose for his regnal era.

MONETARY UNITS

Rin 厘

Sen 銭

Yen 円 or 圓 or 圓

EMPIRE

REFORM COINAGE

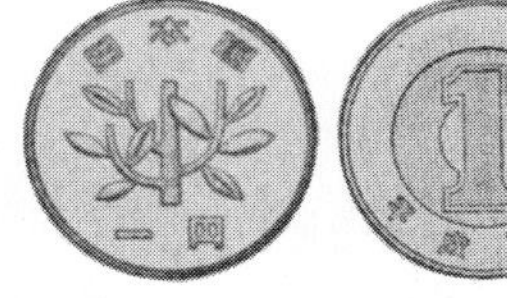

Y# 95.2 YEN

1.0000 g., Aluminum **Ruler:** Akihito (Heisei)

Date	Mintage	VG	F	VF	XF	BU
Yr.13(2001)	7,786,000	—	—	—	—	0.50
Yr.13(2001) Proof	238,000	Value: 3.00				
Yr.15(2003) Proof	275,000	Value: 3.00				
Yr.16(2004)	—	—	—	—	—	0.50
Yr.16(2004) Proof	273,000	Value: 3.00				

Y# 96.2 5 YEN

Brass **Ruler:** Akihito (Heisei)

Date	Mintage	F	VF	XF	Unc	BU
Yr.13(2001)	77,787,000	—	—	—	—	0.35
Yr.13(2001) Proof	238,000	Value: 1.75				
Yr.14(2002)	143,420,000	—	—	—	—	0.35
Yr.14(2002) Proof	242,000	Value: 1.75				
Yr.15(2003)	102,131,000	—	—	—	—	0.35
Yr.15(2003) Proof	275,000	Value: 1.75				
Yr.16(2004)	—	—	—	—	—	0.35
Yr.16(2004) Proof	273,000	Value: 1.75				

Y# 97.2 10 YEN
4.5000 g., Bronze **Ruler:** Akihito (Heisei)

Date	Mintage	F	VF	XF	Unc	BU
Yr.13(2001)	541,786,000	—	—	—	—	0.45
Yr.13(2001) Proof	238,000	Value: 1.75				
Yr.14(2002)	455,425,000	—	—	—	—	0.45
Yr.14(2002) Proof	242,000	Value: 1.75				
Yr.15(2003)	551,131,000	—	—	—	—	0.45
Yr.15(2003) Proof	275,000	Value: 1.75				
Yr.16(2004)	—	—	—	—	—	0.45
Yr.16(2004) Proof	273,000	Value: 1.75				

Y# 101.2 50 YEN
Copper-Nickel **Ruler:** Akihito (Heisei)

Date	Mintage	VG	F	VF	XF	BU
Yr.13(2001)	7,786,000	—	—	—	—	3.00
Yr.13(2001) Proof	238,000	Value: 4.00				
Yr.14(2002)	11,425,000	—	—	—	—	5.00
Yr.14(2002) Proof	242,000	Value: 7.00				
Yr.15(2003)	10,131,000	—	—	—	—	5.00
Yr.15(2003) Proof	275,000	Value: 7.00				
Yr.16(2004)	—	—	—	—	—	5.00
Yr.16(2004) Proof	273,000	Value: 7.00				

Y# 98.2 100 YEN
9.8000 g., Copper-Nickel **Ruler:** Akihito (Heisei)

Date	Mintage	VG	F	VF	XF	BU
Yr.13(2001)	7,786,000	—	—	—	—	7.50
Yr.13(2001) Proof	238,000	Value: 10.00				
Yr.14(2002)	10,425,000	—	—	—	—	5.00
Yr.14(2002) Proof	242,000	Value: 8.00				
Yr.15(2003)	98,131,000	—	—	—	—	2.00
Yr.15(2003) Proof	275,000	Value: 5.00				
Yr.16(2004)	—	—	—	—	—	2.00
Yr.16(2004) Proof	273,000	Value: 5.00				

Y# 125 500 YEN
7.0000 g., Nickel-Brass, 26.5 mm. **Ruler:** Akihito (Heisei) **Obv:** Pawlownia flower and highlighted legends **Rev:** Denomination with latent denomination in the zeros **Edge:** Slanted reeding

Date	Mintage	VG	F	VF	XF	BU
Yr.13(2001)	607,803,000	—	—	—	—	9.00
Yr.13(2001) Proof	238,000	Value: 15.00				
Yr.14(2002)	504,419,000	—	—	—	—	9.00
Yr.14(2002) Proof	242,000	Value: 15.00				
Yr.15(2003)	438,130,000	—	—	—	—	9.00
Yr.15(2003) Proof	275,000	Value: 15.00				
Yr.16(2004)	—	—	—	—	—	9.00
Yr.16(2004) Proof	273,000	Value: 15.00				

Y# 126 500 YEN
7.0000 g., Copper-Zinc-Nickel, 26.5 mm. **Ruler:** Akihito (Heisei) **Subject:** World Cup Soccer - Europe & Africa **Obv:** Four players and map background **Rev:** Games logo **Edge:** Reeded

Date	Mintage	VG	F	VF	XF	BU
Yr.14(2002)	10,000,000	—	—	—	—	10.00

Y# 127 500 YEN
7.0000 g., Copper-Zinc-Nickel, 26.5 mm. **Ruler:** Akihito (Heisei) **Subject:** World Cup Soccer - Asia & Oceania **Obv:** Three players and map background **Rev:** Games logo **Edge:** Reeded

Date	Mintage	VG	F	VF	XF	BU
Yr. 14(2002)	10,000,000	—	—	—	—	11.50

Y# 128 500 YEN
7.0000 g., Copper-Zinc-Nickel, 26.5 mm. **Ruler:** Akihito (Heisei) **Subject:** World Cup Soccer - North & South America **Obv:** Four players and map background **Rev:** Games logo **Edge:** Reeded

Date	Mintage	VG	F	VF	XF	BU
Yr. 14 (2002)	10,000,000	—	—	—	—	11.50

Y# 133 500 YEN
7.0000 g., Copper-Zinc-Nickel, 26.5 mm. **Ruler:** Akihito (Heisei) **Subject:** Expo 2005 - Aichi, Japan **Obv:** Pacific map **Rev:** Expo logo

Date	Mintage	F	VF	XF	Unc	BU
Yr. 17(2005)	8,241,000	—	—	—	—	11.50

Y# 134 500 YEN
15.6000 g., 0.9990 Silver 0.501 oz. ASW, 28 mm. **Ruler:** Akihito (Heisei) **Subject:** Chubu National Airport **Obv:** Aircraft wing in flight over airport **Rev:** Aircraft silhouettes over maps

Date	Mintage	F	VF	XF	Unc	BU
Yr. 17(2005)	50,000	—	—	—	—	75.00

Y# 129 1000 YEN
31.1000 g., 0.9990 Silver 0.9989 oz. ASW, 40 mm. **Ruler:** Akihito (Heisei) **Subject:** World Cup Soccer **Obv:** Trophy **Rev:** Games logo **Edge:** Reeded

Date	Mintage	F	VF	XF	Unc	BU
Yr. 14 (2002) Proof	100,000	Value: 90.00				

Y# 132 1000 YEN
31.1000 g., 0.9990 Silver 0.9989 oz. ASW **Ruler:** Akihito (Heisei) **Subject:** 50th Anniversary of the reversion of the Amami Islands **Obv:** Lily and bird in multicolor enamel **Rev:** Map of the Amami-shoto

Date	Mintage	F	VF	XF	Unc	BU
Yr 15 (2003) Proof	—	Value: 120				

Y# 131 1000 YEN
31.1000 g., 0.9990 Silver 0.9989 oz. ASW **Ruler:** Akihito (Heisei) **Subject:** 5th Winter Asian Games, Aomori **Obv:** Skier and skater **Rev:** Three red apples and multicolor games logo

Date	Mintage	VG	F	VF	XF	BU
Yr.15 (2003) Proof	50,000	Value: 300				

Y# 135 1000 YEN
31.1000 g., 0.9990 Silver 0.9989 oz. ASW, 40 mm. **Ruler:** Akihito (Heisei) **Subject:** Expo 2005 **Obv:** Blue and white enamel Pacific map in wreath **Rev:** Expo logo

Date	Mintage	F	VF	XF	Unc	BU
Yr. 16(2004) Proof	70,000	Value: 120				

Y# 130 10000 YEN
15.6000 g., 0.9990 Gold 0.501 oz. AGW, 26 mm. **Ruler:** Akihito (Heisei) **Subject:** World Cup Soccer **Obv:** Two soccer players **Rev:** Games logo **Edge:** Reeded

Date	Mintage	F	VF	XF	Unc	BU
Yr.14(2002) Proof	100,000	Value: 550				

Y# 136 10000 YEN
15.6000 g., 0.9990 Gold 0.501 oz. AGW, 26 mm. **Ruler:** Akihito (Heisei) **Subject:** Expo 2005 **Obv:** Two owls on globe **Rev:** Expo logo

Date	Mintage	F	VF	XF	Unc	BU
Yr. 16(2004) Proof	70,000	Value: 700				

MINT SETS

KM#	Date	Mintage	Identification	Issue Price	Mkt Val
MS125	2001 (6)	8,000	Y#95.2-98.2, 101.2, 125 Mint exhibition in Fukuoka	16.00	22.00
MS126	2001 (6)	85,000	Y#95.2-98.2, 101.2, 125 Osaka cherry blossoms box	17.00	22.00

KM#	Date	Mintage	Identification	Issue Price	Mkt Val
MS127	2001 (6)	10,000	Y#95.2-98.2, 101.2, 125 Hiroshima cherry blossoms box	17.00	25.00
MS128	2001 (6)	10,000	Y#95.2-98.2, 101.2, 125 12th Tokyo International Coin Convention	17.00	22.00
MS129	2001 (6)	5,000	Y#95.2-98.2, 101.2, 125 Beautiful Future Exposition	17.00	22.00
MS130	2001 (6)	8,000	Y#95.2-98.2, 101.2, 125 Kagoshima Coin and Stamp Show	17.00	22.00
MS131	2001 (6)	5,000	Y#95.2-98.2, 101.2, 125 Tokyo Mint Fair	17.00	25.00
MS132	2001 (6)	5,000	Y#95.2-98.2, 101.2, 125 Yamaguchi Mica Exposition	17.00	30.00
MS133	2001 (6)	250,000	Y#95.2-98.2, 101.2, 125 21st Century Commemorative Respect for the Aged	17.00	20.00
MS134	2001 (6)	200,000	Y#95.2-98.2, 101.2, 125 Ryukyu World Cultural Sites	17.00	20.00
MS135	2001 (6)	10,000	Y#95.2-98.2, 101.2, 125 Birthday folder	18.00	25.00
MS136	2001 (1)	7,000	Y#125 Mint Visit Commemorative	8.00	8.00
MS137	2001 (6)	300,000	Y#95.2-98.2, 101.2, 125 Mint Bureau Box	15.00	20.00
MS138	2001 (6)	3,000	Y#95.2-98.2, 101.2, 125 "Japan Coins"	17.00	22.00
MS139	2001 (2)	3,000	Y#96.2, 125 "Japan Coins" (short set)	8.50	11.00
MS140	2001 (6)	150,000	Y#95.2-98.2, 101.2, 125 World Intangible Heritage - Nogaku	17.00	22.00
MS141	2002 (1)	3,000	Y#125 Mint Visit Commemorative	7.50	8.00
MS142	2002 (6)	7,000	Y#95.2-98.2, 102.2, 125 Birthday folder	18.00	20.00
MS143	2002 (2)	4,000	Y#96.2, 125. "Japan Coins" (short set)	8.50	11.00
MS144	2002 (6)	6,000	Y#95.2-98.2, 101.2, 125 "Japan Coins"	17.00	18.00
MS145	2002 (6)	4,000	Y#95.2-98.2, 101.2, 125 Mint exhibition in Takamatsu	16.00	25.00
MS146	2002 (6)	80,000	Y#95.2-98.2, 101.2, 125 Osaka cherry blossoms	16.00	16.00
MS147	2002 (6)	10,000	Y#95.2-98.2, 101.2, 125 Hiroshima cherry blossoms	16.00	16.00
MS148	2002 (6)	10,000	Y#95.2-98.2, 101.2, 125 13th Tokyo Int'l Coin Convention	16.00	16.00
MS149	2002 (6)	6,000	Y#95.2-98.2, 101.2, 125 Mint exhibition in Sendai	16.00	18.00
MS150	2002 (6)	194,000	Y#95.2-98.2, 101.2, 125 Respect for the Aged	19.00	16.00
MS151	2002 (6)	6,000	Y#95.2-98.2, 101.2, 125 Matsuyama Coin and Stamp Show	16.00	18.00
MS152	2002 (6)	3,000	Y395.2-98.2, 101.2, 125 Tokyo Mint Fair	16.00	150
MS153	2002 (6)	2,000	Y#95.2-98.2, 101,2, 125 Birthday folder (with sound recording function)	25.00	30.00
MS154	2002 (6)	214,800	Y395.2-98.2, 101.2, 125 Mint Bureau box	15.00	16.00
MS155	2003 (6)	8,000	Y#95.2-98.2, 101,2, 125 "Japan Coins"	17.00	15.00
MS156	2003 (6)	7,000	Y#95.2-98.2, 101.2, 125 Birthday folder	18.00	15.00
MS157	2003 (6)	7,000	Y#95.2-98.2, 101.2, 125 Birthday folder (with sound recording function)	25.00	20.00
MS158	2003 (6)	6,000	Y#95.2-98.2, 101.2, 125 Mint exhibition in Okayama	16.00	22.00
MS159	2003 (6)	80,000	Y#95.2-98.2, 101.2, 125 Osaka cherry blossoms	16.00	15.00
MS160	2003 (6)	10,000	Y#95.2-98.2, 101.2, 125 Hiroshima cherry blossoms	16.00	15.00
MS161	2003 (6)	10,000	Y#95.2-98.2, 101.2, 125 14th Tokyo Int'l Coin Convention	16.00	15.00
MS162	2003 (6)	6,000	Y#95.2-98.2, 101.2, 125 First Osaka Coin Show	16.00	15.00
MS163	2003 (6)	235,000	Y#95.2-98.2, 101.2, 125 Birth of Astro Boy	19.00	15.00
MS164	2003 (6)	130,000	Y#95.2-98.2, 101.2, 125 Respect for the Aged	19.00	15.00
MS165	2003 (6)	5,000	Y#95.2-98.2, 101.2, 125 Tokyo Mint Fair - Mint Collection in Omote-sando	17.00	22.00
MS166	2003 (6)	5,000	Y#95.2-98.2, 101.2, 125 Mint exhibition in Sapporo	17.00	20.00
MS167	2003 (6)	5,000	Y#95.2-98.2, 101.2, 125 Yonago Coin and Stamp Show	17.00	17.50
MS168	2003 (6)	205,000	Y#95.2-98.2, 101.2, 125 Mint Bureau box	17.00	15.00
MS169	2003 (6)	100,000	Y#95.2-98.2, 101.2, 125 2003 Central League Champions - Hanshin Tigers	22.00	25.00
MS170	2003 (6)	100,000	Y#95.2-98.2, 101.2, 125 2003 Pacific league Champions - Fukuoka Daiei Hawks	22.00	15.00
MS172	2004	—	Y#95.2-98.2, 101.2, 125 Japan Coins	19.00	—
MS173	2004 (6)	—	Y#95.2-98.2, 101.2, 125 Birthday folder	20.00	—
MS174	2004 (6)	—	Y#95.2-98.2, 101.2, 125 Birthday folder (with sound recording function)	28.50	—
MS175	2004 (6)	4,000	Y#95.2-98.2, 101.2, 125 Mint exhibition in Fukui	18.00	—
MS176	2004 (6)	70,000	Y#95.2-98.2, 101.2, 125 Osaka cherry blossoms	18.00	—
MS177	2004 (6)	10,000	Y#95.2-98.2, 101.2, 125 Hiroshima cherry blossoms	18.00	—
MS178	2004 (6)	10,000	Y#95.2-98.2, 101.2, 125 15th Tokyo Int'l Coin Convention	18.00	—
MS179	2004 (6)	6,000	Y#95.2-98.2, 101.2, 125 Second Osaka Coin Show	18.00	—
MS180	2004 (6)	120,000	Y#95.2-98.2, 101.2, 125 World Intangible Heritage series: Bunraku puppets	19.00	—
MS181	2004 (6)	130,000	Y#95.2-98.2, 101.2, 125 Respect for the Aged	20.00	—
MS182	2004 (6)	5,000	Y#95.2-98.2, 101.2, 125 Mint exhibition in Tosu	18.00	—
MS183	2004 (6)	200,000	Y#95.2-98.2, 101.2, 125 Mint Bureau box	16.00	—
MS184	2004 (6)	5,000	Y#95.2-98.2, 101.2, 125 Gifu Coin and Stamp Show	17.00	—
MS185	2004 (6)	200,000	Y#95.2-98.2, 101.2, 125 30th Birthday of Hello Kitty (cartoon character)	22.00	—
MS186	2004 (6)	5,000	Y#95.2-98.2, 101.2, 125 Tokyo Mint Fair - 40th Anniversary - Issue of Commemorative Coins	17.00	—
MS187	2004 (6)	50,000	Y#95.2-98.2, 101.2, 125 2004 Central League Champions - Chunichi Dragons	21.00	—
MS188	2004 (6)	50,000	Y#95.2-98.2, 101.2, 125 2004 Pacific League Champions - Seibu Lions	21.00	—

PROOF SETS

KM#	Date	Mintage	Identification	Issue Price	Mkt Val
PS32	2001 (6)	138,000	Y#95.2-98.2, 101.2, 125 Mint Bureau Box	62.50	80.00
PS33	2001 (6)	100,000	Y#95.2-98.2, 101.2, 125 Old Type Coin Series	62.50	80.00
PS34	2002 (6)	144,000	Y#95.2-98.2, 101.2, 125 Mint Bureau box	62.50	55.00
PS35	2002 (6)	3,000	Y#95.2-98.2, 101.2, 125 15th Anniversary of Proof Sets	62.50	100
PS36	2002 (6)	95,000	Y#95.2-98.2, 101.2, 125 Techno medal set	62.50	55.00
PS37	2002 (3)	200,000	Y#126-128 World Cup	26.00	20.00
PS38	2002 (2)	50,000	Y#129, 130 World Cup	385	550
PS39	2003 (6)	105,000	Y#95.2-98.2, 101.2, 125 Mint Bureau box, with date plaquette	67.50	70.00
PSA40	2003 (6)	—	Y#95.2-98.2, 101.2, 125 Mint Bureau Box without Date Plaquette	66.00	70.00
PS40	2003 (6)	90,000	Y#95.2-98.2, 101.2, 125 Astro Boy	115	100
PS41	2003 (6)	5,000	Y#95.2-98.2, 101.2, 125 Tokyo Mint Fair - Mint Collection in Omote-Sando	67.50	100
PS42	2003 (6)	70,000	Y#95.2-98.2, 101.2, 125 Mickey Mouse	125	125
PS43	2003 (6)	5,000	Y#95.2-98.2, 101.2, 125 400th Anniversary - Establishment of Government in Edo	67.50	125
PS44	2004 (6)	108,000	Y#95.2-98.2, 101.2, 125 Mint Bureau box with date plaquette	71.00	—
PS45	2004 (6)	—	Y#95.2-98.2, 101.2, 125 Mint Bureau box without date plaquette	70.00	—
PS46	2004 (6)	60,000	Y#95.2-98.2, 101.2, 125 75th Anniversary - Pro Baseball	120	—
PS47	2004 (6)	50,000	Y#95.2-98.2, 101.2, 125 Techno Medal Series 2	71.00	—
PS48	2004 (6)	50,000	Y#95.2-98.2, 101.2, 125 30th Birthday of Hello Kitty (cartoon character)	120	—
PS49	2004 (6)	5,000	Y#95.2-98.2, 101.2, 125 Tokyo Mint Fair - 40th Anniversary - Issue of Commemorative Coins	71.00	—

JERSEY

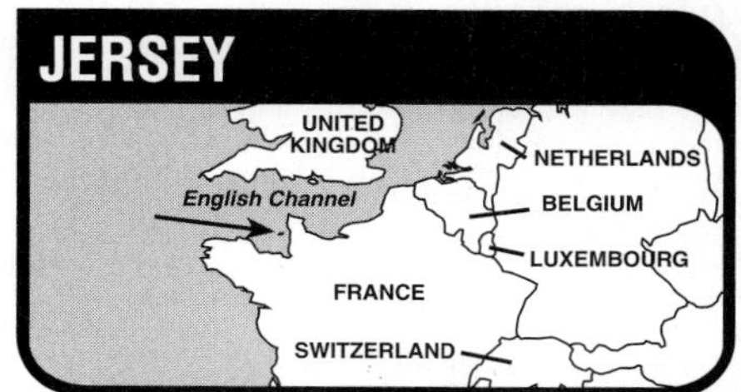

The Bailiwick of Jersey, a British Crown dependency located in the English Channel 12 miles (19 km.) west of Normandy, France, has an area of 45 sq. mi. (117 sq. km.) and a population of 74,000. Capital: St. Helier. The economy is based on agriculture and cattle breeding – the importation of cattle is prohibited to protect the purity of the island's world-famous strain of milk cows.

RULERS

British

BRITISH DEPENDENCY

DECIMAL COINAGE

100 New Pence = 1 Pound

Many of the following coins are also struck in silver, gold, and platinum for collectors

KM# 103 PENNY

Copper Plated Steel **Obv:** Portrait of Queen Elizabeth II **Obv. Designer:** Rank-Broadley

Date	Mintage	F	VF	XF	Unc	BU
2002	1,500,000	—	—	0.10	0.50	—
2003	1,485,000	—	—	0.10	0.50	—

KM# 104 2 PENCE

Copper Plated Steel **Obv:** Portrait of Queen Elizabeth II **Obv. Designer:** Rank-Broadley **Rev:** L'Hermitage, St. Helier

Date	Mintage	F	VF	XF	Unc	BU
2002	1,250,000	—	—	0.15	0.50	—
2003	10,000	—	—	0.15	0.50	—

KM# 105 5 PENCE

Copper-Nickel **Obv:** Portrait of Queen Elizabeth II **Obv. Designer:** Rank-Broadley

Date	Mintage	F	VF	XF	Unc	BU
2002	1,200,000	—	—	0.15	0.50	—
2003	1,002,000	—	—	0.15	0.50	—

KM# 106 10 PENCE

Copper-Nickel **Obv:** Portrait of Queen Elizabeth II **Obv. Designer:** Rank-Broadley

Date	Mintage	F	VF	XF	Unc	BU
2002	500,000	—	—	—	1.00	—
2003	10,000	—	—	—	1.00	—

KM# 57.2 10 PENCE

Copper-Nickel **Obv:** Bust of Queen Elizabeth II right **Rev:** La Houque Bie, Faldouet, St. Martin **Note:** Reduced size.

Date	Mintage	F	VF	XF	Unc	BU
2002	—	—	—	—	1.00	—

KM# 66 20 PENCE

Copper-Nickel **Subject:** 100th Anniversary of Lighthouse at Corbiere **Obv:** Bust of Queen Elizabeth II right **Rev:** Date below bust **Rev. Designer:** Robert Lowe **Shape:** 7-sided

Date	Mintage	F	VF	XF	Unc	BU
2002	—	—	—	0.50	1.00	—

KM# 107 20 PENCE

5.8300 g., 0.9250 Silver .1734 oz. ASW **Obv:** Portrait of Queen Elizabeth II **Obv. Designer:** Rank-Broadley

Date	Mintage	F	VF	XF	Unc	BU
2002	515,000	—	—	—	1.00	—
2003	10,000	—	—	—	1.00	—

KM# 123 50 PENCE
8.0000 g., Copper-Nickel, 27.3 mm. **Subject:** Golden Coronation Anniversary **Obv:** Queen's portrait **Rev:** Coronation scene **Edge:** Plain **Shape:** 7-sided

Date	Mintage	F	VF	XF	Unc	BU
2003	10,000	—	—	—	2.50	—

KM# 123a 50 PENCE
8.0000 g., 0.9250 Silver 0.2379 oz. ASW, 27.3 mm. **Subject:** Golden Coronation Anniversary **Obv:** Queen's portrait **Rev:** Coronation scene **Edge:** Plain **Shape:** 7-sided

Date	Mintage	F	VF	XF	Unc	BU
2003 Proof	15,000	Value: 25.00				

KM# 108 50 PENCE
Copper-Nickel **Obv:** Bust of Queen Elizabeth II right **Obv. Designer:** Rank-Broadley

Date	Mintage	F	VF	XF	Unc	BU
2003	—	—	—	1.00	2.50	—

KM# 101 POUND
Nickel-Brass **Obv:** Portrait of Queen Elizabeth II **Obv. Designer:** Rank-Broadley **Rev:** Schooner, Resolute **Rev. Designer:** Robert Evans **Edge Lettering:** CAESAREA INSULA

Date	Mintage	F	VF	XF	Unc	BU
2003	10,000	—	—	—	4.00	—

KM# 102 2 POUNDS
Bi-Metallic Copper-Nickel center in Brass ring **Obv:** Portrait of Queen Elizabeth II **Obv. Designer:** Rank-Broadley **Rev:** Latent image value in circle of arms **Edge Lettering:** CAESARA INSULA

Date	Mintage	F	VF	XF	Unc	BU
2003	10,000	—	—	—	10.00	—

KM# 111 5 POUNDS
28.2800 g., Copper-Nickel, 38.6 mm. **Subject:** Princess Diana **Obv:** Queen's portrait **Rev:** Diana's cameo portrait above people **Edge:** Reeded

Date	Mintage	F	VF	XF	Unc	BU
2002	—	—	—	—	13.50	—

KM# 111a 5 POUNDS
28.2800 g., 0.9250 Silver 0.841 oz. ASW, 38.6 mm. **Subject:** Princess Dana **Obv:** Queen's portrait **Rev:** Diana's cameo portrait above people **Edge:** Reeded

Date	Mintage	F	VF	XF	Unc	BU
2002 Proof	20,000	Value: 45.00				

KM# 111b 5 POUNDS
39.9400 g., 0.9167 Gold 1.1771 oz. AGW, 38.6 mm. **Subject:** Princess Diana **Obv:** Queen's portrait **Rev:** Diana's cameo portrait above people **Edge:** Reeded

Date	Mintage	F	VF	XF	Unc	BU
2002 Proof	100	Value: 850				

KM# 113 5 POUNDS
28.2800 g., Copper-Nickel, 38.6 mm. **Subject:** Queen Mother **Obv:** Queen's portrait **Rev:** Queen Mother's portrait circa 1918 **Edge:** Reeded

Date	Mintage	F	VF	XF	Unc	BU
2002	—	—	—	—	13.50	—

KM# 113a 5 POUNDS
28.2800 g., 0.9250 Silver 0.841 oz. ASW, 38.6 mm. **Subject:** Queen Mother **Obv:** Queen's portrait **Rev:** Queen Mother's portrait circa 1918 **Edge:** Reeded

Date	Mintage	F	VF	XF	Unc	BU
2002 Proof	15,000	Value: 50.00				

KM# 113b 5 POUNDS
39.9400 g., 0.9166 Gold 1.177 oz. AGW, 38.6 mm. **Subject:** Queen Mother **Obv:** Queen's portrait **Rev:** Queen Mother's portrait circa 1918 **Edge:** Reeded

Date	Mintage	F	VF	XF	Unc	BU
2002 Proof	250	Value: 775				

KM# 115 5 POUNDS
28.2800 g., Copper-Nickel, 38.6 mm. **Subject:** Golden Jubilee **Obv:** Queen's portrait **Rev:** Abbey procession scene **Rev. Designer:** Robert Evans **Edge:** Reeded

Date	Mintage	F	VF	XF	Unc	BU
2002	—	—	—	—	13.50	—

KM# 115a 5 POUNDS
28.2800 g., 0.9250 Silver 0.841 oz. ASW, 38.6 mm. **Subject:** Golden Jubilee **Obv:** Queen's portrait **Rev:** Abbey procession scene **Edge:** Reeded

Date	Mintage	F	VF	XF	Unc	BU
2002 Proof	20,000	Value: 50.00				

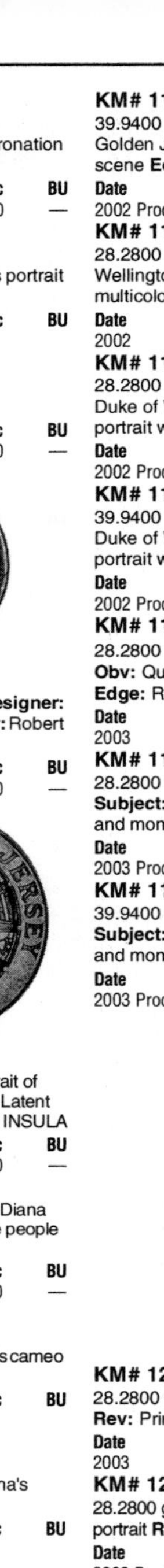

KM# 115b 5 POUNDS
39.9400 g., 0.9166 Gold 1.177 oz. AGW, 38.6 mm. **Subject:** Golden Jubilee **Obv:** Queen's portrait **Rev:** Abbey procession scene **Edge:** Reeded

Date	Mintage	F	VF	XF	Unc	BU
2002 Proof	100	Value: 775				

KM# 117 5 POUNDS
28.2800 g., Copper-Nickel, 38.6 mm. **Subject:** Duke of Wellington **Obv:** Queen's portrait **Rev:** Wellington's portrait with multicolor infantry scene **Edge:** Reeded

Date	Mintage	F	VF	XF	Unc	BU
2002	—	—	—	—	13.50	—

KM# 117a 5 POUNDS
28.2800 g., 0.9250 Silver 0.841 oz. ASW, 38.6 mm. **Subject:** Duke of Wellington **Obv:** Queen's portrait **Rev:** Wellington's portrait with multicolor infantry scene **Edge:** Reeded

Date	Mintage	F	VF	XF	Unc	BU
2002 Proof	15,000	Value: 50.00				

KM# 117b 5 POUNDS
39.9400 g., 0.9166 Gold 1.177 oz. AGW, 38.6 mm. **Subject:** Duke of Wellington **Obv:** Queen's portrait **Rev:** Wellington's portrait with multicolor infantry scene **Edge:** Reeded

Date	Mintage	F	VF	XF	Unc	BU
2002 Proof	200	Value: 775				

KM# 119 5 POUNDS
28.2800 g., Copper-Nickel, 38.6 mm. **Subject:** Golden Jubilee **Obv:** Queen's portrait **Rev:** Honor guard and memorial **Edge:** Reeded

Date	Mintage	F	VF	XF	Unc	BU
2003	—	—	—	—	13.50	—

KM# 119a 5 POUNDS
28.2800 g., 0.9250 Silver 0.841 oz. ASW, 38.6 mm. **Subject:** Golden Jubilee **Obv:** Queen's portrait **Rev:** Honor guard and monument **Edge:** Reeded

Date	Mintage	F	VF	XF	Unc	BU
2003 Proof	20,000	Value: 50.00				

KM# 119b 5 POUNDS
39.9400 g., 0.9166 Gold 1.177 oz. AGW, 38.6 mm. **Subject:** Golden Jubilee **Obv:** Queen's portrait **Rev:** Honor guard and monument **Edge:** Reeded

Date	Mintage	F	VF	XF	Unc	BU
2003 Proof	250	Value: 775				

KM# 121 5 POUNDS
28.2800 g., Copper-Nickel, 38.6 mm. **Obv:** Queen's portrait **Rev:** Prince William wearing coat and tie **Edge:** Reeded

Date	Mintage	F	VF	XF	Unc	BU
2003	—	—	—	—	16.50	—

KM# 121a 5 POUNDS
28.2800 g., 0.9250 Silver 0.841 oz. ASW, 38.6 mm. **Obv:** Queen's portrait **Rev:** Prince William wearing coat and tie **Edge:** Reeded

Date	Mintage	F	VF	XF	Unc	BU
2003 Proof	5,000	Value: 47.50				

KM# 121b 5 POUNDS
39.9400 g., 0.9166 Gold 1.177 oz. AGW, 38.6 mm. **Obv:** Queen's portrait **Rev:** Prince William wearing coat and tie **Edge:** Reeded

Date	Mintage	F	VF	XF	Unc	BU
2003 Proof	200	Value: 850				

KM# 124a 5 POUNDS
28.2800 g., 0.9250 Silver 0.841 oz. ASW, 38.6 mm.

Date	Mintage	F	VF	XF	Unc	BU
2004 Proof	10,000	Value: 85.00				

KM# 124b 5 POUNDS
39.9400 g., 0.9167 Gold 1.1771 oz. AGW, 38.6 mm.

Date	Mintage	F	VF	XF	Unc	BU
2004 Proof	500	Value: 1,000				

KM# 126 5 POUNDS
28.2800 g., Copper-Nickel, 38.6 mm. **Obv:** Queen Elizabeth II **Rev:** Charge of the Light Brigade scene with one blue uniform behind the Earl of Cardigan **Edge:** Reeded

Date	Mintage	F	VF	XF	Unc	BU
2004	—	—	—	—	25.00	—

KM# 126a 5 POUNDS
28.2800 g., 0.9250 Silver 0.841 oz. ASW, 38.6 mm. **Obv:** Queen Elizabeth II **Rev:** Charge of the Light Brigade scene with one blue uniform behind the Earl of Cardigan **Edge:** Reeded

Date	Mintage	F	VF	XF	Unc	BU
2004 Proof	10,000	Value: 85.00				

KM# 126b 5 POUNDS
39.9400 g., 0.9166 Gold 1.177 oz. AGW, 38.6 mm. **Obv:** Queen Elizabeth II **Rev:** Charge of the Light Brigade scene with one blue uniform behind the Earl of Cardigan **Edge:** Reeded

Date	Mintage	F	VF	XF	Unc	BU
2004 Proof	500	Value: 1,000				

KM# 124 5 POUNDS
28.2800 g., Copper-Nickel, 38.6 mm. **Obv:** Queen Elizabeth II **Rev:** British Horsa gliders in flight **Edge:** Reeded **Note:** D-Day

Date	Mintage	F	VF	XF	Unc	BU
2004	—	—	—	—	15.00	—

KM# 127 5 POUNDS
Copper Nickel **Ruler:** Elizabeth II **Subject:** Battle of Trafalgar

Date	Mintage	F	VF	XF	Unc	BU
2005	—	—	—	—	7.50	—

KM# 128 5 POUNDS
Copper Nickel **Ruler:** Elizabeth II **Subject:** 60th Anniversary - End of WW II

Date	Mintage	F	VF	XF	Unc	BU
2005	—	—	—	—	7.50	—

KM# 128a 5 POUNDS
28.2800 g., 0.9250 Silver 0.841 oz. ASW, 38.6 mm. **Ruler:** Elizabeth II **Subject:** WWII Liberation **Obv:** Elizabeth II by Broadley **Rev:** Big Ben Tower **Edge:** Reeded

Date	Mintage	F	VF	XF	Unc	BU
2005 Proof	5,000	Value: 85.00				

KM# 128b 5 POUNDS
39.9400 g., 0.9167 Gold 1.1771 oz. AGW, 38.6 mm. **Ruler:** Elizabeth II **Subject:** WWII Liberation **Obv:** Elizabeth II by Broadley **Rev:** Big Ben Tower **Edge:** Reeded

Date	Mintage	F	VF	XF	Unc	BU
2005 Proof	150	Value: 1,000				

KM# 129 5 POUNDS
Copper Nickel **Ruler:** Elizabeth II **Subject:** WW II Liberation **Rev:** Returning evacuees **Edge:** Reeded

Date	Mintage	F	VF	XF	Unc	BU
2005	—	—	—	—	7.50	—

KM# 129a 5 POUNDS
39.9400 g., 0.9167 Gold 1.1771 oz. AGW, 38.6 mm. **Ruler:** Elizabeth II **Subject:** WWII Liberation **Obv:** Elizabeth II by Broadley **Rev:** Returning evacuees **Edge:** Reeded

Date	Mintage	F	VF	XF	Unc	BU
2005 Proof	150	Value: 1,000				

KM# 114 25 POUNDS
7.9800 g., 0.9166 Gold 0.2352 oz. AGW, 22 mm. **Subject:** Queen Mother **Obv:** Queen's portrait **Rev:** Queen Mother's portrait circa 1918 **Edge:** Reeded

Date	Mintage	F	VF	XF	Unc	BU
2002 Proof	2,500	Value: 300				

KM# 116 25 POUNDS
7.9800 g., 0.9166 Gold 0.2352 oz. AGW, 22 mm. **Subject:** Golden Jubilee **Obv:** Queen's portrait **Rev:** Abbey procession scene **Edge:** Reeded

Date	Mintage	F	VF	XF	Unc	BU
2002 Proof	2,500	Value: 300				

KM# 118 25 POUNDS
7.9800 g., 0.9166 Gold 0.2352 oz. AGW, 22 mm. **Subject:** Duke of Wellington **Obv:** Queen's portrait **Rev:** Wellington's portrait with infantry scene **Edge:** Reeded

Date	Mintage	F	VF	XF	Unc	BU
2002 Proof	2,500	Value: 300				

KM# 112 25 POUNDS
7.9800 g., 0.9167 Gold 0.2352 oz. AGW, 22.05 mm. **Subject:** Princess Diana **Obv:** Queen's portrait **Rev:** Diana's portrait **Edge:** Reeded

Date	Mintage	F	VF	XF	Unc	BU
2002 Proof	2,500	Value: 290				

KM# 120 25 POUNDS
7.9800 g., 0.9166 Gold 0.2352 oz. AGW, 22 mm. **Subject:** Golden Jubilee **Obv:** Queen's portrait **Rev:** Honor guard and monument **Edge:** Reeded

Date	Mintage	F	VF	XF	Unc	BU
2003 Proof	5,000	Value: 300				

KM# 125 25 POUNDS
7.9800 g., 0.9167 Gold 0.2352 oz. AGW, 22 mm. **Obv:** Queen Elizabeth II **Rev:** British Horsa gliders in flight **Edge:** Reeded **Note:** D-Day

Date	Mintage	F	VF	XF	Unc	BU
2004 Proof	500	Value: 325				

KM# 122 50 POUNDS
1000.0000 g., 0.9250 Silver 29.7394 oz. ASW, 100 mm. **Obv:** Queen's portrait **Rev:** Prince William wearing coat and tie **Edge:** Reeded

Date	Mintage	F	VF	XF	Unc	BU
2003 Proof	500	Value: 995				

PIEFORTS

KM#	Date	Mintage	Identification	Mkt Val
P3	2002	100	5 Pounds. 0.9166 Gold. 56.5600 g. 38.6 mm. Queen's portrait. Abbey procession scene. Reeded edge. Underweight piefort	1,400

JORDAN

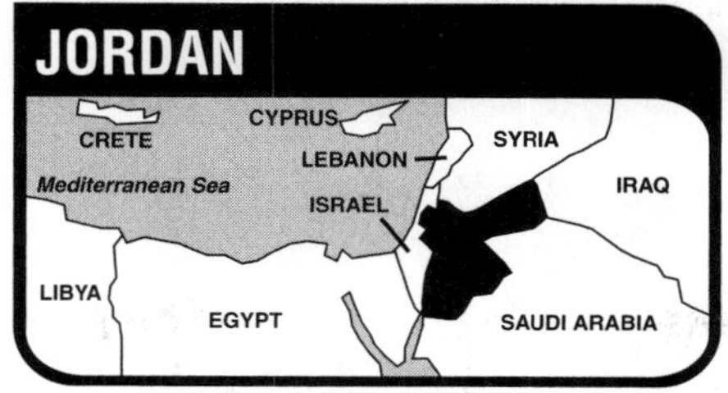

The Hashemite Kingdom of Jordan, a constitutional monarchy in southwest Asia, has an area of 37,738 sq. mi.(91,880 sq. km.) and a population of 3.5 million. Capital: Amman. Agriculture and tourism comprise Jordan's economic base. Chief exports are phosphates, tomatoes and oranges.

TITLES

المملكة الاردنية الهاشمية

el-Mamlaka(t)	el-Urduniya(t)	el-Hashemiya(t)

RULERS
Abdullah Ibn Al-Hussein, 1999-

MONETARY SYSTEM
Commencing 1992
100 Piastres = 1 Dinar

KINGDOM

DECIMAL COINAGE

KM# 74 10 PIASTRES
8.0000 g., Nickel Clad Steel, 27.9 mm. **Ruler:** Abdullah Ibn Al-Hussein **Obv:** King Abdullah II **Edge:** Milled

Date	Mintage	F	VF	XF	Unc	BU
AH1425-2004	—	—	—	—	4.00	5.00

KM# 83 1/4 DINAR
Nickel-Brass **Ruler:** Abdullah Ibn Al-Hussein **Obv:** King Abdullah II **Edge:** Plain

Date	Mintage	F	VF	XF	Unc	BU
AH1425-2004	—	—	—	—	3.00	4.00

KM# 75 3 DINARS
28.5000 g., Brass, 40 mm. **Subject:** Amman: Arabic Culture Capital **Obv:** King's portrait **Rev:** Building **Edge:** Milled

Date	Mintage	F	VF	XF	Unc	BU
AH1423//2002	2,000	—	—	—	40.00	—

KAZAKHSTAN

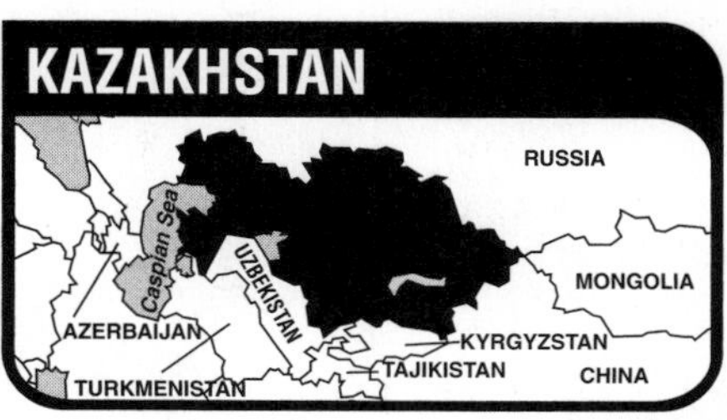

The Republic of Kazakhstan (formerly Kazakhstan S.S.R.) is bordered to the west by the Caspian Sea and Russia, to the north by Russia, in the east by the Peoples Republic of China and in the south by Uzbekistan and Kirghizia. It has an area of 1,049,155 sq. mi. (2,717,300 sq. km.) and a population of 16.7 million. Capital: Astana. Rich in mineral resources including coal, tungsten, copper, lead, zinc and manganese with huge oil and natural gas reserves. Agriculture is very important, (it previously represented 20 percent of the total arable acreage of the combined U.S.S.R.) Non-ferrous metallurgy, heavy engineering and chemical industries are leaders in its economy.

MONETARY SYSTEM
100 Tyin = 1 Tenge

REPUBLIC

DECIMAL COINAGE

KM# 23 TENGE
Brass **Obv:** National emblem **Rev:** Denomination

Date	Mintage	F	VF	XF	Unc	BU
2002	—	—	—	—	0.50	—
2004	—	—	—	—	0.50	—

KM# 64 2 TENGE
1.8200 g., Brass, 16 mm. **Obv:** National arms **Rev:** Value **Edge:** Plain

Date	Mintage	F	VF	XF	Unc	BU
2005	—	—	—	—	0.65	—

KM# 8 3 TENGE
Copper-Nickel

Date	Mintage	F	VF	XF	Unc	BU
2005	—	—	—	—	0.75	—

KM# 24 5 TENGE
Brass **Obv:** National emblem **Rev:** Denomination

Date	Mintage	F	VF	XF	Unc	BU
2002	—	—	—	—	0.50	—
2004	—	—	—	—	0.50	—

KM# 25 10 TENGE
Brass **Obv:** National emblem **Rev:** Denomination

Date	Mintage	F	VF	XF	Unc	BU
2002	—	—	—	—	0.75	—
2004	—	—	—	—	0.75	—

KM# 26 20 TENGE
Copper-Nickel **Obv:** National emblem **Rev:** Denomination

Date	Mintage	F	VF	XF	Unc	BU
2002	—	—	—	—	1.00	—
2004	—	—	—	—	1.00	—

KM# 40 50 TENGE
11.5000 g., Copper-Nickel, 31 mm. **Obv:** Eagle superimposed on ornate 10 **Edge:** Reeded and plain sections

Date	Mintage	F	VF	XF	Unc	BU
2001	—	—	—	—	4.00	5.00

KM# 41 50 TENGE
11.2000 g., Copper Nickel, 31.1 mm. **Subject:** Gabiden Mustafin **Obv:** National arms **Rev:** Mustafin's portrait **Edge:** Segmented reeding

Date	Mintage	F	VF	XF	Unc	BU
ND(2002)	—	—	—	—	4.00	5.00

KM# 27 50 TENGE
Copper-Nickel **Obv:** National emblem **Rev:** Denomination

Date	Mintage	F	VF	XF	Unc	BU
2002	—	—	—	—	2.00	—

KM# 65 50 TENGE
11.5000 g., Copper-Nickel, 31.1 mm. **Subject:** Alken Margulan **Obv:** National arms **Rev:** Portrait **Edge:** Segmented reeding

Date	Mintage	F	VF	XF	Unc	BU
2004	—	—	—	—	4.00	5.00

KM# 54 50 TENGE
11.5000 g., Copper-Nickel, 31.1 mm. **Obv:** National arms above value **Rev:** Painter Abylichan Kasteev (1904-1973) **Edge:** Reeded and plain sections

Date	Mintage	F	VF	XF	Unc	BU
2004	—	—	—	—	4.00	5.00

KM# 58 50 TENGE
11.5000 g., Copper-Nickel, 31.1 mm. **Subject:** 10th Anniversary of the Constitution **Obv:** National arms above value **Rev:** National arms above book **Edge:** Segmented reeding

Date	Mintage	F	VF	XF	Unc	BU
2005	—	—	—	—	4.00	5.00

KM# 39 100 TENGE
6.2300 g., Bi-Metallic Copper-Nickel center in Brass ring, 24.4 mm. **Obv:** National emblem **Rev:** Value **Edge:** Reeding over incuse value

Date	Mintage	F	VF	XF	Unc	BU
2002	—	—	—	—	3.50	4.50
2004	—	—	—	—	3.50	4.50

KM# 49 100 TENGE
6.4000 g., Bi-Metallic Copper-Nickel center in Brass ring, 24.5 mm. **Obv:** Stylized chicken **Rev:** Value **Edge:** Reeded and lettered

Date	Mintage	F	VF	XF	Unc	BU
2003	100,000	—	—	—	4.00	5.00

KM# 50 100 TENGE
6.4000 g., Bi-Metallic Copper-Nickel center in Brass ring, 24.5 mm. **Obv:** Stylized panther **Rev:** Value **Edge:** Reeded and lettered

Date	Mintage	F	VF	XF	Unc	BU
2003	100,000	—	—	—	4.00	5.00

KM# 51 100 TENGE
6.4000 g., Bi-Metallic Copper-Nickel center in Brass ring, 24.5 mm. **Obv:** Stylized wolf's head **Rev:** Value **Edge:** Reeded and lettered

Date	Mintage	F	VF	XF	Unc	BU
2003	100,000	—	—	—	4.00	5.00

KM# 52 100 TENGE
6.4000 g., Bi-Metallic Copper-Nickel center in Brass ring, 24.5 mm. **Obv:** Stylized sheep's head **Rev:** Value **Edge:** Reeded and lettered

Date	Mintage	F	VF	XF	Unc	BU
2003	100,000	—	—	—	4.00	5.00

KM# 57 100 TENGE
6.4000 g., Bi-Metallic Copper-Nickel center in Brass ring, 24.5 mm. **Subject:** 60th Anniversary of the UN **Obv:** UN logo as part of the number 60 **Rev:** Value **Edge:** Reeded and lettered

Date	Mintage	F	VF	XF	Unc	BU
2005	—	—	—	—	5.00	6.00

KM# 37 500 TENGE
23.9000 g., 0.9250 Silver 0.7108 oz. ASW, 37 mm. **Subject:** Wildlife **Obv:** Denomination **Rev:** Female Saiga with two young **Edge:** Plain

Date	Mintage	F	VF	XF	Unc	BU
2001 Proof	—	Value: 50.00				

KM# 38 500 TENGE
23.8100 g., 0.9250 Silver 0.7081 oz. ASW, 36.9 mm. **Subject:** 10 Years of Independence **Obv:** Monument and flag **Rev:** Denomination and arms **Edge:** Plain

Date	Mintage	F	VF	XF	Unc	BU
2001 Proof	3,000	Value: 42.50				

KM# 55 500 TENGE
24.0000 g., 0.9250 Silver 0.7137 oz. ASW, 37 mm. **Obv:** Value **Rev:** Altai Mountain petroglyph **Edge:** Plain

Date	Mintage	F	VF	XF	Unc	BU
2001 Proof	3,000	Value: 45.00				

KM# 42 500 TENGE
23.9000 g., 0.9250 Silver 0.7108 oz. ASW, 37 mm. **Subject:** Music **Obv:** Musician and denomination divided by tree **Rev:** Musical instruments **Edge:** Plain

Date	Mintage	F	VF	XF	Unc	BU
2002 Proof	—	Value: 45.00				

KM# 43 500 TENGE
23.9000 g., 0.9250 Silver 0.7108 oz. ASW, 37 mm. **Subject:** Prehistoric Art **Obv:** Denomination **Rev:** Prehistoric cave art **Edge:** Plain

Date	Mintage	F	VF	XF	Unc	BU
2002 Proof	—	Value: 37.50				

KM# 44 500 TENGE
23.9000 g., 0.9250 Silver 0.7108 oz. ASW, 37 mm. **Subject:** Bighorn Sheep **Obv:** Denomination **Rev:** Kazakhstan Argali Ram **Edge:** Plain

Date	Mintage	F	VF	XF	Unc	BU
2002 Proof	—	Value: 50.00				

KM# 56 500 TENGE
24.0000 g., 0.9250 Silver 0.7137 oz. ASW, 37 mm. **Subject:** Applied Arts **Obv:** Folk Dancer **Rev:** Cultural artifacts **Edge:** Plain

Date	Mintage	F	VF	XF	Unc	BU
2003 Proof	3,000	Value: 45.00				

KM# 53 500 TENGE
24.0000 g., 0.9250 Silver 0.7137 oz. ASW, 37 mm. **Obv:** Value **Rev:** Great Bustard bird standing on ground **Edge:** Plain

Date	Mintage	F	VF	XF	Unc	BU
2003 Proof	3,000	Value: 50.00				

KM# 59 500 TENGE
31.1000 g., 0.9250 Bi-Metallic Blackend silver center in proof silver ring 0.9249 oz., 38.6 mm. **Subject:** "Denga" **Obv:** Black square holed coin design above value **Rev:** Black square holed coin design and metal content statement **Edge:** Reeded

Date	Mintage	F	VF	XF	Unc	BU
2004 Proof	5,000	Value: 50.00				

KM# 60 500 TENGE
24.0000 g., 0.9250 Silver 0.7137 oz. ASW, 37 mm. **Obv:** Value **Rev:** Prehistoric art horseman **Edge:** Plain

Date	Mintage	F	VF	XF	Unc	BU
2005 Proof	3,000	Value: 50.00				

KM# 61 500 TENGE
24.0000 g., 0.9250 Silver 0.7137 oz. ASW, 37 mm. **Obv:** Value **Rev:** Two Gazelles **Edge:** Plain

Date	Mintage	F	VF	XF	Unc	BU
2005 Proof	3,000	Value: 50.00				

KM# 62 500 TENGE
31.1000 g., 0.9250 Silver 0.9249 oz. ASW, 38.6 mm. **Obv:** Horse race and value **Rev:** Gold plated tiger **Edge:** Plain **Shape:** 12-sided

Date	Mintage	F	VF	XF	Unc	BU
2005 Proof	5,000	Value: 50.00				

KM# 63 500 TENGE
31.1000 g., 0.9250 Bi-Metallic Blackend Silver center in Proof Silver ring 0.9249 oz., 38.6 mm. **Subject:** "Drakhma" **Obv:** Old coin design above value **Rev:** Old coin design **Edge:** Reeded

Date	Mintage	F	VF	XF	Unc	BU
2005 Proof	5,000	Value: 50.00				

KENYA

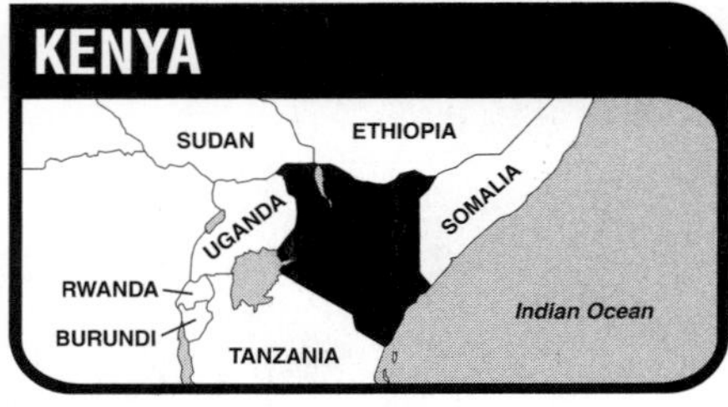

The Republic of Kenya, located on the east coast of Central Africa, has an area of 224,961 sq. mi (582,650 sq. km.) and a population of 20.1 million. Capital: Nairobi. The predominantly agricultural country exports coffee, tea and petroleum products.

Independence was attained on Dec. 12, 1963. Kenya became a republic in 1964. It is a member of the Commonwealth of Nations. The president is Chief of State and Head of Government.

MONETARY SYSTEM
100 Cents = 1 Shilling

REPUBLIC

STANDARD COINAGE

KM# 33 40 SHILLINGS
11.1000 g., Bi-Metallic Copper-Nickel center in Brass ring, 27.4 mm. **Obv:** President Kibaki **Rev:** National arms and value **Edge:** Reeding over lettering **Edge Lettering:** "40 YEARS OF INDEPENDENCE"

Date	Mintage	F	VF	XF	Unc	BU
ND(2003)	—	—	—	—	6.00	7.50

KIRIBATI

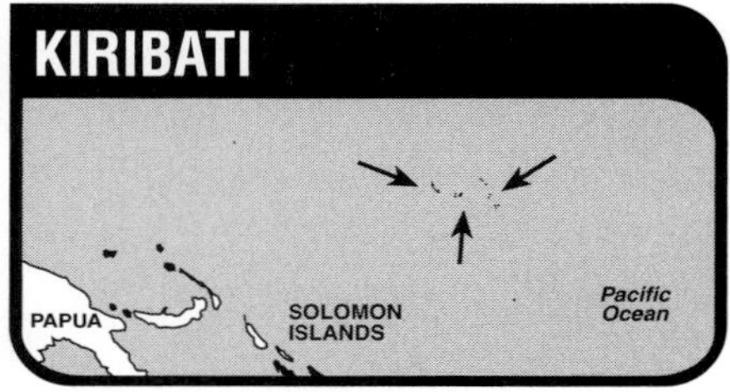

The Republic of Kiribati (formerly the Gilbert Islands), consists of 30 coral atolls and islands spread over more than one million sq. mi. (2,590,000 sq. km.) of the southwest Pacific Ocean, has an area of 332 sq. mi. (717 sq. km.) and a population of 64,200. Capital: Bairiki, on Tarawa. In addition to the Gilbert Islands proper, Kiribati includes Ocean Island, the Central and Southern Line Islands, and the Phoenix Islands, though possession of Canton and Enderbury of the Phoenix Islands is disputed with the United States. Most families engage in subsistence fishing. Copra and phosphates are exported, mostly to Australia and New Zealand.

MONETARY SYSTEM
100 Cents = 1 Dollar

REPUBLIC

DECIMAL COINAGE

KM# 40 5 CENTS
4.2400 g., Brass, 22.9 mm. **Obv:** National arms **Rev:** Gorilla **Edge:** Reeded

Date	Mintage	F	VF	XF	Unc	BU
2003	—	—	—	—	1.00	1.50

KOREA-NORTH

The Democratic Peoples Republic of Korea, situated in northeastern Asia on the northern half of the Korean peninsula between the Peoples Republic of China and the Republic of Korea, has an area of 46,540 sq. mi. (120,540 sq. km.) and a population of 20 million. Capital: Pyongyang. The economy is based on heavy industry and agriculture. Metals, minerals and farm produce are exported.

NOTE: For earlier coinage see Korea.

MONETARY SYSTEM
100 Chon = 1 Won

PEOPLES REPUBLIC

DECIMAL COINAGE

KM# 183 1/2 CHON
2.2100 g., Aluminum, 27 mm. **Obv:** State arms **Rev:** Horse walking left **Edge:** Plain

Date	Mintage	F	VF	XF	Unc	BU
2002	—	—	—	—	1.25	1.50

KM# 184 1/2 CHON
2.2100 g., Aluminum, 27 mm. **Obv:** State arms **Rev:** Orangutan **Edge:** Plain

Date	Mintage	F	VF	XF	Unc	BU
2002	—	—	—	—	1.25	1.50

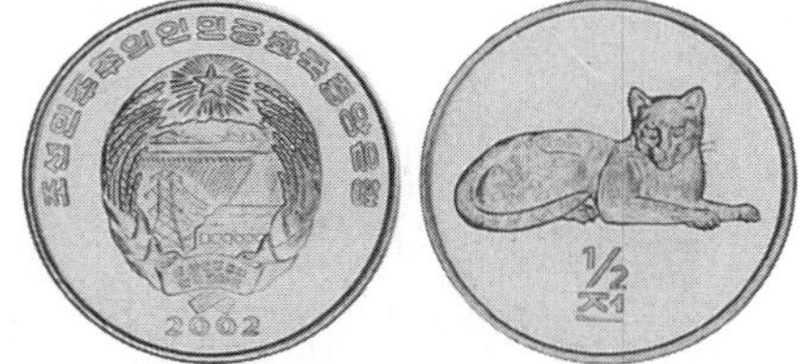

KM# 185 1/2 CHON
2.2100 g., Aluminum, 27 mm. **Obv:** State arms **Rev:** Leopard **Edge:** Plain

Date	Mintage	F	VF	XF	Unc	BU
2002	—	—	—	—	1.25	1.50

KM# 186 1/2 CHON
Aluminum, 27 mm. **Obv:** State arms **Rev:** Two giraffes **Edge:** Plain

Date	Mintage	F	VF	XF	Unc	BU
2002	—	—	—	—	1.25	1.50

KM# 187 1/2 CHON
2.2100 g., Aluminum, 27 mm. **Obv:** State arms **Rev:** Helmeted guineafowl **Edge:** Plain

Date	Mintage	F	VF	XF	Unc	BU
2002	—	—	—	—	1.25	1.50

KM# 188 1/2 CHON
2.2100 g., Aluminum, 27 mm. **Obv:** State arms **Rev:** Mamushi pit viper **Edge:** Plain

Date	Mintage	F	VF	XF	Unc	BU
2002	—	—	—	—	1.25	1.50

KM# 189 1/2 CHON
2.2100 g., Aluminum, 27 mm. **Obv:** State arms **Rev:** Bighorn sheep **Edge:** Plain

Date	Mintage	F	VF	XF	Unc	BU
2002	—	—	—	—	1.25	1.50

KM# 190 1/2 CHON
2.2100 g., Aluminum, 27 mm. **Obv:** State arms **Rev:** Hippopotamus **Edge:** Plain

Date	Mintage	F	VF	XF	Unc	BU
2002	—	—	—	—	1.25	1.50

KM# 191 1/2 CHON
2.2100 g., Aluminum, 27 mm. **Subject:** FAO **Obv:** State arms **Rev:** Ancient ship **Edge:** Plain

Date	Mintage	F	VF	XF	Unc	BU
2002	—	—	—	—	1.25	1.50

KM# 192 1/2 CHON
2.2100 g., Aluminum, 27 mm. **Subject:** FAO **Obv:** State arms **Rev:** Archaic ship **Edge:** Plain

Date	Mintage	F	VF	XF	Unc	BU
2002	—	—	—	—	1.25	1.50

KM# 193 1/2 CHON
2.2100 g., Aluminum, 27 mm. **Subject:** FAO **Obv:** State arms **Rev:** Modern train **Edge:** Plain

Date	Mintage	F	VF	XF	Unc	BU
2002	—	—	—	—	1.25	1.50

KM# 194 1/2 CHON
2.2100 g., Aluminum, 27 mm. **Subject:** FAO **Obv:** State arms **Rev:** Jet airliner **Edge:** Plain

Date	Mintage	F	VF	XF	Unc	BU
2002	—	—	—	—	1.25	1.50

KM# 195 CHON
4.5700 g., Brass, 21.7 mm. **Subject:** FAO **Obv:** State arms **Rev:** Antique steam locomotive **Edge:** Plain

Date	Mintage	F	VF	XF	Unc	BU
2002	—	—	—	—	1.50	1.75

KM# 196 CHON
4.5700 g., Brass, 21.7 mm. **Subject:** FAO **Obv:** State arms **Rev:** Antique automobile **Edge:** Plain

Date	Mintage	F	VF	XF	Unc	BU
2002	—	—	—	—	1.50	1.75

KM# 197 2 CHON
6.0400 g., Copper Nickel, 24.2 mm. **Subject:** FAO **Obv:** State arms **Rev:** Antique touring car **Edge:** Plain

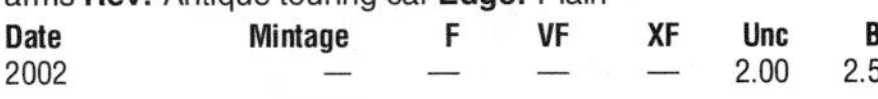

Date	Mintage	F	VF	XF	Unc	BU
2002	—	—	—	—	2.00	2.50

KM# 236a WON
7.0000 g., Aluminum, 40 mm. **Obv:** State arms **Rev:** "Hyonmu" **Edge:** Plain

Date	Mintage	F	VF	XF	Unc	BU
2001 Proof	—	Value: 15.00				

KM# 157a WON
29.0500 g., Brass, 40.2 mm. **Obv:** State arms **Rev:** Cruise ship **Edge:** Plain

Date	Mintage	F	VF	XF	Unc	BU
2001 Proof	—	Value: 17.50				

KM# 162.2 WON
7.0000 g., Aluminum, 40 mm. **Obv:** State arms, date above value **Rev:** Radiant Korean map and landmarks **Edge:** Plain

Date	Mintage	F	VF	XF	Unc	BU
2001 Proof	—	Value: 15.00				

KM# 351 WON
7.0000 g., Aluminum, 40 mm. **Obv:** State arms, date and value below **Rev:** North Korean Arch of Triumph **Edge:** Plain

Date	Mintage	F	VF	XF	Unc	BU
2001 Proof	—	Value: 15.00				

KM# 352 WON
28.6000 g., Brass, 40.1 mm. **Obv:** State arms, value below **Rev:** North Korean Arch of Triumph **Edge:** Plain

Date	Mintage	F	VF	XF	Unc	BU
2001 Proof	—	Value: 17.50				

KM# 353 WON
6.4500 g., Aluminum, 40 mm. **Obv:** State arms, value below **Rev:** N. Korean landmarks and tourists above ship **Edge:** Plain

Date	Mintage	F	VF	XF	Unc	BU
2001 Proof	—	Value: 15.00				

KM# 354 WON
27.6300 g., Brass, 40 mm. **Obv:** State arms, date and value below **Rev:** N. Korean landmarks and tourists above ship **Edge:** Plain

Date	Mintage	F	VF	XF	Unc	BU
2001 Proof	—	Value: 17.50				

KM# 355 WON
6.7500 g., Aluminum, 40 mm. **Obv:** State arms, value below **Rev:** Temple of Heaven above Hong Kong city view below **Edge:** Plain

Date	Mintage	F	VF	XF	Unc	BU
ND Proof	—	Value: 15.00				

KM# 356 WON
28.1000 g., Brass, 40 mm. **Obv:** State arms, date and value below **Rev:** Temple of Heaven above, Hong Kong city view below **Edge:** Plain

Date	Mintage	F	VF	XF	Unc	BU
2001 Proof	—	Value: 17.50				

KM# 294a WON
6.7500 g., Aluminum, 40 mm. **Obv:** State arms **Rev:** Antique ceramics **Edge:** Plain

Date	Mintage	F	VF	XF	Unc	BU
2001 Proof	—	Value: 15.00				

KM# 358 WON
6.7500 g., Aluminum, 40 mm. **Obv:** State arms **Rev:** Old fort **Edge:** Plain

Date	Mintage	F	VF	XF	Unc	BU
2001 Proof	—	Value: 15.00				

KM# 358a WON
28.1000 g., Brass, 40 mm. **Obv:** State arms **Rev:** Old fort **Edge:** Plain

Date	Mintage	F	VF	XF	Unc	BU
2001 Proof	—	Value: 17.50				

KM# 359 WON
7.0000 g., Aluminum, 40.1 mm. **Obv:** State arms **Rev:** Old couple above dates1945-2000 **Edge:** Plain

Date	Mintage	F	VF	XF	Unc	BU
2001 Proof	—	Value: 15.00				

KM# 359a WON
27.8000 g., Brass, 40.1 mm. **Obv:** State arms **Rev:** Old couple above dates 1945-2000 **Edge:** Plain

Date	Mintage	F	VF	XF	Unc	BU
2001 Proof	—	Value: 17.50				

KM# 360 WON
27.8000 g., Brass, 40.1 mm. **Obv:** State arms **Rev:** Blue Dragon **Edge:** Plain

Date	Mintage	F	VF	XF	Unc	BU
2001 Proof	—	Value: 17.50				

KM# 361 WON
7.0000 g., Aluminum, 40.1 mm. **Obv:** State arms **Rev:** Deng Xiaoping 1904-1997 **Edge:** Plain

Date	Mintage	F	VF	XF	Unc	BU
2001 Proof	—	Value: 15.00				

KM# 361a WON
27.8000 g., Brass, 40.1 mm. **Obv:** State arms **Rev:** Deng Xiaoping 1904-1997 **Edge:** Plain

Date	Mintage	F	VF	XF	Unc	BU
2001 Proof	—	Value: 17.50				

KM# 362 WON
7.0000 g., Aluminum, 40.1 mm. **Obv:** State arms **Rev:** Children flying a kite **Edge:** Plain

Date	Mintage	F	VF	XF	Unc	BU
2001 Proof	—	Value: 15.00				

KM# 362a WON
27.8000 g., Brass, 40.1 mm. **Obv:** State arms **Rev:** Children flying a kite **Edge:** Plain

Date	Mintage	F	VF	XF	Unc	BU
2001 Proof	—	Value: 17.50				

KM# 363 WON
7.0000 g., Aluminum, 40.1 mm. **Obv:** State arms **Rev:** Children on seesaw **Edge:** Plain

Date	Mintage	F	VF	XF	Unc	BU
2001 Proof	—	Value: 15.00				

KM# 363a WON

27.8000 g., Brass, 40.1 mm. **Obv:** State arms **Rev:** Children on seesaw **Edge:** Plain

Date	Mintage	F	VF	XF	Unc	BU
2001 Proof	—	Value: 17.50				

KM# 364 WON

7.0000 g., Aluminum, 40.1 mm. **Obv:** State arms **Rev:** Children wrestling **Edge:** Plain

Date	Mintage	F	VF	XF	Unc	BU
2001 Proof	—	Value: 15.00				

KM# 364a WON

27.8000 g., Brass, 40.1 mm. **Obv:** State arms **Rev:** Children wrestling **Edge:** Plain

Date	Mintage	F	VF	XF	Unc	BU
2001 Proof	—	Value: 17.50				

KM# 365 WON

7.0000 g., Aluminum, 40.1 mm. **Obv:** State arms **Rev:** Girl on swing **Edge:** Plain

Date	Mintage	F	VF	XF	Unc	BU
2001 Proof	—	Value: 15.00				

KM# 365a WON

27.8000 g., Brass, 40.1 mm. **Obv:** State arms **Rev:** Girl on swing **Edge:** Plain

Date	Mintage	F	VF	XF	Unc	BU
2001 Proof	—	Value: 17.50				

KM# 366 WON

7.0000 g., Aluminum, 40.1 mm. **Obv:** State arms **Rev:** Girls jumping rope **Edge:** Plain

Date	Mintage	F	VF	XF	Unc	BU
2001 Proof	—	Value: 15.00				

KM# 366a WON

27.8000 g., Brass, 40.1 mm. **Obv:** State arms **Rev:** Girls jumping rope **Edge:** Plain

Date	Mintage	F	VF	XF	Unc	BU
2001 Proof	—	Value: 17.50				

KM# 367 WON

8.7000 g., Aluminum, 40.4 mm. **Obv:** State arms **Rev:** "Kumdang-2 Injection" in center square on leaves **Edge:** Plain

Date	Mintage	F	VF	XF	Unc	BU
2001 Proof	—	Value: 15.00				

KM# 367a WON

26.5400 g., Brass, 40.2 mm. **Obv:** State arms **Rev:** "Kumdang-2 Injection" in center square on leaves **Edge:** Plain

Date	Mintage	F	VF	XF	Unc	BU
2001 Proof	—	Value: 17.50				

KM# 368 WON

27.6100 g., Brass, 40.2 mm. **Obv:** State arms **Rev:** Kim Il Sung 1912-1994 **Edge:** Plain

Date	Mintage	F	VF	XF	Unc	BU
2001 Proof	—	Value: 17.50				

KM# 369 WON

6.5500 g., Aluminum, 40.4 mm. **Obv:** State arms **Rev:** Train at left, couple below jet plane at right **Edge:** Plain

Date	Mintage	F	VF	XF	Unc	BU
2001 Proof	—	Value: 15.00				

KM# 370 WON

27.5600 g., Brass, 40.1 mm. **Obv:** State arms **Rev:** Train at left, couple below jet plane at right **Edge:** Plain

Date	Mintage	F	VF	XF	Unc	BU
2001 Proof	—	Value: 17.50				

KM# 371 WON

5.0500 g., Aluminum, 35 mm. **Obv:** State arms **Rev:** Hong Kong city view **Edge:** Plain

Date	Mintage	F	VF	XF	Unc	BU
2001 Proof	—	Value: 10.00				

KM# 372 WON

6.4000 g., Aluminum, 40 mm. **Obv:** State arms **Rev:** King Tangun **Edge:** Plain

Date	Mintage	F	VF	XF	Unc	BU
2001 Proof	—	Value: 15.00				

KM# 372a WON

27.7000 g., Brass, 40 mm. **Obv:** State arms **Rev:** King Tangun **Edge:** Plain

Date	Mintage	F	VF	XF	Unc	BU
2001 Proof	—	Value: 17.50				

KM# 373 WON

6.9000 g., Aluminum, 40 mm. **Subject:** 1996 Olympics **Obv:** State arms **Rev:** Two green gymnasts and multicolor flame **Edge:** Plain

Date	Mintage	F	VF	XF	Unc	BU
2001 Proof	—	Value: 15.00				

KM# 374 WON

7.0000 g., Aluminum, 40 mm. **Obv:** State arms **Rev:** Taedong Gatehouse **Edge:** Plain

Date	Mintage	F	VF	XF	Unc	BU
2001 Proof	—	Value: 15.00				

KM# 375 WON

8.5000 g., Aluminum, 40.2 mm. **Obv:** State arms **Rev:** Tourists above volcano crater **Edge:** Plain

Date	Mintage	F	VF	XF	Unc	BU
2001 Proof	—	Value: 15.00				

KM# 238a WON

7.1400 g., Aluminum, 40.1 mm. **Obv:** State arms **Rev:** Tiger and cub **Edge:** Plain

Date	Mintage	F	VF	XF	Unc	BU
2001 Proof	—	Value: 15.00				

KM# 376 WON

7.1000 g., Aluminum, 40.1 mm. **Subject:** 1996 Olympics **Obv:** State arms **Rev:** Horse jumping **Edge:** Plain

Date	Mintage	F	VF	XF	Unc	BU
2001 Proof	—	Value: 15.00				

KM# 377 WON

7.0000 g., Aluminum, 40.1 mm. **Subject:** 1996 Olympics **Obv:** State arms **Rev:** Four runners **Edge:** Plain

Date	Mintage	F	VF	XF	Unc	BU
2001 Proof	—	Value: 15.00				

KM# 378 WON

6.8400 g., Aluminum, 40.1 mm. **Obv:** State arms **Rev:** Monument behind multicolor flags and flowers **Edge:** Plain

Date	Mintage	F	VF	XF	Unc	BU
2001 Proof	—	Value: 15.00				

KM# 379 WON

6.6000 g., Aluminum, 40.1 mm. **Obv:** State arms **Rev:** Olympic diver **Edge:** Plain

Date	Mintage	F	VF	XF	Unc	BU
2001 Proof	—	Value: 15.00				

KM# 380 WON

6.9100 g., Aluminum, 40.1 mm. **Obv:** State arms **Rev:** Olympic handball player **Edge:** Plain

Date	Mintage	F	VF	XF	Unc	BU
2001 Proof	—	Value: 15.00				

KM# 381 WON

7.1100 g., Aluminum, 40.2 mm. **Obv:** State arms **Rev:** Olympic high bar gymnast **Edge:** Plain

Date	Mintage	F	VF	XF	Unc	BU
2001 Proof	—	Value: 15.00				

KM# 381a WON

28.8200 g., Brass, 40.1 mm. **Obv:** State arms **Rev:** Olympic high bar gymnast **Edge:** Plain

Date	Mintage	F	VF	XF	Unc	BU
2001 Proof	—	Value: 17.50				

KM# 382 WON

6.5000 g., Aluminum, 40.1 mm. **Obv:** State arms **Rev:** Olympic archer **Edge:** Plain

Date	Mintage	F	VF	XF	Unc	BU
2001 Proof	—	Value: 15.00				

KM# 382a WON

27.4100 g., Brass, 40.2 mm. **Obv:** State arms **Rev:** Olympic archer **Edge:** Plain

Date	Mintage	F	VF	XF	Unc	BU
2001 Proof	—	Value: 17.50				

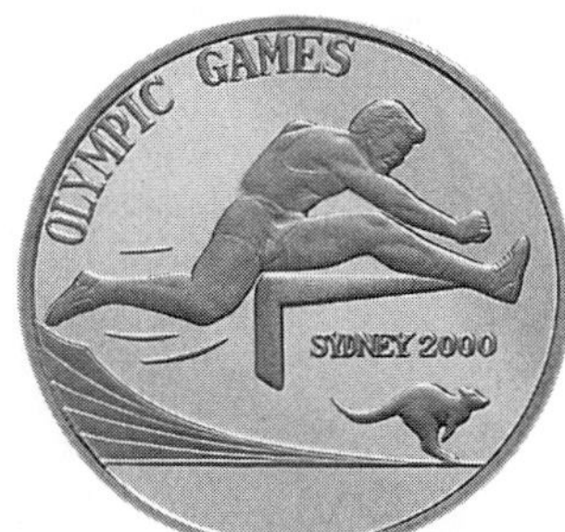

KM# 383 WON

7.1000 g., Aluminum, 40.1 mm. **Obv:** State arms **Rev:** Olympic hurdler **Edge:** Plain

Date	Mintage	F	VF	XF	Unc	BU
2001 Proof	—	Value: 15.00				

KM# 383a WON

28.0000 g., Brass, 40.1 mm. **Obv:** State arms **Rev:** Olympic hurdler **Edge:** Plain

Date	Mintage	F	VF	XF	Unc	BU
2001 Proof	—	Value: 17.50				

KM# 384 WON

7.1500 g., Aluminum, 40.1 mm. **Obv:** State arms **Rev:** Kim Il Sung's birthplace side view **Edge:** Plain

Date	Mintage	F	VF	XF	Unc	BU
2001 Proof	—	Value: 15.00				

KM# 385 WON

7.0000 g., Aluminum, 40.1 mm. **Obv:** State arms **Rev:** Mt. Kumgang Fairy playing flute **Edge:** Plain

Date	Mintage	F	VF	XF	Unc	BU
2001 Proof	—	Value: 15.00				

KM# 385a WON

28.1600 g., Brass, 40.2 mm. **Obv:** State arms **Rev:** Mt. Kumgang Fairy playing flute **Edge:** Plain

Date	Mintage	F	VF	XF	Unc	BU
2001 Proof	—	Value: 17.50				

KM# 290 WON

28.2000 g., Brass, 40.1 mm. **Obv:** National arms **Rev:** Kim Jong Il **Edge:** Plain

Date	Mintage	F	VF	XF	Unc	BU
2001 Proof	—	Value: 20.00				

KM# 291 WON

28.2000 g., Brass, 40.1 mm. **Obv:** National arms **Rev:** Woman between dates 1917-1949 **Edge:** Plain

Date	Mintage	F	VF	XF	Unc	BU
2001 Proof	—	Value: 20.00				

KM# 293 WON

28.2000 g., Brass, 40.2 mm. **Obv:** National arms **Rev:** Olympic runners **Edge:** Crude reeding

Date	Mintage	F	VF	XF	Unc	BU
2001 Proof	—	Value: 20.00				

KM# 294 WON

28.2000 g., Brass, 40.2 mm. **Obv:** National arms **Rev:** Antique porcelain objects **Edge:** Plain

Date	Mintage	F	VF	XF	Unc	BU
2001 Proof	—	Value: 20.00				

KM# 157 WON

6.7000 g., Aluminum, 40 mm. **Subject:** Seafaring Ships **Obv:** State arms **Rev:** Cruise ship left, conjoined busts in cameo upper right **Edge:** Plain

Date	Mintage	F	VF	XF	Unc	BU
ND(2001) Proof	—	Value: 9.00				

KM# 158 WON

16.2000 g., Brass, 35 mm. **Subject:** First Nobel Prize Winner in Literature **Obv:** State arms **Rev:** Half bust Sully Prudhomme seated left, shelves and books behind **Edge:** Plain

Date	Mintage	F	VF	XF	Unc	BU
ND(2001) Proof	—	Value: 10.00				

KM# 158a WON

17.0000 g., Copper-Nickel, 35 mm. **Subject:** First Nobel Prize Winner in Literature - Sully Prudhomme **Obv:** State arms **Rev:** Seated half bust of Prudhomme, shelves and books behind **Edge:** Plain

Date	Mintage	F	VF	XF	Unc	BU
ND(2001) Proof	2,000	Value: 100				

KM# 159 WON

16.2000 g., Brass, 35 mm. **Subject:** First Nobel Prize in Physics **Obv:** State arms **Rev:** Bust of Wilhelm C. Rontgen at left facing half right, seated at desk in lab scene at right **Edge:** Plain

Date	Mintage	F	VF	XF	Unc	BU
ND(2001) Proof	—	Value: 10.00				

KM# 159a WON

17.0000 g., Copper-Nickel, 35 mm. **Subject:** First Nobel Prize Winner in Physics - Wilhelm C. Roentgen **Obv:** State arms **Rev:** Bust of Roentgen at left, seated in lab at right **Edge:** Plain

Date	Mintage	F	VF	XF	Unc	BU
ND(2001) Proof	2,000	Value: 100				

KM# 160 WON

16.2000 g., Brass, 35 mm. **Subject:** Nipponia Nippon **Obv:** State arms **Rev:** Two nest building Japanese ibis **Edge:** Plain

Date	Mintage	F	VF	XF	Unc	BU
2001 Proof	—	Value: 14.00				

KM# 160a WON

17.0000 g., Copper-Nickel, 35 mm. **Subject:** Wildlife **Obv:** State arms **Rev:** Two nesting Japanese Ibis birds **Edge:** Plain

Date	Mintage	F	VF	XF	Unc	BU
2001 Proof	200	Value: 100				

KM# 160b WON

5.3500 g., Aluminum, 35.1 mm. **Obv:** State arms **Rev:** Two nest building Japanese Ibis birds **Edge:** Plain

Date	Mintage	F	VF	XF	Unc	BU
2001 Proof	—	Value: 15.00				

KM# 202 WON

17.0000 g., Copper-Nickel, 35 mm. **Subject:** School Ships **Obv:** State arms **Rev:** SS Krusenstern **Edge:** Plain

Date	Mintage	F	VF	XF	Unc	BU
ND(2001) Proof	200	Value: 100				

KM# 204 WON

17.0000 g., Copper-Nickel, 35 mm. **Subject:** Wildlife **Obv:** State arms **Rev:** Two standing Japanese Ibis birds **Edge:** Plain

Date	Mintage	F	VF	XF	Unc	BU
2001 Proof	100	Value: 150				

KM# 207 WON

17.0000 g., Copper-Nickel, 35 mm. **Subject:** Wildlife **Obv:** State arms **Rev:** Two Korean Longtail Gorals **Edge:** Plain

Date	Mintage	F	VF	XF	Unc	BU
2001 Proof	200	Value: 100				

KM# 207a WON

16.0500 g., Brass, 35 mm. **Obv:** State arms **Rev:** Two Longtail Gorals **Edge:** Plain

Date	Mintage	F	VF	XF	Unc	BU
2001 Proof	—	Value: 18.50				

KM# 207b WON

5.3500 g., Aluminum, 35.1 mm. **Obv:** State arms **Rev:** Two Longtail Gorals **Edge:** Plain

Date	Mintage	F	VF	XF	Unc	BU
2001 Proof	—	Value: 15.00				

KM# 209 WON

17.0000 g., Copper-Nickel, 35 mm. **Subject:** First Nobel Prize Winner in Medicine - Emil A. von Behring **Obv:** State arms **Rev:** von Behring and another man in lab scene **Edge:** Plain

Date	Mintage	F	VF	XF	Unc	BU
ND(2001) Proof	2,000	Value: 100				

KM# 210 WON

17.0000 g., Copper-Nickel, 35 mm. **Subject:** First Nobel Prize Winner in Peace - Henri Dunant **Obv:** State arms **Rev:** Bust of Henri Dunant facing at left, war wounded at right **Edge:** Plain

Date	Mintage	F	VF	XF	Unc	BU
ND(2001) Proof	2,000	Value: 100				

KM# 211 WON

17.0000 g., Copper-Nickel, 35 mm. **Subject:** First Nobel Prize Winner in Chemistry - Jacobus Van't Hoff **Obv:** State arms **Rev:** Van't Hoff and another man in lab scene **Edge:** Plain

Date	Mintage	F	VF	XF	Unc	BU
ND(2001) Proof	2,000	Value: 100				

KM# 212 WON

17.0000 g., Copper-Nickel, 35 mm. **Subject:** First Nobel Prize Winner in Peace - Frederic Passy **Obv:** State arms **Rev:** Bust of Passy at right with allegorical scene at left **Edge:** Plain

Date	Mintage	F	VF	XF	Unc	BU
ND(2001) Proof	2,000	Value: 100				

KM# 232 WON

28.1100 g., Brass, 40 mm. **Obv:** State emblem **Rev:** "Dryocopus Javensis" (White-bellied woodpecker) **Edge:** Plain

Date	Mintage	F	VF	XF	Unc	BU
2001 Proof	—	Value: 25.00				

KM# 233 WON

28.1100 g., Brass, 40 mm. **Obv:** State emblem **Rev:** "Lyrurus Tetrix" (Black grouse) **Edge:** Plain

Date	Mintage	F	VF	XF	Unc	BU
2001 Proof	—	Value: 25.00				

KM# 234 WON

28.1100 g., Brass, 40 mm. **Obv:** State emblem **Rev:** "Syrrhaptes Paradoxus" (Sand grouse) **Edge:** Plain

Date	Mintage	F	VF	XF	Unc	BU
2001 Proof	—	Value: 25.00				

KM# 235 WON

28.1100 g., Brass, 40 mm. **Obv:** State emblem **Rev:** "Pitta Brachyura" (Fairy Pitta bird) **Edge:** Plain

Date	Mintage	F	VF	XF	Unc	BU
2001 Proof	—	Value: 25.00				

KM# 236 WON

28.1100 g., Brass, 40 mm. **Obv:** State emblem **Rev:** Mythical "Hyonmu" **Edge:** Plain

Date	Mintage	F	VF	XF	Unc	BU
2001 Proof	—	Value: 25.00				

KM# 237 WON
28.1100 g., Brass, 40 mm. **Obv:** State emblem **Rev:** Blue Dragon **Edge:** Plain

Date	Mintage	F	VF	XF	Unc	BU
2001 Proof	—	Value: 25.00				

KM# 238 WON
28.1100 g., Brass, 40 mm. **Obv:** State emblem **Rev:** Two tigers **Edge:** Plain

Date	Mintage	F	VF	XF	Unc	BU
2001 Proof	—	Value: 25.00				

KM# 239 WON
28.1100 g., Brass, 40 mm. **Obv:** State emblem **Rev:** Brontosaurus **Edge:** Plain

Date	Mintage	F	VF	XF	Unc	BU
2001 Proof	—	Value: 25.00				

KM# 247 WON
26.9500 g., Brass, 40 mm. **Obv:** State arms **Rev:** Soldier watching an air raid on a Yalu River bridge **Edge:** Plain

Date	Mintage	F	VF	XF	Unc	BU
2001 Proof	—	Value: 20.00				

KM# 248 WON
7.0000 g., Aluminum, 40 mm. **Obv:** State arms **Rev:** Multicolor rabbit and hearts **Edge:** Plain **Note:** Year of the Rabbit

Date	Mintage	F	VF	XF	Unc	BU
2001 Proof	—	Value: 17.50				

KM# 305 WON
28.2000 g., Brass, 40.2 mm. **Obv:** National arms **Rev:** Tomb of King Kong Min **Edge:** Plain

Date	Mintage	F	VF	XF	Unc	BU
2002 Proof	—	Value: 20.00				

KM# 306 WON
28.2000 g., Brass, 40.2 mm. **Obv:** National arms **Rev:** Two horses within circle of animals **Edge:** Plain

Date	Mintage	F	VF	XF	Unc	BU
2002 Proof	—	Value: 20.00				

KM# 308 WON
28.2000 g., Brass, 40.2 mm. **Subject:** Arirang **Obv:** National arms **Rev:** Performers and flying cranes **Edge:** Plain

Date	Mintage	F	VF	XF	Unc	BU
2002 Proof	—	Value: 20.00				

KM# 310 WON
28.2000 g., Brass, 40.2 mm. **Obv:** National arms **Rev:** Tomb of King Tongmyong **Edge:** Plain

Date	Mintage	F	VF	XF	Unc	BU
2002 Proof	—	Value: 20.00				

KM# 313 WON
28.2000 g., Brass, 40.2 mm. **Subject:** Arirang **Obv:** National arms **Rev:** Dancer with upheld arms **Edge:** Plain

Date	Mintage	F	VF	XF	Unc	BU
2002 Proof	—	Value: 20.00				

KM# 388 WON
7.1000 g., Aluminum, 40 mm. **Obv:** State arms **Rev:** Arirang dancer Silhouette **Edge:** Plain

Date	Mintage	F	VF	XF	Unc	BU
2002 Proof	—	Value: 15.00				

KM# 389 WON
6.7000 g., Aluminum, 40 mm. **Obv:** State arms **Rev:** Arirang dancer **Edge:** Plain

Date	Mintage	F	VF	XF	Unc	BU
2002 Proof	—	Value: 15.00				

KM# 390 WON
6.9000 g., Aluminum, 40 mm. **Obv:** State arms **Rev:** Arirang dancer with cranes flying above **Edge:** Plain

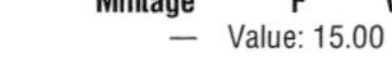
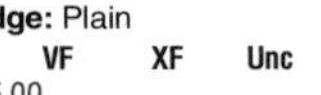

Date	Mintage	F	VF	XF	Unc	BU
2002 Proof	—	Value: 15.00				

KM# 391 WON
7.1000 g., Aluminum, 40 mm. **Obv:** State arms **Rev:** Arirang ribbon dancer **Edge:** Plain

Date	Mintage	F	VF	XF	Unc	BU
2002 Proof	—	Value: 15.00				

KM# 392 WON
7.0000 g., Aluminum, 40 mm. **Obv:** State arms **Rev:** May Day Stadium **Edge:** Plain

Date	Mintage	F	VF	XF	Unc	BU
2002 Proof	—	Value: 15.00				

KM# 392a WON
28.5000 g., Brass, 40.1 mm. **Obv:** State arms **Rev:** May Day Stadium **Edge:** Plain

Date	Mintage	F	VF	XF	Unc	BU
2002 Proof	—	Value: 17.50				

KM# 393 WON
7.1000 g., Aluminum, 40 mm. **Obv:** State arms **Rev:** Woman floating above stadium **Edge:** Plain

Date	Mintage	F	VF	XF	Unc	BU
2002 Proof	—	Value: 15.00				

KM# 393a WON
28.2000 g., Brass, 40 mm. **Obv:** State arms **Rev:** Woman floating above stadium **Edge:** Plain

Date	Mintage	F	VF	XF	Unc	BU
2002 Proof	—	Value: 17.50				

KM# 394 WON
27.5000 g., Brass, 40 mm. **Obv:** State arms **Rev:** Ribbon dancer with Korea shaped ribbon **Edge:** Plain

Date	Mintage	F	VF	XF	Unc	BU
2002 Proof	—	Value: 17.50				

KM# 395 WON
27.5000 g., Brass, 40 mm. **Obv:** State arms **Rev:** Dancer in the shape of Korea **Edge:** Plain

Date	Mintage	F	VF	XF	Unc	BU
2002 Proof	—	Value: 17.50				

KM# 396 WON
7.0000 g., Aluminum, 40 mm. **Obv:** State arms **Rev:** Jongmongju and Sonjukgyo **Edge:** Plain

Date	Mintage	F	VF	XF	Unc	BU
2002 Proof	—	Value: 15.00				

KM# 397 WON
7.0000 g., Aluminum, 40 mm. **Obv:** State arms **Rev:** Victorious athletes **Edge:** Plain

Date	Mintage	F	VF	XF	Unc	BU
2002 Proof	—	Value: 15.00				

KM# 397a WON
28.2400 g., Brass, 40 mm. **Obv:** State arms **Rev:** Victorious athletes **Edge:** Plain

Date	Mintage	F	VF	XF	Unc	BU
2002 Proof	—	Value: 17.50				

KM# 398 WON
7.1000 g., Aluminum, 40 mm. **Obv:** State arms **Rev:** Two horses within circle of animals **Edge:** Plain

Date	Mintage	F	VF	XF	Unc	BU
2002 Proof	—	Value: 15.00				

KM# 399 WON
4.8600 g., Aluminum, 35 mm. **Obv:** State arms **Rev:** Goose-stepping horse **Edge:** Plain

Date	Mintage	F	VF	XF	Unc	BU
2002 Proof	—	Value: 12.50				

KM# 399a WON
16.9300 g., Brass, 35 mm. **Obv:** State arms **Rev:** Goose-stepping horse **Edge:** Plain

Date	Mintage	F	VF	XF	Unc	BU
2002 Proof	—	Value: 15.00				

KM# 400 WON
5.1000 g., Aluminum, 35 mm. **Obv:** State arms **Rev:** Two wrestlers **Edge:** Plain

Date	Mintage	F	VF	XF	Unc	BU
2002 Proof	—	Value: 12.50				

KM# 400a WON
16.5000 g., Brass, 35 mm. **Obv:** State arms **Rev:** Two wrestlers **Edge:** Plain

Date	Mintage	F	VF	XF	Unc	BU
2002 Proof	—	Value: 15.00				

KM# 323 WON
6.9400 g., Aluminum, 40 mm. **Obv:** State arms **Rev:** Turtle shaped armoured ship of 1592 **Edge:** Plain

Date	Mintage	F	VF	XF	Unc	BU
2003 Proof	—	Value: 15.00				

KM# 323a WON
28.1000 g., Brass, 40.2 mm. **Obv:** National arms **Rev:** Turtle-shaped armoured ship of 1592 **Edge:** Plain

Date	Mintage	F	VF	XF	Unc	BU
2003 Proof	—	Value: 20.00				

KM# 319 WON
9.6200 g., Aluminum, 40 mm. **Obv:** State arms **Rev:** Helmeted head with two antenna-like horns on the helmet **Edge:** Plain

Date	Mintage	F	VF	XF	Unc	BU
2003 Proof	—	Value: 15.00				

KM# 319a WON
28.2000 g., Brass, 40.2 mm. **Obv:** National arms **Rev:** Helmeted head with two antenna-like horns on helmet **Edge:** Plain

Date	Mintage	F	VF	XF	Unc	BU
2003 Proof	—	Value: 20.00				

KM# 403a WON
22.1000 g., Brass, 40 mm. **Obv:** State arms **Rev:** Kang Kam Chan (948-1032) in winged helmet **Edge:** Plain

Date	Mintage	F	VF	XF	Unc	BU
2003 Proof	—	Value: 17.50				

KM# 404 WON
9.6300 g., Aluminum, 40 mm. **Obv:** State arms **Rev:** King wearing a horned helmet **Edge:** Plain

Date	Mintage	F	VF	XF	Unc	BU
2003 Proof	—	Value: 15.00				

KM# 404a WON
22.2500 g., Brass, 40 mm. **Obv:** State arms **Rev:** King wearing a horned helmet **Edge:** Plain

Date	Mintage	F	VF	XF	Unc	BU
2003 Proof	—	Value: 17.50				

KM# 405 WON
7.0000 g., Aluminum, 40 mm. **Obv:** State arms **Rev:** Ram within circle of animals **Edge:** Plain

Date	Mintage	F	VF	XF	Unc	BU
2003 Proof	—	Value: 15.00				

KM# 405a WON
28.4400 g., Brass, 40 mm. **Obv:** State arms **Rev:** Ram within circle of animals **Edge:** Plain

Date	Mintage	F	VF	XF	Unc	BU
2003 Proof	—	Value: 17.50				

KM# 406 WON
10.1500 g., Aluminum, 40 mm. **Obv:** State arms **Rev:** Children kicking a shuttlecock **Edge:** Plain

Date	Mintage	F	VF	XF	Unc	BU
2003 Proof	—	Value: 15.00				

KM# 406a WON
24.6300 g., Brass, 40 mm. **Obv:** State arms **Rev:** Children kicking a shuttlecock **Edge:** Plain

Date	Mintage	F	VF	XF	Unc	BU
2003 Proof	—	Value: 17.50				

KM# 407a WON
23.1000 g., Brass, 40 mm. **Obv:** State arms **Rev:** Children playing jacks **Edge:** Plain

Date	Mintage	F	VF	XF	Unc	BU
2003 Proof	—	Value: 17.50				

KM# 408a WON
24.5600 g., Brass, 40 mm. **Obv:** State arms **Rev:** Children spinning tops **Edge:** Plain

Date	Mintage	F	VF	XF	Unc	BU
2003 Proof	—	Value: 17.50				

KM# 410a WON
24.6400 g., Brass, 40 mm. **Obv:** State arms **Rev:** Large dome building **Edge:** Plain

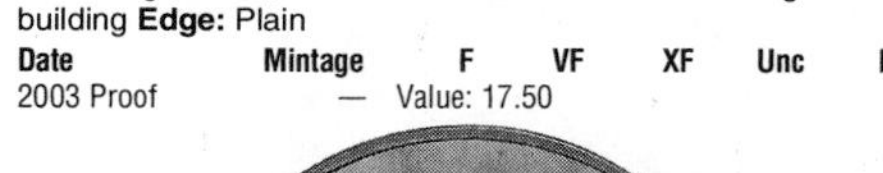

Date	Mintage	F	VF	XF	Unc	BU
2003 Proof	—	Value: 17.50				

KM# 264 WON
28.4700 g., Brass, 40 mm. **Obv:** State arms **Rev:** Sheep within circle of animals **Edge:** Plain

Date	Mintage	F	VF	XF	Unc	BU
2003 Proof	—	Value: 22.00				

KM# 265 WON
17.7000 g., Brass, 23.2 x 40.1 mm. **Obv:** State arms **Rev:** Callithrix Jacchus monkey **Edge:** Plain

Date	Mintage	F	VF	XF	Unc	BU
2004	—	Value: 25.00				

KM# 266 WON
17.7000 g., Brass, 23.2 x 40.1 mm. **Obv:** State arms **Rev:** Cercopjthecus Mitis monkey **Edge:** Plain

Date	Mintage	F	VF	XF	Unc	BU
2004 Proof	—	Value: 25.00				

KM# 267 WON
17.7000 g., Brass, 23.2 x 40.1 mm. **Obv:** State arms **Rev:** Two Saguinus Midas monkeys **Edge:** Plain

Date	Mintage	F	VF	XF	Unc	BU
2004 Proof	—	Value: 25.00				

KM# 330 WON
26.4500 g., Brass, 45 mm. **Obv:** National arms **Rev:** Mountain cabin **Edge:** Plain **Note:** Similar to KM# 411

Date	Mintage	F	VF	XF	Unc	BU
2004 Proof	—	Value: 20.00				

KM# 331 WON
26.4500 g., Brass, 45 mm. **Obv:** National arms **Rev:** Sung's birth place, front view **Edge:** Plain **Note:** Similar to KM# 412

Date	Mintage	F	VF	XF	Unc	BU
2004 Proof	—	Value: 20.00				

KM# 332 WON
26.4500 g., Brass, 45 mm. **Obv:** National arms **Rev:** Sung's birthplace, side view **Edge:** Plain **Note:** Similar to KM# 413

Date	Mintage	F	VF	XF	Unc	BU
2004 Proof	—	Value: 20.00				

KM# 333 WON

26.4500 g., Brass, 45 mm. **Obv:** National arms **Rev:** Kim Il Sung as a young soldier **Edge:** Plain

Date	Mintage	F	VF	XF	Unc	BU
2004 Proof	—	Value: 20.00				

KM# 334 WON

26.4500 g., Brass, 45 mm. **Obv:** National arms **Rev:** Kim Il Sung as a General **Edge:** Plain

Date	Mintage	F	VF	XF	Unc	BU
2004 Proof	—	Value: 20.00				

KM# 335 WON

26.4500 g., Brass, 45 mm. **Obv:** National arms **Rev:** Sung as General facing slightly left **Edge:** Plain

Date	Mintage	F	VF	XF	Unc	BU
2004 Proof	—	Value: 20.00				

KM# 336 WON

26.4500 g., Brass, 45 mm. **Obv:** National arms **Rev:** Orchids **Edge:** Plain **Note:** Similar to KM# 414

Date	Mintage	F	VF	XF	Unc	BU
2004 Proof	—	Value: 20.00				

KM# 337 WON

26.4500 g., Brass, 45 mm. **Obv:** National arms **Rev:** Peony flower **Edge:** Plain **Note:** Similar to KM# 415

Date	Mintage	F	VF	XF	Unc	BU
2004 Proof	—	Value: 20.00				

KM# 338 WON

26.4500 g., Brass, 45 mm. **Obv:** National arms **Rev:** Rose of Sharon flowers **Edge:** Plain Note: Similar to KM# 416

Date	Mintage	F	VF	XF	Unc	BU
2004 Proof	—	Value: 20.00				

KM# 411 WON

9.9200 g., Aluminum, 45 mm. **Obv:** State arms **Rev:** Mountain cabin **Edge:** Plain

Date	Mintage	F	VF	XF	Unc	BU
2004 Proof	—	Value: 15.00				

KM# 412 WON

10.0000 g., Aluminum, 45 mm. **Obv:** State arms **Rev:** Kim Il Sung's birthplace, front view **Edge:** Plain

Date	Mintage	F	VF	XF	Unc	BU
2004 Proof	—	Value: 15.00				

KM# 413 WON

10.0000 g., Aluminum, 45 mm. **Obv:** State arms **Rev:** Kim Il Sung's birthplace, side view **Edge:** Plain

Date	Mintage	F	VF	XF	Unc	BU
2004 Proof	—	Value: 15.00				

KM# 414 WON

10.1000 g., Aluminum, 45 mm. **Obv:** State arms **Rev:** Orchids **Edge:** Plain

Date	Mintage	F	VF	XF	Unc	BU
2004 Proof	—	Value: 15.00				

KM# 415 WON

10.1000 g., Aluminum, 45 mm. **Obv:** State arms **Rev:** Peony flower **Edge:** Plain

Date	Mintage	F	VF	XF	Unc	BU
2004 Proof	—	Value: 15.00				

KM# 416 WON

9.9300 g., Aluminum, 45 mm. **Obv:** State arms **Rev:** Rose of Sharon flowers **Edge:** Plain

Date	Mintage	F	VF	XF	Unc	BU
2004 Proof	—	Value: 15.00				

KM# 249 2 WON

7.0000 g., 0.9990 Silver 0.2248 oz. ASW, 30 mm. **Obv:** State arms **Rev:** Two multicolor pandas **Edge:** Plain

Date	Mintage	F	VF	XF	Unc	BU
2003 Proof	—	Value: 30.00				

KM# 417 2 WON

24.6600 g., Brass, 31.6x45.75 mm. **Obv:** State arms **Rev:** Deng Xiaoping standing in land rover, saluting and dates 1904-2004 **Edge:** Plain **Shape:** Rectangle

Date	Mintage	F	VF	XF	Unc	BU
ND(2004) Proof	—	Value: 18.00				

KM# 339 3 WON

12.5500 g., Aluminum, 50.1 mm. **Obv:** Korean map **Rev:** King Sejong the Great **Edge:** Plain

Date	Mintage	F	VF	XF	Unc	BU
2004 Proof	—	Value: 20.00				

KM# 339a 3 WON

40.5300 g., Brass, 50.2 mm. **Obv:** Korean map **Rev:** Sejong the Great **Edge:** Plain

Date	Mintage	F	VF	XF	Unc	BU
2004 Proof	—	Value: 25.00				

KM# 203 5 WON

15.0000 g., 0.9990 Silver 0.4818 oz. ASW, 35 mm. **Subject:** School Ships **Obv:** State arms **Rev:** SS Krusenstern **Edge:** Plain

Date	Mintage	F	VF	XF	Unc	BU
ND(2001) Proof	500	Value: 75.00				

KM# 205 5 WON

15.0000 g., 0.9990 Silver 0.4818 oz. ASW, 35 mm. **Subject:** Wildlife **Obv:** State arms **Rev:** Two standing Japanese Ibis birds **Edge:** Plain

Date	Mintage	F	VF	XF	Unc	BU
2001 Proof	100	Value: 200				

KM# 206 5 WON

15.0000 g., 0.9990 Silver 0.4818 oz. ASW, 35 mm. **Subject:** Wildlife **Obv:** State arms **Rev:** Two nesting Japanese Ibis birds **Edge:** Plain

Date	Mintage	F	VF	XF	Unc	BU
2001 Proof	3,000	Value: 50.00				

KM# 208 5 WON

15.0000 g., 0.9990 Silver 0.4818 oz. ASW, 35 mm. **Subject:** Wildlife **Obv:** State arms **Rev:** Two Korean Longtail Gorals **Edge:** Plain

Date	Mintage	F	VF	XF	Unc	BU
2001 Proof	3,000	Value: 50.00				

KM# 219 5 WON

14.9600 g., 0.9990 Silver 0.4805 oz. ASW, 35 mm. **Obv:** State arms **Rev:** Dragon ship **Edge:** Plain

Date	Mintage	F	VF	XF	Unc	BU
2001 Proof	5,000	Value: 35.00				

KM# 226 5 WON

20.0000 g., 0.9990 Silver 0.6424 oz. ASW, 33.8 mm. **Subject:** Olympics **Obv:** State arms **Rev:** Hurdler **Edge:** Reeded

Date	Mintage	F	VF	XF	Unc	BU
2001 proof	—	Value: 35.00				

KM# 240 5 WON

14.9400 g., 0.9990 Silver 0.4799 oz. ASW, 35 mm. **Obv:** State emblem **Rev:** "Orca" (Killer Whale) **Edge:** Plain

Date	Mintage	F	VF	XF	Unc	BU
2001 Proof	—	Value: 60.00				

KM# 241 5 WON

14.9200 g., 0.9990 Silver 0.4792 oz. ASW, 35 mm. **Obv:** State emblem **Rev:** Orca and Eco-Tourists in boat **Edge:** Plain

Date	Mintage	F	VF	XF	Unc	BU
2001 Proof	—	Value: 60.00				

KM# 242 5 WON

14.8700 g., 0.9990 Silver 0.4776 oz. ASW, 35 mm. **Obv:** State emblem **Rev:** "Pottwal" (Sperm Whale) **Edge:** Plain

Date	Mintage	F	VF	XF	Unc	BU
2001 Proof	—	Value: 60.00				

KM# 243 5 WON

14.9500 g., 0.9990 Silver 0.4802 oz. ASW, 35 mm. **Obv:** State emblem **Rev:** "Buckelwal" (Humpback Whale) **Edge:** Plain

Date	Mintage	F	VF	XF	Unc	BU
2001 Proof	—	Value: 60.00				

KM# 244 5 WON

14.9300 g., 0.9990 Silver 0.4795 oz. ASW, 35 mm. **Obv:** State emblem **Rev:** "Groenlandwal" (Greenland Whale) **Edge:** Plain

Date	Mintage	F	VF	XF	Unc	BU
2001 Proof	—	Value: 60.00				

KM# 245 5 WON

14.9500 g., 0.9990 Silver 0.4802 oz. ASW, 35 mm. **Obv:** State emblem **Rev:** "Blauwal" (Blue Whale) **Edge:** Plain

Date	Mintage	F	VF	XF	Unc	BU
2001 Proof	—	Value: 60.00				

KM# 246 5 WON

14.9600 g., 0.9990 Silver 0.4805 oz. ASW, 35 mm. **Obv:** State emblem **Rev:** "Grindwal" (Pilot Whale) **Edge:** Plain

Date	Mintage	F	VF	XF	Unc	BU
2001 Proof	—	Value: 60.00				

KM# 250 5 WON

14.9600 g., 0.9990 Silver 0.4805 oz. ASW, 35 mm. **Subject:** Return of Hong Kong to China **Obv:** State emblem **Rev:** City view **Edge:** Plain

Date	Mintage	F	VF	XF	Unc	BU
2001 Proof	—	Value: 16.00				

KM# 251 5 WON

14.9000 g., 0.9990 Silver 0.4786 oz. ASW, 35 mm. **Subject:** Year of the Horse **Obv:** State emblem **Rev:** Horse striding to the right **Edge:** Plain

Date	Mintage	F	VF	XF	Unc	BU
2002 Proof	—	Value: 20.00				

KM# 252 5 WON

14.9200 g., 0.9990 Silver 0.4792 oz. ASW, 35 mm. **Subject:** Korean Games **Obv:** State emblem **Rev:** Two wrestlers **Edge:** Plain

Date	Mintage	F	VF	XF	Unc	BU
2002 Proof	—	Value: 16.00				

KM# 303 5 WON

15.0000 g., 0.9990 Silver 0.4818 oz. ASW, 35 mm. **Obv:** National arms **Rev:** Janggo dancer **Edge:** Segmented reeding

Date	Mintage	F	VF	XF	Unc	BU
2002 Proof	—	Value: 30.00				

KM# 304 5 WON

15.0000 g., 0.9990 Silver 0.4818 oz. ASW, 35 mm. **Obv:** National arms **Rev:** Li Dynasty Knight **Edge:** Segmented reeding

Date	Mintage	F	VF	XF	Unc	BU
2002 Proof	—	Value: 30.00				

KM# 327 5 WON

20.0000 g., 0.9990 Silver 0.6424 oz. ASW, 35 mm. **Obv:** National arms **Rev:** "Turtle Boat " of 1592 **Edge:** Segmented reeding

Date	Mintage	F	VF	XF	Unc	BU
2003 Proof	—	Value: 30.00				

KM# 328 5 WON

20.0000 g., 0.9990 Silver 0.6424 oz. ASW, 35 mm. **Obv:** National arms **Rev:** Olympic fencers **Edge:** Segmented reeding

Date	Mintage	F	VF	XF	Unc	BU
2003 Proof	—	Value: 30.00				

KM# 329 5 WON

20.0000 g., 0.9990 Silver 0.6424 oz. ASW, 35 mm. **Obv:** National arms **Rev:** Three wild horses **Edge:** Segmented reeding

Date	Mintage	F	VF	XF	Unc	BU
2003 Proof	—	Value: 30.00				

KM# 220 7 WON

20.0000 g., 0.9990 Silver 0.6424 oz. ASW, 38 mm. **Subject:** 2002 Olympics **Obv:** State emblem **Rev:** Two speed skaters **Edge:** Plain

Date	Mintage	F	VF	XF	Unc	BU
2001 Proof	10,000	Value: 40.00				

KM# 221 7 WON

20.0000 g., 0.9990 Silver 0.6424 oz. ASW, 38 mm. **Subject:** Endangered Wildlife **Obv:** State emblem **Rev:** White-tailed sea Eagle **Edge:** Plain

Date	Mintage	F	VF	XF	Unc	BU
2001 Proof	10,000	Value: 35.00				

KM# 292 10 WON

31.0000 g., 0.9990 Silver 0.9957 oz. ASW, 40.2 mm. **Obv:** National arms **Rev:** Kim Il Sung and dates 1912-1994 **Edge:** Plain

Date	Mintage	F	VF	XF	Unc	BU
2001 Proof	—	Value: 35.00				

KM# 295 10 WON

31.0000 g., 0.9990 Silver 0.9957 oz. ASW, 40.2 mm. **Obv:** National arms **Rev:** Mountain cabin **Edge:** Plain

Date	Mintage	F	VF	XF	Unc	BU
2001 Proof	—	Value: 35.00				

KM# 296 10 WON

31.0000 g., 0.9990 Silver 0.9957 oz. ASW, 40.2 mm. **Obv:** National arms **Rev:** "KUMDANG - 2 INJECTION" in center of leaves **Edge:** Plain

Date	Mintage	F	VF	XF	Unc	BU
2001 Proof	—	Value: 35.00				

KM# 297 10 WON

31.0000 g., 0.9990 Silver 0.9957 oz. ASW, 40.2 mm. **Obv:** National arms **Rev:** Train scene and a couple below a jet liner **Edge:** Plain

Date	Mintage	F	VF	XF	Unc	BU
2001 Proof	—	Value: 35.00				

KM# 298 10 WON

31.0000 g., 0.9990 Silver 0.9957 oz. ASW, 40.2 mm. **Obv:** National arms **Rev:** Cruise ship **Edge:** Plain

Date	Mintage	F	VF	XF	Unc	BU
2001 Proof	—	Value: 35.00				

KM# 299 10 WON

31.0000 g., 0.9990 Silver 0.9957 oz. ASW, 40.2 mm. **Obv:** National arms **Rev:** Old fortress **Edge:** Plain

Date	Mintage	F	VF	XF	Unc	BU
2001 Proof	—	Value: 35.00				

KM# 300 10 WON
31.0000 g., 0.9990 Silver 0.9957 oz. ASW, 40.2 mm.
Obv: National arms **Rev:** Landmarks, flag and tourist couple above cruise ship **Edge:** Plain

Date	Mintage	F	VF	XF	Unc	BU
2001 Proof	—	Value: 35.00				

KM# 301 10 WON
31.0000 g., 0.9990 Silver 0.9957 oz. ASW, 40.2 mm.
Obv: National arms **Rev:** Kim Il Sung with diplomat **Edge:** Plain

Date	Mintage	F	VF	XF	Unc	BU
2001 Proof	—	Value: 35.00				

KM# 302 10 WON
31.0000 g., 0.9990 Silver 0.9957 oz. ASW, 40.1 mm. **Obv:** National arms **Rev:** Old building **Edge:** Plain

Date	Mintage	F	VF	XF	Unc	BU
2001 Proof	—	Value: 35.00				

KM# 357 10 WON
31.0000 g., 0.9990 Silver 0.9957 oz. ASW, 40.2 mm. **Obv:** State arms **Rev:** Antique ceramic items **Edge:** Plain

Date	Mintage	F	VF	XF	Unc	BU
2001 Proof	—	Value: 35.00				

KM# 386 10 WON
30.7600 g., 0.9990 Silver 0.988 oz. ASW, 40.1 mm. **Obv:** State arms **Rev:** Woman with dates 1917-1949 **Edge:** Plain

Date	Mintage	F	VF	XF	Unc	BU
2001 Proof	—	Value: 35.00				

KM# 387 10 WON
30.7600 g., 0.9990 Silver 0.988 oz. ASW, 40.1 mm. **Obv:** State arms **Rev:** Kim Il Sung facing bust **Edge:** Plain

Date	Mintage	F	VF	XF	Unc	BU
2001 Proof	—	Value: 35.00				

KM# 227 10 WON
31.0600 g., 0.9250 Silver 0.9237 oz. ASW, 39.9 mm. **Subject:** General Ri Sun Sin **Obv:** State emblem **Rev:** Helmeted portrait **Edge:** Reeded

Date	Mintage	F	VF	XF	Unc	BU
2001	—	—	—	—	35.00	—

KM# 253 10 WON
31.1100 g., 0.9990 Silver 0.9992 oz. ASW, 40.2 mm. **Obv:** State emblem **Rev:** Deng Xiaoping, 1904-1997 **Edge:** Plain

Date	Mintage	F	VF	XF	Unc	BU
2001	—	Value: 25.00				

KM# 152 10 WON
31.0000 g., 0.9990 Silver .9957 oz. ASW, 39.8 mm.
Subject: Asian Money Fair **Obv:** State arms **Rev:** Two snakes
Edge: Reeded and plain sections

Date	Mintage	F	VF	XF	Unc	BU
2001 Proof	—	Value: 50.00				

KM# 153 10 WON
31.0000 g., 0.9990 Silver .9957 oz. ASW, 39.8 mm. **Subject:** Tortoise-Serpent **Obv:** State arms **Rev:** Mythical creature **Edge:** Reeded and plain sections

Date	Mintage	F	VF	XF	Unc	BU
2001 Proof	—	Value: 50.00				

KM# 255 10 WON
30.9400 g., 0.9990 Silver 0.9937 oz. ASW, 40.2 mm.
Subject: Jongmongju and Sonjukgyo **Obv:** State emblem
Rev: Head above pavilion and bridge **Edge:** Plain

Date	Mintage	F	VF	XF	Unc	BU
2002 Proof	—	Value: 25.00				

KM# 254 10 WON
30.7700 g., 0.9990 Silver 0.9883 oz. ASW, 40.15 mm. **Obv:** State emblem **Rev:** King Tangun and his tomb **Edge:** Plain

Date	Mintage	F	VF	XF	Unc	BU
2002 Proof	—	Value: 25.00				

KM# 231 10 WON
31.0000 g., 0.9990 Silver 0.9957 oz. ASW, 39.9 mm.
Subject: Kim Ill Sung **Obv:** State emblem **Rev:** Smiling portrait
Edge: Segmented reeding

Date	Mintage	F	VF	XF	Unc	BU
2002 Proof	—	Value: 40.00				

KM# 401 10 WON
31.0000 g., 0.9990 Silver 0.9957 oz. ASW, 40.1 mm. **Obv:** State arms **Rev:** Arirang dancer **Edge:** Plain

Date	Mintage	F	VF	XF	Unc	BU
2002 Proof	—	Value: 35.00				

KM# 402 10 WON
31.0000 g., 0.9990 Silver 0.9957 oz. ASW, 40.1 mm. **Obv:** State arms **Rev:** Arirang ribbon dancer **Edge:** Plain

Date	Mintage	F	VF	XF	Unc	BU
2002 Proof	—	Value: 35.00				

KM# 307 10 WON
31.0000 g., 0.9990 Silver 0.9957 oz. ASW, 40.1 mm. **Obv:** National arms **Rev:** Two horses within a circle of animals **Edge:** Plain

Date	Mintage	F	VF	XF	Unc	BU
2002 Proof	—	Value: 35.00				

KM# 309 10 WON
31.0000 g., 0.9990 Silver 0.9957 oz. ASW, 40.2 mm. **Subject:** Arirang **Obv:** National arms **Rev:** Performers and flying cranes **Edge:** Plain

Date	Mintage	F	VF	XF	Unc	BU
2002 Proof	—	Value: 35.00				

KM# 311 10 WON
31.0000 g., 0.9990 Silver 0.9957 oz. ASW, 40.2 mm. **Obv:** National arms **Rev:** Tomb of King Tongmyong **Edge:** Plain

Date	Mintage	F	VF	XF	Unc	BU
2002 Proof	—	Value: 35.00				

KM# 312 10 WON
31.0000 g., 0.9990 Silver 0.9957 oz. ASW, 40.2 mm. **Obv:** National arms **Rev:** Tomb of King Kong Min **Edge:** Plain

Date	Mintage	F	VF	XF	Unc	BU
2002 Proof	—	Value: 35.00				

KM# 314 10 WON
31.0000 g., 0.9990 Silver 0.9957 oz. ASW, 40.2 mm. **Subject:** Arirang **Obv:** National arms **Rev:** Show logo **Edge:** Plain

Date	Mintage	F	VF	XF	Unc	BU
2002 Proof	—	Value: 35.00				

KM# 315 10 WON
31.0000 g., 0.9990 Silver 0.9957 oz. ASW, 40.2 mm. **Obv:** National arms **Rev:** Korean map shaped dancer **Edge:** Plain

Date	Mintage	F	VF	XF	Unc	BU
2002 Proof	—	Value: 35.00				

KM# 316 10 WON
31.0000 g., 0.9990 Silver 0.9957 oz. ASW, 40.2 mm. **Obv:** National arms **Rev:** Korean map shaped ribbon dancer **Edge:** Plain

Date	Mintage	F	VF	XF	Unc	BU
2002 Proof	—	Value: 35.00				

KM# 317 10 WON
31.0000 g., 0.9990 Silver 0.9957 oz. ASW, 40.2 mm. **Obv:** National arms **Rev:** Three victorious athletes in embrace **Edge:** Plain

Date	Mintage	F	VF	XF	Unc	BU
2002 Proof	—	Value: 35.00				

KM# 318 10 WON
31.0000 g., 0.9990 Silver 0.9957 oz. ASW, 40.2 mm. **Obv:** National arms **Rev:** Woman floating above arena **Edge:** Plain

Date	Mintage	F	VF	XF	Unc	BU
2002 Proof	—	Value: 35.00				

KM# 320 10 WON
31.0000 g., 0.9990 Silver 0.9957 oz. ASW, 40.2 mm. **Obv:** National arms **Rev:** Helmeted head with two antenna-like horns on helmet **Edge:** Plain **Note:** Similar to KM# 319

Date	Mintage	F	VF	XF	Unc	BU
2003 Proof	—	Value: 35.00				

KM# 321 10 WON
31.0000 g., 0.9990 Silver 0.9957 oz. ASW, 40.2 mm. **Obv:** National arms **Rev:** Helmeted head, helmet with horns **Edge:** Plain **Note:** Similar to KM# 404

Date	Mintage	F	VF	XF	Unc	BU
2003 Proof	—	Value: 35.00				

KM# 322 10 WON
31.0000 g., 0.9990 Silver 0.9957 oz. ASW, 40.2 mm. **Obv:** National arms **Rev:** Kang Kam Chan (948-1031) wearing a winged helmet **Edge:** Plain **Note:** Similar to KM# 403a

Date	Mintage	F	VF	XF	Unc	BU
2003 Proof	—	Value: 35.00				

KM# 324 10 WON
31.0000 g., 0.9990 Silver 0.9957 oz. ASW, 40.2 mm. **Obv:** National arms **Rev:** Turtle-shaped armoured ship of 1592 **Edge:** Plain **Note:** Similar to KM# 323

Date	Mintage	F	VF	XF	Unc	BU
2003 Proof	—	Value: 35.00				

KM# 325 10 WON

31.0000 g., 0.9990 Silver 0.9957 oz. ASW, 40.2 mm. **Obv:** National arms **Rev:** Children playing jacks **Edge:** Plain **Note:** Similar to KM# 407a

Date	Mintage	F	VF	XF	Unc	BU
2003 Proof	—	Value: 35.00				

KM# 326 10 WON

31.0000 g., 0.9990 Silver 0.9957 oz. ASW, 40.2 mm. **Obv:** National arms **Rev:** Children kicking a shuttlecock **Edge:** Plain **Note:** Similar to KM# 406

Date	Mintage	F	VF	XF	Unc	BU
2003 Proof	—	Value: 35.00				

KM# 409 10 WON

30.9400 g., 0.9990 Silver 0.9937 oz. ASW, 40 mm. **Obv:** State arms **Rev:** Children spinning tops **Edge:** Plain **Note:** Similar to KM# 408a

Date	Mintage	F	VF	XF	Unc	BU
2003 Proof	—	Value: 35.00				

KM# 418 10 WON

31.0000 g., 0.9990 Silver 0.9957 oz. ASW, 39.7 mm. **Obv:** State arms **Rev:** Ibis standing in water **Edge:** Segmented reeding

Date	Mintage	F	VF	XF	Unc	BU
2004 Proof	—	Value: 35.00				

KM# 342 10 WON

31.0000 g., 0.9990 Silver 0.9957 oz. ASW, 40 mm. **Obv:** National arms **Rev:** Domed building **Edge:** Plain **Note:** Similar to KM# 410a

Date	Mintage	F	VF	XF	Unc	BU
2004 Proof	—	Value: 35.00				

KM# 343 10 WON

31.0000 g., 0.9990 Silver 0.9957 oz. ASW, 40 mm. **Obv:** National arms **Rev:** Pigeon on branch **Edge:** Segmented reeding

Date	Mintage	F	VF	XF	Unc	BU
2004 Proof	—	Value: 35.00				

KM# 344 10 WON

31.0000 g., 0.9990 Silver 0.9957 oz. ASW, 40 mm. **Obv:** National arms **Rev:** Two Leiothrix birds **Edge:** Segmented reeding

Date	Mintage	F	VF	XF	Unc	BU
2004 Proof	—	Value: 35.00				

KM# 345 10 WON

31.0000 g., 0.9990 Silver 0.9957 oz. ASW, 40 mm. **Obv:** National arms **Rev:** Two cranes standing in water **Edge:** Segmented reeding

Date	Mintage	F	VF	XF	Unc	BU
2004 Proof	—	Value: 35.00				

KM# 346 10 WON

31.0000 g., 0.9990 Silver 0.9957 oz. ASW, 40 mm. **Obv:** National arms **Rev:** Curlew bird **Edge:** Segmented reeding

Date	Mintage	F	VF	XF	Unc	BU
2004 Proof	—	Value: 35.00				

KM# 347 10 WON

31.0000 g., 0.9990 Silver 0.9957 oz. ASW, 40 mm. **Obv:** National arms **Rev:** Goshawk on branch **Edge:** Segmented reeding

Date	Mintage	F	VF	XF	Unc	BU
2004 Proof	—	Value: 35.00				

KM# 420 10 WON

30.9100 g., 0.9990 Silver 0.9928 oz. ASW, 40 mm. **Subject:** End of WWII 60th Anniversary **Obv:** State arms **Rev:** Multicolor radiant map, doves, rainbow and inscription **Edge:** Plain

Date	Mintage	F	VF	XF	Unc	BU
2005 Proof	—	Value: 35.00				

KM# 256 20 WON

42.0600 g., 0.9990 Silver 1.3509 oz. ASW, 45.1 mm. **Obv:** State emblem **Rev:** Flowers type I **Edge:** Plain **Note:** Similar to KM# 416

Date	Mintage	F	VF	XF	Unc	BU
2004 Proof	—	Value: 45.00				

KM# 257 20 WON

42.0100 g., 0.9990 Silver 1.3493 oz. ASW, 45.1 mm. **Obv:** State emblem **Rev:** Flowers type II **Edge:** Plain **Note:** Similar to KM# 415

Date	Mintage	F	VF	XF	Unc	BU
2004 Proof	—	Value: 45.00				

KM# 258 20 WON

41.9200 g., 0.9990 Silver 1.3464 oz. ASW, 45.1 mm. **Obv:** State emblem **Rev:** Flowers type III **Edge:** Plain **Note:** Similar to KM# 414

Date	Mintage	F	VF	XF	Unc	BU
2004 Proof	—	Value: 45.00				

KM# 259 20 WON

42.0000 g., 0.9990 Silver 1.349 oz. ASW, 45.1 mm. **Obv:** State emblem **Rev:** Kim Il Sung's birth place, side view **Edge:** Plain **Note:** Similar to KM# 413

Date	Mintage	F	VF	XF	Unc	BU
2004 Proof	—	Value: 45.00				

KM# 260 20 WON

41.6200 g., 0.9990 Silver 1.3368 oz. ASW, 45.1 mm. **Obv:** State emblem **Rev:** Mountain cabin **Edge:** Plain **Note:** Similar to KM# 411

Date	Mintage	F	VF	XF	Unc	BU
2004 Proof	—	Value: 45.00				

KM# 261 20 WON

41.9100 g., 0.9990 Silver 1.3461 oz. ASW, 45.1 mm. **Obv:** State emblem **Rev:** Kim Il Sung's birth place, front view **Edge:** Plain **Note:** Similar to KM# 412

Date	Mintage	F	VF	XF	Unc	BU
2004 Proof	—	Value: 45.00				

KM# 340 20 WON

31.0000 g., 0.9990 Silver 0.9957 oz. ASW, 39.8 mm. **Obv:** National arms **Rev:** Kim Jong Il and Putin **Edge:** Segmented reeding

Date	Mintage	F	VF	XF	Unc	BU
2004 Proof	—	Value: 45.00				

KM# 341 20 WON

31.0000 g., 0.9990 Silver 0.9957 oz. ASW, 39.8 mm. **Obv:** National arms **Rev:** Kim Jong Il **Edge:** Segmented reeding

Date	Mintage	F	VF	XF	Unc	BU
2004 Proof	—	Value: 45.00				

KM# 419 20 WON

31.0000 g., 0.9990 Silver 0.9957 oz. ASW, 39.75 mm. **Subject:** Historic Pyongyang Meeting **Obv:** State arms **Rev:** Kim Jong Il standing face to face with Kim Dae Jung shaking hands, English legend **Edge:** Segmented reeding

Date	Mintage	F	VF	XF	Unc	BU
2004 Proof	—	Value: 45.00				

KM# 262 50 WON

69.6300 g., 0.9990 Silver 2.2364 oz. ASW, 50 mm. **Obv:** Korean map **Rev:** King Sejong the Great and books **Edge:** Plain

Date	Mintage	F	VF	XF	Unc	BU
2004 Proof	—	Value: 65.00				

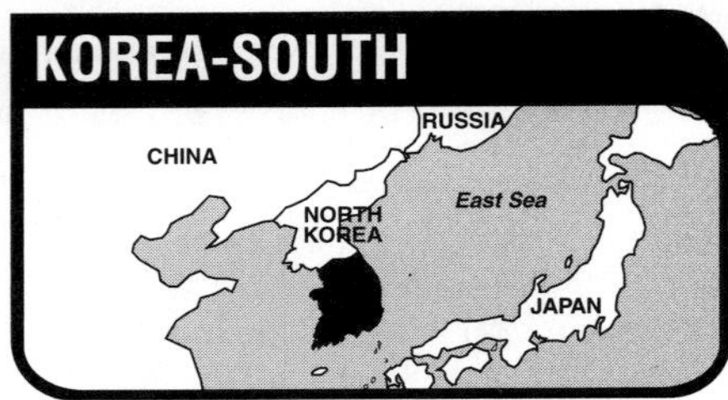

The Republic of Korea, situated in northeastern Asia on the southern half of the Korean peninsula between North Korea and the Korean Strait, has an area of 38,025 sq. mi. (98,480 sq. km.) and a population of 42.5 million. Capital: Seoul. The economy is based on agriculture and light and medium industry. Some of the world's largest oil tankers are built here. Automobiles, plywood, electronics, and textile products are exported.

NOTE: For earlier coinage see Korea.

REPUBLIC

REFORM COINAGE

10 Hwan = 1 Won

KM# 31 WON

0.7290 g., Aluminum, 17.2 mm. **Obverse:** Rose of Sharon (hibiscus syriacus)

Date	Mintage	F	VF	XF	Unc
2001	—	—	—	—	0.15

KM# 32 5 WON

2.9500 g., Brass, 20.4 mm. **Obverse:** Iron-clad turtle boat

Date	Mintage	F	VF	XF	Unc
2001	—	—	—	0.10	0.20
2003	—	—	—	0.10	0.20

KM# 33.2 10 WON

Brass **Obverse:** Pagoda at Pul Guk Temple **Reverse:** Thick numbers in denomination

Date	Mintage	F	VF	XF	Unc
2001	—	—	—	0.10	0.35
2002	—	—	—	0.10	0.35
2003	—	—	—	0.10	0.35

KM# 34 50 WON

4.1600 g., Copper-Nickel, 21.16 mm. **Series:** F.A.O. **Note:** Die varieties exist.

Date	Mintage	F	VF	XF	Unc
2001	—	—	—	0.10	0.35
2002	—	—	—	0.10	0.35
2003	—	—	—	0.10	0.35

KM# 35.2 100 WON

5.4200 g., Copper-Nickel, 24 mm. **Obverse:** Admiral Yi Soon-shin **Reverse:** Modified design

Date	Mintage	F	VF	XF	Unc
2001	—	—	0.15	0.25	0.55
2003	—	—	0.15	0.25	0.55

KM# 27 500 WON

7.7000 g., Copper-Nickel, 26.5 mm. **Obverse:** Manchurian crane

Date	Mintage	F	VF	XF	Unc
2001	—	—	—	1.00	2.50
2003	—	—	—	1.00	2.50

KM# 89 1000 WON

12.0000 g., Brass, 32 mm. **Mint:** Seoul **Series:** World Cup Soccer **Obverse:** FIFA World Cup logo **Reverse:** Mascot soccer player **Edge:** Reeded

Date	Mintage	F	VF	XF	Unc
2001	102,000	—	—	—	8.50

KM# 90 10000 WON

31.1035 g., 0.9990 Silver 1.0000 oz. ASW, 35 mm. **Mint:** Seoul **Series:** World Cup Soccer **Subject:** Gwangju Stadium **Obverse:** Multicolor soccer logo **Reverse:** Player heading the ball **Edge:** Reeded

Date	Mintage	F	VF	XF	Unc
2001 Proof	37,000	Value: 40.00			

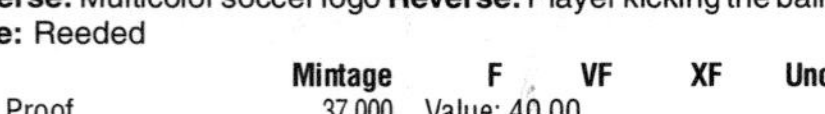

KM# 91 10000 WON

31.1035 g., 0.9990 Silver 1.0000 oz. ASW, 35 mm. **Mint:** Seoul **Series:** World Sup Soccer **Subject:** Busan Stadium **Obverse:** Multicolor soccer logo **Reverse:** Player kicking the ball **Edge:** Reeded

Date	Mintage	F	VF	XF	Unc
2001 Proof	37,000	Value: 40.00			

KM# 93 10000 WON

31.1035 g., 0.9990 Silver 1.0000 oz. ASW, 35 mm. **Mint:** Seoul **Series:** World Cup Soccer **Subject:** Daegu Stadium **Obverse:** Multicolor soccer logo **Reverse:** Player controlling the ball **Edge:** Reeded

Date	Mintage	F	VF	XF	Unc
2001 Proof	37,000	Value: 40.00			

KM# 92 10000 WON

31.1035 g., 0.9990 Silver 1.0000 oz. ASW, 35 mm. **Mint:** Seoul **Series:** World Cup Soccer **Subject:** Daegu Stadium **Obverse:** Multicolor soccer logo **Reverse:** Player controlling the ball **Edge:** Reeded

Date	Mintage	F	VF	XF	Unc
2001 Proof	37,000	Value: 35.00			

KM# 94 20000 WON

15.5518 g., 0.9990 Gold .5000 oz. AGW, 28 mm. **Mint:** Seoul **Series:** World Cup Soccer **Obverse:** Soccer logo **Reverse:** World Cup soccer trophy **Edge:** Reeded

Date	Mintage	F	VF	XF	Unc
2001 Proof	20,000	Value: 335			

KM# 97 20000 WON

20.7000 g., Silver, 35 mm. **Obverse:** Blue circle with APEC, 2005 Korea at bottom at upper center, Vista Pacific Economic Cooperation and value below **Reverse:** APEC on World map at upper center, building below with Korean words below it

Date	Mintage	F	VF	XF	Unc
2005 Proof	10,000	Value: 35.00			

KM# 95 30000 WON

31.1035 g., 0.9990 Gold 1.0000 oz. AGW, 35 mm. **Mint:** Seoul **Series:** World Cup Soccer **Obverse:** Soccer logo **Reverse:** Nude soccer player **Edge:** Reeded

Date	Mintage	F	VF	XF	Unc
2001 Proof	12,000	Value: 650			

MINT SETS

KM#	Date	Mintage	Identification	Issue Price	Mkt Val
MS8	2001 (7)	—	KM#27, 31, 32, 33.2, 34, 35.2, 89	10.00	12.50

PROOF SETS

KM#	Date	Mintage	Identification	Issue Price	Mkt Val
PS10	2001 (6)	2,002	KM#90-95	—	1,000

KUWAIT

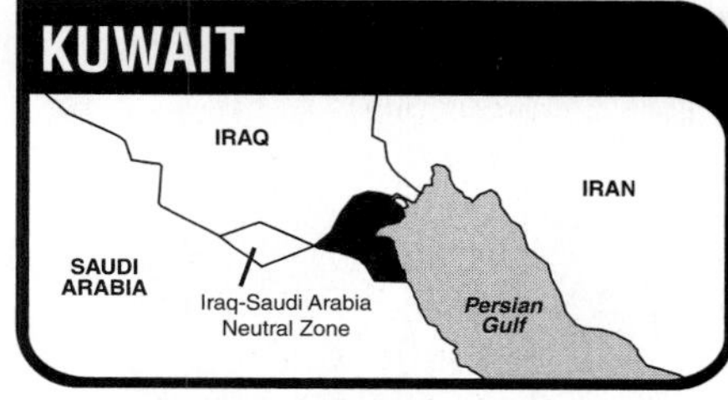

The State of Kuwait, a constitutional monarchy located on the Arabian Peninsula at the northwestern corner of the Persian Gulf, has an area of 6,880 sq. mi. (17,820 sq. km.) and a population of 1.7 million. Capital: Kuwait. Petroleum, the basis of the economy, provides 95 percent of the exports.

TITLES

al-Kuwait

RULERS

LOCAL

Al Sabah Dynasty

Jabir Ibn Ahmad, 1977-2006
Sabah Al Ahmad Al Sabah, 2006-

MONETARY SYSTEM

1000 Fils = 1 Dinar

STATE OF KUWAIT

MODERN COINAGE

KM# 12c 20 FILS

Stainless Steel **Ruler:** Jabir Ibn Ahmad **Obv:** Value **Rev:** Sail boat

Date	Mintage	F	VF	XF	Unc	BU
AH1421-2001	—	—	—	—	1.00	—

KYRGYZSTAN

The Republic of Kyrgyzstan, (formerly Kirghiz S.S.R., a Union Republic of the U.S.S.R.),is an independent state since Aug. 31, 1991, a member of the United Nations and of the C.I.S. It was the last state of the Union Republics to declare its sovereignty. Capital: Bishkek (formerly Frunze).

REPUBLIC

STANDARD COINAGE

KM# 3 10 SOM

28.2800 g., 0.9250 Silver 0.841 oz. ASW, 38.6 mm.
Subject: Tenth Anniversary of Republic **Obv:** National arms **Rev:** Denomination and mountain **Edge:** Reeded

Date	Mintage	F	VF	XF	Unc	BU
2001 Proof	1,000	Value: 60.00				

KM# 4 10 SOM

28.2800 g., 0.9250 Silver 0.841 oz. ASW, 38.6 mm.
Subject: Flora and Fauna **Obv:** National arms **Rev:** Edelweiss flower and mountain **Edge:** Reeded

Date	Mintage	F	VF	XF	Unc	BU
2002 Proof	1,000	Value: 60.00				

KM# 5 10 SOM

28.2800 g., 0.9250 Silver 0.841 oz. ASW, 38.6 mm.
Subject: Flora and Fauna **Obv:** National arms **Rev:** Bighorn sheep and mountain **Edge:** Reeded

Date	Mintage	F	VF	XF	Unc	BU
2002 Proof	1,000	Value: 60.00				

KM# 6 10 SOM

28.2800 g., 0.9250 Silver 0.841 oz. ASW, 38.6 mm.
Subject: 60 Years of Great Victory

Date	Mintage	F	VF	XF	Unc	BU
2005 Proof	1,000	Value: 60.00				

KM# 7 10 SOM

28.2800 g., 0.8250 Silver 0.7501 oz. ASW, 38.6 mm.
Subject: The Great Silk Road: Tashrabat

Date	Mintage	F	VF	XF	Unc	BU
2005 Proof	1,500	Value: 60.00				

LAO

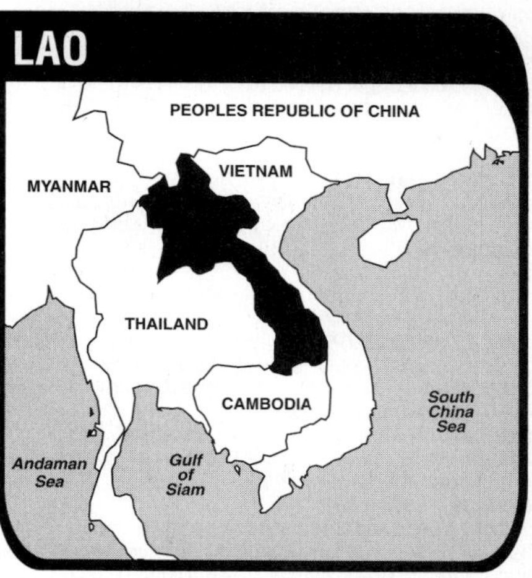

The Lao Peoples Democratic Republic, located on the Indo-Chinese Peninsula between the Socialist Republic of Vietnam and the Kingdom of Thailand, has an area of 91,428 sq. mi. (236,800 km.) and a population of 3.6 million. Capital Vientiane. Agriculture employs 95 per cent of the people. Tin, lumber and coffee are exported.

NOTE: For earlier coinage see French Indo-China.

RULERS

Sisavang Vong, 1904-1959
Savang Vatthana, 1959-1975

MONETARY SYSTEM

100 Cents = 1 Piastre

Commencing 1955

100 Att = 1 Kip

MINT MARKS

(a) - Paris, privy marks only
Key - Havana
None - Berlin

PEOPLES DEMOCRATIC REPUBLIC

STANDARD COINAGE

100 Att = 1 Kip

KM# 85 1000 KIP

31.5000 g., 0.9990 Silver 1.0117 oz. ASW, 38.5 mm. **Subject:** Olympics **Obv:** State arms **Rev:** Freestyle skier **Edge:** Reeded

Date	Mintage	F	VF	XF	Unc	BU
2001 Proof	—	Value: 40.00				

KM# 96 1000 KIP

31.4500 g., 0.9990 Silver 1.0101 oz. ASW, 38.5 mm.
Obv: National arms **Rev:** Soccer player **Edge:** Reeded

Date	Mintage	F	VF	XF	Unc	BU
2001 Proof	—	Value: 40.00				

KM# 74 5000 KIP
20.0000 g., 0.9250 Silver .5948 oz. ASW, 39 mm.
Subject: Silver Dragon Fish **Obv:** State emblem **Rev:** Fish turning to right **Edge:** Reeded

Date	Mintage	F	VF	XF	Unc	BU
2000-2001 Proof	10,000	Value: 40.00				

Note: Latent image date

KM# 75 5000 KIP
20.0000 g., 0.9250 Silver .5948 oz. ASW, 39 mm. **Subject:** Red Dragon Fish **Obv:** State emblem **Rev:** Red colored fish **Edge:** Reeded

Date	Mintage	F	VF	XF	Unc	BU
2000-2001 Proof	10,000	Value: 40.00				

Note: Latent image date

KM# 76 5000 KIP
20.0000 g., 0.9250 Silver .5948 oz. ASW, 39 mm.
Subject: Golden Dragon Fish **Obv:** State emblem **Rev:** Jumping fish below gold cameo **Edge:** Reeded

Date	Mintage	F	VF	XF	Unc	BU
2000-2001 Proof	Est. 4,000	Value: 50.00				

Note: Latent image date

KM# 86 15000 KIP
20.0000 g., 0.9250 Silver 0.5948 oz. ASW, 38.7 mm.
Subject: Year of the Horse **Obv:** State emblem **Rev:** Multicolor horse **Edge:** Reeded

Date	Mintage	F	VF	XF	Unc	BU
2002 Proof	9,500	Value: 40.00				

KM# 87 15000 KIP
20.0000 g., 0.9250 Silver 0.5948 oz. ASW, 38.7 mm.
Subject: Year of the Horse **Obv:** State emblem **Rev:** Horse with multicolor holographic background **Edge:** Reeded

Date	Mintage	F	VF	XF	Unc	BU
2002 Proof	9,500	Value: 45.00				

KM# 94 15000 KIP
20.0000 g., 0.9990 Silver 0.6424 oz. ASW, 38.7 mm. **Obv:** State emblem **Rev:** Multicolor Golden Monkey **Edge:** Reeded

Date	Mintage	F	VF	XF	Unc	BU
2004 Proof	2,300	Value: 45.00				

KM# 83 50000 KIP
7.7750 g., 0.9990 Gold 0.2497 oz. AGW, 32.2 mm.
Obv: National arms **Rev:** Red Dragon Fish **Edge:** Reeded

Date	Mintage	F	VF	XF	Unc	BU
2000-2001 Proof	3,000	Value: 180				

KM# 88 60000 KIP
155.5175 g., 0.9250 Silver 4.625 oz. ASW, 65 mm.
Subject: Year of the Horse **Obv:** State emblem **Rev:** Multicolor horse **Edge:** Reeded

Date	Mintage	F	VF	XF	Unc	BU
2002 Proof	1,000	Value: 200				

KM# 78 100000 KIP
15.5518 g., 0.9999 Gold .4999 oz. AGW, 27 mm.
Subject: Golden Dragon Fish **Obv:** State emblem
Rev: Multicolored holographic jumping fish **Edge:** Reeded

Date	Mintage	F	VF	XF	Unc	BU
2000-2001 Proof	3,000	Value: 400				

Note: Latent image date

KM# 89 100000 KIP
15.5518 g., 0.9999 Gold 0.5 oz. AGW, 27 mm. **Subject:** Year of the Horse **Obv:** State emblem **Rev:** Horse **Edge:** Reeded

Date	Mintage	F	VF	XF	Unc	BU
2002	2,000	Value: 375				

KM# 95 100000 KIP
15.5518 g., 0.9990 Gold 0.4995 oz. AGW, 27 mm. **Obv:** State emblem **Rev:** Black Gibbon on holographic background **Edge:** Reeded

Date	Mintage	F	VF	XF	Unc	BU
2004 Proof	888	Value: 385				

KM# 90 1000000 KIP
155.5175 g., 0.9999 Gold 4.9995 oz. AGW, 55 mm.
Subject: Year of the Horse **Obv:** State emblem **Rev:** Horse with multicolor holographic background **Edge:** Reeded

Date	Mintage	F	VF	XF	Unc	BU
2002 Proof	500	Value: 3,250				

PROOF SETS

KM#	Date	Mintage	Identification	Issue Price	Mkt Val
PS7	2000-2001 (3)	3,500	KM#74-76	138	200
PS8	2000-2001 (3)	500	KM#74-76	214	300
PS9	2000-2001 (2)	800	KM#78, 83	—	575

The Republic of Latvia, the central Baltic state in east Europe, has an area of 24,749 sq. mi. (43,601 sq. km.) and a population of *2.6 million. Capital: Riga. Livestock raising and manufacturing are the chief industries. Butter, bacon, fertilizers and telephone equipment are exported.

MONETARY SYSTEM
100 Santimu = 1 Lats

MODERN REPUBLIC
1991-present

STANDARD COINAGE
100 Santimu = 1 Lats

KM# 15 SANTIMS
Copper Plated Iron

Date	Mintage	F	VF	XF	Unc	BU
2005	—	—	—	—	0.25	0.35

KM# 54 LATS
4.7500 g., Copper-Nickel, 21.7 mm. **Obv:** National arms **Rev:** Stork above denomination **Edge Lettering:** "LATVIJAS BANKA" twice

Date	Mintage	F	VF	XF	Unc	BU
2001	—	—	—	—	5.50	6.00

KM# 51 LATS
31.4700 g., 0.9250 Silver 0.9359 oz. ASW, 38.6 mm.
Series: Roots - Heaven **Obv:** Stylized Roots pattern
Rev: Woman holding the sun **Edge:** Plain

Date	Mintage	F	VF	XF	Unc	BU
2001 Proof	—	Value: 50.00				

KM# 49 LATS
31.4700 g., 0.9250 Silver .9359 oz. ASW, 38.6 mm. **Subject:** Hanseatic City of Cesis **Obv:** City arms **Rev:** Castle and ship **Edge Lettering:** "LATVIJAS REPUBLIKA.LATVIJAS BANKA"

Date	Mintage	F	VF	XF	Unc	BU
2001 Proof	25,000	Value: 50.00				

KM# 50 LATS
31.4700 g., 0.9250 Silver .9359 oz. ASW **Series:** Ice Hockey **Obv:** National arms **Rev:** Hockey player

Date	Mintage	F	VF	XF	Unc	BU
2001 Proof	25,000	Value: 50.00				

KM# 52 LATS
31.4700 g., 0.9250 Silver 0.9359 oz. ASW, 38.6 mm.
Series: Roots - Destiny **Obv:** Stylized Roots pattern **Rev:** Apple tree and landscape **Edge:** Plain

Date	Mintage	F	VF	XF	Unc	BU
2002 Proof	—	Value: 50.00				

KM# 53 LATS
31.4700 g., 0.9250 Silver 0.9359 oz. ASW, 38.6 mm.
Subject: Hanseatic City of Kuldiga **Obv:** City arms **Rev:** City view and ships **Edge:** Lettered

Date	Mintage	F	VF	XF	Unc	BU
2002 Proof	—	Value: 50.00				

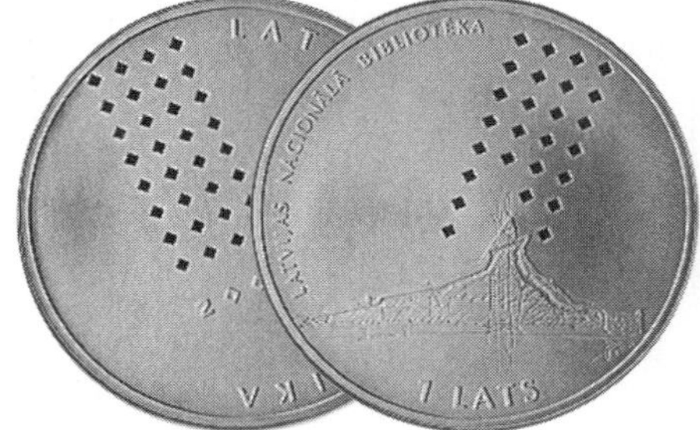

KM# 55 LATS
31.4700 g., 0.9250 Silver 0.9359 oz. ASW, 38.6 mm. **Subject:** National Library **Obv:** Country name and diamonds pattern **Rev:** Library building sketch and diamonds design **Edge Lettering:** "GAISMU SAUCA-GAISMA AUSA"

Date	Mintage	F	VF	XF	Unc	BU
2002 Proof	5,000	Value: 50.00				

KM# 56 LATS
15.0000 g., 0.9250 Silver 0.4461 oz. ASW, 28 mm.
Subject: "Fortune" **Obv:** Totally gold plated. Sun above country name **Rev:** Waning moon, date and value **Edge:** Plain

Date	Mintage	F	VF	XF	Unc	BU
2002 Proof	—	Value: 35.00				

KM# 57 LATS
31.4700 g., 0.9250 Silver 0.9359 oz. ASW, 38.6 mm. **Subject:** Olympics 2004 **Obv:** National arms **Rev:** Ancient wrestlers **Edge:** Lettered **Edge Lettering:** LATVIJAS BANKA repeated twice

Date	Mintage	F	VF	XF	Unc	BU
2002 Proof	—	Value: 50.00				

KM# 58 LATS
4.8000 g., Copper Nickel, 21.8 mm. **Obv:** National arms **Rev:** Ant above value **Edge:** Lettered **Edge Lettering:** LATVIJAS BANKA

Date	Mintage	F	VF	XF	Unc	BU
2003	—	—	—	—	5.00	6.00

KM# 60 LATS
31.4700 g., 0.9250 Silver 0.9359 oz. ASW, 38.6 mm. **Obv:** Crowned arms of Courland above a partially built ship **Rev:** Hemp weighing scene with Iron foundry and brick wall in background **Edge:** Lettered **Edge Lettering:** "REPUBLIKA LATVIJAS BANKA LATVIJA" **Note:** Western Latvia formerly Courland

Date	Mintage	F	VF	XF	Unc	BU
2003 Proof	—	Value: 50.00				

KM# 61 LATS
4.8000 g., Copper-Nickel, 21.7 mm. **Obv:** National arms **Rev:** Child with shovel above value **Edge:** Lettered **Edge Lettering:** "LATVIJAS BANKA" twice

Date	Mintage	F	VF	XF	Unc	BU
2004	—	—	—	—	5.50	6.00

KM# 62 LATS
17.1500 g., Bi-Metallic Dark Blue Niobium 7.15g center in .900 Silver 10g ring, 34 mm. **Obv:** Heraldic Rose **Rev:** Astronomical Clock **Edge:** Plain

Date	Mintage	F	VF	XF	Unc	BU
2004	—	—	—	—	50.00	55.00

KM# 63 LATS
31.4700 g., 0.9250 Silver 0.9359 oz. ASW, 38.6 mm. **Obv:** National arms **Rev:** World Cup Soccer player **Edge:** "LATVIJA" three times

Date	Mintage	F	VF	XF	Unc	BU
2004 Proof	—	Value: 50.00				

KM# 64 LATS
31.4700 g., 0.9250 Silver 0.9359 oz. ASW, 38.6 mm. **Subject:** Latvian European Union Membership **Obv:** National arms askew **Rev:** "P.S. LATVIJA-ES 2004" above value **Edge:** Lettered **Edge Lettering:** "LATVIJAS BANKA" twice

Date	Mintage	F	VF	XF	Unc	BU
2004 Proof	—	Value: 50.00				

KM# 65 LATS
14.8400 g., Copper-Nickel, 21.7 mm. **Obv:** National arms **Rev:** Chicken above value **Edge:** Lettered **Edge Lettering:** :LATVIJAS BANKA" twice

Date	Mintage	F	VF	XF	Unc	BU
2005	—	—	—	—	5.50	6.00

KM# 66 LATS
4.8500 g., Copper-Nickel, 21.7 mm. **Obv:** National arms **Rev:** Pretzel **Edge Lettering:** "LATVIJAS BANKA"

Date	Mintage	F	VF	XF	Unc	BU
2005	—	—	—	—	4.00	5.00

KM# 59 5 LATI
1.2442 g., 0.9999 Gold 0.04 oz. AGW, 13.92 mm. **Obv:** Latvian maiden **Rev:** National arms above value **Edge:** Reeded **Note:** Remake of the popular KM-9 design

Date	Mintage	F	VF	XF	Unc	BU
2003 Proof	—	Value: 60.00				

LEBANON

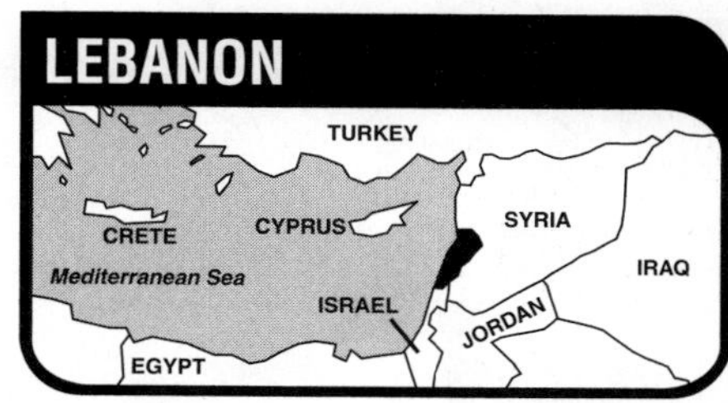

The Republic of Lebanon, situated on the eastern shore of the Mediterranean Sea between Syria and Israel, has an area of 4,015 sq. mi. (10,400 sq. km.) and a population of 3.5 million. Capital: Beirut. The economy is based on agriculture, trade and tourism. Fruit, other foodstuffs and textiles are exported.

TITLES

الجمهورية اللبنانية

al-Jomhuriya(t) al-Lubnaniya(t)

MINT MARKS
(a) - Paris, privy marks only
(u) - Utrecht, privy marks only

MONETARY SYSTEM
100 Piastres = 1 Livre (Pound)

REPUBLIC

STANDARD COINAGE

KM# 40 25 LIVRES
2.8200 g., Nickel Plated Steel, 20.5 mm. **Obv:** Denomination on tree **Rev:** Denomination in square design **Edge:** Plain

Date	Mintage	F	VF	XF	Unc	BU
2002	—	—	—	—	1.00	2.00

KM# 38a 100 LIVRES
4.0500 g., Stainless Steel, 22.5 mm. **Obv:** Value on tree **Rev:** Value above date **Edge:** Plain

Date	Mintage	F	VF	XF	Unc	BU
2003	—	—	—	—	1.50	2.50

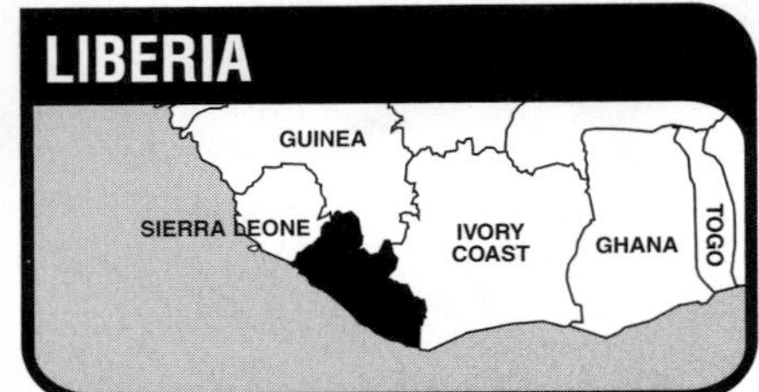

The Republic of Liberia, located on the southern side of the West African bulge between Sierra Leone and Ivory Coast, has an area of 38,250 sq. mi. (111,370 sq. km) and a population of 2.2 million. Capital: Monrovia. The major industries are agriculture, mining and lumbering. Iron ore, diamonds, rubber, coffee and coca are exported.

MINT MARKS

B - Bern, Switzerland
H - Heaton, Birmingham
(l) - London
(s) - San Francisco, U.S.
FM - Franklin Mint, U.S.A.*
PM - Pobjoy Mint

MONETARY SYSTEM

100 Cents = 1 Dollar

REPUBLIC

STANDARD COINAGE

100 Cents = 1 Dollar

KM# 618 5 CENTS

5.0200 g., Copper-Nickel, 23.8 mm. **Obv:** National arms **Rev:** Chimpanzee family **Edge:** Plain

Date	Mintage	F	VF	XF	Unc	BU
2003	—	—	—	—	1.50	2.00

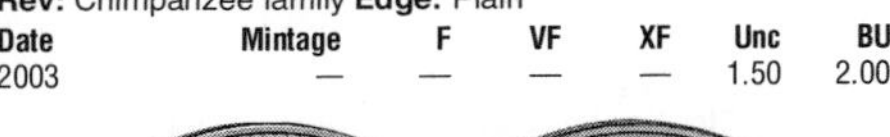

KM# 568 5 DOLLARS

14.6300 g., Copper-Nickel, 33.1 mm. **Subject:** Battle of Gettysburg **Obv:** National arms **Rev:** Generals Meade and Lee, cannon and crossed flags **Edge:** Reeded

Date	Mintage	F	VF	XF	Unc	BU
2001B	—	—	—	—	12.00	—

KM# 494 5 DOLLARS

8.5000 g., 0.9999 Silver .2733 oz. ASW, 30 mm. **Subject:** Soccer **Obv:** National arms **Rev:** Soccer player **Edge:** Reeded

Date	Mintage	F	VF	XF	Unc	BU
2002 Proof	3,000	Value: 30.00				

KM# 664 5 DOLLARS

6.4000 g., Bi-Metallic Brass center in Copper-Nickel ring, 25.7 mm. **Obv:** National arms **Rev:** Pope and cathedral **Edge:** Reeded

Date	Mintage	F	VF	XF	Unc	BU
2005	—	—	—	—	12.00	—

KM# 491 10 DOLLARS

25.2500 g., 0.9250 Silver .7509 oz. ASW, 36.8 mm. **Subject:** Illusion **Obv:** National arms **Rev:** Male-female portrait **Edge:** Plain **Shape:** 10-sided

Date	Mintage	F	VF	XF	Unc	BU
2001 Proof	5,000	Value: 35.00				

KM# 513 10 DOLLARS

Copper-Nickel, 38.6 mm. **Subject:** Hungarian Revolution of 1848 **Obv:** Liberian arms **Rev:** Multicolor heroic scene **Edge:** Reeded

Date	Mintage	F	VF	XF	Unc	BU
2001 Proof	9,999	Value: 10.00				

KM# 537 10 DOLLARS

28.5000 g., Copper-Nickel, 38.6 mm. **Subject:** "Moments of Freedom" Series **Obv:** National arms **Rev:** Multicolor Buddha, spelled "Budha" on the coin **Edge:** Reeded

Date	Mintage	F	VF	XF	Unc	BU
2001 Proof	9,999	Value: 10.00				

KM# 538 10 DOLLARS

28.5000 g., Copper-Nickel, 38.6 mm. **Subject:** "Moments of Freedom" Series **Obv:** National arms **Rev:** Multicolor Battle of Marathon scene **Edge:** Reeded

Date	Mintage	F	VF	XF	Unc	BU
2001 Proof	9,999	Value: 10.00				

KM# 539 10 DOLLARS

28.5000 g., Copper-Nickel, 38.6 mm. **Series:** "Moments of Freedom" **Obv:** National arms **Rev:** Multicolor founding of Liberia design **Edge:** Reeded

Date	Mintage	F	VF	XF	Unc	BU
2001 Proof	9,999	Value: 10.00				

KM# 540 10 DOLLARS

28.5000 g., Copper-Nickel, 38.6 mm. **Series:** "Moments of Freedom" **Obv:** National arms **Rev:** Multicolor portrait of Constantine I **Edge:** Reeded

Date	Mintage	F	VF	XF	Unc	BU
2001 Proof	9,999	Value: 10.00				

KM# 541 10 DOLLARS

28.5000 g., Copper-Nickel, 38.6 mm. **Series:** "Moments of Freedom" **Obv:** National arms **Rev:** Multicolor William Tell statue **Edge:** Reeded

Date	Mintage	F	VF	XF	Unc	BU
2001 Proof	9,999	Value: 10.00				

KM# 542 10 DOLLARS

28.5000 g., Copper-Nickel, 38.6 mm. **Series:** "Moments of Freedom" **Obv:** National arms **Rev:** Multicolor Galileo portrait **Edge:** Reeded

Date	Mintage	F	VF	XF	Unc	BU
2001 Proof	9,999	Value: 10.00				

KM# 544 10 DOLLARS

28.5000 g., Copper-Nickel, 38.6 mm. **Series:** "Moments of Freedom" **Subject:** Fall of Berlin Wall **Obv:** National arms **Rev:** Multicolor Brandenburg Gate scene **Edge:** Reeded

Date	Mintage	F	VF	XF	Unc	BU
2001 Proof	9,999	Value: 10.00				

KM# 545 10 DOLLARS

28.5000 g., Copper-Nickel, 38.6 mm. **Series:** "Moments of Freedom" **Obv:** National arms **Rev:** Multicolor Dalai Lama portrait **Edge:** Reeded

Date	Mintage	F	VF	XF	Unc	BU
2001 Proof	9,999	Value: 10.00				

KM# 546 10 DOLLARS

28.5000 g., Copper Nickel, 38.6 mm. **Subject:** "Moments of Freedom" Series **Obv:** National arms **Rev:** Multicolor Sitting Bull portrait **Edge:** Reeded

Date	Mintage	F	VF	XF	Unc	BU
2001 Proof	9,999	Value: 10.00				

KM# 547 10 DOLLARS
28.5000 g., Copper-Nickel, 38.6 mm. **Series:** "Moments of Freedom" **Obv:** National arms **Rev:** Multicolor Declaration of Independence scene **Edge:** Reeded

Date	Mintage	F	VF	XF	Unc	BU
2001 Proof	9,999	Value: 10.00				

KM# 548 10 DOLLARS
28.5000 g., Copper-Nickel, 38.6 mm. **Series:** "Moments of Freedom" **Subject:** Women's Rights **Obv:** National arms **Rev:** Multicolor allegorical woman **Edge:** Reeded

Date	Mintage	F	VF	XF	Unc	BU
2001 Proof	9,999	Value: 10.00				

KM# 549 10 DOLLARS
28.5000 g., Copper-Nickel, 38.6 mm. **Series:** "Moments of Freedom" **Obv:** National arms **Rev:** Multicolor Gandhi portrait **Edge:** Reeded

Date	Mintage	F	VF	XF	Unc	BU
2001 Proof	9,999	Value: 10.00				

KM# 550 10 DOLLARS
28.5000 g., Copper-Nickel, 38.6 mm. **Series:** "Moments of Freedom" **Subject:** Spanish Civil War **Obv:** National arms **Rev:** Multicolor picture of a soldier at the moment he is shot in battle **Edge:** Reeded

Date	Mintage	F	VF	XF	Unc	BU
2001 Proof	9,999	Value: 10.00				

KM# 551 10 DOLLARS
28.5000 g., Copper-Nickel, 38.6 mm. **Series:** "Moments of Freedom" **Subject:** End of Holocaust **Obv:** National arms **Rev:** Multicolor inmates behind wire fence scene **Edge:** Reeded

Date	Mintage	F	VF	XF	Unc	BU
2001 Proof	9,999	Value: 10.00				

KM# 552 10 DOLLARS
28.5000 g., Copper-Nickel, 38.6 mm. **Series:** "Moments of Freedom" **Subject:** End of WWII **Obv:** National arms **Rev:** Multicolor Iwo Jima flag raising scene **Edge:** Reeded

Date	Mintage	F	VF	XF	Unc	BU
2001 Proof	9,999	Value: 10.00				

KM# 553 10 DOLLARS
28.5000 g., Copper-Nickel, 38.6 mm. **Series:** "Moments of Freedom" **Subject:** United Nations **Obv:** National arms **Rev:** Multicolor UN logo and dove **Edge:** Reeded

Date	Mintage	F	VF	XF	Unc	BU
2001 Proof	9,999	Value: 10.00				

KM# 554 10 DOLLARS
28.5000 g., Copper-Nickel, 38.6 mm. **Series:** "Moments of Freedom" **Obv:** National arms **Rev:** Multicolor Solzhenitsyn portrait **Edge:** Reeded

Date	Mintage	F	VF	XF	Unc	BU
2001 Proof	9,999	Value: 10.00				

KM# 555 10 DOLLARS
28.5000 g., Copper-Nickel, 38.6 mm. **Series:** "Moments of Freedom" **Obv:** National arms **Rev:** Multicolor Spartacus and troops **Edge:** Reeded

Date	Mintage	F	VF	XF	Unc	BU
2001 Proof	9,999	Value: 10.00				

KM# 556 10 DOLLARS
28.5000 g., Copper-Nickel, 38.6 mm. **Series:** "Moments of Freedom" **Subject:** Czechoslovakia 1968 **Obv:** National arms **Rev:** Multicolor Soviet tank in Prague **Edge:** Reeded

Date	Mintage	F	VF	XF	Unc	BU
2001 Proof	9,999	Value: 10.00				

KM# 557 10 DOLLARS
28.5000 g., Copper Nickel, 38.6 mm. **Subject:** "Moments of Freedom" Series - French Revolution **Obv:** National arms. **Rev:** Multicolor Bastille scene. **Edge:** Reeded.

Date	Mintage	F	VF	XF	Unc	BU
2001 Proof	9,999	Value: 10.00				

KM# 558 10 DOLLARS
28.5000 g., Copper-Nickel, 38.6 mm. **Series:** "Moments of Freedom" **Obv:** National arms **Rev:** Multicolor Nelson Mandela and fist **Edge:** Reeded

Date	Mintage	F	VF	XF	Unc	BU
2001 Proof	9,999	Value: 10.00				

KM# 559 10 DOLLARS
28.5000 g., Copper-Nickel, 38.6 mm. **Series:** "Moments of Freedom" **Subject:** Freedom of Communication **Obv:** National arms **Rev:** Multicolor circuit board and world globe **Edge:** Reeded

Date	Mintage	F	VF	XF	Unc	BU
2001 Proof	9,999	Value: 10.00				

KM# 510 10 DOLLARS
33.2400 g., Gold-Plated Copper, 40.1 mm. **Subject:** American Eagle **Obv:** National arms **Rev:** Multicolor holographic eagle **Edge:** Reeded **Note:** The American Mint is not an actual mint.

Date	Mintage	F	VF	XF	Unc	BU
2001	20,000	—	—	—	35.00	—

KM# 511 10 DOLLARS
27.6100 g., Copper-Nickel, 40.1 mm. **Subject:** American Eagle **Obv:** Multicolor holographic Statue of Liberty **Obv. Legend:** LIBERTY 10 DOLLARS **Rev:** Multicolor holographic eagle **Rev. Legend:** AMERICAN EAGLE 10 DOLLARS **Edge:** Reeded **Note:** There is not a country name or symbol to be found on this coin. The American Mint is not an actual mint.

Date	Mintage	F	VF	XF	Unc	BU
ND(2001)	20,000	—	—	—	30.00	—

KM# 543 10 DOLLARS
28.5000 g., Copper-Nickel, 38.6 mm. **Series:** "Moments of Freedom" **Subject:** Liberation of Vienna **Obv:** National arms **Rev:** Multicolor Sultan and battle scene **Edge:** Reeded **Note:** Vienna was never captured by the Turks.

Date	Mintage	F	VF	XF	Unc	BU
2001 Proof	9,999	Value: 10.00				

KM# 493 10 DOLLARS
770.0000 g., Copper, 100 mm. **Subject:** "The Wreck of the Princess Louisa" **Obv:** National arms **Rev:** Sailing ship **Edge:** Reeded **Note:** Illustration reduced. With an encased glass shard recovered from the wreck site of the Princess Louisa.

Date	Mintage	F	VF	XF	Unc	BU
2001	2,000	—	—	—	200	—

KM# 654 10 DOLLARS
15.3300 g., Copper-Nickel, 33.2 mm. **Obv:** National arms **Rev:** "GEORGE W. BUSH..." No value at bottom **Edge:** Reeded

Date	Mintage	F	VF	XF	Unc	BU
2002	—	—	—	—	10.00	—

KM# 705 10 DOLLARS
31.1035 g., 0.9990 Silver 0.999 oz. ASW, 38.6 mm. **Subject:** 2002 World Football Championship - Japan - South Korea **Obv:** National arms **Rev:** Pagoda superimposed on a soccer ball, legend around **Edge:** Reeded

Date	Mintage	F	VF	XF	Unc	BU
2002 Proof	—	Value: 45.00				

KM# 602 10 DOLLARS
25.0000 g., 0.9250 Silver 0.7435 oz. ASW, 38.6 mm. **Obv:** National arms **Rev:** Icarus and Daedalus in flight **Edge:** Reeded

Date	Mintage	F	VF	XF	Unc	BU
2003 Proof	—	Value: 35.00				

KM# 603 10 DOLLARS
25.0000 g., 0.9250 Silver 0.7435 oz. ASW, 38.6 mm. **Obv:** National arms **Rev:** First parachute design by Leonardo da Vinci **Edge:** Reeded

Date	Mintage	F	VF	XF	Unc	BU
2003 Proof	—	Value: 35.00				

KM# 604 10 DOLLARS
25.0000 g., 0.9250 Silver 0.7435 oz. ASW, 38.6 mm. **Obv:** National arms **Rev:** Montgolfier ballon **Edge:** Reeded

Date	Mintage	F	VF	XF	Unc	BU
2003 Proof	—	Value: 35.00				

KM# 605 10 DOLLARS
25.0000 g., 0.9250 Silver 0.7435 oz. ASW, 38.6 mm. **Obv:** National arms **Rev:** Otto v. Lillenthal **Edge:** Reeded

Date	Mintage	F	VF	XF	Unc	BU
2003 Proof	—	Value: 35.00				

KM# 606 10 DOLLARS
25.0000 g., 0.9250 Silver 0.7435 oz. ASW, 38.6 mm. **Obv:** National arms **Rev:** Wright Brothers **Edge:** Reeded

Date	Mintage	F	VF	XF	Unc	BU
2003 Proof	—	Value: 35.00				

KM# 607 10 DOLLARS
25.0000 g., 0.9250 Silver 0.7435 oz. ASW, 38.6 mm. **Obv:** National arms **Rev:** Mach 1- Bell X **Edge:** Reeded

Date	Mintage	F	VF	XF	Unc	BU
2003 Proof	—	Value: 35.00				

KM# 608 10 DOLLARS
25.0000 g., 0.9250 Silver 0.7435 oz. ASW, 38.6 mm. **Obv:** National arms **Rev:** The Concorde **Edge:** Reeded

Date	Mintage	F	VF	XF	Unc	BU
2003 Proof	—	Value: 35.00				

KM# 611 10 DOLLARS
62.2070 g., 0.9990 Silver 1.998 oz. ASW, 50 mm. **Obv:** National arms left of window design with Tiffany Glass inlay **Rev:** Window design with Tiffany Glass inlay **Edge:** Plain

Date	Mintage	F	VF	XF	Unc	BU
2004	999	—	—	—	85.00	—

KM# 514 20 DOLLARS
31.1035 g., 0.9990 Silver 0.999 oz. ASW, 38.2 mm. **Subject:** Bush-Cheney Inauguration **Obv:** White House **Rev:** Conjoined busts of President Bush and Vice President Cheney right **Edge:** Reeded

Date	Mintage	F	VF	XF	Unc	BU
2001 Proof	—	Value: 40.00				

KM# 643 20 DOLLARS
15.5500 g., 0.9990 Silver 0.4994 oz. ASW, 30.4 mm. **Obv:** St. Peter's Basilica **Rev:** Pope John Paul II **Edge:** Reeded

Date	Mintage	F	VF	XF	Unc	BU
2001S Proof	—	Value: 25.00				

KM# 650 20 DOLLARS
19.9100 g., 0.9990 Silver 0.6395 oz. ASW, 40 mm. **Obv:** National arms **Rev:** Charles Lindbergh and the Spirit of St. Louis **Edge:** Reeded

Date	Mintage	F	VF	XF	Unc	BU
2001 Proof	—	Value: 40.00				

KM# 616 20 DOLLARS
31.2000 g., 0.9990 Gold Plated Silver 1.0021 oz. ASW AGW, 38.7 mm. **Obv:** National arms **Rev:** "Scorpio" diamond-studded scorpion **Edge:** Reeded

Date	Mintage	F	VF	XF	Unc	BU
2002 Proof	—	Value: 60.00				

KM# 617 20 DOLLARS
31.2000 g., 0.9990 Gold Plated Silver 1.0021 oz. ASW AGW, 38.7 mm. **Obv:** National arms **Rev:** "Sagittarius" diamond-studded **Edge:** Reeded

Date	Mintage	F	VF	XF	Unc	BU
2002 Proof	—	Value: 60.00				

KM# 495 50 DOLLARS
907.0000 g., 0.9990 Silver 29.1315 oz. ASW, 100 mm. **Subject:** Wreck of the Princess Louisa **Obv:** National arms, denomination and date **Rev:** Ship under sail **Edge:** Reeded **Note:** Each coin has a cob coin recovered from the wreck site encased in a hole with clear resin. Illustration reduced.

Date	Mintage	F	VF	XF	Unc	BU
2001	500	—	—	—	325	—

PATTERNS

Including off metal strikes

KM#	Date	Mintage	Identification	Mkt Val
Pn58	2001	—	10 Dollars. Copper Nickel. 29.2500 g. 38.2 mm. National arms. "9-11" Flag raising scene. Plain edge.	100

KM#	Date	Mintage	Identification	Mkt Val
Pn59	2001	—	20 Dollars. Silver-Plated Base Metal. 5.3100 g. 20 mm. National arms. "9-11" Flag raising scene. Plain edge.	60.00

KM#	Date	Mintage	Identification	Mkt Val
Pn60	2001	—	100 Dollars. Gold-Plated Base Metal. 3.4200 g. 16 mm. National arms. "9-11" Flag raising scene. Plain edge.	40.00

LIBYA

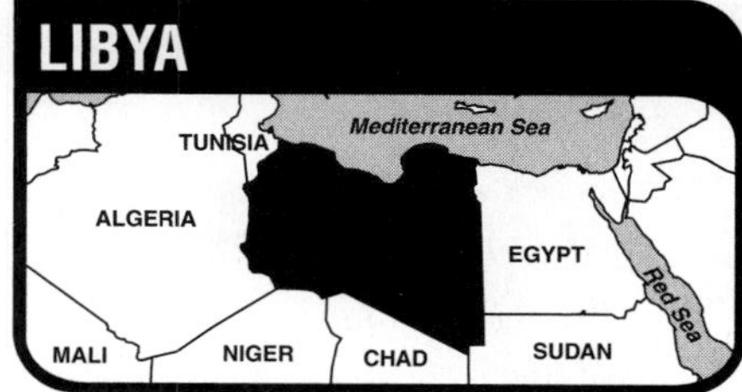

The Socialist People's Libyan Arab Jamahariya, located on the north-central coast of Africa between Tunisia and Egypt, has an area of 679,358 sq. mi. (1,759,540 sq. km.) and a population of 3.9 million. Capital: Tripoli. Crude oil, which accounts for 90 per cent of the export earnings, is the mainstay of the economy.

TITLES

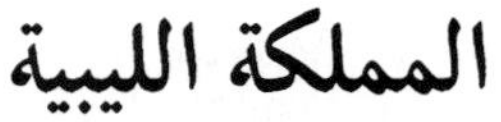

al-Mamlaka(t) al-Libiya(t)

al-Jomhuriya(t) al-Arabiya(t) al-Libiya(t)

MONETARY SYSTEM

10 Milliemes = 1 Piastre
100 Piastres = 1 Pound

SOCIALIST PEOPLE'S REPUBLIC

STANDARD COINAGE

1000 Dirhams = 1 Dinar

KM# 26 1/4 DINAR
11.1500 g., Nickel-Brass, 28 mm. **Obv:** Libyan knight on horse **Rev:** Nonumeric value above two crossed wheat ears all within an ornamental frame **Edge:** Ten alternating reeded and plain flat sections **Shape:** 10-sided

Date	Mintage	F	VF	XF	Unc	BU
1369(2001-02)	—	—	—	—	50.00	—

LITHUANIA

The Republic of Lithuania, southernmost of the Baltic states in east Europe, has an area of 25,174 sq. mi.(65,201 sq. km.) and a population of *3.6 million. Capital: Vilnius. The economy is based on livestock raising and manufacturing. Hogs, cattle, hides and electric motors are exported.

Lithuania declared its independence March 11, 1990 and it was recognized by the United States on Sept. 2, 1991, followed by the Soviet government in Moscow on Sept. 6. They were seated in the UN General Assembly on Sept. 17, 1991.

MODERN REPUBLIC

1991-present

STANDARD COINAGE

100 Centas = 1 Litas

KM# 147 50 LITU
28.2800 g., 0.9250 Silver 0.841 oz. ASW, 38.6 mm. **Subject:** 1905 Lithuanian Congress **Obv:** Lithuanian Knight **Rev:** Legend and inscription **Edge:** Ornamented

Date	Mintage	F	VF	XF	Unc	BU
2005 Proof	1,500	Value: 50.00				

REFORM COINAGE

100 Centas = 1 Litas

KM# 106 10 CENTU
2.6000 g., Brass, 16 mm. **Obv:** Lithuanian knight **Rev:** Denomination **Edge:** Milled

Date	Mintage	F	VF	XF	Unc	BU
2003	—	—	—	—	0.40	—
2003 Proof	10,000	Value: 0.75				

KM# 107 20 CENTU
4.8000 g., Brass, 20 mm. **Obv:** Lithuanian knight **Rev:** Denomination **Edge:** Milled

Date	Mintage	F	VF	XF	Unc	BU
2003	—	—	—	—	0.75	—
2003 Proof	10,000	Value: 1.00				

KM# 108 50 CENTU
6.0000 g., Brass

Date	Mintage	F	VF	XF	Unc	BU
2003	—	—	—	—	1.00	—
2003 Proof	10,000	Value: 1.50				

KM# 111 LITAS
Copper-Nickel **Obv:** Lithuanian knight **Rev:** Denomination **Edge:** Reeded

Date	Mintage	F	VF	XF	Unc	BU
2001	—	—	—	—	1.25	—
2002	—	—	—	—	1.25	—
2003	—	—	—	—	1.25	—
2003 Proof	10,000	Value: 2.00				

KM# 137 LITAS
6.1500 g., Copper-Nickel, 22.2 mm. **Subject:** 425th Anniversary - University of Vilnius **Obv:** Lithuanian knight above value **Rev:** Old university buildings **Edge:** Segmented reeding

Date	Mintage	F	VF	XF	Unc	BU
2004	200,000	—	—	—	5.00	—

KM# 142 LITAS
6.4100 g., Copper-Nickel, 22.35 mm. **Obv:** Lithuanian Knight **Rev:** Vilnius Ducal Palace **Edge:** Segmented reeding

Date	Mintage	F	VF	XF	Unc	BU
2005	1,000,000	—	—	—	3.50	—

KM# 112 2 LITAI
Bi-metallic; Copper-Nickel center in Brass ring **Obv:** Lithuanian knight **Rev:** Denomination **Edge:** Segmented reeding

Date	Mintage	F	VF	XF	Unc	BU
2001	—	—	—	—	2.75	—
2002	—	—	—	—	2.75	—
2003	—	—	—	—	2.75	—
2003 Proof	10,000	Value: 3.00				

KM# 132 5 LITAI
28.2800 g., 0.9250 Silver 0.841 oz. ASW, 38.6 mm. **Series:** Endangered Wildlife **Obv:** Knight on horse **Rev:** Barn owl in flight **Edge Lettering:** LIETUVOS BANKAS

Date	Mintage	F	VF	XF	Unc	BU
2002 Proof	3,000	Value: 45.00				

KM# 113 5 LITAI
Bi-metallic; Copper-Nickel center in Brass ring **Obv:** Lithuanian knight **Rev:** Denomination **Edge Lettering:** PENKI LITAI

Date	Mintage	F	VF	XF	Unc	BU
2003	—	—	—	—	5.00	—
2003 Proof	10,000	Value: 6.00				

KM# 131 10 LITU
13.1500 g., Copper-Nickel, 28.7 mm. **Obv:** National arms above an aerial harbor view **Rev:** Klaipeda (Memel) city arms and city view **Edge Lettering:** KLAIPEDAI - 75 (twice)

Date	Mintage	F	VF	XF	Unc	BU
2002 Proof	5,000	Value: 15.00				

KM# 130 50 LITU
28.2800 g., 0.9250 Silver 0.841 oz. ASW, 38.61 mm. **Subject:** Jonas Basanavicius (1851-1927) **Obv:** Mounted knight left **Rev:** Jonas Basanavlcius **Edge Lettering:** KAD AUSRAI AUSTANT PRAVISTU IR LIETUVOS DVASIA

Date	Mintage	F	VF	XF	Unc	BU
2001 Proof	2,000	Value: 47.50				

KM# 129 50 LITU
28.2800 g., 0.9250 Silver .8410 oz. ASW, 38.61 mm. **Subject:** Motiejus Valancius' 200th Birthday **Obv:** National arms and church landscape **Rev:** Bishop's portrait **Edge Lettering:** LIETUVISKAS ZODIS RASTAS IR TIKEJMAS TAUTOS GYVASTIS

Date	Mintage	F	VF	XF	Unc	BU
2001 Proof	2,000	Value: 47.50				

KM# 133 50 LITU
28.2800 g., 0.9250 Silver 0.8410 oz. ASW **Obv:** Republic of Lithuania coat of arms **Rev:** Trakai Island Castle **Edge Lettering:** ISTORIJOS IR ARCHITEKTUROS PAMINKLAI

Date	Mintage	F	VF	XF	Unc	BU
2002 Proof	1,500	Value: 50.00				

KM# 134 50 LITU
28.2800 g., 0.9250 Silver 0.841 oz. ASW, 38.6 mm. **Obv:** Lithuanian knight above value **Rev:** Vilnius Cathedral **Edge Lettering:** ISTORIJOS IR ARCHITEKTUROS PAMINKLAI

Date	Mintage	F	VF	XF	Unc	BU
2003 Proof	1,500	Value: 50.00				

KM# 135 50 LITU
28.2800 g., 0.9250 Silver 0.841 oz. ASW, 38.6 mm. **Subject:** Olympics **Obv:** Lithuanian knight above value **Rev:** Stylized cyclists **Edge Lettering:** XXVIII OLIMPIADOS ZAIDYNEMS

Date	Mintage	F	VF	XF	Unc	BU
2003 Proof	2,000	Value: 47.50				

KM# 138 50 LITU
28.2800 g., 0.9250 Silver 0.841 oz. ASW, 38.6 mm. **Subject:** 425th Anniversary - University of Vilnius **Obv:** Lithuanian Knight **Rev:** Old university buildings **Edge:** Lettered

Date	Mintage	F	VF	XF	Unc	BU
2004 Proof	2,000	Value: 37.50				

KM# 139 50 LITU
28.2800 g., 0.9250 Silver 0.841 oz. ASW, 38.6 mm. **Obv:** Lithuanian knight **Rev:** Pazaislis Monastery **Edge:** Lettered **Edge Lettering:** ISTORIJOS IR ARCHITEKTUROS PAMINKLAI

Date	Mintage	F	VF	XF	Unc	BU
2004 Proof	1,500	Value: 45.00				

KM# 140 50 LITU
28.2800 g., 0.9250 Silver 0.841 oz. ASW, 38.6 mm. **Subject:** First Lithuanian Statute of 1529 **Obv:** Lithuanian Knight **Rev:** King Sigismond the Old and Chancellor Gostaustas **Edge:** Lettered **Edge Lettering:** "BUKIME TEISES VERGAI, KAD GALETUME NAUDOTIS LAISVEMIS"

Date	Mintage	F	VF	XF	Unc	BU
2004 Proof	1,000	Value: 50.00				

KM# 141 50 LITU
28.2800 g., 0.9250 Silver 0.841 oz. ASW, 38.6 mm. **Subject:** Curonian Spit **Obv:** Lithuanian Knight **Rev:** Shifting sand dunes design **Edge:** Ornamented pattern from Neringa emblem

Date	Mintage	F	VF	XF	Unc	BU
2004 Proof	2,000	Value: 40.00				

KM# 143 50 LITU
28.2800 g., 0.9250 Silver 0.841 oz. ASW, 38.6 mm. **Obv:** Denar coin with Lithuanian knight **Rev:** Kernavé hill fort **Edge Lettering:** ISTORIJOS IR ARCHITEKTUROS PAMINKLAI

Date	Mintage	F	VF	XF	Unc	BU
2005 Proof	2,000	Value: 40.00				

KM# 144 50 LITU
28.2800 g., 0.9250 Silver 0.841 oz. ASW, 38.6 mm. **Subject:** 150th Anniversary - National Museum **Obv:** Trio of ancient Lithuanian coins **Rev:** Man blowing horn **Edge Lettering:** PRO PUBLICO BONO

Date	Mintage	F	VF	XF	Unc	BU
2005 Proof	1,500	Value: 40.00				

KM# 145 50 LITU
28.2800 g., 0.9250 Silver 0.841 oz. ASW, 38.6 mm. **Subject:** Lithuanian knight, cross **Rev:** Cardinal Vincentas Sladkevicius **Edge Lettering:** LET OUR LIFE BE BUILT ON GOODNESS AND HOPE

Date	Mintage	F	VF	XF	Unc	BU
2005 Proof	2,000	Value: 42.50				

KM# 136 200 LITU
15.0000 g., Bi-Metallic .900 Gold 7.9g. center in a .925 Silver 7.1g. ring, 27 mm. **Subject:** 750th Anniversary - King Mindaugas **Obv:** Lithuanian Knight **Rev:** Seated King Mindaugas **Edge Lettering:** LIETUVOS KARALYSTE 1253

Date	Mintage	F	VF	XF	Unc	BU
2003 Proof	2,000	Value: 450				

KM# 146 500 LITU
31.1000 g., 0.9999 Gold 0.9998 oz. AGW, 32.5 mm. **Subject:** Vilnius Ducal Palace **Obv:** Lithuanian Knight **Rev:** Vilnius Ducal Palace **Edge:** Plain

Date	Mintage	F	VF	XF	Unc	BU
2005 Proof	1,000	Value: 950				

MINT SETS

KM#	Date	Mintage	Identification	Issue Price	Mkt Val
MS4	2003 (6)	10,000	KM#106-108, 111-113	7.50	14.50

LUXEMBOURG

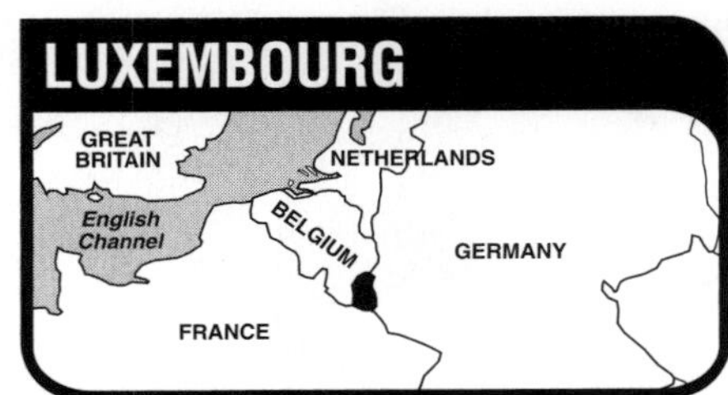

The Grand Duchy of Luxembourg is located in western Europe between Belgium, Germany and France, has an area of 1,103 sq. mi. (2,586 sq. km.) and a population of 377,100. Capital: Luxembourg. The economy is based on steel.

RULERS
Henri, 2000-

MINT MARKS
(u) - Utrecht, privy marks only

GRAND DUCHY

EURO COINAGE

European Economic Community Issues

KM# 75 EURO CENT
2.2700 g., Copper Plated Steel, 16.2 mm. **Ruler:** Henri **Obv:** Prince's portrait **Obv. Designer:** Yvette Gastauer-Claire **Rev:** Denominaton and globe **Rev. Designer:** Luc Luycx **Edge:** Plain

Date	Mintage	F	VF	XF	Unc	BU
2002(u)	34,512,000	—	—	—	0.35	—
2003	1,500,000	—	—	—	0.50	—
2004	21,000,000	—	—	—	0.35	—
2005	—	—	—	—	0.35	—
2006	—	—	—	—	0.35	—

KM# 76 2 EURO CENTS
3.0300 g., Copper Plated Steel, 18.7 mm. **Ruler:** Henri **Obv:** Prince's portrait **Obv. Designer:** Yvette Gastauer-Claire **Rev:** Denomination and globe **Rev. Designer:** Luc Luycx **Edge:** Grooved

Date	Mintage	F	VF	XF	Unc	BU
2002(u)	35,912,000	—	—	—	0.50	—
2003	1,500,000	—	—	—	0.65	—
2004	20,000,000	—	—	—	0.50	—
2005	—	—	—	—	0.50	—
2006	—	—	—	—	0.50	—

KM# 77 5 EURO CENTS
3.8600 g., Copper Plated Steel, 21.2 mm. **Ruler:** Henri **Obv:** Prince's portrait **Obv. Designer:** Yvette Gastauer-Claire **Rev:** Denomination and globe **Rev. Designer:** Luc Luycx **Edge:** Plain

Date	Mintage	F	VF	XF	Unc	BU
2002(u)	28,912,000	—	—	—	0.75	—
2003	4,500,000	—	—	—	1.00	—
2004	16,000,000	—	—	—	0.75	—
2005	—	—	—	—	0.75	—
2006	—	—	—	—	0.75	—

KM# 78 10 EURO CENTS
4.0700 g., Brass, 19.7 mm. **Ruler:** Henri **Obv:** Prince's portrait **Obv. Designer:** Yvette Gastauer-Claire **Rev:** Denomination and map **Rev. Designer:** Luc Luycx **Edge:** Reeded

Date	Mintage	F	VF	XF	Unc	BU
2002(u)	25,112,000	—	—	—	0.75	—
2003	3,500,000	—	—	—	1.00	—
2004	12,000,000	—	—	—	0.75	—
2005	—	—	—	—	0.75	—
2006	—	—	—	—	0.75	—

KM# 79 20 EURO CENTS

5.7300 g., Brass, 22.1 mm. **Ruler:** Henri **Obv:** Prince's portrait **Obv. Designer:** Yvette Gastauer-Claire **Rev:** Denomination and map **Rev. Designer:** Luc Luycx **Edge:** Notched

Date	Mintage	F	VF	XF	Unc	BU
2002	25,712,000	—	—	—	1.00	—
2003	1,500,000	—	—	—	1.25	—
2004	14,000,000	—	—	—	1.00	—
2005	—	—	—	—	1.00	—
2006	—	—	—	—	1.00	—

KM# 80 50 EURO CENTS

7.8100 g., Brass, 24.1 mm. **Ruler:** Henri **Obv:** Prince's portrait **Obv. Designer:** Yvette Gastauer-Claire **Rev:** Denomination and map **Rev. Designer:** Luc Luycx **Edge:** Reeded

Date	Mintage	F	VF	XF	Unc	BU
2002(u)	21,912,000	—	—	—	1.25	—
2003	2,500,000	—	—	—	1.50	—
2004	10,000,000	—	—	—	1.25	—
2005	—	—	—	—	1.25	—
2006	—	—	—	—	1.25	—

KM# 81 EURO

7.5000 g., Bi-Metallic Copper-Nickel center in Brass ring, 23.2 mm. **Ruler:** Henri **Obv:** Prince's portrait **Obv. Designer:** Yvette Gastauer-Claire **Rev:** Denomination and map **Rev. Designer:** Luc Luycx **Edge:** Reeded and plain sections

Date	Mintage	F	VF	XF	Unc	BU
2002(u)	21,313,000	—	—	—	2.50	—
2003	1,500,000	—	—	—	2.75	—
2004	9,000,000	—	—	—	2.50	—
2005	—	—	—	—	2.50	—
2006	—	—	—	—	2.50	—

KM# 82 2 EUROS

8.5200 g., Bi-Metallic Brass center in Copper-Nickel ring, 25.7 mm. **Ruler:** Henri **Obv:** Prince's portrait **Obv. Designer:** Yvette Gastauer-Claire **Rev:** Denomination and map **Rev. Designer:** Luc Luycx **Edge:** Reeded with 2's and stars

Date	Mintage	F	VF	XF	Unc	BU
2002(u)	148,512,000	—	—	—	3.75	—
2003	3,500,000	—	—	—	4.50	—
2004	7,552,000	—	—	—	4.00	—
2005	—	—	—	—	4.00	—
2006	—	—	—	—	4.00	—

KM# 85 2 EUROS

8.5200 g., Bi-Metallic Brass center in Copper-Nickel ring, 25.7 mm. **Ruler:** Henri **Obv:** Grand Duke and crowned monogram **Rev:** Value and map

Date	Mintage	F	VF	XF	Unc	BU
2004	—	—	—	—	5.50	—

KM# 87 2 EUROS

8.5200 g., Bi-Metallic Brass center in Copper-Nickel ring, 25.7 mm. **Obv:** Grand Dukes Henri and Adolph **Rev:** Value and map **Edge:** Reeding over stars and 2's

Date	Mintage	F	VF	XF	Unc	BU
2005	—	—	—	—	5.00	—

KM# 88 2 EUROS

8.5000 g., Bi-Metallic, 25.7 mm. **Ruler:** Henri **Obv:** Grand Duke and son **Rev:** Value **Edge:** Reeding over 2's and stars

Date	Mintage	F	VF	XF	Unc	BU
2006	1,000,000	—	—	—	5.00	—

KM# 84 5 EURO

6.2200 g., 0.9990 Gold 0.1998 oz. AGW, 20 mm. **Ruler:** Henri **Subject:** European Central Bank **Obv:** Grand Duke Henri **Rev:** Building

Date	Mintage	F	VF	XF	Unc	BU
2003 Proof	20,000	Value: 225				

KM# 83 25 EURO

22.8500 g., 0.9250 Silver 0.6795 oz. ASW, 37 mm. **Ruler:** Henri **Subject:** European Court System **Obv:** Grand Duke Henri **Rev:** Sword-scale on law book

Date	Mintage	F	VF	XF	Unc	BU
2002 Proof	20,000	Value: 100				

KM# 86 25 EURO

22.8500 g., 0.9250 Silver 0.6795 oz. ASW, 37 mm. **Ruler:** Henri **Subject:** European Parliament **Obv:** Grand Duke Henri

Date	Mintage	F	VF	XF	Unc	BU
2004 Proof	20,000	Value: 100				

MINT SETS

KM#	Date	Mintage	Identification	Issue Price	Mkt Val
MS7	2005 (9)	20,000	KM#75-82, 87	40.00	45.00
MS8	2006 (9)	15,000	KM#75-82, 88	40.00	45.00

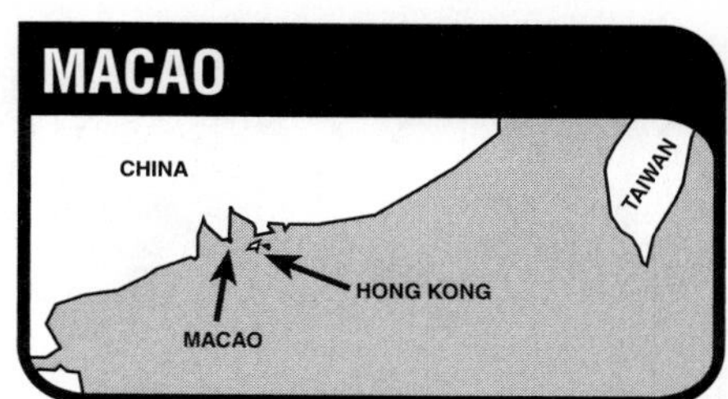

The Province of Macao, a Chinese province located in the South China Sea 40 miles southwest of Hong Kong, consists of the peninsula of Macao and the islands of Taipa and Coloane. It has an area of 6.2 sq. mi. (16 sq. km.) and a population of 500,000. Capital: Macao. Macao's economy is based on light industry, commerce, tourism, fishing, and gold trading - Macao is one of the entirely free markets for gold in the world. Cement, textiles, fireworks, vegetable oils, and metal products are exported.

In December of 1999, Macao became a special administrative zone of China.

MONETARY SYSTEM

100 Avos = 1 Pataca

SPECIAL ADMINISTRATIVE REGION

STANDARD COINAGE

100 Avos = 1 Pataca

KM# 102 100 PATACAS

28.2800 g., 0.9250 Silver .8410 oz. ASW **Subject:** Year of the Snake **Obv:** Church facade **Rev:** Snake

Date	Mintage	F	VF	XF	Unc	BU
2001 Proof	4,000	Value: 55.00				

KM# 107 100 PATACAS

28.2800 g., 0.9250 Silver 0.841 oz. ASW, 38.6 mm. **Subject:** Year of the Horse **Obv:** Church of St. Paul facade **Rev:** Horse above denomination **Edge:** Reeded

Date	Mintage	F	VF	XF	Unc	BU
2002 Proof	4,000	Value: 55.00				

KM# 103 250 PATACAS

3.9900 g., 0.9167 Gold .1176 oz. AGW **Subject:** Year of the Snake **Obv:** Church facade **Rev:** Snake

Date	Mintage	F	VF	XF	Unc	BU
2001 Proof	2,500	Value: 125				

KM# 108 250 PATACAS

3.9900 g., 0.9167 Gold 0.1176 oz. AGW, 19.3 mm. **Subject:** Year of the Horse **Obv:** Church of St. Paul facade **Rev:** Horse above denomination **Edge:** Reeded

Date	Mintage	F	VF	XF	Unc	BU
2002 Proof	2,500	Value: 125				

KM# 119 250 PATACAS

3.9900 g., 0.9167 Gold 0.1176 oz. AGW, 19.3 mm. **Subject:** Year of the Goat **Obv:** Church facade **Rev:** Goat above value **Edge:** Reeded

Date	Mintage	F	VF	XF	Unc	BU
2003 Proof	2,500	Value: 125				

KM# 104 500 PATACAS

7.9900 g., 0.9167 Gold .2355 oz. AGW **Subject:** Year of the Snake **Obv:** Church facade **Rev:** Snake

Date	Mintage	F	VF	XF	Unc	BU
2001 Proof	2,500	Value: 250				

KM# 109 500 PATACAS

7.9800 g., 0.9167 Gold 0.2352 oz. AGW, 22.05 mm. **Subject:** Year of the Horse **Obv:** Church of St. Paul facade **Rev:** Horse above denomination **Edge:** Reeded

Date	Mintage	F	VF	XF	Unc	BU
2002 Proof	2,500	Value: 250				

KM# 120 500 PATACAS

7.9800 g., 0.9167 Gold 0.2352 oz. AGW, 22 mm. **Subject:** Year of the Goat **Obv:** Church facade **Rev:** Goat above value **Edge:** Reeded

Date	Mintage	F	VF	XF	Unc	BU
2003 Proof	2,500	Value: 250				

KM# 105 1000 PATACAS
16.9760 g., 0.9167 Gold .4709 oz. AGW **Subject:** Year of the Snake **Obv:** Church facade **Rev:** Snake

Date	Mintage	F	VF	XF	Unc	BU
2001 Proof	4,000	Value: 450				

KM# 110 1000 PATACAS
15.9700 g., 0.9167 Gold 0.4707 oz. AGW, 28.4 mm. **Subject:** Year of the Horse **Obv:** Church of St. Paul facade **Rev:** Horse above denomination **Edge:** Reeded

Date	Mintage	F	VF	XF	Unc	BU
2002 Proof	4,000	Value: 450				

KM# 118 1000 PATACAS
28.2800 g., 0.9250 Silver 0.841 oz. ASW, 38.6 mm. **Subject:** Year of the Goat **Obv:** Church facade **Rev:** Goat above value **Edge:** Reeded

Date	Mintage	F	VF	XF	Unc	BU
2003 Proof	4,000	Value: 55.00				

KM# 121 1000 PATACAS
15.9760 g., 0.9170 Gold .4711 oz. AGW **Subject:** Year of the Goat **Obv:** Church facade **Rev:** Goat above value **Edge:** Reeded

Date	Mintage	F	VF	XF	Unc	BU
2003 Proof	4,000	Value: 450				

PROOF SETS

KM#	Date	Mintage	Identification	Issue Price	Mkt Val
PS16	2001 (3)	2,500	KM#103-105	849	825
PS17	2002 (3)	4,000	KM#108-110	849	825
PS18	2003 (3)	2,500	KM#119-121	849	825

MACEDONIA

The Republic of Macedonia is land-locked, and is bordered in the north by Yugoslavia, to the east by Bulgaria, in the south by Greece and to the west by Albania and has an area of 9,781 sq. mi. (25,713 sq. km.) and a population at the 1991 census was 2,038,847, of which the predominating ethnic groups were Macedonians. The capital is Skopje.

On Nov. 20, 1991 parliament promulgated a new constitution, and declared its independence on Nov.20, 1992, but failed to secure EC and US recognition owing to Greek objections to use of the name *Macedonia*. On Dec. 11, 1992, the UN Security Council authorized the expedition of a small peacekeeping force to prevent hostilities spreading into Macedonia.

There is a 120-member single-chamber National Assembly.

REPUBLIC

STANDARD COINAGE

KM# 2 DENAR
Brass **Obv:** Sar Planina sheepdog standing left

Date	Mintage	F	VF	XF	Unc	BU
2001	12,874,000	—	0.20	0.35	1.50	2.50

KM# 3 2 DENARI
Brass **Obv:** Trout above waterline

Date	Mintage	F	VF	XF	Unc	BU
2001	11,672,000	—	0.25	0.50	1.25	2.00

KM# 4 5 DENARI
Brass **Obv:** European lynx

Date	Mintage	F	VF	XF	Unc	BU
2001	6,921,000	—	0.35	0.75	1.75	2.50

KM# 13 10 DENARI
10.0000 g., 0.9160 Gold 0.2945 oz. AGW, 27 mm.
Subject: 10th Anniversary of Independence **Obv:** Map of Macedonia in form of the flag **Rev:** Vine

Date	Mintage	F	VF	XF	Unc	BU
2001	1,000	—	—	—	—	275

KM# 22 60 DENARI
6.0000 g., 0.9160 Gold 0.1767 oz. AGW, 23.8 mm.
Subject: 100th Anniversary - Statehood **Obv:** Monument at Krusevo **Rev:** Djorce Petrov

Date	Mintage	F	VF	XF	Unc	BU
2003	500	—	—	—	—	175

KM# 23 60 DENARI
6.0000 g., 0.9160 Gold 0.1767 oz. AGW, 23.8 mm.
Subject: 100th Anniversary - Statehood **Obv:** Monument at Krusevo **Rev:** Krste Petkov-Misirkov

Date	Mintage	F	VF	XF	Unc	BU
2003	500	—	—	—	—	175

KM# 24 60 DENARI
6.0000 g., 0.9160 Gold 0.1767 oz. AGW, 23.8 mm.
Subject: 100th Anniversary - Statehood **Obv:** Monument at Krusevo **Rev:** Metodije Andonov

Date	Mintage	F	VF	XF	Unc	BU
2003	500	—	—	—	—	175

KM# 25 60 DENARI
6.0000 g., 0.9160 Gold 0.1767 oz. AGW, 23.8 mm.
Subject: 100th Anniversary - Statehood **Obv:** Monument at Krusevo **Rev:** Mihailo Apostolski

Date	Mintage	F	VF	XF	Unc	BU
2003	500	—	—	—	—	175

KM# 26 60 DENARI
6.0000 g., 0.9160 Gold 0.1767 oz. AGW, 23.8 mm.
Subject: 100th Anniversary - Statehood **Obv:** Monument at Krusevo **Rev:** Blaze Koneski

Date	Mintage	F	VF	XF	Unc	BU
2003	500	—	—	—	—	175

KM# 21 60 DENARI
8.0000 g., 0.9160 Gold 0.2356 oz. AGW, 23.8 mm.
Subject: 50th Anniversary of seperation from Greece **Obv:** The Monifest **Rev:** Monastery of S. Prohor Pcinski

Date	Mintage	F	VF	XF	Unc	BU
2004	500	—	—	—	—	200

KM# 14 100 DENARI
16.0000 g., 0.9250 Silver 0.4758 oz. ASW, 32 mm.
Subject: 100th Anniversary of Statehood **Obv:** Monument at Krusevo **Rev:** Cherry tree canon

Date	Mintage	F	VF	XF	Unc	BU
2003	500	—	—	—	—	450

KM# 14a 100 DENARI
18.0000 g., 0.9160 Gold 0.5301 oz. AGW, 32 mm.
Subject: 100th Anniversary of Statehood **Obv:** Monument at Krusevo **Rev:** Cherry tree canon

Date	Mintage	F	VF	XF	Unc	BU
2003	500	—	—	—	—	475

KM# 15 100 DENARI
6.0000 g., 0.9160 Gold 0.1767 oz. AGW, 23.8 mm.
Subject: 100th Anniversary of Statehood **Obv:** Monument at Krusevo **Rev:** Goce Delcev

Date	Mintage	F	VF	XF	Unc	BU
2003	500	—	—	—	—	175

KM# 16 100 DENARI
6.0000 g., 0.9160 Gold 0.1767 oz. AGW, 23.8 mm.
Subject: 100th Anniversary of Statehood **Obv:** Monument at Krusevo **Rev:** Piti Guli

Date	Mintage	F	VF	XF	Unc	BU
2003	500	—	—	—	—	175

KM# 17 100 DENARI
6.0000 g., 0.9160 Gold 0.1767 oz. AGW, 23.8 mm.
Subject: 100th Anniversary of Statehood **Obv:** Monument at Krusevo **Rev:** Jane Sandanski

Date	Mintage	F	VF	XF	Unc	BU
2003	500	—	—	—	—	175

KM# 18 100 DENARI
6.0000 g., 0.9160 Gold 0.1767 oz. AGW, 23.8 mm.
Subject: 100th Anniversary of Statehood **Obv:** Monument at Krusevo **Rev:** Dame Gruev

Date	Mintage	F	VF	XF	Unc	BU
2003	500	—	—	—	—	175

KM# 19 100 DENARI
6.0000 g., 0.9160 Gold 0.1767 oz. AGW, 23.8 mm.
Subject: 100th Anniversary of Statehood **Obv:** Monument at Krusevo **Rev:** Nikola Karev

Date	Mintage	F	VF	XF	Unc	BU
2003	500	—	—	—	—	175

MADAGASCAR

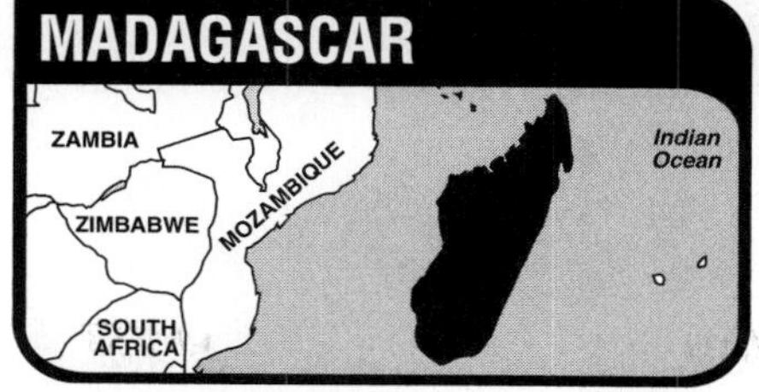

The Democratic Republic of Madagascar, an independent member of the French Community located in the Indian Ocean 250 miles (402 km.) off the southeast coast of Africa, has an area of 226,656 sq. mi. (587,040 sq. km.) and a population of 10 million. Capital: Antananarivo. The economy is primarily agricultural; large bauxite deposits are being developed. Coffee, vanilla, graphite, and rice are exported.

MONETARY SYSTEM
100 Centimes = 1 Franc

MINT MARKS
(a) - Paris, privy marks only
SA - Pretoria

REPUBLIC OF MADAGASCAR
Madagasikara Republic
STANDARD COINAGE

KM# 28 10 FRANCS (2 Ariary)
4.3400 g., Bronze (Red To Yellow), 21.9 mm. **Obv:** Monkey **Rev:** Value in buffalo horns **Edge:** Plain

Date	Mintage	F	VF	XF	Unc	BU
2003	—	—	—	—	2.50	3.50

KM# 29 ARIARY
4.9300 g., Stainless Steel, 22 mm. **Obv:** Flower **Rev:** Steer **Edge:** Plain

Date	Mintage	F	VF	XF	Unc	BU
2004(a)	—	—	—	—	2.00	3.00

KM# 30 2 ARIARY
3.2300 g., Copper Plated Steel, 21 mm. **Obv:** Plant **Rev:** Steer **Edge:** Reeded

Date	Mintage	F	VF	XF	Unc	BU
2003(a)	—	—	—	—	2.00	3.00

MALAWI

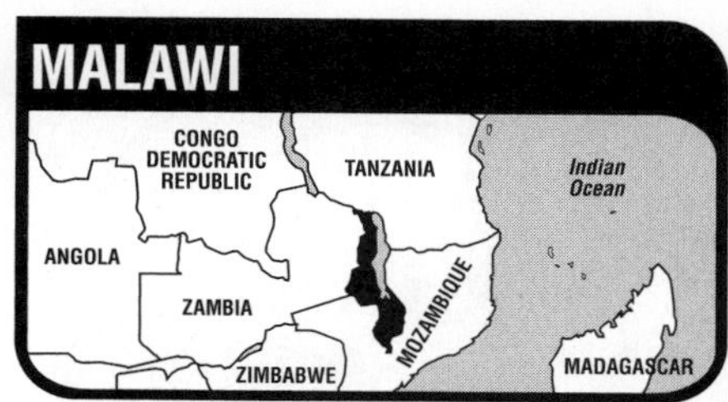

The Republic of Malawi (formerly Nyasaland), located in southeastern Africa to the west of Lake Malawi (Nyasa), has an area of 45,745 sq. mi. (118,480 sq. km.) and a population of 7 million. Capital: Lilongwe. The economy is predominantly agricultural. Tobacco, tea, peanuts and cotton are exported.

REPUBLIC
DECIMAL COINAGE
100 Tambala = 1 Kwacha

KM# 28 KWACHA
Brass Plated Steel **Obv:** Portrait of President Bakili Muluzi

Date	Mintage	F	VF	XF	Unc	BU
2003	—	—	—	—	7.00	9.00

KM# 39 10 KWACHA
29.1000 g., Copper-Nickel, 38.7 mm. **Subject:** Soccer World Championship **Obv:** National arms **Rev:** Two soccer players **Edge:** Reeded

Date	Mintage	F	VF	XF	Unc	BU
2002 Proof	—	Value: 50.00				

KM# 42 10 KWACHA
19.7400 g., 0.9990 Silver 0.634 oz. ASW, 29.9 mm.
Subject: Athens Olympics **Obv:** National arms **Rev:** Two rowers **Edge:** Reeded

Date	Mintage	F	VF	XF	Unc	BU
2003 Proof	—	Value: 40.00				

KM# 43 50 KWACHA
141.5100 g., 0.9990 Silver with Gold Plated center 4.5451 oz. ASW, 65 mm. **Subject:** Republic of China **Obv:** Large building above value **Rev:** 11th President and Vice President of the Republic of China **Edge:** Reeded

Date	Mintage	F	VF	XF	Unc	BU
2004 Proof	—	Value: 85.00				

MALAYSIA

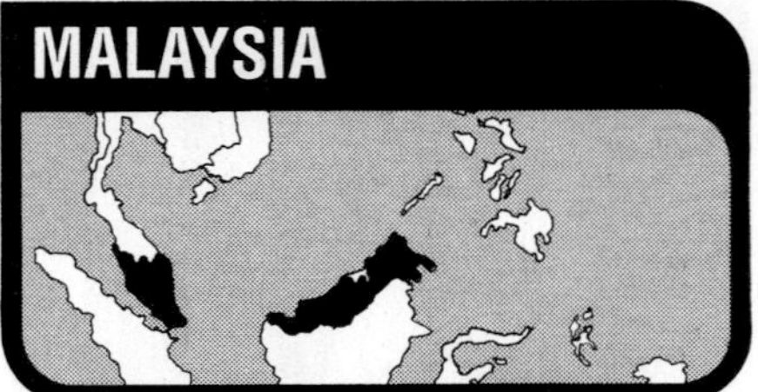

The independent limited constitutional monarchy of Malaysia, which occupies the southern part of the Malay Peninsula in Southeast Asia and the northern part of the island of Borneo, has an area of 127,316 sq. mi. (329,750 sq. km.) and a population of 15.4 million. Capital: Kuala Lumpur. The economy is based on agriculture, mining and forestry. Rubber, tin, timber and palm oil are exported.

Malaysia came into being on Sept. 16, 1963, as a federation of Malaya (Johore, Kelantan, Kedah, Perlis, Trengganu, Negri-Sembilan, Pahang, Perak, Selangor, Penang, Malacca), Singapore, Sabah (British North Borneo) and Sarawak. Following two serious racial riots involving Malays and Chinese, Singapore withdrew from the federation on Aug. 9, 1965. Malaysia is a member of the Commonwealth of Nations.

CONSTITUTIONAL MONARCHY

STANDARD COINAGE

100 Sen = 1 Ringgit (Dollar)

KM# 49 SEN
Bronze Clad Steel **Rev:** Drum

Date	Mintage	F	VF	XF	Unc	BU
2001	213,645,000	—	—	—	0.15	0.25
2002	185,220,000	—	—	—	0.15	0.25
2003	—	—	—	—	0.15	0.25
2004	—	—	—	—	0.15	0.25
2005	—	—	—	—	0.15	0.25

KM# 50 5 SEN
Copper-Nickel **Rev:** Top with string

Date	Mintage	F	VF	XF	Unc	BU
2001	94,617,472	—	—	—	0.15	0.25
2002	85,316,000	—	—	—	0.15	0.25
2003	—	—	—	—	0.15	0.25
2004	—	—	—	—	0.15	0.25
2005	—	—	—	—	0.15	0.25

KM# 51 10 SEN
Copper-Nickel **Rev:** Ceremonial table

Date	Mintage	F	VF	XF	Unc	BU
2001	313,422,000	—	—	—	0.25	0.40
2002	290,451,948	—	—	—	0.25	0.40
2003	—	—	—	—	0.25	0.40
2004	—	—	—	—	0.25	0.40
2005	—	—	—	—	0.25	0.40

KM# 52 20 SEN
Copper-Nickel **Rev:** Basket containing food and utensils

Date	Mintage	F	VF	XF	Unc	BU
2001	278,802,000	—	—	—	0.35	0.50
2002	131,279,881	—	—	—	0.35	0.50
2003	—	—	—	—	0.35	0.50
2004	—	—	—	—	0.35	0.50
2005	—	—	—	—	0.35	0.50

KM# 77 25 SEN
9.1400 g., Brass, 30 mm. **Series:** Endangered Species **Obv:** Seal and value **Rev:** Sumatran Rhinocerus **Edge:** Reeded

Date	Mintage	F	VF	XF	Unc	BU
2003	—	—	—	—	5.00	7.50

KM# 78 25 SEN
9.1400 g., Brass, 30 mm. **Series:** Endangered Species **Obv:** Seal and value **Rev:** Asian Elephant **Edge:** Reeded

Date	Mintage	F	VF	XF	Unc	BU
2003	—	—	—	—	5.00	7.50

KM# 79 25 SEN
9.1400 g., Brass, 30 mm. **Series:** Endangered Species **Obv:** Seal and value **Rev:** Orangutan **Edge:** Reeded

Date	Mintage	F	VF	XF	Unc	BU
2003	—	—	—	—	5.00	7.50

KM# 80 25 SEN
9.1400 g., Brass, 30 mm. **Series:** Endangered Species **Obv:** Seal and value **Rev:** Sumatran Tiger **Edge:** Reeded

Date	Mintage	F	VF	XF	Unc	BU
2003	—	—	—	—	5.00	7.50

KM# 81 25 SEN
9.1400 g., Brass, 30 mm. **Series:** Endangered Species **Obv:** Seal and value **Rev:** Slow Loris lemur (nycticebus coucang) on branch **Edge:** Reeded

Date	Mintage	F	VF	XF	Unc	BU
2003	—	—	—	—	5.00	7.50

KM# 82 25 SEN
9.1400 g., Brass, 30 mm. **Series:** Endangered Species **Obv:** Seal and value **Rev:** Barking Deer (muntiacus muntjak) **Edge:** Reeded

Date	Mintage	F	VF	XF	Unc	BU
2003	—	—	—	—	5.00	7.50

KM# 83 25 SEN
9.1400 g., Brass, 30 mm. **Series:** Endangered Species **Obv:** Seal and value **Rev:** Tapir (tapirus indicus) **Edge:** Reeded

Date	Mintage	F	VF	XF	Unc	BU
2003	—	—	—	—	5.00	7.50

KM# 84 25 SEN
9.1400 g., Brass, 30 mm. **Series:** Endangered Species **Obv:** Seal and value **Rev:** Serow (capricornis sumatrensis) **Edge:** Reeded

Date	Mintage	F	VF	XF	Unc	BU
2003	—	—	—	—	5.00	7.50

KM# 85 25 SEN
9.1400 g., Brass, 30 mm. **Subject:** Endangered Species **Obv:** Bank seal and value **Rev:** Sambar Deer **Edge:** Reeded

Date	Mintage	F	VF	XF	Unc	BU
2003	—	—	—	—	5.00	7.50

KM# 86 25 SEN

9.1400 g., Brass, 30 mm. **Subject:** Endangered Species **Obv:** Bank seal and value **Rev:** Proboscis Monkey **Edge:** Reeded

Date	Mintage	F	VF	XF	Unc	BU
2003	—	—	—	—	5.00	7.50

KM# 87 25 SEN

9.1400 g., Brass, 30 mm. **Subject:** Endangered Species **Obv:** Bank seal and value **Rev:** Gaur (wild bovine) **Edge:** Reeded

Date	Mintage	F	VF	XF	Unc	BU
2003	—	—	—	—	5.00	7.50

KM# 88 25 SEN

9.1400 g., Brass, 30 mm. **Subject:** Endangered Species **Obv:** Bank seal and value **Rev:** Clouded Leopard **Edge:** Reeded

Date	Mintage	F	VF	XF	Unc	BU
2003	—	—	—	—	5.00	7.50

KM# 89 25 SEN

9.1400 g., Brass, 30 mm. **Obv:** Value **Rev:** Straw-headed Bulbul bird **Edge:** Reeded

Date	Mintage	F	VF	XF	Unc	BU
2004	—	—	—	—	5.00	7.50

KM# 90 25 SEN

9.1400 g., Brass, 30 mm. **Obv:** Value **Rev:** Great Argus bird **Edge:** Reeded

Date	Mintage	F	VF	XF	Unc	BU
2004	—	—	—	—	5.00	7.50

KM# 91 25 SEN

9.1400 g., Brass, 30 mm. **Obv:** Value **Rev:** Collared Kingfisher **Edge:** Reeded

Date	Mintage	F	VF	XF	Unc	BU
2004	—	—	—	—	5.00	7.50

KM# 92 25 SEN

9.1400 g., Brass, 30 mm. **Obv:** Value **Rev:** White-Bellied Sea Eagle **Edge:** Reeded

Date	Mintage	F	VF	XF	Unc	BU
2004	—	—	—	—	5.00	7.50

KM# 93 25 SEN

9.1600 g., Brass, 30 mm. **Obv:** Value **Rev:** Asian Fairy Bluebird **Edge:** Reeded

Date	Mintage	F	VF	XF	Unc	BU
2004	40,000	—	—	—	8.50	12.50

KM# 94 25 SEN

9.1600 g., Brass, 30 mm. **Obv:** Value **Rev. Designer:** Rhinoceros Hornbill bird **Edge:** Reeded

Date	Mintage	F	VF	XF	Unc	BU
2004	40,000	—	—	—	8.50	12.50

KM# 95 25 SEN

9.1600 g., Brass, 30 mm. **Obv:** Value **Rev:** Nicobar Pigeon **Edge:** Reeded

Date	Mintage	F	VF	XF	Unc	BU
2004	40,000	—	—	—	8.50	12.50

KM# 96 25 SEN

9.1600 g., Brass, 30 mm. **Obv:** Value **Rev:** Two Crested Wood Partridges **Edge:** Reeded

Date	Mintage	F	VF	XF	Unc	BU
2004	40,000	—	—	—	8.50	12.50

KM# 97 25 SEN

9.1600 g., Brass, 30 mm. **Obv:** Value **Rev:** Black and Red Broadbill bird **Edge:** Reeded

Date	Mintage	F	VF	XF	Unc	BU
2004	40,000	—	—	—	8.50	12.50

KM# 98 25 SEN

9.1600 g., Brass, 30 mm. **Obv:** Value and logo **Rev:** Green Imperial Pigeon on branch **Edge:** Reeded

Date	Mintage	F	VF	XF	Unc	BU
2004	40,000	—	—	—	8.50	12.50

KM# 99 25 SEN

9.1600 g., Brass, 30 mm. **Obv:** Value and logo **Rev:** Great Egret **Edge:** Reeded

Date	Mintage	F	VF	XF	Unc	BU
2004	40,000	—	—	—	8.50	12.50

KM# 100 25 SEN

9.1600 g., Brass, 30 mm. **Obv:** Value and logo **Rev:** Brown Shrike on branch **Edge:** Reeded

Date	Mintage	F	VF	XF	Unc	BU
2004	40,000	—	—	—	8.50	12.50

KM# 53 50 SEN

Copper-Nickel **Rev:** Ceremonial kite

Date	Mintage	F	VF	XF	Unc	BU
2001	67,371,000	—	—	—	0.65	0.85
2002	61,928,000	—	—	—	0.65	0.85
2003	—	—	—	—	0.65	0.85
2004	—	—	—	—	0.65	0.85
2005	—	—	—	—	0.65	0.85

KM# 71 RINGGIT

16.8000 g., Copper Nickel, 33.7 mm. **Subject:** XXI SEA Games **Obv:** Games logo **Rev:** Cartoon mascot **Edge:** Reeded

Date	Mintage	F	VF	XF	Unc	BU
2001	200,000	—	—	—	3.00	5.00

KM# 74 RINGGIT

16.8000 g., Copper-Nickel, 33.7 mm. **Subject:** Coronation of Agong XII **Obv:** King's portrait **Rev:** National arms **Edge:** Reeded **Note:** Prev. KM#72.

Date	Mintage	F	VF	XF	Unc	BU
ND(2002)	100,000	—	—	—	4.00	6.00

KM# 72 10 RINGGIT

21.7000 g., 0.9250 Silver 0.6453 oz. ASW, 35.7 mm. **Subject:** XXI SEA Games **Obv:** Games logo **Rev:** Cartoon mascot **Edge:** Reeded

Date	Mintage	F	VF	XF	Unc	BU
2001 Proof	3,000	Value: 45.00				

KM# 75 10 RINGGIT

21.7000 g., 0.9250 Silver 0.6453 oz. ASW, 35.7 mm. **Subject:** Coronation of Agong XII **Obv:** King's portrait **Rev:** National arms **Edge:** Reeded

Date	Mintage	F	VF	XF	Unc	BU
ND(2002) Proof	10,000	Value: 45.00				

KM# 73 100 RINGGIT

8.6000 g., 0.9160 Gold 0.2533 oz. AGW, 22 mm. **Subject:** XXI SEA Games **Obv:** Games logo **Rev:** Cartoon mascot **Edge:** Reeded

Date	Mintage	F	VF	XF	Unc	BU
2001 Proof	500	Value: 350				

KM# 76 100 RINGGIT

8.6000 g., 0.9160 Gold 0.2533 oz. AGW, 22 mm. **Subject:** Coronation of Agong XII **Obv:** King's portrait **Rev:** National arms **Edge:** Reeded

Date	Mintage	F	VF	XF	Unc	BU
ND(2002) Proof	300	Value: 350				

MALI

The Republic of Mali, a landlocked country in the interior of West Africa southwest of Algeria, has an area of 482,077 sq. mi. (1,240,000 sq. km.) and a population of 8.1 million. Capital: Bamako. Livestock, fish, cotton and peanuts are exported.

MINT MARKS
(a) - Paris, privy marks only

REPUBLIC

STANDARD COINAGE

KM# 17 1500 CFA FRANCS - 1 AFRICA
7.3000 g., Nickel Plated Steel, 25.9 mm. **Obv:** Gazelle and tree **Rev:** Elephant head on map **Edge:** Plain

Date	Mintage	F	VF	XF	Unc	BU
2003	1,200	—	—	—	20.00	—

KM# 17a 1500 CFA FRANCS - 1 AFRICA
0.9990 Silver, 25.9 mm. **Edge:** Plain

Date	Mintage	F	VF	XF	Unc	BU
2003	5	—	—	—	120	—

MALTA

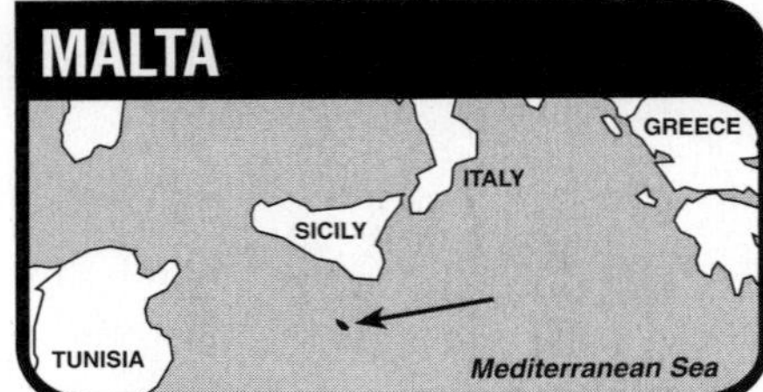

The Republic of Malta, an independent parliamentary democracy, is situated in the Mediterranean Sea between Sicily and North Africa. With the islands of Gozo and Comino, Malta has an area of 124 sq. mi. (320 sq. km.) and a population of 386,000.Capital: Valletta. Malta has no proven mineral resources, an agriculture insufficient to its needs, and a small, but expanding, manufacturing facility. Clothing, textile yarns and fabrics, and knitted wear are exported.

Malta became a republic on Dec. 13, 1974, but remained a member of the Commonwealth of Nations. The president is Chief of State. The prime minister is the Head of Government.

REPUBLIC

DECIMAL COINAGE

10 Mils = 1 Cent; 100 Cents = 1 Pound

KM# 5 2 MILS
Aluminum **Obv:** Maltese cross **Shape:** Scalloped

Date	Mintage	F	VF	XF	Unc	BU
2005	—	—	—	—	4.00	—

REFORM COINAGE

1982 - Present

100 Cents = 1 Lira

KM# 93 CENT
Copper-Zinc **Obv. Designer:** Galea Bason **Rev:** Common weasel

Date	Mintage	F	VF	XF	Unc	BU
2001	—	—	0.15	0.25	0.50	—
2005	—	—	0.15	0.25	0.50	—

KM# 94 2 CENTS
Copper-Zinc **Obv. Designer:** Galea Bason

Date	Mintage	F	VF	XF	Unc	BU
2002	—	—	0.15	0.25	0.45	—
2005	—	—	0.15	0.25	0.45	—

KM# 95 5 CENTS
Copper-Nickel **Obv. Designer:** Galea Bason **Rev:** Fresh-water crab

Date	Mintage	F	VF	XF	Unc	BU
2001	—	—	0.25	0.45	1.00	2.00
2005	—	—	0.25	0.45	1.00	2.00
2006	—	—	0.25	0.45	1.00	2.00

KM# 96 10 CENTS
Copper-Nickel **Obv:** Crowned shield **Obv. Designer:** Galea Bason **Rev:** Dolphin fish

Date	Mintage	F	VF	XF	Unc	BU
2005	—	—	0.40	0.75	1.50	—
2006	—	—	0.40	0.75	1.50	—

KM# 97 25 CENTS
Copper-Nickel **Obv:** Crowned shield **Obv. Designer:** Galea Bason **Rev:** Ghirlanda flower

Date	Mintage	F	VF	XF	Unc	BU
2005	—	—	1.00	1.50	2.50	—
2006	—	—	1.00	1.50	2.50	—

KM# 98 50 CENTS
Copper-Nickel **Obv:** Similar to 5 Cents, KM#95 **Obv. Designer:** Galea Bason **Rev:** Tulliera plant

Date	Mintage	F	VF	XF	Unc	BU
2001	—	—	1.75	2.25	10.00	—
2005	—	—	1.75	2.25	10.00	—
2006	—	—	1.75	2.25	10.00	—

KM# 99 LIRA
Nickel **Obv. Designer:** Galea Bason **Rev. Designer:** Noel Galea

Date	Mintage	F	VF	XF	Unc	BU
2005	—	—	—	4.00	6.00	10.00
2006	—	—	—	4.00	6.00	10.00

KM# 117 5 LIRI
28.2800 g., 0.9250 Silver 0.841 oz. ASW, 38.6 mm. **Obv:** National arms **Rev:** Enrico Mizzi right **Edge:** Reeded

Date	Mintage	F	VF	XF	Unc	BU
2001 Proof	2,000	Value: 52.50				

KM# 118 5 LIRI
28.2800 g., 0.9250 Silver 0.841 oz. ASW, 38.6 mm. **Obv:** National arms **Rev:** Nicolo Isouard left **Edge:** Reeded

Date	Mintage	F	VF	XF	Unc	BU
2002 Proof	2,000	Value: 52.50				

KM# 120 5 LIRI
28.2800 g., 0.9250 Silver 0.841 oz. ASW, 38.6 mm. **Obv:** National arms **Rev:** Sir Adriano Dingli as Grand Commander of the St. Michael and George Order **Edge:** Reeded

Date	Mintage	F	VF	XF	Unc	BU
2003 Proof	2,000	Value: 52.50				

KM# 121 5 LIRI
28.2800 g., 0.9250 Silver 0.841 oz. ASW, 38.6 mm. **Obv:** National arms **Rev:** Painter Giuseppe Cali with palette **Edge:** Reeded

Date	Mintage	F	VF	XF	Unc	BU
2004 Proof	2,000	Value: 57.50				

KM# 119 10 LIRI
1.2400 g., 0.9990 Gold 0.0398 oz. AGW, 13.92 mm. **Obv:** National arms **Rev:** Xprunara sailboat **Edge:** Reeded

Date	Mintage	F	VF	XF	Unc	BU
2002 Prooflike	25,000	—	—	—	—	50.00

KM# 122 25 LIRI
3.9940 g., 0.9167 Gold 0.1177 oz. AGW, 19.3 mm. **Subject:** Accession to the European Union **Obv:** National arms **Rev:** Maltese flag under European Union star circle **Edge:** Reeded

Date	Mintage	F	VF	XF	Unc	BU
2004 Proof	6,000	Value: 195				

MINT SETS

KM#	Date	Mintage	Identification	Issue Price	Mkt Val
MS26	2005 (8)	—	KM#5, 93-99	—	30.00
MS27	2006	—	KM#95-99	—	—

MARTINIQUE

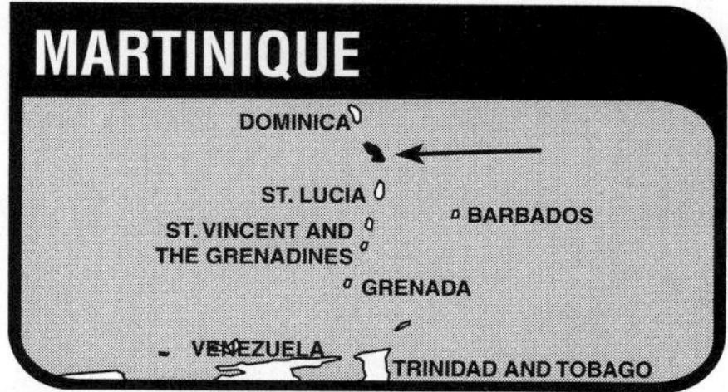

The French Overseas Department of Martinique, located in the Lesser Antilles of the West Indies between Dominica and Saint Lucia, has an area of 425 sq. mi.(1,100 sq. km.) and a population of 290,000. Capital: Fort-de-France. Agriculture and tourism are the major sources of income. Bananas, sugar, and rum are exported.

The official currency of Martinique is the Euro.

FRENCH TERRITORY

ESSAIS

KM# E5 1/4 EURO
7.8000 g., 0.9990 Silver 0.2505 oz. ASW, 27.2 mm. **Obv:** Louis O. Roty **Rev:** Woman holding torch **Edge:** Reeded

Date	Mintage	F	VF	XF	Unc	BU
2004 Proof	2,000	Value: 20.00				

KM# E6 1-1/2 EURO
31.1600 g., 0.9990 Silver 1.0008 oz. ASW, 39.1 mm. **Obv:** Martinique arms **Rev:** War ship Cuirasse Dunkerque **Edge:** Reeded

Date	Mintage	F	VF	XF	Unc	BU
2004 Proof	2,000	Value: 30.00				

KM# E7 20 EURO
7.8000 g., 0.9990 Gold 0.2505 oz. AGW, 27 mm.
Obv: Martinique arms **Rev:** Great Egret **Edge:** Reeded

Date	Mintage	F	VF	XF	Unc	BU
2004 Proof	300	Value: 300				

MAURITANIA

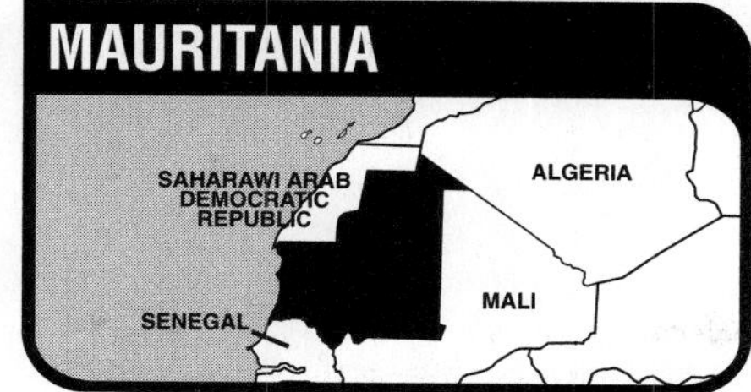

The Islamic Republic of Mauritania, located in northwest Africa bounded by Western Sahara, Mali, Algeria, Senegal and the Atlantic Ocean, has an area of 397,955 sq. mi.(1,030,700 sq. km.) and a population of 1.9 million. Capital: Nouakchott. The economy centers on herding, agriculture, fishing and mining. Iron ore, copper concentrates and fish products are exported.

On June 28, 1973, in a move designed to emphasize its non-alignment with France, Mauritania converted its currency from the old French-supported C.F.A. franc unit to a new unit called the Ouguiya.

MONETARY SYSTEM
5 Khoums = 1 Ouguiya

REPUBLIC

STANDARD COINAGE

KM# 3 5 OUGUIYA
Copper-Nickel-Aluminum

Date	Mintage	VG	F	VF	XF	Unc
AH1424-2003	—	—	—	0.50	1.00	2.00

KM# 4 10 OUGUIYA
Copper-Nickel

Date	Mintage	VG	F	VF	XF	Unc
AH1424-2003	—	—	—	0.75	1.50	2.50

MAURITIUS

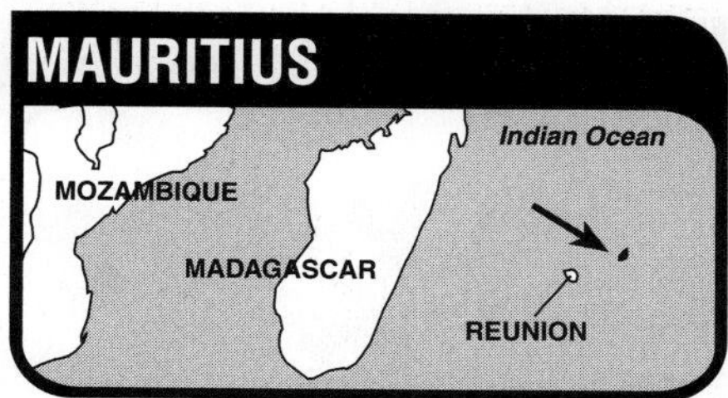

The Republic of Mauritius, is located in the Indian Ocean 500 miles (805 km.) east of Madagascar, has an area of 790 sq. mi. (1,860 sq. km.) and a population of 1 million. Capital: Port Louis. Sugar provides 90 percent of the export revenue.

Mauritius became independent on March 12, 1968. It is a member of the Commonwealth of Nations.

MINT MARKS
SA - Pretoria Mint

MONETARY SYSTEM
100 Cents = 1 Rupee

COMMONWEALTH

REFORM COINAGE

KM# 52 5 CENTS
Copper Plated Steel **Obv:** Bust of Sir Seewoosagur Ramgoolam right

Date	Mintage	F	VF	XF	Unc	BU
2003	—	—	—	—	0.30	0.50

KM# 53 20 CENTS
Nickel Plated Steel **Obv:** Bust of Sir Seewoosagur Ramgoolam right

Date	Mintage	F	VF	XF	Unc	BU
2001	—	—	—	—	0.50	0.75
2003	—	—	—	—	0.50	0.75

KM# 54 1/2 RUPEE
Nickel Plated Steel **Obv:** Bust of Sir Seewoosagur Ramgoolam right **Rev:** Stag left

Date	Mintage	F	VF	XF	Unc	BU
2002	—	—	—	—	1.50	2.50
2003	—	—	—	—	1.50	2.50

KM# 55 RUPEE
Copper-Nickel **Obv:** Bust of Sir Seewoosagur Ramgoolam right

Date	Mintage	F	VF	XF	Unc	BU
2002	—	—	—	—	1.65	2.75

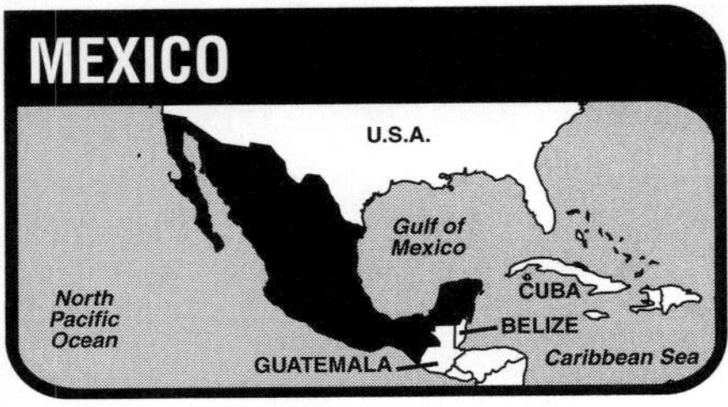

UNITED STATES

The United States of Mexico, located immediately south of the United States has an area of 759,529 sq. mi. (1,967,183 sq. km.) and an estimated population of 100 million. Capital: Mexico City. The economy is based on agriculture, manufacturing and mining. Oil, cotton, silver, coffee, and shrimp are exported.

REFORM COINAGE

1 New Peso = 1000 Old Pesos

KM# 546 5 CENTAVOS
Stainless Steel

Date	Mintage	F	VF	XF	Unc	BU
2001Mo	34,811,000	—	—	0.15	0.20	0.25
2002Mo	14,901,000	—	—	0.15	0.20	0.25

KM# 547 10 CENTAVOS
Stainless Steel

Date	Mintage	F	VF	XF	Unc	BU
2001	618,061,000	—	—	0.20	0.25	0.30
2002	463,968,000	—	—	0.20	0.25	0.30
2003Mo	378,938,000	—	—	0.20	0.25	0.30

KM# 548 20 CENTAVOS
Aluminum-Bronze **Shape:** 12-sided

Date	Mintage	F	VF	XF	Unc	BU
2001	234,360,000	—	—	0.25	0.35	0.40
2002Mo	229,256,000	—	—	0.25	0.35	0.40
2003Mo	149,518,000	—	—	0.25	0.35	0.40

KM# 549 50 CENTAVOS
Aluminum-Bronze **Shape:** Scalloped

Date	Mintage	F	VF	XF	Unc	BU
2001	199,006,000	—	—	0.45	0.75	1.00
2002	94,552,000	—	—	0.45	0.75	1.00
2003Mo	124,522,000	—	—	0.45	0.75	1.00

KM# 603 PESO
Bi-Metallic Stainless-steel ring in Aluminum Bronze center
Note: Similar to KM#550 but without N.

Date	Mintage	F	VF	XF	Unc	BU
2001Mo	208,576,000	—	—	—	1.25	2.25
2002Mo	119,541,000	—	—	—	1.25	2.25
2003Mo	169,320,000	—	—	—	1.25	2.25

KM# 604 2 PESOS
Bi-Metallic Aluminumn-Bronze center in Stainless Steel ring
Note: Similar to KM#551, but denomination without N.

Date	Mintage	F	VF	XF	Unc	BU
2001Mo	74,563,000	—	—	—	2.35	2.50
2002Mo	74,547,000	—	—	—	2.35	2.50
2003Mo	39,814,000	—	—	—	2.35	2.50

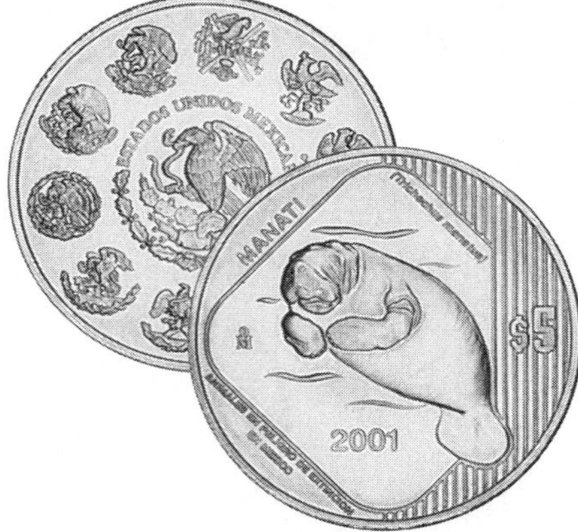

KM# 651 5 NUEVOS PESOS
31.1710 g., 0.9990 Silver 1.0012 oz. ASW, 40 mm.
Series: Endangered Wildlife **Obv:** National arms past and present **Rev:** West Indian Manati **Edge:** Reeded

Date	Mintage	F	VF	XF	Unc	BU
2001	50,000	—	—	—	30.00	—

KM# 653 5 NUEVOS PESOS
31.1710 g., 0.9990 Silver 1.0012 oz. ASW, 40 mm. **Subject:** Aguila Arpia **Obv:** National arms past and present **Rev:** Harpie Eagle

Date	Mintage	F	VF	XF	Unc	BU
2001	50,000	—	—	—	30.00	—

KM# 654 5 NUEVOS PESOS
31.1710 g., 0.9990 Silver 1.0012 oz. ASW, 40 mm.
Series: Endangered Wildlife **Subject:** Oso Negro **Obv:** National arms past and present **Rev:** Black bear

Date	Mintage	F	VF	XF	Unc	BU
2001	50,000	—	—	—	30.00	—

KM# 658 5 NUEVOS PESOS
31.1710 g., 0.9990 Silver 1.0012 oz. ASW, 40 mm.
Series: Endangered Wildlife **Obv:** National arms past and present **Rev:** Jaguar resting

Date	Mintage	F	VF	XF	Unc	BU
2001	50,000	—	—	—	30.00	—

KM# 659 5 NUEVOS PESOS
31.1710 g., 0.9990 Silver 1.0012 oz. ASW, 40 mm.
Series: Endangered Wildlife **Obv:** National arms past and present **Rev:** Black-tailed Prairie dog

Date	Mintage	F	VF	XF	Unc	BU
2001	50,000	—	—	—	30.00	—

KM# 660 5 NUEVOS PESOS
31.1710 g., 0.9990 Silver 1.0012 oz. ASW, 40 mm.
Series: Endangered Wildlife **Obv:** National arms past and present **Rev:** Volcano Rabbit

Date	Mintage	F	VF	XF	Unc	BU
2001	50,000	—	—	—	30.00	—

KM# 605 5 PESOS
Bi-Metallic Aluminumn-Bronze center in Stainless Steel ring
Note: Similar to KM#552 but deonomination without N.

Date	Mintage	F	VF	XF	Unc	BU
2001Mo	79,169,000	—	—	3.00	4.00	5.00
2002Mo	34,754,000	—	—	3.00	4.00	5.00
2003Mo	54,676,000	—	—	3.00	4.00	5.00

KM# 678 5 PESOS
27.0000 g., 0.9250 Silver 0.803 oz. ASW, 40 mm. **Subject:** Ibero-America: Acapulco Galleon **Obv:** Mexican arms encircled by ten coats of arms **Rev:** Spanish galleon with Pacific Ocean background and trading scene in foreground **Edge:** Reeded

Date	Mintage	F	VF	XF	Unc	BU
2003Mo Proof	5,000	Value: 65.00				

KM# 636 10 PESOS
Bi-Metallic Copper-Nickel center in Brass ring **Subject:** Millennium Series **Rev:** Aztec carving

Date	Mintage	F	VF	XF	Unc	BU
2001Mo	44,768,000	—	—	—	5.00	6.50
2002Mo	—	—	—	—	5.00	6.50
2003Mo	—	—	—	—	5.00	6.50
2004Mo	—	—	—	—	5.00	6.50
2005Mo	—	—	—	—	5.00	6.50

KM# 616 10 PESOS
Bi-Metallic Copper-Nickel-Brass center within Brass ring **Obv:** National emblem **Rev:** Aztec design

Date	Mintage	F	VF	XF	Unc	BU
2002	44,721,000	—	—	—	5.00	6.50

KM# 679 10 PESOS
31.1040 g., 0.9990 Silver 0.999 oz. ASW, 40 mm. **Obv:** Mexican arms **Rev:** Zacatecas arms **Edge:** Reeded

Date	Mintage	F	VF	XF	Unc	BU
2003Mo Proof	10,000	Value: 55.00				

KM# 680 10 PESOS
31.1040 g., 0.9990 Silver 0.999 oz. ASW, 40 mm.
Subject: Mexican States: Yucatan **Obv:** Mexican arms
Rev: Yucatan arms **Edge:** Reeded

Date	Mintage	F	VF	XF	Unc	BU
2003Mo Proof	10,000	Value: 55.00				

KM# 681 10 PESOS
31.1040 g., 0.9990 Silver 0.999 oz. ASW, 40 mm.
Subject: Mexican States: Veracruz-Llave **Obv:** Mexican arms
Rev: Veracruz-Llave arms **Edge:** Reeded

Date	Mintage	F	VF	XF	Unc	BU
2003Mo Proof	10,000	Value: 55.00				

KM# 682 10 PESOS
31.1040 g., 0.9990 Silver 0.999 oz. ASW, 40 mm.
Subject: Mexican States: Tlaxcala **Obv:** Mexican arms
Rev: Tlaxcala arms **Edge:** Reeded

Date	Mintage	F	VF	XF	Unc	BU
2003Mo Proof	10,000	Value: 55.00				

KM# 683 10 PESOS
31.1040 g., 0.9990 Silver 0.999 oz. ASW, 40 mm.
Subject: Mexican State: Tamaulipas **Obv:** Mexican arms
Rev: Tamaulipas arms **Edge:** Reeded

Date	Mintage	F	VF	XF	Unc	BU
2004Mo Proof	10,000	Value: 55.00				

KM# 684 10 PESOS
31.1040 g., 0.9990 Silver 0.999 oz. ASW, 40 mm.
Subject: Mexican States: Tabasco **Obv:** Mexican arms
Rev: Tabasco arms **Edge:** Reeded

Date	Mintage	F	VF	XF	Unc	BU
2004Mo Proof	10,000	Value: 55.00				

KM# 687 10 PESOS
31.1040 g., 0.9990 Silver 0.999 oz. ASW, 40 mm. **Obv:** Mexican arms **Rev:** San Luis Potosi arms **Edge:** Reeded **Note:** Mexican States: San Luis Potosi

Date	Mintage	F	VF	XF	Unc	BU
2004Mo Proof	10,000	Value: 55.00				

KM# 686 10 PESOS
31.1040 g., 0.9990 Silver 0.999 oz. ASW, 40 mm. **Obv:** Mexican arms **Rev:** Sinaloa arms **Edge:** Reeded **Note:** Mexican States: Sinaloa

Date	Mintage	F	VF	XF	Unc	BU
2004Mo Proof	10,000	Value: 55.00				

KM# 685 10 PESOS
31.1040 g., 0.9990 Silver 0.999 oz. ASW, 40 mm. **Obv:** Mexican arms **Rev:** Sonora arms **Edge:** Reeded **Note:** Mexican States: Sonora

Date	Mintage	F	VF	XF	Unc	BU
2004Mo Proof	10,000	Value: 55.00				

KM# 733 10 PESOS
Bi-Metallic **Obv:** Mexican arms **Rev:** Quintero Arteaga arms

Date	Mintage	F	VF	XF	Unc	BU
2004 Proof	—	Value: 55.00				

KM# 735 10 PESOS
31.1040 g., 0.9990 Silver 0.999 oz. ASW, 40 mm. **Obv:** Mexican arms **Rev:** Quintara Roo arms

Date	Mintage	F	VF	XF	Unc	BU
2004 Proof	—	Value: 55.00				

KM# 737 10 PESOS
31.1040 g., 0.9990 Silver 0.999 oz. ASW, 40 mm. **Obv:** Mexican arms **Rev:** Pueblo Arms

Date	Mintage	F	VF	XF	Unc	BU
2004 Proof	—	Value: 55.00				

KM# 739 10 PESOS
31.1040 g., 0.9990 Bi-Metallic 0.999 oz., 40 mm. **Obv:** Mexican arms **Rev:** Oaxaca arms

Date	Mintage	F	VF	XF	Unc	BU
2004 Proof	—	Value: 55.00				

KM# 741 10 PESOS
31.1040 g., 0.9990 Silver 0.999 oz. ASW, 40 mm. **Obv:** Mexican arms **Rev:** Nuevo Leon arms

Date	Mintage	F	VF	XF	Unc	BU
2004 Proof	—	Value: 55.00				

KM# 743 10 PESOS
31.1040 g., 0.9990 Silver 0.999 oz. ASW, 40 mm. **Obv:** Mexican arms **Rev:** Nayarit arms

Date	Mintage	F	VF	XF	Unc	BU
2004 Proof	—	Value: 55.00				

KM# 745 10 PESOS
31.1040 g., 0.9990 Silver 0.999 oz. ASW, 40 mm. **Obv:** Mexican arms **Rev:** Morelos arms

Date	Mintage	F	VF	XF	Unc	BU
2004 Proof	—	Value: 55.00				

KM# 747 10 PESOS
31.1040 g., 0.9990 Silver 0.999 oz. ASW, 40 mm. **Obv:** Mexican arms **Rev:** State of Mexico arms

Date	Mintage	F	VF	XF	Unc	BU
2004 Proof	—	Value: 55.00				

KM# 749 10 PESOS
31.1040 g., 0.9990 Silver 0.999 oz. ASW, 40 mm. **Obv:** Mexican arms **Rev:** Jalisco arms

Date	Mintage	F	VF	XF	Unc	BU
2004 Proof	—	Value: 55.00				

KM# 751 10 PESOS
31.1040 g., 0.9990 Silver 0.999 oz. ASW, 40 mm. **Obv:** Mexican arms **Rev:** Coahuilla arms

Date	Mintage	F	VF	XF	Unc	BU
2005 Proof	—	Value: 55.00				

KM# 753 10 PESOS
31.1040 g., 0.9990 Silver 0.999 oz. ASW, 40 mm. **Obv:** Mexican arms **Rev:** Chihuahua arms

Date	Mintage	F	VF	XF	Unc	BU
2005 Proof	—	Value: 55.00				

KM# 755 10 PESOS
31.1040 g., 0.9990 Silver 0.999 oz. ASW, 40 mm. **Obv:** Mexican arms **Rev:** Baja California del Norte arms

Date	Mintage	F	VF	XF	Unc	BU
2005 Proof	—	Value: 55.00				

KM# 637 20 PESOS
Bi-Metallic Copper-Nickel center within Brass ring **Subject:** Xiuhtecuhtli **Rev:** Aztec with torch

Date	Mintage	F	VF	XF	Unc	BU
2001	2,478,000	—	—	—	15.00	17.50

KM# 638 20 PESOS
Bi-Metallic Copper-Nickel center within Brass ring **Rev:** Octavio Paz

Date	Mintage	F	VF	XF	Unc	BU
2001	2,515,000	—	—	—	15.00	17.50

KM# 704 20 PESOS
62.4000 g., 0.9990 Silver 2.0042 oz. ASW, 48.1 mm. **Obv:** Eagle and snake **Rev:** Skeletal Don Quijote on horse **Edge:** Plain

Date	Mintage	F	VF	XF	Unc	BU
2005Mo Proof	10,000	Value: 75.00				

KM# 696 100 PESOS
29.1690 g., Bi-Metallic .999 Gold 17.154g center in .999 Silver 12.015g ring, 34.5 mm. **Obv:** Mexican arms **Rev:** Zacatecas arms **Edge:** Segmented reeding

Date	Mintage	F	VF	XF	Unc	BU
2003Mo Proof	244,900	Value: 445				

KM# 697 100 PESOS
29.1690 g., Bi-Metallic .999 Gold 17.154g center in .999 Silver 12.015g ring, 34.5 mm. **Obv:** Mexican arms **Rev:** Yucatan arms **Edge:** Segmented reeding

Date	Mintage	F	VF	XF	Unc	BU
2003Mo Proof	235,763	Value: 445				

KM# 698 100 PESOS
29.1690 g., Bi-Metallic .999 Gold 17.154g center in .999 Silver 12.015g ring, 34.5 mm. **Obv:** Mexican arms **Rev:** Veracruz-Llave arms **Edge:** Segmented reeding

Date	Mintage	F	VF	XF	Unc	BU
2003Mo Proof	248,810	Value: 445				

KM# 699 100 PESOS
29.1690 g., Bi-Metallic .999 Gold 17.154g center in .999 Silver 12.015g ring, 34.5 mm. **Obv:** Mexican arms **Rev:** Tlaxcala arms **Edge:** Segmented reeding

Date	Mintage	F	VF	XF	Unc	BU
2003Mo Proof	248,976	Value: 445				

KM# 688 100 PESOS
Bi-Metallic .925 Silver 20.1753g center in Aluminum-Bronze ring, 39.9 mm. **Obv:** Mexican arms **Rev:** Zacatecas arms **Edge:** Segmented reeding

Date	Mintage	F	VF	XF	Unc	BU
2003Mo	250,000	—	—	—	45.00	—

KM# 689 100 PESOS
Bi-Metallic .925 Silver 20.1753g center in Aluminum-Bronze ring, 39.9 mm. **Obv:** Mexican arms **Rev:** Yucatan arms **Edge:** Segmented reeding

Date	Mintage	F	VF	XF	Unc	BU
2003Mo	250,000	—	—	—	45.00	—

KM# 690 100 PESOS
Bi-Metallic .925 Silver 20.1753g center in Aluminum-Bronze ring, 39.9 mm. **Obv:** Mexican arms **Rev:** Veracruz-Llave arms **Edge:** Segmented reeding

Date	Mintage	F	VF	XF	Unc	BU
2003Mo	250,000	—	—	—	45.00	—

KM# 691 100 PESOS
Bi-Metallic .925 Silver 20.1753g center in Aluminum-Bronze ring, 39.9 mm. **Obv:** Mexican arms **Rev:** Tlaxcala arms **Edge:** Segmented reeding

Date	Mintage	F	VF	XF	Unc	BU
2003Mo	250,000	—	—	—	25.00	—

KM# 692 100 PESOS
33.8250 g., Bi-Metallic .925 Silver 20.1753g center in Aluminum-Bronze ring, 39.9 mm. **Obv:** Mexican arms **Rev:** Tamaulipas arms **Edge:** Segmented reeding

Date	Mintage	F	VF	XF	Unc	BU
2004Mo	250,000	—	—	—	25.00	—

KM# 693 100 PESOS
33.8250 g., Bi-Metallic .925 Silver 20.1753g center in Aluminum-Bronze ring, 39.9 mm. **Obv:** Mexican arms **Rev:** Tabasco arms **Edge:** Segmented reeding

Date	Mintage	F	VF	XF	Unc	BU
2004Mo	250,000	—	—	—	25.00	—

KM# 694 100 PESOS
33.8250 g., Bi-Metallic .925 Silver 20.1753g center in Aluminum-Bronze ring, 39.9 mm. **Obv:** Mexican arms **Rev:** Sonora arms **Edge:** Segmented reeding

Date	Mintage	F	VF	XF	Unc	BU
2004Mo	250,000	—	—	—	25.00	—

KM# 695 100 PESOS
33.8250 g., Bi-Metallic .925 Silver 20.1753g center in Aluminum-Bronze ring, 39.9 mm. **Obv:** Mexican arms **Rev:** Sinaloa arms **Edge:** Segmented reeding

Date	Mintage	F	VF	XF	Unc	BU
2004Mo	250,000	—	—	—	25.00	—

KM# 700 100 PESOS
29.1690 g., Bi-Metallic .999 Gold 17.154g center in .999 Silver 12.015g ring, 34.5 mm. **Obv:** Mexican arms **Rev:** Tamaulipas arms **Edge:** Segmented reeding

Date	Mintage	F	VF	XF	Unc	BU
2004Mo Proof	1,000	Value: 445				

KM# 701 100 PESOS
29.1690 g., Bi-Metallic .999 Gold 17.154g center in .999 Silver 12.015g ring, 34.5 mm. **Obv:** Mexican arms **Rev:** Tabasco arms **Edge:** Segmented reeding

Date	Mintage	F	VF	XF	Unc	BU
2004Mo Proof	1,000	Value: 445				

KM# 702 100 PESOS
29.1690 g., Bi-Metallic .999 Gold 17.154g center in .999 Silver 12.015g ring, 34.5 mm. **Obv:** Mexican arms **Rev:** Sonora arms **Edge:** Segmented reeding

Date	Mintage	F	VF	XF	Unc	BU
2004Mo Proof	1,000	Value: 445				

KM# 703 100 PESOS
29.1690 g., Bi-Metallic .999 Gold 17.154g center in .999 Silver 12.015g ring, 34.5 mm. **Obv:** Mexican arms **Rev:** Sinaloa arms **Edge:** Segmented reeding

Date	Mintage	F	VF	XF	Unc	BU
2004Mo Proof	1,000	Value: 445				

KM# 734 100 PESOS
Bi-Metallic .925 Silver 20.1753g center in Aluminum-Bronze ring **Obv:** Mexican arms **Rev:** Quintero Arteaga arms

Date	Mintage	F	VF	XF	Unc	BU
2004	—	—	—	—	30.00	—

KM# 736 100 PESOS
Bi-Metallic .925 Silver 20.1753g center in Aluminum-Bronze ring **Obv:** Mexican arms **Rev:** Quintara Roo arms

Date	Mintage	F	VF	XF	Unc	BU
2004	—	—	—	—	30.00	—

KM# 738 100 PESOS
Bi-Metallic .925 Silver 20.1753g center in Aluminum-Bronze ring **Obv:** Mexican arms **Rev:** Pueblo arms

Date	Mintage	F	VF	XF	Unc	BU
2004	—	—	—	—	30.00	—

KM# 740 100 PESOS
Bi-Metallic .925 Silver 20.1753g center in Aluminum-Bronze ring **Obv:** Mexican arms **Rev:** Oaxaca arms

Date	Mintage	F	VF	XF	Unc	BU
2004	—	—	—	—	30.00	—

KM# 742 100 PESOS
Bi-Metallic .925 Silver 20.1753g center in Aluminum-Bronze ring **Obv:** Mexican arms **Rev:** Nuevo Leon arms

Date	Mintage	F	VF	XF	Unc	BU
2004	—	—	—	—	30.00	—

KM# 744 100 PESOS
Bi-Metallic .925 Silver 20.1753g center in Aluminum-Bronze ring **Obv:** Mexican arms **Rev:** Nayarit arms

Date	Mintage	F	VF	XF	Unc	BU
2004	—	—	—	—	30.00	—

KM# 746 100 PESOS
Bi-Metallic .925 Silver 20.1753g center in Aluminum-Bronze ring **Obv:** Mexican arms **Rev:** Morelos Arms

Date	Mintage	F	VF	XF	Unc	BU
2004	—	—	—	—	30.00	—

KM# 748 100 PESOS
Bi-Metallic .925 Silver 20.1753g center in Aluminum-Bronze ring **Obv:** Mexican arms **Rev:** State of Mexico arms

Date	Mintage	F	VF	XF	Unc	BU
2004	—	—	—	—	30.00	—

KM# 750 100 PESOS
Bi-Metallic .925 Silver 20.1753g center in Aluminum-Bronze ring **Obv:** Mexican arms **Rev:** Jalisco arms

Date	Mintage	F	VF	XF	Unc	BU
2004	—	—	—	—	30.00	—

KM# 705 100 PESOS
33.7400 g., Bi-Metallic .925 Silver center in Aluminum-Bronze ring, 39 mm. **Obv:** Eagle and snake **Rev:** Sekeletal Don Quijote on horse **Edge:** Segmented reeding

Date	Mintage	F	VF	XF	Unc	BU
2005Mo	—	—	—	—	25.00	—

KM# 712 100 PESOS
33.8253 g., Bi-Metallic .925 Silver ring in Brass ring, 39.9 mm. **Obv:** Mexican arms **Rev:** Chiapas state arms **Edge:** Segmented reeding

Date	Mintage	F	VF	XF	Unc	BU
2005Mo	—	—	—	—	45.00	—

KM# 713 100 PESOS
33.8253 g., Bi-Metallic .925 Silver ring in Brass ring, 39.9 mm. **Obv:** Mexican arms **Rev:** Federal District arms **Edge:** Segmented reeding

Date	Mintage	F	VF	XF	Unc	BU
2005Mo	—	—	—	—	45.00	—

KM# 714 100 PESOS
33.8253 g., Bi-Metallic .925 Silver ring in Brass ring, 39.9 mm. **Obv:** Mexican arms **Rev:** Durango arms **Edge:** Segmented reeding

Date	Mintage	F	VF	XF	Unc	BU
2005Mo	—	—	—	—	45.00	—

KM# 715 100 PESOS
33.8253 g., Bi-Metallic .925 Silver ring in Brass ring, 39.9 mm. **Obv:** Mexican arms **Rev:** Guanajuato arms **Edge:** Segmented reeding

Date	Mintage	F	VF	XF	Unc	BU
2005Mo	—	—	—	—	45.00	—

KM# 716 100 PESOS
33.8253 g., Bi-Metallic .925 Silver ring in Brass ring, 39.9 mm. **Obv:** Mexican arms **Rev:** Guerrero state arms **Edge:** Segmented reeding

Date	Mintage	F	VF	XF	Unc	BU
2005Mo	—	—	—	—	45.00	—

KM# 717 100 PESOS
33.8253 g., Bi-Metallic .925 Silver ring in Brass ring, 39.9 mm. **Obv:** Mexican arms **Rev:** Hidalgo state arms **Edge:** Segmented reeding

Date	Mintage	F	VF	XF	Unc	BU
2005Mo	—	—	—	—	45.00	—

KM# 719 100 PESOS
33.8250 g., Bi-Metallic .925 Silver 20.1753g center in Aluminum-Bronze ring, 39.9 mm. **Subject:** Aguascalientes City **Obv:** Mexican eagle **Rev:** Cathedral **Edge:** Segmented reeding

Date	Mintage	F	VF	XF	Unc	BU
2005Mo	—	—	—	—	30.00	—

KM# 721 100 PESOS
33.8250 g., Bi-Metallic .925 Silver 20.1753g center in Aluminum-Bronze ring, 39.9 mm. **Obv:** Mexican eagle **Rev:** Aguascalientes arms **Edge:** Segmented reeding

Date	Mintage	F	VF	XF	Unc	BU
2005Mo	—	—	—	—	30.00	—

KM# 723 100 PESOS
33.8250 g., Bi-Metallic .925 Silver 20.1753g center in Aluminum-Bronze ring, 39.9 mm. **Obv:** Mexican eagle **Rev:** Baja California arms **Edge:** Segmented reeding

Date	Mintage	F	VF	XF	Unc	BU
2005Mo	—	—	—	—	30.00	—

KM# 725 100 PESOS
33.8250 g., Bi-Metallic .925 Silver 20.1753g center in Aluminum-Bronze ring, 39.9 mm. **Obv:** Mexican eagle **Rev:** Baja California Sur arms **Edge:** Segmented reeding

Date	Mintage	F	VF	XF	Unc	BU
2005Mo	—	—	—	—	30.00	—

KM# 727 100 PESOS
33.8250 g., Bi-Metallic .925 Silver 20.1753g center in Aluminum-Bronze ring, 39.9 mm. **Obv:** Mexican eagle **Rev:** Campeche arms **Edge:** Segmented reeding

Date	Mintage	F	VF	XF	Unc	BU
2005Mo	—	—	—	—	30.00	—

KM# 729 100 PESOS
33.8250 g., Bi-Metallic .925 Silver 20.1753g center in Aluminum-Bronze ring, 39.9 mm. **Obv:** Mexican eagle **Rev:** Colima arms **Edge:** Segmented reeding

Date	Mintage	F	VF	XF	Unc	BU
2005Mo	—	—	—	—	30.00	—

KM# 730 100 PESOS
33.8250 g., Bi-Metallic .925 Silver 20.1753g center in Aluminum-Bronze ring, 39.9 mm. **Subject:** Monetary Reform Centennial **Obv:** Mexican eagle **Rev:** Radiant Liberty Cap design **Edge:** Segmented reeding

Date	Mintage	F	VF	XF	Unc	BU
2005Mo	—	—	—	—	30.00	—

KM# 731 100 PESOS
33.8250 g., Bi-Metallic .925 Silver 20.1753g center in Aluminum-Bronze ring, 39.9 mm. **Subject:** Mexico City Mint's 470th Anniversary **Obv:** Mexican eagle **Rev:** Screw press **Edge:** Segmented reeding

Date	Mintage	F	VF	XF	Unc	BU
2005Mo	—	—	—	—	30.00	—

KM# 732 100 PESOS
33.8250 g., Bi-Metallic .925 Silver 20.1753g center in Aluminum-Bronze ring, 39.9 mm. **Subject:** Bank of Mexico's 80th Anniversary **Obv:** Mexican eagle **Rev:** Back design of the 1925 hundred peso note **Edge:** Segmented reeding

Date	Mintage	F	VF	XF	Unc	BU
2005Mo	—	—	—	—	30.00	—

KM# 757 100 PESOS
Bi-Metallic **Subject:** Baja California **Rev:** Ram's head

Date	Mintage	F	VF	XF	Unc	BU
2005	—	—	—	—	—	18.00

KM# 752 100 PESOS
Bi-Metallic .925 Silver 20.1753g center in Aluminum-Bronze ring **Obv:** Mexican arms **Rev:** Coahuilla arms

Date	Mintage	F	VF	XF	Unc	BU
2005	—	—	—	—	30.00	—

KM# 754 100 PESOS
Bi-Metallic .925 Silver 20.1753g center in Aluminum-Bronze ring **Obv:** Mexican arms **Rev:** Chihuahua arms

Date	Mintage	F	VF	XF	Unc	BU
2005	—	—	—	—	30.00	—

KM# 756 100 PESOS
Bi-Metallic .925 Silver 20.1753g center in Aluminum-Bronze ring **Obv:** Mexican arms **Rev:** Baja California del Norte arms

Date	Mintage	F	VF	XF	Unc	BU
2005	—	—	—	—	30.00	—

KM# 760 100 PESOS
Bi-Metallic **Subject:** Estado de Campeche **Rev:** Jade Mask

Date	Mintage	F	VF	XF	Unc	BU
2006	—	—	—	—	—	18.00

KM# 762 100 PESOS
Bi-Metallic **Subject:** Estado de Baja California Sur **Rev:** Deer, sunset and cactus, map superimposed

Date	Mintage	F	VF	XF	Unc	BU
2006	—	—	—	—	—	18.00

KM# 764 100 PESOS
Bi-Metallic **Subject:** Benito Juarez Garcia **Rev:** Bust facing

Date	Mintage	F	VF	XF	Unc	BU
2006	—	—	—	—	—	18.00

SILVER BULLION COINAGE

Libertad Series

KM# 609 1/20 ONZA (1/20 Troy Ounce of Silver)
1.5551 g., 0.9990 Silver .0500 oz. ASW **Obv:** Mexican eagle **Rev:** Winged Victory

Date	Mintage	F	VF	XF	Unc	BU
2001	25,000	—	—	—	—	12.00
2001 Proof	1,500	Value: 15.00				
2002	45,000	—	—	—	—	8.00
2002 Proof	2,800	Value: 13.00				
2003	—	—	—	—	—	8.00
2003 Proof	—	Value: 13.00				
2004	—	—	—	—	—	8.00
2004 Proof	—	Value: 13.00				
2005	—	—	—	—	—	8.00
2005 Proof	—	Value: 12.00				

KM# 610 1/10 ONZA (1/10 Troy Ounce of Silver)
3.1103 g., 0.9990 Silver .1000 oz. ASW **Obv:** Mexican eagle **Rev:** Winged Victory

Date	Mintage	F	VF	XF	Unc	BU
2001	25,000	—	—	—	—	14.00
2001 Proof	1,500	Value: 18.00				
2002	35,000	—	—	—	—	10.00

Date	Mintage	F	VF	XF	Unc	BU
2002 Proof	2,800	Value: 15.00				
2003	—	—	—	—	—	10.00
2003 Proof	—	Value: 15.00				
2004	—	—	—	—	—	10.00
2004 Proof	—	Value: 15.00				
2005	—	—	—	—	—	10.00
2005 Proof	—	Value: 14.00				

KM# 611 1/4 ONZA (1/4 Troy Ounce of Silver)
7.7758 g., 0.9990 Silver .2500 oz. ASW **Obv:** Mexican eagle **Rev:** Winged Victory

Date	Mintage	F	VF	XF	Unc	BU
2001	25,000	—	—	—	—	18.00
2001 Proof	1,000	Value: 22.00				
2002	35,000	—	—	—	—	13.00
2002 Proof	2,800	Value: 20.00				
2003	—	—	—	—	—	13.00
2003 Proof	—	Value: 20.00				
2004	—	—	—	—	—	13.00
2004 Proof	—	Value: 20.00				
2005	—	—	—	—	—	13.00
2005 Proof	—	Value: 18.00				

KM# 612 1/2 ONZA (1/2 Troy Ounce of Silver)
15.5517 g., 0.9990 Silver .5000 oz. ASW **Obv:** Mexican eagle **Rev:** Winged Victory

Date	Mintage	F	VF	XF	Unc	BU
2001	20,000	—	—	—	—	22.00
2001 Proof	1,000	Value: 30.00				
2002	35,000	—	—	—	—	18.00
2002 Proof	2,800	Value: 25.00				
2003	—	—	—	—	—	18.00
2003 Proof	—	Value: 25.00				
2004	—	—	—	—	—	18.00
2004 Proof	—	Value: 25.00				
2005	—	—	—	—	—	18.00
2005 Proof	—	Value: 22.00				

KM# 639 ONZA (Troy Ounce of Silver)
31.1000 g., 0.9990 Silver 1.0000 oz. ASW **Subject:** Libertad **Obv:** Modern Mexican eagle within circle of obsolete versions **Edge:** Reeded edge **Note:** Mule

Date	Mintage	F	VF	XF	Unc	BU
2001	650,000	—	—	—	—	20.00
2001 Proof	2,000	Value: 50.00				
2002	850,000	—	—	—	—	18.00
2002 Proof	3,800	Value: 50.00				
2003Mo	—	—	—	—	—	18.00
2003Mo Proof	—	Value: 50.00				
2004Mo	—	—	—	—	—	18.00
2004Mo Proof	—	Value: 45.00				
2005	—	—	—	—	—	18.00
2005 Proof	—	Value: 45.00				

KM# 614 2 ONZAS (2 Troy Ounces of Silver)
62.2070 g., 0.9990 Silver 2.0000 oz. ASW **Subject:** Libertad **Obv:** Mexican eagle within circle of obsolete versions **Rev:** Winged Victory

Date	Mintage	F	VF	XF	Unc	BU
2001	1,700	—	—	—	—	50.00
2001 Proof	500	Value: 60.00				
2002	8,700	—	—	—	—	45.00
2002 Proof	1,000	Value: 55.00				
2003	—	—	—	—	—	45.00
2003 Proof	—	Value: 55.00				
2004	—	—	—	—	—	40.00
2004 Proof	—	Value: 50.00				
2005	—	—	—	—	—	40.00
2005 Proof	—	Value: 50.00				

KM# 615 5 ONZAS (5 Troy Ounces of Silver)
155.5175 g., 0.9990 Silver 5.0000 oz. ASW **Subject:** Libertad **Obv:** Mexican eagle within circle of obsolete versions **Rev:** Winged Victory

Date	Mintage	F	VF	XF	Unc	BU
2001	4,000	—	—	—	—	95.00
2001 Proof	600	Value: 200				
2002	5,200	—	—	—	—	95.00
2002 Proof	1,000	Value: 200				
2003	—	—	—	—	—	85.00
2003 Proof	—	Value: 110				
2004	—	—	—	—	—	85.00
2004 Proof	—	Value: 110				
2005	—	—	—	—	—	85.00
2005 Proof	—	Value: 110				

KM# 677 KILO (32.15 Troy Ounces of Silver)
999.9775 g., 0.9990 Silver 32.1178 oz. ASW, 110 mm. **Subject:** Collector Bullion **Obv:** Current Mexican emblem within circle of obsolete versions **Rev:** Winged Victory statue **Edge:** Reeded

Date	Mintage	F	VF	XF	Unc	BU
2002Mo Prooflike	1,100	—	—	—	—	750
2003Mo Proof	3,000	Value: 650				
2004Mo Prooflike	—	—	—	—	—	650
2005Mo Proof	—	Value: 675				

GOLD BULLION COINAGE

KM# 671 1/20 ONZA (1/20 Ounce of Pure Gold)
1.5551 g., 0.9990 Gold .05 oz. AGW, 16 mm. **Obv:** Mexican arms **Rev:** Winged Victory facing left **Edge:** Reeded **Note:** Design similar to KM#609. Value estimates do not include the high taxes and surcharges added to the issue prices by the Mexican Government.

Date	Mintage	F	VF	XF	Unc	BU
2002Mo	5,000	—	—	—	BV+30%	—
2004Mo	—	—	—	—	BV+30%	—
2005Mo	—	—	—	—	BV+30%	—
2006Mo	—	—	—	—	BV+30%	—

KM# 672 1/10 ONZA (1/10 Ounce of Pure Gold)
3.1103 g., 0.9990 Gold 0.0999 oz. AGW, 20 mm. **Obv:** Mexican arms **Rev:** Winged Victory facing left **Edge:** Reeded **Note:** Design similar to KM#610. Value estimates do not include the high taxes and surcharges added to the issue prices by the Mexican Government.

Date	Mintage	F	VF	XF	Unc	BU
2002Mo	5,000	—	—	—	BV+20%	—
2004Mo	—	—	—	—	BV+20%	—
2005Mo	—	—	—	—	BV+20%	—

KM# 673 1/4 ONZA (1/4 Ounce of Pure Gold)
7.7758 g., 0.9990 Gold .25 oz. AGW, 26.9 mm. **Obv:** Mexican arms **Rev:** Winged Victory facing left **Edge:** Reeded **Note:** Design similar to KM#611. Value estimates do not include the high taxes and surcharges added to the issue prices by the Mexican Government.

Date	Mintage	F	VF	XF	Unc	BU
2002Mo	—	—	—	—	BV+12%	—
2004Mo	—	—	—	—	BV+12%	—
2004Mo Proof	—	—	—	—	—	—
2005Mo	—	—	—	—	BV+12%	—
2005Mo Proof	—	—	—	—	—	—

KM# 674 1/2 ONZA (1/2 Ounce of Pure Gold)
15.5517 g., 0.9990 Gold 0.4995 oz. AGW, 32.9 mm. **Obv:** Mexican arms **Rev:** Winged Victory facing left **Edge:** Reeded **Note:** Design similar to KM#612. Value estimates do not include the high taxes and surcharges added to the issue prices by the Mexican Government.

Date	Mintage	F	VF	XF	Unc	BU
2002Mo	—	—	—	—	BV+8%	—
2004Mo	—	—	—	—	BV+8%	—
2005Mo	—	—	—	—	BV+8%	—
2005 Proof	—	—	—	—	—	—
2006Mo	—	—	—	—	BV+8%	—

KM# 675 ONZA (Ounce of Pure Gold)
31.1035 g., 0.9990 Gold 0.999 oz. AGW, 40 mm. **Obv:** Mexican arms **Rev:** Winged Victory facing left **Edge:** Reeded **Note:** Design similar to KM#639. Value estimates do not include the high taxes and surcharges added to the issue prices by the Mexican Government.

Date	Mintage	F	VF	XF	Unc	BU
2002Mo	—	—	—	—	BV+3%	—
2004Mo	—	—	—	—	BV+3%	—
2005Mo	—	—	—	—	BV+3%	—
2006Mo	—	—	—	—	BV+3%	—

BANK SETS

Hard Case Sets unless otherwise noted.

KM#	Date	Mintage	Identification	Issue Price	Mkt Val
BS38	2001 (10)	—	KM#546-549, 603-605, 636-638 Set in folder	—	30.00
BS39	2002 (8)	—	KM#546-549, 603-605, 616 Set in folder	—	30.00
BS40	2003 (6)	—	KM#547-549, 603-605 Set in folder	—	30.00

The Republic of Moldova (formerly the Moldavian S.S.R.) is bordered in the north, east and south by the Ukraine and on the west by Romania. It has an area of 13,000 sq.mi. (33,700 sq.km.) and a population of 4.4 million. The capital is Chisinau. Agricultural products are mainly cereals, grapes, tobacco, sugar beets and fruits. Food processing, clothing, building materials and agricultural machinery manufacturing dominate industry.

MONETARY SYSTEM
100 Bani = 1 Leu

REPUBLIC

DECIMAL COINAGE

KM# 1 BAN
0.0700 g., Aluminum, 14.5 mm. **Obv:** Heraldic eagle **Rev:** Value and date **Edge:** Plain

Date	Mintage	F	VF	XF	Unc	BU
2004	—	—	—	—	0.25	0.50

KM# 2 5 BANI
0.7800 g., Aluminum, 16 mm. **Obv:** Heraldic eagle **Rev:** Value and date **Edge:** Plain

Date	Mintage	F	VF	XF	Unc	BU
2001	—	—	—	—	0.30	0.50
2002	—	—	—	—	0.30	0.50
2003	—	—	—	—	0.30	0.50
2005	—	—	—	—	0.30	0.50

KM# 7 10 BANI
0.8400 g., Aluminum, 16.6 mm. **Obv:** Heraldic eagle **Rev:** Value and date **Edge:** Plain

Date	Mintage	F	VF	XF	Unc	BU
2001	—	—	—	—	0.40	0.60
2002	—	—	—	—	0.40	0.60
2003	—	—	—	—	0.40	0.60
2005	—	—	—	—	0.40	0.60

KM# 3 25 BANI
0.9200 g., Aluminum, 17.5 mm. **Obv:** Heraldic eagle **Rev:** Value and date **Edge:** Plain

Date	Mintage	F	VF	XF	Unc	BU
2001	—	—	—	—	0.50	0.75
2002	—	—	—	—	0.50	0.75
2003	—	—	—	—	0.50	0.75
2004	—	—	—	—	0.50	0.75

KM# 10 50 BANI
3.1000 g., Brass-Clad Steel, 19 mm. **Obv:** Heraldic eagle **Rev:** Denomination and grapevine **Edge:** Reeded

Date	Mintage	F	VF	XF	Unc	BU
2003	—	—	—	—	1.50	2.00
2005	—	—	—	—	1.50	2.00

KM# 12 10 LEI
13.5000 g., 0.9250 Silver 0.4015 oz. ASW, 24.5 mm. **Obv:** National arms above value **Rev:** European wildcat **Edge:** Plain

Date	Mintage	F	VF	XF	Unc	BU
2001 Proof	1,000	Value: 50.00				

KM# 13 10 LEI
13.5000 g., 0.9250 Silver 0.4015 oz. ASW, 24.5 mm. **Obv:** National arms above value **Rev:** Eurasian Green Woodpecker **Edge:** Plain

Date	Mintage	F	VF	XF	Unc	BU
2001 Proof	1,000	Value: 50.00				

KM# 19 10 LEI
13.4500 g., 0.9250 Silver 0.4 oz. ASW, 24.5 mm. **Obv:** National arms above value **Rev:** European Mink **Edge:** Plain

Date	Mintage	F	VF	XF	Unc	BU
2003 Proof	500	Value: 50.00				

KM# 20 10 LEI
13.4500 g., 0.9250 Silver 0.4 oz. ASW, 24.5 mm. **Obv:** National arms above value **Rev:** Two Black Storks **Edge:** Plain

Date	Mintage	F	VF	XF	Unc	BU
2003 Proof	500	Value: 45.00				

KM# 22 10 LEI
13.5000 g., 0.9250 Silver 0.4015 oz. ASW, 24.5 mm. **Obv:** National arms above value **Rev:** Wood Marten **Edge:** Plain

Date	Mintage	F	VF	XF	Unc	BU
2004 Proof	500	Value: 50.00				

KM# 17 50 LEI
16.5000 g., 0.9250 Silver 0.4907 oz. ASW, 30 mm. **Obv:** National arms above value **Rev:** Constantin Brancusi (1876-1957) and building **Edge:** Plain

Date	Mintage	F	VF	XF	Unc	BU
2001 Proof	1,000	Value: 35.00				

KM# 18 50 LEI
16.5000 g., 0.9250 Silver 0.4907 oz. ASW, 30 mm. **Obv:** National arms above value **Rev:** Vasile Alecsandri (1821-90) with book and landscape **Edge:** Plain

Date	Mintage	F	VF	XF	Unc	BU
2001 Proof	1,000	Value: 35.00				

KM# 21 50 LEI
16.5000 g., 0.9250 Silver 0.4907 oz. ASW, 29.8 mm. **Obv:** National arms above value **Rev:** Dimitrie Cantemir **Edge:** Plain

Date	Mintage	F	VF	XF	Unc	BU
2003 Proof	500	Value: 35.00				

KM# 14 50 LEI
16.5500 g., 0.9250 Silver 0.4922 oz. ASW, 29.9 mm. **Obv:** National arms above value **Rev:** Miron Costin (1633-91) in fur hat with books at right **Edge:** Plain

Date	Mintage	F	VF	XF	Unc	BU
2003 Proof	500	Value: 50.00				

KM# 23 50 LEI
16.5000 g., 0.9250 Silver 0.4907 oz. ASW, 30 mm. **Obv:** National arms **Rev:** Mitropolitul Dosoftei holding staff **Edge:** Plain

Date	Mintage	F	VF	XF	Unc	BU
2004 Proof	500	Value: 40.00				

KM# 16 100 LEI
31.1000 g., 0.9250 Silver 0.9249 oz. ASW, 37 mm. **Subject:** 10th Anniversary of Independence **Obv:** National arms **Rev:** Arch monument **Edge:** Plain

Date	Mintage	F	VF	XF	Unc	BU
2001 Proof	1,000	Value: 55.00				

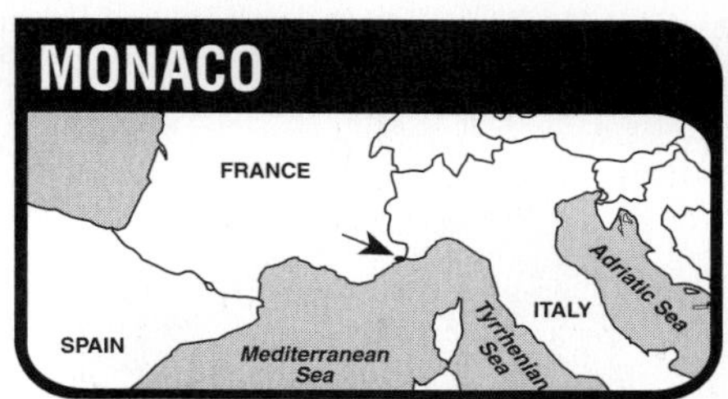

The Principality of Monaco, located on the Mediterranean coast nine miles from Nice, has an area of 0.58 sq. mi. (1.9 sq. km.) and a population of 26,000. Capital: Monaco-Ville. The economy is based on tourism and the manufacture of cosmetics, gourmet foods and highly specialized electronics. Monaco also derives its revenue from a tobacco monopoly and the sale of postage stamps for philatelic purpose. Gambling in Monte Carlo accounts for only a small fraction of the country's revenue.

RULERS
Rainier III, 1949-2005
Albert II, 2005-

MINT MARKS
M - Monaco
A – Paris

MINT PRIVY MARKS
(a) - Paris (privy marks only)
Horseshoe - 2001 and 2002
Heart - 2003
French Horn - 2004
(p) - Thunderbolt - Poissy

MONETARY SYSTEM
10 Centimes = 1 Decime
10 Decimes = 1 Franc

PRINCIPALITY

EURO COINAGE

KM# 167 EURO CENT
2.2700 g., Copper Plated Steel, 16.2 mm. **Ruler:** Rainier III **Obv:** Crowned arms **Obv. Designer:** Robert Cochet **Rev:** Denomination and globe **Rev. Designer:** Luc Luycx **Edge:** Plain

Date	Mintage	F	VF	XF	Unc	BU
2001	327,200	—	—	—	20.00	30.00
2001 Proof	3,500	Value: 75.00				
2002	Est. 40,000	—	—	—	—	65.00
Note: Initially available only in sets						
2003	—	—	—	—	—	—
2004 Proof	14,999	Value: 25.00				
2005 Proof	35,000	Value: 50.00				

KM# 168 2 EURO CENTS
3.0300 g., Copper Plated Steel, 18.7 mm. **Ruler:** Rainier III **Obv:** Crowned arms **Obv. Designer:** Robert Cochet **Rev:** Denomination and globe **Rev. Designer:** Luc Luycx **Edge:** Grooved

Date	Mintage	F	VF	XF	Unc	BU
2001	373,400	—	—	—	15.00	25.00
2001 Proof	3,500	Value: 85.00				
2002	Est. 40,000	—	—	—	—	65.00
Note: Initially available only in sets						
2003	—	—	—	—	—	—
2004 Proof	14,999	Value: 35.00				
2005 Proof	35,000	Value: 50.00				

KM# 169 5 EURO CENTS
3.8600 g., Copper-Nickel Plated Steel, 21.2 mm. **Ruler:** Rainier III **Obv:** Crowned arms **Obv. Designer:** Robert Cochet **Rev:** Denomination and globe **Rev. Designer:** Luc Luycx **Edge:** Plain

Date	Mintage	F	VF	XF	Unc	BU
2001	300,000	—	—	—	20.00	30.00
2001 Proof	3,500	Value: 95.00				
2002	Est. 40,000	—	—	—	—	70.00
Note: Initially available only in sets						
2003	—	—	—	—	—	—
2004 Proof	14,999	Value: 45.00				
2005 Proof	—	Value: 55.00				

KM# 170 10 EURO CENTS
4.0700 g., Brass, 19.7 mm. **Ruler:** Rainier III **Obv:** Charging knight **Obv. Designer:** R. Baron **Rev:** Map and denomination **Rev. Designer:** Luc Luycx **Edge:** Reeded

Date	Mintage	F	VF	XF	Unc	BU
2001	300,000	—	—	—	15.00	20.00
2001 Proof	3,500	Value: 110				
2002	367,200	—	—	—	8.00	12.00
2003	—	—	—	—	12.00	16.00
2004 Proof	14,999	Value: 50.00				

KM# 171 20 EURO CENTS
5.7300 g., Brass, 22.1 mm. **Ruler:** Rainier III **Obv:** Charging knight **Obv. Designer:** R. Baron **Rev:** Map and denomination **Rev. Designer:** R. Baron **Edge:** Notched

Date	Mintage	F	VF	XF	Unc	BU
2001	366,400	—	—	—	15.00	20.00
2001 Proof	3,500	Value: 120				
2002	336,000	—	—	—	12.00	16.00
2003	—	—	—	—	12.00	16.00
2004 Proof	14,999	Value: 60.00				

KM# 172 50 EURO CENTS
7.8100 g., Brass **Ruler:** Rainier III **Obv:** Charging knight **Obv. Designer:** R. Baron **Rev:** Map and denomination **Rev. Designer:** Luc Luycx **Edge:** Reeded

Date	Mintage	F	VF	XF	Unc	BU
2001	300,000	—	—	—	15.00	20.00
2001 Proof	3,500	Value: 130				
2002	324,000	—	—	—	8.00	12.00
2003	—	—	—	—	12.00	16.00
2004 Proof	14,999	Value: 65.00				

KM# 173 EURO
7.5000 g., Bi-Metallic Copper- Nickel center in Brass ring, 23.2 mm. **Ruler:** Rainier III **Obv:** Conjoined heads of Prince Rainier and Crown Prince Albert right **Obv. Designer:** Pierre Rodier **Rev:** Denomination and map **Rev. Designer:** Luc Luycx **Edge:** Reeded and plain sections

Date	Mintage	F	VF	XF	Unc	BU
2001	971,200	—	—	—	10.00	12.00
2001 Proof	3,500	Value: 145				
2002	472,500	—	—	—	11.00	14.00
2003	—	—	—	—	13.50	18.50
2004 Proof	14,999	Value: 75.00				

KM# 174 2 EUROS
8.5200 g., Bi-Metallic Brass center in Copper-Nickel ring, 25.7 mm. **Ruler:** Rainier III **Obv:** Prince Rainier's portrait right **Obv. Designer:** Pierre Rodier **Rev:** Denomination and map **Rev. Designer:** Luc Luycx **Edge:** Reeding over "2's" and stars

Date	Mintage	F	VF	XF	Unc	BU
2001	899,800	—	—	—	14.00	16.00
2001 Proof	3,500	Value: 165				
2002	456,000	—	—	—	15.00	18.00
2003	—	—	—	—	17.50	22.50
2004 Proof	14,999	Value: 95.00				

KM# 180 5 EURO
12.0000 g., 0.9000 Silver 0.3472 oz. ASW, 29 mm. **Ruler:** Rainier III **Obv:** Bust of Prince Rainier III right **Rev:** Saint standing

Date	Mintage	F	VF	XF	Unc	BU
2004 Proof	14,999	Value: 125				

KM# 178 10 EURO
25.0000 g., 0.9250 Silver 0.7435 oz. ASW, 37 mm. **Ruler:** Rainier III **Obv:** Overlaping busts of Prince Rainier III and Crown Prince Albert right **Rev:** Arms

Date	Mintage	F	VF	XF	Unc	BU
2003 Proof	4,000	Value: 465				

KM# 177 20 EURO
18.0000 g., 0.9250 Gold 0.5353 oz. AGW, 32 mm. **Ruler:** Rainier III **Obv:** Prince Rainier III right **Rev:** Arms

Date	Mintage	F	VF	XF	Unc	BU
2002 Proof	10,000	Value: 1,100				

KM# 179 100 EURO
29.0000 g., 0.9000 Gold 0.8391 oz. AGW **Ruler:** Rainier III **Obv:** Bust of Prince Rainier III right **Rev:** Knight on horseback

Date	Mintage	F	VF	XF	Unc	BU
2003 Proof	1,000	Value: 3,250				

MINT SETS

KM#	Date	Mintage	Identification	Issue Price	Mkt Val
MS1	2001 (8)	20,000	KM#167-174, exercise caution, as privately packaged and deceptively false sets are known	35.00	400
MS2	2002 (8)	40,000	KM#167-174, exercise caution, as partial sets, privately packaged and deceptively false sets are known	35.00	375

PROOF SETS

KM#	Date	Mintage	Identification	Issue Price	Mkt Val
PS1	2001 (8)	3,500	KM#167-174	—	925
PS2	2004 (9)	14,999	KM#167-174, 180	—	575
PS3	2005 (3)	35,000	KM#167-169	—	150

MONGOLIA

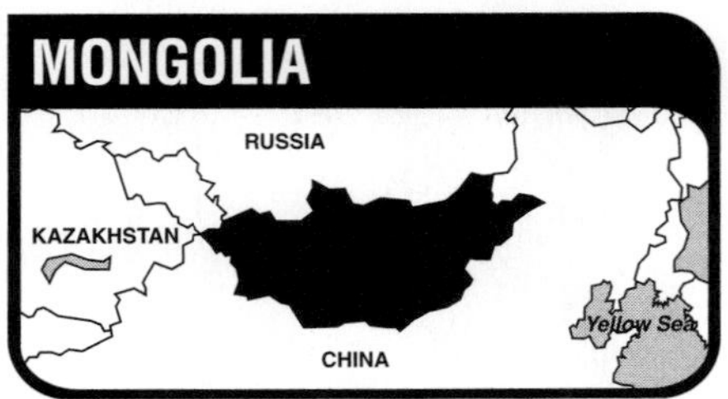

The State of Mongolia, (formerly the Mongolian Peoples Republic) a landlocked country in central Asia between Russia and the People's Republic of China, has an area of 604,250 sq. mi. (1,565,000 sq. km.) and a population of 2.26 million. Capital: Ulaan Baatar. Animal herds and flocks are the chief economic asset. Wool, cattle, butter, meat and hides are exported.

For earlier issues see Russia - Tannu Tuva.

MONETARY SYSTEM
100 Mongo = 1 Tugrik

STATE OF MONGOLIA

DECIMAL COINAGE

KM# 189 500 TUGRIK
25.0000 g., 0.9250 Silver .7435 oz. ASW, 38.7 mm. **Subject:** Protoceratops Andrewsi **Obv:** National arms above denomination **Rev:** Dinosaur **Edge:** Reeded

Date	Mintage	F	VF	XF	Unc	BU
2001 Proof	2,500	Value: 40.00				

KM# 190 500 TUGRIK
25.0000 g., 0.9250 Silver .7435 oz. ASW **Subject:** Velociraptor Mongoliensis **Obv:** National arms above denomination **Rev:** Dinosaur

Date	Mintage	F	VF	XF	Unc	BU
2001 Proof	2,500	Value: 40.00				

KM# 191 500 TUGRIK
25.0000 g., 0.9250 Silver .7435 oz. ASW **Series:** Olympics **Obv:** National arms above denomination **Rev:** Speed skater

Date	Mintage	F	VF	XF	Unc	BU
2001 Proof	15,000	Value: 32.50				

KM# 192 500 TUGRIK
25.0000 g., 0.9250 Silver .7435 oz. ASW **Series:** Olympics **Obv:** National arms above denomination **Rev:** Three cross-country skiers

Date	Mintage	F	VF	XF	Unc	BU
2001 Proof	20,000	Value: 32.50				

KM# 195 500 TUGRIK
Copper-Nickel, 22.1 mm. **Subject:** Sukhe-Bataar **Obv:** National emblem and denomination **Rev:** Bataars portrait **Edge:** Plain

Date	Mintage	F	VF	XF	Unc	BU
2001	—	—	—	—	2.50	3.00

KM# 200 500 TUGRIK
25.5700 g., 0.9250 Silver 0.7604 oz. ASW, 38.5 mm. **Subject:** Marco Polo, Homeward **Obv:** National emblem above value **Rev:** Five-masted sailing junk **Edge:** Reeded

Date	Mintage	F	VF	XF	Unc	BU
2003 Proof	5,000	Value: 45.00				

KM# 205 500 TUGRIK
25.0000 g., 0.9250 Silver 0.7435 oz. ASW, 38.6 mm. **Obv:** National emblem above value **Rev:** Kublai Khan and Marco Polo with the "paitzu" passport medallion in foreground **Edge:** Reeded

Date	Mintage	F	VF	XF	Unc	BU
2003 Proof	5,000	Value: 50.00				

KM# 206 500 TUGRIK
1.2440 g., 0.9999 Gold 0.04 oz. AGW, 13.92 mm. **Obv:** National emblem above value **Rev:** Five masted sailing junk **Edge:** Reeded

Date	Mintage	F	VF	XF	Unc	BU
2003 Proof	25,000	Value: 50.00				

KM# 207 500 TUGRIK
1.2440 g., 0.9999 Gold .04 oz. AGW, 13.92 mm. **Obv:** National emblem above value **Rev:** Kublai Khan and Marco Polo with the "paitzu" passport medallion in the foreground **Edge:** Reeded

Date	Mintage	F	VF	XF	Unc	BU
2003 Proof	25,000	Value: 50.00				

KM# 204 500 TUGRIK
25.0000 g., 0.9250 Silver 0.7435 oz. ASW, 38 mm.
Obv: National arms and value **Rev:** Wolf with full moon background **Edge:** Reeded

Date	Mintage	F	VF	XF	Unc	BU
2003 Proof	10,000	Value: 45.00				

KM# 208 500 TUGRIK
25.0000 g., 0.9250 Silver 0.7435 oz. ASW, 38 mm.
Obv: National emblem above value **Rev:** Holographic fish eagle catching fish **Edge:** Reeded

Date	Mintage	F	VF	XF	Unc	BU
2004 Proof	5,000	Value: 50.00				

KM# 209 500 TUGRIK
24.9300 g., 0.9250 Bi-Metallic Niobium Leopard shape center in .925 Silver oval 0.7414 oz., 30 mm. **Obv:** National arms above value **Rev:** Snow Leopard **Edge:** Reeded

Date	Mintage	F	VF	XF	Unc	BU
2005 Proof	5,000	Value: 70.00				

KM# 210 500 TUGRIK
31.1035 g., 0.9990 Silver 0.999 oz. ASW, 35x35 mm. **Obv:** Bronze plated horse and rider on antiqued silver with national emblem and value **Rev:** Bronze plated horse and rider on antiqued silver above date **Edge:** Reeded **Shape:** Square

Date	Mintage	F	VF	XF	Unc	BU
2005	2,500	—	—	—	50.00	55.00

KM# 210a 500 TUGRIK
31.1035 g., 0.9990 Silver 0.999 oz. ASW, 35x35 mm. **Obv:** Gold plated horse and rider with national emblem and value **Rev:** Gold plated horse and rider above date **Edge:** Reeded

Date	Mintage	F	VF	XF	Unc	BU
2005 Proof	2,500	Value: 60.00				

KM# 199 1000 TUGRIK
31.1100 g., 0.9250 Silver 0.9252 oz. ASW, 38.6 mm. **Obv:** National emblem above value **Obv. Inscription:** Denomination spelled "TOGROG" **Rev:** Head of Chinggis Khan facing **Edge:** Reeded

Date	Mintage	F	VF	XF	Unc	BU
2002	17,000	—	—	—	35.00	40.00

KM# 198 5000 TUGRIK
155.5000 g., 0.9990 Silver 4.9944 oz. ASW, 40x90 mm. **Subject:** Year of the Horse **Obv:** National emblem, denomination and Palace Museum **Rev:** Five multicolor running horses **Edge:** Plain **Note:** Round-cornered rectangle.

Date	Mintage	F	VF	XF	Unc	BU
2002 Proof	—	Value: 175				

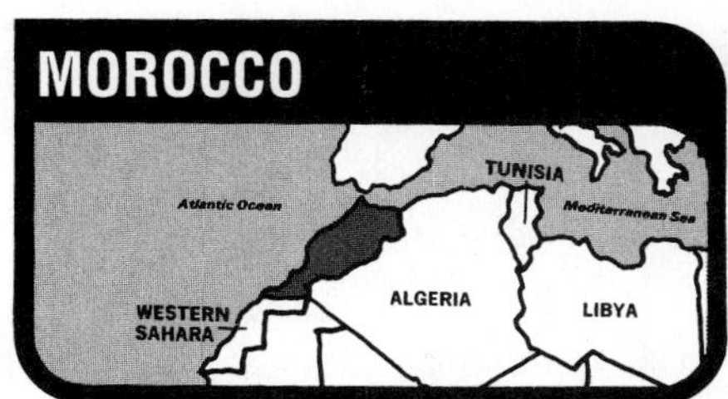

The Kingdom of Morocco, situated on the northwest corner of Africa, has an area of 432,620 sq. mi. (710,850 sq. km.) and a population of 36 million. Capital: Rabat. The economy is essentially agricultural. Phosphates, fresh and preserved vegetables, canned fish, and raw materials are exported.

KINGDOM

Mohammed VI
AH1420 / 1999AD

REFORM COINAGE

100 Santimat = 1 Dirham

Y# 116 1/2 DIRHAM
4.0000 g., Copper-Nickel, 21 mm. **Obv:** National arms **Rev:** World globe and satellite **Edge:** Reeded

Date	Mintage	F	VF	XF	Unc
AH1423-2002	—	—	—	—	1.50

Y# 112 5 SANTIMAT
2.5000 g., Brass, 17.5 mm. **Obv:** National arms **Rev:** Value and flower **Edge:** Plain

Date	Mintage	F	VF	XF	Unc
AH1423-2002	—	—	—	—	0.30

Y# 114 10 SANTIMAT
3.0000 g., Brass, 19.8 mm. **Obv:** National arms **Rev:** Value and design **Edge:** Reeded

Date	Mintage	F	VF	XF	Unc
2002-1423	—	—	—	—	0.75

Y# 115 20 SANTIMAT
4.0000 g., Brass, 23 mm. **Obv:** National arms **Rev:** Value and design **Edge:** Reeded

Date	Mintage	F	VF	XF	Unc
2002-1423	—	—	—	—	1.00

Y# 117 DIRHAM
6.0000 g., Copper-Nickel, 24 mm. **Obv:** Mohammed VI **Rev:** National arms above value **Edge:** Reeded

Date	Mintage	F	VF	XF	Unc
AH1423-2002	—	—	—	—	2.50

Y# 118 2 DIRHAMS
7.3000 g., Copper-Nickel, 25.9 mm. **Obv:** Mohammed VI **Rev:** National arms above value **Edge:** Reeded

Date	Mintage	F	VF	XF	Unc
2002-1423	—	—	—	—	3.50

Y# 109 5 DIRHAMS
7.5300 g., Bi-Metallic Brass center in Copper-Nickel ring Brass center in Copper-Nickel ring, 25 mm. **Obv:** King Mohammed VI **Rev:** Coat of Arms **Edge:** Segmented reeding

Date	Mintage	F	VF	XF	Unc
AH1423-2002	—	—	—	—	7.00

Y# 110 10 DIRHAMS
9.0000 g., Bi-Metallic Copper-Nickel center in Brass ring Copper-Nickel center in Brass ring, 26.9 mm. **Obv:** King Mohammed VI **Rev:** Coat of arms **Edge:** Reeded

Date	Mintage	F	VF	XF	Unc
AH1423-2002	—	—	—	—	8.00

Y# 107 250 DIRHAMS
25.0000 g., 0.9250 Silver 0.7435 oz. ASW, 37 mm. **Subject:** Inauguration of Mohammed VI 2nd Anniversary **Obv:** King's portrait **Rev:** National arms **Edge:** Reeded

Date	Mintage	F	VF	XF	Unc
AH1422-2001	—	—	—	—	50.00

Y# 95 250 DIRHAMS
25.0000 g., 0.9250 Silver 0.7435 oz. ASW, 37 mm. **Subject:** World Children's Day **Obv:** King's portrait **Rev:** Children standing on open book with a globe background **Edge:** Reeded

Date	Mintage	F	VF	XF	Unc
AH1422-2001	—	—	—	—	50.00
AH1422-2001 Proof	—	Value: 80.00			

Y# 95a 250 DIRHAMS
25.0000 g., 0.9999 Gold .8037 oz. AGW, 37 mm. **Subject:** World Children's Day **Obv:** King's portrait **Rev:** Two children on an open book and a world globe **Edge:** Reeded **Note:** Previous Y#95.

Date	Mintage	F	VF	XF	Unc
AH1422-2001 Proof	2,800	Value: 520			

Y# 108 250 DIRHAMS
25.0000 g., 0.9250 Silver 0.7435 oz. ASW, 37 mm. **Subject:** Mohammed VI's Inauguration 3rd Anniversary **Obv:** King's portrait **Rev:** National arms, legend differs slightly from the legend of Y-107 **Edge:** Reeded

Date	Mintage	F	VF	XF	Unc
AH1423-2002	—	—	—	—	45.00
AH1423-2002 Proof	—	Value: 75.00			

Y# 113 250 DIRHAMS
25.0000 g., 0.9250 Silver 0.7435 oz. ASW, 37 mm. **Obv:** King Mohammed VI **Rev:** Crown above radiant flowers **Edge:** Reeded

Date	Mintage	F	VF	XF	Unc
ND (2002) Proof	—	Value: 75.00			

Y# 119 250 DIRHAMS
25.0000 g., Silver, 37 mm. **Subject:** Birth of Crown Prince Moulay Al Hassan **Obv:** Head of Mohammed VI left **Rev:** National arms

Date	Mintage	F	VF	XF	Unc
ND(2003) Proof	—	Value: 75.00			

Y# 120 250 DIRHAMS
25.0000 g., Silver, 37 mm. **Subject:** 50th Anniversary - Kingdom **Obv:** 3 ruler's heads right **Rev:** National arms

Date	Mintage	F	VF	XF	Unc
AH1424-2003	—	—	—	—	45.00
AH1424-2003 Proof	—	Value: 75.00			

Y# 111 250 DIRHAMS
25.0000 g., 0.9250 Silver 0.7435 oz. ASW, 37 mm. **Subject:** Anniversary of king's reign **Obv:** Mohammed VI **Rev:** National arms **Edge:** Reeded **Note:** Virtually identical to Y-107 and Y-108.

Date	Mintage	F	VF	XF	Unc
AH1424-2003	—	—	—	—	50.00

Y# 121 250 DIRHAMS
25.0000 g., Silver, 37 mm. **Subject:** Year of Handicapped Persons **Obv:** Head of Mohammed VI left **Rev:** 4 stylized figures

Date	Mintage	F	VF	XF	Unc
AH1425-2004	—	—	—	—	50.00

Y# 122 250 DIRHAMS
25.0000 g., Silver, 37 mm. **Subject:** 5th Anniversary of Mohammed VI's Reign **Obv:** Head of Mohammed VI left **Rev:** National arms

Date	Mintage	F	VF	XF	Unc
AH1425-2004	—	—	—	—	50.00

Y# 123 250 DIRHAMS
25.0000 g., Silver, 37 mm. **Subject:** 30th Anniversary - Green March **Obv:** Head of Mohammed VI left **Rev:** Men marching left with flags aloft

Date	Mintage	F	VF	XF	Unc
AH1426-2005	—	—	—	—	50.00

MOROCCO

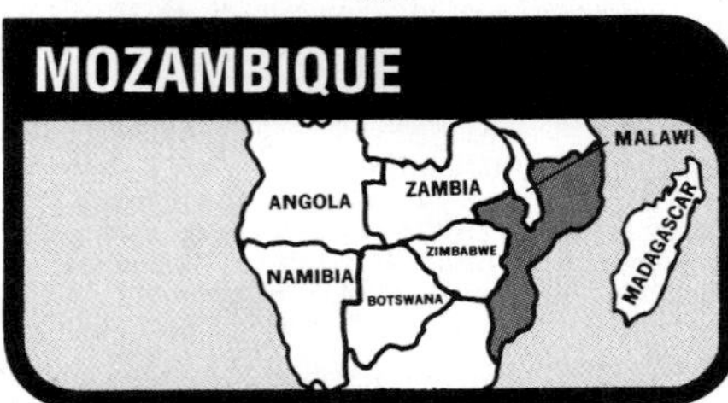

The Republic of Mozambique, a former overseas province of Portugal, stretches for 1,430 miles (2,301 km.) along the southeast coast of Africa, has an area of 302,330 sq. mi. (801,590 sq. km.) and a population of 14.1 million, 99 % of whom are native Africans of the Bantu tribes. Capital: Maputo. Agriculture is the chief industry. Cashew nuts, cotton, sugar, copra and tea are exported.

Mozambique became a member of the Commonwealth of Nations in November 1995. The President is Head of State; the Prime Minister is Head of Government.

PEOPLE'S REPUBLIC

REFORM COINAGE

100 Centavos = 1 Metical; 1994

KM# 130 1000 METICAIS
25.7100 g., 0.9800 Silver 0.8101 oz. ASW, 38.5 mm. **Subject:** Pedro De Covilha, 1498 **Obv:** National arms **Rev:** Sailing ship **Edge:** Reeded

Date	Mintage	F	VF	XF	Unc	BU
2003 Proof	—	Value: 40.00				

KM# 131 10000 METICAIS
8.0400 g., Bi-Metallic Stainless Steel center in Brass ring, 26.6 mm. **Obv:** National arms **Rev:** Rhino **Edge:** Segmented reeding

Date	Mintage	F	VF	XF	Unc	BU
2003	—	—	—	—	10.00	12.00

Nagorno-Karabakh, an ethnically Armenian enclave inside Azerbaijan (pop., 1991 est.: 193,000), SW region. It occupies an area of 1,700 sq mi (4,400 square km) on the NE flank of the Karabakh Mountain Range, with the capital city of Stepanakert.

Russia annexed the area from Persia in 1813, and in 1923 it was established as an autonomous province of the Azerbaijan S.S.R. In 1988 the region's ethnic Armenian majority demonstrated against Azerbaijani rule, and in 1991, after the breakup of the U.S.S.R. brought independence to Armenia and Azerbaijan, war broke out between the two ethnic groups. On January 8, 1992 the leaders of Nagorno-Karabakh declared independence as the Republic of Mountainous Karabakh (RMK). Since 1994, following a cease-fire, ethnic Armenians have held Karabakh, though officially it remains part of Azerbaijan. Karabakh remains sovereign, but the political and military condition is volatile and tensions frequently flare into skirmishes.

Its marvelous nature and geographic situation, have all facilitated Karabakh to be a center of science, poetry and, especially, of the musical culture of Azerbaijan.

MONETARY SYSTEM
100 Luma = 1 Dram

REPUBLIC

STANDARD COINAGE

KM# 6 50 LUMA
0.9500 g., Aluminum, 19.8 mm. **Obv:** National arms **Rev:** Horse cantering left **Edge:** Plain

Date	Mintage	F	VF	XF	Unc	BU
2004	—	—	—	—	0.50	1.25

KM# 7 50 LUMA
0.9500 g., Aluminum, 19.8 mm. **Obv:** National arms **Rev:** Antelope leaping right **Edge:** Plain

Date	Mintage	F	VF	XF	Unc	BU
2004	—	—	—	—	0.50	1.25

KM# 8 DRAM
1.1300 g., Aluminum, 21.8 mm. **Obv:** National arms **Rev:** Pheasant right **Edge:** Plain

Date	Mintage	F	VF	XF	Unc	BU
2004	—	—	—	—	0.75	1.25

KM# 9 DRAM
1.1200 g., Aluminum, 21.8 mm. **Obv:** National arms **Rev:** 1/2-length St. Gregory facing **Edge:** Plain

Date	Mintage	F	VF	XF	Unc	BU
2004	—	—	—	—	0.75	1.25

KM# 10 DRAM

1.1300 g., Aluminum, 21.8 mm. **Obv:** National arms **Rev:** Cheetah facing **Edge:** Plain

Date	Mintage	F	VF	XF	Unc	BU
2004	—	—	—	—	0.75	1.25

KM# 11 5 DRAMS

4.4000 g., Brass, 21.8 mm. **Obv:** National arms **Rev:** Church **Edge:** Plain

Date	Mintage	F	VF	XF	Unc	BU
2004	—	—	—	—	1.00	1.50

KM# 12 5 DRAMS

4.5000 g., Brass, 21.8 mm. **Obv:** National arms **Rev:** Monument faces **Edge:** Plain

Date	Mintage	F	VF	XF	Unc	BU
2004	—	—	—	—	1.00	1.50

KM# 23 1000 DRAMS

31.4300 g., 0.9990 Silver 1.0095 oz. ASW, 38.9 mm. **Obv:** National arms **Rev:** Archer **Edge:** Plain

Date	Mintage	F	VF	XF	Unc	BU
2003 Proof	—	Value: 60.00				

KM# 19 1000 DRAMS

31.3700 g., 0.9990 Silver 1.0076 oz. ASW, 38.9 mm. **Obv:** National arms **Rev:** Leopard **Edge:** Plain

Date	Mintage	F	VF	XF	Unc	BU
2004 Proof	—	Value: 60.00				

KM# 19a 1000 DRAMS

31.3700 g., 0.9990 Gold Plated Silver 1.0076 oz. ASW AGW, 38.9 mm. **Obv:** National arms **Rev:** Leopard **Edge:** Plain

Date	Mintage	F	VF	XF	Unc	BU
2004 Proof	—	Value: 75.00				

KM# 20 1000 DRAMS

31.3700 g., 0.9990 Silver 1.0076 oz. ASW, 38.9 mm. **Obv:** National arms **Rev:** Standing Bear **Edge:** Plain

Date	Mintage	F	VF	XF	Unc	BU
2004 Proof	—	Value: 60.00				

KM# 20a 1000 DRAMS

31.3700 g., 0.9990 Gold Plated Silver 1.0076 oz. ASW AGW, 38.9 mm. **Obv:** National arms **Rev:** Standing Bear **Edge:** Plain

Date	Mintage	F	VF	XF	Unc	BU
2004 Proof	—	Value: 75.00				

KM# 21 1000 DRAMS

31.3700 g., 0.9990 Silver 1.0076 oz. ASW, 38.9 mm. **Obv:** National arms **Rev:** Eagle head **Edge:** Plain

Date	Mintage	F	VF	XF	Unc	BU
2004 Proof	—	Value: 60.00				

KM# 21a 1000 DRAMS

31.3700 g., 0.9990 Gold Plated Silver 1.0076 oz. ASW AGW, 38.9 mm. **Obv:** National arms **Rev:** Eagle head **Edge:** Plain

Date	Mintage	F	VF	XF	Unc	BU
2004 Proof	—	Value: 75.00				

KM# 22 1000 DRAMS

31.1200 g., 0.9990 Silver 0.9995 oz. ASW, 38.9 mm. **Obv:** National arms **Rev:** 1918 Genocide Victims Monument **Edge:** Plain

Date	Mintage	F	VF	XF	Unc	BU
2004 Proof	—	Value: 50.00				

NAMIBIA

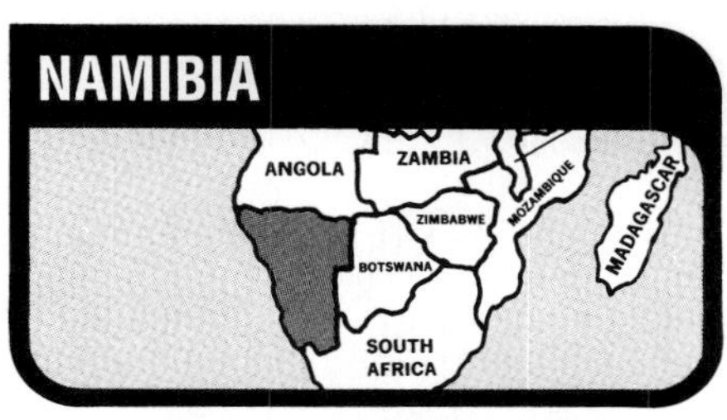

The Republic of Namibia, once the German colonial territory of German South West Africa, and later South West Africa, is situated on the Atlantic coast of southern Africa, bounded on the north by Angola, on the east by Botswana, and on the south by South Africa. It has an area of 318,261 sq. mi. (824,290 sq. km.) and a population of *1.4 million. Capital: Windhoek. Diamonds, copper, lead, zinc, and cattle are exported.

On June 17, 1985 the Transitional Government of National Unity was installed. Negotiations were held in 1988 between Angola, Cuba, and South Africa reaching a peaceful settlement on Aug. 5, 1988. By April 1989 Cuban troops were to withdraw from Angola and South African troops from Namibia. The Transitional Government resigned on Feb. 28, 1988 for the upcoming elections of the constituent assembly in Nov. 1989. Independence was finally achieved on March 12, 1990 within the Commonwealth of Nations. The President is the Head of State; the Prime Minister is Head of Government.

MONETARY SYSTEM

100 Cents = 1 Namibia Dollar
1 Namibia Dollar = 1 South African Rand

REPUBLIC

DECIMAL COINAGE

KM# 1 5 CENTS

Nickel Plated Steel **Obv:** National arms

Date	Mintage	F	VF	XF	Unc	BU
2002	—	—	—	0.20	0.50	0.75

KM# 2 10 CENTS

Nickel Plated Steel **Obv:** National arms

Date	Mintage	F	VF	XF	Unc	BU
2002	—	—	—	0.35	1.00	1.25

NAURU ISLAND

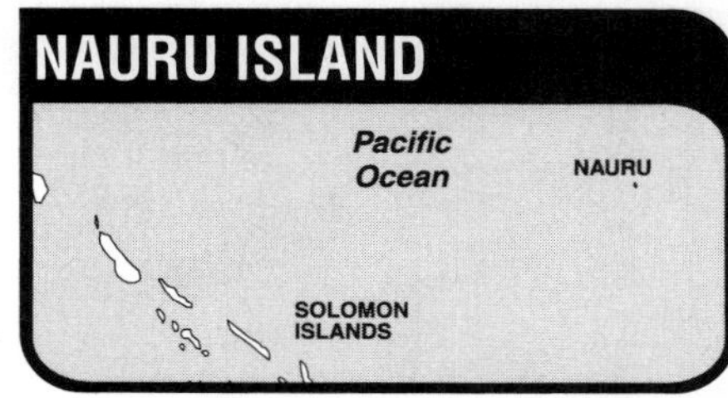

The Republic of Nauru, formerly Pleasant Island, is an island republic in the western Pacific Ocean west of the Gilbert Islands. It has an area of 8-1/2 sq. mi. and a population of 7,254. It is known for its phosphate deposits.

MONETARY SYSTEM

100 Cents = 1 (Australian) Dollar

REPUBLIC

DECIMAL COINAGE

KM# 13 10 DOLLARS

31.2500 g., 0.9990 Silver 71.5 x 72 1.0037 oz. ASW, 72 mm. **Subject:** First Euro Coinage **Obv:** National arms, matte finish **Rev:** Denomination, inscription and partially gold-plated 1 euro reverse coin design, Proof finish **Edge:** Plain **Shape:** Like a map

Date	Mintage	F	VF	XF	Unc	BU
2002 Proof	—	Value: 55.00				

KM# 14 10 DOLLARS

34.6000 g., 0.9250 Silver with gold plated or gold attachment 1.029 oz. ASW, 38.5 mm. **Subject:** Brandenburg Gate **Obv:** National arms **Rev:** Gold color 1mm thick model of the Brandenburg Gate mounted on the center surface **Edge:** Plain

Date	Mintage	F	VF	XF	Unc	BU
2002 Proof/Matte	—	Value: 110				

KM# 15 10 DOLLARS

31.1000 g., 0.9990 Silver 0.9989 oz. ASW, 40 mm. **Obv:** National arms **Rev:** Blue Whale on mother of pearl insert **Edge:** Plain

Date	Mintage	F	VF	XF	Unc	BU
2002 Proof	2,000	Value: 60.00				

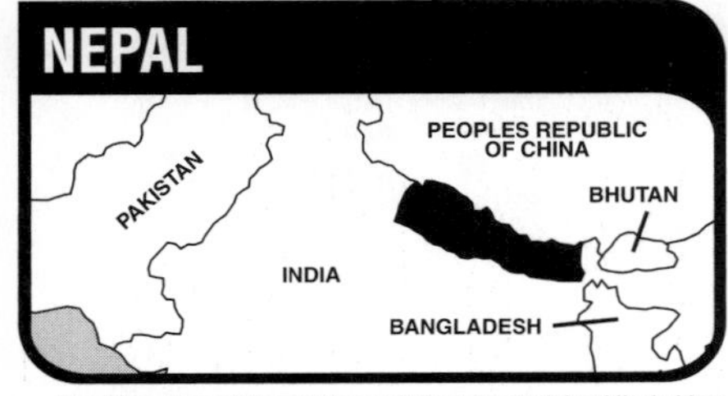

The Kingdom of Nepal, the world's only surviving Hindu kingdom, is a landlocked country occupying the southern slopes of the Himalayas. It has an area of 56,136 sq. mi. (140,800 sq. km.) and a population of 18 million. Capital: Kathmandu. Nepal has deposits of coal, copper, iron and cobalt, but they are largely unexploited. Agriculture is the principal economic activity. Rice, timber and jute are exported, with tourism being the other major foreign exchange earner.

On June 2, 2001 tragedy struck the royal family when Crown Prince Dipendra used an assault rifle to kill his father, mother and other members of the royal family as the result of a dispute over his current lady friend. He died 48 hours later, as King, from self inflicted gunshot wounds. Gyanendra began his second reign as King (his first was a short time as a toddler, 1950-51).

DATING

Bikram Samvat Era (VS)

From 1888AD most copper coins were dated in the Bikram Samvat (VS) era. To convert take VS date - 57 =AD date. Coins with this era have VS before the year in the listing. With the exception of a few gold coins struck in 1890 & 1892, silver and gold coins only changed to the VS era in 1911AD, but now this era is used for all coins struck in Nepal.

RULERS

SHAH DYNASTY

त्रिभुवनवीर विक्रम

Tribhuvana Bir Bikram
VS2058- / 2001- AD (second reign)

वीरेन्द्र वीर विक्रम

Birendra Bir Bikram
VS2028-2058 /1971-2001AD

ऐश्वर्य राज्य लक्ष्मी देवी

Queen of Birendra Bir Bikram: Aishvarya Rajya Lakshmi
VS2028-2058 /1971-2001AD

Dipendra Bir Bikram
VS2058 / 2001AD (reign of 48 hours)

ज्ञानेन्द्र वीर विक्रम

Gyanendra Bir Bikram
VS2058-/2001-AD

NUMERALS

Nepal has used more variations of numerals on their coins than any other nation. The most common are illustrated in the numeral chart in the introduction. The chart below illustrates some variations encompassing the last four centuries.

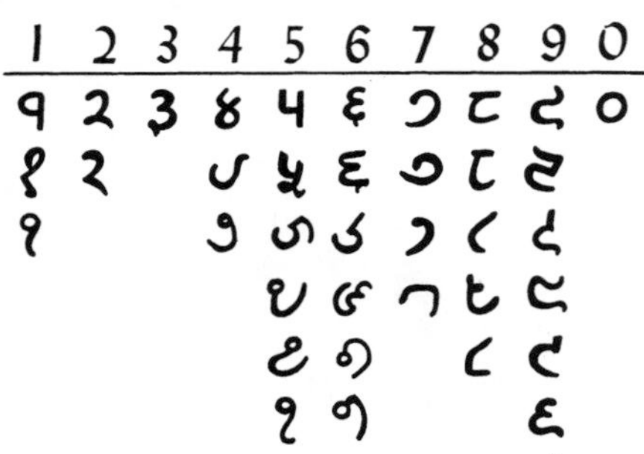

NUMERICS

Half	आधा
One	एक
Two	दुइ
Four	चार
Five	पाच
Ten	दसा
Twenty	विसा
Twenty-five	पचीसा
Fifty	पचासा
Hundred	सय

DENOMINATIONS

Paisa	पैसा
Dam	दाम
Mohar	मोहरु
Rupee	रुपैयाँ
Ashrapi	असार्फी
Asarphi (Asarfi)	अश्रफी

SHAH DYNASTY

KINGDOM

Gyanendra Bir Bikram

VS2058- / 2001- AD

DECIMAL COINAGE

100 Paisa = 1 Rupee

KM# 1173 10 PAISA
Aluminum, 17 mm. **Obv:** Royal crown **Edge:** Plain

Date	Mintage	F	VF	XF	Unc
VS2058 (2001)	—	—	—	—	1.00

KM# 1148 25 PAISA
Aluminum, 20 mm. **Obv:** Royal crown **Edge:** Plain

Date	Mintage	F	VF	XF	Unc
VS2058 (2001)	—	—	—	—	0.50
VS2059 (2002)	—	—	—	—	0.50

KM# 1149 50 PAISA
Aluminum, 22.5 mm. **Obv:** Royal crown **Edge:** Plain

Date	Mintage	F	VF	XF	Unc
VS2058 (2001)	—	—	—	—	0.50

Date	Mintage	F	VF	XF	Unc
VS2059 (2002)	—	—	—	—	0.50
VS2060 (2003)	—	—	—	—	0.50
VS2061 (2004)	—	—	—	—	0.50

KM# 1150.3 RUPEE
Brass, 30 mm. **Rev:** 3mm "1", small temple **Edge:** Reeded

Date	Mintage	F	VF	XF	Unc
VS2058 (2001)	—	—	—	—	1.00
VS2059 (2002)	—	—	—	—	1.00

KM# 1150.2 RUPEE
Copper Plated Steel **Edge:** Plain **Note:** Magnetic.

Date	Mintage	F	VF	XF	Unc
VS2058 (2001)	—	—	—	—	1.00
VS2059 (2002)	—	—	—	—	1.00
VS2060 (2003)	—	—	—	—	1.00

KM# 1150.1 RUPEE
Brass **Rev:** 4 millimeter "1", large temple **Edge:** Reeded **Note:** Non-magnetic.

Date	Mintage	F	VF	XF	Unc
VS2058 (2001)	—	—	—	—	1.00

KM# 1170 2 RUPEES
4.9400 g., Brass, 25 mm. **Obv:** Traditional square design **Rev:** People with flag celebrating 50 Years of Democracy **Edge:** Plain

Date	Mintage	F	VF	XF	Unc
VS2058(2001)	—	—	—	—	0.50

KM# 1151.2 2 RUPEES
Brass Plated Steel, 25 mm. **Rev:** Thick dots, larger central trident **Edge:** Plain

Date	Mintage	F	VF	XF	Unc
VS2058 (2001)	—	—	—	—	1.25
VS2059 (2002)	—	—	—	—	1.25

KM# 1151.1 2 RUPEES
Brass Plated Steel, 25 mm. **Obv:** Three domed building **Rev:** Thin dots, small central trident **Edge:** Plain **Note:** Edge varieties exist. Prev. KM#1151.

Date	Mintage	F	VF	XF	Unc
VS2058 (2001)	—	—	—	—	1.25
VS2060(2003) (2003)	—	—	—	—	1.25

KM# 1151.1a 2 RUPEES
6.7000 g., Silver, 25 mm. **Rev:** Thin dots, small central trident **Edge:** Plain

Date	Mintage	F	VF	XF	Unc
VS2060(2003)	—	—	—	—	100

KM# 1164 5 RUPEE
8.5300 g., Copper-Nickel, 29.2 mm. **Obv:** King wearing coronation crown **Rev:** Traditional design **Edge:** Plain

Date	Mintage	F	VF	XF	Unc
VS2058 (2001)	—	—	—	—	3.50

KM# 1159 25 RUPEE
8.3600 g., Copper Nickel, 29.1 mm. **Obv:** King's portrait **Rev:** Sword in round design **Edge:** Plain

Date	Mintage	F	VF	XF	Unc
VS2059 (2002)	—	—	—	—	4.00

KM# 1160 50 RUPEE
20.1000 g., Brass, 37.7 mm. **Subject:** 50th Anniversary of Scouting in Nepal **Obv:** Traditional design **Rev:** Scouting emblem **Edge:** Plain

Date	Mintage	F	VF	XF	Unc
VS2059 (2002)	—	—	—	—	9.00

KM# 1157 100 RUPEE
20.0000 g., Brass, 38.7 mm. **Subject:** Buddha **Obv:** Traditional design **Rev:** Seated Buddha teaching five seated monks **Edge:** Reeded

Date	Mintage	F	VF	XF	Unc
VS2058 (2001)	30,000	—	—	—	10.00

KM# 1162 200 RUPEE
18.1000 g., 0.5000 Silver 0.291 oz. ASW, 29.6 mm. **Subject:** 50th Anniversary of Civil Service **Obv:** Traditional square design **Rev:** Crown above flags and value **Edge:** Plain

Date	Mintage	F	VF	XF	Unc
VS2058 (2001)	—	—	—	—	20.00

KM# 1161 200 RUPEE
18.1000 g., 0.5000 Silver 0.291 oz. ASW, 29.6 mm. **Subject:** 50th Anniversary of the Nepal Chamber of Commerce **Obv:** Traditional design **Rev:** Chamber of Commerce emblem **Edge:** Plain

Date	Mintage	F	VF	XF	Unc
VS2059 (2002)	—	—	—	—	20.00

KM# 1171 250 RUPEE
18.0000 g., 0.5000 Silver 0.2894 oz. ASW, 29 mm. **Subject:** 2600th Anniversary of Bhagawan Mahavir **Obv:** Traditional square design **Rev:** Haloed Mahavir above value **Edge:** Plain

Date	Mintage	F	VF	XF	Unc
VS2058 (2001)	—	—	—	—	25.00

KM# 1176 250 RUPEE
17.8300 g., 0.5000 Silver 0.2866 oz. ASW, 31.6 mm. **Obv:** Traditional design **Rev:** Swastika **Edge:** Reeded

Date	Mintage	F	VF	XF	Unc
VS2060 (2003)	—	—	—	—	25.00

KM# 1174 300 RUPEE
Silver, 31.8 mm. **Subject:** Economic Growth Through Export **Rev:** Two joined hands in front of globe **Edge:** Reeded

Date	Mintage	F	VF	XF	Unc
VS2060 (2003)	—	—	—	—	20.00

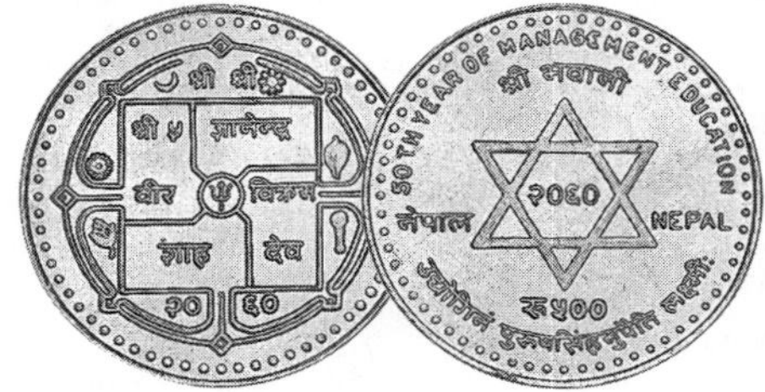

KM# 1177 500 RUPEE
23.0000 g., 0.9000 Silver 0.6655 oz. ASW, 31.7 mm. **Subject:** Management Education 50th Anniversary **Obv:** Traditional design **Rev:** Six point star outline **Edge:** Reeded

Date	Mintage	F	VF	XF	Unc
VS2060 (2003)	—	—	—	—	25.00

KM# 1163 500 RUPEE
23.3400 g., 0.9000 Silver 0.6754 oz. ASW, 32 mm. **Subject:** 50th Anniversary of the Conquest of Mt. Everest **Obv:** Traditional design **Rev:** Mountain and map above value **Edge:** Reeded

Date	Mintage	F	VF	XF	Unc
VS2060 (2003)	—	—	—	—	25.00

KM# 1175 1000 RUPEE
35.0000 g., Silver, 40 mm. **Subject:** 100 Years - Rotary Club **Edge:** Reeded

Date	Mintage	F	VF	XF	Unc
VS2062 (2005)	—	—	—	—	45.00

KM# 1158 1500 RUPEE
20.0000 g., 0.9250 Silver 0.5948 oz. ASW, 38.7 mm. **Subject:** Buddha **Obv:** Traditional design **Rev:** Seated Buddha teaching five seated monks **Edge:** Reeded

Date	Mintage	F	VF	XF	Unc
VS2058 (2001) Proof	15,000	Value: 31.50			

KM# 1172 2000 RUPEE
31.2000 g., 0.7200 Silver 0.7222 oz. ASW, 40 mm. **Obv:** King Gyanendra Bir Bikram wearing coronation crown **Rev:** Upright sword above value in circular design **Edge:** Reeded

Date	Mintage	F	VF	XF	Unc
VS2058 (2001)	—	—	—	—	40.00

ASARFI GOLD COINAGE

(Asarphi)

Fractional designations are approximate for this series. Actual Gold Weight (AGW) is used to identify each type.

KM# 1153 0.3G ASARPHI
0.3000 g., 0.9999 Gold 0.0096 oz. AGW, 7 mm. **Subject:** Buddha **Obv:** Traditional design **Rev:** Seated Buddha **Edge:** Plain

Date	Mintage	VF	XF	Unc	BU
VS2058 (2001)	30,000	—	—	—	16.00

KM# 1154 1/25-OZ. ASARFI
1.2441 g., 0.9999 Gold 0.04 oz. AGW, 13.92 mm. **Subject:** Buddha **Obv:** Traditional design **Rev:** Seated Buddha **Edge:** Reeded

Date	Mintage	VF	XF	Unc	BU
VS2058 (2001)	25,000	—	—	—	30.00

KM# 1155 1/10-OZ. ASARFI
3.1104 g., 0.9999 Gold 0.1 oz. AGW, 17.95 mm. **Subject:** Buddha **Obv:** Traditional design **Rev:** Seated Buddha **Edge:** Reeded

Date	Mintage	VF	XF	Unc	BU
VS2058 (2001)	15,000	—	—	—	55.00

KM# 1156 1/2-OZ. ASARFI
15.5518 g., 0.9999 Gold 0.5 oz. AGW, 27 mm. **Subject:** Buddha **Obv:** Traditional design **Rev:** Seated Buddha **Edge:** Reeded

Date	Mintage	VF	XF	Unc	BU
VS2058 (2001)	2,500	Value: 315			

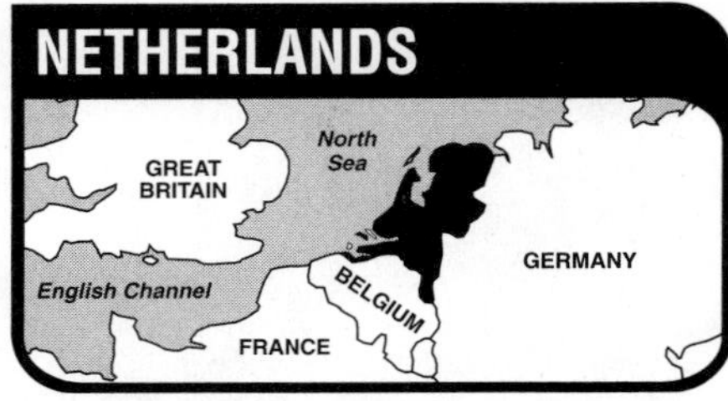

The Kingdom of the Netherlands, a country of western Europe fronting on the North Sea and bordered by Belgium and Germany, has an area of 15,770 sq. mi. (41,500 sq. km.) and a population of 16.1 million. Capital: Amsterdam, but the seat of government is at The Hague. The economy is based on dairy farming and a variety of industrial activities. Chemicals, yarns and fabrics, and meat products are exported.

NOTE: All of the modern coins struck at the Utrecht Mint bear the caduceus mint mark of that facility. They also bear the mint-masters' marks.

RULERS

Beatrix, 1980—

MINT PRIVY MARKS

Utrecht

Date	Privy Mark
1806-present	Caduceus

MINTMASTER'S PRIVY MARKS

Utrecht Mint

Date	Privy Mark
2001	Wine tendril w/grapes
2002	Wine tendril w/grapes and star
2003	Sails of a clipper

NOTE: A star adjoining the privy mark indicates that the piece was struck at the beginning of the term of office of a successor. (The star was used only if the successor had not chosen his own mark yet.)

NOTE: Since October, 1999, the Dutch Mint has taken the title of Royal Dutch Mint.

MONETARY SYSTEM

Until January 29, 2002

100 Cents = 1 Gulden

Since January 1, 2002

100 Euro Cents = 1 Euro

KINGDOM OF THE NETHERLANDS

DECIMAL COINAGE

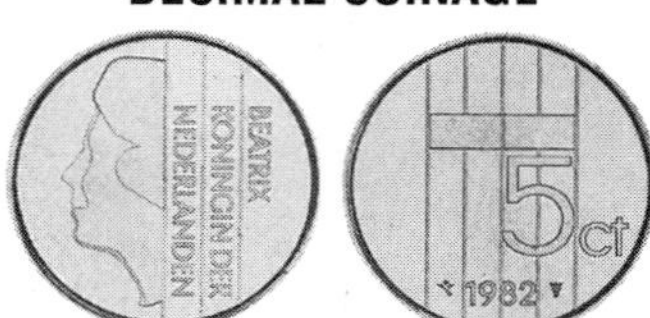

KM# 202 5 CENTS

3.5000 g., Bronze, 21 mm. **Obv:** Head left **Rev:** Value and vertical lines **Designer:** Bruno Ninaber von Eybew

Date	Mintage	F	VF	XF	Unc	BU
2001	30,000,000	—	—	—	—	0.40
2001 Proof	17,000	Value: 4.00				

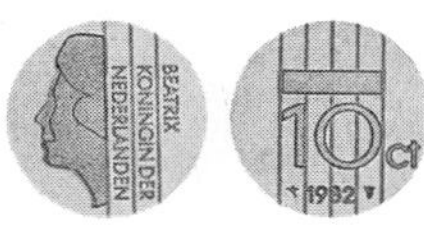

KM# 203 10 CENTS

1.5000 g., Nickel, 15 mm. **Obv:** Head left **Rev:** Value and vertical lines **Edge:** Reeded **Designer:** Bruno Ninaber von Eybew

Date	Mintage	F	VF	XF	Unc	BU
2001	25,900,000	—	—	—	—	0.50
2001 Proof	17,000	Value: 4.00				

KM# 204 25 CENTS

3.0000 g., Nickel, 19 mm. **Obv:** Half head silhouette of Queen Beatrix left, 3-line inscription vertically at right **Obv. Inscription:** Beatrix/Konincin Der/Nederlanden **Rev:** Vertical and horizontal lines **Edge:** Reeded **Designer:** Bruno Ninaber van Eyber

Date	Mintage	F	VF	XF	Unc	BU
2001	11,800,000	—	—	—	0.20	0.60
2001 Proof	17,000	Value: 6.00				

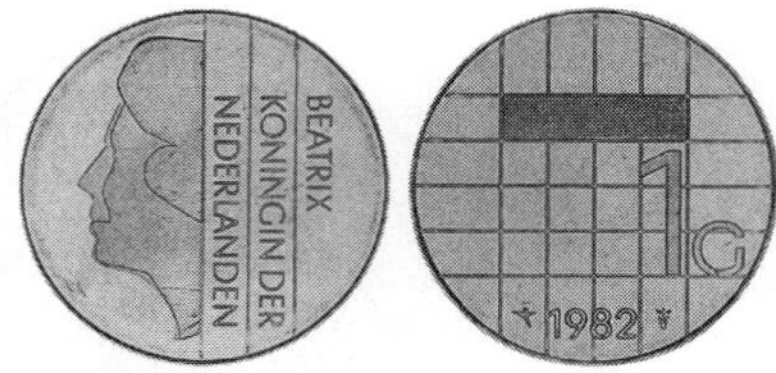

KM# 205 GULDEN

6.0000 g., Nickel, 25 mm. **Obv:** Head left **Rev:** Vertical and horizontal lines **Edge Lettering:** GOD * ZIJ * MET * ONS * **Designer:** Bruno Ninaber von Eybew

Date	Mintage	F	VF	XF	Unc	BU
2001	22,700,000	—	—	—	—	1.25
2001 Proof	17,000	Value: 7.50				

KM# 205b GULDEN

13.2000 g., 0.9990 Gold .4243 oz. AGW **Edge Lettering:** GOD*ZIJ*MET*ONS* **Note:** Prev. KM#205a.

Date	Mintage	F	VF	XF	Unc	BU
2001 Prooflike	25,000	—	—	—	—	325

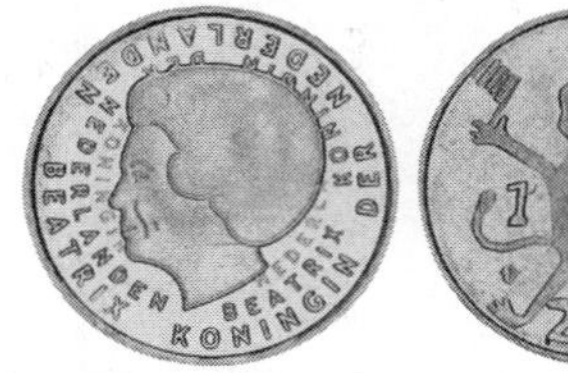

KM# 233 GULDEN

6.0400 g., Nickel, 25 mm. **Obv:** Queen's portrait **Obv. Designer:** Geerten Verheus and Michael Raedecker **Rev:** Child art design **Rev. Designer:** Tim van Melis **Edge Lettering:** GOD ZIJ MET ONS

Date	Mintage	F	VF	XF	Unc	BU
2001	16,045,000	—	—	—	—	4.00
2001 Prooflike	32,000	—	—	—	—	6.00

KM# 233a GULDEN

7.1000 g., 0.9250 Silver .3926 oz. ASW, 25 mm. **Obv:** Queen's portrait **Rev:** Child art design **Edge Lettering:** GOD * ZIJ * MET * ONS *

Date	Mintage	F	VF	XF	Unc	BU
2001 Prooflike	360	—	—	—	—	800

Note: Given as gifts to workers at the mint

KM# 233b GULDEN

13.2000 g., 0.9990 Gold .4240 oz. AGW, 25 mm. **Obv:** Queen's portrait **Obv. Designer:** G. Verheus and M. Raedecker **Rev:** Child art design **Rev. Designer:** T. van Malis **Note:** 98 of 100 pieces melted down, with 2 known in museum collections.

Date	Mintage	F	VF	XF	Unc	BU
2001 Prooflike	100	—	—	—	—	2,750

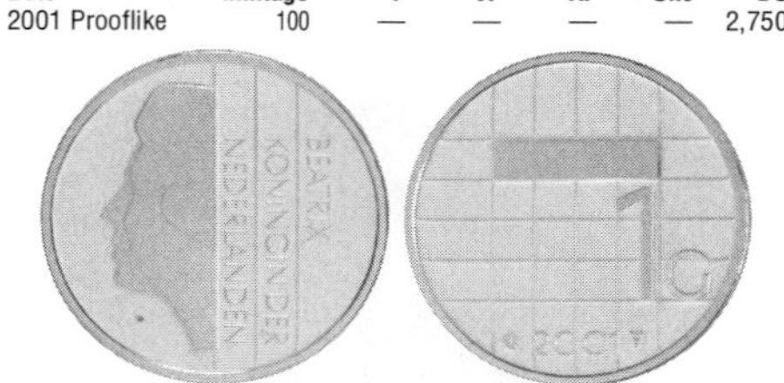

KM# 205a GULDEN

7.1000 g., 0.9250 Silver 0.2111 oz. ASW **Edge Lettering:** GOD* ZIJ*MET*OMS*

Date	Mintage	F	VF	XF	Unc	BU
2001 Prooflike	200,000	—	—	—	17.50	—

KM# 205c GULDEN

13.2000 g., 0.9990 Gold 0.424 oz. AGW **Edge:** Plain

Date	Mintage	F	VF	XF	Unc	BU
2001 Prooflike	Est. 500	—	—	—	—	550

KM# 206 2-1/2 GULDEN

10.0000 g., Nickel, 29 mm. **Obv:** Head left **Rev:** Value with horizontal, vertical and diagonal lines **Edge Lettering:** GOD * ZIJ * MET * ONS * **Designer:** Bruno Ninaber van Eyben

Date	Mintage	F	VF	XF	Unc	BU
2001	600,000	—	—	—	—	4.00
2001 Proof	17,000	Value: 16.00				

KM# 210 5 GULDEN

9.2500 g., Bronze Clad Nickel, 23.5 mm. **Obv:** Head left **Rev:** Value with horizontal, vertical and diagonal lines **Edge:** GOD * ZIJ * MET * ONS * **Designer:** Bruno Ninaber van Eyben

Date	Mintage	F	VF	XF	Unc	BU
2001	400,000	—	—	—	—	3.50
2001 Proof	17,000	Value: 15.50				

EURO COINAGE

European Economic Community Issues

KM# 234 EURO CENT

2.3000 g., Copper Plated Steel, 16.2 mm. **Obv:** Head of Queen Beatrix left **Obv. Designer:** Bruno Ninaber van Eybew **Rev:** Denomination and globe **Rev. Designer:** Luc Luyckx **Edge:** Plain

Date	Mintage	F	VF	XF	Unc	BU
2001	179,300,000	—	—	—	0.35	—
2001 Prooflike	Inc. above	—	—	—	—	—
2002	19,000,000	—	—	—	1.00	—
2002 Prooflike	Inc. above	—	—	—	—	—
2003	58,100,000	—	—	—	0.50	—
2003 Prooflike	Inc. above	—	—	—	—	—
2004	113,900,000	—	—	—	0.50	—
2004 Proof	5,000	—	—	—	—	—
2005	557,351	—	—	—	1.50	—
2005 Proof	5,964	—	—	—	—	—
2006	—	—	—	—	1.50	—

KM# 235 2 EURO CENTS

3.0000 g., Copper Plated Steel, 18.7 mm. **Obv:** Head of Queen Beatrix left **Obv. Designer:** Bruno Ninaber van Eybew **Rev:** Denomination and globe **Rev. Designer:** Luc Luyckx **Edge:** Grooved

Date	Mintage	F	VF	XF	Unc	BU
2001	145,800,000	—	—	—	0.50	—
2001 Prooflike	Inc. above	—	—	—	—	—
2002	71,500,000	—	—	—	0.50	—
2002 Prooflike	Inc. above	—	—	—	—	—
2003	151,200,000	—	—	—	0.50	—
2003 Prooflike	Inc. above	—	—	—	—	—
2004	115,700,000	—	—	—	0.50	—
2004 Proof	5,000	—	—	—	—	—
2005	557,351	—	—	—	1.50	—
2005 Proof	5,964	—	—	—	—	—
2006	—	—	—	—	1.50	—

KM# 236 5 EURO CENTS

3.9000 g., Copper Plated Steel, 21.2 mm. **Obv:** Head of Queen Beatrix left **Obv. Designer:** Bruno Ninaber van Eybew **Rev:** Denomination and globe **Rev. Designer:** Luc Luycx **Edge:** Plain

Date	Mintage	F	VF	XF	Unc	BU
2001	205,900,000	—	—	—	0.50	—
2001 Prooflike	Inc. above	—	—	—	—	—
2002	107,000,000	—	—	—	1.25	—
2002 Prooflike	Inc. above	—	—	—	—	—
2003	1,400,000	—	—	—	1.50	—
2003 Prooflike	Inc. above	—	—	—	—	—
2004	380,000	—	—	—	2.00	—
2004 Proof	5,000	—	—	—	—	—
2005	80,527,351	—	—	—	1.00	—
2005 Proof	5,964	—	—	—	—	—
2006	—	—	—	—	1.00	—

KM# 237 10 EURO CENTS
4.1000 g., Brass, 19.7 mm. **Obv:** Head of Queen Beatrix left **Obv. Designer:** Bruno Ninaber van Eybew **Rev:** Denomination and map **Rev. Designer:** Luc Luycx

Date	Mintage	F	VF	XF	Unc	BU
2001	193,500,000	—	—	—	0.75	—
2001 Prooflike	Inc. above	—	—	—	—	—
2002	19,000,000	—	—	—	1.50	—
2002 Prooflike	Inc. above	—	—	—	—	—
2003	1,200,000	—	—	—	1.50	—
2003 Prooflike	Inc. above	—	—	—	—	—
2004	330,000	—	—	—	2.00	—
2004 Proof	5,000	—	—	—	—	—
2005	427,351	—	—	—	1.75	—
2005 Proof	5,964	—	—	—	—	—
2006	—	—	—	—	1.75	—

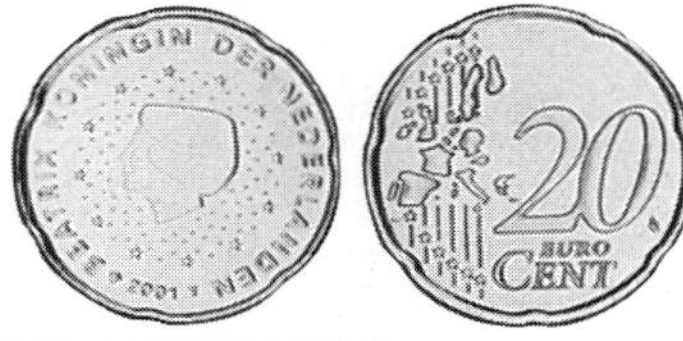

KM# 238 20 EURO CENTS
5.7000 g., Brass, 22.2 mm. **Obv:** Head of Queen Beatrix left **Obv. Designer:** Bruno Ninaber van Eybew **Rev:** Denomination and map **Rev. Designer:** Luc Luycx **Edge:** Notched

Date	Mintage	F	VF	XF	Unc	BU
2001	97,600,000	—	—	—	1.00	—
2001 Prooflike	Inc. above	—	—	—	—	—
2002	40,000,000	—	—	—	1.75	—
2002 Prooflike	Inc. above	—	—	—	—	—
2003	58,200,000	—	—	—	1.75	—
2003 Prooflike	Inc. above	—	—	—	—	—
2004	20,500,000	—	—	—	2.00	—
2004 Proof	5,000	—	—	—	—	—
2005	427,351	—	—	—	2.50	—
2005 Proof	5,964	—	—	—	—	—
2006	—	—	—	—	2.50	—

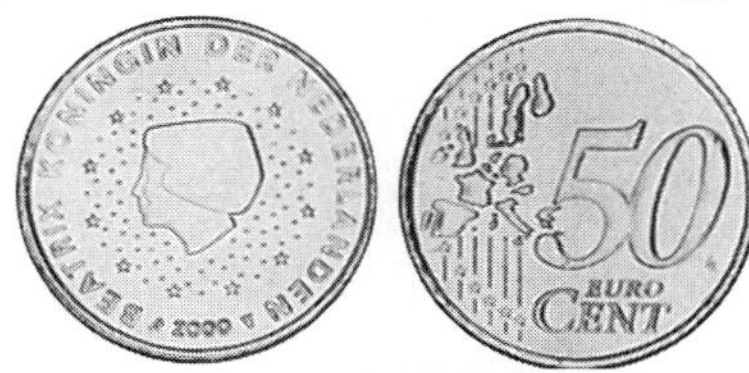

KM# 239 50 EURO CENTS
7.8000 g., Brass, 24.2 mm. **Obv:** Head of Queen Beatrix left **Obv. Designer:** Bruno Ninaber van Eybew **Rev:** Denomination and map **Rev. Designer:** Luc Luycx **Edge:** Notched

Date	Mintage	F	VF	XF	Unc	BU
2001	94,500,000	—	—	—	1.25	—
2001 Prooflike	Inc. above	—	—	—	—	—
2002	45,000,000	—	—	—	1.25	—
2002 Prooflike	Inc. above	—	—	—	—	—
2003	1,200,000	—	—	—	2.00	—
2003 Prooflike	Inc. above	—	—	—	—	—
2004	332,000	—	—	—	2.25	—
2004 Proof	5,000	—	—	—	—	—
2005	427,351	—	—	—	2.00	—
2006	—	—	—	—	2.00	—

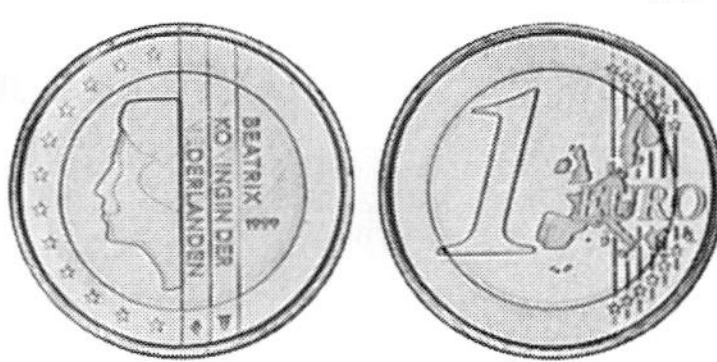

KM# 240 EURO
7.5000 g., Bi-Metallic Copper-Nickel center in Brass ring, 23.2 mm. **Obv:** Queen's profile left **Obv. Designer:** Bruno Ninaber van Eybew **Rev:** Denomination and map **Rev. Designer:** Luc Luycx **Edge:** Plain and reeded sections

Date	Mintage	F	VF	XF	Unc	BU
2001	67,900,000	—	—	—	2.50	—
2001 Prooflike	Inc. above	—	—	—	—	—
2002	100,000,000	—	—	—	3.25	—
2002 Prooflike	Inc. above	—	—	—	—	—
2003	1,400,000	—	—	—	3.25	—
2003 Prooflike	Inc. above	—	—	—	—	—
2004	257,000	—	—	—	5.00	—
2004 Proof	5,000	—	—	—	—	—
2005	327,351	—	—	—	4.00	—
2005 Proof	5,964	—	—	—	—	—
2006	—	—	—	—	4.00	—

KM# 241 2 EURO
8.5000 g., Bi-Metallic Brass center in Copper-Nickel ring, 25.7 mm. **Obv:** Queen's profile left **Obv. Designer:** Bruno Ninaber van Eybew **Rev:** Denomination and map **Rev. Designer:** Luc Luycx **Edge:** Reeded **Edge Lettering:** "GOD*ZIJ*MET*ONS*"

Date	Mintage	F	VF	XF	Unc	BU
2001	140,500,000	—	—	—	4.00	—
2001 Prooflike	Inc. above	—	—	—	—	—
2002	98,500,000	—	—	—	4.00	—
2002 Prooflike	Inc. above	—	—	—	—	—
2003	1,200,000	—	—	—	5.00	—
2003 Prooflike	Inc. above	—	—	—	—	—
2004	257,000	—	—	—	7.00	—
2004 Proof	5,000	—	—	—	—	—
2005	327,351	—	—	—	6.00	—
2005 Proof	5,964	—	—	—	—	—
2006	—	—	—	—	6.00	—

KM# 245 5 EURO
11.9900 g., 0.9250 Silver 0.3566 oz. ASW, 29 mm. **Subject:** Vincent Van Gogh **Obv:** Queen's portrait **Rev:** Van Gogh's portrait **Edge:** Lettered **Edge Lettering:** GOD ZIJ MET ONS **Designer:** K. Martens

Date	Mintage	F	VF	XF	Unc	BU
ND(2003)	1,000,000	—	—	—	6.00	—
ND(2003) Prooflike	100,000	—	—	—	—	17.00

KM# 252 5 EURO
11.9000 g., 0.9250 Silver 0.3539 oz. ASW **Ruler:** Beatrix **Obv:** Queen Beatrix head left **Rev:** Names of old and new member countries

Date	Mintage	F	VF	XF	Unc	BU
2004	1,000,000	—	—	—	—	10.00
2004 Proof	37,000	Value: 30.00				

KM# 253 5 EURO
11.9000 g., 0.9250 Silver 0.3539 oz. ASW **Ruler:** Beatrix **Subject:** 50th Anniversary - End of colonization of Netherlands Antilles **Obv:** Queen Beatrix head left **Rev:** Fruit **Edge Lettering:** GOD*ZIJ*MET*ONS*

Date	Mintage	F	VF	XF	Unc	BU
2004	600,000	—	—	—	—	10.00
2004 Proof	27,000	Value: 30.00				

KM# 254 5 EURO
11.9100 g., 0.9250 Silver 0.3542 oz. ASW, 29 mm. **Subject:** 60th Anniversary of Liberation **Obv:** Queen's image **Rev:** Value and dots **Edge:** Lettered

Date	Mintage	F	VF	XF	Unc	BU
2005	630,000	—	—	—	12.00	15.00
2005 Proof	40,000	Value: 45.00				

KM# 255 5 EURO
11.9100 g., 0.9250 Silver 0.3542 oz. ASW, 29 mm. **Ruler:** Beatrix **Obv:** Queen's silhouette centered on a world globe **Rev:** Value above Australia on a world globe **Edge Lettering:** "GOD ZIJ MET ONS"

Date	Mintage	F	VF	XF	Unc	BU
2006	—	—	—	—	15.00	18.00

KM# 243 10 EURO
17.8000 g., 0.9250 Silver 0.5294 oz. ASW, 33 mm. **Subject:** Crown Prince's Wedding **Obv:** Head of Queen Beatrix left **Rev:** Two facing silhouettes **Edge:** Plain **Designer:** H. van Houwalingen

Date	Mintage	F	VF	XF	Unc	BU
2002	1,000,000	—	—	—	15.00	30.00
2002 Prooflike	80,000	—	—	—	—	35.00

KM# 244 10 EURO
6.7200 g., 0.9000 Gold 0.1944 oz. AGW, 22.5 mm. **Subject:** Crown Prince's Wedding **Obv:** Head of Queen Beatrix right **Rev:** Two facing silhouettes of Willem Alexander and Maxima **Edge:** Reeded **Designer:** J. van Houwalingen

Date	Mintage	F	VF	XF	Unc	BU
2002 Prooflike	33,000	—	—	—	—	145

KM# 246 10 EURO
6.7200 g., 0.9000 Gold 0.1944 oz. AGW, 22.5 mm. **Subject:** Vincent Van Gogh **Obv:** Queen's portrait **Rev:** Van Gogh's portrait **Edge:** Reeded **Designer:** K. Martens

Date	Mintage	F	VF	XF	Unc	BU
ND(2003) Prooflike	20,000	—	—	—	—	160

KM# 247 10 EURO
6.7200 g., 0.9000 Gold 0.1944 oz. AGW, 22.5 mm. **Ruler:** Beatrix **Subject:** New EEC members **Obv:** Head of Queen Beatrix half left **Rev:** Value, legend around **Edge:** Reeded **Designer:** M. Mieras and H. Mieras

Date	Mintage	F	VF	XF	Unc	BU
2004 Proof	6,000	Value: 165				

KM# 251 10 EURO
Gold **Ruler:** Beatrix **Subject:** 50 Years of Domestic Autonomy, 1954-2004 (for Netherlands Antilles) **Obv:** Small head facing left **Edge:** Reeded **Designer:** R. L. Luijters

Date	Mintage	F	VF	XF	Unc	BU
2004 Proof	3,800	Value: 185				

KM# 248 10 EURO
0.9250 Silver **Ruler:** Beatrix **Obv:** Queen Beatrix head left **Rev:** Multi-views of Prince Willem-Alexander, Princess Catherina-Amalia and Princess Maxima

Date	Mintage	F	VF	XF	Unc	BU
2004	1,000,000	—	—	—	—	18.00
2004 Proof	50,000	Value: 30.00				

KM# 261 10 EURO
17.8000 g., 0.9250 Silver 0.5294 oz. ASW, 33 mm. **Ruler:** Beatrix **Subject:** Silver Jubilee of Reign **Obv:** Queen's photo **Rev:** Queen taking oath photo

Date	Mintage	F	VF	XF	Unc	BU
2005	1,000,000	—	—	—	—	20.00
2005 Proof	59,754	Value: 45.00				

KM# 264 10 EURO
6.7200 g., 0.9000 Gold 0.1944 oz. AGW, 22.5 mm. **Ruler:** Beatrix **Subject:** 60th Anniversary of Liberation **Obv:** Queen and dots **Rev:** Value and dots

Date	Mintage	F	VF	XF	Unc	BU
2005 Proof	6,000	Value: 200				

KM# 249 20 EURO
8.5000 g., 0.9000 Gold 0.2460 oz. AGW, 25 mm. **Ruler:** Beatrix **Subject:** Birth of Crown-Princess - Catharina-Amalia - July 12, 2003 **Obv:** Bust of Queen Beatrix left **Rev:** Holographic images: left, Princess Maxima; front, Princess Catharina-Amalia; right, Prince Willem-Alexander **Edge:** Reeded

Date	Mintage	F	VF	XF	Unc	BU
2004 Proof	7,000	Value: 300				

KM# 262 20 EURO
8.5000 g., 0.9000 Gold 0.246 oz. AGW, 25 mm. **Ruler:** Beatrix **Subject:** Silver Jubilee of Reign **Obv:** Queen's photo **Rev:** Queen taking oath photo

Date	Mintage	F	VF	XF	Unc	BU
2005 Proof	5,001	Value: 345				

KM# 250 50 EURO

13.4400 g., 0.9000 Gold 0.3889 oz. AGW, 27 mm. **Ruler:** Beatrix **Subject:** Birth of Crown-Princess - Catharina-Amalia - July 12, 2003 **Obv:** Bust of Queen Beatrix left **Rev:** Holographic images: left, Princess Maxima; front, Princess Catharina-Amalia; right, Prince Willem-Alexander **Edge:** Reeded

Date	Mintage	F	VF	XF	Unc	BU
2004 Proof	3,500	Value: 500				

KM# 263 50 EURO

13.4400 g., 0.9000 Gold 0.3889 oz. AGW, 27 mm. **Ruler:** Beatrix **Subject:** Silver Jubilee of Reign **Obv:** Queen's photo **Rev:** Queen taking oath photo

Date	Mintage	F	VF	XF	Unc	BU
2005 Proof	3,500	Value: 575				

TRADE COINAGE

KM# 190.2 DUCAT

3.4940 g., 0.9830 Gold .1106 oz. AGW **Obv:** Knight with left leg bent, larger letters in legend **Rev:** Decorated square with text

Date	Mintage	F	VF	XF	Unc	BU
2001 Proof	7,500	Value: 95.00				
2002 Proof	3,400	Value: 110				
2003 Proof	3,800	Value: 110				
2004 Proof	2,400	Value: 145				
2005 Proof	2,243	Value: 145				
2006 Proof	2,500	Value: 145				

KM# 211 2 DUCAT

6.9880 g., 0.9830 Gold .2209 oz. AGW, 26 mm. **Obv:** Knight standing **Rev:** Decorated square with text

Date	Mintage	F	VF	XF	Unc	BU
2002 Proof	6,650	Value: 150				
2003 Proof	4,500	Value: 165				
2004 Proof	2,000	Value: 185				
2005 Proof	3,500	Value: 180				
2006 Proof	2,000	Value: 180				

SILVER BULLION COINAGE

KM# 242 SILVER DUCAT

28.2500 g., 0.8730 Silver 0.7929 oz. ASW, 40 mm. **Obv:** Standing knight with sword and arms **Rev:** Crowned arms **Edge:** Reeded **Note:** Utrecht coin design circa 1659 based on KM#48.

Date	Mintage	F	VF	XF	Unc	BU
2001 Proof	9,000	Value: 40.00				

KM# 232 SILVER DUCAT

28.2500 g., 0.8730 Silver .7948 oz. ASW, 40 mm. **Obv:** Crowned arms of the Netherlands **Rev:** Standing knight with the arms of Overijssel **Edge:** Reeded

Date	Mintage	F	VF	XF	Unc	BU
2002 Proof	—	Value: 45.00				

KM# 256 SILVER DUCAT

28.2500 g., 0.8730 Silver 0.7929 oz. ASW, 40 mm. **Ruler:** Beatrix **Obv:** Standing Knight with Gelderland arms **Rev:** Crowned arms **Edge:** Reeded

Date	Mintage	F	VF	XF	Unc	BU
2002 Proof	9,400	Value: 45.00				

KM# 257 SILVER DUCAT

28.2500 g., 0.8730 Silver 0.7929 oz. ASW, 40 mm. **Ruler:** Beatrix **Obv:** Standing Knight with Holland arms **Rev:** Crowned arms **Edge:** Reeded

Date	Mintage	F	VF	XF	Unc	BU
2003 Proof	4,100	Value: 45.00				

KM# 258 SILVER DUCAT

28.2500 g., 0.8730 Silver 0.7929 oz. ASW, 40 mm. **Ruler:** Beatrix **Obv:** Standing Knight with Zeeland arms **Rev:** Crowned arms **Edge:** Reeded

Date	Mintage	F	VF	XF	Unc	BU
2004 Proof	2,500	Value: 45.00				

KM# 259 SILVER DUCAT

28.2500 g., 0.8730 Silver 0.7929 oz. ASW, 40 mm. **Ruler:** Beatrix **Obv:** Standing Knight with Friesland arms **Rev:** Crowned arms **Edge:** Reeded

Date	Mintage	F	VF	XF	Unc	BU
2005 Proof	4,000	Value: 45.00				

KM# 260 SILVER DUCAT

28.2500 g., 0.8730 Silver 0.7929 oz. ASW, 40 mm. **Obv:** Standing Knight with Groningen arms **Rev:** Crowned arms **Edge:** Reeded

Date	Mintage	F	VF	XF	Unc	BU
2006 Proof	2,500	Value: 45.00				

PATTERNS

Including off metal strikes

KM#	Date	Mintage	Identification	Mkt Val
Pn162	2001	—	Gulden. Nickel. Medal rotation	—
Pn165	2001	—	2 Euro Cents. Nickel.	100
Pn166	2001	—	Euro. Brass. KM240	—

MINT SETS

KM#	Date	Mintage	Identification	Issue Price	Mkt Val
MS4	2001 (6)	85,000	KM#202-206, 210	12.00	15.00
MS5	2001 (8)	68,000	KM#234-241 Charity set, Disabled Sports	15.00	17.00
MS6	2002 (8)	105,000	KM#234-241 Charity set, Blind Escort Dogs Fund	15.00	17.00
MS7	2002 (8)	59,500	KM#234-241 Last FDC set	15.00	17.00
MS8	2002 (8)	25,000	KM#234-241 plus bear medal Baby set	15.50	25.00
MS9	2002 (8)	10,000	KM#234-241 plus medal Wedding Set	15.50	35.00
MS10	2002 (8)	3,500	KM#234-241 plus medal Queen Beatrix set	20.00	110
MS11	2002 (8)	2,002	KM#234-241 plus medal 10th Day of the Mint	22.00	150
MS12	2002 (8)	10,000	KM#234-241 plus medal VOC set I	22.00	35.00
MS13	2002 (8)	10,000	KM#234-241 plus medal VOC set II	22.00	25.00
MS14	2002 (8)	10,000	KM#234-241 plus medal VOC set III	22.00	25.00
MS15	2002 (8)	10,000	KM#234-241 plus medal VOC set IV	22.00	25.00
MS16	2002 (8)	3,000	KM#234-241 plus medal BVC	30.00	40.00
MS17A	2002 (8)	2,500	KM#234-241 VVV - Irisgiftset	20.00	40.00
MS17	2002 (1)	9,200	KM#243 plus stamp	30.00	30.00
MS18	2002 (8)	1,000	KM#234-241 plus medal Theo Peters (Christmas)	99.00	99.00
MS19	2003 (8)	75,000	KM#234-241 Charity set, Epilepsy fund	15.50	17.00
MS20	2003 (8)	15,000	KM#234-241 Information set Denmark	20.00	40.00
MS21	2003 (8)	10,000	KM#234-241 VVV - Irisgiftset	15.50	17.00
MS22	2003 (8)	10,000	KM#234-241 plus medal VOC set V	22.00	25.00
MS23	2003 (8)	10,000	KM#234-241 plus medal VOC set VI	42.00	45.00
MS24	2003 (8)	2,003	KM#234-241 plus medal Day of the Mint	25.00	120
MS25	2003 (8)	1,000	KM#234-241 plus bi-color medal Theo Peters Jubilee set	—	30.00
MS26	2003 (8)	100	KM#234-241 plus silver medal Theo Peters Jubilee set	70.00	70.00
MS27	2003 (8)	25	KM#234-241 plus golden medal Theo Peters Jubilee set	400	410
MS28	2003 (8)	25,000	KM#234-241 plus bear medal Baby set	20.00	25.00
MS29	2003 (8)	15,000	KM#234-241 plus medal Wedding set	20.00	25.00
MS30	2003 (8)	1,000	KM#234-241 plus silver medal Theo Peters Christmas set	—	30.00
MS31	2003 (8)	150	KM#234-241 plus silver medal Theo Peters Christmas set	70.00	70.00
MS32	2003 (8)	50	KM#234-241 plus golden medal Theo Peters Christmas set	400	400
MS33	2003	3,500	KM#234-241 plus medal Mintmasters I	20.00	60.00
MS34	2003 (8)	1,000	KM#234-241 World Money Fair	20.00	110
MS35	2003 (8)	15,000	KM234-241 Information Set Hungaria	20.00	40.00
MS36	2003 (8)	20,000	KM#234-241 plus silver medal Royal Birth of Princess Catharina-Amalia	22.00	25.00
MS37	2003 (16)	10,000	KM#234-241 and Luxembourg KM#75-81, 40 Benelux Set	40.00	45.00
MS38	2003 (40)	10,000	KM#224-231 plus Germany KM#207-214 plus Spain KM#1040-1047 plus Belgium KM#224-231 and Austria KM#3082-3089 Charles V Set	85.00	85.00
MS39	2004 (8)	3,500	KM#234-241 plus medal Mintmasters II	20.00	60.00

PROOF SETS

KM#	Date	Mintage	Identification	Issue Price	Mkt Val
PS54	2001 (6)	17,000	KM#202-206, 210 Booklet 5 Guilder	50.00	60.00
PS55	2001 (2)	500	KM#190.2, 242 Gold and Silver Ducat	50.00	60.00
PS56	2002 (2)	—	KM#190.2, 211 Golden Ducats	—	230
PS57	2002 (3)	—	KM#190.2, 211, 232 Golden Ducats and Silver Ducat	—	270
PS58	2003 (2)	—	KM#190.2, 211 Golden ducats in wooden box	230	230
PS59	2003 (8)	2,000	KM#234-241 Frigate "The Netherland" and silber medal and numbered ingot	85.00	125

PROOF-LIKE SETS (PL)

KM#	Date	Mintage	Identification	Issue Price	Mkt Val
PL3	2001 (8)	16,500	KM#234-241	50.00	50.00
PL4	2002 (2)	—	KM#243, 244 Wedding set (10 Euro in silver and gold) in plastic box	145	150
PL5	2002 (2)	—	KM#243, 244 Wedding set in wooden box	145	160
PL6	2002 (8)	16,500	KM#234-241	50.00	50.00
PL7	2003 (8)	16,500	KM#234-241	50.00	50.00

SELECT SETS (FLEUR DE COIN)

KM#	Date	Mintage	Identification	Issue Price	Mkt Val
SS90	2001 (6)	120,000	KM#202-206, 210 Introduction to Euro Coins	15.00	16.00
SS91	2001 (6)	3,400	KM#202-206, 210 Queen Julianna Medal	17.50	40.00
SS92	2001 (6)	100	KM#202-206, 210 Queen Julianna Medal; some coins dated 2000 in error	17.50	150
SS93	2001 (6)	1,000	KM#202-206, 210 BOLEGO - VOK	—	60.00
SS94	2001 (7)	1,000	KM#202-206, 210, 2 Stuiver coin from the wreck of the De Akerendam II	125	145
SS95	2001 (6)	1,000	KM#202-206, 210 United Provinces, Groningen Medal	40.00	40.00
SS96	2001 (6)	21,000	KM#202-206, 210 Baby set plus bear medal	15.50	17.50
SS97	2001 (6)	1,015	KM#202-206, 210 Onderlinge "'s-Grabenhage"	70.00	70.00

SPECIMEN FDC SETS (FLEUR DE COIN)

KM#	Date	Mintage	Identification	Issue Price	Mkt Val
SS95A	2001 (6)	1,000	KM202-206, 210 United Provinces, Utrecht Medal	40.00	40.00

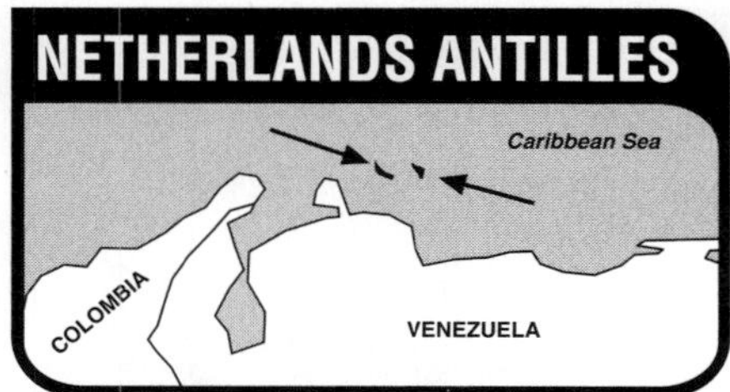

The Netherlands Antilles, comprises two groups of islands in the West Indies: Aruba (until 1986), Bonaire and Curacao and their dependencies near the Venezuelan coast and St. Eustatius, Saba, and the southern part of St. Martin (*St. Maarten*) southeast of Puerto Rico. The island group has an area of 371 sq. mi. (960 sq. km.) and a population of 225,000. Capital: Willemstad. Chief industries are the refining of crude oil and tourism. Petroleum products and phosphates are exported.

RULERS

Beatrix, 1980-

MINT MARKS

Y – York Mint
Utrecht Mint
(privy marks only)

Date	Privy Mark
2001	Wine tendril with grapes
2002	Wine tendril with grapes and star
2003	Sails of a clipper

MONETARY SYSTEM

100 Cents = 1 Gulden

KINGDOM

DECIMAL COINAGE

KM# 32 CENT

0.7000 g., Aluminum, 14 mm. **Obv:** Orange blossom **Rev:** Geometric design **Edge:** Reeded

Date	Mintage	F	VF	XF	Unc	BU
2001	12,806,500	—	—	—	0.25	0.50
2002 In sets only	6,000	—	—	—	1.00	1.25
2003	19,604,000	—	—	—	0.25	0.50
2004	—	—	—	—	0.25	0.50
2005	—	—	—	—	0.25	0.50

KM# 33 5 CENTS

1.1600 g., Aluminum, 16 mm. **Obv:** Orange blossom **Edge:** Reeded

Date	Mintage	F	VF	XF	Unc	BU
2001	2,006,500	—	—	—	0.60	0.75
2002 In sets only	6,000	—	—	—	2.00	2.50
2003	—	—	—	—	0.60	0.75
2004	—	—	—	—	0.50	0.75
2005	—	—	—	—	0.50	0.75

KM# 34 10 CENTS

3.0000 g., Nickel Bonded Steel, 18 mm. **Obv:** Orange blossom **Rev:** Geometric design **Edge:** Reeded

Date	Mintage	F	VF	XF	Unc	BU
2001	11,500	—	—	—	1.25	2.00
2002 In sets only	6,000	—	—	—	2.00	3.00
2003	2,104,000	—	—	—	1.00	1.75
2004	—	—	—	—	1.00	1.75
2005	—	—	—	—	1.00	1.75

KM# 35 25 CENTS

3.5000 g., Nickel Bonded Steel, 20.2 mm. **Obv:** Orange blossom **Rev:** Geometric design **Edge:** Reeded

Date	Mintage	F	VF	XF	Unc	BU
2001	11,500	—	—	—	1.25	1.50
2002 In set only	6,000	—	—	—	2.00	3.00
2003	1,404,000	—	—	—	1.25	1.50
2004	—	—	—	—	1.25	1.50
2005	—	—	—	—	1.25	1.50

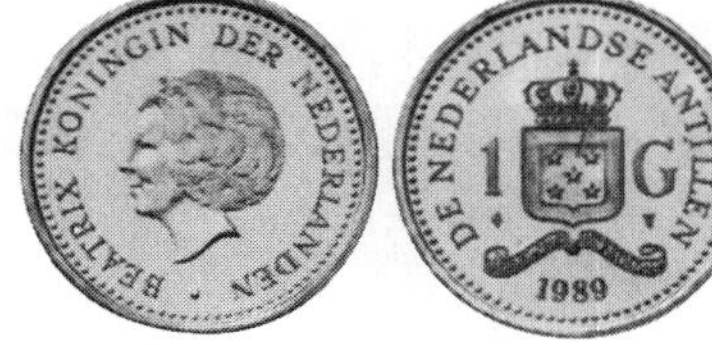

KM# 36 50 CENTS

5.0000 g., Aureate Steel, 24 mm. **Obv:** Orange blossom (citrus sinensis), geometric design **Rev:** Value, pearls, shells **Edge:** Plain **Shape:** 4-sided

Date	Mintage	F	VF	XF	Unc	BU
2001	11,500	—	—	—	3.00	4.00
2002 In sets only	6,000	—	—	—	4.50	6.00
2003	9,000	—	—	—	3.00	4.00
2004	—	—	—	—	3.00	4.00
2005	—	—	—	—	3.00	4.00

KM# 37 GULDEN

6.0000 g., Aureate Steel **Obv:** Queen Beatrix **Rev:** Arms **Edge Lettering:** GOD * ZIJ * MET * ONS *

Date	Mintage	F	VF	XF	Unc	BU
2001	11,500	—	—	—	3.00	4.00
2002 In sets only	6,000	—	—	—	5.00	6.00
2003	504,000	—	—	—	3.00	4.00
2004	—	—	—	—	3.00	4.00
2005	—	—	—	—	3.00	4.00

KM# 38 2-1/2 GULDEN

9.0000 g., Aureate Steel, 28 mm. **Obv:** Queen Beatrix **Rev:** Arms **Edge Lettering:** GOD * ZIJ * MET * ONS *

Date	Mintage	F	VF	XF	Unc	BU
2001	11,500	—	—	—	5.00	6.00
2002	6,000	—	—	—	7.00	8.00
Note: In sets only						
2003	9,000	—	—	—	5.00	6.00
2004	—	—	—	—	5.00	6.00
2005	—	—	—	—	5.00	6.00

KM# 43 5 GULDEN

11.0000 g., Brass Plated Steel, 26 mm. **Obv:** Head of Queen Beatrix left **Rev:** Crowned arms divide denomination **Edge Lettering:** GOD * ZIJ * MET * ONS *

Date	Mintage	F	VF	XF	Unc	BU
2001	9,500	—	—	—	4.00	5.00
2002 In sets only	6,000	—	—	—	5.00	6.00
2003	7,000	—	—	—	4.00	5.00
2004	—	—	—	—	4.00	5.00
2005	—	—	—	—	4.00	5.00

KM# 74 5 GULDEN

11.9000 g., 0.9250 Silver 0.3539 oz. ASW, 29 mm. **Ruler:** Beatrix **Subject:** 50th Anniversary - End to Dutch Colonial Rule **Obv:** Queen left **Rev:** Triangular signatures around value **Edge Lettering:** GOD*ZY*MET*ONS* **Designer:** Ans Mezas-Hummelink

Date	Mintage	F	VF	XF	Unc	BU
2004 Proof	4,000	Value: 30.00				

KM# 76 5 GULDEN

11.9000 g., 0.9250 Silver 0.3539 oz. ASW, 29 mm. **Ruler:** Beatrix **Subject:** Queen's Silver Jubilee **Obv:** Queen left **Rev:** Child art and value

Date	Mintage	F	VF	XF	Unc	BU
2005 Proof	4,000	Value: 32.00				

KM# 49 10 GULDEN

31.1035 g., 0.9250 Silver .9250 oz. ASW, 40 mm. **Ruler:** Beatrix **Series:** Gold Trade Coins: Sulla Aureus **Obv:** National arms and denomination **Rev:** Bust of Sulla facing two gold inserts replicating the aureus coin issued by Manlius and Sulla in 82-81 BC **Edge:** Plain

Date	Mintage	F	VF	XF	Unc	BU
2001 Proof	589	Value: 50.00				

KM# 50 10 GULDEN

31.1035 g., 0.9250 Silver .9250 oz. ASW, 40 mm. **Ruler:** Beatrix **Series:** Gold Trade Coins: Constantin I Solidus **Obv:** National arms and denomination **Rev:** Bust of Constantin I the Great facing, two gold inserts replicating a solidus coin issued during his reign **Edge:** Plain

Date	Mintage	F	VF	XF	Unc	BU
2001 Proof	578	Value: 50.00				

KM# 51 10 GULDEN

31.1035 g., 0.9250 Silver .9250 oz. ASW, 40 mm. **Ruler:** Beatrix **Series:** Gold Trade Coins: Clovis I Tremissisfiorino d'oro **Obv:** National arms and denomination **Rev:** Bust of Clovis I facing two gold inserts replicating the tremissisfioeino d'oro coin issued during his reign **Edge:** Plain

Date	Mintage	F	VF	XF	Unc	BU
2001 Proof	566	Value: 50.00				

KM# 52 10 GULDEN

31.1035 g., 0.9250 Silver .9250 oz. ASW, 40 mm. **Ruler:** Beatrix **Series:** Gold Trade Coins: Cosimo de'Medici Fiorino d'oro **Obv:** National arms and denomination **Rev:** Bust of Cosimo de'Medici facing two gold inserts replicating the Fiorino d'oro coin issued during his reign **Edge:** Plain

Date	Mintage	F	VF	XF	Unc	BU
2001 Proof	575	Value: 50.00				

KM# 53 10 GULDEN

31.1035 g., 0.9250 Silver .9250 oz. ASW, 40 mm. **Ruler:** Beatrix **Series:** Gold Trade Coins: Dandolo Ducato d'Oro **Obv:** National arms and denomination **Rev:** Bust of Dandolo facing two gold inserts replicating the Ducato d'oro coin issued during his reign **Edge:** Plain

Date	Mintage	F	VF	XF	Unc	BU
2001 Proof	490	Value: 50.00				

KM# 54 10 GULDEN

31.1035 g., 0.9250 Silver .9250 oz. ASW, 40 mm. **Ruler:** Beatrix **Series:** Gold Trade Coins: Philips IV Ecu d'or la chaise **Obv:** National arms and denomination **Rev:** Bust of Philips IV facing two gold inserts replicating the Ecu d'or la chaise coin issued during his reign **Edge:** Plain

Date	Mintage	F	VF	XF	Unc	BU
2001 Proof	460	Value: 50.00				

KM# 55 10 GULDEN

31.1035 g., 0.9250 Silver .9250 oz. ASW, 40 mm. **Ruler:** Beatrix **Series:** Gold Trade Coins: Edward III Nobel **Obv:** National arms and denomination **Rev:** Bust of Edward III facing two gold inserts replicating the nobel coin issued during his reign **Edge:** Plain

Date	Mintage	F	VF	XF	Unc	BU
2001 Proof	575	Value: 50.00				

KM# 56 10 GULDEN
31.1035 g., 0.9250 Silver .9250 oz. ASW, 40 mm. **Ruler:** Beatrix **Series:** Gold Trade Coins: Carolus IV Rhine Gold Guilder **Obv:** National arms and denomination **Rev:** Bust of Carolus IV facing two gold inserts replicating the Rhine Gold Guilder coin issued during his reign **Edge:** Plain

Date	Mintage	F	VF	XF	Unc	BU
2001 Proof	430	Value: 50.00				

KM# 57 10 GULDEN
31.1035 g., 0.9250 Silver .9250 oz. ASW, 40 mm. **Ruler:** Beatrix **Series:** Gold Trade Coins: John II Franc d'or a cheval **Obv:** National arms and denomination **Rev:** Bust of John II the Good facing two gold inserts replicating the Franc d'or a cheval coin issued during his reign **Edge:** Plain

Date	Mintage	F	VF	XF	Unc	BU
2001 Proof	464	Value: 50.00				

KM# 58 10 GULDEN
31.1035 g., 0.9250 Silver .9250 oz. ASW, 40 mm. **Ruler:** Beatrix **Series:** Gold Trade Coins: Philip the Good Adriesguilder **Obv:** National arms and denomination **Rev:** Bust of Philip the Good facing two gold inserts replicating the Adriesguilder coin issued during his reign **Edge:** Plain

Date	Mintage	F	VF	XF	Unc	BU
2001 Proof	250	Value: 50.00				

KM# 59 10 GULDEN
31.1035 g., 0.9250 Silver .9250 oz. ASW, 40 mm. **Ruler:** Beatrix **Series:** Gold Trade Coins: Louis XI Ecu d'or au soleil **Obv:** National arms and denomination **Rev:** Bust of Louis XI facing two gold inserts replicating the Ecu d'or au soleil coin issued during his reign **Edge:** Plain

Date	Mintage	F	VF	XF	Unc	BU
2001 Proof	450	Value: 50.00				

KM# 60 10 GULDEN
31.1035 g., 0.9250 Silver .9250 oz. ASW, 40 mm. **Ruler:** Beatrix **Series:** Gold Trade Coins: Elisabeth I Sovereign **Obv:** National arms and denomination **Rev:** Bust of Elisabeth I facing two gold inserts replicating the Sovereign coin issued during her reign **Edge:** Plain

Date	Mintage	F	VF	XF	Unc	BU
2001 Proof	450	Value: 50.00				

KM# 61 10 GULDEN
31.1035 g., 0.9250 Silver .9250 oz. ASW, 40 mm. **Ruler:** Beatrix **Series:** Gold Trade Coins: Carolus V Carolus Guilder **Obv:** National arms and denomination **Rev:** Bust of Carolus V facing two gold inserts replicating the Carolus Guilder coin issued during his reign **Edge:** Plain

Date	Mintage	F	VF	XF	Unc	BU
2001 Proof	440	Value: 50.00				

KM# 62 10 GULDEN
31.1035 g., 0.9250 Silver .9250 oz. ASW, 40 mm. **Ruler:** Beatrix **Series:** Gold Trade Coins: Philips II Real **Obv:** National arms and denomination **Rev:** Bust of Philips II facing two gold inserts replicating the Real coin issued during his reign **Edge:** Plain

Date	Mintage	F	VF	XF	Unc	BU
2001 Proof	440	Value: 50.00				

KM# 63 10 GULDEN
31.1035 g., 0.9250 Silver .9250 oz. ASW, 40 mm. **Ruler:** Beatrix **Series:** Gold Trade Coins: Maurits Ducat **Obv:** National arms and denomination **Rev:** Bust of Maurits (Orange-Nassau) facing two gold inserts replicating the Ducat coin issued during his reign **Edge:** Plain

Date	Mintage	F	VF	XF	Unc	BU
2001 Proof	443	Value: 50.00				

KM# 64 10 GULDEN
31.1035 g., 0.9250 Silver .9250 oz. ASW, 40 mm. **Ruler:** Beatrix **Series:** Gold Trade Coins: Isabella and Albrecht Double Albertin **Obv:** National arms and denomination **Rev:** Bust of Isabella and Albrecht facing two gold inserts replicating Double Albertin issued during their reign **Edge:** Plain

Date	Mintage	F	VF	XF	Unc	BU
2001 Proof	490	Value: 50.00				

KM# 65 10 GULDEN
31.1035 g., 0.9250 Silver .9250 oz. ASW, 40 mm. **Ruler:** Beatrix **Series:** Gold Trade Coins: William III Golden Rider **Obv:** National arms and denomination **Rev:** Bust of William III facing two gold inserts replicating Golden Rider issued during his reign **Edge:** Plain

Date	Mintage	F	VF	XF	Unc	BU
2001 Proof	440	Value: 50.00				

KM# 66 10 GULDEN
31.1035 g., 0.9250 Silver .9250 oz. ASW, 40 mm. **Ruler:** Beatrix **Series:** Gold Trade Coins: Louis XIII Louis d'or **Obv:** National arms and denomination **Rev:** Bust of Louis XIII facing two gold inserts replicating Louis d'or issued during his reign **Edge:** Plain

Date	Mintage	F	VF	XF	Unc	BU
2001 Proof	440	Value: 50.00				

KM# 67 10 GULDEN
31.1035 g., 0.9250 Silver .9250 oz. ASW, 40 mm. **Ruler:** Beatrix **Series:** Gold Trade Coins: Catharina the Great Rubel **Obv:** National arms and denomination **Rev:** Bust of Catharina the Great facing two gold inserts replicating a Rubel coin issued during her reign **Edge:** Plain

Date	Mintage	F	VF	XF	Unc	BU
2001 Proof	560	Value: 50.00				

KM# 68 10 GULDEN
31.1035 g., 0.9250 Silver .9250 oz. ASW, 40 mm. **Ruler:** Beatrix **Series:** Gold Trade Coins: Maria Theresia Double Sovereign **Obv:** National arms and denomination **Rev:** Bust of Maria Theresia facing two gold inserts replicating a double sovereign coin issued during her reign **Edge:** Plain

Date	Mintage	F	VF	XF	Unc	BU
2001 Proof	440	Value: 50.00				

KM# 69 10 GULDEN
31.1035 g., 0.9250 Silver .9250 oz. ASW, 40 mm. **Ruler:** Beatrix **Series:** Gold Trade Coins: Napolean Bonaparte 20 Franc **Obv:** National arms and denomination **Rev:** Bust of Napolean Bonaparte facing two gold inserts replicating a 20 franc coin issued during his rule **Edge:** Plain

Date	Mintage	F	VF	XF	Unc	BU
2001 Proof	555	Value: 50.00				

KM# 70 10 GULDEN
31.1035 g., 0.9250 Silver .9250 oz. ASW, 40 mm. **Ruler:** Beatrix **Series:** Gold Trade Coins: Wilhelmina Golden 10 Guilder **Obv:** National arms and denomination **Rev:** Bust of Wilhelmina facing two gold inserts replicating a Golden 10 Guilder issued during her reign **Edge:** Plain

Date	Mintage	F	VF	XF	Unc	BU
2001 Proof	440	Value: 50.00				

KM# 71 10 GULDEN
31.1035 g., 0.9250 Silver .9250 oz. ASW, 40 mm. **Ruler:** Beatrix **Series:** Gold Trade Coins: George III Sovereign **Obv:** National arms and denomination **Rev:** Bust of George III facing two gold inserts replicating a gold sovereign coin issued during his reign **Edge:** Plain

Date	Mintage	F	VF	XF	Unc	BU
2001 Proof	440	Value: 50.00				

KM# 72 10 GULDEN
31.1035 g., 0.9250 Silver .9250 oz. ASW, 40 mm. **Ruler:** Beatrix **Series:** Gold Trade Coins: Albert I Belgium 20 Franc **Obv:** National arms and denomination **Rev:** Bust of Albert I facing two gold inserts replicating a Belgian 20 franc coin issued during his reign **Edge:** Plain

Date	Mintage	F	VF	XF	Unc	BU
2001 Proof	490	Value: 50.00				

KM# 75 10 GULDEN
6.7200 g., 0.9000 Gold 0.1944 oz. AGW **Ruler:** Beatrix **Subject:** 50th Anniversary - End to Dutch Colonial Rule **Obv:** Queen left **Rev:** Triangular signatures around value **Edge:** Reeded **Designer:** Ans Mezas-Hummelink

Date	Mintage	F	VF	XF	Unc	BU
2004 Proof	1,000	Value: 180				

KM# 77 10 GULDEN
6.7200 g., 0.9000 Gold 0.1944 oz. AGW, 22.5 mm. **Ruler:** Beatrix **Subject:** Queen's Silver Jubilee **Obv:** Queen left **Rev:** Child art and value

Date	Mintage	F	VF	XF	Unc	BU
2005 Proof	1,500	Value: 175				

MINT SETS

KM#	Date	Mintage	Identification	Issue Price	Mkt Val
MS22	2001 (8)	6,500	KM#32-38, 43	15.00	18.50
MS23	2002 (8)	6,000	KM#32-38, 43	15.00	27.50
MS24	2003 (8)	4,000	KM#32-38, 43	15.00	20.00
MS25	2004 (8)	—	KM32-38, 43	15.00	20.00
MS26	2005 (8)	—	KM32-38, 43	17.00	17.50

NEW CALEDONIA

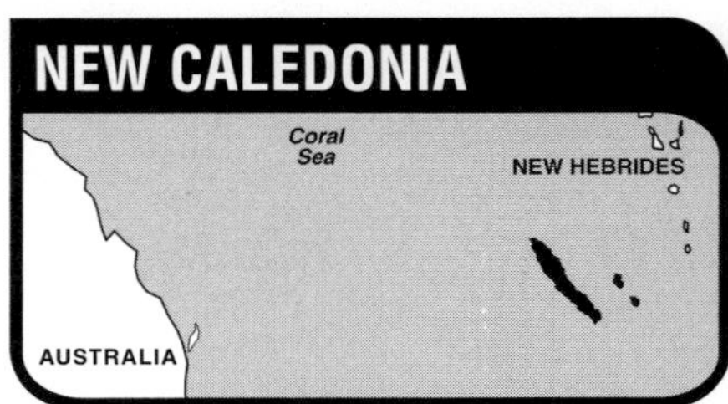

The French Overseas Territory of New Caledonia, is a group of about 25 islands in the South Pacific. They are situated about 750 miles (1,207 km.) east of Australia. The territory, which includes the dependencies of Isle des Pins, Loyalty Islands, Isle Huon, Isles Belep, Isles Chesterfield, Isle Walpole, Wallis and Futuna Islands and has a total land area of 7,358 sq. mi.(19,060 sq. km.) and a population of *156,000. Capital: Noumea. The islands are rich in minerals; New Caledonia has some of the world's largest known deposit of nickel. Nickel, nickel castings, coffee and copra are exported.

MINT MARKS
Paris, privy marks only

MONETARY SYSTEM
100 Centimes = 1 Franc

FRENCH OVERSEAS TERRITORY

DECIMAL COINAGE

KM# 10 FRANC
Aluminum **Obv:** Legend added **Obv. Legend:** I. E. O. M. **Rev:** Kagu bird (Rhynochetos jubatus) **Designer:** G.B.L. Bazor

Date	Mintage	F	VF	XF	Unc	BU
2001(a)	100,000	—	—	0.15	0.50	1.00
2002(a)	1,200,000	—	—	0.15	0.50	1.00
2003(a)	2,000,000	—	—	0.15	0.50	1.00
2004(a)	1,200,000	—	—	0.15	0.50	1.00
2005(a)	700,000	—	—	0.15	0.50	0.50

KM# 14 2 FRANCS
Aluminum **Obv:** Legend added **Obv. Legend:** I. E. O. M. **Rev:** Kagu bird (Rhynochetos jubatus)

Date	Mintage	F	VF	XF	Unc	BU
2001(a)	800,000	—	—	0.25	0.75	2.00
2002(a)	1,200,000	—	—	0.25	0.75	2.00
2003(a)	2,400,000	—	—	0.20	0.65	2.00
2004(a)	200,000	—	—	0.20	0.65	2.00
2005(a)	530,000	—	—	0.20	0.65	2.00

KM# 16 5 FRANCS
Aluminum **Obv:** Legend added **Obv. Legend:** I. E. O. M. **Rev:** Kagu bird (Rhynochetos jubatus) **Designer:** G.B.L. Bazor

Date	Mintage	F	VF	XF	Unc	BU
2001(a)	600,000	—	—	0.50	1.50	3.00
2002(a)	480,000	—	—	0.50	1.50	3.00
2003(a)	700,000	—	—	0.40	1.25	2.75
2004(a)	1,000,000	—	—	0.40	1.25	2.75
2005(a)	360,000	—	—	0.40	1.25	2.75

KM# 11 10 FRANCS
Nickel **Obv:** Legend added **Obv. Legend:** I. E. O. M. **Rev:** Pirogue **Designer:** R. Joly

Date	Mintage	F	VF	XF	Unc	BU
2001(a)	100,000	—	—	0.65	1.25	2.75
2002(a)	200,000	—	—	0.65	1.25	2.75
2003(a)	800,000	—	—	0.65	1.25	2.75
2004(a)	600,000	—	—	0.65	1.25	2.75
2005(a)	64,000	—	—	0.65	1.25	2.75

KM# 12 20 FRANCS
Nickel **Obv:** Legend added **Obv. Legend:** I. O. E. M. **Rev:** Three zebus heads left **Designer:** R. Joly

Date	Mintage	F	VF	XF	Unc	BU
2001(a)	150,000	—	—	1.00	1.75	3.50
2002(a)	250,000	—	—	1.00	1.75	3.50
2003(a)	250,000	—	—	1.00	1.75	3.50
2004(a)	500,000	—	—	1.00	1.75	3.50
2005(a)	300,000	—	—	1.00	1.75	3.50

KM# 13 50 FRANCS
Nickel **Obv:** Legend added **Obv. Legend:** I. E. O. M. **Designer:** R. Joly

Date	Mintage	F	VF	XF	Unc	BU
2001(a)	100,000	—	—	1.25	2.50	3.50
2002(a)	—	—	—	1.25	2.50	3.50
2003(a)	75,000	—	—	1.25	2.50	3.50
2004(a)	150,000	—	—	1.25	2.50	3.50
2005(a)	54,000	—	—	1.25	2.50	3.50

KM# 15 100 FRANCS
Nickel-Bronze **Designer:** R. Joly

Date	Mintage	F	VF	XF	Unc	BU
2001(a)	100,000	—	—	1.50	3.00	5.00
2002(a)	620,000	—	—	1.50	3.00	5.00
2003(a)	500,000	—	—	1.50	3.00	5.00
2004(a)	500,000	—	—	1.50	3.00	5.00
2005(a)	180,000	—	—	1.50	3.00	5.00

MINT SETS

KM#	Date	Mintage	Identification	Issue Price	Mkt Val
MS1	2001 (7)	3,000	KM#10-16	—	35.00
MS2	2002 (7)	5,000	KM#10-16	—	32.00
MS3	2004 (7)	3,000	KM#10-16	—	35.00

NEW ZEALAND

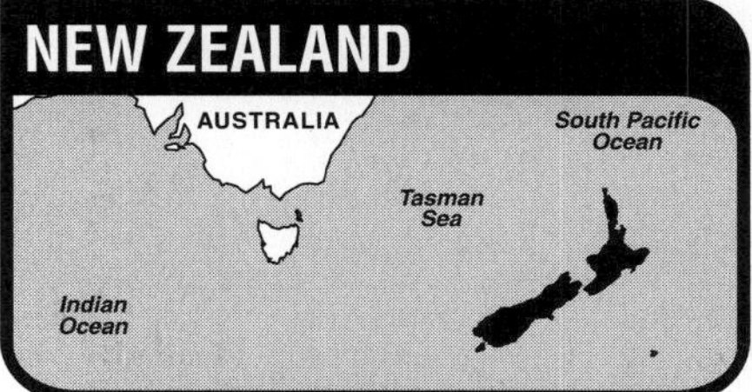

New Zealand, a parliamentary state located in the Southwest Pacific 1,250 miles (2,011 km.) east of Australia, has an area of 103,883 sq. mi. (268,680 sq. km.) and a population of *3.4 million. Capital: Wellington. Wool, meat, dairy products and some manufactured items are exported.

RULERS
British

MINTS
(L) – British Royal Mint (Llantrisant)
(C) – Royal Australian Mint (Canberra)
(O) – Royal Canadian Mint
(N) – Norwegian Mint
(P) – South African Mint (Pretoria)

COMMONWEALTH OF NEW ZEALAND

DECIMAL COINAGE

100 Cents = 1 Dollar

KM# 116 5 CENTS
Copper-Nickel **Obv:** Rank-Broadley portrait of Queen Elizabeth II **Rev:** Tuatara **Rev. Designer:** James Berry

Date	Mintage	F	VF	XF	Unc	BU
2001(l)	20,000,000	—	—	0.10	1.00	—
2001(l) Proof	2,000	Value: 3.00				
2002(l)	40,500,000	—	—	0.10	0.50	—
2002(l) Proof	2,000	Value: 3.00				
2003	—	—	—	—	0.50	—
2003 Proof	—	Value: 3.00				
2004	—	—	—	—	0.40	—
2004 Proof	3,500	Value: 3.00				
2005	—	—	—	—	0.30	—
2005 Proof	—	Value: 3.00				

KM# 117 10 CENTS
Copper-Nickel **Obv:** Rank-Broadley portrait of Queen Elizabeth II **Rev:** Koruru **Rev. Designer:** James Berry

Date	Mintage	F	VF	XF	Unc	BU
2001(l)	10,000,000	—	—	0.10	0.50	—
2001(l) Proof	2,000	Value: 4.00				
2002(l)	10,000,000	—	—	0.10	0.50	—
2002(l) Proof	2,000	Value: 4.00				
2003(l)	—	—	—	0.10	0.50	—
2003(l) Proof	—	Value: 4.00				
2004	—	—	—	—	0.50	—
2004 Proof	3,500	Value: 4.00				
2005	—	—	—	—	0.50	—
2005 Proof	—	Value: 4.00				

KM# 117a 10 CENTS
Copper Plated Steel, 20.5 mm.

Date	Mintage	F	VF	XF	Unc	BU
2006	—	—	—	—	0.20	—

KM# 118 20 CENTS
Copper-Nickel **Obv:** Rank-Broadley portrait of Queen Elizabeth II **Rev:** Similar to KM#81

Date	Mintage	F	VF	XF	Unc	BU
2001	—	—	—	—	0.50	—
2001(l) Proof	2,000	Value: 10.00				
2002(l)	7,000,000	—	—	—	0.50	—
2002(l) Proof	2,000	Value: 10.00				
2003(l)	—	—	—	—	0.50	—
2003 Proof	—	Value: 10.00				
2004	—	—	—	—	0.50	—
2004 Proof	3,500	Value: 10.00				
2005	—	—	—	—	0.50	—
2005 Proof	—	Value: 10.00				

KM# 118a 20 CENTS
Nickel Plated Steel, 21.75 mm.

Date	Mintage	F	VF	XF	Unc	BU
2006	—	—	—	—	0.40	—

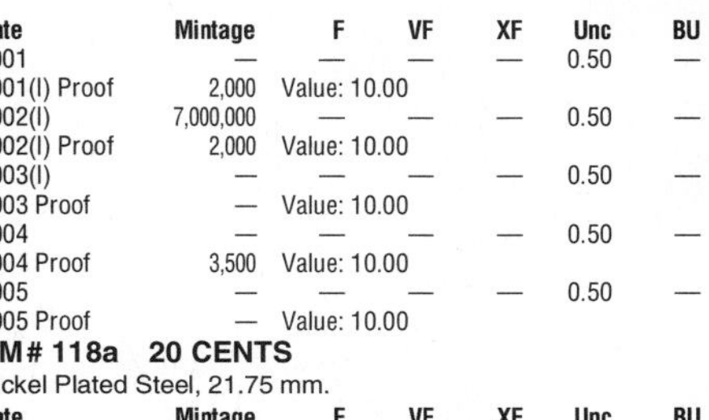

KM# 119 50 CENTS
Copper-Nickel **Obv:** Rank-Broadley portrait of Queen Elizabeth II **Rev:** H.M.S. Endeavour **Rev. Designer:** James Berry

Date	Mintage	F	VF	XF	Unc	BU
2001(l)	5,000,000	—	—	—	1.00	—
2001(l) Proof	2,000	Value: 5.00				
2002(l)	3,000,000	—	—	0.50	1.00	—
2002(l) Proof	2,000	Value: 5.00				
2003(l)	—	—	—	0.50	1.00	—
2003(l) Proof	—	Value: 5.00				
2004	—	—	—	—	1.00	—
2004 Proof	3,500	Value: 5.00				
2005	—	—	—	—	1.00	—
2005 Proof	—	Value: 5.00				

KM# 119a 50 CENTS
Nickel Plated Steel, 24.75 mm.

Date	Mintage	F	VF	XF	Unc	BU
2006	—	—	—	—	0.75	—

KM# 135 50 CENTS
13.6100 g., Copper-Nickel, 31.75 mm. **Subject:** Lord of the Rings **Obv:** Elizabeth II **Rev:** Hobbit Frodo Baggins **Edge:** Reeded

Date	Mintage	F	VF	XF	Unc	BU
2003 In sets only	—	—	—	—	4.00	—

KM# 136 50 CENTS
13.6100 g., Copper-Nickel, 31.75 mm. **Subject:** Lord of the Rings **Obv:** Elizabeth II **Rev:** Gandalf the Grey **Edge:** Reeded

Date	Mintage	F	VF	XF	Unc	BU
2003 In sets only	—	—	—	—	4.00	—

KM# 137 50 CENTS

13.6100 g., Copper-Nickel, 31.75 mm. **Subject:** Lord of the Rings **Obv:** Elizabeth II **Rev:** Aragon **Edge:** Reeded

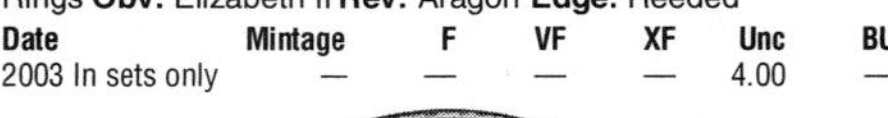

Date	Mintage	F	VF	XF	Unc	BU
2003 In sets only	—	—	—	—	4.00	—

KM# 138 50 CENTS

13.6100 g., Copper-Nickel, 31.75 mm. **Subject:** Lord of the Rings **Obv:** Elizabeth II **Rev:** Gollum **Edge:** Reeded

Date	Mintage	F	VF	XF	Unc	BU
2003 In sets only	—	—	—	—	4.00	—

KM# 139 50 CENTS

13.6100 g., Copper-Nickel, 31.75 mm. **Subject:** Lord of the Rings **Obv:** Elizabeth II **Rev:** Sauron, dark lord of Mordor **Edge:** Reeded

Date	Mintage	F	VF	XF	Unc	BU
2003 In sets only	—	—	—	—	4.00	—

KM# 140 50 CENTS

13.6100 g., Copper-Nickel, 31.75 mm. **Subject:** Lord of the Rings **Obv:** Elizabeth II **Rev:** Saruman the White **Edge:** Reeded

Date	Mintage	F	VF	XF	Unc	BU
2003 In sets only	—	—	—	—	4.00	—

KM# 120 DOLLAR

Aluminum-Bronze **Obv:** Head of Queen Elizabeth II right **Obv. Designer:** Rank-Broadley **Rev:** Kiwi bird **Rev. Designer:** R. Maurice Conly

Date	Mintage	F	VF	XF	Unc	BU
2001	—	—	—	—	1.00	2.00
2001 Proof	2,000	Value: 5.00				
2002(I)	8,000,000	—	—	—	1.00	2.00
2002(I) Proof	2,000	Value: 5.00				
2003(I)	—	—	—	—	1.00	2.00
2003(I) Proof	—	Value: 5.00				
2004	—	—	—	—	1.00	2.00
2004 Proof	3,500	Value: 5.00				
2005	—	—	—	—	1.00	2.00
2005 Proof	—	Value: 5.00				

KM# 141 DOLLAR

28.2800 g., Nickel-Brass, 38.61 mm. **Subject:** Lord of the Rings **Obv:** Elizabeth II **Rev:** Inscribed ring around value **Edge:** Reeded

Date	Mintage	F	VF	XF	Unc	BU
2003	—	—	—	—	15.00	—

KM# 141a DOLLAR

28.2100 g., 0.9250 Silver 0.841 oz. ASW, 38.61 mm. **Obv:** Elizabeth II **Rev:** Gold-plated ring and edge **Edge:** Reeded

Date	Mintage	F	VF	XF	Unc	BU
2003 Proof	150,000	Value: 30.00				

KM# 142 DOLLAR

28.2800 g., Nickel-Brass, 38.61 mm. **Subject:** Lord of the Rings **Obv:** Elizabeth II **Rev:** Hobbit Frodo Baggins **Edge:** Reeded

Date	Mintage	F	VF	XF	Unc	BU
2003 In sets only	—	—	—	—	10.00	—

KM# 143 DOLLAR

28.2800 g., Nickel-Brass, 38.61 mm. **Subject:** Lord of the Rings **Obv:** Elizabeth II **Rev:** Sauron, dark lord of Mordor **Edge:** Reeded

Date	Mintage	F	VF	XF	Unc	BU
2003 In sets only	—	—	—	—	10.00	—

KM# 121 2 DOLLARS

Aluminum-Bronze **Obv:** Head of Queen Elizabeth II right **Obv. Designer:** Rank-Broadley **Rev:** Kotuku, white heron **Rev. Designer:** R. Maurice Conley

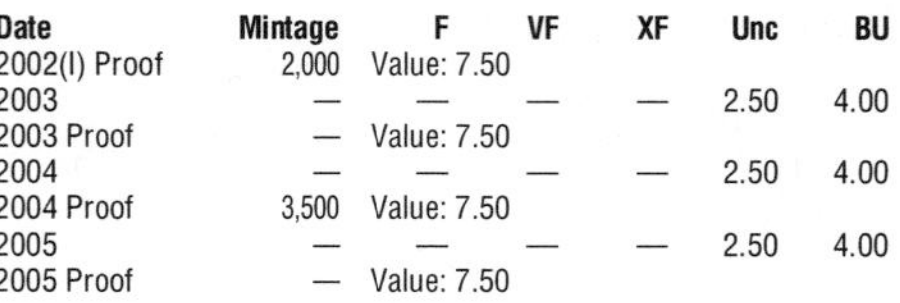

Date	Mintage	F	VF	XF	Unc	BU
2001(I)	3,000,000	—	—	—	2.50	4.00
2001 Proof	2,000	Value: 7.50				
2002(I)	6,000,000	—	—	—	2.50	4.00
2002(I) Proof	2,000	Value: 7.50				
2003	—	—	—	—	2.50	4.00
2003 Proof	—	Value: 7.50				
2004	—	—	—	—	2.50	4.00
2004 Proof	3,500	Value: 7.50				
2005	—	—	—	—	2.50	4.00
2005 Proof	—	Value: 7.50				

KM# 128 5 DOLLARS

28.2800 g., Copper-Nickel, 38.6 mm. **Subject:** Kereru Bird **Obv:** Rank-Broadley **Rev:** Pigeon on branch **Edge:** Reeded

Date	Mintage	F	VF	XF	Unc	BU
2001(I)	7,500	—	—	—	12.50	—
2001 Proof	—	Value: 35.00				

KM# 149 5 DOLLARS

28.2800 g., Copper-Nickel, 38.6 mm. **Subject:** Royal Visit (canceled after coin issue) **Obv:** Elizabeth II **Rev:** Queen with flowers and two girls **Edge:** Reeded

Date	Mintage	F	VF	XF	Unc	BU
2001	—	—	—	—	—	20.00

KM# 149a 5 DOLLARS

28.2800 g., 0.9250 Silver 0.841 oz. ASW, 38.6 mm. **Subject:** Royal Visit (canceled after coin issue) **Obv:** Elizabeth II **Rev:** Queen with flowers and two girls **Edge:** Reeded

Date	Mintage	F	VF	XF	Unc	BU
2001 Proof	2,000	Value: 65.00				

KM# 128a 5 DOLLARS

28.2800 g., 0.9990 Silver .9083 oz. ASW **Obv:** Queen's head right **Obv. Designer:** Rank-Broadley **Rev:** Pigeon on branch

Date	Mintage	F	VF	XF	Unc	BU
2001 Proof	4,500	Value: 35.00				

KM# 131 5 DOLLARS

28.2800 g., Copper-Nickel, 38.6 mm. **Subject:** Architectural Heritage **Obv:** Bust of Queen Elizabeth II right **Obv. Designer:** Rank-Broadley **Rev:** Auckland Sky Tower **Edge:** Reeded

Date	Mintage	F	VF	XF	Unc	BU
2002(I)	3,000	—	—	—	12.50	—

Note: 500 of which are issued in Numismatic-Philatelic covers.

KM# 131a 5 DOLLARS

28.2800 g., 0.9250 Silver 0.841 oz. ASW, 38.6 mm. **Subject:** Architectural Heritage **Obv:** Bust of Queen Elizabeth II right **Obv. Designer:** Rank-Broadley **Rev:** Auckland Sky Tower **Edge:** Reeded

Date	Mintage	F	VF	XF	Unc	BU
2002(I)	2,000	Value: 37.50				

Note: 500 of which are issued in Numismatic-Philatelic covers

KM# 145 5 DOLLARS
27.2200 g., Copper-Nickel, 38.74 mm. **Obv:** Queen Elizabeth II **Rev:** Two Hector's Dolphins jumping out of the water **Edge:** Reeded

Date	Mintage	F	VF	XF	Unc	BU
2002	4,000	—	—	—	25.00	—

KM# 147 5 DOLLARS
28.2300 g., 0.9250 Silver 0.8395 oz. ASW, 38.6 mm. **Subject:** 50th Anniversary of Coronation **Obv:** Gold plated bust of Elizabeth II **Rev:** Crown above fern and flowers **Edge:** Reeded

Date	Mintage	F	VF	XF	Unc	BU
2003 Proof	25,000	Value: 50.00				

KM# 132 5 DOLLARS
26.7000 g., Copper-Nickel, 38.6 mm. **Obv:** Queen's portrait **Rev:** Giant Kokopu fish **Edge:** Reeded

Date	Mintage	F	VF	XF	Unc	BU
2003	8,000	—	—	—	12.00	20.00

KM# 133 5 DOLLARS
26.7200 g., Copper-Nickel, 38.6 mm. **Subject:** Chatham Island Taiko **Obv:** Queen's portrait **Rev:** Bird **Edge:** Reeded

Date	Mintage	F	VF	XF	Unc	BU
2004(2003)	3,000	—	—	—	40.00	—
2004(2003) Proof	3,500	Value: 40.00				

KM# 146 5 DOLLARS
27.2200 g., Copper-Nickel, 38.74 mm. **Obv:** Queen Elizabeth II **Rev:** Fiordland Crested Penguin **Edge:** Reeded

Date	Mintage	F	VF	XF	Unc	BU
2005(2004)	4,000	—	—	—	25.00	30.00

KM# 148 5 DOLLARS
27.2200 g., Copper-Nickel, 38.74 mm. **Obv:** Elizabeth II **Rev:** New Zealand Falcon on tree stump **Edge:** Reeded

Date	Mintage	F	VF	XF	Unc	BU
2006	4,000	—	—	—	—	25.00

KM# 129 10 DOLLARS
3.8879 g., 0.9990 Gold .1250 oz. AGW, 18 mm. **Obv:** Queen's portrait **Rev:** Salvage ship "Claymore" **Edge:** Reeded

Date	Mintage	F	VF	XF	Unc	BU
2001 Proof	600	Value: 125				

KM# 130 10 DOLLARS
7.7759 g., 0.9990 Gold .2500 oz. AGW, 22 mm. **Obv:** Queen's portrait **Rev:** R.M.S. Niagara **Edge:** Reeded

Date	Mintage	F	VF	XF	Unc	BU
2001 Proof	600	Value: 225				

KM# 144 10 DOLLARS
39.9400 g., 0.9166 Gold 1.177 oz. AGW, 38.61 mm. **Subject:** Lord of the Rings **Obv:** Elizabeth II **Rev:** Inscribed ring around value **Edge:** Reeded

Date	Mintage	F	VF	XF	Unc	BU
2003 Proof	—	Value: 1,000				

MINT SETS

KM#	Date	Mintage	Identification	Issue Price	Mkt Val
MS50	2001 (7)	5,000	KM#116-121, 128	18.50	20.00
MS51	2002 (7)	4,000	KM#116-121, 128	18.00	20.00
MS52	2003 (7)	5,000	KM#116-121, 128	18.00	20.00
MS53	2003 (6)	—	KM#135, 136, 137, 138, 139, 140 Light vs Dark Set	19.95	25.00
MS54	2003 (3)	—	KM141, 142, 143 Battle for the Ring Set	29.95	35.00

PROOF SETS

KM#	Date	Mintage	Identification	Issue Price	Mkt Val
PS45	2001 (7)	2,000	KM#116-121, 128	49.25	60.00
PS46	2001 (2)	600	KM#129-130	400	450
PS47	2002 (7)	—	KM#116-121, 128	60.00	55.00
PS48	2003 (7)	—	KM#116-121, 132a	60.00	55.00
PS49	2004 (7)	3,500	KM#116-121, 133 Chatham Islands Taiko	—	—

NICARAGUA

The Republic of Nicaragua, situated in Central America between Honduras and Costa Rica, has an area of 50,193 sq. mi. (129,494 sq. km.) and a population of *3.7 million. Capital: Managua. Agriculture, mining (gold and silver) and hardwood logging are the principal industries. Cotton, meat, coffee and sugar are exported.

MONETARY SYSTEM
100 Centavos = 1 Cordoba

REPUBLIC

DECIMAL COINAGE

KM# 97 5 CENTAVOS
3.0000 g., Copper Plated Steel, 18.5 mm. **Obv:** National arms **Rev:** Denomination **Edge:** Plain

Date	Mintage	F	VF	XF	Unc	BU
2002	—	—	—	—	0.25	0.50

KM# 98 10 CENTAVOS
4.0000 g., Brass Plated Steel, 20.5 mm. **Obv:** National arms **Rev:** Denomination **Edge:** Reeded and plain sections

Date	Mintage	F	VF	XF	Unc	BU
2002	—	—	—	—	0.45	0.85

KM# 99 25 CENTAVOS
5.0000 g., Brass Plated Steel, 23.25 mm. **Obv:** National arms **Rev:** Denomination **Edge:** Reeded and plain sections

Date	Mintage	F	VF	XF	Unc	BU
2002	—	—	—	—	0.65	1.25

KM# 89 CORDOBA
Nickel Clad Steel **Obv:** National emblem **Rev:** Denomination

Date	Mintage	F	VF	XF	Unc	BU
2002	—	—	—	—	2.50	3.00

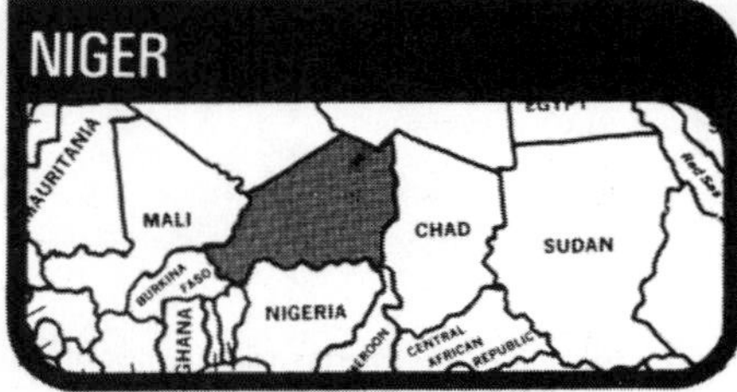

The Republic of Niger, located in West Africa's Sahara region 1,000 miles (1,609 km.) from the Mediterranean shore, has an area of 489,191 sq. mi. (1,267,000 sq. km.) and a population of *7.4 million. Capital: Niamey. The economy is based on subsistence agriculture and raising livestock. Peanuts, peanut oil, and livestock are exported.

REPUBLIC

DECIMAL COINAGE

KM# 12 3000 CFA FRANCS - 2 AFRICA
9.9300 g., Brass, 27.5 mm. **Obv:** Lion **Rev:** Elephant head on map **Edge:** Plain

Date	Mintage	F	VF	XF	Unc	BU
2003	1,200	—	—	—	35.00	—

KM# 12a 3000 CFA FRANCS - 2 AFRICA
0.9990 Silver, 27.5 mm. **Edge:** Plain

Date	Mintage	F	VF	XF	Unc	BU
2003	5	—	—	—	150	—

KM# 14 6000 CFA FRANCS - 4 AFRICA
10.1000 g., Bi-Metallic Copper-Nickel center in Brass ring, 28.3 mm. **Obv:** President Tandja, map and lion cub **Rev:** Elephant head on map **Edge:** Plain

Date	Mintage	F	VF	XF	Unc	BU
2005	500	—	—	—	50.00	—

KM# 16 6000 CFA FRANCS - 4 AFRICA
10.1000 g., Bi-Metallic Copper-Nickel center in Brass ring, 28.3 mm. **Obv:** Mosquito and "STOP MALARIA" **Rev:** Elephant head on Central African map **Edge:** Plain

Date	Mintage	F	VF	XF	Unc	BU
2005	1,200	—	—	—	45.00	—

KM# 16a 6000 CFA FRANCS - 4 AFRICA
11.0000 g., 0.9990 Bi-Metallic .999 Silver center in .999 Gold ring 0.3533 oz., 28.3 mm. **Obv:** Mosquito and "STOP MALARIA" **Rev:** Elephant head on map **Edge:** Plain

Date	Mintage	F	VF	XF	Unc	BU
2005	10	—	—	—	450	—

KM# 16b 6000 CFA FRANCS - 4 AFRICA
13.2000 g., 0.9990 Silver 0.424 oz. ASW, 28.3 mm. **Obv:** Mosquito and "STOP MALARIA" **Rev:** Elephant head on map **Edge:** Plain

Date	Mintage	F	VF	XF	Unc	BU
2005	10	—	—	—	400	—

KM# 15 150000 CFA FRANCS - 100 AFRICA
13.2000 g., 0.9990 Silver 0.424 oz. ASW, 28.4 mm. **Obv:** President Tandja, map and lion cub **Rev:** Elephant head on map **Edge:** Plain

Date	Mintage	F	VF	XF	Unc	BU
2005	25	—	—	—	250	—

KM# 15a 150000 CFA FRANCS - 100 AFRICA
13.2000 g., 0.9990 Gold Plated Silver 0.424 oz. ASW AGW, 28.4 mm. **Obv:** President Tandja, map and lion cub **Rev:** Elephant head on map **Edge:** Plain

Date	Mintage	F	VF	XF	Unc	BU
2005	25	—	—	—	250	—

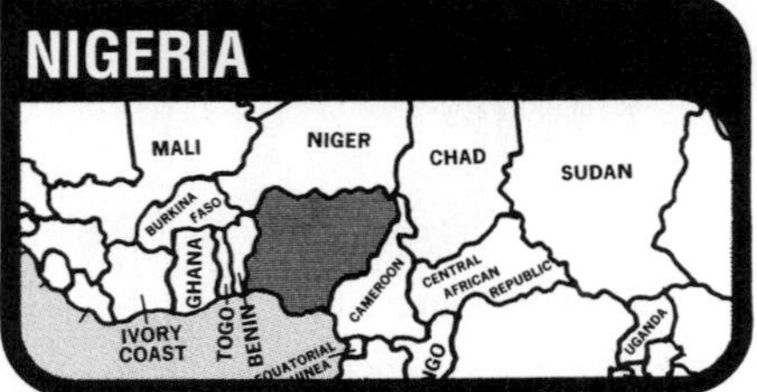

Nigeria, situated on the Atlantic coast of West Africa has an area of 356,669 sq. mi. (923,770 sq. km.).

REPUBLIC

DECIMAL COINAGE

KM# 17 KOBO
4.6700 g., Brass, 23.2 mm. **Obv:** National arms **Rev:** Monkey musicians **Edge:** Reeded

Date	Mintage	F	VF	XF	Unc	BU
2003	—	—	—	—	0.50	0.85

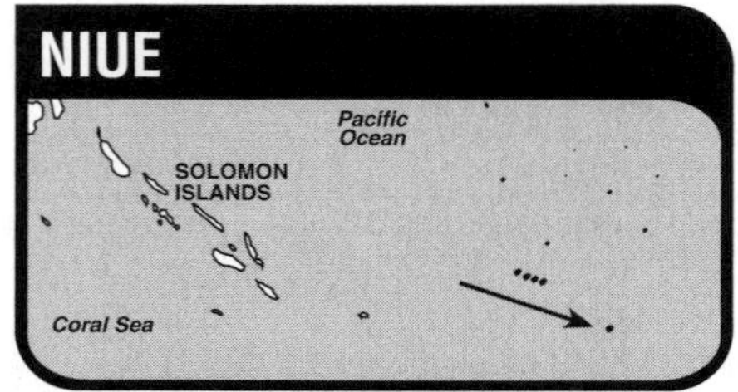

Niue, or Savage Island, a dependent state of New Zealand is located in the Pacific Ocean east of Tonga and southeast of Samoa. The size is 100 sq. mi. (260 sq. km.) with a population of *2,000. Chief village and port is Alofi. Bananas and copra are exported.

MINT MARKS
PM - Pobjoy Mint

NEW ZEALAND DEPENDENT STATE

DECIMAL COINAGE

KM# 123 DOLLAR
28.2800 g., Copper-Nickel, 38.6 mm. **Subject:** Snoopy as an Ace **Obv:** Queen's portrait **Rev:** Snoopy flying his dog house **Edge:** Reeded

Date	Mintage	F	VF	XF	Unc	BU
2001	100,000	—	—	—	4.00	6.00

KM# 128 DOLLAR
28.2800 g., Copper-Nickel, 38.6 mm. **Series:** Pokemon **Obv:** National arms **Rev:** "Bulbasaur" **Edge:** Reeded

Date	Mintage	F	VF	XF	Unc	BU
2001	100,000	—	—	—	3.50	5.00

KM# 129 DOLLAR
7.7700 g., 0.9990 Silver .2496 oz. ASW, 22 mm. **Series:** Pokemon **Obv:** National arms **Rev:** "Bulbasaur" **Edge:** Reeded

Date	Mintage	F	VF	XF	Unc	BU
2001 Proof	20,000	Value: 8.00				

KM# 131 DOLLAR
28.2800 g., Copper-Nickel, 38.6 mm. **Series:** Pokemon **Obv:** National arms **Rev:** "Charmander" **Edge:** Reeded

Date	Mintage	F	VF	XF	Unc	BU
2001	100,000	—	—	—	3.50	5.00

KM# 132 DOLLAR
7.7700 g., 0.9990 Silver .2496 oz. ASW, 22 mm. **Series:** Pokemon **Obv:** National arms **Rev:** "Charmander" **Edge:** Reeded

Date	Mintage	F	VF	XF	Unc	BU
2001 Proof	20,000	Value: 8.00				

KM# 134 DOLLAR
28.2800 g., Copper-Nickel, 38.6 mm. **Series:** Pokemon **Obv:** National arms **Rev:** "Meowth" **Edge:** Reeded

Date	Mintage	F	VF	XF	Unc	BU
2001	100,000	—	—	—	3.50	5.00

KM# 135 DOLLAR
7.7700 g., 0.9990 Silver .2496 oz. ASW, 22 mm. **Series:** Pokemon **Obv:** National arms **Rev:** "Meowth" **Edge:** Reeded

Date	Mintage	F	VF	XF	Unc	BU
2001 Proof	20,000	Value: 8.00				

KM# 137 DOLLAR
28.2800 g., Copper-Nickel, 38.6 mm. **Series:** Pokemon **Obv:** National arms **Rev:** "Pikachu" **Edge:** Reeded

Date	Mintage	F	VF	XF	Unc	BU
2001	100,000	—	—	—	3.50	5.00

KM# 138 DOLLAR
7.7700 g., 0.9990 Silver .2496 oz. ASW, 22 mm. **Series:** Pokemon **Obv:** National arms **Rev:** "Pikachu" **Edge:** Reeded

Date	Mintage	F	VF	XF	Unc	BU
2001 Proof	20,000	Value: 8.00				

KM# 140 DOLLAR
28.2800 g., Copper-Nickel, 38.6 mm. **Series:** Pokemon **Obv:** National arms **Rev:** "Squirtle" **Edge:** Reeded

Date	Mintage	F	VF	XF	Unc	BU
2001	100,000	—	—	—	3.50	5.00

KM# 141 DOLLAR

7.7700 g., 0.9990 Silver .2496 oz. ASW, 22 mm. **Series:** Pokemon **Obv:** National arms **Rev:** "Squirtle" **Edge:** Reeded

Date	Mintage	F	VF	XF	Unc	BU
2001 Proof	20,000	Value: 8.00				

KM# 146 DOLLAR

28.2800 g., Copper-Nickel, 38.6 mm. **Subject:** Pokemon Series **Obv:** National arms **Rev:** Pikachu **Edge:** Reeded

Date	Mintage	F	VF	XF	Unc	BU
2002PM	100,000	—	—	—	3.50	5.00

KM# 151 DOLLAR

28.2800 g., Copper-Nickel, 38.6 mm. **Subject:** Pokemon Series **Obv:** National arms **Rev:** Pichu **Edge:** Reeded

Date	Mintage	F	VF	XF	Unc	BU
2002PM	100,000	—	—	—	3.50	5.00

KM# 156 DOLLAR

28.2800 g., Copper-Nickel, 38.6 mm. **Subject:** Pokemon Series **Obv:** National arms **Rev:** Mewtwo **Edge:** Reeded

Date	Mintage	F	VF	XF	Unc	BU
2002PM	100,000	—	—	—	3.50	5.00

KM# 161 DOLLAR

28.2800 g., Copper-Nickel, 38.6 mm. **Subject:** Pokemon Series **Obv:** National arms **Rev:** Entei **Edge:** Reeded

Date	Mintage	F	VF	XF	Unc	BU
2002PM	100,000	—	—	—	3.50	5.00

KM# 166 DOLLAR

28.2800 g., Copper Nickel, 38.6 mm. **Subject:** Pokemon Series **Obv:** National arms **Rev:** Celebi **Edge:** Reeded

Date	Mintage	F	VF	XF	Unc	BU
2002PM	100,000	—	—	—	3.50	5.00

KM# 124 10 DOLLARS

28.2800 g., 0.9250 Silver .8410 oz. ASW, 38.6 mm. **Subject:** Snoopy as an Ace **Obv:** Queen's portrait **Rev:** Snoopy flying his dog house **Edge:** Reeded

Date	Mintage	F	VF	XF	Unc	BU
2001 Proof	10,000	Value: 20.00				

KM# 130 10 DOLLARS

28.2800 g., 0.9250 Silver .8410 oz. ASW, 38.6 mm. **Series:** Pokeman **Obv:** National arms **Rev:** "Bulbasaur" **Edge:** Reeded

Date	Mintage	F	VF	XF	Unc	BU
2001 Proof	10,000	Value: 14.00				

KM# 133 10 DOLLARS

28.2800 g., 0.9250 Silver .8410 oz. ASW, 38.6 mm. **Series:** Pokeman **Obv:** National arms **Rev:** "Charmander" **Edge:** Reeded

Date	Mintage	F	VF	XF	Unc	BU
2001 Proof	10,000	Value: 14.00				

KM# 136 10 DOLLARS

28.2800 g., 0.9250 Silver .8410 oz. ASW, 38.6 mm. **Series:** Pokeman **Obv:** National arms **Rev:** "Meowth" **Edge:** Reeded

Date	Mintage	F	VF	XF	Unc	BU
2001 Proof	10,000	Value: 14.00				

KM# 139 10 DOLLARS

28.2800 g., 0.9250 Silver .8410 oz. ASW, 38.6 mm. **Series:** Pokeman **Obv:** National arms **Rev:** "Pikachu" **Edge:** Reeded

Date	Mintage	F	VF	XF	Unc	BU
2001 Proof	10,000	Value: 14.00				

KM# 142 10 DOLLARS

28.2800 g., 0.9250 Silver .8410 oz. ASW, 38.6 mm. **Series:** Pokeman **Obv:** National arms **Rev:** "Squirtle" **Edge:** Reeded

Date	Mintage	F	VF	XF	Unc	BU
2001 Proof	10,000	Value: 14.00				

KM# 147 10 DOLLARS

28.2800 g., 0.9250 Silver 0.841 oz. ASW, 38.6 mm. **Subject:** Pokémon Series **Obv:** National arms **Rev:** Pikachu **Edge:** Reeded

Date	Mintage	F	VF	XF	Unc	BU
2002PM Proof	10,000	Value: 14.00				

KM# 152 10 DOLLARS

28.2800 g., 0.9250 Silver 0.841 oz. ASW, 38.6 mm. **Subject:** Pokémon Series **Obv:** National arms **Rev:** Pichu **Edge:** Reeded

Date	Mintage	F	VF	XF	Unc	BU
2002PM Proof	10,000	Value: 14.00				

KM# 157 10 DOLLARS

28.2800 g., 0.9250 Silver 0.841 oz. ASW, 38.6 mm. **Subject:** Pokémon Series **Rev:** Mewtwo **Edge:** Reeded

Date	Mintage	F	VF	XF	Unc	BU
2002PM Proof	10,000	Value: 14.00				

KM# 162 10 DOLLARS

28.2800 g., 0.9250 Silver 0.841 oz. ASW, 38.6 mm. **Subject:** Pokémon Series **Obv:** National arms **Rev:** Entei **Edge:** Reeded

Date	Mintage	F	VF	XF	Unc	BU
2002PM Proof	10,000	Value: 14.00				

KM# 167 10 DOLLARS

28.2800 g., 0.9250 Silver 0.841 oz. ASW, 38.6 mm. **Subject:** Pokémon Series **Obv:** National arms **Rev:** Celebi **Edge:** Reeded

Date	Mintage	F	VF	XF	Unc	BU
2002PM Proof	10,000	Value: 14.00				

KM# 125 20 DOLLARS

1.2400 g., 0.9999 Gold .0399 oz. AGW, 13.9 mm. **Subject:** Snoopy as an Ace **Obv:** Queen's portrait **Rev:** Snoopy flying his dog house **Edge:** Reeded

Date	Mintage	F	VF	XF	Unc	BU
2001 Proof	10,000	Value: 32.00				

KM# 148 20 DOLLARS

1.2400 g., 0.9999 Gold 0.0399 oz. AGW, 13.92 mm. **Subject:** Pokémon Series **Obv:** National arms **Rev:** Pikachu **Edge:** Reeded

Date	Mintage	F	VF	XF	Unc	BU
2002PM Proof	10,000	Value: 30.00				

KM# 153 20 DOLLARS

1.2400 g., 0.9999 Gold 0.0399 oz. AGW, 13.9 mm. **Subject:** Pokémon Series **Obv:** National arms **Rev:** Pichu **Edge:** Reeded

Date	Mintage	F	VF	XF	Unc	BU
2002PM Proof	10,000	Value: 30.00				

KM# 158 20 DOLLARS

1.2400 g., 0.9999 Gold 0.0399 oz. AGW, 13.92 mm. **Subject:** Pokémon Series **Rev:** Mewtwo **Edge:** Reeded

Date	Mintage	F	VF	XF	Unc	BU
2002PM Proof	10,000	Value: 30.00				

KM# 163 20 DOLLARS

, 13.9 mm. **Subject:** Pokémon Series **Obv:** National arms **Rev:** Entei **Edge:** Reeded

Date	Mintage	F	VF	XF	Unc	BU
2002PM Proof	10,000	Value: 30.00				

KM# 168 20 DOLLARS

1.2400 g., 0.9999 Gold 0.0399 oz. AGW, 13.9 mm. **Subject:** Pokémon Series **Obv:** National arms **Rev:** Celebi **Edge:** Reeded

Date	Mintage	F	VF	XF	Unc	BU
2002PM Proof	10,000	Value: 30.00				

KM# 126 50 DOLLARS

3.1100 g., 0.9999 Gold .1000 oz. AGW, 17.9 mm. **Subject:** Snoopy as an Ace **Obv:** Queen's portrait **Rev:** Snoopy flying his dog house **Edge:** Reeded

Date	Mintage	F	VF	XF	Unc	BU
2001 Proof	7,500	Value: 70.00				

KM# 149 50 DOLLARS

3.1100 g., 0.9999 Gold 0.1 oz. AGW, 17.9 mm. **Subject:** Pokémon Series **Obv:** National arms **Rev:** Pikachu **Edge:** Reeded

Date	Mintage	F	VF	XF	Unc	BU
2002PM Proof	7,500	Value: 65.00				

KM# 154 50 DOLLARS

3.1100 g., 0.9999 Gold 0.1 oz. AGW, 17.9 mm. **Subject:** Pokémon Series **Obv:** National arms **Rev:** Pichu **Edge:** Reeded

Date	Mintage	F	VF	XF	Unc	BU
2002PM Proof	7,500	Value: 65.00				

KM# 159 50 DOLLARS

3.1100 g., 0.9999 Gold 0.1 oz. AGW, 17.9 mm. **Subject:** Pokémon Series **Obv:** National arms **Rev:** Mewtwo **Edge:** Reeded

Date	Mintage	F	VF	XF	Unc	BU
2002PM Proof	7,500	Value: 65.00				

KM# 164 50 DOLLARS

3.1100 g., 0.9999 Gold 0.1 oz. AGW, 17.9 mm. **Subject:** Pokémon Series **Obv:** National arms **Rev:** Entei **Edge:** Reeded

Date	Mintage	F	VF	XF	Unc	BU
2002PM Proof	7,500	Value: 65.00				

KM# 169 50 DOLLARS

3.1100 g., 0.9999 Gold 0.1 oz. AGW, 17.9 mm. **Subject:** Pokémon Series **Obv:** National arms **Rev:** Celebi **Edge:** Reeded

Date	Mintage	F	VF	XF	Unc	BU
2002PM Proof	7,500	Value: 65.00				

KM# 127 100 DOLLARS

6.2200 g., 0.9999 Gold .2000 oz. AGW, 22 mm. **Subject:** Snoopy as an Ace **Obv:** Queen's portrait **Rev:** Snoopy flying his dog house **Edge:** Reeded

Date	Mintage	F	VF	XF	Unc	BU
2001 Proof	5,000	Value: 145				

KM# 150 100 DOLLARS

6.2200 g., 0.9999 Gold 0.2 oz. AGW, 22 mm. **Subject:** Pokémon Series **Obv:** National arms **Rev:** Pikachu **Edge:** Reeded

Date	Mintage	F	VF	XF	Unc	BU
2002PM Proof	5,000	Value: 130				

KM# 155 100 DOLLARS

6.2200 g., 0.9999 Gold 0.2 oz. AGW, 22 mm. **Subject:** Pokémon Series **Obv:** National arms **Rev:** Pichu **Edge:** Reeded

Date	Mintage	F	VF	XF	Unc	BU
2002PM Proof	5,000	Value: 130				

KM# 160 100 DOLLARS

6.2200 g., 0.9999 Gold 0.2 oz. AGW, 22 mm. **Subject:** Pokémon Series **Obv:** National arms **Rev:** Mewtwo **Edge:** Reeded

Date	Mintage	F	VF	XF	Unc	BU
2002PM Proof	5,000	Value: 130				

KM# 165 100 DOLLARS

6.2200 g., 0.9999 Gold 0.2 oz. AGW, 22 mm. **Subject:** Pokémon Series **Obv:** National arms **Rev:** Entei **Edge:** Reeded

Date	Mintage	F	VF	XF	Unc	BU
2002PM Proof	5,000	Value: 130				

KM# 170 100 DOLLARS

6.2200 g., 0.9999 Gold 0.2 oz. AGW, 22 mm. **Subject:** Pokémon Series **Obv:** National arms **Rev:** Celebi **Edge:** reeded

Date	Mintage	F	VF	XF	Unc	BU
2002PM Proof	5,000	Value: 130				

The Kingdom of Norway (*Norge, Noreg*), a constitutional monarchy located in northwestern Europe, has an area of 150,000sq. mi. (324,220 sq. km.), including the island territories of Spitzbergen (Svalbard) and Jan Mayen, and a population of *4.2 million. Capital: Oslo (Christiania). The diversified economic base of Norway includes shipping, fishing, forestry, agriculture, and manufacturing. Nonferrous metals, paper and paperboard, paper pulp, iron, steel and oil are exported.

RULERS
Harald V, 1991-

MINT MARKS
(h) - Crossed hammers – Kongsberg

MONETARY SYSTEM
100 Ore = 1 Krone (30 Skilling)

KINGDOM

DECIMAL COINAGE

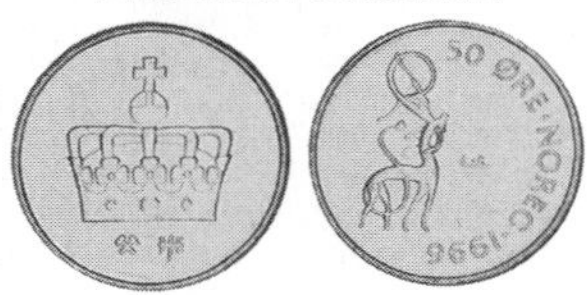

KM# 460 50 ORE

3.6000 g., Bronze **Obv:** Crown **Rev:** Stylized animal, denomination **Designer:** Grazyna Jolanta Linday

Date	Mintage	VG	F	VF	XF	BU
2001 without star	16,848,250	—	—	—	—	0.40
2001 with star	13,291,750	—	—	—	—	0.40
2001 Proof	—	Value: 10.00				
2002	—	—	—	—	—	0.40
2002 Proof	—	Value: 10.00				
2003	—	—	—	—	—	0.40
2003 Proof	—	Value: 10.00				
2004	—	—	—	—	—	0.40
2004 Proof	—	Value: 10.00				
2005	—	—	—	—	—	0.40
2005 Proof	—	Value: 10.00				
2006	—	—	—	—	—	0.40

KM# 462 KRONE

4.3000 g., Copper-Nickel **Obv:** Monogram cross **Rev:** Bird on vine above date and denomination

Date	Mintage	VG	F	VF	XF	BU
2001 without star	43,128,650	—	—	—	—	0.65
2001 with star	7,355,350	—	—	—	—	0.75
2001 Proof	—	Value: 10.00				
2002	—	—	—	—	—	0.65
2002 Proof	—	Value: 10.00				
2003	—	—	—	—	—	0.65
2003 Proof	—	Value: 10.00				
2004	—	—	—	—	—	0.65
2004 Proof	—	Value: 10.00				
2005	—	—	—	—	—	0.65
2005 Proof	—	Value: 10.00				
2006	—	—	—	—	—	0.65

KM# 463 5 KRONER

7.8500 g., Copper-Nickel **Subject:** Order of St. Olaf **Rev:** Denomination and date

Date	Mintage	VG	F	VF	XF	BU
2001	460,000	—	—	—	—	1.50
2001 Proof	—	Value: 12.50				
2002	—	—	—	—	—	1.50
2002 Proof	—	Value: 12.50				
2003	—	—	—	—	—	1.50
2003 Proof	—	Value: 12.50				
2004	—	—	—	—	—	1.50
2004 Proof	—	Value: 12.50				
2005	—	—	—	—	—	1.50
2005 Proof	—	Value: 12.50				
2006	—	—	—	—	—	1.50

KM# 457 10 KRONER

6.8000 g., Copper-Zinc-Nickel **Rev:** Church rooftop **Designer:** Ingrid Austlid Rise

Date	Mintage	VG	F	VF	XF	BU
2001 without star	9,837,500	—	—	—	—	3.50
2001 with star	10,000	—	—	—	—	7.50
2001 Proof	—	Value: 10.00				
2002	—	—	—	—	—	3.50
2002 Proof	—	Value: 10.00				
2003	—	—	—	—	—	3.50
2003 Proof	—	Value: 10.00				
2004	—	—	—	—	—	3.50
2004 Proof	—	Value: 10.00				
2005	—	—	—	—	—	3.50
2005 Proof	—	Value: 10.00				
2006	—	—	—	—	—	3.50

KM# 478 20 KRONER (5 Speciedaler)

9.9000 g., Copper-Zinc-Nickel, 27.5 mm. **Ruler:** Harald V **Subject:** First Norwegian Railroad **Obv:** King Harald V **Rev:** Switch track and value **Edge:** Plain

Date	Mintage	F	VF	XF	Unc	BU
2005	10,000	—	—	—	17.50	20.00

KM# 453 20 KRONER

Copper-Zinc-Nickel **Designer:** Ingrid Austlid Rise

Date	Mintage	VG	F	VF	XF	BU
2001	4,178,010	—	—	—	—	6.50
2001 Proof	—	Value: 25.00				
2002	—	—	—	—	—	6.50
2002 Proof	—	Value: 25.00				
2003	—	—	—	—	—	6.50
2003 Proof	—	Value: 25.00				
2005	—	—	—	—	—	6.50
2005 Proof	—	Value: 25.00				

KM# 471 20 KRONER

9.7300 g., Nickel-Brass, 27.4 mm. **Ruler:** Harald V **Subject:** Niels Henrik Abel **Obv:** King's portrait **Rev:** Mathematical graphs **Edge:** Plain

Date	Mintage	F	VF	XF	Unc	BU
2002	—	—	—	—	10.00	12.50

KM# 469 100 KRONER

33.6000 g., 0.9250 Silver .9992 oz. ASW, 39 mm. **Subject:** Nobel Peace Prize Centennial **Obv:** National arms **Rev:** Nobel's portrait **Edge:** Plain

Date	Mintage	F	VF	XF	Unc	BU
2001 Proof	Est. 50,000	Value: 60.00				

KM# 472 100 KRONER

33.8000 g., 0.9250 Silver 1.0052 oz. ASW, 39 mm. **Ruler:** Harald V **Subject:** 1905 Liberation **Obv:** Three kings **Rev:** Farm field **Edge:** Plain

Date	Mintage	F	VF	XF	Unc	BU
2003 Proof	65,000	Value: 70.00				

KM# 474 100 KRONER

33.8000 g., 0.9250 Silver 1.0052 oz. ASW, 39 mm. **Ruler:** Harald V **Subject:** 1905 Liberation **Obv:** Three kings **Rev:** Off shore ocean oil well **Edge:** Plain

Date	Mintage	F	VF	XF	Unc	BU
2004 Proof	65,000	Value: 70.00				

KM# 476 100 KRONER

33.8000 g., 0.9250 Silver 1.0052 oz. ASW, 39 mm. **Ruler:** Harald V **Obv:** Three kings **Rev:** Circuit board **Edge:** Plain

Date	Mintage	F	VF	XF	Unc	BU
2005 Proof	—	Value: 70.00				

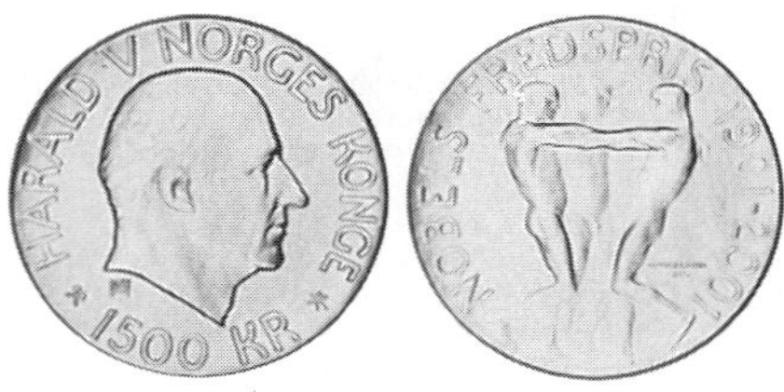

KM# 470 1500 KRONER

16.9600 g., 0.9170 Gold .5000 oz. AGW, 27 mm. **Ruler:** Harald V **Subject:** Nobel Peace Prize Centennial **Obv:** King's portrait **Rev:** Reverse design of the prize medal **Edge:** Plain

Date	Mintage	VG	F	VF	XF	BU
ND(2001) Matte Proof	7,500	Value: 385				

KM# 473 1500 KRONER

16.9600 g., 0.9170 Gold 0.5 oz. AGW, 27 mm. **Ruler:** Harald V **Subject:** 1905 Liberation **Obv:** Three kings **Rev:** Various leaf types **Edge:** Plain

Date	Mintage	F	VF	XF	Unc	BU
2003 Proof	10,000	Value: 500				

KM# 475 1500 KRONER

16.9600 g., 0.9170 Gold 0.5 oz. AGW, 27 mm. **Ruler:** Harald V **Subject:** 1905 Liberation **Obv:** Three kings **Rev:** Liquid drops on hard surface **Edge:** Plain

Date	Mintage	F	VF	XF	Unc	BU
2004 Proof	10,000	Value: 500				

KM# 477 1500 KRONER

16.9600 g., 0.9170 Gold 0.5 oz. AGW, 27 mm. **Obv:** Three kings **Rev:** Binary language **Edge:** Plain

Date	Mintage	F	VF	XF	Unc	BU
2005 Proof	—	Value: 500				

MINT SETS

KM#	Date	Mintage	Identification	Issue Price	Mkt Val
MS59	2001 (5)	55,000	KM453, 457, 460, 462, 463. Folder.	20.00	22.00
MS60	2001 (5)	30,000	KM453, 457, 460, 462, 463. Baby gift set.	18.00	20.00
MS61	2001 (5)	2,000	KM453, 457, 460, 462, 463 plus medal.	27.00	27.00
MS62	2001 (5)	—	KM453, 457, 460, 462, 463. Sandhill.	—	20.00

OMAN

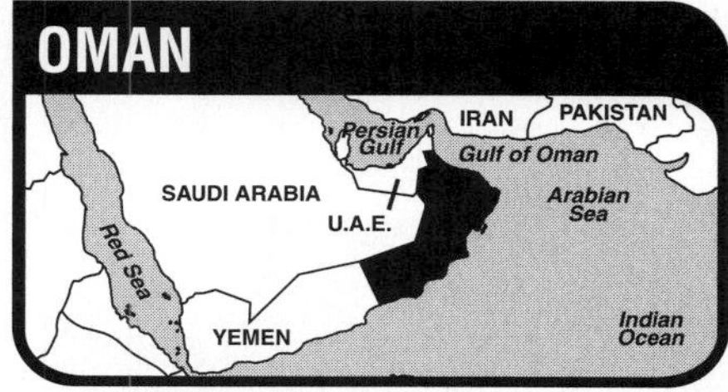

The Sultanate of Oman (formerly Muscat and Oman), an independent monarchy located in the southeastern part of the Arabian Peninsula, has an area of 82,030 sq. mi. (212,460 sq. km.) and a population of *1.3 million. Capital: Muscat. The economy is based on agriculture, herding and petroleum. Petroleum products, dates, fish and hides are exported.

TITLES

مسقط
Muscat

عمان
Oman

SULTANATE

REFORM COINAGE

1000 Baisa = 1 Omani Rial

KM# 154 OMANI RIAL
28.2800 g., 0.9250 Silver 0.841 oz. ASW, 38.6 mm. **Subject:** 31st National Day and Environment Year **Obv:** National arms **Rev:** Multicolor map design **Edge:** Reeded

Date	Mintage	F	VF	XF	Unc	BU
2001	500	—	—	—	60.00	—
2001 Proof	105	Value: 100				

KM# 154a OMANI RIAL
37.8000 g., 0.9160 Gold 1.1132 oz. AGW, 38.6 mm. **Subject:** 31st National Day and Environment Year **Obv:** National arms **Rev:** Multicolor map design **Edge:** Reeded

Date	Mintage	F	VF	XF	Unc	BU
2001	350	—	—	—	850	—
2001 Proof	105	Value: 950				

KM# 155 OMANI RIAL
28.2800 g., 0.9250 Silver 0.841 oz. ASW, 38.6 mm. **Obv:** National arms **Rev:** Arab sailing ship and route on map **Edge:** Reeded

Date	Mintage	F	VF	XF	Unc	BU
2003 Proof	—	Value: 50.00				

PAKISTAN

The Islamic Republic of Pakistan, located on the Indian subcontinent between India and Afghanistan, has an area of 310,404 sq. mi. (803,940 sq. km.) and a population of130 million. Capital: Islamabad. Pakistan is mainly an agricultural land although the industrial base is expanding rapidly. Yarn, textiles, cotton, rice, medical instruments, sports equipment and leather are exported.

TITLE

پاکستان
Pakistan

ISLAMIC REPUBLIC

DECIMAL COINAGE

100 Paisa (Pice) = 1 Rupee

KM# 62 RUPEE
4.0000 g., Bronze, 20 mm. **Obv:** Portrait of Mohammad Ali Jinnah **Rev:** Mosque and denomination **Edge:** Milled

Date	Mintage	F	VF	XF	Unc	BU
2001	—	0.20	0.25	0.35	0.65	0.75
2002	—	0.20	0.25	0.35	0.65	0.75
2003	—	0.20	0.25	0.35	0.65	0.75
2004	—	0.20	0.25	0.35	0.65	0.75
2005	—	0.20	0.25	0.35	0.65	0.75

KM# 64 2 RUPEES
4.0000 g., Nickel-Brass, 22.5 mm. **Obv:** National emblem **Rev:** Clouds above mosque **Edge:** Reeded

Date	Mintage	F	VF	XF	Unc	BU
2001	—	0.20	0.30	0.45	0.85	1.00
2002	—	0.20	0.30	0.45	0.85	1.00
2003	—	0.20	0.30	0.45	0.85	1.00
2004	—	0.20	0.30	0.45	0.85	1.00
2005	—	0.20	0.30	0.45	0.85	1.00

KM# 65 5 RUPEES
6.5000 g., Copper-Nickel, 24 mm. **Obv:** National emblem **Rev:** Value in pentagon **Edge:** Reeded

Date	Mintage	F	VF	XF	Unc	BU
2002	—	0.50	1.00	1.50	3.00	3.25
2003	—	0.50	1.00	1.50	3.00	3.25
2004	—	0.50	1.00	1.50	3.00	3.25

KM# 66 10 RUPEES
7.5000 g., Copper-Nickel, 27 mm. **Obv:** National emblem, date and value **Rev:** Flowers and inscription **Rev. Inscription:** Year of Fatima Jinnah **Edge:** Reeded

Date	Mintage	F	VF	XF	Unc	BU
2003	200,000	—	—	4.00	6.50	7.50

PALAU

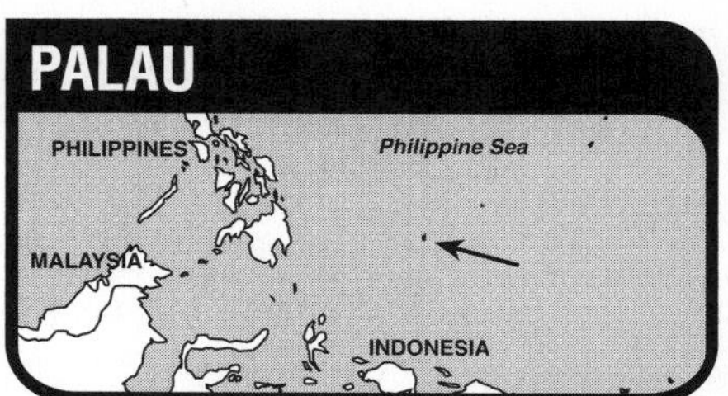

The Republic of Palau, a group of about 100 islands and islets, is generally considered a part of the Caroline Islands. It is located about 1,000 miles southeast of Manila and about the same distance southwest of Saipan and has an area of 179 sq. mi. and a population of 12,116. Capital: Koror.

REPUBLIC

COLLECTOR COINAGE

KM# 60 DOLLAR
26.8000 g., Copper-Nickel, 37.2 mm. **Obv:** Seated Mermaid with raised arm **Rev:** Two glittering fish **Edge:** Reeded

Date	Mintage	F	VF	XF	Unc	BU
2001 Proof	—	Value: 30.00				

KM# 61 DOLLAR
26.8000 g., Copper-Nickel, 37.2 mm. **Obv:** Prone Mermaid **Rev:** Two glittering fish **Edge:** Reeded

Date	Mintage	F	VF	XF	Unc	BU
2001 Proof	—	Value: 35.00				

KM# 62 DOLLAR
26.8000 g., Copper-Nickel, 37.2 mm. **Subject:** Marine Life Protection **Obv:** Figurehead mermaid **Rev:** Black and white striped fish **Edge:** Reeded

Date	Mintage	F	VF	XF	Unc	BU
2001 Proof	—	Value: 30.00				

KM# 86 DOLLAR
1.2441 g., 0.9999 Gold 0.04 oz. AGW, 13.94 mm. **Obv:** Prone Mermaid **Rev:** Two fish (like KM-61)

Date	Mintage	F	VF	XF	Unc	BU
2001 Proof	—	Value: 35.00				

KM# 87 DOLLAR
1.2441 g., 0.9999 Gold 0.04 oz. AGW, 13.94 mm. **Obv:** Seated Mermaid with raised right arm **Rev:** Two fish (like KM-60)

Date	Mintage	F	VF	XF	Unc	BU
2001 Proof	—	Value: 35.00				

KM# 88 DOLLAR
1.2441 g., 0.9999 Gold 0.04 oz. AGW, 13.94 mm. **Obv:** Figurehead Mermaid **Rev:** Jellyfish (like KM-52)

Date	Mintage	F	VF	XF	Unc	BU
2001 Proof	—	Value: 35.00				

KM# 89 DOLLAR
1.2441 g., 0.9999 Gold 0.04 oz. AGW, 13.94 mm. **Obv:** Figurehead Mermaid **Rev:** Angelfish (like KM-62)

Date	Mintage	F	VF	XF	Unc	BU
2001 Proof	—	Value: 35.00				

KM# 52 DOLLAR
26.8600 g., Copper Nickel, 37.3 mm. **Subject:** Marine Life Protection **Obv:** Mermaid figurehead **Rev:** Multicolor jellyfish **Edge:** Reeded

Date	Mintage	F	VF	XF	Unc	BU
2001 Proof	—	Value: 30.00				

KM# 56 DOLLAR
26.8000 g., Copper-Nickel, 37.2 mm. **Subject:** Marine Life Protection **Obv:** Mermaid figurehead **Rev:** Multicolor fish scene **Edge:** Reeded

Date	Mintage	F	VF	XF	Unc	BU
2002 Proof	—	Value: 30.00				

KM# 57 DOLLAR
26.8000 g., Copper-Nickel, 37.2 mm. **Subject:** Marine Life Protection **Obv:** Mermaid figurehead on approaching ship **Rev:** Multicolor reflective fish scene under an acrylic layer **Edge:** Reeded

Date	Mintage	F	VF	XF	Unc	BU
2002 Proof	—	Value: 30.00				

KM# 90 DOLLAR
1.2441 g., 0.9999 Gold 0.04 oz. AGW, 13.94 mm. **Obv:** Figurehead Mermaid **Rev:** Sperm Whales (like KM-64)

Date	Mintage	F	VF	XF	Unc	BU
2002 Proof	—	Value: 35.00				

KM# 91 DOLLAR
1.2441 g., 0.9999 Gold 0.04 oz. AGW, 13.94 mm. **Obv:** Figurehead Mermaid **Rev:** Pufferfish (like KM-57)

Date	Mintage	F	VF	XF	Unc	BU
2002 Proof	—	Value: 35.00				

KM# 92 DOLLAR
1.2441 g., 0.9999 Gold 0.04 oz. AGW, 13.94 mm. **Obv:** Seated Mermaid with both arms raised **Rev:** Jellyfish (like KM-65)

Date	Mintage	F	VF	XF	Unc	BU
2002 Proof	—	Value: 35.00				

KM# 93 DOLLAR
1.2441 g., 0.9999 Gold 0.04 oz. AGW, 13.94 mm. **Obv:** Figurehead Mermaid **Rev:** Doctorfish (like KM-63)

Date	Mintage	F	VF	XF	Unc	BU
2002 Proof	—	Value: 35.00				

KM# 94 DOLLAR
1.2441 g., 0.9999 Gold 0.04 oz. AGW, 13.94 mm. **Obv:** Figurehead mermaid **Rev:** Lionfish

Date	Mintage	F	VF	XF	Unc	BU
2002 Proof	—	Value: 35.00				

KM# 63 DOLLAR
26.8000 g., Copper-Nickel, 37.2 mm. **Subject:** Marine Life Protection **Obv:** Figurehead mermaid **Rev:** Purple fish **Edge:** Reeded

Date	Mintage	F	VF	XF	Unc	BU
2002 Proof	—	Value: 30.00				

KM# 64 DOLLAR
26.8000 g., Copper-Nickel, 37.2 mm. **Subject:** Marine Life Protection **Obv:** Figurehead mermaid **Rev:** Multicolor whales **Edge:** Reeded

Date	Mintage	F	VF	XF	Unc	BU
2002 Proof	—	Value: 30.00				

KM# 65 DOLLAR
26.8000 g., Copper-Nickel, 37.2 mm. **Subject:** Marine Life Protection **Obv:** Mermaid washing her hair **Rev:** Multicolor jellyfish **Edge:** Reeded

Date	Mintage	F	VF	XF	Unc	BU
2002 Proof	—	Value: 30.00				

KM# 66 DOLLAR
26.8000 g., Copper-Nickel, 37.2 mm. **Subject:** Marine Life Protection **Obv:** Mermaid under sun **Rev:** Orange crab **Edge:** Reeded

Date	Mintage	F	VF	XF	Unc	BU
2003 Proof	—	Value: 32.00				

KM# 67 DOLLAR
26.8000 g., Copper-Nickel, 37.2 mm. **Subject:** Marine Life Protection **Obv:** Mermaid riding turtle **Rev:** Two glittering fish **Edge:** Reeded

Date	Mintage	F	VF	XF	Unc	BU
2003 Proof	—	Value: 30.00				

KM# 68 DOLLAR
26.8000 g., Copper-Nickel, 37.2 mm. **Subject:** Marine Life Protection **Obv:** Mermaid seated on a clam shell **Rev:** Multicolor Orca **Edge:** Reeded

Date	Mintage	F	VF	XF	Unc	BU
2003 Proof	—	Value: 30.00				

KM# 69 DOLLAR
26.8000 g., Copper-Nickel, 37.2 mm. **Subject:** Marine Life Protection **Obv:** Mermaid playing shell guitar **Rev:** Green fish **Edge:** Reeded

Date	Mintage	F	VF	XF	Unc	BU
2003 Proof	—	Value: 30.00				

KM# 95 DOLLAR
1.2441 g., 0.9999 Gold 0.04 oz. AGW, 13.94 mm. **Obv:** Mermaid riding a dolphin **Rev:** Starfish

Date	Mintage	F	VF	XF	Unc	BU
2003 Proof	—	Value: 35.00				

KM# 96 DOLLAR
1.2441 g., 0.9999 Gold 0.04 oz. AGW, 13.94 mm. **Obv:** Mermaid sitting on a shell **Rev:** Orca (like KM-68) **Edge:** Reeded Proof

Date	Mintage	F	VF	XF	Unc	BU
2003 Proof	—	Value: 35.00				

KM# 98 DOLLAR
1.2441 g., 0.9999 Gold 0.04 oz. AGW, 13.94 mm. **Obv:** Mermaid riding a turtle **Rev:** Amphipron fish (like KM-67)

Date	Mintage	F	VF	XF	Unc	BU
2003 Proof	—	Value: 35.00				

KM# 97 DOLLAR
1.2441 g., 0.9999 Gold 0.04 oz. AGW, 13.94 mm. **Obv:** Mermaid under radiant sun **Rev:** Crab (like KM-66)

Date	Mintage	F	VF	XF	Unc	BU
2003 Proof	—	Value: 35.00				

KM# 100 DOLLAR
1.2441 g., 0.9999 Gold 0.04 oz. AGW, 13.94 mm. **Obv:** Mermaid and two dolphins **Rev:** Dolphin head (like KM-72)

Date	Mintage	F	VF	XF	Unc	BU
2004 Proof	—	Value: 35.00				

KM# 99 DOLLAR
1.2441 g., 0.9999 Gold 0.04 oz. AGW, 13.94 mm. **Obv:** Mermaid under radiant sun **Rev:** Clownfish (like KM-71)

Date	Mintage	F	VF	XF	Unc	BU
2004 Proof	—	Value: 35.00				

KM# 70 DOLLAR
26.8000 g., Copper-Nickel, 37.2 mm. **Subject:** Marine Life Protection **Obv:** Mermaid seated on rock **Rev:** School of blue fish **Edge:** Reeded

Date	Mintage	F	VF	XF	Unc	BU
2004 Proof	—	Value: 30.00				

KM# 71 DOLLAR
26.8000 g., Copper-Nickel, 37.2 mm. **Subject:** Marine Life Protection **Obv:** Mermaid, right rear side view **Rev:** Orange and white fish **Edge:** Reeded

Date	Mintage	F	VF	XF	Unc	BU
2004 Proof	—	Value: 30.00				

KM# 72 DOLLAR
26.8000 g., Copper-Nickel, 37.2 mm. **Subject:** Marine Life Protection **Obv:** Mermaid and two dolphins **Rev:** Multicolor dolphin **Edge:** Reeded

Date	Mintage	F	VF	XF	Unc	BU
2004 Proof	—	Value: 30.00				

KM# 101 DOLLAR
1.2441 g., 0.9999 Gold 0.04 oz. AGW, 13.94 mm. **Obv:** Mermaid sitting in a shell listening to a conch shell **Rev:** Sea Horse

Date	Mintage	F	VF	XF	Unc	BU
2005 Proof	—	Value: 35.00				

KM# 75 5 DOLLARS
25.0000 g., 0.9000 Silver, 37.2 mm. **Subject:** Marine Life Protection **Obv:** Neptune behind Polynesian ship **Rev:** Black and white striped fish **Edge:** Reeded

Date	Mintage	F	VF	XF	Unc	BU
2001 Proof	—	Value: 60.00				

KM# 76 5 DOLLARS
Silver, 37.2 mm. **Subject:** Marine Life Protection **Obv:** Neptune riding seahorse **Rev:** Large greenish fish **Edge:** Reeded

Date	Mintage	F	VF	XF	Unc	BU
2001 Proof	—	Value: 60.00				

KM# 115 5 DOLLARS
25.0000 g., 0.9000 Silver 0.7234 oz. ASW, 37.2 mm. **Obv:** Neptune waist deep in water(like KM-75) above value with mermaid to the left and behind **Rev:** Multicolor irridescent fish scene **Edge:** Reeded

Date	Mintage	F	VF	XF	Unc	BU
2001 Proof	—	Value: 60.00				

KM# 53 5 DOLLARS
25.0000 g., 0.9000 Silver .7234 oz. ASW, 37.2 mm. **Series:** Marine Life Protection **Obv:** Neptune **Rev:** Multicolor jellyfish **Edge:** Reeded

Date	Mintage	F	VF	XF	Unc	BU
2001	—	—	—	—	60.00	—

KM# 77 5 DOLLARS
25.0000 g., 0.9000 Silver, 37.2 mm. **Subject:** Marine Life Protection **Obv:** Neptune in shell boat **Rev:** Purple Doctor fish **Edge:** Reeded

Date	Mintage	F	VF	XF	Unc	BU
2002 Proof	—	Value: 60.00				

KM# 78 5 DOLLARS
25.0000 g., 0.9000 Silver, 37.2 mm. **Subject:** Marine Life Protection **Obv:** Neptune in sea chariot **Rev:** Multicolor whales **Edge:** Reeded

Date	Mintage	F	VF	XF	Unc	BU
2002 Proof	—	Value: 60.00				

KM# 79 5 DOLLARS
25.0000 g., 0.9000 Silver, 37.2 mm. **Subject:** Marine Life Protection **Obv:** Zeus **Rev:** Multicolor puffer fish **Edge:** Reeded

Date	Mintage	F	VF	XF	Unc	BU
2002 Proof	—	Value: 60.00				

KM# 80 5 DOLLARS
25.0000 g., 0.9000 Silver, 37.2 mm. **Subject:** Marine Life Protection **Obv:** Neptune standing behind Polynesian ship **Rev:** Multicolor Jellyfish **Edge:** Reeded

Date	Mintage	F	VF	XF	Unc	BU
2002 Proof	—	Value: 60.00				

KM# 102 5 DOLLARS
25.0000 g., 0.9000 Silver 0.7234 oz. ASW, 32 mm.
Obv: Neptune in sea chariot with two merhorses **Rev:** Two multicolor reflective fish

Date	Mintage	F	VF	XF	Unc	BU
2002 Proof	—	Value: 60.00				

KM# 103 5 DOLLARS
25.0000 g., 0.9000 Silver 0.7234 oz. ASW, 32 mm.
Obv: Neptune standing in waves **Rev:** Multicolor starfish

Date	Mintage	F	VF	XF	Unc	BU
2003 Proof	—	Value: 60.00				

KM# 104 5 DOLLARS
25.0000 g., 0.9000 Silver 0.7234 oz. ASW, 32 mm. **Obv:** Neptune standing in sea chariot **Rev:** Two multicolor reflective fish

Date	Mintage	F	VF	XF	Unc	BU
2003 Proof	—	Value: 60.00				

KM# 105 5 DOLLARS
25.0000 g., 0.9000 Silver 0.7234 oz. ASW, 32 mm. **Subject:** Three mermaids in Neptune's beard **Rev:** Multicolor Orca

Date	Mintage	F	VF	XF	Unc	BU
2003 Proof	—	Value: 60.00				

KM# 106 5 DOLLARS
25.0000 g., 0.9000 Silver 0.7234 oz. ASW, 32 mm. **Obv:** Neptune in sea chariot **Rev:** Multicolor Napoleon Fish

Date	Mintage	F	VF	XF	Unc	BU
2003 Proof	—	Value: 60.00				

KM# 107 5 DOLLARS
25.0000 g., 0.9000 Silver 0.7234 oz. ASW, 32 mm. **Obv:** Neptune seated behind mermaid **Rev:** Multicolor school of fish

Date	Mintage	F	VF	XF	Unc	BU
2004 Proof	—	Value: 60.00				

KM# 108 5 DOLLARS
25.0000 g., 0.9000 Silver 0.7234 oz. ASW, 32 mm.
Obv: Standing Neptune and ship **Rev:** Multicolor Porcupine fish

Date	Mintage	F	VF	XF	Unc	BU
2004 Proof	—	Value: 60.00				

KM# 109 5 DOLLARS
25.0000 g., 0.9000 Silver 0.7234 oz. ASW, 32 mm. **Obv:** Neptune in sea chariot **Rev:** Multicolor Loggerhead turtle

Date	Mintage	F	VF	XF	Unc	BU
2004 Proof	—	Value: 60.00				

KM# 110 5 DOLLARS
25.0000 g., 0.9000 Silver 0.7234 oz. ASW, 32 mm.
Obv: Neptune and merhorse **Rev:** Multicolor dolphin head

Date	Mintage	F	VF	XF	Unc	BU
2004 Proof	—	Value: 60.00				

KM# 81 5 DOLLARS
25.0000 g., 0.9000 Silver, 37.2 mm. **Subject:** Marine Life Protection **Obv:** Neptune with treasure chest **Rev:** Orange and white fish **Edge:** Reeded

Date	Mintage	F	VF	XF	Unc	BU
2004 Proof	—	Value: 60.00				

KM# 111 5 DOLLARS
25.0000 g., 0.9000 Silver 0.7234 oz. ASW, 32 mm. **Obv:** Neptune cavorting with two mermaids **Rev:** Multicolor sea horse

Date	Mintage	F	VF	XF	Unc	BU
2005 Proof	—	Value: 60.00				

KM# 113 5 DOLLARS
25.0000 g., 0.9000 Silver 0.7234 oz. ASW, 32 mm.
Obv: Neptune with two pet mermaids **Rev:** Multicolor fish with tree ring-like stripes **Edge:** Reeded

Date	Mintage	F	VF	XF	Unc	BU
2005 Proof	—	Value: 60.00				

KM# 114 5 DOLLARS
25.0000 g., 0.9000 Silver 0.7234 oz. ASW, 32 mm.
Obv: Neptune in shell boat visiting with dolphin **Rev:** Multicolor reef fish scene **Edge:** Reeded

Date	Mintage	F	VF	XF	Unc	BU
2006 Proof	—	Value: 60.00				

PANAMA

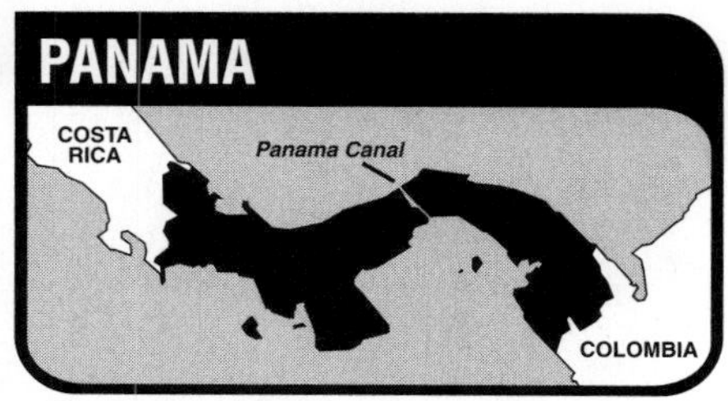

The Republic of Panama, a Central American Country situated between Costa Rica and Colombia, has an area of 29,762 sq. mi. (78,200 sq. km.) and a population of *2.4 million. Capital: Panama City. The Panama Canal is the country's biggest asset; servicing world related transit trade and international commerce. Bananas, refined petroleum, sugar and shrimp are exported.

MINT

(RCM) Royal Canadian Mint

MONETARY SYSTEM

100 Centesimos = 1 Balboa

REPUBLIC

DECIMAL COINAGE

KM# 125 CENTESIMO

Copper Plated Zinc

Date	Mintage	F	VF	XF	Unc	BU
2001 (RCM)	160,000,000	—	—	—	0.25	0.50

KM# 133 5 CENTESIMOS

5.0000 g., Copper Nickel, 21.2 mm. **Subject:** Sara Sotillo **Obv:** National arms **Rev:** Portrait **Edge:** Plain

Date	Mintage	F	VF	XF	Unc	BU
2001 (RCM)	8,000,000	—	—	—	0.25	0.30

KM# 127 1/10 BALBOA

Copper-Nickel Clad Copper **Obv:** National arms **Rev:** Balboa's portrait

Date	Mintage	F	VF	XF	Unc	BU
2001 (RCM)	15,000,000	—	—	—	0.35	0.50

KM# 135 25 CENTESIMOS

5.5600 g., Copper-Nickel Clad Copper, 24.2 mm. **Obv:** National arms **Rev:** Tower and Spanish ruins of Old Panama City **Edge:** Reeded

Date	Mintage	F	VF	XF	Unc	BU
2003 (RCM)	6,000,000	—	—	—	1.50	2.50
2003 (RCM) Proof	2,000	Value: 15.00				

KM# 128 1/4 BALBOA

Copper-Nickel Clad Copper **Obv:** National arms **Rev:** Balboa's portrait

Date	Mintage	F	VF	XF	Unc	BU
2001 (RCM)	12,000,000	—	—	—	0.60	0.75

KM# 129 1/2 BALBOA

Copper-Nickel Clad Copper **Obv:** National arms **Rev:** Balboa's portrait

Date	Mintage	F	VF	XF	Unc	BU
2001 (RCM)	600,000	—	—	1.00	2.00	3.50

KM# 134 BALBOA

22.7700 g., Copper-Nickel, 38 mm. **Obv:** President Mireya Moscoso **Rev:** Flag and canal scene **Edge:** Reeded

Date	Mintage	F	VF	XF	Unc	BU
1999(2004) (RCM)	348,000	—	—	—	4.00	6.00
1999(2004) (RCM)(P)	2,000	Value: 50.00				

PAPUA NEW GUINEA

Papua New Guinea occupies the eastern half of the island of New Guinea. It lies north of Australia near the equator and borders on West Irian. The country, which includes nearby Bismark archipelago, Buka and Bougainville, has an area of 178,260 sq. mi. (461,690 sq. km.).and a population of 3.7 million that is divided into more than 1,000 separate tribes speaking more than 700 mutually unintelligible languages. Capital: Port Moresby. The economy is agricultural, and exports copra, rubber, cocoa, coffee, tea, gold and copper

Guinea is a member of the Commonwealth of Nations. Elizabeth II is Head of State, as Queen of Papua New Guinea.

COMMONWEALTH

STANDARD COINAGE

100 Toea = 1 Kina

KM# 1 TOEA

Bronze **Obv:** Paradise bird **Rev:** Birdwing butterfly (o. paradisea)

Date	Mintage	F	VF	XF	Unc	BU
2002	—	—	—	—	0.35	1.00

KM# 2 2 TOEA

Bronze **Obv:** Bird of Paradise **Rev:** Butterfly cod, sometimes called the lionfish

Date	Mintage	F	VF	XF	Unc	BU
2001	—	—	—	—	0.50	1.00

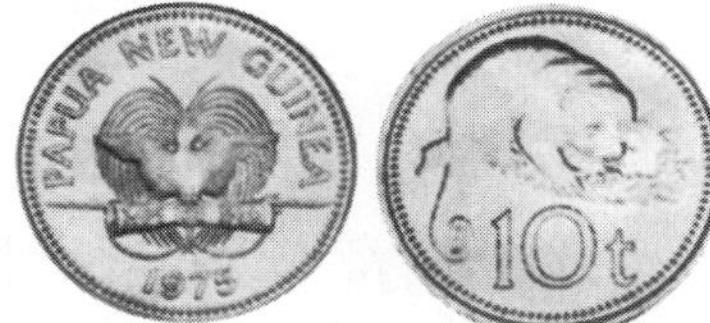

KM# 4 10 TOEA

Copper-Nickel **Rev:** Cuscus

Date	Mintage	F	VF	XF	Unc	BU
2001	—	—	—	—	1.50	2.00
2002	—	—	—	—	1.50	2.00

KM# 6 KINA

Copper-Nickel **Rev:** Sea and river crocodiles

Date	Mintage	F	VF	XF	Unc	BU
2002	—	—	—	—	3.50	6.00

The Republic of Paraguay, a landlocked country in the heart of South America surrounded by Argentina, Bolivia and Brazil, has an area of 157,048 sq. mi. (406,750 sq. km.) and a population of *4.5 million, 95 percent of whom are of mixed Spanish and Indian descent. Capital: Asuncion. The country is predominantly agrarian, with no important mineral deposits or oil reserves. Meat, timber, hides, oilseeds, tobacco and cotton account for 70 percent of Paraguay's export revenue.

During the Triple Alliance War (1864-1870) in which Paraguay faced Argentina, Brazil and Uruguay, Asuncion's ladies gathered in an Assembly on Feb. 24, 1867 and decided to give up their jewelry in order to help the national defense. The President of the Republic, Francisco Solano Lopez accepted the offering and ordered one twentieth of it be used to mint the first Paraguayan gold coins according to the Decree of the 11th of Sept.1867.

Two dies were made, one by Bouvet, and another by an American, Leonard Charles, while only the die made by Bouvet was eventually used.

REPUBLIC

REFORM COINAGE

100 Centimos = 1 Guarani

KM# 197 GUARANI
27.0000 g., 0.9250 Silver 0.803 oz. ASW, 39.7 mm. **Subject:** 50th Anniversary of the Central Bank **Obv:** The Gun Ship Paraguay **Rev:** Bank building **Edge:** Reeded

Date	Mintage	F	VF	XF	Unc	BU
2002 Proof	—	Value: 55.00				

KM# 195 500 GUARANIES
Brass **Obv:** Bust of General Bernardino Caballero facing **Rev:** Central Bank of Paraguay above denomination

Date	Mintage	F	VF	XF	Unc	BU
2002	15,000	—	—	—	2.50	3.00

The Republic of Peru, located on the Pacific coast of South America, has an area of 496,225 sq. mi. (1,285,220sq. km.) and a population of *21.4 million. Capital: Lima. The diversified economy includes mining, fishing and agriculture. Fishmeal, copper, sugar, zinc and iron ore are exported.

MINT MARKS
(monogram), LIMA = Lima

REPUBLIC

REFORM COINAGE

1/M Intis = 1 Nuevo Sol; 100 (New) Centimos = 1 Nuevo Sol

KM# 303.4 CENTIMO
Brass **Obv:** Oval wreath above arms, accent mark above "u" **Rev:** Without Braille dots, no Chavez

Date	Mintage	F	VF	XF	Unc	BU
2001LM	—	—	—	—	0.25	0.40
2002LM	—	—	—	—	0.25	0.40
2004LM	—	—	—	—	0.25	0.40

KM# 304.4 5 CENTIMOS
Brass **Obv:** Oval wreath above arms, accent above "u" **Rev:** Without Braille dots, with accent above "e"

Date	Mintage	F	VF	XF	Unc	BU
2001LM	—	—	—	—	0.35	0.50
2002LM	—	—	—	—	0.35	0.50

KM# 305.4 10 CENTIMOS
Brass **Obv:** Oval wreath above arms, accent above "u" **Rev:** Without braille dots, accent above "e" **Note:** LIMA monogram mint mark.

Date	Mintage	F	VF	XF	Unc	BU
2001LM	—	—	—	—	0.65	0.85
2002LM	—	—	—	—	0.65	0.85
2003	—	—	—	—	0.65	0.85
2004	—	—	—	—	0.65	0.85

KM# 306.3 20 CENTIMOS
Brass **Obv:** Oval wreath above arms, accent above "u" **Rev:** Small braille dots, accent above "e"

Date	Mintage	F	VF	XF	Unc	BU
2001LM	—	—	—	—	0.85	1.20
2002LM	—	—	—	—	0.85	1.20
2004LM	—	—	—	—	0.85	1.20

KM# 306.4 20 CENTIMOS
Brass **Obv:** Oval wreath above arms, accent above "u" **Rev:** Without braille dots, accent above "e"

Date	Mintage	F	VF	XF	Unc	BU
2001	—	—	—	—	0.85	1.20
2002	—	—	—	—	0.85	1.20
2004	—	—	—	—	0.85	1.20

KM# 307.4 50 CENTIMOS
Copper-Nickel **Obv:** Oval wreath above arms, accent above "u" **Rev:** Without braille, accent above "e" **Note:** Mint mark in monogram.

Date	Mintage	F	VF	XF	Unc	BU
2001LM	—	—	—	—	1.50	1.75
2002LM	—	—	—	—	1.50	1.75
2003LM	—	—	—	—	1.50	1.75
2004LM	—	—	—	—	1.50	1.75

KM# 308.4 NUEVO SOL
Copper-Nickel **Obv:** Oval wreath above arms, accent above "u" **Rev:** Without braille, accent above "e"

Date	Mintage	F	VF	XF	Unc	BU
2001 LIMA	—	—	—	—	4.00	4.50
2002 LIMA	—	—	—	—	4.00	4.50
2003 LIMA	—	—	—	—	4.00	4.50
2004 LIMA	—	—	—	—	4.00	4.50

KM# 329 NUEVO SOL
33.6250 g., 0.9250 Silver 1 oz. ASW, 37 mm. **Subject:** 450th Anniversary - San Marcos University **Obv:** National arms above value **Rev:** University seal and building **Edge:** Reeded

Date	Mintage	F	VF	XF	Unc	BU
2001LIMAE Proof	—	Value: 55.00				

KM# 330 NUEVO SOL
33.6250 g., 0.9250 Silver 1 oz. ASW, 37 mm. **Subject:** 50th Anniversary - Numismatic Society of Peru **Obv:** National arms above value **Rev:** Stylized design **Edge:** Reeded

Date	Mintage	F	VF	XF	Unc	BU
2001LIMAE Proof	—	Value: 45.00				

KM# 331 NUEVO SOL
33.6250 g., 0.9250 Silver 1 oz. ASW, 37 mm. **Subject:** 200th Anniversary - von Humboldt's visit to Peru **Obv:** National arms above value **Rev:** Alexander von Humboldt seated **Edge:** Reeded

Date	Mintage	F	VF	XF	Unc	BU
2002LIMAE Proof	—	Value: 55.00				

KM# 332 NUEVO SOL
33.6250 g., 0.9250 Silver 1 oz. ASW, 37 mm. **Subject:** 125th Anniversary of the Inmaculate Jesuitas - Lima College **Obv:** National arms above value **Rev:** Statue and crowned arms **Edge:** Reeded

Date	Mintage	F	VF	XF	Unc	BU
2003LIMAE Proof	—	Value: 50.00				

KM# 333 NUEVO SOL
33.6250 g., 0.9250 Silver 1 oz. ASW, 37 mm. **Subject:** 180th Anniversary of Peru's Congress **Obv:** National arms above value **Rev:** Statue in front of building **Edge:** Reeded

Date	Mintage	F	VF	XF	Unc	BU
2003LIMAE Proof	—	Value: 55.00				

KM# 313.2 2 NUEVOS SOLES
Bi-Metallic Brass center in Steel ring **Obv:** Large wreath and shield

Date	Mintage	F	VF	XF	Unc	BU
2002 LIMA	—	—	—	—	4.50	5.00
2003 LIMA	—	—	—	—	4.50	5.00
2004 LIMA	—	—	—	—	4.50	5.00

KM# 316.2 5 NUEVOS SOLES
Bi-Metallic Brass center in Streel ring **Obv:** Large wreath and shield

Date	Mintage	F	VF	XF	Unc	BU
2001 LIMA	—	—	—	—	6.50	7.00
2002 LIMA	—	—	—	—	6.50	7.00

PHILIPPINES

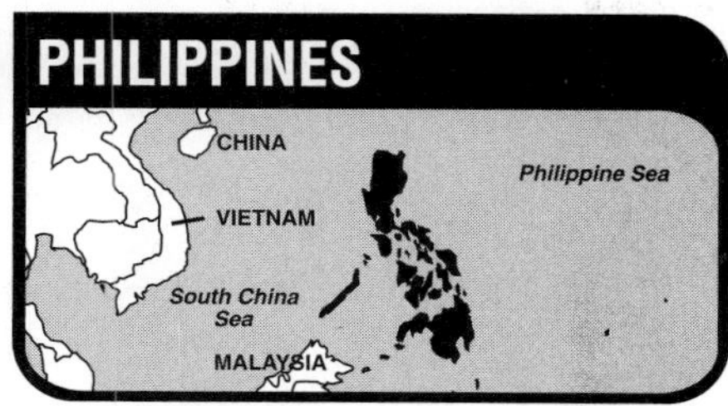

The Republic of the Philippines, an archipelago in the western Pacific 500 miles (805 km.) from the southeast coast of Asia, has an area of 115,830 sq. mi. (300,000 sq. km.) and a population of *64.9 million. Capital: Manila. The economy of the 7,000-island group is based on agriculture, forestry and fishing. Timber, coconut products, sugar and hemp are exported.

MINT MARKS
BSP - Bangko Sentral Pilipinas
M, MA - Manila

REPUBLIC

REFORM COINAGE

100 Sentimos = 1 Piso

KM# 273 SENTIMO
Copper Plated Steel **Obv:** Denomination **Rev:** Central bank seal

Date	Mintage	F	VF	XF	Unc	BU
2005	—	—	—	—	0.35	0.50

KM# 268 5 SENTIMOS
Copper Plated Steel **Rev. Legend:** 1993 BANGKO CENTRAL NG PILIPINAS **Note:** Hole punched out of center.

Date	Mintage	F	VF	XF	Unc	BU
2005	—	—	—	—	0.50	0.75

KM# 270 10 SENTIMOS
2.4600 g., Bronze Plated Steel, 16.9 mm. **Obv:** Value and date **Rev:** Central Bank seal **Edge:** Reeded

Date	Mintage	F	VF	XF	Unc	BU
2002	—	—	—	—	0.25	0.40
2005	—	—	—	—	0.25	0.40

KM# 271 25 SENTIMOS
3.8000 g., Brass, 20 mm. **Obv:** Value **Rev:** Central Bank seal **Edge:** Plain

Date	Mintage	F	VF	XF	Unc	BU
2001	—	—	—	—	1.00	1.25
2002	—	—	—	—	1.00	1.25
2003	—	—	—	—	1.00	1.25
2004	—	—	—	—	1.00	1.25
2005	—	—	—	—	1.00	1.25

KM# 269 PISO
Copper-Nickel **Obv:** Jose Rizal **Rev:** Bank seal, date 1993

Date	Mintage	F	VF	XF	Unc	BU
2001	—	—	—	—	1.25	1.75
2005	—	—	—	—	1.25	1.75

KM# 272 5 PISO
7.6700 g., Nickel-Brass, 26.7 mm. **Obv:** Aguinaldo **Rev:** Central Bank seal **Edge:** Plain

Date	Mintage	F	VF	XF	Unc	BU
2001BSP	—	—	—	—	1.50	3.50
2003	—	—	—	—	1.50	3.00
2004	—	—	—	—	1.50	3.00
2005	—	—	—	—	1.50	3.00

KM# 278 10 PISO
8.7000 g., Bi-Metallic Brass center in Copper-Nickel ring, 26.5 mm. **Obv:** Conjoined busts of Mobini and Bonifacio facing right **Rev:** Bank seal **Edge:** Plain and reeded sections

Date	Mintage	F	VF	XF	Unc	BU
2001	—	—	—	—	3.00	4.50
2002	—	—	—	—	3.00	4.50
2003	—	—	—	—	3.00	4.50
2005	—	—	—	—	3.00	4.50

MINT SETS

KM#	Date	Mintage	Identification	Issue Price	Mkt Val
MS39	2005 (7)	—	KM#268-273, 278 plus medal	—	—

PITCAIRN ISLANDS

A small volcanic island, along with the uninhabited islands of Oeno, Henderson, and Ducie, constitute the British Colony of Pitcairn Islands. The main island has an area of about 2 sq. mi. (5 sq. km.) and a population of *68. It is located 1350 miles southeast of Tahiti. The islanders subsist on fishing, garden produce and crops. The sale of postage stamps and carved curios to passing ships brings cash income.

New Zealand currency has been used since July 10, 1967.

BRITISH COLONY

REGULAR COINAGE

KM# 12 5 DOLLARS
31.1000 g., 0.9990 Silver 0.9989 oz. ASW, 40 mm. **Obv:** Elizabeth II **Rev:** Humpback Whale on mother of pearl insert **Edge:** Plain

Date	Mintage	F	VF	XF	Unc	BU
2002 Proof	2,000	Value: 60.00				

POLAND

The Republic of Poland, located in central Europe, has an area of 120,725 sq. mi. (312,680 sq. km.) and a population of *38.2 million. Capital: Warszawa (Warsaw). The economy is essentially agricultural; but industrial activity provides the products for foreign trade. Machinery, coal, coke, iron, steel and transport equipment are exported.

MINT MARKS
MV, MW, MW-monogram - Warsaw Mint, 1965-
CHI - Valcambi, Switzerland

Other letters appearing with date denote the Mintmaster at the time the coin was struck.

REPUBLIC
Democratic

REFORM COINAGE

100 Old Zlotych = 1 Grosz; 10,000 Old Zlotych = 1 Zloty

As far back as 1990, production was initiated for the new 1 Grosz - 1 Zlotych coins for a forthcoming monetary reform. It wasn't announced until the Act of July 7, 1994 and was enacted on January 1, 1995.

Y# 276 GROSZ
Brass

Date	Mintage	F	VF	XF	Unc	BU
2001	210,000,020	—	—	—	0.10	0.20
2002	240,000,000	—	—	—	0.10	0.20
2003	250,000,000	—	—	—	0.10	0.20
2004	300,000,000	—	—	—	0.10	0.20
2005	375,000,000	—	—	—	0.10	0.20

Y# 277 2 GROSZE
Brass

Date	Mintage	F	VF	XF	Unc	BU
2001	86,100,000	—	—	—	0.15	0.25
2002	83,910,000	—	—	—	0.15	0.25
2003	80,000,000	—	—	—	0.15	0.25
2004	100,000,000	—	—	—	0.15	0.25
2005	163,003,250	—	—	—	0.15	0.25

Y# 278 5 GROSZY
Brass

Date	Mintage	F	VF	XF	Unc	BU
2001	67,368,000	—	—	—	0.25	0.45
2002	67,200,000	—	—	—	0.25	0.45
2003	48,000,000	—	—	—	0.25	0.45
2004	62,500,000	—	—	—	0.25	0.45
2005	113,000,000	—	—	—	0.25	0.45

Y# 279 10 GROSZY
Copper-Nickel

Date	Mintage	F	VF	XF	Unc	BU
2001	62,820,000	—	—	—	0.40	0.60
2002	10,500,000	—	—	—	0.40	0.60
2003	31,500,000	—	—	—	0.40	0.60
2004	70,500,000	—	—	—	0.40	0.60
2005	94,000,000	—	—	—	0.40	0.60

Y# 280 20 GROSZY
Copper-Nickel

Date	Mintage	F	VF	XF	Unc	BU
2001	41,980,001	—	—	—	0.65	0.85
2002	10,500,000	—	—	—	0.65	0.85
2003	20,400,000	—	—	—	0.65	0.85
2004	40,000,025	—	—	—	0.65	0.85
2005	37,000,000	—	—	—	0.65	0.85

Y# 408 2 ZLOTE
8.1500 g., Brass **Subject:** Wieliczka Salt Mine **Obv:** Crowned eagle **Rev:** Ancient salt miners

Date	Mintage	F	VF	XF	Unc	BU
2001	500,000	—	—	—	3.00	—

Y# 410 2 ZLOTE
8.1500 g., Brass **Subject:** Amber Route **Obv:** Crowned eagle **Rev:** Ancient Roman coin and map with route marked in stars

Date	Mintage	F	VF	XF	Unc	BU
2001	500,000	—	—	—	3.00	—

Y# 412 2 ZLOTE
8.1500 g., Brass, 27 mm. **Subject:** 15 Years of the Constitutional Court **Obv:** Crowned eagle **Rev:** Crowned eagle head and scale **Edge:** "*NBP*" eight times

Date	Mintage	F	VF	XF	Unc	BU
2001	500,000	—	—	—	3.00	—

Y# 414 2 ZLOTE
8.1500 g., Brass, 27 mm. **Obv:** Crowned eagle **Rev:** Flying Swallowtail butterfly **Edge:** "*NBP*" eight times

Date	Mintage	F	VF	XF	Unc	BU
2001	600,000	—	—	—	6.00	—

Y# 418 2 ZLOTE
8.1500 g., Brass, 27 mm. **Subject:** Cardinal Stefan Wyszynski **Obv:** Polish eagle **Rev:** Cardinal wearing mitre **Edge:** "NBP" eight times

Date	Mintage	F	VF	XF	Unc	BU
2001	1,200,000	—	—	—	3.00	—

Y# 423 2 ZLOTE
8.1500 g., Brass, 26.8 mm. **Subject:** Jan III Sobieski **Obv:** Polish eagle **Rev:** Half bust of Sobieski facing **Edge Lettering:** *NBP* repeated

Date	Mintage	F	VF	XF	Unc	BU
2001	500,000	—	—	—	3.00	—

Y# 426 2 ZLOTE
8.1500 g., Brass, 26.8 mm. **Subject:** Henryk Wieniawski **Obv:** Polish eagle **Rev:** Bust of Wieniawski facing right **Edge Lettering:** *NBP* repeated

Date	Mintage	F	VF	XF	Unc	BU
2001	600,000	—	—	—	3.00	—

Y# 421 2 ZLOTE
8.1000 g., Brass, 26.8 mm. **Subject:** Michal Siedlecki **Obv:** Eagle **Rev:** Portrait and art work **Edge:** "NBP" eight times

Date	Mintage	F	VF	XF	Unc	BU
2001	600,000	—	—	—	3.00	—

Y# 422 2 ZLOTE
Brass **Subject:** Koledicy **Obv:** Eagle **Rev:** Christmas celebration scene

Date	Mintage	F	VF	XF	Unc	BU
2001	600,000	—	—	—	3.00	—

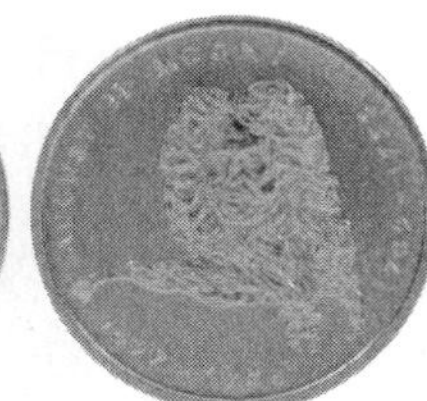

Y# 439 2 ZLOTE
8.1000 g., Brass, 26.8 mm. **Subject:** August II (1697-1706, 1709-1733) **Obv:** Crowned eagle **Rev:** Portrait **Edge:** "NBP*" repeatedly

Date	Mintage	F	VF	XF	Unc	BU
2002MW	620,000	—	—	—	3.00	—

Y# 427 2 ZLOTE
8.1000 g., Brass, 26.7 mm. **Obv:** Crowned eagle **Rev:** Two pond turtles **Edge:** Lettered **Edge Lettering:** "NBP" repeatedly

Date	Mintage	F	VF	XF	Unc	BU
2002	750,000	—	—	—	6.00	7.50

Y# 431 2 ZLOTE
8.1500 g., Brass, 27 mm. **Subject:** Bronislaw Malinowski **Obv:** Crowned eagle **Rev:** Portrait and Trobriand Islanders **Edge Lettering:** "NBP" eight times

Date	Mintage	F	VF	XF	Unc	BU
2002	680,000	—	—	—	3.50	—

Y# 433 2 ZLOTE
8.1500 g., Brass, 27 mm. **Subject:** World Cup Soccer **Obv:** Crowned eagle **Rev:** Two soccer players **Edge Lettering:** "NBP" eight times

Date	Mintage	F	VF	XF	Unc	BU
2002	1,000,000	—	—	—	3.50	—

Y# 440 2 ZLOTE
8.1300 g., Brass, 26.7 mm. **Subject:** Gen. Wladyslaw Anders **Obv:** Crowned eagle **Rev:** Military portrait and cross **Edge:** "NBP" repeated eight times

Date	Mintage	F	VF	XF	Unc	BU
2002MW	680,000	—	—	—	3.00	—

Y# 443 2 ZLOTE
8.1500 g., Brass, 26.8 mm. **Subject:** Zamek W. Malborku **Obv:** Crowned eagle **Rev:** Castle **Edge:** "*NBP* "repeatedly

Date	Mintage	F	VF	XF	Unc	BU
2002MW	680,000	—	—	—	3.00	—

Y# 444 2 ZLOTE
8.1300 g., Brass, 26.8 mm. **Subject:** Jan Matejko **Obv:** Denomination, crowned eagle and artist's palette **Rev:** Jester behind portrait **Edge:** "NBP" repeatedly

Date	Mintage	F	VF	XF	Unc	BU
2002MW	700,000	—	—	—	3.00	—

Y# 445 2 ZLOTE
8.1300 g., Brass, 26.8 mm. **Subject:** Eels **Obv:** Crowned eagle **Rev:** Two eels **Edge:** "NBP" repeatedly

Date	Mintage	F	VF	XF	Unc	BU
2003MW	—	—	—	—	5.00	—

Y# 447 2 ZLOTE
8.1500 g., Brass, 26.8 mm. **Subject:** City of Poznan (Posen) **Obv:** Crowned eagle **Rev:** Clock face and tower between two goat heads **Edge:** NBP repeated eight times

Date	Mintage	F	VF	XF	Unc	BU
2003MW	—	—	—	—	4.50	—

Y# 451 2 ZLOTE
8.2100 g., Brass, 26.8 mm. **Subject:** Easter Monday Festival **Obv:** Crowned eagle **Rev:** Festival scene **Edge:** Lettered **Edge Lettering:** NBP eight times

Date	Mintage	F	VF	XF	Unc	BU
2003MW	—	—	—	—	3.00	—

Y# 455 2 ZLOTE
8.1400 g., Brass, 26.7 mm. **Subject:** Petroleum and Gas Industry 150th Anniversary **Obv:** Crowned eagle **Rev:** Portrait and refinery **Edge:** "NBP" repeated eight times

Date	Mintage	F	VF	XF	Unc	BU
2003MW	—	—	—	—	3.50	—

Y# 456 2 ZLOTE
8.1400 g., Brass, 26.7 mm. **Subject:** General B. S. Maczek **Obv:** Crowned eagle **Rev:** Military uniformed portrait **Edge:** "NBP" repeated eight times

Date	Mintage	F	VF	XF	Unc	BU
2003MW	600,000	—	—	—	3.00	—

Y# 446 2 ZLOTE
7.7500 g., Brass, 26.7 mm. **Subject:** Children **Obv:** Children and square design above crowned eagle, date and denomination **Rev:** Children on square design **Edge:** "NBP" repeatedly **Note:** minted with center hole

Date	Mintage	F	VF	XF	Unc	BU
2003MW	—	—	—	—	4.50	—

Y# 465 2 ZLOTE
8.1700 g., Aluminum-Bronze, 26.7 mm. **Obv:** Small Polish eagle with large cross background **Rev:** Pope in prayer with cross background **Edge:** Lettered **Edge Lettering:** "NBP" repeated

Date	Mintage	F	VF	XF	Unc	BU
2003MW	—	—	—	—	3.00	—

Y# 479 2 ZLOTE
8.1500 g., Brass, 27 mm. **Subject:** 80th Anniversary of the Modern Zloty Currency **Obv:** Crowned eagle above value **Rev:** Reverse design of the 1 Zloty Y-15 **Edge:** Lettered **Edge Lettering:** "NBP" eight times

Date	Mintage	F	VF	XF	Unc	BU
2004MW	800,000	—	—	—	3.00	—

Y# 481 2 ZLOTE
8.1500 g., Brass, 27 mm. **Subject:** Poland Joining the European Union **Obv:** Crowned eagle above value **Rev:** Polish map and stars **Edge:** Lettered **Edge Lettering:** "NBP" eight times

Date	Mintage	F	VF	XF	Unc	BU
2004MW	1,000,000	—	—	—	3.00	—

Y# 484 2 ZLOTE
8.1500 g., Brass, 27 mm. **Subject:** Dolnoslaskie (Lower Silesian) District **Obv:** Crowned eagle on map **Rev:** Silesian eagle on shield **Edge:** Lettered **Edge Lettering:** "NBP" eight times

Date	Mintage	F	VF	XF	Unc	BU
2004MW	700,000	—	—	—	3.00	—

Y# 485 2 ZLOTE
8.1500 g., Brass, 27 mm. **Subject:** Kujawsko-Pomorskie District **Obv:** Crowned eagle on map **Rev:** Shield with crowned half eagle and griffin **Edge:** Lettered **Edge Lettering:** "NBP" eight times

Date	Mintage	F	VF	XF	Unc	BU
2004MW	750,000	—	—	—	3.00	—

Y# 486 2 ZLOTE
8.1500 g., Brass, 27 mm. **Subject:** Lubuskie District **Obv:** Crowned eagle on map **Rev:** Shield with half eagle and two stars **Edge:** Lettered **Edge Lettering:** "NBP" eight times

Date	Mintage	F	VF	XF	Unc	BU
2004MW	820,000	—	—	—	3.00	—

Y# 487 2 ZLOTE
8.1500 g., Brass, 27 mm. **Subject:** Lodzkie District **Obv:** Crowned eagle on map **Rev:** Shield with two creatures above an eagle **Edge:** Lettered **Edge Lettering:** "NBP" eight times

Date	Mintage	F	VF	XF	Unc	BU
2004MW	920,000	—	—	—	3.00	—

Y# 488 2 ZLOTE
8.1500 g., Brass, 27 mm. **Subject:** Malopolskie District **Obv:** Crowned eagle on map **Rev:** Shield with crowned eagle **Edge:** Lettered **Edge Lettering:** "NBP" eight times

Date	Mintage	F	VF	XF	Unc	BU
2004MW	920,000	—	—	—	3.00	—

Y# 489 2 ZLOTE
8.1500 g., Brass, 27 mm. **Subject:** Mazowieckie District **Obv:** Crowned eagle on map **Rev:** Uncrowned eagle on shield **Edge:** Lettered **Edge Lettering:** "NBP" eight times

Date	Mintage	F	VF	XF	Unc	BU
2004MW	920,000	—	—	—	3.00	—

Y# 490 2 ZLOTE
8.1500 g., Brass, 27 mm. **Subject:** Podkarpackie District **Obv:** Crowned eagle on map **Rev:** Shield with iron cross above griffin and lion **Edge:** Lettered **Edge Lettering:** "NBP" eight times

Date	Mintage	F	VF	XF	Unc	BU
2004MW	920,000	—	—	—	3.00	—

Y# 491 2 ZLOTE
8.1500 g., Brass, 27 mm. **Subject:** Podlaskie District **Obv:** Crowned eagle on map **Rev:** Shield with Polish eagle above Lithuanian knight **Edge:** Lettered **Edge Lettering:** "NBP" eight times

Date	Mintage	F	VF	XF	Unc	BU
2004MW	900,000	—	—	—	3.00	—

Y# 492 2 ZLOTE
8.1500 g., Brass, 27 mm. **Subject:** Pomorskie District **Obv:** Crowned eagle on map **Rev:** Griffin on shield **Edge:** Lettered **Edge Lettering:** "NBP" eight times

Date	Mintage	F	VF	XF	Unc	BU
2004MW	900,000	—	—	—	3.00	—

Y# 493 2 ZLOTE
8.1500 g., Brass, 27 mm. **Subject:** Slaskie (Silesia) District **Obv:** Crowned eagle on map **Rev:** Eagle on shield **Edge:** Lettered **Edge Lettering:** "NBP" eight times

Date	Mintage	F	VF	XF	Unc	BU
2004MW	960,000	—	—	—	3.00	—

Y# 464 2 ZLOTE
8.1300 g., Brass, 26.8 mm. **Obv:** Crowned eagle **Rev:** Two dolphins **Edge:** Lettered **Edge Lettering:** "NBP" repeated

Date	Mintage	F	VF	XF	Unc	BU
2004MW	—	—	—	—	4.00	—

Y# 521 2 ZLOTE
8.1500 g., Brass, 26.8 mm. **Obv:** Crowned Polish eagle **Rev:** 2 Zlote ship coin design of 1936 **Edge:** Lettered **Edge Lettering:** "NBP" repeatedly

Date	Mintage	F	VF	XF	Unc	BU
2005MW	—	—	—	—	3.50	—

Y# 522 2 ZLOTE
8.1500 g., Brass, 26.8 mm. **Subject:** Japan's Aichi Expo **Obv:** Crowned Polish eagle **Rev:** Two cranes flying over Mt. Fuji with rising sun background **Edge:** Lettered **Edge Lettering:** "NBP" repeatedly

Date	Mintage	F	VF	XF	Unc	BU
2005MW	—	—	—	—	3.50	—

Y# 283 2 ZLOTE
Bi-Metallic Copper-Nickel center in Brass ring

Date	Mintage	F	VF	XF	Unc	BU
2005	—	—	—	—	4.00	4.50

Y# 473 2 ZLOTY
8.1500 g., Brass, 27 mm. **Obv:** Crowned eagle **Rev:** Stanislaus Leszcywski **Edge:** Lettered **Edge Lettering:** "NBP" repeated eight times

Date	Mintage	F	VF	XF	Unc	BU
2003MW	600,000	—	—	—	3.50	—

Y# 477 2 ZLOTY
8.1500 g., Brass, 27 mm. **Obv:** Crowned eagle and artists palette **Rev:** Self portrait of Jacek Malczewski **Edge:** Lettered **Edge Lettering:** "NPB" repeated eight times

Date	Mintage	F	VF	XF	Unc	BU
2003MW	600,000	—	—	—	3.50	—

Y# 496 2 ZLOTY
8.1500 g., Brass, 27 mm. **Subject:** Warsaw Uprising 60th Anniversary **Obv:** Crowned eagle **Rev:** Resistance symbol on brick wall **Edge:** Lettered **Edge Lettering:** "NBP" eight times

Date	Mintage	F	VF	XF	Unc	BU
2004MW	900,000	—	—	—	3.00	—

Y# 499 2 ZLOTY
8.1500 g., Brass, 27 mm. **Obv:** Crowned eagle **Rev:** Gen. Stanislaw F. Sosabowski **Edge:** Lettered **Edge Lettering:** "NBP" eight times

Date	Mintage	F	VF	XF	Unc	BU
2004MW	850,000	—	—	—	3.00	—

Y# 501 2 ZLOTY
8.1500 g., Brass, 27 mm. **Subject:** Polish Police 85th Anniversary **Obv:** Crowned eagle **Rev:** Police badge **dge:** Lettered **Edge Lettering:** "NBP" eight times

Date	Mintage	F	VF	XF	Unc	BU
2004MW	760,000	—	—	—	3.00	—

Y# 503 2 ZLOTY
8.1500 g., Brass, 27 mm. **Subject:** Polish Senate **Obv:** Crowned eagle **Rev:** Senate eagle and speaker's staff **Edge:** Lettered **Edge Lettering:** "NBP" eight times

Date	Mintage	F	VF	XF	Unc	BU
2004MW	760,000	—	—	—	3.00	—

Y# 505 2 ZLOTY
8.1500 g., Brass, 27 mm. **Obv:** Crowned eagle **Rev:** Aleksander Czekanowski (1833-1876) **Edge:** Lettered **Edge Lettering:** "NBP" eight times

Date	Mintage	F	VF	XF	Unc	BU
2004MW	700,000	—	—	—	3.00	—

Y# 507 2 ZLOTY
8.1500 g., Brass, 27 mm. **Obv:** Crowned eagle **Rev:** Harvest fest couple in folk costume **Edge:** Lettered **Edge Lettering:** "NBP" eight times

Date	Mintage	F	VF	XF	Unc	BU
2004MW	850,000	—	—	—	3.00	—

Y# 509 2 ZLOTY
8.1500 g., Brass, 27 mm. **Subject:** Warsaw Fine Arts Academy Centennial **Obv:** Crowned eagle **Rev:** Painter's hands **Edge:** Lettered **Edge Lettering:** "NBP" eight times

Date	Mintage	F	VF	XF	Unc	BU
2004MW	850,000	—	—	—	3.00	—

Y# 512 2 ZLOTY
8.1500 g., Brass, 27 mm. **Obv:** Crowned eagle and artists palette **Rev:** Stanislaw Wyspianski (1869-1907) **Edge:** Lettered **Edge Lettering:** "NBP" eight times

Date	Mintage	F	VF	XF	Unc	BU
2004MW	900,000	—	—	—	3.00	—

Y# 516 2 ZLOTY
8.1500 g., Brass, 27 mm. **Subject:** Olympics **Obv:** Crowned eagle **Rev:** Ancient runners **Edge:** Lettered **Edge Lettering:** "NBP" eight times

Date	Mintage	F	VF	XF	Unc	BU
2004MW	1,000,000	—	—	—	3.00	—

Y# 520 2 ZLOTY
8.1500 g., Brass, 26.8 mm. **Obv:** Crowned eagle **Rev:** Eagle Owl on nest with chicks **Edge:** Lettered **Edge Lettering:** "NBP" repeated eight times

Date	Mintage	F	VF	XF	Unc	BU
2005MW	—	—	—	—	3.50	—

Y# 524 2 ZLOTY
8.1300 g., Brass, 26.7 mm. **Subject:** Obrony Jasnej Cory **Obv:** Polish eagle above value **Rev:** Monk **Edge:** Lettered **Edge Lettering:** "NBP" repeatedly

Date	Mintage	F	VF	XF	Unc	BU
2005MW	—	—	—	—	4.00	—

Y# 525 2 ZLOTY
8.1300 g., Brass, 26.7 mm. **Obv:** Polish eagle above value **Rev:** Pope John Paul II **Edge:** Lettered **Edge Lettering:** "NBP" repeatedly

Date	Mintage	F	VF	XF	Unc	BU
2005MW	—	—	—	—	4.00	—

Y# 527 2 ZLOTY
8.2000 g., Brass, 26.7 mm. **Obv:** Eagle above value **Rev:** Konstanty Ildefons Galczynski **Edge Lettering:** "NBP" repeatedly

Date	Mintage	F	VF	XF	Unc	BU
2005MW	—	—	—	—	3.00	—

Y# 528 2 ZLOTY
8.2000 g., Brass, 26.7 mm. **Obv:** Eagle and value above wall **Rev:** Kolobrzeg light house **Edge Lettering:** "NBP" repeatedly

Date	Mintage	F	VF	XF	Unc	BU
2005MW	—	—	—	—	3.00	—

Y# 529 2 ZLOTY
8.2000 g., Brass, 26.7 mm. **Obv:** Eagle and value above wall **Rev:** Wloclawek Cathedral **Edge Lettering:** "NBP" repeatedly

Date	Mintage	F	VF	XF	Unc	BU
2005MW	—	—	—	—	3.00	—

Y# 530 2 ZLOTY
8.2000 g., Brass, 26.7 mm. **Obv:** Eagle above value **Rev:** Stanislaw August Poniatowski **Edge Lettering:** "NBP" repeatedly

Date	Mintage	F	VF	XF	Unc	BU
2005MW	—	—	—	—	3.00	—

Y# 284 5 ZLOTYCH
Bi-Metallic Brass center in Copper-Nickel ring

Date	Mintage	F	VF	XF	Unc	BU
2005	5,000,000	—	—	—	0.70	8.00

Y# 406 10 ZLOTYCH
14.1400 g., 0.9250 Silver .4205 oz. ASW **Subject:** Year 2001 **Obv:** Crowned eagle **Rev:** Printed circuit board

Date	Mintage	F	VF	XF	Unc	BU
2001 Proof	35,000	Value: 27.50				

Y# 413 10 ZLOTYCH
14.1400 g., 0.9250 Silver .4205 oz. ASW, 32 mm. **Subject:** 15 Years of the Constitutional Court **Obv:** Crowned eagle suspended from a judge's neck chain **Rev:** Crowned eagle head and balance scale **Edge Lettering:** "TRYBUNAL KONSTYTUCYJNY W SLUZBIE PANSTWA PRAWA"

Date	Mintage	F	VF	XF	Unc	BU
2001 Proof	25,000	Value: 22.50				

Y# 419 10 ZLOTYCH
14.1400 g., 0.9250 Silver .4205 oz. ASW, 32 mm. **Subject:** Cardinal Stefan Wyszynski **Obv:** Polish eagle above ribbon **Rev:** Portrait with raised hands **Edge Lettering:** "100.ROCZNIA URODZIN"

Date	Mintage	F	VF	XF	Unc	BU
2001 Proof	60,000	Value: 27.50				

Y# 425 10 ZLOTYCH
14.2100 g., 0.9250 Silver 0.4226 oz. ASW, 32 mm. **Subject:** Jan III Sobieski **Obv:** Polish eagle above denomination **Rev:** 3/4 bust Jan III Sobieski lower left, army in background **Edge:** Plain

Date	Mintage	F	VF	XF	Unc	BU
2001 Proof	24,000	Value: 30.00				

Y# 458 10 ZLOTYCH
14.1400 g., 0.9250 Silver 0.4205 oz. ASW, 32 mm. **Obv:** Polish eagle **Rev:** Jan Sobieski, type II **Edge:** Plain

Date	Mintage	F	VF	XF	Unc	BU
2001MW Proof	17,000	Value: 35.00				

Y# 459 10 ZLOTYCH
14.1400 g., 0.9250 Silver 0.4205 oz. ASW, 32 mm. **Obv:** Three violins **Rev:** Henryk Wieniawski **Edge:** Plain

Date	Mintage	F	VF	XF	Unc	BU
2001MW Proof	28,000	Value: 35.00				

Y# 460 10 ZLOTYCH
14.1400 g., 0.9250 Silver 0.4205 oz. ASW, 32 mm. **Obv:** Polish eagle above fish **Rev:** Michal Siedlecki **Edge:** Plain

Date	Mintage	F	VF	XF	Unc	BU
2001MW Proof	26,000	Value: 35.00				

Y# 461 10 ZLOTYCH
14.1400 g., 0.9250 Silver 0.4205 oz. ASW, 32 mm. **Obv:** Polish eagle above value **Rev:** August II **Edge:** Plain

Date	Mintage	F	VF	XF	Unc	BU
2002MW Proof	30,000	Value: 27.50				

Y# 432 10 ZLOTYCH
14.1400 g., 0.9250 Silver 0.4205 oz. ASW, 32 mm. **Subject:** Bronislaw Malinowski **Obv:** Portrait and crowned eagle **Rev:** Trobriand Islands village scene **Edge Lettering:** "etnolog, antropolog kultury"

Date	Mintage	F	VF	XF	Unc	BU
2002 Proof	33,500	Value: 20.00				

Y# 434 10 ZLOTYCH
14.1400 g., 0.9250 Silver 0.4205 oz. ASW, 32 mm. **Subject:** World Cup Soccer **Obv:** Crowned eagle **Rev:** Soccer player **Edge Lettering:** "etnolog, antropolog kultury"

Date	Mintage	F	VF	XF	Unc	BU
2002 Proof	55,000	Value: 20.00				

Y# 435 10 ZLOTYCH
14.1400 g., 0.9250 Silver 0.4205 oz. ASW, 32 mm. **Subject:** World Cup Soccer **Obv:** Amber soccer ball inset entering goal net **Rev:** Two soccer players with amber soccer ball inset **Edge Lettering:** "etnolog, antropolog kultury"

Date	Mintage	F	VF	XF	Unc	BU
2002 Proof	65,000	Value: 25.00				

Y# 437 10 ZLOTYCH
14.1400 g., 0.9250 Silver 0.4205 oz. ASW, 32 mm. **Subject:** Pope John Paul II **Obv:** Polish eagle and two views of praying Pope **Rev:** Pope facing radiant Holy Door **Edge:** Plain

Date	Mintage	F	VF	XF	Unc	BU
2002 Proof	80,000	Value: 27.50				

Y# 441 10 ZLOTYCH
14.2000 g., 0.9250 Silver 0.4223 oz. ASW, 32 mm. **Subject:** Gen. Wladyslaw Anders **Obv:** Crowned eagle, cross and multicolor flowers **Rev:** Military portrait **Edge:** Plain

Date	Mintage	F	VF	XF	Unc	BU
2002MW Proof	40,000	Value: 35.00				

Y# 450 10 ZLOTYCH
14.1400 g., 0.9250 Silver 0.4205 oz. ASW, 32 mm. **Subject:** August II (1697-1706, 1709-1735) **Obv:** Crowned eagle above value **Rev:** Portrait and Order of the White Eagle **Edge:** Plain

Date	Mintage	F	VF	XF	Unc	BU
2002MW Proof	—	Value: 25.00				

Y# 453 10 ZLOTYCH
14.1400 g., 0.9250 Silver 0.4205 oz. ASW, 32 mm. **Subject:** Great Orchestra of Christmas Charity **Obv:** Large inscribed heart **Rev:** Boy playing flute **Edge:** Plain

Date	Mintage	F	VF	XF	Unc	BU
2003MW	47,000	—	—	—	—	25.00

Y# 468 10 ZLOTYCH
14.1400 g., 0.9250 Silver 0.4205 oz. ASW, 32 mm. **Obv:** Tanks on battlefield **Rev:** General Maczek (1892-1994) **Edge:** Plain

Date	Mintage	F	VF	XF	Unc	BU
2003MW Proof	44,000	Value: 25.00				

Y# 469 10 ZLOTYCH
14.1400 g., 0.9250 Silver 0.4205 oz. ASW, 32 mm. **Subject:** Gas and Oil Industry **Obv:** Crowned eagle and highway leading to city view **Rev:** Portrait and refinery **Edge:** Plain

Date	Mintage	F	VF	XF	Unc	BU
2003MW Proof	43,000	Value: 25.00				

Y# 474 10 ZLOTYCH

14.1400 g., 0.9250 Silver 0.4205 oz. ASW, 32 mm. **Obv:** Crowned eagle **Rev:** Stanislaus I and wife's portrait **Edge:** Plain

Date	Mintage	F	VF	XF	Unc	BU
2003MW Proof	45,000	Value: 25.00				

Y# 475 10 ZLOTYCH

14.1400 g., 0.9250 Silver 0.4205 oz. ASW, 32 mm. **Obv:** Crowned eagle **Rev:** Half-length figure of Stanislaus I with his wife in background **Edge:** Plain

Date	Mintage	F	VF	XF	Unc	BU
2003MW Proof	40,000	Value: 25.00				

Y# 448 10 ZLOTYCH

14.1400 g., 0.9250 Silver 0.4205 oz. ASW, 32 mm. **Subject:** City of Poznan (Posen) **Obv:** Old coin design and door **Rev:** Old coin design and city view **Edge:** Plain

Date	Mintage	F	VF	XF	Unc	BU
2003MW Proof	—	Value: 25.00				

Y# 480 10 ZLOTYCH

14.1400 g., 0.9250 Silver 0.4205 oz. ASW, 32 mm. **Subject:** 80th Anniversary of the Modern Zloty Currency **Obv:** Man wearing glasses behind obverse design of 1 zloty Y-15 **Rev:** Reverse design of 1 Zloty Y-15 **Edge:** Plain

Date	Mintage	F	VF	XF	Unc	BU
2004MW Proof	55,000	Value: 25.00				

Y# 482 10 ZLOTYCH

14.1400 g., 0.9250 Silver 0.4205 oz. ASW, 32 mm. **Subject:** Poland Joining the European Union **Obv:** Crowned eagle in blue circle with yellow stars **Rev:** Multicolor European Union and Polish flags **Edge:** Plain

Date	Mintage	F	VF	XF	Unc	BU
2004MW Proof	78,000	Value: 25.00				

Y# 497 10 ZLOTYCH

14.1400 g., 0.9250 Silver 0.4205 oz. ASW, 32 mm. **Subject:** Warsaw Uprising 60th Anniversary **Obv:** Crowned eagle and value on resistance symbol **Rev:** Polish soldier wearing captured German helmet **Edge:** Plain

Date	Mintage	F	VF	XF	Unc	BU
2004MW Proof	92,000	Value: 25.00				

Y# 500 10 ZLOTYCH

14.1400 g., 0.9250 Silver 0.4205 oz. ASW, 32 mm. **Obv:** Polish paratrooper badge **Rev:** Gen. Sosabowski and descending paratrooper **Edge:** Plain

Date	Mintage	F	VF	XF	Unc	BU
2004MW Proof	56,000	Value: 25.00				

Y# 502 10 ZLOTYCH

14.1400 g., 0.9250 Silver 0.4205 oz. ASW, 32 mm. **Subject:** Polish Police 85th Anniversary **Obv:** Crowned eagle **Rev:** Seal partially overlapping police badge **Edge:** Plain

Date	Mintage	F	VF	XF	Unc	BU
2004MW Proof	65,000	Value: 25.00				

Y# 506 10 ZLOTYCH

14.1400 g., 0.9250 Silver 0.4205 oz. ASW, 32 mm. **Obv:** Siberian landscape above crowned eagle and value **Rev:** Aleksander Czekanowski (1833-1876) **Edge:** Plain

Date	Mintage	F	VF	XF	Unc	BU
2004MW Proof	45,000	Value: 25.00				

Y# 510 10 ZLOTYCH

14.1400 g., 0.9250 Silver 0.4205 oz. ASW, 32 mm. **Subject:** Warsaw Fine Arts Academy Centennial **Obv:** Crowned eagle in city square **Rev:** Art studio **Edge:** Plain

Date	Mintage	F	VF	XF	Unc	BU
2004MW	75,000	—	—	—	—	25.00

Y# 517 10 ZLOTYCH

14.1400 g., 0.9250 Silver 0.4205 oz. ASW, 32 mm. **Subject:** Olympics **Obv:** Woman and crowned eagle **Rev:** Fencers in front of Parthenon **Edge:** Plain

Date	Mintage	F	VF	XF	Unc	BU
2004MW Proof	70,000	Value: 25.00				

Y# 518 10 ZLOTYCH

14.1400 g., 0.9250 Silver 0.4205 oz. ASW, 32 mm. **Subject:** Olympics **Obv:** Crowned eagle in gold plated center **Rev:** Ancient athlete within gold plated circle **Edge:** Plain

Date	Mintage	F	VF	XF	Unc	BU
2004MW Proof	90,000	Value: 35.00				

Y# 523 10 ZLOTYCH

14.2300 g., 0.9250 Silver 0.4232 oz. ASW, 43.2 x 29.2 mm. **Subject:** Japan's Aichi Expo **Obv:** Frederic Chopin Monument **Rev:** Two cranes **Edge:** Plain **Shape:** Fan

Date	Mintage	F	VF	XF	Unc	BU
2005 Proof	—	Value: 30.00				

Y# 526 10 ZLOTYCH

14.1400 g., 0.9250 Silver Gold plated reverse 0.4205 oz. ASW, 32.1 mm. **Obv:** Polish eagle above hands **Rev:** Pope John Paul II and church **Edge:** Plain

Date	Mintage	F	VF	XF	Unc	BU
2005MW Proof	—	Value: 30.00				

Y# 409 20 ZLOTYCH

28.2800 g., 0.9250 Silver .8410 oz. ASW, 38.6 mm. **Subject:** Wieliezce Salt Mine **Obv:** Crowned eagle and rock **Rev:** Ancient salt miners **Edge:** Plain

Date	Mintage	F	VF	XF	Unc	BU
2001 Proof	25,000	Value: 55.00				

Y# 411 20 ZLOTYCH

28.2800 g., 0.9250 Silver .8410 oz. ASW, 38.6 mm. **Subject:** Amber Route **Obv:** Crowned eagle and two ancient Roman silver cups **Rev:** Piece of amber mounted above an ancient Roman coin design and map with the route marked with stars **Edge:** Plain

Date	Mintage	F	VF	XF	Unc	BU
2001	30,000	—	—	—	80.00	—

Note: Antiqued finish

Y# 415 20 ZLOTYCH

28.2800 g., 0.9250 Silver .8410 oz. ASW, 38.6 mm. **Obv:** Crowned eagle between two flags **Rev:** Flying Swallowtail butterfly **Edge:** Plain

Date	Mintage	F	VF	XF	Unc	BU
2001 Proof	27,000	Value: 50.00				

Y# 424 20 ZLOTYCH

28.7700 g., 0.9250 Silver 0.8556 oz. ASW, 38.6 mm. **Subject:** Christmas **Obv:** Ornate city view **Rev:** Celebration scene including an attached zirconia star **Edge:** Plain **Note:** Antiqued finish.

Date	Mintage	F	VF	XF	Unc	BU
2001	55,000	—	—	—	35.00	—

Y# 457 20 ZLOTYCH

28.2800 g., 0.9250 Silver 0.841 oz. ASW, 38.6 mm. **Obv:** Crowned eagle and castle **Rev:** Malborku castle and ceramic applique **Edge:** Plain **Note:** Antiqued finish

Date	Mintage	F	VF	XF	Unc	BU
2002MW Antiqued finish	51,000	—	—	—	35.00	—

Y# 442 20 ZLOTYCH

28.0500 g., 0.9250 Silver 0.8342 oz. ASW **Subject:** Jan Matejko **Obv:** Seated figure with crowned eagle at lower right **Rev:** Portrait with multicolor artist's palette **Edge:** Plain **Shape:** Rectangular **Note:** Actual size 40 x 37.9mm.

Date	Mintage	F	VF	XF	Unc	BU
2002MW Proof	57,000	Value: 40.00				

Y# 428 20 ZLOTYCH

28.2800 g., 0.9250 Silver 0.841 oz. ASW, 38.6 mm. **Obv:** Crowned eagle **Rev:** Two pond turtles **Edge:** Plain

Date	Mintage	F	VF	XF	Unc	BU
2002 Proof	35,000	Value: 45.00				

Y# 449 20 ZLOTYCH

28.4700 g., 0.9250 Silver 0.8467 oz. ASW, 38.6 mm. **Obv:** Crowned eagle **Rev:** Eels and world globe **Edge:** Plain

Date	Mintage	F	VF	XF	Unc	BU
2003MW Proof	—	Value: 40.00				

Y# 452 20 ZLOTYCH

28.2800 g., 0.9250 Silver 0.841 oz. ASW, 38.6 mm. **Subject:** Easter Monday Festival **Obv:** Crowned eagle on lace curtain above lamb and multicolor Easter eggs **Rev:** Festival scene **Edge:** Plain

Date	Mintage	F	VF	XF	Unc	BU
2003MW Proof	44,000	Value: 36.00				

Y# 471 20 ZLOTYCH

28.2800 g., 0.9250 Silver 0.841 oz. ASW, 40 x 40 mm. **Obv:** Standing Pope John Paul II **Rev:** Pope"s portrait **Edge:** Plain **Shape:** Square

Date	Mintage	F	VF	XF	Unc	BU
2003MW Proof	83,000	Value: 35.00				

Y# 478 20 ZLOTYCH

28.2800 g., 0.9250 Silver 0.841 oz. ASW, 28 mm. **Obv:** "Death" allegory closing an old man's eyes **Rev:** Self portrait of Jacek Malczewski **Edge:** Plain **Shape:** Rectangular

Date	Mintage	F	VF	XF	Unc	BU
2003MW Proof	64,000	Value: 35.00				

Y# 498 20 ZLOTYCH

28.2800 g., 0.9250 Silver 0.841 oz. ASW, 38.6 mm. **Subject:** Lodz Ghetto (1940-1944) **Obv:** Silhouette on wall **Rev:** Child with a pot **Edge:** Plain

Date	Mintage	F	VF	XF	Unc	BU
2004MW	64,000	—	—	—	—	35.00

Y# 504 20 ZLOTYCH

28.2800 g., 0.9250 Silver 0.841 oz. ASW, 38.6 mm. **Subject:** Polish Senate **Obv:** Crowned eagle above Senate chamber **Rev:** Senate eagle and speaker's staff **Edge:** Plain

Date	Mintage	F	VF	XF	Unc	BU
2004MW Proof	67,000	Value: 35.00				

Y# 508 20 ZLOTYCH

28.2800 g., 0.9250 Silver 0.841 oz. ASW, 38.6 mm. **Obv:** Crowned eagle in harvest wreath **Rev:** Harvest fest parade **Edge:** Plain

Date	Mintage	F	VF	XF	Unc	BU
2004MW Proof	74,000	Value: 35.00				

Y# 513 20 ZLOTYCH

28.2800 g., 0.9250 Silver 0.841 oz. ASW, 40x28 mm. **Obv:** Mother and children **Rev:** Stanislaw Wyspianski (1869-1907) **Edge:** Plain

Date	Mintage	F	VF	XF	Unc	BU
2004MW Proof	80,000	Value: 35.00				

Y# 515 20 ZLOTYCH

28.2800 g., 0.9250 Silver 0.841 oz. ASW, 38.6 mm. **Obv:** Crowned eagle **Rev:** Two porpoises **Edge:** Plain

Date	Mintage	F	VF	XF	Unc	BU
2004MW Proof	56,000	Value: 35.00				

Y# 416 100 ZLOTYCH

8.0000 g., 0.9000 Gold .2315 oz. AGW, 21 mm. **Subject:** Wladyslaw I (1320-33) **Obv:** Crowned eagle **Rev:** Crowned portrait **Edge:** Plain

Date	Mintage	F	VF	XF	Unc	BU
2001 Proof	2,000	Value: 225				

Y# 417 100 ZLOTYCH

8.0000 g., 0.9000 Gold .2315 oz. AGW, 21 mm. **Subject:** Boleslaw III (1102-1138) **Obv:** Polish eagle **Rev:** Portrait **Edge:** Plain

Date	Mintage	F	VF	XF	Unc	BU
2001 Proof	2,000	Value: 220				

Y# 462 100 ZLOTYCH

8.0000 g., 0.9000 Gold 0.2315 oz. AGW, 21 mm. **Obv:** Polish eagle **Rev:** Jan Sobieski III **Edge:** Plain

Date	Mintage	F	VF	XF	Unc	BU
2001MV Proof	2,200	Value: 225				

Y# 436 100 ZLOTYCH

8.0000 g., 0.9000 Gold 0.2315 oz. AGW, 21 mm. **Subject:** World Cup Soccer **Obv:** Crowned eagle with world background **Rev:** Soccer player **Edge:** Plain

Date	Mintage	F	VF	XF	Unc	BU
2002 Proof	4,500	Value: 225				

Y# 429 100 ZLOTYCH

8.0000 g., 0.9000 Gold 0.2315 oz. AGW, 21 mm. **Obv:** Crowned eagle **Rev:** Bust of crowned King Kazimierz III (1333-1370) **Edge:** Plain

Date	Mintage	F	VF	XF	Unc	BU
2002 Proof	2,400	Value: 225				

Y# 430 100 ZLOTYCH

8.0000 g., 0.9000 Gold 0.2315 oz. AGW, 21 mm. **Obv:** Crowned eagle **Rev:** Bust of crowned King Wladyslaw II Jagiello (1386-1434) half left **Edge:** Plain

Date	Mintage	F	VF	XF	Unc	BU
2002 Proof	2,200	Value: 225				

Y# 454 100 ZLOTYCH

8.0000 g., 0.9000 Gold 0.2315 oz. AGW, 21 mm. **Obv:** Crowned eagle **Rev:** King Wladyslaw III (1434-1444) **Edge:** Plain

Date	Mintage	F	VF	XF	Unc	BU
2003MW Proof	2,000	Value: 225				

Y# 466 100 ZLOTYCH

8.0000 g., 0.9000 Gold 0.2315 oz. AGW, 21 mm. **Subject:** 750th Anniversary - City Charter **Obv:** Door knocker and church **Rev:** Clock face and tower **Edge:** Plain

Date	Mintage	F	VF	XF	Unc	BU
2003MW Proof	2,100	Value: 225				

Y# 467 100 ZLOTYCH

8.0000 g., 0.9000 Gold 0.2315 oz. AGW, 21 mm. **Obv:** Crowned eagle **Rev:** Kazimierz IV (1447-1492) **Edge:** Plain

Date	Mintage	F	VF	XF	Unc	BU
2003MW Proof	2,300	Value: 225				

Y# 476 100 ZLOTYCH

8.0000 g., 0.9000 Gold 0.2315 oz. AGW, 21 mm. **Obv:** Crowned eagle **Rev:** Stanislaus I and eagle **Edge:** Plain

Date	Mintage	F	VF	XF	Unc	BU
2003MW Proof	2,500	Value: 225				

Y# 494 100 ZLOTYCH

8.0000 g., 0.9000 Gold 0.2315 oz. AGW, 21 mm. **Obv:** Crowned eagle **Rev:** King Przemysl II (1295-1296) **Edge:** Plain

Date	Mintage	F	VF	XF	Unc	BU
2004MW Proof	3,400	Value: 225				

Y# 495 100 ZLOTYCH

8.0000 g., 0.9000 Gold 0.2315 oz. AGW, 21 mm. **Obv:** Crowned eagle **Rev:** King Zygmunt I (1506-1548) **Edge:** Plain

Date	Mintage	F	VF	XF	Unc	BU
2004MW Proof	3,400	Value: 225				

Y# 407 200 ZLOTYCH

Tri-Metallic Gold with Palladium center, Gold with Silver ring, Gold with Copper outer limit, 27 mm. **Subject:** Year 2001 **Obv:** Crowned eagle in a swirl **Rev:** Couple looking into the future **Edge:** Plain

Date	Mintage	F	VF	XF	Unc	BU
2001 Proof	4,000	Value: 200				

Y# 420 200 ZLOTYCH

15.5000 g., 0.9000 Gold .4485 oz. AGW, 27 mm. **Subject:** Cardinal Stefan Wyszynski **Obv:** Pillar divides arms and eagle **Rev:** Cardinal's portrait **Edge Lettering:** "100 ROCZNIA URODZIN"

Date	Mintage	F	VF	XF	Unc	BU
2001 Proof	4,500	Value: 350				

Y# 463 200 ZLOTYCH

15.5000 g., 0.9000 Gold 0.4485 oz. AGW, 27 mm. **Obv:** Standing violinist **Rev:** Henry Wieniawski **Edge:** Lettered **Edge Lettering:** "XII MIEDZYNARODOWY KONKURS SKRZYPCOWY IM HENRYKA WIENIAWSKIEGO"

Date	Mintage	F	VF	XF	Unc	BU
2001MW Proof	2,000	Value: 365				

Y# 438 200 ZLOTYCH

15.5000 g., 0.9000 Gold 0.4485 oz. AGW, 27 mm. **Subject:** Pope John Paul II **Obv:** Bust of Pope at right facing left, small eagle in background **Rev:** Pope facing radiant Holy Door **Edge:** Plain

Date	Mintage	F	VF	XF	Unc	BU
2002 Proof	5,000	Value: 350				

Y# 470 200 ZLOTYCH

15.5000 g., 0.9000 Gold 0.4485 oz. AGW, 27 mm. **Subject:** Gas and Oil Industry **Obv:** Crowned eagle, oil wells and refinery **Rev:** Scientist at work **Edge:** Plain

Date	Mintage	F	VF	XF	Unc	BU
2003MW Proof	2,100	Value: 375				

Y# 472 200 ZLOTYCH

15.5000 g., 0.9000 Gold 0.4485 oz. AGW, 27 mm. **Obv:** Standing Pope John Paul II **Rev:** Seated Pope **Edge:** Plain

Date	Mintage	F	VF	XF	Unc	BU
2003MW Proof	4,900	Value: 375				

Y# 483 200 ZLOTYCH

15.5000 g., 0.9000 Gold 0.4485 oz. AGW, 27 mm. **Subject:** Poland Joining the European Union **Obv:** Polish euro coin design elements **Rev:** Polish euro coin design elements **Edge:** Plain

Date	Mintage	F	VF	XF	Unc	BU
2004MW Proof	4,400	Value: 350				

Y# 511 200 ZLOTYCH

15.5000 g., 0.9000 Gold 0.4485 oz. AGW, 27 mm. **Subject:** Warsaw Fine Arts Academy Centennial **Obv:** Campus view **Rev:** Statue and building **Edge:** Plain

Date	Mintage	F	VF	XF	Unc	BU
2004MW Proof	5,000	Value: 350				

Y# 519 200 ZLOTYCH

15.5000 g., 0.9000 Gold 0.4485 oz. AGW, 27 mm. **Subject:** Olympics **Obv:** Woman and crowned eagle **Rev:** Ancient runners painted on pottery **Edge:** Plain

Date	Mintage	F	VF	XF	Unc	BU
2004MW Proof	6,000	Value: 350				

PORTUGAL

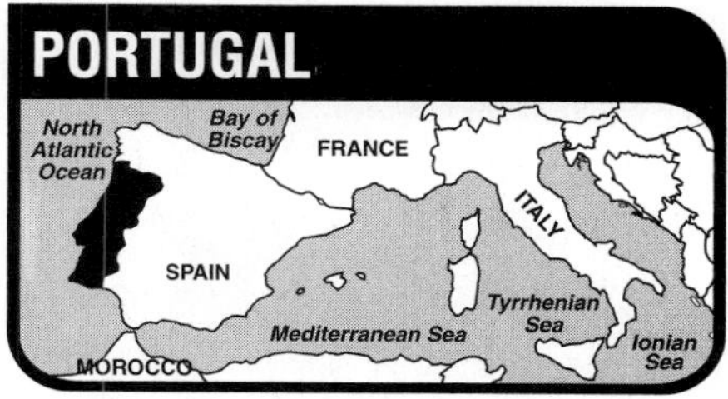

The Portuguese Republic, located in the western part of the Iberian Peninsula in southwestern Europe, has an area of 35,553 sq. mi. (92,080 sq. km.) and a population of *10.5 million. Capital: Lisbon. Portugal's economy is based on agriculture, tourism, minerals, fisheries and a rapidly expanding industrial sector. Textiles account for 33% of the exports and Portuguese wine is world famous. Portugal has become Europe's number one producer of copper and the world's largest producer of cork.

RULERS

Republic, 1910 to date

MONETARY SYSTEM

100 Cents = 1 Euro

REPUBLIC

DECIMAL COINAGE

KM# 631a ESCUDO

4.6000 g., 0.9167 Gold 0.1356 oz. AGW, 16 mm. **Subject:** Last Escudo **Obv:** Similar to KM#631 but with addition of "Au" above top left shield corner **Rev:** Same as KM#631 **Edge:** Plain

Date	Mintage	F	VF	XF	Unc	BU
2001INCM	50,000	—	—	—	115	—

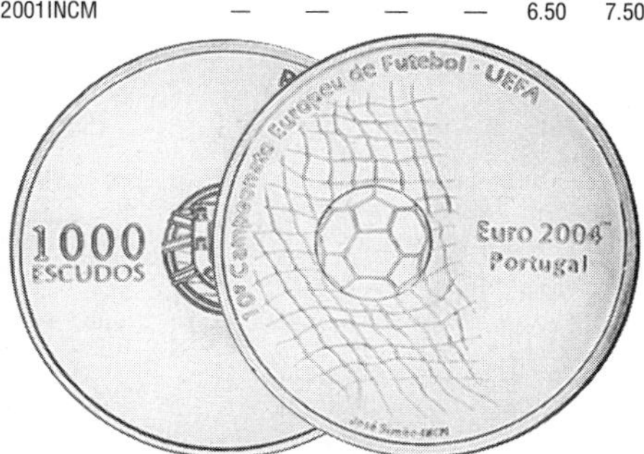

KM# 733 500 ESCUDOS

13.9600 g., 0.5000 Silver .2244 oz. ASW, 30.1 mm. **Subject:** Porto, European Culture Capital **Obv:** National arms and denomination **Rev:** Stylized design **Edge:** Reeded

Date	Mintage	F	VF	XF	Unc	BU
2001INCM	—	—	—	—	6.50	7.50

KM# 734 1000 ESCUDOS

26.9500 g., 0.5000 Silver .4332 oz. ASW, 40 mm. **Obv:** National arms and denomination **Rev:** Soccer ball **Edge:** Reeded

Date	Mintage	F	VF	XF	Unc	BU
2001	—	—	—	—	13.50	15.00

EURO COINAGE

European Economic Community Issues

KM# 740 EURO CENT

2.2700 g., Copper Plated Steel, 16.2 mm. **Obv:** Royal seal of 1134, country name in cross **Obv. Designer:** Vitor Santos **Rev:** Denomination and globe **Rev. Designer:** Luc Luycx **Edge:** Plain

Date	Mintage	F	VF	XF	Unc	BU
2002INCM	278,000,000	—	—	—	0.35	0.50

KM# 741 2 EURO CENTS

3.0300 g., Copper Plated Steel, 18.7 mm. **Obv:** Royal seal of 1134, country name in cross **Obv. Designer:** Vitor Santos **Rev:** Denomination and globe **Rev. Designer:** Luc Luycx **Edge:** Grooved

Date	Mintage	F	VF	XF	Unc	BU
2002INCM	322,000,000	—	—	—	0.50	0.65
2003INCM	—	—	—	—	0.50	0.65

KM# 742 5 EURO CENTS

3.8600 g., Copper Plated Steel, 21.2 mm. **Obv:** Royal seal of 1134, country name in cross **Obv. Designer:** Vitor Santos **Rev:** Denomination and globe **Rev. Designer:** Luc Luycx **Edge:** Plain

Date	Mintage	F	VF	XF	Unc	BU
2002INCM	234,000,000	—	—	—	0.75	1.00
2003INCM	—	—	—	—	0.75	1.00

KM# 743 10 EURO CENTS

4.0700 g., Brass, 19.7 mm. **Obv:** Royal seal of 1142, country name in circular design **Obv. Designer:** Vitor Santos **Rev:** Denomination and map **Rev. Designer:** Luc Luycx **Edge:** Reeded

Date	Mintage	F	VF	XF	Unc	BU
2002INCM	220,000,000	—	—	—	0.75	1.00
2003INCM	—	—	—	—	0.75	1.00

KM# 744 20 EURO CENTS

5.7300 g., Brass, 22.1 mm. **Obv:** Royal seal of 1142, country name in circular design **Obv. Designer:** Vitor Santos **Rev:** Denomination and map **Rev. Designer:** Luc Luycx **Edge:** Notched

Date	Mintage	F	VF	XF	Unc	BU
2002INCM	144,000,000	—	—	—	1.25	1.50
2003INCM	—	—	—	—	1.25	1.50

KM# 745 50 EURO CENTS

7.8100 g., Brass, 24.2 mm. **Obv:** Royal seal of 1142, country name in circular design **Obv. Designer:** Vitor Santos **Rev:** Denomination and map **Rev. Designer:** Luc Luycx **Edge:** Reeded

Date	Mintage	F	VF	XF	Unc	BU
2002INCM	152,000,000	—	—	—	1.50	2.00
2003INCM	—	—	—	—	1.50	2.00

KM# 746 EURO

7.5000 g., Bi-Metallic Copper-Nickel center in Brass ring, 23.2 mm. **Obv:** Royal seal of 1144, country name in looped design **Obv. Designer:** Vitor Santos **Rev:** Denomination and map **Rev. Designer:** Luc Luycx **Edge:** Reeded and plain sections

Date	Mintage	F	VF	XF	Unc	BU
2002INCM	96,000,000	—	—	—	2.75	3.50
2003INCM	—	—	—	—	2.75	3.50

KM# 747 2 EUROS

8.5200 g., Bi-Metallic Brass center in Copper-Nickel ring, 25.7 mm. **Obv:** Royal seal fo 1144, country name in looped design **Obv. Designer:** Vitor Santos **Rev:** Denomination and map **Rev. Designer:** Luc Luycx **Edge:** Reeding over castles and shields

Date	Mintage	F	VF	XF	Unc	BU
2002INCM	59,000,000	—	—	—	4.25	5.00
2003INCM	—	—	—	—	4.25	5.00

KM# 749 5 EURO

14.0000 g., 0.5000 Silver 0.2251 oz. ASW, 30 mm. **Subject:** 150th Anniversary - First Portuguese Postage Stamp **Obv:** National arms and value **Rev:** Partial postal stamp design **Edge:** Reeded

Date	Mintage	F	VF	XF	Unc	BU
2003INCM	300,000	—	—	—	30.00	32.50

KM# 749a 5 EURO

14.0000 g., 0.9250 Silver 0.4164 oz. ASW, 30 mm. **Obv:** National arms and value **Rev:** Partial postal stamp design

Date	Mintage	F	VF	XF	Unc	BU
2003INCM Proof	20,000	Value: 40.00				

KM# 749b 5 EURO

17.5000 g., 0.9166 Gold 0.5157 oz. AGW, 30 mm. **Obv:** National arms and value **Rev:** Partial postal stamp design

Date	Mintage	F	VF	XF	Unc	BU
2003INCM Proof	—	Value: 400				

KM# 754 5 EURO

14.0000 g., 0.5000 Silver 0.2251 oz. ASW, 30 mm. **Subject:** Convent of Christ **Obv:** National arms above value **Rev:** Ornate convent window **Edge:** Reeded

Date	Mintage	F	VF	XF	Unc	BU
2004INCM	300,000	—	—	—	30.00	32.50

KM# 754a 5 EURO

14.0000 g., 0.9250 Silver 0.4164 oz. ASW, 30 mm. **Subject:** Convent of Christ **Obv:** National arms above value **Rev:** Ornate convent window **Edge:** Reeded

Date	Mintage	F	VF	XF	Unc	BU
2004INCM Proof	10,000	Value: 50.00				

KM# 755 5 EURO

14.0000 g., 0.5000 Silver 0.2251 oz. ASW, 30 mm. **Subject:** Historic City of Evora **Obv:** National arms and value on city map silhouette **Rev:** Architectural highlights **Edge:** Reeded

Date	Mintage	F	VF	XF	Unc	BU
2004INCM	300,000	—	—	—	30.00	32.50

KM# 755a 5 EURO

14.0000 g., 0.9250 Silver 0.4164 oz. ASW, 30 mm. **Subject:** Historic City of Evora **Obv:** National arms and value on city map silhouette **Rev:** Architectural highlights **Edge:** Reeded

Date	Mintage	F	VF	XF	Unc	BU
2004INCM Proof	10,000	Value: 50.00				

KM# 760 5 EURO

14.0000 g., 0.5000 Silver 0.2251 oz. ASW, 30 mm. **Obv:** National arms and value **Rev:** Angra do Heroismo harbor view **Edge:** Reeded

Date	Mintage	F	VF	XF	Unc	BU
2005	—	—	—	—	30.00	32.50

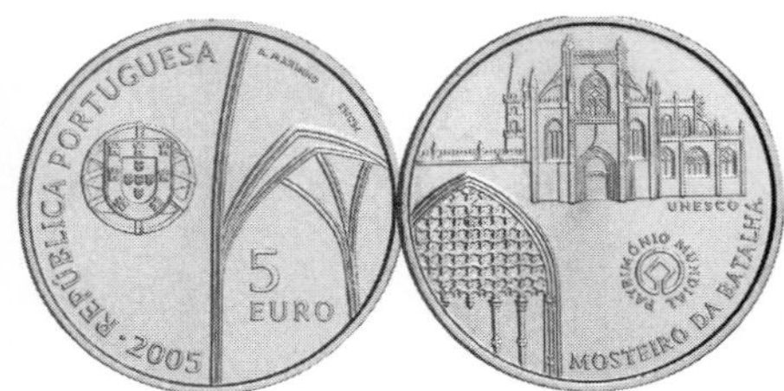

KM# 761 5 EURO
14.0000 g., 0.5000 Silver 0.2251 oz. ASW, 30 mm. **Obv:** National arms and value **Rev:** Batalha Monastery **Edge:** Reeded

Date	Mintage	F	VF	XF	Unc	BU
2005	—	—	—	—	30.00	32.50

KM# 762 5 EURO
14.0000 g., 0.5000 Silver 0.2251 oz. ASW, 30 mm. **Obv:** National arms and value **Rev:** Pope John XXI **Edge:** Reeded

Date	Mintage	F	VF	XF	Unc	BU
2005	—	—	—	—	30.00	32.50

KM# 750 8 EURO
21.1000 g., 0.5000 Silver 0.9249 oz. ASW, 36 mm. **Obv:** National arms, value and flag-covered globe **Rev:** Flag-covered globe and "Euro 2004" soccer games logo **Edge:** Reeded

Date	Mintage	F	VF	XF	Unc	BU
2003INCM	1,500,000	—	—	—	35.00	37.50

KM# 750a 8 EURO
31.1000 g., 0.9250 Silver 0.9249 oz. ASW, 36 mm. **Obv:** National arms, value and flag-covered globe **Rev:** Flag-covered globe and "Euro 2004" soccer games logo

Date	Mintage	F	VF	XF	Unc	BU
2003INCM Proof	—	Value: 45.00				

KM# 750b 8 EURO
31.1000 g., 0.9166 Gold 0.9165 oz. AGW, 36 mm. **Obv:** National arms, value and flag-covered globe **Rev:** Flag-covered globe and "Euro 2004" soccer games logo

Date	Mintage	F	VF	XF	Unc	BU
2003INCM Proof	—	Value: 650				

KM# 751 8 EURO
21.1000 g., 0.5000 Silver 0.9249 oz. ASW, 36 mm. **Obv:** National arms and value below many bubbles **Rev:** "Euro 2004" soccer games logo below many hearts **Edge:** Reeded

Date	Mintage	F	VF	XF	Unc	BU
2003INCM	1,500,000	—	—	—	35.00	37.50

KM# 751a 8 EURO
31.1000 g., 0.9250 Silver 0.9249 oz. ASW, 36 mm.
Obv: National arms and value below many bubbles **Rev:** "Euro 2004" soccer games logo below many hearts

Date	Mintage	F	VF	XF	Unc	BU
2003INCM Proof	—	Value: 45.00				

KM# 751b 8 EURO
31.1000 g., 0.9166 Gold 0.9165 oz. AGW, 36 mm.
Obv: National arms and value below many bubbles **Rev:** "Euro 2004" soccer games logo below many hearts

Date	Mintage	F	VF	XF	Unc	BU
2003INCM Proof	—	Value: 650				

KM# 752 8 EURO
21.1000 g., 0.5000 Silver 0.9249 oz. ASW, 36 mm.
Obv: National arms and value **Rev:** "Euro 2004" soccer games logo in center with partial text background **Edge:** Reeded

Date	Mintage	F	VF	XF	Unc	BU
2003INCM	1,500,000	—	—	—	35.00	37.50

KM# 752a 8 EURO
31.1000 g., 0.9250 Silver 0.9249 oz. ASW, 36 mm.
Obv: National arms and value **Rev:** "Euro 2004" soccer games logo in center with partial text background

Date	Mintage	F	VF	XF	Unc	BU
2003INCM Proof	—	Value: 45.00				

KM# 752b 8 EURO
31.1000 g., 0.9166 Gold 0.9165 oz. AGW, 36 mm.
Obv: National arms and value **Rev:** "Euro 2004" soccer games logo in center with partial text background

Date	Mintage	F	VF	XF	Unc	BU
2003INCM Proof	—	Value: 650				

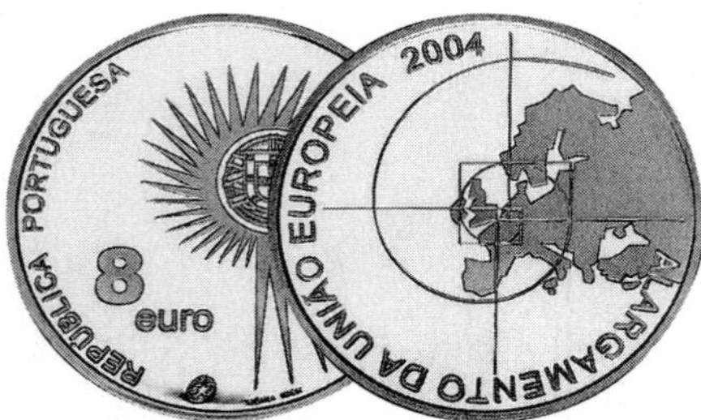

KM# 753 8 EURO
21.2200 g., 0.5000 Silver 0.3411 oz. ASW, 36 mm.
Subject: Expansion of the European Union **Obv:** Radiant national arms and value **Rev:** European map **Edge:** Reeded

Date	Mintage	F	VF	XF	Unc	BU
2004INCM	300,000	—	—	—	20.00	22.50

KM# 753a 8 EURO
31.1000 g., 0.9250 Silver 0.9249 oz. ASW, 36 mm.
Subject: Expansion of the European Union **Obv:** Radiant national arms and value **Rev:** European map **Edge:** Reeded

Date	Mintage	F	VF	XF	Unc	BU
2004INCM Proof	35,000	Value: 50.00				

KM# 756 8 EURO
21.0000 g., 0.5000 Silver 0.3376 oz. ASW, 36 mm.
Subject: Euro 2004 Soccer **Obv:** National arms **Rev:** Stylized goal keeper **Edge:** Reeded

Date	Mintage	F	VF	XF	Unc	BU
2004INCM	1,500,000	—	—	—	12.50	15.00

KM# 756a 8 EURO
31.1000 g., 0.9250 Silver 0.9249 oz. ASW, 36 mm.
Subject: Euro 2004 Soccer **Obv:** National arms **Rev:** Stylized goal keeper **Edge:** Reeded

Date	Mintage	F	VF	XF	Unc	BU
2004INCM	30,000	—	—	—	—	30.00
2004INCM Proof	15,000	Value: 50.00				

KM# 756b 8 EURO
31.1000 g., 0.9166 Gold 0.9165 oz. AGW, 36 mm.
Subject: Euro 2004 Soccer **Obv:** National arms **Rev:** Stylized goal keeper **Edge:** Reeded

Date	Mintage	F	VF	XF	Unc	BU
2004INCM Proof	10,000	Value: 650				

KM# 757 8 EURO
21.0000 g., 0.9250 Silver 0.6245 oz. ASW, 36 mm.
Subject: Euro 2004 Soccer **Obv:** National arms **Rev:** Face of player making shot **Edge:** Reeded

Date	Mintage	F	VF	XF	Unc	BU
2004INCM	1,500,000	—	—	—	12.50	15.00

KM# 757a 8 EURO
31.1000 g., 0.9250 Silver 0.9249 oz. ASW, 36 mm.
Subject: Euro 2004 Soccer **Obv:** National arms **Rev:** Face of player making a shot **Edge:** Reeded

Date	Mintage	F	VF	XF	Unc	BU
2004INCM	30,000	—	—	—	—	30.00
2004INCM Proof	15,000	Value: 50.00				

KM# 757b 8 EURO
31.1000 g., 0.9166 Gold 0.9165 oz. AGW, 36 mm.
Subject: Euro 2004 Soccer **Obv:** National arms **Rev:** Face of player making a shot **Edge:** Reeded

Date	Mintage	F	VF	XF	Unc	BU
2004INCM Proof	10,000	Value: 650				

KM# 758 8 EURO
21.0000 g., 0.5000 Silver 0.3376 oz. ASW, 36 mm.
Subject: Euro 2004 Soccer **Obv:** National arms **Rev:** Symbolic explosion of a goal **Edge:** Reeded

Date	Mintage	F	VF	XF	Unc	BU
2004INCM	1,500,000	—	—	—	12.50	15.00

KM# 758a 8 EURO
31.1000 g., 0.9250 Silver 0.9249 oz. ASW, 36 mm.
Subject: Euro 2004 Soccer **Obv:** National arms **Rev:** Symbolic explosion of a goal **Edge:** Reeded

Date	Mintage	F	VF	XF	Unc	BU
2004INCM	30,000	—	—	—	—	30.00
2004INCM Proof	15,000	Value: 50.00				

KM# 758b 8 EURO
31.1000 g., 0.9166 Gold 0.9165 oz. AGW, 36 mm.
Subject: Euro 2004 Soccer **Obv:** National arms **Rev:** Symbolic explosion of a goal **Edge:** Reeded

Date	Mintage	F	VF	XF	Unc	BU
2004INCM Proof	10,000	Value: 650				

KM# 748 10 EURO
27.0000 g., 0.5000 Silver 0.434 oz. ASW, 40 mm.
Subject: Nautica **Obv:** National arms in inner ring, symbols all around **Rev:** Sailing ship and sextant **Edge:** Reeded

Date	Mintage	F	VF	XF	Unc	BU
2003INCM	350,000	—	—	—	20.00	22.50

KM# 748a 10 EURO
27.0000 g., 0.9250 Silver 0.803 oz. ASW, 40 mm. **Edge:** Reeded

Date	Mintage	F	VF	XF	Unc	BU
2003INCM Proof	10,000	Value: 50.00				

KM# 759 10 EURO
27.0000 g., 0.5000 Silver 0.434 oz. ASW, 40 mm.
Subject: Olympics **Obv:** National arms above value **Rev:** Sail above Olympic rings **Edge:** Reeded

Date	Mintage	F	VF	XF	Unc	BU
2004INCM	350,000	—	—	—	25.00	27.50

KM# 759a 10 EURO
27.0000 g., 0.9250 Silver 0.803 oz. ASW, 40 mm.
Subject: Olympics **Obv:** National arms above value **Rev:** Sail above Olympic rings **Edge:** Reeded

Date	Mintage	F	VF	XF	Unc	BU
2004INCM Proof	15,000	Value: 55.00				

QATAR

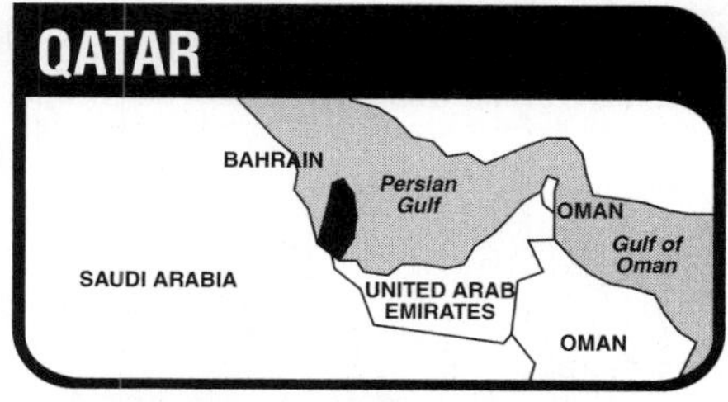

The State of Qatar, an emirate in the Persian Gulf between Bahrain and Trucial Oman, has an area of 4,247sq. mi. (11,000 sq. km.) and a population of *469,000. Capital: Doha. Oil is the chief industry and export.

TITLES

Daulat Qatar

RULERS

Al-Thani Dynasty

Hamad bin Khalifah, 1995-

MONETARY SYSTEM

100 Dirhem = 1 Riyal

EMIRATE

STANDARD COINAGE

KM# 4 25 DIRHAMS

Copper-Nickel **Ruler:** Khalifah Bin Hamad **Rev:** Dhow

Date	Mintage	F	VF	XF	Unc	BU
AH1424 - 2003	—	—	0.25	0.65	1.75	2.50

KM# 9 50 DIRHAMS

6.5000 g., Copper-Nickel, 24 mm. **Ruler:** Hamad bin Khalifah **Obv:** Denomination **Rev:** Dhow and palm trees **Edge:** Reeded

Date	Mintage	F	VF	XF	Unc	BU
AH1424-2002	—	—	—	—	2.00	3.00
AH1424-2003	—	—	—	—	2.00	3.00

ROMANIA

Romania (formerly the Socialist Republic of Romania), a country in southeast Europe, has an area of 91,699 sq. mi. (237,500 sq. km.) and a population of 23.2 million. Capital: Bucharest. Machinery, foodstuffs, raw minerals and petroleum products are exported. Heavy industry and oil have become increasingly important to the economy since 1959.

MONETARY SYSTEM

100 Bani = 1 Leu

REPUBLIC

STANDARD COINAGE

KM# 115 LEU

Copper Clad Steel **Rev:** Coat of arms

Date	Mintage	F	VF	XF	Unc	BU
2002 Proof	1,500	Value: 5.00				
2003 Proof	2,000	Value: 5.00				
2004 Proof	2,000	Value: 5.00				
2005 Proof	—	Value: 6.00				
2005	—	—	—	—	1.00	—

KM# 114 5 LEI

Nickel Plated Steel **Edge:** Plain

Date	Mintage	F	VF	XF	Unc	BU
2002 Proof	1,500	Value: 5.00				
2003 Proof	2,000	Value: 5.00				
2004 Proof	—	Value: 5.00				
2005 Proof	—	Value: 5.00				

KM# 116 10 LEI

Nickel-Clad Steel

Date	Mintage	F	VF	XF	Unc	BU
2002 Proof	1,500	Value: 6.00				
2003 Proof	2,000	Value: 6.00				

KM# 109 20 LEI

5.0000 g., Brass Clad Steel, 24 mm. **Obv:** Bust of King Stefan Cel Mare **Edge:** Plain **Designer:** Constantin Dumitrescu
Note: Date varieties exist.

Date	Mintage	F	VF	XF	Unc	BU
2002 Proof	1,500	Value: 7.50				
2003 Proof	2,000	Value: 7.50				

KM# 159 50 LEI

15.5510 g., 0.9990 Silver 0.4995 oz. ASW, 31.1 mm.
Series: Romanian Aviation **Obv:** AVIONUL VUIA 1 - 1906 airplane **Rev:** Portrait of Traian Vuia **Edge:** Plain **Shape:** Octagonal

Date	Mintage	F	VF	XF	Unc	BU
2001 Proof	500	Value: 70.00				

KM# 160 50 LEI

15.5510 g., 0.9990 Silver 0.4995 oz. ASW, 31.1 mm.
Series: Romanian Aviation **Obv:** Avionul Coanda 1910, world's first (?) jet airplane **Rev:** Portrait of Henri Coanda **Edge:** Plain **Shape:** Octagonal

Date	Mintage	F	VF	XF	Unc	BU
2001 Proof	500	Value: 70.00				

KM# 161 50 LEI

15.5510 g., 0.9990 Silver 0.4995 oz. ASW, 31.1 mm.
Series: Romanian Aviation **Obv:** IAR CV-11 airplane **Rev:** Elie Carafoli portrait **Edge:** Plain **Shape:** Octagonal

Date	Mintage	F	VF	XF	Unc	BU
2001 Proof	500	Value: 70.00				

KM# 195 50 LEI

15.5510 g., 0.9990 Silver 0.4995 oz. ASW, 29.5 mm.
Subject: National Parks: Retezzf **Shape:** Triangle

Date	Mintage	F	VF	XF	Unc	BU
2002 Proof	—	Value: 85.00				

KM# 196 50 LEI

15.5510 g., 0.9990 Silver 0.4995 oz. ASW, 29.5 mm.
Subject: National Parks: Pictrosul Mare **Shape:** Triangle

Date	Mintage	F	VF	XF	Unc	BU
2002 Proof	—	Value: 85.00				

KM# 197 50 LEI

15.5510 g., 0.9990 Silver 0.4995 oz. ASW, 29.5 mm.
Subject: National Parks: Piztra Crzivtvi **Shape:** Triangle

Date	Mintage	F	VF	XF	Unc	BU
2002 Proof	—	Value: 85.00				

KM# 110 50 LEI

5.9000 g., Brass Clad Steel, 26 mm. **Obv:** Bust of Prince Alexandru Ioan Cuza **Edge:** Plain **Designer:** Vasile Gabor

Date	Mintage	F	VF	XF	Unc	BU
2002 Proof	1,500	Value: 8.00				
2003 Proof	2,000	Value: 8.00				

KM# 167 50 LEI

15.5510 g., 0.9990 Silver 0.4995 oz. ASW **Subject:** Wildlife **Obv:** National arms in triangular design **Rev:** Chamois **Edge:** Plain **Shape:** Rounded triangle

Date	Mintage	F	VF	XF	Unc	BU
2002 Proof	500	Value: 80.00				

KM# 168 50 LEI

15.5510 g., 0.9990 Silver 0.4995 oz. ASW, 27 mm.
Subject: Wildlife **Obv:** National arms in triangular design **Rev:** Eagle **Edge:** Plain **Shape:** Rounded triangle

Date	Mintage	F	VF	XF	Unc	BU
2002 Proof	500	Value: 80.00				

KM# 169 50 LEI

15.5510 g., 0.9990 Silver 0.4995 oz. ASW **Subject:** Wildlife **Obv:** National arms in triangular design **Rev:** Lynx **Edge:** Plain **Shape:** Rounded triangle

Date	Mintage	F	VF	XF	Unc	BU
2002 Proof	500	Value: 80.00				

KM# 186 50 LEI

15.5510 g., 0.9990 Silver 0.4995 oz. ASW, 26.8 mm. **Subject:** Birds **Obv:** Stylized water drop **Rev:** Pelicans **Edge:** Plain

Date	Mintage	F	VF	XF	Unc	BU
2003 Proof	500	Value: 75.00				

KM# 187 50 LEI

15.5510 g., 0.9990 Silver 0.4995 oz. ASW, 26.8 mm.
Subject: Birds **Obv:** Stylized water drop **Rev:** Egret **Edge:** Plain

Date	Mintage	F	VF	XF	Unc	BU
2003 Proof	500	Value: 75.00				

KM# 188 50 LEI
15.5510 g., 0.9990 Silver 0.4995 oz. ASW, 26.8 mm. **Subject:** Birds **Obv:** Stylized water drop **Rev:** Common Kingfisher **Edge:** Plain

Date	Mintage	F	VF	XF	Unc	BU
2003 Proof	500	Value: 75.00				

KM# 111 100 LEI
8.7500 g., Nickel Plated Steel **Obv:** Bust of Prince Mihai Viteazul **Edge Lettering:** ROMANIA **Designer:** Vasile Gabor

Date	Mintage	F	VF	XF	Unc	BU
2002 Proof	1,500	Value: 8.00				
2003 Proof	2,000	Value: 8.00				
2004 Proof	2,000	Value: 8.00				
2005 Proof	2,000	Value: 9.00				
2005	—	—	—	—	2.50	—

KM# 165 100 LEI
1.2240 g., 0.9990 Gold 0.0393 oz. AGW **Subject:** History of Gold **Obv:** National arms in ornamental circle above value **Rev:** Eagle of Apahida **Edge:** Plain

Date	Mintage	F	VF	XF	Unc	BU
2003 Proof	2,000	Value: 100				

KM# 166 100 LEI
1.2240 g., 0.9990 Gold 0.0393 oz. AGW, 14 mm. **Subject:** History of Gold **Obv:** National arms and country name above two stylized birds and value **Rev:** Jeweled double headed eagle pendant

Date	Mintage	F	VF	XF	Unc	BU
2004 Proof	1,000	Value: 150				

KM# 170 500 LEI
6.2200 g., 0.9990 Gold, 12 mm. **Subject:** History of Gold **Rev:** "Big clip" of Pietroasa

Date	Mintage	F	VF	XF	Unc	BU
2001	250	—	—	—	—	165

KM# 171 500 LEI
6.2200 g., 0.9990 Gold 0.1998 oz. AGW **Subject:** History of Gold **Rev:** "Medium Clip" of Pietroasa

Date	Mintage	F	VF	XF	Unc	BU
2001	250	—	—	—	—	165

KM# 172 500 LEI
6.2200 g., 0.9990 Gold 0.1998 oz. AGW **Subject:** History of Gold **Rev:** 12-sided golden bowl

Date	Mintage	F	VF	XF	Unc	BU
2001	250	—	—	—	—	165

KM# 173 500 LEI
6.2200 g., 0.9990 Gold 0.1998 oz. AGW **Subject:** History of Gold **Rev:** Pitcher

Date	Mintage	F	VF	XF	Unc	BU
2001	250	—	—	—	—	165

KM# 174 500 LEI
6.2200 g., 0.9990 Gold 0.1998 oz. AGW **Subject:** Christian Monuments **Rev:** Bistritz Monastery

Date	Mintage	F	VF	XF	Unc	BU
2002	250	—	—	—	—	165

KM# 175 500 LEI
6.2200 g., 0.9990 Gold 0.1998 oz. AGW **Subject:** Christian Monuments **Rev:** Coltea Church

Date	Mintage	F	VF	XF	Unc	BU
2002	250	—	—	—	—	165

KM# 176 500 LEI
6.2200 g., 0.9990 Gold 0.1998 oz. AGW, 23 mm. **Subject:** Christian Monuments **Rev:** Mogosoaia Palace **Shape:** Square

Date	Mintage	F	VF	XF	Unc	BU
2001	250	—	—	—	—	165

KM# 145 500 LEI
3.7000 g., Aluminum, 25 mm. **Obv:** Denomination **Rev:** National arms **Edge:** Lettered **Edge Lettering:** ROMANIA (three times)

Date	Mintage	F	VF	XF	Unc	BU
2001	—	—	—	0.75	2.00	—
2002 Proof	1,500	Value: 7.00				
2003 Proof	2,000	Value: 7.00				
2004 Proof	2,000	Value: 7.00				
2005 Proof	2,000	Value: 8.00				
2005	—	—	—	—	3.00	—

KM# 177 500 LEI
31.1030 g., 0.9990 Silver 0.999 oz. ASW, 37 mm. **Subject:** Ciprian Porumbescu, Composer, Birth Anniversary **Obv:** Partial piano and violin left of National arms and value **Rev:** Portrait and musical score **Edge:** Plain

Date	Mintage	F	VF	XF	Unc	BU
2003 Proof	500	Value: 60.00				

KM# 178 500 LEI
31.1030 g., 0.9990 Silver 0.999 oz. ASW, 37 mm. **Subject:** Bishopric of Ramnic, 500th Anniversary **Obv:** National arms and value above inscription **Rev:** Bishopric's coat-of-arms **Edge:** Plain

Date	Mintage	F	VF	XF	Unc	BU
2003 Proof	500	Value: 60.00				

KM# 179 500 LEI
31.1030 g., 0.9990 Silver 0.999 oz. ASW, 37 mm. **Subject:** Romanian Numismatic Society Centennial **Obv:** Cornucopia above value **Rev:** Minerva and torch

Date	Mintage	F	VF	XF	Unc	BU
2003 Proof	1,000	Value: 50.00				

KM# 180 500 LEI
31.1030 g., 0.9990 Silver 0.999 oz. ASW, 37 mm. **Subject:** 140th Anniversary - University of Bucharest **Obv:** National arms, value and date at left. University emblem at right **Rev:** Prince Alexandru Ion Cuza cameo and crowned arms above University Building **Edge:** Plain

Date	Mintage	F	VF	XF	Unc	BU
2004 Proof	500	Value: 60.00				

KM# 193 500 LEI
31.1035 g., 0.9990 Silver 0.999 oz. ASW, 37 mm. **Obv:** Cernavoda bridge **Rev:** Bridge builder Anghel Saligny **Edge:** Plain

Date	Mintage	F	VF	XF	Unc	BU
2004 Proof	500	Value: 60.00				

KM# 163 500 LEI
31.1030 g., 0.9990 Silver 0.999 oz. ASW, 37 mm. **Subject:** Feudal art **Obv:** National arms and value left of church tower **Rev:** Cotroceni Monastery church **Edge:** plain, ten sided

Date	Mintage	F	VF	XF	Unc	BU
2004 Proof	500	Value: 60.00				

KM# 164 500 LEI
31.1030 g., 0.9990 Silver 0.999 oz. ASW, 37 mm. **Subject:** Fuedal art **Obv:** National arms, bell and value **Rev:** St. Trei Ierarhi church in Iasi **Edge:** Plain, ten sided

Date	Mintage	F	VF	XF	Unc	BU
2004 Proof	500	Value: 60.00				

KM# 194 500 LEI
31.1035 g., 0.9990 Silver 0.999 oz. ASW, 37 mm. **Subject:** 125th Anniversary - National Bank **Obv:** National arms and coin design of 5 Lei dated 1880 **Rev:** Bank building **Edge:** Plain

Date	Mintage	F	VF	XF	Unc	BU
2005 Proof	—	Value: 60.00				

KM# 153 1000 LEI
2.0000 g., Aluminum, 22.2 mm. **Subject:** Constantin Brancoveanu **Obv:** Denomination above arms **Rev:** Portrait **Edge:** Reeded and plain sections

Date	Mintage	VG	F	VF	XF	Unc
2001	—	—	—	—	0.25	2.50
2002	—	—	—	—	0.25	2.50
2002 Proof	1,500	Value: 12.00				
Note: In proof sets only						
2003	—	—	—	—	0.25	2.50
2003 Proof	2,000	Value: 12.00				
Note: In proof sets only						
2004	—	—	—	—	0.25	2.50
2004 Proof	2,000	Value: 12.00				
Note: In proof sets only						
2005	—	—	—	—	0.25	2.50
2005 Proof	—	Value: 13.00				
Note: In proof sets only						

KM# 156 1000 LEI
15.5510 g., 0.9990 Gold .4995 oz. AGW, 27 mm. **Subject:** 1900th Anniversary of the First Roman-Dacian War **Obv:** Traian's column **Rev:** Monument and cameo portraits of Trajan and King Decebal **Edge:** Plain

Date	Mintage	VG	F	VF	XF	Unc
2001 Proof	500	Value: 450				

KM# 181 2000 LEI
25.0000 g., Bi-Metallic .999 Silver, 10g center in .999 Gold, 15g ring, 35 mm. **Subject:** Ion Heliade Radulescu (1802-1872) **Obv:** Lyre at left, natioal arms at right in divided circle design **Rev:** Ion Heliade Radulescu above signature **Edge:** Reeded

Date	Mintage	F	VF	XF	Unc	BU
2002 Proof	500	Value: 575				

KM# 158 5000 LEI
2.5200 g., Aluminum, 23.5 mm. **Obv:** Denomination and country name **Rev:** National arms and date **Edge:** Plain **Shape:** 12-sided

Date	Mintage	F	VF	XF	Unc	BU
2001	—	—	—	—	0.50	—
2002	—	—	—	—	0.50	—
2002 Proof	1,500	Value: 15.00				
2003	—	—	—	—	0.25	—
2003 Proof	2,000	Value: 15.00				
2004	—	—	—	—	0.25	—
2004 Proof	2,000	Value: 16.00				
2005	—	—	—	—	0.25	—
2005 Proof	2,000	Value: 17.00				

KM# 162 5000 LEI
31.1035 g., 0.9990 Gold 0.999 oz. AGW, 35 mm. **Subject:** Constantin Brancusi 125th Anniversary of Birth **Obv:** National arms, denomination and sculpture **Rev:** Bearded portrait and signature **Edge:** Plain

Date	Mintage	F	VF	XF	Unc	BU
2001 Proof	500	Value: 800				

KM# 183 5000 LEI
31.1030 g., 0.9990 Gold 0.999 oz. AGW, 35 mm. **Subject:** Ion Luca Caragiale, playright (1852-1912) **Obv:** National arms, value and masks of Comedy and Tragedy **Rev:** Portrait **Edge:** Plain

Date	Mintage	F	VF	XF	Unc	BU
2002 Proof	250	Value: 800				

KM# 184 5000 LEI
31.1030 g., 0.9990 Gold 0.999 oz. AGW, 35 mm. **Subject:** Bran Castle (1378-2003) **Obv:** Two coats of arms on shield above value **Rev:** Castle view **Edge:** Plain

Date	Mintage	F	VF	XF	Unc	BU
2003 Proof	250	Value: 800				

KM# 185 5000 LEI
31.1030 g., 0.9990 Gold 0.999 oz. AGW, 35 mm. **Subject:** Stephen the Great **Obv:** National arms, value above coin design in wall **Rev:** Portrait of Stephen and Putna Monastery

Date	Mintage	F	VF	XF	Unc	BU
2004 Proof	250	Value: 800				

REFORM COINAGE - 2005

KM# 189 BAN
2.4000 g., Copper-Plated-Steel, 16.8 mm. **Subject:** Monetary Reform of 2005 **Obv:** National arms **Rev:** Value **Edge:** Plain

Date	Mintage	F	VF	XF	Unc	BU
2005	—	—	—	—	0.30	0.50
2005 Proof	—	Value: 2.50				

KM# 198 BAN
2.4000 g., Brass Plated Steel, 16.75 mm. **Obv:** National arms **Rev:** Value **Edge:** Plain

Date	Mintage	F	VF	XF	Unc	BU
2005	—	—	—	—	—	0.20

KM# 190 5 BANI
2.8100 g., Copper Plated Steel, 18.2 mm. **Subject:** Monetary Reform of 2005 **Obv:** National arms **Rev:** Value **Edge:** Reeded

Date	Mintage	F	VF	XF	Unc	BU
2005	—	—	—	—	0.50	0.75
2005 Proof	—	Value: 5.00				

KM# 199 5 BANI
2.7800 g., Copper Plated Steel, 18.25 mm. **Obv:** National arms **Rev:** Value **Edge:** Reeded

Date	Mintage	F	VF	XF	Unc	BU
2005	—	—	—	—	—	0.25

KM# 191 10 BANI
4.0000 g., Nickel Plated Steel, 20.4 mm. **Subject:** Monetary Reform of 2005 **Obv:** National arms **Rev:** Value **Edge:** Segmented reeding

Date	Mintage	F	VF	XF	Unc	BU
2005	—	—	—	—	0.65	0.85
2005 Proof	—	Value: 7.00				

KM# 200 10 BANI
4.0000 g., Nickel Plated Steel, 20.5 mm. **Obv:** National arms **Rev:** Value **Edge:** Reeded

Date	Mintage	F	VF	XF	Unc	BU
2005	—	—	—	—	—	0.30

KM# 192 50 BANI
6.1200 g., Brass, 23.6 mm. **Subject:** Monetary Reform of 2005 **Obv:** National arms **Rev:** Value **Edge:** Lettered **Edge Lettering:** "ROMANIA' twice

Date	Mintage	F	VF	XF	Unc	BU
2005	—	—	—	—	0.85	1.00
2005 Proof	—	Value: 10.00				

KM# 201 50 BANI
6.1000 g., Brass, 23.75 mm. **Obv:** National arms **Rev:** Value **Edge:** Plain

Date	Mintage	F	VF	XF	Unc	BU
2005	—	—	—	—	—	0.40

MINT SETS

KM#	Date	Mintage	Identification	Issue Price	Mkt Val
MS1	2005 (9)	—	KM#111, 115, 145, 153, 158, 198-201 plus medal	—	20.00

PROOF SETS

KM#	Date	Mintage	Identification	Issue Price	Mkt Val
PS4	2001 (3)	500	KM#159,160,161	80.00	250
PS5	2002 (9)	1,500	KM#109-111, 114-116, 145, 153, 158	20.00	50.00
PS6	2003 (9)	2,000	KM#109-111, 114-116, 145, 153, 158	20.00	50.00
PS7	2003 (3)	500	KM#186-188	—	225

Russia, formerly the central power of the Union of Soviet Socialist Republics and now of the Commonwealth of Independent States occupies the northern part of Asia and the eastern part of Europe, has an area of 17,075,400 sq. km. Capital: Moscow. Exports include iron and steel, crude oil, timber, and nonferrous metals.

In the fall of 1991, events moved swiftly in the Soviet Union. Estonia, Latvia and Lithuania won their independence and were recognized by Moscow, Sept. 6. The Commonwealth of Independent States was formed Dec. 8, 1991 in Mensk by Belarus, Russia and Ukraine. It was expanded at a summit Dec. 21, 1991 to include 11 of the 12 remaining republics (excluding Georgia) of the old U.S.S.R.

RUSSIAN FEDERATION
Issued by БАНК РОССИИ (Bank Russia)

REFORM COINAGE
January 1, 1998

1,000 Old Roubles = 1 New Rouble

Y# 600 KOPEK
Nickel **Obv:** St. George **Rev:** Denomination

Date	Mintage	F	VF	XF	Unc	BU
2001 M	—	—	—	—	0.25	0.35
2001 SP	—	—	—	—	0.25	0.35
2002 M	—	—	—	—	0.25	0.35
2002 SP	—	—	—	—	0.25	0.35
2003 SP	—	—	—	—	0.25	0.35
2003 M	—	—	—	—	0.25	0.35
2004 SP	—	—	—	—	0.25	0.35
2004 M	—	—	—	—	0.25	0.35

Y# 601 5 KOPEKS
Nickel **Obv:** St. George **Rev:** Denomination **Edge:** Plain

Date	Mintage	F	VF	XF	Unc	BU
2001 M	—	—	—	—	0.35	0.50
2001 SP	—	—	—	—	0.35	0.50
2002	—	—	—	—	15.00	17.00
2002 M	—	—	—	—	0.35	0.50
2002 SP	—	—	—	—	0.35	0.50
2003	—	—	—	—	10.00	12.00
2003 M	—	—	—	—	0.35	0.50
2003 SP	—	—	—	—	0.35	0.50
2004 M	—	—	—	—	0.35	0.50
2004 SP	—	—	—	—	0.35	0.50
2005 SP	—	—	—	—	0.35	0.50

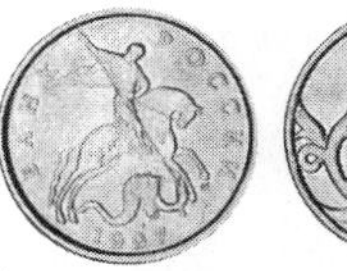

Y# 602 10 KOPEKS
Brass **Obv:** St. George **Rev:** Denomination

Date	Mintage	F	VF	XF	Unc	BU
2001 M	—	—	—	—	0.50	0.75
2001 SP	—	—	—	—	0.50	0.75
2002 M	—	—	—	—	0.50	0.75
2002 SP	—	—	—	—	0.50	0.75
2003 M	—	—	—	—	0.50	0.75
2003 SP	—	—	—	—	0.50	0.75

Date	Mintage	F	VF	XF	Unc	BU
2004 M	—	—	—	—	0.50	0.75
2004 SP	—	—	—	—	0.50	0.75
2005 SP	—	—	—	—	0.50	0.75

Y# 603 50 KOPEKS
Brass **Obv:** St. George **Rev:** Denomination **Edge:** Reeded

Date	Mintage	F	VF	XF	Unc	BU
2001 M Rare	—	—	—	—	—	—
2002 SP	—	—	—	—	0.75	1.00
2002 M	—	—	—	—	0.75	1.00
2003 SP	—	—	—	—	0.75	1.00
2003 M	—	—	—	—	0.75	1.00
2004 M	—	—	—	—	0.75	1.00
2004 SP	—	—	—	—	0.75	1.00

Y# 745 ROUBLE
17.4000 g., 0.9000 Silver 0.5035 oz. ASW, 32.8 mm. **Obv:** Double-headed eagle **Rev:** Altai Argali sheep **Edge:** Reeded

Date	Mintage	F	VF	XF	Unc	BU
2001(sp) Proof	7,500	Value: 35.00				

Y# 746 ROUBLE
17.4000 g., 0.9000 Silver 0.5035 oz. ASW, 32.8 mm. **Obv:** Double-headed eagle **Rev:** Two Eurasian Beavers **Edge:** Reeded

Date	Mintage	F	VF	XF	Unc	BU
2001(sp) Proof	7,500	Value: 40.00				

Y# 732 ROUBLE
17.4300 g., 0.9000 Silver 0.5043 oz. ASW, 32.8 mm. **Subject:** Sturgeon **Obv:** Double-headed eagle **Rev:** Sakhalin sturgeon and other fish **Edge:** Reeded

Date	Mintage	F	VF	XF	Unc	BU
2001 Proof	7,500	Value: 40.00				

Y# 604 ROUBLE
3.2500 g., Copper-Nickel-Zinc, 20.6 mm. **Rev:** Denomination **Edge:** Reeded

Date	Mintage	F	VF	XF	Unc	BU
2001 M Rare	—	—	—	—	—	—

Y# 731 ROUBLE

3.2100 g., Copper-Nickel, 20.7 mm. **Obv:** Double-headed eagle **Rev:** Stylized design above hologram **Edge:** Reeded

Date	Mintage	F	VF	XF	Unc	BU
2001 (SP)	100,000,000	—	—	—	1.50	2.00

Y# 797 ROUBLE

3.2500 g., Copper Nickel **Obv:** Curved bank name below eagle

Date	Mintage	F	VF	XF	Unc	BU
2002	—	—	—	—	1.00	1.50

Y# 758 ROUBLE

17.4400 g., 0.9000 Silver 0.5046 oz. ASW, 33 mm. **Obv:** Double-headed eagle **Rev:** Chinese Goral **Edge:** Reeded

Date	Mintage	F	VF	XF	Unc	BU
2002 (SP) Proof	10,000	Value: 35.00				

Y# 759 ROUBLE

17.4400 g., 0.9000 Silver 0.5046 oz. ASW, 33 mm. **Obv:** Double-headed eagle **Rev:** Sei Whale **Edge:** Reeded

Date	Mintage	F	VF	XF	Unc	BU
2002 (SP) Proof	10,000	Value: 35.00				

Y# 760 ROUBLE

17.4400 g., 0.9000 Silver 0.5046 oz. ASW, 33 mm. **Subject:** Golden Eagle **Obv:** Double-headed eagle **Rev:** Eagle with nestling **Edge:** Reeded

Date	Mintage	F	VF	XF	Unc	BU
2002 (SP) Proof	10,000	Value: 35.00				

Y# 770 ROUBLE

8.5300 g., 0.9250 Silver 0.2537 oz. ASW, 25 mm. **Subject:** Ministry of Education **Obv:** Double-headed eagle **Rev:** Seedling and open book **Edge:** Reeded

Date	Mintage	F	VF	XF	Unc	BU
2002(m) Proof	3,000	Value: 50.00				

Y# 771 ROUBLE

8.5300 g., 0.9250 Silver 0.2537 oz. ASW, 25 mm. **Subject:** Ministry of Finances **Obv:** Double-headed eagle **Rev:** Caduceus in monogram **Edge:** Reeded

Date	Mintage	F	VF	XF	Unc	BU
2002 (SP) Proof	3,000	Value: 50.00				

Y# 772 ROUBLE

8.5300 g., 0.9250 Silver 0.2537 oz. ASW, 25 mm. **Subject:** Ministry of Economic Developement **Obv:** Double-headed eagle **Rev:** Crowned two headed eagle with cornucopia and caduceus **Edge:** Reeded

Date	Mintage	F	VF	XF	Unc	BU
2002 (SP) Proof	3,000	Value: 50.00				

Y# 773 ROUBLE

8.5300 g., 0.9250 Silver 0.2537 oz. ASW, 25 mm. **Subject:** Ministry of Foreign Affairs **Obv:** Double-headed eagle **Rev:** Crowned two-headed eagle above crossed **Edge:** Reeded

Date	Mintage	F	VF	XF	Unc	BU
2002 (SP) Proof	3,000	Value: 50.00				

Y# 774 ROUBLE

8.5300 g., 0.9250 Silver 0.2537 oz. ASW, 25 mm. **Subject:** Ministry of Internal Affairs **Obv:** Double-headed eagle **Rev:** Crowned two-headed eagle with round breast **Edge:** Reeded

Date	Mintage	F	VF	XF	Unc	BU
2002 (SP) Proof	3,000	Value: 50.00				

Y# 775 ROUBLE

8.5300 g., 0.9250 Silver 0.2537 oz. ASW, 25 mm. **Subject:** Ministry of Justice **Obv:** Double-headed eagle **Rev:** Crowned double-headed eagle with column on breast shield **Edge:** Reeded

Date	Mintage	F	VF	XF	Unc	BU
2002 (SP) Proof	3,000	Value: 50.00				

Y# 776 ROUBLE

8.5300 g., 0.9250 Silver 0.2537 oz. ASW, 25 mm. **Subject:** Russian Armed Forces **Obv:** Double-headed eagle **Rev:** Double-headed eagle with crowned top pointed breast shield **Edge:** Reeded

Date	Mintage	F	VF	XF	Unc	BU
2002(m) Proof	3,000	Value: 50.00				

Y# 833 ROUBLE

3.2500 g., Copper-Nickel-Zinc, 20.6 mm. **Obv:** Two headed eagle above curved inscription **Rev:** Value and flower **Edge:** Reeded

Date	Mintage	F	VF	XF	Unc	BU
2002 (SP)	—	—	—	—	1.00	1.50
2005(m)	—	—	—	—	0.75	1.25

Y# A834 ROUBLE

7.7800 g., 0.9250 Silver 0.2314 oz. ASW, 0.25 mm. **Subject:** St. Petersburg **Obv:** Double-headed eagle **Rev:** Angel on steeple of Cathedral in fortress

Date	Mintage	F	VF	XF	Unc	BU
2002 Proof	5,000	Value: 15.00				

Y# 835 ROUBLE

7.7800 g., 0.9250 Silver 0.2314 oz. ASW, 25 mm. **Subject:** St. Petersburg **Obv:** Double-headed eagle **Rev:** Sphinx

Date	Mintage	F	VF	XF	Unc	BU
2002 Proof	5,000	Value: 15.00				

Y# 836 ROUBLE

7.7800 g., 0.9250 Silver 0.2314 oz. ASW, 25 mm. **Subject:** St. Petersburg **Obv:** Double-headed eagle **Rev:** Small ship

Date	Mintage	F	VF	XF	Unc	BU
2002 Proof	5,000	Value: 15.00				

Y# 837 ROUBLE

7.7800 g., 0.9250 Silver 0.2314 oz. ASW, 25 mm. **Subject:** St. Petersburg **Obv:** Double-headed eagle **Rev:** Lion

Date	Mintage	F	VF	XF	Unc	BU
2002 Proof	5,000	Value: 15.00				

Y# 838 ROUBLE

7.7800 g., 0.9250 Silver 0.2314 oz. ASW, 25 mm. **Subject:** St. Petersburg **Obv:** Double-headed eagle **Rev:** Horse sculpture

Date	Mintage	F	VF	XF	Unc	BU
2002 Proof	5,000	Value: 15.00				

Y# 839 ROUBLE

7.7800 g., 0.9250 Silver 0.2314 oz. ASW, 25 mm. **Subject:** St. Petersburg **Obv:** Double-headed eagle **Rev:** Griffin

Date	Mintage	F	VF	XF	Unc	BU
2002 Proof	5,000	Value: 15.00				

Y# 814 ROUBLE

17.4000 g., 0.9000 Silver 0.5035 oz. ASW, 32.8 mm. **Obv:** Double-headed eagle **Rev:** Two Arctic foxes **Edge:** Reeded

Date	Mintage	F	VF	XF	Unc	BU
2003 (SP) Proof	10,000	Value: 30.00				

Y# 816 ROUBLE

17.4000 g., 0.9000 Silver 0.5035 oz. ASW, 32.8 mm. **Obv:** Double-headed eagle **Rev:** Pygmy Cormorant drying it's wings **Edge:** Reeded

Date	Mintage	F	VF	XF	Unc	BU
2003 (SP) Proof	10,000	Value: 30.00				

Y# 815 ROUBLE

17.4000 g., 0.9000 Silver 0.5035 oz. ASW, 32.8 mm. **Obv:** Double-headed eagle **Rev:** Chinese Softshell turtle **Edge:** Reeded

Date	Mintage	F	VF	XF	Unc	BU
2003 (SP) Proof	10,000	Value: 30.00				

Y# 828 ROUBLE

17.2800 g., 0.9000 Silver 0.4499 oz. ASW, 33 mm. **Obv:** Two headed eagle **Rev:** Amur Forest Cat on branch **Edge:** Reeded

Date	Mintage	F	VF	XF	Unc	BU
2004 (SP) Proof	10,000	Value: 40.00				

Y# 881 ROUBLE

7.4300 g., 0.9000 Silver 0.215 oz. ASW, 32.8 mm. **Obv:** Double-headed eagle **Rev:** Natterjack Toad **Edge:** Reeded

Date	Mintage	F	VF	XF	Unc	BU
2005 Proof	—	Value: 25.00				

Y# 882 ROUBLE

7.0100 g., 0.9250 Silver 0.2085 oz. ASW, 32.8 mm. **Obv:** Double-headed eagle **Rev:** Two Marbled Murrelet sea birds **Edge:** Reeded

Date	Mintage	F	VF	XF	Unc	BU
2005 Proof	—	Value: 25.00				

Y# 883 ROUBLE

7.0100 g., 0.9250 Silver 0.2085 oz. ASW, 32.8 mm. **Obv:** Double-headed eagle **Rev:** Asiatic Wild Dog **Edge:** Reeded

Date	Mintage	F	VF	XF	Unc	BU
2005 Proof	—	Value: 25.00				

Y# 884 ROUBLE

7.0100 g., 0.9250 Silver 0.2085 oz. ASW, 32.8 mm. **Obv:** Double-headed eagle **Rev:** Volkhov Whitefish **Edge:** Reeded

Date	Mintage	F	VF	XF	Unc	BU
2005 Proof	—	Value: 25.00				

Y# 675 2 ROUBLES

5.2000 g., Copper-Nickel, 23 mm. **Subject:** Yuri Gagarin **Obv:** Denomination and date **Rev:** Uniformed portrait **Edge:** Segmented reeding

Date	Mintage	F	VF	XF	Unc	BU
2001	—	—	—	—	15.00	18.00
2001(m)	10,000,000	—	—	—	2.00	3.00
2001(sp)	10,000,000	—	—	—	2.00	3.00

Y# 605 2 ROUBLES

Copper-Nickel-Zinc **Rev:** Denomination **Edge:** Alternating reeded and smooth

Date	Mintage	F	VF	XF	Unc	BU
2001(m)	—	—	—	—	5.00	6.00

Y# 730 2 ROUBLES

17.0000 g., 0.9250 Silver .5056 oz. ASW, 33 mm. **Subject:** V.I. Dal **Obv:** Double-headed eagle **Rev:** Portrait, book, signature, figures **Edge:** Reeded

Date	Mintage	F	VF	XF	Unc	BU
2001(m) Proof	7,500	Value: 40.00				

Y# 747 2 ROUBLES

17.0000 g., 0.9250 Silver 0.5056 oz. ASW, 33 mm. **Subject:** Zodiac Signs **Obv:** Double-headed eagle **Rev:** Virgo **Edge:** Reeded

Date	Mintage	F	VF	XF	Unc	BU
2002(m) Proof	20,000	Value: 25.00				

Y# 761 2 ROUBLES

17.0000 g., 0.9250 Silver 0.5056 oz. ASW, 33 mm. **Subject:** Zodiac Signs **Obv:** Double-headed eagle **Rev:** Capricorn **Edge:** Reeded

Date	Mintage	F	VF	XF	Unc	BU
2002 (SP) Proof	20,000	Value: 22.50				

Y# 762 2 ROUBLES

17.0000 g., 0.9250 Silver 0.5056 oz. ASW, 33 mm. **Subject:** Zodiac Signs **Obv:** Double-headed eagle **Rev:** Sagittarius **Edge:** Reeded

Date	Mintage	F	VF	XF	Unc	BU
2002 (SP) Proof	20,000	Value: 22.50				

Y# 766 2 ROUBLES

17.0000 g., 0.9250 Silver 0.5056 oz. ASW, 33 mm. **Subject:** Zodiac Signs **Obv:** Double-headed eagle **Rev:** Scorpion **Edge:** Reeded

Date	Mintage	F	VF	XF	Unc	BU
2002(m) Proof	20,000	Value: 22.50				

Y# 768 2 ROUBLES

17.0000 g., 0.9250 Silver 0.5056 oz. ASW, 33 mm. **Subject:** Zodiac Signs **Obv:** Double-headed eagle **Rev:** Balance scale **Edge:** Reeded

Date	Mintage	F	VF	XF	Unc	BU
2002 (SP) Proof	20,000	Value: 22.50				

Y# 793 2 ROUBLES

17.0000 g., 0.9250 Silver 0.5056 oz. ASW, 33 mm. **Subject:** L.P. Orlova **Obv:** Double-headed eagle **Rev:** Actress' portrait **Edge:** Reeded

Date	Mintage	F	VF	XF	Unc	BU
2002(m) Proof	10,000	Value: 25.00				

Y# 742 2 ROUBLES

17.0000 g., 0.9250 Silver 0.5056 oz. ASW, 33 mm. **Subject:** Zodiac Signs: Leo **Obv:** Double-headed eagle **Rev:** Lion and symbol **Edge:** Reeded

Date	Mintage	F	VF	XF	Unc	BU
2002 Proof	20,000	Value: 22.50				

Y# 798 2 ROUBLES

5.1000 g., Copper Nickel **Obv:** Curved bank name below eagle

Date	Mintage	F	VF	XF	Unc	BU
2002	—	—	—	—	1.50	2.00

Y# 834 2 ROUBLES

5.1000 g., Copper-Nickel, 23 mm. **Obv:** Two headed eagle above curved inscription **Rev:** Value and flower **Edge:** Segmented reeding

Date	Mintage	F	VF	XF	Unc	BU
2002 (SP)	—	—	—	—	4.00	5.00

Y# 803 2 ROUBLES

17.1000 g., 0.9250 Silver 0.5085 oz. ASW, 32.8 mm. **Subject:** Zodiac signs **Obv:** Double-headed eagle **Rev:** Pisces - 2 fish **Edge:** Reeded

Date	Mintage	F	VF	XF	Unc	BU
2003 (SP) Proof	20,000	Value: 35.00				

Y# 804 2 ROUBLES

17.1000 g., 0.9250 Silver 0.5085 oz. ASW, 32.8 mm. **Subject:** Zodiac signs **Obv:** Double-headed eagle **Rev:** Aquarius kneeling and pouring water from jar **Edge:** Reeded

Date	Mintage	F	VF	XF	Unc	BU
2003(m) Proof	20,000	Value: 35.00				

Y# 820 2 ROUBLES

17.0000 g., 0.9250 Silver 0.5056 oz. ASW, 33 mm. **Obv:** Double-headed eagle **Rev:** Crab and Cancer zodiac symbol **Edge:** Reeded

Date	Mintage	F	VF	XF	Unc	BU
2003 (SP) Proof	20,000	Value: 25.00				

Y# 840 2 ROUBLES

16.8100 g., 0.9250 Silver 0.4999 oz. ASW, 33 mm. **Rev:** Guil Yarovsky

Date	Mintage	F	VF	XF	Unc	BU
2003(m) Proof	10,000	Value: 20.00				

Y# 841 2 ROUBLES

16.8100 g., 0.9250 Silver 0.4999 oz. ASW, 33 mm. **Rev:** Fedor Tyutchev

Date	Mintage	F	VF	XF	Unc	BU
2003(sp) Proof	10,000	Value: 20.00				

Y# 844 2 ROUBLES

17.0000 g., 0.9250 Silver 0.5056 oz. ASW, 33 mm. **Subject:** Zodiac Signs **Rev:** Aries

Date	Mintage	F	VF	XF	Unc	BU
2003 Proof	20,000	Value: 22.50				

Y# 845 2 ROUBLES

17.0000 g., 0.9250 Silver 0.5056 oz. ASW **Subject:** Zodiac Signs **Rev:** Taurus

Date	Mintage	F	VF	XF	Unc	BU
2003 Proof	20,000	Value: 22.50				

Y# 846 2 ROUBLES

17.0000 g., 0.9250 Silver 0.5056 oz. ASW, 33 mm. **Subject:** Zodiac Signs **Rev:** Gemini

Date	Mintage	F	VF	XF	Unc	BU
2003 Proof	20,000	Value: 22.50				

Y# 842 2 ROUBLES

16.8100 g., 0.9250 Silver 0.4999 oz. ASW, 33 mm. **Rev:** V. P. Tchkalov

Date	Mintage	F	VF	XF	Unc	BU
2004(m) Proof	7,000	Value: 20.00				

Y# 843 2 ROUBLES

16.8100 g., 0.9250 Silver 0.4999 oz. ASW, 33 mm. **Rev:** Mikhail Glinka

Date	Mintage	F	VF	XF	Unc	BU
2004(m) Proof	7,000	Value: 20.00				

Y# 733 3 ROUBLES

34.8800 g., 0.9000 Silver 1.0093 oz. ASW, 39 mm. **Subject:** 200th Anniversary of Navigation School **Obv:** Double-headed eagle **Rev:** Navigational tools and building **Edge:** Reeded

Date	Mintage	F	VF	XF	Unc	BU
2001 Proof	5,000	Value: 40.00				

Y# 734 3 ROUBLES

34.8800 g., 0.9000 Silver 1.0093 oz. ASW, 39 mm. **Subject:** First Moscow Savings Bank **Obv:** Double-headed eagle **Rev:** Beehive above building **Edge:** Reeded

Date	Mintage	F	VF	XF	Unc	BU
2001 Proof	17,500	Value: 40.00				

Y# 735 3 ROUBLES

34.8800 g., 0.9000 Silver 1.0093 oz. ASW, 39 mm. **Subject:** State Labor Savings Bank **Obv:** Double-headed eagle **Rev:** Dam, passbook and tractor **Edge:** Reeded

Date	Mintage	F	VF	XF	Unc	BU
2001 Proof	17,500	Value: 40.00				

Y# 736 3 ROUBLES

34.8800 g., 0.9000 Silver 1.0093 oz. ASW, 39 mm. **Subject:** Savings Bank of the Russian Federation **Obv:** Double-headed eagle **Rev:** Chevrons above building **Edge:** Reeded

Date	Mintage	F	VF	XF	Unc	BU
2001 Proof	17,500	Value: 40.00				

Y# 737 3 ROUBLES

34.8800 g., 0.9000 Silver 1.0093 oz. ASW, 39 mm. **Subject:** 10th Anniversary - Commonwealth of Independent States **Obv:** Double-headed eagle **Rev:** Hologram below logo **Edge:** Reeded

Date	Mintage	F	VF	XF	Unc	BU
2001 Proof	7,500	Value: 45.00				

Y# 677 3 ROUBLES

34.8800 g., 0.9000 Silver 1.0093 oz. ASW, 39 mm. **Subject:** 225 Years - Bolshoi Theater **Obv:** Double-headed eagle **Rev:** Five men, one with pole ax **Edge:** Reeded

Date	Mintage	F	VF	XF	Unc	BU
2001 Proof	7,500	Value: 40.00				

Y# 680 3 ROUBLES

34.8800 g., 0.9000 Silver 1.0093 oz. ASW, 39 mm. **Subject:** 40th Anniversary of Manned Space Flight **Obv:** Double-headed eagle **Rev:** Uniformed portrait of Yuri Gagarin holding dove **Edge:** Reeded

Date	Mintage	F	VF	XF	Unc	BU
2001 Proof	7,500	Value: 40.00				

Y# 682 3 ROUBLES

34.8800 g., 0.9000 Silver 1.0093 oz. ASW, 39 mm. **Subject:** Siberian Exploration **Obv:** Double-headed eagle **Rev:** Men riding horses, deer and sleds **Edge:** Reeded

Date	Mintage	F	VF	XF	Unc	BU
2001 Proof	5,000	Value: 45.00				

Y# 778 3 ROUBLES

34.8800 g., 0.9000 Silver 1.0093 oz. ASW, 39 mm. **Subject:** Kideksha **Obv:** Double-headed eagle **Rev:** Three churches on river bank **Edge:** Reeded

Date	Mintage	F	VF	XF	Unc	BU
2002 (SP) Proof	10,000	Value: 40.00				

Y# 779 3 ROUBLES

34.8800 g., 0.9000 Silver 1.0093 oz. ASW, 39 mm. **Subject:** Iversky Monastery, Valdaiy **Obv:** Double-headed eagle **Rev:** Building complex on an island in Lake Valdaiy **Edge:** Reeded

Date	Mintage	F	VF	XF	Unc	BU
2002 (SP) Proof	10,000	Value: 40.00				

Y# 780 3 ROUBLES

34.8800 g., 0.9000 Silver 1.0093 oz. ASW, 39 mm. **Subject:** Miraculous Savior Church **Obv:** Double-headed eagle **Rev:** Church with separate bell tower **Edge:** Reeded

Date	Mintage	F	VF	XF	Unc	BU
2002(m) Proof	5,000	Value: 45.00				

Y# 781 3 ROUBLES

34.8800 g., 0.9000 Silver 1.0093 oz. ASW, 39 mm. **Subject:** Works of Dionissy **Obv:** Double-headed eagle **Rev:** "The Crucifix" **Edge:** Reeded

Date	Mintage	F	VF	XF	Unc	BU
2002 (SP) Proof	10,000	Value: 40.00				

Y# 755 3 ROUBLES

34.8800 g., 0.9000 Silver 1.0093 oz. ASW, 39 mm. **Subject:** Admiral Nakhimov **Obv:** Double-headed eagle **Rev:** Monument, Admiral with cannon and naval battle scene **Edge:** Reeded

Date	Mintage	F	VF	XF	Unc	BU
2002 (SP) Proof	10,000	Value: 40.00				

Y# 787 3 ROUBLES

34.8800 g., 0.9000 Silver 1.0093 oz. ASW, 39 mm. **Subject:** World Cup Soccer **Obv:** Double-headed eagle **Rev:** Soccer ball center in circle of players **Edge:** Reeded

Date	Mintage	F	VF	XF	Unc	BU
2002 (SP) Proof	25,000	Value: 25.00				

Y# 756 3 ROUBLES

34.8800 g., 0.9000 Silver 1.0093 oz. ASW, 39 mm. **Subject:** Hermitage **Obv:** Double-headed eagle **Rev:** Statues and arch **Edge:** Reeded

Date	Mintage	F	VF	XF	Unc	BU
2002 (SP) Proof	10,000	Value: 40.00				

Y# 738 3 ROUBLES

34.8800 g., 0.9000 Silver 1.0093 oz. ASW, 39 mm. **Subject:** Olympics **Obv:** Double-headed eagle **Rev:** Two cross-country skiers **Edge:** Reeded

Date	Mintage	F	VF	XF	Unc	BU
2002 Proof	25,000	Value: 40.00				

Y# 744 3 ROUBLES

34.8800 g., 0.9000 Silver 1.0093 oz. ASW, 39 mm. **Subject:** St. John's Nunnery, St. Petersburg **Obv:** Double-headed eagle **Rev:** Nunnery and cameo portraits of John of Kronstadt **Edge:** Reeded

Date	Mintage	F	VF	XF	Unc	BU
2002 Proof	5,000	Value: 45.00				

Y# 801 3 ROUBLES

34.8000 g., 0.9000 Silver 1.007 oz. ASW, 38.7 mm. **Subject:** Veborg **Obv:** Double-headed eagle **Rev:** Sailing ships and buildings **Edge:** Reeded

Date	Mintage	F	VF	XF	Unc	BU
2003(sp) Proof	10,000	Value: 50.00				

Y# 802 3 ROUBLES

34.7500 g., 0.9000 Silver 1.0055 oz. ASW, 38.7 mm. **Subject:** Lunar Calendar **Obv:** National emblem **Rev:** Mountain goat in crescent **Edge:** Reeded

Date	Mintage	F	VF	XF	Unc	BU
2003(m) Proof	15,000	Value: 50.00				

Y# 805 3 ROUBLES

34.8400 g., 0.9000 Silver 1.0081 oz. ASW, 38.8 mm. **Subject:** Zodiac signs **Obv:** Double-headed eagle **Rev:** Leo - Lion **Edge:** Reeded

Date	Mintage	F	VF	XF	Unc	BU
2003(m) Proof	30,000	Value: 45.00				

Y# 806 3 ROUBLES
34.7400 g., 0.9000 Silver 1.0052 oz. ASW, 38.8 mm. **Subject:** St. Daniel's Monastery **Obv:** Double-headed eagle **Rev:** Statue and monastery **Edge:** Reeded

Date	Mintage	F	VF	XF	Unc	BU
2003(m) Proof	10,000	Value: 45.00				

Y# 807 3 ROUBLES
34.7400 g., 0.9000 Silver 1.0052 oz. ASW, 38.8 mm. **Subject:** World Biathlon Championships **Obv:** Double-headed eagle **Rev:** Rifleman and archer on skis **Edge:** Reeded

Date	Mintage	F	VF	XF	Unc	BU
2003(m) Proof	7,500	Value: 35.00				

Y# 808 3 ROUBLES
34.7400 g., 0.9000 Silver 1.0052 oz. ASW, 38.8 mm. **Obv:** Double-headed eagle **Rev:** Ipatiyevsky Monastery in Kostroma **Edge:** Reeded

Date	Mintage	F	VF	XF	Unc	BU
2003(m) Proof	10,000	Value: 40.00				

Y# 809 3 ROUBLES
34.7400 g., 0.9000 Silver 1.0052 oz. ASW, 38.8 mm. **Subject:** First Kamchatka Expedition **Obv:** Double-headed eagle **Rev:** Natives drying fish, tall ship in background **Edge:** Reeded

Date	Mintage	F	VF	XF	Unc	BU
2003 (SP) Proof	10,000	Value: 35.00				

Y# 810 3 ROUBLES
34.7400 g., 0.9000 Silver 1.0052 oz. ASW, 38.8 mm. **Subject:** Zodiac signs **Obv:** Double-headed eagle **Rev:** Virgo - Stars and seated allegorical woman **Edge:** Reeded **Note:** Similar to 2 Roubles, KM747

Date	Mintage	F	VF	XF	Unc	BU
2003 (SP)	30,000	Value: 30.00				

Y# 811 3 ROUBLES
34.7400 g., 0.9000 Silver 1.0052 oz. ASW, 38.8 mm. **Subject:** Zodiac signs **Obv:** Double-headed eagle **Rev:** Libra - scale and stars **Edge:** Reeded **Note:** Similar to 2 Roubles, KM768

Date	Mintage	F	VF	XF	Unc	BU
2003(m) Proof	30,000	Value: 30.00				

Y# 812 3 ROUBLES
34.7400 g., 0.9000 Silver 1.0052 oz. ASW, 38.8 mm. **Subject:** Diveyevsky Monastery **Obv:** Double-headed eagle **Rev:** Cameo portrait above churches **Edge:** Reeded

Date	Mintage	F	VF	XF	Unc	BU
2003 (SP) Proof	10,000	Value: 40.00				

Y# 813 3 ROUBLES
34.7400 g., 0.9000 Silver 1.0052 oz. ASW, 38.8 mm. **Subject:** Zodiac Signs **Obv:** Double-headed eagle **Rev:** Scorpio - scorpion and stars **Edge:** Reeded **Note:** Similar to 2 Roubles, KM766

Date	Mintage	F	VF	XF	Unc	BU
2003(m) Proof	30,000	Value: 30.00				

Y# 885 3 ROUBLES
34.8000 g., 0.9000 Silver 1.007 oz. ASW, 38.7 mm. **Subject:** City of Pskov 1100th Anniversary **Obv:** Double-headed eagle **Rev:** Pskov walled city view **Edge:** Reeded

Date	Mintage	F	VF	XF	Unc	BU
2003 (SP) Proof	—	Value: 55.00				

Y# 847 3 ROUBLES
34.5600 g., 0.9000 Silver 1 oz. ASW, 39 mm. **Rev:** St. Trinity Monastery

Date	Mintage	F	VF	XF	Unc	BU
2003(sp) Proof	10,000	Value: 25.00				

Y# 848 3 ROUBLES
34.5600 g., 0.9000 Silver 1 oz. ASW, 39 mm. **Subject:** Zodiac Signs **Rev:** Archer

Date	Mintage	F	VF	XF	Unc	BU
2003(sp) Proof	30,000	Value: 30.00				

Y# 849 3 ROUBLES
34.5600 g., 0.9000 Silver 1 oz. ASW, 39 mm. **Subject:** Zodiac Signs **Rev:** Capricorn

Date	Mintage	F	VF	XF	Unc	BU
2003(m) Proof	30,000	Value: 30.00				

Y# 850 3 ROUBLES
34.5600 g., 0.9000 Silver 1 oz. ASW, 39 mm. **Subject:** Lunar Calendar **Rev:** Monkey

Date	Mintage	F	VF	XF	Unc	BU
2004(m) Proof	15,000	Value: 35.00				

Y# 851 3 ROUBLES
34.5600 g., 0.9000 Silver 1 oz. ASW, 39 mm. **Subject:** Zodiac Signs **Rev:** Aquarius

Date	Mintage	F	VF	XF	Unc	BU
2004(sp) Proof	30,000	Value: 30.00				

Y# 852 3 ROUBLES
34.5600 g., 0.9000 Silver 1 oz. ASW, 39 mm. **Rev:** Tomsk

Date	Mintage	F	VF	XF	Unc	BU
2004(m) Proof	8,000	Value: 25.00				

Y# 853 3 ROUBLES
34.5600 g., 0.9000 Silver 1 oz. ASW, 39 mm. **Subject:** Zodiac Signs **Rev:** Pisces

Date	Mintage	F	VF	XF	Unc	BU
2004(m) Proof	30,000	Value: 30.00				

Y# 854 3 ROUBLES
34.5600 g., 0.9000 Silver 1 oz. ASW, 39 mm. **Rev:** Epiphany Cathedral, Moscow

Date	Mintage	F	VF	XF	Unc	BU
2004(m) Proof	8,000	Value: 25.00				

Y# 855 3 ROUBLES
34.5600 g., 0.9000 Silver 1 oz. ASW, 39 mm. **Subject:** Zodiac Signs **Rev:** Aries

Date	Mintage	F	VF	XF	Unc	BU
2004(sp) Proof	30,000	Value: 30.00				

Y# 856 3 ROUBLES
34.5600 g., 0.9000 Silver 1 oz. ASW, 39 mm. **Rev:** Soccer

Date	Mintage	F	VF	XF	Unc	BU
2004(sp) Proof	10,000	Value: 22.50				

Y# 857 3 ROUBLES
34.5600 g., 0.9000 Silver 1 oz. ASW, 39 mm. **Subject:** Zodiac Signs **Rev:** Taurus

Date	Mintage	F	VF	XF	Unc	BU
2004(sp) Proof	30,000	Value: 30.00				

Y# 858 3 ROUBLES
34.5600 g., 0.9000 Silver 1 oz. ASW, 39 mm. **Rev:** Olympic torch

Date	Mintage	F	VF	XF	Unc	BU
2004(m) Proof	20,000	Value: 25.00				

Y# 859 3 ROUBLES
34.5600 g., 0.9000 Silver 1 oz. ASW, 39 mm. **Subject:** Zodiac Signs **Rev:** Gemini

Date	Mintage	F	VF	XF	Unc	BU
2004(m) Proof	30,000	Value: 30.00				

Y# 860 3 ROUBLES
34.5600 g., 0.9000 Silver 1 oz. ASW, 39 mm. **Subject:** Zodiac Signs **Rev:** Cancer

Date	Mintage	F	VF	XF	Unc	BU
2004(sp) Proof	30,000	Value: 30.00				

Y# 861 3 ROUBLES
34.5600 g., 0.9000 Silver 1 oz. ASW, 39 mm. **Rev:** Church of the Sign of the Holy Mother of God

Date	Mintage	F	VF	XF	Unc	BU
2004(m) Proof	8,000	Value: 25.00				

Y# 862 3 ROUBLES
34.5600 g., 0.9000 Silver 1 oz. ASW, 39 mm. **Rev:** Transfiguration icon

Date	Mintage	F	VF	XF	Unc	BU
2004(m) Proof	8,000	Value: 25.00				

Y# 863 3 ROUBLES
34.5600 g., 0.9000 Silver 1 oz. ASW, 39 mm. **Rev:** Peter I's monetary reform

Date	Mintage	F	VF	XF	Unc	BU
2004(sp) Proof	8,000	Value: 75.00				

Y# 799 5 ROUBLES
6.4500 g., Copper-Nickel Clad Copper, 25 mm. **Obv:** Curved bank name below eagle **Edge:** Segmented reeding

Date	Mintage	F	VF	XF	Unc	BU
2002	—	—	—	—	2.00	3.00

Y# 829 5 ROUBLES
47.2400 g., 0.9000 Bi-Metallic Gold And Silver .900 Silver 21.34g center in .900 Gold 25.9g ring 1.3669 oz., 39.5 mm. **Obv:** Double-headed eagle **Rev:** Uglich city view **Edge:** Reeded

Date	Mintage	F	VF	XF	Unc	BU
2004 (SP) Proof	5,000	Value: 850				

Y# 676 10 ROUBLES
8.2200 g., Bi-Metallic Copper-Nickel center in Brass ring, 27 mm. **Subject:** Yuri Gagarin **Obv:** Denomination with latent image in zero, and date **Rev:** Helmeted portrait **Edge:** Reeding over denomination

Date	Mintage	F	VF	XF	Unc	BU
2001(m)	10,000,000	—	—	—	3.50	5.00
2001(m)	10,000,000	—	—	—	3.50	5.00
2001(sp)	10,000,000	—	—	—	3.50	5.00
2001(sp)	10,000,000	—	—	—	3.50	5.00

Y# 686 10 ROUBLES
1.6100 g., 0.9990 Gold .0517 oz. AGW, 12 mm. **Subject:** Bolshoi Theater 225 Years **Obv:** Double-headed eagle **Rev:** Building above number 225 **Edge:** Reeded

Date	Mintage	F	VF	XF	Unc	BU
2001 Proof	3,000	Value: 55.00				

Y# 739 10 ROUBLES
8.2200 g., Bi-Metallic Copper-Nickel center in Brass ring, 27 mm. **Subject:** Ancient Towns - Derbent **Obv:** Denomination in wreath **Rev:** City arms above walled city view **Edge:** Reeding over denomination

Date	Mintage	F	VF	XF	Unc	BU
2002	5,000,000	—	—	—	3.00	4.00

Y# 740 10 ROUBLES

8.2200 g., Bi-Metallic Copper-Nickel center in Brass ring, 27 mm. **Subject:** Ancient Towns - Kostroma **Obv:** Denomination in wreath **Rev:** Cupola, city arms and river view **Edge:** Reeding over denomination

Date	Mintage	F	VF	XF	Unc	BU
2002	5,000,000	—	—	—	3.00	4.00

Y# 741 10 ROUBLES

8.2200 g., Bi-Metallic Copper-Nickel center in Brass ring, 27 mm. **Subject:** Ancient Towns - Staraya Russa **Obv:** Denomination in wreath **Rev:** City arms and cathedral **Edge:** Reeding over denomination

Date	Mintage	F	VF	XF	Unc	BU
2002	5,000,000	—	—	—	3.00	4.00

Y# 748 10 ROUBLES

8.2200 g., Bi-Metallic Copper-Nickel center in Brass ring, 27 mm. **Subject:** Ministry of Education **Obv:** Denomination **Rev:** Seedling and open book **Edge:** Reeding over denomination

Date	Mintage	F	VF	XF	Unc	BU
2002(m)	5,000,000	—	—	—	2.00	2.50

Y# 749 10 ROUBLES

8.2200 g., Bi-Metallic Copper-Nickel center in Brass ring, 27 mm. **Subject:** Ministry of Finance **Obv:** Denomination **Rev:** Caduceus in monogram **Edge:** Reeding over denomination

Date	Mintage	F	VF	XF	Unc	BU
2002 (SP)	5,000,000	—	—	—	2.00	2.50

Y# 750 10 ROUBLES

8.2200 g., Bi-Metallic Copper-Nickel center in Brass ring, 27 mm. **Subject:** Ministry of Economic Developement **Obv:** Denomination **Rev:** Crowned double-headed eagle with cornucopia and Caduceus **Edge:** Reeding over denomination

Date	Mintage	F	VF	XF	Unc	BU
2002 (SP)	5,000,000	—	—	—	2.00	2.50

Y# 751 10 ROUBLES

8.2200 g., Bi-Metallic Copper-Nickel center in Brass ring, 27 mm. **Subject:** Ministry of Foreign Affairs **Obv:** Denomination **Rev:** Crowned double-headed eagle above crossed palms **Edge:** Reeding over denomination

Date	Mintage	F	VF	XF	Unc	BU
2002 (SP)	5,000,000	—	—	—	2.00	2.50

Y# 752 10 ROUBLES

8.2200 g., Bi-Metallic Copper-Nickel center in Brass ring, 27 mm. **Subject:** Ministry of Internal Affairs **Obv:** Denomination **Rev:** Crowned double-headed eagle with round breast shield **Edge:** Reeding over denomination

Date	Mintage	F	VF	XF	Unc	BU
2002 (SP)	5,000,000	—	—	—	2.00	2.50

Y# 753 10 ROUBLES

8.2200 g., Bi-Metallic Copper-Nickel center in Brass ring, 27 mm. **Subject:** Ministry of Justice **Obv:** Denomination **Rev:** Crowned double-headed eagle with column on breast shield **Edge:** Reeding over denomination

Date	Mintage	F	VF	XF	Unc	BU
2002 (SP)	5,000,000	—	—	—	2.00	2.50

Y# 754 10 ROUBLES

8.2200 g., Bi-Metallic Copper-Nickel center in Brass ring, 27 mm. **Subject:** Russian Armed Forces **Obv:** Denomination **Rev:** Crowned double-headed eagle with crowned pointed top shield **Edge:** Reeding over denomination

Date	Mintage	F	VF	XF	Unc	BU
2002(m)	5,000,000	—	—	—	2.00	2.50

Y# 817 10 ROUBLES

8.3400 g., Bi-Metallic Copper-nickel center in Brass ring, 27 mm. **Obv:** Value **Rev:** Murom city view and arms **Edge:** Reeded and lettered

Date	Mintage	F	VF	XF	Unc	BU
2003 (SP)	5,000,000	—	—	—	3.00	3.50

Y# 818 10 ROUBLES

8.3400 g., Bi-Metallic Copper-Nickel center in Brass ring, 27 mm. **Obv:** Value **Rev:** Kasimov city view and arms **Edge:** Reeded and lettered

Date	Mintage	F	VF	XF	Unc	BU
2003 (SP)	5,000,000	—	—	—	3.00	3.50

Y# 819 10 ROUBLES

8.3400 g., Bi-Metallic Copper-Nickel center in Brass ring, 27 mm. **Obv:** Value **Rev:** Dorogobush monument, city view and arms **Edge:** Reeded and lettered

Date	Mintage	F	VF	XF	Unc	BU
2003(m)	5,000,000	—	—	—	3.00	3.50

Y# 800 10 ROUBLES

8.4400 g., Bi-Metallic Copper-Nickel center in Brass ring, 27.1 mm. **Obv:** Value **Rev:** Coat of arms above walled city **Edge:** Reeding over lettering

Date	Mintage	F	VF	XF	Unc	BU
2003 (SP)	—	—	—	—	3.00	3.50

Y# 824 10 ROUBLES

8.1300 g., Bi-Metallic Copper-Nickel center in Brass ring, 27 mm. **Subject:** Town of Ryazhsk **Obv:** Value **Rev:** City view **Edge:** Reeded and lettered

Date	Mintage	F	VF	XF	Unc	BU
2004	—	—	—	—	3.00	3.50

Y# 825 10 ROUBLES

8.1300 g., Bi-Metallic Copper-Nickel center in Brass ring, 27 mm. **Subject:** Town of Dmitrov **Obv:** Value **Rev:** City view **Edge:** Reeded and lettered

Date	Mintage	F	VF	XF	Unc	BU
2004	—	—	—	—	3.00	3.50

Y# 826 10 ROUBLES

8.1300 g., Bi-Metallic Copper-Nickel center in Brass ring, 27 mm. **Subject:** Town of Kem **Obv:** Value **Rev:** City view **Edge:** Reeded and lettered

Date	Mintage	F	VF	XF	Unc	BU
2004	—	—	—	—	3.00	3.50

Y# 827 10 ROUBLES

8.4000 g., Bi-Metallic Copper-Nickel center in Brass ring, 27 mm. **Obv:** Value **Rev:** WWII eternal flame monument **Edge:** Reeded and Lettered

Date	Mintage	F	VF	XF	Unc	BU
2005 (SP)	—	—	—	—	3.00	5.00

Y# 886 10 ROUBLES

8.2300 g., Bi-Metallic Copper-Nickel center in Brass ring, 27 mm. **Obv:** Moscow coat of arms **Rev:** Value **Edge:** Reeded and lettered

Date	Mintage	F	VF	XF	Unc	BU
2005	—	—	—	—	3.00	4.00

Y# 887 10 ROUBLES

8.2300 g., Bi-Metallic Copper-Nickel center in Brass ring, 27 mm. **Obv:** Leningrad Oblast coat of arms **Rev:** Value **Edge:** Reeded and lettered

Date	Mintage	F	VF	XF	Unc	BU
2005	—	—	—	—	3.00	4.00

Y# 888 10 ROUBLES
8.2300 g., Bi-Metallic Copper-Nickel center in Brass ring, 27 mm. **Obv:** Tverskaya Oblast coat of arms **Rev:** Value **Edge:** Reeded and lettered

Date	Mintage	F	VF	XF	Unc	BU
2005	—	—	—	—	3.00	4.00

Y# 889 10 ROUBLES
8.2300 g., Bi-Metallic Copper-Nickel center in Brass ring, 27 mm. **Obv:** Krasnodarskiy Kray coat of arms **Rev:** Value **Edge:** Reeded and lettered

Date	Mintage	F	VF	XF	Unc	BU
2005	—	—	—	—	3.00	4.00

Y# 890 10 ROUBLES
8.2300 g., Bi-Metallic Copper-Nickel center in Brass ring, 27 mm. **Obv:** Orlovskaya Oblast coat of arms **Rev:** Value **Edge:** Reeded and lettered

Date	Mintage	F	VF	XF	Unc	BU
2005	—	—	—	—	3.00	4.00

Y# 891 10 ROUBLES
8.2300 g., Bi-Metallic Copper-Nickel center in Brass ring, 27 mm. **Obv:** Tatarstan Republic coat of arms **Rev:** Value **Edge:** Reeded and lettered

Date	Mintage	F	VF	XF	Unc	BU
2005	—	—	—	—	3.00	4.00

Y# 794 25 ROUBLES
173.1300 g., 0.9000 Silver 5.0096 oz. ASW, 60.2 mm. **Subject:** Foundation of Russian Savings Banks **Obv:** Double-headed eagle **Rev:** Czar Nicholas I and document **Edge:** Reeded

Date	Mintage	F	VF	XF	Unc	BU
2001(m) Proof	10,500	Value: 120				

Y# 678 25 ROUBLES
173.2900 g., 0.9000 Silver 5.0143 oz. ASW, 60 mm. **Subject:** Bolshoi Theater 225 Years **Obv:** Double-headed eagle **Rev:** Dancing couple scene **Edge:** Reeded **Note:** Illustration reduced.

Date	Mintage	F	VF	XF	Unc	BU
2001 Proof	2,000	Value: 135				

Y# 683 25 ROUBLES
173.2900 g., 0.9000 Silver 5.0143 oz. ASW, 60 mm. **Subject:** Siberian Exploration **Obv:** Double-headed eagle **Rev:** Standing king and river boats **Edge:** Reeded **Note:** Illustration reduced.

Date	Mintage	F	VF	XF	Unc	BU
2001 Proof	1,000	Value: 145				

Y# 687 25 ROUBLES
3.2000 g., 0.9990 Gold .1028 oz. AGW, 16 mm. **Subject:** Bolshoi Theater 225 Years **Obv:** Double-headed eagle **Rev:** Ballerina **Edge:** Reeded

Date	Mintage	F	VF	XF	Unc	BU
2001 Proof	2,500	Value: 140				

Y# 785 25 ROUBLES
173.2900 g., 0.9000 Silver 5.0143 oz. ASW, 60 mm. **Subject:** Admiral Nakhimov **Obv:** Double-headed eagle **Rev:** Admiral watching naval battle **Edge:** Reeded **Note:** Illustration reduced.

Date	Mintage	F	VF	XF	Unc	BU
2002 (SP) Proof	2,000	Value: 150				

Y# 790 25 ROUBLES
173.2900 g., 0.9000 Silver 5.0143 oz. ASW, 60 mm. **Subject:** Hermitage **Obv:** Double-headed eagle **Rev:** Staircase viewed through door way **Edge:** Reeded **Note:** Illustration reduced.

Date	Mintage	F	VF	XF	Unc	BU
2002 (SP) Proof	2,000	Value: 150				

Y# 777 25 ROUBLES
173.2900 g., 0.9000 Silver 5.0143 oz. ASW, 60 mm. **Subject:** Czar Alexander I **Obv:** Double-headed eagle **Rev:** Portrait and Imperial eagle above document text establishing government ministries **Edge:** Reeded

Date	Mintage	F	VF	XF	Unc	BU
2002(m) Proof	1,500	Value: 165				

Y# 743 25 ROUBLES
3.2000 g., 0.9990 Gold 0.1028 oz. AGW, 16 mm. **Subject:** Zodiac Signs: Leo **Obv:** Double-headed eagle **Rev:** Lion and symbol **Edge:** Reeded

Date	Mintage	F	VF	XF	Unc	BU
2002 Proof	10,000	Value: 120				

Y# 763 25 ROUBLES
3.2000 g., 0.9990 Gold 0.1028 oz. AGW, 16 mm. **Subject:** Zodiac - Capricorn **Obv:** Double-headed eagle **Edge:** Reeded

Date	Mintage	F	VF	XF	Unc	BU
2002(m)	10,000	—	—	—	—	120

Y# 764 25 ROUBLES
3.2000 g., 0.9990 Gold 0.1028 oz. AGW, 16 mm. **Subject:** Zodiac Signs **Obv:** Double-headed eagle **Rev:** Virgo, seated woman **Edge:** Reeded

Date	Mintage	F	VF	XF	Unc	BU
2002 (SP)	10,000	—	—	—	—	120

Y# 765 25 ROUBLES
3.2000 g., 0.9990 Gold 0.1028 oz. AGW, 16 mm. **Subject:** Zodiac Signs **Obv:** Double-headed eagle **Rev:** Sagittarius the archer **Edge:** Reeded

Date	Mintage	F	VF	XF	Unc	BU
2002 (SP)	10,000	—	—	—	—	120

Y# 767 25 ROUBLES
3.2000 g., 0.9990 Gold 0.1028 oz. AGW, 16 mm. **Subject:** Zodiac - Scorpio **Obv:** Double-headed eagle **Rev:** Scorpion **Edge:** Reeded

Date	Mintage	F	VF	XF	Unc	BU
2002(m)	10,000	—	—	—	—	120

Y# 769 25 ROUBLES
3.2000 g., 0.9990 Gold .1028 oz. AGW **Subject:** Zodiac Signs **Obv:** Double-headed eagle **Rev:** Libra, balance scale **Edge:** Reeded

Date	Mintage	F	VF	XF	Unc	BU
2002 (SP)	10,000	—	—	—	—	120

Y# 821 25 ROUBLES
3.2000 g., 0.9990 Gold 0.1028 oz. AGW, 16 mm. **Obv:** Double-headed eagle **Rev:** Crab and Cancer zodiac symbol **Edge:** Reeded

Date	Mintage	F	VF	XF	Unc	BU
2003 (SP)	50,000	—	—	—	—	120

Y# 864 25 ROUBLES
172.8000 g., 0.9000 Silver 5.0001 oz. ASW, 60 mm.
Rev: St. Sercius Monastery

Date	Mintage	F	VF	XF	Unc	BU
2003 Proof	2,000	Value: 150				

Y# 865 25 ROUBLES
172.8000 g., 0.9000 Silver 5.0001 oz. ASW, 60 mm.
Rev: Shlisselburg

Date	Mintage	F	VF	XF	Unc	BU
2003(m) Proof	2,000	Value: 125				

Y# 866 25 ROUBLES
172.8000 g., 0.9000 Silver 5.0001 oz. ASW, 60 mm.
Rev: Kamchatka

Date	Mintage	F	VF	XF	Unc	BU
2003	2,000	Value: 150				

Y# 830 25 ROUBLES
177.9600 g., 0.9000 Bi-Metallic Gold And Silver .900 Silver 172.78g planchet with .900 Gold 5.18g insert 5.1494 oz., 60 mm. **Subject:** Monetary reform of Peter the Great **Obv:** Double-headed eagle **Rev:** Gold insert replicating the obverse and reverse designs of a 1704 one rouble coin **Edge:** Reeded **Note:** Illustration reduced.

Date	Mintage	F	VF	XF	Unc	BU
2004 (SP) Proof	1,000	Value: 300				

Y# 867 25 ROUBLES
172.8000 g., 0.9000 Silver 5.0001 oz. ASW, 60 mm.
Rev: Valaam Church

Date	Mintage	F	VF	XF	Unc	BU
2004	1,500	Value: 150				

Y# 679 50 ROUBLES
8.7500 g., 0.9990 Gold .2532 oz. AGW, 22.6 mm.
Subject: Bolshoi Theater 225 Years **Obv:** Double-headed eagle **Rev:** Dueling figures **Edge:** Reeded

Date	Mintage	F	VF	XF	Unc	BU
2001 Proof	2,000	Value: 185				

Y# 684 50 ROUBLES
8.7500 g., 0.9000 Gold .2532 oz. AGW, 22.6 mm.
Subject: Siberian Exploration **Obv:** Double-headed eagle **Rev:** Portrait and boat **Edge:** Reeded

Date	Mintage	F	VF	XF	Unc	BU
2001 Proof	1,500	Value: 185				

Y# 757 50 ROUBLES
8.6444 g., 0.9000 Gold 0.2501 oz. AGW, 22.6 mm.
Subject: Olympics **Obv:** Double-headed eagle **Rev:** Figure skater and flying eagle **Edge:** Reeded

Date	Mintage	F	VF	XF	Unc	BU
2002 Proof	3,000	Value: 250				

Y# 782 50 ROUBLES
7.8900 g., 0.9990 Gold 0.2534 oz. AGW, 22.6 mm.
Subject: Works of Dionissy **Obv:** Double-headed eagle **Rev:** Virgin of Odygitriya **Edge:** Reeded

Date	Mintage	F	VF	XF	Unc	BU
2002(m) Proof	1,500	Value: 225				

Y# 786 50 ROUBLES
8.7500 g., 0.9000 Gold 0.2532 oz. AGW, 22.6 mm.
Subject: Admiral Nakhimov **Obv:** Double-headed eagle **Rev:** Portrait above flags and anchor **Edge:** Reeded

Date	Mintage	F	VF	XF	Unc	BU
2002 (SP) Proof	1,500	Value: 225				

Y# 788 50 ROUBLES
8.7500 g., 0.9000 Gold 0.2532 oz. AGW, 22.6 mm.
Subject: World Cup Soccer **Obv:** Double-headed eagle **Rev:** Player kicking soccer ball **Edge:** Reeded

Date	Mintage	F	VF	XF	Unc	BU
2002(m) Proof	3,000	Value: 200				

Y# 822 50 ROUBLES
7.8900 g., 0.9990 Gold 0.2534 oz. AGW, 22.6 mm.
Obv: Double-headed eagle **Rev:** Seated "Virgo" and zodiac symbol **Edge:** Reeded

Date	Mintage	F	VF	XF	Unc	BU
2003(sp)	30,000	—	—	—	—	200

Y# 823 50 ROUBLES
7.8900 g., 0.9990 Gold 0.2534 oz. AGW, 22.6 mm.
Obv: Double-headed eagle **Rev:** Balance scale Libra and zodiac symbol **Edge:** Reeded

Date	Mintage	F	VF	XF	Unc	BU
2003(m)	30,000	—	—	—	—	200

Y# 868 50 ROUBLES
8.6400 g., 0.9000 Gold 0.25 oz. AGW, 23 mm. **Rev:** Peter I monetary reform

Date	Mintage	F	VF	XF	Unc	BU
2003(m) Proof	1,500	Value: 220				

Y# 869 50 ROUBLES
8.6400 g., 0.9000 Gold 0.25 oz. AGW, 23 mm. **Rev:** Ski race

Date	Mintage	F	VF	XF	Unc	BU
2003(m) Proof	1,500	Value: 220				

Y# 870 50 ROUBLES
8.6400 g., 0.9000 Gold .2500 oz. AGW, 23 mm. **Rev:** Soccer player

Date	Mintage	F	VF	XF	Unc	BU
2004(sp) Proof	1,000	Value: 225				

Y# 871 50 ROUBLES
8.6400 g., 0.9000 Gold 0.25 oz. AGW, 23 mm. **Rev:** Olympic athletes

Date	Mintage	F	VF	XF	Unc	BU
2004(m) Proof	2,000	Value: 220				

Y# 872 50 ROUBLES
8.6400 g., 0.9000 Gold 0.25 oz. AGW, 23 mm. **Rev:** Virgin of the Son Icon

Date	Mintage	F	VF	XF	Unc	BU
2004(m) Proof	1,500	Value: 220				

Y# 795 100 ROUBLES
1111.1200 g., 0.9000 Silver 32.151 oz. ASW, 100 mm. **Subject:** The Bark Sedov **Obv:** Double-headed eagle **Rev:** Cameo portrait and sailing ship **Edge:** Reeded **Note:** Illustration reduced.

Date	Mintage	F	VF	XF	Unc	BU
2001(m) Proof	500	Value: 800				

Y# 681 100 ROUBLES
1111.1000 g., 0.9000 Silver 32.1504 oz. ASW, 100 mm.
Subject: Yuri Gagarin **Obv:** Double-headed eagle **Rev:** Astronaut and rocket in space **Edge:** Reeded **Note:** Illustration reduced.

Date	Mintage	F	VF	XF	Unc	BU
2001 Proof	750	Value: 800				

Y# 689 100 ROUBLES
1111.1000 g., 0.9000 Silver 32.1504 oz. ASW, 100 mm. **Subject:** Bolshoi Theater 225 Years **Obv:** Double-headed eagle **Rev:** Casino gambling scene **Edge:** Reeded **Note:** Illustration reduced.

Date	Mintage	F	VF	XF	Unc	BU
2001 Proof	500	Value: 1,000				

Y# 685 100 ROUBLES
17.4500 g., 0.9000 Gold .5049 oz. AGW, 30 mm.
Subject: Siberian Exploration **Obv:** Double-headed eagle **Rev:** Two portraits and sailboat **Edge:** Reeded

Date	Mintage	F	VF	XF	Unc	BU
2001 Proof	1,000	Value: 360				

Y# 688 100 ROUBLES
15.7200 g., 0.9990 Gold .5049 oz. AGW, 30 mm.
Subject: Bolshoi Theater 225 Years **Obv:** Double-headed eagle **Rev:** Three dancers with swords **Edge:** Reeded

Date	Mintage	F	VF	XF	Unc	BU
2001 Proof	1,500	Value: 360				

Y# 783 100 ROUBLES
1111.1200 g., 0.9000 Silver 32.151 oz. ASW, 100 mm. **Subject:** Works of Dionissy **Obv:** Double-headed eagle **Rev:** St. Ferapont Monastery in the center of a fresco covered cross **Edge:** Reeded **Note:** Illustration reduced.

Date	Mintage	F	VF	XF	Unc	BU
2002 (SP) Prooflike	500	—	—	—	—	900

Y# 789 100 ROUBLES
1111.1200 g., 0.9000 Silver 32.151 oz. ASW, 100 mm. **Subject:** World Cup Soccer **Obv:** Double-headed eagle **Rev:** Soccer ball design with map and players **Edge:** Reeded **Note:** Illustration reduced.

Date	Mintage	F	VF	XF	Unc	BU
2002 (SP) Proof	500	Value: 900				

Y# 791 100 ROUBLES
1111.1200 g., 0.9000 Silver 32.151 oz. ASW, 100 mm.
Subject: Hermitage **Obv:** Double-headed eagle **Rev:** Statues and arches **Edge:** Reeded **Note:** Illustration reduced.

Date	Mintage	F	VF	XF	Unc	BU
2002 (SP) Proof	1,000	Value: 800				

Y# 792 100 ROUBLES
17.4500 g., 0.9000 Gold 0.5049 oz. AGW, 30 mm.
Subject: Hermitage **Obv:** Double-headed eagle **Rev:** Ancient battle scene sculpted on comb **Edge:** Reeded

Date	Mintage	F	VF	XF	Unc	BU
2002 (SP) Proof	1,000	Value: 360				

Y# 873 100 ROUBLES
1111.1200 g., 0.9000 Silver 32.151 oz. ASW, 100 mm.
Rev: St. Petersburg

Date	Mintage	F	VF	XF	Unc	BU
2003(m) Proof	1,000	Value: 500				

Y# 874 100 ROUBLES
17.4500 g., 0.9000 Gold 0.5049 oz. AGW, 30 mm.
Rev: Petrozavodsk

Date	Mintage	F	VF	XF	Unc	BU
2003(m) Proof	1,000	Value: 375				

Y# 875 100 ROUBLES
17.4500 g., 0.9000 Gold 0.5049 oz. AGW, 30 mm. **Rev:** Kamchatka

Date	Mintage	F	VF	XF	Unc	BU
2003(sp) Proof	1,500	Value: 375				

Y# 832 100 ROUBLES
17.2800 g., 0.9000 Gold 0.5 oz. AGW, 30 mm. **Subject:** 2nd Kamchatka Expedition **Obv:** Double-headed eagle **Rev:** Shaman and two seated men **Edge:** Reeded

Date	Mintage	F	VF	XF	Unc	BU
2004 (SP) Proof	1,500	Value: 360				

Y# 831 100 ROUBLES
1000.0000 g., 0.9000 Silver 28.9357 oz. ASW, 100 mm.
Obv: Double-headed eagle **Rev:** Panel of icons painted by Theophanes the Greek **Edge:** Reeded **Note:** Illustration reduced.

Date	Mintage	F	VF	XF	Unc	BU
2004 (SP) Proof	500	Value: 750				

Y# 876 100 ROUBLES
1111.1200 g., 0.9000 Silver 32.151 oz. ASW, 100 mm.
Rev: Annunciation Cathedral Iconostasis

Date	Mintage	F	VF	XF	Unc	BU
2004(sp) Proof	500	Value: 700				

Y# 877 200 ROUBLES
3342.3899 g., 0.9000 Silver 96.7142 oz. ASW, 130 mm.
Rev: Peter I monetrary reform

Date	Mintage	F	VF	XF	Unc	BU
2003(sp) Proof	300	Value: 4,000				

Y# 796 1000 ROUBLES
0.9990 Gold, 50 mm. **Subject:** The Bark Sedov **Obv:** Double-headed eagle **Rev:** Four-masted ship sailing to the left **Edge:** Reeded

Date	Mintage	F	VF	XF	Unc	BU
2001(m) Proof	250	—	—	—	—	—

Y# 878 1000 ROUBLES
156.4000 g., 0.9990 Gold 5.0233 oz. AGW, 50 mm. **Rev:** Cronstadt

Date	Mintage	F	VF	XF	Unc	BU
2003(m) Proof	250	Value: 4,000				

Y# 784 10000 ROUBLES
1001.1000 g., 0.9990 Gold 32.1539 oz. AGW, 100 mm.
Subject: Works of Dionissy **Obv:** Double-headed eagle **Rev:** Interior view of the carved portal of the Virgin of the Nativity Church **Edge:** Reeded **Note:** Illustration reduced.

Date	Mintage	F	VF	XF	Unc	BU
2002 (SP) Prooflike	100	—	—	—	—	22,500

Y# 879 10000 ROUBLES
1001.1000 g., 0.9990 Gold 32.1539 oz. AGW, 100 mm.
Rev: St. Petersburg area map

Date	Mintage	F	VF	XF	Unc	BU
2003 Proof	200	Value: 25,000				

Y# 880 10000 ROUBLES
1001.1000 g., 0.9990 Gold 32.1539 oz. AGW, 100 mm.
Rev: Church of the Transfiguration of the Savior, Novgorod

Date	Mintage	F	VF	XF	Unc	BU
2004 Proof	100	Value: 25,000				

MINT SETS

KM#	Date	Mintage	Identification	Issue Price	Mkt Val
MS44	2002 (7)	—	Y#600-603, 797-799, plus mint medal	7.50	10.00

RWANDA

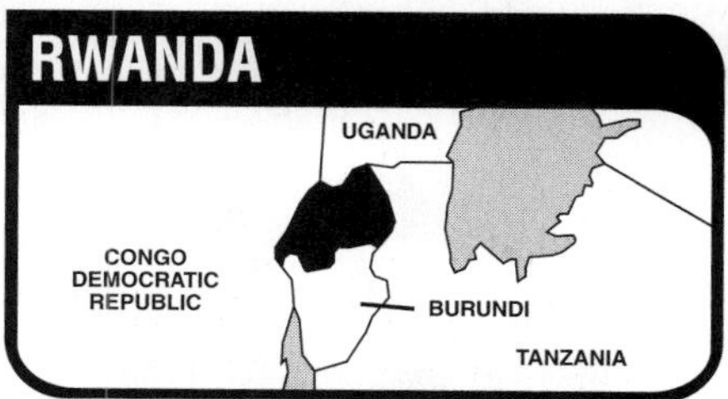

The Republic of Rwanda, located in central Africa between the Republic of the Congo and Tanzania, has an area of 10,169 sq. mi. (26,340 sq. km.) and a population of 7.3 million. Capital: Kigali. The economy is based on agriculture and mining. Coffee and tin are exported.

MONETARY SYSTEM
100 Centimes = 1 Franc

REPUBLIC

STANDARD COINAGE

KM# 22 FRANC
0.0700 g., Aluminum, 16 mm. **Obv:** National arms **Rev:** Sorghum plant **Edge:** Plain

Date	Mintage	F	VF	XF	Unc	BU
2003	—	—	—	—	0.25	0.50

KM# 23 5 FRANCS
2.9600 g., Brass Plated Steel, 20 mm. **Obv:** National arms **Rev:** Coffee plant **Edge:** Plain

Date	Mintage	F	VF	XF	Unc	BU
2003	—	—	—	—	0.50	0.75

KM# 24 10 FRANCS
5.0000 g., Brass Plated Steel, 23.9 mm. **Obv:** National arms **Rev:** Banana tree **Edge:** Plain

Date	Mintage	F	VF	XF	Unc	BU
2003	—	—	—	—	1.00	1.25

KM# 25 20 FRANCS
3.5000 g., Nickel Clad Steel, 20 mm. **Obv:** National arms **Rev:** Coffee plant seedling **Edge:** Reeded

Date	Mintage	F	VF	XF	Unc	BU
2003	—	—	—	—	1.75	2.00

KM# 26 50 FRANCS
5.8000 g., Nickel Clad Steel, 24 mm. **Obv:** National arms **Rev:** Corn **Edge:** Reeded

Date	Mintage	F	VF	XF	Unc	BU
2003	—	—	—	—	4.50	5.00

SAHARAWI ARAB D.R.

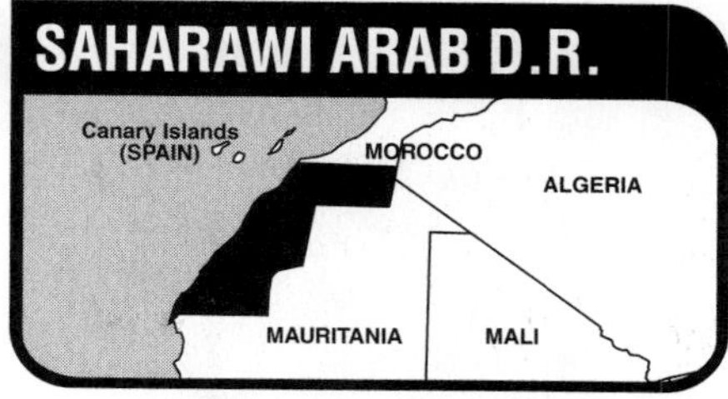

The Saharawi Arab Democratic Republic, located in northwest Africa has an area of 102,703 sq. mi. and a population (census taken 1974) of 76,425. Formerly known as Spanish Sahara, the area is bounded on the north by Morocco, on the east and southeast by Mauritania, on the northeast by Algeria, and on the west by the Atlantic Ocean. Capital: El Aaium. Agriculture, fishing and mining are the two main industries. Exports are barley, livestock and phosphates.

DEMOCRATIC REPUBLIC

NON-CIRCULATING COLLECTOR COINAGE

KM# 51 500 PESETAS
Bi-Metallic Stainless Steel center in Brass ring, 26 mm. **Obv:** National arms **Rev:** Two Fennec foxes **Edge:** Segmented reeding

Date	Mintage	F	VF	XF	Unc	BU
2004	5,000	—	—	—	30.00	35.00

KM# 51a 500 PESETAS
Bi-Metallic .999Silver center in .999 Gold plated .999 Silver ring, 26 mm. **Obv:** National arms **Rev:** Two Fennec foxes **Edge:** Segmented reeded

Date	Mintage	F	VF	XF	Unc	BU
2004	25	—	—	—	235	—

KM# 51b 500 PESETAS
0.9990 Silver, 26 mm. **Obv:** National arms **Rev:** Two Fennec foxes **Edge:** Segmented reeding

Date	Mintage	F	VF	XF	Unc	BU
2004	25	—	—	—	210	—

KM# 52 500 PESETAS
Bi-Metallic Stainless Steel center in Brass ring, 26 mm. **Obv:** National arms **Rev:** Independence map **Edge:** Segmented reeding

Date	Mintage	F	VF	XF	Unc	BU
2004	5,000	—	—	—	30.00	35.00

KM# 52a 500 PESETAS
Bi-Metallic .999 Silver center in .999 Gold plated .999 Silver ring, 26 mm. **Obv:** National arms **Rev:** Independence map **Edge:** Segmented reeding

Date	Mintage	F	VF	XF	Unc	BU
2004	25	—	—	—	235	—

KM# 52b 500 PESETAS
0.9990 Silver, 26 mm. **Obv:** National arms **Rev:** Independence map **Edge:** Segmented reeding

Date	Mintage	F	VF	XF	Unc	BU
2004	25	—	—	—	210	—

KM# 54 1000 PESETAS
19.9400 g., 0.9990 Silver 0.6404 oz. ASW, 38.1 mm. **Obv:** National arms **Rev:** Soccer player and stadium **Edge:** Plain

Date	Mintage	F	VF	XF	Unc	BU
2002 Proof	—	Value: 30.00				

SAINT HELENA

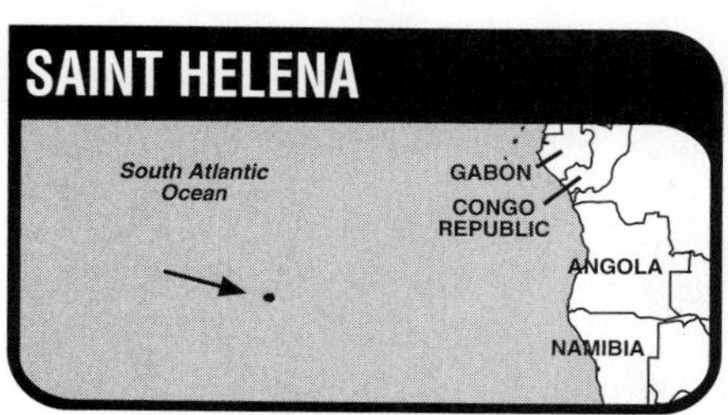

Saint Helena, a British colony located about 1,150 miles (1,850 km.) from the west coast of Africa, has an area of 47 sq. mi. (410 sq. km.) and a population of *7,000. Capital: Jamestown. Flax, lace, and rope are produced for export. Ascension and Tristan da Cunha are dependencies of Saint Helena.

MONETARY SYSTEM
12 Pence = 1 Shilling
100 Pence = 1 Pound

BRITISH COLONY

STANDARD COINAGE

KM# 19 50 PENCE
38.6000 g., Copper-Nickel, 38.6 mm. **Subject:** Queen's 75th Birthday **Obv:** Queen's crowned portrait **Rev:** Queen's uncrowned portrait **Edge:** Reeded

Date	Mintage	VG	F	VF	XF	Unc
2001	—	—	—	—	—	8.00

KM# 19a 50 PENCE
28.2800 g., 0.9250 Silver 0.841 oz. ASW, 38.6 mm. **Subject:** 75th Birthday of Queen Elizabeth II **Edge:** Reeded

Date	Mintage	F	VF	XF	Unc	BU
2001 Proof	10,000	Value: 50.00				

KM# 19b 50 PENCE
47.5400 g., 0.9166 Gold 1.401 oz. AGW, 38.6 mm. **Subject:** 75th Birthday of Queen Elizabeth II **Edge:** Reeded

Date	Mintage	F	VF	XF	Unc	BU
2001 Proof	75	Value: 975				

KM# 20 50 PENCE
28.5500 g., Copper-Nickel, 38.6 mm. **Subject:** Queen Victoria's Death **Obv:** Queen's crowned portrait **Rev:** Queen Victoria and ship **Edge:** Reeded

Date	Mintage	VG	F	VF	XF	Unc
2001	—	—	—	—	—	8.00

KM# 20a 50 PENCE
28.2800 g., 0.9250 Silver 0.841 oz. ASW, 38.6 mm. **Subject:** Centennial - Death of Queen Victoria **Obv:** Bust of Queen Elizabeth II right **Rev:** Young Queen Victoria in foreground, 3-masted ship in back **Edge:** Reeded

Date	Mintage	F	VF	XF	Unc	BU
2001 Proof	10,000	Value: 50.00				

KM# 20b 50 PENCE
47.5400 g., 0.9166 Gold 1.401 oz. AGW, 38.6 mm.
Subject: Centennial - Death of Queen Victoria **Obv:** Bust of Queen Elizabeth II right **Rev:** Young Queen Victoria in foreground, 3-masted ship in background **Edge:** Reeded

Date	Mintage	F	VF	XF	Unc	BU
2001 Proof	100	Value: 950				

KM# 23 50 PENCE
28.2800 g., Copper-Nickel, 38.6 mm. **Subject:** 50th Anniversary - Queen Elizabeth II's Accession **Obv:** Queen Elizabeth II **Rev:** Crown on pillow **Edge:** Reeded

Date	Mintage	F	VF	XF	Unc	BU
ND(2002)	—	—	—	—	10.00	—

KM# 23a 50 PENCE
28.2800 g., 0.9250 Silver 0.841 oz. ASW, 38.6 mm. **Subject:** 50th Anniversary - Queen Elizabeth's Accession **Obv:** Queen Elizabeth II **Rev:** Crown on pillow **Edge:** Reeded

Date	Mintage	F	VF	XF	Unc	BU
ND(2002) Proof	10,000	Value: 50.00				

KM# 24 50 PENCE
28.2800 g., Copper-Nickel, 38.6 mm. **Subject:** To Celebrate a Life of Duty, Dignity and Love, 1900-2002 **Obv:** Bust of Queen Elizabeth II right **Rev:** Queen Mother as a young and elderly lady **Edge:** Reeded

Date	Mintage	F	VF	XF	Unc	BU
ND(2002)	—	—	—	—	10.00	—

KM# 24a 50 PENCE
28.2800 g., 0.9250 Silver 0.841 oz. ASW, 38.6 mm.
Subject: To Celebrate a Life of Duty, Dignity and Love, 1900-2002 **Obv:** Bust of Queen Elizabeth II right **Rev:** Queen Mother as a young and elderly lady **Edge:** Reeded

Date	Mintage	F	VF	XF	Unc	BU
ND(2002) Proof	10,000	Value: 50.00				

KM# 25 50 PENCE
28.2800 g., Copper-Nickel, 38.6 mm. **Subject:** 500th Anniversary - Discovery of St. Helena **Obv:** Queen Elizabeth II **Rev:** Joao Da Nova and ship above 1502 date **Edge:** Reeded

Date	Mintage	F	VF	XF	Unc	BU
ND(2002)	—	—	—	—	10.00	—

KM# 25a 50 PENCE
28.2800 g., 0.9250 Silver 0.841 oz. ASW, 38.6 mm. **Subject:** 500th Anniversary - Discovery of St. Helena **Obv:** Queen Elizabeth II **Rev:** Joao Da Nova and ship above 1502 date **Edge:** Reeded

Date	Mintage	F	VF	XF	Unc	BU
ND(2002) Proof	5,000	Value: 50.00				

KM# 26 50 PENCE
28.2800 g., Copper-Nickel, 38.6 mm. **Obv:** Queen Elizabeth II **Rev:** Edmund Halley, the ship HMS Paramour and a comet **Edge:** Reeded

Date	Mintage	F	VF	XF	Unc	BU
ND(2002)	—	—	—	—	10.00	—

KM# 26a 50 PENCE
28.2800 g., 0.9250 Silver 0.841 oz. ASW, 38.6 mm. **Obv:** Queen Elizabeth II **Rev:** Edmund Halley, the ship HMS Paramour and a comet **Edge:** Reeded

Date	Mintage	F	VF	XF	Unc	BU
ND(2002) Proof	5,000	Value: 50.00				

KM# 27 50 PENCE
28.2800 g., Copper-Nickel, 38.6 mm. **Obv:** Queen Elizabeth II **Rev:** Captain Cook and the HMS Resolution **Edge:** Reeded

Date	Mintage	F	VF	XF	Unc	BU
ND(2002)	—	—	—	—	10.00	—

KM# 27a 50 PENCE
28.2800 g., 0.9250 Silver 0.841 oz. ASW, 38.6 mm. **Obv:** Queen Elizabeth II **Rev:** Captain Cook and the HMS Resolution **Edge:** Reeded

Date	Mintage	F	VF	XF	Unc	BU
ND(2002) Proof	5,000	Value: 50.00				

KM# 28 50 PENCE
28.2800 g., Copper-Nickel, 38.6 mm. **Obv:** Queen Elizabeth II **Rev:** Napoleon and the ship HMS Northumberland **Edge:** Reeded

Date	Mintage	F	VF	XF	Unc	BU
ND(2002)	—	—	—	—	10.00	—

KM# 29 50 PENCE
28.2800 g., Copper-Nickel, 38.6 mm. **Obv:** Queen Elizabeth II **Rev:** 1947 Royal Visitors; King George VI and Queen Elizabeth with Princesses Elizabeth and Margaret plus the HMS Vanguard **Edge:** Reeded

Date	Mintage	F	VF	XF	Unc	BU
ND(2002)	—	—	—	—	10.00	—

KM# 29a 50 PENCE
28.2800 g., 0.9250 Silver 0.841 oz. ASW, 38.6 mm. **Obv:** Queen Elizabeth II **Rev:** 1947 Royal Visitors: King George VI and queen Elizabeth with Princesses Elizabeth and Margaret plus the HMS Vanguard **Edge:** Reeded

Date	Mintage	F	VF	XF	Unc	BU
ND(2002) Proof	5,000	Value: 50.00				

KM# 30 50 PENCE
28.2800 g., Copper-Nickel, 38.6 mm. **Subject:** 50th Anniversary of Queen Elizabeth's Coronation **Obv:** Queen Elizabeth II **Rev:** Crowned Queen with scepter and orb **Edge:** Reeded

Date	Mintage	F	VF	XF	Unc	BU
ND(2003)	—	—	—	—	10.00	—

KM# 30a 50 PENCE
28.2800 g., 0.9250 Silver 0.841 oz. ASW, 38.6 mm. **Subject:** 50th Anniversary - Queen Elizabeth's Coronation **Obv:** Queen Elizabeth II **Rev:** Crowned Queen with scepter and orb **Edge:** Reeded

Date	Mintage	F	VF	XF	Unc	BU
ND(2003) Proof	5,000	Value: 50.00				

KM# 30b 50 PENCE
39.9400 g., 0.9166 Gold 1.177 oz. AGW, 38.6 mm. **Subject:** 50th Anniversary of Queen's Coronation **Obv:** Queen Elizabeth II **Rev:** Crowned Queen with scepter and orb **Edge:** Reeded

Date	Mintage	F	VF	XF	Unc	BU
ND(2003) Proof	50	Value: 975				

KM# 31 50 PENCE
28.2800 g., Copper-Nickel, 38.6 mm. **Subject:** 50th Anniversary of Coronation **Obv:** Queen Elizabeth II **Rev:** Coronation implements **Edge:** Reeded

Date	Mintage	F	VF	XF	Unc	BU
ND(2003)	—	—	—	—	10.00	—

KM# 31a 50 PENCE
28.2800 g., 0.9250 Silver 0.841 oz. ASW, 38.6 mm. **Subject:** 50th Anniversary - Queen Elizabeth II's Coronation **Obv:** Queen Elizabeth II **Edge:** Reeded

Date	Mintage	F	VF	XF	Unc	BU
ND(2003) Proof	5,000	Value: 50.00				

KM# 31b 50 PENCE
39.9400 g., 0.9166 Gold 1.177 oz. AGW, 38.6 mm.
Subject: 50th Anniversary of Coronation **Obv:** Queen Elizabeth II **Rev:** Coronation implements **Edge:** Reeded

Date	Mintage	F	VF	XF	Unc	BU
ND(2003) Proof	50	Value: 975				

KM# 28a 50 PENCE
28.2800 g., 0.9250 Silver 0.841 oz. ASW, 38.6 mm. **Obv:** Queen Elizabeth II **Rev:** Napoleon and the ship HMS Northumberland **Edge:** Reeded

Date	Mintage	F	VF	XF	Unc	BU
ND(2002) Proof	5,000	Value: 50.00				

PIEFORTS

KM#	Date	Mintage	Identification	Mkt Val
P3	ND(2002)	500	50 Pence. 0.9250 Silver. 56.5600 g. 38.6 mm. Reeded edge. Proof.	100

SAINT HELENA - ASCENSION

STANDARD COINAGE

100 Pence = 1 Pound

KM# 26 2 POUNDS
11.8100 g., Aluminum-Bronze, 28.3 mm. **Obv:** Elizabeth II **Rev:** National arms above value **Edge:** Reeded and lettered **Edge Lettering:** "500TH ANNIVERSARY"

Date	Mintage	F	VF	XF	Unc	BU
2002	—	—	—	6.00	10.00	12.50

KM# 25 2 POUNDS
11.9000 g., Bi-Metallic Copper-Nickel center in Brass ring, 28.3 mm. **Obv:** Elizabeth II **Rev:** Coat of Arms **Edge:** Reeded and lettered **Edge Lettering:** "LOYAL AND FAITHFUL"

Date	Mintage	F	VF	XF	Unc	BU
2003	—	—	—	9.00	15.00	17.50

SAMOA

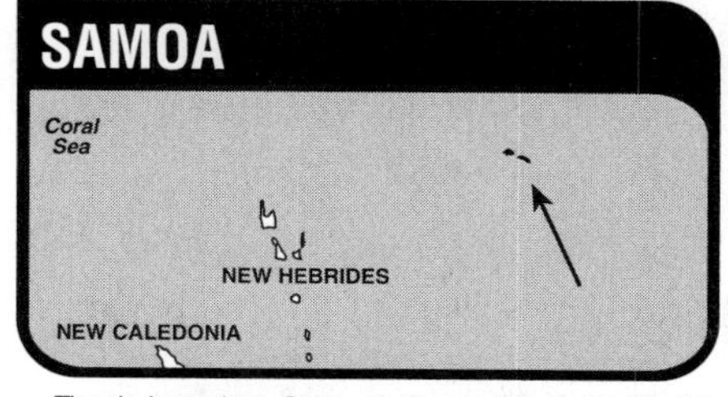

The Independent State of Samoa (formerly Western Samoa), located in the Pacific Ocean 1,600 miles (2,574 km.) northeast of New Zealand, has an area of 1,097 sq. mi. (2,860 sq. km.) and a population of *182,000. Capital: Apia. The economy is based on agriculture, fishing and tourism. Copra, cocoa and bananas are exported.

Samoa is a member of the Commonwealth of Nations. The Chief Executive is Chief of State. The prime minister is the Head of Government. The present Head of State, Malietoa Tanumafili II, holds his position for life. The Legislative Assembly will elect future Heads of State for 5-year terms.

Samoa, which had used New Zealand coinage, converted to a decimal coinage in 1967.

RULERS
Malietoa Tanumafili II, 1962—

MONETARY SYSTEM
100 Sene = 1 Tala

BRITISH ADMINISTRATION

STANDARD COINAGE

KM# 131 5 SENE
2.8400 g., Copper-Nickel, 19.5 mm. **Obv:** Malietoa Tanumafili II head left **Obv. Designer:** T.H. Paget **Rev:** Pineapple and value **Rev. Designer:** James Berry **Edge:** Reeded **Note:** "Western" dropped from country name

Date	Mintage	F	VF	XF	Unc	BU
2002	—	—	—	—	0.65	0.85

KM# 132 10 SENE
5.6500 g., Copper-Nickel, 23.6 mm. **Obv:** T.H. Paget **Rev:** Taro leaves and value **Rev. Designer:** James Berry **Edge:** Reeded **Note:** "Western" dropped from country name

Date	Mintage	F	VF	XF	Unc	BU
2002	—	—	—	—	1.00	1.25

KM# 133 20 SENE
11.4000 g., Copper-Nickel, 28.45 mm. **Obv:** Malietoa Tanumafili II head left **Obv. Designer:** T.H. Paget **Rev:** Breadfruits and value **Rev. Designer:** James Berry **Edge:** Reeded **Note:** "Western" dropped from country name

Date	Mintage	F	VF	XF	Unc	BU
2002	—	—	—	—	1.50	1.75

KM# 134 50 SENE
14.1300 g., Copper-Nickel, 32.3 mm. **Obv:** King's head left **Rev:** Banana tree and value **Edge:** Reeded **Note:** "Western" dropped from country name

Date	Mintage	F	VF	XF	Unc	BU
2002	—	—	—	—	3.25	3.50

KM# 135 TALA
9.5000 g., Brass, 30 mm. **Obv:** Malietoa Tanumafili II head left **Obv. Designer:** T.H. Paget **Rev:** National arms **Rev. Designer:** Nelson Eustis **Edge:** Reeded **Note:** "Western" dropped from country name

Date	Mintage	F	VF	XF	Unc	BU
2002	—	—	—	—	4.50	5.00

KM# 137 10 TALA
31.1000 g., 0.9990 Silver 0.9989 oz. ASW, 40 mm. **Obv:** National arms **Rev:** Bowhead Whale on mother of pearl insert **Edge:** Plain

Date	Mintage	F	VF	XF	Unc	BU
2002 Proof	2,000	Value: 60.00				

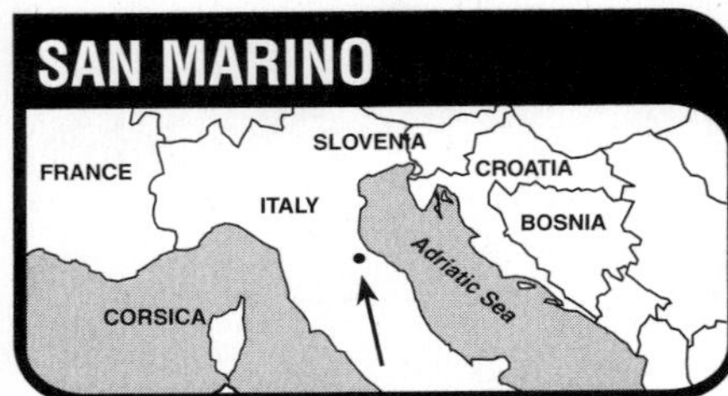

The Republic of San Marino, the oldest and smallest republic in the world is located in north central Italy entirely surrounded by the Province of Emilia-Romagna. It has an area of 24 sq. mi. (60 sq. km.) and a population of *23,000. Capital: San Marino. The principal economic activities are farming, livestock raising, cheese making, tourism and light manufacturing. Building stone, lime, wheat, hides and baked goods are exported. The government derives most of its revenue from the sale of postage stamps for philatelic purposes.

San Marino has its own coinage, but Italian and Vatican City coins and currency are also in circulation.

MINT MARKS

M - Milan

R – Rome

MONETARY SYSTEM

100 Centesimi = 1 Lira

REPUBLIC

STANDARD COINAGE

KM# 424 10 LIRE

1.6000 g., Aluminum, 23.3 mm. **Obv:** Three towers **Rev:** Wheat stalks **Edge:** Plain

Date	Mintage	F	VF	XF	Unc	BU
2001	—	—	—	—	0.35	—

KM# 425 20 LIRE

3.6000 g., Aluminum-Bronze, 21.8 mm. **Obv:** Three towers **Rev:** Two dolphins **Edge:** Plain

Date	Mintage	F	VF	XF	Unc	BU
2001	—	—	—	—	0.75	1.50

KM# 426 50 LIRE

4.5000 g., Stainless Steel, 19.2 mm. **Obv:** Three towers **Rev:** Tree **Edge:** Plain

Date	Mintage	F	VF	XF	Unc	BU
2001	—	—	—	—	0.85	—

KM# 427 100 LIRE

4.5000 g., Copper-Nickel, 22 mm. **Obv:** Three towers **Rev:** Two hands **Edge:** Plain and reeded sections

Date	Mintage	F	VF	XF	Unc	BU
2001	—	—	—	—	1.25	—

KM# 428 200 LIRE

5.0000 g., Aluminum-Bronze, 24 mm. **Obv:** Three towers **Rev:** Broken chain, leaves and vines **Edge:** Reeded

Date	Mintage	F	VF	XF	Unc	BU
2001	—	—	—	—	1.50	—

KM# 429 500 LIRE

Bi-Metallic Aluminum-Bronze center in Stainless Steel ring, 25.8 mm. **Obv:** Three towers **Rev:** Three different plant stalks **Edge:** Reeded and plain sections **Note:** 6.8 grams.

Date	Mintage	F	VF	XF	Unc	BU
2001	—	—	—	—	2.00	—

KM# 430 1000 LIRE

8.8000 g., Bi-Metallic Stainless-Steel center in Aluminum-Bronze ring, 27 mm. **Obv:** Three towers **Rev:** Circle of birds **Edge:** Reeded and plain sections

Date	Mintage	F	VF	XF	Unc	BU
2001	—	—	—	—	7.50	—

KM# 436 5000 LIRE

18.0000 g., 0.8350 Silver .4832 oz. ASW, 32 mm. **Subject:** Last Lire Coinage **Obv:** National arms **Rev:** Six old coin designs **Edge:** Lettered

Date	Mintage	F	VF	XF	Unc	BU
2001 Proof	20,000	Value: 20.00				

KM# 431 5000 LIRE

18.0000 g., 0.8350 Silver .4832 oz. ASW, 32 mm. **Obv:** Three towers **Rev:** Dove on laurel branch **Edge:** Reeded and plain sections

Date	Mintage	F	VF	XF	Unc	BU
2001	—	—	—	—	15.00	—

KM# 437 10000 LIRE

22.0000 g., 0.8350 Silver .5906 oz. ASW, 34 mm. **Subject:** Last Lire Coinage **Obv:** National arms **Rev:** Six old coin designs **Edge:** Reeded and plain sections

Date	Mintage	F	VF	XF	Unc	BU
2001 Proof	20,000	Value: 30.00				

KM# 438 10000 LIRE

22.0000 g., 0.8350 Silver .5906 oz. ASW, 34 mm. **Subject:** 2nd International Chambers of Commerce Convention **Obv:** National arms. **Rev:** Mercury running by a computer. **Edge:** Reeded and plain sections.

Date	Mintage	F	VF	XF	Unc	BU
2001 Proof	20,000	Value: 20.00				

KM# 432 10000 LIRE

22.0000 g., 0.8350 Silver .5906 oz. ASW, 34 mm. **Subject:** Ferrari **Obv:** Three towers **Rev:** Race car with "FERRARI" background **Edge:** Reeded and plain sections

Date	Mintage	F	VF	XF	Unc	BU
2001 Proof	20,000	Value: 25.00				

KM# 433 1/2 SCUDO

1.6100 g., 0.9000 Gold .0466 oz. AGW, 13.8 mm. **Subject:** Cavaliere **Obv:** National arms **Rev:** Horse and rider **Edge:** Reeded

Date	Mintage	F	VF	XF	Unc	BU
2001 Proof	4,500	Value: 37.50				

KM# 434 SCUDO

3.2200 g., 0.9000 Gold .0932 oz. AGW, 16 mm. **Subject:** Tiziano **Obv:** National arms **Rev:** Bearded male portrait **Edge:** Reeded

Date	Mintage	F	VF	XF	Unc	BU
2001 Proof	4,500	Value: 70.00				

KM# 435 2 SCUDI

6.4400 g., 0.9000 Gold .1863 oz. AGW, 21 mm. **Subject:** Flora **Obv:** National arms **Rev:** Portrait **Edge:** Reeded

Date	Mintage	F	VF	XF	Unc	BU
2001 Proof	4,500	Value: 125				

KM# 457 2 SCUDI

6.4516 g., 0.9000 Gold 0.1867 oz. AGW, 21 mm. **Obv:** National arms **Rev:** Cimabue's " Madonna and Child" **Edge:** Reeded

Date	Mintage	F	VF	XF	Unc	BU
2002R Proof	3,000	Value: 135				

KM# 459 2 SCUDI

6.4516 g., 0.9000 Gold 0.1867 oz. AGW, 21 mm. **Obv:** National arms **Rev:** Nostradamus above value **Edge:** Reeded

Date	Mintage	F	VF	XF	Unc	BU
2003R Proof	7,500	Value: 145				

KM# 464 2 SCUDI

6.4516 g., 0.9000 Gold 0.1867 oz. AGW, 21 mm. **Subject:** The Domagnano Treasure **Obv:** Crowned arms **Rev:** Gothic Eagle Brooch, same as on the German KM-113 5 Mark coin of 1952 **Edge:** Reeded

Date	Mintage	F	VF	XF	Unc	BU
2004R Proof	6,500	Value: 155				

KM# 439 5 SCUDI
16.9655 g., 0.9166 Gold .5000 oz. AGW, 28 mm. **Subject:** San Marino's World Bank Membership **Obv:** National arms **Rev:** Orchid and bee **Edge:** Reeded

Date	Mintage	F	VF	XF	Unc	BU
2001 Proof	4,000	Value: 320				

EURO COINAGE

KM# 440 EURO CENT
2.2700 g., Copper Plated Steel, 16.2 mm. **Obv:** "Il Montale" **Obv. Designer:** M. Frantisek Chochola **Rev:** Denomination and globe **Rev. Designer:** Luc Luycx **Edge:** Plain

Date	Mintage	F	VF	XF	Unc	BU
2002	120,000	—	—	—	—	40.00
2003	70,000	—	—	—	—	42.00
2004R	—	—	—	—	—	20.00
2005R	—	—	—	—	—	20.00
2006R	—	—	—	—	—	18.00

KM# 441 2 EURO CENTS
3.0300 g., Copper Plated Steel, 18.7 mm. **Obv:** Stefano Gallietti, Liberty fighter **Obv. Designer:** M. Frantisek Chochola **Rev:** Denomination and globe **Rev. Designer:** Luc Luycx **Edge:** Grooved

Date	Mintage	F	VF	XF	Unc	BU
2002	120,000	—	—	—	—	40.00
2003	70,000	—	—	—	—	42.00
2004R	—	—	—	—	—	20.00
2005R	—	—	—	—	—	20.00
2006R	—	—	—	—	—	18.00

KM# 442 5 EURO CENTS
3.8600 g., Copper Plated Steel, 21.2 mm. **Obv:** "Guaita" tower **Obv. Designer:** M. Frantisek Chochola **Rev:** Denomination and globe **Rev. Designer:** Luc Luycx **Edge:** Plain

Date	Mintage	F	VF	XF	Unc	BU
2002	120,000	—	—	—	—	40.00
2003	70,000	—	—	—	—	42.00
2004R	—	—	—	—	—	20.00
2005R	—	—	—	—	—	20.00
2006R	—	—	—	—	—	18.00

KM# 443 10 EURO CENTS
4.0700 g., Brass, 19.7 mm. **Obv:** Building Basilica del Santo Marinus **Obv. Designer:** M. Frantisek Chochola **Rev:** Map and denomination **Rev. Designer:** Luc Luycx **Edge:** Reeded

Date	Mintage	F	VF	XF	Unc	BU
2002	120,000	—	—	—	—	40.00
2003	70,000	—	—	—	—	42.00
2004R	—	—	—	—	—	22.00
2005R	—	—	—	—	—	22.00
2006R	—	—	—	—	—	20.00

KM# 444 20 EURO CENTS
5.7300 g., Brass, 22.1 mm. **Obv:** St. Marinus from a portrait by van Guercino **Obv. Designer:** M. Frantisek Chochola **Rev:** Map and denomination **Rev. Designer:** Luc Luycx **Edge:** Notched

Date	Mintage	F	VF	XF	Unc	BU
2002	302,400	—	—	—	18.00	20.00
2003	430,000	—	—	—	15.00	18.00
2004R	—	—	—	—	15.00	18.00
2005R	—	—	—	—	15.00	18.00
2006R	—	—	—	—	15.00	18.00

KM# 445 50 EURO CENTS
7.8100 g., Brass, 24.2 mm. **Obv:** Fortress of San Marino **Obv. Designer:** M. Frantisek Chochola **Rev:** Map and denomination **Rev. Designer:** Luc Luycx **Edge:** Reeded

Date	Mintage	F	VF	XF	Unc	BU
2002	230,400	—	—	—	20.00	22.50
2003	415,000	—	—	—	17.50	20.00
2004R	—	—	—	—	17.50	20.00
2005R	—	—	—	—	17.50	20.00
2006R	—	—	—	—	15.00	18.00

KM# 446 EURO
7.5000 g., Bi-Metallic Copper-Nickel center in Brass ring, 23.2 mm. **Obv:** Crowned arms **Obv. Designer:** M. Frantisek Chochola **Rev:** Denomination and map **Rev. Designer:** Luc Luycx **Edge:** Reeded and plain sections

Date	Mintage	F	VF	XF	Unc	BU
2002	360,800	—	—	—	22.00	25.00
2003	70,000	—	—	—	—	45.00
2004R	—	—	—	—	—	25.00
2005R	—	—	—	—	—	25.00
2006R	—	—	—	—	—	20.00

KM# 447 2 EURO
8.5200 g., Bi-Metallic Brass center in Copper-Nickel ring, 25.7 mm. **Obv:** Goverment building "Domus Magna Comunis" **Obv. Designer:** M. Frantisek Chochola **Rev:** Denomination and map **Rev. Designer:** Luc Luycx **Edge:** Reeded with 2's and stars

Date	Mintage	F	VF	XF	Unc	BU
2002	255,760	—	—	—	25.00	28.00
2003	70,000	—	—	—	—	45.00
2004R	—	—	—	—	—	28.00
2005R	—	—	—	—	—	28.00
2006R	—	—	—	—	—	22.00

KM# 467 2 EURO
8.5000 g., Bi-Metallic Brass center in Copper-Nickel ring, 25.75 mm. **Obv:** National arms **Rev:** Bartolomeo Borghesi **Edge:** Alternating stars and 2's

Date	Mintage	F	VF	XF	Unc	BU
2004R	110,000	—	—	—	17.50	30.00

KM# 469 2 EURO
8.5000 g., Bi-Metallic, 25.75 mm. **Obv:** Galileo Galilei at telescope

Date	Mintage	F	VF	XF	Unc	BU
2005R	130,000	—	—	—	35.00	45.00

KM# 448 5 EURO
18.0000 g., 0.9250 Silver 0.5353 oz. ASW, 32 mm. **Subject:** Welcome Euro **Obv:** Three plumed towers **Rev:** Circle of roses

Date	Mintage	F	VF	XF	Unc	BU
2002 Proof	37,000	Value: 75.00				

KM# 450 5 EURO
18.0000 g., 0.9250 Silver 0.5353 oz. ASW, 32 mm. **Subject:** 1600th Anniversary of Ravenna **Obv:** National arms **Rev:** Bas-relief wall design **Edge:** Reeded

Date	Mintage	F	VF	XF	Unc	BU
2002R Proof	—	Value: 60.00				

KM# 453 5 EURO
18.0000 g., 0.9250 Silver 0.5353 oz. ASW, 32 mm. **Subject:** 2004 Olympics **Obv:** Stylized three towers **Rev:** Ancient Olympians **Edge:** Reeded

Date	Mintage	F	VF	XF	Unc	BU
2003R Proof	37,766	Value: 50.00				

KM# 452 5 EURO
18.0000 g., 0.9250 Silver 0.5353 oz. ASW, 32 mm. **Obv:** National arms **Rev:** Allegorical depiction of Independence, Tolerance and Liberty

Date	Mintage	F	VF	XF	Unc	BU
2003R	—	—	—	—	35.00	40.00

KM# 468 5 EURO
18.0000 g., 0.9250 Silver 0.5353 oz. ASW, 32 mm. **Obv:** Three towers **Rev:** Antonio Onofri and value

Date	Mintage	F	VF	XF	Unc	BU
2004R	—	—	—	—	45.00	50.00
2005R	—	—	—	—	45.00	50.00

KM# 458 5 EURO
18.0000 g., 0.9250 Silver 0.5353 oz. ASW, 32 mm. **Obv:** National arms **Rev:** Value behind Bartolomeo Borghesi

Date	Mintage	F	VF	XF	Unc	BU
2004R	—	—	—	—	—	35.00
2004R Proof	—	Value: 45.00				

KM# 462 5 EURO
18.0000 g., 0.9250 Silver 0.5353 oz. ASW, 32 mm. **Obv:** Three stylized plumed towers **Rev:** Two soccer players

Date	Mintage	F	VF	XF	Unc	BU
2004R Proof	35,000	Value: 45.00				

KM# 472 5 EURO
18.0000 g., 0.9250 Silver 0.5353 oz. ASW, 32 mm. **Obv:** Portrait of Melchiorie Delfico

Date	Mintage	F	VF	XF	Unc	BU
2006R	65,000	—	—	—	—	35.00

KM# 449 10 EURO
22.0000 g., 0.9250 Silver 0.6543 oz. ASW, 34 mm. **Subject:** Welcome Euro **Obv:** Three plumed towers **Rev:** Infant sleeping in flower

Date	Mintage	F	VF	XF	Unc	BU
2002 Proof	37,000	Value: 100				

KM# 451 10 EURO
22.0000 g., 0.9250 Silver 0.6543 oz. ASW, 34 mm. **Subject:** 1600th Anniversary of Ravenna **Obv:** National arms **Rev:** Wall painting

Date	Mintage	F	VF	XF	Unc	BU
2002R Proof	—	Value: 95.00				

KM# 454 10 EURO
22.0000 g., 0.9250 Silver 0.6543 oz. ASW, 34 mm. **Subject:** 2004 Olympics **Obv:** Three stylized towers **Rev:** Modern Olympians **Edge:** Segmented reeding

Date	Mintage	F	VF	XF	Unc	BU
2003R Proof	37,766	Value: 75.00				

KM# 463 10 EURO
22.0000 g., 0.9250 Silver 0.6543 oz. ASW, 34 mm. **Obv:** Three stylized plumed towers **Rev:** Two soccer players

Date	Mintage	F	VF	XF	Unc	BU
2004R Proof	30,000	Value: 60.00				

KM# 460 20 EURO
6.4510 g., 0.9000 Gold 0.1867 oz. AGW, 21 mm. **Subject:** 1600th Anniversary of Ravenna **Obv:** National arms **Rev:** Bas-relief wall design **Edge:** Reeded

Date	Mintage	F	VF	XF	Unc	BU
2002R Proof	4,550	Value: 375				

KM# 455 20 EURO
6.4516 g., 0.9000 Gold 0.1867 oz. AGW, 21 mm. **Obv:** Three plumes **Rev:** Giotto's "Presentation of Jesus at the Temple" **Edge:** Reeded

Date	Mintage	F	VF	XF	Unc	BU
2003R Proof	7,300	Value: 245				

KM# 465 20 EURO
6.4510 g., 0.9000 Gold 0.1867 oz. AGW, 21 mm. **Obv:** Three plumes **Rev:** Marco Polo meeting Kublai Khan **Edge:** Reeded

Date	Mintage	F	VF	XF	Unc	BU
2004R Proof	7,300	Value: 255				

KM# 470 20 EURO
6.4510 g., 0.9000 Gold 0.1867 oz. AGW, 21 mm. **Subject:** International Day of Peace **Obv:** Stylized faces and leaves

Date	Mintage	F	VF	XF	Unc	BU
2005R Proof	5,300	Value: 300				

KM# 461 50 EURO
16.1290 g., 0.9000 Gold 0.4667 oz. AGW, 28 mm. **Subject:** 1600th Anniversary of Ravenna **Obv:** National arms **Rev:** Wall painting **Edge:** Reeded

Date	Mintage	F	VF	XF	Unc	BU
2002R Proof	4,550	Value: 775				

KM# 456 50 EURO
16.1290 g., 0.9000 Gold 0.4667 oz. AGW, 28 mm. **Obv:** Three plumes **Rev:** Giotto's "The Pentecost" **Edge:** Reeded

Date	Mintage	F	VF	XF	Unc	BU
2003R Proof	7,300	Value: 500				

KM# 466 50 EURO
16.1290 g., 0.9000 Gold 0.4667 oz. AGW, 28 mm. **Obv:** Three plumes **Rev:** Marco Polo **Edge:** Reeded

Date	Mintage	F	VF	XF	Unc	BU
2004R Proof	7,300	Value: 525				

KM# 471 50 EURO
16.1290 g., 0.9000 Gold 0.4667 oz. AGW, 28 mm. **Subject:** International Day of Peace **Obv:** Group of people gathering

Date	Mintage	F	VF	XF	Unc	BU
2005R Proof	5,300	Value: 500				

MINT SETS

KM#	Date	Mintage	Identification	Issue Price	Mkt Val
MS61	2001 (8)	2,000	KM424-431	18.00	25.00
MS62	2002 (8)	120,000	KM440 - 447	—	300
MS63	2003 (9)	—	KM#440-447, 452	55.00	350
MS64	2004 (9)	—	KM#440-447, 458	55.00	220
MS65	2005 (9)	—	KM#440-447, 468	55.00	225
MS66	2006 (9)	65,000	KM#440-447, 472	—	185

PROOF SETS

KM#	Date	Mintage	Identification	Issue Price	Mkt Val
PS14	2001 (3)	4,500	KM433-435	179	180
PS15	2002 (2)	37,000	KM448-449	—	175
PS16	2002 (2)	4,550	KM#460-461	—	1,150
PS17	2003 (2)	7,300	KM#455-456	—	750
PS18	2004 (2)	7,300	KM#465-466	—	780
PS19	2005 (2)	5,300	KM#470-471	—	800

UNITED KINGDOMS

The Kingdom of Saudi Arabia, an independent and absolute hereditary monarchy comprising the former sultanate of Nejd, the old kingdom of Hejaz, Asir and Al Hasa, occupies four-fifths of the Arabian peninsula. The kingdom has an area of 830,000 sq. mi. (2,149,690 sq. km.) and a population of *16.1 million. Capital: Riyadh. The economy is based on oil, which provides 85 percent of Saudi Arabia's revenue.

TITLES

العربية السعودية

Al-Arabiya(t) as-Sa'udiya(t)

المملكة العربية السعودية

Al-Mamlaka(t) al-'Arabiya(t) as-Sa'udiya(t)

RULERS

al Sa'ud Dynasty

Fahad bin Abd Al-Aziz, AH1403-1426/1982-2005AD
Abdullah bin Abdul Aziz, AH1426-/2005AD

KINGDOM

REFORM COINAGE

5 Halala = 1 Ghirsh; 100 Halala = 1 Riyal

KM# 62 10 HALALA (2 Ghirsh)
Copper-Nickel

Date	Mintage	F	VF	XF	Unc	BU
AH1423 (2002)	—	—	0.30	0.60	1.25	—

KM# 63 25 HALALA (1/4 Riyal)
Copper-Nickel

Date	Mintage	F	VF	XF	Unc	BU
AH1423 (2002)	—	—	0.40	0.70	1.50	—

KM# 64 50 HALALA (1/2 Riyal)
Copper-Nickel

Date	Mintage	F	VF	XF	Unc	BU
AH1423 (2002)	—	0.20	0.50	2.25	3.50	—

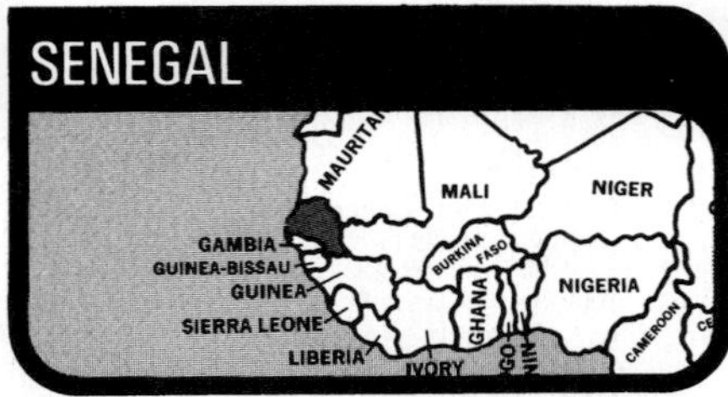

The Republic of Senegal, located on the bulge of West Africa between Mauritania and Guinea-Bissau, has an area of 75,750 sq. mi. (196,190 sq. km.) and a population of *7.5 million. Capital: Dakar. The economy is primarily agricultural. Peanuts and products, phosphates, and canned fish are exported.

Senegal is a member of a monetary union of autonomous republics called the Monetary Union of West African States (*Union Monetaire Ouest-Africaine*). The other members are Ivory Coast, Benin, Burkina Faso (Upper Volta), Niger, Mauritania and Togo. Mali was a member, but seceded in 1962. Some of the member countries have issued coinage in addition to the common currency issued by the Monetary Union of West African States.

REPUBLIC

INSTITUT MONETAIRE

KM# 11 3000 CFA FRANCS - 2 AFRICA
9.9300 g., Brass, 27.6 mm. **Subject:** West African Development Institute **Obv:** Bush baby **Rev:** Elephant on map **Edge:** Plain

Date	Mintage	F	VF	XF	Unc	BU
2003	1,200	—	—	—	30.00	—

KM# 11a 3000 CFA FRANCS - 2 AFRICA
0.9990 Silver, 27.5 mm. **Edge:** Plain

Date	Mintage	F	VF	XF	Unc	BU
2003	5	—	—	—	130	—

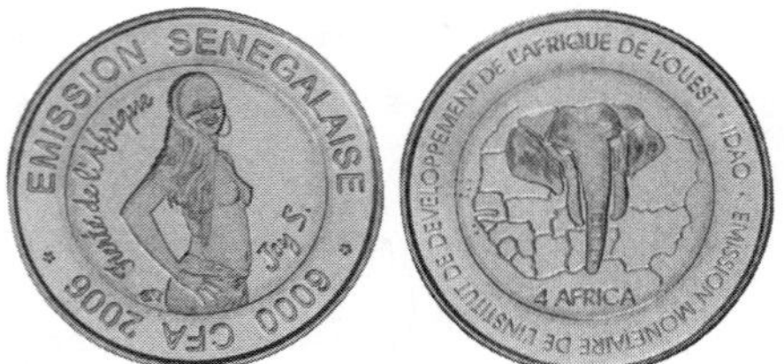

KM# 12 6000 CFA FRANCS - 4 AFRICA
10.0000 g., Bi-Metallic Copper-Nickel center in Brass ring, 28.4 mm. **Subject:** Bare-breasted African girl **Rev:** Elephant head on partial African map **Edge:** Plain

Date	Mintage	F	VF	XF	Unc	BU
2006	2,006	—	—	—	80.00	—

KM# 12a 6000 CFA FRANCS - 4 AFRICA
11.1000 g., Bi-Metallic Copper center in Brass ring, 28.4 mm. **Obv:** Bare-breasted African girl **Rev:** Elephant head on partial African map **Edge:** Plain

Date	Mintage	F	VF	XF	Unc	BU
2006	100	—	—	—	180	—

KM# 12b 6000 CFA FRANCS - 4 AFRICA
14.0000 g., 0.9990 Silver 0.4497 oz. ASW, 28 mm. **Obv:** Bare-breasted African girl **Rev:** Elephant head on partial African map **Edge:** Plain

Date	Mintage	F	VF	XF	Unc	BU
2006	25	—	—	—	420	—

KM# 12c 6000 CFA FRANCS - 4 AFRICA
14.0000 g., 0.9990 Gold Plated Silver 0.4497 oz. ASW AGW, 28 mm. **Obv:** Bare-breasted African girl **Rev:** Elephant head on partial African map **Edge:** Plain

Date	Mintage	F	VF	XF	Unc	BU
2006	25	—	—	—	480	—

KM# 13 6000 CFA FRANCS - 4 AFRICA
14.0000 g., 0.9990 Silver 0.4497 oz. ASW, 28 mm. **Obv:** Bare-breasted African girl **Rev:** Elephant head on full African map **Edge:** Plain

Date	Mintage	F	VF	XF	Unc	BU
2006	25	—	—	—	480	—

KM# 13a 6000 CFA FRANCS - 4 AFRICA
14.0000 g., 0.9990 Gold Plated Silver 0.4497 oz. ASW AGW, 28 mm. **Obv:** Topless girl **Rev:** Elephant head on full African map **Edge:** Plain

Date	Mintage	F	VF	XF	Unc	BU
2006	25	—	—	—	540	—

Serbia, a former inland Balkan kingdom has an area of 34,116 sq. mi. (88,361 sq. km.). Capital: Belgrade.

MINT MARKS
БП - (BP) Budapest

MONETARY SYSTEM
100 Para = 1 Dinara

DENOMINATIONS
ПАРА = Para
ПАРЕ = Pare
ДИНАР = Dinar
ДИНАРА = Dinara

REPUBLIC

STANDARD COINAGE

KM# 34 DINAR
4.3300 g., Copper-Zinc-Nickel, 20 mm. **Obv:** National Bank emblem **Rev:** Bank building **Edge:** Reeded

Date	Mintage	F	VF	XF	Unc	BU
2003	10,320,000	—	—	0.25	1.00	1.50
2004	—	—	—	0.25	1.00	1.50

KM# 39 DINAR
4.2600 g., Copper-Zinc-Nickel, 20 mm. **Obv:** Coat of arms **Rev:** National Bank of Serbia **Edge:** Alternating reeded and plain sections

Date	Mintage	F	VF	XF	Unc	BU
2005	—	—	—	0.25	1.00	1.50

KM# 35 2 DINARA
5.2400 g., Copper-Zinc-Nickel, 22 mm. **Obv:** National Bank emblem **Rev:** Gracanica monastery **Edge:** Reeded

Date	Mintage	F	VF	XF	Unc	BU
2003	4,688,500	—	—	0.50	2.00	2.50

KM# 36 5 DINARA
6.2300 g., Copper-Zinc-Nickel, 24 mm. **Obv:** National Bank emblem **Rev:** Krusedol Monastery **Edge:** Reeded

Date	Mintage	F	VF	XF	Unc	BU
2003	15,170,000	—	0.50	1.00	2.25	3.25

KM# 40 5 DINARA
6.1300 g., Copper-Zinc-Nickel, 24 mm. **Obv:** Coat of arms **Rev:** Krusedol Monastery **Edge:** Alternating reeded and plain sections

Date	Mintage	F	VF	XF	Unc	BU
2005	—	—	—	0.75	2.00	3.00

KM# 37 10 DINARA
7.7700 g., Copper-Zinc-Nickel, 26 mm. **Obv:** National Bank emblem **Rev:** Studenica Monastery **Edge:** Reeded

Date	Mintage	F	VF	XF	Unc	BU
2003	10,160,500	—	0.50	1.00	2.50	3.50

KM# 41 10 DINARA
7.7700 g., Copper-Zinc-Nickel, 26 mm. **Obv:** Coat of arms **Rev:** Studenica Monastery **Edge:** Alternating reeded and plain sections

Date	Mintage	F	VF	XF	Unc	BU
2005	—	—	—	0.75	2.25	3.25

KM# 38 20 DINARA
9.0000 g., Copper-Zinc-Nickel, 28 mm. **Obv:** National Bank emblem **Rev:** Temple of St. Sava **Edge:** Reeded

Date	Mintage	F	VF	XF	Unc	BU
2003	25,491,500	—	—	0.75	2.00	3.00

MINT SETS

KM#	Date	Mintage	Identification	Issue Price	Mkt Val
MS1	2003 (5)	—	KM34-38	—	10.00
MS2	2005 (3)	—	KM39-41	—	10.00

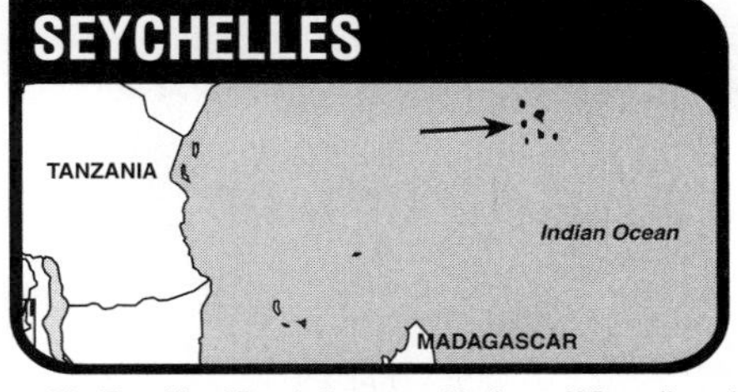

The Republic of Seychelles, an archipelago of 85 granite and coral islands situated in the Indian Ocean 600 miles (965 km.) northeast of Madagascar, has an area of 156sq. mi. (455 sq. km.) and a population of *70,000. Among these islands are the Aldabra Islands, the Farquhar Group, and Ile Desroches, which the United Kingdom ceded to the Seychelles upon its independence. Capital: Victoria, on Mahe. The economy is based on fishing, a plantation system of agriculture, and tourism. Copra, cinnamon and vanilla are exported.

Seychelles is a member of the Commonwealth of Nations. The president is the Head of State and of the Government.

MINT MARKS
PM - Pobjoy Mint
None - British Royal Mint

MONETARY SYSTEM
100 Cents = 1 Rupee

REPUBLIC

STANDARD COINAGE

KM# 47.2 5 CENTS
Brass **Obv:** Altered coat of arms

Date	Mintage	F	VF	XF	Unc	BU
2003	—	—	—	0.10	0.30	0.50

KM# 48.2 10 CENTS
Brass **Obv:** Altered coat of arms **Rev:** Yellowfin tuna

Date	Mintage	F	VF	XF	Unc	BU
2003	—	—	0.10	0.25	1.00	1.50

KM# 49.4 25 CENTS
Stainless Steel

Date	Mintage	F	VF	XF	Unc	BU
2003	—	—	—	—	2.50	3.00

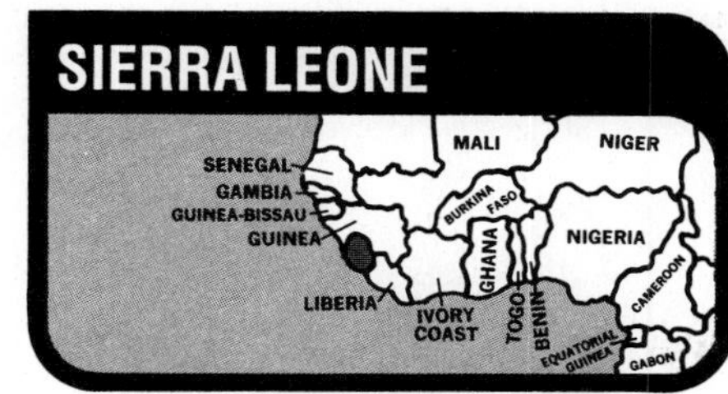

The Republic of Sierra Leone is located in western Africa between Guinea and Liberia, has an area of 27,699 sq. mi. (71,740 sq. km.) and a population of *4.1 million. Capital: Freetown. The economy is predominantly agricultural but mining contributes significantly to export revenues. Diamonds, iron ore, palm kernels, cocoa, and coffee are exported.

Sierra Leone is a member of the Commonwealth of Nations. The president is Chief of State and Head of Government.

MONETARY SYSTEM
Commencing 1964
100 Cents = 1 Leone = 1 Dollar
NOTE: Sierra Leone's official currency is the Leone.

REPUBLIC

STANDARD COINAGE

KM# 295 20 LEONES
3.9200 g., Copper-Nickel, 21.7 mm. **Obv:** Value **Rev:** Chimpanzee facing **Edge:** Plain

Date	Mintage	F	VF	XF	Unc	BU
2003	—	—	—	—	0.50	1.00

KM# 302 100 LEONES
28.2800 g., Copper-Nickel, 38.6 mm. **Subject:** 40th Anniversary - Bank of Sierra Leone **Obv:** Bank President Kabbah **Rev:** Lion **Edge:** Reeded

Date	Mintage	F	VF	XF	Unc	BU
ND (2004)	5,000	—	—	—	15.00	18.00

KM# 296 500 LEONES
7.2000 g., Bi-Metallic Stainless Steel center in Brass ring, 24 mm. **Obv:** Building **Rev:** Kai Londo **Edge:** Plain **Shape:** 10-sided

Date	Mintage	F	VF	XF	Unc	BU
2004	—	—	—	—	7.50	9.00

DOLLAR DENOMINATED COINAGE

KM# 198 DOLLAR
28.2800 g., Copper-Nickel, 38.6 mm. **Subject:** Year of the Snake **Obv:** National arms **Rev:** Snake **Edge:** Reeded

Date	Mintage	F	VF	XF	Unc	BU
2001	—	—	—	—	10.00	12.00

KM# 206 DOLLAR
Copper-Nickel **Subject:** P'an Ku **Obv:** National arms **Rev:** Dragon

Date	Mintage	F	VF	XF	Unc	BU
2001	—	—	—	—	10.00	12.00

KM# 214 DOLLAR
Copper-Nickel **Subject:** P'an Ku **Obv:** National arms **Rev:** Dragon and three animals

Date	Mintage	F	VF	XF	Unc	BU
2001	—	—	—	—	10.00	12.00

KM# 222 DOLLAR
28.2800 g., Copper-Nickel, 38.6 mm. **Series:** The Big Five **Obv:** National arms **Rev:** Rhino **Edge:** Reeded

Date	Mintage	F	VF	XF	Unc	BU
2001	—	—	—	—	10.00	12.00

KM# 225 DOLLAR
28.2800 g., Copper-Nickel **Series:** The Big Five **Obv:** National arms **Rev:** Lion

Date	Mintage	F	VF	XF	Unc	BU
2001	—	—	—	—	10.00	12.00

KM# 228 DOLLAR
28.2800 g., Copper-Nickel **Series:** The Big Five **Obv:** National arms **Rev:** Leopard

Date	Mintage	F	VF	XF	Unc	BU
2001	—	—	—	—	10.00	12.00

KM# 231 DOLLAR
28.2800 g., Copper-Nickel **Series:** The Big Five **Obv:** National arms **Rev:** Elephants

Date	Mintage	F	VF	XF	Unc	BU
2001	—	—	—	—	10.00	12.00

KM# 234 DOLLAR
28.2800 g., Copper-Nickel **Series:** The Big Five **Obv:** National arms **Rev:** Buffalo

Date	Mintage	F	VF	XF	Unc	BU
2001	—	—	—	—	10.00	12.00

KM# 237 DOLLAR
28.2800 g., Copper-Nickel **Series:** The Big Five **Obv:** National arms **Rev:** All five animals

Date	Mintage	F	VF	XF	Unc	BU
2001	—	—	—	—	10.00	12.00

KM# 241 DOLLAR
28.2800 g., Copper-Nickel, 38.6 mm. **Series:** Big Cats **Obv:** National arms **Rev:** Male and female lions **Edge:** Reeded

Date	Mintage	F	VF	XF	Unc	BU
2001	—	—	—	—	12.50	15.00

KM# 241a DOLLAR
28.2800 g., Copper-Nickel, 38.6 mm. **Series:** Big Cats **Rev:** Colorized lions **Edge:** Reeded

Date	Mintage	F	VF	XF	Unc	BU
2001	—	—	—	—	—	15.00

KM# 242 DOLLAR
28.2800 g., Copper-Nickel, 38.6 mm. **Series:** Big Cats **Rev:** Tiger **Edge:** Reeded

Date	Mintage	F	VF	XF	Unc	BU
2001	—	—	—	—	10.00	12.00

KM# 242a DOLLAR
28.2800 g., Copper-Nickel, 38.6 mm. **Series:** Big Cats **Rev:** Colorized tiger **Edge:** Reeded

Date	Mintage	F	VF	XF	Unc	BU
2001	—	—	—	—	—	15.00

KM# 243 DOLLAR
28.2800 g., Copper-Nickel, 38.6 mm. **Series:** Big Cats **Rev:** Cheetah **Edge:** Reeded

Date	Mintage	F	VF	XF	Unc	BU
2001	—	—	—	—	10.00	12.00

KM# 243a DOLLAR
28.2800 g., Copper-Nickel, 38.6 mm. **Series:** Big Cats **Rev:** Colorized cheetah **Edge:** Reeded

Date	Mintage	F	VF	XF	Unc	BU
2001	—	—	—	—	—	15.00

KM# 244 DOLLAR
28.2800 g., Copper-Nickel, 38.6 mm. **Series:** Big Cats **Rev:** Cougar **Edge:** Reeded

Date	Mintage	F	VF	XF	Unc	BU
2001	—	—	—	—	10.00	12.00

KM# 244a DOLLAR
28.2800 g., Copper-Nickel, 38.6 mm. **Series:** Big Cats **Rev:** Colorized cougar **Edge:** Reeded

Date	Mintage	F	VF	XF	Unc	BU
2001	—	—	—	—	—	15.00

KM# 245 DOLLAR
28.2800 g., Copper-Nickel, 38.6 mm. **Series:** Big Cats **Rev:** Black panther **Edge:** Reeded

Date	Mintage	F	VF	XF	Unc	BU
2001	—	—	—	—	10.00	12.00

KM# 245a DOLLAR
28.2800 g., Copper-Nickel, 38.6 mm. **Series:** Big Cats **Rev:** Colorized black panther **Edge:** Reeded

Date	Mintage	F	VF	XF	Unc	BU
2001	—	—	—	—	—	15.00

KM# 256 DOLLAR
28.2800 g., Copper-Nickel, 38.6 mm. **Subject:** Year of the Horse **Obv:** National arms **Rev:** Horse **Edge:** Reeded

Date	Mintage	F	VF	XF	Unc	BU
2002	—	—	—	—	10.00	12.00

KM# 264 DOLLAR
28.2800 g., Copper-Nickel, 38.6 mm. **Subject:** RMS Titanic **Obv:** National arms **Rev:** Titanic at dock **Edge:** Reeded

Date	Mintage	F	VF	XF	Unc	BU
2002	—	—	—	—	10.00	12.00

KM# 268 DOLLAR
28.2800 g., Copper-Nickel, 38.6 mm. **Subject:** Queen's Golden Jubilee **Obv:** National arms **Rev:** Queen Elizabeth II and Prince Philip visiting blacksmiths in Sierra Leone **Edge:** Reeded

Date	Mintage	F	VF	XF	Unc	BU
2002	—	—	—	—	10.00	12.00

KM# 269 DOLLAR
28.2800 g., Copper-Nickel, 38.6 mm. **Subject:** Queen's Golden Jubilee **Obv:** National arms **Rev:** Queen Elizabeth II with her two sons **Edge:** Reeded

Date	Mintage	F	VF	XF	Unc	BU
2002	—	—	—	—	10.00	12.00

KM# 276 DOLLAR
28.2800 g., Copper-Nickel, 38.6 mm. **Subject:** British Queen Mother **Obv:** National arms **Rev:** Queen Mother with dog in garden **Edge:** Reeded

Date	Mintage	F	VF	XF	Unc	BU
2002	—	—	—	—	10.00	12.00

KM# 279 DOLLAR
28.2800 g., Copper-Nickel, 38.6 mm. **Subject:** British Queen Mother **Obv:** National arms **Rev:** Queen Mother with daughters **Edge:** Reeded

Date	Mintage	F	VF	XF	Unc	BU
2002	—	—	—	—	10.00	12.00

KM# 282 DOLLAR

28.2800 g., Copper-Nickel, 38.6 mm. **Subject:** Queen Elizabeth's Golden Jubilee **Obv:** National arms **Rev:** The Queen and a young Prince Charles **Edge:** Reeded

Date	Mintage	F	VF	XF	Unc	BU
2002	—	—	—	—	10.00	12.00

KM# 285 DOLLAR

28.2800 g., Copper-Nickel, 38.6 mm. **Subject:** Queen Elizabeth's Golden Jubilee **Obv:** National arms **Rev:** Queen and Prince Philip **Edge:** Reeded

Date	Mintage	F	VF	XF	Unc	BU
2002	—	—	—	—	10.00	12.00

KM# 291 DOLLAR

28.2800 g., Copper-Nickel, 38.6 mm. **Subject:** Olympics **Obv:** National arms **Rev:** Ancient archer **Edge:** Reeded

Date	Mintage	F	VF	XF	Unc	BU
2003	—	—	—	—	10.00	12.00
2004	—	—	—	—	10.00	12.00

KM# 288 DOLLAR

28.2800 g., Copper-Nickel, 38.6 mm. **Subject:** Olympics **Obv:** National arms **Rev:** Victory goddess Nike **Edge:** Reeded **Note:** The Leone is the official currency of Sierra Leone

Date	Mintage	F	VF	XF	Unc	BU
2003	—	—	—	—	10.00	12.00
2004	—	—	—	—	10.00	12.00

KM# 297 DOLLAR

28.2800 g., Copper-Nickel, 38.6 mm. **Obv:** National arms **Rev:** Nelson Mandela **Edge:** Reeded

Date	Mintage	F	VF	XF	Unc	BU
2004	—	—	—	—	15.00	16.50

KM# 300 DOLLAR

28.2800 g., Copper-Nickel, 38.6 mm. **Obv:** National arms **Rev:** Ronald Reagan **Edge:** Reeded

Date	Mintage	F	VF	XF	Unc	BU
2004	—	—	—	—	15.00	16.50

KM# 304 DOLLAR

28.4200 g., Copper-Nickel, 38.6 mm. **Obv:** National arms **Rev:** Giraffe **Edge:** Reeded

Date	Mintage	F	VF	XF	Unc	BU
2005	—	—	—	—	10.00	12.00

KM# 305 DOLLAR

28.4200 g., Copper-Nickel, 38.6 mm. **Obv:** National arms **Rev:** Crocodile **Edge:** Reeded

Date	Mintage	F	VF	XF	Unc	BU
2005	—	—	—	—	10.00	12.00

KM# 306 DOLLAR

28.4200 g., Copper-Nickel, 38.6 mm. **Obv:** National arms **Rev:** Hippo in water **Edge:** Reeded

Date	Mintage	F	VF	XF	Unc	BU
2005	—	—	—	—	10.00	12.00

KM# 307 DOLLAR

28.6200 g., 0.9250 Silver 0.8511 oz. ASW, 38.5 mm. **Obv:** National arms **Rev:** Giraffe **Edge:** Reeded

Date	Mintage	F	VF	XF	Unc	BU
2005 Proof	—	Value: 50.00				

KM# 199 10 DOLLARS

28.2800 g., 0.9250 Silver .8410 oz. ASW, 38.6 mm. **Subject:** Year of the Snake **Obv:** National arms **Rev:** Snake on bamboo **Edge:** Reeded

Date	Mintage	F	VF	XF	Unc	BU
2001 Proof	Est. 25,000	Value: 50.00				

KM# 207 10 DOLLARS

28.2800 g., 0.9250 Silver .8410 oz. ASW **Subject:** P'an Ku **Obv:** National arms **Rev:** Dragon

Date	Mintage	F	VF	XF	Unc	BU
2001	Est. 5,000	Value: 47.50				

KM# 215 10 DOLLARS

28.2800 g., 0.9250 Silver .8410 oz. ASW **Subject:** P'an Ku **Obv:** National arms **Rev:** Dragon and three animals

Date	Mintage	F	VF	XF	Unc	BU
2001 Proof	Est. 5,000	Value: 47.50				

KM# 223 10 DOLLARS

28.2800 g., 0.9250 Silver .8410 oz. ASW, 38.6 mm. **Series:** The Big Five **Obv:** National arms **Rev:** Rhino **Edge:** Reeded

Date	Mintage	F	VF	XF	Unc	BU
2001 Proof	—	Value: 45.00				

KM# 226 10 DOLLARS

28.2800 g., 0.9250 Silver .8410 oz. ASW **Series:** The Big Five **Obv:** National arms **Rev:** Lion

Date	Mintage	F	VF	XF	Unc	BU
2001 Proof	Est. 10,000	Value: 45.00				

KM# 229 10 DOLLARS

28.2800 g., 0.9250 Silver .8410 oz. ASW **Series:** The Big Five **Obv:** National arms **Rev:** Leopard

Date	Mintage	F	VF	XF	Unc	BU
2001 Proof	Est. 10,000	Value: 45.00				

KM# 232 10 DOLLARS

28.2800 g., 0.9250 Silver .8410 oz. ASW **Series:** The Big Five **Obv:** National arms **Rev:** Elephants

Date	Mintage	F	VF	XF	Unc	BU
2001 Proof	Est. 10,000	Value: 45.00				

KM# 235 10 DOLLARS
28.2800 g., 0.9250 Silver .8410 oz. ASW **Series:** The Big Five **Obv:** National arms **Rev:** Buffalo

Date	Mintage	F	VF	XF	Unc	BU
2001 Proof	Est. 10,000	Value: 45.00				

KM# 238 10 DOLLARS
28.2800 g., 0.9250 Silver .8410 oz. ASW **Series:** The Big Five **Obv:** National arms **Rev:** All five animals

Date	Mintage	F	VF	XF	Unc	BU
2001 Proof	Est. 10,000	Value: 45.00				

KM# 246 10 DOLLARS
28.2800 g., 0.9250 Silver .8410 oz. ASW, 38.6 mm. **Series:** Big Cats **Obv:** National arms **Rev:** Male and female lions **Edge:** Reeded

Date	Mintage	F	VF	XF	Unc	BU
2001 Proof	10,000	Value: 45.00				

KM# 246a 10 DOLLARS
28.2800 g., 0.9250 Silver .8410 oz. ASW, 38.6 mm. **Series:** Big Cats **Obv:** National arms **Rev:** Male and female lions **Edge:** Reeded

Date	Mintage	F	VF	XF	Unc	BU
2001 Proof	—	Value: 50.00				

KM# 247 10 DOLLARS
28.2800 g., 0.9250 Silver .8410 oz. ASW, 38.6 mm. **Series:** Big Cats **Rev:** Tiger **Edge:** Reeded

Date	Mintage	F	VF	XF	Unc	BU
2001 Proof	—	Value: 45.00				

KM# 247a 10 DOLLARS
28.2800 g., 0.9250 Silver .8410 oz. ASW, 38.6 mm. **Series:** Big Cats **Rev:** Multicolor tiger **Edge:** Reeded

Date	Mintage	F	VF	XF	Unc	BU
2001 Proof	—	Value: 50.00				

KM# 248 10 DOLLARS
28.2800 g., 0.9250 Silver .8410 oz. ASW, 38.6 mm. **Series:** Big Cats **Rev:** Cheetah head facing **Edge:** Reeded

Date	Mintage	F	VF	XF	Unc	BU
2001 Proof	10,000	Value: 45.00				

KM# 248a 10 DOLLARS
28.2800 g., 0.9250 Silver .8410 oz. ASW, 38.6 mm. **Series:** Big Cats **Rev:** Multicolor cheetah **Edge:** Reeded

Date	Mintage	F	VF	XF	Unc	BU
2001 Proof	—	Value: 50.00				

KM# 249 10 DOLLARS
28.2800 g., 0.9250 Silver .8410 oz. ASW, 38.6 mm. **Series:** Big Cats **Rev:** Cougar **Edge:** Reeded

Date	Mintage	F	VF	XF	Unc	BU
2001 Proof	10,000	Value: 45.00				

KM# 249a 10 DOLLARS
28.2800 g., 0.9250 Silver .8410 oz. ASW, 38.6 mm. **Series:** Big Cats **Rev:** Multicolored cougar **Edge:** Reeded

Date	Mintage	F	VF	XF	Unc	BU
2001 Proof	—	Value: 50.00				

KM# 250 10 DOLLARS
28.2800 g., 0.9250 Silver .8410 oz. ASW, 38.6 mm. **Series:** Big Cats **Rev:** Black panther **Edge:** Reeded

Date	Mintage	F	VF	XF	Unc	BU
2001 Proof	10,000	Value: 45.00				

KM# 250a 10 DOLLARS
28.2800 g., 0.9250 Silver .8410 oz. ASW, 38.6 mm. **Series:** Big Cats **Rev:** Multicolored black panther **Edge:** Reeded

Date	Mintage	F	VF	XF	Unc	BU
2001 Proof	—	Value: 50.00				

KM# 277 10 DOLLARS
28.2800 g., 0.9250 Gold Clad Silver 0.841 oz., 38.6 mm. **Subject:** British Queen Mother **Obv:** National arms **Rev:** Queen Mother in garden with dog **Edge:** Reeded

Date	Mintage	F	VF	XF	Unc	BU
2002 Proof	10,000	Value: 47.50				

KM# 280 10 DOLLARS
28.2800 g., 0.9250 Gold Clad Silver 0.841 oz., 38.6 mm. **Subject:** British Queen Mother **Obv:** National arms **Rev:** Queen Mother and daughters **Edge:** Reeded

Date	Mintage	F	VF	XF	Unc	BU
2002 Proof	10,000	Value: 47.50				

KM# 257 10 DOLLARS
28.2800 g., 0.9250 Silver .8410 oz. ASW, 38.6 mm. **Subject:** Year of the Horse **Obv:** National arms **Rev:** Horse **Edge:** Reeded

Date	Mintage	F	VF	XF	Unc	BU
2002 Proof	5,000	Value: 50.00				

KM# 265 10 DOLLARS
28.2800 g., 0.9250 Silver 0.841 oz. ASW, 38.6 mm. **Subject:** RMS Titanic **Obv:** National arms **Rev:** Titanic at dock **Edge:** Reeded

Date	Mintage	F	VF	XF	Unc	BU
2002 Proof	10,000	Value: 47.50				

KM# 270 10 DOLLARS
28.2800 g., 0.9250 Gold Clad Silver 0.841 oz., 38.6 mm. **Subject:** Queen's Golden Jubilee **Obv:** National arms **Rev:** Queen Elizabeth II and Prince Philip visiting blacksmiths in Sierra Leone **Edge:** Reeded

Date	Mintage	F	VF	XF	Unc	BU
2002 Proof	10,000	Value: 50.00				

KM# 271 10 DOLLARS
28.2800 g., 0.9250 Gold Clad Silver 0.841 oz., 38.6 mm. **Subject:** Queen's Golden Jubilee **Obv:** National arms **Rev:** Queen Elizabeth II, Prince Charles and Princess Anne **Edge:** Reeded

Date	Mintage	F	VF	XF	Unc	BU
2002 Proof	10,000	Value: 50.00				

KM# 283 10 DOLLARS
28.2800 g., 0.9250 Gold Clad Silver 0.841 oz., 38.6 mm. **Subject:** Queen Elizabeth's Golden Jubilee **Obv:** National arms **Rev:** Queen and young Prince Charles **Edge:** Reeded

Date	Mintage	F	VF	XF	Unc	BU
2002 Proof	10,000	Value: 47.50				

KM# 286 10 DOLLARS
28.2800 g., 0.9250 Gold Clad Silver 0.841 oz., 38.6 mm. **Subject:** Queen Elizabeth's Golden Jubilee **Obv:** National arms **Rev:** Queen and Prince Philip **Edge:** Reeded

Date	Mintage	F	VF	XF	Unc	BU
2002 Proof	10,000	Value: 47.50				

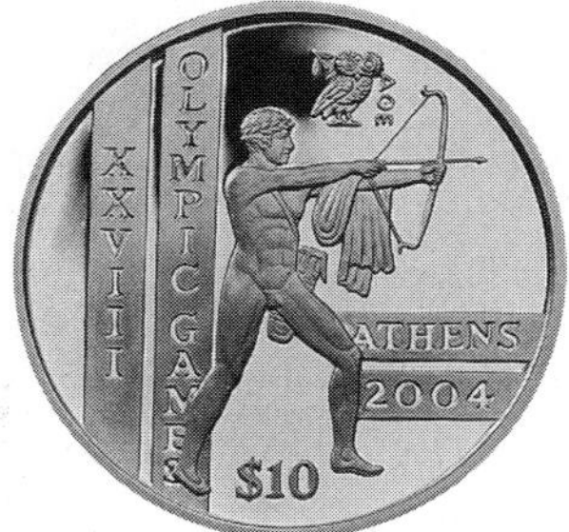

KM# 292 10 DOLLARS
28.2800 g., 0.9250 Silver 0.841 oz. ASW, 38.6 mm. **Subject:** Olympics **Obv:** National arms **Rev:** Ancient archer **Edge:** Reeded

Date	Mintage	F	VF	XF	Unc	BU
2003 Proof	10,000	Value: 45.00				
2004 Proof	10,000	Value: 45.00				

KM# 289 10 DOLLARS
28.2800 g., 0.9250 Silver 0.841 oz. ASW, 38.6 mm. **Subject:** Olympics **Obv:** National arms **Rev:** Victory goddess Nike **Edge:** Reeded **Note:** The leone is the official currency of Sierra Leone

Date	Mintage	F	VF	XF	Unc	BU
2003 Proof	10,000	Value: 45.00				
2004 Proof	10,000	Value: 45.00				

KM# 298 10 DOLLARS
28.2800 g., 0.9250 Silver 0.841 oz. ASW, 38.6 mm. **Obv:** National arms **Rev:** Nelson Mandela **Edge:** Reeded

Date	Mintage	F	VF	XF	Unc	BU
2004 Proof	10,000	Value: 50.00				

KM# 301 10 DOLLARS
28.2800 g., 0.9250 Silver 0.841 oz. ASW, 38.6 mm. **Obv:** National arms **Rev:** Ronald Reagan **Edge:** Reeded

Date	Mintage	F	VF	XF	Unc	BU
2004 Proof	10,000	Value: 50.00				

KM# 200 20 DOLLARS
1.2441 g., 0.9990 Gold .0400 oz. AGW, 13.9 mm. **Subject:** Year of the Snake **Obv:** National arms **Rev:** Snake **Edge:** Reeded

Date	Mintage	F	VF	XF	Unc	BU
2001 Proof	Est. 50,000	Value: 60.00				

KM# 208 20 DOLLARS
1.2441 g., 0.9990 Gold .0400 oz. AGW **Subject:** P'an Ku **Obv:** National arms **Rev:** Dragon

Date	Mintage	F	VF	XF	Unc	BU
2001 Proof	Est. 5,000	Value: 60.00				

KM# 216 20 DOLLARS
1.2441 g., 0.9990 Gold .0400 oz. AGW **Subject:** P'an Ku **Obv:** National arms **Rev:** Dragon and three animals

Date	Mintage	F	VF	XF	Unc	BU
2001 Proof	Est. 5,000	Value: 60.00				

KM# 258 20 DOLLARS
1.2400 g., 0.9990 Gold .0398 oz. AGW, 13.92 mm. **Subject:** Year of the Horse **Obv:** National arms **Rev:** Horse **Edge:** Reeded

Date	Mintage	F	VF	XF	Unc	BU
2002 Proof	5,000	Value: 55.00				

KM# 272 30 DOLLARS
6.2200 g., 0.3750 Gold 0.075 oz. AGW, 22 mm. **Subject:** Queen's Golden Jubilee **Obv:** National arms **Rev:** Queen Elizabeth II and Prince Philip **Edge:** Reeded

Date	Mintage	F	VF	XF	Unc	BU
2002 Proof	5,000	Value: 95.00				

KM# 273 30 DOLLARS
6.2200 g., 0.3750 Gold 0.075 oz. AGW, 22 mm. **Subject:** Queen's Golden Jubilee **Obv:** National arms **Rev:** Queen Elizabeth II, Prince Charles and Princess Anne **Edge:** Reeded

Date	Mintage	F	VF	XF	Unc	BU
2002 Proof	5,000	Value: 95.00				

KM# 201 50 DOLLARS
3.1103 g., 0.9990 Gold .1000 oz. AGW, 18 mm. **Subject:** Year of the Snake **Obv:** National arms **Rev:** Snake **Edge:** Reeded

Date	Mintage	F	VF	XF	Unc	BU
2001 Proof	Est. 10,000	Value: 95.00				

KM# 209 50 DOLLARS
3.1103 g., 0.9990 Gold .1000 oz. AGW **Subject:** P'an Ku **Obv:** National arms **Rev:** Dragon

Date	Mintage	F	VF	XF	Unc	BU
2001 Proof	Est. 5,000	Value: 95.00				

KM# 217 50 DOLLARS
3.1103 g., 0.9990 Gold .1000 oz. AGW **Subject:** P'an Ku **Obv:** National arms **Rev:** Dragon and three animals

Date	Mintage	F	VF	XF	Unc	BU
2001 Proof	Est. 5,000	Value: 95.00				

KM# 266 50 DOLLARS
155.5500 g., 0.9999 Silver 5.0005 oz. ASW, 65 mm. **Subject:** RMS Titanic **Obv:** National arms **Rev:** Titanic at dock **Edge:** Reeded

Date	Mintage	F	VF	XF	Unc	BU
2002 Proof	2,000	Value: 150				

KM# 259 50 DOLLARS
3.1100 g., 0.9990 Gold .0999 oz. AGW, 17.95 mm. **Subject:** Year of the Horse **Obv:** National arms **Rev:** Horse **Edge:** Reeded

Date	Mintage	F	VF	XF	Unc	BU
2002 Proof	5,000	Value: 95.00				

KM# 202 100 DOLLARS
6.2200 g., 0.9990 Gold .2000 oz. AGW, 22 mm. **Subject:** Year of the Snake **Obv:** National arms **Rev:** Snake **Edge:** Reeded

Date	Mintage	F	VF	XF	Unc	BU
2001 Proof	—	Value: 175				

KM# 210 100 DOLLARS
6.2200 g., 0.9990 Gold .2000 oz. AGW **Subject:** P'an Ku **Obv:** National arms **Rev:** Dragon

Date	Mintage	F	VF	XF	Unc	BU
2001 Proof	Est. 10,000	Value: 175				

KM# 218 100 DOLLARS
6.2200 g., 0.9990 Gold .2000 oz. AGW **Subject:** P'an Ku **Obv:** National arms **Rev:** Dragon and three animals

Date	Mintage	F	VF	XF	Unc	BU
2001 Proof	Est. 10,000	Value: 175				

KM# 224 100 DOLLARS
6.2200 g., 0.9990 Gold .2000 oz. AGW, 22 mm. **Series:** The Big Five **Obv:** National arms **Rev:** Rhino **Edge:** Reeded

Date	Mintage	F	VF	XF	Unc	BU
2001 Proof	Est. 5,000	Value: 175				

KM# 227 100 DOLLARS
6.2200 g., 0.9990 Gold .2000 oz. AGW **Series:** The Big Five **Obv:** National arms **Rev:** Lion

Date	Mintage	F	VF	XF	Unc	BU
2001 Proof	Est. 5,000	Value: 175				

KM# 230 100 DOLLARS
6.2200 g., 0.9990 Gold .2000 oz. AGW **Series:** The Big Five **Obv:** National arms **Rev:** Leopard

Date	Mintage	F	VF	XF	Unc	BU
2001 Proof	Est. 5,000	Value: 175				

KM# 233 100 DOLLARS
6.2200 g., 0.9990 Gold .2000 oz. AGW **Series:** The Big Five **Obv:** National arms **Rev:** Elephants

Date	Mintage	F	VF	XF	Unc	BU
2001 Proof	Est. 5,000	Value: 175				

KM# 236 100 DOLLARS
6.2200 g., 0.9990 Gold .2000 oz. AGW **Series:** The Big Five **Obv:** National arms **Rev:** Buffalo

Date	Mintage	F	VF	XF	Unc	BU
2001 Proof	Est. 5,000	Value: 175				

KM# 239 100 DOLLARS
6.2200 g., 0.9990 Gold .2000 oz. AGW **Series:** The Big Five **Obv:** National arms **Rev:** All five animals

Date	Mintage	F	VF	XF	Unc	BU
2001 Proof	Est. 5,000	Value: 175				

KM# 251 100 DOLLARS
6.2200 g., 0.9990 Gold .1998 oz. AGW, 22 mm. **Series:** Big Cats **Obv:** National arms **Rev:** Male and female lions **Edge:** Reeded

Date	Mintage	F	VF	XF	Unc	BU
2001 Proof	5,000	Value: 175				

KM# 252 100 DOLLARS
6.2200 g., 0.9990 Gold .1998 oz. AGW, 22 mm. **Series:** Big Cats **Rev:** Tiger **Edge:** Reeded

Date	Mintage	F	VF	XF	Unc	BU
2001 Proof	5,000	Value: 175				

KM# 253 100 DOLLARS
6.2200 g., 0.9990 Gold .1998 oz. AGW, 22 mm. **Series:** Big Cats **Rev:** Cheetah **Edge:** Reeded

Date	Mintage	F	VF	XF	Unc	BU
2001 Proof	5,000	Value: 175				

KM# 254 100 DOLLARS
6.2200 g., 0.9990 Gold .1998 oz. AGW, 22 mm. **Series:** Big Cats **Rev:** Cougar **Edge:** Reeded

Date	Mintage	F	VF	XF	Unc	BU
2001 Proof	5,000	Value: 175				

KM# 255 100 DOLLARS
6.2200 g., 0.9990 Gold .1998 oz. AGW, 22 mm. **Series:** Big Cats **Rev:** Black panther **Edge:** Reeded

Date	Mintage	F	VF	XF	Unc	BU
2001 Proof	5,000	Value: 175				

KM# 278 100 DOLLARS
6.2200 g., 0.9999 Gold 0.2 oz. AGW, 22 mm. **Subject:** British Queen Mother **Obv:** National arms **Rev:** Queen Mother in garden with dog **Edge:** Reeded

Date	Mintage	F	VF	XF	Unc	BU
2002 Proof	2,000	Value: 175				

KM# 281 100 DOLLARS
6.2200 g., 0.9999 Gold 0.2 oz. AGW, 22 mm. **Subject:** British Queen Mother **Obv:** National arms **Rev:** Queen Mother with daughters **Edge:** Reeded

Date	Mintage	F	VF	XF	Unc	BU
2002 Proof	2,000	Value: 175				

KM# 260 100 DOLLARS
6.2200 g., 0.9990 Gold .1998 oz. AGW, 22 mm. **Subject:** Year of the Horse **Obv:** National arms **Rev:** Horse **Edge:** Reeded

Date	Mintage	F	VF	XF	Unc	BU
2002 Proof	2,000	Value: 175				

KM# 274 100 DOLLARS
6.2200 g., 0.9999 Gold 0.2 oz. AGW, 22 mm. **Subject:** Queen's Golden Jubilee **Obv:** National arms **Rev:** Queen Elizabeth II and Prince Philip **Edge:** Reeded

Date	Mintage	F	VF	XF	Unc	BU
2002 Proof	2,002	Value: 175				

KM# 275 100 DOLLARS
6.2200 g., 0.9999 Gold 0.2 oz. AGW, 22 mm. **Subject:** Queen's Golden Jubilee **Obv:** National arms **Rev:** Queen Elizabeth II, Prince Charles and Princess Anne **Edge:** Reeded

Date	Mintage	F	VF	XF	Unc	BU
2002 Proof	5,000	Value: 175				

KM# 284 100 DOLLARS
6.2200 g., 0.9999 Gold 0.2 oz. AGW, 22 mm. **Subject:** Queen Elizabeth's Golden Jubilee **Obv:** National arms **Rev:** Queen and young Prince Charles **Edge:** Reeded

Date	Mintage	F	VF	XF	Unc	BU
2002 Proof	2,002	Value: 175				

KM# 287 100 DOLLARS
6.2200 g., 0.9999 Gold 0.2 oz. AGW, 22 mm. **Subject:** Queen Elizabeth's Golden Jubilee **Obv:** National arms **Rev:** Queen and Prince Philip **Edge:** Reeded

Date	Mintage	F	VF	XF	Unc	BU
2002 Proof	2,002	Value: 175				

KM# 293 100 DOLLARS
6.2200 g., 0.9999 Gold 0.2 oz. AGW, 22 mm. **Subject:** Olympics **Obv:** National arms **Rev:** Ancient archer **Edge:** Reeded

Date	Mintage	F	VF	XF	Unc	BU
2003 Proof	5,000	Value: 175				
2004 Proof	5,000	Value: 175				

KM# 290 100 DOLLARS
6.2200 g., 0.9999 Gold 0.2 oz. AGW, 22 mm. **Subject:** Olympics **Obv:** National arms **Rev:** Victory goddess Nike **Edge:** Reeded **Note:** The leone is the official currency of Sierra Leone

Date	Mintage	F	VF	XF	Unc	BU
2003 Proof	5,000	Value: 175				
2004 Proof	5,000	Value: 175				

KM# 267 150 DOLLARS
1000.0000 g., 0.9999 Silver 32.1475 oz. ASW, 85 mm. **Subject:** RMS Titanic **Obv:** National arms **Rev:** Titanic at dock **Edge:** Reeded

Date	Mintage	F	VF	XF	Unc	BU
2002 Proof	500	Value: 450				

KM# 203 250 DOLLARS
15.5118 g., 0.9990 Gold .5000 oz. AGW, 30 mm. **Subject:** Year of the Snake **Obv:** National arms **Rev:** Snake **Edge:** Reeded

Date	Mintage	F	VF	XF	Unc	BU
2001 Proof	Est. 5,000	Value: 350				

KM# 211 250 DOLLARS
15.5518 g., 0.9990 Gold .5000 oz. AGW **Subject:** P'an Ku **Obv:** National arms **Rev:** Dragon

Date	Mintage	F	VF	XF	Unc	BU
2001 Proof	Est. 2,000	Value: 350				

KM# 219 250 DOLLARS
15.5518 g., 0.9990 Gold .5000 oz. AGW **Subject:** P'an Ku **Obv:** National arms **Rev:** Dragon and three animals

Date	Mintage	F	VF	XF	Unc	BU
2001 Proof	Est. 2,000	Value: 350				

KM# 261 250 DOLLARS
15.5500 g., 0.9990 Gold .4994 oz. AGW, 30 mm. **Subject:** Year of the Horse **Obv:** National arms **Rev:** Horse **Edge:** Reeded

Date	Mintage	F	VF	XF	Unc	BU
2002 Proof	2,000	Value: 350				

KM# 204 500 DOLLARS
31.1035 g., 0.9990 Gold 1.000 oz. AGW, 32.7 mm. **Subject:** Year of the Snake **Obv:** National arms **Rev:** Snake **Edge:** Reeded

Date	Mintage	F	VF	XF	Unc	BU
2001 Proof	Est. 1,000	Value: 675				

KM# 212 500 DOLLARS
31.1035 g., 0.9990 Gold 1.0000 oz. AGW **Subject:** P'an Ku **Obv:** National arms **Rev:** Dragon

Date	Mintage	F	VF	XF	Unc	BU
2001 Proof	Est. 1,000	Value: 675				

KM# 220 500 DOLLARS
31.1035 g., 0.9990 Gold 1.0000 oz. AGW **Subject:** P'an Ku **Obv:** National arms **Rev:** Dragon and three animals

Date	Mintage	F	VF	XF	Unc	BU
2001 Proof	Est. 1,000	Value: 675				

KM# 262 500 DOLLARS
31.1000 g., 0.9990 Gold .9989 oz. AGW, 32.7 mm. **Subject:** Year of the Horse **Obv:** National arms **Rev:** Horse **Edge:** Reeded

Date	Mintage	F	VF	XF	Unc	BU
2002 Proof	1,000	Value: 675				

KM# 294 500 DOLLARS
31.1000 g., 0.9999 Gold 0.9998 oz. AGW, 32.7 mm. **Obv:** National arms **Rev:** Multicolor Astro Boy cartoon **Edge:** Reeded **Note:** The leone is Sierra Leone's official currency

Date	Mintage	F	VF	XF	Unc	BU
2003 Proof	2,003	Value: 675				

KM# 299 500 DOLLARS
31.1035 g., 0.9999 Gold 0.9999 oz. AGW, 32.7 mm. **Obv:** National arms **Rev:** Nelson Mandela **Edge:** Reeded

Date	Mintage	F	VF	XF	Unc	BU
2004 Proof	—	Value: 675				

KM# 205 2500 DOLLARS
155.5175 g., 0.9990 Gold 5.0000 oz. AGW, 50 mm. **Subject:** Year of the Snake **Obv:** National arms **Rev:** Snake **Edge:** Reeded

Date	Mintage	F	VF	XF	Unc	BU
2001 Proof	Est. 250	Value: 3,450				

KM# 213 2500 DOLLARS
155.5175 g., 0.9990 Gold 5.0000 oz. AGW **Subject:** P'an Ku **Obv:** National arms **Rev:** Dragon

Date	Mintage	F	VF	XF	Unc	BU
2001 Proof	Est. 250	Value: 3,450				

KM# 263 2500 DOLLARS
155.5100 g., 0.9990 Gold 4.9948 oz. AGW, 50 mm. **Subject:** Year of the Horse **Obv:** National arms **Rev:** Horse **Edge:** Reeded

Date	Mintage	F	VF	XF	Unc	BU
2002 Proof	250	Value: 3,450				

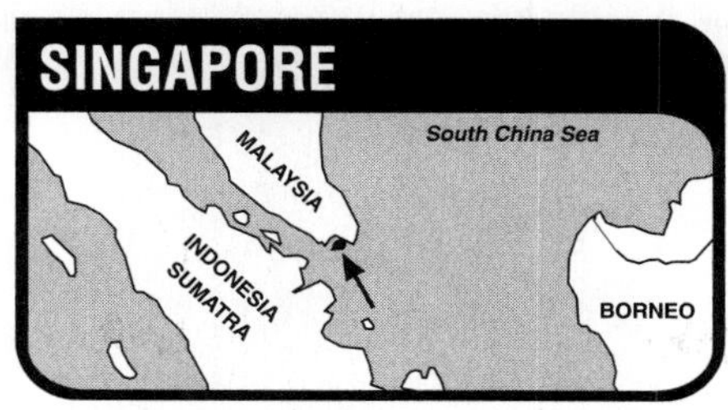

The Republic of Singapore, a member of the Commonwealth of Nations situated off the southern tip of the Malay peninsula, has an area of 224 sq. mi. (633 sq. km.) and a population of *2.7 million. Capital: Singapore. The economy is based on entrepot trade, manufacturing and oil. Rubber, petroleum products, machinery and spices are exported.

The President is Chief of State. The prime minister is Head of Government.

MINT MARKS

sm = ***"sm"*** - Singapore Mint monogram

MONETARY SYSTEM

100 Cents = 1 Dollar

REPUBLIC

STANDARD COINAGE

100 Cents = 1 Dollar

KM# 98 CENT
Copper Plated Zinc **Edge:** Plain **Note:** Similar to KM#49 but motto ribbon on arms curves down at center.

Date	Mintage	F	VF	XF	Unc	BU
2001sm	40,000,000	—	—	—	0.10	0.15

KM# 99 5 CENTS
Aluminum-Bronze **Edge:** Reeded **Note:** Similar to KM#50 but motto ribbon on arms curves down at center.

Date	Mintage	F	VF	XF	Unc	BU
2001	13,000,000	—	—	—	0.20	0.30
2003sm	—	—	—	—	0.20	0.30

KM# 184 DOLLAR
Copper-Nickel, 24.66 mm. **Subject:** Old World Charm - Balestier **Obv:** National arms **Rev:** Old buildings **Edge:** Reeded

Date	Mintage	F	VF	XF	Unc	BU
2004 Prooflike	—	—	—	—	—	10.00

KM# 184a DOLLAR
0.9990 Silver, 24.6 mm. **Subject:** Old World Charm - Balestier

Date	Mintage	F	VF	XF	Unc	BU
2004 Proof	8,000	Value: 25.00				

KM# 186 DOLLAR
0.3000 g., 0.9999 Gold 0.0096 oz. AGW, 7 mm. **Subject:** Year of the Monkey **Obv:** National arms **Rev:** Seated monkey **Edge:** Plain

Date	Mintage	F	VF	XF	Unc	BU
2004	8,000	—	—	—	30.00	—

KM# 190 DOLLAR
Copper-Nickel, 24.6 mm. **Subject:** Old World Charm - Jalan Besar

Date	Mintage	F	VF	XF	Unc	BU
2004 Prooflike	—	—	—	—	—	10.00

KM# 190a DOLLAR
0.9990 Silver, 24.6 mm. **Subject:** Old World Charm - Jalan Besar

Date	Mintage	F	VF	XF	Unc	BU
2004 Proof	8,000	Value: 25.00				

KM# 191 DOLLAR
Copper-Nickel, 24.6 mm. **Subject:** Old World Charm - Joo Chiat

Date	Mintage	F	VF	XF	Unc	BU
2004 Prooflike	—	—	—	—	—	10.00

KM# 191a DOLLAR
0.9990 Silver, 24.6 mm. **Subject:** Old World Charm - Joo Chiat

Date	Mintage	F	VF	XF	Unc	BU
2004 Proof	8,000	Value: 25.00				

KM# 192 DOLLAR
Copper Nickel, 24.6 mm. **Subject:** Old World Charm - Tanjong Katong

Date	Mintage	F	VF	XF	Unc	BU
2004 Prooflike	—	—	—	—	—	10.00

KM# 192a DOLLAR
0.9990 Silver, 24.6 mm. **Subject:** Old World Charm - Tanjong Katong

Date	Mintage	F	VF	XF	Unc	BU
2004 Proof	8,000	Value: 25.00				

KM# 104.1 5 DOLLARS
Copper-Nickel **Obv:** National arms above latent image **Rev:** Flower above value **Edge:** Plain

Date	Mintage	F	VF	XF	Unc	BU
2001sm	—	—	—	—	10.00	—

Note: In mint sets only

KM# 177a 5 DOLLARS
20.0000 g., 0.9250 Silver .5948 oz. ASW, 38.6 mm. **Subject:** Productivity Movement **Obv:** National arms **Rev:** Spiral design **Edge:** Reeded

Date	Mintage	F	VF	XF	Unc	BU
2001 Proof	10,000	Value: 50.00				

KM# 177 5 DOLLARS
Copper-Nickel, 38.6 mm. **Subject:** Productivity Movement **Obv:** National arms **Rev:** Spiral design **Edge:** Reeded

Date	Mintage	F	VF	XF	Unc	BU
2001	20,000	—	—	—	12.50	15.00

KM# 181 5 DOLLARS
20.0000 g., Copper Nickel, 38.7 mm. **Subject:** Esplanade Theaters on the Bay **Obv:** National arms **Rev:** Stylized symbolic design **Edge:** Reeded

Date	Mintage	F	VF	XF	Unc	BU
2002	—	—	—	—	13.50	16.50

KM# 181a 5 DOLLARS
20.0000 g., 0.9990 Silver 0.6424 oz. ASW, 38.7 mm. **Subject:** Esplanade Theaters on the Bay **Obv:** National arms **Rev:** Stylized symbolic design **Edge:** Reeded

Date	Mintage	F	VF	XF	Unc	BU
2002 Proof	10,000	Value: 45.00				

KM# 179 10 DOLLARS
28.0000 g., Copper-Nickel, 40.7 mm. **Subject:** Year of the Snake **Obv:** National arms **Rev:** Snake **Edge:** Reeded

Date	Mintage	F	VF	XF	Unc	BU
2001	—	—	—	—	15.00	20.00

KM# 180 10 DOLLARS
62.2060 g., 0.9990 Silver 1.998 oz. ASW, 40.7 mm. **Subject:** Year of the Snake **Obv:** National arms **Rev:** Snake **Edge:** Reeded

Date	Mintage	F	VF	XF	Unc	BU
2001 Proof	38,000	Value: 75.00				

KM# 182 10 DOLLARS
28.0000 g., Copper-Nickel, 40.7 mm. **Subject:** Year of the Horse **Obv:** National arms **Rev:** Horse **Edge:** Reeded

Date	Mintage	F	VF	XF	Unc	BU
2002	—	—	—	—	15.00	20.00

KM# 182a 10 DOLLARS
62.2070 g., 0.9990 Silver 1.998 oz. ASW, 40.7 mm. **Subject:** Year of the Horse **Obv:** National arms **Rev:** Horse **Edge:** Reeded

Date	Mintage	F	VF	XF	Unc	BU
2002 Proof	35,000	Value: 75.00				

KM# 185 10 DOLLARS
31.1040 g., 0.9999 Gold 0.9999 oz. AGW, 32.12 mm. **Subject:** Suzhou Industrial Park **Obv:** National arms **Rev:** "Harmony" Sculpture **Edge:** Lettered edge

Date	Mintage	F	VF	XF	Unc	BU
2004 Proof	500	Value: 750				

KM# 187 10 DOLLARS
62.2060 g., 0.9990 Silver 1.998 oz. ASW, 40.7 mm. **Subject:** Year of the Monkey **Obv:** National arms **Rev:** Seated monkey **Edge:** Reeded

Date	Mintage	F	VF	XF	Unc	BU
2004 Proof	35,000	Value: 75.00				

KM# 189 10 DOLLARS
28.0000 g., Copper-Nickel, 40.7 mm. **Subject:** Suzhou Industrial Park **Obv:** National arms **Rev:** "Harmony Sculpture" **Edge:** Reeded

Date	Mintage	F	VF	XF	Unc	BU
2004sm	7,000	—	—	—	20.00	—

KM# 178 250 DOLLARS
31.1035 g., 0.9990 Gold 0.999 oz. AGW, 32.1 mm. **Subject:** Year of the Snake **Obv:** National arms **Rev:** Stylized snake **Edge:** Reeded

Date	Mintage	F	VF	XF	Unc	BU
2001 Proof	7,000	Value: 825				

KM# 183 250 DOLLARS
31.1035 g., 0.9999 Gold 0.9999 oz. AGW, 32.12 mm. **Subject:** Year of the Horse **Obv:** National arms **Rev:** Horse **Edge:** Reeded

Date	Mintage	F	VF	XF	Unc	BU
2002 Proof	7,600	Value: 825				

KM# 188 250 DOLLARS
31.1030 g., 0.9999 Gold 0.9999 oz. AGW, 32.12 mm. **Subject:** Year of the Monkey **Obv:** National arms **Rev:** Seated monkey **Edge:** Reeded

Date	Mintage	F	VF	XF	Unc	BU
2004 Proof	7,000	Value: 675				

PROOF SETS

KM#	Date	Mintage	Identification	Issue Price	Mkt Val
PS55	2001 (2)	3,000	KM#179-180 plus copper-nickel ingot	—	85.00
PS56	2001 (3)	2,000	KM#178-180 plus copper-nickel ingot	—	685

SLOVAKIA

The Republic of Slovakia has an area of 18,923 sq. mi. (49,035 sq. km.) and a population of 4.9 million. Capital: Bratislava. Textiles, steel, and wood products are exported.

MINT MARK

Kremnica Mint

REPUBLIC

STANDARD COINAGE

100 Halierov = 1 Slovak Koruna (Sk)

KM# 17 10 HALIEROV
Aluminum, 17 mm. **Obv:** Slovak shield **Rev:** 19th century wooden belfry from Zemplin **Edge:** Plain **Designer:** Drahomir Zobek

Date	Mintage	F	VF	XF	Unc	BU
2001	20,330,000	—	—	—	0.35	—
2001 Proof	12,500	Value: 2.50				
2002	37,640,000	—	—	—	0.35	—
2002 Proof	16,100	Value: 1.50				
2003	—	—	—	—	0.35	—

KM# 18 20 HALIEROV
Aluminum, 19.5 mm. **Obv:** Slovak shield **Rev:** Tatra Mountain peak of Krivan **Edge:** Reeded **Designer:** Drahomir Zobek

Date	Mintage	F	VF	XF	Unc	BU
2001	21,920,000	—	—	—	0.45	—
2001 Proof	12,500	Value: 2.50				
2002	36,300,000	—	—	—	0.45	—
2002 Proof	16,100	Value: 1.50				
2003	—	—	—	—	0.45	—

KM# 35 50 HALIEROV
2.8000 g., Copper Plated Steel, 18.7 mm. **Obv:** Slovak shield **Rev:** Watch tower of Devin Castle **Edge:** Milled and plain **Designer:** Drahomir Zobek

Date	Mintage	F	VF	XF	Unc	BU
2001	10,400,000	—	—	—	0.60	—
2001 Proof	12,500	Value: 2.50				
2002	11,000,000	—	—	—	0.60	—
2002 Proof	16,100	Value: 1.50				
2003	—	—	—	—	0.60	—
2005	—	—	—	—	0.60	—

KM# 12 KORUNA
Bronze Clad Steel, 21 mm. **Subject:** 15th Century of Madonna and Child **Obv:** Slovak shield **Edge:** Milled **Designer:** Drahomir Zobek

Date	Mintage	F	VF	XF	Unc	BU
2001	12,500	—	—	—	1.50	—
Note: In sets only						
2001 Proof	—	Value: 3.00				
2002	11,000,000	—	—	—	1.50	—
2002 Proof	16,100	Value: 2.50				
2003	14,000	—	—	—	1.50	—

Date	Mintage	F	VF	XF	Unc	BU
Note: In sets only						
2005	—	—	—	—	1.50	—

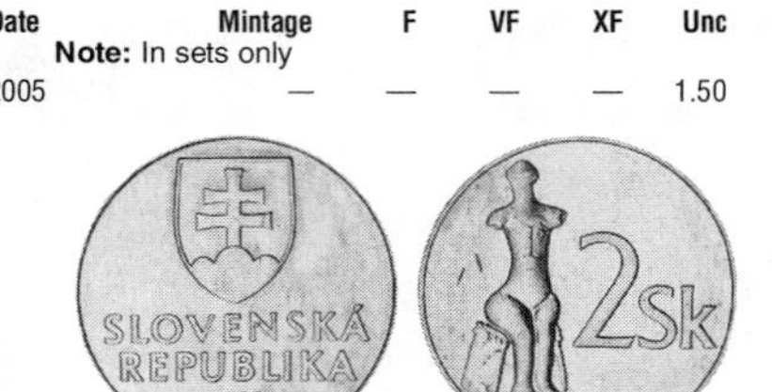

KM# 13 2 KORUNA
4.4000 g., Nickel Clad Steel, 21.5 mm. **Obv:** Slovak shield **Rev:** 4th century B.C. Venus statue **Designer:** Drahomir Zobek

Date	Mintage	F	VF	XF	Unc	BU
2001	10,668,000	—	—	—	0.85	—
2001 Proof	12,500	Value: 5.00				
2002	10,312,000	—	—	—	0.85	—
2002 Proof	16,100	Value: 2.50				
2003	—	—	—	—	0.85	—
2005	—	—	—	—	0.85	—

KM# 14 5 KORUNA
5.4000 g., Nickel Clad Steel, 24.75 mm. **Obv:** Slovak shield **Rev:** 1st century Celtic coin of BIATEC **Edge:** Milled **Designer:** Drahomir Zobek

Date	Mintage	F	VF	XF	Unc	BU
2001 Proof	12,500	Value: 6.00				
2002 Proof	16,100	Value: 5.00				
2003	14,000	—	—	—	2.00	—
Note: In sets only						
2005	—	—	—	—	2.00	—

KM# 11.1 10 KORUNA
6.6000 g., Brass, 26.5 mm. **Obv:** Slovak shield **Rev:** 11th century bronze cross **Designer:** Drahomir Zobek

Date	Mintage	F	VF	XF	Unc	BU
2001 Proof	12,500	Value: 12.50				
2002 Proof	16,100	Value: 10.00				
2003	14,000	—	—	—	4.00	—
Note: In sets only						
2005	—	—	—	—	4.00	—

KM# 67 20 KORUN
24.4800 g., 0.9250 Silver .7280 oz. ASW, 27.1 x 50.6 mm. **Series:** Banknotes **Obv:** Prince Pribina (800-861) **Rev:** Nitra Castle **Edge:** Plain

Date	Mintage	F	VF	XF	Unc	BU
2003 Proof	6,000	Value: 20.00				

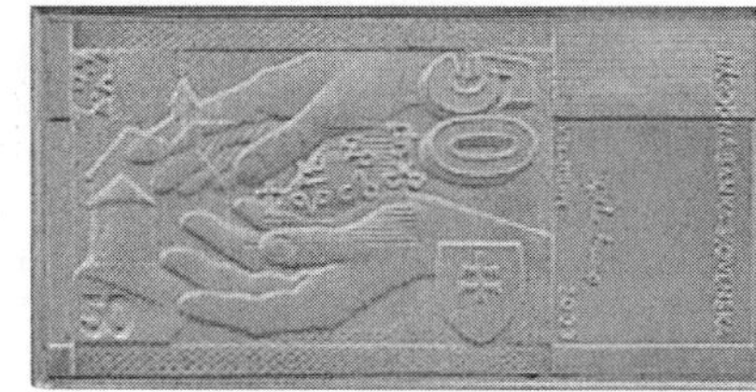

KM# 68 50 KORUN
26.6300 g., 0.9250 Silver 0.792 oz. ASW, 28.2 x 52.8 mm. **Series:** Banknotes **Obv:** Saints Cyril and Methodius (814-885) **Rev:** Two hands **Edge:** Plain

Date	Mintage	F	VF	XF	Unc	BU
2003 Proof	6,000	Value: 25.00				

KM# 69 100 KORUN
28.8700 g., 0.9250 Silver 0.8586 oz. ASW, 29.3 x 55 mm. **Series:** Banknotes **Obv:** The Levoca Madonna **Rev:** St. James Church in Levoca **Edge:** Plain

Date	Mintage	F	VF	XF	Unc	BU
2003 Proof	—	Value: 30.00				

KM# 59 200 KORUN
20.0000 g., 0.7500 Silver .4823 oz. ASW, 34 mm. **Subject:** Alexander Dubcek **Obv:** National arms and tree **Rev:** Portrait **Edge Lettering:** "BUDSKOST SLOBODA DEMOKRACIA"

Date	Mintage	F	VF	XF	Unc	BU
2001	12,800	—	—	—	15.00	—
2001 Proof	3,000	Value: 50.00				
Note: Unc. examples without edge lettering exist. Value $800.						

KM# 60 200 KORUN
20.0000 g., 0.7500 Silver 0.4823 oz. ASW, 34 mm. **Subject:** L'udovit Fulla **Obv:** Two examples of modern art **Rev:** Portrait and denomination **Edge:** Lettered

Date	Mintage	F	VF	XF	Unc	BU
2002	10,600	—	—	—	20.00	—
2002 Proof	1,600	Value: 35.00				

KM# 62 200 KORUN
20.3500 g., 0.7500 Silver 0.4907 oz. ASW, 34 mm. **Subject:** UNESCO World Heritage site - Vlkolínec **Obv:** Log building **Rev:** Wooden tower and denomination **Edge Lettering:** WORLD HERITAGE PATRIMONE MONDIAL

Date	Mintage	F	VF	XF	Unc	BU
2002	11,500	—	—	—	15.00	—
2002 Proof	2,800	Value: 35.00				

KM# 65 200 KORUN
20.0000 g., 0.7500 Silver 0.4823 oz. ASW, 33.9 mm. **Subject:** Imrich Karvas **Obv:** Building, national arms and value **Rev:** Portrait **Edge:** Lettered **Edge Lettering:** NARODOHOSPODAR HUMANIST EUROPAN

Date	Mintage	F	VF	XF	Unc	BU
2003	9,800	—	—	—	15.00	—
2003 Proof	3,000	Value: 30.00				

KM# 70 200 KORUN
31.2100 g., 0.9250 Silver 0.9282 oz. ASW, 30.4 x 57.2 mm. **Series:** Banknotes **Obv:** Anton Bernolak (1762-1813) **Rev:** Trnava 18th Century city view **Edge:** Plain

Date	Mintage	F	VF	XF	Unc	BU
2003 Proof	6,000	Value: 35.00				

KM# 66 200 KORUN
20.0000 g., 0.7500 Silver 0.4823 oz. ASW, 34 mm. **Obv:** Matica Slovenska building **Rev:** Jozef Skultety bust, value **Edge:** Lettered **Edge Lettering:** VYTRVALOST A VERNOST NARODNEMU IDEALU

Date	Mintage	F	VF	XF	Unc	BU
2003	8,800	—	—	—	15.00	—
2003 Proof	2,700	Value: 30.00				

KM# 75 200 KORUN
20.0000 g., 0.7500 Silver 0.4823 oz. ASW, 34 mm. **Obv:** Kempelen's Chess Machine (1770) **Rev:** Inventor Wolfgang Kemelen (1734-1804) above Bratislava city view **Edge:** "VYNALEZCA - TECHNIK - KONSTRUKTER"

Date	Mintage	F	VF	XF	Unc	BU
2004	8,000	—	—	—	15.00	—
2004 Proof	3,200	Value: 35.00				

KM# 76 200 KORUN
20.0000 g., 0.7500 Silver 0.4823 oz. ASW, 34 mm. **Obv:** St. Aegidius Church and Bardejov Town Hall **Rev:** Aerial view of Bardejov circa 1768 **Edge:** Lettered **Edge Lettering:** "WORLD HERITAGE - PATRIMOINE MONDIAL"

Date	Mintage	F	VF	XF	Unc	BU
2004	8,400	—	—	—	15.00	—
2004 Proof	3,600	Value: 35.00				

KM# 77 200 KORUN
18.0000 g., 0.9000 Silver 0.5208 oz. ASW, 34 mm. **Obv:** "The Segner Wheel" model **Rev:** Portrait of Segner wearing a fur hat **Edge:** Lettered **Edge Lettering:** "VYNALEZCA - FYZIK - MATEMATIK - PEDAGOG"

Date	Mintage	F	VF	XF	Unc	BU
2004	10,000	—	—	—	15.00	—
2004 Proof	5,000	Value: 30.00				

KM# 78 200 KORUN
20.0000 g., 0.7500 Silver 0.4823 oz. ASW, 34 mm. **Subject:** Slovakian entry into the European Union **Obv:** Circle of stars in arch above national arms **Rev:** Map in arch above value **Edge:** Lettered **Edge Lettering:** " ROZSIRENIE EUROPSKEJ UNIE O DESAT KRAJIN "

Date	Mintage	F	VF	XF	Unc	BU
2004	10,100	—	—	—	15.00	—
2004 Proof	4,700	Value: 30.00				

KM# 81 200 KORUN
18.0000 g., 0.9000 Silver 0.5208 oz. ASW, 34 mm. **Subject:** Leopold I Coronation **Obv:** Value and partial castle view **Rev:** Coin design of Leopold I in large size legend **Edge Lettering:** "BRATISLAVSKE KORUNOVACIE"

Date	Mintage	F	VF	XF	Unc	BU
2005	10,000	—	—	—	—	20.00
2005 Proof	5,000	Value: 40.00				

KM# 82 200 KORUN
18.0000 g., 0.9000 Silver 0.5208 oz. ASW, 34 mm. **Subject:** Treaty of Pressburg **Obv:** Primate's Palace behind French military standard **Rev:** Napoleon and Francis I of Austria **Edge Lettering:** "26 DECEMBER. 5 MIVOSE AN 14"

Date	Mintage	F	VF	XF	Unc	BU
2005	10,000	—	—	—	—	20.00
2005 Proof	5,000	Value: 40.00				

KM# 56 500 KORUN
33.6300 g., 0.9250 Silver 1.0001 oz. ASW, 40 mm. **Subject:** Mala Fatra National Park **Obv:** National arms center of beetle cross **Rev:** Orchid with mountain background **Edge Lettering:** OCHRANA PRIRODY A KRAJINY

Date	Mintage	F	VF	XF	Unc	BU
2001	10,200	—	—	—	40.00	—
2001 Proof	1,800	Value: 60.00				

KM# 57 500 KORUN
31.1035 g., 0.9990 Silver 1.0000 oz. ASW, 45 mm. **Subject:** Third Millennium **Obv:** "The Universe" **Rev:** Three hands **Edge:** Plain **Shape:** 3-sided **Designer:** Patrik Kovacovsky

Date	Mintage	F	VF	XF	Unc	BU
2001	13,000	—	—	—	45.00	—
2001 Proof	4,000	Value: 65.00				

KM# 71 500 KORUN
33.6300 g., 0.9250 Silver 1.0001 oz. ASW, 31.5 x 59.4 mm. **Series:** Banknotes **Obv:** Ludovit Stur (1815-1856) **Rev:** Bratislava Castle view **Edge:** Plain

Date	Mintage	F	VF	XF	Unc	BU
2003 Proof	6,000	Value: 40.00				

KM# 84 500 KORUN
33.6300 g., 0.9250 Silver 1.0001 oz. ASW, 40 mm. **Subject:** Muranska Planina National Park **Obv:** Wildflowers and castle ruins **Rev:** Two wild horses **Edge Lettering:** "OCHRANA PRIRODY A KRAJINY"

Date	Mintage	F	VF	XF	Unc	BU
2006	8,500	—	—	—	—	40.00
2006 Proof	5,000	Value: 60.00				

KM# 63 1000 KORUN
62.2070 g., 0.9990 Silver 1.998 oz. ASW, 43.6 x 43.6 mm. **Subject:** 10th Anniversary of Republic **Obv:** National arms between hands **Rev:** Denomination above map **Edge:** Segmented reeding **Shape:** Square

Date	Mintage	F	VF	XF	Unc	BU
2003 Proof	10,000	Value: 65.00				

KM# 72 1000 KORUN
43.9100 g., Bi-Metallic Gold And Silver .925 Silver 43.91g with .999 Gold .28g insert, 32.6 x 61.6 mm. **Series:** Banknotes **Obv:** Andrej Hlinka (1864-1938) **Rev:** The Madonna Protector and church of Liptovske Sliace **Edge:** Plain **Note:** Illustration reduced.

Date	Mintage	F	VF	XF	Unc	BU
2003 Proof	6,000	Value: 60.00				

KM# 58 5000 KORUN
Tri-Metallic 31.1035, .999 Silver, 1.00 oz ASW with 6.22, .999 Gold, .20 oz AGW and .31, .999 Platinum, .10 oz. APW, 50 mm. **Series:** Third Millennium **Obv:** "The Universe" **Rev:** Three hands **Edge:** Plain **Shape:** Triangular **Designer:** Patrik Kovacovsky

Date	Mintage	F	VF	XF	Unc	BU
2001 Proof	8,000	Value: 400				

KM# 61 5000 KORUN
9.5000 g., 0.9000 Gold 0.2749 oz. AGW, 26 mm. **Subject:** Vikolinec Village **Obv:** Enclosed communal well **Rev:** Window and fence **Edge:** Reeded

Date	Mintage	F	VF	XF	Unc	BU
2002 Proof	7,200	Value: 325				

KM# 73 5000 KORUN
47.6340 g., Bi-Metallic Gold And Silver .925 Silver 46.65g with two .9999 Gold inserts .964g in total, 33.4 x 63.8 mm. **Series:** Banknotes **Obv:** Milan R. Stefanik **Rev:** Stefanik's grave monument **Edge:** Plain **Note:** Illustration reduced.

Date	Mintage	F	VF	XF	Unc	BU
2003 Proof	6,000	Value: 85.00				

KM# 80 5000 KORUN
9.5000 g., 0.9000 Gold 0.2749 oz. AGW, 26 mm. **Subject:** Historic Town of Bardejov **Obv:** National arms and value left of Town Hall **Rev:** Zachariah in window frame left of St. Aegidius Church **Edge:** Reeded

Date	Mintage	F	VF	XF	Unc	BU
2004 Proof	9,000	Value: 300				

KM# 83 5000 KORUN
9.5000 g., 0.9000 Gold 0.2749 oz. AGW, 26 mm. **Subject:** Leopold I Coronation **Obv:** Mounted Herald with Bratislava Castile in background **Rev:** Leopold I and Crown of St. Stephan **Edge:** Reeded

Date	Mintage	F	VF	XF	Unc	BU
2005 Proof	7,500	Value: 350				

KM# 64 10000 KORUN
17.1050 g., Bi-Metallic 1.555g, .999 Palladium round center in a 15.55g, .900 Gold square, 29.5 x 29.5 mm. **Subject:** 10th Anniversary of the Republic **Obv:** Girls portrait above national arms **Rev:** Bratislava castle above denomination **Edge:** Segmented reeding **Shape:** Square

Date	Mintage	F	VF	XF	Unc	BU
2003 Proof	6,000	Value: 750				

KM# 79 10000 KORUN
24.8828 g., Bi-Metallic .999 Gold 12.4414g 23mm round center in .999 Palladium 12.4414g 40mm pentagon, 40 mm. **Subject:** Slovakian entry into the European Union **Obv:** National arms above date in center **Rev:** European map with entry date **Edge:** Plain

Date	Mintage	F	VF	XF	Unc	BU
2004 Proof	7,200	Value: 800				

MINT SETS

KM#	Date	Mintage	Identification	Issue Price	Mkt Val
MS9	2001 (7)	—	KM#11.1-14, 17-18, 35, plus medal	—	12.00
MS10	2002 (7)	—	KM#11.1-14, 17-18, 35, plus medal	—	12.00
MS11	2003 (7)	—	KM#11.1-14, 17-18, 35, plus medal	—	12.00

PROOF SETS

KM#	Date	Mintage	Identification	Issue Price	Mkt Val
PS2	2001 (7)	12,500	KM#11.1-14, 17-18, 35	—	30.00
PS3	2002 (7)	16,500	KM#11.1-14, 17-18, 35	—	25.00

SLOVENIA

The Republic of Slovenia is located northwest of Yugoslavia in the valleys of the Danube River. It has an area of 7,819 sq. mi. and a population of *1.9 million. Capital: Ljubljana. Agriculture is the main industry with large amounts of hops and fodder crops grown as well as many varieties of fruit trees. Sheep raising, timber production and the mining of mercury from one of the country's oldest mines are also very important to the economy.

MINT MARKS
Based on last digit in date.
(K) - Kremnitz (Slovakia): open 4, upturned 5
(BP) - Budapest (Hungary): closed 4, down-turned 5

REPUBLIC

STANDARD COINAGE

100 Stotinow = 1 Tolar

KM# 7 10 STOTINOV
Aluminum **Rev:** Proteus anguineus **Edge:** Plain **Note:** Varieties exist.

Date	Mintage	F	VF	XF	Unc	BU
2001 Proof	—	Value: 3.00				
2002 Proof	—	Value: 3.00				
2003 Proof	—	Value: 3.00				

KM# 8 20 STOTINOV
Aluminum **Obv:** Value within square **Rev:** Long-eared owl (asio otus) **Edge:** Plain

Date	Mintage	F	VF	XF	Unc	BU
2001 Proof	—	Value: 4.00				
2002 Proof	—	Value: 4.00				
2003 Proof	—	Value: 4.00				

KM# 3 50 STOTINOV
Aluminum **Rev:** Bee (apis mellifera) **Edge:** Plain

Date	Mintage	F	VF	XF	Unc	BU
2001 Proof	—	Value: 6.00				
2002 Proof	—	Value: 6.00				
2003 Proof	—	Value: 6.00				

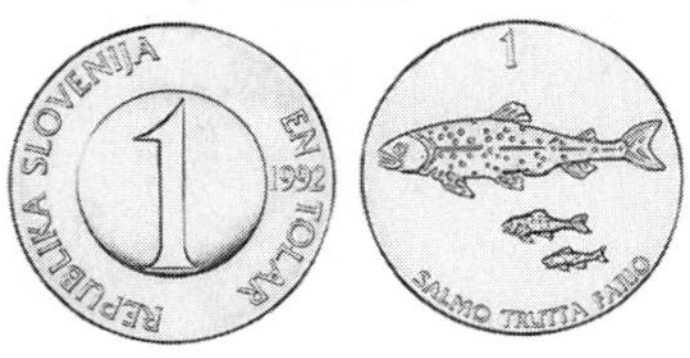

KM# 4 TOLAR
Brass **Rev:** 3 brown trout (salma trutta fario) **Edge:** Reeded **Note:** Date varieties exist: 1994 = closed or open "4"; 1995 = serif up and serif down in "5".

Date	Mintage	F	VF	XF	Unc	BU
2001	—	—	—	—	0.75	1.25
2001 Proof	—	Value: 5.00				
2002 Proof	—	Value: 5.00				
2003 Proof	—	Value: 5.00				
2004 Proof	—	Value: 5.00				

KM# 5 2 TOLARJA

Brass **Rev:** Barn swallow in flight (hirundo rustica) **Edge:** Reeded **Note:** Date varieties exist: 1994 = closed or open "4"; 1995 = serif up and serif down in "5".

Date	Mintage	F	VF	XF	Unc	BU
2001	—	—	—	—	0.75	1.50
2001 Proof	—	Value: 7.00				
2002 Proof	—	Value: 7.00				
2003 Proof	—	Value: 7.00				
2004 Proof	—	Value: 7.00				
2005	—	—	—	—	0.60	1.20

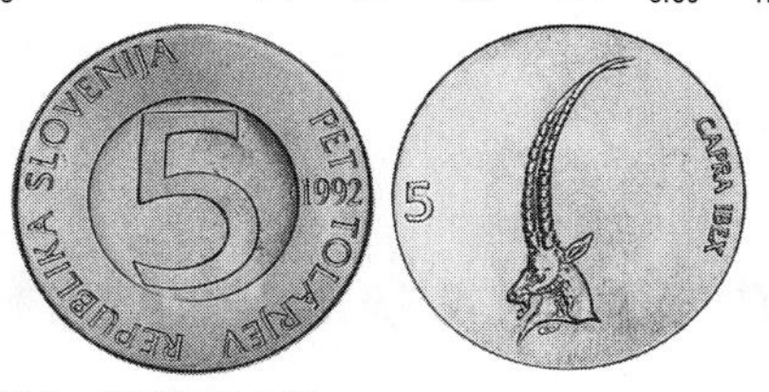

KM# 6 5 TOLARJEV

Brass **Rev:** Head and horns of ibex (capra ibex) **Edge:** Reeded **Note:** Date varieties exist: 1994 = closed or open "4"; 1995 = serif up and serif down in "5".

Date	Mintage	F	VF	XF	Unc	BU
2001 Proof	—	Value: 8.00				
2002 Proof	—	Value: 8.00				
2003 Proof	—	Value: 8.00				

KM# 41 10 TOLARJEV

5.7500 g., Copper Nickel **Obv:** Denomination **Rev:** Saddled horse (equus) **Edge:** Reeded

Date	Mintage	F	VF	XF	Unc	BU
2001	—	—	—	—	3.00	4.00
2001 Proof	—	Value: 10.00				
2002	—	—	—	—	3.00	4.00
2002 Proof	—	Value: 10.00				
2003 Proof	—	Value: 10.00				
2004	—	—	—	—	3.00	4.00
2004 Proof	—	Value: 10.00				
2005	—	—	—	—	3.00	4.00
2005 Proof	—	Value: 10.00				

KM# 51 20 TOLARJEV

6.8500 g., Copper-Nickel, 24 mm. **Obv:** Value **Rev:** White Stork standing **Edge:** Reeded

Date	Mintage	F	VF	XF	Unc	BU
2003	—	—	—	—	3.50	4.50
2003 Proof	—	Value: 11.50				
2004	—	—	—	—	3.50	4.50
2004 Proof	—	Value: 6.00				
2005	—	—	—	—	3.50	4.50
2005 Proof	—	Value: 6.00				

KM# 52 50 TOLARJEV

8.0000 g., Copper-Nickel, 26 mm. **Obv:** Value **Rev:** Stylized bull **Edge:** Reeded and plain sections

Date	Mintage	F	VF	XF	Unc	BU
2003	—	—	—	—	4.00	5.00
2003 Proof	—	Value: 12.00				

Date	Mintage	F	VF	XF	Unc	BU
2004	—	—	—	—	4.00	5.00
2004 Proof	—	Value: 12.00				
2005	—	—	—	—	4.00	5.00
2005 Proof	—	Value: 12.00				

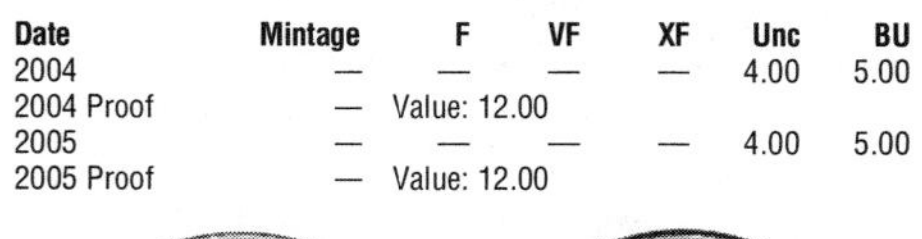

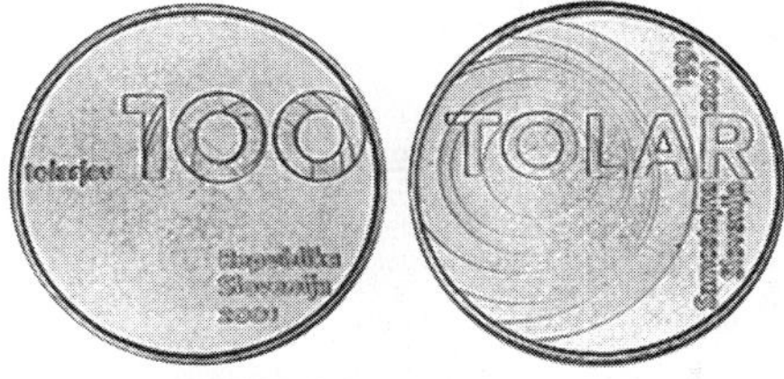

KM# 42 100 TOLARJEV

9.1000 g., Copper-Nickel, 28 mm. **Subject:** 10th Anniversary of Slovenia and the Tolar **Obv:** Denomination **Rev:** Tree rings and inscription **Edge:** Reeded

Date	Mintage	F	VF	XF	Unc	BU
2001	500,000	—	—	—	3.00	4.00
2001 Proof	—	Value: 10.00				

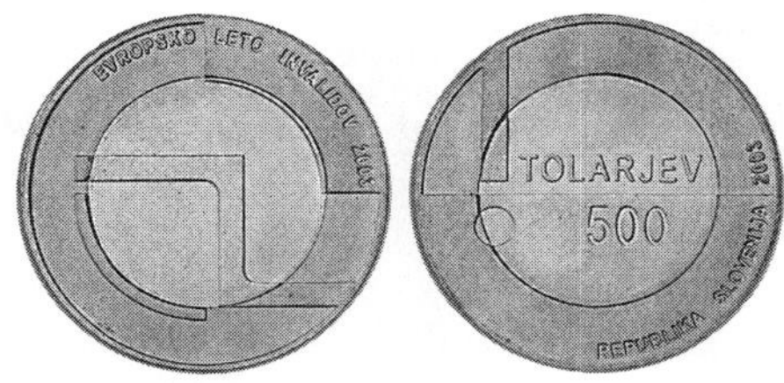

KM# 45 500 TOLARJEV

8.5400 g., Bi-Metallic Copper-Nickel center in Brass ring, 28.1 mm. **Subject:** Soccer **Obv:** Denomination **Rev:** Soccer player and radiant sun **Edge:** Reeded

Date	Mintage	F	VF	XF	Unc	BU
2002	500,000	—	—	—	5.50	7.50
2002 Proof	—	Value: 12.50				

KM# 50 500 TOLARJEV

8.7200 g., Bi-Metallic Copper-Nickel center in Brass ring, 27.9 mm. **Subject:** European Year of the Disabled **Obv:** Value **Rev:** Stylized wheelchair **Edge:** Reeded

Date	Mintage	F	VF	XF	Unc	BU
2003	200,000	—	—	—	6.00	8.00
2003 Proof	—	Value: 13.50				

KM# 57 500 TOLARJEV

8.6000 g., Bi-Metallic Copper-Nickel center in Brass ring, 28 mm. **Obv:** Value **Rev:** Jurij Vega facial profile behind mathematical graph **Edge:** Reeded

Date	Mintage	F	VF	XF	Unc	BU
2004	200,000	—	—	—	6.00	8.00

KM# 63 500 TOLARJEV

8.6500 g., Bi-Metallic Copper-Nickel center in Brass ring, 27.9 mm. **Obv:** Perched falcon **Rev:** Two partial suns **Edge:** Reeded

Date	Mintage	F	VF	XF	Unc	BU
2005	—	—	—	—	6.25	8.50

KM# 43 2000 TOLARJEV

15.0000 g., 0.9250 Silver 0.4461 oz. ASW, 32 mm. **Subject:** 10th Anniversary of Slovenia and the Tolar **Obv:** Denomination **Rev:** Tree rings and inscription **Edge:** Reeded

Date	Mintage	F	VF	XF	Unc	BU
2001 Proof	3,000	Value: 35.00				

KM# 46 2500 TOLARJEV

15.0000 g., 0.9250 Silver 0.4461 oz. ASW, 32 mm. **Subject:** Soccer **Obv:** Denomination **Rev:** Soccer player and radiant sun **Edge:** Reeded

Date	Mintage	F	VF	XF	Unc	BU
2002 Proof	2,500	Value: 35.00				

KM# 48 2500 TOLARJEV

15.0000 g., 0.9250 Silver 0.4461 oz. ASW, 32 mm. **Subject:** 35th Chess Olympiad **Obv:** Rearing horse and reflection **Rev:** Chess pieces in starting positions **Edge:** Reeded **Designer:** MNiljenko Licul and Jan Cernaj

Date	Mintage	F	VF	XF	Unc	BU
2002 Proof	1,000	Value: 40.00				

KM# 53 2500 TOLARJEV

15.0000 g., 0.9250 Silver 0.4461 oz. ASW, 32 mm. **Subject:** European Year of the Disabled **Obv:** Value **Rev:** Stylized wheel chair **Edge:** Reeded

Date	Mintage	F	VF	XF	Unc	BU
2003 Proof	1,500	Value: 30.00				

KM# 55 5000 TOLARJEV

15.0000 g., 0.9250 Silver 0.4461 oz. ASW, 32 mm. **Subject:** 60th Anniversary of the Slovenian Assembly **Obv:** Value in partial star design **Rev:** Dates in partial star design **Edge:** Reeded

Date	Mintage	F	VF	XF	Unc	BU
2003 Proof	1,500	Value: 35.00				

KM# 58 5000 TOLARJEV
15.0000 g., 0.9250 Silver 0.4461 oz. ASW, 32 mm. **Obv:** Value **Rev:** Facial profile of Jurij Vega behind mathematical graph **Edge:** Reeded

Date	Mintage	F	VF	XF	Unc	BU
2004 Proof	1,500	Value: 50.00				

KM# 60 5000 TOLARJEV
15.0000 g., 0.9250 Silver 0.4461 oz. ASW, 32 mm. **Subject:** 1000th Anniversary Town of Bled **Obv:** Value **Rev:** Castle and towers silhouette **Edge:** Reeded

Date	Mintage	F	VF	XF	Unc	BU
2004	1,500	—	—	—	50.00	50.00

KM# 62 5000 TOLARJEV
15.1000 g., 0.9250 Silver 0.4491 oz. ASW, 32 mm. **Subject:** Slovenian Film Centennial **Obv:** Value above a director's clapboard **Rev:** Film segment **Edge:** Reeded

Date	Mintage	F	VF	XF	Unc	BU
2005 Proof	—	Value: 45.00				

KM# 64 5000 TOLARJEV
15.1000 g., 0.9250 Silver 0.4491 oz. ASW, 32 mm. **Obv:** Perched falcon **Rev:** Two partial suns **Edge:** Reeded

Date	Mintage	F	VF	XF	Unc	BU
2005 Proof	—	Value: 45.00				

KM# 44 20000 TOLARJEV
7.0000 g., 0.9000 Gold 0.2025 oz. AGW, 24 mm. **Subject:** 10th Anniversary of Slovenia and the Tolar **Obv:** Denomination **Rev:** Tree rings and inscription **Edge:** Reeded

Date	Mintage	F	VF	XF	Unc	BU
2001 Proof	1,000	Value: 275				

KM# 47 20000 TOLARJEV
7.0000 g., 0.9000 Gold 0.2025 oz. AGW, 24 mm. **Subject:** World Cup Soccer **Obv:** Value **Rev:** Soccer player and rising sun **Edge:** Reeded

Date	Mintage	F	VF	XF	Unc	BU
2002 Proof	1,500	Value: 275				

KM# 49 20000 TOLARJEV
7.0000 g., 0.9000 Gold 0.2025 oz. AGW, 24 mm. **Subject:** 35th Chess Olympiad **Obv:** Rearing horse and reflection **Rev:** Chess pieces in starting positions **Edge:** Reeded

Date	Mintage	F	VF	XF	Unc	BU
2002 Proof	500	Value: 300				

KM# 54 25000 TOLARJEV
7.0000 g., 0.9000 Gold 0.2025 oz. AGW, 24 mm. **Subject:** European Year of the Disabled **Obv:** Value **Rev:** Stylized wheel chair **Edge:** Reeded

Date	Mintage	F	VF	XF	Unc	BU
2003 Proof	300	Value: 300				

KM# 56 25000 TOLARJEV
7.0000 g., 0.9000 Gold 0.2025 oz. AGW, 24 mm. **Subject:** 60th Anniversary of the Slovenian Assembly **Obv:** Value in partial star design **Rev:** Dates in partial star design **Edge:** Reeded

Date	Mintage	F	VF	XF	Unc	BU
2003 Proof	300	Value: 300				

KM# 59 25000 TOLARJEV
7.0000 g., 0.9000 Gold 0.2025 oz. AGW, 24 mm. **Subject:** 250th Anniversary of Jurij Vega's Birth **Obv:** Value **Rev:** Mathematical graph over facial profile **Edge:** Reeded

Date	Mintage	F	VF	XF	Unc	BU
2004	300	—	—	—	—	300

KM# 61 25000 TOLARJEV
7.0000 g., 0.9000 Gold 0.2025 oz. AGW, 24 mm. **Subject:** 1000th Anniversary Town of Bled **Obv:** Value **Rev:** Castle and towers silouette **Edge:** Reeded

Date	Mintage	F	VF	XF	Unc	BU
2004	300	—	—	—	—	300

PROOF SETS

KM#	Date	Mintage	Identification	Issue Price	Mkt Val
PS13	2001 (8)	—	KM#3, 4, 5, 6, 7, 8, 41, 42	—	55.00
PS14	2002 (8)	—	KM#3, 4, 5, 6, 7, 8, 41, 45	—	58.00
PS15	2003 (10)	—	KM#3, 4, 5, 6, 7, 8, 41, 50, 51, 52	—	80.00

SOLOMON ISLANDS

The Solomon Islands, located in the southwest Pacific east of Papua New Guinea, has an area of 10,983 sq. mi. (28,450 sq. km.) and a population of *324,000. Capital: Honiara. The most important islands of the Solomon chain are Guadalcanal (scene of some of the fiercest fighting of World War II), Malaitia, New Georgia, Florida, Vella Lavella, Choiseul, Rendova, San Cristobal, the Lord Howe group, the Santa Cruz islands, and the Duff group. Copra is the only important cash crop but it is hoped that timber will become an economic factor.

Solomon Islands is a member of the Commonwealth of Nations. Queen Elizabeth II is Head of State, as Queen of the Solomon Islands.

RULERS
British, until 1978

MONETARY SYSTEM
100 Cents = 1 Dollar

COMMONWEALTH NATION

STANDARD COINAGE

KM# 83 2 DOLLARS
62.2700 g., 0.9990 Silver 2 oz. ASW, 50.3 mm. **Subject:** Regional Assistance Mission to Solomon Islands **Obv:** Elizabeth II **Rev:** Dove outline over multicolor islands in a sea of country names **Edge:** Reeded

Date	Mintage	F	VF	XF	Unc	BU
2005 Proof	2,500	Value: 125				

KM# 75 5 DOLLARS
28.2800 g., Copper-Nickel, 38.6 mm. **Obv:** Queen's portrait **Rev:** F-117A Nighthawk Stealth fighter plane **Edge:** Reeded

Date	Mintage	F	VF	XF	Unc	BU
2003	—	—	—	—	6.00	8.00

KM# 76 5 DOLLARS
28.2800 g., Copper-Nickel, 38.6 mm. **Obv:** Queen's portrait **Rev:** Concorde supersonic airliner **Edge:** Reeded

Date	Mintage	F	VF	XF	Unc	BU
2003	—	—	—	—	6.00	8.00

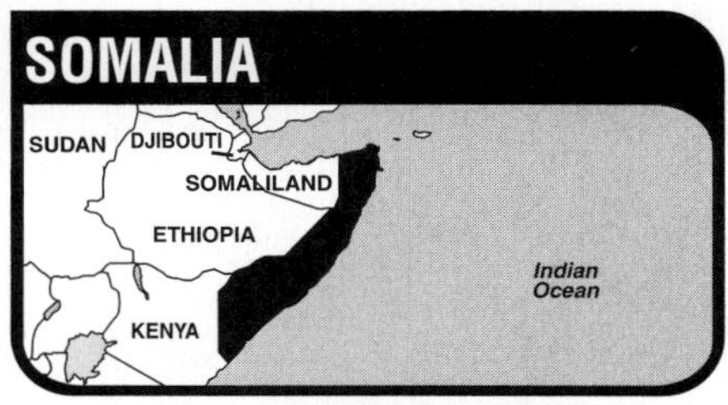

The Somali Democratic Republic, comprised of the former Italian Somaliland, is located on the coast of the eastern projection of the African continent commonly referred to as the "Horn". It has an area of 178,201 sq. mi. (461,657 sq. km.) and a population of *8.2 million. Capital: Mogadishu. The economy is pastoral and agricultural. Livestock, bananas and hides are exported.

The Northern Somali National Movement (SNM) declared a secession of the northwestern Somaliland Republic on May 17, 1991, which is not recognized by the Somali Democratic Republic.

TITLES

Al-Jumhuriya(t)as - Somaliya(t)

REPUBLIC OF SOMALIA

STANDARD COINAGE

100 Centesimi = 1 Somalo

KM# 120 5 SHILLINGS

1.2400 g., Aluminum, 22 mm. **Obv:** Adult and juvenile elephants **Rev:** Value **Edge:** Plain

Date	Mintage	F	VF	XF	Unc	BU
2005	—	—	—	—	1.25	1.50

KM# 45 5 SHILLING / SCELLINI

Aluminum **Series:** F.A.O. **Obv:** National arms **Rev:** Elephant

Date	Mintage	F	VF	XF	Unc	BU
2002	—	—	—	—	1.50	1.75

KM# 103 25 SHILLINGS / SCELLINI

4.3700 g., Brass, 21.8 mm. **Subject:** Soccer **Obv:** National arms **Rev:** Soccer player **Edge:** Plain

Date	Mintage	F	VF	XF	Unc	BU
2001	—	—	—	—	1.25	1.50

KM# 111 50 SHILLINGS

3.9000 g., Nickel-Clad Steel, 21.9 mm. **Obv:** National arms **Rev:** Mandrill **Edge:** Plain

Date	Mintage	F	VF	XF	Unc	BU
2002	—	—	—	—	0.85	1.25

KM# 109 100 SHILLINGS

10.5000 g., 0.9990 Silver 0.3372 oz. ASW, 30.1 mm. **Subject:** Soccer **Obv:** National arms **Rev:** Multicolor soccer player and Brandenburg Gate **Edge:** Reeded

Date	Mintage	F	VF	XF	Unc	BU
2001 Proof	—	Value: 25.00				

KM# 112 100 SHILLINGS

3.5400 g., Brass, 18.8 mm. **Obv:** National arms above value **Rev:** Queen of Sheba **Edge:** Plain

Date	Mintage	F	VF	XF	Unc	BU
2002	—	—	—	—	1.50	2.50

KM# 110 250 SHILLINGS

31.1500 g., 0.9990 Silver 1.0005 oz. ASW, 39.9 mm. **Subject:** Queen of Sheba **Obv:** National arms **Rev:** Queen's portrait **Edge:** Reeded

Date	Mintage	F	VF	XF	Unc	BU
2002	—	—	—	—	35.00	40.00

KM# 121 250 SHILLINGS

20.1200 g., Silver-Plated Base Metal, 38.5 mm. **Obv:** National arms **Rev:** Multicolor Pope John Paul II and mountains **Edge:** Reeded

Date	Mintage	F	VF	XF	Unc	BU
2005 Proof	—	Value: 18.00				

KM# 123 250 SHILLINGS

20.1200 g., Silver-Plated Base Metal, 38.5 mm. **Obv:** National arms **Rev:** Multicolor Pope John Paul II kissing book **Edge:** Reeded

Date	Mintage	F	VF	XF	Unc	BU
2005 Proof	—	Value: 18.00				

KM# 125 250 SHILLINGS

20.1200 g., Silver-Plated Base Metal, 38.5 mm. **Obv:** National arms **Rev:** Multicolor Pope John Paul II with flowers **Edge:** Reeded

Date	Mintage	F	VF	XF	Unc	BU
2005 Proof	—	Value: 18.00				

KM# 127 250 SHILLINGS

20.1200 g., Silver-Plated Base Metal, 38.5 mm. **Obv:** National arms **Rev:** Multicolor Pope John Paul II saying mass **Edge:** Reeded

Date	Mintage	F	VF	XF	Unc	BU
2005 Proof	—	Value: 18.00				

KM# 129 250 SHILLINGS

20.1200 g., Silver-Plated Base Metal, 38.5 mm. **Obv:** National arms **Rev:** Multicolor Pope John Paul II with cardinals **Edge:** Reeded

Date	Mintage	F	VF	XF	Unc	BU
2005 Proof	—	Value: 18.00				

KM# 131 250 SHILLINGS

20.1200 g., Silver-Plated Base Metal, 38.5 mm. **Obv:** National arms **Rev:** Pope John Paul II with red vestments **Edge:** Reeded

Date	Mintage	F	VF	XF	Unc	BU
2005 Proof	—	Value: 18.00				

KM# 133 250 SHILLINGS

20.1200 g., Silver-Plated Base Metal, 38.5 mm. **Obv:** National arms **Rev:** Pope John Paul II in white with skull cap **Edge:** Reeded

Date	Mintage	F	VF	XF	Unc	BU
2005 Proof	—	Value: 18.00				

KM# 135 250 SHILLINGS
20.1200 g., Silver-Plated Base Metal, 38.5 mm. **Obv:** National arms **Rev:** Multicolor Pope John Paul II leaning head on staff **Edge:** Reeded

Date	Mintage	F	VF	XF	Unc	BU
2005 Proof	—	Value: 18.00				

KM# 137 250 SHILLINGS
20.1200 g., Silver-Plated Base Metal, 38.5 mm. **Obv:** National arms **Rev:** Multicolor Pope John Paul II with staff facing left **Edge:** Reeded

Date	Mintage	F	VF	XF	Unc	BU
2005 Proof	—	Value: 18.00				

KM# 139 250 SHILLINGS
20.1200 g., Silver-Plated Base Metal, 38.5 mm. **Obv:** National arms **Rev:** Multicolor Pope John Paul II with staff facing half right **Edge:** Reeded

Date	Mintage	F	VF	XF	Unc	BU
2005 Proof	—	Value: 18.00				

KM# 122 500 SHILLINGS
18.8400 g., Silver-Plated Base Metal, 34.1 mm. **Obv:** National arms **Rev:** Multicolor Pope John Paul II and mountains **Edge:** Plain **Shape:** Square with round corners

Date	Mintage	F	VF	XF	Unc	BU
2005 Proof	—	Value: 20.00				

KM# 124 500 SHILLINGS
18.8400 g., Silver-Plated Base Metal, 34.1 mm. **Obv:** National arms **Rev:** Multicolor Pope John Paul II kissing book **Edge:** Plain **Shape:** Square with round corners

Date	Mintage	F	VF	XF	Unc	BU
2005 Proof	—	Value: 20.00				

KM# 126 500 SHILLINGS
18.8400 g., Silver-Plated Base Metal, 34.1 mm. **Obv:** National arms **Rev:** Multicolor Pope John Paul II with flowers **Edge:** Plain **Shape:** Square with round corners

Date	Mintage	F	VF	XF	Unc	BU
2005 Proof	—	Value: 20.00				

KM# 128 500 SHILLINGS
18.1400 g., Silver-Plated Base Metal, 34.1 mm. **Obv:** National arms **Rev:** Multicolor Pope John Paul II saying mass **Edge:** Plain **Shape:** Square with round corners

Date	Mintage	F	VF	XF	Unc	BU
2005 Proof	—	Value: 20.00				

KM# 130 500 SHILLINGS
18.8400 g., Silver-Plated Base Metal, 34.1 mm. **Obv:** National arms **Rev:** Multicolor Pope John Paul II with cardinals **Edge:** Plain **Shape:** Square with round corners

Date	Mintage	F	VF	XF	Unc	BU
2005 Proof	—	Value: 20.00				

KM# 132 500 SHILLINGS
18.8400 g., Silver-Plated Base Metal, 34.1 mm. **Obv:** National arms **Rev:** Pope John Paul II with red vestments **Edge:** Plain **Shape:** Square with round corners

Date	Mintage	F	VF	XF	Unc	BU
2005 Proof	—	Value: 20.00				

KM# 134 500 SHILLINGS
18.8400 g., Silver-Plated Base Metal, 34.1 mm. **Obv:** National arms **Rev:** Pope John Paul II in white with skull cap **Edge:** Plain **Shape:** Square with round corners

Date	Mintage	F	VF	XF	Unc	BU
2005 Proof	—	Value: 20.00				

KM# 136 500 SHILLINGS
18.8400 g., Silver-Plated Base Metal, 34.1 mm. **Obv:** National arms **Rev:** Multicolor Pope John Paul II leaning head on staff **Edge:** Plain **Shape:** Square with round corners

Date	Mintage	F	VF	XF	Unc	BU
2005 Proof	—	Value: 20.00				

KM# 138 500 SHILLINGS
18.8400 g., Silver-Plated Base Metal, 34.1 mm. **Obv:** National arms **Rev:** Multicolor Pope John Paul II with staff facing left **Edge:** Plain **Shape:** Square with round corners

Date	Mintage	F	VF	XF	Unc	BU
2005 Proof	—	Value: 20.00				

KM# 140 500 SHILLINGS
18.8400 g., Silver-Plated Base Metal, 34.1 mm. **Obv:** National arms **Rev:** Multicolor Pope John Paul II with staff facing half right **Edge:** Plain **Shape:** Square with round corners

Date	Mintage	F	VF	XF	Unc	BU
2005 Proof	—	Value: 20.00				

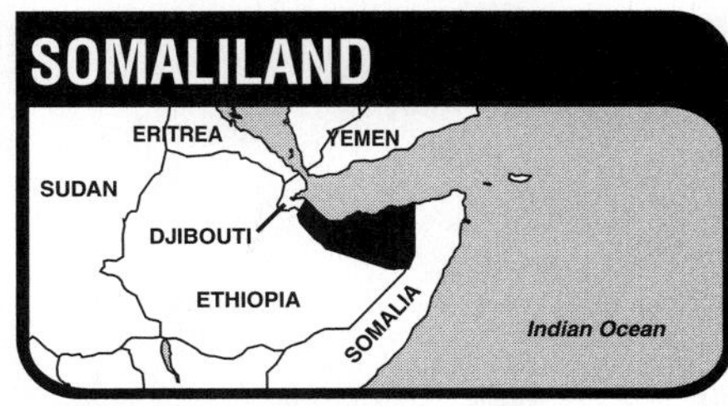

The Somaliland Republic, comprising of the former British Somaliland Protectorate is located on the coast of the northeastern projection of the African continent commonly referred to as the "Horn" on the southwestern end of the Gulf of Aden. Bordered by Ethiopia to west and south and Somalia to the east. It has an area of 68,000* sq. mi. (176,000* sq. km). Capital: Hargeysa. It is mostly arid and mountainous except for the gulf shoreline.

The northern Somali National Movement (SNM) declared a secession of the Somaliland Republic on May 17, 1991, which is not recognized by the Somali Democratic Republic.

REPUBLIC

SHILLING COINAGE

KM# 4 5 SHILLINGS

1.4500 g., Aluminum, 21.9 mm. **Obv:** Value **Rev:** Sir Richard F. Burton **Edge:** Plain

Date	Mintage	F	VF	XF	Unc	BU
2002	—	—	—	—	1.50	1.75

KM# 5 5 SHILLINGS

1.4500 g., Aluminum, 21.9 mm. **Obv:** Value **Rev:** Rooster **Edge:** Plain

Date	Mintage	F	VF	XF	Unc	BU
2002	—	—	—	—	1.00	1.25

KM# 3 10 SHILLINGS

3.5100 g., Brass, 17.7 mm. **Obv:** Vervet monkey **Rev:** Value **Edge:** Plain

Date	Mintage	F	VF	XF	Unc	BU
2002	—	—	—	—	0.75	1.25

KM# 7 10 SHILLINGS

4.8000 g., Stainless Steel, 24.9 mm. **Obv:** Value **Rev:** Aquarius the water carrier **Edge:** Plain

Date	Mintage	F	VF	XF	Unc	BU
2006	—	—	—	—	1.25	1.50

KM# 8 10 SHILLINGS

4.8000 g., Stainless Steel, 24.9 mm. **Obv:** Value **Rev:** Pisces the two fish **Edge:** Plain

Date	Mintage	F	VF	XF	Unc	BU
2006	—	—	—	—	1.25	1.50

KM# 9 10 SHILLINGS

4.8000 g., Stainless Steel, 24.9 mm. **Obv:** Value **Rev:** Aries the ram **Edge:** Plain

Date	Mintage	F	VF	XF	Unc	BU
2006	—	—	—	—	1.25	1.50

KM# 10 10 SHILLINGS

4.8000 g., Stainless Steel, 24.9 mm. **Obv:** Value **Rev:** Taurus the bull **Edge:** Plain

Date	Mintage	F	VF	XF	Unc	BU
2006	—	—	—	—	1.25	1.50

KM# 11 10 SHILLINGS

4.8000 g., Stainless Steel, 24.9 mm. **Obv:** Value **Rev:** Gemini twins **Edge:** Plain

Date	Mintage	F	VF	XF	Unc	BU
2006	—	—	—	—	1.25	1.50

KM# 12 10 SHILLINGS

4.8000 g., Stainless Steel, 24.9 mm. **Obv:** Value **Rev:** Cancer the crab **Edge:** Plain

Date	Mintage	F	VF	XF	Unc	BU
2006	—	—	—	—	1.25	1.50

KM# 13 10 SHILLINGS

4.8000 g., Stainless Steel, 24.9 mm. **Obv:** Value **Rev:** Leo the lion **Edge:** Plain

Date	Mintage	F	VF	XF	Unc	BU
2006	—	—	—	—	1.25	1.50

KM# 14 10 SHILLINGS

4.8000 g., Stainless Steel, 24.9 mm. **Obv:** Value **Rev:** Virgo as a winged woman **Edge:** Plain

Date	Mintage	F	VF	XF	Unc	BU
2006	—	—	—	—	1.25	1.50

KM# 15 10 SHILLINGS

4.8000 g., Stainless Steel, 24.9 mm. **Obv:** Value **Rev:** Libra balance scale **Edge:** Plain

Date	Mintage	F	VF	XF	Unc	BU
2006	—	—	—	—	1.25	1.50

KM# 16 10 SHILLINGS

4.8000 g., Stainless Steel, 24.9 mm. **Obv:** Value **Rev:** Scorpio the scorpion **Edge:** Plain

Date	Mintage	F	VF	XF	Unc	BU
2006	—	—	—	—	1.25	1.50

KM# 17 10 SHILLINGS

4.8000 g., Stainless Steel, 24.9 mm. **Obv:** Value **Rev:** Sagittarius the archer **Edge:** Plain

Date	Mintage	F	VF	XF	Unc	BU
2006	—	—	—	—	1.25	1.50

KM# 18 10 SHILLINGS

4.8000 g., Stainless Steel, 24.9 mm. **Obv:** Value **Rev:** Capricorn the goat **Edge:** Plain

Date	Mintage	F	VF	XF	Unc	BU
2006	—	—	—	—	1.25	1.50

KM# 6 20 SHILLINGS

3.8700 g., Stainless Steel, 21.8 mm. **Obv:** Value **Rev:** Greyhound dog **Edge:** Plain

Date	Mintage	F	VF	XF	Unc	BU
2002	—	—	—	—	1.50	2.00

KM# 2 1000 SHILLINGS

31.2700 g., 0.9990 Silver 1.0043 oz. ASW, 38.8 mm. **Obv:** National arms **Rev:** Bust of Richard F. Burton half right **Edge:** Reeded

Date	Mintage	F	VF	XF	Unc	BU
2002	—	—	—	—	40.00	45.00

The Republic of South Africa, located at the southern tip of Africa, has an area of 471,445 sq. mi. (1,221,043 sq. km.) and a population of *30.2 million. Capitals: Administrative, Pretoria; Legislative, Cape Town; Judicial, Bloemfontein. Manufacturing, mining and agriculture are the principal industries. Exports include wool, diamonds, gold, and metallic ores.

The apartheid era ended April 27, 1994 with the first democratic election for all people of South Africa. Nelson Mandela was inaugurated President May 10, 1994, and South Africa was readmitted into the Commonwealth of Nations.

South African coins and currency bear inscriptions in tribal languages, Afrikaans and English.

MONETARY SYSTEM

100 Cents = 1 Rand

REPUBLIC

STANDARD COINAGE

KM# 221 CENT

1.5100 g., Copper Plated Steel, 14.9 mm. **Obv:** National arms **Obv. Designer:** A.L. Sutherland **Rev:** Two Cape Sparrows **Rev. Designer:** W. Lumley **Edge:** Plain

Date	Mintage	F	VF	XF	Unc	BU
2001	—	—	—	—	0.35	0.50

KM# 222 2 CENTS

3.0000 g., Copper Plated Steel, 17.9 mm. **Obv:** National arms **Rev:** African Fish Eagle catching fish **Edge:** Plain **Designer:** A.L. Sutherland

Date	Mintage	F	VF	XF	Unc	BU
2001	—	—	—	—	0.50	0.75

KM# 242 2-1/2 CENTS

1.4140 g., 0.9250 Silver 0.0421 oz. ASW, 16.3 mm. **Obv:** National arms **Rev:** Dolphin **Edge:** Reeded

Date	Mintage	F	VF	XF	Unc	BU
2001 Proof	—	Value: 25.00				

KM# 282 2-1/2 CENTS

1.4140 g., 0.9250 Silver 0.0421 oz. ASW, 16.3 mm. **Obv:** Protea flower **Rev:** Southern Right Whale **Edge:** Plain

Date	Mintage	F	VF	XF	Unc	BU
2002 Proof	3,000	Value: 25.00				

KM# 285 2-1/2 CENTS
1.4140 g., 0.9250 Silver 0.0421 oz. ASW, 16.3 mm. **Obv:** Protea flower **Rev:** Martial and Bateleur Eagles **Edge:** Plain

Date	Mintage	F	VF	XF	Unc	BU
2003 Proof	—	Value: 15.00				

KM# 283 2-1/2 CENTS
1.4140 g., 0.9250 Silver 0.0421 oz. ASW, 16.3 mm. **Obv:** Protea flower **Rev:** Spotted Owl **Edge:** Plain

Date	Mintage	F	VF	XF	Unc	BU
2004 Proof	2,000	Value: 20.00				

KM# 223 5 CENTS
4.4300 g., Copper Plated Steel, 21 mm. **Obv:** National arms **Obv. Designer:** A.L. Sutherland **Rev:** Crane standing on shore **Rev. Designer:** G. Richard **Edge:** Plain

Date	Mintage	F	VF	XF	Unc	BU
2001	—	—	—	—	0.50	1.00

KM# 243 5 CENTS
8.4560 g., 0.9250 Silver 0.2515 oz. ASW, 26.7 mm. **Obv:** Water buffalo head **Rev:** Two buffalo drinking water **Edge:** Reeded

Date	Mintage	F	VF	XF	Unc	BU
2001 Proof	—	Value: 20.00				

KM# 268 5 CENTS
4.5000 g., Copper Plated Steel, 21 mm. **Obv:** National arms **Obv. Designer:** A.L. Sutherland **Rev:** Blue Crane **Rev. Designer:** G. Richard **Edge:** Plain **Note:** Change in legend.

Date	Mintage	F	VF	XF	Unc	BU
2002	—	—	—	—	0.50	1.00
2002 Proof	—	Value: 2.00				

KM# 291 5 CENTS
4.4300 g., Copper-Plated-Steel, 21 mm. **Obv:** National arms, "Aforika Borwa" **Rev:** Crane and value **Edge:** Plain

Date	Mintage	F	VF	XF	Unc	BU
2005	—	—	—	—	—	0.50

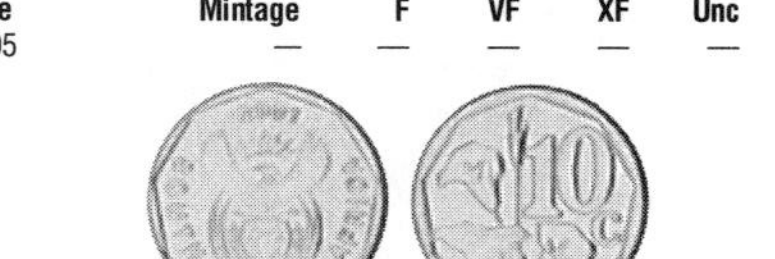

KM# 224 10 CENTS
2.0000 g., Brass Plated Steel, 15.9 mm. **Obv:** National arms **Obv. Designer:** A.L. Sutherland **Rev:** Arum Lily and denomination **Rev. Designer:** R.C. McFarlane **Edge:** Reeded

Date	Mintage	F	VF	XF	Unc	BU
2001	—	—	—	—	0.60	0.85

KM# 244 10 CENTS
16.8630 g., 0.9250 Silver 0.5015 oz. ASW, 32.7 mm. **Obv:** Water buffalo and country name **Rev:** Two water buffalo bulls facing off **Edge:** Reeded

Date	Mintage	F	VF	XF	Unc	BU
2001 Proof	—	Value: 25.00				

KM# 269 10 CENTS
2.0000 g., Copper Plated Steel, 16 mm. **Obv:** National arms; Tsonga legend **Obv. Legend:** AFRIKA DZONGA **Obv. Designer:** A.L. Sutherland **Rev:** Arum Lily **Rev. Designer:** R.C. McFarlane **Edge:** Reeded **Note:** Change in legend.

Date	Mintage	F	VF	XF	Unc	BU
2002	—	—	—	—	0.60	1.00
2002 Proof	—	Value: 3.00				

KM# 292 10 CENTS
2.0000 g., Brass Plated Steel, 16 mm. **Obv:** National arms **Obv. Legend:** Afrika Borwe **Rev:** Lily and value **Edge:** Reeded **Shape:** Round

Date	Mintage	F	VF	XF	Unc	BU
2005	—	—	—	—	—	0.60

KM# 225 20 CENTS
3.4500 g., Brass Plated Steel, 19 mm. **Obv:** National arms **Obv. Designer:** A.L. Sutherland **Rev:** S. Erasmus **Edge:** Reeded

Date	Mintage	F	VF	XF	Unc	BU
2001	—	—	—	—	0.75	1.00

KM# 245 20 CENTS
33.7260 g., 0.9250 Silver 1.003 oz. ASW, 38.3 mm. **Obv:** Water buffalo and country name **Rev:** Two water buffalo facing viewer **Edge:** Reeded

Date	Mintage	F	VF	XF	Unc	BU
2001 Proof	—	Value: 50.00				

KM# 270 20 CENTS
3.5000 g., Bronze Plated Steel, 19 mm. **Obv:** National arms **Obv. Designer:** A.L. Sutherland **Rev:** Protea flower **Rev. Designer:** S. Erasmus **Edge:** Reeded **Note:** Change in legend.

Date	Mintage	F	VF	XF	Unc	BU
2002	—	—	—	—	0.75	1.25
2002 Proof	—	Value: 4.00				

KM# 293 20 CENTS
3.4500 g., Brass Plated Steel, 19 mm. **Obv:** National arms **Obv. Legend:** Suid Afrika **Rev:** Protea flower and value **Edge:** Reeded **Shape:** Round

Date	Mintage	F	VF	XF	Unc	BU
2005	—	—	—	—	—	0.75

KM# 226 50 CENTS
4.9000 g., Brass Plated Steel, 22 mm. **Obv:** National arms **Obv. Designer:** A.L. Sutherland **Rev:** Grass-like plant and denomination **Rev. Designer:** C. Cogle **Edge:** Reeded

Date	Mintage	F	VF	XF	Unc	BU
2001	—	—	—	—	1.00	1.25

KM# 246 50 CENTS
76.4020 g., 0.9250 Silver 2.2722 oz. ASW, 50 mm. **Obv:** Water buffalo and country name **Rev:** Water buffalo head and denomination **Edge:** Reeded

Date	Mintage	F	VF	XF	Unc	BU
2001 Proof	—	Value: 80.00				

KM# 287 50 CENTS
4.9200 g., Brass Plated Steel **Obv:** National arms **Rev:** Soccer player

Date	Mintage	F	VF	XF	Unc	BU
2002	—	—	—	—	2.25	2.50

KM# 271 50 CENTS
5.0000 g., Bronze Plated Steel, 22 mm. **Obv:** National arms **Obv. Designer:** A.L. Sutherland **Rev:** Strelitzia plant **Rev. Designer:** C. Cogle **Edge:** Reeded **Note:** Change in legend.

Date	Mintage	F	VF	XF	Unc	BU
2002	—	—	—	—	1.00	1.50
2002 Proof	—	Value: 5.00				

KM# 276 50 CENTS
4.9200 g., Brass Plated Steel, 21.9 mm. **Obv:** National arms **Obv. Designer:** A.L. Sutherland **Rev:** Cricket player diving towards the wicket **Edge:** Reeded

Date	Mintage	F	VF	XF	Unc	BU
2003	—	—	—	—	2.25	2.50

KM# 294 50 CENTS

4.9000 g., Brass Plated Steel, 22 mm. **Obv:** National arms **Obv. Legend:** uMzantsi Afrika **Rev:** Plant and value **Edge:** Reeded **Shape:** Round

Date	Mintage	F	VF	XF	Unc	BU
2005	—	—	—	—	—	1.00

KM# 227 RAND

4.0000 g., Nickel Plated Steel, 20 mm. **Obv:** National arms **Obv. Designer:** A.L. Sutherland **Rev:** Springbok and denomination **Rev. Designer:** L. Lotriet **Edge:** Reeded and plain sections

Date	Mintage	F	VF	XF	Unc	BU
2001	—	—	—	—	1.75	2.75

KM# 231 RAND

15.0000 g., 0.9250 Silver 0.4461 oz. ASW, 32.7 mm. **Subject:** Tourism **Obv:** Protea flower **Rev:** Steam locomotive and flower **Edge:** Reeded

Date	Mintage	F	VF	XF	Unc	BU
2001 Proof	3,000	Value: 30.00				

KM# 247 RAND

3.1103 g., 0.9999 Gold 0.1 oz. AGW, 16.5 mm. **Obv:** National arms **Obv. Designer:** A.L. Sutherland **Rev:** Sotho "healer" **Edge:** Reeded

Date	Mintage	F	VF	XF	Unc	BU
2001 Proof	—	Value: 110				

KM# 272 RAND

4.0000 g., Nickel Plated Copper, 20 mm. **Obv:** National arms **Obv. Designer:** A.L. Sutherland **Rev:** Springbok **Rev. Designer:** L. Lotriet **Edge:** Reeded **Note:** Change in legend.

Date	Mintage	F	VF	XF	Unc	BU
2002	—	—	—	—	1.75	2.50
2002 Proof	—	Value: 6.00				

KM# 275 RAND

3.9700 g., Nickel-Plated Steel, 19.9 mm. **Subject:** Johannesburg World Summit on Sustainable Development **Obv:** National arms **Obv. Designer:** A.L. Sutherland **Rev:** World globe and logo **Edge:** Reeded and plain sections

Date	Mintage	F	VF	XF	Unc	BU
2002	—	—	—	—	3.00	4.00

KM# 277 RAND

15.0000 g., 0.9250 Silver 0.4461 oz. ASW, 32.7 mm. **Subject:** Soccer **Obv:** Protea flower **Obv. Designer:** A.L. Sutherland **Rev:** Goalkeeper in action **Edge:** Reeded

Date	Mintage	F	VF	XF	Unc	BU
2002	—	—	—	—	30.00	32.50

KM# 298 RAND

15.0500 g., 0.9250 Silver 0.4476 oz. ASW, 32.8 mm. **Obv:** Protea flower **Rev:** Cricket player **Edge:** Reeded

Date	Mintage	F	VF	XF	Unc	BU
2003	—	—	—	—	—	30.00

KM# 288 RAND

15.0000 g., 0.9250 Silver 0.4461 oz. ASW, 32.7 mm. **Subject:** 10th Anniversary of South African Democracy **Obv:** Protea flower **Rev:** Flora and fawna **Edge:** Reeded

Date	Mintage	F	VF	XF	Unc	BU
2004 Proof	6,000	Value: 25.00				

KM# 295 RAND

4.0000 g., Nickel Plated Steel, 20 mm. **Obv:** National arms **Obv. Legend:** ISewula Afrika iNingizimu Afrika **Rev:** Springbok and value **Edge:** Segmented reeding **Shape:** Round

Date	Mintage	F	VF	XF	Unc	BU
2005	—	—	—	—	—	1.75

KM# 228 2 RAND

5.4300 g., Nickel Plated Steel, 23 mm. **Obv:** National arms; Xhosha legend **Obv. Legend:** UMZANSTI AFRIKA **Rev:** Greater Kudu and denomination **Edge:** Reeded and plain sections **Designer:** A.L. Sutherland

Date	Mintage	F	VF	XF	Unc	BU
2001	—	—	—	—	2.00	3.00

KM# 248 2 RAND

33.6260 g., 0.9250 Silver 1 oz. ASW, 38.7 mm. **Obv:** National arms **Rev:** Dolphins **Edge:** Reeded

Date	Mintage	F	VF	XF	Unc	BU
2001 Proof	—	Value: 50.00				

KM# 249 2 RAND

7.7770 g., 0.9999 Gold 0.25 oz. AGW, 22 mm. **Obv:** National arms **Obv. Designer:** A.L. Sutherland **Rev:** Gondwana theoretical landmass and dinosaur **Edge:** Reeded

Date	Mintage	F	VF	XF	Unc	BU
2001 Proof	—	Value: 195				

KM# 280 2 RAND

33.8000 g., 0.9250 Silver 1.0052 oz. ASW, 38.7 mm. **Obv:** National arms and country name in eight languages **Rev:** Southern Right Whale **Edge:** Reeded

Date	Mintage	F	VF	XF	Unc	BU
2002 Proof	3,000	Value: 40.00				

KM# 273 2 RAND

5.5000 g., Nickel Plated Copper, 23 mm. **Obv:** National arms **Rev:** Kudu **Edge:** Reeded and plain sections **Designer:** A.L. Sutherland **Note:** Change in legend.

Date	Mintage	F	VF	XF	Unc	BU
2002	—	—	—	—	2.00	3.50
2002 Proof	—	Value: 8.00				
2003	—	—	—	—	2.00	3.50

KM# 286 2 RAND

33.7300 g., 0.9250 Silver 1.0031 oz. ASW, 38.7 mm. **Obv:** National arms and country name in ten languages **Rev:** Martial and Bateleur Eagles **Edge:** Reeded

Date	Mintage	F	VF	XF	Unc	BU
2003 Proof	—	Value: 45.00				

KM# 284 2 RAND

33.6260 g., 0.9250 Silver 1 oz. ASW, 38.7 mm. **Obv:** National arms and country name in ten languages **Rev:** Owl face and value **Edge:** Reeded

Date	Mintage	F	VF	XF	Unc	BU
2004 Proof	3,000	Value: 45.00				

KM# 296 2 RAND

5.4300 g., Nickel Plated Steel, 23 mm. **Obv:** National arms **Obv. Legend:** Ningizimu Afrika Afurika Tshipembe **Rev:** Greater Kudu and value **Edge:** Segmented reeding **Shape:** Round

Date	Mintage	F	VF	XF	Unc	BU
2005	—	—	—	—	—	2.00

KM# 229 5 RAND
6.9400 g., Nickel Plated Steel, 26 mm. **Obv:** National arms; Zulu legend **Obv. Legend:** ININGIZIMU AFRIKA **Rev:** Black Wildebeest and denomination **Edge:** Reeded and plain sections **Designer:** A.L. Sutherland

Date	Mintage	F	VF	XF	Unc	BU
2001	—	—	—	—	4.50	5.50

KM# 274 5 RAND
7.0000 g., Nickel Plated Copper, 26 mm. **Obv:** National arms; Venda legend left, Ndebele legend right **Obv. Legend:** AFURIKA TSHIPEMBE - ISEWULA AFRIKA **Rev:** Black Wildebeest **Edge:** Reeded and plain sections **Designer:** A.L. Sutherland **Note:** Change in legend.

Date	Mintage	F	VF	XF	Unc	BU
2002	—	—	—	—	4.50	6.00
2002 Proof	—	Value: 10.00				

KM# 278 5 RAND
3.1104 g., 0.9999 Gold 0.1 oz. AGW, 16.5 mm. **Obv:** Protea flower **Rev:** Soccer player heading the ball **Edge:** Reeded

Date	Mintage	F	VF	XF	Unc	BU
2002	—	—	—	—	110	120

KM# 281 5 RAND
9.5400 g., Bi-Metallic Brass center in Copper-Nickel ring, 26 mm. **Obv:** National arms; Tsonga legend left, Zulu legend right **Obv. Legend:** AFRIKA DZONGA - NINGIZIMU AFRIKA **Rev:** Black Wildebeest and value **Edge:** Security type with lettering **Edge Lettering:** "SARB R5" repeated ten times

Date	Mintage	F	VF	XF	Unc	BU
2004	—	—	—	—	5.00	6.50

KM# 289 5 RAND
3.1100 g., 0.9999 Gold 0.1 oz. AGW, 16.5 mm. **Subject:** 10th Anniversary of South African Democracy **Obv:** Protea flower **Rev:** Inscription covered flag **Edge:** Reeded

Date	Mintage	F	VF	XF	Unc	BU
2004 Proof	1,000	Value: 100				

KM# 297 5 RAND
9.5400 g., Bi-Metallic Brass center in Copper-Nickel ring, 26 mm. **Obv:** National arms **Obv. Legend:** Afrika Dzonga South Africa **Rev:** Wildebeest and value **Edge:** Security type with lettering **Edge Lettering:** "SARB R5" repeated ten times

Date	Mintage	F	VF	XF	Unc	BU
2005	—	—	—	—	—	5.00

KM# 279 25 RAND
31.1035 g., 0.9999 Gold 0.9999 oz. AGW, 32.7 mm. **Obv:** Protea flower **Rev:** Soccer player kicking ball **Edge:** Reeded

Date	Mintage	F	VF	XF	Unc	BU
2002	—	—	—	—	650	—

KM# 290 25 RAND
31.1035 g., 0.9999 Gold 0.9999 oz. AGW, 32.7 mm. **Subject:** 10th Anniversary of South African Democracy **Obv:** Protea flower **Rev:** Two images of Nelson Mandela **Edge:** Reeded

Date	Mintage	F	VF	XF	Unc	BU
2004 Proof	5,000	Value: 650				

BULLION COINAGE

Mint mark: GRC - Gold Reef City

KM# 262 1/10 PROTEA
3.1103 g., 0.9999 Gold 0.1 oz. AGW, 16.5 mm. **Obv:** Protea flower **Rev:** Lion and partial shield **Edge:** Reeded

Date	Mintage	F	VF	XF	Unc	BU
2001 Proof	—	Value: 110				

KM# 263 PROTEA
31.1035 g., 0.9999 Gold 0.9999 oz. AGW, 32.7 mm. **Obv:** Protea flower **Rev:** Child on sandy beach and partial sun **Edge:** Reeded

Date	Mintage	F	VF	XF	Unc	BU
2001 Proof	—	Value: 675				

NATURA GOLD BULLION COINAGE

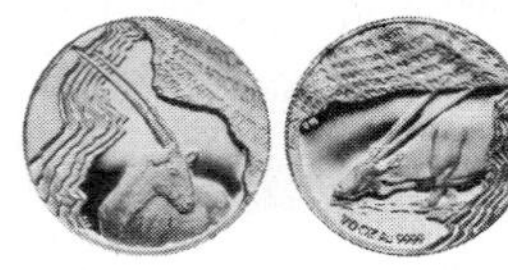

KM# 264 1/10 OUNCE
3.1103 g., 0.9999 Gold 0.1 oz. AGW, 16.5 mm. **Obv:** Gemsbok head **Rev:** Gemsbok drinking **Edge:** Reeded

Date	Mintage	F	VF	XF	Unc	BU
2001 Proof	—	Value: 110				

KM# 265 1/4 OUNCE
7.7770 g., 0.9999 Gold 0.25 oz. AGW, 22 mm. **Obv:** Gemsbok head **Rev:** Two Gemsbok males facing off **Edge:** Reeded

Date	Mintage	F	VF	XF	Unc	BU
2001 Proof	—	Value: 195				

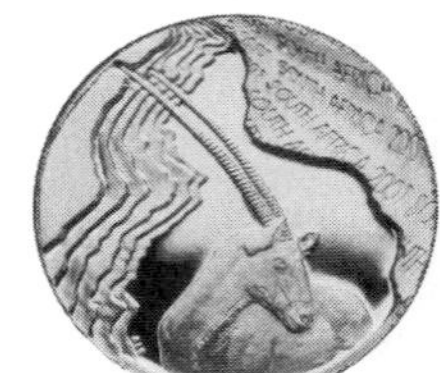

KM# 266 1/2 OUNCE
15.5518 g., 0.9990 Gold 0.4995 oz. AGW, 27 mm. **Obv:** Gemsbok head **Rev:** Gemsbok grazing **Edge:** Reeded

Date	Mintage	F	VF	XF	Unc	BU
2001 Proof	—	Value: 320				

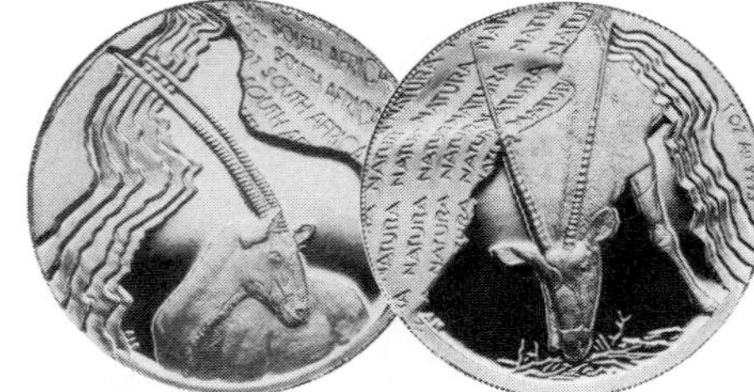

KM# 267 OUNCE
31.1035 g., 0.9990 Gold 0.999 oz. AGW, 32.7 mm. **Obv:** Gemsbok head **Rev:** Gemsbok grazing **Edge:** Reeded

Date	Mintage	F	VF	XF	Unc	BU
2001 Proof	—	Value: 650				

MINT SETS

KM#	Date	Mintage	Identification	Issue Price	Mkt Val
MS38	2002 (7)	—	KM#268-274 plus 1- and 2-cent medals	30.00	32.50

PROOF SETS

KM#	Date	Mintage	Identification	Issue Price	Mkt Val
PS170	2002 (7)	—	KM#268-274 plus 1- and 2-cent medals	40.00	42.50

S. GEORGIA & THE S. SANDWICH IS.

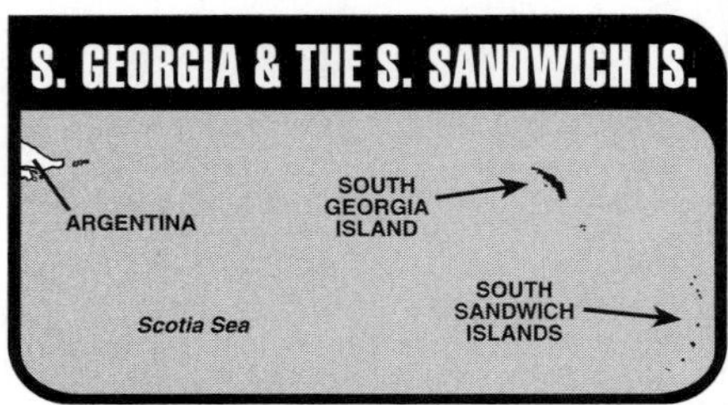

South Georgia and the South Sandwich Islands are a dependency of the Falkland Islands, and located about 800 miles east of them. South Georgia is 1,450 sq. mi. (1,770 sq. km.), South Sandwich Islands is 120 sq. mi. (311 sq. km.) Fishing and Antarctic research are the main industries. The islands were claimed for Great Britain in 1775 by Captain James Cook.

RULERS
British since 1775

BRITISH ADMINISTRATION

STANDARD COINAGE

KM# 7 2 POUNDS
28.2800 g., Copper-Nickel, 38.6 mm. **Subject:** Sir Ernest H. Shackleton **Obv:** Queen's portrait **Rev:** Portrait and ship "Endurance" **Edge:** Reeded

Date	Mintage	F	VF	XF	Unc	BU
2001	—	—	—	—	10.00	12.00

KM# 7a 2 POUNDS
28.2800 g., 0.9250 Silver .8410 oz. ASW

Date	Mintage	F	VF	XF	Unc	BU
2001 Proof	Est. 10,000	Value: 50.00				

KM# 9 2 POUNDS
Copper-Nickel **Subject:** Sir Joseph Banks **Obv:** Queen's portrait **Rev:** Cameo portrait and ship

Date	Mintage	F	VF	XF	Unc	BU
2001	—	—	—	—	10.00	12.00

KM# 9a 2 POUNDS
28.2800 g., 0.9250 Silver .8410 oz. ASW

Date	Mintage	F	VF	XF	Unc	BU
2001 Proof	Est. 10,000	Value: 50.00				

KM# 11 2 POUNDS
28.2800 g., Copper-Nickel, 38.6 mm. **Subject:** Queen Elizabeth II's Golden Jubilee **Obv:** Bust of Queen Elizabeth II right **Rev:** Young crowned portrait. **Edge:** Reeded

Date	Mintage	F	VF	XF	Unc	BU
2002	—	—	—	—	10.00	12.00

KM# 11a 2 POUNDS
28.2800 g., 0.9250 Gold Clad Silver 0.841 oz., 38.6 mm. **Subject:** Queen Elizabeth II's Golden Jubilee **Obv:** Bust of Queen Elizabeth II right **Rev:** Young crowned portrait **Edge:** Reeded

Date	Mintage	F	VF	XF	Unc	BU
2002 Proof	10,000	Value: 50.00				

KM# 13 2 POUNDS
28.2800 g., Copper-Nickel, 38.6 mm. **Subject:** Queen Elizabeth II's Golden Jubilee **Obv:** Bust of Queen Elizabeth II right **Rev:** National arms **Edge:** Reeded

Date	Mintage	F	VF	XF	Unc	BU
2002	—	—	—	—	10.00	12.00

KM# 13a 2 POUNDS
28.2800 g., 0.9250 Gold Clad Silver 0.841 oz., 38.6 mm. **Subject:** Queen Elizabeth II's Golden Jubilee **Obv:** Bust of Queen Elizabeth II right **Rev:** National arms **Edge:** Reeded

Date	Mintage	F	VF	XF	Unc	BU
2002 Proof	10,000	Value: 50.00				

KM# 15 2 POUNDS
28.2800 g., Copper-Nickel, 38.6 mm. **Subject:** Diana, Princess of Wales - The Work Continues **Obv:** Crowned bust of Queen Elizabeth II right **Obv. Designer:** Ian Rank-Broadley **Rev:** Head of Diana half left **Edge:** Reeded

Date	Mintage	VG	F	VF	XF	Unc
2002	—	—	—	—	8.50	10.00

KM# 18 2 POUNDS
28.2800 g., Copper-Nickel, 38.6 mm. **Obv:** Queen Elizabeth II **Rev:** Capt. Cook, ship and map **Edge:** Reeded

Date	Mintage	F	VF	XF	Unc	BU
2003PM	—	—	—	—	10.00	12.00

KM# 18a 2 POUNDS
28.2800 g., 0.9250 Silver 0.841 oz. ASW, 38.6 mm. **Obv:** Queen Elizabeth II **Rev:** Capt. Cook, ship and map **Edge:** Reeded

Date	Mintage	F	VF	XF	Unc	BU
2003PM Proof	—	Value: 47.50				

KM# 17 2 POUNDS
28.2800 g., Copper-Nickel, 38.6 mm. **Subject:** Prince William's 21st Birthday **Obv:** Queen's portrait **Rev:** Crowned arms of the Crown Prince's first son **Edge:** Reeded

Date	Mintage	F	VF	XF	Unc	BU
2003PM	—	—	—	—	10.00	12.00

KM# 17a 2 POUNDS
28.2800 g., 0.9250 Silver 0.841 oz. ASW, 38.6 mm. **Subject:** Prince William's 21st Birthday **Obv:** Queen's portrait **Rev:** Crowned arms of the Crowned Prince's first son **Edge:** Reeded

Date	Mintage	F	VF	XF	Unc	BU
2003PM Proof	—	Value: 50.00				

KM# 20 2 POUNDS
28.2800 g., Copper-Nickel, 38.6 mm. **Obv:** Elizabeth II **Rev:** Sir Ernest Shackleton and icebound ship **Edge:** Reeded

Date	Mintage	F	VF	XF	Unc	BU
2004	—	—	—	—	15.00	16.50

KM# 20a 2 POUNDS
28.2800 g., 0.9250 Silver 0.841 oz. ASW, 38.6 mm. **Obv:** Elizabeth II **Rev:** Sir Ernest Shackleton and icebound ship **Edge:** Reeded

Date	Mintage	F	VF	XF	Unc	BU
2004 Proof	10,000	Value: 50.00				

KM# 21 2 POUNDS
28.2800 g., Copper-Nickel, 38.6 mm. **Subject:** Centennial of Grytviken **Obv:** Elizabeth II **Rev:** Portrait above ship in harbor **Edge:** Reeded

Date	Mintage	F	VF	XF	Unc	BU
2004	—	—	—	—	15.00	16.50

KM# 21a 2 POUNDS
28.2800 g., 0.9250 Silver 0.841 oz. ASW, 38.6 mm. **Subject:** Centennial of Grytviken **Obv:** Elizabeth II **Rev:** Portrait above ship in harbor **Edge:** Reeded

Date	Mintage	F	VF	XF	Unc	BU
2004 Proof	—	Value: 50.00				

KM# 19 10 POUNDS
155.5100 g., 0.9990 Silver 4.9948 oz. ASW, 65 mm. **Obv:** Queen Elizabeth II **Rev:** Capt. Cook, ship and map **Edge:** Reeded

Date	Mintage	F	VF	XF	Unc	BU
2003PM Proof	2,003	Value: 175				

KM# 8 20 POUNDS
6.2200 g., 0.9999 Gold .2000 oz. AGW, 22 mm. **Obv:** Queen's portrait **Rev:** Sir Ernest H. Shackleton and ship **Edge:** Reeded

Date	Mintage	F	VF	XF	Unc	BU
2001 Proof	Est. 2,000	Value: 175				

KM# 10 20 POUNDS
6.2200 g., 0.9999 Gold .2000 oz. AGW **Obv:** Queen's portrait **Rev:** Sir Joseph Banks cameo and ship

Date	Mintage	F	VF	XF	Unc	BU
2001 Proof	Est. 2,000	Value: 175				

KM# 16 20 POUNDS
6.2200 g., 0.9999 Gold 0.2 oz. AGW, 22 mm. **Subject:** Princess Diana **Obv:** Queen's portrait **Rev:** Diana's portrait **Edge:** reeded

Date	Mintage	F	VF	XF	Unc	BU
2002PM Proof	—	Value: 175				

KM# 12 20 POUNDS
6.2200 g., 0.9990 Gold 0.1998 oz. AGW, 22 mm. **Subject:** Queen Elizabeth II's Golden Jubilee **Obv:** Bust of Queen Elizabeth II right **Rev:** Young crowned portrait of the Queen **Edge:** Reeded

Date	Mintage	F	VF	XF	Unc	BU
2002 Proof	2,002	Value: 175				

KM# 14 20 POUNDS
6.2200 g., 0.9990 Gold 0.1998 oz. AGW, 22 mm. **Subject:** Queen Elizabeth II's Golden Jubilee **Obv:** Bust of Queen Elizabeth II right **Rev:** National arms **Edge:** Reeded

Date	Mintage	F	VF	XF	Unc	BU
2002 Proof	2,002	Value: 175				

The Spanish State, forming the greater part of the Iberian Peninsula of southwest Europe, has an area of 195,988 sq. mi. (504,714 sq. km.) and a population of 39.4 million including the Balearic and the Canary Islands. Capital: Madrid. The economy is based on agriculture, industry and tourism. Machinery, fruit, vegetables and chemicals are exported.

RULERS
Juan Carlos I, 1975-

MINT MARKS.
Crowned M – Madrid

KINGDOM
1949 - Present

DECIMAL COINAGE
Peseta System

100 Centimos = 1 Peseta

KM# 832 PESETA
Aluminum **Edge:** Plain

Date	Mintage	F	VF	XF	Unc	BU
2001	—	—	—	0.10	0.30	0.50

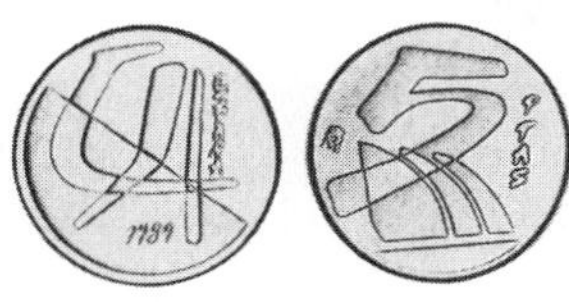

KM# 833 5 PESETAS
Aluminum-Bronze **Edge:** Plain

Date	Mintage	F	VF	XF	Unc	BU
2001	—	—	—	0.10	0.25	0.35

KM# 1013 25 PESETAS
Nickel-Brass, 19.5 mm. **Subject:** Navarra **Obv:** King's portrait **Rev:** Crown, denomination and order **Edge:** Plain

Date	Mintage	F	VF	XF	Unc	BU
2001	—	—	—	—	2.00	3.00

KM# 1016 100 PESETAS
9.8000 g., Aluminum-Bronze, 24.4 mm. **Ruler:** Juan Carlos I **Subject:** 132nd Anniversary of the Peseta **Obv:** Head of King Juan Carlos I left **Rev:** Seated allegorical figure from an old coin design **Edge:** Ornamented

Date	Mintage	F	VF	XF	Unc	BU
2001	—	—	—	—	1.50	2.00

KM# 924 500 PESETAS
Copper-Aluminum-Nickel **Obv:** Conjoined busts of King Juan Carlos I and Sofia facing left

Date	Mintage	F	VF	XF	Unc	BU
2001	—	—	—	—	6.00	8.00

KM# 1038 2000 PESETAS
27.0000 g., 0.9250 Silver 0.803 oz. ASW, 40 mm. **Ruler:** Juan Carlos I **Subject:** Segovia Mint's 500th Anniversary **Obv:** Hammer coining scene **Rev:** Segovia Mint 8 reales coin design of 1588 **Edge:** Reeded

Date	Mintage	F	VF	XF	Unc	BU
2001Crowned M Proof	15,000	Value: 55.00				

KM# 1017 2000 PESETAS
18.0000 g., 0.9250 Silver .5353 oz. ASW, 32.9 mm. **Subject:** 132nd Anniversary of the Peseta **Obv:** Portraits of King and Queen **Rev:** Seated allegorical design from the 1869 Spanish coin series **Edge:** Plain

Date	Mintage	F	VF	XF	Unc	BU
2001	—	—	—	—	18.00	23.00

EURO COINAGE

European Economic Community Issues

KM# 1040 EURO CENT
2.2700 g., Copper Plated Steel, 16.2 mm. **Obv:** Cathedral of Santiago de Compostela **Obv. Designer:** Garcilano Rollan **Rev:** Denomination and globe **Rev. Designer:** Luc Luycx **Edge:** Plain

Date	Mintage	F	VF	XF	Unc	BU
2001	79,541,000	—	—	—	1.00	1.25
2002	112,000,000	—	—	—	0.60	0.75
2003	200,000,000	—	—	—	0.50	0.65
2004Crowned M	—	—	—	—	0.50	0.65
2005Crowned M	—	—	—	—	0.50	0.65

KM# 1041 2 EURO CENTS
3.0300 g., Copper Plated Steel, 18.7 mm. **Obv:** Cathedral of Santiago de Compostela **Obv. Designer:** Garcilano Rollan **Rev:** Denomination and globe **Rev. Designer:** Luc Luycx **Edge:** Grooved

Date	Mintage	F	VF	XF	Unc	BU
2001	417,701,000	—	—	—	0.45	0.60
2002	192,000,000	—	—	—	2.00	2.50
2003	400,000,000	—	—	—	0.50	0.65
2004Crowned M	—	—	—	—	0.50	0.65
2005Crowned M	—	—	—	—	0.50	0.65

KM# 1042 5 EURO CENTS
3.8600 g., Copper Plated Steel, 21.2 mm. **Obv:** Cathedral of Santiago de Compostela **Obv. Designer:** Garcilano Rollan **Rev:** Denomination and globe **Rev. Designer:** Luc Luycx **Edge:** Plain

Date	Mintage	F	VF	XF	Unc	BU
2001	233,820,500	—	—	—	0.65	0.75
2002	147,000,000	—	—	—	1.50	2.00
2003	400,000,000	—	—	—	0.65	0.75
2004Crowned M	—	—	—	—	0.65	0.75
2005Crowned M	—	—	—	—	0.65	0.75

KM# 1043 10 EURO CENTS
4.0700 g., Brass, 19.7 mm. **Obv:** Cervantes **Rev:** Denomination and map **Edge:** Reeded

Date	Mintage	F	VF	XF	Unc	BU
2001	116,468,000	—	—	—	0.75	1.00
2002	125,000,000	—	—	—	0.75	1.00
2003	150,000,000	—	—	—	0.75	1.00
2004Crowned M	—	—	—	—	0.75	1.00
2005Crowned M	—	—	—	—	0.75	1.00

KM# 1044 20 EURO CENTS
5.7300 g., Brass, 22.1 mm. **Obv:** Cervantes **Obv. Designer:** Begoña Castellanos **Rev:** Denomination and map **Rev. Designer:** Luc Luycx **Edge:** Notched

Date	Mintage	F	VF	XF	Unc	BU
2001	108,525,000	—	—	—	1.25	1.50
2002	124,000,000	—	—	—	1.25	1.50
2003	400,000,000	—	—	—	1.00	1.25
2004Crowned M	—	—	—	—	1.00	1.25
2005Crowned M	—	—	—	—	1.00	1.25

KM# 1045 50 EURO CENTS
7.8100 g., Brass, 24.2 mm. **Obv:** Cervantes **Obv. Designer:** Begoña Castellanos **Rev:** Denomination and map **Rev. Designer:** Luc Luycx **Edge:** Reeded

Date	Mintage	F	VF	XF	Unc	BU
2001	343,882,500	—	—	—	1.25	1.50
2002	171,000,000	—	—	—	3.50	5.00
2003	400,000,000	—	—	—	1.25	1.50
2004Crowned M	—	—	—	—	1.25	1.50
2005Crowned M	—	—	—	—	1.25	1.50

KM# 1046 EURO
7.5000 g., Bi-Metallic Copper-Nickel center in Brass ring, 23.2 mm. **Obv:** King's portrait **Obv. Designer:** Luiz Jose Diaz **Rev:** Denomination and map **Rev. Designer:** Luc Luycx **Edge:** Reeded and plain sections

Date	Mintage	F	VF	XF	Unc	BU
2001	284,551,500	—	—	—	3.00	3.50
2002	65,000,000	—	—	—	4.50	5.00
2003	350,000,000	—	—	—	3.00	3.50
2004Crowned M	—	—	—	—	3.00	3.50
2005Crowned M	—	—	—	—	3.00	3.50

KM# 1047 2 EUROS
8.5200 g., Bi-Metallic Brass center in Copper-Nickel ring, 25.7 mm. **Obv:** King's portrait **Obv. Designer:** Luis Jose Diaz **Rev:** Denomination and stars **Rev. Designer:** Luc Luycx **Edge:** Reeded **Edge Lettering:** 2's and stars

Date	Mintage	F	VF	XF	Unc	BU
2001	133,623,500	—	—	—	4.75	5.00
2002	65,000,000	—	—	—	5.00	6.00
2003	150,000,000	—	—	—	4.75	5.00
2004Crowned M	—	—	—	—	4.75	5.00
2005Crowned M	—	—	—	—	4.75	5.00

KM# 1063 2 EUROS
8.5200 g., Bi-Metallic Brass center in Copper-Nickel ring, 25.7 mm. **Ruler:** Juan Carlos I **Obv:** Don Juan caricature **Rev:** Value and map **Edge:** Reeding over stars and 2's **Note:** Mint mark: Crowned M.

Date	Mintage	F	VF	XF	Unc	BU
2005	—	—	—	—	5.00	6.00

KM# 1048 10 EURO
27.0000 g., 0.9250 Silver 0.803 oz. ASW, 40 mm. **Ruler:** Juan Carlos I **Subject:** Spanish Presidency of the European Union **Obv:** Head of King Juan Carlos I left **Rev:** Map of Europe **Edge:** Reeded

Date	Mintage	F	VF	XF	Unc	BU
2002 Proof	30,000	Value: 50.00				

KM# 1050 10 EURO
27.0000 g., 0.9250 Silver 0.803 oz. ASW, 40 mm. **Ruler:** Juan Carlos I **Subject:** Annexation of Minorca **Obv:** Portraits of king and queen **Rev:** Annexation scene **Edge:** Reeded **Note:** Mint mark: Crowned M.

Date	Mintage	F	VF	XF	Unc	BU
2002 Proof	30,000	Value: 50.00				

KM# 1052 10 EURO

27.0000 g., 0.9250 Silver 0.803 oz. ASW, 40 mm.
Ruler: Juan Carlos I **Obv:** Juan Carlos I **Rev:** School Ship "Elcano" **Edge:** Reeded

Date	Mintage	F	VF	XF	Unc	BU
2003Crowned M Proof	50,000	Value: 50.00				

KM# 1053 10 EURO

27.0000 g., 0.9250 Silver 0.803 oz. ASW, 40 mm.
Ruler: Juan Carlos I **Obv:** Juan Carlos I **Rev:** Miguel Lopez de Legazpi **Edge:** Reeded

Date	Mintage	F	VF	XF	Unc	BU
2003Crowned M Proof	25,000	Value: 50.00				

KM# 1054 10 EURO

27.0000 g., 0.9250 Silver 0.803 oz. ASW, 40 mm.
Ruler: Juan Carlos I **Obv:** Salvador Dali **Rev:** Leda and the Swan **Edge:** Reeded

Date	Mintage	F	VF	XF	Unc	BU
2003Crowned M Proof	25,000	Value: 50.00				

KM# 1055 10 EURO

27.0000 g., 0.9250 Silver 0.803 oz. ASW, 40 mm.
Ruler: Juan Carlos I **Obv:** Salvador Dali **Rev:** Dali's painting "El gran masturbador" of 1929 **Edge:** Reeded

Date	Mintage	F	VF	XF	Unc	BU
2004Crowned M Proof	25,000	Value: 50.00				

KM# 1056 10 EURO

27.0000 g., 0.9250 Silver 0.803 oz. ASW, 40 mm.
Ruler: Juan Carlos I **Obv:** Salvador Dali **Rev:** Dali's self portrait with bacon strip **Edge:** Reeded

Date	Mintage	F	VF	XF	Unc	BU
2004Crowned M Proof	25,000	Value: 50.00				

KM# 1059 10 EURO

27.0000 g., 0.9250 Silver 0.803 oz. ASW, 40 mm.
Ruler: Juan Carlos I **Obv:** King and Queen left **Rev:** St. James and value **Edge:** Reeded

Date	Mintage	F	VF	XF	Unc	BU
2004Crowned M Proof	20,000	Value: 50.00				

KM# 1060 10 EURO

27.0000 g., 0.9250 Silver 0.803 oz. ASW, 40 mm. **Ruler:** Juan Carlos I **Obv:** King and Queen left **Rev:** Isabel I the Catholic (1451-1504) **Edge:** Reeded

Date	Mintage	F	VF	XF	Unc	BU
2004Crowned M Proof	20,000	Value: 50.00				

KM# 1064 10 EURO

27.0000 g., 0.9250 Silver 0.803 oz. ASW, 40 mm. **Ruler:** Juan Carlos I **Subject:** 2006 Winter Olympics **Obv:** Juan Carlos **Rev:** Skier **Edge:** Reeded

Date	Mintage	F	VF	XF	Unc	BU
2005Crowned M Proof	25,000	Value: 45.00				

KM# 1065 10 EURO

27.0000 g., 0.9250 Silver 0.803 oz. ASW, 40 mm. **Ruler:** Juan Carlos I **Subject:** European Peace and Freedom **Obv:** Juan Carlos **Rev:** European map on clasped hands **Edge:** Reeded

Date	Mintage	F	VF	XF	Unc	BU
2005Crowned M Proof	40,000	Value: 40.00				

KM# 1049 12 EURO

18.0000 g., 0.9250 Silver 0.5353 oz. ASW, 33 mm.
Ruler: Juan Carlos I **Subject:** Spanish European Union Presidency **Obv:** Conjoined busts of Juan Carlos I and Queen Sofia left **Rev:** Distorted star design **Edge:** Reeded

Date	Mintage	F	VF	XF	Unc	BU
2002Crowned M	1,500,000	—	—	—	20.00	22.50
2002Crowned M Special select	25,000	—	—	—	—	30.00
2002Crowned M Proof	50,000	Value: 50.00				

KM# 1051 12 EURO

18.0000 g., 0.9250 Silver 0.5353 oz. ASW, 33 mm.
Ruler: Juan Carlos I **Subject:** 25th Anniversary of Constitution **Obv:** Jugate portraits of the king and queen **Rev:** National arms above denomination **Edge:** Plain

Date	Mintage	F	VF	XF	Unc	BU
2003Crowned M	1,469,000	—	—	—	25.00	27.50

KM# 1067 12 EURO

18.0000 g., 0.9250 Silver 0.5353 oz. ASW, 33 mm. **Ruler:** Juan Carlos I **Subject:** Don Quixote **Obv:** Juan Carlos and Sofia **Rev:** Man seated on books **Edge:** Reeded

Date	Mintage	F	VF	XF	Unc	BU
2005Crowned M	4,000,000	—	—	—	22.50	25.00

KM# 1057 50 EURO

168.7500 g., 0.9250 Silver with removeable gold plated silver insert 5.0185 oz. ASW, 73 mm. **Ruler:** Juan Carlos I **Obv:** Dali's "Dream State' painting **Rev:** Dali's "Rhinocerotic Disintegration..." painting **Edge:** Reeded **Note:** Illustration reduced.

Date	Mintage	F	VF	XF	Unc	BU
2004Crowned M Proof	12,000	Value: 175				

KM# 1061 50 EURO
168.7300 g., 0.9250 Silver 5.0179 oz. ASW, 73 mm.
Ruler: Juan Carlos I **Obv:** Isabella I (1451-1504) and castle **Rev:** Surrender of Grenada scene **Edge:** Reeded
Note: Illustration reduced.

Date	Mintage	F	VF	XF	Unc	BU
2004Crowned M Proof	8,000	Value: 180				

KM# 1062 200 EURO
13.5000 g., 0.9990 Gold 0.4336 oz. AGW, 30 mm. **Ruler:** Juan Carlos I **Obv:** Ferdinand and Isabella on shield **Rev:** Ferdinand and Isabella facing portraits coin design **Edge:** Reeded

Date	Mintage	F	VF	XF	Unc	BU
2004Crowned M Proof	5,000	Value: 540				

KM# 1066 200 EURO
13.5000 g., 0.9990 Gold 0.4336 oz. AGW, 30 mm. **Ruler:** Juan Carlos I **Subject:** European Peace and Freedom **Obv:** Juan Carlos **Rev:** European map on clasped hands **Edge:** Reeded

Date	Mintage	F	VF	XF	Unc	BU
2005Crowned M Proof	4,000	Value: 650				

KM# 1058 400 EURO
27.0000 g., 0.9990 Gold 0.8672 oz. AGW, 38 mm.
Ruler: Juan Carlos I **Obv:** Salvador Dali **Rev:** Dali's painting "Girl at the Window" **Edge:** Reeded

Date	Mintage	F	VF	XF	Unc	BU
2004Crowned M Proof	5,000	Value: 975				

MINT SETS

KM#	Date	Mintage	Identification	Issue Price	Mkt Val
MS27	2000-2001 (8)	—	KM#832-833, 924, 991-992 (both dated 2000), 1012-1013, 1016	15.50	20.00

PROOF SETS

KM#	Date	Mintage	Identification	Issue Price	Mkt Val
PS35	2003 (3)	—	KM#1186, 1187, 1188	—	320

SRI (SHRI) LANKA

The Democratic Socialist Republic of Sri Lanka (formerly Ceylon) situated in the Indian Ocean 18 miles (29 km.) southeast of India, has an area of 25,332 sq. mi.(65,610 sq. km.) and a population of *16.9 million. Capital: Colombo. The economy is chiefly agricultural. Tea, coconut products and rubber are exported.

Sri Lanka remains a member of the Commonwealth of Nations. The president is Chief of State. The prime minister is Head of Government. The present leaders of the country have reverted the country name back to Sri Lanka.

DEMOCRATIC SOCIALIST REPUBLIC

DECIMAL COINAGE

100 Cents = 1 Rupee

KM# 141.2a 25 CENTS
Nickel Clad Steel **Edge:** Reeded

Date	Mintage	F	VF	XF	Unc	BU
2001	10,000,000	—	—	0.10	0.25	0.40
2002	10,000,000	—	—	0.10	0.25	0.40

KM# 135.2a 50 CENTS
Nickel Clad Steel **Edge:** Reeded

Date	Mintage	F	VF	XF	Unc	BU
2001	30,000,000	—	0.10	0.25	0.65	0.85
2002	10,000,000	—	0.10	0.25	0.65	0.85

KM# 166 RUPEE
7.1300 g., Copper Nickel, 25.4 mm. **Subject:** Air Force's 50th Anniversary **Obv:** National arms on air force insignia **Rev:** Two jets above propeller plane **Edge:** Reeded

Date	Mintage	F	VF	XF	Unc	BU
2001 Proof	2,000	Value: 100				

KM# 136.2a RUPEE
Nickel Clad Steel **Edge:** Reeded

Date	Mintage	F	VF	XF	Unc	BU
2002	50,000,000	—	0.25	0.50	1.00	1.25

KM# 147 2 RUPEES
Copper-Nickel

Date	Mintage	F	VF	XF	Unc	BU
2001	10,000,000	—	0.30	0.60	1.35	1.65
2002	40,000,000	—	0.30	0.60	1.35	1.65

KM# 167 2 RUPEES
8.2500 g., Copper Nickel, 28.5 mm. **Subject:** Colombo Plan's 50th Anniversary **Obv:** Denomination **Rev:** Gear wheel **Edge:** Reeded

Date	Mintage	F	VF	XF	Unc	BU
2001	10,000,000	—	—	—	2.00	3.00

KM# 148.2 5 RUPEES
Aluminum-Bronze **Edge:** Lettered **Edge Lettering:** CBSL - Central Bank of Sri Lanka

Date	Mintage	F	VF	XF	Unc	BU
2002	30,000,000	—	0.35	0.65	2.25	2.75

KM# 168 5 RUPEES
9.5200 g., Aluminum-Bronze, 23.4 mm. **Subject:** 250th Annniversary of the "Upasampada" Rite **Obv:** Value **Rev:** Half-length figure of Phra Upali Nahimi

Date	Mintage	F	VF	XF	Unc	BU
2003	—	—	—	—	3.00	4.00

KM# 169 5 RUPEES
9.5200 g., Aluminum-Bronze, 23.4 mm. **Subject:** 250th Anniversary - Upasampada **Obv:** Value **Rev:** Welivita Sri Saranankara Sangharaja Mahimi standing behind shield **Edge:** Reeded and lettered

Date	Mintage	F	VF	XF	Unc	BU
2003	—	—	—	—	3.00	4.00

SUDAN

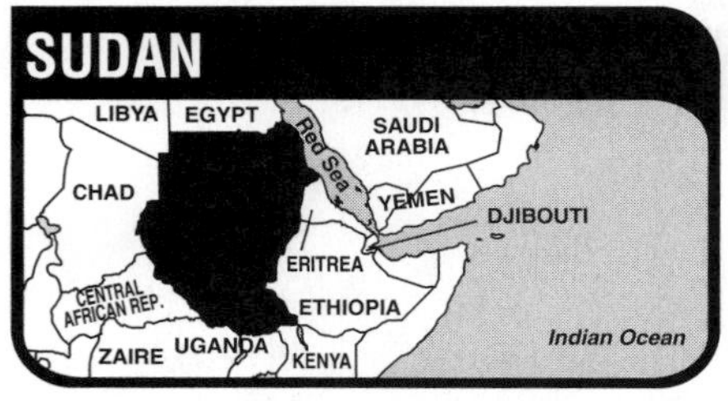

The Democratic Republic of the Sudan, located in northeast Africa on the Red Sea between Egypt and Ethiopia, has an area of 967,500 sq. mi. (2,505,810 sq. km.) and a population of *24.5 million. Capital: Khartoum. Agriculture and livestock raising are the chief occupations. Cotton, gum arabic and peanuts are exported.

REPUBLIC

REFORM COINAGE

100 Qurush (Piastres) = 1 Dinar

KM# 119 5 DINARS
Brass, 19 mm. **Note:** Reduced size

Date	Mintage	F	VF	XF	Unc	BU
AH1424-2003	—	—	1.00	2.00	4.50	7.00

KM# 120.1 10 DINARS
Brass, 22 mm. **Rev:** A above N in Sudan **Note:** Reduced size; legend below building is away from the rim.

Date	Mintage	F	VF	XF	Unc	BU
AH1424-2002	—	—	1.50	3.00	6.50	9.00
AH1424-2003	—	—	1.50	3.00	6.50	9.00

KM# 120.2 10 DINARS
Brass, 22 mm. **Rev:** A to right of N in Sudan **Note:** Reduced size; legend below building touches rim.

Date	Mintage	F	VF	XF	Unc	BU
AH1424-2003	—	—	1.50	3.00	6.50	9.00

KM# 121 50 DINARS
Copper-Nickel, 24 mm. **Rev:** Central Bank building

Date	Mintage	F	VF	XF	Unc	BU
AH1419-2002	—	—	2.50	5.00	10.00	12.50
AH1423-2003	—	—	2.50	5.00	10.00	12.50

SURINAME

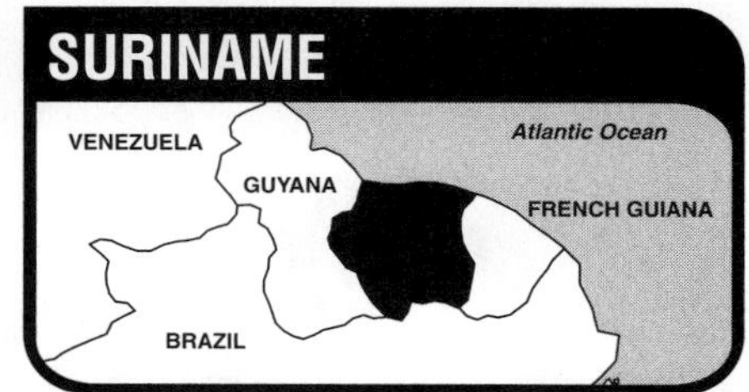

The Republic of Suriname also known as Dutch Guiana, located on the north central coast of South America between Guyana and French Guiana has an area of 63,037 sq. mi. (163,270 sq. km.) and a population of *433,000.Capital: Paramaribo. The country is rich in minerals and forests, and self-sufficient in rice, the staple food crop. The mining, processing and exporting of bauxite is the principal economic activity.

Lieutenants of Amerigo Vespucci sighted the Guiana coast in 1499. Spanish explorers of the 16th century, disappointed at finding no gold, departed leaving the area to be settled by the British in 1652. The colony prospered and the Netherlands acquired it in 1667 in exchange for the Dutch rights in Nieuw Nederland (state of New York). During the European wars of the 18th and 19th centuries, which were fought in part in the new world, Suriname was occupied by the British from 1781-1784 and 1796-1814.Suriname became an autonomous part of the Kingdom of the Netherlands on Dec. 15, 1954. Full independence was achieved on Nov. 25, 1975. In 1980, a coup installed a military government, which has since been dissolved.

MINT MARKS

(u) - Utrecht (privy marks only)

MONETARY SYSTEM

After January, 2004

1 Dollar = 100 Cents

REPUBLIC

MODERN COINAGE

KM# 11b CENT

Copper Plated Steel **Obv:** Arms **Rev:** Geometric design

Date	Mintage	F	VF	XF	Unc	BU
2004(u)	4,000	—	—	—	—	1.50

Note: In sets only

KM# 12.1b 5 CENTS

Copper Plated Steel, 18 mm. **Obv:** Arms **Rev:** Geometric design **Shape:** Square

Date	Mintage	F	VF	XF	Unc	BU
2004(u)	4,000	—	—	—	—	1.50

Note: In sets only

KM# 13a 10 CENTS

Nickel Plated Steel, 15 mm. **Obv:** Arms **Rev:** Geometric design **Edge:** Reeded

Date	Mintage	F	VF	XF	Unc	BU
2004(u)	4,000	—	—	—	—	2.50

Note: In sets only

KM# 14a 25 CENTS

Nickel Plated Steel, 20 mm. **Obv:** Arms **Rev:** Geometric design **Edge:** Reeded

Date	Mintage	F	VF	XF	Unc	BU
2004(u)	4,000	—	—	—	—	4.00

Note: In sets only

KM# 23 100 CENTS

Copper-Nickel, 23 mm. **Obv:** Arms **Rev:** Geometric design **Edge:** Reeded

Date	Mintage	F	VF	XF	Unc	BU
2004(u)	4,000	—	—	—	—	8.00

Note: In sets only

KM# 24 250 CENTS

Copper-Nickel, 28 mm. **Obv:** Arms **Rev:** Geometric design

Date	Mintage	F	VF	XF	Unc	BU
2004(u)	4,000	—	—	—	—	12.50

Note: In sets only

MINT SETS

KM#	Date	Mintage	Identification	Issue Price	Mkt Val
MS1	2004 (6)	4,000	KM#11b, 12.1b, 13a, 14a, 23, 24	25.00	26.00

SWAZILAND

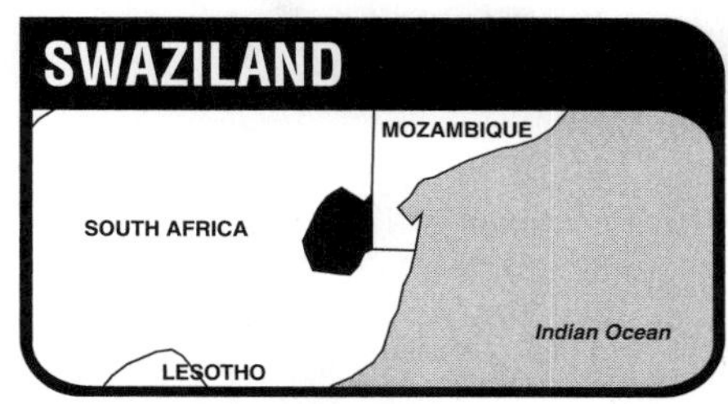

The Kingdom of Swaziland, located in southeastern Africa, has an area of 6,704 sq. mi. (17,360 sq. km.) and a population of *756,000. Capital: Mbabane (administrative); Lobamba (legislative). The diversified economy includes mining, agriculture, and light industry. Asbestos, iron ore, wood pulp, and sugar are exported.

The Kingdom is a member of the Commonwealth of Nations. King Mswati III is Head of State. The prime minister is Head of Government.

RULERS

King Msawati III, 1986-

KINGDOM

DECIMAL COINAGE

100 Cents = 1 Lilangeni (plural emelangeni)

KM# 48 5 CENTS

Nickel Plated Steel **Obv:** King Msawati III **Obv. Legend:** Arum Lily **Shape:** Scalloped

Date	Mintage	F	VF	XF	Unc	BU
2001	—	—	—	—	0.50	0.75
2002	—	—	—	—	0.50	0.75

KM# 49 10 CENTS

Copper-Nickel **Obv:** King Msawati III **Rev:** Sugar cane **Shape:** Scalloped

Date	Mintage	F	VF	XF	Unc	BU
2001	—	—	—	—	0.50	0.75
2002	—	—	—	—	0.50	0.75

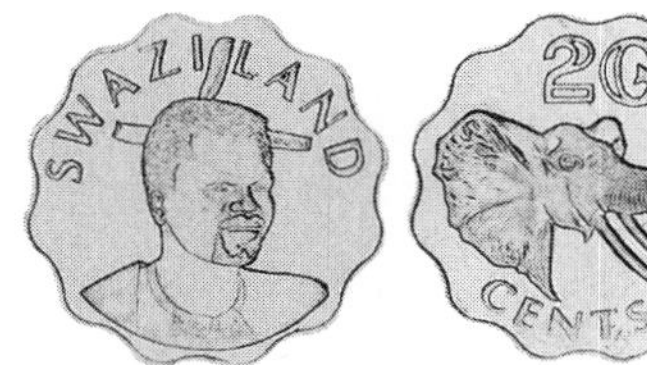

KM# 50 20 CENTS

Copper-Nickel **Obv:** King Msawati III **Rev:** Elephant **Shape:** Scalloped **Note:** "Lg bust and legend": right tusk closer to rim; "Sm bust and legend": right tusk further from rim.

Date	Mintage	F	VF	XF	Unc	BU
2001	—	—	0.40	0.80	2.50	4.50
Note: Small bust and legend						
2002	—	—	0.40	0.80	2.50	4.50
Note: Small bust and legend						
2003	—	—	0.40	0.80	2.50	4.50
Note: Small bust and legend						

KM# 52 50 CENTS

Copper-Nickel **Obv:** King Msawati III **Rev:** Arms

Date	Mintage	F	VF	XF	Unc	BU
2001	—	—	—	—	3.75	4.50
2003	—	—	—	—	3.75	4.50

KM# 45 LILANGENI

Brass

Date	Mintage	F	VF	XF	Unc	BU
2002	—	—	—	1.50	3.25	3.75
2003	—	—	—	1.50	3.25	3.75

KM# 46 2 EMALANGENI

Brass

Date	Mintage	F	VF	XF	Unc	BU
2003 sm. bust	—	—	—	—	3.75	4.25

KM# 47 5 EMALANGENI

Brass

Date	Mintage	F	VF	XF	Unc	BU
2003 sm. bust	—	—	—	—	6.00	7.00

SWEDEN

The Kingdom of Sweden, a limited constitutional monarchy located in northern Europe between Norway and Finland, has an area of 173,732 sq. mi. (449,960 sq. km.) and a population of *8.5 million. Capital: Stockholm. Mining, lumbering and a specialized machine industry dominate the economy. Machinery, paper, iron and steel, motor vehicles and wood pulp are exported.

RULERS
Carl XVI Gustaf, 1973-

MINT OFFICIALS INITIALS

Letter	Date	Name
D	1986-	Bengt Dennis

MONETARY SYSTEM
100 Ore = 1 Krona

KINGDOM

REFORM COINAGE

KM# 878 50 ORE
Bronze

Date	Mintage	F	VF	XF	Unc	BU
2001 B	30,120,532	—	—	0.10	0.15	0.25
2002 B	—	—	—	0.10	0.15	0.25
2003 B	—	—	—	0.10	0.15	0.25
2004 B	—	—	—	0.10	0.15	0.25
2005 B	—	—	—	0.10	0.15	0.25

KM# 894 KRONA
6.9800 g., Copper-Nickel, 24.9 mm. **Ruler:** Carl XVI Gustaf **Obv:** King's new portrait **Rev:** Crown and denomination **Edge:** Reeded

Date	Mintage	F	VF	XF	Unc	BU
2001 B	23,905,454	—	—	—	0.65	1.00
2002 B	—	—	—	—	0.65	1.00
2003 B	—	—	—	—	0.65	1.00
2004 B	—	—	—	—	0.65	1.00
2005 B	—	—	—	—	0.65	1.00

KM# 853a 5 KRONOR
Copper-Nickel Clad Nickel, 28.5 mm.

Date	Mintage	F	VF	XF	Unc	BU
2001 B	6,001,481	—	—	—	1.00	1.25
2002 B	—	—	—	—	1.00	1.25
2003 B	—	—	—	—	1.00	1.25

KM# 895 10 KRONOR
6.5700 g., Copper-Aluminum-Zinc, 20.4 mm. **Ruler:** Carl XVI Gustaf **Obv:** King's new portrait **Rev:** Three crowns and denomination **Edge:** Reeded and plain sections

Date	Mintage	F	VF	XF	Unc	BU
2001B	4,171,757	—	—	—	1.75	2.00
2002B	—	—	—	—	1.75	2.00
2003B	—	—	—	—	1.75	2.00
2004B	—	—	—	—	1.75	2.00
2005B	—	—	—	—	1.75	2.00

KM# 896 200 KRONOR
27.2500 g., 0.9250 Silver .8104 oz. ASW, 36 mm. **Ruler:** Carl XVI Gustaf **Subject:** 25th Wedding Anniversary **Obv:** Conjoined busts of King Carl Gustaf XVI and Queen Silvia **Rev:** National arms **Edge:** Plain

Date	Mintage	F	VF	XF	Unc	BU
ND(2001)	50,000	—	—	—	35.00	45.00

KM# 902 200 KRONOR
Silver **Ruler:** Carl XVI Gustaf **Subject:** 30th Anniversary of Reign

Date	Mintage	F	VF	XF	Unc	BU
2003	—	—	—	—	35.00	45.00

KM# 904 200 KRONOR
Silver **Ruler:** Carl XVI Gustaf **Subject:** 700th Anniversary, St. Birgitta

Date	Mintage	F	VF	XF	Unc	BU
2003	—	—	—	—	35.00	45.00

KM# 906 200 KRONOR
Silver **Ruler:** Carl XVI Gustaf **Subject:** Centennial of the end of the Union between Norway and Sweden

Date	Mintage	F	VF	XF	Unc	BU
2005	—	—	—	—	35.00	45.00

KM# 903 2000 KRONOR
Gold **Ruler:** Carl XVI Gustaf **Subject:** 30th Anniversary of Reign

Date	Mintage	F	VF	XF	Unc	BU
2003	—	—	—	—	260	—

KM# 905 2000 KRONOR
Gold **Ruler:** Carl XVI Gustaf **Subject:** 700th Anniversary St. Birgitta

Date	Mintage	F	VF	XF	Unc	BU
2003	—	—	—	—	260	—

KM# 907 2000 KRONOR
Gold **Ruler:** Carl XVI Gustaf **Subject:** Centennial of the end of the Union between Norway and Sweden

Date	Mintage	F	VF	XF	Unc	BU
2005	—	—	—	—	260	—

MINT SETS

KM#	Date	Mintage	Identification	Issue Price	Mkt Val
MS107	2002 (4)	—	KM#853a, 878, 894, 895 plus medal	—	—

SWITZERLAND

The Swiss Confederation, located in central Europe north of Italy and south of Germany, has an area of 15,941 sq. mi. (41,290 sq. km.) and a population of *6.6 million. Capital: Bern. The economy centers about a well developed manufacturing industry. Machinery, chemicals, watches and clocks, and textiles are exported.

The Swiss Constitutions of 1848 and 1874 established a union modeled upon that of the United States.

MINT MARK
B - Bern

MONETARY SYSTEM
100 Rappen (Centimes) = 1 Franc

CONFEDERATION

DECIMAL COINAGE

KM# 46 RAPPEN
Bronze **Edge:** Plain

Date	Mintage	F	VF	XF	Unc	BU
2001B	1,522,000	—	—	—	0.25	0.50
2001B Proof	6,000	Value: 1.00				
2002B	2,024,000	—	—	—	0.25	0.50
2002B Proof	5,500	Value: 1.00				
2003B	1,522,000	—	—	—	0.25	0.50
2003B Proof	5,500	Value: 1.00				
2004B	1,522,000	—	—	—	0.25	0.50
2004B Proof	5,000	Value: 1.00				
2005B	1,524,000	—	—	—	0.25	0.50
2005B Proof	4,500	Value: 1.00				

KM# 26c 5 RAPPEN
Aluminum-Brass

Date	Mintage	F	VF	XF	Unc	BU
2001B	5,022,000	—	—	—	0.25	0.50
2001B Proof	6,000	Value: 1.50				
2002B	12,024,000	—	—	—	0.25	0.50
2002B Proof	6,000	Value: 1.50				
2003B	10,022,000	—	—	—	0.25	0.50
2003B Proof	5,500	Value: 1.50				
2004B	10,022,000	—	—	—	0.25	0.50
2004B Proof	5,000	Value: 1.50				
2005B	13,024,000	—	—	—	0.25	0.50
2005B Proof	4,500	Value: 1.50				

KM# 27 10 RAPPEN
Copper-Nickel **Edge:** Plain **Note:** Retired from legal tender status as of January 1, 2004, and removed from circulation.

Date	Mintage	F	VF	XF	Unc	BU
2001B	7,022,000	—	—	—	0.25	0.50
2001B Proof	6,000	Value: 1.50				
2002B	15,024,000	—	—	—	0.25	0.50
2002B Proof	6,000	Value: 1.50				
2003B	12,022,000	—	—	—	0.25	0.50
2003B Proof	5,500	Value: 1.50				
2004B	5,022,000	—	—	—	0.25	0.50
2004B Proof	5,000	Value: 1.50				
2005B	7,024,000	—	—	—	0.25	0.50
2005B Proof	4,500	Value: 1.50				

KM# 29a 20 RAPPEN
Copper-Nickel **Edge:** Plain

Date	Mintage	F	VF	XF	Unc	BU
2001B	7,022,000	—	—	—	0.50	1.00
2001B Proof	6,000	Value: 2.25				
2002B	12,024,000	—	—	—	0.50	1.00
2002B Proof	6,000	Value: 2.25				
2003B	10,022,000	—	—	—	0.30	1.00
2003B Proof	5,500	Value: 2.25				
2004B	10,022,000	—	—	—	0.30	1.00
2004B Proof	5,000	Value: 2.25				
2005B	6,024,000	—	—	—	0.30	1.00
2005B Proof	4,500	Value: 2.25				

KM# 23a.3 1/2 FRANC
Copper-Nickel **Obv:** Helvetia standing with lance and shield, 23 stars

Date	Mintage	F	VF	XF	Unc	BU
2001B	6,022,000	—	—	—	2.00	3.00
2001B Proof	6,000	Value: 4.50				
2002B	2,024,000	—	—	—	2.00	3.00
2002B Proof	6,000	Value: 4.50				
2003B	2,022,000	—	—	—	2.00	3.00
2003B Proof	5,500	Value: 4.50				
2004B	2,022,000	—	—	—	2.00	3.00
2004B Proof	5,000	Value: 4.50				
2005B	1,024,000	—	—	—	2.00	3.00
2005B Proof	4,500	Value: 4.50				

KM# 24a.3 FRANC
Copper-Nickel **Obv:** Helvetia standing with lance and shield, 23 stars **Edge:** Reeded **Designer:** A. Bovy

Date	Mintage	F	VF	XF	Unc	BU
2001B	3,022,000	—	—	—	2.50	4.00
2001B Proof	6,000	Value: 5.00				
2002B	1,024,000	—	—	—	2.50	4.00
2002B Proof	6,000	Value: 5.00				
2003B	2,022,000	—	—	—	2.50	4.00
2003B Proof	5,500	Value: 5.00				
2004B	2,022,000	—	—	—	2.50	4.00
2004B Proof	5,000	Value: 5.00				
2005B	1,024,000	—	—	—	2.50	4.00
2005B Proof	4,500	Value: 5.00				

KM# 21a.3 2 FRANCS
Copper-Nickel **Obv:** Helvetia standing with staff and shield, 23 stars

Date	Mintage	F	VF	XF	Unc	BU
2001B	4,022,000	—	—	—	4.50	7.50
2001B Proof	6,000	Value: 9.00				
2002B	1,024,000	—	—	—	4.50	7.50
2002B Proof	6,000	Value: 9.00				
2003B	1,022,000	—	—	—	4.50	7.50
2003B Proof	5,500	Value: 9.00				
2004B	1,022,000	—	—	—	4.50	7.50
2004B Proof	5,000	Value: 9.00				
2005B	2,024,000	—	—	—	4.50	7.50
2005B Proof	4,500	Value: 9.00				

KM# 40a.4 5 FRANCS
Copper-Nickel **Edge:** Raised lettering

Date	Mintage	F	VF	XF	Unc	BU
2001B	1,022,000	—	—	—	6.50	9.50
2001B Proof	6,000	Value: 15.00				
2002B	1,024,000	—	—	—	6.50	9.50
2002B Proof	6,000	Value: 15.00				
2003B	1,022,000	—	—	—	6.50	9.50
2003B Proof	5,500	Value: 15.00				
2004B	522,000	—	—	—	6.50	9.50
2004B Proof	5,000	Value: 15.00				
2005B	524,000	—	—	—	6.50	9.50
2005B Proof	4,500	Value: 15.00				

COMMEMORATIVE COINAGE

KM# 92 5 FRANCS
15.0000 g., Bi-Metallic Gold center in Copper-Nickel ring, 33 mm. **Subject:** Zurcher Sechselauten **Obv:** Denomination **Rev:** Burning strawman **Edge:** Reeded

Date	Mintage	F	VF	XF	Unc	BU
2001B	170,000	—	—	—	5.50	8.00
2001B Proof	20,000	Value: 18.00				

KM# 98 5 FRANCS
15.0000 g., Bi-Metallic Gold center in Copper-Nickel ring, 33 mm. **Subject:** Escalade 1602-2002 **Obv:** Denomination **Rev:** Swirling ladders design **Edge:** Reeded **Note:** Weight can vary 14.8-15 g.

Date	Mintage	F	VF	XF	Unc	BU
2002B	108,000	—	—	—	5.50	8.00
2002B Proof	9,000	Value: 18.00				

KM# 103 5 FRANCS
15.0000 g., Bi-Metallic Gold center in Copper-Nickel ring, 33 mm. **Subject:** Chalandamarz **Obv:** Value **Rev:** Boys inverting pots **Edge:** Reeded

Date	Mintage	F	VF	XF	Unc	BU
2003B	78,800	—	—	—	6.00	8.50
2003B Proof	6,500	Value: 35.00				

KM# 107 10 FRANCS
15.0000 g., Bi-Metallic Copper-Nickel center in Aluminum-Bronze ring, 33 mm. **Obv:** Value **Rev:** Matterhorn mountain **Edge:** Segmented reeding

Date	Mintage	F	VF	XF	Unc	BU
2004B	Est. 98,000	—	—	—	12.00	14.00
2004B Proof	Est. 13,000	Value: 32.00				

KM# 111 10 FRANCS
15.0000 g., Bi-Metallic Copper-Nickel center in Aluminum-Bronze ring, 33 mm. **Obv:** Value **Rev:** Jungfrau mountain **Edge:** Segmented reeding

Date	Mintage	F	VF	XF	Unc	BU
2005B	Est. 96,000	—	—	—	12.00	14.00
2005B Proof	Est. 12,500	Value: 32.00				

KM# 114 10 FRANCS
15.0000 g., Bi-Metallic Copper-Nickel center in Aluminum-Bronze ring, 33 mm. **Obv:** Value **Rev:** Piz Bernina mountain **Edge:** Segmented reeding

Date	Mintage	F	VF	XF	Unc	BU
2006B	96,000	—	—	—	8.00	10.00
2006B Proof	12,000	Value: 30.00				

KM# 93 20 FRANCS
20.0000 g., 0.9250 Silver .5369 oz. ASW, 32.6 mm. **Subject:** Mustair Cloister **Obv:** Church floor plan **Rev:** Walled cloister **Edge:** "DOMINUS PROVIDEBIT" and 13 stars

Date	Mintage	F	VF	XF	Unc	BU
2001B	100,000	—	—	—	22.00	28.00
2001B Proof	15,000	Value: 45.00				

KM# 94 20 FRANCS
20.0000 g., 0.8350 Silver .5369 oz. ASW **Subject:** Johanna Spyri **Obv:** Denomination and handwritten background **Rev:** Portrait

Date	Mintage	F	VF	XF	Unc	BU
2001B	100,000	—	—	—	22.00	28.00
2001B Proof	15,000	Value: 45.00				

KM# 99 20 FRANCS
20.0000 g., 0.8350 Silver 0.5369 oz. ASW, 33 mm. **Obv:** St. Gall and bear cub **Rev:** St. Gall Cloister **Edge:** Lettered

Date	Mintage	F	VF	XF	Unc	BU
2002B	50,000	—	—	—	22.00	28.00
2002B Proof	6,500	Value: 50.00				

KM# 100 20 FRANCS
20.0000 g., 0.8350 Silver 0.5369 oz. ASW, 33 mm. **Subject:** REGA **Obv:** Denomination, inscription and cross above rotating propeller **Rev:** Rescue helicopter in flight **Edge:** Lettered

Date	Mintage	F	VF	XF	Unc	BU
2002B	55,000	—	—	—	22.00	28.00
2002B Proof	7,000	Value: 50.00				

KM# 101 20 FRANCS
20.0000 g., 0.8350 Silver 0.5369 oz. ASW, 33 mm.
Subject: Expo '02 **Obv:** Denomination and date in center
Rev: Child at water's edge **Edge:** Lettered

Date	Mintage	F	VF	XF	Unc	BU
2002B	61,100	—	—	—	22.00	28.00
2002B Proof	10,000	Value: 45.00				

KM# 104 20 FRANCS
19.9700 g., 0.8350 Silver 0.5361 oz. ASW, 32.5 mm.
Subject: St. Moritz Ski Championships **Obv:** Value in snow storm
Rev: Skier in snow storm **Edge:** Lettered, 13 stars
Edge Lettering: DOMINUS PROVIDEBIT

Date	Mintage	F	VF	XF	Unc	BU
2003B	55,000	—	—	—	22.00	28.00
2003B Proof	7,000	Value: 50.00				

KM# 106 20 FRANCS
20.0000 g., 0.8350 Silver 0.5369 oz. ASW, 33 mm.
Subject: Bern, Old Town **Obv:** Stylized clock tower and buildings
Rev: Stylized aerial view of Berner Altstadt **Edge:** Lettered
Edge Lettering: DOMINUS PROVIDEBIT

Date	Mintage	F	VF	XF	Unc	BU
2003B	50,000	—	—	—	22.50	30.00
2003B Proof	6,000	Value: 50.00				

KM# 108 20 FRANCS
20.0000 g., 0.8350 Silver 0.5369 oz. ASW, 33 mm. **Obv:** Value
Rev: The Three Castles of Bellinzona **Edge:** Lettered with 13 stars **Edge Lettering:** "DOMINUS PROVIDEBIT"

Date	Mintage	F	VF	XF	Unc	BU
2004B	70,000	—	—	—	22.00	28.00
2004B Proof	8,000	Value: 50.00				

KM# 109 20 FRANCS
20.0000 g., 0.8350 Silver 0.5369 oz. ASW, 33 mm. **Obv:** Value
Rev: Chillon Castle **Edge:** Lettered with 13 stars
Edge Lettering: "DOMINUS PROVIDEBIT"

Date	Mintage	F	VF	XF	Unc	BU
2004B	70,000	—	—	—	22.00	28.00
2004B Proof	8,000	Value: 50.00				

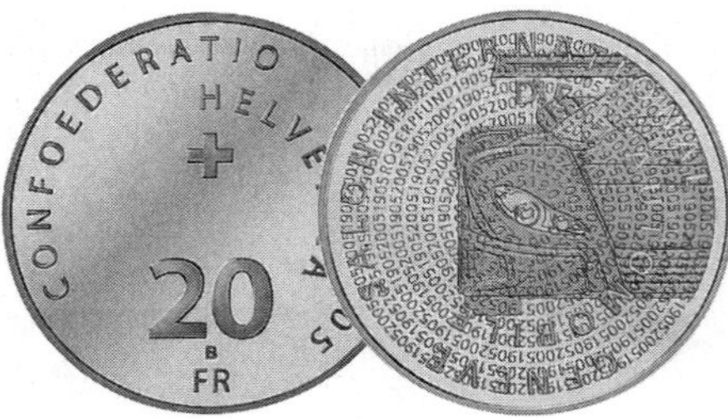

KM# 112 20 FRANCS
20.0000 g., 0.8350 Silver 0.5369 oz. ASW, 33 mm. **Subject:** Geneva Motor Show **Obv:** Value **Rev:** Partial view of prototype car **Edge:** Lettered **Edge Lettering:** "DOMINUS PROVIDEBIT"

Date	Mintage	F	VF	XF	Unc	BU
2005B	65,000	—	—	—	22.00	28.00
2005B Proof	25,000	Value: 50.00				

KM# 115 20 FRANCS
20.0000 g., 0.8350 Silver 0.5369 oz. ASW, 33 mm. **Obv:** Value
Rev: 1906 Post Bus **Edge Lettering:** 'DOMINUS PROVIDEBIT"

Date	Mintage	F	VF	XF	Unc	BU
2006B	65,000	—	—	—	20.00	25.00
2006B Proof	8,000	Value: 50.00				

KM# 95 50 FRANCS
11.2900 g., 0.9000 Gold .3267 oz. AGW, 25 mm.
Obv: Landscape and denomination **Rev:** Heidi and goat running
Edge: Lettered **Designer:** Albrecht Schnider

Date	Mintage	F	VF	XF	Unc	BU
2001B Proof	7,000	Value: 275				

KM# 102 50 FRANCS
11.2900 g., 0.9000 Gold 0.3267 oz. AGW, 25 mm.
Subject: Expo '02 **Obv:** Denomination **Rev:** Aerial view of landscape **Edge:** Lettered

Date	Mintage	F	VF	XF	Unc	BU
2002B Proof	5,000	Value: 265				

KM# 105 50 FRANCS
11.2900 g., 0.9000 Gold 0.3267 oz. AGW, 25 mm. **Obv:** Skier and value **Rev:** St. Moritz city view **Edge:** Lettered

Date	Mintage	F	VF	XF	Unc	BU
2003B Proof	4,000	Value: 265				

KM# 110 50 FRANCS
11.2900 g., 0.9000 Gold 0.3267 oz. AGW, 25 mm. **Obv:** Value
Rev: Matterhorn mountain **Edge:** Lettered with 13 stars
Edge Lettering: "DOMINUS PROVIDEBIT"

Date	Mintage	F	VF	XF	Unc	BU
2004B Proof	6,000	Value: 265				

KM# 113 50 FRANCS
11.2900 g., 0.9000 Gold 0.3267 oz. AGW, 25 mm. **Subject:** Geneva Motor Show **Obv:** Value **Rev:** Partial view of an antique car **Edge:** Lettered **Edge Lettering:** DOMINUS PROVIDEBIT

Date	Mintage	F	VF	XF	Unc	BU
2005B Proof	10,000	Value: 275				

KM# 116 50 FRANCS
11.2900 g., 0.9000 Gold 0.3267 oz. AGW, 25 mm. **Obv:** Value
Rev: Swiss Guardsman **Edge Lettering:** "Dominus Providebit"

Date	Mintage	F	VF	XF	Unc	BU
2006B Proof	6,000	Value: 350				

COMMEMORATIVE COINAGE

KM# S61 50 FRANCS
25.0000 g., 0.9000 Silver .7235 oz. ASW **Subject:** Uri Festival

Date	Mintage	F	VF	XF	Unc	BU
2001 Proof	1,500	Value: 75.00				

KM# S63 50 FRANCS
25.0000 g., 0.9000 Silver .7235 oz. ASW **Subject:** Zurich Festival

Date	Mintage	F	VF	XF	Unc	BU
2002 Proof	1,500	Value: 75.00				

KM# S62 500 FRANCS
0.9000 Gold .3762 oz. AGW **Issuer:** Uri Festival

Date	Mintage	F	VF	XF	Unc	BU
2001 Proof	125	Value: 750				

KM# S64 500 FRANCS
13.0000 g., 0.9000 Gold .3762 oz. AGW **Subject:** Zurich Festival

Date	Mintage	F	VF	XF	Unc	BU
2002 Proof	150	Value: 800				

KM# S66 500 FRANCS
13.0000 g., 0.9000 Gold .3762 oz. AGW **Issuer:** Basel Festival

Date	Mintage	F	VF	XF	Unc	BU
2003 Proof	150	Value: 750				

KM# S68 500 FRANCS
15.5000 g., 0.9000 Gold .4485 oz. AGW **Issuer:** Fribourg Festival

Date	Mintage	F	VF	XF	Unc	BU
2004 Proof	150	Value: 850				

ESSAIS

KM#	Date	Mintage	Identification	Mkt Val
E13	2001	—	20 Francs. Silver. KM#93	225
E14	2002	700	5 Francs. Brass. KM#98	140
E15	2003	700	5 Francs. Bi-Metallic. KM#103	140
E16	2004	700	10 Francs. Bi-Metallic. KM#107.	180

MINT SETS

KM#	Date	Mintage	Identification	Issue Price	Mkt Val
MS35	2001 (9)	22,000	KM#21a.3, 23a.3, 24a.3, 26c, 27, 29a, 40a.4, 46, 92 Zurich Sechselauten	—	24.00
MS36	2002 (9)	22,000	KM#21a.3, 23a.3, 24a.3, 26c, 27, 29a, 40a.4, 46, 98 Escalade	—	20.00
MS37	2002 (9)	2,000	KM#21a.3, 23a.3, 24a.3, 26c, 27, 29a, 40a.4, 46, 98 Includes a medal and different cover (intended as a birth year set for 2002 from the mint)	—	95.00
MS38	2003 (9)	18,000	KM#21a.3, 23a.3, 24a.3, 26c, 27, 29a, 40a.4, 46, 103, Chalandamarz.	—	24.00
MS39	2004 (9)	18,000	KM#21a.3, 23a.3, 24a.3, 26c, 27, 29a, 40a.4, 46, 107, Matterhorn.	—	42.00

PROOF SETS

KM#	Date	Mintage	Identification	Issue Price	Mkt Val
PS30	2001 (9)	6,000	KM#21a.3, 23a.3, 24a.3, 26c, 27, 29a, 40a.4, 46, 92 Zurich Sechselauten	—	60.00
PS31	2002 (9)	6,000	KM#21a.3, 23a.3, 24a.3, 26c, 27, 29a, 40a.4, 46, 98 Escalade	—	65.00
PS32	2003 (9)	5,500	KM#21a.3, 23a.3, 24a.3, 26c, 27, 29a, 40a.4, 46, 103 Chatandamarz	—	65.00

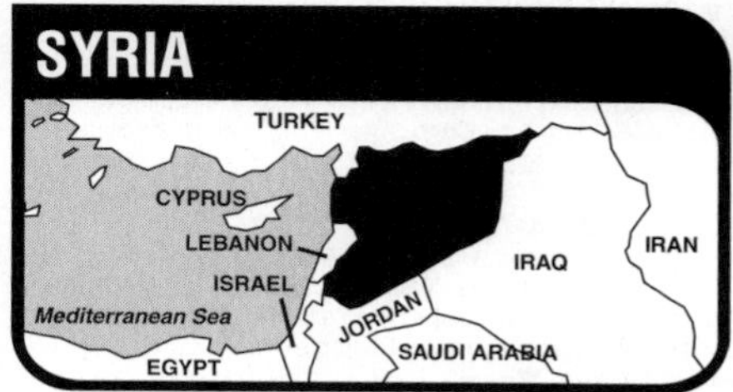

The Syrian Arab Republic, located in the Near East at the eastern end of the Mediterranean Sea, has an area of 71,498 sq. mi. (185,180 sq. km.) and a population of *12 million. Capital: Greater Damascus. Agriculture and animal breeding are the chief industries. Cotton, crude oil and livestock are exported.

TITLES

الجمهورية السورية

al-Jumhuriya(t) al-Suriya(t)

الجمهورية لعربية السورية

al-Jumhuriya(t) al-Arabiya(t) as-Suriya(t)

SYRIAN ARAB REPUBLIC

STANDARD COINAGE

KM# 129 5 POUNDS
7.5300 g., Nickel-Clad Steel, 24.5 mm. **Obv:** National arms **Rev:** Old fort and latent image above value **Edge:** Reeded and lettered **Edge Lettering:** "CENTRAL BANK 5 SYP"

Date	Mintage	F	VF	XF	Unc	BU
AH1424-2003	—	—	—	—	1.00	1.50

KM# 130 10 POUNDS
9.5300 g., Copper-Nickel-Zinc, 27.4 mm. **Obv:** National arms **Rev:** Ancient ruins with latent image **Edge:** Reeded and lettered **Edge Lettering:** "10 SYRIAN POUNDS"

Date	Mintage	F	VF	XF	Unc	BU
2003-AH1424	—	—	—	—	2.00	3.00

KM# 131 25 POUNDS
8.3000 g., Copper-Nickel-Zinc, 24.9 mm. **Obv:** National arms **Rev:** Building and latent image **Edge:** Reeded and lettered **Edge Lettering:** "CENTRAL BANK OF SYRIA 25"

Date	Mintage	F	VF	XF	Unc	BU
AH1424-2003	—	—	—	—	4.50	6.00

The Republic of Tajikistan (Tadjiquistan), was formed from those regions of Bukhara and Turkestan where the population consisted mainly of Tajiks. It is bordered in the north and west by Uzbekistan and Kyrgyzstan, in the east by China and in the south by Afghanistan. It has an area of 55,240 sq. miles (143,100 sq. km.) and a population of 5.95 million. It includes 2 provinces of Khudzand and Khatlon together with the Gorno-Badakhshan Autonomous Region with a population of 5,092,603. Capital: Dushanbe. Tajikistan was admitted as a constituent republic of the Soviet Union on Dec. 5, 1929. In August 1990 the Tajik Supreme Soviet adopted a declaration of republican sovereignty, and in Dec. 1991 the republic became a member of the CIS.

After demonstrations and fighting, the Communist government was replaced by a Revolutionary Coalition Council on May 7, 1992. Following further demonstrations President Nabiev was ousted on Sept. 7, 1992. Civil war broke out, and the government resigned on Nov. 10, 1992. On Nov. 30, 1992 it was announced that a CIS peacekeeping force would be sent to Tajikistan. A state of emergency was imposed in Jan. 1993. A ceasefire was signed in 1996 and a peace agreement signed in June 1997.

MONETARY SYSTEM
1 Ruble = 100 Tanga

REPUBLIC

DECIMAL COINAGE

KM# 2 5 DRAMS
2.0500 g., Brass Clad Steel, 16.5 mm. **Obv:** Crown **Rev:** Denomination **Edge:** Plain

Date	Mintage	F	VF	XF	Unc	BU
2001	—	—	—	—	0.50	0.75

KM# 3 10 DRAMS
2.4700 g., Brass Clad Steel, 17.5 mm. **Obv:** Crown **Rev:** Denomination **Edge:** Plain

Date	Mintage	F	VF	XF	Unc	BU
2001	—	—	—	—	0.75	1.00

KM# 4 20 DRAMS
2.7300 g., Brass Clad Steel, 18.5 mm. **Obv:** Crown **Rev:** Denomination **Edge:** Plain

Date	Mintage	F	VF	XF	Unc	BU
2001	—	—	—	—	1.00	1.25

KM# 5 25 DRAMS
2.8000 g., Brass, 19.1 mm. **Obv:** Crown **Rev:** Denomination **Edge:** Plain

Date	Mintage	F	VF	XF	Unc	BU
2001	—	—	—	—	1.50	1.75

KM# 6 50 DRAMS
3.5500 g., Brass, 21 mm. **Obv:** Crown **Rev:** Denomination **Edge:** Plain

Date	Mintage	F	VF	XF	Unc	BU
2001	—	—	—	—	1.75	2.00

KM# 7 SOMONI
5.1500 g., Copper-Nickel-Zinc, 23.9 mm. **Obv:** King's bust 1/2 right **Rev:** Denomination **Edge:** Reeded and plain sections

Date	Mintage	F	VF	XF	Unc	BU
2001	—	—	—	—	3.50	5.00

KM# 8 3 SOMONI
6.3200 g., Copper-Nickel-Zinc, 25.5 mm. **Obv:** National arms **Rev:** Denomination **Edge:** Lettered

Date	Mintage	F	VF	XF	Unc	BU
2001	—	—	—	—	5.00	7.00

KM# 10 3 SOMONI
Bi-Metallic, 25.5 mm. **Subject:** 80th Year - Dushanbe City

Date	Mintage	F	VF	XF	Unc	BU
2004	1,000	—	—	—	13.50	15.00

KM# 10a 3 SOMONI
6.9800 g., 0.9250 Silver 0.2076 oz. ASW, 25.5 mm. **Subject:** 80th Anniversary of Republic **Obv:** Value below arms **Rev:** Statue in arch

Date	Mintage	F	VF	XF	Unc	BU
2004 Proof	1,000	Value: 30.00				

KM# 9 5 SOMONI
7.1000 g., Copper-Nickel-Zinc, 26.4 mm. **Obv:** Turbaned portrait **Rev:** Denomination **Edge:** Reeded and plain sections with a star

Date	Mintage	F	VF	XF	Unc	BU
2001	—	—	—	—	7.50	9.00

KM# 11 5 SOMONI
6.9400 g., Bi-Metallic Copper-Nickel center in Brass ring, 26.5 mm. **Subject:** 10th Anniversary - Constitution **Obv:** Arms above value **Rev:** Flag and book **Edge:** Lettered

Date	Mintage	F	VF	XF	Unc	BU
2004	—	—	—	—	8.00	10.00

KM# 11a 5 SOMONI
8.5500 g., 0.9250 Silver 0.2558 oz. ASW, 26.5 mm.
Subject: 10th Anniversary - Constitution **Obv:** Arms above value
Rev: Flag and book

Date	Mintage	F	VF	XF	Unc	BU
2004 Proof	2,000	Value: 35.00				

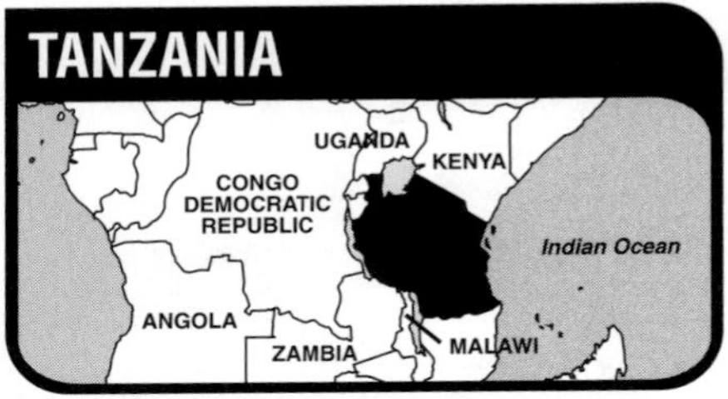

The United Republic of Tanzania, located on the east coast of Africa between Kenya and Mozambique, consists of Tanganyika and the islands of Zanzibar and Pemba. It has an area of 364,900 sq. mi. (945,090 sq. km.) and a population of *25.2 million. Capital: Dar es Salaam (Haven of Peace). The chief exports are cotton, coffee, diamonds, sisal, cloves, petroleum products, and cashew nuts.

Tanzania is a member of the Commonwealth of Nations. The President is Chief of State.

REPUBLIC

STANDARD COINAGE

100 Senti = 1 Shilingi

KM# 56 500 SHILLINGS
31.4600 g., 0.9250 Silver 0.9356 oz. ASW, 38.6 mm.
Obv: National arms **Rev:** African dhow **Edge:** Reeded

Date	Mintage	F	VF	XF	Unc	BU
2001 Proof	—	Value: 40.00				

The Kingdom of Thailand (formerly Siam), a constitutional monarchy located in the center of mainland Southeast Asia between Burma and Laos, has an area of 198,457 mi. (514,000 sq. km.) and a population of *55.5 million. Capital: Bangkok. The economy is based on agriculture and mining. Rubber, rice, teakwood, tin and tungsten are exported.

RULERS
Rama IX (Phra Maha Bhumifhol Adulyadej), 1946-

KINGDOM OF THAILAND

DECIMAL COINAGE

25 Satang = 1 Salung; 100 Satang = 1 Baht

Y# 187 25 SATANG = 1/4 BAHT
Aluminum-Bronze **Ruler:** Rama IX **Edge:** Reeded

Date	Mintage	F	VF	XF	Unc	BU
BE2545 (2002)	—	—	—	—	0.10	—

Y# 203 50 SATANG = 1/2 BAHT
Brass **Ruler:** Rama IX

Date	Mintage	F	VF	XF	Unc	BU
BE2544 (2001)	—	—	—	—	0.10	—
BE2545 (2002)	—	—	—	—	0.10	—
BE2547 (2004)	—	—	—	—	0.10	—

Y# 183 BAHT
Copper-Nickel **Ruler:** Rama IX **Edge:** Reeded **Note:** Circulation coinage. Varieties exist.

Date	Mintage	F	VF	XF	Unc	BU
BE2544 (2001)	—	—	—	—	0.10	—

Y# 373 10 BAHT
8.5000 g., Bi-Metallic Brass center in Copper-Nickel ring, 25.6 mm.
Ruler: Rama IX **Subject:** Department of Lands Centennial
Obv: Portraits of Kings Chulalongkorn and Bhumibol Adulyadej
Rev: Department seal **Edge:** Alternating reeded and plain

Date	Mintage	F	VF	XF	Unc	BU
BE2544(2001)	—	—	—	—	2.50	—

Y# 381 10 BAHT
8.5500 g., Bi-Metallic Brass center in Copper-Nickel ring, 25.8 mm. **Ruler:** Rama IX **Subject:** Centennial of Irrigation Department **Obv:** Portraits of Kings Rama V and Rama IX **Rev:** Department logo **Edge:** Alternating reeded and plain

Date	Mintage	F	VF	XF	Unc	BU
BE2545(2002)	—	—	—	—	2.00	—

Y# 382 10 BAHT
8.5500 g., Bi-Metallic Brass center in Copper-Nickel ring, 25.8 mm. **Ruler:** Rama IX **Subject:** Department of Internal Trade 60th Anniversary **Obv:** King's portrait **Rev:** Department logo **Edge:** Alternating reeded and plain

Date	Mintage	F	VF	XF	Unc	BU
BE2545(2002)	—	—	—	—	2.00	—

Y# 383 10 BAHT
8.5500 g., Bi-Metallic Brass center in Copper-Nickel ring, 25.8 mm. **Ruler:** Rama IX **Subject:** State Highway Department 90th Anniversary **Obv:** Portraits of Kings Rama VI and Rama IX **Rev:** Department logo **Edge:** Alternating reeded and plain

Date	Mintage	F	VF	XF	Unc	BU
BE2545(2002)	—	—	—	—	2.00	—

Y# 384 10 BAHT
8.5500 g., Bi-Metallic Brass center in Copper-Nickel ring, 25.8 mm. **Ruler:** Rama IX **Subject:** Vajira Hospital 90th Anniversary **Obv:** Portraits of Kings Rama VI and Rama IX **Rev:** Hospital logo **Edge:** Alternating reeded and plain

Date	Mintage	F	VF	XF	Unc	BU
BE2545(2002)	—	—	—	—	2.00	—

Y# 385 10 BAHT
8.5500 g., Bi-Metallic Brass center in Copper-Nickel ring, 25.8 mm. **Ruler:** Rama IX **Subject:** 20th World Scouting Jamboree **Obv:** King's portrait wearing a scouting uniform **Rev:** Jamboree logo **Edge:** Alternating reeded and plain

Date	Mintage	F	VF	XF	Unc	BU
BE2545(2002)	—	—	—	—	2.00	—

Y# 387 10 BAHT
8.5500 g., Bi-Metallic Brass center in Copper-Nickel ring, 25.8 mm. **Ruler:** Rama IX **Subject:** King's 75th Birthday **Obv:** King's portrait **Rev:** Royal crown in radiant oval **Edge:** Alternating reeded and plain

Date	Mintage	F	VF	XF	Unc	BU
BE2545(2002)	—	—	—	—	2.00	—

Y# 400 10 BAHT
8.5500 g., Bi-Metallic Brass center in Copper-Nickel ring, 25.8 mm. **Ruler:** Rama IX **Obv:** King facing left **Rev:** APEC logo **Edge:** Segmented reeding

Date	Mintage	F	VF	XF	Unc	BU
BE2546-2003	—	—	—	—	3.00	—

Y# 405 10 BAHT
8.5400 g., Bi-Metallic, 25.9 mm. **Ruler:** Rama IX
Subject: "CITES COP" **Obv:** Woman **Rev:** "CITES" logo
Edge: Segmented reeding

Date	Mintage	F	VF	XF	Unc	BU
ND(2003)	—	—	—	—	2.00	—

Y# 391 10 BAHT
8.5000 g., Bi-Metallic Brass center in Copper-Nickel ring, 25.9 mm. **Ruler:** Rama IX **Subject:** Inspector General's Department Centennial **Obv:** King's portrait **Rev:** Department seal **Edge:** Alternating reeded and plain

Date	Mintage	F	VF	XF	Unc	BU
BE2546(2003)	—	—	—	—	1.75	—

Y# 392 10 BAHT
8.5000 g., Bi-Metallic Brass center in Copper-Nickel ring, 25.9 mm. **Ruler:** Rama IX **Subject:** 80th Birthday of Princess **Obv:** Bust of Princess half right **Rev:** Crowned emblem and denomination **Edge:** Alternating reeded and plain

Date	Mintage	F	VF	XF	Unc	BU
BE2546(2003)	—	—	—	—	1.75	—

Y# 396 10 BAHT

8.5500 g., Bi-Metallic Brass center in Copper-Nickel ring, 25.9 mm. **Ruler:** Rama IX **Subject:** 90th Anniversary of the Government Savings Bank **Obv:** Uniformed bust of King Rama VI half right **Rev:** Bank emblem **Edge:** Alternating reeded and plain

Date	Mintage	F	VF	XF	Unc	BU
BE2546(2003)	—	—	—	—	2.00	—

Y# 402 10 BAHT

8.4400 g., Bi-Metallic Brass center in Copper-Nickel ring, 25.9 mm. **Ruler:** Rama IX **Obv:** King wearing glasses **Rev:** Treasury Department seal **Edge:** Segmented reeding

Date	Mintage	F	VF	XF	Unc	BU
ND (BE2548-2005)	—	—	—	—	2.50	—

Y# 406 10 BAHT

8.4400 g., Bi-Metallic Brass center in Copper-Nickel ring, 25.9 mm. **Ruler:** Rama IX **Subject:** 60th Anniversary of Reign **Obv:** Rama IX **Rev:** Royal Crown on display **Edge:** Segmented reeding

Date	Mintage	F	VF	XF	Unc	BU
2549 (2006)	—	—	—	—	—	2.50

Y# 374 20 BAHT

15.1000 g., Copper-Nickel, 31.9 mm. **Ruler:** Rama IX **Subject:** Chulalongkorn University 84th Anniversary **Obv:** Portraits of Kings Chulalongkorn, Vjiravudh, and Bhumibol Adulyadej **Rev:** University emblem dividing denomination **Edge:** Reeded

Date	Mintage	F	VF	XF	Unc	BU
BE2544(2001)	—	—	—	—	3.50	—
BE2544(2001) Proof	—	Value: 12.50				

Y# 375 20 BAHT

15.1000 g., Copper-Nickel **Ruler:** Rama IX **Subject:** Civil Service Comission 72nd Anniversary **Obv:** Conjoined busts of Kings Prajadhipok and Bhumibol Adulyadej left **Rev:** Civil service emblem dividing denomination **Edge:** Reeded

Date	Mintage	F	VF	XF	Unc	BU
BE2544(2001)	—	—	—	—	3.50	—
BE2544(2001) Proof	—	Value: 12.50				

Y# 393 20 BAHT

5.0000 g., Copper-Nickel, 31.9 mm. **Ruler:** Rama IX **Subject:** 80th Birthay of Princess **Obv:** Bust of Princess half right **Rev:** Crowned emblem and value **Edge:** Reeded

Date	Mintage	F	VF	XF	Unc	BU
BE2546(2003)	—	—	—	—	3.50	—
BE2546(2003) Proof	—	Value: 12.50				

Y# 386 20 BAHT

15.0000 g., Copper Nickel, 32 mm. **Ruler:** Rama IX **Subject:** Centennial of Thai Banknotes **Obv:** Portraits of Kings Rama V and Rama IX **Rev:** Coat of arms in center of seal **Edge:** Reeded

Date	Mintage	F	VF	XF	Unc	BU
2545(2002)	—	—	—	—	3.50	—
2545(2002) Proof	—	Value: 12.00				

Y# 388 20 BAHT

15.0000 g., Copper-Nickel, 32 mm. **Ruler:** Rama IX **Subject:** King's 75th Birthday **Rev:** Royal crown in radiant oval **Edge:** Reeded

Date	Mintage	F	VF	XF	Unc	BU
BE2545(2002)	—	—	—	—	3.50	—
BE2545(2002) Proof	—	Value: 12.00				

Y# 397 20 BAHT

15.0000 g., Copper-Nickel, 31.9 mm. **Ruler:** Rama IX **Subject:** Centennial of the National Police **Obv:** Kings Rama VI and IX **Rev:** National Police emblem **Edge:** Reeded

Date	Mintage	F	VF	XF	Unc	BU
BE2545(2002)	—	—	—	—	3.50	—

Y# 398 20 BAHT

15.0000 g., Copper-Nickel, 31.9 mm. **Ruler:** Rama IX **Subject:** 50th Birthday of the Crown Prince **Obv:** Crown Prince **Rev:** Crowned monogram **Edge:** Reeded

Date	Mintage	F	VF	XF	Unc	BU
BE2545(2002)	—	—	—	—	3.50	—

Y# 388 20 BAHT

15.0000 g., Copper-Nickel, 32 mm. **Ruler:** Rama IX **Subject:** King's 75th Birthday **Rev:** Royal crown in radiant oval **Edge:** Reeded

Date	Mintage					
BE2545(2002)	—	—	—	—	3.50	—
	—	Value: 12.00				

Y# 403 20 BAHT

15.0200 g., Copper-Nickel, 31.9 mm. **Ruler:** Rama IX **Obv:** King wearing glasses **Rev:** Treasury Department seal **Edge:** Reeded

Date	Mintage	F	VF	XF	Unc	BU
ND (BE2548-2005)	—	—	—	—	4.00	—

Y# 407 20 BAHT

15.0200 g., Copper Nickel, 31.9 mm. **Ruler:** Rama IX **Subject:** 60th Anniversary of Reign **Obv:** Rama IX **Rev:** Royal Crown on display **Edge:** Reeded

Date	Mintage	F	VF	XF	Unc	BU
2549 (2006)	—	—	—	—	—	4.00
2549 (2006) Proof	—	Value: 15.00				

Y# 404 50 BAHT

21.0000 g., Copper-Nickel, 35.9 mm. **Ruler:** Rama IX **Subject:** Air Force **Obv:** King in uniform **Rev:** Crowned wings in wreath **Edge:** Reeded

Date	Mintage	F	VF	XF	Unc	BU
2546 (2003)	—	—	—	—	12.00	—

Y# 389 600 BAHT

22.1500 g., 0.9250 Silver 0.6587 oz. ASW, 35 mm. **Ruler:** Rama IX **Subject:** King's 75th Birthday **Obv:** King's portrait **Rev:** Royal crown in radiant oval **Edge:** Reeded

Date	Mintage	F	VF	XF	Unc	BU
BE2545(2002)	—	—	—	—	25.00	—
BE2545(2002) Proof	—	Value: 35.00				

Y# 394 600 BAHT

22.1500 g., 0.9250 Silver 0.6587 oz. ASW, 35 mm. **Ruler:** Rama IX **Subject:** 80th Birthday of Princess **Obv:** Bust of Princess half right **Rev:** Crowned emblem and value **Edge:** Reeded

Date	Mintage	F	VF	XF	Unc	BU
BE2546(2003)	—	—	—	—	35.00	—
BE2546(2003) Proof	—	Value: 125				

Y# 401 600 BAHT

22.1500 g., 0.9250 Silver 0.6587 oz. ASW, 35 mm. **Ruler:** Rama IX **Subject:** Queen's Birthday **Obv:** Crowned monogram **Rev:** Queen Sirikit wearing orders **Edge:** Reeded

Date	Mintage	F	VF	XF	Unc	BU
BE2547(2004) Proof	—	Value: 40.00				

Y# 408 600 BAHT

22.1500 g., 0.9250 Silver 0.6587 oz. ASW, 35 mm. **Ruler:** Rama IX **Subject:** 60th Anniversary of Reign **Obv:** Rama IX **Rev:** Royal Crown on display **Edge:** Reeded

Date	Mintage	F	VF	XF	Unc	BU
2549 (2006)	—	—	—	—	—	35.00
2549 (2006) Proof	—	Value: 125				

Y# 390 7500 BAHT

15.0000 g., 0.9000 Gold 0.434 oz. AGW, 26 mm. **Ruler:** Rama IX **Subject:** King's 75th Birthday **Obv:** King's portrait **Rev:** Royal crown in radiant oval **Edge:** Reeded

Date	Mintage	F	VF	XF	Unc	BU
BE2545(2002)	—	—	—	—	325	—
BE2545(2002) Proof	—	Value: 425				

Y# 395 9000 BAHT

15.0000 g., 0.9000 Gold 0.434 oz. AGW, 26 mm. **Ruler:** Rama IX **Subject:** 80th Birthday of Princess **Obv:** Bust of Princess half right **Rev:** Crowned emblem and value **Edge:** Reeded

Date	Mintage	F	VF	XF	Unc	BU
BE2546 (2003)	—	—	—	—	400	—
BE2546 (2003) Proof	—	Value: 700				

TOGO

The Republic of Togo (formerly part of German Togoland), situated on the Gulf of Guinea in West Africa between Ghana and Dahomey, has an area of 21,622 sq. mi. (56,790 sq. km.) and a population of *3.4 million. Capital: Lome. Agriculture and herding, the production of dyewoods, and the mining of phosphates and iron ore are the chief industries. Copra, phosphates and coffee are exported.

MINT MARKS
(a) - Paris, privy marks only

MONETARY SYSTEM
100 Centimes = 1 Franc

REPUBLIC

INSTITUT MONETAIRE

KM# 20 6000 CFA FRANCS - 4 AFRICA
10.1000 g., Bi-Metallic Copper-Nickel center in Brass ring, 28.3 mm. **Obv:** Elephants fighting **Rev:** Elephant head on map **Edge:** Plain

Date	Mintage	F	VF	XF	Unc	BU
2003	1,200	—	—	—	35.00	—

KM# 20a 6000 CFA FRANCS - 4 AFRICA
13.2000 g., 0.9990 Silver, 28.3 mm. **Edge:** Plain

Date	Mintage	F	VF	XF	Unc	BU
2003	5	—	—	—	135	—

KM# 20b 6000 CFA FRANCS - 4 AFRICA
11.0000 g., 0.9990 Bi-Metallic .999 Silver center in .999 Gold ring 0.3533 oz., 28.3 mm. **Obv:** Elephants fighting **Rev:** Elephant head on map **Edge:** Plain

Date	Mintage	F	VF	XF	Unc	BU
2003	5	—	—	—	450	—

KM# 21 6000 CFA FRANCS - 4 AFRICA
10.1000 g., Bi-Metallic Copper-Nickel center in Brass ring, 28.3 mm. **Obv:** Native woman **Rev:** Elephant head on map **Edge:** Plain

Date	Mintage	F	VF	XF	Unc	BU
2003	1,200	—	—	—	35.00	—

KM# 21a 6000 CFA FRANCS - 4 AFRICA
13.2000 g., 0.9990 Silver, 28.3 mm. **Edge:** Plain

Date	Mintage	F	VF	XF	Unc	BU
2003	5	—	—	—	135	—

KM# 21b 6000 CFA FRANCS - 4 AFRICA
11.0000 g., 0.9990 Bi-Metallic .999 Silver center in .999 Gold ring 0.3533 oz., 28.3 mm. **Obv:** Topless female **Rev:** Elephant head on map **Edge:** Plain

Date	Mintage	F	VF	XF	Unc	BU
2003	5	—	—	—	450	—

KM# 22 6000 CFA FRANCS - 4 AFRICA
10.1000 g., Bi-Metallic Copper-Nickel center in Brass ring, 28.3 mm. **Obv:** President left of map **Rev:** Elephant head on map **Edge:** Plain

Date	Mintage	F	VF	XF	Unc	BU
ND(2003)	500	—	—	—	40.00	—

KM# 30 6000 CFA FRANCS - 4 AFRICA
0.9990 Silver, 28.4 mm. **Obv:** President **Rev:** Elephant head on full Africa map within Presidential legend

Date	Mintage	F	VF	XF	Unc	BU
2003	5	—	—	—	480	—

KM# 30a 6000 CFA FRANCS - 4 AFRICA
Bi-Metallic .999 Silver center in .999 Gold plated .999 Silver ring, 28.4 mm. **Obv:** President **Rev:** Elephant head on full Africa map within Presidential legend

Date	Mintage	F	VF	XF	Unc	BU
2003	5	—	—	—	480	—

KM# 32 6000 CFA FRANCS - 4 AFRICA
0.9990 Silver, 28.4 mm. **Obv:** Fighting Elephants **Rev:** Elephant head on full Africa map with Presidential legend

Date	Mintage	F	VF	XF	Unc	BU
2003	5	—	—	—	480	—

KM# 32a 6000 CFA FRANCS - 4 AFRICA
Bi-Metallic .999 Silver center in .999 Gold plated .999 Silver ring, 28.4 mm. **Obv:** Fighting elephants **Rev:** Elephant head on full Africa map with Presidential legend

Date	Mintage	F	VF	XF	Unc	BU
2003	5	—	—	—	480	—

KM# 33 6000 CFA FRANCS - 4 AFRICA
0.9990 Silver, 28.4 mm. **Obv:** Topless girl **Rev:** Elephant head on full Africa map with Presidential legend

Date	Mintage	F	VF	XF	Unc	BU
2003	5	—	—	—	480	—

KM# 33a 6000 CFA FRANCS - 4 AFRICA
Bi-Metallic .999 Silver center in .999 Gold plated .999 Silver ring, 28.4 mm. **Obv:** Topless girl **Rev:** Elephant head on full Africa map with Presidential legend

Date	Mintage	F	VF	XF	Unc	BU
2003	5	—	—	—	480	—

KM# 23 150000 CFA FRANCS - 100 AFRICA
13.2000 g., 0.9990 Silver, 28.4 mm. **Obv:** President and map **Rev:** Elephant head on map

Date	Mintage	F	VF	XF	Unc	BU
ND(2003)	25	—	—	—	250	—

KM# 23a 150000 CFA FRANCS - 100 AFRICA
13.2000 g., 0.9990 Gold Plated Silver, 28.4 mm.

Date	Mintage	F	VF	XF	Unc	BU
ND(2003)	25	—	—	—	265	—

KM# 31 150000 CFA FRANCS - 100 AFRICA
0.9990 Silver **Obv:** President **Rev:** Elephant head on full Africa map within Presidential legend

Date	Mintage	F	VF	XF	Unc	BU
2003	5	—	—	—	480	—

KM# 31a 150000 CFA FRANCS - 100 AFRICA
Bi-Metallic .999 Silver center in .999 Gold plated .999 Silver ring **Obv:** President **Rev:** Elephant head on full Africa map within Presidential legend

Date	Mintage	F	VF	XF	Unc	BU
2003	5	—	—	—	480	—

STANDARD COINAGE

100 Centimes = 1 Franc

KM# 29 500 FRANCS
7.0500 g., 0.9990 Silver 0.2264 oz. ASW, 30 mm. **Obv:** National arms above value **Rev:** Multicolor tiger **Edge:** Plain

Date	Mintage	F	VF	XF	Unc	BU
2001 Proof	—	Value: 50.00				

KM# 18 500 FRANCS
6.9300 g., 0.9990 Silver 0.2226 oz. ASW, 29.7 mm. **Obv:** National arms **Rev:** "Gorch Fock" sailing school ship **Edge:** Plain

Date	Mintage	F	VF	XF	Unc	BU
ND(2000) Proof	—	Value: 35.00				

KM# 17 1000 FRANCS
14.9500 g., 0.9990 Silver 0.4802 oz. ASW, 35 mm. **Obv:** National arms **Rev:** Adler von Lubeck sailing ship **Edge:** Plain

Date	Mintage	F	VF	XF	Unc	BU
2001 Proof	—	Value: 50.00				

KM# 35 1000 FRANCS
14.7000 g., 0.9990 Silver 0.4721 oz. ASW, 36 mm. **Subject:** World Cup Soccer - Bern 1954 **Obv:** National arms **Rev:** Portrait and tower **Edge:** Plain

Date	Mintage	F	VF	XF	Unc	BU
2001 Proof	—	Value: 40.00				

KM# 36 1000 FRANCS
19.9100 g., 0.9990 Silver 0.6395 oz. ASW, 38.1 mm. **Subject:** World Cup Soccer - France 1938 **Obv:** National arms **Rev:** Eiffel Tower behind soccer player kicking ball **Edge:** Reeded

Date	Mintage	F	VF	XF	Unc	BU
2001 Proof	—	Value: 40.00				

KM# 37 1000 FRANCS
19.9700 g., 0.9990 Silver 0.6414 oz. ASW, 40 mm. **Subject:** World Cup Soccer - USA 1994 **Obv:** National arms **Rev:** Soccer player **Edge:** Reeded

Date	Mintage	F	VF	XF	Unc	BU
2002 Proof	—	Value: 40.00				

KM# 38 1000 FRANCS
30.7300 g., 0.9990 Silver 0.987 oz. ASW, 39 mm. **Subject:** Year of the Monkey **Obv:** Native Chieftan **Rev:** Gold plated Monkey **Edge:** Reeded

Date	Mintage	F	VF	XF	Unc	BU
ND (2004) Proof	—	Value: 50.00				

KM# 39 1000 FRANCS
62.2400 g., 0.9999 Silver 2.0009 oz. ASW, 50 mm.
Subject: Year of the Monkey **Obv:** Gold plated World Globe center **Rev:** Gold plated center with holographic monkey **Edge:** Reeded and lettered sections **Edge Lettering:** "PAN ASIA BANK TAIWAN" in English and Chinese

Date	Mintage	F	VF	XF	Unc	BU
ND (2004) Proof	—	Value: 60.00				

KM# 24 1000 FRANCS
31.1035 g., 0.9990 Silver 0.999 oz. ASW, 40 mm. **Obv:** National arms **Rev:** Convex horsewoman left **Edge:** Plain

Date	Mintage	F	VF	XF	Unc	BU
2004	2,500	—	—	—	—	55.00

KM# 25 1000 FRANCS
31.1035 g., 0.9990 Silver 0.999 oz. ASW, 40 mm. **Obv:** National arms **Rev:** Concave horsewoman right **Edge:** Plain

Date	Mintage	F	VF	XF	Unc	BU
2004	2,500	—	—	—	—	55.00

KM# 26 1000 FRANCS
1.2440 g., 0.9999 Gold 0.04 oz. AGW, 13.92 mm. **Obv:** National arms **Rev:** Convex Nike **Edge:** Plain

Date	Mintage	F	VF	XF	Unc	BU
2004 Proof	5,000	Value: 60.00				

KM# 27 1000 FRANCS
1.2440 g., 0.9999 Gold 0.04 oz. AGW, 13.92 mm. **Obv:** National arms **Rev:** Concave Nike **Edge:** Plain

Date	Mintage	F	VF	XF	Unc	BU
2004 Proof	5,000	Value: 60.00				

KM# 34 1000 FRANCS
30.9200 g., 0.9990 Silver 0.9931 oz. ASW, 39 mm. **Obv:** Native chieftan **Rev:** Gold plated Baboon **Edge:** Reeded

Date	Mintage	F	VF	XF	Unc	BU
ND (2004) Proof	—	Value: 50.00				

ESSAIS

KM#	Date	Mintage	Identification	Mkt Val
E17	ND(2003)	2	150000 Cfa Francs - 100 Africa. Bi-Metallic. President and map. Elephant head on map.	250

TOKELAU ISLANDS

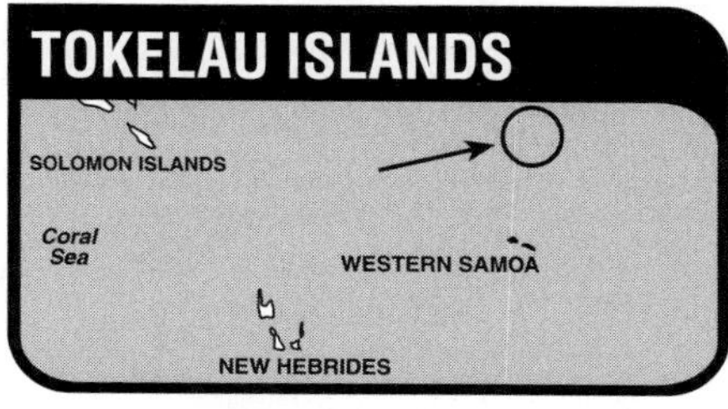

Tokelau or Union Islands, a New Zealand Territory located in the South Pacific 2,100 miles (3,379 km.) northeast of New Zealand and 300 miles (483 km.) north of Samoa, has an area of 4 sq. mi. (10 sq. km.) and a population of *2,000. Geographically, the group consists of four atolls - Atafu, Nukunono, Fakaofo and Swains – but the last belongs to American Samoa (and the United States claims the other three). The people are of Polynesian origin; Samoan is the official language. The New Zealand Minister for Foreign Affairs governs the islands; councils of family elders handle local government at the village level. The chief settlement is Fenuafala, on Fakaofo. It is connected by wireless with the offices of the New Zealand Administrative Center, located at Apia, Western Samoa. Subsistence farming and the production of copra for export are the main occupations. Revenue is also derived from the sale of postage stamps and, since 1978,coins.

NEW ZEALAND TERRITORY

STANDARD COINAGE

KM# 30 5 TALA
31.1000 g., 0.9990 Silver 0.9989 oz. ASW, 40 mm. **Obv:** Elizabeth II **Rev:** Fin Whale on mother of pearl insert **Edge:** Plain

Date	Mintage	F	VF	XF	Unc	BU
2002 Proof	2,000	Value: 60.00				

TONGA

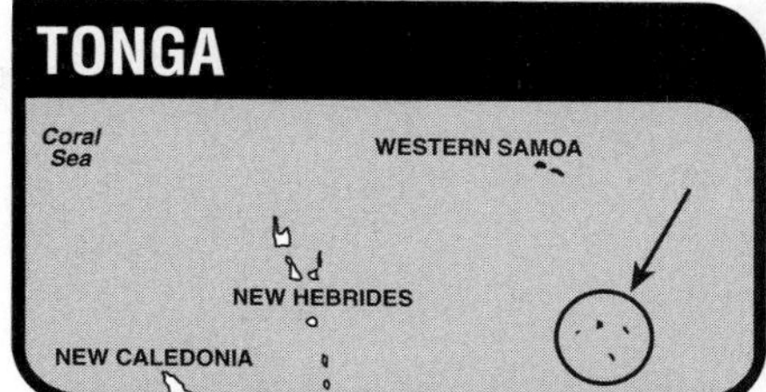

The Kingdom of Tonga (or Friendly Islands) is an archipelago situated in the southern Pacific Ocean south of Western Samoa and east of Fiji comprised of 150 islands. Tonga has an area of 270 sq. mi. (748 sq. km.) and a population of *100,000. Capital: Nuku'alofa. Primarily agricultural, the kingdom exports bananas and copra.

The monarchy is a member of the Commonwealth of Nations. King Taufa'ahau is Head of State and Government.

KINGDOM

DECIMAL COINAGE

100 Senti = 1 Pa'anga; 100 Pa'anga = 1 Hau

KM# 178 PA'ANGA
31.1000 g., 0.9990 Silver 0.9989 oz. ASW, 40 mm.
Ruler: King Taufa'ahau IV **Obv:** National arms **Rev:** Right Whale on mother of pearl insert **Edge:** Plain

Date	Mintage	F	VF	XF	Unc	BU
2002 Proof	2,000	Value: 60.00				

TRANSNISTRIA

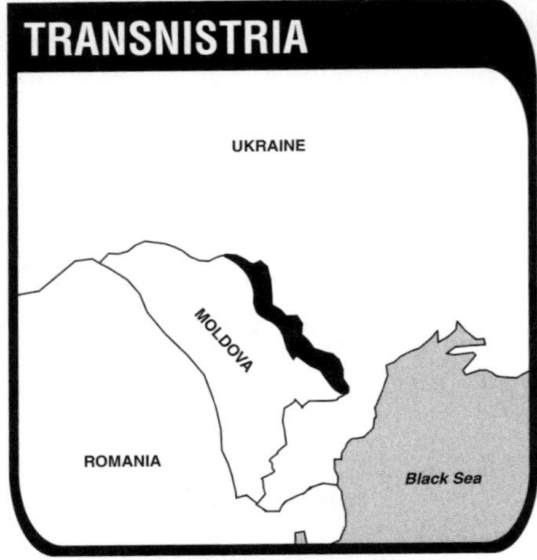

The Transnistria Moldavian Republic was formed in 1990, even before the separation of Moldavia from Russia. It has an area of 11,544 sq. mi. (29,900 sq. km.) and a population of 700,000. Capital: Tiraspol.

Transnistria has a president, parliament, army and police forces, but as yet it is lacking international recognition.

MOLDAVIAN REPUBLIC

STANDARD COINAGE

1 Rublei = 100 Kopeek

KM# 2 5 KOPEEK
0.7000 g., Aluminum, 17.9 mm. **Obv:** State arms **Rev:** Denomination between wheat stalks **Edge:** Plain

Date	Mintage	F	VF	XF	Unc	BU
2005	—	—	—	—	0.50	0.65

KM# 3 10 KOPEEK
1.0000 g., Aluminum, 20 mm. **Obv:** State arms **Rev:** Denomination between wheat stalks **Edge:** Plain

Date	Mintage	F	VF	XF	Unc	BU
2005	—	—	—	—	0.75	0.90

KM# 5 25 KOPEEK
2.1500 g., Aluminum-Bronze, 17 mm. **Obv:** State arms **Rev:** Denomination between wheat stalks **Edge:** Plain

Date	Mintage	F	VF	XF	Unc	BU
2002	—	—	—	—	1.00	1.20

KM# 7 100 RUBLEI
14.1600 g., 0.9250 Silver - Billon 0.4211 oz. ASW, 32 mm. **Subject:** City of Tiraspol **Obv:** State arms **Rev:** Statue and buildings **Edge:** Plain

Date	Mintage	F	VF	XF	Unc	BU
2002 Proof	—	Value: 45.00				

KM# 8 100 RUBLEI
14.1600 g., 0.9250 Silver 0.4211 oz. ASW, 32 mm. **Subject:** City of Tiraspol **Obv:** State arms **Rev:** Cameo portrait above fortress **Edge:** Plain

Date	Mintage	F	VF	XF	Unc	BU
2002 Proof	—	Value: 45.00				

KM# 9 100 RUBLEI
14.1600 g., 0.9250 Silver 0.4211 oz. ASW, 32 mm. **Subject:** K. K. Gedroets **Obv:** State arms **Rev:** Portrait with plants, beaker and book **Edge:** Plain

Date	Mintage	F	VF	XF	Unc	BU
2002 Proof	500	Value: 45.00				

KM# 10 100 RUBLEI
14.0400 g., 0.9250 Silver 0.4175 oz. ASW, 32 mm. **Subject:** 10th Anniversary - Trans-Dniester Republican Bank **Obv:** State arms **Rev:** Colorized monogram in wreath with "1992" at top **Edge:** Plain

Date	Mintage	F	VF	XF	Unc	BU
2002 Proof	500	Value: 45.00				

KM# 11 100 RUBLEI
14.1400 g., 0.9250 Silver 0.4205 oz. ASW, 32 mm. **Obv:** State arms **Rev:** Upupa Epops bird on branch **Edge:** Plain

Date	Mintage	F	VF	XF	Unc	BU
2003 Proof	500	Value: 45.00				

KM# 12 100 RUBLEI
14.1400 g., 0.9250 Silver 0.4205 oz. ASW, 32 mm. **Obv:** State arms **Rev:** City of Bendery arms **Edge:** Plain

Date	Mintage	F	VF	XF	Unc	BU
2003 Proof	500	Value: 45.00				

KM# 13 100 RUBLEI
14.1400 g., 0.9250 Silver 0.4205 oz. ASW, 32 mm. **Subject:** 80th Anniversary of Nationhood **Obv:** National arms **Rev:** Map and multicolor flag **Edge:** Plain

Date	Mintage	F	VF	XF	Unc	BU
2004 Proof	500	Value: 45.00				

KM# 14 100 RUBLEI
14.1400 g., 0.9250 Silver 0.4205 oz. ASW, 32 mm. **Obv:** State arms **Rev:** Two deer; a doe and her fawn **Edge:** Plain

Date	Mintage	F	VF	XF	Unc	BU
2004 Proof	1,000	Value: 35.00				

KM# 15 100 RUBLEI
14.1400 g., 0.9250 Silver 0.4205 oz. ASW, 32 mm. **Obv:** National arms **Rev:** Eurasian Griffon bird on rock **Edge:** Plain

Date	Mintage	F	VF	XF	Unc	BU
2005 Proof	1,000	Value: 35.00				

TRINIDAD & TOBAGO

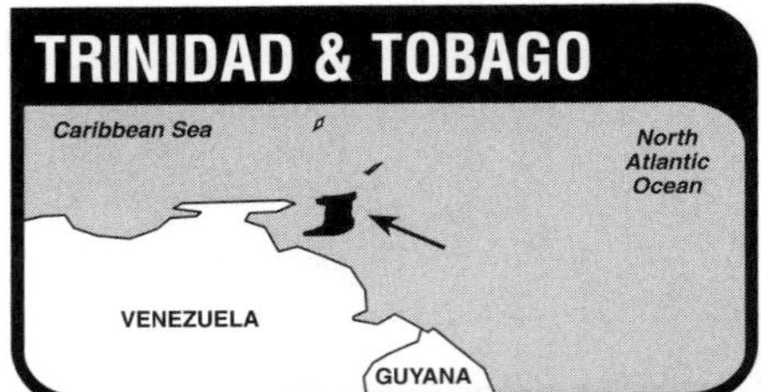

The Republic of Trinidad and Tobago is situated 7 miles (11 km.) off the coast of Venezuela, has an area of 1,981 sq. mi. (5,130 sq. km.) and a population of *1.2 million. Capital: Port-of-Spain. The island of Trinidad contains the world's largest natural asphalt bog. Birds of Paradise live on little Tobago, the only place outside of their native New Guinea where they can be found in a wild state. Petroleum and petroleum products are the mainstay of the economy. Petroleum products, crude oil and sugar are exported.

Trinidad and Tobago is a member of the Commonwealth of Nations. The President is Chief of State. The Prime Minister is Head of Government.

MONETARY SYSTEM
100 Cents = 1 Dollar

REPUBLIC

STANDARD COINAGE

KM# 30 5 CENTS
Bronze **Rev:** Great bird of paradise

Date	Mintage	F	VF	XF	Unc	BU
2001	—	—	—	0.10	0.25	0.50

KM# 31 10 CENTS
Copper-Nickel **Rev:** Hibiscus **Edge:** Reeded

Date	Mintage	F	VF	XF	Unc	BU
2002	—	—	—	—	0.50	1.00

TRISTAN DA CUNHA

Tristan da Cunha is the principal island and group name of a small cluster of volcanic islands located in the South Atlantic midway between the Cape of Good Hope and South America, and 1,500 miles (2,414 km.) south-southwest of the British colony of St. Helena. The other islands are inaccessible, Gough, and the three Nightingale Islands. The group, which comprises a dependency of St. Helena, has a total area of 40 sq. mi. (104 sq. km.) and a population of less than 300. There is a village of 60 houses called Edinburgh. Potatoes are the staple subsistence crop.

MONETARY SYSTEM

25 Pence = 1 Crown

ST. HELENA DEPENDENCY

STANDARD COINAGE

KM# 13 50 PENCE

29.6000 g., Copper-Nickel, 38.7 mm. **Subject:** Centennial of Queen Victoria's Death **Obv:** Queen Elizabeth's portrait **Obv. Designer:** Raphael Maklouf **Rev:** Queen Victoria's portrait **Edge:** Reeded

Date	Mintage	F	VF	XF	Unc	BU
2001	—	—	—	—	8.00	10.00

KM# 13a 50 PENCE

28.2800 g., 0.9250 Silver 0.841 oz. ASW, 38.6 mm. **Subject:** Centennial of Queen Victoria's Death **Obv:** Queen Elizabeth II **Rev:** Queen Victoria **Edge:** Reeded

Date	Mintage	F	VF	XF	Unc	BU
2001 Proof	10,000	Value: 50.00				

KM# 13b 50 PENCE

47.5400 g., 0.9166 Gold 1.401 oz. AGW, 38.6 mm. **Subject:** Centennial of Queen Victoria's Death **Obv:** Queen Elizabeth II **Rev:** Queen Victoria **Edge:** Reeded

Date	Mintage	F	VF	XF	Unc	BU
2001 Proof	100	Value: 975				

KM# 12 50 PENCE

29.1000 g., Copper-Nickel, 38.6 mm. **Subject:** Queen Elizabeth's 75th Birthday **Obv:** Queen's portrait in profile **Obv. Designer:** Raphael Maklouf **Rev:** Queen's portrait facing viewer **Edge:** Reeded

Date	Mintage	F	VF	XF	Unc	BU
2001	—	—	—	—	7.00	8.00

KM# 12a 50 PENCE

28.2800 g., 0.9250 Silver 0.841 oz. ASW, 38.6 mm. **Subject:** Queen's 75th Birthday **Obv:** Queen Elizabeth II above value **Rev:** Queen above date **Edge:** Reeded

Date	Mintage	F	VF	XF	Unc	BU
2001 Proof	10,000	Value: 40.00				

KM# 12b 50 PENCE

47.5400 g., 0.9166 Gold 1.401 oz. AGW, 38.6 mm.

Date	Mintage	F	VF	XF	Unc	BU
2001 Proof	75	Value: 1,000				

KM# 14 CROWN

24.1200 g., 0.9250 Silver 0.7173 oz. ASW, 38.5 mm. **Obv:** Elizabeth II **Rev:** Pope John Paul II **Edge:** Reeded

Date	Mintage	F	VF	XF	Unc	BU
2005	—	—	—	—	25.00	27.50
2005 Proof	—	Value: 30.00				

PIEFORTS

KM#	Date	Mintage	Identification	Mkt Val
P1	2001	500	50 Pence. 0.9250 Silver. 56.5400 g. 38.6 mm.	100
P2	2001	500	50 Pence. 0.9250 Silver. 56.5600 g. 38.6 mm. Reeded edge. Proof KM-13a.	100

TUNISIA

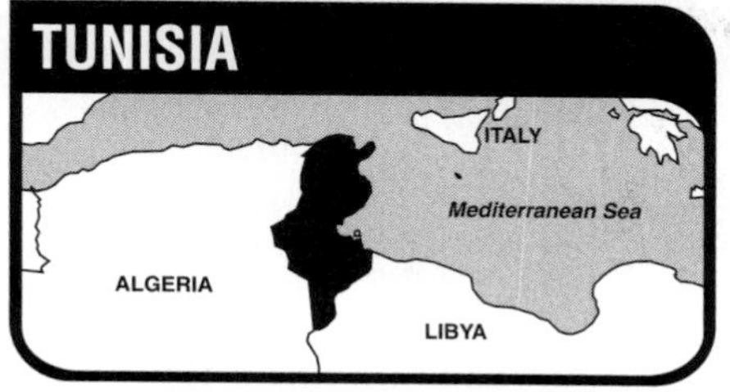

The Republic of Tunisia, located on the northern coast of Africa between Algeria and Libya, has an area of 63,170sq. mi. (163,610 sq. km.) and a population of *7.9 million. Capital: Tunis. Agriculture is the backbone of the economy. Crude oil, phosphates, olive oil, and wine are exported.

TITLES

المملكة التونسية

al-Mamlaka al-Tunisiya

الجمهورية التونسية

al-Jumhuriya al-Tunisiya

al-Amala al-Tunisiya
(Tunisian Protectorate)

REPUBLIC

DECIMAL COINAGE

1000 Millim = 1 Dinar

KM# 350 5 DINARS

10.0000 g., Bi-Metallic Copper-Nickel center in Brass ring Copper-Nickel center in Brass ring, 29 mm. **Obv:** National arms **Rev:** Former president Habib Bourguiba **Edge:** Six reeded and six plain sections **Shape:** 12-sided

Date	Mintage	F	VF	XF	Unc
AH1423-2002	—	—	—	—	6.00

KM# 352 100 DINARS

38.0000 g., 0.9000 Gold 1.0996 oz. AGW, 40 mm. **Subject:** United Nations **Obv:** National arms above value **Rev:** UN logo on stylized hand **Edge:** Reeded

Date	Mintage	F	VF	XF	Unc
AH1424-2003 Proof	—	Value: 775			

TURKEY

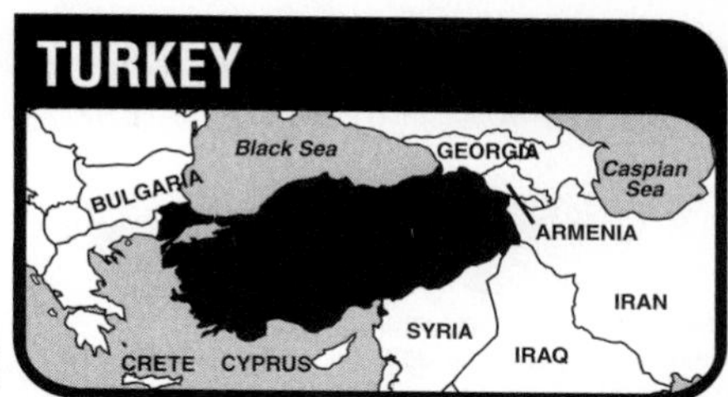

The Republic of Turkey, a parliamentary democracy of the Near East located partially in Europe and partially in Asia between the Black and the Mediterranean Seas, has an area of 301,382 sq. mi. (780,580 sq. km.) and a population of *55.4 million. Capital: Ankara. Turkey exports cotton, hazelnuts, and tobacco, and enjoys a virtual monopoly in meerschaum.

REPUBLIC

DECIMAL COINAGE

Western numerals and Latin alphabet

40 Para = 1 Kurus; 100 Kurus = 1 Lira

KM# 1104 25000 LIRA (25 Bin Lira)

2.7000 g., Copper-Zinc, 17 mm. **Obv:** Bust of Kemal Atatürk **Rev:** Denomination **Edge:** Plain

Date	Mintage	F	VF	XF	Unc
2001	—	—	—	—	2.50

KM# 1105 50000 LIRA (50 Bin Lira)

3.2000 g., Copper-Nickel-Zinc, 17.75 mm. **Obv:** Ataturk's portrait **Rev:** Denomination **Edge:** Plain

Date	Mintage	F	VF	XF	Unc
2001	—	—	—	—	3.00
2002	—	—	—	—	3.00

KM# 1106 100000 LIRA (100 Bin Lira)

4.6000 g., Copper-Nickel-Zinc, 21 mm. **Obv:** Ataturk wearing hat **Rev:** Denomination **Edge:** Plain

Date	Mintage	F	VF	XF	Unc
2001	—	—	—	—	3.50
2002	—	—	—	—	3.50
2003	—	—	—	—	3.50

KM# 1137 250000 LIRA

6.4200 g., Copper-Nickel-Zinc, 23.4 mm. **Obv:** Portrait **Rev:** Denomination **Edge Lettering:** "T.C." six times dividing reeded sections

Date	Mintage	F	VF	XF	Unc
2002	—	—	—	—	1.75
2003	—	—	—	—	1.75

KM# 1161 500000 LIRA

4.6000 g., Copper-Nickel, 21 mm. **Obv:** Value **Rev:** One sheep **Edge:** Plain

Date	Mintage	F	VF	XF	Unc
2002	—	—	—	—	2.50

KM# 1162 750000 LIRA
6.4000 g., Copper-Nickel, 23.5 mm. **Obv:** Value **Rev:** Ram **Edge:** Plain

Date	Mintage	F	VF	XF	Unc
2002	—	—	—	—	3.50

KM# 1163 1000000 LIRA
12.0000 g., Copper-Nickel, 31.9 mm. **Obv:** Value **Rev:** Turbaned bust of Yunus Emre half left **Edge:** Reeded

Date	Mintage	F	VF	XF	Unc
2002	—	—	—	—	5.00

KM# 1170 1000000 LIRA
31.4200 g., 0.9250 Silver 0.9344 oz. ASW, 38.6 mm. **Subject:** Mevlana Celaleddin-I Rumi **Obv:** Value and date in wreath **Rev:** Turbaned bust **Edge:** Reeded

Date	Mintage	F	VF	XF	Unc
2002 Proof	—	Value: 45.00			

KM# 1139 1000000 LIRA
11.8700 g., Bi-Metallic Brass center in Copper-Nickel ring Brass center in Copper-Nickel ring, 32.1 mm. **Subject:** Foundation of the Mint **Obv:** National arms above building and denomination **Rev:** Legend and date inscription **Edge:** Plain **Note:** This coin type is produced by a machine outside the money museum at the Istanbul Mint. Visitors pay 1 mio lira, press a button and strike a coin with the actual date of their visit. Many other dates exist in unknown and unregistered quantities.

Date	Mintage	F	VF	XF	Unc
06 Mayis 2002	—	—	—	—	15.00
19 Kasim 2002	—	—	—	—	15.00
28 Kasim 2002	—	—	—	—	15.00
10 Mayis 2002	—	—	—	—	15.00
17 Jan 2003	—	—	—	—	15.00
18 Jan 2003	—	—	—	—	15.00

KM# 1107 3000000 LIRA
31.4700 g., 0.9250 Silver .9359 oz. ASW, 38.6 mm. **Series:** Olympics **Obv:** Denomination **Rev:** Long jumper and logo **Edge:** Reeded

Date	Mintage	F	VF	XF	Unc
2002 Proof	—	Value: 35.00			

KM# 1110 5000000 LIRA
67.0000 g., Bronze, 50 mm. **Subject:** Children's Day **Obv:** Legend and inscription **Rev:** Dancing children **Edge:** Plain

Date	Mintage	F	VF	XF	Unc
2001 Matte	1,583	—	—	—	20.00

KM# 1142 7500000 LIRA
31.2500 g., 0.9250 Silver 0.9294 oz. ASW, 38.5 mm. **Obv:** Mathematical formula **Rev:** 1/2-length figure of Cahit Arf, mathematician, facing **Edge:** Reeded

Date	Mintage	F	VF	XF	Unc
2001 Proof	—	Value: 42.50			

KM# 1143 7500000 LIRA
31.2500 g., 0.9250 Silver 0.9294 oz. ASW, 38.5 mm. **Obv:** Ornamented circle design **Rev:** 1/2-length bust of Mimar Koca Sinan, Architect, facing **Edge:** Reeded

Date	Mintage	F	VF	XF	Unc
2001 Proof	—	Value: 42.50			

KM# 1144 7500000 LIRA
31.2500 g., 0.9250 Silver 0.9294 oz. ASW, 38.5 mm. **Subject:** Koca Yusuf Baspehlivan **Obv:** Two figures wrestling **Rev:** Portrait on circular background **Edge:** Reeded

Date	Mintage	F	VF	XF	Unc
2001 Proof	—	Value: 40.00			

KM# 1120 7500000 LIRA
15.4000 g., 0.9250 Silver 0.458 oz. ASW **Subject:** Bird Series - Saz Horozu **Obv:** Denomination **Rev:** Purple swamphen on ground **Edge:** Plain **Shape:** 4-sided **Note:** 28.1 x 28.1mm

Date	Mintage	F	VF	XF	Unc
2001 Proof	—	Value: 22.50			

KM# 1121 7500000 LIRA
15.4000 g., 0.9250 Silver 0.458 oz. ASW **Subject:** Bird Series - Toy **Obv:** Denomination **Rev:** Greater Bustard on ground **Edge:** Plain **Shape:** 4-sided **Note:** 28.1 x 28.1mm

Date	Mintage	F	VF	XF	Unc
2001 Proof	—	Value: 22.50			

KM# 1122 7500000 LIRA
15.4000 g., 0.9250 Silver 0.458 oz. ASW **Subject:** Bird Series - Yaz Ordegi **Obv:** Denomination **Rev:** White-headed duck on ground **Edge:** Plain **Shape:** 4-sided **Note:** 28.1 x 28.1mm

Date	Mintage	F	VF	XF	Unc
2001 Proof	—	Value: 22.50			

KM# 1123 7500000 LIRA
15.4000 g., 0.9250 Silver 0.458 oz. ASW **Subject:** Bird Series - Dikkuyruk **Obv:** Denomination **Rev:** Marbled teal on water **Edge:** Plain **Shape:** 4-sided **Note:** 28.1 x 28.1mm

Date	Mintage	F	VF	XF	Unc
2001 Proof	—	Value: 22.50			

KM# 1124 7500000 LIRA
15.4000 g., 0.9250 Silver 0.458 oz. ASW **Subject:** Bird Series - Yesil Arikusu **Obv:** Denomination **Rev:** Bee-eater on branch **Edge:** Plain **Shape:** 4-sided **Note:** 28.1 x 28.1mm

Date	Mintage	F	VF	XF	Unc
2001 Proof	—	Value: 22.50			

KM# 1125 7500000 LIRA
15.4000 g., 0.9250 Silver 0.458 oz. ASW **Subject:** Bird Series - Kucuk Karabatak **Obv:** Denomination **Rev:** Three pygmy cormorants **Edge:** Plain **Shape:** 4-sided **Note:** 28.1 x 28.1mm

Date	Mintage	F	VF	XF	Unc
2001 Proof	—	Value: 24.00			

KM# 1126 7500000 LIRA
15.4000 g., 0.9250 Silver 0.458 oz. ASW **Subject:** Bird Series - Kizil Akbaba **Obv:** Denomination **Rev:** Eurasian griffon **Edge:** Plain **Shape:** 4-sided **Note:** 28.1 x 28.1mm

Date	Mintage	F	VF	XF	Unc
2001 Proof	—	Value: 22.50			

KM# 1127 7500000 LIRA
15.4000 g., 0.9250 Silver 0.458 oz. ASW **Subject:** Bird Series - Sah Kartal **Obv:** Denomination **Rev:** Two imperial eagles **Edge:** Plain **Shape:** 4-sided **Note:** 28.1 x 28.1mm

Date	Mintage	F	VF	XF	Unc
2001 Proof	—	Value: 25.00			

KM# 1128 7500000 LIRA

15.4000 g., 0.9250 Silver 0.458 oz. ASW **Subject:** Bird Series - Ala Sigireik **Obv:** Denomination **Rev:** Rosy starling on ground **Edge:** Plain **Shape:** 4-sided **Note:** 28.1 x 28.1mm

Date	Mintage	F	VF	XF	Unc
2001 Proof	—	Value: 22.50			

KM# 1129 7500000 LIRA

15.4000 g., 0.9250 Silver 0.458 oz. ASW **Subject:** Bird Series - Izmir Yalicapkini **Obv:** Denomination **Rev:** White-throated kingfisher on stump **Edge:** Plain **Shape:** 4-sided **Note:** 28.1 x 28.1mm

Date	Mintage	F	VF	XF	Unc
2001 Proof	—	Value: 22.50			

KM# 1130 7500000 LIRA

15.4000 g., 0.9250 Silver 0.458 oz. ASW **Subject:** Bird Series - Turac **Obv:** Denomination **Rev:** Black francolin birds on the ground **Edge:** Plain **Shape:** 4-sided **Note:** 28.1 x 28.1mm

Date	Mintage	F	VF	XF	Unc
2001 Proof	—	Value: 22.50			

KM# 1131 7500000 LIRA

15.4000 g., 0.9250 Silver 0.458 oz. ASW **Subject:** Bird Series - Kelaynak **Obv:** Denomination **Rev:** Two Bald Ibis birds on ground **Edge:** Plain **Shape:** 4-sided **Note:** 28.1 x 28.1mm

Date	Mintage	F	VF	XF	Unc
2001 Proof	—	Value: 22.50			

KM# 1132 7500000 LIRA

15.4000 g., 0.9250 Silver 0.458 oz. ASW, 28.1x28.1 mm. **Subject:** Bird Series - Sakalli Akbaba **Obv:** Denomination **Rev:** Bearded vulture **Edge:** Plain **Shape:** 4-sided **Note:** 28.1 x 28.1mm

Date	Mintage	F	VF	XF	Unc
2001 Proof	—	Value: 24.00			

KM# 1133 7500000 LIRA

15.4000 g., 0.9250 Silver 0.458 oz. ASW **Subject:** Bird Series - Tepeli Pelikan **Obv:** Denomination **Rev:** Dalmatian pelican on rock **Edge:** Plain **Shape:** Square **Note:** 28.1 x 28.1mm

Date	Mintage	F	VF	XF	Unc
2001 Proof	—	Value: 24.00			

KM# 1134 7500000 LIRA

15.4000 g., 0.9250 Silver 0.458 oz. ASW **Subject:** Bird Series - Ishakkusu **Obv:** Denomination **Rev:** European scops owl on branch **Edge:** Plain **Shape:** 4-sided **Note:** 28.1 x 28.1mm

Date	Mintage	F	VF	XF	Unc
2001 Proof	—	Value: 24.00			

KM# 1117 7500000 LIRA

31.4700 g., 0.9250 Silver .9359 oz. ASW **Subject:** Iznik Tabak **Obv:** Two peacocks **Rev:** Circle of flowers

Date	Mintage	F	VF	XF	Unc
2001 Proof	1,349	Value: 35.00			

KM# 1135 7500000 LIRA

31.0300 g., 0.9250 Silver 0.9228 oz. ASW, 38.5 mm. **Subject:** Mevlana Celaleddin-i Rumi **Obv:** Dancer **Rev:** Portrait **Edge:** Reeded

Date	Mintage	F	VF	XF	Unc
2001 Proof	—	Value: 32.00			

KM# 1145 7500000 LIRA

15.6100 g., 0.9250 Silver 0.4642 oz. ASW, 27.9 x 38.6 mm. **Series:** Flowers **Obv:** Value **Rev:** Paeonia turcica **Edge:** Reeded **Shape:** Oval

Date	Mintage	F	VF	XF	Unc
2002 Proof	—	Value: 17.50			

KM# 1146 7500000 LIRA

15.6100 g., 0.9250 Silver 0.4642 oz. ASW, 27.9 x 38.6 mm. **Series:** Flowers **Obv:** Value **Rev:** Orchis anatolica **Edge:** Reeded **Shape:** Oval

Date	Mintage	F	VF	XF	Unc
2002 Proof	—	Value: 17.50			

KM# 1147 7500000 LIRA

15.6100 g., 0.9250 Silver 0.4642 oz. ASW, 27.9 x 38.6 mm. **Series:** Flowers **Obv:** Value **Rev:** Iris pamphylica **Edge:** Reeded **Shape:** Oval

Date	Mintage	F	VF	XF	Unc
2002 Proof	—	Value: 17.50			

KM# 1148 7500000 LIRA

15.6100 g., 0.9250 Silver 0.4642 oz. ASW, 27.9 x 38.6 mm. **Series:** Flowers **Obv:** Value **Rev:** Gladiolus anatolicus **Edge:** Reeded **Shape:** Oval

Date	Mintage	F	VF	XF	Unc
2002 Proof	—	Value: 17.50			

KM# 1149 7500000 LIRA

15.6100 g., 0.9250 Silver 0.4642 oz. ASW, 27.9 x 38.6 mm. **Series:** Flowers **Obv:** Value **Rev:** Crocus sativus **Edge:** Reeded **Shape:** Oval

Date	Mintage	F	VF	XF	Unc
2002 Proof	—	Value: 17.50			

KM# 1150 7500000 LIRA

15.6100 g., 0.9250 Silver 0.4642 oz. ASW, 27.9 x 38.6 mm. **Series:** Flowers **Obv:** Value **Rev:** Campanula betulifolia **Edge:** Reeded **Shape:** Oval

Date	Mintage	F	VF	XF	Unc
2002 Proof	—	Value: 17.50			

KM# 1151 7500000 LIRA
15.6100 g., 0.9250 Silver 0.4642 oz. ASW, 27.9 x 38.6 mm.
Series: Flowers **Rev:** Centaurea tchihatcheffii **Edge:** Reeded
Shape: Oval

Date	Mintage	F	VF	XF	Unc
2002 Proof	—	Value: 17.50			

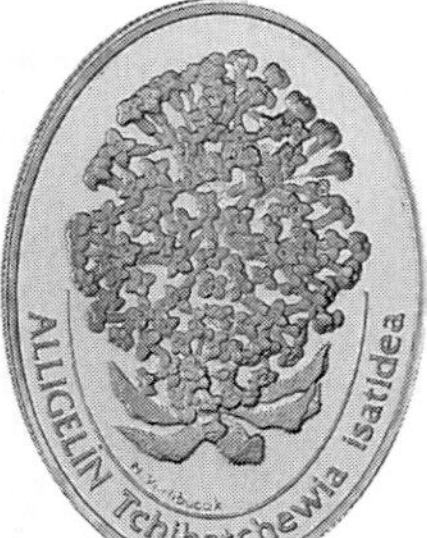

KM# 1152 7500000 LIRA
15.6100 g., 0.9250 Silver 0.4642 oz. ASW, 27.9 x 38.6 mm.
Series: Flowers **Obv:** Value **Rev:** Tchihatchewia isatidea
Edge: Reeded **Shape:** Oval

Date	Mintage	F	VF	XF	Unc
2002 Proof	—	Value: 17.50			

KM# 1153 7500000 LIRA
15.6100 g., 0.9250 Silver 0.4642 oz. ASW, 27.9 x 38.6 mm.
Series: Flowers **Obv:** Value **Rev:** Linum anatolicum **Edge:**
Reeded **Shape:** Oval

Date	Mintage	F	VF	XF	Unc
2002 Proof	—	Value: 17.50			

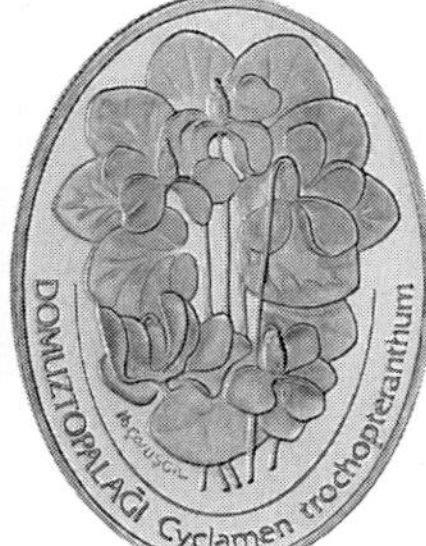

KM# 1154 7500000 LIRA
15.6100 g., 0.9250 Silver 0.4642 oz. ASW, 27.9 x 38.6 mm.
Series: Flowers **Obv:** Value **Rev:** Cyclamen trochopteranthum
Edge: Reeded **Shape:** Oval

Date	Mintage	F	VF	XF	Unc
2002 Proof	—	Value: 17.50			

KM# 1155 7500000 LIRA
15.6100 g., 0.9250 Silver 0.4642 oz. ASW, 27.9 x 38.6 mm.
Series: Flowers **Obv:** Value **Rev:** Tulipa orphanidea
Edge: Reeded **Shape:** Oval

Date	Mintage	F	VF	XF	Unc
2002 Proof	—	Value: 17.50			

KM# 1156 7500000 LIRA
15.6100 g., 0.9250 Silver 0.4642 oz. ASW, 27.9 x 38.6 mm.
Obv: Value **Rev:** Stenbergia candida **Edge:** Reeded
Shape: Oval

Date	Mintage	F	VF	XF	Unc
2002 Proof	—	Value: 17.50			

KM# 1157 7500000 LIRA
15.6100 g., 0.9250 Silver 0.4642 oz. ASW, 27.9 x 38.6 mm.
Series: Flowers **Obv:** Value **Rev:** Arum maculatum **Edge:**
Reeded **Shape:** Oval

Date	Mintage	F	VF	XF	Unc
2002 Proof	—	Value: 17.50			

KM# 1159 10000000 LIRA
31.4200 g., 0.9250 Silver 0.9344 oz. ASW, 38.6 mm.
Subject: Bogazici'nde Yalilar **Obv:** Value **Rev:** Waterfront
buildings **Edge:** Reeded

Date	Mintage	F	VF	XF	Unc
2001 Proof	—	Value: 45.00			

KM# 1118 10000000 LIRA
31.4700 g., 0.9250 Silver .9359 oz. ASW, 38.6 mm.
Subject: Divrigi Ulu Camii **Obv:** Art work in center **Rev:** Ornate
door **Edge:** Reeded

Date	Mintage	F	VF	XF	Unc
2001 Matte	15,000	—	—	—	42.50

KM# 1140 10000000 LIRA
31.4600 g., 0.9250 Silver 0.9356 oz. ASW, 38.6 mm.
Subject: 75th Anniversary of Turkish Radio **Obv:** Large mint
mark **Rev:** Radio microphone **Edge:** Reeded

Date	Mintage	F	VF	XF	Unc
2002 Proof	—	Value: 40.00			

KM# 1160 10000000 LIRA
31.4200 g., 0.9250 Silver 0.9344 oz. ASW, 38.6 mm.
Obv: Turkish mint symbol **Rev:** Ayasofya Mosque and
surrounding buildings **Edge:** Reeded

Date	Mintage	F	VF	XF	Unc
2002 Proof	—	Value: 45.00			

REFORM DECIMAL COINAGE

2005 - 100,000 Old Lira = 1 New Lira

KM# 1164 NEW KURUS
2.7200 g., Brass, 17 mm. **Obv:** Head left **Rev:** Value **Edge:** Plain

Date	Mintage	F	VF	XF	Unc
2005	—	—	—	—	0.15

KM# 1165 5 NEW KURUS
2.9500 g., Copper-Nickel, 17.1 mm. **Obv:** Head left **Rev:** Value
Edge: Plain

Date	Mintage	F	VF	XF	Unc
2005	—	—	—	—	0.25

KM# 1166 10 NEW KURUS
3.8300 g., Copper-Nickel, 19.4 mm. **Obv:** Head right **Rev:** Value **Edge:** Plain

Date	Mintage	F	VF	XF	Unc
2005	—	—	—	—	0.45

KM# 1167 25 NEW KURUS
5.3000 g., Copper-Nickel, 21.5 mm. **Obv:** Head facing front **Rev:** Value **Edge:** Reeded

Date	Mintage	F	VF	XF	Unc
2005	—	—	—	—	1.00

KM# 1168 50 NEW KURUS
7.0000 g., Copper-Nickel, 23.8 mm. **Obv:** Head right **Rev:** Value **Edge:** Reeded

Date	Mintage	F	VF	XF	Unc
2005	—	—	—	—	2.00

KM# 1169 NEW LIRA
8.4500 g., Bi-Metallic Brass center in Copper-Nickel ring Brass center in Copper-Nickel ring, 26 mm. **Obv:** Head left **Rev:** Value **Edge:** Segmented Reeding

Date	Mintage	F	VF	XF	Unc
2005	—	—	—	—	3.50

KM# 1171 5 NEW LIRA
12.0000 g., Bi-Metallic Brass center in Copper-Nickel ring, 32 mm. **Subject:** 23rd Universiade in red holder **Obv:** Stylized bird **Rev:** Logo

Date	Mintage	F	VF	XF	Unc
ND (2005)	10,000	—	—	—	10.00

KM# 1172 5 NEW LIRA
12.0000 g., Bi-Metallic Copper-Nickel center in Brass ring, 32 mm. **Subject:** 23rd Universiade in blue holder **Obv:** Stylized bird **Rev:** Logo

Date	Mintage	F	VF	XF	Unc
ND (2005)	10,000	—	—	—	10.00

KM# 1173 20 NEW LIRA
31.3600 g., 0.9250 Silver 0.9326 oz. ASW, 38.6 mm. **Obv:** Value in wreath **Rev:** Aegean Carpet **Edge:** Reeded

Date	Mintage	F	VF	XF	Unc
2005 Proof	5,000	Value: 40.00			

KM# 1174 20 NEW LIRA
31.4300 g., 0.9250 Silver 0.9347 oz. ASW, 38.6 mm. **Obv:** Value in wreath **Rev:** Mostar Bridge **Edge:** Reeded

Date	Mintage	F	VF	XF	Unc
2005 Proof	5,000	Value: 40.00			

KM# 1175 20 NEW LIRA
23.4500 g., 0.9250 Silver 0.6974 oz. ASW, 38.6 mm. **Obv:** Value in wreath **Rev:** Angora Goat **Edge:** Reeded

Date	Mintage	F	VF	XF	Unc
2005 Proof	5,000	Value: 30.00			

KM# 1176 20 NEW LIRA
23.4600 g., 0.9250 Silver 0.6977 oz. ASW, 38.6 mm. **Obv:** Value in wreath **Rev:** Long-eared Desert Hedgehog **Edge:** Reeded

Date	Mintage	F	VF	XF	Unc
2005 Proof	5,000	Value: 30.00			

KM# 1177 20 NEW LIRA
23.4100 g., 0.9250 Silver 0.6962 oz. ASW, 38.6 mm. **Obv:** Value in wreath **Rev:** Anatolian Mouflon **Edge:** Reeded

Date	Mintage	F	VF	XF	Unc
2005 Proof	5,000	Value: 30.00			

KM# 1178 20 NEW LIRA
23.4300 g., 0.9250 Silver 0.6968 oz. ASW, 38.6 mm. **Obv:** Value in wreath **Rev:** Striped Hyena **Edge:** Reeded

Date	Mintage	F	VF	XF	Unc
2005 Proof	5,000	Value: 30.00			

KM# 1179 20 NEW LIRA
23.4300 g., 0.9250 Silver 0.6968 oz. ASW, 38.6 mm. **Obv:** Value in wreath **Rev:** Hazel Dormouse **Edge:** Reeded

Date	Mintage	F	VF	XF	Unc
2005 Proof	5,000	Value: 30.00			

KM# 1180.1 20 NEW LIRA
23.5000 g., 0.9250 Silver 0.6989 oz. ASW, 38.6 mm. **Obv:** Value in wreath **Rev:** Angora Cat with plain eyes **Edge:** Reeded

Date	Mintage	F	VF	XF	Unc
2005 Proof	5,000	Value: 30.00			

KM# 1180.2 20 NEW LIRA
23.5000 g., 0.9250 Silver 0.6989 oz. ASW, 38.6 mm. **Obv:** Value in wreath **Rev:** Cat with mismatched colored eyes **Edge:** Reeded

Date	Mintage	F	VF	XF	Unc
2005 Proof	—	Value: 35.00			

KM# 1181 20 NEW LIRA

23.3700 g., 0.9990 Silver 0.7506 oz. ASW, 38.6 mm.
Obv: Value in wreath **Rev:** Anatolian Leopard **Edge:** Reeded

Date	Mintage	F	VF	XF	Unc
2005 Proof	5,000	Value: 30.00			

KM# 1182 20 NEW LIRA
23.2500 g., 0.9250 Silver 0.6914 oz. ASW, 38.6 mm.
Obv: Value in wreath **Rev:** Kangal Dog **Edge:** Reeded

Date	Mintage	F	VF	XF	Unc
2005 Proof	—	Value: 30.00			

KM# 1183 20 NEW LIRA
23.4600 g., 0.9250 Silver 0.6977 oz. ASW, 38.6 mm.
Obv: Value in wreath **Rev:** Five-toed Jerboa **Edge:** Reeded

Date	Mintage	F	VF	XF	Unc
2005 Proof	5,000	Value: 30.00			

KM# 1184 20 NEW LIRA
23.2600 g., 0.9250 Silver 0.6917 oz. ASW, 38.6 mm.
Obv: Value in wreath **Rev:** Grizzly Bear **Edge:** Reeded

Date	Mintage	F	VF	XF	Unc
2005 Proof	5,000	Value: 30.00			

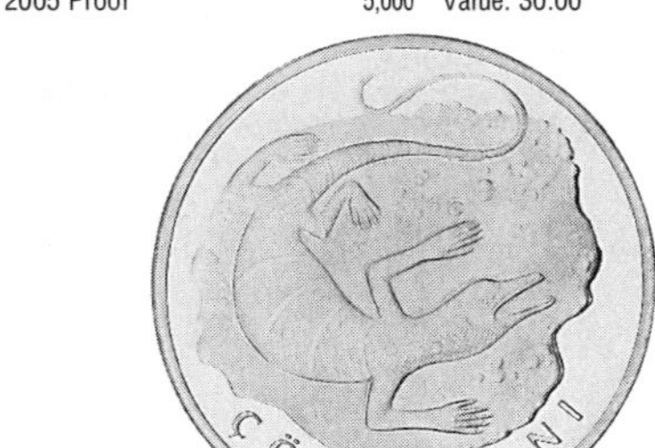

KM# 1185 20 NEW LIRA
23.5300 g., 0.9250 Silver 0.6998 oz. ASW, 38.6 mm.
Obv: Value in wreath **Rev:** Desert Monitor **Edge:** Reeded

Date	Mintage	F	VF	XF	Unc
2005 Proof	5,000	Value: 30.00			

TURKS & CAICOS ISLANDS

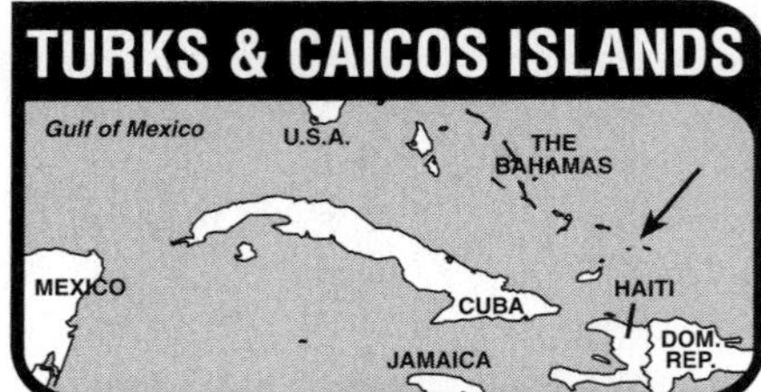

The Colony of the Turks and Caicos Islands, a British colony situated in the West Indies at the eastern end of the Bahama Islands, has an area of 166 sq. mi. (430 sq.km.) and a population of *10,000. Capital: Cockburn Town, on Grand Turk. The principal industry of the colony is the production of salt, which is gathered by raking. Salt, crayfish, and conch shells are exported.

RULERS
British

MONETARY SYSTEM
1 Crown = 1 Dollar U.S.A.

CROWN COLONY

STANDARD COINAGE

KM# 233 5 CROWNS
26.4300 g., Copper-Nickel, 39.2 mm. **Subject:** Royal Navy Submarines **Obv:** Bust of Queen Elizabeth II right **Obv. Designer:** Ian Rank-Broadley **Rev:** Old and modern submarines **Edge:** Reeded

Date	Mintage	F	VF	XF	Unc	BU
2001	—	—	—	3.00	7.50	8.50

KM# 236 20 CROWNS
31.2000 g., 0.9990 Silver 1.0021 oz. ASW, 38.9 mm. **Obv:** Bust of Queen Elizabeth II right **Obv. Designer:** Ian Rank-Broadley **Rev:** Queen Victoria **Edge:** Reeded

Date	Mintage	F	VF	XF	Unc	BU
2001 Proof	—	Value: 40.00				

KM# 245 20 CROWNS
31.1600 g., 0.9990 Silver 1.0008 oz. ASW, 39 mm.
Obv: Elizabeth II **Rev:** Richard II (1377-1399) **Edge:** Reeded

Date	Mintage	F	VF	XF	Unc	BU
2002 Proof	—	Value: 40.00				

KM# 246 20 CROWNS
Hafnium, 38.6 mm. **Subject:** H.M. Queen Elizabeth, The Queen Mother **Obv:** Head of Queen Elizabeth II right **Rev:** Bust of young Queen Mother with crown and necklace **Edge:** Reeded

Date	Mintage	F	VF	XF	Unc	BU
2002	—	—	—	—	—	—

TUVALU

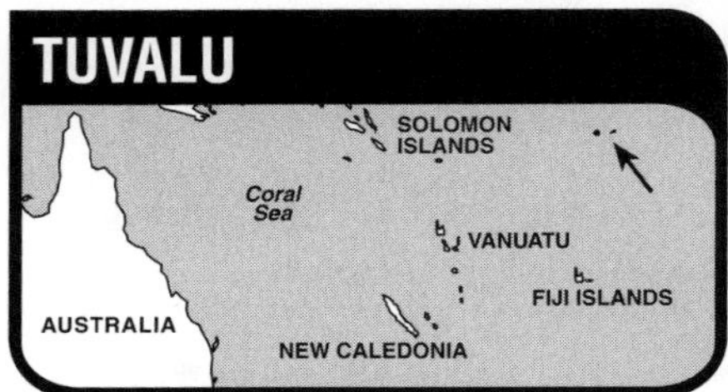

Tuvalu (formerly the Ellice or Lagoon Islands of the Gilbert and Ellice Islands), located in the South Pacific north of the Fiji Islands, has an area of 10 sq. mi. (26 sq.km.) and a population of *9,000. Capital: Funafuti. The independent state includes the islands of Nanumanga, Nanumea, Nui, Niutao, Viatupa, Funafuti, Nukufetau, Nukulailai and Nurakita. The latter four islands were claimed by the United States until relinquished by the Feb. 7, 1979, Treaty of Friendship signed by the United States and Tuvalu. The principal industries are copra production and phosphate mining.

Tuvalu is a member of the Commonwealth of Nations. Elizabeth II is Head of State as Queen of Tuvalu.

MONETARY SYSTEM
100 Cents = 1 Dollar

PARLIMENTARY DEMOCRACY

STANDARD COINAGE

KM# 40 DOLLAR
20.0000 g., Brass, 38.7 mm. **Subject:** Dinosaurs **Obv:** Head of Queen Elizabeth II right **Obv. Designer:** Raphael Maklouf **Rev:** Giganotosaurus **Edge:** Reeded

Date	Mintage	F	VF	XF	Unc	BU
2002	50,000	—	—	—	12.00	15.00

KM# 41 DOLLAR
20.0000 g., Brass, 38.7 mm. **Subject:** Dinosaurs **Obv:** Head of Queen Elizabeth II right **Rev:** Dromaeosaurus **Edge:** Reeded

Date	Mintage	F	VF	XF	Unc	BU
2002	50,000	—	—	—	12.00	15.00

KM# 42 DOLLAR
, 38.7 mm. **Subject:** Dinosaurs **Obv:** Head of Queen Elizabeth II right **Rev:** Seismosaurus **Edge:** Reeded

Date	Mintage	F	VF	XF	Unc	BU
2002	50,000	—	—	—	12.00	15.00

KM# 43 DOLLAR
20.0000 g., Brass, 38.7 mm. **Subject:** Dinosaurs **Obv:** Head of Queen Elizabeth II right **Rev:** Stegosaurus **Edge:** Reeded

Date	Mintage	F	VF	XF	Unc	BU
2002	50,000	—	—	—	12.00	15.00

KM# 49 5 DOLLARS
62.5000 g., 0.9990 Silver 2.0074 oz. ASW, 49.9 mm.
Subject: Dinosaurs **Obv:** Queen Elizabeth II **Rev:** Giganotosaurus **Edge:** Reeded

Date	Mintage	F	VF	XF	Unc	BU
2002 Proof	1,000	Value: 35.00				

KM# 50 5 DOLLARS
62.5000 g., 0.9990 Silver 2.0074 oz. ASW, 49.9 mm.
Subject: Dinosaurs **Obv:** Queen Elizabeth II
Rev: Dromaeosaurus **Edge:** Reeded

Date	Mintage	F	VF	XF	Unc	BU
2002 Proof	1,000	Value: 35.00				

KM# 51 5 DOLLARS
62.5000 g., 0.9990 Silver 2.0074 oz. ASW, 49.9 mm.
Subject: Dinosaurs **Obv:** Queen Elizabeth II **Rev:** Stegosaurus
Edge: Reeded

Date	Mintage	F	VF	XF	Unc	BU
2002 Proof	1,000	Value: 35.00				

KM# 52 5 DOLLARS
62.5000 g., 0.9990 Silver 2.0074 oz. ASW, 49.9 mm.
Subject: Dinosaurs **Obv:** Queen Elizabeth II **Rev:** Seismosaurus
Edge: Reeded

Date	Mintage	F	VF	XF	Unc	BU
2002 Proof	1,000	Value: 35.00				

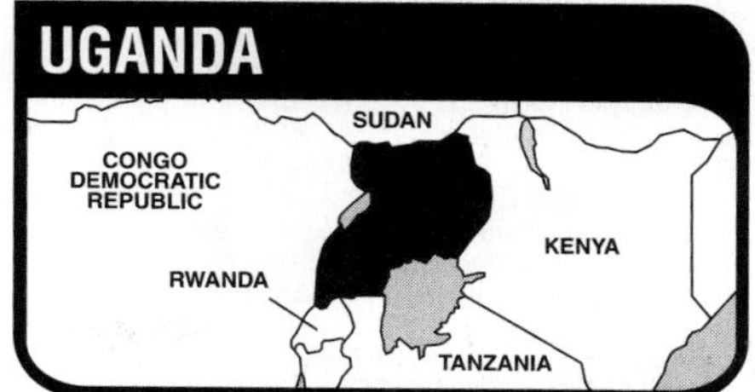

The Republic of Uganda, a former British protectorate located astride the equator in east-central Africa, has an area of 91,134 sq. mi. (236,040 sq. km.) and a population of *17 million. Capital: Kampala. Agriculture, including livestock, is the basis of the economy; there is some mining of copper, tin, gold and lead. Coffee, cotton, copper and tea are exported.

Uganda is a member of the Commonwealth of Nations. The president is Chief of State and Head of Government.

MONETARY SYSTEM
100 Cents = 1 Shilling

REPUBLIC

STANDARD COINAGE

KM# 77 1000 SHILLINGS
19.8400 g., Copper-Nickel, 38.6 mm. **Subject:** Colourful Big Five of Africa **Obv:** National arms **Rev:** Multicolor rhinocerous stamp design **Edge:** Reeded

Date	Mintage	F	VF	XF	Unc	BU
2001 Proof	—	Value: 37.50				

KM# 78 1000 SHILLINGS
19.8400 g., Copper-Nickel, 38.6 mm. **Subject:** Colourful Big Five of Africa **Obv:** National arms **Rev:** Multicolor lion stamp design **Edge:** Reeded

Date	Mintage	F	VF	XF	Unc	BU
2001 Proof	—	Value: 37.50				

KM# 79 1000 SHILLINGS
19.8400 g., Copper-Nickel, 38.6 mm. **Subject:** Coulourful Big Five of Africa **Obv:** National arms **Rev:** Multicolor water buffalo stamp design **Edge:** Reeded

Date	Mintage	F	VF	XF	Unc	BU
2001 Proof	—	Value: 37.50				

KM# 80 1000 SHILLINGS
19.8400 g., Copper-Nickel, 38.6 mm. **Subject:** Colourful Big Five of Africa **Obv:** National arms **Rev:** Multicolor leopard stamp design **Edge:** Reeded

Date	Mintage	F	VF	XF	Unc	BU
2001 Proof	—	Value: 37.50				

KM# 81 1000 SHILLINGS
19.8400 g., Copper-Nickel, 38.6 mm. **Subject:** Colourful Big Five of Africa **Obv:** National arms **Rev:** Multicolor elephant stamp design **Edge:** Reeded

Date	Mintage	F	VF	XF	Unc	BU
2001 Proof	—	Value: 37.50				

KM# 82 1000 SHILLINGS
24.8300 g., 0.9990 Silver 0.7975 oz. ASW, 38.6 mm.
Subject: World of Football **Obv:** National arms **Rev:** Soccer ball globe **Edge:** Reeded

Date	Mintage	F	VF	XF	Unc	BU
2002 Proof	—	Value: 30.00				

KM# 83 1000 SHILLINGS
24.8300 g., 0.9990 Silver 0.7975 oz. ASW, 38.6 mm.
Subject: World of Football **Obv:** National arms **Rev:** Soccer ball in net **Edge:** Reeded

Date	Mintage	F	VF	XF	Unc	BU
2002 Proof	—	Value: 30.00				

KM# 84 1000 SHILLINGS
24.8300 g., 0.9990 Silver 0.7975 oz. ASW, 38.6 mm. **Subject:** World of Football **Obv:** National arms **Rev:** Goalie catching ball, red kicker insert at right **Edge:** Reeded

Date	Mintage	F	VF	XF	Unc	BU
2002 Proof	—	Value: 30.00				

KM# 85 1000 SHILLINGS
24.8300 g., 0.9990 Silver 0.7975 oz. ASW, 38.6 mm. **Subject:** World of Football **Obv:** National arms **Rev:** Two players going after the ball, red runner insert at left **Edge:** Reeded

Date	Mintage	F	VF	XF	Unc	BU
2002 Proof	—	Value: 30.00				

KM# 86 1000 SHILLINGS
24.8300 g., 0.9990 Silver 0.7975 oz. ASW, 38.6 mm. **Subject:** World of Football **Obv:** National arms **Rev:** Player kicking ball, blue kicker insert at right **Edge:** Reeded

Date	Mintage	F	VF	XF	Unc	BU
2002 Proof	—	Value: 30.00				

KM# 101 1000 SHILLINGS
29.4400 g., Silver Plated Bronze (Specific gravity 8.8675), 38.5 mm. **Subject:** Gorillas **Obv:** National arms **Rev:** Seated gorilla **Edge:** Reeded

Date	Mintage	F	VF	XF	Unc	BU
2002 Proof	—	Value: 20.00				

KM# 102 1000 SHILLINGS
29.4400 g., Silver Plated Bronze (Specific gravity 8.8675), 38.5 mm. **Subject:** Gorillas **Obv:** National arms **Rev:** Gorilla eating **Edge:** Reeded

Date	Mintage	F	VF	XF	Unc	BU
2002 Proof	—	Value: 20.00				

KM# 103 1000 SHILLINGS
29.4400 g., Silver Plated Bronze (Specific gravity 8.8675), 38.5 mm. **Subject:** Gorillas **Obv:** National arms **Rev:** Gorilla on all fours **Edge:** Reeded

Date	Mintage	F	VF	XF	Unc	BU
2002 Proof	—	Value: 25.00				

KM# 104 1000 SHILLINGS
29.4400 g., Silver Plated Bronze (Specific gravity 8.8675), 38.5 mm. **Subject:** Gorillas **Obv:** National arms **Rev:** Gorilla female with infant **Edge:** Reeded

Date	Mintage	F	VF	XF	Unc	BU
2002 Proof	—	Value: 25.00				

KM# 105 1000 SHILLINGS
29.2000 g., Silver Plated Bronze (Specific gravity 9.0123), 38.6 mm. **Subject:** Pope John Paul II **Obv:** Ugandan National Arms **Rev:** Pope saying mass, design of Zambian 1000 Kwacha KM-160 **Edge:** Reeded **Note:** Muling error

Date	Mintage	F	VF	XF	Unc	BU
2003 Proof	—	Value: 300				

KM# 106 1000 SHILLINGS
29.1600 g., Silver Plated Bronze (Specific gravity 8.8096), 38.6 mm. **Subject:** Marine Life **Obv:** National arms **Rev:** Multicolor sea horses **Edge:** Reeded

Date	Mintage	F	VF	XF	Unc	BU
2002 Proof	—	Value: 25.00				

KM# 107 1000 SHILLINGS
29.1600 g., Silver Plated Bronze (Specific gravity 8.8096), 38.6 mm. **Subject:** Marine Life **Obv:** National arms **Rev:** Multicolor Hammerhead sharks **Edge:** Reeded

Date	Mintage	F	VF	XF	Unc	BU
2002 Proof	—	Value: 20.00				

KM# 108 1000 SHILLINGS
29.1600 g., Silver Plated Bronze (Specific gravity 8.8096), 38.6 mm. **Subject:** Marine Life **Obv:** National arms **Rev:** Multicolor Stingray **Edge:** Reeded

Date	Mintage	F	VF	XF	Unc	BU
2002 Proof	—	Value: 20.00				

KM# 109 1000 SHILLINGS
29.1600 g., Silver Plated Bronze (Specific gravity 8.8096), 38.6 mm. **Subject:** Marine Life **Obv:** National arms **Rev:** Multicolor Seal **Edge:** Reeded

Date	Mintage	F	VF	XF	Unc	BU
2002 Proof	—	Value: 20.00				

KM# 110 1000 SHILLINGS
29.1600 g., Silver Plated Bronze (Specific gravity 8.8096), 38.6 mm. **Subject:** Marine Life **Obv:** National arms **Rev:** Multicolor sea turtle **Edge:** Reeded

Date	Mintage	F	VF	XF	Unc	BU
2002 Proof	—	Value: 22.50				

KM# 111 1000 SHILLINGS
29.1600 g., Silver Plated Bronze (Specific gravity 8.8096), 38.6 mm. **Subject:** Marine Life **Obv:** National arms **Rev:** Multicolor dolphins **Edge:** Reeded

Date	Mintage	F	VF	XF	Unc	BU
2002 Proof	—	Value: 25.00				

KM# 112 1000 SHILLINGS
29.1600 g., Silver Plated Bronze (Specific gravity 8.8096), 38.6 mm. **Subject:** Marine Life **Obv:** National arms **Rev:** Multicolor octopus **Edge:** Reeded

Date	Mintage	F	VF	XF	Unc	BU
2002 Proof	—	Value: 22.50				

KM# 113 1000 SHILLINGS
29.1600 g., Silver Plated Bronze (Specific gravity 8.8096), 38.6 mm. **Subject:** Marine Life **Obv:** National arms **Rev:** Multicolor red fish **Edge:** Reeded

Date	Mintage	F	VF	XF	Unc	BU
2002 Proof	—	Value: 25.00				

KM# 114 1000 SHILLINGS
29.1600 g., Silver Plated Bronze (Specific gravity 8.8096), 38.6 mm. **Subject:** Marine Life **Obv:** National arms **Rev:** Multicolor black fish with white dots **Edge:** Reeded

Date	Mintage	F	VF	XF	Unc	BU
2002 Proof	—	Value: 25.00				

KM# 115 1000 SHILLINGS
29.1600 g., Silver Plated Bronze (Specific gravity 8.8096), 38.6 mm. **Subject:** Marine Life **Obv:** National arms **Rev:** Multicolor yellow and black striped fish **Edge:** Reeded

Date	Mintage	F	VF	XF	Unc	BU
2002 Proof	—	Value: 25.00				

KM# 75 2000 SHILLINGS
49.9000 g., 0.9990 Silver 1.4840 oz. ASW, 50 mm. **Subject:** Illusion: "Spirit of the Mountain" **Obv:** Ugandan arms above Queen Elizabeth's portrait **Rev:** Landscape that looks like a male portrait **Edge:** Reeded

Date	Mintage	F	VF	XF	Unc	BU
2001 Proof	—	Value: 42.50				

KM# 121 2000 SHILLINGS
25.0000 g., 0.9250 Silver 0.7435 oz. ASW, 38.6 mm. **Subject:** Queen Elizabeth's 75th Birthday **Obv:** Ugandan arms above Queen Elizabeth II **Rev:** Queen accepting flowers from children **Edge:** Reeded

Date	Mintage	F	VF	XF	Unc	BU
2001 Proof	2,000	Value: 35.00				

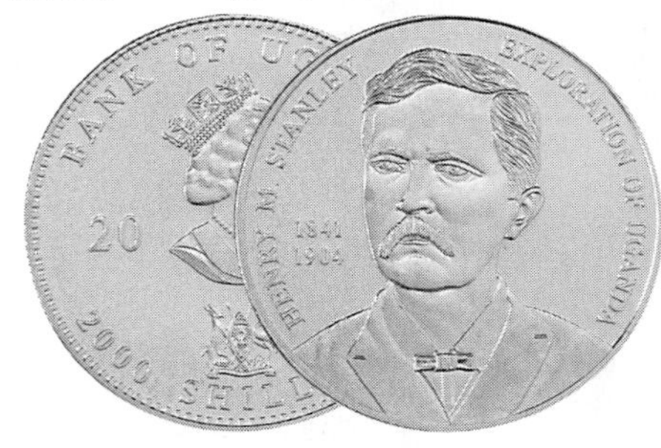

KM# 100 2000 SHILLINGS
31.4000 g., 0.9990 Silver 1.0085 oz. ASW, 38.8 mm. **Obv:** Bust of Queen Elizabeth II divides date above the Ugandan arms **Rev:** Bust of Henry M. Stanley facing **Edge:** Reeded

Date	Mintage	F	VF	XF	Unc	BU
2002	—	—	—	—	35.00	37.50

KM# 117 4000 SHILLINGS
1.5300 g., Gold, 16 mm. **Subject:** Famous Places **Obv:** National arms **Rev:** Matterhorn Mountain **Edge:** Plain

Date	Mintage	F	VF	XF	Unc	BU
ND Proof	—	Value: 75.00				

KM# 87 5000 SHILLINGS
33.7300 g., 0.8500 Silver 0.9218 oz. ASW, 38.65 mm. **Subject:** "The Big Five" **Obv:** National arms **Rev:** Rhinoceros **Edge:** Reeded

Date	Mintage	F	VF	XF	Unc	BU
2002 Proof	—	Value: 45.00				

KM# 88 5000 SHILLINGS
33.7300 g., 0.8500 Silver 0.9218 oz. ASW, 38.65 mm. **Subject:** "The Big Five" **Obv:** National arms **Rev:** Lion **Edge:** Reeded

Date	Mintage	F	VF	XF	Unc	BU
2002 Proof	—	Value: 45.00				

KM# 89 5000 SHILLINGS
33.7300 g., 0.8500 Silver 0.9218 oz. ASW, 38.65 mm.
Subject: "The Big Five" **Obv:** National arms **Rev:** Cape Buffalo **Edge:** Reeded

Date	Mintage	F	VF	XF	Unc	BU
2002 Proof	—	Value: 45.00				

KM# 90 5000 SHILLINGS
33.7300 g., 0.8500 Silver 0.9218 oz. ASW, 38.65 mm. **Subject:** "The Big Five" **Obv:** National arms **Rev:** Leopard **Edge:** Reeded

Date	Mintage	F	VF	XF	Unc	BU
2002 Proof	—	Value: 45.00				

KM# 91 5000 SHILLINGS
33.7300 g., 0.8500 Silver 0.9218 oz. ASW, 38.65 mm. **Subject:** "The Big Five" **Obv:** National arms **Rev:** Elephant **Edge:** Reeded

Date	Mintage	F	VF	XF	Unc	BU
2002 Proof	—	Value: 45.00				

KM# 96 5000 SHILLINGS
31.1035 g., 0.9990 Silver 0.999 oz. ASW, 40.6 mm. **Subject:** Matthew Flinders **Obv:** Bust of Queen Elizabeth II right dividing date above Ugandan arms **Rev:** Multicolor bust of Flinders half left at right with ship and harbor scene at left **Edge:** Plain **Shape:** As a map of Australia

Date	Mintage	F	VF	XF	Unc	BU
2002 Proof	2,500	Value: 47.50				

KM# 97 5000 SHILLINGS
31.1035 g., 0.9990 Silver 0.999 oz. ASW, 40.6 mm. **Obv:** Bust of Queen Elizabeth II right dividing date above Ugandan arms **Rev:** Multicolor cameo of Matthew Flinders at right, ship on calm seas at left **Edge:** Plain **Shape:** As a map

Date	Mintage	F	VF	XF	Unc	BU
2002 Proof	2,500	Value: 47.50				

KM# 98 5000 SHILLINGS
31.1035 g., 0.9990 Silver 0.999 oz. ASW, 40.6 mm. **Obv:** Bust of Queen Elizabeth II right dividing date above Ugandan arms **Rev:** Multicolor busts of Baudin at left and Matthew Flinders at right facing center **Edge:** Plain **Shape:** As a map

Date	Mintage	F	VF	XF	Unc	BU
2002 Proof	2,500	Value: 47.50				

KM# 99 5000 SHILLINGS
31.1035 g., 0.9990 Silver 0.999 oz. ASW, 40.6 mm. **Subject:** Bust of Queen Elizabeth II right dividing date above Ugandan arms **Rev:** Multicolor bust of Matthew Flinders on Australian map showing his route around Australia **Edge:** Plain **Shape:** As a map

Date	Mintage	F	VF	XF	Unc	BU
2002 Proof	2,500	Value: 47.50				

KM# 76 12000 SHILLINGS
6.2207 g., 0.9999 Gold .2000 oz. AGW, 22 mm. **Subject:** Illusion: "Spirit of the Mountain" **Obv:** Ugandan arms above Queen Elizabeth's portrait **Rev:** Landscape that looks like a male portrait **Edge:** Reeded

Date	Mintage	F	VF	XF	Unc	BU
2001 Proof	—	Value: 195				

UKRAINE

Ukraine (formerly the Ukrainian Soviet Socialist Republic) is bordered by Russia to the east, Russia and Belarus to the north, Poland, Slovakia and Hungary to the west, Romania and Moldova to the southwest and in the south by the Black Sea and the Sea of Azov. It has an area of 233,088 sq. mi. (603,700 sq. km.) and a population of 51.9 million. Capital: Kyiv (Kiev). Coal, grain, vegetables and heavy industrial machinery are major exports.

MONETARY SYSTEM
(1) Kopiyka
(2) Kopiyky КОПІЙКИ
(5 and up) Kopiyok КОПІЙОК
100 Kopiyok = 1 Hrynia ГРИВЕНЬ

REPUBLIC

REFORM COINAGE

KM# 6 KOPIYKA
1.5000 g., Stainless Steel, 16 mm. **Edge:** Plain

Date	Mintage	F	VF	XF	Unc	BU
2001	—	—	—	0.35	0.75	—
2002	—	—	—	0.35	0.75	—
2003	—	—	—	0.35	0.75	—
2004	—	—	—	0.35	0.75	—
2005	—	—	—	0.35	0.75	—

KM# 4b 2 KOPIYKY
1.8000 g., Stainless Steel, 17.3 mm. **Edge:** Plain

Date	Mintage	F	VF	XF	Unc	BU
2001	—	—	0.20	0.50	1.00	—
2002	—	—	0.20	0.50	1.00	—
2003	—	—	0.20	0.50	1.00	—
2004	—	—	0.20	0.50	1.00	—
2005	—	—	0.20	0.50	1.00	—

KM# 7 5 KOPIYOK
4.3000 g., Stainless Steel, 24 mm. **Edge:** Reeded

Date	Mintage	F	VF	XF	Unc	BU
2001	—	—	0.50	3.00	6.00	—
2003	—	—	—	0.50	1.00	—
2004	—	—	—	0.50	1.00	—
2005	—	—	—	0.50	1.00	—

KM# 1.1b 10 KOPIYOK
Aluminum-Bronze

Date	Mintage	F	VF	XF	Unc	BU
2001	—	—	2.00	5.00	6.00	—
2002	—	—	0.60	1.25	2.50	—
2003	—	—	0.50	1.00	2.25	—
2004	—	—	0.50	1.00	2.25	—
2005	—	—	0.50	1.00	2.25	—

KM# 2.1b 25 KOPIYOK
Aluminum-Bronze

Date	Mintage	F	VF	XF	Unc	BU
2001	—	—	0.80	3.00	6.00	—

KM# 3.3b 50 KOPIYOK
Aluminum-Bronze

Date	Mintage	F	VF	XF	Unc	BU
2001	—	—	2.00	4.00	8.00	—

KM# 8b HRYVNIA
6.9000 g., Aluminum-Bronze

Date	Mintage	F	VF	XF	Unc	BU
2001	—	—	—	2.50	4.50	—
2002	—	—	—	3.50	6.50	—
2003	—	—	—	2.50	4.50	—
2004	—	—	—	3.50	6.50	—

KM# 208 HRYVNIA
6.8000 g., Aluminum-Bronze, 26 mm. **Subject:** 60th Anniversary - Victory over the Nazis **Obv:** National arms above value **Rev:** Uniform lapel with Soviet military medals group **Edge:** Lettered **Edge Lettering:** Date and denomination

Date	Mintage	F	VF	XF	Unc	BU
2004	5,000,000	—	—	—	3.00	—

KM# 209 HRYVNIA
6.7400 g., Aluminum-Bronze, 26 mm. **Obv:** National arms above value **Rev:** Volodimir Veliky holding church model building and staff **Edge:** Lettered **Edge Lettering:** Date and denomination

Date	Mintage	F	VF	XF	Unc	BU
2004	10,000,000	—	—	—	2.50	—
2005	—	—	—	—	3.00	—

KM# 228 HRYVNIA
6.8000 g., Aluminum-Bronze, 26 mm. **Subject:** WW II Victory 60th Anniversary **Obv:** Value **Rev:** Soldiers in a"V" of search lights **Edge:** Reeded

Date	Mintage	F	VF	XF	Unc	BU
2005	5,000,000	—	—	—	3.00	—

KM# 106 2 HRYVNI
12.8000 g., Copper-Nickel-Zinc, 31 mm. **Series:** Olympics - Salt Lake City, 2002 **Obv:** National arms and denomination **Rev:** Stylized ice dancing couple **Edge:** Reeded

Date	Mintage	F	VF	XF	Unc	BU
2001	30,000	—	—	—	7.00	—

KM# 111 2 HRYVNI
12.8000 g., Copper-Nickel-Zinc, 31 mm. **Series:** Flora and Fauna **Obv:** Denomination **Rev:** Lynx and offspring **Edge:** Reeded

Date	Mintage	F	VF	XF	Unc	BU
2001	30,000	—	—	—	15.00	—

KM# 136 2 HRYVNI
12.8000 g., Copper-Nickel-Zinc, 31 mm. **Subject:** Mykolaiv Zoo **Obv:** Man running alongside large cat **Rev:** Twelve animals **Edge:** Reeded

Date	Mintage	F	VF	XF	Unc	BU
2001	30,000	—	—	—	22.50	—

KM# 137 2 HRYVNI
12.8000 g., Copper-Nickel-Zinc, 31 mm. **Obv:** Arms and denomination divided by wavy line graph **Rev:** Bust of mathematician Mikhaylo Ostrohradsky half left **Edge:** Reeded

Date	Mintage	F	VF	XF	Unc	BU
2001	30,000	—	—	—	8.00	—

KM# 138 2 HRYVNI
12.8000 g., Copper-Nickel-Zinc, 31 mm. **Subject:** Larix Polonica **Obv:** Denomination in wreath **Rev:** Pine branch with cone **Edge:** Reeded

Date	Mintage	F	VF	XF	Unc	BU
2001	30,000	—	—	—	11.50	—

KM# 139 2 HRYVNI
12.8000 g., Copper-Nickel-Zinc, 31 mm. **Subject:** Volodymyr Dal **Obv:** Books **Rev:** Head of Volodymyr Dal facing at right **Edge:** Reeded

Date	Mintage	F	VF	XF	Unc	BU
2001	30,000	—	—	—	7.50	—

KM# 147 2 HRYVNI
12.8000 g., Copper-Nickel-Zinc, 31 mm. **Series:** Olympics - Salt lake City, 2002 **Obv:** National arms and denomination on ice design **Rev:** Stylized hockey player **Edge:** Reeded

Date	Mintage	F	VF	XF	Unc	BU
2001	30,000	—	—	—	6.50	—

KM# 149 2 HRYVNI
12.8000 g., Copper-Nickel-Zinc, 31 mm. **Obv:** National arms and denomination **Rev:** Bust of Mykhaylo Drahomanov (1841-95) right **Edge:** Reeded

Date	Mintage	F	VF	XF	Unc	BU
2001	30,000	—	—	—	8.00	—

KM# 133 2 HRYVNI
12.8000 g., Copper-Nickel-Zinc, 31 mm. **Subject:** Kindness to Children **Obv:** National arms above denomination **Rev:** Two children frolicking under fountain of knowledge **Edge:** Reeded

Date	Mintage	F	VF	XF	Unc	BU
2001	100,000	—	—	—	7.50	—

KM# 134 2 HRYVNI
12.8000 g., Copper-Nickel-Zinc, 31 mm. **Subject:** 5th Anniversary of Constitution **Obv:** National arms above denomination **Rev:** Building above book **Edge:** Reeded

Date	Mintage	F	VF	XF	Unc	BU
2001	30,000	—	—	—	12.50	—

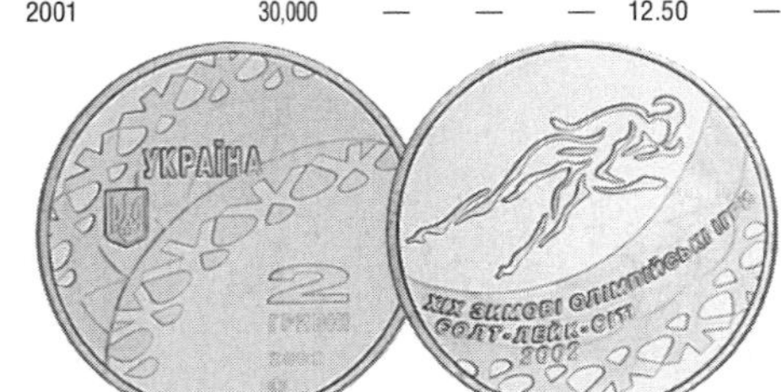

KM# 150 2 HRYVNI
12.8000 g., Copper-Nickel-Zinc, 31 mm. **Series:** Olympics - Salt lake City, 2002 **Obv:** National arms and denomination on ice design **Rev:** Speed skater **Edge:** Reeded

Date	Mintage	F	VF	XF	Unc	BU
2002	30,000	—	—	—	6.50	—

KM# 155 2 HRYVNI
12.8000 g., Copper-Nickel-Zinc, 31 mm. **Series:** Flora and Fauna **Obv:** Value **Rev:** Eurasian Eagle Owl **Edge:** Reeded

Date	Mintage	F	VF	XF	Unc	BU
2002	30,000	—	—	—	20.00	—

KM# 154 2 HRYVNI
12.8000 g., Copper-Nickel-Zinc, 31 mm. **Obv:** Musical score and value **Rev:** Composer Mykola Lysenko **Edge:** Reeded

Date	Mintage	F	VF	XF	Unc	BU
2002	30,000	—	—	—	8.00	—

KM# 166 2 HRYVNI
12.8000 g., Copper-Nickel-Zinc, 31 mm. **Subject:** Leonid Glibov, writer (1827-1893) **Obv:** National arms and value **Rev:** 1/2-length bust of Leonid Glibov half right **Edge:** Reeded

Date	Mintage	F	VF	XF	Unc	BU
2002	30,000	—	—	—	8.00	—

KM# 156 2 HRYVNI
12.8000 g., Copper-Nickel-Zinc, 31 mm. **Subject:** Olympics - Athens, 2004 **Obv:** Two ancient figures above value **Rev:** Swimmer **Edge:** Reeded

Date	Mintage	F	VF	XF	Unc	BU
2003 Prooflike	30,000	—	—	—	7.50	—

KM# 167 2 HRYVNI
12.8000 g., Copper-Nickel-Zinc, 31 mm. **Series:** Flora and Fauna **Obv:** National arms and value **Rev:** European Bison **Edge:** Reeded

Date	Mintage	F	VF	XF	Unc	BU
2003	50,000	—	—	—	12.00	—

KM# 168 2 HRYVNI

12.8000 g., Copper-Nickel-Zinc, 31 mm. **Obv:** National arms and value **Rev:** Long-snouted Sea Horse **Edge:** Reeded

Date	Mintage	F	VF	XF	Unc	BU
2003	50,000	—	—	—	15.00	—

KM# 169 2 HRYVNI

12.8000 g., Copper-Nickel-Zinc, 31 mm. **Obv:** National arms, value and world globe **Rev:** V. I. Vernadsky (1863-1945) in thoughtful pose **Edge:** Reeded

Date	Mintage	F	VF	XF	Unc	BU
2003	30,000	—	—	—	7.50	—

KM# 170 2 HRYVNI

12.8000 g., Copper-Nickel-Zinc, 31 mm. **Obv:** National arms above book and value **Rev:** Head of bearded V. Korolenko half right above dates (1853-1921) **Edge:** Reeded

Date	Mintage	F	VF	XF	Unc	BU
2003	30,000	—	—	—	7.50	—

KM# 171 2 HRYVNI

12.8000 g., Copper-Nickel-Zinc, 31 mm. **Obv:** National arms **Rev:** Bust of V. Chernovol (1937-1999) half left **Edge:** Reeded

Date	Mintage	F	VF	XF	Unc	BU
2003	30,000	—	—	—	7.50	—

KM# 178 2 HRYVNI

1.2400 g., 0.9999 Gold 0.0399 oz. AGW, 13.92 mm. **Obv:** National arms **Rev:** Salamander **Edge:** Plain

Date	Mintage	F	VF	XF	Unc	BU
2003 Proof	10,000	Value: 65.00				

KM# 179 2 HRYVNI

12.8000 g., Copper-Nickel-Zinc, 31 mm. **Obv:** Value, arms, date and musical symbol **Rev:** Singer Boris Gmyrya **Edge:** Reeded

Date	Mintage	F	VF	XF	Unc	BU
2003	30,000	—	—	—	7.50	—

KM# 180 2 HRYVNI

12.8000 g., Copper-Nickel-Zinc, 31 mm. **Subject:** 70th Anniversary National Aviation University **Obv:** World globe behind arms, value and date **Rev:** Wright Brothers biplane **Edge:** Reeded

Date	Mintage	F	VF	XF	Unc	BU
2003	30,000	—	—	—	11.00	—

KM# 181 2 HRYVNI

12.8000 g., Copper-Nickel-Zinc, 31 mm. **Obv:** Musical stringed instrument and ornamental design **Rev:** Ostap Veresay playing stringed instrument **Edge:** Reeded

Date	Mintage	F	VF	XF	Unc	BU
2003	30,000	—	—	—	8.00	—

KM# 182 2 HRYVNI

12.8000 g., Copper-Nickel-Zinc, 31 mm. **Subject:** Olympics **Obv:** Two ancient women with seedlings **Rev:** Boxer **Edge:** Reeded

Date	Mintage	F	VF	XF	Unc	BU
2003	30,000	—	—	—	6.50	—

KM# 183 2 HRYVNI

12.8000 g., Copper-Nickel-Zinc, 31 mm. **Obv:** Children and books **Rev:** Teacher Vasyl O. Sukhomlynsky **Edge:** Reeded

Date	Mintage	F	VF	XF	Unc	BU
2003	30,000	—	—	—	7.50	—

KM# 184 2 HRYVNI

12.8000 g., Copper-Nickel-Zinc, 31 mm. **Obv:** Ornamental shawl, national arms and value **Rev:** Andrey Malishko **Edge:** Reeded

Date	Mintage	F	VF	XF	Unc	BU
2003	30,000	—	—	—	7.50	—

KM# 201 2 HRYVNI

12.8000 g., Copper-Nickel-Zinc, 31 mm. **Subject:** Flora and fauna **Obv:** Value in wreath **Rev:** Two Azovka dolphins **Edge:** Reeded

Date	Mintage	F	VF	XF	Unc	BU
2004	30,000	—	—	—	9.00	—

KM# 202 2 HRYVNI

12.8000 g., Copper-Nickel-Zinc, 31 mm. **Subject:** Football World Cup - 2006 **Obv:** Soccer ball in net **Rev:** Two soccer players **Edge:** Reeded

Date	Mintage	F	VF	XF	Unc	BU
2004	50,000	—	—	—	6.00	—

KM# 203 2 HRYVNI

12.8000 g., Copper-Nickel-Zinc, 31 mm. **Obv:** Stylized dancer **Rev:** Serhiy Lyfar (1904-1986) **Edge:** Reeded

Date	Mintage	F	VF	XF	Unc	BU
2004	30,000	—	—	—	6.00	—

KM# 210 2 HRYVNI

12.8000 g., Copper-Nickel-Zinc, 31 mm. **Subject:** 170th Anniversary - Kiev University **Obv:** National arms in center above value dividing scientific items **Rev:** University building main entrance **Edge:** Reeded

Date	Mintage	F	VF	XF	Unc	BU
2004	50,000	—	—	—	6.00	—

KM# 211 2 HRYVNI

12.8000 g., Copper-Nickel-Zinc, 31 mm. **Obv:** Boy standing in small boat **Rev:** Alexander Dovzhenko **Edge:** Reeded

Date	Mintage	F	VF	XF	Unc	BU
2004	30,000	—	—	—	6.00	—

KM# 212 2 HRYVNI
12.8000 g., Copper-Nickel-Zinc, 31 mm. **Obv:** Winged pens **Rev:** Nickolay Bazhan **Edge:** Reeded

Date	Mintage	F	VF	XF	Unc	BU
2004	30,000	—	—	—	6.00	—

KM# 213 2 HRYVNI
12.8000 g., Copper-Nickel-Zinc, 31 mm. **Obv:** Two reclining figures **Rev:** Michael Kotsubinsky **Edge:** Reeded

Date	Mintage	F	VF	XF	Unc	BU
2004	30,000	—	—	—	6.00	—

KM# 214 2 HRYVNI
12.8000 g., Copper-Nickel-Zinc, 31 mm. **Obv:** National arms, value and drawn curtain **Rev:** Maria Zankovetskaya **Edge:** Reeded

Date	Mintage	F	VF	XF	Unc	BU
2004	30,000	—	—	—	6.00	—

KM# 215 2 HRYVNI
12.8000 g., Copper-Nickel-Zinc, 31 mm. **Obv:** National arms above building and value **Rev:** Michael Maximovich **Edge:** Reeded

Date	Mintage	F	VF	XF	Unc	BU
2004	30,000	—	—	—	6.00	—

KM# 216 2 HRYVNI
12.8000 g., Copper-Nickel-Zinc, 31 mm. **Obv:** National arms and value on artists palette **Rev:** Michael Deregus **Edge:** Reeded

Date	Mintage	F	VF	XF	Unc	BU
2004	30,000	—	—	—	6.00	—

KM# 217 2 HRYVNI
12.8000 g., Copper-Nickel-Zinc, 31 mm. **Obv:** National arms and value in atomic design **Rev:** Nuclear reactor **Edge:** Reeded

Date	Mintage	F	VF	XF	Unc	BU
2004	30,000	—	—	—	9.00	—

KM# 227 2 HRYVNI
1.2400 g., 0.9999 Gold 0.0399 oz. AGW, 13.92 mm. **Obv:** National arms **Rev:** Flying Stork **Edge:** Plain

Date	Mintage	F	VF	XF	Unc	BU
2004 Proof	10,000	Value: 60.00				

KM# 330 2 HRYVNI
12.8000 g., Copper-Nickel-Zinc, 31 mm. **Subject:** 200th Anniversary of Kharkiv University **Obv:** National arms and solar system **Rev:** University buildings **Edge:** Reeded

Date	Mintage	F	VF	XF	Unc	BU
2004	50,000	—	—	—	6.00	—

KM# 331 2 HRYVNI
12.8000 g., Copper-Nickel-Zinc, 31 mm. **Obv:** National arms above National Academy of Law arms and date **Rev:** Building **Edge:** Reeded

Date	Mintage	F	VF	XF	Unc	BU
2004	30,000	—	—	—	7.50	—

KM# 332 2 HRYVNI
12.8000 g., Copper-Nickel-Zinc, 31 mm. **Obv:** National arms, value and man on horse **Rev:** Yuri Fedkovych **Edge:** Reeded

Date	Mintage	F	VF	XF	Unc	BU
2004	30,000	—	—	—	7.50	—

KM# 346 2 HRYVNI
12.8000 g., Copper-Nickel-Zinc, 31 mm. **Obv:** Musical G Clef symbol and value below national arms **Rev:** Musician Boris Liatoshynsky **Edge:** Reeded

Date	Mintage	F	VF	XF	Unc	BU
2005	20,000	—	—	—	5.00	—

KM# 347 2 HRYVNI
12.8000 g., Copper-Nickel-Zinc, 31 mm. **Obv:** Light passing through the lens of an eye **Rev:** Volodymyr P. Filatov **Edge:** Reeded

Date	Mintage	F	VF	XF	Unc	BU
2005	20,000	—	—	—	5.00	—

KM# 348 2 HRYVNI
12.8000 g., Copper-Nickel-Zinc, 31 mm. **Obv:** Books between stylized horsemen **Rev:** Ulas Samchuk **Edge:** Reeded

Date	Mintage	F	VF	XF	Unc	BU
2005	20,000	—	—	—	5.00	—

KM# 349 2 HRYVNI
12.8000 g., Copper-Nickel-Zinc, 31 mm. **Obv:** National arms in flower circle **Rev:** Pavlo Virsky **Edge:** Reeded

Date	Mintage	F	VF	XF	Unc	BU
2005	20,000	—	—	—	5.00	—

KM# 350 2 HRYVNI
12.8000 g., Copper-Nickel-Zinc, 31 mm. **Obv:** Roses and grapes **Rev:** Poet Maksym Rylsky **Edge:** Reeded

Date	Mintage	F	VF	XF	Unc	BU
2005	20,000	—	—	—	5.00	—

KM# 351 2 HRYVNI
1.2400 g., 0.9999 Gold 0.0399 oz. AGW, 13.9 mm. **Obv:** National arms **Rev:** Scythian horseman depicted on golden plaque **Edge:** Plain

Date	Mintage	F	VF	XF	Unc	BU
2005	15,000	—	—	—	65.00	—

KM# 352 2 HRYVNI
12.8000 g., Copper-Nickel-Zinc, 31 mm. **Obv:** "Solar Wind" depiction **Rev:** Astronomer Serhiy Vsekhsviatsky **Edge:** Reeded

Date	Mintage	F	VF	XF	Unc	BU
2005	20,000	—	—	—	5.00	—

KM# 353 2 HRYVNI
12.8000 g., Copper-Nickel-Zinc, 31 mm. **Obv:** National arms **Rev:** Kyivmiskbud Company buildings **Edge:** Reeded

Date	Mintage	F	VF	XF	Unc	BU
2005	20,000	—	—	—	5.00	—

KM# 354 2 HRYVNI
12.8000 g., Copper-Nickel-Zinc, 31 mm. **Obv:** Zhukovsky Aerospace University building on book outline **Rev:** Airplane, computor monitor and books **Edge:** Reeded

Date	Mintage	F	VF	XF	Unc	BU
2005	30,000	—	—	—	5.00	—

KM# 356 2 HRYVNI
12.8000 g., Copper-Nickel-Zinc, 31 mm. **Obv:** Theatrical masks **Rev:** Oleksander Korniychuk **Edge:** Reeded

Date	Mintage	F	VF	XF	Unc	BU
2005	20,000	—	—	—	5.00	—

KM# 357 2 HRYVNI
12.8000 g., Copper-Nickel-Zinc, 31 mm. **Obv:** National arms above value **Rev:** Spalax (mole rat) **Edge:** Reeded

Date	Mintage	F	VF	XF	Unc	BU
2005	60,000	—	—	—	5.00	—

KM# 359 2 HRYVNI
12.8000 g., Copper-Nickel-Zinc, 31 mm. **Obv:** National arms **Rev:** Tairov Wine Institute building and cameo portrait **Edge:** Reeded

Date	Mintage	F	VF	XF	Unc	BU
2005	20,000	—	—	—	5.00	—

KM# 360 2 HRYVNI
12.8000 g., Copper-Nickel-Zinc, 31 mm. **Obv:** Georgian and Ukrainian style ornamentation **Rev:** Poet David Guramishvili **Edge:** Reeded

Date	Mintage	F	VF	XF	Unc	BU
2005	30,000	—	—	—	5.00	—

KM# 361 2 HRYVNI
12.8000 g., Copper-Nickel-Zinc, 31 mm. **Obv:** National arms **Rev:** Writer Dmytro Yavornytsky **Edge:** Reeded

Date	Mintage	F	VF	XF	Unc	BU
2005	30,000	—	—	—	5.00	—

KM# 375 2 HRYVNI
12.8000 g., Copper-Nickel-Zinc, 31 mm. **Obv:** Steam train, factory, National arms and value **Rev:** Oleksiy Alchevsky **Edge:** Reeded

Date	Mintage	F	VF	XF	Unc	BU
2005	20,000	—	—	—	5.00	—

KM# 376 2 HRYVNI
12.8000 g., Copper-Nickel-Zinc, 31 mm. **Obv:** Ameba and National arms **Rev:** Illia Mechnikov **Edge:** Reeded

Date	Mintage	F	VF	XF	Unc	BU
2005	20,000	—	—	—	5.00	—

KM# 377 2 HRYVNI
12.8000 g., Copper-Nickel-Zinc, 31 mm. **Obv:** National arms **Rev:** Vsevolod Holubovych **Edge:** Reeded

Date	Mintage	F	VF	XF	Unc	BU
2005	20,000	—	—	—	5.00	—

KM# 378 2 HRYVNI
12.8000 g., Copper-Nickel-Zinc, 31 mm. **Obv:** National arms **Rev:** Volodymyr Vynnychenko **Edge:** Reeded

Date	Mintage	F	VF	XF	Unc	BU
2005	20,000	—	—	—	5.00	—

KM# 383 2 HRYVNI
12.8000 g., Copper-Nickel-Zinc, 31 mm. **Subject:** Kyiv National University of Economics **Obv:** National arms, value and graph **Rev:** University building **Edge:** Reeded

Date	Mintage	F	VF	XF	Unc	BU
2006	60,000	—	—	—	5.00	—

KM# 384 2 HRYVNI
12.8000 g., Copper-Nickel-Zinc, 31 mm. **Obv:** National arms **Rev:** Viacheslav Prokopovych **Edge:** Reeded

Date	Mintage	F	VF	XF	Unc	BU
2006	30,000	—	—	—	5.00	—

KM# 385 2 HRYVNI
12.8000 g., Copper-Nickel-Zinc, 31 mm. **Obv:** Peasant couple **Rev:** Heurhii Narbut silhouette **Edge:** Reeded

Date	Mintage	F	VF	XF	Unc	BU
2006	30,000	—	—	—	5.00	—

KM# 386 2 HRYVNI
12.8000 g., Copper-Nickel-Zinc, 31 mm. **Obv:** Large jet plane **Rev:** Oleh K. Antonov **Edge:** Reeded

Date	Mintage	F	VF	XF	Unc	BU
2006	45,000	—	—	—	5.00	—

KM# 107 5 HRYVEN
9.4000 g., Bi-Metallic Brass center in Copper-Nickel ring, 28 mm. **Subject:** New Millennium **Obv:** Spiral design **Rev:** Mother and child **Edge:** Segmented reeding

Date	Mintage	F	VF	XF	Unc	BU
2001	50,000	—	—	—	15.00	—

KM# 112 5 HRYVEN
16.5400 g., Copper-Nickel-Zinc, 35 mm. **Subject:** Ostrozhska Academy **Obv:** Denomination, old writing and printing artifacts **Rev:** Teaching scene **Edge:** Reeded

Date	Mintage	F	VF	XF	Unc	BU
2001	30,000	—	—	—	14.00	—

KM# 129 5 HRYVEN
16.5400 g., Copper-Nickel-Zinc, 35 mm. **Subject:** 10th Anniversary - National Bank **Obv:** National arms between two arches **Rev:** Large building central entrance **Edge:** Reeded

Date	Mintage	F	VF	XF	Unc	BU
2001	50,000	—	—	—	12.00	—

KM# 132 5 HRYVEN
16.5400 g., Copper-Nickel-Zinc, 35 mm. **Subject:** 10th Anniversary - National Independence **Obv:** National arms **Rev:** Building on map **Edge:** Reeded

Date	Mintage	F	VF	XF	Unc	BU
2001	100,000	—	—	—	10.00	—

KM# 135 5 HRYVEN
16.5400 g., Copper-Nickel-Zinc, 35 mm. **Subject:** 1100th Anniversary - Poltava **Obv:** National arms above denomination **Rev:** Buildings above arms **Edge:** Reeded

Date	Mintage	F	VF	XF	Unc	BU
2001	50,000	—	—	—	10.00	—

KM# 140 5 HRYVEN
9.4000 g., Bi-Metallic Brass center in Copper-Nickel ring, 28 mm. **Subject:** 10th Anniversary of Military forces **Obv:** Crossed maces **Rev:** Military decoration in wreath **Edge:** Reeded and plain sections

Date	Mintage	F	VF	XF	Unc	BU
2001	30,000	—	—	—	20.00	—

KM# 148 5 HRYVEN
16.5400 g., Copper-Nickel-Zinc, 35 mm. **Obv:** National arms above gateway **Rev:** Krolivets city arms **Edge:** Reeded

Date	Mintage	F	VF	XF	Unc	BU
2001	30,000	—	—	—	12.50	—

KM# 151 5 HRYVEN
16.5400 g., Copper-Nickel-Zinc, 35 mm. **Subject:** City of Khotyn **Obv:** Denomination **Rev:** Castle **Edge:** Reeded

Date	Mintage	F	VF	XF	Unc	BU
2002	30,000	—	—	—	12.50	—

KM# 152 5 HRYVEN
16.5400 g., Copper-Nickel-Zinc, 35 mm. **Obv:** Sun and flying geese **Rev:** "AN-225 Mrija" cargo jet **Edge:** Reeded

Date	Mintage	F	VF	XF	Unc	BU
2002	30,000	—	—	—	20.00	—

KM# 158 5 HRYVEN
9.4300 g., Bi-Metallic Brass center in Copper-Nickel ring, 28 mm. **Subject:** 70th Anniversary of Dnipro Hydroelectric Power Station **Obv:** Turbine **Rev:** Large dam **Edge:** Reeded and plain sections

Date	Mintage	F	VF	XF	Unc	BU
2002	30,000	—	—	—	10.00	—

KM# 159 5 HRYVEN
16.5400 g., Copper-Nickel-Zinc, 35 mm. **Obv:** National arms **Rev:** Battle scene around Batig in 1652 **Edge:** Reeded

Date	Mintage	F	VF	XF	Unc	BU
2002	30,000	—	—	—	14.00	—

KM# 163 5 HRYVEN
16.5400 g., Copper-Nickel-Zinc, 35 mm. **Subject:** Christmas **Obv:** National arms in star above value **Rev:** Christmas pageant scene **Edge:** Reeded

Date	Mintage	F	VF	XF	Unc	BU
ND(2002)	50,000	—	—	—	22.50	—

KM# 157 5 HRYVEN
16.5400 g., Copper-Nickel, 35 mm. **Subject:** 1100th Anniversary - City of Romny **Obv:** National arms above value **Rev:** City view **Edge:** Reeded

Date	Mintage	F	VF	XF	Unc	BU
2002	30,000	—	—	—	12.50	—

KM# 200 5 HRYVEN
9.4000 g., Bi-Metallic Brass center in Copper-Nickel ring, 28 mm. **Obv:** Bandura strings over ornamental design **Rev:** Bandura, a stringed musical instrument **Edge:** Segmented reeding

Date	Mintage	F	VF	XF	Unc	BU
2003	30,000	—	—	—	14.00	—

KM# 172 5 HRYVEN
16.5400 g., Copper-Nickel-Zinc, 35 mm. **Subject:** Easter **Obv:** Circle of Easter eggs, national arms in center above value **Rev:** Religious celebration **Edge:** Reeded

Date	Mintage	F	VF	XF	Unc	BU
2003	50,000	—	—	—	12.00	—

KM# 173 5 HRYVEN
16.5400 g., Copper-Nickel-Zinc, 35 mm. **Subject:** Antonov AN-2 Biplane **Obv:** National arms sun face and flying geese **Rev:** World's largest biplane **Edge:** Reeded

Date	Mintage	F	VF	XF	Unc	BU
2003	50,000	—	—	—	12.00	—

KM# 185 5 HRYVEN
9.4000 g., Bi-Metallic Brass center in Copper-Nickel ring, 28 mm. **Subject:** 150th Anniversary of the Central Ukrainian Archives **Obv:** Value, signature and seal **Rev:** Hourglass and books **Edge:** Segmented reeding

Date	Mintage	F	VF	XF	Unc	BU
2003	30,000	—	—	—	13.50	—

KM# 186 5 HRYVEN
16.5400 g., Copper-Nickel-Zinc, 35 mm. **Subject:** 2500th Anniversary of the City of Yevpatoria **Obv:** National arms, date and value with partial sun background **Rev:** Ancient amphora and modern city view **Edge:** Reeded

Date	Mintage	F	VF	XF	Unc	BU
2003	30,000	—	—	—	11.50	—

KM# 187 5 HRYVEN
16.5400 g., Copper-Nickel-Zinc, 35 mm. **Subject:** 60th Anniversary - Liberation of Kiev **Obv:** Eternal flame monument **Rev:** Battle scene and map of the offence **Edge:** Reeded

Date	Mintage	F	VF	XF	Unc	BU
2003	30,000	—	—	—	11.50	—

KM# 204 5 HRYVEN
16.5400 g., Copper-Nickel-Zinc, 35 mm. **Subject:** 50th Anniversary - Pivdenne Space Design Office **Obv:** Satellite orbiting Earth **Rev:** Satellite above moonscape **Edge:** Reeded

Date	Mintage	F	VF	XF	Unc	BU
2004	30,000	—	—	—	11.50	—

KM# 205 5 HRYVEN
16.5400 g., Copper-Nickel-Zinc, 35 mm. **Subject:** 2500 Anniversary City of Balaklava **Obv:** National arms between two ancient ships **Rev:** Harbor view above pillar **Edge:** Reeded

Date	Mintage	F	VF	XF	Unc	BU
2004	30,000	—	—	—	10.00	—

KM# 218 5 HRYVEN
16.9400 g., 0.9250 Silver 0.5038 oz. ASW, 33 mm. **Obv:** National arms, value and solar system **Rev:** Kharkov University buildings **Edge:** Reeded

Date	Mintage	F	VF	XF	Unc	BU
2004 Proof	7,000	Value: 35.00				

KM# 219 5 HRYVEN
16.9400 g., 0.9250 Silver 0.5038 oz. ASW, 33 mm. **Obv:** National arms above value dividing scientific items **Rev:** Kiev University building main entrance **Edge:** Reeded

Date	Mintage	F	VF	XF	Unc	BU
2004 Proof	7,000	Value: 35.00				

KM# 220 5 HRYVEN
9.4300 g., Bi-Metallic BRASS center in COPPER-NICKEL ring, 28 mm. **Obv:** National arms in center **Rev:** "UNESCO" building in center **Edge:** Segmented reeding

Date	Mintage	F	VF	XF	Unc	BU
2004	50,000	—	—	—	11.00	—

KM# 221 5 HRYVEN
16.5400 g., Copper-Nickel-Zinc, 35 mm. **Obv:** National arms on ships wheel and anchor **Rev:** Ice Breaker "Captain Belousov" **Edge:** Reeded

Date	Mintage	F	VF	XF	Unc	BU
2004	30,000	—	—	—	11.50	—

KM# 222 5 HRYVEN
16.5400 g., Copper-Nickel-Zinc, 35 mm. **Subject:** Whit Sunday **Obv:** National arms in flower wreath above value **Rev:** Four dancing women and child **Edge:** Reeded

Date	Mintage	F	VF	XF	Unc	BU
2004	50,000	—	—	—	11.00	—

KM# 333 5 HRYVEN
9.4000 g., Bi-Metallic Brass center in Copper-Nickel ring, 28 mm. **Obv:** Horizontal lines across flowery design **Rev:** Cossack style lyre **Edge:** Segmented reeding

Date	Mintage	F	VF	XF	Unc	BU
2004	30,000	—	—	—	10.00	—

KM# 334 5 HRYVEN
16.5400 g., Copper-Nickel-Zinc, 35 mm. **Subject:** 250th Anniversary of Kirovohrad **Obv:** National arms above crossed cannons **Rev:** City arms above city view **Edge:** Reeded

Date	Mintage	F	VF	XF	Unc	BU
2004	30,000	—	—	—	8.00	—

KM# 335 5 HRYVEN
16.5400 g., Copper-Nickel-Zinc, 35 mm. **Obv:** Assumption Cathedral **Rev:** Kharkiv State Industrial Building complex **Edge:** Reeded

Date	Mintage	F	VF	XF	Unc	BU
2004	30,000	—	—	—	8.00	—

KM# 336 5 HRYVEN
9.4000 g., Bi-Metallic Brass center in Copper-Nickel ring, 28 mm. **Subject:** 50th Anniversary of Crimean Union With Ukraine **Obv:** National arms on wheat sheaf on map **Rev:** Crimean arms **Edge:** Segmented reeding

Date	Mintage	F	VF	XF	Unc	BU
2004	30,000	—	—	—	9.50	—

KM# 337 5 HRYVEN
16.5400 g., Copper-Nickel-Zinc, 35 mm. **Obv:** National arms on sun, flying geese at right **Rev:** AN-140 Airliner **Edge:** Reeded

Date	Mintage	F	VF	XF	Unc	BU
2004	50,000	—	—	—	8.00	—

KM# 362 5 HRYVEN
16.5400 g., Copper-Nickel-Zinc, 35 mm. **Obv:** National arms on sun with geese flying right **Rev:** AN-124 jet plane in flight **Edge:** Reeded

Date	Mintage	F	VF	XF	Unc	BU
2005	60,000	—	—	—	9.00	—

KM# 364 5 HRYVEN
16.5400 g., Copper-Nickel-Zinc, 35 mm. **Subject:** City of Korosten 1300th Anniversary **Obv:** National arms **Rev:** Ancient earring below modern building and bridge **Edge:** Reeded

Date	Mintage	F	VF	XF	Unc	BU
2005	30,000	—	—	—	9.00	—

KM# 365 5 HRYVEN
16.5400 g., Copper-Nickel-Zinc, 35 mm. **Subject:** City of Sumy 350th Anniversary **Obv:** National arms **Rev:** City view behind city arms **Edge:** Reeded

Date	Mintage	F	VF	XF	Unc	BU
2005	30,000	—	—	—	9.00	—

KM# 366 5 HRYVEN
16.5400 g., Copper-Nickel-Zinc, 35 mm. **Obv:** National arms on Cossack regalia **Rev:** Wedding scene **Edge:** Reeded

Date	Mintage	F	VF	XF	Unc	BU
2005	45,000	—	—	—	—	9.00

KM# 368 5 HRYVEN
16.5400 g., Copper-Nickel-Zinc, 35 mm. **Subject:** Sorochynsky Fair **Obv:** Writer Mykola V. Hohol and his literary charactor Rudy Panko **Rev:** Farmer with family in ox cart **Edge:** Reeded

Date	Mintage	F	VF	XF	Unc	BU
2005	60,000	—	—	—	—	9.00

KM# 379 5 HRYVEN
16.5400 g., Copper-Nickel-Zinc, 35 mm. **Subject:** 500th Anniversary - Kalmiuska Palanqua Cossack Settlement **Obv:** Cossack in ornamental frame and National arms **Rev:** Soldiers **Edge:** Reeded

Date	Mintage	F	VF	XF	Unc	BU
2005	30,000	—	—	—	8.00	—

KM# 380 5 HRYVEN
16.5400 g., Copper-Nickel-Zinc, 35 mm. **Subject:** Sviatdhirsky Assumption Monastery **Obv:** Madonna and child **Rev:** Hillside monastery **Edge:** Reeded

Date	Mintage	F	VF	XF	Unc	BU
2005	45,000	—	—	—	8.00	—

KM# 387 5 HRYVEN
16.5400 g., Copper-Nickel-Zinc, 35 mm. **Subject:** Vernadsky Antarctic Station **Obv:** Flag and buildings **Rev:** Antarctica map **Edge:** Reeded

Date	Mintage	F	VF	XF	Unc	BU
2006	60,000	—	—	—	8.00	—

KM# 389 5 HRYVEN
16.9300 g., Silver, 33 mm. **Subject:** Zodiac - Ram **Obv:** Sun face **Rev:** Ram **Edge:** Reeded

Date	Mintage	F	VF	XF	Unc	BU
2006 Proof	10,000	Value: 40.00				

KM# 390 5 HRYVEN
16.9300 g., Silver, 33 mm. **Subject:** Kyiv National University of Economics **Obv:** National arms, graph above value **Rev:** University building **Edge:** Reeded

Date	Mintage	F	VF	XF	Unc	BU
2006 Proof	5,000	Value: 40.00				

KM# 388 5 HRYVEN
16.9300 g., Silver, 33 mm. **Subject:** Year of the Dog **Obv:** Value on textile art **Rev:** Stylized dog **Edge:** Reeded

Date	Mintage	F	VF	XF	Unc	BU
2006 Proof	12,000	Value: 32.50				

KM# 113 10 HRYVEN
33.6220 g., 0.9250 Silver .9998 oz. ASW, 38.61 mm.
Obv: National arms **Rev:** Half figure of Ivan Mazepa (1644-1709), palace at left **Edge:** Reeded

Date	Mintage	F	VF	XF	Unc	BU
2001 Proof	5,000	Value: 90.00				

KM# 114 10 HRYVEN
33.6220 g., 0.9250 Silver .9998 oz. ASW, 38.61 mm.
Rev: Mosaic portrait at left and Grand prince Yaroslav the Wise (1015-1054) with scroll at right **Edge:** Reeded

Date	Mintage	F	VF	XF	Unc	BU
2001 Proof	3,000	Value: 600				

KM# 115 10 HRYVEN
33.6220 g., 0.9250 Silver .9998 oz. ASW, 38.61 mm.
Series: Ukranian Flora and Fauna **Obv:** Denomination **Rev:** Lynx with offspring **Edge:** Reeded

Date	Mintage	F	VF	XF	Unc	BU
2001 Proof	3,000	Value: 120				

KM# 130 10 HRYVEN
33.6220 g., 0.9250 Silver .9998 oz. ASW, 38.61 mm. **Subject:** 10th Anniversary - National Bank **Obv:** National arms between arches **Rev:** Large building entrance **Edge:** Reeded

Date	Mintage	F	VF	XF	Unc	BU
2001 Proof	3,000	Value: 80.00				

KM# 131 10 HRYVEN
33.6220 g., 0.9250 Silver .9998 oz. ASW, 38.61 mm.
Series: Olympics **Obv:** National arms and denomination on ice **Rev:** Stylized ice dancing couple **Edge:** Reeded

Date	Mintage	F	VF	XF	Unc	BU
2001 Proof	3,000	Value: 45.00				

KM# 141 10 HRYVEN
33.6220 g., 0.9250 Silver .9998 oz. ASW, 38.61 mm.
Subject: Flora and Fauna **Obv:** National arms and denomination **Rev:** Pine branch with cone **Edge:** Reeded

Date	Mintage	F	VF	XF	Unc	BU
2001 Proof	3,000	Value: 50.00				

KM# 142 10 HRYVEN
33.6220 g., 0.9250 Silver 1.0081 oz. ASW, 38.61 mm.
Subject: Khan Palace in Bakhchisarai **Obv:** Denomination in arch **Rev:** Courtyard view **Edge:** Reeded

Date	Mintage	F	VF	XF	Unc	BU
2001 Proof	3,000	Value: 110				

KM# 143 10 HRYVEN
4.3110 g., 0.9000 Gold 0.1247 oz. AGW, 16 mm. **Subject:** 10 Years Independence **Obv:** National arms **Rev:** Parliament building on map **Edge:** Plain

Date	Mintage	F	VF	XF	Unc	BU
2001 Proof	3,000	Value: 300				

KM# 165 10 HRYVEN
33.6220 g., 0.9250 Silver 1.0000 oz. ASW, 38.61 mm. **Subject:** Olympics **Obv:** Value **Rev:** Stylized hockey player **Edge:** Reeded

Date	Mintage	F	VF	XF	Unc	BU
2001 Proof	15,000	Value: 45.00				

KM# 229 10 HRYVEN
33.6220 g., 0.9250 Silver 0.9999 oz. ASW, 38.6 mm.
Obv: National arms and value **Rev:** Owl on branch **Edge:** Reeded

Date	Mintage	F	VF	XF	Unc	BU
2002 Proof	—	Value: 40.00				

KM# 145 10 HRYVEN
33.6220 g., 0.9250 Silver 1.0000 oz. ASW, 38.61 mm.
Subject: Ivan Sirko **Obv:** National arms **Rev:** Cossack battle scene **Edge:** Reeded

Date	Mintage	F	VF	XF	Unc	BU
2002 Proof	3,000	Value: 85.00				

KM# 146 10 HRYVEN
33.6220 g., 0.9250 Silver 1.0000 oz. ASW, 38.5 mm. **Obv:** National arms and denomination on ice **Rev:** Speed skater **Edge:** Reeded

Date	Mintage	F	VF	XF	Unc	BU
2002 Proof	3,000	Value: 47.50				

KM# 160 10 HRYVEN
33.9500 g., 0.9250 Silver 1.0097 oz. ASW, 38.61 mm. **Obv:** Value encircled by angels **Rev:** Church and tower **Edge:** Reeded

Date	Mintage	F	VF	XF	Unc	BU
2002 Proof	3,000	Value: 120				

KM# 161 10 HRYVEN
33.6220 g., 0.9250 Silver 1.0000 oz. ASW, 38.61 mm.
Subject: Grand Prince Vladimir Monomakh **Obv:** Value within jewelry design **Rev:** Monomakh holding book with buildings and St. George in background **Edge:** Reeded

Date	Mintage	F	VF	XF	Unc	BU
2002 Proof	3,000	Value: 200				

KM# 162 10 HRYVEN
33.6220 g., 0.9250 Silver 1.0000 oz. ASW, 38.61 mm. **Obv:** Value in ornate design **Rev:** Prince of Ukraine, Sviatoslav **Edge:** Reeded

Date	Mintage	F	VF	XF	Unc	BU
2002 Proof	3,000	Value: 180				

KM# 164 10 HRYVEN
33.6220 g., 0.9250 Silver 1.0000 oz. ASW, 38.61 mm.
Subject: Christmas **Obv:** National arms in star above value **Rev:** Christmas pageant scene **Edge:** Reeded

Date	Mintage	F	VF	XF	Unc	BU
ND(2002) Proof	3,000	Value: 180				

KM# 176 10 HRYVEN
33.6220 g., 0.9250 Silver 1.0000 oz. ASW, 38.6 mm.
Subject: Olympics **Obv:** Two ancient women with seedlings **Rev:** Swimmer **Edge:** Reeded

Date	Mintage	F	VF	XF	Unc	BU
2002 Proof	15,000	Value: 47.50				

KM# 177 10 HRYVEN
33.6220 g., 0.9250 Silver 1.0000 oz. ASW, 38.6 mm. **Subject:** Hetman Pylyp Orlik 1672-1742 **Obv:** Michael and crowned lion **Rev:** Pylyp Orlyck unfolding roll of Pacts and Code of Laws **Edge:** Reeded

Date	Mintage	F	VF	XF	Unc	BU
2002 Proof	3,000	Value: 100				

KM# 198 10 HRYVEN
33.6220 g., 0.9250 Silver 1.0000 oz. ASW, 38.6 mm. **Obv:** National arms and value **Rev:** European bison **Edge:** Reeded

Date	Mintage	F	VF	XF	Unc	BU
2003 Proof	2,000	Value: 250				

KM# 189 10 HRYVEN
33.6220 g., 0.9250 Silver 1.0000 oz. ASW, 38.6 mm. **Subject:** Olympics **Obv:** Two ancient women with seedlings **Rev:** Boxer **Edge:** Reeded

Date	Mintage	F	VF	XF	Unc	BU
2003 Proof	15,000	Value: 50.00				

KM# 190 10 HRYVEN
33.6220 g., 0.9250 Silver 1.0000 oz. ASW, 38.6 mm. **Obv:** Fancy art work and sculpture **Rev:** Livadia Palace view **Edge:** Reeded

Date	Mintage	F	VF	XF	Unc	BU
2003 Proof	3,000	Value: 100				

KM# 191 10 HRYVEN
33.6220 g., 0.9250 Silver 1.0000 oz. ASW, 38.6 mm. **Obv:** National arms on sun, flying geese **Rev:** Antonov AN-2 biplane **Edge:** Reeded

Date	Mintage	F	VF	XF	Unc	BU
2003 Proof	3,000	Value: 100				

KM# 192 10 HRYVEN
33.6220 g., 0.9250 Silver 1.0000 oz. ASW, 38.6 mm. **Obv:** Easter eggs around arms above value **Rev:** Easter celebration **Edge:** Reeded

Date	Mintage	F	VF	XF	Unc	BU
2003 Proof	3,000	Value: 100				

KM# 193 10 HRYVEN
33.6220 g., 0.9250 Silver 1.0000 oz. ASW, 38.6 mm. **Obv:** Angels, national arms and value **Rev:** The protection of the Virgin Mary over the Pochayiv Monastery **Edge:** Reeded

Date	Mintage	F	VF	XF	Unc	BU
2003 Proof	Est. 8,000	Value: 120				

KM# 194 10 HRYVEN
33.6220 g., 0.9250 Silver 1.0000 oz. ASW, 38.6 mm. **Obv:** National arms above value **Rev:** Sea horse (Hippocamp) **Edge:** Reeded

Date	Mintage	F	VF	XF	Unc	BU
2003 Proof	2,000	Value: 300				

KM# 195 10 HRYVEN
33.6220 g., 0.9250 Silver 1.0000 oz. ASW, 38.6 mm. **Obv:** National arms **Rev:** 1/2-length figure of Kirill Razumovsky, 1728-1803 **Edge:** Reeded

Date	Mintage	F	VF	XF	Unc	BU
2003 Proof	3,000	Value: 100				

KM# 196 10 HRYVEN
33.6220 g., 0.9250 Silver 1.0000 oz. ASW, 38.6 mm. **Obv:** National arms **Rev:** Half-length figure of Pavlo Polubotok, 1660-1724 **Edge:** Reeded

Date	Mintage	F	VF	XF	Unc	BU
2003 Proof	3,000	Value: 110				

KM# 197 10 HRYVEN
33.6220 g., 0.9250 Silver 1.0000 oz. ASW, 38.6 mm. **Obv:** Map, national arms and value **Rev:** Genoese Fortress in Sudak **Edge:** Reeded

Date	Mintage	F	VF	XF	Unc	BU
2003 Proof	3,000	Value: 100				

KM# 206 10 HRYVEN
33.9100 g., 0.9250 Silver 1.0085 oz. ASW, 38.6 mm. **Subject:** Flora and fauna **Obv:** Value in wreath **Rev:** Two Azovka dolphins **Edge:** Reeded

Date	Mintage	F	VF	XF	Unc	BU
2004 Proof	8,000	Value: 60.00				

KM# 207 10 HRYVEN
33.9100 g., 0.9250 Silver 1.0085 oz. ASW, 38.6 mm. \Subject: Football World Cup - 2006 **Obv:** Soccer ball in net \Rev: Two soccer players **Edge:** Reeded

Date	Mintage	F	VF	XF	Unc	BU
2004 Proof	50,000	Value: 45.00				

KM# 223 10 HRYVEN
33.9100 g., 0.9250 Silver 1.0085 oz. ASW, 38.6 mm.
Obv: National arms on sun, flying geese and value **Rev:** AH-140 Airliner **Edge:** Reeded

Date	Mintage	F	VF	XF	Unc	BU
2004 Proof	10,000	Value: 50.00				

KM# 224 10 HRYVEN
33.9100 g., 0.9250 Silver 1.0085 oz. ASW, 38.6 mm.
Obv: National arms on ships wheel and anchor **Rev:** Ice Breaker "Captain Belousov" **Edge:** Reeded

Date	Mintage	F	VF	XF	Unc	BU
2004 Proof	10,000	Value: 50.00				

KM# 225 10 HRYVEN
33.6220 g., 0.9250 Silver 1. oz. ASW, 38.6 mm. **Subject:** Whit Sunday **Obv:** National arms in wreath above value **Rev:** Four women folk dancers and child **Edge:** Reeded

Date	Mintage	F	VF	XF	Unc	BU
2004 Proof	10,000	Value: 65.00				

KM# 339 10 HRYVEN
33.6220 g., 0.9250 Silver 0.9999 oz. ASW, 38.6 mm.
Subject: Ostrozhsky Family **Obv:** Our Lady of Duben and Elias Icon **Rev:** Three cameo portraits **Edge:** Reeded

Date	Mintage	F	VF	XF	Unc	BU
2004 Proof	3,000	Value: 75.00				

KM# 340 10 HRYVEN
33.6220 g., 0.9250 Silver 0.9999 oz. ASW, 38.6 mm.
Obv: Statue of St. Yura (St. George) on horse killing dragon **Rev:** Cathedral of St. Yura **Edge:** Reeded

Date	Mintage	F	VF	XF	Unc	BU
ND (2004) Proof	8,000	Value: 50.00				

KM# 342 10 HRYVEN
33.6220 g., 0.9250 Silver 0.9999 oz. ASW, 38.6 mm. **Subject:** Defense of Sevastopol 1854-56 **Obv:** National arms and value above fortifications map **Rev:** Cannon and ships **Edge:** Reeded

Date	Mintage	F	VF	XF	Unc	BU
2004 Proof	8,000	Value: 47.50				

KM# 343 10 HRYVEN
33.6220 g., 0.9250 Silver 0.9999 oz. ASW, 38.6 mm. **Subject:** Perejaslav Cossack Rada of 1654 **Obv:** National arms above value **Rev:** Bohdan Khmelnytski and group of men **Edge:** Reeded

Date	Mintage	F	VF	XF	Unc	BU
2004 Proof	8,000	Value: 47.50				

KM# 358 10 HRYVEN
33.6220 g., 0.9250 Silver 0.9999 oz. ASW, 38.6 mm. **Obv:** National arms above value **Rev:** Spalax (mole rat) **Edge:** Reeded

Date	Mintage	F	VF	XF	Unc	BU
2005 Proof	8,000	Value: 47.50				

KM# 367 10 HRYVEN
33.6220 g., 0.9250 Silver 0.9999 oz. ASW, 38.6 mm. **Obv:** National arms on Cossack regalia **Rev:** Wedding scene **Edge:** Reeded

Date	Mintage	F	VF	XF	Unc	BU
2005 Proof	8,000	Value: 47.50				

KM# 370 10 HRYVEN
33.6220 g., 0.9250 Silver 0.9999 oz. ASW, 38.6 mm.
Subject: 60 Years UN Membership **Obv:** National arms, value and olive branch **Rev:** UN logo above map **Edge:** Reeded

Date	Mintage	F	VF	XF	Unc	BU
2005 Proof	5,000	Value: 47.50				

KM# 371 10 HRYVEN
33.6220 g., 0.9250 Silver 0.9999 oz. ASW, 38.6 mm. **Subject:** National Anthem **Obv:** Musical score **Rev:** Coiled legend around holographic flower **Edge:** Reeded

Date	Mintage	F	VF	XF	Unc	BU
2005 Proof	3,000	Value: 50.00				

KM# 372 10 HRYVEN
33.6220 g., 0.9250 Silver 0.9999 oz. ASW, 38.6 mm. **Obv:** Statue **Rev:** Kobylianska Theater in Cherivtsi **Edge:** Reeded

Date	Mintage	F	VF	XF	Unc	BU
2005 Proof	5,000	Value: 47.50				

KM# 373 10 HRYVEN
33.6220 g., 0.9250 Silver 0.9999 oz. ASW, 38.6 mm. **Obv:** Sviatohirska Icon supported by two angels **Rev:** Sviatohirsky Monastery on river bank **Edge:** Reeded

Date	Mintage	F	VF	XF	Unc	BU
2005 Proof	8,000	Value: 47.50				

KM# 381 10 HRYVEN
33.8600 g., 0.9250 Silver 1.007 oz. ASW, 38.6 mm. **Subject:** Baturyn Hetman Capital City **Obv:** Value between 2 groups **Rev:** Four portraits above city view **Edge:** Reeded

Date	Mintage	F	VF	XF	Unc	BU
2005 Proof	5,000	Value: 50.00				

KM# 382 10 HRYVEN
33.8600 g., 0.9250 Silver 1.007 oz. ASW, 38.6 mm. **Subject:** Symyrenko Family **Obv:** Country name **Rev:** Family tree **Edge:** Reeded

Date	Mintage	F	VF	XF	Unc	BU
2005 Proof	5,000	Value: 50.00				

KM# 144 20 HRYVEN
67.2400 g., 0.9250 Silver 2.000 oz. ASW, 50 mm. **Subject:** 10 Years Independence **Obv:** National arms **Rev:** Parliament building on map **Edge:** Segmented reeding

Date	Mintage	F	VF	XF	Unc	BU
2001 Proof	1,000	Value: 4,000				

KM# 174 20 HRYVEN
14.7000 g., Bi-Metallic .916 Gold 6.22g center in .925 Silver8.39g ring, 31 mm. **Subject:** "Kyiv Rus" Culture **Obv:** Old arms of Ukraine, Prince and a cathedral model in his hand and princess **Rev:** Old rus ear-ring **Edge:** Reeded and plain sections

Date	Mintage	F	VF	XF	Unc	BU
2001 Proof	2,000	Value: 300				

KM# 175 20 HRYVEN
14.7000 g., Bi-Metallic .916 Gold 6.22g center in .925 Silver 8.39g ring, 31 mm. **Subject:** Scythian Culture **Obv:** Warrior with a bowl in his hand and to the right, a Queen of Scythia **Rev:** Scythian horse's stylized **Edge:** Reeded and plain sections

Date	Mintage	F	VF	XF	Unc	BU
2001 Proof	2,000	Value: 250				

KM# 153 20 HRYVEN
67.2400 g., 0.9250 Silver 2.000 oz. ASW, 50 mm. **Obv:** Sun and flying geese **Rev:** "AN-225 Mrija" cargo jet **Edge:** Reeded and plain sections

Date	Mintage	F	VF	XF	Unc	BU
2002 Proof	2,002	Value: 500				

KM# 188 20 HRYVEN
67.2400 g., 0.9250 Silver 2.00 oz. ASW, 50 mm. **Subject:** 60th Anniversary - Liberation of Kiev **Obv:** Eternal flame monument **Rev:** Map and battle scene **Edge:** Segmented reeding

Date	Mintage	F	VF	XF	Unc	BU
2003 Proof	2,000	Value: 280				

KM# 226 20 HRYVEN
62.2000 g., 0.9250 Silver 1.8498 oz. ASW, 50 mm.
Obv: National arms above value **Rev:** Taras Shevchenko
Edge: Segmented Reeding

Date	Mintage	F	VF	XF	Unc	BU
2004 Proof	4,000	Value: 140				

KM# 344 20 HRYVEN
67.2440 g., 0.9250 Silver 1.9998 oz. ASW, 50 mm. **Subject:** 2006 Olympic Games **Obv:** Woman holding flame and branch **Rev:** Six athletes around flame **Edge:** Segmented reeding

Date	Mintage	F	VF	XF	Unc	BU
2004 Proof	5,000	Value: 130				

KM# 363 20 HRYVEN
67.2400 g., 0.9250 Silver 1.9997 oz. ASW, 50 mm.
Obv: National arms on sun with geese flying right **Rev:** AN-124 jet plane in flight **Edge:** Segmented reeding

Date	Mintage	F	VF	XF	Unc	BU
2005 Proof	5,000	Value: 150				

KM# 369 20 HRYVEN
67.2400 g., 0.9250 Silver 1.9997 oz. ASW, 50 mm. **Obv:** Writer Mykola V. Hohol and his literary character Rudy Panko
Rev: Farmer leading family in ox cart **Edge:** Segmented reeding

Date	Mintage	F	VF	XF	Unc	BU
2005 Proof	5,000	Value: 150				

KM# 374 20 HRYVEN
67.2400 g., 0.9250 Silver 1.9997 oz. ASW, 50 mm.
Subject: 60th Anniversary of Victory in WWII **Obv:** Cranes flying over value and below arms **Rev:** V-shaped search light beams filled with soldiers. Order of the Patriotic War at bottom left
Edge: Segmented reeding

Date	Mintage	F	VF	XF	Unc	BU
2005 Proof	5,000	Value: 150				

KM# 345 100 HRYVEN
34.5594 g., 0.9000 Gold 1 oz. AGW, 32 mm. **Obv:** National arms above value between two stylized cranes **Rev:** Riders approaching castle gate **Edge:** Segmented reeding

Date	Mintage	F	VF	XF	Unc	BU
2004 Proof	2,000	Value: 800				

KM# 199 100 HRYVNIAS
31.1000 g., 0.9000 Gold 0.8999 oz. AGW, 32 mm. **Subject:** Ancient Scythian Culture **Obv:** National arms above ornamental design and value **Rev:** Ancient craftsmen and jewelry **Edge:** Reeded

Date	Mintage	F	VF	XF	Unc	BU
2003 Proof	1,500	Value: 850				

MINT SETS

KM#	Date	Mintage	Identification	Issue Price	Mkt Val
MS2	2001 (8)	5,000	KM#1.1b, 2.1b, 3.3b, 4b, 6, 7, 8b, 129	—	40.00

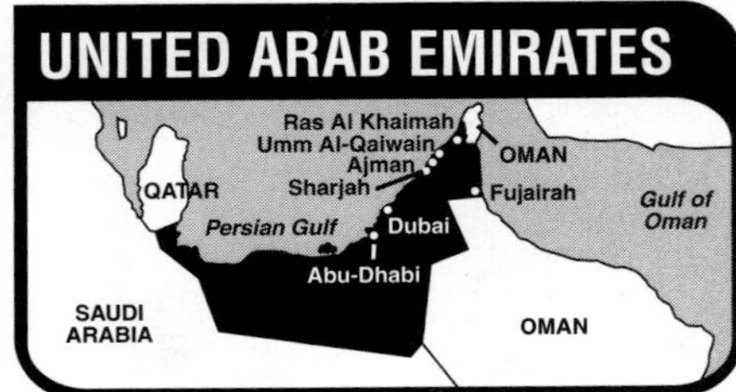

The seven United Arab Emirates (formerly known as the Trucial Sheikhdoms or States), located along the southern shore of the Persian Gulf, are comprised of the Sheikhdoms of Abu Dhabi, Dubai, al-Sharjah, Ajman, Umm al Qaiwain, Ras al-Khaimah and al-Fujairah. They have a combined area of about 32,000 sq. mi. (83,600 sq. km.) and a population of *2.1 million. Capital: Abu Zaby (Abu Dhabi). Since the oil strikes of 1958-60, the economy has centered about petroleum.

TITLES

الامارات العربية المتحدة

al-Imara(t) al-Arabiya(t) al-Muttahida(t)

UNITED EMIRATES

STANDARD COINAGE

KM# 49 DIRHAM
6.3700 g., Copper-Nickel, 24 mm. **Subject:** 25th Anniversary - Armed Forces Unification **Obv:** Denomination **Rev:** Heraldic eagle **Edge:** Reeded

Date	Mintage	F	VF	XF	Unc	BU
ND (2001)	250,000	—	—	—	4.00	—

KM# 51 DIRHAM
6.3300 g., Copper-Nickel, 24 mm. **Subject:** 50 Years of Formal Education **Obv:** Value **Rev:** Symbolic design **Edge:** Reeded

Date	Mintage	F	VF	XF	Unc	BU
ND (2003)	—	—	—	—	4.00	—

KM# 52 DIRHAM
6.4000 g., Copper-Nickel, 24 mm. **Subject:** Abu Dhabi National Bank 35th Anniversary **Obv:** Value **Rev:** Bank building **Edge:** Reeded

Date	Mintage	F	VF	XF	Unc	BU
ND (2003)	—	—	—	—	4.00	—

KM# 54 DIRHAM
6.4000 g., Copper-Nickel, 24 mm. **Subject:** 40th Anniversary of Crude Oil Exports **Obv:** Value **Rev:** "ADCO" logo **Edge:** Reeded

Date	Mintage	F	VF	XF	Unc	BU
ND (2004)	—	—	—	—	4.00	—

KM# 47 50 DIRHAMS
40.2200 g., 0.9250 Silver 1.1961 oz. ASW, 40 mm. **Subject:** 25th Anniversary - Women's Union (1975-2000) **Obv:** Portrait **Rev:** Stylized gazelle **Edge:** Reeded

Date	Mintage	F	VF	XF	Unc	BU
ND(2001) Proof	5,000	Value: 55.00				

KM# 59 50 DIRHAMS
40.0000 g., 0.9250 Silver 1.1896 oz. ASW, 40 mm. **Subject:** 25th Anniversary - Arab Bank of Investment and Foreign Trade **Edge:** Reeded

Date	Mintage	F	VF	XF	Unc	BU
ND(2001) Proof	2,000	Value: 65.00				

KM# 60 50 DIRHAMS
40.0000 g., 0.9250 Silver 1.1896 oz. ASW, 40 mm. **Subject:** 25th Anniversary - Armed Forces Unification **Edge:** Reeded

Date	Mintage	F	VF	XF	Unc	BU
ND(2001) Proof	10,000	Value: 65.00				

KM# 61 50 DIRHAMS
40.0000 g., 0.9250 Silver 1.1896 oz. ASW, 40 mm. **Subject:** 30th Anniversary - Al-Ain National Museum **Edge:** Reeded

Date	Mintage	F	VF	XF	Unc	BU
ND(2002) Proof	5,000	Value: 65.00				

KM# 62 50 DIRHAMS
40.0000 g., 0.9250 Silver 1.1896 oz. ASW, 40 mm. **Subject:** 25th Anniversary - University of the U.A.E. **Edge:** Reeded

Date	Mintage	F	VF	XF	Unc	BU
ND(2002) Proof	5,000	Value: 65.00				

KM# 63 50 DIRHAMS
40.0000 g., 0.9250 Silver 1.1896 oz. ASW, 40 mm. **Subject:** 25 Years - Etisalat Jubilee **Edge:** Reeded

Date	Mintage	F	VF	XF	Unc	BU
ND(2002) Proof	5,000	Value: 65.00				

KM# 64 50 DIRHAMS
40.0000 g., 0.9250 Silver 1.1896 oz. ASW, 40 mm.
Subject: Sheikh Hamdan Bin Rashid Al Maktoum Award for Medical Sciences **Edge:** Reeded

Date	Mintage	F	VF	XF	Unc	BU
ND(2002) Proof	2,000	Value: 65.00				

KM# 65 50 DIRHAMS
40.0000 g., 0.9250 Silver 1.1896 oz. ASW, 40 mm. **Subject:** Al Ahmadia School Foundation Committee **Edge:** Reeded

Date	Mintage	F	VF	XF	Unc	BU
ND(2002) Proof	5,000	Value: 60.00				

KM# 67 50 DIRHAMS
40.0000 g., 0.9250 Silver 1.1896 oz. ASW, 40 mm.
Subject: 20th Anniversary - Establishment of the Administrative Development Institute **Edge:** Reeded

Date	Mintage	F	VF	XF	Unc	BU
ND(2002) Proof	2,000	Value: 65.00				

KM# 68 50 DIRHAMS
40.0000 g., 0.9250 Silver 1.1896 oz. ASW, 40 mm.
Subject: 30th Anniversary - U.A.E. Central Bank **Edge:** Reeded

Date	Mintage	F	VF	XF	Unc	BU
ND(2003) Proof	5,000	Value: 60.00				

KM# 69 50 DIRHAMS
40.0000 g., 0.9250 Silver 1.1896 oz. ASW, 40 mm.
Subject: 58th Annual Meeting of the World Bank Group and the Int'l Money Fund **Obv:** Colored dots **Edge:** Reeded

Date	Mintage	F	VF	XF	Unc	BU
ND(2003) Proof	10,000	Value: 50.00				

KM# 50 50 DIRHAMS
40.0000 g., 0.9250 Silver 1.1896 oz. ASW, 40 mm. **Obv:** Value **Rev:** FIFA 2003 World Youth Soccer Championship **Edge:** Reeded

Date	Mintage	F	VF	XF	Unc	BU
ND(2003) Proof	—	Value: 65.00				

KM# 66 50 DIRHAMS
40.0000 g., 0.9250 Silver 1.1896 oz. ASW, 40 mm.
Subject: Quality Certification for the Ministry of Finance and Industry **Edge:** Reeded

Date	Mintage	F	VF	XF	Unc	BU
ND(2003) Proof	3,000	Value: 65.00				

KM# 70 50 DIRHAMS
40.0000 g., 0.9250 Silver 1.1896 oz. ASW, 40 mm.
Subject: 40th Anniversary - First Oil Export from Abu Dhabi Onshore Oil Fields (ADCO) **Edge:** Reeded

Date	Mintage	F	VF	XF	Unc	BU
ND(2004) Proof	—	Value: 65.00				

KM# 71 50 DIRHAMS
40.0000 g., 0.9250 Silver 1.1896 oz. ASW, 40 mm.
Subject: 25th Anniversary - Sharjah City for Humanitarian Services (SCHS) **Edge:** Reeded

Date	Mintage	F	VF	XF	Unc	BU
ND(2005) Proof	—	Value: 65.00				

UNITED STATES OF AMERICA

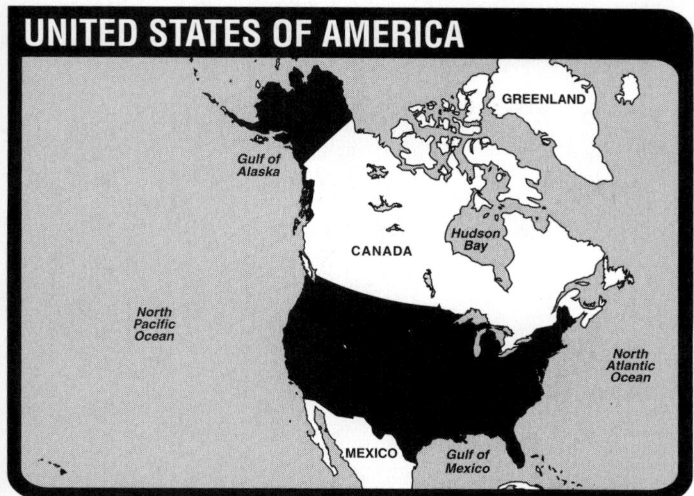

The United States of America as politically organized, under the Articles of Confederation consisted of the 13 original British-American colonies; New Hampshire, Massachusetts, Rhode Island, Connecticut, New York, New Jersey, Pennsylvania, Delaware, Virginia, North Carolina, South Carolina, Georgia and Maryland. Clustered along the eastern seaboard of North American between the forests of Maine and the marshes of Georgia. Under the Article of Confederation, the United States had no national capital: Philadelphia, where the "United States in Congress Assembled", was the "seat of government". The population during this political phase of America's history (1781-1789) was about 3 million, most of whom lived on self-sufficient family farms. Fishing, lumbering and the production of grains for export were major economic endeavors. Rapid strides were also being made in industry and manufacturing by 1775, the (then) colonies were accounting for one-seventh of the world's production of raw iron.

On the basis of the voyage of John Cabot to the North American mainland in 1497, England claimed the entire continent. The first permanent English settlement was established at Jamestown, Virginia, in 1607. France and Spain also claimed extensive territory in North America. At the end of the French and Indian Wars (1763), England acquired all of the territory east of the Mississippi River, including East and West Florida. From 1776 to 1781, the States were governed by the Continental Congress. From 1781 to 1789, they were organized under the Articles of Confederation, during which period the individual States had the right to issue money. Independence from Great Britain was attained with the American Revolution in 1776. The Constitution organized and governs the present United States. It was ratified on Nov. 21, 1788.

MINT MARKS

C – Charlotte, N.C., 1838-61
CC – Carson City, NV, 1870-93
D – Dahlonega, GA, 1838-61
D – Denver, CO, 1906-present
O – New Orleans, LA, 1838-1909
P – Philadelphia, PA, 1793-present
S – San Francisco, CA, 1854-present
W – West Point, NY, 1984-present

CIRCULATION COINAGE

CENT

Lincoln Cent

Lincoln Memorial

KM# 201b COPPER PLATED ZINC 19 mm. **Notes:** The 1983 "doubled die reverse" shows doubling of "United States of America." The 1984 "doubled die" shows doubling of Lincoln's ear on the obverse.

Date	Mintage	XF-40	MS-65	Prf-65
2001P	4,959,600,000	—	.25	—
2001D	5,374,990,000	—	.25	—
2001S	(3,099,096)	—	—	4.00
2002P	3,260,800,000	—	.25	—
2002D	4,028,055,000	—	.25	—
2002S	(3,157,739)	—	—	4.00
2003P	—	—	.25	—
2003D	—	—	.25	—
2003S	(3,116,590)	—	—	4.00
2004P	—	—	.25	—
2004D	—	—	.25	—
2004S	—	—	—	4.00
2005P	—	—	.25	—
2005D	—	—	.25	—
2005S	—	—	—	4.00
2006P	—	—	.25	—
2006D	—	—	.25	—
2006S	—	—	—	4.00

5 CENTS

Jefferson Nickel

Pre-war design resumed

KM# A192 COPPER-NICKEL 21.2 mm. 5.0000 g. **Designer:** Felix Schlag **Notes:** KM#192 design and composition resumed. The 1979-S and 1981-S Type II proofs have clearer mint marks than the Type I proofs of those years.

Date	Mintage	MS-65	Prf-65
2001P	675,704,000	.50	—
2001D	627,680,000	.50	—
2001S	(3,099,096)	—	2.00
2002P	539,280,000	.50	—
2002D	691,200,000	.50	—
2002S	(3,157,739)	—	2.00
2003P	441,840,000	.50	—
2003D	383,040,000	.50	—
2003S	3,116,590	—	2.00

Jefferson - Peace Reverse

Jefferson era peace medal design: two clasped hands, pipe and hatchet

KM# 360 COPPER NICKEL 21.2 mm. 5.0000 g. **Obv. Designer:** Felix Schlag **Rev. Designer:** Norman E. Nemeth

Date	Mintage	MS-65	Prf-65
2004P	361,440,000	.50	—
2004D	372,000,000	.50	—
2004S	—	—	12.50

Jefferson - Keelboat Reverse

Lewis and Clark's Keelboat

KM# 361 COPPER NICKEL 21.2 mm. 5.0000 g. **Obv. Designer:** Felix Schlag **Rev. Designer:** Al Maletsky

Date	Mintage	MS-65	Prf-65
2004P	366,720,000	.50	—
2004D	344,880,000	.50	—
2004S	—	—	12.50

Jefferson large profile - Bison Reverse

Thomas Jefferson large profile right American Bison right

KM# 368 COPPER NICKEL 21.2 mm. 5.0000 g. **Obv. Designer:** Joe Fitzgerald and Don Everhart II **Rev. Designer:** Jamie Franki and Norman E. Nemeth

Date	Mintage	MS-65	Prf-65
2005P	448,320,000	.50	—
2005D	487,680,000	.50	—
2005S	—	—	2.00

Jefferson - Pacific Coastline

Pacific coastline

KM# 369 **COPPER NICKEL** 0 oz. 5.0000 g. **Obv. Designer:** Joe Fitzgerald and Don Everhart **Rev. Designer:** Joe Fitzgerald and Donna Weaver

Date	Mintage	MS-65	Prf-65
2005P	—	.50	—
2005D	—	.50	—
2005S	—	—	2.00

Jefferson large facing portrait - Enhanced Monticello Reverse

Jefferson head facing Monticello, enhanced design

KM# 381 **COPPER-NICKEL** 21 mm. 5.0000 g. **Obv. Designer:** Jamie N. Franki and Donna Weaver **Rev. Designer:** Felix Schlag and John Mercanti

Date	Mintage	MS-65	Prf-65	Date	Mintage	MS-65	Prf-65
2006	—	—	—	2006S	—	—	—
2006D	—	—	—				

DIME

Roosevelt Dime

KM# 195a **COPPER-NICKEL CLAD COPPER** 17.9 mm. 2.2700 g. **Designer:** John R. Sinnock **Notes:** The 1979-S and 1981-S Type II proofs have clearer mint marks than the Type I proofs of those years. On the 1982 no-mint-mark variety, the mint mark was inadvertently left off.

Date	Mintage	MS-65	Prf-65	Date	Mintage	MS-65	Prf-65
2001P	1,369,590,000	1.00	—	2004P	1,328,000,000	1.00	—
2001D	1,412,800,000	1.00	—	2004D	1,159,500,000	1.00	—
2001S	(2,249,496)	—	1.00	2004S	1,804,396	—	4.75
2002P	1,187,500,000	1.00	—	2005P	1,412,000,000	1.00	—
2002D	1,379,500,000	1.00	—	2005D	1,423,500,000	1.00	—
2002S	(2,268,913)	—	2.00	2005S	—	—	2.25
2003P	1,085,500,000	1.00	—	2006P	—	1.00	—
2003D	986,500,000	1.00	—	2006D	—	1.00	—
2003S	(2,076,165)	—	2.00	2006S	—	—	2.25

Roosevelt Dime

KM# A195 **SILVER**

Date	Mintage	Prf-65	Date	Mintage	Prf-65
2001S	(849,600)	5.00	2004S	—	4.50
2002S	(888,826)	5.00	2005S	—	3.50
2003S	1,090,425	4.00	2006S	—	—

QUARTER

50 State Quarters

Kentucky

KM# 322 **COPPER-NICKEL CLAD COPPER**

Date	Mintage	MS-63	MS-65	Prf-65
2001P	353,000,000	.75	.75	—
2001D	370,564,000	.75	.75	—
2001S	(3,009,800)	—	—	6.50

KM# 322a 0.9000 **SILVER** .1808 oz. ASW. 6.2500 g.

Date	Mintage	MS-63	MS-65	Prf-65
2001S	(849,500)	—	—	22.50

New York

KM# 318 **COPPER-NICKEL CLAD COPPER**

Date	Mintage	MS-63	MS-65	Prf-65
2001P	655,400,000	.75	.75	—
2001D	619,640,000	.75	.75	—
2001S	(3,009,800)	—	—	6.50

KM# 318a 0.9000 **SILVER** .1808 oz. ASW. 6.2500 g.

Date	Mintage	MS-63	MS-65	Prf-65
2001S	(849,600)	—	—	22.50

North Carolina

KM# 319 **COPPER-NICKEL CLAD COPPER**

Date	Mintage	MS-63	MS-65	Prf-65
2001P	627,600,000	.75	.75	—
2001D	427,876,000	.75	.75	—
2001S	(3,009,800)	—	—	6.50

KM# 319a 0.9000 **SILVER** .1808 oz. ASW. 6.2500 g.

Date	Mintage	MS-63	MS-65	Prf-65
2001S	(849,600)	—	—	22.50

Rhode Island

KM# 320 **COPPER-NICKEL CLAD COPPER**

Date	Mintage	MS-63	MS-65	Prf-65
2001P	423,000,000	.75	.75	—
2001D	447,100,000	.75	.75	—
2001S	(3,009,800)	—	—	6.50

KM# 320a 0.9000 **SILVER** .1808 oz. ASW. 6.2500 g.

Date	Mintage	MS-63	MS-65	Prf-65
2001S	(849,600)	—	—	22.50

Vermont

KM# 321 **COPPER-NICKEL CLAD COPPER**

Date	Mintage	MS-63	MS-65	Prf-65
2001P	423,400,000	.75	.75	—
2001D	459,404,000	.75	.75	—
2001S	(3,009,800)	—	—	6.50

KM# 321a 0.9000 **SILVER** .1808 oz. ASW. 6.2500 g.

Date	Mintage	MS-63	MS-65	Prf-65
2001S	(849,600)	—	—	22.50

Indiana

KM# 334 **COPPER-NICKEL CLAD COPPER**

Date	Mintage	MS-63	MS-65	Prf-65
2002P	362,600,000	.75	.75	—
2002D	327,200,000	.75	.75	—
2002S	(3,084,185)	—	—	6.00

KM# 334a 0.9000 **SILVER** .1808 oz. ASW. 6.2500 g.

Date	Mintage	MS-63	MS-65	Prf-65
2002S	(892,229)	—	—	18.00

Louisiana

KM# 333 COPPER-NICKEL CLAD COPPER

Date	Mintage	MS-63	MS-65	Prf-65
2002P	362,000,000	.75	.75	—
2002D	402,204,000	.75	.75	—
2002S	(3,084,185)	—	—	6.00

KM# 333a 0.9000 **SILVER** .1808 oz. ASW. 6.2500 g.

Date	Mintage	MS-63	MS-65	Prf-65
2002S	(892,229)	—	—	18.00

Mississippi

KM# 335 COPPER-NICKEL CLAD COPPER

Date	Mintage	MS-63	MS-65	Prf-65
2002P	290,000,000	.75	.75	—
2002D	289,600,000	.75	.75	—
2002S	(3,084,185)	—	—	6.00

KM# 335a 0.9000 **SILVER** .1808 oz. ASW. 6.2500 g.

Date	Mintage	MS-63	MS-65	Prf-65
2002S	(892,229)	—	—	18.00

Ohio

KM# 332 COPPER-NICKEL CLAD COPPER

Date	Mintage	MS-63	MS-65	Prf-65
2002P	217,200,000	.75	.75	—
2002D	414,832,000	.75	.75	—
2002S	(3,084,185)	—	—	6.00

KM# 332a 0.9000 **SILVER** .1808 oz. ASW. 6.2500 g.

Date	Mintage	MS-63	MS-65	Prf-65
2002S	(892,229)	—	—	18.00

Tennessee

KM# 331 COPPER-NICKEL CLAD COPPER

Date	Mintage	MS-63	MS-65	Prf-65
2002P	361,600,000	1.25	1.25	—
2002D	286,468,000	.85	.85	—
2002S	(3,084,185)	—	—	6.00

KM# 331a 0.9000 **SILVER** .1808 oz. ASW. 6.2500 g.

Date	Mintage	MS-63	MS-65	Prf-65
2002S	(892,229)	—	—	18.00

Alabama

KM# 344 COPPER-NICKEL CLAD COPPER

Date	Mintage	MS-63	MS-65	Prf-65
2003P	225,000,000	.75	.75	—
2003D	232,400,000	.75	.75	—
2003S	(3,270,603)	—	—	5.00

KM# 344a 0.9000 **SILVER** .1808 oz. ASW. 6.2500 g.

Date	Mintage	MS-63	MS-65	Prf-65
2003S	—	—	—	9.00

Arkansas

KM# 347 COPPER-NICKEL CLAD COPPER

Date	Mintage	MS-63	MS-65	Prf-65
2003P	228,000,000	.75	.75	—
2003D	229,800,000	.75	.75	—
2003S	(3,270,603)	—	—	5.00

KM# 347a 0.9000 **SILVER** .1808 oz. ASW. 6.2500 g.

Date	Mintage	MS-63	MS-65	Prf-65
2003S	—	—	—	9.00

Illinois

KM# 343 COPPER-NICKEL CLAD COPPER

Date	Mintage	MS-63	MS-65	Prf-65
2003P	225,800,000	.75	.75	—
2003D	237,400,000	.75	.75	—
2003S	(3,270,603)	—	—	5.00

KM# 343a 0.9000 **SILVER** .1808 oz. ASW. 6.2500 g.

Date	Mintage	MS-63	MS-65	Prf-65
2003S	—	—	—	9.00

Maine

KM# 345 COPPER-NICKEL CLAD COPPER

Date	Mintage	MS-63	MS-65	Prf-65
2003P	217,400,000	.75	.75	—
2003D	213,400,000	.75	.75	—
2003S	(3,270,603)	—	—	5.00

KM# 345a 0.9000 **SILVER** .1808 oz. ASW. 6.2500 g.

Date	Mintage	MS-63	MS-65	Prf-65
2003S	—	—	—	9.00

Missouri

KM# 346 COPPER-NICKEL CLAD COPPER

Date	Mintage	MS-63	MS-65	Prf-65
2003P	225,000,000	.75	.75	—
2003D	228,200,000	.75	.75	—
2003S	(3,270,603)	—	—	5.00

KM# 346a 0.9000 **SILVER** .1808 oz. ASW. 6.2500 g.

Date	Mintage	MS-63	MS-65	Prf-65
2003S	—	—	—	9.00

Florida

KM# 356 COPPER-NICKEL CLAD COPPER

Date	Mintage	MS-63	MS-65	Prf-65
2004P	240,200,000	.75	.75	—
2004D	241,600,000	.75	.75	—
2004S	—	—	—	5.00

KM# 356a 0.9000 **SILVER** .1808 oz. ASW. 6.2500 g.

Date	Mintage	MS-63	MS-65	Prf-65
2004S	—	—	—	9.00

Iowa

KM# 358 COPPER-NICKEL CLAD COPPER

Date	Mintage	MS-63	MS-65	Prf-65
2004P	213,800,000	.75	.75	—
2004D	251,800,000	.75	.75	—
2004S	—	—	—	5.00

KM# 358a 0.9000 **SILVER** .1808 oz. ASW. 6.2500 g.

Date	Mintage	MS-63	MS-65	Prf-65
2004S	—	—	—	9.00

Michigan

KM# 355 COPPER-NICKEL CLAD COPPER

Date	Mintage	MS-63	MS-65	Prf-65
2004P	233,800,000	.75	.75	—
2004D	225,800,000	.75	.75	—
2004S	—	—	—	5.00

KM# 355a 0.9000 **SILVER** .1808 oz. ASW. 6.2500 g.

Date	Mintage	MS-63	MS-65	Prf-65
2004S	—	—	—	9.00

Texas

KM# 357 COPPER-NICKEL CLAD COPPER

Date	Mintage	MS-63	MS-65	Prf-65
2004P	278,800,000	.75	.75	—
2004D	263,000,000	.75	.75	—
2004S	—	—	—	5.00

KM# 357a 0.9000 **SILVER** .1808 oz. ASW. 6.2500 g.

Date	Mintage	MS-63	MS-65	Prf-65
2004S	—	—	—	9.00

Wisconsin

KM# 359 COPPER-NICKEL CLAD COPPER

Date	Mintage	MS-63	MS-65	Prf-65
2004P	226,400,000	.75	.75	—
2004D	226,800,000	.75	.75	—
2004D Extra Leaf Low	Est. 9,000	250	800	—
2004D Extra Leaf High	Est. 3,000	400	1,000	—
2004S	—	—	—	5.00

KM# 359a 0.9000 **SILVER** .1808 oz. ASW. 6.2500 g.

Date	Mintage	MS-63	MS-65	Prf-65
2004S	—	—	—	9.00

California

KM# 370 COPPER-NICKEL CLAD COPPER

Date	Mintage	MS-63	MS-65	Prf-65
2005P	257,200,000	.75	.75	—
2005D	263,200,000	.75	.75	—
2005S	—	—	—	5.00

KM# 370a 0.9000 **SILVER** 0.1808 oz. ASW. 6.2500 g.

Date	Mintage	MS-63	MS-65	Prf-65
2005S	—	—	—	9.00

Kansas

KM# 373 COPPER-NICKEL CLAD COPPER

Date	Mintage	MS-63	MS-65	Prf-65
2005P	263,400,000	.75	.75	—
2005D	300,000,000	.75	.75	—
2005S	—	—	—	9.00

KM# 373a 0.9000 **SILVER** 0.1808 oz. ASW. 6.2500 g.

Date	Mintage	MS-63	MS-65	Prf-65
2005S	—	—	—	9.00

Minnesota

KM# 371 COPPER-NICKEL CLAD COPPER

Date	Mintage	MS-63	MS-65	Prf-65
2005P	226,400,000	.75	.75	—
2005D	226,800,000	.75	.75	—
2005S	—	—	—	5.00

KM# 371a 0.9000 **SILVER** 0.1808 oz. ASW. 6.2500 g.

Date	Mintage	MS-63	MS-65	Prf-65
2005S	—	—	—	9.00

Oregon

KM# 372 COPPER-NICKEL CLAD COPPER

Date	Mintage	MS-63	MS-65	Prf-65
2005P	316,200,000	.75	.75	—
2005D	404,000,000	.75	.75	—
2005S	—	—	—	5.00

KM# 372a 0.9000 **SILVER** 0.1808 oz. ASW. 6.2500 g.

Date	Mintage	MS-63	MS-65	Prf-65
2005S	—	—	—	9.00

West Virginia

KM# 374 COPPER-NICKEL CLAD COPPER

Date	Mintage	MS-63	MS-65	Prf-65
2005P	365,400,000	.75	.75	—
2005S	—	—	—	5.00
2005D	356,200,000	.75	.75	—

KM# 374a 0.9000 **SILVER** 0.1808 oz. ASW. 6.2500 g.

Date	Mintage	MS-63	MS-65	Prf-65
2005S	—	—	—	9.00

Colorado

KM# 384 COPPER-NICKEL CLAD COPPER

Date	Mintage	MS-63	MS-65	Prf-65
2006P	—	.75	.75	—
2006D	—	.75	.75	—
2006S	—	—	—	5.00

KM# 384a 0.9000 **SILVER** .1808 oz. ASW. 6.2500 g.

Date	Mintage	MS-63	MS-65	Prf-65
2006S	—	—	—	9.00

Nebraska

KM# 383 COPPER-NICKEL CLAD COPPER

Date	Mintage	MS-63	MS-65	Prf-65
2006P	—	.75	.75	—
2006D	—	.75	.75	—
2006S	—	—	—	5.00

KM# 383a 0.9000 **SILVER** .1808 oz. ASW. 6.2500 g.

Date	Mintage	MS-63	MS-65	Prf-65
2006S	—	—	—	9.00

Nevada

KM# 382 COPPER-NICKEL CLAD COPPER

Date	Mintage	MS-63	MS-65	Prf-65
2006P	—	.75	.75	—
2006D	—	.75	.75	—
2006S	—	—	—	5.00

KM# 382a 0.9000 **SILVER** .1808 oz. ASW. 6.2500 g.

Date	Mintage	MS-63	MS-65	Prf-65
2006S	—	—	—	9.00

North Dakota

KM# 385 COPPER-NICKEL CLAD COPPER

Date	Mintage	MS-63	MS-65	Prf-65
2006P	—	.75	.75	—
2006D	—	.75	.75	—
2006S	—	—	—	5.00

KM# 385a 0.9000 **SILVER** .1808 oz. ASW. 6.2500 g.

Date	Mintage	MS-63	MS-65	Prf-65
2006S	—	—	—	9.00

South Dakota

KM# 386 COPPER-NICKEL CLAD COPPER

Date	Mintage	MS-63	MS-65	Prf-65
2006P	—	.75	.75	—
2006D	—	.75	.75	—
2006S	—	—	—	5.00

KM# 386a 0.9000 **SILVER** .1808 oz. ASW. 6.2500 g.

Date	Mintage	MS-63	MS-65	Prf-65
2006S	—	—	—	9.00

Kennedy Half Dollar

Regular design resumed

KM# A202b COPPER-NICKEL CLAD COPPER 30.6 mm. 11.3400 g. **Notes:** KM#202b design and composition resumed. The 1979-S and 1981-S Type II proofs have clearer mint marks than the Type I proofs of those years.

Date	Mintage	MS-65	Prf-65	Date	Mintage	MS-65	Prf-65
2001P	21,200,000	6.00	—	2004P	2,900,000	10.00	—
2001D	19,504,000	6.00	—	2004D	2,900,000	10.00	—
2001S	(2,235,000)	—	10.00	2004S	—	—	7.00
2002P	3,100,000	15.00	—	2005P	3,800,000	10.00	—
2002D	2,500,000	10.00	—	2005D	3,500,000	10.00	—
2002S	(2,268,913)	—	7.00	2005S	—	—	7.00
2003P	2,500,000	10.00	—	2006P	—	10.00	—
2003D	2,500,000	10.00	—	2006D	—	10.00	—
2003S	2,076,165	—	7.00	2006S	—	—	7.00

Kennedy Half Dollar

KM# B202b SILVER

Date	Mintage	Prf-65	Date	Mintage	Prf-65
2001S	(849,600)	12.50	2004S	—	12.50
2002S	(888,816)	12.50	2005S	—	12.50
2003S	1,040,425	12.50	2006S	—	12.50

DOLLAR

Sacagawea Dollar

Sacagawea bust right, with baby on back Eagle in flight left

KM# 310 COPPER-ZINC-MANGANESE-NICKEL CLAD COPPER 26.4 mm. 8.0700 g.

Date	Mintage	MS-63	Prf-65	Date	Mintage	MS-63	Prf-65
2001P	62,468,000	4.00	—	2004P	2,660,000	2.50	—
2001D	70,909,500	4.00	—	2004D	2,660,000	2.50	—
2001S	(3,084,600)	—	100.00	2004S	—	—	22.50
2002P	3,865,610	2.00	—	2005P	2,520,000	2.50	—
2002D	3,732,000	2.00	—	2005D	2,520,000	2.50	—
2002S	(3,157,739)	—	28.50	2005S	—	—	22.50
2003P	3,090,000	2.50	—	2006P	—	2.50	—
2003D	3,090,000	2.50	—	2006D	—	2.50	—
2003S	(3,116,590)	—	20.00	2006S	—	—	22.50

COMMEMORATIVE COINAGE 2001-PRESENT

All commemorative silver dollar coins of 1982-present have the following specifications: diameter -- 38.1 millimeters; weight -- 26.7300 grams; composition -- 0.9000 silver, 0.7736 ounces actual silver weight. All commemorative $5 coins of 1982-present have the following specificiations: diameter -- 21.6 millimeters; weight -- 8.3590 grams; composition: 0.9000 gold, 0.242 ounces actual gold weight.

Note: In 1982, after a hiatus of nearly 20 years, coinage of commemorative half dollars resumed. Those designated with a 'W' were struck at the West Point Mint. Some issues were struck in copper--nickel. Those struck in silver have the same size, weight and composition as the prior commemorative half--dollar series.

HALF DOLLAR

U. S. CAPITOL VISITOR CENTER. KM# 323 Copper-Nickel Clad Copper 0 oz. 11.3400 g. **Obv. Designer:** Dean McMullen and Marcel Jovine **Rev. Designer:** Alex Shagin

Date	Mintage	Proof	MS-65	Prf-65
2001	99,157	(77,962)	13.50	18.00

FIRST FLIGHT CENTENNIAL. KM# 348 Copper-Nickel Clad Copper 11.3400 g. **Obv. Designer:** John Mercanti **Rev. Designer:** Donna Weaver

Date	Mintage	Proof	MS-65	Prf-65
2003P	—	—	16.00	18.00

DOLLAR

AMERICAN BUFFALO. KM# 325 Designer: James E. Fraser.

Date	Mintage	Proof	MS-65	Prf-65
2001D	197,131	—	130	—
2001P	—	(272,869)	—	150

CAPITOL VISITOR CENTER. KM# 324 Obv. Designer: Marika Somogyi **Rev. Designer:** John Mercanti

Date	Mintage	Proof	MS-65	Prf-65
2001P	66,636	(143,793)	41.50	46.00

WEST POINT MILITARY ACADEMY BICENTENNIAL. KM# 338 Obv. Designer: T. James Ferrell **Rev. Designer:** John Mercanti

Date	Mintage	Proof	MS-65	Prf-65
2002W	103,201	(288,293)	32.50	36.00

WINTER OLYMPICS - SALT LAKE CITY. KM# 336 Obv. Designer: John Mercanti **Rev. Designer:** Donna Weaver

Date	Mintage	Proof	MS-65	Prf-65
2002P	35,388	(142,873)	38.00	40.00

FIRST FLIGHT CENTENNIAL. KM# 349 Obv. Designer: T. James Ferrell **Rev. Designer:** Norman E. Nemeth **Obverse:** Orville and Wilbur Wright **Reverse:** Wright Brothers airplane

Date	Mintage	Proof	MS-65	Prf-65
2003P	—	—	38.50	42.50

125TH ANNIVERSARY OF EDISON'S ELECTRIC LIGHT. KM# 362 Obv. Designer: Donna Weaver **Rev. Designer:** John Mercanti

Date	Mintage	Proof	MS-65	Prf-65
2004P	—	—	43.50	46.00

LEWIS AND CLARK CORPS OF DISCOVERY BICENTENNIAL. KM# 363

Date	Mintage	Proof	MS-65	Prf-65
2004P	—	—	37.50	36.00

CHIEF JUSTICE JOHN MARSHALL, 250TH BIRTH ANNIVERSARY. KM# 375 Obv. Designer: John Mercanti **Rev. Designer:** Donna Weaver

Date	Mintage	Proof	MS-65	Prf-65
2005P	—	—	40.00	41.50

U.S. MARINE CORPS, 230TH ANNIVERSARY. KM# 376

Date	Mintage	Proof	MS-65	Prf-65
2005P	—	—	85.00	90.00

$5 (HALF EAGLE)

CAPITOL VISITOR CENTER. KM# 326 Designer: Elizabeth Jones.

Date	Mintage	Proof	MS-65	Prf-65
2001	6,761	(27,652)	735	375

2002 SALT LAKE CITY WINTER OLYMPICS. KM# 337 Designer: Donna Weaver.

Date	Mintage	Proof	MS-65	Prf-65
2002	10,585	(32,877)	450	350

$10 (EAGLE)

FIRST FLIGHT CENTENNIAL. KM# 350 0.9000 Gold .4839 oz. AGW. 16.7180 g. **Designer:** Donna Weaver

Date	Mintage	Proof	MS-65	Prf-65
2003P	—	—	470	470

AMERICAN EAGLE BULLION COINS

GOLD $50

KM# 219 0.9167 **GOLD** 1 oz. 32.7mm. 33.9310 g. **Obv. Designer:** Augustus Saint-Gaudens **Rev. Designer:** Miley Busiek

Date	Mintage	Unc	Prf.
2001	143,605	715	—
2001W	(24,580)	—	725
2002	222,029	715	—
2002W	(24,242)	—	725
2003	416,032	715	—
2003W	(29,000)	—	725
2004	417,019	715	—
2004W	(28,731)	—	725
2005	356,555	715	—
2005W	34,695	—	725
2006	—	710	—
2006W	—	—	725

PLATINUM $10

KM# 327 0.9995 **PLATINUM** .1000 oz. 3.1100 g. **Obv. Designer:** John Mercanti

Date	Mintage	Unc	Prf.
2001W	(12,193)	—	145

KM# 283 0.9995 **PLATINUM** .1000 oz. 3.1100 g. **Obv. Designer:** John Mercanti **Rev. Designer:** Thomas D. Rogers Sr

Date	Mintage	Unc	Prf.
2001	52,017	145	—
2002	23,005	145	—
2003	22,007	145	—
2004	15,010	165	—
2005	14,013	170	—
2006	—	—	—

KM# 339 0.9995 **PLATINUM** .1000 oz. 3.1100 g. **Obv. Designer:** John Mercanti

Date	Mintage	Unc	Prf.
2002W	(12,365)	—	145

KM# 351 0.9995 **PLATINUM** .1000 oz. 3.1100 g. **Obv. Designer:** John Mercanti **Rev. Designer:** Al Maletsky

Date	Mintage	Unc	Prf.
2003W	(8,161)	—	175

KM# 364 0.9995 **PLATINUM** .1000 oz. 3.1100 g. **Obv. Designer:** John Mercanti

Date	Mintage	Unc	Prf.
2004W	(6,846)	—	350

KM# 377 0.9995 **PLATINUM** 0.0999 oz. 3.1100 g. **Obv. Designer:** John Mercanti **Rev. Designer:** Donna Weaver

Date	Mintage	Unc	Prf.
2005W	8,000	—	210

PLATINUM $25

KM# 328 0.9995 **PLATINUM** .2500 oz. 7.7857 g. **Obv. Designer:** John Mercanti

Date	Mintage	Unc	Prf.
2001W	(8,858)	—	320

KM# 284 0.9995 **PLATINUM** 0.2500 oz. 7.7857 g. **Obv. Designer:** John Mercanti **Rev. Designer:** Thomas D. Rogers Sr

Date	Mintage	Unc	Prf.
2001	21,815	365	—
2002	27,405	350	—
2003	25,207	365	—
2004	18,010	365	—
2005	12,013	365	—
2006	—	—	—

KM# 340 0.9995 **PLATINUM** .2500 oz. 7.7857 g. **Obv. Designer:** John Mercanti

Date	Mintage	Unc	Prf.
2002W	(9,282)	—	320

KM# 352 0.9995 **PLATINUM** .2500 oz. 7.7857 g. **Obv. Designer:** John Mercanti **Rev. Designer:** Al Maletsky

Date	Mintage	Unc	Prf.
2003W	(6,045)	—	385

KM# 365 0.9995 **PLATINUM** .2500 oz. 7.7857 g. **Obv. Designer:** John Mercanti

Date	Mintage	Unc	Prf.
2004W	(5,035)	—	950

KM# 378 0.9995 **PLATINUM** 0.2502 oz. 7.7857 g. **Obv. Designer:** John Mercanti **Rev. Designer:** Donna Weaver

Date	Mintage	Unc	Prf.
2005W	6,424	—	410

PLATINUM $50

KM# 329 0.9995 **PLATINUM** .5000 oz. 15.5520 g. **Obv. Designer:** John Mercanti

Date	Mintage	Unc	Prf.
2001W	(8,268)	—	660

KM# 285 0.9995 **PLATINUM** 0.5000 oz. 15.5520 g. **Obv. Designer:** John Mercanti **Rev. Designer:** Thomas D. Rogers Sr

Date	Mintage	Unc	Prf.
2001	12,815	660	—
2002	24,005	660	—
2003	17,409	660	—
2004	98,040	660	—
2005	9,013	660	—
2006	—	—	—

KM# 341 0.9995 **PLATINUM** .5000 oz. 15.5520 g. **Obv. Designer:** John Mercanti

Date	Mintage	Unc	Prf.
2002W	(8,772)	—	660

KM# 353 0.9995 **PLATINUM** .5000 oz. 15.5520 g. **Obv. Designer:** John Mercanti **Rev. Designer:** Al Maletsky

Date	Mintage	Unc	Prf.
2003W	(6,181)	—	660

KM# 366 0.9995 **PLATINUM** .5000 oz. 15.5520 g. **Obv. Designer:** John Mercanti

Date	Mintage	Unc	Prf.
2004W	(4,886)	—	2,600

KM# 379 0.9995 **PLATINUM** .5000 oz. 15.5520 g. **Obv. Designer:** John Mercanti **Rev. Designer:** Donna Weaver

Date	Mintage	Unc	Prf.
2005W Proof	5,720	—	735

PLATINUM $100

KM# 330 0.9995 **PLATINUM** 1.000 oz. 31.1050 g. **Obv. Designer:** John Mercanti

Date	Mintage	Unc	Prf.
2001W	(8,990)	—	1,275

KM# 342 0.9995 **PLATINUM** 1.000 oz. 31.1050 g. **Obv. Designer:** John Mercanti

Date	Mintage	Unc	Prf.
2002W	(9,834)	—	1,275

KM# 354 0.9995 **PLATINUM** 1.000 oz. 31.1050 g. **Obv. Designer:** John Mercanti **Rev. Designer:** Al Maletsky

Date	Mintage	Unc	Prf.
2003W	(6,991)	—	1,275

KM# 367 0.9995 **PLATINUM** 1.000 oz. 31.1050 g. **Obv. Designer:** John Mercanti **Rev. Designer:** Donna Weaver

Date	Mintage	Unc	Prf.
2004W	(5,833)	—	4,500

KM# 380 0.9995 **PLATINUM** 0.9995 oz. 31.1050 g. **Obv. Designer:** John Mercanti **Rev. Designer:** Donna Weaver

Date	Mintage	Unc	Prf.
2005W	6,700	—	1,345

MINT SETS

Date	Sets Sold	Issue Price	Value
2001	1,066,900	14.95	18.50
2002	1,139,388	14.95	13.75
2003	1,002,555	14.95	23.75
2004	1,160,000	16.95	83.50
2005	—	16.95	22.00
2006	—	16.95	—

MODERN COMMEMORATIVE COIN SETS

Capitol Visitor Center

Date	Price
2001 3 coin set: proof half, silver dollar, gold $5; KM323, 324, 326.	380

American Buffalo

Date	Price
2001 2 coin set: 90% silver unc. & proof $1.; KM325.	270
2001 coin & currency set 90% unc. dollar & replicas of 1899 $5 silver cert.; KM325.	160

Winter Olympics - Salt Lake City

Date	Price
2002 2 coin set: proof 90% silver dollar KM336 & $5.00 Gold KM337	330
2002 4 coin set: 90% silver unc. & proof $1, KM336 & unc. & proof gold $5, KM337.	725

First Flight Centennial

Date	Price
2003 3-coin set includes proof gold ten dollar KM350, proof silver dollar KM349 & proof clad half dollar KM348	475

PROOF SETS

Date	Sets Sold	Issue Price	Value
2001S	2,249,498	19.95	135
2001S 5 quarter set	774,800	13.95	63.50
2001S Silver	849,600	31.95	170
2002S	2,319,766	19.95	38.50
2002S 5 quarter set	764,419	13.95	23.50
2002S Silver	892,229	31.95	63.50
2003 X#207, 208, 209.2	—	44.00	28.75
2003S	2,175,684	19.95	25.00
2003S 5 quarter set	1,225,507	13.95	19.50
2003S Silver	1,142,858	31.95	31.00
2004S 11 pieces	2,275,000	22.95	56.00
2004S 5 quarter set	987,960	15.95	27.00
2004S Silver 11 pieces	1,187,673	37.95	51.50
2004S Silver 5 quarter set	594,137	23.95	30.00
2005S 11 Pieces	—	22.95	26.50
2005S 5 quarter set	—	15.95	18.50
2005S Silver 11 pieces	—	37.95	51.50
2005S Silver 5 quarter set	—	23.95	27.50
2006S 10 pieces clad	—	22.95	—
2006S 5 quarter set	—	15.95	—
2006S Silver 10 pieces	—	37.95	—
2006S Silver 5 quarter set	—	23.95	—

URUGUAY

The Oriental Republic of Uruguay (so called because of its location on the east bank of the Uruguay River) is situated on the Atlantic coast of South America between Argentina and Brazil. This South American country has an area of 68,536 sq. mi. (176,220 sq. km.) and a population of *3 million. Capital: Montevideo. Uruguay's chief economic asset is the rich, rolling grassy plains. Meat, wool, hides and skins are exported.

REPUBLIC

REFORM COINAGE

1,000 Nuevos Pesos = 1 Uruguayan Peso; 100 Centesimos = 1 Uruguayan Peso (UYP)

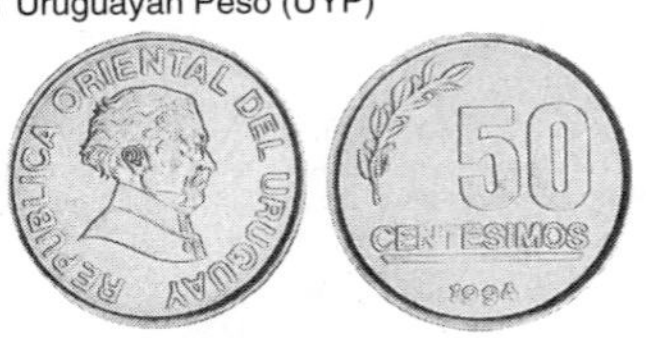

KM# 106 50 CENTESIMOS
Stainless Steel **Note:** Coin rotation.

Date	Mintage	F	VF	XF	Unc	BU
2002	—	—	—	0.35	0.75	1.00

KM# 120 5 PESOS
6.2400 g., Brass, 25.8 mm. **Obv:** Artigas **Rev:** Value **Edge:** Plain

Date	Mintage	F	VF	XF	Unc	BU
2003	—	—	—	—	2.50	3.00

UZBEKISTAN

The Republic of Uzbekistan (formerly the Uzbek S.S.R.), is bordered on the north by Kazakhstan, to the east by Kirghizia and Tajikistan, on the south by Afghanistan and on the west by Turkmenistan. The republic is comprised of the regions of Andizhan, Bukhara, Dzhizak, Ferghana, Kashkadar, Khorezm (Khiva), Namangan, Navoi, Samarkand, Surkhan-.Darya, Syr-Darya, Tashkent and the Karakalpak Autonomous Republic. It has an area of 172,741 sq. mi. (447,400 sq. km.) and a population of 20.3 million. Capital: Tashkent. Crude oil, natural gas, coal, copper, and gold deposits make up the chief resources, while intensive farming, based on artificial irrigation, provides an abundance of cotton.

Monetary System
100 Tiyin = 1 Som

REPUBLIC

STANDARD COINAGE

KM# 12 SOM
2.8300 g., Nickel-Clad Steel, 18.8 mm. **Obv:** National arms **Rev:** Denomination and map **Edge:** Reeded

Date	Mintage	F	VF	XF	Unc	BU
2001	—	—	—	—	1.00	1.25

KM# 13 5 SOM
3.3500 g., Brass Plated Steel, 21.2 mm. **Obv:** National arms **Rev:** Denomination and map **Edge:** Plain

Date	Mintage	F	VF	XF	Unc	BU
2001	—	—	—	—	1.35	1.75

KM# 14 10 SOM
2.7100 g., Nickel-Clad Steel, 19.75 mm. **Obv:** National arms **Rev:** Denomination and map **Edge:** Plain

Date	Mintage	F	VF	XF	Unc	BU
2001	—	—	—	—	2.00	2.50

KM# 15 50 SOM
8.0000 g., Nickel-Clad Steel, 26.2 mm. **Obv:** National arms **Rev:** Denomination and map **Edge:** Plain and reeded sections

Date	Mintage	F	VF	XF	Unc	BU
2001	—	—	—	—	3.50	4.00

KM# 16 50 SOM
7.9000 g., Nickel-Clad Steel, 26.3 mm. **Subject:** 2700th Anniversary of Shahrisabz Town **Obv:** National arms **Rev:** Statue and ruins above value **Edge:** Reeded and plain sections

Date	Mintage	F	VF	XF	Unc	BU
2002	—	—	—	—	3.75	4.50

VATICAN CITY

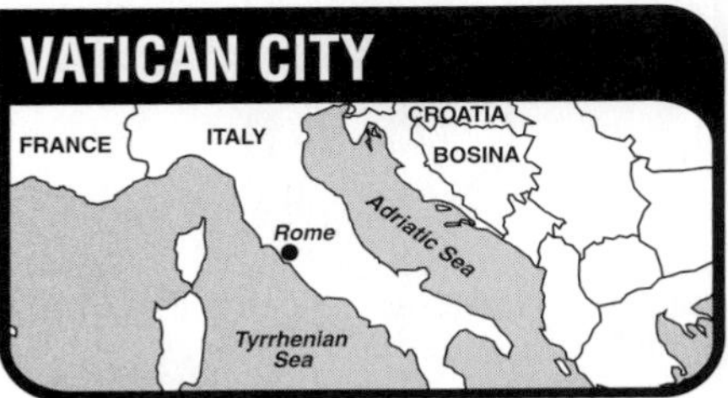

The State of the Vatican City, a papal state on the right bank of the Tiber River within the boundaries of Rome, has an area of 0.17 sq. mi. (0.44 sq. km.) and a population of *775. Capital: Vatican City.

Today the Pope exercises supreme legislative, executive and judicial power within the Vatican City, and the State of the Vatican City is recognized by many nations as an independent sovereign state under the temporal jurisdiction of the Pope, even to the extent of ambassadorial exchange. The Pope, is of course, the head of the Roman Catholic Church.

PONTIFFS
John Paul II, 1978-2005
Sede Vacante, April 2 - 19, 2005
Benedict XVI, 2005-

MINT MARKS
R - Rome

MONETARY SYSTEM
100 Centesimi = 1 Lira (thru 2002)
100 Euro Cent = 1 Euro

DATING
Most Vatican coins indicate the regnal year of the pope preceded by the word *Anno* (or an abbreviation), even if the *anno domini* date is omitted.

CITY STATE

John Paul II

STANDARD COINAGE

100 Centesimi = 1 Lira

Y# 331 10 LIRE
1.6000 g., Aluminum, 23.2 mm. **Obverse:** John Paul I bust left **Reverse:** Papal arms **Edge:** Plain **Designer:** Laura Cretella

Date	Mintage	F	VF	XF	Unc
2001	—	—	0.50	0.75	2.00

Y# 332 20 LIRE
3.5700 g., Brass, 21.2 mm. **Obverse:** Pius XI bust left **Reverse:** Papal arms **Edge:** Plain **Designer:** Laura Cretella

Date	Mintage	F	VF	XF	Unc
2001	—	—	0.50	0.75	2.00

Y# 333 50 LIRE
4.5000 g., Copper-Nickel, 19.2 mm. **Obverse:** Pius XII bust left **Reverse:** Papal arms **Edge:** Plain **Designer:** Laura Cretella

Date	Mintage	F	VF	XF	Unc
2001	—	—	0.50	0.75	2.00

Y# 334 100 LIRE
4.5000 g., Copper-Nickel, 22 mm. **Obverse:** John XXIII bust left **Reverse:** Papal arms **Edge:** Reeded and plain sections **Designer:** Laura Cretella

Date	Mintage	F	VF	XF	Unc
2001	—	—	0.50	1.00	2.50

Y# 335 200 LIRE
5.0000 g., Brass, 22 mm. **Obverse:** Paul VI bust left **Reverse:** Papal arms **Edge:** Reeded **Designer:** Laura Cretella

Date	Mintage	F	VF	XF	Unc
2001	—	—	0.50	1.00	2.25

Y# 336 500 LIRE
6.7700 g., Bi-Metallic Aluminumn-Bronze center in Stainless steel ring, 25.7 mm. **Obverse:** John Paul I bust left **Reverse:** Papal arms **Edge:** Reeded and plain sections **Designer:** Laura Cretella

Date	Mintage	F	VF	XF	Unc
2001	—	—	—	2.50	4.00

Y# 338 1000 LIRE
14.6000 g., 0.8350 Silver .3919 oz. ASW, 31.4 mm. **Subject:** Peace **Obverse:** Dove over earth **Reverse:** Papal arms **Edge Lettering:** "+++ TOTVSTVVS +++ MMI"

Date	Mintage	F	VF	XF	Unc
2001	—	—	—	12.50	25.00

Y# 337 1000 LIRE
8.8500 g., Copper-Nickel, 26.9 mm. **Obverse:** John Paul II bust left **Reverse:** Papal arms **Edge:** Reeded and plain sections **Designer:** Laura Cretella

Date	Mintage	F	VF	XF	Unc
2001/XIV	—	—	—	5.50	7.00

Y# 339 2000 LIRE
16.0000 g., 0.8350 Silver .4295 oz. ASW, 31.4 mm. **Subject:** Dialog for Peace **Obverse:** Pope holding croizer **Reverse:** Dove above crowd **Edge:** Reeded **Designer:** Floriano Bodini

Date	Mintage	F	VF	XF	Unc
2001/XXIII	16,000	—	—	25.00	35.00
2001/XXIII Proof	8,000	Value: 40.00			

Y# 340 5000 LIRE
18.0000 g., 0.8350 Silver .4832 oz. ASW, 32 mm. **Subject:** Easter **Obverse:** Pope praying **Reverse:** Jesus rising **Edge:** Reeded and plain sections **Designer:** Floriano Bodini

Date	Mintage	F	VF	XF	Unc
2001/XXIII Proof	16,000	Value: 30.00			

EURO COINAGE

Y# 341 EURO CENT
2.2700 g., Copper Plated Steel, 16.2 mm. **Obverse:** Pope's portrait **Obv. Designer:** Guido Veroi **Reverse:** Value and globe **Rev. Designer:** Luc Luyckx **Edge:** Plain

Date	Mintage	F	VF	XF	Unc
2002R	80,000	—	—	—	115
2002R Proof	9,000	Value: 175			
2003R	65,000	—	—	—	55.00
2003R Proof	13,000	Value: 145			
2004R	65,000	—	—	—	18.00
2004R Proof	13,000	Value: 145			
2005R	85,000	—	—	—	18.00
2005R Proof	16,000	Value: 140			

Y# 342 2 EURO CENTS
3.0300 g., Copper Plated Steel, 18.7 mm. **Obverse:** Pope's portrait **Obv. Designer:** Guido Veroi **Reverse:** Value and globe **Edge:** Grooved

Date	Mintage	F	VF	XF	Unc
2002R	80,000	—	—	—	115
2002R Proof	9,000	Value: 175			
2003R	65,000	—	—	—	55.00
2003R Proof	13,000	Value: 145			
2004R	65,000	—	—	—	18.00
2004R Proof	13,000	Value: 145			
2005R	85,000	—	—	—	18.00
2005R Proof	16,000	Value: 140			

Y# 343 5 EURO CENTS
3.8600 g., Copper Plated Steel, 21.2 mm. **Obverse:** Pope's portrait **Obv. Designer:** Guido Veroi **Reverse:** Value and globe **Edge:** Plain

Date	Mintage	F	VF	XF	Unc
2002R	80,000	—	—	—	115
2002R Proof	9,000	Value: 175			
2003R	65,000	—	—	—	55.00
2003R Proof	13,000	Value: 145			
2004R	65,000	—	—	—	22.50
2004R Proof	13,000	Value: 145			
2005R	85,000	—	—	—	22.50
2005R Proof	16,000	Value: 140			

Y# 344 10 EURO CENTS
4.0700 g., Brass, 19.7 mm. **Obverse:** Pope's portrait **Obv. Designer:** Guido Veroi **Reverse:** Map and value **Edge:** Reeded

Date	Mintage	F	VF	XF	Unc
2002R	80,000	—	—	—	115
2002R Proof	9,000	Value: 175			
2003R	65,000	—	—	—	55.00
2003R Proof	13,000	Value: 145			
2004R	65,000	—	—	—	25.00
2004R Proof	13,000	Value: 145			
2005R	85,000	—	—	—	25.00
2005R Proof	16,000	Value: 140			

Y# 345 20 EURO CENTS
5.7300 g., Brass, 22.1 mm. **Obverse:** Pope's portrait **Obv. Designer:** Guido Veroi **Reverse:** Map and value **Rev. Designer:** Luc Luycx **Edge:** Notched

Date	Mintage	F	VF	XF	Unc
2002R	80,000	—	—	—	115
2002R Proof	9,000	Value: 175			
2003R	65,000	—	—	—	55.00
2003R Proof	13,000	Value: 145			
2004R	65,000	—	—	—	27.50
2004R Proof	13,000	Value: 145			
2005R	85,000	—	—	—	27.50
2005R Proof	16,000	Value: 140			

Y# 346 50 EURO CENTS
7.8100 g., Brass, 24.2 mm. **Obverse:** Pope's portrait **Obv. Designer:** Guido Veroi **Reverse:** Map and value **Rev. Designer:** Luc Luycx **Edge:** Reeded

Date	Mintage	F	VF	XF	Unc
2002R	80,000	—	—	—	115
2002R Proof	9,000	Value: 175			
2003R	65,000	—	—	—	55.00
2003R Proof	13,000	Value: 145			
2004R	65,000	—	—	—	32.50
2004R Proof	13,000	Value: 145			
2005R	85,000	—	—	—	32.50
2005R Proof	16,000	Value: 140			

Y# 347 EURO
7.5000 g., Bi-Metallic Copper-Nickel center in Brass ring, 23.2 mm. **Obverse:** Pope's portrait **Obv. Designer:** Guido Veroi **Reverse:** Value and map **Rev. Designer:** Luc Luycx **Edge:** Reeded and plain sections

Date	Mintage	F	VF	XF	Unc
2002R	80,000	—	—	—	100
2002R Proof	9,000	Value: 185			
2003R	65,000	—	—	—	55.00
2003R Proof	13,000	Value: 145			
2004R	65,000	—	—	—	45.00
2004R Proof	13,000	Value: 145			
2005R	85,000	—	—	—	45.00
2005R Proof	16,000	Value: 140			

Y# 348 2 EURO
8.5200 g., Bi-Metallic Brass center in Copper-Nickel ring, 25.7 mm. **Obverse:** Pope's portrait **Obv. Designer:** Guido Veroi **Reverse:** Value and map **Rev. Designer:** Luc Luycx **Edge:** Reeded **Edge Lettering:** 2's and stars

Date	Mintage	F	VF	XF	Unc
2002R	80,000	—	—	—	165
2002R Proof	9,000	Value: 215			
2003R	65,000	—	—	—	90.00
2003R Proof	13,000	Value: 185			
2004R	65,000	—	—	—	65.00
2004R Proof	13,000	Value: 185			
2005R	85,000	—	—	—	65.00
2005R Proof	16,000	Value: 180			

Y# 358 2 EURO
8.5000 g., Bi-Metallic Brass center in Copper-nickel ring, 25.75 mm. **Subject:** 75th Anniversary of the Founding of the Vatican City State **Obverse:** St. Peters Square within city walls, dates 1929-2004 **Reverse:** Value and map **Edge:** Reeding over 2's and stars **Designer:** Luciana de Simoni

Date	Mintage	F	VF	XF	Unc
2004R	85,000	—	—	—	15.00

Y# 349 5 EURO
18.0000 g., 0.8350 Silver 0.5353 oz. ASW, 32 mm. **Subject:** 24th Anniversary of Reign **Obverse:** Pope's portrait **Reverse:** Allegorical female and bridge **Edge:** Lettered **Edge Lettering:** +++ TOTUS TUUS +++ MMII

Date	Mintage	F	VF	XF	Unc
2002R Proof	10,000	Value: 125			

Y# 354 5 EURO
18.0000 g., 0.9250 Silver, 34 mm. **Subject:** Year of the Rosary **Obverse:** Pope praying the rosary **Reverse:** "Our Lady of Pompei" presenting rosaries to Saints Dominic and Catherine **Edge:** Reeded **Designer:** Roberto Mauri

Date	Mintage	F	VF	XF	Unc
2003R Proof	10,000	—	—	—	65.00

Y# 359 5 EURO
18.0000 g., 0.9250 Silver 0.5353 oz. ASW, 32 mm. **Subject:** 150th Anniversary of the Proclamation of the Dogma of the Immaculate Conception **Obverse:** Virgin Mary **Reverse:** Two Papal coat of arms **Edge:** Reeded and plain sections **Designer:** Claudia Momoni

Date	Mintage	F	VF	XF	Unc
2004R	13,000	—	—	—	60.00

Y# 350 10 EURO
22.0000 g., 0.8350 Silver 0.5906 oz. ASW, 34 mm. **Subject:** 24th Anniversary of Reign **Reverse:** Risen Christ (Message of peace) **Edge:** Reeded **Designer:** Floriano Bodini

Date	Mintage	F	VF	XF	Unc
2002R Proof	10,000	Value: 80.00			

Y# 355 10 EURO
22.0000 g., 0.9250 Silver 0.6543 oz. ASW, 34 mm. **Subject:** 25th Anniversary of Reign **Obverse:** Pope praying **Reverse:** St. Peter receiving the keys of Rome **Edge:** Reeded **Designer:** Amalia Mistichelli

Date	Mintage	F	VF	XF	Unc
2003R Proof	10,000	Value: 80.00			

Y# 360 10 EURO
22.0000 g., 0.9250 Silver 0.6543 oz. ASW, 34 mm. **Obverse:** Pope praying for peace **Reverse:** Tree of Life rooted in virtues **Edge:** Reeded and plain sections **Designer:** Maria Carmela Colaneri

Date	Mintage	F	VF	XF	Unc
2004R	13,000	—	—	—	75.00

Y# 361 20 EURO
6.0000 g., 0.9170 Gold 0.1769 oz. AGW **Subject:** Roots of Faith **Reverse:** Noah's Ark **Designer:** Floriano Bodini

Date	Mintage	F	VF	XF	Unc
2002	2,800	Value: 1,100			

Y# 351 20 EURO
6.0000 g., 0.9166 Gold 0.1768 oz. AGW, 21 mm. **Reverse:** Moses being found in floating basket **Edge:** Reeded **Designer:** Floriano Bodini

Date	Mintage	F	VF	XF	Unc
2003R Proof	2,800	Value: 1,100			

Y# 363 20 EURO
6.0000 g., 0.9170 Gold, 21 mm. **Reverse:** David slaying Goliath **Designer:** Floriano Bodini

Date	Mintage	F	VF	XF	Unc
2004/XXVIIR Proof	3,050	Value: 1,000			

Y# 362 50 EURO
15.0000 g., 0.9170 Gold 0.4422 oz. AGW **Subject:** Roots of Faith **Reverse:** Sacrifice of Abraham **Designer:** Floriano Bodini

Date	Mintage	F	VF	XF	Unc
2002 Proof	2,800	Value: 1,950			

Y# 352 50 EURO
15.0000 g., 0.9166 Gold 0.442 oz. AGW, 28 mm. **Reverse:** Moses receiving the Ten Commandments **Edge:** Reeded **Designer:** Floriano Bodini

Date	Mintage	F	VF	XF	Unc
2003R Proof	2,800	Value: 1,950			

Y# 364 50 EURO
15.0000 g., 0.9170 Gold .4422 oz. AGW **Reverse:** Judgement of Solomon **Designer:** Floriano Bodini

Date	Mintage	F	VF	XF	Unc
2004/XXVIIR Proof	3,050	Value: 1,850			

Sede Vacante

EURO COINAGE

Y# 365 EURO CENT
2.2700 g., Copper Plated Steel **Obverse:** Arms of Cardinal Jorge Arturo Medina Estevez **Obv. Designer:** Daniela Longo **Reverse:** Value and globe **Rev. Designer:** Luc Luycx

Date	Mintage	F	VF	XF	Unc
MMV (2005)R	60,000	—	—	—	28.00

Y# 366 2 EURO CENTS
3.0300 g., Copper Plated Steel **Obverse:** Arms of Cardinal Jorge Arturo Medina Estevez **Obv. Designer:** Daniela Longo **Reverse:** Value and globe **Rev. Designer:** Luc Luycx

Date	Mintage	F	VF	XF	Unc
MMV (2005)R	60,000	—	—	—	30.00

Y# 367 5 EURO CENTS
3.8600 g., Copper Plated Steel **Obverse:** Arms of Cardinal Jorge Arturo Medina Estevez **Obv. Designer:** Daniela Longo **Reverse:** Value and globe **Rev. Designer:** Luc Luycx

Date	Mintage	F	VF	XF	Unc
MMV (2005)R	60,000	—	—	—	32.00

Y# 368 10 EURO CENTS
4.0700 g., Brass **Obverse:** Arms of Cardinal Jorge Arturo Medina Estevez **Obv. Designer:** Daniela Longo **Reverse:** Map and value **Rev. Designer:** Luc Luycx

Date	Mintage	F	VF	XF	Unc
MMV (2005)R	60,000	—	—	—	35.00

Y# 369 20 EURO CENTS
Brass **Obverse:** Arms of Cardinal Jorge Arturo Medina Estevez **Obv. Designer:** Daniela Longo **Reverse:** Map and value **Rev. Designer:** Luc Luycx

Date	Mintage	F	VF	XF	Unc
MMV (2005)R	60,000	—	—	—	40.00

Y# 370 50 EURO CENTS
7.8100 g., Brass **Obverse:** Arms of Cardinal Jorge Arturo Medina Estevez **Obv. Designer:** Daniela Longo **Reverse:** Map and value **Rev. Designer:** Luc Luycx

Date	Mintage	F	VF	XF	Unc
MMV (2005)R	60,000	—	—	—	45.00

Y# 371 EURO
7.5000 g., Bi-Metallic **Obverse:** Arms of Cardinal Jorge Arturo Medina Estevez **Obv. Designer:** Daniela Longo **Reverse:** Value and map **Rev. Designer:** Luc Luycx

Date	Mintage	F	VF	XF	Unc
MMV (2005)R	60,000	—	—	—	50.00

Y# 372 2 EURO
8.5200 g., Bi-Metallic **Obverse:** Arms of Cardinal Jorge Arturo Medina Estevez **Obv. Designer:** Daniela Longo **Reverse:** Map and value **Rev. Designer:** Luc Luycx

Date	Mintage	F	VF	XF	Unc
MMV (2005)R	60,000	—	—	—	55.00

Y# 373 5 EURO
18.0000 g., 0.9250 Silver 0.5353 oz. ASW, 32 mm. **Obverse:** Dove within square **Reverse:** Arms of Cardinal Jorge Arturo Medina Estevez **Edge:** Reeded **Designer:** Daniela Longo

Date	Mintage	F	VF	XF	Unc
MMV (2005)R Proof	13,440	Value: 200			

Benedict XVI

EURO COINAGE

Y# 375 EURO CENT
Copper-Plated-Steel **Obverse:** Pope's portrait. **Reverse:** Value and globe.

Date	Mintage	F	VF	XF	Unc
2006R	85,000	—	—	—	—
2006R Proof	16,000	Value: 60.00			

Y# 376 2 EURO CENTS
Copper-Plated-Steel **Obverse:** Pope's portrait. **Reverse:** Value and globe.

Date	Mintage	F	VF	XF	Unc
2006R	85,000	—	—	—	—
2006R Proof	16,000	Value: 65.00			

Y# 377 5 EURO CENTS
Copper-Plated-Steel **Obverse:** Pope's portrait **Reverse:** Value and globe

Date	Mintage	F	VF	XF	Unc
2006R	85,000	—	—	—	—
2006R Proof	16,000	Value: 70.00			

Y# 378 10 EURO CENTS
Brass **Obverse:** Pope's portrait **Reverse:** Map and value

Date	Mintage	F	VF	XF	Unc
2006R	85,000	—	—	—	—
2006R Proof	16,000	Value: 80.00			

Y# 379 20 EURO CENTS
Brass **Obverse:** Pope's portrait **Reverse:** Map and value

Date	Mintage	F	VF	XF	Unc
2006R	85,000	—	—	—	—
2006R Proof	16,000	Value: 90.00			

Y# 380 50 EURO CENTS
Brass **Obverse:** Pope's portrait **Reverse:** Map and value

Date	Mintage	F	VF	XF	Unc
2006R	85,000	—	—	—	—
2006R Proof	16,000	Value: 100			

Y# 381 EURO
Bi-Metallic Copper-Nickel center in brass ring. **Obverse:** Pope's portrait **Reverse:** Value and map

Date	Mintage	F	VF	XF	Unc
2006R	85,000	—	—	—	—
2006R Proof	16,000	Value: 110			

Y# 374 2 EURO
Bi-Metallic **Subject:** World Youth Day **Obverse:** Cologne Cathedral **Reverse:** Value and Euro map

Date	Mintage	F	VF	XF	Unc
2005R	—	—	—	—	90.00

Y# 382 2 EURO
Bi-Metallic Brass center in Copper-Nickel ring. **Obverse:** Pope's portrait **Reverse:** Value and map

Date	Mintage	F	VF	XF	Unc
2006R	85,000	—	—	—	—
2006R Proof	16,000	Value: 120			

Y# 383 5 EURO
18.0000 g., 0.9250 Silver **Subject:** Life reborn **Obverse:** Bust left **Reverse:** Children playing among branches of an olive tree

Date	Mintage	F	VF	XF	Unc
2005R Proof	13,000	Value: 100			

Y# 384 10 EURO
22.0000 g., 0.9250 Silver 0.6543 oz. ASW **Subject:** Disciples of Emanaus **Obverse:** Bust left. **Reverse:** Three men seated at table

Date	Mintage	F	VF	XF	Unc
2006R Proof	13,000	Value: 215			

MINT SETS

KM#	Date	Mintage	Identification	Issue Price	Mkt Val
MS107	2001 (8)	26,000	Y#331-338	21.25	200
MS108	2002 (8)	65,000	Y#341-348	12.00	950
MS109	2003 (8)	65,000	Y#341-348	15.00	475
MS110	2004 (8)	85,000	Y#341-348	16.50	250
MS111	2005 (8)	85,000	Y#341-348.	32.50	250
MS112	MMV (2005) (8)	60,000	Y#365-372	—	300

PROOF SETS

KM#	Date	Mintage	Identification	Issue Price	Mkt Val
PS5	2002 (8)	9,000	Y#341-348	75.00	1,450
PS6	2003 (8)	13,000	Y#341-348	78.00	1,200
PS7	2004 (8)	13,000	Y#341-348	—	1,200
PS8	2005 (8)	16,000	Y#341-348, plus silver medal.	150	1,150

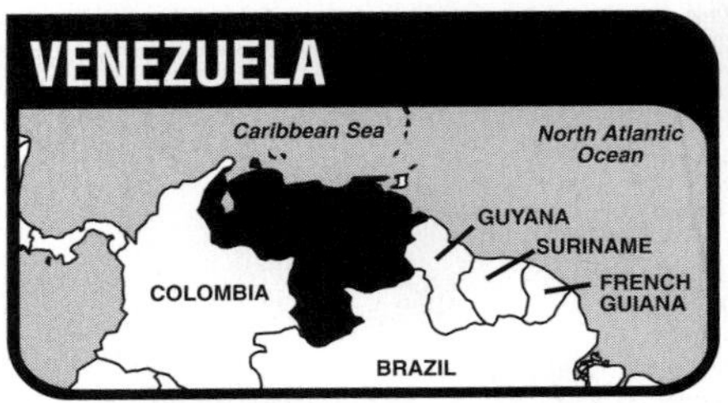

The Republic of Venezuela ("Little Venice"), located on the northern coast of South America between Colombia and Guyana, has an area of 352,145 sq. mi.(912,050 sq. km.) and a population of 20 million. Capital: Caracas. Petroleum and mining provide a significant portion of Venezuela's exports. Coffee, grown on 60,000 plantations, is the chief crop. Metalurgy, refining, oil, iron and steel production are the main employment industries.

GOVERNMENT
Republic, 1823-present

MINT MARKS
(c) - Caracas

ENGRAVER'S INITIALS
W. W. – William Wyon

REPUBLIC

REFORM COINAGE

1896; 100 Centimos = 1 Bolivar

Y# 80a 10 BOLIVARES
1.7390 g., Aluminum-Zinc, 17 mm. **Obv:** National arms and value **Rev:** Bolivar left **Edge:** Reeded

Date	Mintage	F	VF	XF	Unc	BU
2001	—	—	—	—	0.50	0.75

Y# 81a 20 BOLIVARES
3.2650 g., Aluminum-Zinc, 20 mm. **Obv:** National arms and value **Rev:** Bolivar left **Edge:** Plain

Date	Mintage	F	VF	XF	Unc	BU
2001	—	—	—	—	0.65	1.00

Y# 83 100 BOLIVARES
6.8200 g., Nickel Clad Steel, 25 mm. **Obv:** Arms next to value in center **Rev:** Bolivar portrait and mint mark **Edge:** Plain

Date	Mintage	F	VF	XF	Unc	BU
2001(c)	—	—	—	0.60	1.25	1.50
2002(c)	—	—	—	0.60	1.25	1.50

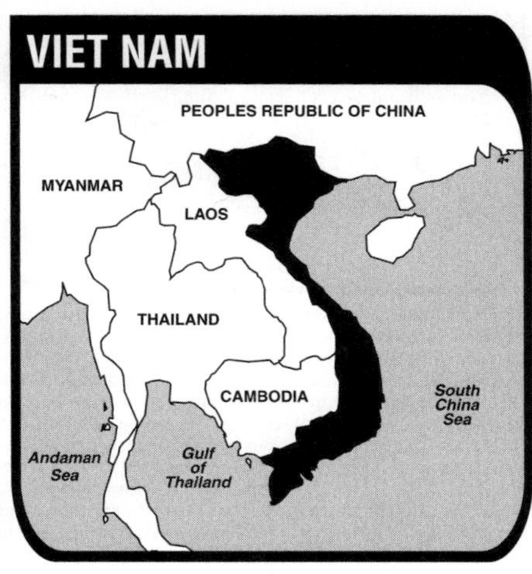

SOCIALIST REPUBLIC

The Socialist Republic of Viet Nam, located in Southeast Asia west of the South China Sea, has an area of 127,300 sq. mi. (329,560 sq. km.) and a population of *66.8 million. Capital: Hanoi. Agricultural products, coal, and mineral ores are exported.

The activities of Communists in South Viet Nam led to the second Indochina war which came to a brief halt in 1973 (when a cease-fire was arranged and U.S. forces withdrew), but it didn't end until April 30, 1975 when South Viet Nam surrendered unconditionally. The two Viet Nams were reunited as the Socialist Republic of Viet Nam on July 2, 1976.

SOCIALIST REPUBLIC

STANDARD COINAGE

KM# 71 200 DONG

3.1500 g., Nickel Clad Steel, 20 mm. **Obv:** State emblem **Rev:** Value

Date	Mintage	F	VF	XF	Unc	BU
2003	—	—	—	—	0.75	1.25

KM# 74 500 DONG

4.5000 g., Nickel-Clad Steel, 22 mm. **Obv:** State emblem **Rev:** Value **Edge:** Segmented reeding

Date	Mintage	F	VF	XF	Unc	BU
2003	—	—	—	—	1.00	1.50

KM# 72 1000 DONG

3.7300 g., Brass Plated Steel, 19 mm. **Obv:** State emblem **Rev:** Bat De Pagoda in Hanoi **Edge:** Reeded

Date	Mintage	F	VF	XF	Unc	BU
2003	—	—	—	—	1.50	2.00

KM# 75 2000 DONG

5.0000 g., Brass Plated Steel, 23.5 mm. **Obv:** State emblem **Rev:** Highland Stilt House in Tay Nguyen above value **Edge:** Segmented reeding

Date	Mintage	F	VF	XF	Unc	BU
2003	—	—	—	—	2.25	2.75

KM# 64 5000 DONG

1.2441 g., 0.9999 Gold 0.04 oz. AGW, 13.92 mm. **Subject:** Year of the Snake **Obv:** National arms **Rev:** Sea snake **Edge:** Reeded

Date	Mintage	F	VF	XF	Unc	BU
2001	—	—	—	—	55.00	75.00

KM# 67 5000 DONG

1.2441 g., 0.9999 Gold 0.04 oz. AGW, 13.9 mm. **Subject:** Year of the Horse **Obv:** State emblem **Rev:** Horse **Edge:** Reeded

Date	Mintage	F	VF	XF	Unc	BU
2002	28,000	—	—	—	35.00	55.00

KM# 73 5000 DONG

7.7700 g., Brass, 25.5 mm. **Obv:** State emblem **Rev:** Chua Mot Cot Pagoda in Hanoi

Date	Mintage	F	VF	XF	Unc	BU
2003	—	—	—	—	3.75	5.00

KM# 57 10000 DONG

20.0000 g., 0.9250 Silver .5948 oz. ASW, 38.7 mm. **Subject:** Year of the Snake **Obv:** Arms, value "10000 DONG" below **Obv. Legend:** "CONG HOA XA HOI CHU NGHIA VIET NAM" **Rev:** Sea snake **Rev. Legend:** "...VIET NAM" **Edge:** Reeded

Date	Mintage	F	VF	XF	Unc	BU
2001 (S) Proof	3,500	Value: 45.00				

KM# 58 10000 DONG

20.0000 g., 0.9250 Silver .5948 oz. ASW **Subject:** Year of the Snake **Obv:** Arms, value "10000 DONG" below **Obv. Legend:** "CONG HOA XA HOI CHU NGHIA VIET NAM" **Rev:** Bamboo viper **Rev. Legend:** "...VIET NAM"

Date	Mintage	F	VF	XF	Unc	BU
2001 (S) Proof	3,500	Value: 45.00				

KM# 59 10000 DONG

20.0000 g., 0.9250 Silver .5948 oz. ASW **Subject:** Year of the Snake **Obv:** Arms, value "10000 DONG" below **Obv. Legend:** "CONG HOA XA HOI CHU NGHIA VIET NAM" **Rev:** Multicolor holographic, cobra in center **Rev. Legend:** "...VIET NAM"

Date	Mintage	F	VF	XF	Unc	BU
2001 (S) Proof	3,500	Value: 40.00				

KM# 61 10000 DONG

20.0000 g., 0.9990 Silver 0.6424 oz. ASW, 38.7 mm. **Subject:** Year of the Horse **Obv:** National arms **Rev:** Horse with octagonal latent image **Edge:** Reeded

Date	Mintage	F	VF	XF	Unc	BU
2001 Proof	3,800	Value: 37.50				

Note: In proof set only

KM# 62 10000 DONG

20.0000 g., 0.9990 Silver 0.6424 oz. ASW, 38.7 mm. **Subject:** Year of the Horse **Obv:** National arms **Rev:** Horse with multicolor accouterments **Edge:** Reeded

Date	Mintage	F	VF	XF	Unc	BU
2001 Proof	3,800	Value: 37.50				

Note: In proof set only

KM# 63 10000 DONG

20.0000 g., 0.9990 Silver 0.6424 oz. ASW, 38.7 mm. **Subject:** Year of the Horse **Obv:** National arms **Rev:** Multicolor holographic horse in center **Edge:** Reeded

Date	Mintage	F	VF	XF	Unc	BU
2001 Proof	3,800	Value: 37.50				

Note: In proof set only

KM# 76 10000 DONG

20.0000 g., 0.9990 Silver 0.6424 oz. ASW, 38.7 mm. **Obv:** State arms **Rev:** Multicolored Grey-shanked Douc Langur monkey **Edge:** Reeded

Date	Mintage	F	VF	XF	Unc	BU
2004 Proof	6,200	Value: 40.00				

KM# 65 20000 DONG

7.7759 g., 0.9999 Gold 0.25 oz. AGW, 22 mm. **Subject:** Year of the Snake **Obv:** National arms **Rev:** Sea snake **Edge:** Reeded

Date	Mintage	F	VF	XF	Unc	BU
2001 (S) Proof	—	Value: 225				

Note: Issued in a replica Faberge egg

KM# 68 20000 DONG

7.7759 g., 0.9999 Gold 0.25 oz. AGW, 22 mm. **Subject:** Year of the Horse **Obv:** State emblem **Rev:** Horse **Edge:** Reeded

Date	Mintage	F	VF	XF	Unc	BU
2002 Proof	1,800	Value: 220				

KM# 66 50000 DONG

15.5518 g., 0.9999 Gold 0.5 oz. AGW, 27 mm. **Subject:** Year of the Snake **Obv:** National arms **Rev:** Multicolor holographic King Cobra **Edge:** Reeded

Date	Mintage	F	VF	XF	Unc	BU
2001 (S) Proof	3,200	Value: 400				

KM# 69 50000 DONG

15.5518 g., 0.9999 Gold 0.5 oz. AGW, 27 mm. **Subject:** Year of the Horse **Obv:** State emblem **Rev:** Multicolor holographic horse **Edge:** Reeded

Date	Mintage	F	VF	XF	Unc	BU
2002 Proof	3,800	Value: 375				

PROOF SETS

KM#	Date	Mintage	Identification	Issue Price	Mkt Val
PS4	2001(S) (3)	3,500	KM#57-59	120	130
PS5	2001(S) (2)	—	KM#59, 66	—	440
PS6	2001(S) (2)	—	KM#65-66	—	625
PS7	2002 (3)	3,800	KM#61-63	—	115

WEST AFRICAN STATES

The West African States, a former federation of eight French colonial territories on the northwest coast of Africa, had area of 1,831,079 sq. mi. (4,742,495 sq. km.) and a population of about 17 million. Capital: Dakar. The constituent territories were Mauritania, Senegal, Dahomey, French Sudan, Ivory Coast, Upper Volta, Niger and French Guinea.

The members of the federation were overseas territories within the French Union until Sept. of 1958 when all but French Guinea approved the constitution of the Fifth French Republic, there by electing to become autonomous members of the new French Community. French Guinea voted to become the fully independent Republic of Guinea. The other seven attained independence in 1960. The French West Africa territories were provided with a common currency, a practice which was continued as the monetary union of the West African States which provides a common currency to the autonomous republics of Dahomey (now Benin), Senegal, Upper Volta (now Burkina Faso), Ivory Coast, Mali, Togo and Niger.

MINT MARKS

(a)- Paris, privy marks only

MONETARY SYSTEM

100 Centimes = 1 Franc

FEDERATION

STANDARD COINAGE

KM# 8 FRANC

Steel **Designer:** R. Joly

Date	Mintage	F	VF	XF	Unc	BU
2001(a)	—	—	—	0.10	0.35	0.60
2002(a)	—	—	—	0.10	0.35	0.60

KM# 2a 5 FRANCS

Aluminum-Nickel-Bronze

Date	Mintage	F	VF	XF	Unc	BU
2001(a)	—	—	0.10	0.20	0.40	0.60
2002(a)	—	—	0.10	0.20	0.40	0.60
2003(a)	—	—	0.10	0.20	0.40	0.60

KM# 10 10 FRANCS

Brass **Series:** F.A.O. **Designer:** R. Joly

Date	Mintage	F	VF	XF	Unc	BU
2002(a)	—	—	0.25	0.50	1.25	1.50
2003(a)	—	—	0.25	0.50	1.25	1.50
2004(a)	—	—	0.25	0.50	1.00	1.50

KM# 9 25 FRANCS

Aluminum-Bronze **Series:** F.A.O.

Date	Mintage	F	VF	XF	Unc	BU
2001(a)	—	—	0.25	0.75	1.75	2.00
2002(a)	—	—	0.25	0.75	1.75	2.00
2003(a)	—	—	0.25	0.75	1.75	2.00
2004(a)	—	—	0.25	0.75	1.50	2.00

KM# 6 50 FRANCS

Copper-Nickel **Series:** F.A.O. **Rev:** Rice, millet, ground nuts, cocoa, coffee; all around value **Designer:** R. Joly

Date	Mintage	F	VF	XF	Unc	BU
2001(a)	—	—	0.35	0.50	1.25	1.50
2002(a)	—	—	0.35	0.50	1.25	1.50
2003(a)	—	—	0.35	0.50	1.25	1.50

KM# 4 100 FRANCS

Nickel **Designer:** R. Joly

Date	Mintage	F	VF	XF	Unc	BU
2001(a)	—	—	0.60	0.85	2.25	2.75
2002(a)	—	—	0.60	0.85	2.25	2.75
2003(a)	—	—	0.60	0.85	2.25	2.75
2004(a)	—	—	0.60	0.75	2.00	2.75

KM# 14 200 FRANCS

6.9000 g., Bi-Metallic Brass center in Copper-Nickel ring, 24.4 mm. **Obv:** Native mask **Rev:** Agricultural produce and value **Edge:** Segmented reeding

Date	Mintage	F	VF	XF	Unc	BU
2003	—	—	—	—	4.00	6.00
2004(a)	—	—	—	—	4.00	6.00

KM# 15 500 FRANCS

10.6000 g., Bi-Metallic Copper-Nickel center in Brass ring, 27.9 mm. **Obv:** Native mask **Rev:** Agricultural produce and value **Edge:** Segmented reeding

Date	Mintage	F	VF	XF	Unc	BU
2003	—	—	—	—	10.00	12.00
2004(a)	—	—	—	—	10.00	12.00
2005(a)	—	—	—	—	10.00	12.00

YEMEN REPUBLIC

The Republic of Yemen, formerly Yemen Arab Republic and Peoples Democratic Republic of Yemen, is located on the southern coast of the Arabian Peninsula. It has an area of 205,020 sq. mi. (531,000 sq. km.) and a population of 12 million. Capital: San'a. The port of Aden is the main commercial center and the area's most valuable natural resource. Recent oil and gas finds and a developing petroleum industry have improved their economic prospects. Agriculture and local handicrafts are the main industries. Cotton, fish, coffee, rock salt and hides are exported.

On May 22, 1990, the Yemen Arab Republic (North Yemen) and Peoples Democratic Republic of Yemen (South Yemen) merged into a unified Republic of Yemen. Disagreements between the two former governments simmered until civil war erupted in 1994, with the northern forces of the old Yemen Arab Republic eventually prevailing.

TITLES

المملكة المتوكلية اليمنية

al-Mamlaka(t) al-Mutawakkiliya(t) al-Yamaniya(t)

REPUBLIC

MILLED COINAGE

KM# 26 5 RIYALS

Stainless Steel **Shape:** 21-sided

Date	Mintage	F	VF	XF	Unc	BU
AH1421-2001	—	—	—	—	1.75	2.25

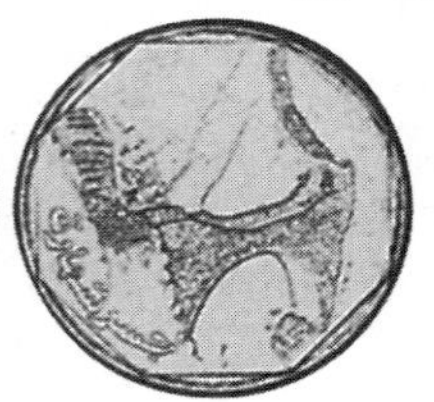

KM# 27 10 RIYALS

Stainless Steel **Rev:** Bridge at Shaharah

Date	Mintage	F	VF	XF	Unc	BU
AH1424-2003	—	—	—	—	2.75	3.50

KM# 29 20 RIALS

7.1000 g., Bi-Metallic Brass plated Steel center in Stainless Steel ring, 29.85 mm. **Obv:** Value **Rev:** Tree **Edge:** Reeded

Date	Mintage	F	VF	XF	Unc	BU
AH1425-2004	—	—	—	—	4.00	5.00

KM# 30 500 RIALS

21.2500 g., Copper-Nickel-Zinc, 35.2 mm. **Subject:** City of Sana'a **Obv:** Value **Rev:** City gate below art work **Edge:** Reeded

Date	Mintage	F	VF	XF	Unc	BU
AH1425-2004	—	—	—	—	30.00	35.00

KM# 31 1000 RIALS

73.3000 g., Pewter Antique silver finish, 60.3 mm. **Subject:** City of Sana'a **Obv:** Value **Rev:** City gate below art work **Edge:** Plain **Note:** Illustration reduced.

Date	Mintage	F	VF	XF	Unc	BU
AH1425-2004	—	—	—	—	45.00	50.00

YUGOSLAVIA

The Federal Republic of Yugoslavia, formerly the Socialist Federal Republic of Yugoslavia, a Balkan country located on the east shore of the Adriatic Sea, has an area of 39,450 sq. mi. (102,173 sq. km.) and a population of 10.5 million. Capital: Belgrade. The chief industries are agriculture, mining, manufacturing and tourism. Machinery, nonferrous metals, meat and fabrics are exported.

The name Yugoslavia appears on the coinage in letters of the Cyrillic alphabet alone until formation of the Federated Peoples Republic of Yugoslavia in 1953, after which both the Cyrillic and Latin alphabets are employed. From 1965, the coin denomination appears in the 4 different languages of the federated republics in letters of both the Cyrillic and Latin alphabets.

DENOMINATIONS

Para ПАРА
Dinar, ДИНАР, Dinara ДИНАРА
Dinari ДИНАРИ, Dinarjev

MONETARY SYSTEM

100 Para = 1 Dinar

FEDERAL REPUBLIC

STANDARD COINAGE

KM# 180 DINAR

4.4000 g., Copper-Zinc-Nickel, 20 mm. **Obv:** National arms **Rev:** Large building and denomination **Edge:** Reeded

Date	Mintage	F	VF	XF	Unc	BU
2002	60,780,000	—	—	—	0.25	0.45

KM# 181 2 DINARA

5.2000 g., Copper-Nickel-Zinc, 21.9 mm. **Obv:** National arms **Rev:** Church and denomination **Edge:** Reeded

Date	Mintage	F	VF	XF	Unc	BU
2002	71,053,000	—	—	—	0.25	0.45

KM# 182 5 DINARA

6.3000 g., Copper-Nickel-Zinc, 24 mm. **Obv:** National arms **Rev:** Domed building and denomination **Edge:** Reeded

Date	Mintage	F	VF	XF	Unc	BU
2002	30,966,000	—	—	—	1.25	1.50

ZAMBIA

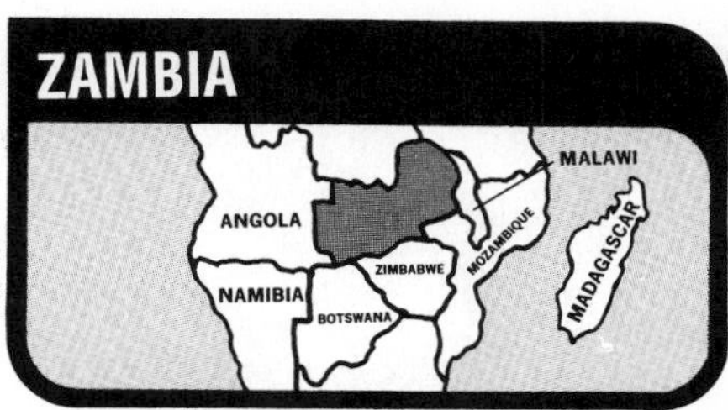

The Republic of Zambia (formerly Northern Rhodesia), a landlocked country in south-central Africa, has an area of 290,586 sq. mi. (752,610 sq. km.) and a population of*7.9 million. Capital: Lusaka. The economy of Zambia is based principally on copper, of which Zambia is the world's third largest producer. Copper, zinc, lead, cobalt and tobacco are exported.

For earlier coinage refer to Rhodesia and Nyasaland.

REPUBLIC

DECIMAL COINAGE

100 Ngwee = 1 Kwacha

KM# 156 500 KWACHA

15.0000 g., 0.9990 Silver 0.4818 oz. ASW, 34.2 mm. **Subject:** Football World Champion - 1954 Germany **Obv:** Queen Elizabeth's cameo portrait above national arms and value **Rev:** Soccer game scene in front of Berlin Wall **Edge:** Plain

Date	Mintage	F	VF	XF	Unc	BU
2001 Proof	—	Value: 35.00				

KM# 174 500 KWACHA

15.0000 g., 0.9990 Silver 0.4818 oz. ASW, 34.2 mm. **Subject:** 1972 Munich Olympics **Obv:** Elizabeth II above Zambian arms **Rev:** Torch runner in stadium **Edge:** Reeded

Date	Mintage	F	VF	XF	Unc	BU
2002 Proof	—	Value: 25.00				

KM# 87 1000 KWACHA

28.9100 g., Copper-Nickel, 38 mm. **Series:** Patrons of the Ocean **Obv:** National arms above Queen Elizabeth's cameo **Rev:** Sea turtle **Edge:** Reeded

Date	Mintage	F	VF	XF	Unc	BU
2001 Proof	—	Value: 12.00				

KM# 88 1000 KWACHA

28.9100 g., Copper-Nickel **Series:** Patrons of the Ocean **Obv:** National arms above cameo of Queen Elizabeth II **Rev:** Coelacanth

Date	Mintage	F	VF	XF	Unc	BU
2001 Proof	—	Value: 12.00				

KM# 89 1000 KWACHA

28.9100 g., Copper-Nickel **Series:** Patrons of the Ocean **Rev:** Sea horse and fish

Date	Mintage	F	VF	XF	Unc	BU
2001 Proof	—	Value: 12.00				

KM# 90 1000 KWACHA

28.9100 g., Copper-Nickel **Series:** Patrons of the Ocean **Obv:** National arms above Queen Elizabeth's cameo **Rev:** Two dolphins

Date	Mintage	F	VF	XF	Unc	BU
2001 Proof	—	Value: 12.00				

KM# 159 1000 KWACHA

31.2200 g., 0.9990 Silver 1.0027 oz. ASW, 38.6 mm. **Obv:** Queen Elizabeth II's head right divides date above national arms **Rev:** Half-length bust of Dr. David Livingstone left **Edge:** Reeded

Date	Mintage	F	VF	XF	Unc	BU
2002	—	—	—	—	35.00	37.50

KM# 74 1000 KWACHA

29.0000 g., Copper-Nickel, 40 mm. **Obv:** Elizabeth II above Zambian arms **Rev:** Dated calendar **Shape:** 7-sided

Date	Mintage	F	VF	XF	Unc	BU
2002 Proof-like	—	—	—	—	—	12.50
2003 Proof-like	—	—	—	—	—	12.50
2004 Proof-like	—	—	—	—	—	12.50

KM# 167 1000 KWACHA

25.0000 g., Copper-Nickel, 38.6 mm. **Subject:** 50th Anniversary of Elizabeth II's Coronation **Obv:** Queen Elizabeth II above Zambian arms **Rev:** Crown on pillow above two crossed scepters **Edge:** Reeded

Date	Mintage	F	VF	XF	Unc	BU
ND(2003)	—	—	—	—	8.00	9.00

KM# 169 1000 KWACHA

25.0000 g., Copper-Nickel, 38.6 mm. **Obv:** Queen Elizabeth II above Zambian arms **Rev:** Prince William on jet ski **Edge:** Reeded

Date	Mintage	F	VF	XF	Unc	BU
2003	—	—	—	—	8.00	9.00

KM# 171 1000 KWACHA

25.0000 g., Copper-Nickel, 38.6 mm. **Obv:** Queen Elizabeth II above Zambian arms **Rev:** Queen Mother **Edge:** Reeded

Date	Mintage	F	VF	XF	Unc	BU
ND(2003)	—	—	—	—	8.00	9.00

KM# 172 1000 KWACHA

25.0000 g., 0.9250 Silver 0.7435 oz. ASW, 38.6 mm. **Obv:** Queen Elizabeth II above Zambian arms **Rev:** Queen Mother **Edge:** Reeded

Date	Mintage	F	VF	XF	Unc	BU
ND(2003) Proof	5,000	Value: 45.00				

KM# 160 1000 KWACHA

29.3000 g., Silver Plated Bronze (Specific gravity 9.099), 38.6 mm. **Subject:** Pope John Paul II **Obv:** National arms **Rev:** Pope saying mass **Edge:** Reeded **Note:** Specific gravity 9.099

Date	Mintage	F	VF	XF	Unc	BU
2003 Proof	—	Value: 20.00				

KM# 118 2000 KWACHA

31.1035 g., 0.9990 Silver 1.0000 oz. ASW, 38.6 mm. **Subject:** Centennial of the Anglo-Japanese Alliance **Obv:** Queen Elizabeth **Rev:** Fantasy Japanese coin design **Edge:** Reeded

Date	Mintage	F	VF	XF	Unc	BU
2002	500	—	—	—	65.00	70.00

KM# 166 4000 KWACHA

25.0000 g., 0.9250 Silver 0.7435 oz. ASW, 38.6 mm. **Subject:** Queen Elizabeth's 75th Birthday **Obv:** Queen Elizabeth II above Zambian arms **Rev:** Queen Elizabeth II wearing a hat **Edge:** Reeded

Date	Mintage	F	VF	XF	Unc	BU
2001 Proof	2,000	Value: 35.00				

KM# 85 4000 KWACHA

25.1000 g., 0.9250 Silver .7465 oz. ASW, 37.9 mm. **Series:** Wildlife Protection **Obv:** British Queen's portrait below arms **Rev:** Lion hologram **Edge:** Reeded **Note:** Lighter weight and smaller diameter than official specifications.

Date	Mintage	F	VF	XF	Unc	BU
2001 Proof	—	Value: 60.00				

KM# 110 4000 KWACHA

20.0000 g., 0.9990 Silver .6424 oz. ASW, 37.9 mm. **Series:** Patrons of the Ocean **Obv:** Zambian arms above Queen Elizabeth's portrait **Rev:** Sea turtle **Edge:** Reeded

Date	Mintage	F	VF	XF	Unc	BU
2001 Proof	—	Value: 40.00				

KM# 111 4000 KWACHA

20.0000 g., 0.9990 Silver .6424 oz. ASW **Series:** Patrons of the Ocean **Obv:** Head of Queen Elizabeth II divides date below national arms **Rev:** Coelacanth fish

Date	Mintage	F	VF	XF	Unc	BU
2001 Proof	—	Value: 50.00				

KM# 112 4000 KWACHA
20.0000 g., 0.9990 Silver .6424 oz. ASW **Series:** Patrons of the Ocean **Obv:** Head of Queen Elizabeth II divides date below national arms **Rev:** Sea horse and fish

Date	Mintage	F	VF	XF	Unc	BU
2001 Proof	—	Value: 40.00				

KM# 113 4000 KWACHA
20.0000 g., 0.9990 Silver .6424 oz. ASW **Series:** Patrons of the Ocean **Obv:** Head of Queen Elizabeth II divides date below national arms **Rev:** Two dolphins

Date	Mintage	F	VF	XF	Unc	BU
2001 Proof	—	Value: 50.00				

KM# 114 4000 KWACHA
50.0000 g., 0.9990 Silver 1.6059 oz. ASW **Subject:** Illusion **Obv:** Zambian arms below Queen Elizabeth's portrait **Rev:** "Cat in the Window" **Edge:** Plain **Note:** 50x50mm

Date	Mintage	F	VF	XF	Unc	BU
2001 Proof	5,000	Value: 55.00				

KM# 175 4000 KWACHA
23.0000 g., 0.9990 Silver 0.7387 oz. ASW, 40 mm. **Obv:** Elizabeth II above Zambian arms **Rev:** Dated calendar **Shape:** Seven sided

Date	Mintage	F	VF	XF	Unc	BU
2002 Proof-like	—	—	—	—	—	50.00
2003 Proof-like	15,000	—	—	—	—	50.00
2004 Proof-like	5,000	—	—	—	—	50.00

KM# 168 4000 KWACHA
25.0000 g., 0.9250 Silver 0.7435 oz. ASW, 38.6 mm. **Subject:** 50th Anniversary of Elizabeth II's Coronation **Obv:** Queen Elizabeth II above Zambian arms **Rev:** Crown on pillow above two crossed scepters **Edge:** Reeded

Date	Mintage	F	VF	XF	Unc	BU
ND(2003) Proof	5,000	Value: 45.00				

KM# 170 4000 KWACHA
25.0000 g., 0.9250 Silver 0.7435 oz. ASW, 38.6 mm.
Obv: Queen Elizabeth II above Zambian arms **Rev:** Prince William on jet ski **Edge:** Reeded

Date	Mintage	F	VF	XF	Unc	BU
2003 Proof	5,000	Value: 45.00				

KM# 117 5000 KWACHA
31.3000 g., 0.9990 Silver 1.0053 oz. ASW, 38.6 mm.
Subject: African Wildlife **Obv:** National arms **Rev:** Elephant mother and calf grazing on grass **Edge:** Reeded

Date	Mintage	F	VF	XF	Unc	BU
2001 Proof	—	Value: 45.00				
2001 Matte	—	—	—	—	25.00	—

KM# 143 5000 KWACHA
28.8600 g., 0.9990 Silver 0.9269 oz. ASW, 38.5 mm. **Subject:** African Wildlife **Obv:** National arms **Rev:** Elephant **Edge:** Reeded

Date	Mintage	F	VF	XF	Unc	BU
2002 Matte	—	—	—	—	40.00	—

KM# 165 5000 KWACHA
31.1000 g., 0.9990 Silver 0.9989 oz. ASW, 38.5 mm. **Obv:** Bust of Queen Elizabeth II right divides date **Rev:** Two African elephants **Edge:** Reeded

Date	Mintage	F	VF	XF	Unc	BU
2003 Matte	—	—	—	—	35.00	—
2003 Proof	—	Value: 30.00				

KM# 94 40000 KWACHA
31.1035 g., 0.9999 Gold 1.0000 oz. AGW, 37.9 mm. **Series:** Wildlife Protection **Obv:** Zambian arms above Queen Elizabeth's portrait **Rev:** Holographic lion picture **Edge:** Reeded

Date	Mintage	F	VF	XF	Unc	BU
2001 Proof	—	Value: 700				

KM# 153.1 40000 KWACHA
47.5400 g., 0.9166 Gold 1.401 oz. AGW, 39 mm. **Subject:** Queen Victoria **Obv:** Head of Queen Elizabeth II in ornate frame divides date above value **Rev:** Crowned Queen Victoria with veil looking left **Edge:** Reeded

Date	Mintage	F	VF	XF	Unc	BU
2001 Proof	1	Value: 1,000				

Note: Medallic die alignment

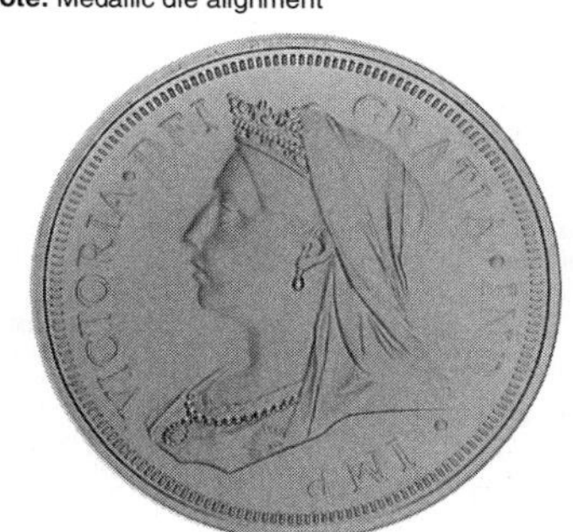

KM# 153.2 40000 KWACHA
47.5400 g., 0.9166 Gold 1.401 oz. AGW, 39 mm. **Subject:** Queen Victoria **Obv:** Head of Queen Elizabeth II right in ornate frame **Rev:** Bust of Queen Victoria left with veil **Edge:** Reeded

Date	Mintage	F	VF	XF	Unc	BU
2001 Matte	1	—	—	—	1,000	—

Note: Coin die alignment

KM# 154.1 40000 KWACHA
47.5400 g., 0.9166 Gold 1.401 oz. AGW, 39 mm. **Subject:** Edward VII **Obv:** Head of Queen Elizabeth II right in ornate frame **Rev:** Bust of King Edward VII right **Edge:** Reeded

Date	Mintage	F	VF	XF	Unc	BU
2001 Proof	1	Value: 1,000				

Note: Medallic die rotation

KM# 154.2 40000 KWACHA
47.5400 g., 0.9166 Gold 1.401 oz. AGW, 39 mm. **Subject:** Edward VII **Obv:** Head of Queen Elizabeth II right in ornate frame **Rev:** Bust of Edward VII right **Edge:** Reeded

Date	Mintage	F	VF	XF	Unc	BU
2001 Matte	1	—	—	—	1,000	—

Note: Coin die alignment

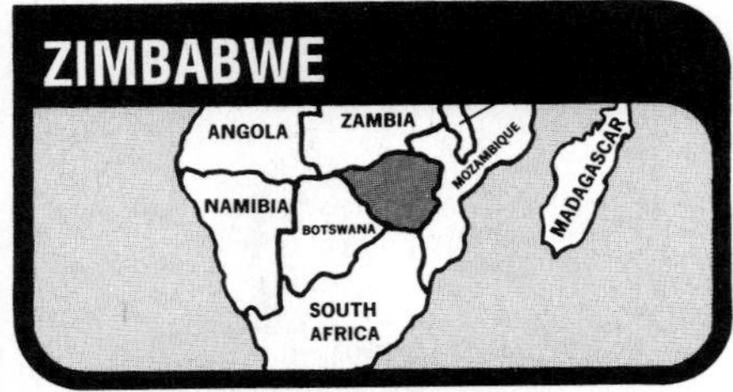

The Republic of Zimbabwe (formerly the Republic of Rhodesia or Southern Rhodesia), located in the east-central part of southern Africa, has an area of 150,804 sq. mi. (390,580sq. km.) and a population of *10.1 million. Capital: Harare (formerly Salisbury). The economy is based on agriculture and mining. Tobacco, sugar, asbestos, copper, chrome, ore and coal are exported.

On April 18, 1980 pursuant to an act of the British Parliament, the colony of Southern Rhodesia became independent as the Republic of Zimbabwe, which remains a member of the British Commonwealth of Nations.

MONETARY SYSTEM
100 Cents = 1 Dollar

REPUBLIC

DECIMAL COINAGE

KM# 3a 10 CENTS
Stainless Steel, 20 mm. **Obv:** National emblem **Rev:** Baobob tree **Edge:** Plain

Date	Mintage	F	VF	XF	Unc	BU
2001	—	—	0.15	0.30	0.75	1.00

KM# 4a 20 CENTS
Stainless Steel, 23 mm. **Obv:** National emblem **Rev:** Bridge **Edge:** Plain

Date	Mintage	F	VF	XF	Unc	BU
2001	—	—	0.20	0.40	1.25	1.50
2002	—	—	0.20	0.40	1.25	1.50

KM# 5a 50 CENTS
Stainless Steel, 26 mm. **Obv:** National emblem **Rev:** Radiant sun landscape **Edge:** Plain

Date	Mintage	F	VF	XF	Unc	BU
2001	—	—	0.40	1.00	1.75	2.00
2002	—	—	0.40	1.00	1.75	2.00

KM# 6a DOLLAR
Stainless Steel, 29 mm. **Obv:** National emblem **Rev:** Ruins between trees with value above **Edge:** Reeded

Date	Mintage	F	VF	XF	Unc	BU
2001	—	—	1.00	1.50	3.00	3.50
2002	—	—	1.00	1.50	3.00	3.50

KM# 12a 2 DOLLARS
Stainless Steel, 24.5 mm. **Obv:** National emblem **Rev:** Pangolin below vallue **Edge:** Reeded

Date	Mintage	F	VF	XF	Unc	BU
2001	—	—	1.25	2.25	5.00	5.50

KM# 13 5 DOLLARS
9.0500 g., Bi-Metallic Stainless Steel center in Brass ring, 27.4 mm. **Obv:** Bird on nest **Rev:** Rhinoceros **Edge:** Reeded

Date	Mintage	F	VF	XF	Unc	BU
2001	—	—	—	—	7.50	8.50
2002	—	—	—	—	7.50	8.50

A GUIDE TO INTERNATIONAL NUMERICS

	ENGLISH	CZECH	DANISH	DUTCH	ESPERANTO	FRENCH
1/4	one-quarter	jeden-ctvrt	én kvart	een-kwart	unu-kvar'ono	un-quart
1/2	one-half	jeden-polovieni or pul	én halve	een-half	unu-du'one	un-demi
1	one	jeden	én	een	unu	un
2	two	dve	to	twee	du	deux
3	three	tri	tre	drie	tri	trois
4	four	ctyri	fire	vier	kvar	quatre
5	five	pet	fem	vijf	kvin	cinq
6	six	sest	seks	zes	ses	six
7	seven	sedm	syv	zeven	sep	sept
8	eight	osm	otte	acht	ok	huit
9	nine	devet	ni	negen	nau	neuf
10	ten	deset	ti	tien	dek	dix
12	twelve	dvanáct	tolv	twaalf	dek du	douze
15	fifteen	patnáct	femten	vijftien	dek kvin	quinze
20	twenty	dvacet	tyve	twintig	du'dek	vingt
24	twenty-four	dvacet-ctyri	fireog tyve	twintig-vier	du'dek kvar	vingt-quatre
25	twenty-five	dvacet-pet	fem og tyve	twintig-vijf	du'dek kvin	vingt-cinq
30	thirty	tricet	tredive	dertig	tri'dek	trente
40	forty	ctyricet	fyrre	veertig	kvar'dek	quarante
50	fifty	padesát	halytreds	vijftig	kvin'dek	cinquante
60	sixty	sedesát	tres	zestig	ses'dek	soixante
70	seventy	sedmdesát	halvfjerds	zeventig	sep'dek	soixante dix
80	eighty	osemdesát	firs	tachtig	ok'dek	quatre-vingt
90	ninety	devadesát	halvfjerds	negentig	nau'dek	quatre-vingt-dix
100	one hundred	jedno sto	et hundrede	een-honderd	unu-cento	un-cent
1000	thousand	tisíc	tusind	duizend	mil	mille

	GERMAN	HUNGARIAN	INDONESIAN	ITALIAN	NORWEGIAN	POLISH
1/4	ein viertel	egy-negyed	satu-suku	uno-guarto	en-fjeerdedel	jeden-c weirc
1/2	einhalb	egy-fél	satu-setengah	uno-mezzo	en-halv	jeden-polowa
1	ein	egy	satu	uno	en	jeden
2	zwei	kettö	dud	due	to	dwa
3	drei	három	tiga	tre	tre	trzy
4	vier	négy	empot	quattro	fire	cztery
5	fünf	öt	lima	cinque	fem	piec'
6	sechs	hat	enam	sei	seks	szes'c'
7	sieben	hét	tudjuh	sette	sju	siedem
8	acht	nyolc	delapan	otto	atte	osiem
9	neun	kilenc	sembilan	nove	ni	dziewiec'
10	zehn	tí z	sepuluh	dieci	ti	dziesiec'
12	zwölf	tizenketto	duabelas	dodici	tolv	dwanas' cie
15	fünfzehn	tizenöt	lima belas	quindici	femten	pietnas'cie
20	zwanzig	húsz	dua pulah	venti	tjue or tyve	dwadzies'cia
24	vierundzwanzig	húsz-négy	dua pulah-empot	venti-quattro	tjue-fire or tyve-fire	dwadzies'cia-cztery
25	fünfundzwanzig	húsz-öt	dua-pulah-lima	venti-cinque	tjue-fem or tyve-fem	dwadzies'cia-piec
30	dreissig	harminc	tigapulah	trenta	tredve	trydzies'ci
40	vierzig	negyven	empat pulah	quaranta	forti	czterdries'ci
50	fünfzig	otven	lima pulah	cinquanta	femti	piec'dziesiat
60	sechzig	hatvan	enam pulah	sessanta	seksti	szes'c'dziesiat
70	siebzig	hetven	tudjuh pulu	settanta	sytti	siedemdziesiat
80	achtzig	nyolvan	delapan puluh	ottonta	atti	osiemdziesiat
90	neunzig	kilencven	sembilan puluh	novanta	nitty	dziewiec'dziesiat
100	ein hundert	egy-száz	satu-seratus	uno-cento	en-hundre	jeden-sto
1000	tausend	ezer	seribu	mille	tusen	tysiac

	PORTUGUESE	ROMANIAN	SERBO-CROATIAN	SPANISH	SWEDEN	TURKISH
1/4	um-quarto	un-sfert	jedan-ceturtina	un-cuarto	en-fjärdedel	bir-ceyrek
1/2	un-meio	o-jumatate	jedan-polovina	un-medio	en-hälft	bir-yarim
1	um	un	jedan	uno	en	bir
2	dois	doi	dva	dos	tva	iki
3	trés	trei	tri	tres	tre	üc
4	quatro	patru	cetiri	cuatro	fyra	dört
5	cinco	cinci	pet	cinco	fem	bes
6	seis	sase	sest	seis	sex	alti
7	sete	sapte	sedam	siete	sju	yedi
8	oito	opt	osam	ocho	atta	sekiz
9	nove	noua	devet	nueve	io	dokuz
10	dez	zece	deset	diez	tio	on
12	doze	doisprezece	dvanaest	doce	tolv	on iki
15	quinze	cincisprezece	petnaest	quince	femton	on bes
20	vinte	douazeci	dvadset	veinte	tjugu	yirmi
24	vinte-quatro	douazeci-patru	dvadesel-citiri	veinticuatro	tjugu-fyra	yirmi-dört
25	vinte-cinco	douazeci-cinci	dvadeset-pet	veinticinco	tjugu-fem	yirmi-bes
30	trinta	treizeci	trideset	treinta	trettio	otuz
40	quarenta	patruzeci	cetrdeset	cuarenta	fyrtio	kirk
50	cinqüenta	cincizeci	padeset	cincuenta	femtio	elli
60	sessenta	saizeci	sezdeset	sesenta	sextio	altmis
70	setenta	saptezeci	sedamdeset	setenta	sjuttio	yetmis
80	oitenta	optzeci	osamdeset	ochenta	attio	seksen
90	noventa	novazeci	devedeset	noventa	nittio	doksan
100	un-cem	o-suta	jedan-sto	cien	en-hundra	bir-yüz
1000	mil	mie	hiljada	mil	tusen	bin

NUMISMATIC SOCIETIES

American Numismatic Association
818 North Cascade Ave.
Colorado Springs, CO 80903
U.S.A.

American Numismatic Society
96 Fulton St.
New York, NY 10038

Amigos de la Casa de la Moneda de Segovia
(Friends of the Segovia Mint)
Apartado 315
40080 Segovia
Spain

Asociación Numismática de Costa Rica
Apartado 2075-1002
San José
Costa Rica

Asociación Numismática Española
Gran via de les Corts Catalanes 627 Pral. 1ª
08010 Barcelonia
Spain

Asociación Numismática de Chile "ANUCH"
Luis Thayer Ojeda 0115
Local 35-36
Providencia, Santiago
Chile

Canadian Numismatic Association
4936 Younge Street, Suite 601
North York, ON M2N 6S3
Canada

Centro Numismatico Buenos Aires
Av. San Juan 2630 (C1232AAV)
Buenos Aires
Argentina

Commission Internationale Numismatique
(C.I.N)
Rutimeyer Strasse 12
CH-4054 Basel
Switzerland

Deutsche Numismatische Gesellschaft
Dr. R. Albert
Hans-Purrman-Allee 26
D-67346 Speyer
Germany

Hellenic Numismatic Society
A.Metaxa 28
p.c 106 81 Athens
Greece

Lithuanian Numismatic Association
P.O. Box 22696
Baltimore, MD 21203
U.S.A.

Malaysia Numismatic Society
G. P.O. 12367
50776 Kuala Lumpur
Malaysia

Nordisk Numismatisk Unions Medlemsblad
%Den Lgl. Mont-og Medaillesamng
Nationalmuseet/Frederiksholms
Kanal 12
DK-1220 Kobenhaven
Denmark

Numismatic Association of Australia
Box 1920
GPO Melbourne
Victoria 3001
Australia

Numismatics International
P.O. Box 570842
Dallas, TX 75357-0842
U.S.A.

Numismatic Society of India
Nisar Ahmed
Banaras Hindu University
Varanasi 221-005
India

Oriental Numismatic Society
Regional Secretary O.N.S.
J. Lingen
Dr. A. Schweitzerstraat 29
2861 XZ BERGAMBACHT
Netherlands
Or
Oriental Numismatic Society
Charlie Karukstis
P.O. Box 1528
Claremont, CA 91711

Polish Numismatic Society
P.O. Box 1873
Chicago, IL 60690
U.S.A.

Royal Numismatic Society
C/o Dept. Coins and Medals
British Museum
Great Russell Street
London, WC1B 3DG
United Kingdom

Royal Numismatic Society of New Zealand
P.O. Box 2023
Wellington 6015
New Zealand

Russian Numismatic Society
RNS Secretary
P.O. Box 3684
Santa Rosa, CA 95402
U.S.A.

Sarawak Philatelic and Numismatic Society
P.O. Box 376
96007 Sibu
Sarawak
Malaysia

Sociedad Numismatica de Mexico
Eugenia 13-301 Col. Napoles
C.P. 03810 Mexico D.F.

Sociedad Numismatica de Puerto Rico
Box 194636
San Juan, Puerto Rico 00919-4636

Sociedad Portuguesa de Numismática
Rue de Costa Cabral 664
4200-211 Porto
Portugal

Sociedade Numismática Brasileira
Rua 24 de Maio, 247 2º And.
Centro San Paulo SP
Brazil

Sodiedade Portugesa de Numismatica
Rua de Costa Cabral, 664
4200 Porto
Portugal

Societe Royale de Numismatique de Belgique
Ave. Leopold 28A
B-1330 Rixensart
Belgium

South Africa Numismatic Society
P.O. Box 1689
Cape Town 8000
South Africa

Turkish Numismatic Society
Haci Emin Efendi Sok. No 7
Murat Apt. Daire 4
Tesvkive Istanbul
Turkey

Ukranian Philatelic and Numismatic Society
P.O. Box 303
Southfields, NY 10975-0303

U.S. Mexican Numismatic Association
USMexNA c/o Don Bailey
P.O. Box 98
Homer, MI 49245-0098

Verband der Deutschen Munzvereine
(Association of German Numismatic Societies)
Reisenbergstr. 58A
D-8000 Munich 60
Germany